New York Math A Edition

TABLE OF CONTENTS

ISBN: 0-07-822594-9

3 4 5 6 7 8 9 10 **071** 07 06 05 04 03 02 01 00

New York

1

Ordering Real Numbers

Use after Lesson 2–8, Glencoe ***Algebra 1***

What YOU'LL LEARN

- To recognize the order of real numbers using rational approximations of irrational numbers.

Why IT'S IMPORTANT

You can determine whether answers to application problems are reasonable if you recognize the order of real numbers.

APPLICATION Photography

An advertisement for a 90mm camera included the following information.

F-stop scale: f2.8–4–5.6–8–11–16–22

Photographers use the numbers in the f-stop scale to regulate the amount of light entering the camera. This controls the brightness of the photograph. Some lenses with different f-stop settings are shown below.

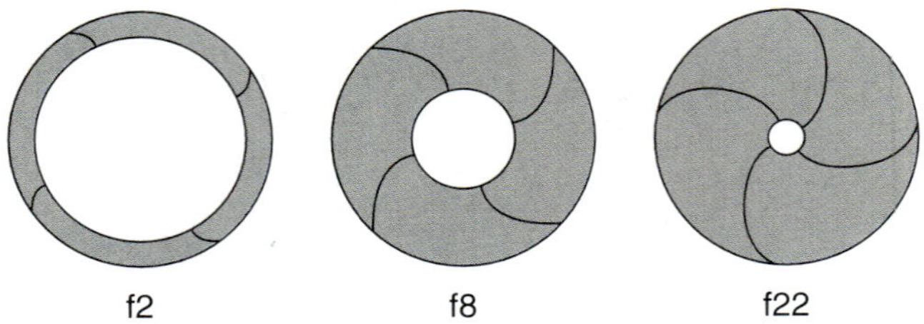

Recall that the set of real numbers includes rational numbers and irrational numbers. Every rational number can be written as a terminating or a repeating decimal. Examples of rational numbers are $2\frac{1}{8}$, -15, $76.\overline{2}$, and 3.945. Irrational numbers are nonterminating and nonrepeating decimals such as $\sqrt{5}$, 9.12673427..., and π (3.14159...).

FYI

An f-stop number is a ratio relating the *aperture* of a camera, the opening that allows light to enter, and the *focal length,* the distance that light travels after passing through the lens.

Some of the f-stop numbers are actually **rational approximations** of irrational numbers. A rational approximation of an irrational number is a rational number that is close to, but not equal to, the value of the irrational number. You can use a calculator to write approximations as decimals.

Irrational Number	Rational Approximation	F-Stop Number
$2\sqrt{2}$	2 [×] 2 [2nd] [$\sqrt{x}$] [=] 2.83	f2.8
$8\sqrt{2}$	8 [×] 2 [2nd] [$\sqrt{x}$] [=] 11.31	f11

There is an infinite number of rational approximations for every irrational number. In the table above, we approximated to the nearest hundredth. Some other rational approximations for $2\sqrt{2}$ are shown below.

$$2\sqrt{2} \approx 2.8 \qquad 2\sqrt{2} \approx 2.828 \qquad 2\sqrt{2} \approx 2.828427$$

The point corresponding to 2.828427... is between 2 and 3 on a number line. To be even more precise, it is between 2.8 and 2.9.

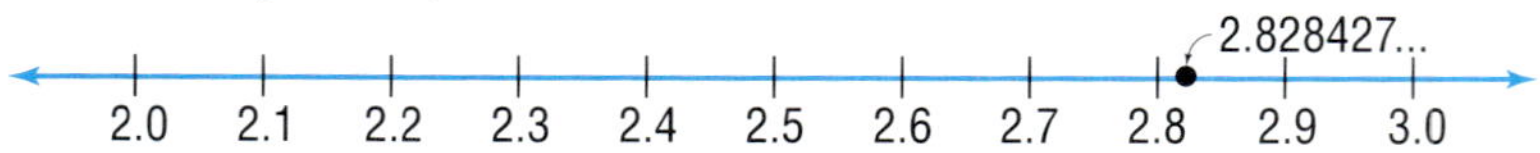

You can use two methods for finding rational approximations for an irrational number without using a calculator. The first finds an approximation to the nearest whole number. The second finds a closer approximation. We will demonstrate both methods in finding rational approximations for $\sqrt{29}$.

Method 1: Perfect Squares

Find two perfect squares closest to 29 and write an inequality. Some perfect squares are 1, 4, 9, 16, 25, 36, 49, ...

$25 < 29 < 36$ *29 is between 25 and 36.*

$\sqrt{25} < \sqrt{29} < \sqrt{36}$ *Find the square root of each number.*

$5 < \sqrt{29} < 6$ *$\sqrt{29}$ is between 5 and 6.*

Since 29 is closer to 25 than to 36, $\sqrt{29}$ is closer to 5 than to 6. The best whole number approximation for $\sqrt{29}$ is 5.

Method 2: Guess and Check

Pick any number to one decimal place and square it to try to get near 29. In this case, you know the number is near 5.

Guess: 5.1
Check: $5.1^2 = 26.01$ Choose a greater number.

Guess: 5.4
Check: $5.4^2 = 29.16$ This is closer. Choose a lesser number.

Guess: 5.3
Check: $5.3^2 = 28.09$

Since 29 is closer to 29.16 than to 28.09, $\sqrt{29}$ is closer to 5.4 than to 5.3. The best approximation to one decimal place for $\sqrt{29}$ is 5.4. *Use a calculator to check.*

Example 1

APPLICATION

Sports

Suppose a basketball player is able to jump 0.502 meter high from a standstill position. The initial velocity v_0 required to reach this height is $\sqrt{9.84}$ meters per second.

a. Find a rational approximation for $\sqrt{9.84}$ to the nearest whole number and to the nearest tenth without using a calculator.

Method 1: Perfect Squares

$9 < 9.84 < 16$ *9.84 is between 9 and 16.*

$\sqrt{9} < \sqrt{9.84} < \sqrt{16}$ *Find the square root of each number.*

$3 < \sqrt{9.84} < 4$ *$\sqrt{9.84}$ is between 3 and 4.*

The best whole number approximation is 3 meters per second. Why?

Method 2: Guess and Check

Guess: 3.1
Check: $3.1^2 = 9.61$ Choose a greater number.

Guess: 3.2
Check: $3.2^2 = 10.24$

$\sqrt{9.84}$ is between 3.1 and 3.2. Since 9.84 is closer to 9.61 than to 10.24, the best approximation to the nearest tenth is 3.1 meters per second.

(continued on the next page)

b. Use a calculator to find a rational approximation of $\sqrt{9.84}$ to the nearest hundredth.

9.84 [2nd] [$\sqrt{x}$] 3.136877428

To the nearest hundredth, $\sqrt{9.84} = 3.14$.

You can use models to compare real numbers.

MODELING MATHEMATICS

Comparing Real Numbers

Materials: geoboard or dot paper; rubber bands

You can use a geoboard to compare the numbers $3\sqrt{2}$ and $\sqrt{8}$.

- Place rubber bands on the geoboard to make a square with an area of 2 square units, as shown at the right. Since the area is the length of the side squared, the length of one side is $\sqrt{2}$ units.

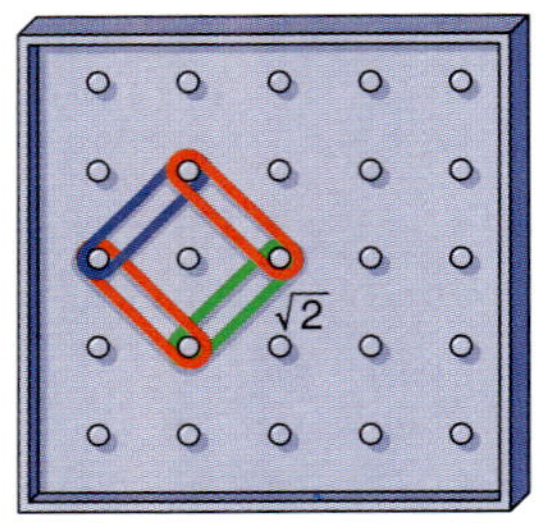

- Use a rubber band to double the length of one side. The length of this segment is $2\sqrt{2}$ units.

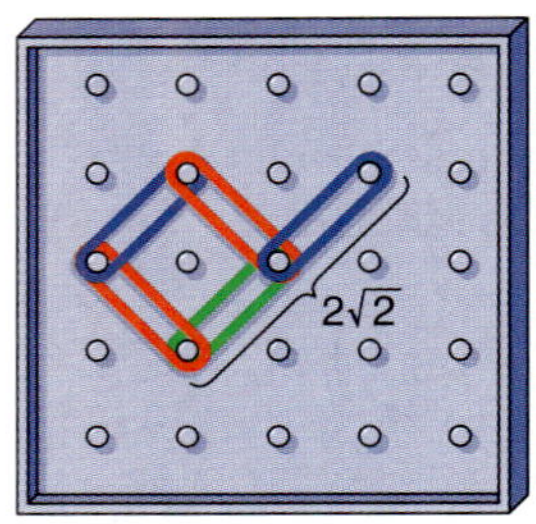

Your Turn

a. Use the method above to show the length $3\sqrt{2}$ on a geoboard.

b. Use rubber bands to make a square having an area of 8 square units.

c. What is the length of one side of your square in part b?

d. Compare the lengths of $3\sqrt{2}$ and $\sqrt{8}$. Which is longer?

e. Write an inequality comparing $3\sqrt{2}$ and $\sqrt{8}$.

Example 2

Replace each __?__ with <, >, or = to make each sentence true.

a. $\sqrt{3}$ __?__ $-\sqrt{5}$

Since any negative number is less than a positive number, $\sqrt{3} > -\sqrt{5}$.

b. $\frac{1}{9}$ __?__ $\frac{1}{\sqrt{19}}$

You can use a calculator to find a rational approximation for each number.

1 [÷] 9 [=] 0.111111111 So, $\frac{1}{9} \approx 0.11$.

19 [2nd] [$\sqrt{x}$] [1/x] 0.229415734 So, $\frac{1}{\sqrt{19}} \approx 0.23$.

Since $0.11 < 0.23$, $\frac{1}{9} < \frac{1}{\sqrt{19}}$.

c. $8.\overline{62}$ ___?___ $\sqrt{52}$

Use the perfect square method to find a rational approximation for $\sqrt{52}$.

$$49 < 52 < 64 \quad \textit{52 is between 49 and 64.}$$
$$\sqrt{49} < \sqrt{52} < \sqrt{64} \quad \textit{Find the square root of each number.}$$
$$7 < \sqrt{52} < 8$$

Since $\sqrt{52}$ is between 7 and 8, it is less than $8.\overline{62}$. Therefore, $8.\overline{62} > \sqrt{52}$.

You can use rational approximations to test the validity of some algebraic statements involving real numbers.

Example 3 **For what values of x is $\frac{1}{\sqrt{x}} > \sqrt{x} > x$ true?**

a. $\frac{1}{2}$ **b.** 0 **c.** −2 **d.** 3

Replace x in $\frac{1}{\sqrt{x}} > \sqrt{x} > x$ with each given value.

a. $x = \frac{1}{2}$

$$\frac{1}{\sqrt{\frac{1}{2}}} > \sqrt{\frac{1}{2}} > \frac{1}{2}$$

Use a calculator to find rational approximations.

$1.41 > 0.71 > 0.5$ ✔ *yes*

b. $x = 0$

$$\frac{1}{\sqrt{0}} > \sqrt{0} > 0$$

$\frac{1}{\sqrt{0}}$ is not a real number.

c. $x = -2$

$$\frac{1}{\sqrt{-2}} > \sqrt{-2} > -2$$

$\frac{1}{\sqrt{-2}}$ and $\sqrt{-2}$ are not real numbers.

d. $x = 3$

$$\frac{1}{\sqrt{3}} > \sqrt{3} > 3$$

Use a calculator to find rational approximations.

$0.58 > 1.73 > 3$ no

So, the inequality is true for $x = \frac{1}{2}$.

CHECK FOR UNDERSTANDING

Communicating Mathematics

Study the lesson. Then complete the following.

1. **State** which is a better approximation for $\sqrt{15}$: 3.872 or 3.873. Explain how you determined your answer.
2. **Determine** whether each statement is *true* or *false*. If false, explain.
   a. Between 2 and 3, there is an infinite number of irrational numbers.
   b. On a number line, if two numbers are an equal distance from 0, then the numbers must be equal.
   c. Every point on the real number line corresponds to an irrational number.

3. **Choose** any rational number. Then write an inequality comparing it with each number below.
   a. your rational number doubled
   b. your rational number squared
   c. your rational number multiplied by an irrational number
4. **Make a conjecture** about the solution set for the inequality in Example 3. How would this set change if the $>$ sign were changed to $\geq$?

MODELING MATHEMATICS

5. Use dot paper to model the numbers $4\sqrt{2}$ and $\sqrt{18}$. (*Note:* A geoboard will be too small.) Write an inequality comparing the two numbers.

Guided Practice

Find a rational approximation for each irrational number to the nearest whole number and to the nearest tenth without using a calculator.

6. $\sqrt{33}$
7. $\sqrt{50}$

Use a calculator to find a rational approximation for each irrational number to the nearest hundredth.

8. $\sqrt{78.1}$
9. $3\sqrt{22}$

Replace each ___?___ with <, >, or = to make each sentence true.

10. 8 ___?___ $\sqrt{62}$
11. $45\frac{2}{11}$ ___?___ $45.\overline{18}$
12. $\frac{1}{7}$ ___?___ $\sqrt{\frac{1}{7}}$
13. For what values of b is $\frac{1}{\sqrt{b}} < b$ true: $-1, 1, 4$?
14. **Construction** The glass of window A lets in $\frac{9}{10}$ of the total sunlight. The glass of window B lets in $\sqrt{\frac{9}{10}}$ of the total sunlight. Which window lets in more sunlight?

EXERCISES

Practice

Find a rational approximation for each irrational number to the nearest whole number and to the nearest tenth without using a calculator.

15. $\sqrt{3}$
16. $\sqrt{15}$
17. $\sqrt{46}$
18. $\sqrt{72}$
19. $3\sqrt{21}$
20. $2\sqrt{11}$

Use a calculator to find a rational approximation for each irrational number to the nearest hundredth.

21. $\sqrt{20.6}$
22. $\sqrt{99}$
23. $7\sqrt{54}$
24. $5\sqrt{38}$
25. $\frac{\sqrt{6}}{42}$
26. $\frac{42}{\sqrt{6}}$

Replace each ___?___ with <, >, or = to make each sentence true.

27. $\frac{1}{6}$ ___?___ $\sqrt{6}$
28. 0.3 ___?___ $\frac{1}{3}$
29. $\frac{2}{9}$ ___?___ $0.\overline{2}$
30. $\frac{3}{\sqrt{9}}$ ___?___ $\frac{3}{9}$
31. $4\frac{1}{2}$ ___?___ $4\sqrt{2}$
32. $5.\overline{72}$ ___?___ $\sqrt{5}$
33. π ___?___ 3.141
34. $\frac{1}{\sqrt{31}}$ ___?___ $\frac{\sqrt{31}}{31}$
35. $\sqrt{10}$ ___?___ $\frac{1}{\sqrt{10}}$

For what values of n is $n^2 > \sqrt{n} > \frac{1}{\sqrt{n}}$ true?

36. $-1, 0, 3$ **37.** $\frac{1}{9}, \frac{1}{2}, 9$ **38.** $2, 4, 8$

Write the numbers in each set in order from least to greatest.

39. $\frac{1}{8}, \sqrt{\frac{1}{8}}, 0.\overline{15}, -15$ **40.** $\sqrt{30}, 5\frac{4}{9}, 13, \frac{1}{\sqrt{30}}$ **41.** $-1.4\overline{6}, 0.2, \sqrt{2}, -\frac{1}{6}$

Graph each set of numbers on a number line.

42. $\sqrt{12}, 4\frac{7}{9}, 1.\overline{1}$ **43.** $13\frac{1}{13}, \sqrt{121}, \frac{47}{\sqrt{10}}$ **44.** $-\sqrt{65}, -6\frac{2}{5}, -3\sqrt{3}$

45. A square has an area of 45 square centimeters. Find the length of a side of the square to the nearest hundredth.

46. Find three values for a that make the inequality $-\sqrt{a} < -\frac{1}{\sqrt{a}}$ true.

Applications and Problem Solving

47. Geometry Find the perimeter of the figure at the right to the nearest hundredth.

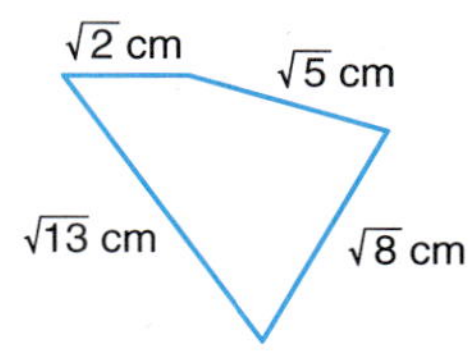

48. Law Enforcement Police use a formula to estimate the speed of a car by measuring the skid marks left on the road. Robert skidded on the wet pavement trying to stop for a red light and caused a minor accident. He told the police officer that he was only driving the speed limit, 35 miles per hour. The police officer measured his skid marks and found that his speed was actually $\sqrt{1026}$ miles per hour. Should the officer give Robert a ticket for speeding? Explain.

49. Sports Major league fastballs can travel over 100 miles per hour. A pitcher throws a baseball that reaches the batter in $\sqrt{\frac{36}{170}}$ second. His second pitch takes $\sqrt{\frac{36}{250}}$ second to reach the batter.

a. Without using a calculator, determine which pitch was faster.

b. Use a calculator to find the difference in the times to the nearest hundredth.

50. Carpentry Joanna and her father are building a bay window for their house. As a support beam, they need a board that measures $3\sqrt{2}$ feet. If they already have a piece of wood that measures 5 feet, will they be able to use it? Explain your answer.

51. Meteorology Meteorologists use the formula $t^2 = \frac{d^3}{216}$ to estimate the amount of time that a storm will last. In this formula, t is the time in hours and d is the diameter of the storm. Suppose that the eye of a hurricane, which causes the greatest amount of destruction, is about 10 miles wide. To the nearest hour, how long will the worst part of the storm last?

52. Physical Science The time it takes for a falling object to cover a certain distance is given by the equation $t = \sqrt{\frac{d}{16}}$ where t is in seconds and d is in feet. If Sally dropped an egg from a window 30 feet above the ground, how long would it take to hit the ground, to the nearest hundredth of a second?

Critical Thinking

53. Determine when the statements $q^2 > r^2$, $\frac{1}{q} < \frac{1}{r}$, $\sqrt{q} > \sqrt{r}$, and $\frac{1}{\sqrt{q}} < \frac{1}{\sqrt{r}}$ are all true for real numbers q and r.

New York

2

Line Graphs and Histograms

Use after Lesson 3–7, Glencoe ***Algebra 1***

What YOU'LL LEARN

- To describe and compare data using broken-line graphs, frequency tables, and histograms.

Why IT'S IMPORTANT

Using frequency tables to make line graphs and histograms will help you to better organize and analyze data recorded from surveys.

APPLICATION
Traffic Control

A new supermarket was built on the corner of High and Oak Streets. The city is considering replacing the stop signs with a traffic light if the number of vehicles passing through the intersection exceeds 20 in a given hour. When is the intersection the busiest? For what hours is a traffic light unnecessary?

To answer these questions, someone must first collect and then record the data. A simple and organized method is to use a **frequency table**. The frequency table below shows the number of vehicles that pass through the intersection each hour for 24 hours beginning at midnight.

The hour 0:00 represents the time between midnight and 1:00 A.M.

Hour	Number of Vehicles	Hour	Number of Vehicles
0:00 (Midnight)	3	12:00 (Noon)	32
1:00	1	13:00	22
2:00	0	14:00	15
3:00	1	15:00	16
4:00	0	16:00	15
5:00	0	17:00	22
6:00	3	18:00	26
7:00	5	19:00	20
8:00	24	20:00	10
9:00	21	21:00	8
10:00	21	22:00	7
11:00	27	23:00	5
		Total Frequency = 304 vehicles	

From the frequency table, you can see that the intersection is the busiest at noon. You can also see that there is probably no need for a traffic light on the intervals 0:00–7:00, 14:00–16:00, and 20:00–23:00 hours. From these results, the city should install the traffic light and have it operating from 8:00 to 20:00 hours, or 8:00 A.M.–8:00 P.M.

You can easily see changes in data using a **line graph**, sometimes called a **broken line graph**. Line graphs usually show how values change over time. The line graph below shows the data from the frequency table.

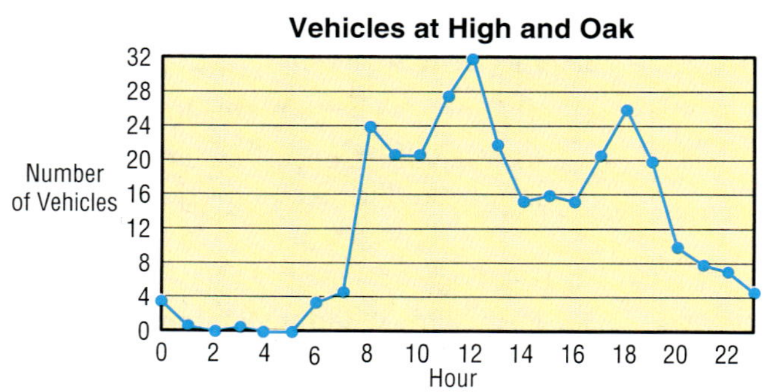

Example 1

APPLICATION
Sales

Mr. Michaels is a sales representative. He recorded how many cars he sold each month in the frequency table shown at the right.

Month	Number of Cars Sold
Jan.	𝍸 IIII
Feb.	III
Mar.	
Apr.	I
May	II
June	𝍸
July	III
Aug.	𝍸 II
Sept.	𝍸 I
Oct.	III
Nov.	IIII
Dec.	𝍸𝍸 II

a. Construct a broken line graph from the data.
b. In what month did Mr. Michaels have the most sales? the least?
c. Between what two months was the greatest change in sales?
d. For what months did Mr. Michaels have an equal number of sales?

a. First, draw a horizontal axis and a vertical axis. Label the axes as shown. Be sure to include the title, Cars Sold, 1999. Then plot the points.

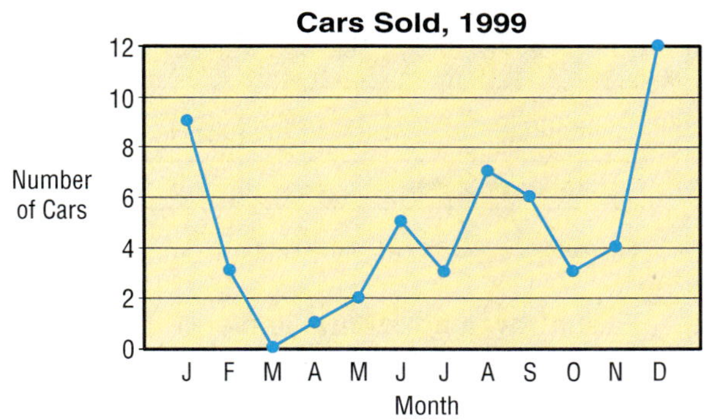

b. Mr. Michaels had the most sales in December and the least in March.

c. Since the segment connecting the data points for November and December is the longest, the greatest change in sales was between these two months.

d. There were an equal number of sales during February, July, and October.

We can use data from frequency tables with intervals of 1 to find measures of central tendency.

Example 2

APPLICATION
Health

Twenty-four students in a health class took a survey reporting how many glasses of water they drank daily. The data was organized in the frequency table shown at the right. Find the mode, the median, and the mean.

Glasses of Water	Number of Students
0	𝍸
1	IIII
2	III
3	𝍸 IIII
4	II
5	
6	
7	
8	I

To find the mode, look for the interval containing the greatest frequency. The greatest number of students, 9, drink three glasses of water a day. Thus, the mode is 3.

To find the median, order the data from least to greatest and record the middle value.

Glasses of Water:
0, 0, 0, 0, 0, 1, 1, 1, 1, 2, 2, 2, 3, 3, 3, 3, 3, 3, 3, 3, 3, 4, 4, 8

Median $= \frac{2+3}{2}$

Since there is an even number of data, the middle value falls between the numbers 2 and 3. Therefore, the median is 2.5.

(continued on the next page)

To find the mean, sum the data and divide by the number of terms.

$$\text{mean} = \frac{\text{total number of glasses}}{\text{number of students}}$$

$$= \frac{8(1) + 7(0) + 6(0) + 5(0) + 4(2) + 3(9) + 2(3) + 1(4) + 0(5)}{24}$$

$$= \frac{53}{24} \text{ or about } 2.21$$

The mean is a little over 2 glasses of water a day.

Another type of graph used to compare numerical data is a **histogram**. A histogram is a bar graph where the data is organized into equal intervals. The entire range of data is covered with no overlapping intervals.

Example 3 APPLICATION Earth Science

The frequency table below shows the number of states whose highest altitude falls within the given intervals. Make a histogram from the data.

Highest Altitude					
Altitude (ft)	0–4999	5000–9999	10,000–14,999	15,000–19,999	20,000–24,999
Number of States	30	8	11	0	1

Source: *The World Almanac*, 1998

First, draw a horizontal and vertical axis. Label the axes as shown. Be sure to include the title, Highest Altitude.

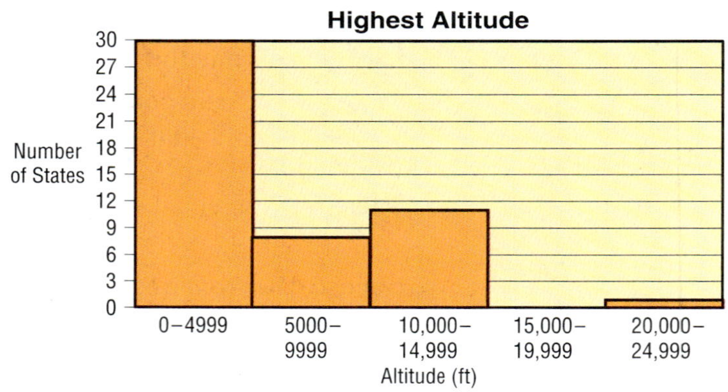

- Equal intervals of 5000 are shown along the horizontal axis.
- Since the intervals are equal, the bar widths are also equal.
- The frequency of data in each interval is represented by the bar height.
- Intervals with a frequency of 0, like 15,000–19,999, have no bar.

CHECK FOR UNDERSTANDING

Communicating Mathematics

Study the lesson. Then complete the following.

1. **Describe** the advantages of using a line graph or histogram rather than a frequency table to display data.
2. **Explain** why you must use equal intervals when making graphs.
3. **Model** the data from Example 2 by making a line graph and histogram. Which type of graph do you think is better for displaying the data. Why?

Guided Practice

4. **Environment** The line graph at the right shows the amount of pollution emitted from 1988–1995.

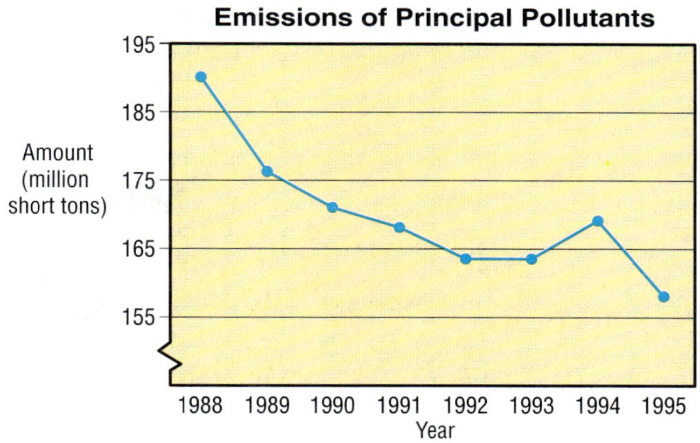

Source: *The World Almanac*, 1998

   a. In which year were the least pollutants emitted?

   b. Between which two years do you find the greatest decrease in pollutants?

   c. Estimate the total amount of pollutants emitted from 1988 to 1995.

5. The frequency table at the right shows the number of movies a sample of 16-year-old students watch per month.

Movie Mania	
Movies per Month	**Number of Students**
1	2
2	6
3	18
4	40
5	12
6	8

   a. Make a histogram from the data.

   b. How many students were in the sample?

   c. Find the mean, median, and mode number of movies this sample of 16-year-old students watch.

   d. How do you think the results would change if the sample was taken at a movie theater?

EXERCISES

Practice

6. A meteorologist was researching temperature fluctuations in a city. The average temperatures recorded for seven days are shown below.

Average Temperatures							
Day	1	2	3	4	5	6	7
Temperature (°F)	37	35	42	40	42	47	48

   a. Construct a line graph from the data.

   b. What is the lowest temperature recorded?

   c. What is the highest temperature recorded?

   d. Between which two days is the greatest change in temperature?

   e. Find the mean, median, and mode of the temperatures.

7. The frequency table at the right shows the number of employees at each salary for a small firm.

Annual Pay	
Salary (dollars)	**Number of Employees**
30,000–39,999	20
40,000–49,999	8
50,000–59,999	4

   a. How large is each interval?

   b. How many employees work for the firm?

   c. What is the mode salary?

   d. Make a histogram from the data.

   e. Is it possible to determine from the histogram how many employees make more than $55,000? Explain.

8. The average times that 18 students spend completing math homework are shown below.

Homework Time (minutes)

35	45	60	45	35	40	30	45	60
35	35	60	45	45	30	35	45	35

   a. Choose intervals of time and make a frequency table of the data. Explain how you chose the interval size.
   b. Make a histogram using your frequency table from part a.
   c. What conclusions can you draw from your graph?
   d. How would doubling the size of the intervals affect the histogram?

Applications and Problem Solving

9. **History** The North Atlantic Treaty Organization (NATO) was formed shortly after WWII by independent nations that made a commitment to maintain peace and defend one another. The span of years in which each member nation entered NATO is shown at the right. Make a histogram from the data.

NATO Entry

Year	Number of Nations
1949–1965	15
1966–1982	1
1983–1999	3

Source: NATO home page

10. **Education** The line graph at the right shows the number of people enrolled in higher education from 1985–1995.

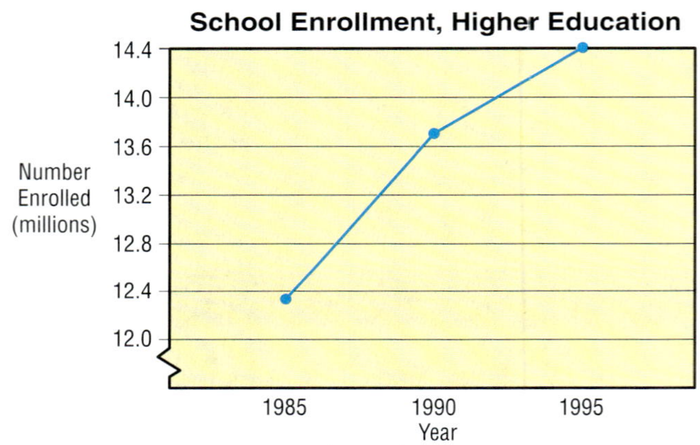

Source: U.S. National Center for Education Statistics

   a. Estimate the change in enrollment between 1985 and 1990.
   b. Estimate the change in enrollment between 1990 and 1995.
   c. If this rate of growth continues, estimate the number of people enrolled in higher education by the year 2000.

11. **Physical Science** In lab, a group of three students made their own equal arm balance scale for weighing objects. The group weighed a nickel ten times and recorded their results (in grams) as shown below.

3.213	3.212	3.212	3.210	3.215
3.210	3.214	3.212	3.211	3.211

   a. Construct a frequency table for the values above with an interval 0.001.
   b. What is the mean weight for the nickel?
   c. Which value is the greatest distance from the mean?
   d. The difference between the value found in part c and the mean is called the *uncertainty*. The actual weight of the nickel lies in the range of values: mean ± uncertainty. What is the range for the nickel's weight?

Critical Thinking

12. Study the information in the table for Exercise 9. How many nations formed NATO in 1949? Explain your answer.

New York

2B Graphing Technology
Making Statistical Graphs

An Extension of Math A Lesson 2, Glencoe ***Algebra 1***

You can use a graphing calculator to create both line graphs and histograms. However, before entering any data to graph, you must clear the statistical memory by pressing STAT 4 2nd L1 2nd L2 ENTER.

Example 1 **Use a graphing calculator to construct a broken line graph from the data on vehicle sales.**

New Vehicle Sales (in millions)						
Year	1992	1993	1994	1995	1996	1997
Sales	12.9	13.9	15.2	15.2	15.5	15.4

Source: U.S. Bureau of Economic Analysis, 1997

First, set your viewing window to [1992, 1997] by [10, 16] with a scale factor of 1 on both axes.

Now enter the data into the memory and draw the graph.

Enter: STAT ENTER *Accesses statistical lists.*

1992 ENTER ... 1997 ENTER *Enters years in L_1.*

▶ 12.9 ENTER ... 15.4 *Enters sales in L_2.*

Choose the type of statistical plot you would like to create.

Enter: 2nd STAT PLOT ENTER *Accesses menu for first statistical graph.*

Use the arrow and ENTER keys to highlight your selections for the graph. Select "On," the line graph icon, "L1" as the Xlist, "L2" as the Ylist, and "•" for the marks.

To create the graph, press GRAPH.

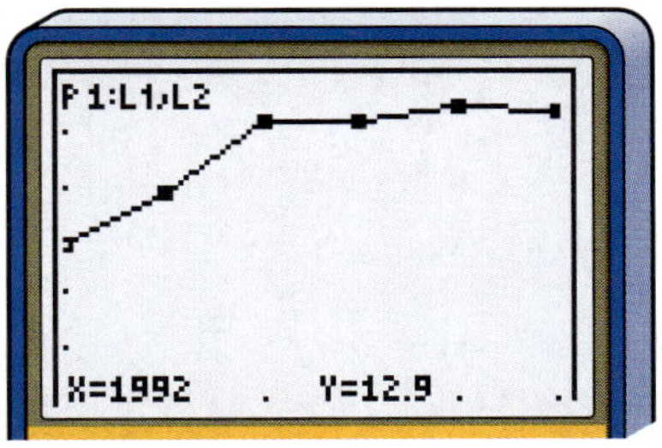

Example 2 **Use a graphing calculator to create a histogram of the number of people enrolled in college for each state.**

APPLICATION
Education

Number of People Enrolled in Colleges by State (in thousands)									
219	29	277	101	1883	243	155	45	31	641
318	61	60	721	286	177	172	178	204	56
261	410	547	275	126	291	43	119	73	64
328	104	1028	373	41	538	177	165	622	72
174	35	247	955	152	35	354	292	86	299

Source: U.S. National Center for Education Statistics, 1996

(continued on the next page)

When you set the viewing window for a histogram, you determine the number of bars (equal intervals) you want to graph. Use the values [0, 2000] by [0, 26] with a scale factor of 200 on the x-axis and 2 on the y-axis. This setting will create 2000 ÷ 200 or 10 bars. The histogram will show the number of states for a given college enrollment.

Now enter the data into the memory and draw the graph.

Enter: STAT ENTER *Accesses statistical lists.*

219 ENTER 29 ENTER 277 ENTER ... 299 ENTER

Enter: 2nd STAT PLOT ENTER *Accesses menu for statistical graph.*

Use the arrow and ENTER keys to highlight "On," the histogram icon, "L1" as the Xlist, and "1" as the frequency.

Press GRAPH to view the histogram.

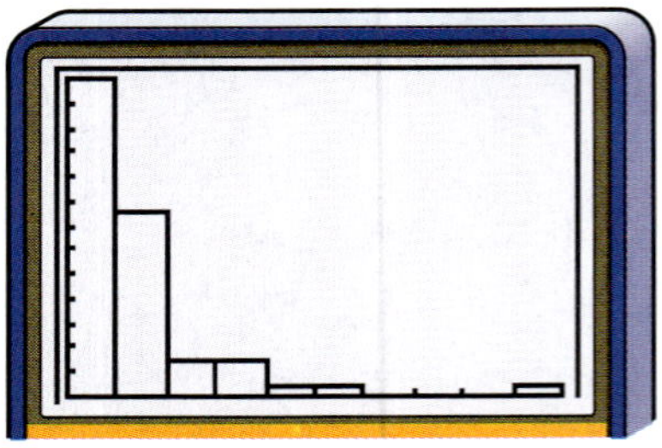

EXERCISES

1. **Tennis** Andre Agassi won the US Open at Shea Stadium in 1999, making him the #1 men's singles tennis player in the world. The table below shows how Agassi's year-end rank fluctuated throughout the 1990s.

Year-End Ranking History									
1990	1991	1992	1993	1994	1995	1996	1997	1998	1999
4	10	9	24	2	2	8	110	6	1

   a. Use a graphing calculator to create a broken line graph from the data.
   b. In which year was Agassi ranked the lowest?
   c. Find Agassi's mode, median, and mean rank.
   d. Explain which measure of central tendency best describes his rank.

2. The table below shows each state's population for the year 1997.

State Populations (in millions)									
32.3	19.4	18.1	14.7	12.0	11.9	9.8	8.1	7.5	6.7
11.2	0.5	1.0	1.7	1.7	2.7	2.9	4.4	5.1	6.1
7.4	0.6	0.9	1.2	1.2	2.6	3.3	4.3	4.7	5.9
5.6	0.6	0.7	1.2	1.2	2.5	3.3	3.9	4.6	5.4
3.2	0.6	0.7	1.7	1.8	2.1	3.8	3.9	5.2	5.4

   a. Use a graphing calculator to create a histogram showing the number of states for a given population.
   b. If a range of values for a histogram is 35 and you want to create 7 bars, what scale factor should you enter? Explain.
   c. Press the TRACE key. The right and left arrow keys allow you to find the frequency of each interval. How many states have populations between 5 and 10 million?

New York

3

Cumulative Frequency and Percentiles

Use after Lesson 5–7, Glencoe ***Algebra 1***

APPLICATION

Testing

What YOU'LL LEARN

- To describe and compare data using cumulative frequency tables, histograms, and percentiles.

Why IT'S IMPORTANT

Using cumulative frequencies to make percentiles will help you to compare data such as standardized test scores and salaries.

A student's score on the SAT is one factor that colleges look at when selecting applicants. The SAT contains a verbal section and a mathematics section. The highest possible score on each section is 800, and the lowest is 200. Colleges may not look at the *raw score*, but rather the **percentile** to make comparisons. Your percentile indicates what percent of all test-takers scored just as well or lower than you.

The teachers in the math department at a certain high school wanted to better prepare their students for the SAT. They administered a sample math SAT test to 160 juniors. The grades were recorded to make the frequency table shown at the right. What score is needed to be in the 90th percentile? *This problem will be solved in Example 2.*

Frequency Table	
Math SAT Scores	Number of Students
201–300	2
301–400	19
401–500	44
501–600	55
601–700	32
701–800	8

From the frequency table above, you can see that 44 students scored in the interval 401–500. How many students scored 500 or less on the sample SAT test? One way to find this answer is to create a **cumulative frequency table**. The cumulative frequency for each interval is the sum of the frequency for that interval and all preceding frequencies.

Cumulative Frequency Table		
Math SAT Scores	Number of Students	Cumulative Number of Students
201–300	2	2
301–400	19	21
401–500	44	65
501–600	55	120
601–700	32	152
701–800	8	160

You can use a **cumulative frequency histogram** to display the data. Equal intervals of 100 are shown on the horizontal axis. The bar height is equal to the cumulative frequency of the data in each interval.

Sample Math SAT Test Scores

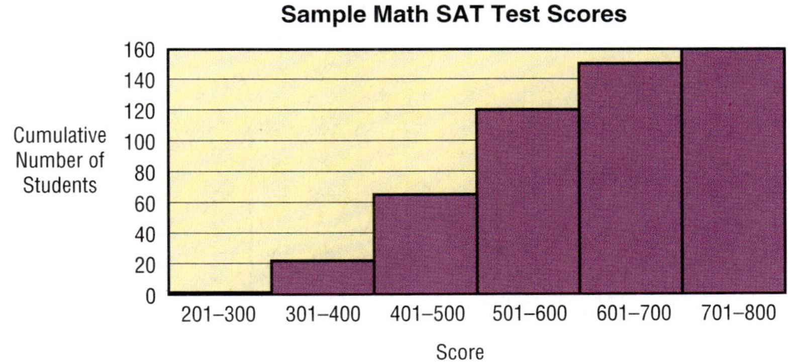

From the cumulative frequency table and histogram, you can see that 65 out of 160 students scored at or below 500.

Example 1

APPLICATION

History

The United Nations (UN) was formed at the end of World War II to maintain international peace and security. The span of years in which each member nation entered the UN is shown in the frequency table. Make a cumulative frequency table and histogram from the data.

United Nations Entry					
Year	1945–1954	1955–1964	1965–1974	1975–1984	1985–1994
Nations	59	55	21	21	29

Source: United Nations home page

Year	Cumulative Number of Nations
1945–1954	59
1955–1964	114
1965–1974	135
1975–1984	156
1985–1994	185

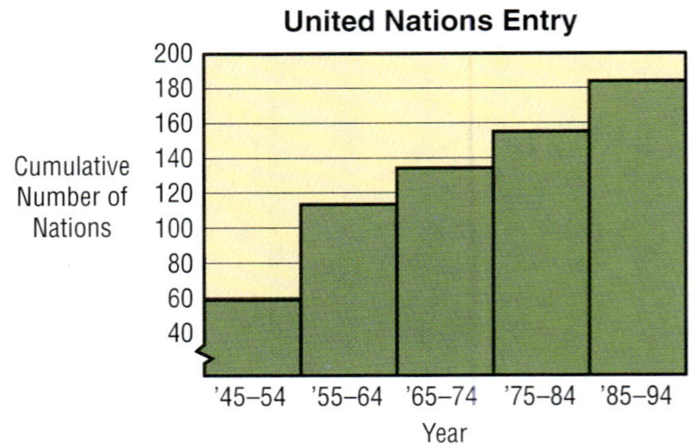

- From 1945 to 1954, 59 nations had entered the UN.
- Through 1964, 59 + 55 or 114 nations had entered.
- Through 1974, 114 + 21 or 135 nations had entered.
- Through 1984, 135 + 21 or 156 nations had entered.
- Through 1994, 156 + 29 or 185 nations had entered.

To calculate and show percentiles, replace the cumulative frequency scale with a percent scale.

Example 2

APPLICATION

Testing

Refer to the application at the beginning of the lesson. Use the cumulative frequency table and histogram to find the score needed to place in the 90th percentile.

Construct a cumulative histogram. Add percentiles to the vertical scale.

- Since 160 represents the total number of students taking the sample SAT test, 100% corresponds with 160.
- Similarly, since 0 students score less than 200, 0% corresponds with 0.
- Label the scale as 25%, 50%, and 75%, representing the four quartiles.

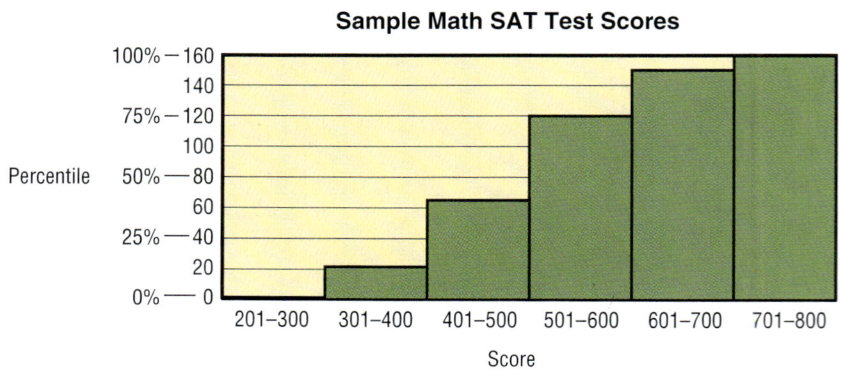

LOOK BACK

You can refer to Lesson 4-4 for more information on using proportions to solve percent problems.

Now find the score needed to place in the 90th percentile. Using the histogram, move up along the vertical axis to the 90th percentile. Then move right on the horizontal axis to find the score. You can estimate that the student needs to score higher than 600. For a more accurate answer, use a proportion to calculate 90% of the total number of students.

$\frac{s}{160} = \frac{90}{100}$ *Let s represent the number of students.*

$100s = 14{,}400$ *Cross multiply.*

$s = 144$ *Divide each side by 100.*

To be in the 90th percentile, the student must score higher than 144 other test-takers out of 160. This places the student's score in the interval 601–700.

CHECK FOR UNDERSTANDING

Communicating Mathematics

Study the lesson. Then complete the following.

1. **Explain** when you would use a frequency table versus a cumulative frequency table.
2. **Describe** the relationship between percentiles and the median.
3. **You Decide** Lionel took a standardized test and scored in the 78th percentile. He told Mia that about 78% of the other test-takers received the same score as he did. Mia said that scoring in the 78th percentile meant he answered 78% of the questions correctly. Who is correct? Explain.

Guided Practice

4. The frequency table at the right shows the age distribution for 20 girls on a high school dance team.

Age	Frequency
14	I
15	III
16	~~IIII~~ II
17	~~IIII~~
18	IIII

   a. Make a cumulative frequency table from the data.
   b. How many girls are at most 15 years old?
   c. How many girls are at least 17 years old?
   d. What is the median age?

5. **Economics** The cumulative frequency table below shows the approximate number of American households at each income interval.

Income of 4-Person Households				
Income (dollars)	under 25,000	25,000–49,999	50,000–74,999	75,000+
Cumulative Number of Households (millions)	3	7.5	11.5	15

Source: *Current Population Reports*, 1997

   a. Make a cumulative histogram from the data showing percentiles.
   b. About how many households participated in this survey?
   c. How many households had an income between \$50,000 and \$74,999?
   d. In which interval would you find the median income?
   e. What percent of households have an income less than \$25,000?

EXERCISES

Practice

6. The cumulative frequency histogram below shows the number of hours each week a sample of 500 students spend exercising.

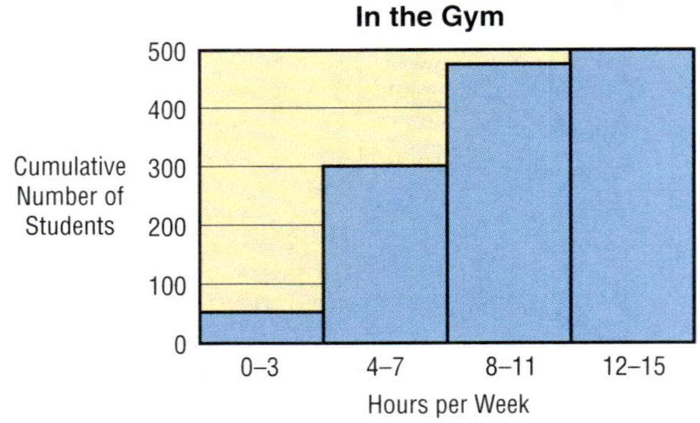

   a. How many students exercise 7 hours or less?

   b. What percent of students taking the survey exercise 7 hours or less?

   c. In which interval would you find the lower quartile? The upper quartile?

7. The frequency table below shows the number of states that entered the United States during the given interval of years.

America's Expansion						
Year	1780–1809	1810–1839	1840–1869	1870–1899	1900–1929	1930–1959
Number of States	17	9	11	8	3	2

   a. Make a cumulative frequency table from the data.

   b. How many states entered the United States before 1870?

   c. From the cumulative frequency table, show how you can find the number of states that entered the United States between 1870 and 1929. Find that number and check your answer using the frequency table above.

   d. What percent of the eventual number of states had been added when New York entered the United States as the 11th state, July 26, 1788?

8. The standardized test scores (out of 100) from a sample of 36 students are shown below.

56	82	76	75	87	86	68	76	74	94	96	86
78	72	85	73	59	85	75	96	78	80	98	74
70	60	88	72	64	92	87	76	76	87	84	63

   a. Make a cumulative frequency histogram from the data showing percentiles.

   b. In what interval is the median?

   c. What score would you need to be in the 75th percentile?

   d. Maria's 9th grade class of 240 students took the same standardized test. She scored 83, placing her in the 75th percentile. How many students in Maria's class have scores less than or equal to her score?

   e. How does Maria's score of 83 in the 75th percentile compare to a sample score in the 75th percentile?

   f. How would you characterize the performance of Maria's class in comparison with the sample? Explain your answer.

Applications and Problem Solving

9. Statistics The table shows the cumulative percent distribution of people in the United States by height.

a. What percent of heights are 5′8″ or less for men? For women?

b. Estimate the median heights for men and women.

c. In what interval is the upper quartile for women? Explain what this means.

Height Under	Cumulative Percent of Men (20–29 years)	Cumulative Percent of Women (20–29 years)
4′8″	0	0.6
5′	0.1	6.0
5′2″	0.5	21.8
5′4″	3.4	48.9
5′6″	11.7	74.0
5′8″	32.0	92.4
5′10″	58.7	98.6
6′	81.2	100
6′+	100	100

Source: U.S. National Center for Health Statistics

10. Travel The cumulative frequency histogram below shows the number of overseas travelers that visited New York from 1994 to 1998.

a. What was the total number of overseas visitors from 1994 to 1998?

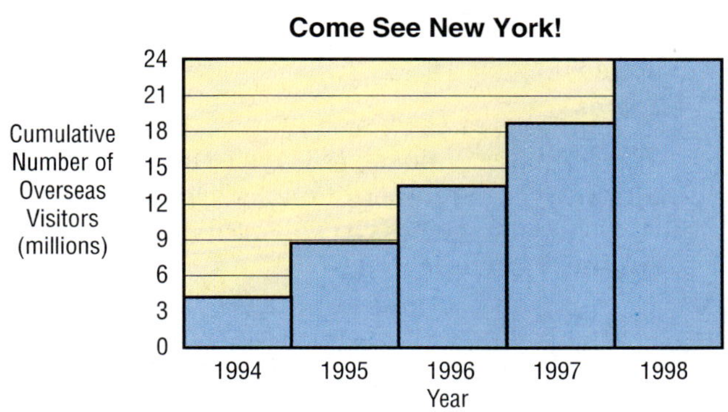

Source: U.S. Department of Commerce

b. Estimate the number of overseas visitors before 1996.

c. Compare your estimate in part b to an estimate of the number of overseas visitors after 1996.

d. Estimate the number of overseas visitors during the year 1996.

11. Government The cumulative frequency table at the right shows the number of New Yorkers who voted in the 1996 presidential election.

Age (years)	Cumulative Number of Voters (millions)
18–24	0.5
25–44	3.0
45–64	5.3
65+	6.8

Source: U.S. Bureau of the Census

a. How many total votes were cast from New York state?

b. How many voters were at least 45 years old?

c. About what percent of the total votes did those aged 18 to 24 cast?

d. If about 19.4 million New Yorkers were registered to vote, what percent of those did vote?

Critical Thinking

12. Jobs *The Occupational Outlook Handbook* compiled by the U.S. Department of Labor is an annual summary of careers with their educational requirements, future employment needs, and earnings. In 1996, the median salary for underwriters was $31,400. The middle 50% earned between $24,000 and $41,000. The handbook also reported that the bottom 10% of underwriters earned less than $18,400 while the top 10% earned at least $52,400.

a. Name the salaries for the 10th, 25th, 50th, 75th, and 90th percentiles.

b. If you were an underwriter earning 63% more than all other underwriters, estimate your salary. Can you determine the exact salary? Explain.

FYI

Some underwriters work for insurance companies analyzing risk, setting rates, and writing policies.

New York

4

Permutations and Combinations

Use after Lesson 7–5, Glencoe ***Algebra 1***

What YOU'LL LEARN

- To determine probabilities using permutations and combinations.

Why IT'S IMPORTANT

You can use permutations and combinations to solve problems involving business and sports.

APPLICATION

Business

An entrepreneur designed a strip mall with 7 different-sized stores. Ten small businesses have shown interest in the mall, and the entrepreneur must decide which business would be best for each store. How many different arrangements are possible?

For the first store, Store A, the entrepreneur can choose one of 10 businesses. There are 9 businesses left to choose for Store B, and so on. One way to organize this problem is to make a *decision chart.* In this case, there are seven decisions to be made, one decision for each store.

Store	A	B	C	D	E	F	G
Number of Choices	10	9	8	7	6	5	4

The number of possible ways to arrange the businesses can be found by multiplying the number of choices for each store: $10 \cdot 9 \cdot 8 \cdot 7 \cdot 6 \cdot 5 \cdot 4 =$ 604,800 arrangements. To solve this problem, we used the **Fundamental Counting Principle**.

Fundamental Counting Principle	**If event *M* can occur in *m* ways and is followed by event *N* that can occur in *n* ways, then the event *M* followed by the event *N* can occur in $m \cdot n$ ways.**

The businesses are in a specific order, so each arrangement is unique. An arrangement or listing in which order is important is called a **permutation**. The symbol ${}_{10}P_7$ denotes the number of permutations in arranging 10 businesses in 7 stores.

$$\begin{aligned}{}_{10}P_7 &= 10 \cdot 9 \cdot 8 \cdot 7 \cdot 6 \cdot 5 \cdot 4 && \text{ways to arrange 10 objects, 7 at a time}\\ &= 10 \cdot 9 \cdot 8 \cdot 7 \cdot 6 \cdot 5 \cdot 4 \cdot \frac{3 \cdot 2 \cdot 1}{3 \cdot 2 \cdot 1} && \frac{3 \cdot 2 \cdot 1}{3 \cdot 2 \cdot 1} = 1\\ &= \frac{10 \cdot 9 \cdot 8 \cdot 7 \cdot 6 \cdot 5 \cdot 4 \cdot 3 \cdot 2 \cdot 1}{3 \cdot 2 \cdot 1}\end{aligned}$$

For all positive integer values of n, n factorial or $n! = n \cdot (n-1) \cdot (n-2) \cdot (n-3) \cdot \ldots \cdot 2 \cdot 1$.

We can simplify the expression in the fraction above using **factorials**.

$$\frac{10 \cdot 9 \cdot 8 \cdot 7 \cdot 6 \cdot 5 \cdot 4 \cdot 3 \cdot 2 \cdot 1}{3 \cdot 2 \cdot 1} = \frac{10!}{3!} \quad \begin{matrix}\leftarrow \text{ten factorial}\\ \leftarrow \text{three factorial}\end{matrix}$$

$${}_{10}P_7 = \frac{10 \cdot 9 \cdot 8 \cdot 7 \cdot 6 \cdot 5 \cdot 4 \cdot 3 \cdot 2 \cdot 1}{3 \cdot 2 \cdot 1} \text{ or } \frac{10!}{3!}$$

In general, ${}_nP_r$ is used to denote the number of permutations of n objects taken r at a time. The formal definition is stated below.

Definition of ${}_nP_r$	**The number of permutations of *n* objects taken *r* at a time is defined as follows.** $${}_nP_r = \frac{n!}{(n-r)!}$$

Example 1

APPLICATION

Employment

The manager of a fast-food chain needs to hire a cashier and a drive-through coordinator. Katie, Bob, Alicia, and Jeremiah all applied for a job. How many possible ways are there for the manager to place the applicants?

A *tree diagram* shows that there are 12 possible arrangements.

Cashier	Drive-Through Coordinator	Outcomes
Katie (K)	Bob	KB
	Alicia	KA
	Jeremiah	KJ
Bob (B)	Katie	BK
	Alicia	BA
	Jeremiah	BJ
Alicia (A)	Jeremiah	AJ
	Katie	AK
	Bob	AB
Jeremiah (J)	Katie	JK
	Bob	JB
	Alicia	JA

An easier method for finding the number of arrangements is to use the definition to find the number of permutations of 4 applicants, taken 2 at a time.

$${}_nP_r = \frac{n!}{(n-r)!}$$ *Definition of permutation*

$${}_4P_2 = \frac{4!}{(4-2)!}$$ *Replace n with 4 and r with 2.*

$${}_4P_2 = \frac{4 \cdot 3 \cdot 2 \cdot 1}{2 \cdot 1} \text{ or } 12$$ *$4! = 4 \cdot 3 \cdot 2 \cdot 1$; $(4-2)! = 2! = 2 \cdot 1$*

There are 12 ways in which the manager can place the 4 applicants in 2 different jobs.

You can also use permutations to find the probability of events occurring.

Example 2

Brett cannot remember the correct order of the five digits in his security code to open his garage door. He does remember that the number code contains the digits 1, 6, 7, 8, 9.

a. How many different codes are possible?

b. What is the probability that the first two digits of the code are even numbers?

a. Since the order of the numbers in the code is important, this situation is a permutation. Find the number of permutations of 5 digits, taken 5 at a time.

$${}_nP_r = \frac{n!}{(n-r)!}$$ *Definition of permutation*

$${}_5P_5 = \frac{5!}{(5-5)!}$$ *Replace n with 5 and r with 5.*

$${}_5P_5 = \frac{5 \cdot 4 \cdot 3 \cdot 2 \cdot 1}{1} \text{ or } 120$$ *By definition, $0! = 1$.*

There are 120 possible codes with the digits 1, 6, 7, 8, and 9.

(continued on the next page)

b. Now find the number of ways in which the first and second digits are even. Use a decision chart to organize this information.

Digit	First	Second	Third	Fourth	Fifth
Number of Choices	2 (even)	1 (even)	3 (odd)	2 (odd)	1 (odd)

Using the Fundamental Counting Principle, we find the number of ways this event can occur is $2 \cdot 1 \cdot 3 \cdot 2 \cdot 1$ or 12. So, there are 12 ways for this event to occur out of 120 possible permutations.

$$P(\text{even, even, odd, odd, odd}) = \frac{12}{120} \quad \begin{matrix} \leftarrow \text{number of favorable outcomes} \\ \leftarrow \text{total number of possible outcomes} \end{matrix}$$

$$= \frac{1}{10}$$

The probability that the first two digits are both even is $\frac{1}{10}$.

Suppose a florist has 10 different flowers and you choose 3 to put in a vase. It does not matter whether you choose (daisy, rose, tulip), (tulip, daisy, rose), or (rose, daisy, tulip). These are 3 different permutations, but all the same **combination**. A combination is an arrangement or listing in which order *does not* matter. There is a quick way to find the number of combinations of 10 flowers, taken 3 at a time. Divide the number of permutations, ${}_{10}P_3$, by the number of ways 3 flowers can be arranged, which is 3!.

$${}_{10}C_3 = \frac{{}_{10}P_3}{3!} \qquad \textit{Dividing by 3! eliminates the outcomes that are the same.}$$

$$= \frac{10!}{(10-3)! \cdot 3!} \text{ or 120 combinations}$$

These results are formally stated in the following definition.

Definition of ${}_nC_r$	**The number of combinations of *n* distinct objects taken *r* at a time is defined as follows.** $${}_nC_r = \frac{n!}{(n-r)!r!}$$

Example 3

APPLICATION

Dining

With her dinner entrée, Eri has a choice of two side items from the list at the right. How many ways can she select two different items?

Side Items	
French fries	mixed vegetables
baked potato	applesauce
cole slaw	baked beans

Since order does not matter, we must find the number of combinations.

$${}_nC_r = \frac{n!}{(n-r)!r!} \qquad \textit{Definition of combination}$$

$${}_6C_2 = \frac{6!}{(6-2)! \cdot 2!} \qquad \textit{Replace n with 6 and r with 2.}$$

$$= \frac{6 \cdot 5 \cdot \cancel{4} \cdot \cancel{3} \cdot \cancel{2} \cdot \cancel{1}}{\cancel{4} \cdot \cancel{3} \cdot \cancel{2} \cdot \cancel{1} \cdot 2 \cdot 1} \qquad 6! = 6 \cdot 5 \cdot 4 \cdot 3 \cdot 2 \cdot 1;\ (6-2)! = 4! = 4 \cdot 3 \cdot 2 \cdot 1;\ 2! = 2 \cdot 1$$

$$= \frac{6 \cdot 5}{2 \cdot 1} \text{ or } 15$$

There are 15 ways Eri can choose two side items from six.

You can use combinations as well as the product of combinations to find the probability of events occurring.

Example 4

APPLICATION
Education

The guidance counselor of Lakewood High School must choose four students out of nine to train as peer counselors. A group of 5 juniors, 3 sophomores, and 1 freshman have applied to fill the positions.

a. How many different ways can he choose four students?

b. What is the probability that he will randomly choose 2 juniors and 2 sophomores?

c. Do you believe the guidance counselor was unfair towards the freshman based on your answer to part b?

a. The order in which the students are chosen does not matter, so we must find the number of combinations of 9 students taken 4 at a time.

$${}_nC_r = \frac{n!}{(n-r)! \cdot r!} \qquad \textit{Definition of combination}$$

$${}_9C_4 = \frac{9!}{(9-4)! \cdot 4!} \qquad \textit{Replace n with 9 and r with 4.}$$

$$= \frac{9 \cdot 8 \cdot 7 \cdot 6 \cdot \cancel{5} \cdot \cancel{4} \cdot \cancel{3} \cdot \cancel{2} \cdot \cancel{1}}{\cancel{5} \cdot 4 \cdot 3 \cdot 2 \cdot 1 \cdot \cancel{4} \cdot \cancel{3} \cdot \cancel{2} \cdot \cancel{1}}$$

$$= \frac{9 \cdot 8 \cdot 7 \cdot 6}{4!} \text{ or } 126$$

There are 126 ways to choose four students out of nine.

b. There are two questions to consider.

- How many ways can 2 juniors be chosen from 5? ${}_5C_2$
- How many ways can 2 sophomores be chosen from 3? ${}_3C_2$

Using the Basic Counting Principle, the answer is the product of two combinations, ${}_5C_2$ and ${}_3C_2$.

$$({}_5C_2)({}_3C_2) = \frac{5!}{(5-2)! \cdot 2!} \cdot \frac{3!}{(3-2)! \cdot 2!}$$

$$= \frac{5!}{3! \cdot 2!} \cdot \frac{3!}{1! \cdot 2!}$$

$$= \frac{5 \cdot \overset{2}{\cancel{4}} \cdot \cancel{3!}}{\cancel{3!} \cdot \underset{1}{\cancel{2}} \cdot 1} \cdot \frac{3 \cdot \cancel{2!}}{\cancel{2!} \cdot 1}$$

$$= 10 \cdot 3 \text{ or } 30$$

There are 30 ways to choose this particular combination out of 126 possible combinations.

$$P(\text{2 juniors, 2 sophomores}) = \frac{30}{126} \qquad \frac{\textit{number of favorable outcomes}}{\textit{total number of possible outcomes}}$$

$$= \frac{5}{21}$$

The probability that the guidance counselor will randomly choose 2 juniors and 2 sophomores is $\frac{5}{21} \approx 24\%$.

c. The probability that a freshman will not be selected is approximately 24%. Since this is a fairly significant number, you cannot assume that the guidance counselor was being unfair.

CHECK FOR UNDERSTANDING

Communicating Mathematics

Study the lesson and then complete the following.

1. **Explain** what the notation 7! means.
2. **Describe** in your own words the difference between a permutation and a combination. Then give an example of each.
3. **Demonstrate** and explain why $nCr = 1$ whenever $n = r$. What does nPr always equal when $n = r$? (*Hint:* Substitute numbers in for n and r.)
4. **Make** a diagram or chart to verify the answer for Example 3.

Guided Practice

Determine whether each situation involves a permutation or combination. Explain your choice.

5. choosing a homecoming queen and king
6. choosing 4 books from a selection of 10 for summer reading
7. choosing digits for a personal identification number

TECHNOLOGY Tip

You can use a graphing calculator to find permutations and combinations. For example, to find ${}_9P_6$ enter
9 [MATH] [◄] 2 6,
and to find ${}_9C_6$ enter
9 [MATH] [◄] 3 6.

Evaluate each expression.

8. ${}_{12}P_3$ 9. ${}_4P_1$ 10. ${}_6C_6$ 11. $({}_3C_2)({}_7C_4)$

Use a calculator to evaluate each expression.

12. ${}_{16}P_5$ 13. ${}_{20}C_8$
14. Julie remembered the 3 digits of her locker combination, 7, 17, 37, but not their order.
    a. What is the maximum number of attempts Julie could make before her locker opens?
    b. What is the probability that 7 is the first digit?
15. **School** The eighth grade class had to choose 4 out of 10 people to serve on the Student Council for next year. How many different groups of students could be selected?

EXERCISES

Practice

Determine whether each situation involves a permutation or combination. Explain your choice.

16. the batting order of the New York Yankees
17. a selection of 5 DVD's from a group of eight
18. a hand of 10 cards from a selection of 52
19. three mannequins in a display window
20. songs played on a CD if "random" is selected and each song plays once
21. the selection of 2 trombones, 3 clarinets, and 2 trumpets for a jazz combo
22. first place and runner-up winners for the table tennis tournament
23. selection of 2 candy bars from six equally-sized bars
24. team captains for the soccer team

Evaluate each expression.

25. ${}_6P_3$ 26. ${}_4P_0$ 27. ${}_8P_5$ 28. $({}_7P_7)({}_7P_1)$
29. $({}_{10}P_5)\,({}_3P_2)$ 30. ${}_5C_0$ 31. ${}_4C_4$ 32. ${}_7C_3$
33. ${}_3C_1$ 34. $({}_6C_2)({}_4C_3)$ 35. $({}_5C_5)({}_2C_1)$ 36. $({}_8C_5)({}_5P_5)$

Use a calculator to evaluate each expression.

37. ${}_{15}P_3$ **38.** ${}_{13}P_6$ **39.** $({}_{20}P_2)({}_{16}P_4)$

40. ${}_{15}C_3$ **41.** ${}_{13}C_6$ **42.** $({}_{20}C_2)({}_{16}C_4)$

43. Refer to Exercises 37–42. What do you notice about the relationship between permutations and combinations?

Applications and Problem Solving

44. Music Arnold Schoenberg was a painter, writer, and composer in the early 20th century. He invented a system of composition in which the twelve pitches of the chromatic scale are played only once. Schoenberg used this technique in his *Suite for Piano.* Upon how many different arrangements could he have based his piece?

45. Travel Akihiro is spending a day in London and has time to see any three of the following seven sites: The National Gallery, St. Paul's Cathedral, The Globe Theater, Westminster Abbey, Buckingham Palace, Piccadilly Circus, and Hyde Park. He will take location into consideration when planning his route. How many different options does Akihiro have?

46. Sports A track coach plans to pick four sprinters out of six for the 1600-meter relay team.

a. How many different teams can he form?

b. The coach must decide in which sequence the four sprinters should run. He timed each and chose the sequence with the best time. How many relays did the four runners have to run so that the coach could collect all the data needed?

47. Business There were six job openings available in the advertising department of a marketing firm. Of the applicants, 35 were men and 15 were women. Five men and one woman were hired.

a. In how many different ways could six applicants be chosen?

b. What is the probability that all men except one will be hired?

c. Was the hiring of five men and only 1 woman fair? Explain your reasoning.

48. Lottery In New York's Pick 10, you can choose any combination of 10 numbers out of 80. Each night, 20 numbers out of 80 are drawn. If your 10 numbers are among the lottery's 20 numbers, you win $500,000.

a. How many possible combinations of 10 are there for you to choose from?

b. When the lottery draws their numbers, how many different combinations of 10 are contained within those 20?

c. What is the probability that when those 20 numbers are drawn, you will be a winner?

49. Government In the United States Senate, a 22-member Budget Committee is being formed from a group of 45 Democrats and 55 Republicans. How many different committees can be formed if there is an equal number of Democrats and Republicans on the committee?

50. Sports The Dolphins are competing against the Electric Eels at a swim meet. Each team entered 4 girls to race the 400-meter crawl. The top three winners receive ribbons.

a. How many different ways can the swimmers place first, second, and third?

b. What is the probability that the first and second place winners are from the Dolphins and the third place winner is from the Electric Eels? Assume that all eight swimmers have the same chance of placing.

Critical Thinking

51. Puzzles Larry is trying to solve a JUMBLE puzzle. He needs to arrange the letters H, P, S, T, A, E, O into a two-word arrangement.

a. How many different arrangements of the letters can he make?

b. Assuming each arrangement has an equal chance of occurring, what is the probability that Larry will form the words "tap shoe" on his first try?

New York

5

Probability

*Use after Lesson 7–5, Glencoe **Algebra 1***

***What* YOU'LL LEARN**

- To use the concept of a random variable in computing probabilities.
- To find the probability of two or more independent or dependent events.
- To find the probability of mutually exclusive or inclusive events.

***Why* IT'S IMPORTANT**

You can use probability to make predictions and to examine how likely it is for an event to occur.

APPLICATION

Meteorology

I remember once listening to someone at a party drone on about the difference between "continually" and "continuously." Later that evening we were watching the news, and the TV weathercaster announced that there was a 50 percent chance of rain for Saturday and a 50 percent chance for Sunday, and concluded that there was therefore a 100 percent chance of rain that weekend. The remark went right by the self-styled grammarian, and even after I explained the mistake to him. . . .

—John Allen Paulos, *Innumeracy*

In the quotation above, the weathercaster predicted a 100% chance of rain for the weekend. Why was the conclusion incorrect?

You can represent this situation with the coin and spinner shown at the right.

- Let heads represent the probability of rain on Saturday.
- Let red on the spinner represent the probability of rain on Sunday.

Since the outcome of tossing the coin does not affect the outcome of spinning the spinner, this is an example of independent events.

The list of all possible outcomes, {TB, TR, HB, HR} is called the **sample space**. Only one of the four outcomes, (HR), matches the weathercaster's prediction. Therefore, the probability of rain on both days is $\frac{1}{4}$.

Note that $P(\text{H})$ is $\frac{1}{2}$, $P(\text{R})$ is $\frac{1}{2}$, and $\frac{1}{2} \cdot \frac{1}{2} = \frac{1}{4}$, which is $P(\text{HR})$. This suggests that the probability of two independent events is the product of the probability of each event.

Probability of Two Independent Events

If two events, *A* and *B*, are independent, then the probability of both events occurring is the product of the probability of *A* and the probability of *B*.

$$P(A \text{ and } B) = P(A) \cdot P(B)$$

Example 1

APPLICATION

Games

In a certain game, rolling the same number on all five dice gives the highest score. What is the probability of rolling the same number on all five dice?

The events are independent since the roll of one die does not affect the outcome of the roll of another die.

There are six ways to roll five dice of the same number, (1, 1, 1, 1, 1), (2, 2, 2, 2, 2), and so on. Using the Fundamental Counting Principal, there are $6 \cdot 6 \cdot 6 \cdot 6 \cdot 6$ or 7776 ways to roll 5 dice. Thus, the probability of rolling 5 dice of the same number is $\frac{6}{7776}$.

$$P\binom{\text{same number}}{\text{on five dice}} = P\binom{\text{any number}}{\text{on die one}} \cdot P\binom{\text{same number}}{\text{on die two}} \cdot P\binom{\text{same number}}{\text{on die three}} \cdot P\binom{\text{same number}}{\text{on die four}} \cdot P\binom{\text{same number}}{\text{on die five}}$$

$$= \frac{6}{6} \cdot \frac{1}{6} \cdot \frac{1}{6} \cdot \frac{1}{6} \cdot \frac{1}{6}$$

$$= \frac{6}{7776}$$

This confirms that the probability of rolling five dice of the same number is $\frac{6}{7776}$ or $\frac{1}{1296}$.

Recall that if an outcome of one event *does* affect the outcome of another event, the events are dependent. For example, suppose you choose a card from a deck, keep it, and then your friend chooses a card. Since you did not replace your card, your friend has fewer cards from which to choose. These events are dependent.

Probability of Two Dependent Events

If two events, *A* and *B*, are dependent, then the probability of both events occurring is the product of the probability of *A* and the probability of *B* after *A* occurs.

$$P(A \text{ and } B) = P(A) \cdot P(B \text{ following } A)$$

Example 2

APPLICATION

Business

Ms. Leary is a buyer for home appliances. She received a shipment of three refrigerators in which one is defective. What is the probability that the last refrigerator she tests is defective?

Let D = the event that the refrigerator is defective.

Let $\overline{D}$ = the event that the refrigerator is not defective.

For test one, $P(\overline{D}) = \frac{\text{number not defective}}{\text{total number of refrigerators}} = \frac{2}{3}$.

For test two, $P(\overline{D}) = \frac{\text{number not defective}}{\text{number of refrigerators remaining}} = \frac{1}{2}$.

For test three, $P(D) = \frac{\text{number defective}}{\text{number of refrigerators remaining}} = \frac{1}{1} = 1$.

$P(\overline{D}, \overline{D}, D) = \frac{2}{3} \cdot \frac{1}{2} \cdot 1 = \frac{2}{6}$ or $\frac{1}{3}$.

The probability that the refrigerator tested last is defective is $\frac{1}{3}$.

In Example 2, the events for which a refrigerator is defective (D) and for which a refrigerator is *not* defective ($\overline{D}$) are called **complements**. For test one only, $P(D) = \frac{1}{3}$ and $P(\overline{D}) = \frac{2}{3}$. The sum of their probabilities equals 1.

Probability of Complements P(A) and P(not A)

The probabilities of *A* and *not A* have the following properties.

1. *P*(*A*) + *P*(*not A*) = 1

2. *P*(*A*) = 1 − *P*(*not A*) or *P*(*not A*) = 1 − *P*(*A*)

Up until now, you have found the probability of multiple events occurring. What if you were asked to find the probability of one event *or* another? Suppose you draw a card from a standard deck of 52. What is the probability of drawing an ace *or* a king? Since a card cannot be both an ace and a king, the events are **mutually exclusive**. The two events cannot occur at the same time. The probability of drawing an ace or a king is found by adding their individual probabilities.

$$P(\text{ace or king}) = P(\text{ace}) + P(\text{king})$$
$$= \frac{4}{52} + \frac{4}{52}$$
$$= \frac{8}{52} \text{ or } \frac{2}{13}$$

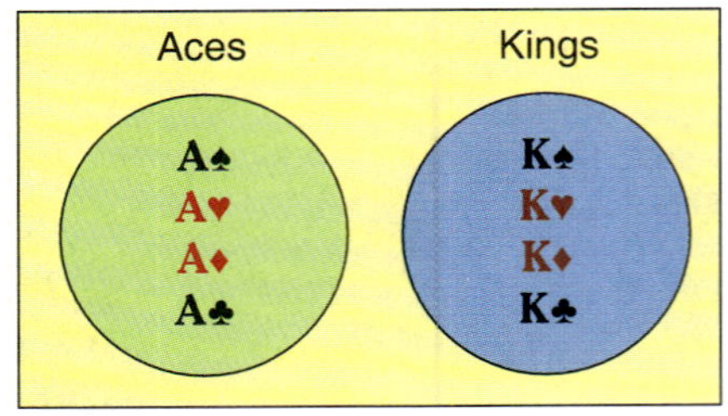

The probability of drawing an ace or a king is $\frac{2}{13}$. Using a Venn diagram verifies this solution.

Probability of Mutually Exclusive Events

If two events, *A* and *B*, are mutually exclusive, then the probability that either *A* or *B* occurs is the sum of their probabilities.

$$P(A \text{ or } B) = P(A) + P(B)$$

What is the probability of drawing an ace or a spade from a deck of cards? Since it is possible to draw a card that is both an ace and a spade, these events are not mutually exclusive. They are called **inclusive** events. In this case, you must adjust the formula for mutually exclusive events.

$P(\text{ace})$	$P(\text{spade})$	$P(\text{ace of spades})$
$\frac{4}{52}$	$\frac{13}{52}$	$\frac{1}{52}$

If you were to use the formula for the probability of mutually exclusive events, the probability of drawing an ace would be counted twice, once for an ace and once for a spade. To find the correct probability, you must subtract $P(\text{ace of spades})$ from the sum of their individual probabilities.

$$P(\text{ace or spade}) = P(\text{ace}) + P(\text{spade}) - P(\text{ace of spades})$$
$$= \frac{4}{52} + \frac{13}{52} - \frac{1}{52}$$
$$= \frac{16}{52} \text{ or } \frac{4}{13}$$

The probability of drawing an ace or a spade is $\frac{4}{13}$. The Venn diagram shows that 16 cards are aces or spades. So the solution checks.

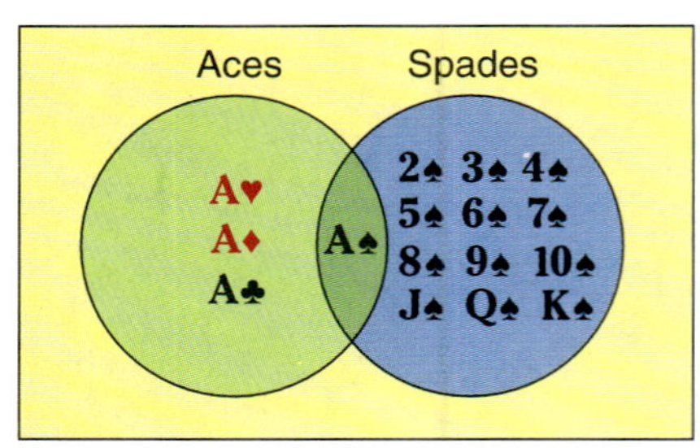

Probability of Inclusive Events

If two events, *A* and *B*, are inclusive, then the probability that either *A* or *B* occurs is the sum of their probabilities decreased by the probability of both occurring.

$$P(A \text{ or } B) = P(A) + P(B) - P(A \text{ and } B)$$

Example 3 **The bar graph below shows the distribution of students on the chess team by class. What is the probability that a chess player chosen at random is either a freshman or a sophomore?**

These are mutually exclusive events because a student cannot be both a freshman and a sophomore.

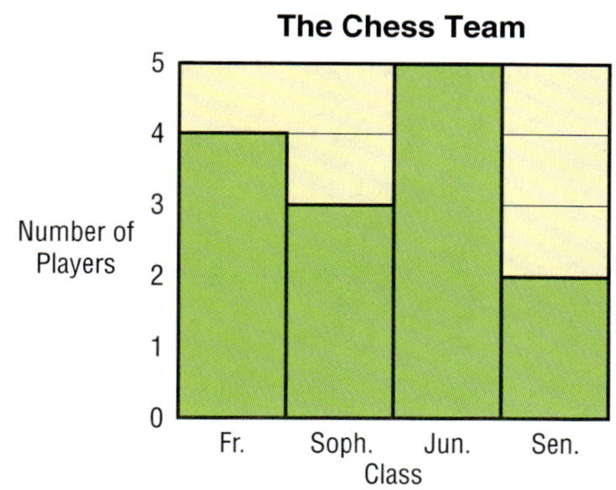

P(freshman or sophomore)

$= P(\text{freshman}) + P(\text{sophomore})$

$= \frac{4}{14} + \frac{3}{14}$

$= \frac{7}{14}$ or $\frac{1}{2}$

The probability of choosing a freshman or a sophomore is $\frac{1}{2}$ or 50%.

Example 4 APPLICATION **Meteorology**

Refer to the application at the beginning of the lesson. What is the probability that it will rain on Saturday or Sunday?

Since it is possible that it will rain on both days, these events are inclusive. You already found that $P(\text{rain on both days}) = \frac{1}{4}$.

P(rain on Saturday or Sunday)

$= P(\text{rain on Saturday}) + P(\text{rain on Sunday}) - P(\text{rain on both days})$

$= \frac{1}{2} + \frac{1}{2} - \frac{1}{4}$ or $\frac{3}{4}$

There is a 75% chance that it will rain on Saturday or Sunday.

CHECK FOR UNDERSTANDING

Communicating Mathematics

Study the lesson. Then complete the following.

1. **Write** an example of independent events and of dependent events.
2. **Explain** why you would find the same probability for mutually exclusive events if you used the formula for inclusive events.
3. **Draw** a Venn diagram to illustrate the events in Example 4.

Guided Practice

Determine whether the events are *independent* or *dependent*. Explain.

4. rolling a red die and then rolling a blue die
5. drawing a name from a hat and then drawing a second name without replacing the first

Determine whether the events are *mutually exclusive* or *inclusive*.

6. A student is selected at random from a group of male and female students in the 9th, 10th, 11th, or 12th grade.
   a. P(9th or 12th grader)
   b. P(10th grader or female)
   c. P(male or female)
   d. P(male or 11th grader)

7. **Sports** North Madison's soccer team has a 60% chance of winning when playing any of the other five teams in its division. If the games are independent, what is the probability that the team will win the division title?

8. **Government** The circle graph below shows for which political parties New York voters are enrolled.

New York Party Lines, 1996

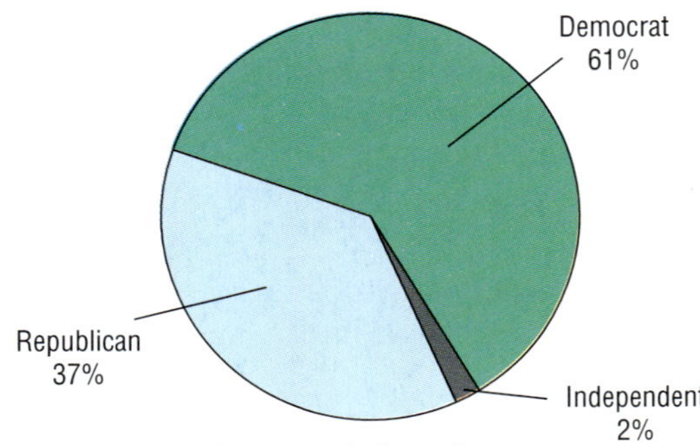

Source: U.S. Census Bureau

   a. If a person is selected at random, what is the probability that he or she is enrolled as an Independent or Republican voter?

   b. If a person is selected at random, what is the probability that he or she is not enrolled as an Independent voter?

   c. If a poll were taken from 500 enrolled voters, about how many would you expect to be Democrats?

EXERCISES

Practice

Determine whether the events are *independent* or *dependent*. Then find the probability.

9. A bag contains colored cubes of equal size. There are 2 orange, 6 yellow, 7 blue, and 3 red cubes in the bag. Once a cube is drawn, it is not replaced.

   a. P(a yellow and then orange)
   b. P(two reds in a row)
   c. P(yellow, then blue, then orange)
   d. P(two blues in a row then red)

10. A die is rolled and a spinner like the one below is spun.

   a. P(3 and D)
   b. P(a prime number and A)
   c. P(an odd number and a vowel)
   d. P(2 and A, B, or C)

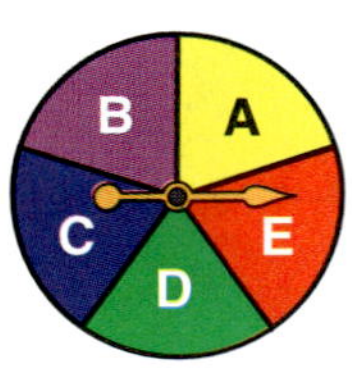

Determine whether the events are *mutually exclusive* or *inclusive*. Then find the probability.

11. A ten-sided die is tossed.

   a. P(odd or less than 6)
   b. P(9 or even)
   c. P(greater than 5 or less than 3)
   d. P(even or odd)
   e. P(less than 8 or less than 2)
   f. P(not 2 or prime)

12. **Geometry** The measures of the interior and exterior angles of a triangle are shown below. Two of the six angles are chosen at random.

   a. P(interior angle or obtuse angle)
   b. P(straight angle or right angle)
   c. P(20° angle or 130° angle)

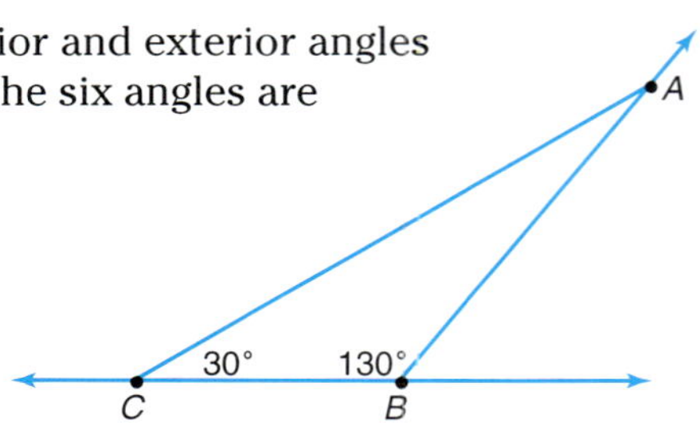

13. The bar graph at the right shows the number of children that ordered each flavor of ice cream at a birthday party.

   a. If a child was chosen at random, what is the probability that he or she ordered vanilla or chocolate ice cream?

   b. If 28 children on a class picnic visit the ice cream store, how many would you expect to order swirl flavor?

14. In a board game, if you roll doubles, you get another turn. What is the probability of rolling two doubles in a row so that you have three consecutive turns?

15. **Transportation** The U.S. Census Bureau conducted a 1998 American Community Survey in Rockland County, New York. The circle graph at the right shows the survey results of how people commute to work.

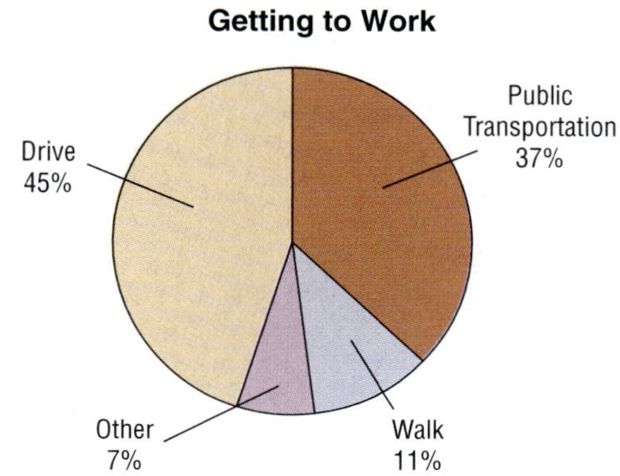

   a. If a person from Rockland County was chosen at random, what is the probability that he or she uses public transportation or walks to work?

   b. If offices are being built in Rockland County to accommodate 400 employees, what is the minimum number of parking spaces an architect should plan for the parking lot?

Applications and Problem Solving

16. **Safety** A carbon monoxide detector system uses two devices, A and B. If carbon monoxide is present, there is a 96% chance that device A will detect it, a 92% chance that device B will detect it, and a 90% chance that both devices will detect it.

   a. Draw a Venn diagram that illustrates this problem.

   b. If carbon monoxide is present, what is the probability that it will be detected?

   c. What is the probability that carbon monoxide would go undetected?

   d. Do devices A and B operate independently of each other? Explain.

17. **Biology** Each person carries two types of genes for eye color. The gene for brown eyes (B) is dominant over the gene for blue eyes (b). That is, if a person has one gene for brown eyes and the other for blue, he or she will have brown eyes. The Punnett square below shows the genes for two parents.

	B	b
b	Bb	bb
b	Bb	bb

   a. What is the probability that this couple's first child has brown eyes?

   b. What is the probability that their two children both have brown eyes?

   c. Find the probability that their two children do not have the same color eyes.

18. **Psychology** In 1983, 260 students who had not taken a probability course were used in the following experiment. They were given a six-sided die with four green and two yellow faces. To win a cash prize, they were to choose the sequence of colors listed below that would be most likely to occur with the first rolls of the die.

YGYYY
YGYYYG
GYYYYY

Psychologists concluded that people's intuitive understanding of probability is not very accurate since more than 63% of the students did not choose the most probable sequence. Which sequence would you choose and why? **Source:** *Psychological Review*

19. **Physics** Two circuits are shown below where one has two switches in series and the other has two switches in parallel. Current will flow if there is at least one closed loop when the switches are activated. Suppose each switch is independent and has an 80% chance of closing when activated.

FYI

In circuit diagrams, the symbol —•—/•— represents a switch and the symbol $\frac{-\,+}{-\,-}$ represents the battery or power source.

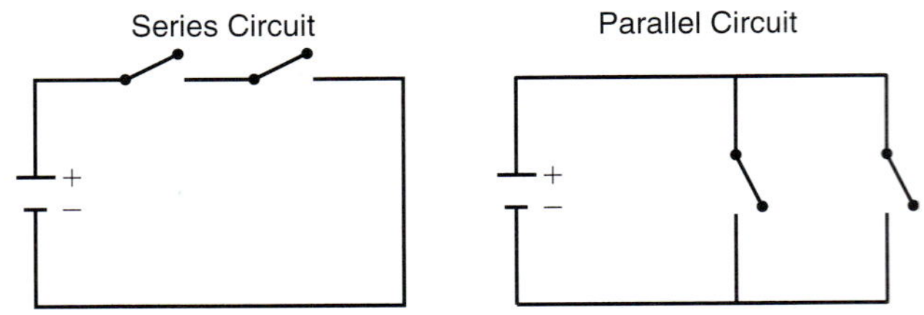

a. What is the probability that current will flow in the series circuit?

b. What is the probability that the current will flow in the parallel circuit? (*Hint:* Use complements.)

20. **Economics** In 1997, minimum wage was $5.15. The table compares the total number of hourly workers with those making $5.15 an hour or less.

Number of Hourly Workers (thousands)			
Age (years)	**Total**	**At $5.15**	**Below $5.15**
16–24	15,793	1145	2080
25+	55,287	970	2043

Source: U.S. Bureau of Labor Statistics

a. If an hourly worker was chosen at random, what is the probability that he or she earns minimum wage? less than minimum wage?

b. What is the probability that a randomly-chosen hourly worker earns less than or equal to minimum wage?

c. If you randomly chose an hourly worker from each age group, which would you expect to be earning no more than minimum wage? Explain.

Critical Thinking

21. A sample of high school students were asked if they *A*) drive a car to school, *B*) play after-school sports, and *C*) have a part-time job. The results of the survey are shown below.

a. How many students were surveyed?

b. How many students said that they drive a car to school?

c. If a high school student is chosen at random, what is the probability that he or she does all three?

d. What is the probability that a randomly-chosen student drives a car to school or plays after-school sports or has a part-time job?

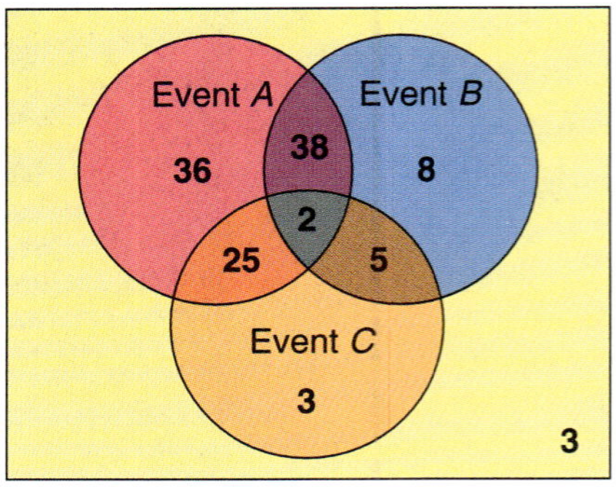

New York

6

Probability Distributions

*Use after Lesson 7–5, Glencoe **Algebra 1***

What YOU'LL LEARN

- To use the concept of a random variable to compute probability distributions.
- To use theoretical and experimental probability to represent and solve problems involving uncertainty.

Why IT'S IMPORTANT

You will use probability distributions to describe and make predictions for a sample population.

APPLICATION

Education

A test has two true and false questions where the correct answers are both false. If a student randomly answers both questions, what is the probability that he or she gets both correct? one correct? zero correct?

A **random variable** is a variable whose value is the numerical outcome of a random event. In the situation above, we can let the random variable Y represent the number of correct answers. Then Y can equal 2, 1, or 0.

Possible Answers		Y = Number Correct
F	F	2
F	T	1
T	F	1
T	T	0

Using the *Fundamental Counting Principle*, there are $2 \cdot 2$ or 4 possible ways the student could answer the questions. The sample space with the number of correct answers, Y, is listed at the left. What is the probability that both answers are correct, or $Y = 2$?

Only one set of answers (F, F) has both questions answered correctly.

$$P(Y = 2) = P(\text{F, F})$$
$$= P(\text{F}) \cdot P(\text{F}) \quad \textit{Independent events}$$
$$= \frac{1}{2} \cdot \frac{1}{2} \text{ or } \frac{1}{4}$$

The probability that the student answers both questions correctly is $\frac{1}{4}$.

What is the probability that only one answer is correct, or $Y = 1$?
Two sets of answers (F, T) and (T, F) have one question answered correctly.

$$P(Y = 1) = P(\text{F, T}) \text{ or } P(\text{T, F})$$
$$= P(\text{F}) \cdot P(\text{T}) + P(\text{T}) \cdot P(\text{F}) \quad \textit{Mutually exclusive events}$$
$$= \frac{1}{2} \cdot \frac{1}{2} + \frac{1}{2} \cdot \frac{1}{2}$$
$$= \frac{1}{4} + \frac{1}{4} \text{ or } \frac{1}{2}$$

The probability that the student only answers one question correctly is $\frac{1}{2}$.

What is the probability that zero answers are correct, or $Y = 0$?

The probability for every possible value of random variable Y is called its **probability distribution**. To find the probability of Y, multiply the number of ways an event can occur by the probability that it will occur.

Properties of Probability Distributions
1. The probability for each value of Y is greater than or equal to 0 and less than or equal to 1.
2. The probabilities for each value of Y add up to 1.
3. The probability for any compound event is equal to the sum of the probabilities of each individual event.

The probability distribution for a random variable can be given in a table or in a probability histogram and used to obtain other data. The probability distribution for the previous problem is shown below.

Probability Distribution Table	
Y = Number of Correct Answers	$P(Y)$
0	0.25
1	0.50
2	0.25

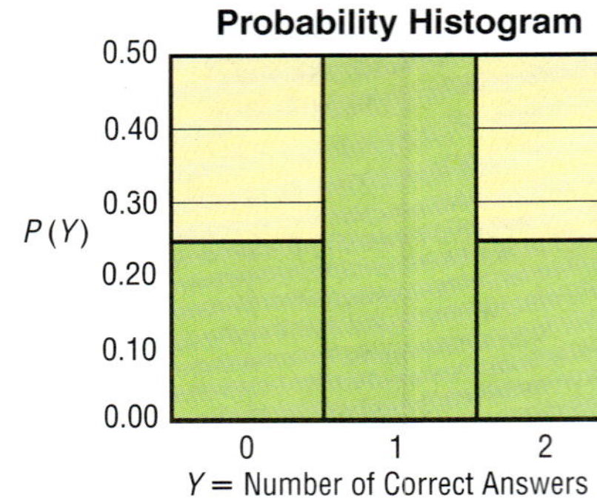

Example 1 **The table below shows the probability distribution of Y, the number of people in a household.**

a. Show that the probability distribution is valid.

b. If a household is chosen at random, what is the probability that five or more people live in it? That is, what is $P(Y \geq 5)$?

c. Make a histogram of the data.

American Households	
Y = Number of People	Probability
1	0.25
2	0.32
3	0.18
4	0.15
5	0.07
6	0.02
7+	0.01

Source: U.S. Census Bureau, 1995

a. For each value of Y, the probability is greater than or equal to 0 and less than or equal to 1.
$0.25 + 0.32 + 0.18 + 0.15 + 0.07 + 0.02 + 0.01 = 1$, so the probabilities add up to 1.

b. $P(Y \geq 5) = P(Y = 5) + P(Y = 6) + P(Y = 7+)$
$= 0.07 + 0.02 + 0.01$ or 0.10

c. First, draw a vertical and horizontal axis. Label the axes as shown.

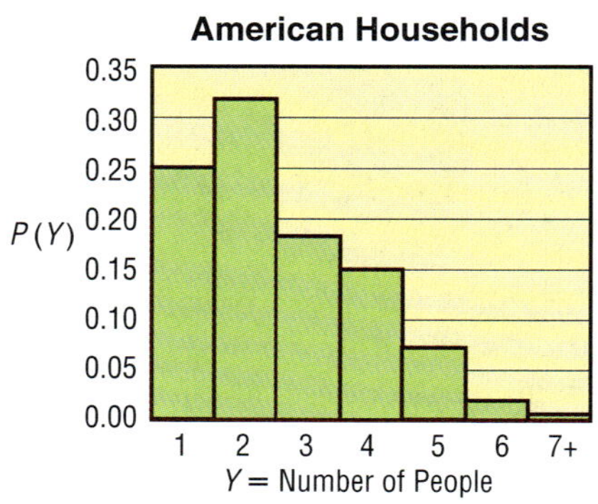

- Remember to include the title, American Households.
- Intervals of 1 are shown along the horizontal axis.
- The bar height represents the probability for values of Y, shown along the vertical axis.

Up to this point in this text, all of the probabilities you have found have been **theoretical probabilities**. They are determined using mathematical methods and provide only an idea of what might happen in a real-world situation. You can never make predictions with complete certainty.

Experimental probability is determined by performing tests or experiments and observing the outcomes. One method for finding experimental probability is **simulation**. In a simulation, a device is used to model the event, and you observe how the model responds to the conditions listed in a given problem. When you repeatedly perform an experiment, collect data, and then analyze the results, you have made an **empirical study**.

Example 2

APPLICATION

Education

A school is considering a transition to block scheduling. Three students are chosen for an advisory board to represent student opinion. Suppose that 75% of all students favor block scheduling and 25% oppose it. Find the probability distribution for Y, the number of students on the advisory board that favor block scheduling.

You could spin a spinner like the one below three times to simulate the students' opinions on the advisory board. The green section (G) represents the probability that a student favors the block. The red section (R) represents the probability that the student opposes the block.

Now spin the spinner three times and record your results. Below are the results of 20 trials.

GGR	GGG	GRG	GRR	GGG
GGG	RGR	GGG	RGG	GRG
RRG	GGG	RGG	GGR	GGG
GRG	GGG	GGG	RGG	RGG

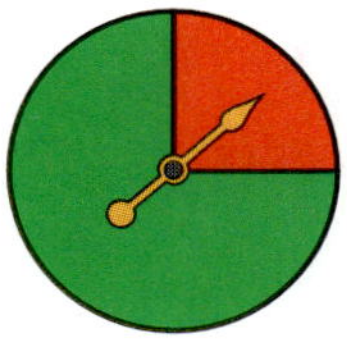

In the simulation, 0 out of 20 trials yielded 0 G. $P(Y = 0) = \frac{0}{20}$ or 0

Three trials yielded 1 G. $P(Y = 1) = \frac{3}{20}$

Nine trials yielded 2 G. $P(Y = 2) = \frac{9}{20}$

Eight trials yielded 3 G. $P(Y = 3) = \frac{8}{20}$ or $\frac{2}{5}$

This probability distribution is based on experimental probabilities.

MODELING MATHEMATICS — An Empirical Study

Materials: number cubes

- Each person should toss a number cube once and record its value.
- Repeat this task 20 times, each time recording the value on the number cube.
- Determine the experimental probability distribution for Y, the value on the number cube.
- Now, combine your results with the rest of the class to find the experimental probability distribution for Y given the new number of trials (*20 · the number of students in your class*).
- Find the theoretical probability for tossing a 2.
- Find the theoretical probability of tossing a 1 or 6.
- Find the theoretical probability of tossing a value less than 4.

Your Turn

a. Compare the experimental and theoretical probabilities. Which pair of probabilities were closer to each other: your individual probabilities or your class's probabilities?

b. What can you conclude about the relationship between the number of experiments in a simulation and the experimental probability?

CHECK FOR UNDERSTANDING

Communicating Mathematics

Study the lesson. Then complete the following.

1. **List** the conditions that must be satisfied in order to have a valid probability distribution.
2. **Explain** why the probability of tossing a coin three times and getting 1 head and 2 tails is the same as the probability of getting 1 tail and 2 heads.
3. **Describe** a situation that could be represented by a simulation. What objects could you use for the experiment?

Guided Practice

4. A fair coin is tossed twice and the number of tails, *Y*, is recorded. This is repeated 50 times and the table below shows the results.

Number of Tails in Two Tosses	0	1	2
Frequency	12	28	10

   a. Write the sample space with all possible outcomes of two coin tosses.
   b. In how many ways can you toss zero tails? one tail? two tails?
   c. Find the theoretical probability distribution for $Y = 0$, $Y = 1$, and $Y = 2$.
   d. Use the table to compute the experimental probability distribution.
   e. Compare the theoretical and experimental probabilities.

5. **Sales** A clothing store manager takes inventory, counting the number of jeans sold each week. After many weeks, the manager has enough data to estimate the sales and make a probability distribution table.

Number of Jeans Sold Each Week	100	200	300	400	500
Probability	0.10	0.15	0.40	0.25	0.10

   a. Define a random variable and list its values.
   b. Show that this is a valid probability distribution.
   c. In a given week, what is the probability that fewer than 400 jeans will sell?
   d. In a given week, what is the probability that more than 100 jeans will sell?

EXERCISES

Practice

6. Two dice are tossed and the sum of the numbers facing up is recorded. The probability histogram at the right shows the distribution of the sums.

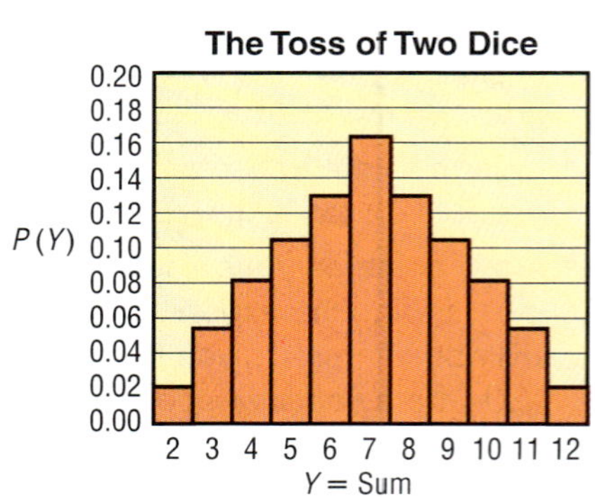

   a. On a random toss, estimate the probability that the sum of the two dice is greater than 8.
   b. On a random toss, estimate the probability that the sum of the two dice is less than 2.
   c. If you tossed the dice, which sum would you most expect? Explain.

7. The table below shows the probability distribution of the number of vehicles per household.

American Households				
Number of Vehicles	0	1	2	3+
Probability	0.098	0.335	0.391	0.176

Source: U.S. Census Bureau, 1995

a. If a household is chosen at random, what is the probability that it will have 2 vehicles?

b. If a house is chosen at random, what is the probability that it will have either 0 or 1 vehicle?

c. If a house is chosen at random, what is the probability that it will have 5 vehicles? Explain.

8. Refer to Example 2 and find the theoretical probability distribution.

a. Write the sample space with all possible outcomes.

b. Do all possible outcomes have an equal chance of occurring? Explain.

c. Find the probability distribution for $Y = 0$, $Y = 1$, $Y = 2$, and $Y = 3$. Then make a probability histogram.

d. Compare these probabilities with the ones obtained from the experiment. Are they similar? What could you do to get experimental probabilities closer to the theoretical probabilities?

Applications and Problem Solving

9. **Grades** The table below shows the grade distribution for a large class, where an A = 4.0, a B = 3.0, a C = 2.0, a D = 1.0, and an F = 0 points.

Y = Grade	0	1.0	2.0	3.0	4.0
Probability	0.05	0.10	0.40	0.40	0.05

a. What is the probability that a student fails the course?

b. What is the probability that a random student from that class receives a grade of a B or better?

10. **Education** A small group of seventh graders participated in a study that tracked the number of years of schooling they eventually completed. The probability distribution of Y, the number of grades completed, is shown in the table below.

LOOK BACK

You can refer to Lesson 3 on pages NY15–19 for more information on cumulative histograms.

Y = Highest Grade Completed	6	7	8	9	10	11	12
Probability	0.005	0.010	0.035	0.070	0.060	0.040	0.780

a. Make a cumulative probability histogram.

b. If a person was randomly chosen from the group, what is the probability that he or she completed at most 11 years of schooling?

c. From the cumulative histogram, show how you can find the probability that a random person completed 12 years of schooling. Find that number and check your answer using the frequency table above.

Critical Thinking

$P(Y = 1)$ is the probability that their first child is a boy.

11. Suppose a married couple has children until they have a boy. Let the random variable Y represent the number of children in their family.

a. Calculate the probability distribution for $Y = 1$, 2, 3, and 4.

b. What is the probability that the couple will have more than 4 children?

Solving Quadratic-Linear Systems

Use after Lesson 11–3, Glencoe ***Algebra 1***

What YOU'LL LEARN

- To solve and apply quadratic-linear systems of equations.

Why IT'S IMPORTANT

You can use quadratic-linear systems to compare and contrast growth in sales.

APPLICATION

Sales

The number of American households (in millions) with home computers can be approximated by the quadratic equation $y = 0.4t^2 + 0.9t + 23$. The number of households with cable television can be approximated by the linear equation $y = 0.5t + 60$. In both equations, $t = 0$ represents 1990. These two equations together are called a **quadratic-linear system**.

$$\left.\begin{aligned} y &= 0.4t^2 + 0.9t + 23 \\ y &= 0.5t + 60 \end{aligned}\right\} \text{ quadratic-linear system}$$

When will the number of households with home computers equal the number of households with cable television? *This problem will be solved in Example 3.*

Like a linear system of equations, the solution of a quadratic-linear system of equations is the ordered pair that satisfies both equations. A quadratic-linear system can have 0, 1, or 2 solutions as shown below.

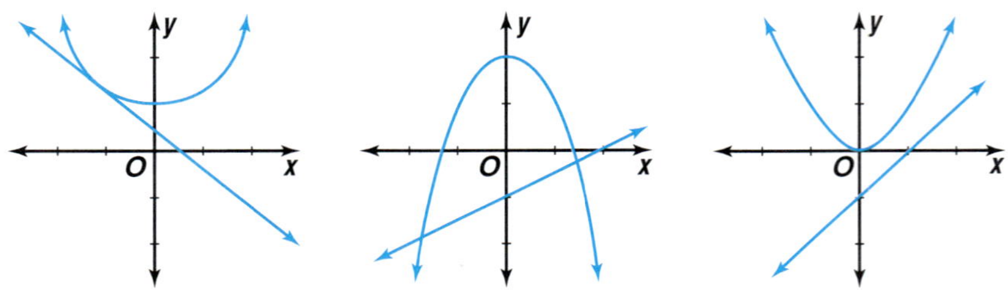

one solution **two solutions** **no solution**

One method for solving a quadratic-linear system is by graphing.

Example 1 **Solve the quadratic-linear system by graphing.**

$\mathbf{y = x^2 - 2x + 1}$

$\mathbf{2x - y = 3}$

Use a table of values to graph the first equation $y = x^2 - 2x + 1$.

x	y
−1	4
0	1
1	0
2	1
3	4

Graph the second equation by using its slope-intercept form, $y = 2x - 3$.

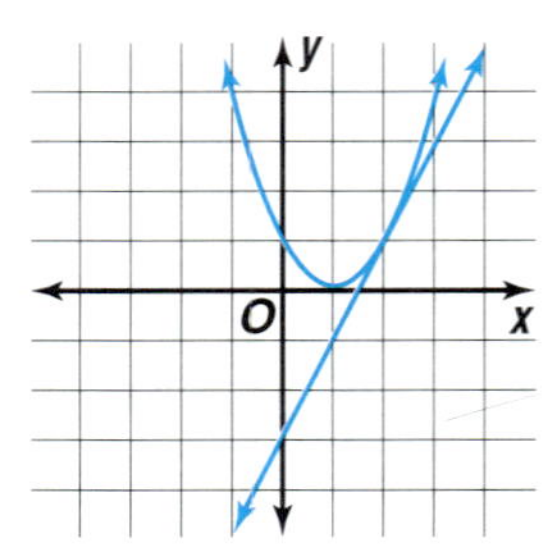

The parabola and line appear to intersect at (2, 1).

Check: Verify that the point at (2, 1) lies on both graphs.

$y = x^2 - 2x + 1$ $\qquad$ $2x - y = 3$

$1 = 2^2 - 2(2) + 1$ *(x, y) = (2, 1)* $\qquad$ $2(2) - 1 = 3$ *(x, y) = (2, 1)*

$1 = 1$ ✔ $\qquad$ $3 = 3$ ✔

Sometimes the exact coordinates of the point where the graphs intersect cannot be easily determined by drawing a graph. You can use a graphing calculator to find a more accurate estimate for the solution.

EXPLORATION — GRAPHING CALCULATOR

Use a graphing calculator to solve the quadratic-linear system of equations.
$y = -1.8x + 3.6$
$y = x^2 - 3x - 1$

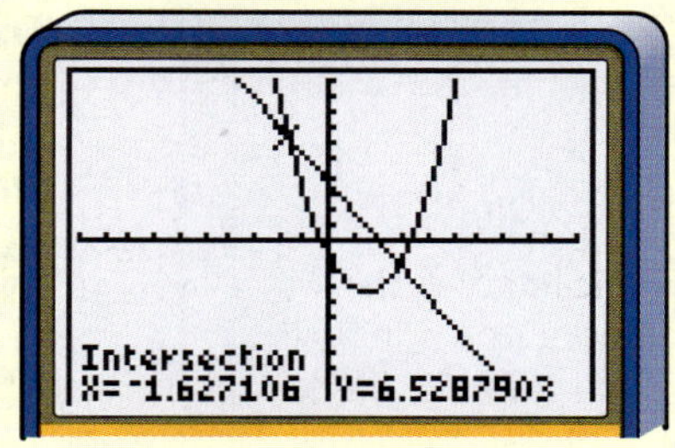

- Graph $y = -1.8x + 3.6$ and $y = x^2 - 3x - 1$ in the standard viewing window.
- To find a point of intersection, select 5:Intersect from the CALC menu.
- Press ENTER ENTER ENTER and the approximate coordinates of the solution will appear. One solution to the nearest hundredth is $(-1.63, 6.53)$. Move the cursor near the other intersection point and repeat this process to find the second solution.

Your Turn

Use a graphing calculator to solve each system of quadratic-linear equations to the nearest hundredth.

a. $y = x^2 - 3.5x + 2.2$
$y = 2x - 5.3625$

b. $y = -0.2x^2 + 0.28x + 1.01$
$y = 0.35x - 1.648$

c. $y = -1.4x - 2.88$
$y = x^2 + 0.4x - 3.14$

LOOK BACK

You can refer to Lessons 8-1 and 8-2 for more information on solving linear systems of equations.

Another method of solving systems of quadratic-linear equations is by using *substitution*. You can use this algebraic method to solve any quadratic-linear system of equations.

Example 2

CONNECTION Geometry

Two corners are cut from a 6-inch by 6-inch square piece of paper. The cuts are x inches from the corners as shown in the figure at the right.

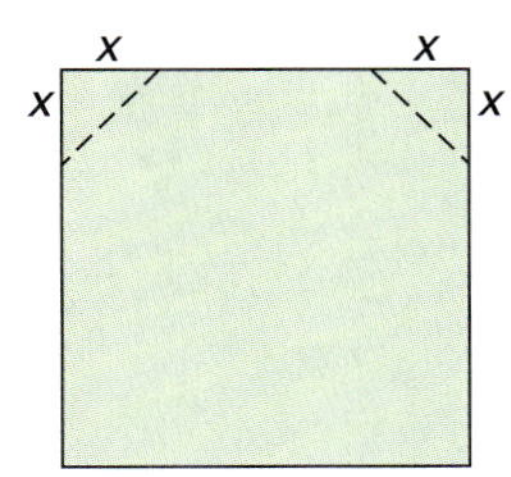

a. Write an equation to represent the area A of the paper after the cuts are made.

b. For what value of x will the resulting area be $\frac{8}{9}$ of the original area?

a. The area of the original piece of paper is $6 \cdot 6$ or 36 square inches. Find the area of each corner that will be cut from the paper.

area of a corner $= \frac{1}{2}bh$ — *Formula for the area of a triangle*

$= \frac{1}{2}x \cdot x$ or $\frac{1}{2}x^2$ — *Replace b with x and h with x.*

(continued on the next page)

The final area is the original area minus the area of the corners.

$$\overbrace{A}^{\text{final area}} = \overbrace{36}^{\text{original area}} - \overbrace{2\left(\tfrac{1}{2}x^2\right)}^{\text{area of corners}}$$

$$A = 36 - x^2$$

The equation representing the area of the paper after the cuts is $A = 36 - x^2$.

b. The resulting area is $\frac{8}{9}$ of the original area. So $A = \frac{8}{9}(36)$, or 32 square inches.

To find x, we can solve the following system of quadratic-linear equations.

$A = 36 - x^2$

$A = 32$

$A = 36 - x^2$	
$32 = 36 - x^2$	*Replace A with 32.*
$x^2 = 4$	*Simplify.*
$x = \pm 2$	*Take the square root of each side.*

Since it does not make sense to have a negative length, the only solution is 2 inches. You can check by graphing the equations.

You can use quadratic-linear systems of equations to make predictions.

Example 3

APPLICATION

Sales

Refer to the application at the beginning of the lesson. Solve the quadratic-linear system of equations to find the year in which the number of households with home computers equals the number with cable television.

$\boldsymbol{y = 0.4t^2 + 0.9t + 23}$

$\boldsymbol{y = 0.5t + 60}$

From the first equation in the system, you know that y is equal to $0.4t^2 + 0.9t + 23$. Since y must have the same value in both equations, you can substitute $0.4t^2 + 0.9t + 23$ for y in the second equation $y = 0.5t + 60$.

$y = 0.5t + 60$	
$0.4t^2 + 0.9t + 23 = 0.5t + 60$	*Substitute $0.4t^2 + 0.9t + 23$ for y.*
$0.4t^2 + 0.4t - 37 = 0$	*Subtract 0.5t and 60 from each side of the equation.*

Now use the quadratic formula to solve for t.

$$t = \frac{-b \pm \sqrt{b^2 - 4ac}}{2a}$$

$$t = \frac{-0.4 \pm \sqrt{0.4^2 - 4(0.4)(-37)}}{2(0.4)} \quad a = 0.4,\ b = 0.4,\ c = -37$$

$$t = \frac{-0.4 \pm \sqrt{59.36}}{0.8}$$

TECHNOLOGY Tip

Use a graphing calculator to check your answer. Graph both equations in the viewing window [0, 15] by [0, 100].

Use a calculator to simplify.

$t = \frac{-0.4 + \sqrt{59.36}}{0.8} \approx 9.13$ $\qquad$ $t = \frac{-0.4 - \sqrt{59.36}}{0.8} \approx -10.13$

The two solutions are approximately 9.13 and -10.13. Since $t = 0$ represents 1990, $t = -10.13$ represents a year before 1990 and $t = 9.13$ represents 1990 + 9.13 or the year 1999. It is more reasonable to think that the number of households with home computers equals the number with cable television in 1999.

CHECK FOR UNDERSTANDING

Communicating Mathematics

Study the lesson and then complete the following.

1. **Describe** a situation in which you would choose to solve a quadratic-linear system graphically rather than algebraically. When is it appropriate to use the graphing calculator to find and/or eliminate solutions?
2. **Explain** what it means when the graphs of a quadratic equation and linear equation never intersect. What is the algebraic solution in such a case?
3. **Sketch** the graphs of a quadratic-linear system of equations if the solutions are (0, 5) and (6, 2).

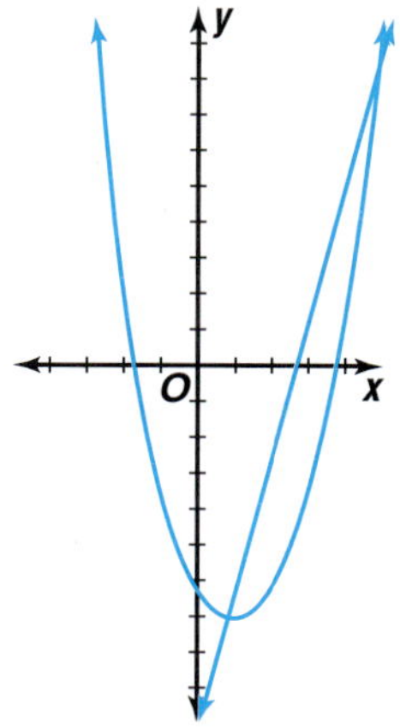

Guided Practice

4. State the solution of the quadratic-linear system of equations graphed at the right.

Solve each quadratic-linear system of equations by graphing. If the system does not have a solution, write *no solution*.

5. $y = x^2 - 4x + 6$
   $y = -x + 4$
6. $y = -3x^2 + 2$
   $y = 2x + 5$

Use substitution to solve each quadratic-linear system of equations. Round answers to the nearest hundredth, if necessary. If the system does not have a solution, write *no solution*.

7. $y = x^2 - 3x - 6$
   $y = 2x$
8. $y = x^2 - 2x + 2$
   $y = x + 1$
9. **Geometry** The formula for the area of a circle is $A = \pi r^2$. The formula for the circumference of a circle is $C = 2\pi r$. For what value of r will the area of a circle equal its circumference?

EXERCISES

Practice

State the solution of each quadratic-linear system of equations. If the system does not have a solution, write *no solution*.

10. 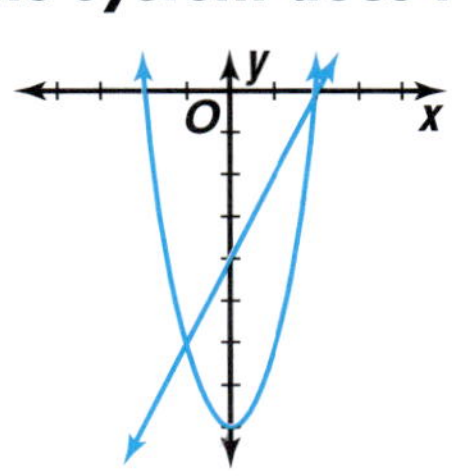

11. 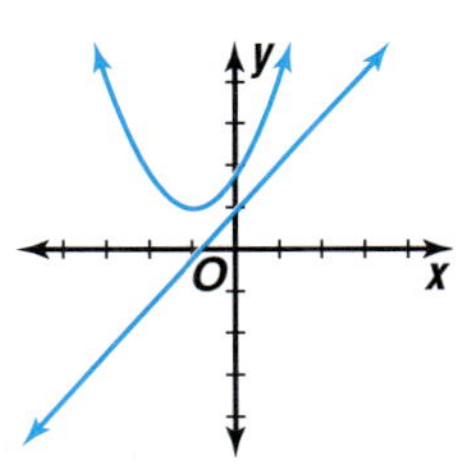

12. 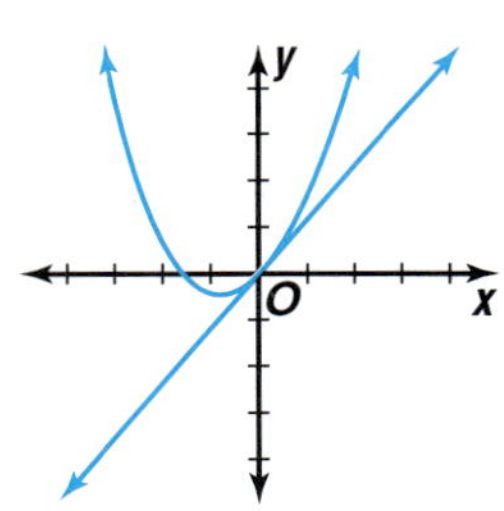

Solve each quadratic-linear system of equations by graphing. If the system does not have a solution, write *no solution*.

13. $y = x^2 - 4x + 4$
$y = -2x + 7$

14. $y = x^2 - 9$
$y = 3x - 9$

15. $y = -x^2 + 2x - 3$
$y = -2x + 1$

16. $y = 2x^2 - x - 3$
$y = -3x + 1$

17. $y = x^2 - 3x$
$y = -2x - 3$

18. $y = (x + 3)^2$
$y = 3x + 19$

Use substitution to solve each quadratic-linear system of equations. Round answers to the nearest hundredth, if necessary. If the system does not have a solution, write *no solution*.

19. $y = x^2 - x - 12$
$y = -10$

20. $y = 4x^2 - 13x - 12$
$y = 11x - 48$

21. $y = -x^2 - 2x$
$x - y = -6$

22. $y = x^2 - 2x - 8$
$y = 4x - 13$

23. $y = x^2 + 8x + 5$
$y = x - 1$

24. $y = x^2 - 6x + 4$
$2x + y = 3$

Applications and Problem Solving

25. **Forensic Science** Police are investigating the shooting of a helicopter. They found a weapon at the scene of the crime that has a suspect's fingerprints on it. Forensic experts have deduced that the weapon is capable of firing with an initial velocity of 960 feet per second. So the height of the bullet t seconds after firing is found by the quadratic function $h(t) = -16t^2 + 960t$. The helicopter was flying at an altitude of 8000 feet at the time of the shot.

   a. Is it possible that this weapon shot the helicopter? Explain your answer.

   b. At what time after the weapon was shot could it have hit the helicopter?

26. **Geometry** Four corners are cut from a rectangular piece of cardboard that measures 5 feet by 3 feet. The cuts are x feet from the corners as shown in the figure at the right. After the cuts are made, the sides of the rectangle are folded to form an open box. The area of the bottom of the box is 3 square feet.

   a. Write two equations to represent the area of the bottom of the box.

   b. What are the dimensions of the box?

   c. What is the volume of the box?

27. **Physics** The distance an object travels at a constant velocity for t seconds is given by $d = vt$. If an object is accelerating, the distance it travels is given by $d = v_i t + \frac{1}{2}at^2$, where v_i is the initial velocity, t is the time in seconds, and a is the acceleration. Suppose a car is speeding at 80 miles per hour. A police car chases after it at the exact moment the speeding car passes by. If the police car began at rest and accelerated 12,000 mph^2, how many seconds would it take to override the speeding car? *(Hint:* Convert hours to seconds.)

28. **Computer games** Ed is creating a computer game where a shuttle flies through outer space. He programs the shuttle to follow a parabolic path using the equation $y = -2x^2 + 8x$ and an asteroid to follow a linear path using the equation $y = 4x - 6$. If his computer screen represents the first quadrant of the coordinate plane, at what point will the two paths cross?

Critical Thinking

29. For the following system, graph each inequality and indicate the solution set.
$y \geq x^2 - 9$
$y \leq x + 3$

EXTRA PRACTICE

NY Lesson 1 **Find a rational approximation for each irrational number to the nearest whole number and to the nearest tenth without using a calculator.**

1. $\sqrt{5}$
2. $\sqrt{11}$
3. $\sqrt{7}$
4. $\sqrt{23}$
5. $\sqrt{70}$
6. $\sqrt{58}$
7. $3\sqrt{14}$
8. $2\sqrt{3}$
9. $4\sqrt{5}$
10. $3\sqrt{17}$
11. $5\sqrt{22}$
12. $2\sqrt{2}$

Use a calculator to find a rational approximation for each irrational number to the nearest hundredth.

13. $\sqrt{13.8}$
14. $\sqrt{125}$
15. $\sqrt{50}$
16. $2\sqrt{10}$
17. $5\sqrt{3}$
18. $2\sqrt{2.45}$
19. $\sqrt{0.78}$
20. $\sqrt{110.5}$
21. $4\sqrt{6}$
22. $\frac{\sqrt{3}}{12}$
23. $\frac{1}{\sqrt{2}}$
24. $\frac{3\sqrt{3}}{2}$

Replace each __?__ with <, >, or = to make each sentence true.

25. $\frac{1}{8}$ __?__ $\sqrt{8}$
26. 0.67 __?__ $\frac{2}{3}$
27. $\frac{4}{9}$ __?__ $0.\overline{4}$
28. $\frac{3}{12}$ __?__ $\frac{1}{3}$
29. $\frac{1}{20}$ __?__ $\sqrt{20}$
30. $2\frac{1}{6}$ __?__ $2\sqrt{6}$
31. $\sqrt{32}$ __?__ $3.\overline{32}$
32. $\frac{\sqrt{2}}{2}$ __?__ $\frac{1}{\sqrt{2}}$
33. $\sqrt{48}$ __?__ $4\sqrt{3}$
34. 3.14 __?__ $\frac{22}{7}$
35. $5\frac{1}{3}$ __?__ $5\sqrt{3}$
36. $\frac{4}{\sqrt{25}}$ __?__ $\frac{4}{25}$
37. $\frac{5}{11}$ __?__ $0.\overline{45}$
38. $\frac{\sqrt{9}}{2}$ __?__ $\frac{9}{2}$
39. 2.166 __?__ $2\frac{1}{6}$
40. $\frac{8}{\sqrt{64}}$ __?__ 1
41. $\frac{100}{99}$ __?__ $\frac{99}{100}$
42. 0.99 __?__ $\frac{0.01}{0.01}$

43. **Physics** The *period* of a pendulum, or the time it takes for a pendulum to swing through one full cycle, is given by the equation $T = 2\pi\sqrt{\frac{L}{9.8}}$ where T is the time in seconds and L is the pendulum's length. Would a pendulum with a length of 4 meters or a length of 6 meters have a longer period?

NY Lesson 2

1. Stocks The line graph at the right shows the closing price per share of a certain stock over a 7-day period. Note that $1\frac{1}{4}$ dollars is equivalent to $1.25.

a. What is the price per share on the sixth day?

b. Between which two days did the price per share increase the most?

c. Which days had a closing price of $1.00 per share?

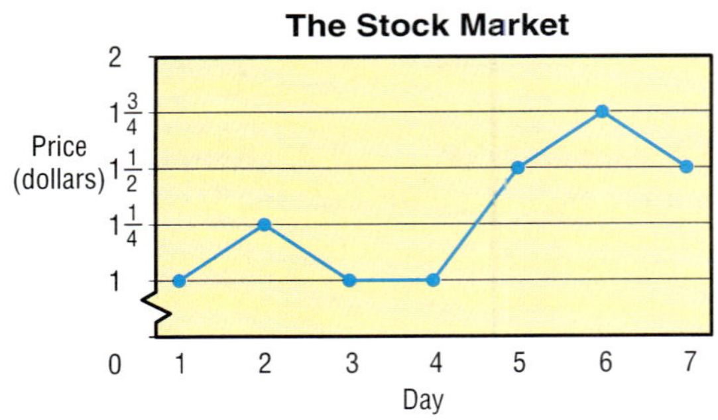

2. During baseball season, Jordan recorded the number of hits he had each game as shown in the frequency table below.

Baseball Season												
Game	1	2	3	4	5	6	7	8	9	10	11	12
Number of Hits	0	0	1	3	2	1	4	3	0	2	5	3

a. Construct a line graph of the data.

b. How many hits per game did Jordan make on average?

c. What is the mode number of hits?

d. What is the median number of hits?

e. How would you characterize Jordan's overall hitting performance?

3. School Josephine's Geometry class took its first test of the school year. Josephine's teacher posted the scores on the blackboard as seen in the frequency table shown at the right.

a. How many students are in Josephine's Geometry class?

b. Which interval of scores contains the least number of students? the greatest?

c. What percent of the students scored in the interval 41–50?

d. How many students scored above a 70 on the test?

Test Score	Number of Students
41–50	1
51–60	0
61–70	4
71–80	7
81–90	5
91–100	3

4. Twenty-five students in gym class were timed in the 400-meter dash. Each of their times was recorded to the nearest tenth of a second as shown in the list below.

Times for the 400-Meter Dash (seconds)

58.6	52.4	57.0	51.8	52.0
54.8	63.6	73.2	70.0	76.0
77.4	74.0	78.6	75.2	76.2
68.0	57.6	59.2	53.8	73.8
79.2	59.8	60.0	78.0	72.2

a. Choose intervals of time and make a frequency table of the data.

b. Make a histogram using your frequency table from part a.

c. What conclusions can you draw from your graph?

NY Lesson 3 **For each frequency table below, make a cumulative frequency table and a cumulative frequency histogram showing percentiles.**

1.

Interval	Frequency	Cumulative Frequency
1–5	IIII	
6–10	II	
11–15	I	
16–20	III	
21–25	II	

2.

Interval	Frequency	Cumulative Frequency
1–15	𝍸 I	
16–30	II	
31–45	𝍸 I	
46–60	III	
61–80	𝍸 III	

3. Students in a club sold magazines to raise money for their club's activities. Below is a list showing the amount of money each student raised.

Student Magazine Sales (dollars)

75.00	52.50	88.00	112.00	74.25	46.00	110.00	98.50	64.00	12.75
225.75	122.00	58.50	66.25	88.25	130.00	82.00	44.50	72.00	74.50
50.00	44.75	90.00	125.00	62.50	36.00	82.00	155.25	27.50	102.00

a. Make a cumulative frequency table of the data with intervals of \$50.00.
b. How many students are in the club?
c. How many students sold less than \$50.00 in magazines?
d. How many students sold at least \$100.00 in magazines?
e. How many students sold \$50.00 to \$99.00 in magazines?
f. Make a cumulative histogram showing percentiles for the data.
g. In what interval is the median sale of magazines?
h. Estimate the amount in sales needed to be in the 75th percentile of students selling magazines.

NY Lesson 4 **Determine whether each situation involves a permutation or combination. Explain your choice.**

1. the order of the four students in a line at the drinking fountain
2. three singers from a group of 10
3. a choice of six books out of 80
4. seven cars in 15 parking spaces

Evaluate each expression.

5. ${}_5P_2$
6. ${}_6P_3$
7. ${}_9P_1$
8. ${}_7P_4$
9. ${}_{10}C_1$
10. ${}_8C_5$
11. ${}_3C_0$
12. ${}_5C_2$
13. $({}_4P_1)({}_{10}P_0)$
14. $({}_4C_4)({}_6C_2)$
15. $({}_5P_1)({}_6C_5)$
16. $({}_7P_2)({}_{12}C_4)$

17. How many ways can a club of 15 members choose a 5-person committee?
18. How many ways can the letters in the word NOTEPAD be arranged?
19. How many ways can 6 children shoot free-throws in basketball practice if Molly always shoots last?

EXTRA PRACTICE

NY Lesson 5 **Suppose you roll two number cubes. Find the probability of each *independent* event.**

1. P(5 and 5)
2. P(two even numbers)
3. P(two numbers less than 4)
4. P(1 and 6)
5. P(a number greater than 2 and 3)
6. P(two numbers less than or equal to 6)

In a bag, there are 2 red marbles, 6 white marbles, and 4 blue marbles. Once a marble is selected, it is not replaced. Find the probability of each *dependent* event.

7. P(a blue marble and then a red marble)
8. P(2 white marbles in a row)
9. P(2 red marbles in a row)
10. P(a blue marble, then a white marble, and then a red marble)
11. P(3 white marbles in a row)
12. P(2 blue marbles and then a red marble)

Determine whether the events are *mutually exclusive* or *inclusive*. Then find the probability.

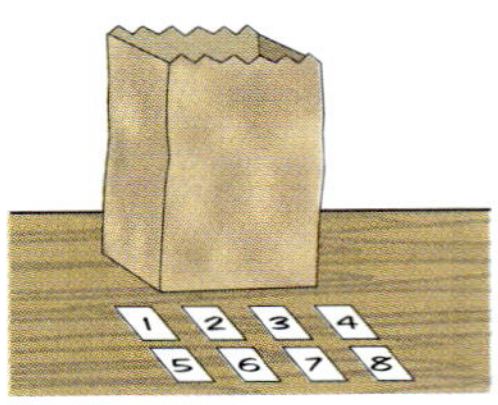

13. After cards numbered 1–8 are placed in the bag shown at the right, one card is drawn.
    a. P(4 or less than 2)
    b. P(odd or prime number)
    c. P(1 or 2 or 3)
    d. P(6 or even)
    e. P(3 or greater than 3)
    f. P(less than 4 or greater than 4)
14. A cookie jar holds 50 cookies, where 20 are chocolate chip and the rest are peanut butter.
    a. If Janette chooses two cookies, what is the probability that both are chocolate chip cookies?
    b. What is the probability that both are peanut butter cookies?
    c. What is the probability that she chooses 1 chocolate chip cookie and 1 peanut butter cookie? (*Hint:* Consider the case where she chooses a chocolate chip cookie first or the case where she chooses a peanut butter cookie first.)
15. **Biology** The gene for tongue curling (T) is dominant as opposed to the gene where you cannot curl your tongue (t). That is, if you can curl your tongue, you have inherited at least one dominant gene. The *Punnett* square below shows the genes for two parents.

	T	**t**
T	TT	Tt
t	Tt	tt

    a. What is the probability that their child will be able to curl his or her tongue?
    b. If they have two children, what is the probability that both will be able to curl their tongues?
    c. What is the probability that neither of the two children will be able to curl their tongues?

NY Lesson 6

1. The table below shows the probability distribution for the number of children under age six in an American family.

American Families			
Number of Children Under Age 6	None	One	Two or more
Probability	0.78	0.15	0.07

Source: U.S. Census Bureau, 1997

   a. Show that this is a valid probability distribution.
   b. If a family is chosen at random, what is the probability that there are two or more children under the age of 6 in it?
   c. If a family is chosen at random, what is the probability that there are no children under the age of 6 in it?
   d. If Jamaal is asked to baby-sit for a random family, what is the probability that he will be caring for at most one child under the age of 6?

2. The spinner at the right is spun twice and the number of times it lands on yellow, Y, is recorded. This is repeated 30 times and the results are recorded in the table below.

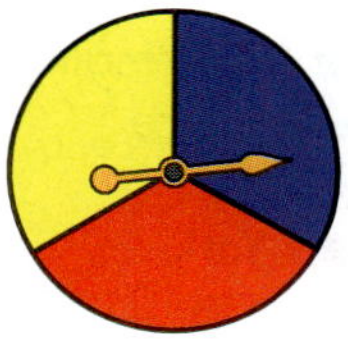

Y = Number of Yellow Spins	Frequency
0	15
1	12
2	3

   a. Write the sample space of the two spins.
   b. In how many ways can you spin a yellow twice, once, or no times at all?
   c. Find the theoretical and experimental probabilities for $Y = 0$, $Y = 1$, and $Y = 2$.
   d. Compare the probabilities found in part c.

NY Lesson 7

State the solution of each quadratic-linear system of equations. If the system does not have a solution, write *no solution*.

1. 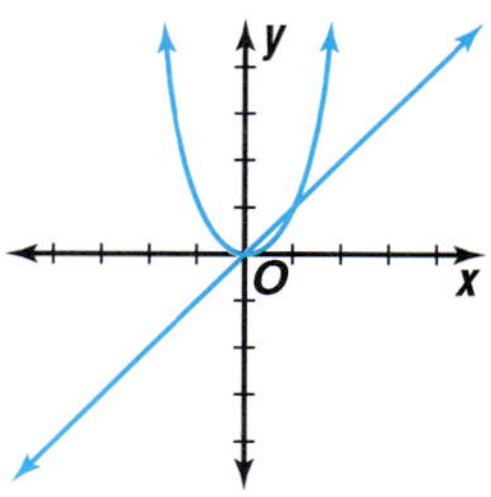

2. 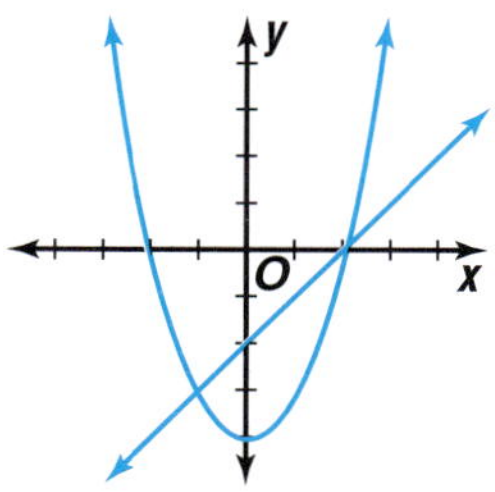

3. 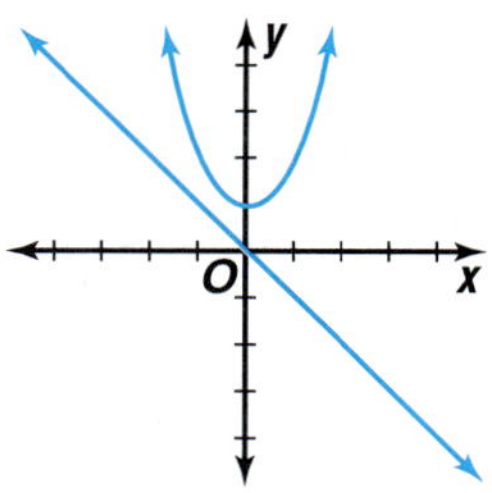

Solve the quadratic-linear system of equations by graphing. If the system does not have a solution, write *no solution*.

4. $y = -x^2 + 2$
   $y = x$

5. $y = x^2 - x + 1$
   $y = 0.25x$

6. $y = x^2 - 4x + 1$
   $y = -3$

7. $y = (x + 1)(x - 1)$
   $y - x = 1$

Use substitution to solve each quadratic-linear system of equations. If the system does not have a solution, write *no solution*.

8. $y = x^2 + 4x + 16$
   $y = -3x + 4$

9. $y = 2x^2 + 2x - 7$
   $y = x - 6$

10. $y = x^2 + 2x - 5$
    $y = 2x - 8$

11. $y = (x - 2)^2$
    $y = 2x - 1$

EXTRA PRACTICE

NEW YORK CONSULTANTS

Each of the New York Consultants reviewed both *Algebra 1* and *Geometry*, New York Editions. They read the New York lessons and gave suggestions for improving the Student Editions. They also reviewed the Pacing and Correlation Guide to ensure complete coverage of the Learning Standards of the *Math A Core Curriculum*.

Steven Balasiano
Mathematics Instructional Specialist
Office of the Superintendent of Brooklyn High Schools
Brooklyn, New York

Sharon Cichocki
Mathematics Teacher
Hamburg High School
Hamburg, New York

Sr. Joan Harnett, O.P.
Department of Mathematics and Computer Science
Manhattan College
Riverdale, New York

Joseph Kavanaugh
Academic Head of Mathematics
Scotia-Glenville High School
Scotia, New York

Donald J. Norton
Chairperson of Secondary Mathematics (Retired)
Lindenhurst High School
Lindenhurst, New York

C. Vincent Pané, Ed.D.
Associate Professor of Education
Molloy College
Rockville Centre, New York

Nicholas J. Restivo
Director of Mathematics, PreK-12
Mineola Schools
Mineola, New York

NEW YORK INDEX

Glencoe McGraw-Hill

A Division of The McGraw-Hill Companies

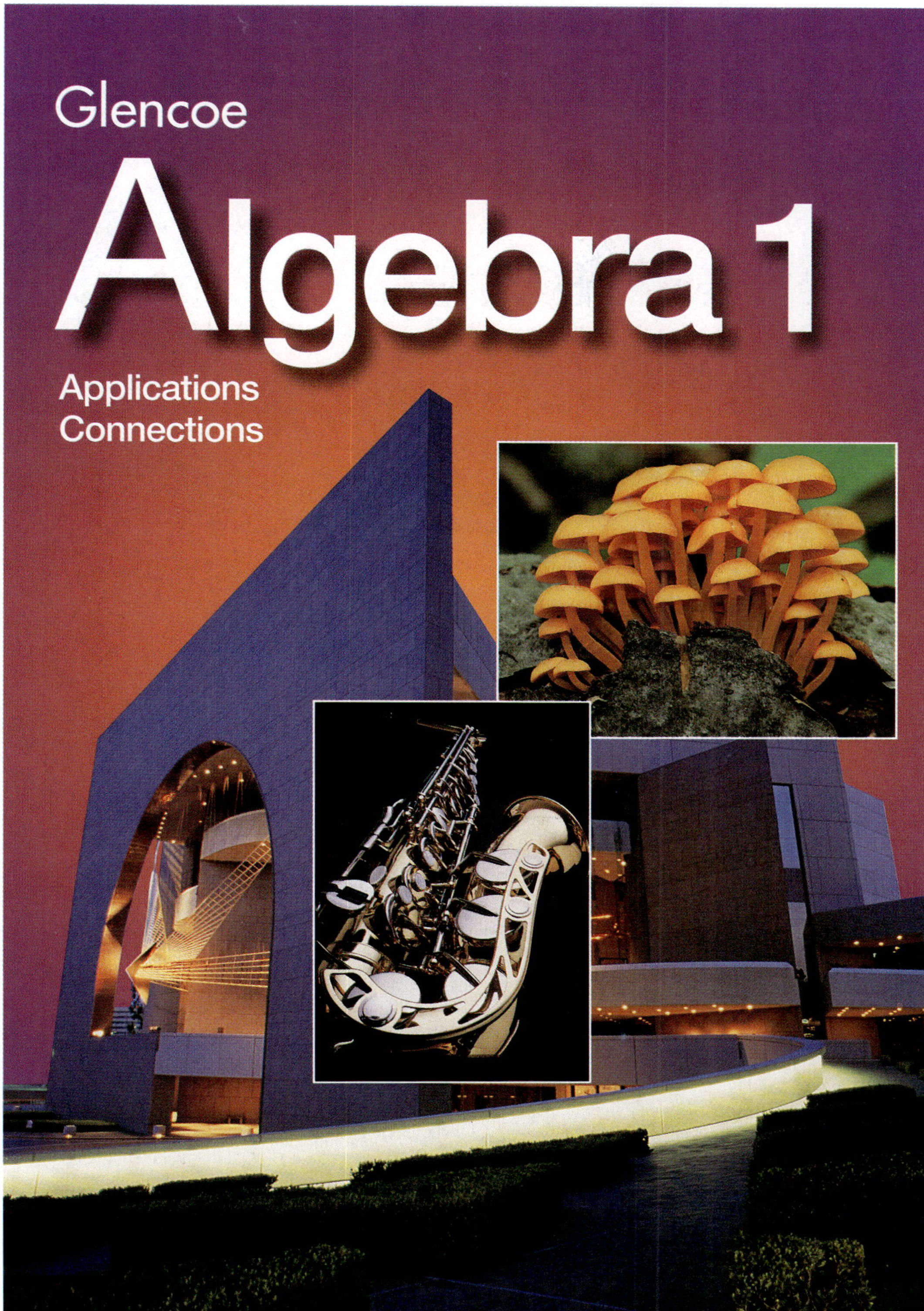

GLENCOE

McGraw-Hill

New York, New York   Columbus, Ohio   Woodland Hills, California   Peoria, Illinois

Glencoe/McGraw-Hill
A Division of The McGraw-Hill Companies

2001 Impression

Send all inquiries to:
Glencoe/McGraw-Hill
8787 Orion Place
Columbus, OH 43240-4027

ISBN: 0-07-821225-1

2 3 4 5 6 7 8 9 10 071/043 08 07 06 05 04 03 02 01 00

WHY IS ALGEBRA IMPORTANT?

Why do I need to study algebra? When am I ever going to have to use algebra in the real world?

Many people, not just algebra students, wonder why mathematics is important. ***Algebra 1*** is designed to answer those questions through **integration, applications,** and **connections.**

INTEGRATION
Geometry

Did you know that algebra and geometry are closely related? Topics from all branches of mathematics, like geometry and statistics, are integrated throughout the text.

You'll learn how to find the complement and supplement of an angle and how to find the measure of the third angle of a triangle. (Lesson 3–4, pages 162–164)

APPLICATION
Nutrition

I can't believe that a double cheeseburger has that much fat! Real-world uses of mathematics are presented.

The number of grams of fat in a double cheeseburger is determined by solving an open sentence. (Lesson 1–5, page 32)

CONNECTION
Biology

What does biology have to do with mathematics? Mathematical topics are connected to other subjects that you study.

Punnett squares, which are models that show the possible ways that genes combine, are connected to squaring a binomial. (Lesson 9–8, page 542)

Authors

William Collins teaches mathematics at James Lick High School in San Jose, California. He has served as the mathematics department chairperson at James Lick and Andrew Hill High Schools. Mr. Collins received his B.A. in mathematics and philosophy from Herbert H. Lehman College in Bronx, New York, and his M.S. in mathematics education from California State University, Hayward. Mr. Collins is a member of the Association of Supervision and Curriculum Development and the National Council of Teachers of Mathematics, and is active in several professional mathematics organizations at the state level. He is also currently serving on the Teacher Advisory Panel of the *Mathematics Teacher.*

"In this era of educational reform and change, it is good to be part of a program that will set the pace for others to follow. This program integrates the ideas of the NCTM Standards with real tools for the classroom, so that algebra teachers and students can expect success every day."

Gilbert Cuevas is a professor of mathematics education at the University of Miami in Miami, Florida. Dr. Cuevas received his B.A. in mathematics and M.Ed. and Ph.D., both in educational research, from the University of Miami. He also holds a M.A.T. in mathematics from Tulane University. Dr. Cuevas is a member of many mathematics, science, and research associations on the local, state, and national levels and has been an author and editor of several National Council of Teachers of Mathematics (NCTM) publications. He is also a frequent speaker at NCTM conferences, particularly on the topics of equity and mathematics for all students.

Alan G. Foster is a former mathematics teacher and department chairperson at Addison Trail High School in Addison, Illinois. He obtained his B.S. from Illinois State University and his M.A. in mathematics from the University of Illinois. Mr. Foster is a past president of the Illinois Council of Teachers of Mathematics (ICTM) and was a recipient of the ICTM's T.E. Rine Award for Excellence in the Teaching of Mathematics. He also was a recipient of the 1987 Presidential Award for Excellence in the Teaching of Mathematics for Illinois. Mr. Foster was the chairperson of the MATHCOUNTS question writing committee in 1990 and 1991. He frequently speaks and conducts workshops on the topic of cooperative learning.

Berchie Gordon is the mathematics/science coordinator for the Northwest Local School District in Cincinnati, Ohio. Dr. Gordon has taught mathematics at every level from junior high school to college. She received her B.S. in mathematics from Emory University in Atlanta, Georgia, her M.A.T. in education from Northwestern University in Evanston, Illinois, and her Ph.D. in curriculum and instruction at the University of Cincinnati. Dr. Gordon has developed and conducted numerous inservice workshops in mathematics and computer applications. She has also served as a consultant for IBM, and has traveled throughout the country making presentations on graphing calculators to teacher groups.

"Using this textbook, you will learn to think mathematically for the 21st century, solve a variety of problems based on real-world applications, and learn the appropriate use of technological devices so you can use them as tools for problem solving."

BEATRICE MOORE-HARRIS is an educational specialist at the Region IV Education Service Center in Houston, Texas. She is also the Southwest Regional Director of the Benjamin Banneker Association. Ms. Moore-Harris received her B.A. from Prairie View A&M University in Prairie View, Texas. She has also done graduate work there, at Texas Southern University in Houston, Texas, and at Tarleton State University in Stephenville, Texas. Ms. Moore-Harris is a consultant for the National Council of Teachers of Mathematics (NCTM) and serves on the Editorial Board of the NCTM's *Mathematics Teaching in the Middle School.*

> *"This program will bring algebra to life by engaging you in motivating, challenging, and worthwhile mathematical tasks that mirror real-life situations. Opportunities to use technology, manipulatives, language, and a variety of other tools are an integral part of this program, which allows all students full access to the algebra curriculum."*

JAMES RATH has 30 years of classroom experience in teaching mathematics at every level of the high school curriculum. He is a former mathematics teacher and department chairperson at Darien High School in Darien, Connecticut. Mr. Rath earned his B.A. in philosophy from The Catholic University of America and his M.Ed. and M.A. in mathematics from Boston College. He has also been a Visiting Fellow in the mathematics department at Yale University in New Haven, Connecticut.

DORA SWART is a mathematics teacher and department chairperson at W.F. West High School in Chehalis, Washington. She received her B.A. in mathematics education at Eastern Washington University in Cheney, Washington, and has done graduate work at Central Washington University in Ellensburg, Washington, and Seattle Pacific University in Seattle, Washington. Ms. Swart is a member of the National Council of Teachers of Mathematics, the Western Washington Mathematics Curriculum Leaders, and the Association of Supervision and Curriculum Development. She has developed and conducted numerous inservices and presentations to teachers in the Pacific Northwest.

> *"Glencoe's algebra series provides the best opportunity for you to learn algebra well. It explores mathematics through hands-on learning, technology, applications, and connections to the world around us. Mathematics can unlock the door to your success—this series is the key."*

LESLIE J. WINTERS is the former secondary mathematics specialist for the Los Angeles Unified School District and is currently supervising student teachers at California State University, Northridge. Mr. Winters received bachelor's degrees in mathematics and secondary education from Pepperdine University and the University of Dayton, and master's degrees from the University of Southern California and Boston College. He is a past president of the California Mathematics Council-Southern Section, and received the 1983 Presidential Award for Excellence in the Teaching of Mathematics and the 1988 George Polya Award for being the Outstanding Mathematics Teacher in the state of California.

Consultants, Writers, and Reviewers

Consultants

Cindy J. Boyd
Mathematics Teacher
Abilene High School
Abilene, Texas

Gail Burrill
National Center for Research/Mathematical & Science Education
University of Wisconsin
Madison, Wisconsin

David Foster
Glencoe Author and Mathematics Consultant
Morgan Hill, California

Eva Gates
Independent Mathematics Consultant
Pearland, Texas

Joan Gell
Mathematics Department Chairman
Palos Verdes High School
Palos Verdes Estates, California

Daniel Marks
Consultant, Real-World Applications
Associate Professor of Mathematics
Auburn University at Montgomery
Montgomery, Alabama

Melissa McClure
Consultant, Tech Prep
Mathematics Consultant
Teaching for Tomorrow
Fort Worth, Texas

Dr. Luis Ortiz-Franco
Consultant, Diversity
Associate Professor of Mathematics
Chapman University
Orange, California

Writers

David Foster
Writer, Investigations
Glencoe Author and Mathematics Consultant
Morgan Hill, California

Jeri Nichols-Riffle
Writer, Graphing Technology
Assistant Professor
Teacher Education/Mathematics and Statistics
Wright State University
Dayton, Ohio

Reviewers

Susan J. Barr
Mathematics Department Chairperson
Dublin Coffman High School
Dublin, Ohio

William Biernbaum
Mathematics Teacher
Platteview High School
Springfield, Nebraska

John R. Blickenstaff
Mathematics Teacher
Martinsville High School
Martinsville, Indiana

Wayne Boggs
Mathematics Supervisor
Ephrata High School
Ephrata, Pennsylvania

Donald L. Boyd
Mathematics Teacher
South Charlotte Middle School
Charlotte, North Carolina

Judith B. Brigman
Mathematics Teacher
South Florence High School
Florence, South Carolina

William A. Brinkman
Mathematics Department Chairperson
Paynesville High School
Paynesville, Minnesota

Louis A. Bruno
Mathematics Department Chairperson
Somerset Area Senior High School
Somerset, Pennsylvania

Luajean Nipper Bryan
Mathematics Teacher
McMinn County High School
Athens, Tennessee

Kenneth Burd, Jr.
Mathematics Teacher
Hershey Senior High School
Hershey, Pennsylvania

Todd W. Busse
Mathematics/Science Teacher
Wenatchee High School
Wenatchee, Washington

Esther Corn
Mathematics Department Chairperson
Renton High School
Renton, Washington

Kimberly C. Cox
Mathematics Teacher
Stonewall Jackson High School
Manassas, Virginia

Janis Frantzen
Mathematics Department Chairperson
McCullough High School
The Woodlands, Texas

Vicki Fugleberg
Mathematics Teacher
May-Port CG School
Mayville, North Dakota

Sabine Goetz
Mathematics Teacher
Hewitt-Trussville Junior High
Trussville, Alabama

Dee Dee Hays
Mathematics Teacher
Henry Clay High School
Lexington, Kentucky

Ralph Jacques
Mathematics Department Chairperson
Biddeford High School
Biddeford, Maine

Dixie T. Johnson
Mathematics Department Chairperson
Paul Blazer High School
Ashland, Kentucky

Jane Housman Jones
Mathematics/Technology Teacher
du Pont Manual High School
Louisville, Kentucky

Rebecca A. Luna
Mathematics Teacher
Austin Junior High School
San Juan, Texas

Sandra A. Nagy
Mathematics Resource Teacher
Mesa Schools
Mesa, Arizona

Linda Palmer
Mathematics Teacher
Clark High School
Plano, Texas

Cynthia H. Ray
Mathematics Teacher
Ravenswood High School
Ravenswood, West Virginia

Hazel Russell
Mathematics Teacher
Riverside Middle School
Fort Worth, Texas

Bernita Jones
Mathematics Department Chairperson
Turner High School
Kansas City, Kansas

Nancy W. Kinard
Mathematics Teacher
Palm Beach Gardens High School
Palm Beach Gardens, Florida

Frances J. MacDonald
Area Mathematics Coordinator, K–12
Pompton Lakes School District
Pompton Lakes, New Jersey

Roger O'Brien
Mathematics Supervisor
Polk County Schools
Bartow, Florida

Deborah Patonai Phillips
Mathematics Department Head
St. Vincent-St. Mary High School
Akron, Ohio

Carrol W. Rich
Mathematics Teacher
High Point Central
High Point, North Carolina

Judith Ryder
Mathematics Teacher
South Charlotte Middle School
Charlotte, North Carolina

Cheryl M. Jones
Mathematics Department Coordinator
Winnetonka High School
Kansas City, Missouri

Margaret M. Kirk
Mathematics Teacher
Welborn Middle School
High Point, North Carolina

George R. Murphy
Mathematics Department Chairperson
Pine-Richland High School
Gibsonia, Pennsylvania

Barbara S. Owens
Mathematics Teacher
Davidson Middle School
Davidson, North Carolina

Kristine Powell
Mathematics Teacher
Lehi Junior High School
Lehi, Utah

Mary Richards
Mathematics Teacher
Clyde A. Erwin High School
Asheville, North Carolina

Donna Schmitt
Reviewer, Technology
Mathematics and Computer Science Teacher
Dubuque Senior High School
Dubuque, Iowa

Mabel S. Sechrist
Mathematics Teacher
Mineral Springs Middle School
Winston-Salem, North Carolina

Diane Baish Stamy
Mathematics Chairperson
Big Spring School District
Newville, Pennsylvania

Robert L. Thompson
Mathematics Teacher
Raines High School
Jacksonville, Florida

John J. Turechek
Mathematics Department Chairperson
Bunnell High School
Stratford, Connecticut

Jan S. Wessell
Mathematics Supervisor
New Hanover County Schools
Wilmington, North Carolina

Kathy Zwanzig
Middle School Algebra Resource Teacher
Jefferson County Public Schools
Louisville, Kentucky

Richard K. Sherry
Mathematics Department Chairman
Roosevelt Junior High School
Altoona, Pennsylvania

Carolyn Stanley
Mathematics Department Chairperson
Tidewater Academy
Wakefield, Virginia

Linda K. Tinga
Mathematics Teacher
Laney High School
Wilmington, North Carolina

Tonya Dessert Urbatsch
Mathematics Curriculum Coordinator
Davenport Community Schools
Davenport, Iowa

Ted Wiecek
Mathematics Department Chairperson
Wells Community Academy
Chicago, Illinois

Catherine C. Sperando
Mathematics Teacher
Shades Valley High School
Birmingham, Alabama

Richard P. Strausz
Math/Computer Coordinator
Farmington Schools
Farmington, Michigan

Kimberly Troise
Mathematics Teacher
A. C. Reynolds High School
Asheville, North Carolina

Anthony J. Weisse
Mathematics Teacher
Central High School
LaCrosse, Wisconsin

Rosalyn Zeid
Mathematics Director
Union High School
Union, New Jersey

Table of Contents

CHAPTER 2 Exploring Rational Numbers 70

CHAPTER 3 Solving Linear Equations 140

INTEGRATION

Content Integration

What does geometry have to do with algebra? Believe it or not, you can study most math topics from more than one point of view. Here are some examples.

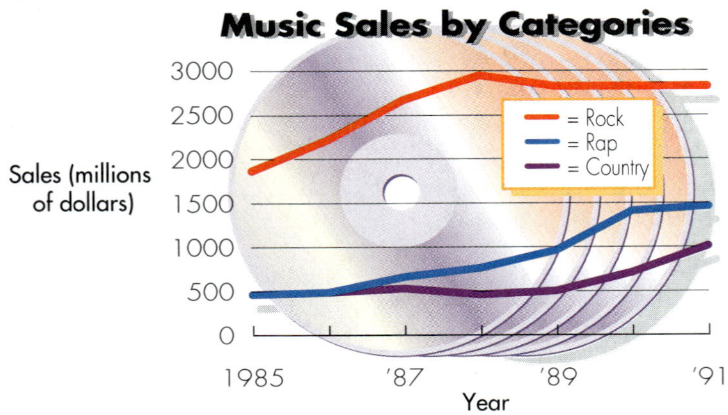

Source: The Recording Industry Association of America

◀ **Probability** You'll model the roll of two dice with relations and line plots. (Lesson 5–2, Exercise 45)

▲ **Problem Solving** You'll interpret graphs and learn how to sketch graphs of real-world situations. (Lesson 1–9, page 62)

LOOK BACK

You can refer to Lesson 1-7 for information on the distributive property.

Source: Lesson 9–6, page 529

Look Back features refer you to skills and concepts that have been taught earlier in the book.

Discrete Mathematics ▶ You'll investigate patterns and sequences and use them to solve a variety of problems. (Lesson 1–2, pages 12–18)

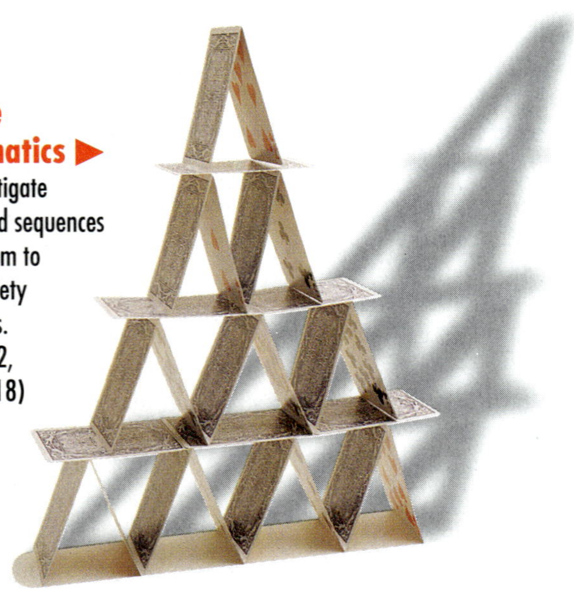

Statistics You'll learn how to display data about the speeds of the fastest animals on a line plot. (Lesson 2–2, page 80) ▶

Geometry You'll use your algebra skills to find the missing measures of similar triangles. (Lesson 4–2, pages 201–205)

CHAPTER 6 Analyzing Linear Equations 322

CHAPTER 7 Solving Linear Inequalities 382

APPLICATIONS

Real-Life Applications

Have you ever wondered if you'll ever actually use math? Every lesson in this book is designed to help show you where and when math is used in the real world. Since you'll explore many interesting topics, we believe you'll discover that math is relevant and exciting. Here are some examples.

Top Five List, FYI, and **Fabulous Firsts** contain interesting facts that enhance the applications.

Top Five List

Selling Prices of Paintings

1. *Portrait du Dr. Gachet* by van Gogh, $75,000,000
2. *Au Moulin de la Galette* by Renoir, $71,000,000
3. *Les Noces de Pierrette* by Picasso, $51,700,000
4. *Irises* by van Gogh, $49,000,000
5. *Yo Picasso* by Picasso, $43,500,000

Source: Lesson 9–4, page 514

Football You'll see how punting a football is related to angle measure. (Lesson 3–4, page 162)

Carpentry You'll study an industrial technology application that involves computing with rational numbers. (Lesson 2–7, Exercise 47)

◄ Recreation Games from several world cultures that are similar to hopscotch will illustrate multiplying a polynomial by a monomial. (Lesson 9–6, page 529)

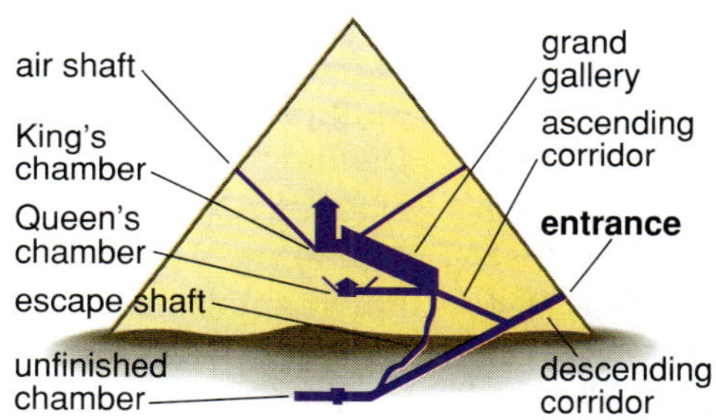

▲ World Cultures The Great Pyramid of Khufu is the setting for an application involving systems of linear equations. (Lesson 8–3, Exercise 42)

fabulous FIRSTS

Elmer Simms Campbell (1906–1971)

Elmer Simms Campbell was the first African-American cartoonist to work for national publications. He contributed cartoons and other art work to several magazines, as well as syndicated features in 145 newspapers.

Source: Lesson 8–3, page 469

Space Science You'll discuss the extreme temperatures encountered during a walk in space as you learn about absolute value. (Lesson 2–3, page 85)

Mathematics and SOCIETY

Teen Talk Dolls

What do dolls have to do with mathematics? Actual reprinted articles illustrate how mathematics is a part of our society. (Lesson 3–7, page 183)

CHAPTER 8 Solving Systems of Linear Equations and Inequalities 450

CHAPTER 9 Exploring Polynomials 494

CHAPTER 10 Using Factoring 556

CHAPTER 11 Exploring Quadratic and Exponential Functions 608

CONNECTIONS

Interdisciplinary Connections

Did you realize that mathematics is used in biology? in history? in geography? Yes, it may be hard to believe, but mathematics is frequently connected to other subjects that you are studying.

GLOBAL CONNECTIONS

About 15,000 years ago, an important application of the lever appeared as hunters used an *atlatl,* the Aztec word for spear-thrower. This simple device was a handle that provided extra mechanical advantage by adding length to the hunter's arm. This enabled the hunter to use less motion to get greater results when hunting.

Source: Lesson 7–2, page 392

◀ **Global Connections** features introduce you to a variety of world cultures.

Health You'll write inequalities to model target heart rates and exercise. (Lesson 7–8, Exercise 47)

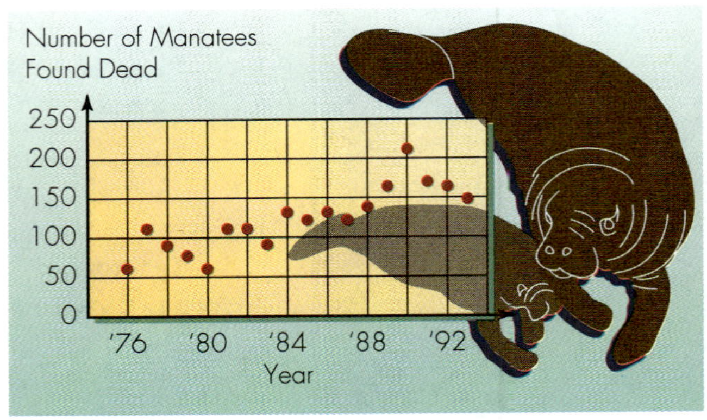

▲ **Biology** You'll study the mortality rates of Florida's manatees, an endangered species. (Lesson 5–2, page 262)

CAREER CHOICES

A **zoologist** studies animals, their origin, life process, behavior, and diseases. They are usually identified by the animal group in which they specialize, for example herpetology (reptiles), ornithology (birds), and ichthyology (fish).

Zoology requires a minimum of a bachelor's degree. Many college positions in this field require a Ph.D. degree.

For more information, see:

Occupational Outlook Handbook, 1994–95, U.S. Department of Labor.

Source: Lesson 5–2, page 264

◀ **Career Choices** features include information on interesting careers.

Geography In 1994, the population of New York was surpassed by Texas. This situation is modeled as a system of linear equations. (Lesson 8–2, page 462)

▲ **Art** A Mondrian painting entitled *Composition with Red, Yellow, and Blue* is used to model polynomials. (Lesson 9–3, page 514)

Math Journal exercises give you the opportunity to assess yourself and write about your understanding of key math concepts. (Lesson 7–1, Exercise 6)

MATH JOURNAL

6. Sometimes statements we make can be translated into inequalities. For example, *In some states, you have to be at least 16 years old to have a driver's license* can be expressed as $a \geq 16$, and *Tomás cannot lift more than 72 pounds* can be translated into $w \leq 72$. Following these examples, write three statements that deal with your everyday life. Then translate each into a corresponding inequality.

TECHNOLOGY

Do you know how to use computers and graphing calculators? If you do, you'll have a much better chance of being successful in today's high-tech society and workplace.

GRAPHING CALCULATORS

There are several ways in which graphing calculators are integrated.

- **Introduction to Graphing Calculators** On pages 2–3, you'll get acquainted with the basic features and functions of a graphing calculator.
- **Graphing Technology Lessons** In Lesson 5–2A, you'll learn how to plot points using a graphing calculator.
- **Graphing Calculator Explorations** You'll learn how to use a graphing calculator to find the mean and median in Lesson 3–7.
- **Graphing Calculator Programs** In Lesson 3–5, Exercise 39 includes a graphing calculator program that can be used to solve equations of the form $ax + b = cx + d$.
- **Graphing Calculator Exercises** Many exercises are designed to be solved using a graphing calculator. For example, see Exercises 40–42 in Lesson 7–8.

COMPUTER SOFTWARE

- **Spreadsheets** On page 297 of Lesson 5–6, a spreadsheet is used to help write an equation that models a relation.
- **BASIC Programs** The program on page 8 of Lesson 1–1 is designed to evaluate expressions.
- **Graphing Software** Graphing software, on page 471 in Lesson 8–3, is used to graph and solve systems of linear equations.

Technology Tips, such as this one on page 216 of Lesson 4–4, are designed to help you make more efficient use of technology through practical hints and suggestions.

TECHNOLOGY Tip

Most calculators have a key labeled [%]. To find 28% of 58.4 on a scientific calculator, enter:

28 [2nd] [%] [×] 58.4 [=] 16.352.

SYMBOLS AND MEASURES

Symbols

$=$	is equal to
$\neq$	is not equal to
$>$	is greater than
$<$	is less than
$\geq$	is greater than or equal to
$\leq$	is less than or equal to
$\approx$	is approximately equal to
$\sim$	is similar to
$\times$ or $\cdot$	times
$\div$	divided by
$-$	negative or minus
$+$	positive or plus
$\pm$	positive or negative
$-a$	opposite or additive inverse of a
$\lvert a \rvert$	absolute value of a
$a \stackrel{?}{=} b$	Does a equal b?
$a : b$	ratio of a to b
$\sqrt{a}$	square root of a
$P(A)$	probability of A
O	origin
π	pi
$\%$	percent
$0.1\overline{2}$	decimal 0.12222...
$^\circ$	degree
$f(x)$	f of x, the value of f at x
(a, b)	ordered pair a, b
$\overline{AB}$	line segment $\overline{AB}$
$\widehat{AB}$	arc AB
$\overrightarrow{AB}$	ray AB
$\overleftrightarrow{AB}$	line AB
AB	measure of $\overline{AB}$
$\angle$	angle
Δ	triangle
$\cos A$	cosine of A
$\sin A$	sine of A
$\tan A$	tangent of A
( )	parentheses; *also* ordered pairs
[ ]	brackets; *also* matrices
{ }	braces; *also* sets
$\varnothing$	empty set

Measures

mm	millimeter
cm	centimeter
m	meter
km	kilometer
g	gram
kg	kilogram
mL	milliliter
L	liter
in.	inch
ft	foot
yd	yard
mi	mile
in^2 or sq in.	square inch
s	second
min	minute
h	hour

GETTING ACQUAINTED WITH THE GRAPHING CALCULATOR

What is it? What does it do? How is it going to help me learn math?

These are just a few of the questions many students ask themselves when they first see a graphing calculator. Some students may think, "Oh, no! Do we *have* to use one?", while others may think, "All right! We get to use these neat calculators!" There are as many thoughts and feelings about graphing calculators as there are students, but one thing is for sure: a graphing calculator *can* help you learn mathematics.

So what is a graphing calculator? Very simply, it is a calculator that draws graphs. This means that it will do all of the things that a "regular" calculator will do, *plus* it will draw graphs of simple or very complex equations. In algebra, this capability is nice to have because the graphs of some complex equations take a lot of time to sketch by hand. Some are even considered impossible to draw by hand. This is where a graphing calculator can be very useful.

But a graphing calculator can do more than just calculate and draw graphs. You can program it, work with matrices, and make statistical graphs and computations, just to name a few things. If you need to generate random numbers, you can do that on the graphing calculator. If you need to find the absolute value of numbers, you can do that, too. It's really a very powerful tool—so powerful that it is often called a pocket computer. But don't let that intimidate you. A graphing calculator can save you time and make doing mathematics easier.

As you may have noticed, graphing calculators have some keys that other calculators do not. The keys located on the bottom half of the calculator are probably familiar to you as they are the keys found on basic scientific calculators. The keys located just below the screen are the graphing keys. You will also notice the up, down, left, and right arrow keys. These allow you to move the cursor around on the screen and to "trace" graphs that have been plotted. The other keys located on the top half of the calculator access the special features such as statistical and matrix computations.

There are some keystrokes that can save you time when using the graphing calculator. A few of them are listed below.

- Any yellow commands written above the calculator keys are accessed with the [2nd] key, which is also yellow. Similarly, any green characters above the keys are accessed with the [ALPHA] key, which is also green.
- [2nd] [ENTRY] copies the previous calculation so you can edit and use it again.
- Pressing [ON] while the calculator is graphing stops the calculator from completing the graph.
- [2nd] [QUIT] will return you to the home (or text) screen.
- [2nd] [A-LOCK] locks the [ALPHA] key, which is like pressing "shift lock" or "caps locks" on a typewriter or computer. The result is that all caps will be typed and you do not have to hold the shift key down. (This is handy for programming.)
- [2nd] [OFF] turns the calculator off.

Some commonly used mathematical functions are shown in the table below. As with any scientific calculator, the graphing calculator observes the order of operations.

Mathematical Operation	Examples	Keys	Display
evaluate expressions	Find 2 + 5.	2 [+] 5 [ENTER]	2+5 7
exponents	Find 3^5.	3 [^] 5 [ENTER]	3^5 243
multiplication	Evaluate 3(9.1 + 0.8).	3 [×] [(] 9.1 [+] .8 [)] [ENTER]	3(9.1+.8) 29.7
roots	Find $\sqrt{14}$.	[2nd] [√] 14 [ENTER]	√ 14 3.741657387
opposites	Enter −3.	[(−)] 3	−3

Graphing

Before graphing, we must instruct the calculator how to set up the axes in the coordinate plane. To do this, we define a **viewing window.** The viewing window for a graph is the portion of the coordinate grid that is displayed on the **graphics screen** of the calculator. The viewing window is written as [left, right] by [bottom, top] or [Xmin, Xmax] by [Ymin, Ymax]. A viewing window of [−10, 10] by [−10, 10] is called the **standard viewing window** and is a good viewing window to start with to graph an equation. The standard viewing window can be easily obtained by pressing [ZOOM] 6. Try this. Move the arrow keys around and observe what happens. You are seeing a portion of the coordinate plane that includes the region from -10 to 10 on the x-axis and from -10 to 10 on the y-axis. Move the cursor, and you can see the coordinates of the points for the current position of the cursor.

Any viewing window can be set manually by pressing the WINDOW key. The window screen will appear and display the current settings for your viewing window. First press ENTER. Then, using the arrow and ENTER keys, move the cursor to edit the window settings. Xscl and Yscl refer to the x-scale and y-scale. This is the number of tick marks placed on the x- and y-axes. Xscl=1 means that there will be a tick mark for every unit of one along the x-axis. The standard viewing window would appear as follows.

Xmin = -10
Xmax = 10
Xscl = 1
Ymin = -10
Ymax = 10
Yscl = 1

Graphing equations is as simple as defining a viewing window, entering the equations in the Y= list, and pressing GRAPH. It is often important to view enough of a graph so you can see all of the important characteristics of the graph and understand its behavior. The term **complete graph** refers to a graph that shows all of the important characteristics such as intercepts or maximum and minimum values.

Example: Graph $y = x - 14$ in the standard viewing window.

Enter: Y= X,T,θ,n − 14 GRAPH

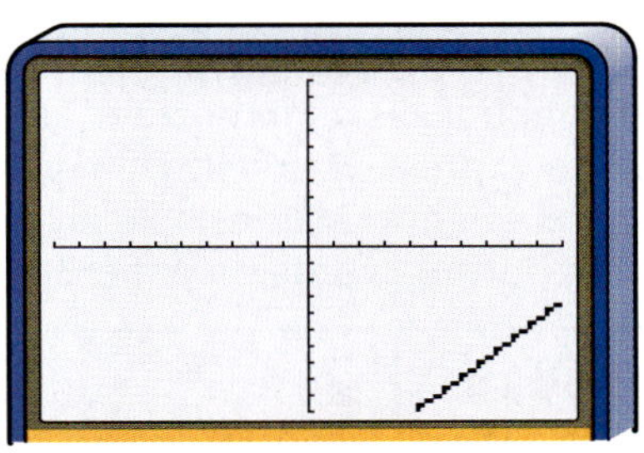

We see only a small portion of the graph. Why?

The graph of $y = x - 14$ is a line that crosses the x-axis at 14 and the y-axis at -14. The important features of the graph are plotted off the screen and so the graph is not complete. A better viewing window for this graph would be $[-20, 20]$ by $[-20, 20]$, which includes both intercepts. This is considered a complete graph.

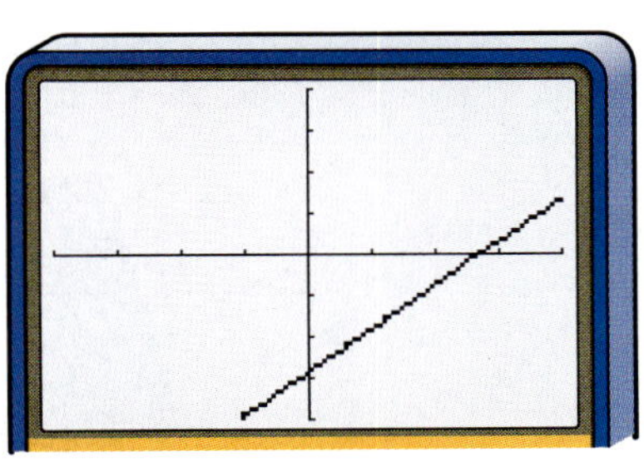

Programming

Programming features allow us to write and execute a series of commands to perform tasks that may be too complex or cumbersome to perform otherwise. Each program is given a name. Commands begin with a colon (:), followed by an expression or an instruction. Most of the features of the calculator are accessible from program mode.

When you press PRGM, you see three menus: EXEC, EDIT, and NEW. EXEC allows you to execute a stored program by selecting the name of the program from the menu. EDIT allows you to edit or change an existing program and NEW allows you to create a new program. To break during program execution, press ON. The following example illustrates how to create and execute a new program that stores an expression as Y and evaluates the expression for a designated value of X.

1. Enter PRGM ▶ ▶ ENTER to create a new program.
2. Type EVAL ENTER to name the program. (Make sure that the caps lock is on.) You are now in the program editor, which allows you to enter commands. The colon (:) in the first column of the line indicates that this is the beginning of the command line.
3. The first command lines will ask the user to designate a value for x. Enter PRGM ▶ 3 2nd A-LOCK " ENTER THE VALUE FOR X " ALPHA ENTER PRGM ▶ 1 X,T,θ,n ENTER.
4. The expression to be evaluated for the value of x is $x - 7$. To store the expression as Y, enter X,T,θ,n − 7 STO▶ ALPHA Y ENTER.
5. Finally, we want to display the value for the expression. Enter PRGM ▶ 3 ALPHA Y ENTER.
6. Now press 2nd QUIT to return to the home screen.
7. To execute the program, press PRGM. Then press the down arrow to locate the program name and press ENTER, or press the number or letter next to the progam name. The program asks for a value for x. You will input any value for which the expression is defined and press ENTER. To immediately re-execute the program, simply press ENTER when Done appears on the screen.

While a graphing calculator cannot do everything, it can make some things easier. To prepare for whatever lies ahead, you should try to learn as much as you can. The future will definitely involve technology, and using a graphing calculator is a good start toward becoming familiar with technology. Who knows? Maybe one day you will be designing the next satellite, building the next skyscraper, or helping students learn mathematics with the aid of a graphing calculator!

CHAPTER 1

Exploring Expressions, Equations, and Functions

Objectives

In this chapter, you will:

- translate verbal expressions into mathematical expressions,
- solve problems by looking for a pattern,
- use mathematical properties to evaluate expressions,
- solve open sentences, and
- use and interpret stem-and-leaf plots, tables, graphs, and functions.

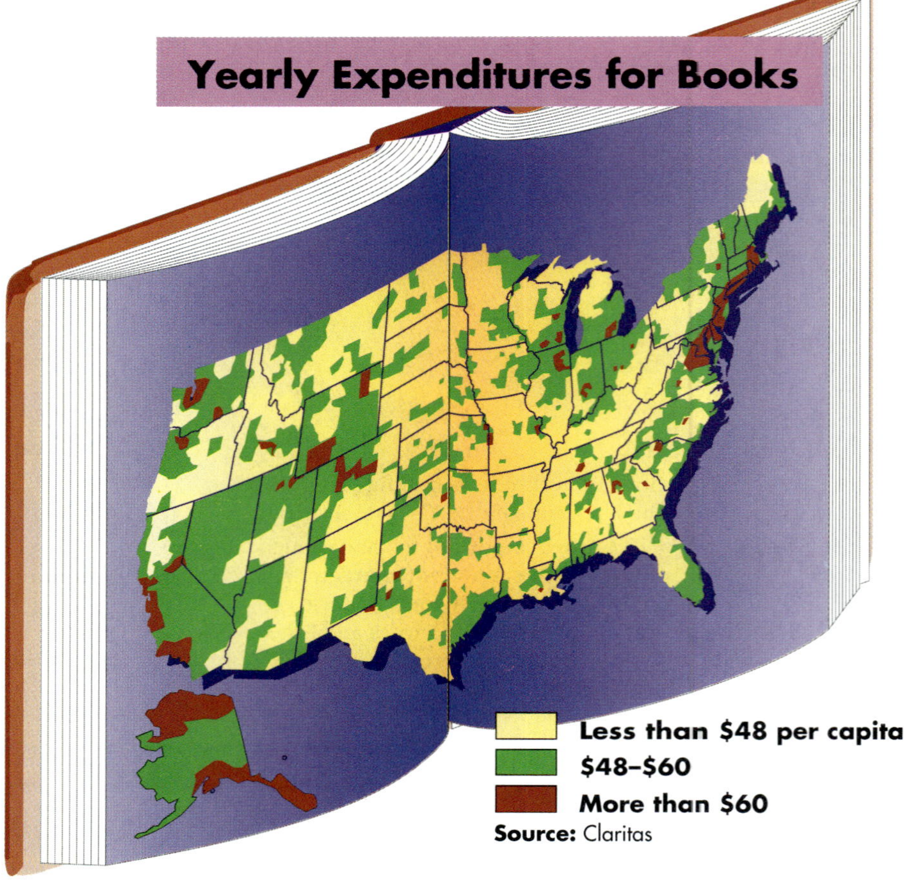

TIME Line

The writing and publishing of books is an important part of our economy. Do you like to express yourself? Do you share your thoughts by writing poems or short stories? Would you like to eventually make a living putting words on paper?

1650 B.C. The Rhind Papyrus shows solutions of simple equations.

A.D. 786 The Grand Mosque of Cordoba, Spain, is completed.

400 B.C. Theodorus of Cyrene demonstrates that the square roots of some numbers are irrational.

PEOPLE IN THE NEWS

When **Wendy Isdell** was in her eighth grade Algebra 1 class, she got an idea for a short story. Later, she wrote an outline and completed a first draft. The following year, she entered the finished story in the Virginia Young Authors' Contest and won first place in the state competition. Wendy sent her story to Free Spirit Publishing in Minneapolis, and her book *A Gebra Named Al* was published during her senior year in high school.

Wendy's Algebra 1 and 2, geometry, trigonometry, chemistry, Earth science, and physical science classes have provided background for the information in her book. She hopes to make a living as a professional writer.

Chapter Project

Choose a poet and read 10 of his or her poems.

- Describe some patterns that you see in these poems.
- Count the number of words in each poem. Make a stem-and-leaf plot of the number of words in the poems. Does the poet seem to write poems with about the same number of words? Are one or more of the poems exceptionally long or short for this poet?
- Make a graph that models one of the poems. Write a paragraph that describes the relationship between the graph and the poem.

1455 The Gutenberg Bible is printed in Mainz, Germany.

1881 French impressionist painter Auguste Renoir completes the *Boating Party Lunch*.

1663 The first known work on probability is published.

1993 Toni Morrison becomes the first African American to receive the Nobel Prize for Literature.

1–1

Variables and Expressions

APPLICATION

Health

What YOU'LL LEARN

- To translate verbal expressions into mathematical expressions and vice versa.

Why IT'S IMPORTANT

You can use expressions to solve problems involving health, recycling, and geometry.

Many people enjoy going to the beach in the summer. Unfortunately, the ultraviolet radiation in direct sunlight causes skin cancer. In recent years, the number of skin cancer cases has increased. Many sunbathers use sunscreen lotions to protect themselves in the sun.

The Sun Protection Factor (SPF) scale gives numbers that represent the length of time you can stay in the sun without burning if you have lotion on. Let's say you can stay in the sun with no sunscreen for 10 minutes without burning. If you put on SPF 5 lotion, you can stay in the sun for 10 minutes × 5 or 50 minutes, or a little less than one hour. Use the table below to see the pattern.

10 × 5 and 10 × 15 are numerical expressions.

No Sunscreen	With Sunscreen	
Minutes in Sun Without Burning	SPF Number	Minutes in Sun Without Burning
10	5	10 × 5
10	15	10 × 15
5	4	5 × 4
15	8	15 × 8
m	s	$m \times s$

CAREER CHOICES

A **registered nurse (RN)** cares for the injured and sick, administers medications, and provides for the physical and emotional needs of his or her patients.

Nursing requires graduation from an accredited nursing school and passing a national licensing examination. About 20% of the 3.8 million new jobs in health care will be for RNs.

For more information, contact:

National League for Nursing
250 Hudson St.
New York, NY 10014.

The letters m and s are called **variables,** and $m \times s$ is an **algebraic expression.** In algebra, variables are symbols that are used to represent unspecified numbers. Any letter may be used as a variable. We selected m because it is the first letter of the word "minutes" and s because it is the first letter of "SPF".

An algebraic expression consists of one or more numbers and variables along with one or more arithmetic operations. Here are some other examples of algebraic expressions.

$x - 2 \qquad \frac{a}{b} + 3 \qquad t \times 2s \qquad 7mn \div 3k$

The symbol "×" as shown in $x \times y$ is often avoided because it may be confused with the variable "x."

In algebraic expressions, a raised dot or parentheses are often used to indicate multiplication. Here are ways to represent the product of x and y.

$xy \qquad x \cdot y \qquad x(y) \qquad (x)(y) \qquad (x)y \qquad x \times y$

In each of the multiplication expressions, the quantities being multiplied are called **factors,** and the result is called the **product.**

It is often necessary to translate verbal expressions into algebraic expressions.

Verbal Expression	Algebraic Expression
7 less than the product of 3 and a number x	$3x - 7$
the product of 7 and s divided by the product of 8 and y	$7s \div 8y$
four years younger than Sarah (S = Sarah's age)	$S - 4$
half as big as last night's crowd (c = size of last night's crowd)	$\frac{c}{2}$

Example 1 **Write an algebraic expression for each verbal expression.**

a. three times a number x subtracted from 24

$24 - 3x$

b. 5 greater than half of a number t

$\frac{t}{2} + 5$ or $\frac{1}{2}t + 5$

Another important skill is translating algebraic expressions into verbal expressions.

Example 2 **Write a verbal expression for each algebraic expression.**

a. $(3 + b) \div y$

the sum of 3 and b divided by y

b. $5y + 10x$

the product of 5 and y plus the product of 10 and x

An expression like x^n is called a **power.** The variable x is called the **base,** and n is called the **exponent.** The exponent indicates the number of times the base is used as a factor.

x^2 means $x \cdot x$. 12^4 means $12 \cdot 12 \cdot 12 \cdot 12$.

Symbols	Words	Meaning
5^1	5 to the first power	5
5^2	5 to the second power or 5 squared	$5 \cdot 5$
5^3	5 to the third power or 5 cubed	$5 \cdot 5 \cdot 5$
5^4	5 to the fourth power	$5 \cdot 5 \cdot 5 \cdot 5$
$3a^5$	three times a to the fifth power	$3 \cdot a \cdot a \cdot a \cdot a \cdot a$
x^n	x to the nth power	$\underbrace{x \cdot x \cdot x \cdot \ldots \cdot x}_{n \text{ factors}}$
	An expression of the form x^n is read as "x to the nth power."	

Example 3

INTEGRATION **Geometry**

Write a power that represents the number of smallest squares in the large square.

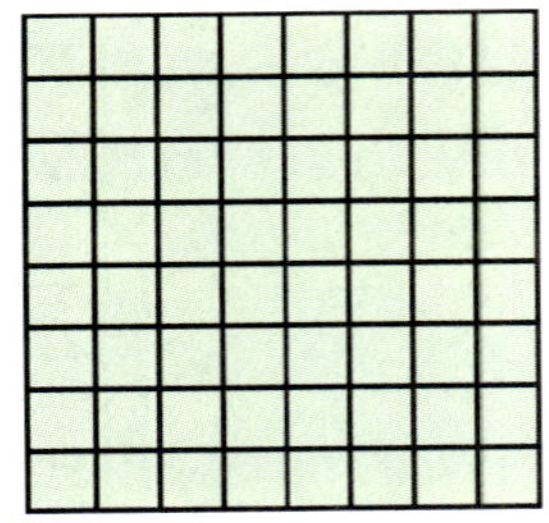

There are 8 squares on each side.

The total number of squares is $8^2 = 8 \cdot 8$ or 64.

You can use the x^2 key on a calculator to square a number.

Enter: 8 [x^2] 64

To **evaluate** an expression means to find its value.

Example 4

Evaluate 3^4.

$$3^4 = 3 \cdot 3 \cdot 3 \cdot 3$$
$$= 81$$

You can use the [y^x] key on a calculator to raise a number to a power.

Enter: 3 [y^x] 4 [=] 81

EXPLORATION PROGRAMMING

BASIC is a computer language. The symbols used in BASIC are similar to those used in algebra.

+ means add.	/ means divide.
− means subtract.	↑ means exponent.
* means multiply.	

Numerical variables in BASIC are represented by capital letters. The program at the right can be used to add, subtract, multiply, divide, and find powers.

```
10 INPUT A,B
20 PRINT "A + B ="; A + B
30 PRINT "A - B ="; A - B
40 PRINT "A * B ="; A * B
50 PRINT "A / B ="; A / B
60 PRINT "A ↑ B ="; A ↑ B
```

Your Turn

a. Let $a = 10$ and $b = 3$. Use the program to find $10 + 3$, $10 - 3$, 10×3, $10 \div 3$, and 10^3.

b. Let $a = 9$ and $b = 3$. Use the program to find $9 + 3$, $9 - 3$, 9×3, $9 \div 3$, and 9^3.

c. Let $a = 5.2$ and $b = 2$. Use the program to find $5.2 + 2$, $5.2 - 2$, 5.2×2, $5.2 \div 2$, and 5.2^2.

CHECK FOR UNDERSTANDING

Communicating Mathematics

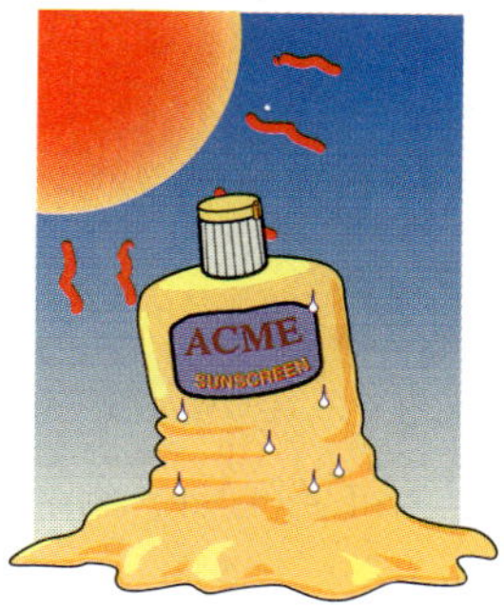

Study the lesson. Then complete the following.

1. **Describe** how you would compute the length of time you could sunbathe using an SPF 20 sunscreen lotion if you can stay in the sun for 15 minutes without burning.
2. Can you find the volume of a cube if you only know the length of a side, s? How?
3. **Describe** what x^7 means.
4. **Explain** the difference between numerical expressions and algebraic expressions.
5. **You Decide** Darcy and Tonya are studying for an exam. Darcy says, "The square of a number is always greater than the number." Tonya disagrees. Who is correct? Explain your answer.

Guided Practice

Write an algebraic expression for each verbal expression.

6. the product of the fourth power of a and the second power of b
7. six less than three times the square of y

Write a verbal expression for each algebraic expression.

8. 7^5
9. $3x^2 + 4$

Write each expression as an expression with exponents.

10. $4 \cdot 4 \cdot 4$
11. $a \cdot a \cdot a \cdot a \cdot a \cdot a \cdot a$

Evaluate each expression.

12. 6^2
13. 2^5
14. **Geometry** The area of a circle can be found by multiplying the number π times the square of the radius. If the radius of the circle is r, write an expression that represents the area of the circle.

EXERCISES

Practice

Write an algebraic expression for each verbal expression.

15. the sum of k and 20
16. the product of 16 and p
17. a to the seventh power
18. 49 increased by twice a number
19. two thirds of the square of a number
20. the product of 5 and m plus half of n
21. 8 pounds heavier than his brother (b = brother's weight)
22. 3 times as many wins as last season (w = last season's wins)

Write a verbal expression for each algebraic expression.

23. $4m^5$
24. $\frac{x^2}{2}$
25. $c^2 + 23$
26. $\frac{1}{2}n^3$
27. $2(4)(5)^2$
28. $3x^2 - 2x$

Write each expression as an expression with exponents.

29. $8 \cdot 8$

30. $10 \cdot 10 \cdot 10 \cdot 10 \cdot 10$

31. $4 \cdot 4 \cdot 4 \cdot 4 \cdot 4 \cdot 4 \cdot 4$

32. $t \cdot t \cdot t$

33. $z \cdot z \cdot z \cdot z \cdot z$

34. $d \cdot d \cdot d \cdot d \cdot d \cdot d \cdot d \cdot d \cdot d \cdot d$

Evaluate each expression.

35. 7^2

36. 9^2

37. 4^3

38. 5^3

39. 2^4

40. 3^5

Write an algebraic expression for each verbal expression.

41. triple the difference of 55 and the cube of w

42. four times the sum of r and s, increased by twice the difference of r and s

43. the sum of a and b, increased by the quotient of a and b

44. the perimeter of a square if the length of a side is s

45. the amount of money in Karen's savings account if she has y dollars and adds x dollars per week for 10 weeks

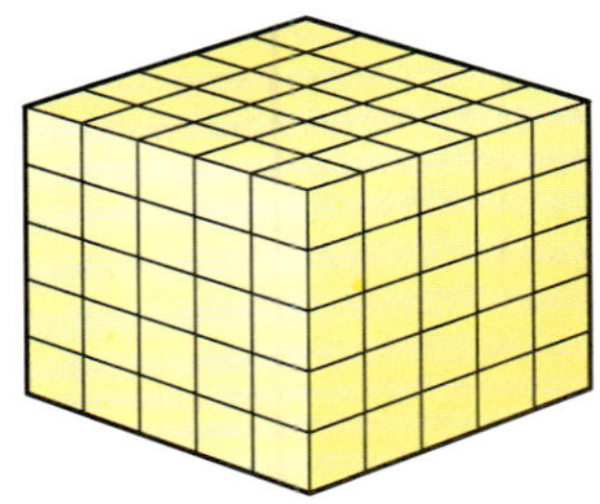

46. **Geometry** Write an expression that represents the total number of small cubes in the large cube shown at the right. Then evaluate the expression.

Critical Thinking

47. Evaluate 4^2 and 2^4.

a. What do you notice? From this example, can you say that the same relationship exists between 2^5 and 5^2? What about between 3^4 and 4^3?

b. In general, do you think that $a^b = b^a$ for positive whole numbers a and b? Support your answer.

Applications and Problem Solving

48. **Babysitting** According to a magazine, in New York City, the average teenage babysitter makes \$7 per hour for a Saturday night. In Atlanta, the average teenage babysitter makes only \$3 per hour. **Source:** *SmartMoney magazine*

a. Write an expression representing the amount of money that the average teenage babysitter in New York City makes for working x hours on a Saturday night.

b. Write an expression representing the amount of money that the average teenage babysitter in Atlanta makes for working x hours on a Saturday night.

c. Write an expression representing the difference between the amount that the New York babysitter makes and the Atlanta babysitter makes for working x hours on a Saturday night.

49. Recycling The alarming amount of garbage produced by our society requires that everyone work to recycle. According to a certain magazine, each person in the United States produces an average of 3.5 pounds of trash a day.

a. Write an expression representing the pounds of trash produced in a day by a family that has x members.

b. Write an expression representing the pounds of trash produced in a day by a family that has y members.

c. Write an expression representing the pounds of trash produced in one day by both of the families in parts a and b.

Source: *Vitality*

50. Geometry The surface area of a rectangular prism is the sum of the product of twice the length ℓ and the width w and the product of twice the length and the height h and the product of twice the width and the height. Write an expression that represents the surface area of this type of prism.

Mathematics and SOCIETY

International Mathematical Olympiad

The excerpt below appeared in an article in a magazine on August 1, 1994.

IF THE UNITED STATES SENDS SIX KIDS TO THE International Mathematical Olympiad in Hong Kong, where a perfect individual score is 42, and together they score 252, does the country have reason to cheer? If you can't answer that one, then you desperately need a remedial course in arithmetic (or perhaps just new batteries in your calculator). The U.S. team members, all public high-school students, started out by competing against 350,000 of their peers on the American High School Mathematics Examination, aced two tougher exams, and prepped for a month at the U.S. Naval Academy. Only then did they board a plane and became the first squad in the Math Olympiad's 35-year history to get perfect scores across the board, outstripping 68 other nations to win the competition. . . . "They showed the world!" suggests the justifiably proud U.S. coach, Walter Mientka, a math professor at the University of Nebraska at Lincoln. ■

Source: *Time magazine*

1. Do you think this type of international contest is a good idea? Why or why not?
2. Would you like to represent your country in this competition? Why or why not?
3. How do you feel about the math courses you have had in school? What factors have influenced the way you feel?

1–2 Patterns and Sequences

What YOU'LL LEARN

- To extend sequences.

Why IT'S IMPORTANT

You can use patterns to extend sequences and solve problems.

APPLICATION

Handicrafts

The photograph at the right shows a Hopi woman completing a basket. Baskets are important in the Hopi culture since they can serve either a functional or a spiritual purpose. Looking at the inside of the basket, we can see a pattern. Following this pattern in a clockwise direction, what color would you expect to find on the first diamond shape that cannot be seen in the photo?

GLOBAL CONNECTIONS

Many American Indians play traditional games passed down through the generations. In one such game, markers made from bone, pottery, or shell are marked and tumbled in a small basket. The array of the markers is the basis for scoring. Five or six of a kind would win.

Example 1 **Study the pattern below.**

1 2 3 4 5 6

a. Draw the next three figures in the pattern.
b. Draw the 35th square in the pattern.

a. The pattern consists of squares with one corner shaded. The corner that is shaded is rotated in a clockwise direction. The next three figures are drawn below.

7 8 9

You may find a different pattern. For example, the seventh square may be the same as the fifth square, the eighth square may be the same as the fourth square, and the ninth square may be the same as the third square.

b. The pattern repeats after every 4 designs. Since 32 is the greatest number less than 35 that is divisible by 4, the 33rd square will be the same as the first square.

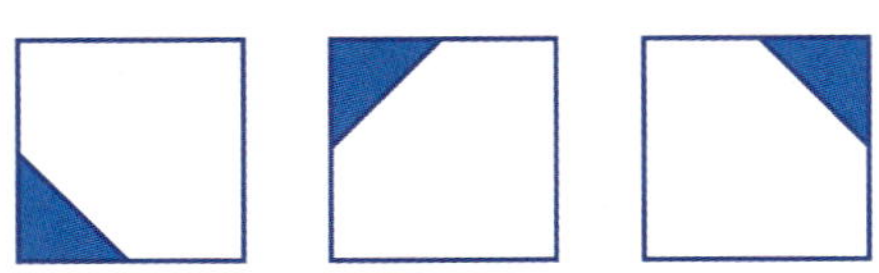

33 34 35

The 35th square will have its upper right corner shaded.

The numbers 2, 4, 6, 8, 10, and 12 form a pattern called a **sequence.** A sequence is a set of numbers in a specific order. The numbers in the sequence are called **terms.**

Example 2 **Find the next three terms in each sequence.**

a. 7, 13, 19, 25, . . .

Study the pattern in the sequence.

7, 13, 19, 25,...

+ 6 + 6 + 6

Each term is 6 more than the term before it.

$25 + 6 = 31$

$31 + 6 = 37$

$37 + 6 = 43$

The next three terms are 31, 37, and 43.

b. 243, 81, 27, 9, . . .

Study the pattern in the sequence.

243, 81, 27, 9,...

$\times \frac{1}{3}$ $\times \frac{1}{3}$ $\times \frac{1}{3}$

Each term is $\frac{1}{3}$ of the term before it.

$9 \times \frac{1}{3} = 3$

$3 \times \frac{1}{3} = 1$

$1 \times \frac{1}{3} = \frac{1}{3}$

The next three terms are 3, 1, and $\frac{1}{3}$.

One of the most-used strategies in problem solving is **look for a pattern.** When using this strategy, you will often need to make a table to organize the information.

Example 3 **What is the number of diagonals in a 10-sided polygon?**

INTEGRATION Geometry

Drawing a 10-sided polygon and all its diagonals would be difficult. Another way to solve the problem is to study the number of diagonals for polygons with fewer sides and then look for a pattern.

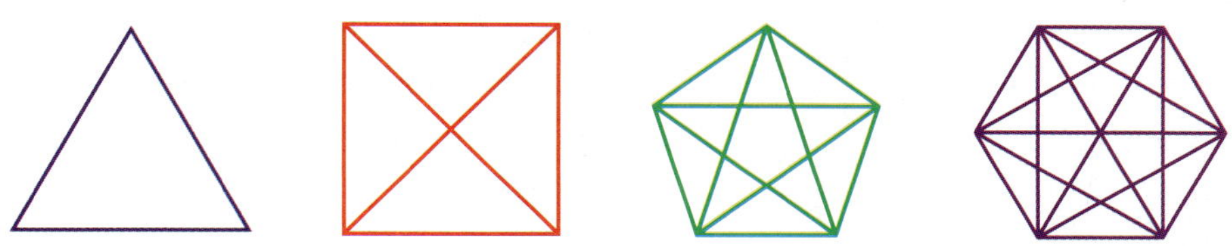

triangle	quadrilateral	pentagon	hexagon
3 sides	4 sides	5 sides	6 sides
0 diagonals	2 diagonals	5 diagonals	9 diagonals

(continued on the next page)

Use a chart to see the pattern.

Number of Sides	3	4	5	6	7	8	9	10
Number of Diagonals	0	2	5	9	?	?	?	?

+ 2   + 3   + 4

Use the pattern to complete the chart.

Recognizing patterns is important, but it does not always guarantee finding the correct answer. You may wish to check this answer by drawing a 10-sided polygon and its diagonals.

Number of Sides	3	4	5	6	7	8	9	10
Number of Diagonals	0	2	5	9	14	20	27	35

+ 2   + 3   + 4   **+ 5**   **+ 6**   **+ 7**   **+ 8**

A 10-sided polygon has 35 diagonals.

Sometimes a pattern can lead to a general rule that can be written as an algebraic expression. This is an example of **inductive reasoning.** Inductive reasoning is used to *make* a rule after seeing several examples.

Example 4 **Study the following pattern. Write an algebraic expression for the perimeter of the pattern consisting of *n* trapezoids.**

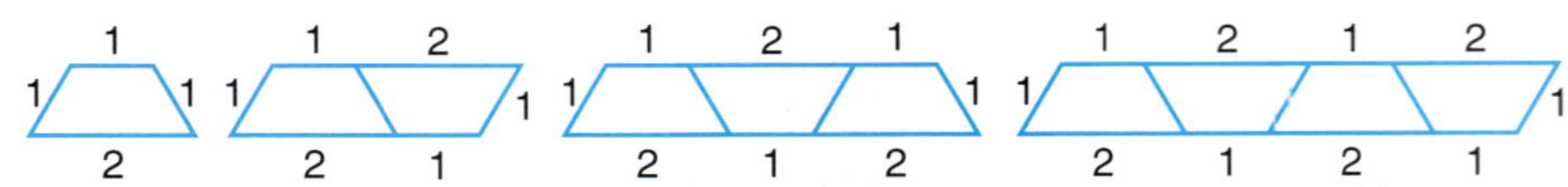

1 trapezoid $P = 5$ units

2 trapezoids $P = 8$ units

3 trapezoids $P = 11$ units

4 trapezoids $P = 14$ units

Use a chart to look for a pattern.

Number of Trapezoids	1	2	3	4	5	6	n
Perimeter	5	8	11	14	?	?	?

+ 3   + 3   + 3

Notice that each trapezoid adds 3 units to the perimeter.

For 1 trapezoid, the perimeter is $3 \cdot 1 + 2$, or 5 units.
For 2 trapezoids, the perimeter is $3 \cdot 2 + 2$, or 8 units.
For 3 trapezoids, the perimeter is $3 \cdot 3 + 2$, or 11 units.
For 4 trapezoids, the perimeter is $3 \cdot 4 + 2$, or 14 units.

Extend this pattern.

For 5 trapezoids, the perimeter should be $3 \cdot 5 + 2$, or 17 units.
For 6 trapezoids, the perimeter should be $3 \cdot 6 + 2$, or 20 units.
For n trapezoids, the perimeter should be $3 \cdot n + 2$, or $3n + 2$ units.

The algebraic expression $3n + 2$ represents the perimeter of this pattern with n trapezoids.

Deductive reasoning is a type of logic that *uses* a rule to make a conclusion. Suppose your teacher says there will be a quiz every Tuesday and today is Tuesday. Then you know by deductive reasoning that you will have a quiz today. You did not observe a pattern to make your conclusion. Is Example 4 inductive or deductive reasoning?

MODELING MATHEMATICS

Looking for Patterns

Materials: string scissors

If you use a pair of scissors to cut a piece of string in the normal way, you will have 2 pieces of string. What happens if you loop the string around one of the cutting edges of the scissors and cut?

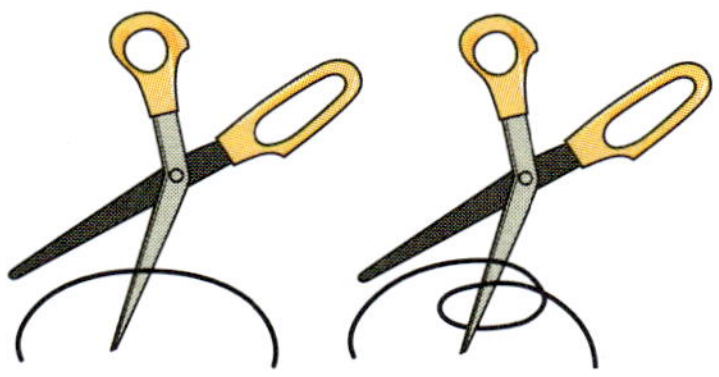

0 loop 1 loop

Your Turn

a. Make a piece of string loop once around your scissors as shown above. Cut the string. How many pieces do you have?

b. Make 2 loops and cut. How many pieces do you have?

c. Continue making loops and cutting until you see a pattern. Describe the pattern and write the sequence.

d. How many pieces would you have if you made 20 loops? Explain whether you used inductive or deductive reasoning to determine your answer.

e. Now tie the ends of the string together before you loop the string around the scissors. Investigate to determine how many pieces you would have if you made 10 loops with this string.

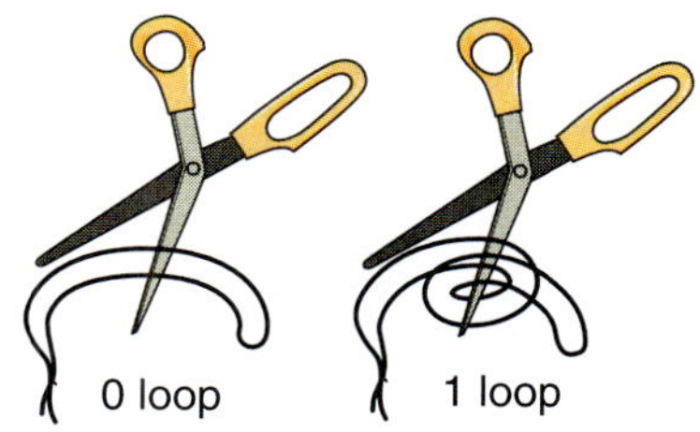

CHECK FOR UNDERSTANDING

Communicating Mathematics

Study the lesson. Then complete the following.

1. **Explain** the difference between inductive and deductive reasoning. Then give an example of each.
2. **Write** a sequence that has 22 as its fourth term.
3. **You Decide** Chi-Yo studies the sequence 1, 2, and 4. She notices that the second number is 1 more than the first, and the third number is 2 more than the second. She concludes that the next number in the sequence is $4 + 3$ or 7. Alonso disagrees. He notices that each number is twice the number before it. He says the next number in the sequence is 8. Who is correct? Explain.

MODELING MATHEMATICS

4. Refer to the Modeling Mathematics activity above. Suppose the ends of a string are *not* tied together.
   a. The string is looped around the scissors 50 times, and the string is cut. How many pieces will you have?
   b. The string is looped around the scissors y times, and the string is cut. How many pieces will you have?

Guided Practice

Give the next two items for each pattern.

5.

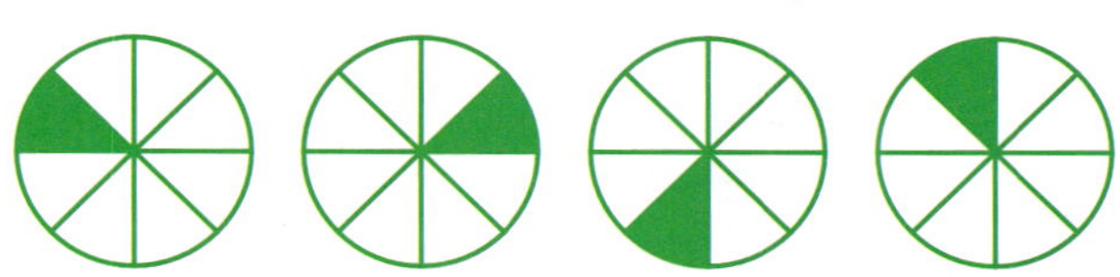

6. 85, 76, 67, 58,...

7. $1x + 1, 2x + 1, 3x + 1, 4x + 1, \ldots$

8. Consider the following pattern.

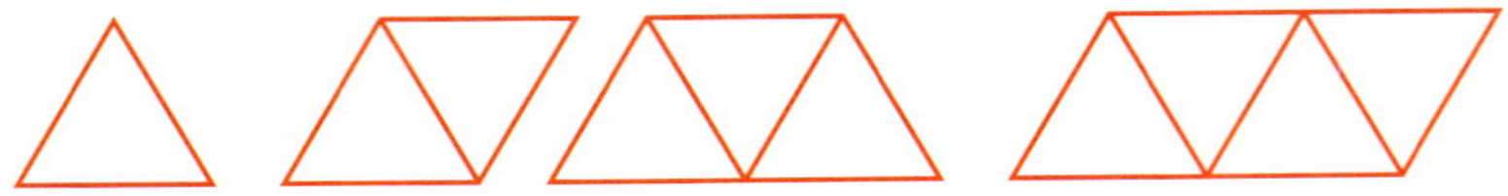

a. Suppose the length of each side of the triangles is 1 unit. What is the perimeter of each figure in the pattern?

b. Draw the next figure in the pattern. What is the perimeter of this figure?

c. What is the perimeter of the tenth figure in this pattern?

d. What is the perimeter of the nth figure in this pattern?

9. a. Copy and complete the following table.

4^1	4^2	4^3	4^4	4^5
4	16			

b. If you found the value of 4^6, what number do you think will be in the ones place? Check your conjecture.

c. Find the number in the ones place for the value of 4^{225}. Explain your reasoning.

EXERCISES

Practice **Give the next two items for each pattern.**

10.

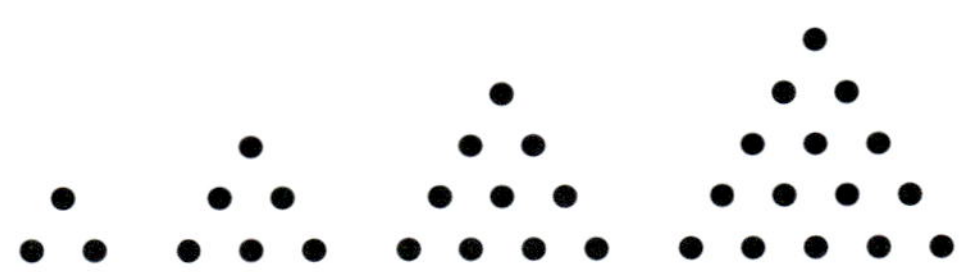

11.

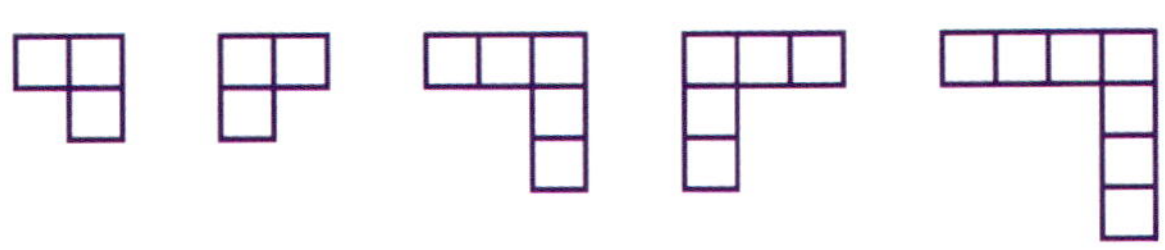

12.

13. 3, 6, 12, 24, ...

14. 4, 5.5, 7, 8.5, ...

15. 1, 4, 9, 16, ...

16. 9, 7, 10, 8, 11, 9, 12, ...

17. $a + 1, a + 3, a + 5, \ldots$

18. $x - 1y, x - 2y, x - 3y, \ldots$

19. a. Draw the next three figures in the following pattern.

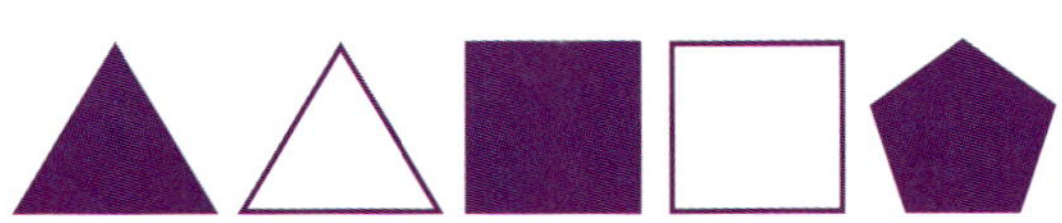

b. What is the color of the 38th figure? Explain your reasoning.

c. How many sides will the 19th figure have? Explain your reasoning.

20. **a.** Copy and complete the following table.

3^1	3^2	3^3	3^4	3^5	3^6
3	9				

b. Write the sequence of numbers representing the numbers in the ones place.

c. What are the next six numbers in this sequence?

d. Find the number in the ones place for the value of 3^{100}. Explain your reasoning. State the type of reasoning that you used.

21. **a.** Copy and find each sum.

$1 = 1$
$1 + 3 = ?$
$1 + 3 + 5 = ?$
$1 + 3 + 5 + 7 = ?$
$1 + 3 + 5 + 7 + 9 = ?$

b. Pythagoras is credited with a discovery about the sum of consecutive odd numbers such as those shown in part a. What did he discover?

c. What is the sum of the first 100 odd numbers?

d. What is the sum of the first x odd numbers?

22. If y represents the counting numbers 1, 2, 3, 4, ..., then the algebraic expression $2y$ represents the terms of a sequence. To find the first term of the sequence, replace y with 1 and find $2 \cdot 1$.

a. How could you find the second term of the sequence?

b. Write the first ten terms of the sequence.

c. Describe the terms of this sequence.

d. A sequence contains all numbers less than 50 that are divisible by 5. So, 35 is in the sequence. Is this an example of inductive or deductive reasoning? Explain.

23. **a.** Use a calculator to find each product.

i. $999{,}999 \times 2$ **ii.** $999{,}999 \times 3$
iii. $999{,}999 \times 4$ **iv.** $999{,}999 \times 5$

b. Without using a calculator, find the product of 999,999 and 9.

24. **a.** Copy and complete the following table.

10^1	10^2	10^3	10^4	10^5
10	100			

b. Use the pattern to find the value of 10^0.

25. If n represents the counting numbers 1, 2, 3, 4, ..., then the algebraic expression $3n + 1$ represents the terms of a sequence. Write the first five terms of the sequence.

Critical Thinking

26. A special sequence is called the *Fibonacci sequence.* It is named after Leonardo Fibonacci from Italy who presented it in 1201. This sequence is very intriguing because the numbers in the sequence are often found in nature. The first six terms of the sequence are listed below. Give the next six numbers in the sequence. 1, 1, 2, 3, 5, 8, ...

Applications and Problem Solving

27. **Transportation** Olga has part of a bus schedule. She wishes to take the bus to go to the mall, but she cannot leave until after 1:00 P.M. What is the earliest time Olga can catch the bus?

Bus Schedule
Departures 8:25 A.M. 9:13 A.M. 10:01 A.M. 10:49 A.M.

28. Sales Paula needs to make a tower of soup cans as a display in a supermarket. Each layer of the tower will be in the shape of a rectangle as shown at the left. The length and width of each layer will be one less than the layer below it.

a. How many cans will be needed for the fourth layer? What type of reasoning did you use?

b. What is the total number of cans needed for an 8-layer tower?

c. A 10-layer tower used 570 cans. Paula has 10 crates holding 70 cans each. Can she make a 10-layer tower? What type of reasoning did you use to make your conclusion?

29. Recreation The house of cards at the right used 26 cards to build four stories.

a. How many cards are needed to build a similar house that is eight stories high?

b. Plan another way to construct a house of cards. Make a drawing showing four stories of your house.

c. Write a sequence that represents the number of cards needed to build 1, 2, 3, and 4 stories of your house.

d. How many cards will you need to build eight stories of your house?

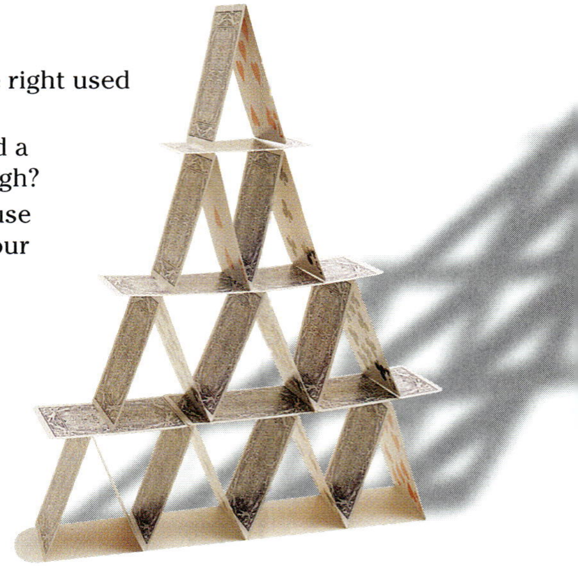

FYI

In 1992, Bryan Berg broke a world record by building the tallest house of cards. He used 208 decks to build 75 stories.

Mixed Review

30. Write an algebraic expression for *eight less than the square of q*. (Lesson 1–1)

31. Write a verbal expression for $\frac{x^3}{9}$. (Lesson 1–1)

32. Write $m \cdot m \cdot m \cdot m \cdot m \cdot m \cdot m \cdot m \cdot m$ as an algebraic expression with exponents. (Lesson 1–1)

33. Geometry Write an expression that represents the total number of small cubes in the large cube at the right. Then evaluate the expression. (Lesson 1–1)

34. Write an algebraic expression for the amount of mileage on Seth's car if the car initially has 20,000 miles and Seth adds an average of x miles per month for 2 years. (Lesson 1–1)

35. Science When water freezes, its volume is increased by one eleventh. In other words, the volume of the ice would equal the sum of the volume of the water and the product of $\frac{1}{11}$ and the volume of the water. Suppose x cubic inches of water is placed in a freezer. Write an expression for the volume of the ice that is formed. (Lesson 1–1)

1–3 Order of Operations

What YOU'LL LEARN

- To use the order of operations to evaluate real number expressions.

Why IT'S IMPORTANT

You use the order of operations to evaluate expressions and solve equations.

APPLICATION

Investments

Bobbie Jackson is investing money in stocks to help pay for her child's college education. She buys one share of Kein stock at \$16. She also purchases five shares of Tainer stock at \$35 each. The expression below represents the amount of money Ms. Jackson spends for the stock purchase.

cost of 1 share of Kein stock → 16; *cost of 1 share of Tainer stock* → 35

$$16 + 5 \cdot 35$$

number of Tainer stocks → 5

Numerical and algebraic expressions often contain more than one operation. A rule is needed to let you know which operation to perform first. This rule is called the **order of operations.**

To find the total amount of money Ms. Jackson invests, evaluate the expression $16 + 5 \cdot 35$. Which of the following methods is correct?

Method 1

$16 + 5 \cdot 35 = 16 + 175$ *Multiply first.*

$= 191$ *Then add.*

Method 2

$16 + 5 \cdot 35 = 21 \cdot 35$ *Add first.*

$= 735$ *Then multiply.*

The answers are not the same because a different order of operations was used in each method. Since numerical expressions must have only one value, the following order of operations has been established.

Order of Operations

1. **Simplify the expressions inside grouping symbols, such as parentheses, brackets, and braces, and as indicated by fraction bars.**
2. **Evaluate all powers.**
3. **Do all multiplications and divisions from left to right.**
4. **Do all additions and subtractions from left to right.**

Based on the context of the problem and the order of operations, Method 1 is correct. Therefore, Ms. Jackson invested $16 + 5 \cdot 35$ or \$191 in the stock market.

Other expressions can be evaluated by using the order of operations.

Example 1 **Evaluate $5 \times 7 - 6 \div 2 + 3^2$.**

Evaluate $5 \times 7 - 6 \div 2 + 3^2$	$= 5 \times 7 - 6 \div 2 + 9$	*Evaluate 3^2.*
	$= 35 - 6 \div 2 + 9$	*Multiply 5 by 7.*
	$= 35 - 3 + 9$	*Divide 6 by 2.*
	$= 32 + 9$	*Subtract 3 from 35.*
	$= 41$	*Add 32 and 9.*

In mathematics, grouping symbols such as parentheses ( ), brackets [ ], and braces { } are used to clarify or change the order of operations. They indicate that the expression within the grouping symbol is to be evaluated first. When more than one grouping symbol is used, start evaluating within the innermost grouping symbols.

Example 2 **Evaluate $8[6^2 - 3(2 + 5)] \div 8 + 3$.**

$8[6^2 - 3(2 + 5)] \div 8 + 3$	$= 8[6^2 - 3(7)] \div 8 + 3$	*Add 2 + 5, the innermost group.*
	$= 8[36 - 3(7)] \div 8 + 3$	*Evaluate 6^2.*
	$= 8[36 - 21] \div 8 + 3$	*Multiply 3 by 7.*
	$= 8[15] \div 8 + 3$	*Subtract 21 from 36.*
	$= 120 \div 8 + 3$	*Multiply 8 by 15.*
	$= 15 + 3$	*Divide 120 by 8.*
	$= 18$	*Add 15 and 3.*

Algebraic expressions can be evaluated when the values of the variables are known. First, replace the variables by their values. Then, calculate the value of the numerical expression.

Example 3 **The figure at the right is a rectangle.**

INTEGRATION
Geometry

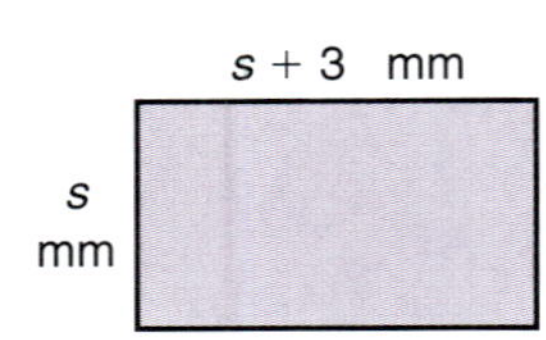

a. Find the perimeter of the rectangle when $s = 5$.
b. Find the area of the rectangle.

a. The perimeter of the rectangle is the sum of 2 times the measure of the width (s) and 2 times the measure of the length ($s + 3$).

$P = 2s + 2(s + 3)$	
$= 2(5) + 2(5 + 3)$	*Replace the variable s with 5.*
$= 2(5) + 2(8)$	*Add 5 and 3.*
$= 10 + 2(8)$	*Multiply 2 and 5.*
$= 10 + 16$	*Multiply 2 and 8.*
$= 26$	*Add 10 and 16.*

The perimeter is 26 mm.

b. The area is the product of the width (s) and the length ($s + 3$).

$$\begin{aligned} A &= s(s + 3) \\ &= 5(5 + 3) && \textit{Replace the variable s with 5.} \\ &= 5(8) && \textit{Add 5 and 3.} \\ &= 40 && \textit{Multiply 5 and 8.} \end{aligned}$$

The area is 40 mm^2. *Area is expressed in units squared.*

EXPLORATION — GRAPHING CALCULATORS

You can use a graphing calculator to evaluate algebraic expressions. Use a calculator to evaluate $\frac{0.25x^2}{7x^3}$ when $x = 0.75$.

Enter: .75 [STO▸] [X,T,θ,n] [2nd] [:] [( ] .25 [X,T,θ,n] [x^2] [ )] [÷] [( ] 7 [X,T,θ,n] [^] 3 [ )] [ENTER] 0.0476190476

Your Turn

a. Evaluate the expression when $x = 24.076$.

b. Evaluate $\frac{2x^2}{(x^2 - x)}$ when $x = 27.89$.

c. Work through some of the examples in this lesson using a graphing calculator.

The fraction bar is another grouping symbol. It indicates that the numerator and denominator should each be treated as a single value.

$$\frac{2 \times 3}{1 + 2} \text{ means } (2 \times 3) \div (1 + 2) \text{ or } 2.$$

Example 4 **Evaluate $\frac{x^3 + y^3}{x^2 - y^2}$ when $x = 4.2$ and $y = 1.8$.**

$$\frac{x^3 + y^3}{x^2 - y^2} = \frac{(4.2)^3 + (1.8)^3}{(4.2)^2 - (1.8)^2}$$

Estimate: $\frac{4^3 + 2^3}{4^2 - 2^2} = \frac{64 + 8}{16 - 4} = \frac{72}{12}$ *or 6*

Use a scientific calculator.

Enter: [( ] 4.2 [y^x] 3 [+] 1.8 [y^x] 3 [ )] [÷]
[( ] 4.2 [x^2] [−] 1.8 [x^2] [ )] [=] 5.55

Is the answer reasonable?

CHECK FOR UNDERSTANDING

Communicating Mathematics

Study the lesson. Then complete the following.

1. When evaluating the expression $4 + 7 \cdot 2$, what would you do first?
2. **Name** two types of grouping symbols and explain how you may use them.
3. **Explain** any errors in the following expression.

$$\begin{aligned} 2[5 + (30 \div 6)]^2 &= 2(5 + 5^2) \\ &= 2(5 + 25) \\ &= 2(30) \\ &= 60 \end{aligned}$$

Guided Practice

Evaluate each expression.

4. $15 + 3 \cdot 2$
5. $5^3 + 3(4^2)$
6. $\dfrac{38 - 12}{2 \cdot 13}$
7. $12 \div 3 \cdot 5 - 4^2$

Evaluate each expression when $w = 12$, $x = 5$, $y = 6$, and $z = 4$.

8. $wx - yz$
9. $2w + x^2 - yz$
10. Use two or more of the variables in Exercises 8–9 and their assigned values to write an expression whose value is 18.
11. If $a = 1.5$, which is less, $a^2 - a$ or 1?
12. **Geometry** Find the area of the rectangle when $t = 6$ inches.

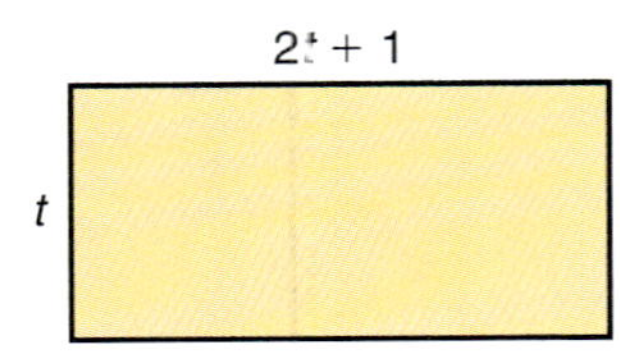

EXERCISES

Practice

Evaluate each expression.

13. $3 + 2 \cdot 3 + 5$
14. $(4 + 5)7$
15. $29 - 3(9 - 4)$
16. $50 - (15 + 9)$
17. $15 \div 3 \cdot 5 - 4^2$
18. $4(11 + 7) - 9 \cdot 8$
19. $\dfrac{(4 \cdot 3)^2 \cdot 5}{(9 + 3)}$
20. $[7(2) - 4] + [9 + 8(4)]$
21. $\dfrac{6 + 4^2}{3^2(4)}$
22. $(5 - 1)^3 + (11 - 2)^2 + (7 - 4)^3$
23. $\dfrac{2 \cdot 8^2 - 2^2 \cdot 8}{2 \cdot 8}$
24. $7(0.2 + 0.5) - 0.6$

Evaluate each expression when $v = 5$, $x = 3$, $a = 7$, and $b = 5$.

25. $(v + 1)(v^2 - v + 1)$
26. $\dfrac{x^2 - x + 6}{x + 3}$
27. $[a + 7(b - 3)]^2 \div 3$
28. $v^2 - (x^3 - 4b)$
29. $(2v)^2 + ab - 3x$
30. $\dfrac{a^2 - b^2}{v^3}$

Write an algebraic expression for each verbal expression. Then, evaluate the expression when $r = 2$, $s = 5$, and $t = \frac{1}{2}$.

31. the square of r increased by $3s$

32. t times the sum of four times s and r

33. the sum of r and s times the square of t

34. r to the fifth power decreased by t

INTEGRATION
Geometry

A formula for the perimeter of each figure is given. Find the perimeter when $a = 5$, $b = 6$, and $c = 8.5$.

35. triangle
$P = a + b + c$

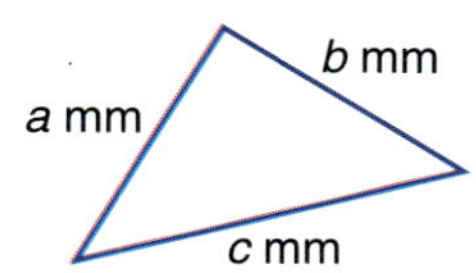

36. square
$P = 4c$

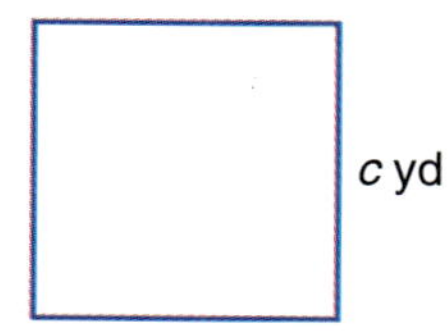

37. parallelogram
$P = 2(a + b)$

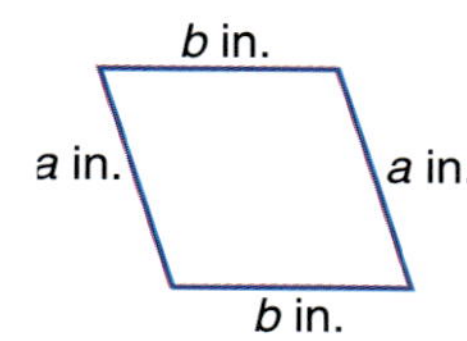

Graphing Calculator

Use a graphing calculator to evaluate each expression to the nearest hundredth.

38. $5(2)^4 + 3$

39. $\frac{(5 \cdot 7)^2 + 5}{(9 \cdot 3^2) - 7}$

40. $4.79\,(0.05)^2 + 0.375\,(6.34)^3$

41. $1 - 2u + 3u^2$ when $u = 1.35$

Critical Thinking

42. Patterns Consider the value of the expression $\frac{2x - 1}{2x}$ for various values of x.

a. Copy and complete the chart below.

x	$\frac{1}{2}$	1	10	50	100
$\frac{2x-1}{2x}$					

b. Describe the pattern that is emerging.

c. What would the approximate value of the expression be if x were a very large number?

43. Consider the following sequence of numbers.

4 2 5 3 2

a. Insert operation symbols and parentheses in the sequence so that its value is 2.

b. Insert operation symbols and parentheses in the sequence so that the answer is the largest possible number.

Applications and Problem Solving

44. Accounting Alicia and Travis are selling tickets for a school talent show. Bleacher seats cost \$3.00, and floor seats cost \$4.00. Alicia sells 30 bleacher seat tickets and 25 floor seat tickets. Travis sells 65 bleacher seat tickets.

a. Write an expression to show how much money Alicia and Travis have collected for the tickets.

b. How much money have they collected?

45. **World Landmarks** The Great Pyramid of Cheops in Egypt is considered to be one of the Seven Wonders of the World. It is also the largest pyramid in the world. The area of its base is 4050 square meters. The volume of any pyramid is one-third the product of the area of the base B and its height h.

Pyramid	Height (meters)
Great Pyramid of Cheops in Egypt	147
Bent Pyramid in Egypt	101
Inca Pyramid in Peru	75
Pyramid of the Sun in Mexico	60
Step Pyramid of Djoser in Egypt	60
Pyramid of the Sun in Peru	50

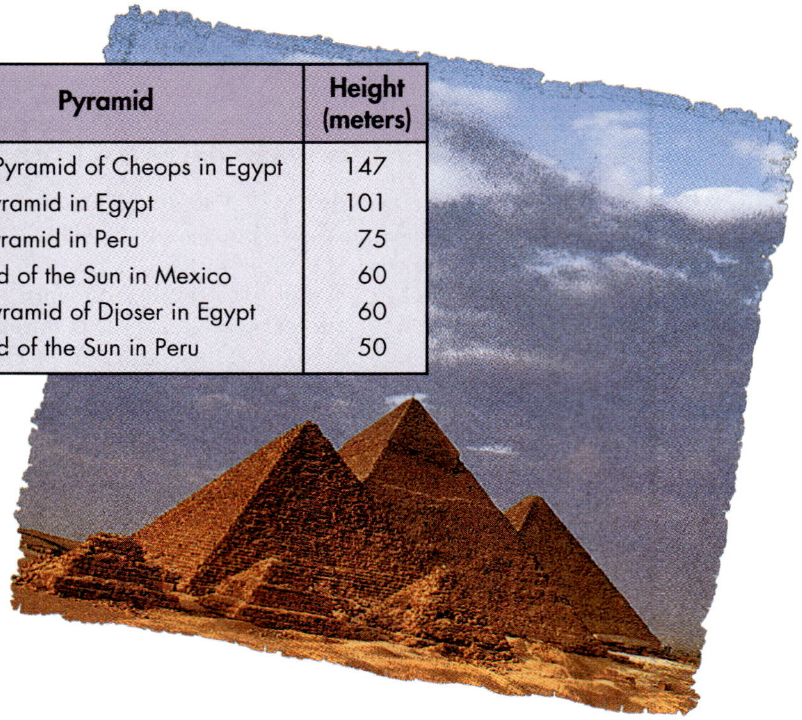

a. Write an expression that represents the volume of a pyramid.

b. Find the volume of the Great Pyramid of Cheops.

Mixed Review

46. Find the next two terms in the sequence 2, 4, 8, 16, ... (Lesson 1–2)

47. Find the next two terms in the sequence 2, 5.5, 9, 12.5, ... (Lesson 1–2)

48. Find the next two items in the pattern a, a^2b, a^3b^2c, $a^4b^3c^2d$, ... (Lesson 1–2)

49. Ishi wants to save her money to buy a drum set from her uncle. Her uncle is willing to sell her the drums for \$525. She has already saved \$357, and she plans to add \$1 on June 1, \$2 on June 2, \$3 on June 3, and so on. On what day will Ishi be able to buy the drums? (Lesson 1–2)

50. Write an algebraic expression for *h to the fifth power*. (Lesson 1–1)

51. The price of tickets for the spring concert is \$3 more than last year. If last year's tickets cost t dollars, write an expression for the cost of the tickets this year. (Lesson 1–1)

52. Evaluate 11^2. (Lesson 1–1)

53. Write a verbal expression for $9 + 2y$. (Lesson 1–1)

1–4 Integration: Statistics
Stem-and-Leaf Plots

What YOU'LL LEARN

- To display and interpret data on a stem-and-leaf plot.

Why IT'S IMPORTANT

Stem-and-leaf plots are a useful way to display data.

APPLICATION
Consumerism

Carmela Perez sells artificial joints to hospitals. She does a lot of highway driving and frequently works with the doctors who perform operations to replace joints. Her present car is old, and she needs to buy a new one. Before deciding which car to buy, she wants to find out the miles-per-gallon (MPG) ratios of the cars she likes. This information will help her decide which cars to investigate in detail before she chooses one to buy. The MPG ratios for 25 cars are listed below.

31	30	28	26	22	31	26	34	47
32	18	33	26	23	18	29	13	40
31	42	17	22	50	12	41		

Which MPG ratio occurs most frequently? Which is the highest MPG ratio? Which is the lowest?

Each day when you read newspapers or magazines, watch television, or listen to the radio, you are bombarded with numerical information about food, sports, the economy, politics, and so on. Interpreting this numerical information, or **data,** is important to your understanding of the world around you. A branch of mathematics called **statistics** helps provide you with methods of collecting, organizing, and interpreting data.

Graphs are often used to display data. The misuse of graphs can lead to false assumptions. One way that graphs are often used to mislead the reader is by labeling the vertical and horizontal scales inconsistently. All of the interval marks should represent the same units. If either of the scales does not begin at zero, this should be indicated by a broken or jagged line. For example, suppose Ana wants to convince her parents that her math grades are improving. Which graph below seems to show the greatest improvement in Ana's grades?

Graph A

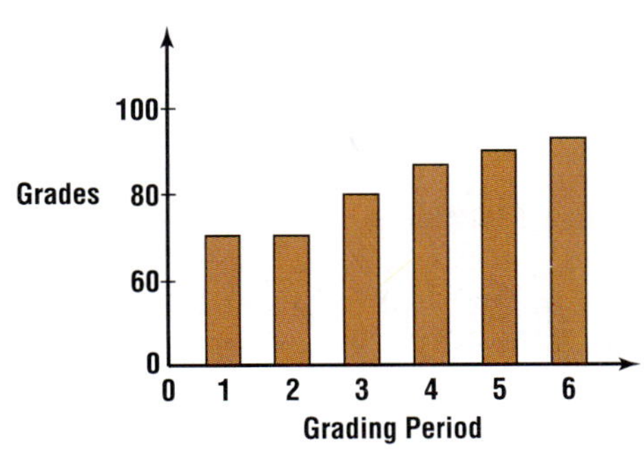

Graph B

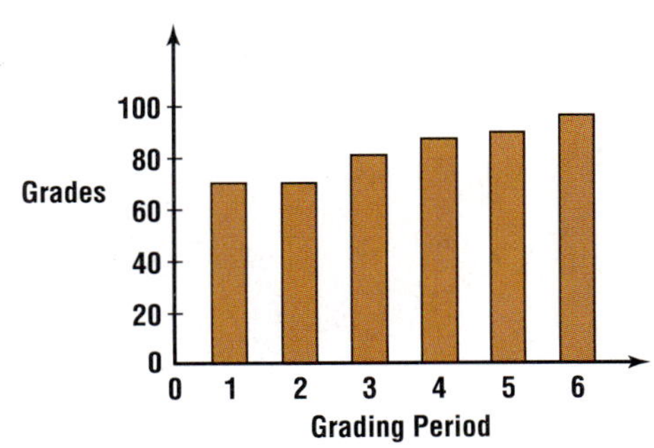

Graph A seems to show the greatest improvement. However, it is misleading. Notice the vertical axis. The distance from 0 to 60 is the same as the distance from 80 to 100. This is an incorrect representation of the data and can lead to the wrong conclusions.

A stem may have one or more digits. A leaf usually has just one digit.

Another way to organize and display data is by using a **stem-and-leaf plot.** In a stem-and-leaf plot, the greatest common place value of the data is used to form the *stems.* The numbers in the next greatest place-value position are then used to form the *leaves.* In the list on the previous page, the greatest place value is tens. Thus, 31 miles per gallon would have stem 3 and leaf 1.

To make the stem-and-leaf plot, first make a vertical list of the stems. Since the mileage data range from 12 to 50, the stems range from 1 to 5. Then, plot each number by placing the units digit (leaf) to the right of its correct stem. Thus, the mileage 31 is plotted by placing leaf 1 to the right of stem 3. Include a key with the plot. The complete stem-and-leaf plot is shown below.

Stem	Leaf
1	8 8 3 7 2
2	8 6 2 6 6 3 9 2
3	1 0 1 4 2 3 1
4	7 0 2 1
5	0 *3|1 = 31 ← Key*

A second stem-and-leaf plot can be made to arrange the leaves in numerical order from least to greatest as shown below. This will make it easier for Ms. Perez to analyze the data.

Stem	Leaf
1	2 3 7 8 8
2	2 2 3 6 6 6 8 9
3	0 1 1 1 2 3 4
4	0 1 2 7
5	0 *3|1 = 31*

Example 1

APPLICATION

Consumerism

Use the information in the stem-and-leaf plot shown above to answer each question.

a. Which MPG ratio did Ms. Perez plot most frequently?
26 and 31 (each three times)

b. What are the highest and lowest MPG ratios?
50 and 12

c. Each line of the stem-and-leaf plot represents an interval of the data. In which mileage interval did Ms. Perez find the most cars?
20–29 miles per gallon (8 cars)

d. How many cars have a ratio of between 20 and 39 miles per gallon?
15 cars

e. If you were Ms. Perez, which cars might you investigate more closely? Why?
Ms. Perez might want to investigate the cars represented in the last two lines of the stem-and-leaf plot, since she should get more miles per gallon with these cars than the other cars.

Sometimes the data for a stem-and-leaf plot are numbers that mostly begin with the same digit. In this case, use the digits in the first two places to form the stems.

Example 2 APPLICATION **Health**

The weights (in pounds) of the students in a health and nutrition class are listed below. Make a stem-and-leaf plot of the student weights and answer the questions.

102	117	119	147	135	148	122	137	103
116	147	152	117	149	108	123	130	123
147	112	133	99	101	135	138	155	118
142	103	159	131	137	156	149	120	98

Since the data range from 159 to 98 pounds, the stems range from 15 to 9.

Notice that the numbers in the stem can be placed in ascending or descending order.

Stem	Leaf
15	9 6 5 2
14	9 9 8 7 7 7 2
13	8 7 7 5 5 3 1 0
12	3 3 2 0
11	9 8 7 7 6 2
10	8 3 3 2 1
9	9 8

12|3 = 123

a. What does 14|8 represent on the plot?
It represents 148 pounds.

b. Which interval has the most students in it?
130–139 pounds (8 students)

c. What is the difference between the lowest and highest weight?
159−98 or 61 pounds

d. Which weight occurred most frequently?
147 pounds (3 students)

fabulous FIRSTS

Dr. Antonia C. Novello (1944–)

In 1989, Dr. Antonia C. Novello became the first woman and the first Hispanic American to become U.S. Surgeon General. She was appointed by President George Bush.

A *back-to-back stem-and-leaf plot* can also be used to compare two related sets of data.

Example 3 **Kyle and Mikito wanted to compare boys' and girls' heights. They measured the height (in inches) of every student in their class. The data they collected and stem-and-leaf plot they made are shown below.**

Boys' Heights (in.)		Girls' Heights (in.)	
65	60	72	64
63	70	57	60
69	72	61	63
71	66	65	62
73	71	59	61
59	58	61	71

(continued on the next page)

In this case, the heights of the boys and the heights of the girls are to be compared. To compare these numbers most effectively, use a back-to-back stem-and-leaf plot.

Boys	Stem	Girls
3 2 1 1 0	7	1 2
9 6 5 3 0	6	0 1 1 1 2 3 4 5
9 8	5	7 9 *5 | 7 = 57*

a. **What is the height of the shortest boy? the shortest girl?**
   The shortest boy is 58 inches tall. The shortest girl is 57 inches tall.

b. **What is the difference in height between the shortest boy and the tallest girl?**
   72 − 58 or 14 inches

c. **What does 6 | 3 represent in each plot?**
   63 inches

d. **What is the greatest number of boys who are the same height? What is the greatest number of girls who are the same height?**
   There are 2 boys who are 71 inches tall and 3 girls who are 61 inches tall.

e. **What patterns, if any, do you see in the data?**
   The boys appear to be slightly taller than the girls. Seven boys are 65 inches or taller, while only 2 of the girls are that tall.

CHECK FOR UNDERSTANDING

Communicating Mathematics

Study the lesson. Then complete the following.

1. **Describe** the information you can determine by looking at a stem-and-leaf plot.
2. **Name** two or three ways in which a graph can be misleading.
3. **List** the steps used to make a stem-and-leaf plot.

MATH JOURNAL

4. **Assess Yourself** Write a paragraph about your use of stem-and-leaf plots. Begin the paragraph by completing this sentence: "I can use stem-and-leaf plots to ____________ ." Think of the ways in which you deal with numbers: earnings from a job, number of assignments turned in, test scores, attendance at club meetings, and so on.

Guided Practice

Suppose the number 25,678 is rounded to 25,700 and plotted using stem 25 and leaf 7. Write the stem and leaf for each number below if the numbers are part of the same set of data.

5. 12,221
6. 6323
7. 126,896
8. Write the stems that would be used for a plot of the following set of data.

57, 43, 34, 12, 29, 8

9. Use the stem-and-leaf plot below to answer each question.

Number of Prom Tickets Sold During a 20-Day Period

Stem	Leaf
3	1 3 5
4	5 5 6 7
5	0 0 1 1 2 3 3
6	3 4 4 4
7	1 5

5 | 1 = 51

a. What does the entry 3 | 5 represent?
b. What was the least number of tickets sold?
c. What was the greatest number of tickets sold during the 20-day period?
d. What was the total number of tickets sold?

10. **Architecture** The *World Almanac* lists 23 tall buildings in Denver, Colorado. Each number below represents the number of floors for one of these buildings.

54	52	43	41	40	36	35	31
32	34	42	32	29	26	28	33
31	30	30	29	27	26	56	

a. Make a stem-and-leaf plot of these data.
b. What was the least number of floors?
c. What was the greatest number of floors?
d. How many buildings had 35 floors or more?
e. How many buildings were in the 20–29 floor range?

EXERCISES

Practice

Suppose the number 178,651 is rounded to 179,000 and plotted using stem 17 and leaf 9. Write the stem and leaf for each number below if the numbers are part of the same set of data.

11. 133,271
12. 44,589
13. 442,672
14. 99,278
15. 1,112,750
16. 8443

Suppose the number 0.0478 is rounded to 0.048 and plotted using stem 4 and leaf 8. Write the stem and leaf for each number below if the numbers are part of the same set of data.

17. 0.14278
18. 0.00997
19. 1.114

Write the stems that would be used for a plot of each set of data.

20. 123, 436, 507, 449, 278, 489, 134, 770, 98, 110, 398
21. 12,367; 24,003; 27,422; 9447; 39,550; 38,045; 40,196
22. 37.2, 8.9, 12.74, 33.5, 27, 17.001, 13.5, 29.6

Critical Thinking

23. **Manufacturing** A video game company tests its products before selling them in stores. Its latest product is an inexpensive space detective adventure. The company would like to know whether to market the game to teens or young adults. A group of 25 teens and 25 young adults rated the game after playing it. The players rated the game for features like graphics, level of difficulty, and player interaction. The ratings consisted of a score between 1 (Trash it, man!) and 60 (Excellent, dude!). The players' ratings are listed below.

Teens (13–19 years old)	19 45 22 44 30 35 41 43 18 35 21 43 30 57 17 27 20 35 15 41 57 22 33 41 55
Young Adults (20–25 years old)	51 43 36 51 42 33 27 48 42 31 48 26 48 31 38 26 45 13 37 25 52 12 44 12 37

a. Should this game be sold to teens or young adults (or to both groups)?

b. Write a memo to the company with a recommendation. Be sure to give reasons for your decision.

Applications and Problem Solving

24. **Geology** According to the *Universal Almanac,* there were 40 major earthquakes from June, 1990, to June, 1994. The stem-and-leaf plot below shows the magnitude of each earthquake in Richter scale units.

Stem	Leaf
5	1 4 4 5 6 9 9
6	0 0 1 2 2 2 2 4 4 5 8 8 8 8 8 8
7	0 0 1 2 2 2 2 2 3 4 5 5 5 6 7 7
8	0 $7\|3 = 7.3$

a. What was the most frequent magnitude of the earthquakes?

b. What was the highest Richter scale value recorded for an earthquake?

c. How many more earthquakes had magnitudes in the 6.0–6.9 range than in the 5.0–5.9 range?

d. What was the magnitude of the weakest earthquake?

Top Five List

Longest rivers in the world

1. Nile, 4145 miles
2. Amazon, 4007 miles
3. Yangtze-Kiang, 3915 miles
4. Mississippi-Missouri-Red Rock, 3710 miles
5. Yenisey-Angara-Selenga, 3442 miles

25. Economics The table at the right shows the average acreage per farm for six western states in 1980 and 1993 according to the *Universal Almanac.*

State	1980	1993
Arizona	5080	4557
Colorado	1358	1286
Montana	2601	2445
Nevada	3100	3708
New Mexico	3467	3274
Wyoming	3846	3742

a. Round each number to the nearest hundred. Then make a back-to-back stem-and-leaf plot of the average farm sizes for 1980 and 1993 for these six states.

b. Which interval shows the most common farm size found in 1980 for these six states? in 1993?

c. Write a statement about the information the stem-and-leaf plot presents.

26. Geography The numbers below show the lengths (in miles) of 30 major rivers in North America as listed in the *World Almanac.*

424	313	444	301	659	652	314	538
377	800	883	525	360	512	500	722
865	360	390	425	309	336	430	692
540	610	800	350	300	420		

a. Round each number to the nearest ten. Then make a stem-and-leaf plot of the data.

b. What is the difference in length between the shortest and longest rivers?

c. How many rivers are less than 400 miles long?

Mixed Review

27. Evaluate $3 \cdot 6 - \frac{12}{4}$. (Lesson 1–3)

28. Evaluate $9a - 4^2 + b^2 \div 2$ when $a = 3$ and $b = 6$. (Lesson 1–3)

29. Weather The time between seeing lightning flash and hearing the bang of thunder it produces can be used to approximate the distance from the lightning. The distance in miles from lightning can be approximated by dividing the number of seconds between seeing the lightning and hearing the thunder by 5. Lightning within three miles can be dangerous and is a warning to take shelter.

a. Suppose there are s seconds between seeing the lightning and hearing the thunder. Write an algebraic expression for the distance from the lightning. (Lesson 1–1)

b. Fernando counted 10 seconds between seeing lightning and hearing thunder. How far away was the lightning? Is Fernando in danger? (Lesson 1–3)

30. Find the next two terms in the sequence $\frac{1}{2}, \frac{3}{4}, \frac{5}{8}, \frac{7}{16}, \frac{9}{32}, \ldots$. (Lesson 1–2)

31. Give the next two items for the following pattern. (Lesson 1–2)

1–5 Open Sentences

***What* YOU'LL LEARN**

- To solve open sentences by performing arithmetic operations.

***Why* IT'S IMPORTANT**

You can use open sentences to solve problems involving nutrition, biology, and weather.

FYI

The largest hamburger in the world was made in Seymour, Wisconsin, on August 2, 1989. It was 21 feet in diameter and weighed 5520 pounds.

APPLICATION

Nutrition

The grams of fat found in cheeseburgers sold by various fast food chains are listed in the stem-and-leaf plot at the right.

Stem	Leaf
1	3 3 3 6 9
2	0 5 8 9
3	6 9
4	6
6	3

$4|6 = 46$

Obviously, some of the fast food chains are selling burgers with more than the usual amount of fat. Some students at Middletown High School have formed a consumer awareness club and are concerned about the high content of fat in this particular cheeseburger. They decide to write a letter to the company recommending a way to reduce the fat of their cheeseburger to 37 grams.

The students know that a one-ounce slice of American cheese has about 7 grams of fat and that ground beef has about 6 grams of fat per ounce. The students need to determine the number of ounces of ground beef that can be used to make a cheeseburger with a fat content of 37 grams.

Let b represent the number of ounces of beef that will go into the cheeseburger. This problem can be represented by the equation below.

$$6b + 7 = 37$$

The number 6 represents the amount of fat in one ounce of ground beef. The 7 represents the number of grams of fat in one slice of cheese. The 37 represents the total number of grams of fat for a cheeseburger.

Mathematical statements with one or more variables, or unknown numbers, are called **open sentences.** An open sentence is neither true nor false until the variable has been replaced by a value. Finding a replacement for the variable that results in a true sentence is called **solving the open sentence.** This replacement is called a **solution** of the open sentence.

Replace b in $6b + 7 = 37$ with the values 3, 4, 5, and 6. Then see whether each replacement results in a true or false sentence.

Replace b with:	$6b + 7 = 37$	True or False?
3	$6(3) + 7 \stackrel{?}{=} 37 \rightarrow 25 \neq 37$	false
4	$6(4) + 7 \stackrel{?}{=} 37 \rightarrow 31 \neq 37$	false
5	$6(5) + 7 \stackrel{?}{=} 37 \rightarrow 37 = 37$	true
6	$6(6) + 7 \stackrel{?}{=} 37 \rightarrow 43 \neq 37$	false

Since $b = 5$ makes the sentence $6b + 7 = 37$ true, the solution for $6b + 7 = 37$ is 5. The students can write a letter suggesting that the chain reduce the amount of fat to 37 grams by using 5 ounces of ground beef in their cheeseburger.

A set of numbers from which replacements for a variable may be chosen is called a **replacement set.** A **set** is a collection of objects or numbers. Sets are often shown by using braces { }. Each object or number in a set is called an **element,** or member. Sets are usually named by capital letters. Set A has three elements; they are 1, 3, and 5.

$A = \{1, 3, 5\}$ $\quad$ $B = \{2, 4, 5\}$ $\quad$ $C = \{1, 2, 3, 4, 5\}$

The **solution set** of an open sentence is the set of all replacements for the variable that make the sentence true.

Example 1 **Find the solution set for $y + 5 \leq 7$ if the replacement set is {0, 1, 2, 3, 4}.**

The symbol ≤ means "less than or equal to." The symbol ≥ means "greater than or equal to."

Replace y with:	$y + 5 \leq 7$	True or False?
0	$0 + 5 \stackrel{?}{\leq} 7 \rightarrow 5 \leq 7$	true
1	$1 + 5 \stackrel{?}{\leq} 7 \rightarrow 6 \leq 7$	true
2	$2 + 5 \stackrel{?}{\leq} 7 \rightarrow 7 \leq 7$	true
3	$3 + 5 \stackrel{?}{\leq} 7 \rightarrow 8 \not\leq 7$	false
4	$4 + 5 \stackrel{?}{\leq} 7 \rightarrow 9 \not\leq 7$	false

Therefore, the solution set for $y + 5 \leq 7$ is {0, 1, 2}.

A sentence that contains an equals sign, =, is called an **equation.** A sentence having the symbols <, ≤, >, or ≥ is called an **inequality.** Which of the open sentences below are equations? Which ones are inequalities?

Mathematical Sentence	Equation or Inequality?
$2x + 10 = 50$	equation
$3a \leq 43$	inequality
$y - 6 > 12$	inequality

Sometimes you can solve an equation by simply applying the order of operations.

Example 2 Solve $\frac{5(3 + 5)}{3 \cdot 2 + 2} = d$.

$\frac{5(3 + 5)}{3 \cdot 2 + 2} = d$

$\frac{5(8)}{6 + 2} = d$

$\frac{40}{8} = d$ *Evaluate the numerator and denominator.*

$5 = d$ *Divide.*

The solution is 5.

Example 3

APPLICATION

Nutrition

Refer to the application at the beginning of the lesson. Solve for the number of grams of fat *f* in a cheeseburger that has one slice of cheese and four ounces of ground beef. Assume that the bun and toppings contain no fat.

$f = 6b + 7$ *f = grams of fat and b = ounces of beef*

$f = 6(4) + 7$ *Replace b with 4.*

$f = 24 + 7$ *Evaluate using the order of operations.*

$f = 31$

The cheeseburger has about 31 grams of fat.

CHECK FOR UNDERSTANDING

Communicating Mathematics

Study the lesson. Then complete the following.

1. **Explain** why an open sentence always has at least one variable.
2. **Explain** the difference between an expression and an open sentence.
3. **Define** in your own words the phrase *solution set of an open mathematical sentence.*
4. **Explain** how to find the solution set for $7 + 2n > 31$ if the replacement set for n is $\{10, 11, 12, 13\}$.

MATH JOURNAL

5. Make up an inequality with a replacement set. Find the solution set and explain how you obtained it.

Guided Practice

State whether each equation is *true* or *false* for the value of the variable given.

6. $7(x^2) - 15 \div 5 = 25, x = 2$
7. $\frac{7a + a}{(9 \cdot 3) - 7} = 4, a = 5$

Find the solution set for each inequality, given the replacement set.

8. $3x + 2 > 2; \{0, 1, 2\}$
9. $2y^2 - 1 > 0; \{1, 3, 5\}$

Solve each equation for *y* if *x* is replaced with 6.

10. $x - 2 = y$
11. $2x^2 + 3 = y$

12. **Diet** During a lifetime, the average American drinks 15,579 glasses of milk, 6220 glasses of fruit juice, and 18,995 glasses of soft drinks.
   a. Write an equation for the total number of glasses of milk, juice, and soft drinks that the average American drinks in a lifetime.
   b. What is the total number of glasses of milk, juice, and soft drinks consumed by the average American in a lifetime?

EXERCISES

Practice

State whether each equation is *true* or *false* for the value of the variable given.

13. $a + \frac{3}{4} = \frac{3}{2} + \frac{1}{4}, a = \frac{1}{2}$

14. $\frac{3 + 15}{x} = \frac{1}{2}(x), x = 6$

15. $y^6 = 4^3, y = 2$

16. $3x^2 - 4(5) = 6, x = 3$

17. $\frac{5^2 - 2y}{5^2 - 6} \leq 1, y = 3$

18. $a^5 \div 8 \div a^2 \div a < \frac{1}{2}, a = 2$

Find the solution set for each inequality if the replacement sets are $x = \left\{\frac{1}{2}, \frac{3}{4}, 1, \frac{5}{4}\right\}$ and $y = \{5, 10, 15, 20\}$.

19. $y - 2 < 6$

20. $y + 2 > 7$

21. $8x + 1 < 8$

22. $2x > 1$

23. $\frac{y}{5} \geq 2$

24. $3x \leq 4$

Solve each equation.

25. $y = \frac{14 - 8}{2}$

26. $4(6) + 3 = a$

27. $\frac{21 - 3}{12 - 3} = x$

28. $d = 3\frac{1}{2} \div 2$

29. $s = 4\frac{1}{2} + \frac{1}{3}$

30. $x = 5^2 - 2^3$

Critical Thinking

31. Find five pairs of values for p and q such that the open sentence $q + 2 > 3p$ is true.

Applications and Problem Solving

32. **Weather Forecasting** The graph at the right shows the states with the most tornadoes.

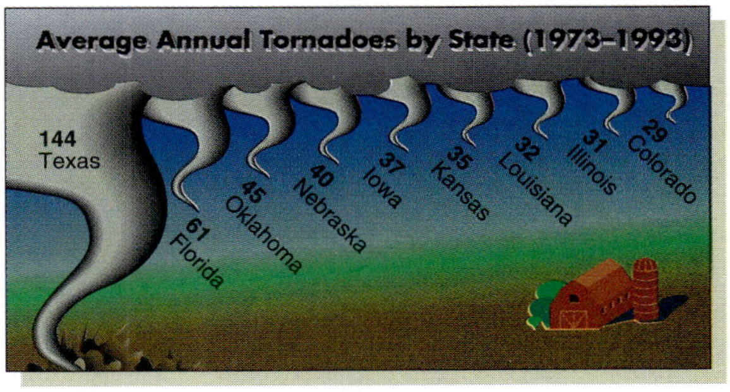

Source: National Severe Storm Forecast Center

   a. Write an equation that estimates the number of tornadoes Texas will have in the next three years. Justify why your equation will provide a good estimate.
   b. At this rate, how many tornadoes will Texas have in the next three years?
   c. Make up another problem using the data in the graph.

33. **Nutrition** A person must burn 3500 calories to lose one pound of weight.
   a. Write an equation that represents the number of calories a person would have to burn a day to lose 4 pounds in two weeks.
   b. How many calories would the person have to burn each day?

34. **Biology** Insects are the largest class of animals in the world with at least 800,000 species. The fastest-moving insect is the large tropical cockroach. It scurries at speeds of up to 3.36 miles per hour, which is about 2.3 feet per second.

a. Write an equation that represents how many miles the roach can travel in 1.5 hours.

b. How many miles can the roach travel in 1.5 hours?

c. Can the roach travel 100 feet in less than a minute? Explain.

Mixed Review

35. Write the stems that would be used to form a stem-and-leaf plot for the following set of data. (Lesson 1–4)

2.7, 5.9, 2.0, 7.7, 5.2, 6.0, 5.4, 9.9, 5.4

36. **Hockey** The stem-and leaf plot at the right shows the greatest number of goals scored by a professional hockey player during any one season. Mario Lemieux is credited with the fourth greatest number of goals in a season. How many goals did Lemieux score during that season? (Lesson 1–4)

Stem	Leaf
7	1 2 3 6 6 6
8	5 6 7
9	2

$7|2 = 72$

37. Evaluate $5(13 - 7) - 22$. (Lesson 1–3)

38. Write the next two expressions for the pattern $2a + 1$, $4a + 3$, $6a + 5$, $8a + 7$, ... (Lesson 1–2)

39. Write a verbal expression for $x^5 - 5$. (Lesson 1–1)

40. **Geometry** Write an algebraic expression for the perimeter of the triangle at the right. (Lesson 1–1)

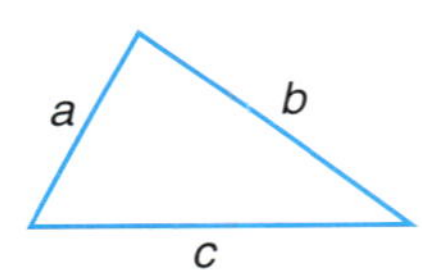

SELF TEST

Write an algebraic expression for each verbal expression. (Lesson 1–1)

1. the sum of three times a and the square of b
2. w to the fifth power minus 37
3. **Patterns** Each Tuesday morning at Central High School, the first seven bells ring at 8:00, 8:43, 8:47, 9:30, 9:34, 10:17, and 10:21 A.M. Give the times of the other morning bells. (Lesson 1–2)

Evaluate each expression. (Lesson 1–3)

4. $5(8 - 3) + 7 \cdot 2$
5. $6(4^3 + 2^2)$
6. $(9 - 2 \cdot 3)^3 - 27 + 9 \cdot 2$

Make a stem-and-leaf plot for each set of data. (Lesson 1–4)

7. 67, 85, 54, 48, 89, 77
8. 236, 450, 748, 254, 755, 347, 97, 386

Find the solution set for each open sentence if the replacement set is {4, 5, 6, 7, 8}. (Lesson 1–5)

9. $x + 2 > 7$
10. $9x - 20 = x^2$

1–6 Identity and Equality Properties

What YOU'LL LEARN

- To recognize and use the properties of identity and equality, and
- to determine the multiplicative inverse of a number.

Why IT'S IMPORTANT

You can use the identity and equality properties to evaluate expressions and solve equations.

APPLICATION

Football

According to the graph at the right, the price of Super Bowl tickets increased by \$0 from 1975 to 1977. Also, from 1981 to 1983, ticket prices stayed at \$40. The open sentences below represent each situation.

Super Bowl Ticket Prices 1967–1995

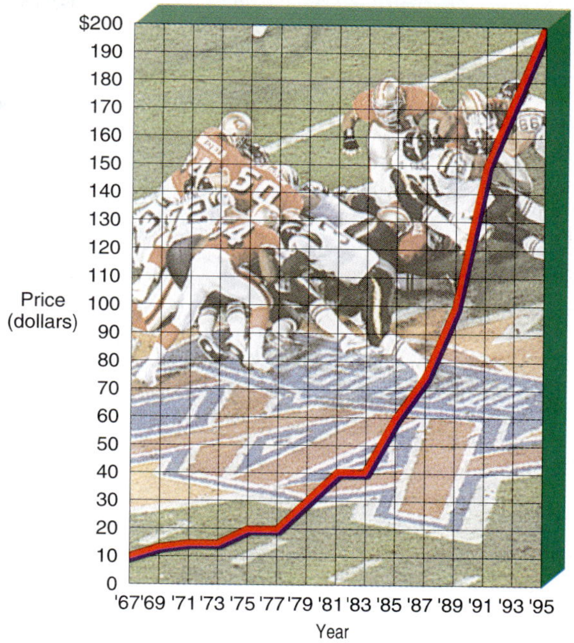

price increase

1975 price → $20 + a = 20$ ← *1977 price*

1981 price → $40 + a = 40$ ← *1983 price*

The solution for each equation is 0. Super Bowl ticket prices increased \$0 during each time period.

Equations such as these can be summarized in algebraic terms. The sum of any number and 0 is equal to that number. Zero is called the **additive identity.**

Additive Identity Property	**For any number a, $a + 0 = 0 + a = a$.**

The equations below also represent the ticket prices from 1975 to 1977 and from 1981 to 1983. The variable m represents the number of times of increase.

number of times of increase

1975 price → $20 \cdot m = 20$ ← *1977 price*

1981 price → $40 \cdot m = 40$ ← *1983 price*

The solution for each equation is 1. Since the product of any number and 1 is equal to the number, 1 is called the **multiplicative identity.**

Multiplicative Identity Property	For any number a, $a \cdot 1 = 1 \cdot a = a$.

Suppose you purchase a number of Super Bowl tickets for \$200 each. If you sell three of them at face value (\$200), your profit is \$0. The following equation describes the situation.

profit per ticket

number of tickets → ↓ ↓ ← *total profit*

$$3 \cdot 0 = p$$

In this equation, one of the factors is 0 and the value of p is 0. This equation suggests the following property.

Multiplicative Property of Zero	For any number a, $a \cdot 0 = 0 \cdot a = 0$.

Two numbers whose product is 1 are called **multiplicative inverses** or **reciprocals.** Zero has no reciprocal because any number times 0 is 0.

Multiplicative Inverse Property	For every nonzero number $\frac{a}{b}$, where $a, b \neq 0$, there is exactly one number $\frac{b}{a}$ such that $\frac{a}{b} \cdot \frac{b}{a} = 1$.

Example 1 **Name the multiplicative inverse of each number or variable. Assume that no variable equals zero.**

a. 5

Since $5 \cdot \frac{1}{5} = 1$, $\frac{1}{5}$ is the multiplicative inverse of 5.

b. x

Since $x \cdot \frac{1}{x} = 1$, the multiplicative inverse is $\frac{1}{x}$.

$x \neq 0$; why?

c. $\frac{2}{3}$

Using the property, the multiplicative inverse is $\frac{3}{2}$.

At the beginning of algebra class, Ms. Escalante gave each of her students a single strip of paper 8 inches long. She instructed the students to divide their paper strips any way they wished.

Staci left her strip as one 8-inch strip.

Amad cut his strip to form a 6-inch strip and a 2-inch strip.

Liam cut his strip to form a 5-inch strip and a 3-inch strip.

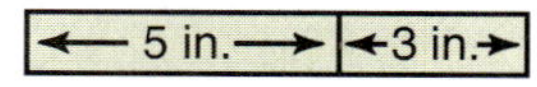

Using the strips of paper, we know the following to be true.

$8 = 8 \qquad 6 + 2 = 6 + 2 \qquad 3 + 5 = 3 + 5$

The **reflexive property of equality** says that any quantity is equal to itself.

Reflexive Property of Equality	**For any number a, $a = a$.**

Many mathematical statements and algebraic properties are written in *if-then* form. In an if-then statement, the **hypothesis** is the part following *if*, and the **conclusion** is the part following *then*.

$$\text{If } \underbrace{8 = 6 + 2}_{\text{hypothesis}}, \text{ then } \underbrace{6 + 2 = 8}_{\text{conclusion}}.$$

$$\text{If } \overbrace{3 + 5 = 6 + 2}, \text{ then } \overbrace{6 + 2 = 3 + 5}.$$

The **symmetric property of equality** says that if one quantity equals a second quantity, then the second quantity also equals the first.

Symmetric Property of Equality	**For any numbers a and b, if $a = b$, then $b = a$.**

A third property can also be shown using the paper strips.

If $3 + 5 = 8$ and $8 = 6 + 2$, then $3 + 5 = 6 + 2$.

If $8 = 3 + 5$ and $3 + 5 = 6 + 2$, then $8 = 6 + 2$.

Identify the hypothesis and conclusion in each statement.

The **transitive property of equality** says that if one quantity equals a second quantity and the second quantity equals a third quantity, then the first and third quantities are equal.

Transitive Property of Equality	**For any numbers a, b, and c, if $a = b$ and $b = c$, then $a = c$.**

We know that $5 + 3 = 6 + 2$. Since $5 + 3$ is equal to 8, we can substitute 8 for $5 + 3$ to get $8 = 6 + 2$. The **substitution property of equality** says that a quantity may be substituted for its equal in any expression.

Substitution Property of Equality	**If $a = b$, then a may be replaced by b in any expression.**

You can use the properties of identity and equality to justify each step when evaluating an expression.

Example 2

APPLICATION
Sales

The pep club at Roosevelt High School is selling submarine sandwiches, lemonade, and apples at the district swim meet. Each sandwich costs $2.00 to make and sells for $3.00. Each glass of lemonade costs $0.25 to make and sells for $1.00. Each apple costs the club $0.25, and the members have decided to sell apples for $0.25 each. Write an expression that represents the profit for 80 sandwiches, 150 glasses of lemonade, and 40 apples. Evaluate the expression, indicating the property used in each step.

sandwiches (*sold*, *profit*) — *lemonade* (*sold*, *profit*) — *apples* (*sold*, *profit*)

$$80(3.00 - 2.00) + 150(1.00 - 0.25) + 40(0.25 - 0.25)$$

$= 80(1) + 150(0.75) + 40(0)$	*Substitution (=)*
$= 80 + 150(0.75) + 40(0)$	*Identity (×)*
$= 80 + 112.50 + 40(0)$	*Substitution (=)*
$= 80 + 112.50 + 0$	*Multiplicative prop. of 0*
$= 192.50 + 0$	*Substitution (=)*
$= 192.50$	*Identity (+)*

The club would make a profit of $192.50.

CHECK FOR UNDERSTANDING

Communicating Mathematics

Study the lesson. Then complete the following.

1. **Define** the term *identity* in your own words.
2. **Explain** whether or not 1 can be the additive identity.
3. **Explain** why 0 does *not* have a multiplicative inverse.
4. **Name** the multiplicative inverse of 1.

MATH JOURNAL

5. Write two if-then statements and identify the hypothesis and conclusion in each.

Guided Practice

Name the multiplicative inverse of each number or variable. Assume that no variable represents zero.

6. 7
7. $\frac{9}{2}$
8. c

Match the expressions in the left-hand column with the properties in the right-hand column.

9. $0 \cdot 36 = 0$
10. $1(68) = 68$
11. $14 + 16 = 14 + 16$
12. $(9 - 7)(5) = 2(5)$
13. $\frac{3}{4} \times \frac{4}{3} = 1$
14. $0 + g = g$
15. If $8 + 1 = 9$, then $9 = 8 + 1$.

a. Additive identity property
b. Multiplicative identity property
c. Multiplicative property of 0
d. Multiplicative inverse property
e. Reflexive property (=)
f. Symmetric property (=)
g. Substitution property (=)

Name the property used in each step.

16. $$\begin{aligned}\left(14 \cdot \tfrac{1}{14} + 8 \cdot 0\right) \cdot 12 &= (1 + 8 \cdot 0) \cdot 12\\ &= (1 + 0) \cdot 12\\ &= 1 \cdot 12\\ &= 12\end{aligned}$$

Evaluate each expression. Name the property used in each step.

17. $6(12 - 48 \div 4) + 9 \cdot 1$
18. $3 + 5(4 - 2^2) - 1$

19. **History** On November 19, 1863, Abraham Lincoln gave his Gettysburg Address as part of a ceremony to dedicate a portion of that Pennsylvania battlefield as a cemetery. The speech began "Four score and seven years ago,...." (*Hint:* A score equals twenty.)
   a. Write an expression to represent four score and seven.
   b. Evaluate the expression. Name the property used in each step.
   c. How many years is that?

EXERCISES

Practice

Name the multiplicative inverse of each number or variable. Assume that no variable represents zero.

20. 9

21. $\frac{1}{9}$

22. $\frac{1}{4}$

23. p

24. $\frac{2}{a}$

25. $1\frac{1}{2}$

Name the property or properties illustrated by each statement.

26. If $7 \cdot 2 = 14$, then $14 = 7 \cdot 2$.

27. $8 + (3 + 9) = 8 + 12$

28. $(10 - 8)(5) = 2(5)$

29. $mnp = 1mnp$

30. $\left(\frac{3}{4}\right)\left(\frac{4}{3}\right) = 1$

31. $3\left(5^2 \cdot \frac{1}{25}\right) = 3$

32. $0 + 23 = 23$

33. If $6 = 9 - 3$, then $9 - 3 = 6$.

34. $5(0) = 0$

35. $32 + 21 = 32 + 21$

36. If $4 \cdot 2 = 8$ and $8 = 6 + 2$, then $4 \cdot 2 = 6 + 2$.

Name the property used in each step.

37.
$$\begin{aligned} 2(3 \cdot 2 - 5) + 3 \cdot \tfrac{1}{3} &= 2(6 - 5) + 3 \cdot \tfrac{1}{3} \\ &= 2(1) + 3 \cdot \tfrac{1}{3} \\ &= 2 + 3 \cdot \tfrac{1}{3} \\ &= 2 + 1 \\ &= 3 \end{aligned}$$

38.
$$\begin{aligned} 26 \cdot 1 - 6 + 5(12 \div 4 - 3) &= 26 \cdot 1 - 6 + 5(3 - 3) \\ &= 26 \cdot 1 - 6 + 5(0) \\ &= 26 - 6 + 5(0) \\ &= 26 - 6 + 0 \\ &= 20 + 0 \\ &= 20 \end{aligned}$$

39.
$$\begin{aligned} 7(5 \cdot 3^2 - 11 \cdot 4) &= 7(5 \cdot 9 - 11 \cdot 4) \\ &= 7(45 - 44) \\ &= 7 \cdot 1 \\ &= 7 \end{aligned}$$

Evaluate each expression. Name the property used in each step.

40. $4(16 \div 4^2)$

41. $(15 - 8) \div 7 \cdot 25$

42. $(8 \cdot 3 - 19 + 5) + (3^2 + 8 \cdot 4)$

43. $(2^5 - 5^2) + (4^2 - 2^4)$

44. $8[6^2 - 3(11)] \div 8 \cdot \frac{1}{3}$

45. $5^3 + 9\left(\frac{1}{3}\right)^2$

Critical Thinking

46. Think about the relationship "is less than," represented by the symbol $<$. Does $<$ work with each of the following? Explain why or why not. Give examples that support your reasoning.

a. reflexive property

b. symmetric property

c. the transitive property

Applications and Problem Solving

47. Entertainment The students in Mr. Toshio's class are planning an ice cream party. They have selected the ice cream flavors shown in the table below. The prices listed are for $\frac{1}{2}$- cup servings. A survey of the students shows that 12 students want vanilla, 15 want chocolate, and 10 want chocolate chip cookie dough.

Flavor	Price
Vanilla	21¢
Chocolate	23¢
Chocolate Chip Cookie Dough	67¢

a. Write an expression that represents how much it will cost to purchase ice cream for the class if each student gets a 1-cup serving.

b. Evaluate the expression. Name the property used in each step.

c. What is the total cost?

48. Postal Rates Patricia wants to mail a package to her cousin in Los Angeles. The cost of first class mail is \$0.32 for the first ounce and \$0.23 for each additional ounce or fraction of an ounce. Patricia's package weighs 14.4 ounces.

a. Write an expression that represents the cost to mail the package.

b. Evaluate the expression. Name the property used in each step.

c. How much will Patricia need to pay in postage?

d. Complete the following statement and identify the hypothesis and conclusion.
If Patricia's package weighs 17.1 ounces, then she must pay __?__ in postage.

Mixed Review

49. *True or False*: $15 \div 3 + 7 < 13$. (Lesson 1–5)

50. Solve $m = (18 - 3) \div (3^2 - 2^2)$. (Lesson 1–5)

51. *True or False*: $(2n^2 + 6) \div 4 < 5$, when $n = 3$. (Lesson 1–5)

52. When is a back-to-back stem-and-leaf plot used? (Lesson 1–4)

53. Write the first and last names of ten of your classmates. Make a stem-and-leaf plot showing the number of letters in these ten names. (Lesson 1–4)

54. Evaluate $5(7 - 2) - 3^2$. (Lesson 1–3)

55. Evaluate $xy - 2y$ when $x = 6$ and $y = 9$. (Lesson 1–3)

56. Find the next two terms in the sequence 1, 4, 7, 10, ... (Lesson 1–2)

57. Write an algebraic expression for the number of months in y years. (Lesson 1–1)

MODELING MATHEMATICS

A Preview of Lesson 1–7

1–7A The Distributive Property

Materials: algebra tiles product mat

Throughout your study of mathematics, you have used rectangles to model multiplication. For example, the figure below shows the multiplication $2(3 + 1)$ as a rectangle that is 2 units wide and $3 + 1$ units long. The model shows that the expression $2(3 + 1)$ is equal to $2 \cdot 3 + 2 \cdot 1$. The sentence $2(3 + 1) = 2 \cdot 3 + 2 \cdot 1$ illustrates the distributive property.

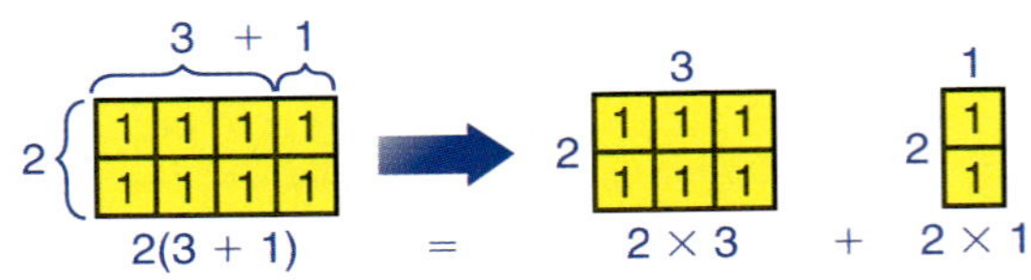

You can use special tiles called **algebra tiles** to form rectangles that model multiplication. A 1-tile is a square that is 1 unit long and 1 unit wide. Its area is 1 square unit. An x-tile is a rectangle that is 1 unit wide and x units long. Its area is x square units.

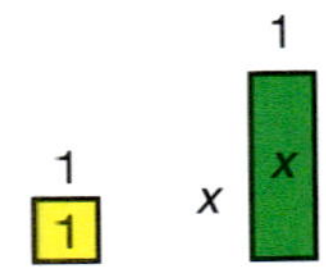

Activity **Find the product $3(x + 2)$ by using algebra tiles. First, model $3(x + 2)$ as the area of a rectangle.**

Step 1 The rectangle has a width of 3 units and a length of $x + 2$ units. Use your algebra tiles to mark off the dimensions on a product mat.

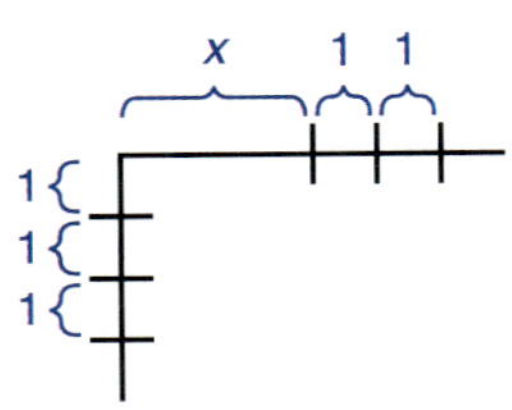

Step 2 Using the marks as a guide, make the rectangle with algebra tiles.

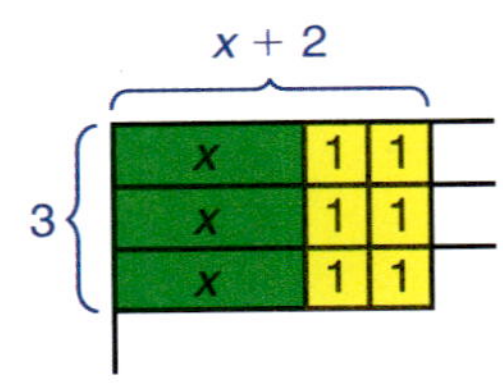

The rectangle has 3 x-tiles and 6 1-tiles. The area of the rectangle is $x + 1 + 1 + x + 1 + 1 + x + 1 + 1$, or $3x + 6$. Thus, $3(x + 2) = 3x + 6$.

Model **Find each product by using algebra tiles.**

1. $2(x + 1)$
2. $5(x + 2)$
3. $2(2x + 1)$
4. $2(3x + 3)$

Draw **Tell whether each statement is true or false. Justify your answer with algebra tiles and a drawing.**

5. $3(x + 3) = 3x + 3$
6. $x(3 + 2) = 3x + 2x$

Write

7. **You Decide** Helen says that $3(x + 4) = 3x + 4$, but Adita says that $3(x + 4) = 3x + 12$.
   a. Which classmate is correct?
   b. Use words and/or models to give an explanation that demonstrates the correct equation.

1–7 The Distributive Property

What YOU'LL LEARN

- To use the distributive property to simplify expressions.

APPLICATION
Food Service

In the school cafeteria, each student can pick one hot or cold entree and one salad from the following in order to get a "Meal Deal" lunch at a special low price.

Hot Lunch	Cold Lunch	Salads
• Tacos • Meat loaf and mashed potatoes • Steamed veggies and rice • Spaghetti 	• Submarine sandwich • Turkey club sandwich • Tuna salad with tomato 	• Tossed salad • Fruit salad 

Why IT'S IMPORTANT

You can use the distributive property to evaluate expressions and solve equations.

Jenine wants to know how many different lunches are possible. She can make a table to represent all the possible combinations.

Hot Lunch				
	Entree			
Salads	Tacos	Meat Loaf	Veggies	Spaghetti
Tossed	x	x	x	x
Fruit	x	x	x	x

Cold Lunch			
	Entree		
Salads	Submarine	Club Sandwich	Tuna Salad
Tossed	x	x	x
Fruit	x	x	x

There are $2 \cdot 4$ or 8 possible hot lunches.
There are $2 \cdot 3$ or 6 possible cold lunches.
There are $(2 \cdot 4) + (2 \cdot 3)$ possible lunches from which students can choose.
Note that $(2 \cdot 4) + (2 \cdot 3) = 8 + 6$ or 14.

Jenine can also represent this problem by using the following table.

	Entree						
	Hot Lunch				Cold Lunch		
Salads	Taco	Meat Loaf	Veggie	Spaghetti	Sub	Club Sand.	Tuna
Tossed	×	×	×	×	×	×	×
Fruit	×	×	×	×	×	×	×

According to this table, there are 2 types of salads times the total number of entrees, 4 + 3, or 7.

$$2(4 + 3) = 2 \cdot 7 \text{ or } 14$$

Either way you look at it, there are 14 possible lunches. That's because the following is true.

$$2(4 + 3) = 2 \cdot 4 + 2 \cdot 3$$

This is an example of the **distributive property.**

Distributive Property	**For any numbers *a*, *b*, and *c*,** $a(b + c) = ab + ac$ **and** $(b + c)a = ba + ca$; $a(b - c) = ab - ac$ **and** $(b - c)a = ba - ca$.

Notice that it doesn't matter whether a is placed on the right or the left of the expression in parentheses.

The symmetric property of equality allows the distributive property to be written as follows.

$$\text{If } a(b + c) = ab + ac, \text{ then } ab + ac = a(b + c).$$

Example 1

INTEGRATION

Geometry

The Oak Grove High School Spirit Club wants to make a banner for the championship football game. The students have two large pieces of paper to use for the banner. One piece is 5 feet by 13 feet, and the other is 5 feet by 10 feet. They plan to use both pieces for the banner. Find the total area of the banner.

The total area of the banner can be found in two ways.

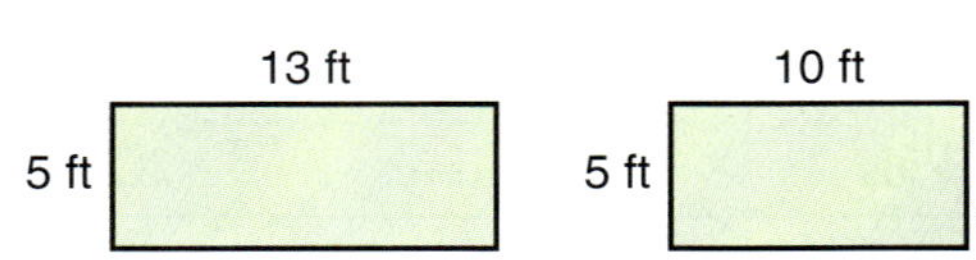

Method 1: Add the areas of the smaller rectangles.

$$\begin{aligned} A &= w\ell_1 + w\ell_2 \\ &= 5(13) + 5(10) \\ &= 65 + 50 \\ &= 115 \end{aligned}$$

Method 2: Multiply the width by the length.

$A = w\ell$

$= 5(13 + 10)$ *$w = 5, l = 13 + 10$*

$= 5(23)$

$= 115$

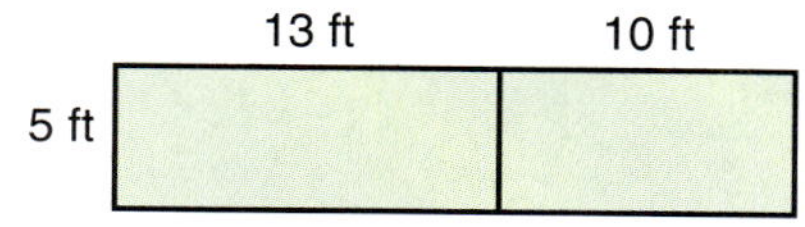

The area is 115 square feet.

You can use the distributive property to multiply in your head.

Example 2 Use the distributive property to find each product.

a. $\mathbf{7 \cdot 98}$

$7 \cdot 98 = 7(100 - 2)$

$= 700 - 14$

$= 686$

b. $\mathbf{8(6.5)}$

$8(6.5) = 8(6 + 0.5)$

$= 48 + 4$

$= 52$

A **term** is a number, a variable, or a product or quotient of numbers and variables. Some examples of terms are x^3, $\frac{1}{4}a$, and $4y$. The expression $9y^2 + 13y^2 + 3$ has three terms.

Like terms are terms that contain the same variables, with corresponding variables having the same power. In the expression $8x^2 + 2x^2 + 5a + a$, $8x^2$ and $2x^2$ are like terms, and $5a$ and a are also like terms.

We can use the distributive property and properties of equality to show that $3x + 8x = 11x$. In this expression, $3x$ and $8x$ are like terms.

$3x + 8x = (3 + 8)x$ *Distributive property*

$= 11x$ *Substitution (=)*

The expressions $3x + 8x$ and $11x$ are called **equivalent expressions** because they denote the same number. An expression is in **simplest form** when it is replaced by an equivalent expression having no like terms and no parentheses.

Example 3 Simplify $\frac{1}{4}x^2 + 2x^2 + \frac{11}{4}x^2$.

In this expression, $\frac{1}{4}x^2$, $2x^2$, and $\frac{11}{4}x^2$ are like terms.

$\frac{1}{4}x^2 + 2x^2 + \frac{11}{4}x^2 = \left(\frac{1}{4} + 2 + \frac{11}{4}\right)x^2$ *Distributive property*

$= 5x^2$ *Substitution (=)*

The **coefficient** of a term is the numerical factor. For example, in $23ab$, the coefficient is 23. In xy, the coefficient is 1 since, by the multiplicative identity property, $1 \cdot xy = xy$. Like terms may also be defined as terms that are the same or that differ only in their coefficients.

Example 4 **Name the coefficient in each term.**

a. $145x^2y$ The coefficient is 145.

b. ab^2 The coefficient is 1 since $ab^2 = 1ab^2$.

c. $\frac{4a^2}{5}$ The coefficient is $\frac{4}{5}$ because $\frac{4a^2}{5}$ can be written as $\frac{4}{5} \cdot a^2$.

Example 5 **Simplify each expression.**

a. $4w^4 + w^4 + 3w^2 - 2w^2$

Remember that $w^4 = 1w^4$.

$$4w^4 + w^4 + 3w^2 - 2w^2$$
$$= (4 + 1)w^4 + (3 - 2)w^2$$
$$= 5w^4 + 1w^2$$
$$= 5w^4 + w^2$$

b. $\frac{a^3}{4} + 2a^3$

Remember that $\frac{a^3}{4} = \frac{1}{4}a^3$.

$$\frac{a^3}{4} + 2a^3 = \frac{1}{4}a^3 + 2a^3$$
$$= \left(\frac{1}{4} + 2\right)a^2$$
$$= 2\frac{1}{4}a^3$$

CHECK FOR UNDERSTANDING

Communicating Mathematics

Study the lesson. Then complete the following.

1. **Explain** why the equation $2(a - 3) = 2a - 3$ is *not* a true sentence.
2. **Write** an expression that meets the following conditions.
   - **a.** It has four terms,
   - **b.** three terms are like terms, and
   - **c.** one has a coefficient of 1.
3. **Describe** how you would simplify $3(2x - 4)$.

MODELING MATHEMATICS

4. **Draw** a rectangular model or use tiles to represent $4(x + 1)$.

Guided Practice

Match an expression in the left-hand column with the equivalent expression in the right-hand column.

5. $8(10 + 4)$	**a.** $(4 + x)2$
6. $(12 - 3)6$	**b.** $8 \cdot 10 + 8 \cdot 4$
7. $(4 \cdot 2) + (x \cdot 2)$	**c.** $2x - 2$
8. $2(x + 5)$	**d.** $2x + 10$
9. $2(x - 1)$	**e.** $(12)(6) - (3)(6)$

Use the distributive property to rewrite each expression without parentheses.

10. $3(2x + 6)$ **11.** $2(a - b)$

Use the distributive property to find each product.

12. $15 \cdot 99$ **13.** $28\left(2\frac{1}{7}\right)$

Name the coefficient of each term.

14. $2.5cd$

15. $7a^2b$

16. $\frac{3b}{5}$

Name the like terms in each expression.

17. $4y^4 + 3y^3 + y^4$

18. $3a^2 + 4c + a + 3b + c + 9a^2$

Simplify each expression, if possible. If not possible, write *in simplest form.*

19. $t^2 + 2t^2 + 4t$

20. $25x^2 + 5x$

21. $16a^2b + 7a^2b + 3ab^2$

22. $7p + q - p + \frac{2q}{3}$

23. **Employment** Maria and Mark are salesclerks at a local department store. Each earns $5.35 per hour. Maria works 24 hours per week, and Mark works 32 hours per week. Write two expressions to represent the amount the two of them earn per week.

EXERCISES

Practice

Use the distributive property to rewrite each expression without parentheses.

24. $2(4 + t)$

25. $(g - 9)5$

26. $5(x + 3)$

27. $8(3m + 6)$

28. $28\left(y - \frac{1}{7}\right)$

29. $a(5 - b)$

Use the distributive property to find each product.

30. $5 \cdot 97$

31. $\left(3\frac{1}{17}\right) \times 17$

32. $16(102)$

33. $24(2.5)$

34. $999 \cdot 6$

35. 3×215

Simplify each expression, if possible. If not possible, write *in simplest form.*

36. $15x + 18x$

37. $14a^2 + 13b^2 + 27$

38. $10n + 3n^2 + 9n^2$

39. $5a + 7a + 10b + 5b$

40. $7(3x^2y - 4xy^2 + xy)$

41. $13p^2 + p$

42. $5(6a + 4b - 3b)$

43. $3(x + 2y) - 2y$

44. $\frac{2}{3}\left(c - \frac{3}{4}\right) + c(1 + b)$

45. $a + \frac{a}{5} + \frac{2}{5}a$

46. $4(3g + 2) + 2(g + 3)$

47. $3(x + y) + 2(x + y) + 4x$

Programming

48. The program at the right tests values of A, B, and C to determine if the distributive property holds for division. That is, does $\frac{A + B}{C} = \frac{A}{C} + \frac{B}{C}$?

```
Program: DISTPROP
: Prompt A,B,C
: If(A + B)/C = A/C + B/C
: Then
: Disp "YES, IT HOLDS."
: Else
: Disp "TRY AGAIN."
: END
```

a. Run the program for 10 different sets of values for A, B, and C. Does the property hold?

b. How could you change the program to test if $(A + B)^C = A^C + B^C$? Does the distributive property hold for powers?

Critical Thinking

49. If $2(b + c) = 2b + 2c$, does $2 + (b \cdot c) = (2 + b)(2 + c)$? Choose values for b and c to show that these may be true or find *counterexamples* to show that they are not.

Applications and Problem Solving

50. **Economics** According to *American Demographics,* the average 13- to 15-year-old male received \$16.15 per week for allowance in 1993. The average 16- to 19-year-old female received \$32.45 per week. Toni was 17 years old, and her brother Carlos was 14 in 1993. Assume that they got the average amount for their weekly allowance.
   a. Write two expressions to represent the amount their parents paid in allowance during the month of February.
   b. What was the amount their parents paid in allowance during that month?

51. **Geometry** The largest permanently installed theater screen has an area of 6768 square feet. It is in Jakarta, Indonesia. The movie screen below represents a typical movie screen in U.S. movie theaters.
   a. Write an expression for the perimeter of the movie screen below and then simplify the expression.

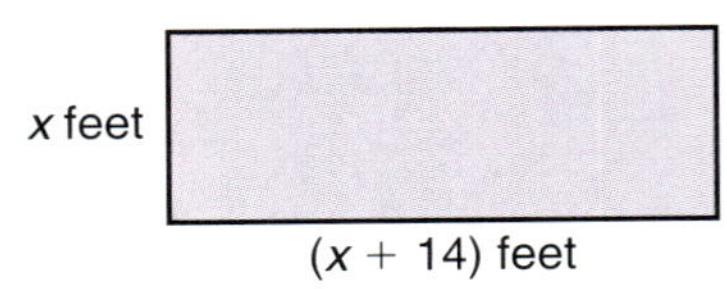

   b. Evaluate the expression if $x = 17$.
   c. Find the area of the movie screen if $x = 17$.

Mixed Review

52. Name the property illustrated by the following statement: *If* $19 - 3 = 16$*, then* $16 = 19 - 3$. (Lesson 1–6)
53. Name the property illustrated by $9 \times 0 = 0$. (Lesson 1–6)
54. Find the solution set for inequality $3x - 5 > 7$ if the replacement set is $\{2, 3, 4, 5, 6\}$. (Lesson 1–5)
55. **Physics** Sound travels 1129 feet per second through air. (Lesson 1–5)
   a. Write an equation that represents how many feet sound can travel in 2 seconds when it is traveling through air.
   b. How many feet can sound travel in 2 seconds when traveling through air?
56. Make a stem-and-leaf plot for the following set of data. (Lesson 1–4)
   37, 45, 36, 51, 55, 29, 45, 58, 36
57. Evaluate $\frac{4^2 - 2^3}{24 - 2(10)}$. (Lesson 1–3)
58. What are the next two expressions for the pattern $5a$, $10a^2$, $15a^3$, $20a^4$, ...? (Lesson 1–2)
59. **Culture** Each year in the Chinese calendar is named for one of 12 animals. Every 12 years, the same animal is named. If 1992 was the Year of the Monkey, how many years in the 20th century were Years of the Monkey? (Lesson 1–2)
60. Write an algebraic expression for *37 less than 2 times a number k.* (Lesson 1–1)

1–8 Commutative and Associative Properties

What YOU'LL LEARN

- To recognize and use the commutative and associative properties to simplify expressions.

Why IT'S IMPORTANT

You can use the communitative and associative properties to evaluate expressions and solve equations.

APPLICATION

Networks

The map below shows the location of Leticia's house and school. It also shows the time in minutes that it takes Leticia to walk around her neighborhood.

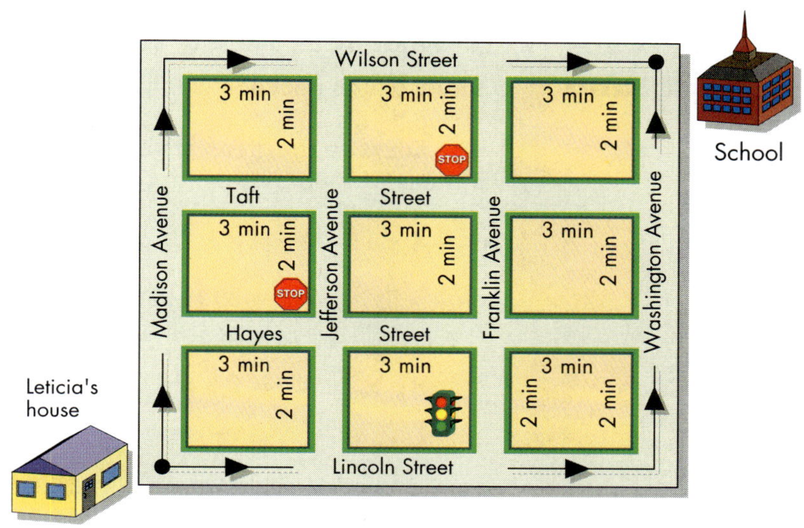

Yesterday, Leticia walked to school by way of Lincoln Street and Washington Avenue. She took $3 + 3 + 3 + 2 + 2 + 2$ or 15 minutes to walk to school. Today, Leticia walked to school by way of Madison Avenue and Wilson Street. She took $2 + 2 + 2 + 3 + 3 + 3$ or 15 minutes. The time it took Leticia to walk to school is the same for both days.

$$3 + 3 + 3 + 2 + 2 + 2 = 2 + 2 + 2 + 3 + 3 + 3$$

In this equation, the addends are the same, but their order is different. The **commutative property** says that the order in which you add or multiply two numbers does not change their sum or product.

Commutative Property	**For any numbers *a* and *b*, $a + b = b + a$ and $a \cdot b = b \cdot a$.**

One easy way to find the sum or product of numbers is to group or *associate* the numbers. The **associative property** says that the way you group three numbers when adding or multiplying does not change their sum or product.

Associative Property	**For any numbers *a*, *b*, and *c*, $(a + b) + c = a + (b + c)$ and $(ab)c = a(bc)$.**

You can group 11 + 12 + 7 + 9 + 7 + 6 to make mental addition easy.

$$
\begin{aligned}
11 + 12 + 7 + 9 + 7 + 6 &= 11 + 9 + 7 + 6 + 7 + 12 && \textit{Commutative } (+)\\
&= (11 + 9) + (7 + 6 + 7) + 12 && \textit{Associative } (+)\\
&= 20 + 20 + 12\\
&= 52
\end{aligned}
$$

The commutative and associative properties can be used with the other properties you have studied when evaluating and simplifying expressions.

Example 1

APPLICATION

Marketing

Juan Martinez is a product manager for a cereal company. Part of his job is to determine what size box should be used to package the company's Toasty Oatsies cereal. Juan can choose from among the following sizes: 8″ by 11″ by $2\frac{1}{2}$″, $8\frac{1}{2}$″ by 10″ by 2″, or $7\frac{7}{8}$″ by 11″ by 3″. Juan wants to know which package will hold the most cereal.

The box with the greatest volume will hold the most cereal. To find the volume of each box, multiply the length times the width times the height.

Why has the order of the factors changed?

$$
\begin{aligned}
8 \times 11 \times 2\tfrac{1}{2} &= 8 \times 2\tfrac{1}{2} \times 11 && \textit{Commutative } (\times)\\
&= 20 \times 11 && \textit{Substitution } (=)\\
&= 220\\
8\tfrac{1}{2} \times 10 \times 2 &= 8\tfrac{1}{2} \times 2 \times 10 && \textit{Commutative } (\times)\\
&= 17 \times 10 && \textit{Substitution } (=)\\
&= 170\\
7\tfrac{7}{8} \times 11 \times 3 &= 7\tfrac{7}{8} \times (11 \times 3) && \textit{Associative } (\times)\\
&= 7\tfrac{7}{8} \times 33 && \textit{Substitution } (=)\\
&= \tfrac{63}{8} \times 33\\
&= \tfrac{2079}{8} \text{ or } 259\tfrac{7}{8}
\end{aligned}
$$

The box that is $7\frac{7}{8}$″ by 11″ by 3″ has the greatest volume.

The chart below summarizes the properties you can use to simplify expressions.

The following properties are true for any numbers *a*, *b*, and *c*.		
	Addition	**Multiplication**
Commutative	$a + b = b + a$	$ab = ba$
Associative	$(a + b) + c = a + (b + c)$	$(ab)c = a(bc)$
Identity	0 is the identity. $a + 0 = 0 + a = a$	1 is the identity. $a \cdot 1 = 1 \cdot a = a$
Zero		$a \cdot 0 = 0 \cdot a = 0$
Distributive	$a(b + c) = ab + ac$ and $(b + c)a = ba + ca$	
Substitution	If $a = b$, then a may be substituted for b.	

Example 2 **a. Write an algebraic expression for the verbal expression *the sum of two and the square of t increased by the sum of t squared and 3.***

b. Then simplify the algebraic expression, indicating all of the properties used.

a. *the sum of two and the square of t* → $2 + t^2$; *increased by* → $+$; *the sum of t squared and 3* → $t^2 + 3$

b.

$2 + t^2 + t^2 + 3$	$= t^2 + t^2 + 2 + 3$	*Commutative (+)*
	$= (t^2 + t^2) + (2 + 3)$	*Associative (+)*
	$= (1 \cdot t^2 + 1 \cdot t^2) + (2 + 3)$	*Multiplicative identity*
	$= (1 + 1)t^2 + (2 + 3)$	*Distributive property*
	$= 2t^2 + 5$	*Substitution (=)*

CHECK FOR UNDERSTANDING

Communicating Mathematics

Study the lesson. Then complete the following.

1. **Illustrate** the associative property of multiplication with a numerical equation.
2. **Explain** how a property or properties can be used to find the product of 5(6.5)(2) without using a calculator or paper and pencil.
3. **Explain** the difference between the commutative and associative properties.
4. **Write** a short explanation as to whether or *not* there is a commutative property of division. Consider these examples.

   $5 \div 3 = 1\frac{2}{3}$ $\qquad$ $3 \div 5 = \frac{3}{5}$

Math Journal

5. **Assess Yourself** Are the values of the following verbal expressions *sometimes, always,* or *never* equal? Explain.
   - *the product of nine and the square of t, multiplied by two*
   - *nine times the product of the square of t and two*

Guided Practice

Name the property illustrated by each statement.

6. $(6 + 4) + 2 = 6 + (4 + 2)$
7. $7 + 6 = 6 + 7$
8. $(2 + 5) + x = 7 + x$
9. $7(ab) = (7a)b$
10. Name the property used in each step.
    - a. $ab(a + b) = (ab)a + (ab)b$
    - b. $\quad = a(ab) + (ab)b$
    - c. $\quad = (a \cdot a)b + a(b \cdot b)$
    - d. $\quad = a^2b + ab^2$

Simplify.

11. $4a + 2b + a$
12. $3p + 2q + 2p + 8q$
13. $3(4x + y) + 2x$
14. $6(0.4x + 0.2y) + 0.5x$
15. Write an algebraic expression for the verbal expression *the product of six and the square of z, increased by the sum of seven, z^2, and 6.* Then simplify, indicating the properties used.

EXERCISES

Practice

Name the property illustrated by each statement.

16. $67 + 3 = 3 + 67$

17. $1 \cdot b^2 = b^2$

18. $10x + 10y = 10(x + y)$

19. $(5 \cdot m) \cdot n = 5 \cdot (m \cdot n)$

20. $(3x^2) \cdot 0 = 0$

21. $4(a + 5b) = 4a + 20b$

22. $(2 + 3)a + 7 = 5a + 7$

23. $fh + 2g = hf + 2g$

24. $7a + \left(\frac{1}{2}b + c\right) = \left(7a + \frac{1}{2}b\right) + c$

25. $(5x^2 + x + 3) + 15 = (5x^2 + x) + (3 + 15)$

26. Name the property used in each step.

a. $3c + 5(2 + c) = 3c + 5(2) + 5c$

b. $= 3c + 5c + 5(2)$

c. $= (3c + 5c) + 5(2)$

d. $= (3 + 5)c + 5(2)$

e. $= 8c + 10$

Simplify.

27. $4x + 5y + 6x$

28. $8a + 3b + a$

29. $5x + 3y + 2x + 7y$

30. $4 + 6(ac + 2b) + 2ac$

31. $2(3x + y) + 4x$

32. $4y^4 + 3y^2 + y^4$

33. $16a^2 + 16 + 16a^2$

34. $3.2(x + y) + 2.3(x + y) + 4x$

35. $\frac{1}{4}x + 2x + 2\frac{3}{4}x$

36. $0.5[3x + 4(3 + 2x)]$

37. $\frac{3}{4} + \frac{2}{3}(m + 2n) + m$

38. $\frac{3}{5}\left(\frac{1}{2}p + 2q\right) + 2p$

Write an algebraic expression for each verbal expression. Then simplify, indicating the properties used.

39. twice the sum of s and t decreased by s

40. half of the sum of p and $2q$ increased by three-fourths q

41. five times the product of x and y increased by $3xy$

42. four times the sum of a and b increased by twice the sum of a and $2b$

43. Find the following product.

$$\frac{1}{2} \cdot \frac{2}{3} \cdot \frac{3}{4} \cdot \ldots \cdot \frac{98}{99} \cdot \frac{99}{100}$$

Recall that an ellipsis "..." means "to continue the pattern." Write a sentence or two explaining how you found the product.

Critical Thinking

44. Is subtraction commutative? Write a short explanation that includes examples to support your answer.

45. Suppose the operation ✱ is defined for all numbers a and b as a ✱ $b = a + 2b$. Is the operation ✱ commutative? Give examples to support your answer.

Applications and Problem Solving

46. Chemistry Chemists use water to dilute acid. One important rule of chemistry is to always pour the acid into the water. Pouring water into acid could produce spattering and burns.

a. Would you say that combining acid and water is commutative?

b. Give an example from your life that is commutative.

c. Give an example from your life that is not commutative.

FYI

In 1994, the roller coaster with the greatest and fastest drop was the Steel Phantom at the Kennywood Amusement Park in West Mifflin, PA. It has a vertical drop of 225 ft with a design speed of 80 mph.

47. Physics The pressure you experience as you ride a roller coaster is produced by the fast changes in direction. This pressure is what pins you down to the back or bottom of your seat. This pressure is known as *g-force*. The formula used to evaluate the g-force is, $G = \frac{(speed)^2}{32.2 \times radius\ of\ the\ curve}$, where the speed is in feet per second, and the radius of the curve is in feet. The acceleration of gravity in $\frac{\text{ft}}{\text{sec}^2}$ is 32.2.

a. If you are riding the Steel Phantom at 60 feet per second (about 40 mph) and the car is turning a curve with a radius of 30 feet, what g-force will you experience?

b. The g-force has an effect on your weight. For example, if you weigh 100 pounds and experience a g-force of 2 g's, your weight at that moment feels like 2×100 or 200 pounds. What will your weight feel like while taking the curve at 60 feet per second?

Mixed Review

48. Name the coefficient of $\frac{4m^2}{5}$. (Lesson 1–7)

49. Environment According to the U.S. Environmental Protection Agency, a typical family of four uses 100 gallons of water flushing the toilet, 80 gallons of water showering and bathing, and 8 gallons of water using the bathroom sink each day. Write two expressions that represent the amount of water a typical family of four uses for these purposes in d days. (Lesson 1–7)

50. Name the property illustrated by the following statement.
If $a + b = c$ and $a = b$, then $a + a = c$. (Lesson 1–6)

51. Name the multiplicative inverse of $\frac{2}{3}$. (Lesson 1–6)

52. *True or False:* $\frac{3k-3}{7} + 13 < 17$, when $k = 8$. (Lesson 1–5)

53. Weather The following data represents the average daily temperature in Fahrenheit for Santiago, Chile, for two weeks during the month of February. Organize the data using a stem-and-leaf plot. (Lesson 1–4)

101, 95, 100, 100, 99, 101, 97,
99, 97, 100, 103, 101, 101, 99

54. Evaluate $(25 - 4) \div (2^2 - 1^3)$. (Lesson 1–3)

55. Find the next two items in the sequence. (Lesson 1–2)

▲ ▼ ▼ ▲ ▲ ▲ ▼ ▼ ▼

56. Write an algebraic expression for *five times p to the sixth power.* (Lesson 1–1)

1–9 A Preview of Graphs and Functions

***What* YOU'LL LEARN**

- To interpret graphs in real-world settings, and
- to sketch graphs for given functions.

***Why* IT'S IMPORTANT**

You need to know how to sketch and interpret graphs in order to study trends and display data.

APPLICATION

Economics

The dollar value of a car begins to decrease immediately after it is sold. This is called *depreciation.* Mathematically, depreciation can be defined by the following open sentence.

$$\text{depreciation} = \text{original cost of car} - \text{value of car when sold}$$

The table below shows how a typical \$15,000 car depreciates over a period of five years. From the table, you can see that as the age of the car increases, the value decreases. Why do you think this happens?

Age of Car (year)	Approximate Value of Car
0	\$15,000
1	11,000
2	8000
3	6000
4	5000
5	4000

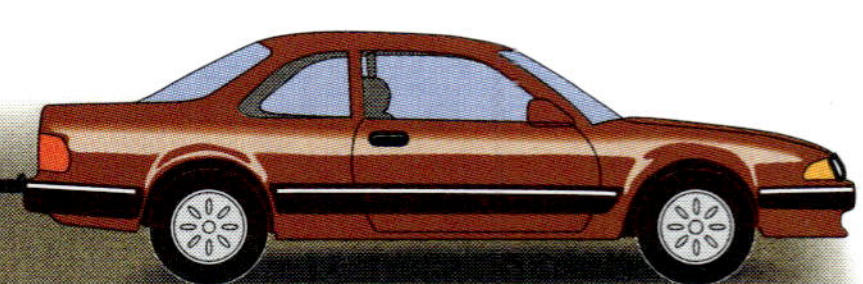

This information can also be presented in a graph. The graph below shows the relationship between the current value of the car and the age of the car.

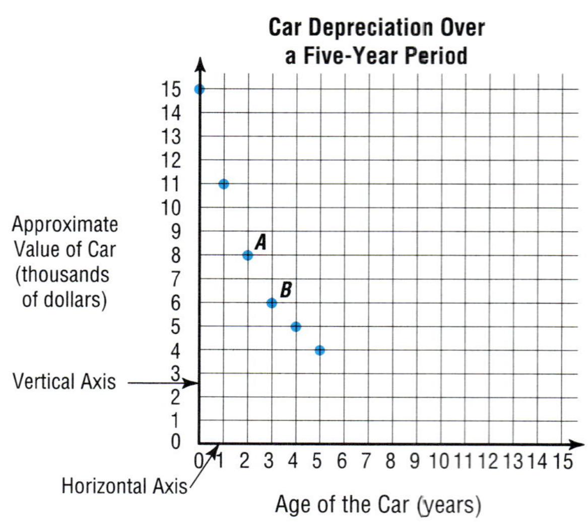

The value of the car is said to be a **function** of the age of the car. A function is a relationship between input and output. In a function, the output depends on the input. There is exactly one output for each input.

There are two number lines on the graph. The line that represents the current value of the car is the **vertical axis.** The line that represents the age of the car is the **horizontal axis.**

Notice that there are six points shown on the graph. Each point represents the dollar value of the car (in thousands) at the end of each year. For example, after year 1, the value is $11,000. You can express this relationship as (1, 11). What do points A and B represent?

$A(2, 8)$ means that at the end of year 2 the value of the car is about $8000.

$B(3, 6)$ means that at the end of year 3 the value of the car is about $6000.

(1, 11), (2, 8), and (3, 6) are called **ordered pairs.** The order in which the pair of numbers is written is important. Ordered pairs are used to locate points on the graph. The first number in an ordered pair corresponds to the horizontal axis, and the second number in an ordered pair corresponds to the vertical axis. The ordered pair (0, 0) corresponds to the **origin**.

Many real-world situations can be modeled using functions.

Example 1 APPLICATION Sales

Shim owns a farm market. The amount a customer pays for sweet corn depends on the number of ears that are purchased. Shim sells a dozen ears of corn for $3.00.

a. Make a table showing the price of various purchases of sweet corn.

Number of Dozen	Ears of Corn	Price
$\frac{1}{2}$	6	$1.50
1	12	$3.00
$1\frac{1}{2}$	18	$4.50
2	24	$6.00

b. Write four ordered pairs that represent the number of ears of corn and the price of the corn.

Four ordered pairs can be determined from the chart. These ordered pairs are (6, 1.50), (12, 3.00), (18, 4.50), and (24, 6.00).

c. Describe a set of axes that could be used to graph the number of ears of corn and the price of the corn.

Let the horizontal axis represent the number of ears of corn, and let the vertical axis represent the price of the corn.

d. Draw a graph that shows the relationship between the number of ears of corn and the price.

Graph the four points described by the ordered pairs.

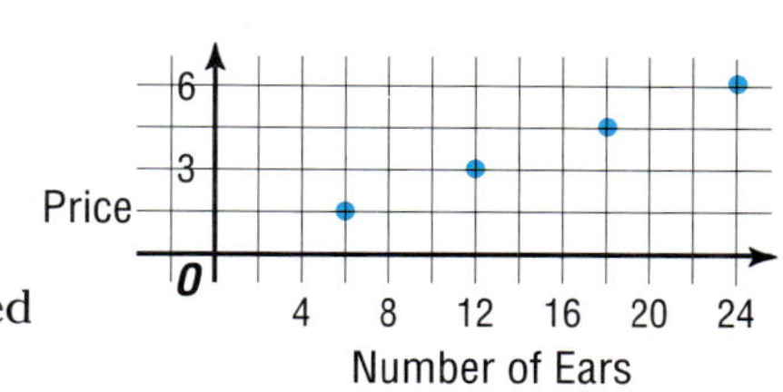

e. As you read the graph from left to right, describe the trend you see. Explain.

The graph goes upward, because the price increases as the number of ears increases. The price is a function of the number of ears purchased.

In Example 1, the price a customer pays depends on the number of ears purchased. Therefore, the number of ears purchased is called the **independent variable** or **quantity,** and the price is called the **dependent variable** or **quantity.** Usually the independent variable is graphed on the horizontal axis and the dependent variable is graphed on the vertical axis.

You can use a graph without scales on either axis to show the general shape of the graph that models a situation.

Example 2 **For a certain time, Lucinda jogs up a hill at a steady speed. Then she runs down the hill and picks up her speed.**

a. What happens to her speed when Lucinda jogs at a steady pace? when Lucinda runs down the hill?

The speed remains the same when her jogging pace is steady. The speed increases when she runs downhill.

b. Identify the independent and dependent quantities.

Time is the independent quantity, and speed is the dependent quantity.

c. Match the graph to the situation.

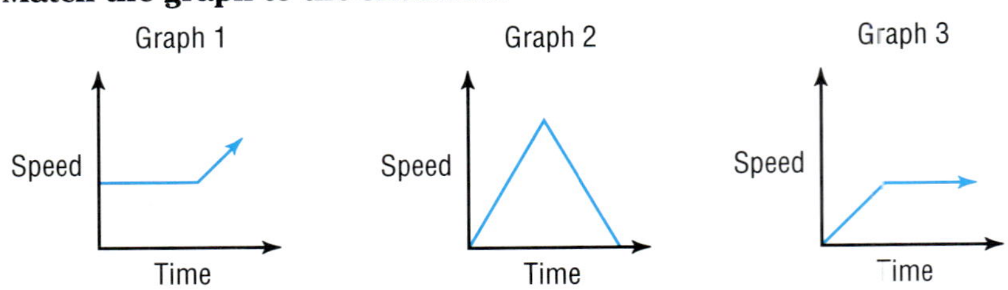

Graph 1 shows a steady speed (a horizontal line), followed by an increase in speed (a line that goes up) the longer she exercises.

A **relation** is a set of ordered pairs. The set of first numbers of the ordered pairs is the **domain** of the relation. The domain contains values of the independent variable. The set of second numbers of the ordered pairs is the **range** of the relation. The range contains values of the dependent variable.

Example 3 **Ryan is not feeling well and has missed a day of school. The graph shows Ryan's temperature as a function of the time of day.**

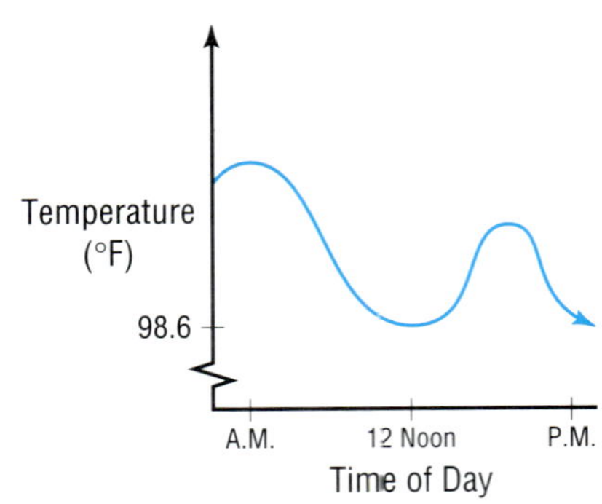

a. Write a story about Ryan's illness.

When Ryan got up in the morning, he had a high fever. As the morning went on, his temperature went down. By noon it was almost normal, but his temperature went up again after lunch. Then his mom gave him some medication. By evening his fever was gone, and his temperature was back to normal.

b. Identify a reasonable domain and range for this problem.

The domain includes the 24 hours in a day. A reasonable range would include all of the temperatures between the highest and lowest temperature a person can have and still be alive.

CHECK FOR UNDERSTANDING

Communicating Mathematics

Study the lesson. Then complete the following.

1. **Explain** why the order of the numbers in an ordered pair is important.

2. Refer to the application at the beginning of the lesson. Extend the graph to predict the value of the car after 6 years and after 10 years.

3. Use the graph at the right to answer the following questions.

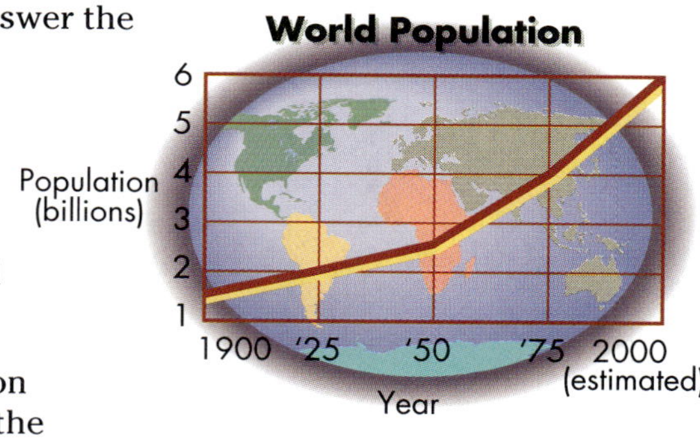

   a. **Describe** the information that the graph shows.

   b. **Identify** the variable represented along each axis.

   c. **Identify** two points on the graph and write the ordered pair for each point. Explain what each point represents.

   d. **Explain** what the ordered pair (2000, 6.2) represents.

   e. **Write** a statement that explains the function in the graph.

"I really look forward to your cheery little visits."

4. **Write** a story that explains what the graph in the cartoon at the left might represent. Identify the independent and dependent variables in your story.

Guided Practice

5. Match each description with the most appropriate graph.

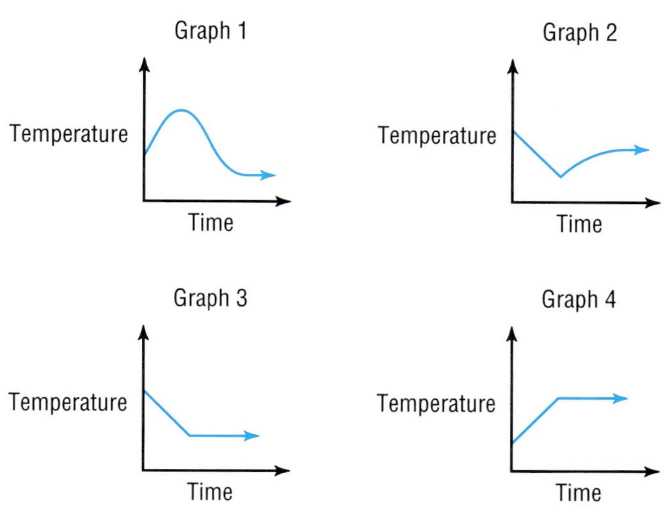

   a. In August, you enter a hot house and turn on the air conditioner.

   b. In January, you enter a cold house and turn up the thermostat to 68° F.

   c. You put ice cubes in your fruit punch and then drink it slowly.

   d. You put a cup of water in the microwave and heat it for one minute.

6. Sketch a reasonable graph for the following statement. *How hard you hit your thumb with a hammer impacts on how much it hurts.* Name the independent and dependent variables.

7. The basketball coach at City College is recruiting basketball players. The graphs below describe two of the players being recruited.

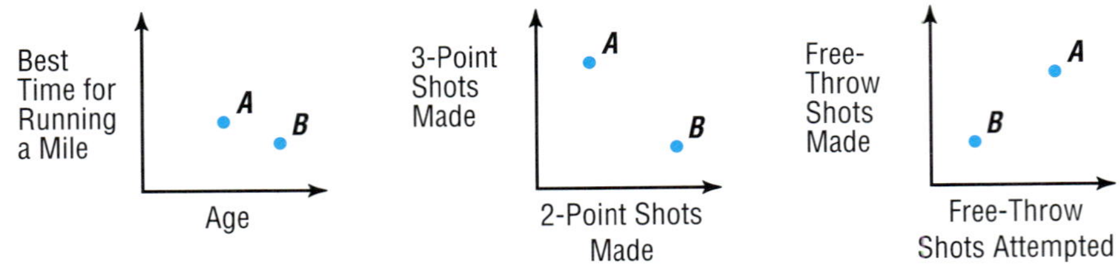

Determine whether each statement is *true* or *false*. Explain your reasoning.

a. The younger player is faster than the older player.

b. One player made more 2-point and more 3-point shots than the other.

c. The older player made more 2-point shots.

d. The younger player tried and made more free-throw shots.

EXERCISES

Practice

8. Identify the graph that matches the following statement. Explain your answer.

A bus frequently stops to pick up passengers.

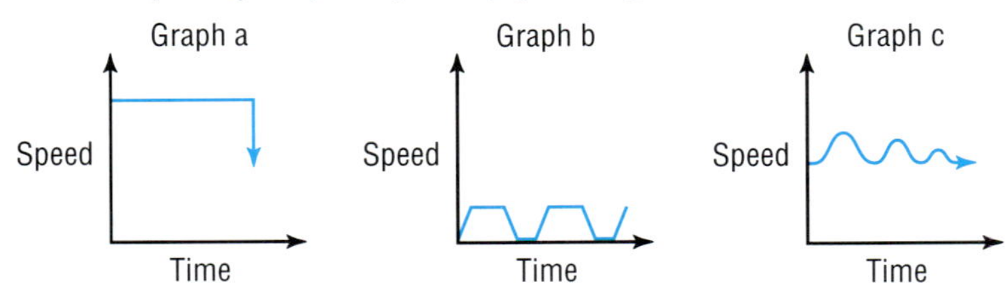

9. Identify the graph that represents annual income as a function of age. Explain your answer.

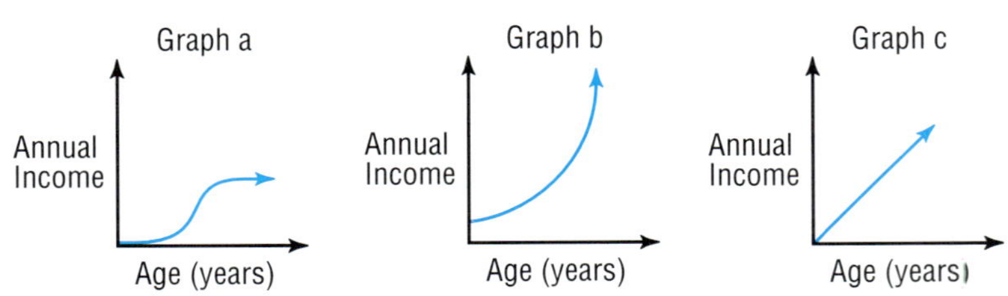

10. The graph at the right shows the amount of money in Jorge's savings account as a function of time.

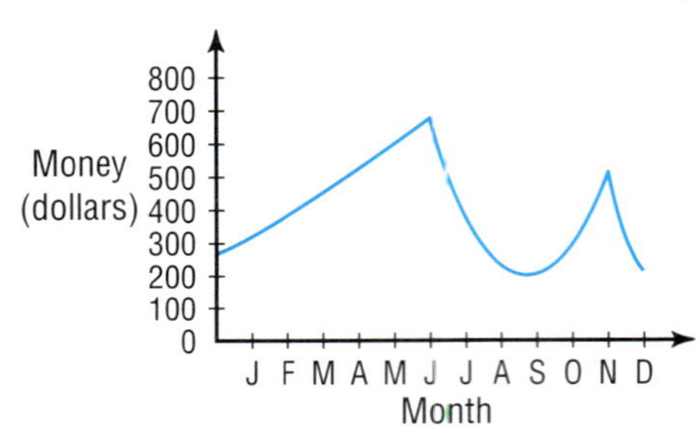

a. Describe what is happening to Jorge's money. Explain why the graph rises and falls at particular points.

b. Describe the elements in the domain and range.

11. Match each table of data to the most appropriate graph.

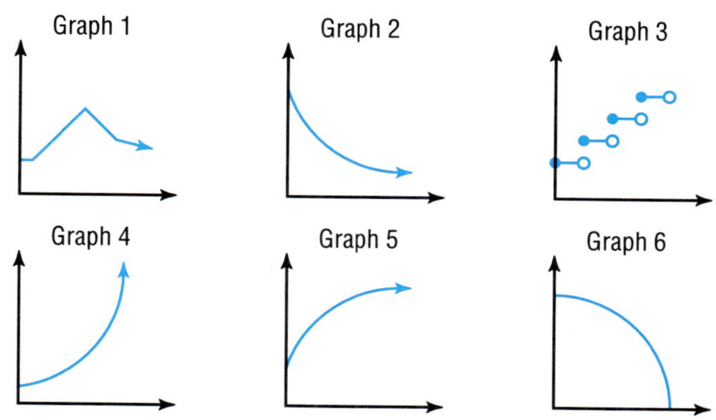

a. Primary Seismic Wave

Distance from Epicenter (km)	1000	2000	3000	4000	5000	6000	7000
Time (minutes)	2	4	5.8	7.2	8.5	9.7	10.8

b. Cost of First-Class Postage Stamps

Year	1983	1985	1987	1989	1991	1993	1995
Cost of Stamp	22¢	25¢	25¢	25¢	29¢	29¢	32¢

c. Immigration into the United States

Year	1987	1988	1989	1990	1991	1992	1993
Legal Admissions (millions)	0.6	0.6	1.1	1.5	1.8	1.0	0.9

d. Development of Human Fetus

Time (weeks)	4	8	12	16	20	24	28
Mass (grams)	0.5	1	28	110	300	650	1200

e. Height of Falling Object

Time (seconds)	0	0.5	1.0	1.5	2.0	2.5	3.0
Height (feet)	200	196	184	164	136	100	56

f. Cooling of Boiling Water

Time (minutes)	0	1	2	3	4	5	6
Temperature (°F)	100	50	25	12.5	6.25	3.125	1.5625

Sketch a reasonable graph for each situation.

12. Rashaad likes to trade basketball cards. During the first two weeks of the month, he added lots of cards to his collection. Then, he lost some cards and sold others.

13. A radio-controlled car moves along and then crashes against a wall.

14. Phyllis is riding her bike at a steady pace. Then she has a flat tire. She walks to a gas station to have the tire repaired. When the tire is fixed, she continues her ride.

15. The height of a football that was thrown into the end zone for a touchdown compared to the distance the football is from the end zone.

Critical Thinking

16. Which of the sports listed will produce a graph like the one below? Explain why you chose the sport you did and give reasons why you did not choose the other sports.

Archery	High Jumping
Biking	Javelin Throwing
Fishing	Pole Vaulting
Golf	Skateboarding
High Diving	Sky Diving

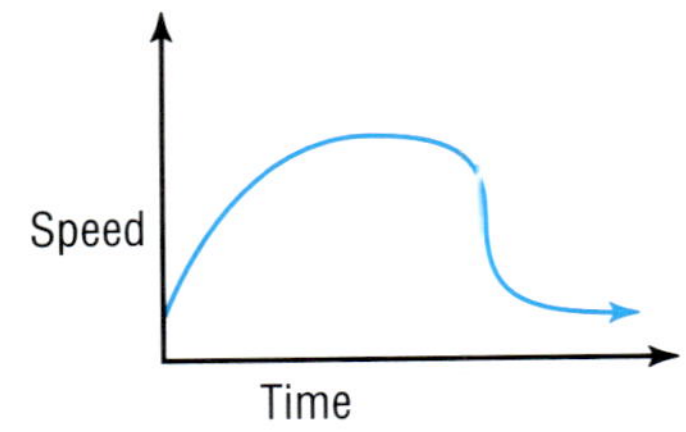

Applications and Problem Solving

17. Charities The graph at the right shows the amount of money raised by the Muscular Dystrophy Association over a 14-year period.

Source: Muscular Dystrophy Association

a. Name the independent and dependent variables.

b. What does the ordered pair (1991, 45) represent?

c. Write a statement about the amount of money raised from 1981 to 1986.

d. Write a statement about the amount of money raised from 1987 to 1994.

e. Use the information to predict the amount of money raised each year since 1994. Research to see if your prediction is correct.

18. Music Business The graph at the right shows the sales in millions of dollars for different music categories. Write two conclusions you can make from the information presented in the graph.

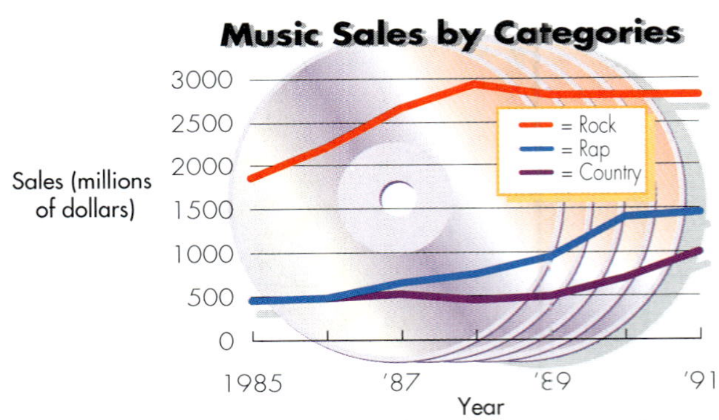

Source: The Recording Industry Association of America

Mixed Review

19. Simplify $5p + 7q + 9 + 4q + 2p$. (Lesson 1–8)

20. Simplify $9a + 14(a + 3)$. (Lesson 1–7)

21. Evaluate $14(1) - 27(0)$. (Lesson 1–6)

22. *True or False:* $5m + 6^2 = 56$, when $m = 4$. (Lesson 1–5)

23. Geometry The volume of a cone equals one-third the area of the base B times the height h. Write an algebraic expression for the volume of a cone. (Lesson 1–1)

CHAPTER 1 HIGHLIGHTS

VOCABULARY

After completing this chapter, you should be able to define each term, property, or phrase and give an example or two of each.

Algebra

additive identity (p. 37)
algebraic expression (p. 6)
algebra tiles (p. 44)
associative property (p. 51)
base (p. 7)
coefficient (p. 47)
commutative property (p. 51)
dependent variable (p. 58)
distributive property (p. 46)
domain (p. 58)
equation (p. 33)
equivalent expressions (p. 47)
evaluate (p. 8)
exponent (p. 7)
factors (p. 6)
function (p. 56)
horizontal axis (p. 56)
independent variable (p. 58)
inequality (p. 33)
like terms (p. 47)
multiplicative identity (p. 38)
multiplicative inverse (p. 38)
multiplicative property of zero (p. 38)
open sentence (p. 32)
order of operations (p. 19)
ordered pairs (p. 57)
power (p. 7)
product (p. 6)
range (p. 58)
reciprocal (p. 38)
reflexive property of equality (p. 39)
relation (p. 58)
replacement set (p. 33)
simplest form (p. 47)
solution (p. 32)
solution set (p. 33)
solving the open sentence (p. 32)
substitution property of equality (p. 39)
symmetric property of equality (p. 39)
term (pp. 13, 47)
transitive property of equality (p. 39)
variable (p. 6)
vertical axis (p. 56)

Discrete Mathematics

element (p. 33)
set (p. 33)
sequence (p. 13)

Statistics

data (p. 25)
statistics (p. 25)
stem-and-leaf plots (p. 25)

Problem Solving

look for a pattern (p. 13)

UNDERSTANDING AND USING THE VOCABULARY

Choose the letter of the term that best matches each statement or phrase.

1. For any number a, $a + 0 = 0 + a = a$.
2. For any number a, $a \cdot 1 = 1 \cdot a = a$.
3. For any number a, $a \cdot 0 = 0 \cdot a = 0$.
4. For any number a, there is exactly one number $\frac{1}{a}$ such that $a \cdot \frac{1}{a} = \frac{1}{a} \cdot a = 1$.
5. For any number a, $a = a$.
6. For any numbers a and b, if $a = b$, then $b = a$.
7. For any numbers a and b, if $a = b$, then b may be substituted for a.
8. For any numbers a, b, and c, if $a = b$ and $b = c$, then $a = c$.
9. For any numbers a, b, and c, $a(b + c) = ab + ac$.

a. additive identity property
b. distributive property
c. multiplicative identity property
d. multiplicative inverse property
e. multiplicative property of zero
f. reflexive property
g. substitution property
h. symmetric property
i. transitive property

CHAPTER 1 STUDY GUIDE AND ASSESSMENT

SKILLS AND CONCEPTS

OBJECTIVES AND EXAMPLES

Upon completing this chapter, you should be able to:

- translate verbal expressions into mathematical expressions and vice versa (Lesson 1–1)

Write an algebraic expression for the sum of twice a number x and fifteen.

$$2x + 15$$

Write a verbal expression for $4x^2 - 13$.
four times a number x squared minus thirteen

REVIEW EXERCISES

Use these exercises to review and prepare for the chapter test.

Write an algebraic expression for each verbal expression.

10. the sum of a number x and twenty-one
11. a number x to the fifth power
12. the difference of three times a number x and 8
13. five times the square of a number x

Write a verbal expression for each algebraic expression.

14. $2p^2$
15. $3m^5$
16. $\frac{1}{2}x + 2$
17. $4m^2 - 2m$

- solve problems by extending sequences (Lesson 1–2)

Give the next two items for each sequence.

3, 7, 15, 31, . . .

3 7 15 31 63 127

+4 +8 +16 +32 +64

The next two terms are 63 and 127.

Give the next two items for each pattern.

18. 

19. 2, 4, 8, 16, . . .
20. 1, 1, 2, 3, 5, . . .
21. $x + y, 2x + y, 3x + y, \ldots$

Consider the following sequence.
10, 100, 1000, 10,000, . . .

22. Give the next two terms of the sequence.
23. Express the first four terms in the sequence as a power of 10.
24. What are the 9th and 13th terms?

- use the order of operations to evaluate real number expressions (Lesson 1–3)

$$\begin{aligned}&5 \times 2^2 - 15 \div 3 + 4\\ &= 5 \times 4 - 15 \div 3 + 4\\ &= 20 - 15 \div 3 + 4\\ &= 20 - 5 + 4\\ &= 15 + 4\\ &= 19\end{aligned}$$

$$\begin{aligned}&[3(6) - 4^2]^3 \times 15 \div 5\\ &= [3(6) - 16]^3 \times 15 \div 5\\ &= [18 - 16]^3 \times 15 \div 5\\ &= [2]^3 \times 15 \div 5\\ &= 8 \times 15 \div 5\\ &= 120 \div 5\\ &= 24\end{aligned}$$

Evaluate each expression.

25. $3 + 2 \times 4$
26. $(10 - 6) \div 8$
27. $18 - 4^2 + 7$
28. $0.8(0.02 + 0.05) - 0.006$
29. $(3 \times 1)^3 - (4 + 6) \div (9.1 + 0.9)$

Evaluate each expression when $x = 0.1$, $t = 3$, and $y = 2$.

30. $t^2 + 3y$
31. xty^3
32. $ty \div x$
33. the product of y and x plus t raised to the second power

OBJECTIVES AND EXAMPLES

- display and interpret data on a stem-and-leaf plot (Lesson 1–4)

Stem	Leaf
2	6 8
3	3 5 6 8 9
4	0 2 3 4 4 4 5 6 7 7 8 8 9
5	0 1 2 2 2 3 3 4 6 7
6	1 3 5 9
7	0 3 *2 | 6 = 26*

The highest entry is 73. The lowest entry is 26. The total number of entries is 36. Most of the data is in the interval 40–49.

REVIEW EXERCISES

The ages (in years) at the time of death for the presidents of the United States are listed below.

67, 90, 83, 85, 73, 80, 78, 79, 68, 71, 53, 65, 74, 64, 77, 56, 66, 63, 70, 49, 56, 67, 71, 58, 60, 72, 67, 57, 60, 90, 63, 88, 78, 46, 64, 81

34. Make a stem-and-leaf plot of the data.

35. How old was the oldest president at death?

36. How old was the youngest president at death?

37. Does the total number of entries match the number of presidents? Explain.

38. In which interval did most of the ages fall?

- solve open sentences by performing arithmetic operations (Lesson 1–5)

State whether each sentence is true or false.

$x + 3 \geq 5$, $x = 1$

$1 + 3 \geq 5$

$4 \geq 5$

false

$5^2 - 3y \leq 1$, $y = 8$

$5^2 - 3(8) \leq 1$

$25 - 24 \leq 1$

$1 \leq 1$

true

State whether each sentence is *true* or *false* for the value of the variable given.

39. $x + 13 = 22$, $x = 8$

40. $2b + 2 < b^3$, $b = 2$

41. $(y + 4) \div (y + 2) \leq 2$, $y = 2$

42. Find the solution set for $3x + 1 \leq 13$ if the replacement set is {2, 4, 6, 8}.

Solve each equation.

43. $y = 4\frac{1}{2} + 3^2$

44. $y = 5[2(4) - 1^3]$

- recognize and use the properties of identity and equality (Lesson 1–6)

$36 + 7 \times 1 + 5(2 - 2)$

$= 36 + 7 \times 1 + 5(0)$ *Substitution (=)*

$= 36 + 7 + 5(0)$ *Multiplicative identity*

$= 36 + 7$ *Multiplicative prop. of zero*

$= 42$ *Substitution (=)*

Name the multiplicative inverse of each number or variable.

45. 3 **46.** y **47.** 0.2

Name the property illustrated by each statement.

48. $xy = 1xy$

49. $0 + 22x = 22x$

50. Evaluate $2[3 \div (19 - 4^2)]$ and name the property used in each step.

- use the distributive property to simplify expressions (Lesson 1–7)

$5(t + 3)$

$= 5(t) + 5(3)$

$= 5t + 15$

$2x^2 + 4x^2 + 7x$

$= (2 + 4)x^2 + 7x$

$= 6x^2 + 7x$

Use the distributive property to rewrite each expression without parentheses.

51. $2(4 + 7)$ **52.** $4(x + 1)$ **53.** $3\left(\frac{1}{3} - p\right)$

Use the distributive property to find each product.

54. 6×103 **55.** 3×98 **56.** $12(1.5)$

Simplify each expression.

57. $3m + 5m + 12n - 4n$ **58.** $2p(1 + 16r)$

OBJECTIVES AND EXAMPLES

- when simplifying expressions recognize and use the commutative and associative properties (Lesson 1–8)

$3x + 7xy + 9x$

$= 3x + 9x + 7xy$ *Commutative (+)*

$= (3 + 9)x + 7xy$ *Distributive*

$= 12x + 7xy$ *Substitution (=)*

REVIEW EXERCISES

Name the property illustrated by each statement.

59. $7(p + q) = 7(q + p)$
60. $3 + (x + y) = (3 + x) + y$
61. $(b + a)c = c(b + a)$
62. $2(mn) = (2m)n$
63. Simplify $2x + 2y + 3x + 3y$.

Write an algebraic expression for each verbal expression. Then simplify, indicating the properties used.

64. five times the sum of x and y decreased by $2x$
65. twice the product of p and q increased by pq

- interpret graphs in real-world settings (Lesson 1–9)

Sketch a graph for the following statement.

As a band gets more popular, their prices increase to a point and then level off.

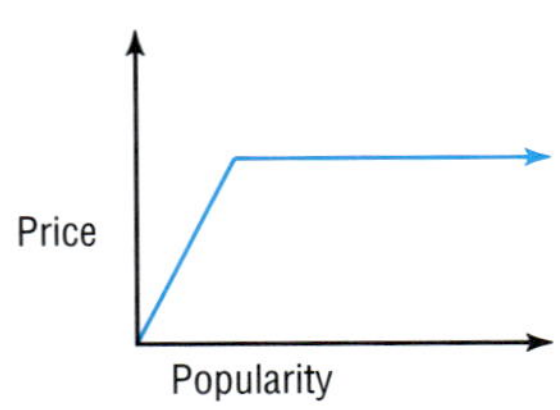

Match each description with the most appropriate graph.

Graph a

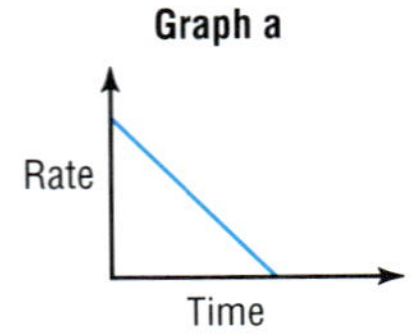

Graph b

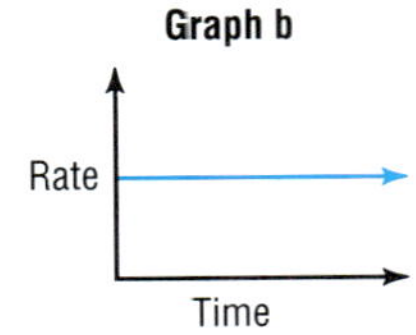

Graph c

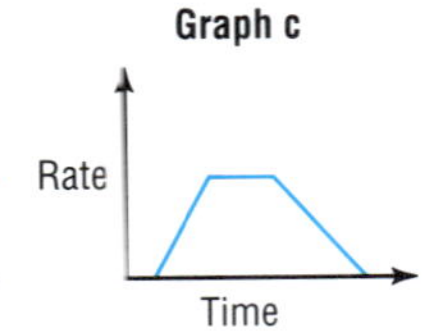

66. the speed of light
67. an airplane taking off, then landing
68. a car approaching a stop sign

APPLICATIONS AND PROBLEM SOLVING

69. **Food and Nutrition** There are 80 Calories in one serving of skim milk and 8 servings in a half gallon. (Lesson 1–1)
    a. Write an expression that describes how many Calories you get if you drink s servings of skim milk.
    b. How many Calories do you consume if you drink 4 servings of skim milk a day?
    c. How many Calories are in a half gallon of skim milk?

70. **Investments** The equation $I = prt$ describes simple interest on a savings account, where I is the amount of interest, p is the amount deposited, r is the annual interest rate, and t is the time in years. (Lesson 1–3)
    a. Solve for I if $p = 100$, $r = 0.05$, and $t = 2$.
    b. If you deposit \$200 in a savings account that earns 6% interest ($6\% = 0.06$), how much money will be in your account after the first year?

71. **Geometry** The triangle inequality states that if you have a triangle, then the sum of any two of its sides must be greater than its third side. (Lesson 1–5)
    a. Verify that a triangle with sides of length 3, 4, and 5 units satisfies the triangle inequality.
    b. Suppose you want to construct a triangle such that two of the sides are 3 feet and 6 feet long. What is the minimum length of the third side? (Use x for the length of the third side.)

A practice test for Chapter 1 is provided on page 787.

ALTERNATIVE ASSESSMENT

COOPERATIVE LEARNING PROJECT

Operating a Music Store In this chapter, you learned how to model verbal sentences with algebraic sentences. The basic principles of modeling verbal sentences involve being able to determine whether or not you have an equality or an inequality and determining what your variables are.

In this project, imagine that you and your friends plan to open a new music store that will sell only compact discs. After some research, you find that the monthly rent for your store will be \$500 and that you can expect to spend about \$200 a month for utilities. Assume that your inventory of compact discs must be at least 400 different titles with 4 discs per title and that the wholesale cost for compact discs is \$8.00 per disc.

Outline the costs for starting your business and plan how much in CD sales you would need to show a profit each month.

Follow these steps to organize your business.

- Determine the cost to open your new business.
- Determine your monthly overhead costs.
- Find a price for which you will sell your CDs.
- Write an algebraic model that describes the number of CDs you have to sell in order to break even each month.
- Draw a graph to show that if sales increase over time, the profits will also increase.
- Write several paragraphs describing your plan and incorporate your algebraic models and graphs to help support it.

THINKING CRITICALLY

- Does the distributive property also apply to multiplication? In other words, does the product $a(bc) = (ab)(ac)$? Why or why not?
- Create a sequence of numbers in which there is more than one pattern. Explain why this is possible.

PORTFOLIO

Do you organize your work so that you and anyone else reading it can tell what you were thinking? Find an example of your work that you have done that is well organized and list the qualities that make it so. Then find an example of your work that isn't as well organized and list what you could have done to make it more so. Place both of these in your portfolio.

SELF EVALUATION

Are you confident with your knowledge of mathematics? Most math students would rather not try to solve a math problem than try to and get the wrong answer.

Assess yourself. How confident are you? Would you rather not attempt a problem, or are you willing to give your best effort and learn from the outcome? Describe how you can become more confident in your problem solving both in mathematics and in your daily life.

LONG-TERM PROJECT

In•ves•ti•ga•tion

the Greenhouse Effect

MATERIALS NEEDED

- lamp with a 100-watt bulb
- stopwatch
- thermometer
- plastic zipper-style sandwich bag
- ruler

The *greenhouse effect* refers to the warming of Earth by the sun. The main culprit in the greenhouse effect is carbon dioxide (CO_2). Carbon dioxide in the atmosphere works like the panes of glass on a greenhouse. Glass is transparent to visible light, allowing the sun's rays to warm Earth's surface. But when the surface gives off excess heat, the hot air stays in the greenhouse, which continues to keep the air warm. Similarly, CO_2 in the atmosphere absorbs the sun's infrared rays, allowing some of the excess heat to stay in the atmosphere rather than escaping into space. How much heat is retained depends on how much CO_2 is in the air.

Over the last 200 years, the amount of CO_2 in our atmosphere has increased, raising Earth's average temperature. Some scientists predict that if global warming continues and Earth's average temperature goes up an additional 3° to 8°F, we could see a marked increase in the number of weather-related disasters like heat waves, droughts, floods, and hurricanes.

In this Investigation, you will use mathematics to analyze aspects of the greenhouse effect and report your findings. As a scientist commissioned to explore the greenhouse effect, you will conduct two experiments. The first experiment is a *control experiment* that will be used to compare data with the second experiment, called the *greenhouse experiment*. Both experiments will involve temperature as a *function* of distance.

Make an Investigation Folder in which you can store all of your work on this Investigation for future use.

CONTROL EXPERIMENT

Test	Distances Between Thermometer and Bulb	First Temperature	Second Temperature	Difference in Temperatures
1				
2				
3				
4				

CONTROL EXPERIMENT

1. Begin by copying the chart above onto a sheet of paper.
2. Set your lamp about 5 inches away from the thermometer. Make sure the lamp is turned off.
3. Measure and record the temperature and the distance between the thermometer and the bulb.
4. Turn the lamp on and leave it on for five minutes. Use the stopwatch to keep accurate time.
5. Record the new temperature and find the difference of the temperatures.
6. Let the thermometer and bulb cool to room temperature and repeat the process, moving the lamp a little farther from the thermometer. Conduct the test a total of four times at four different distances. Make sure you let the thermometer cool to room temperature between each test.

GREENHOUSE EXPERIMENT

7. Begin by making a chart like the one you made for the Control Experiment.
8. Make sure that the thermometer has cooled to room temperature. Then record the temperature.
9. Put the thermometer in the plastic bag and close the bag. Make sure that the bulb of the thermometer does not touch the bag. Then place the thermometer the same distance from the lamp as you did in the control experiment (about 5 inches). Record the distance between the thermometer and the lamp bulb. Then turn the lamp on and leave it on for five minutes.
10. Record the new temperature. Then find the difference of the temperatures.
11. Conduct four tests, using the same distances you used in the control experiment. Make sure you take the thermometer out of the bag and let it cool to room temperature between each test. Be sure to take accurate readings and measurements.

You will continue working on this Investigation throughout Chapters 2 and 3.

Be sure to keep your chart and materials in your Investigation Folder.

The Greenhouse Effect Investigation

Working on the Investigation Lesson 2–2, p. 83

Working on the Investigation Lesson 2–6, p. 111

Working on the Investigation Lesson 3–2, p. 154

Working on the Investigation Lesson 3–6, p. 177

Closing the Investigation

End of Chapter 3, 184

CHAPTER 2

Exploring Rational Numbers

Objectives

In this chapter, you will:

- display and interpret statistical data on line plots,
- add, subtract, multiply, and divide rational numbers,
- find square roots, and
- write equations and formulas.

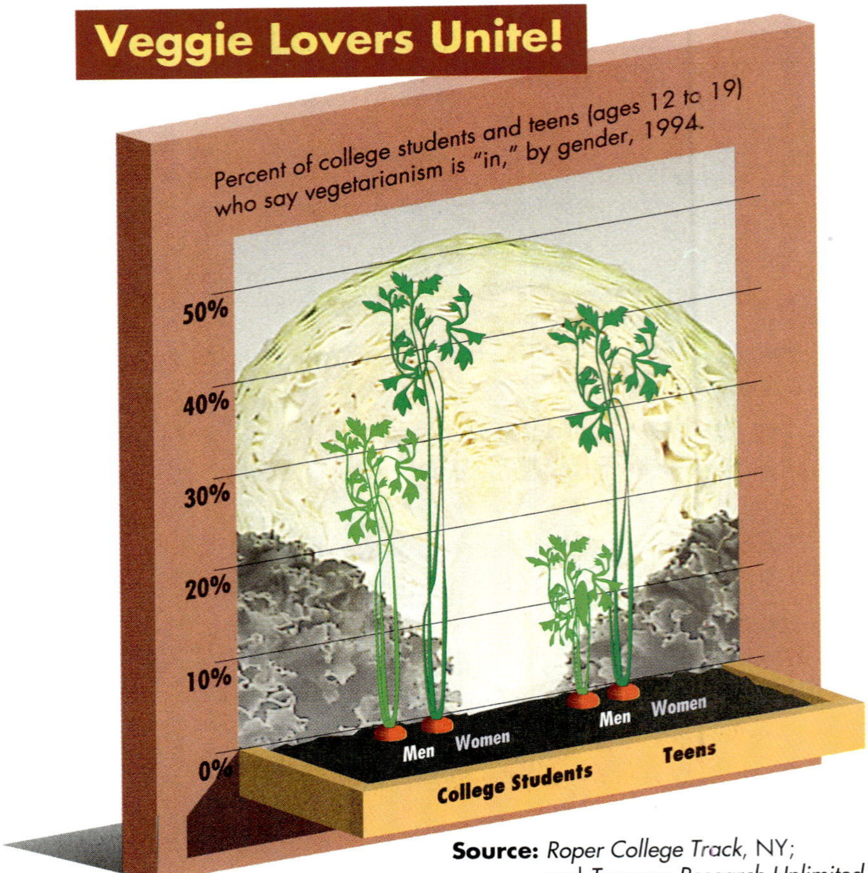

Source: *Roper College Track*, NY; and *Teenage Research Unlimited*

Hamburgers and pepperoni pizzas have been teen diet staples for decades. But lately there is a growing trend toward meatless meals. Why do teens switch to "veggie values" and go for tofu and eggplant? Are there benefits to a diet without meat? Are there dangers to a diet without meat?

TIME Line

1000 B.C. Chinese counting boards originate.

1814 African American Elijah McCoy receives a patent for a locomotive lubricator for which the phrase is coined, "the real McCoy."

A.D. 1565 The first potatoes from the New World arrive in Spain.

1790 The metric system is developed by a group of French scientists.

PEOPLE IN THE NEWS

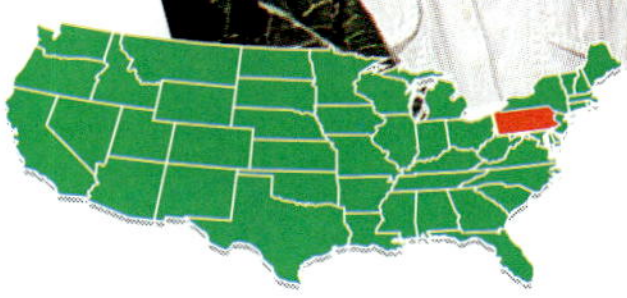

The concern for animals is one reason teenagers give up eating meat. Groups like Earth 2000, a teens-only advocacy group founded by **Danny Seo,** want the focus of their generation to be "no animal cruelty, no meat." Danny and members of Earth 2000 cite teen celebrities like Michael Stipe, Eddie Vedder, and Jennie Garth as vegetarian role models.

Danny also cites health reasons for maintaining a meatless diet, such as cutting back on the intake of fat. In a balanced vegetarian diet, only about one third of the calories come from fat.

Chapter Project

What would you eat if you didn't eat meat? Research nutrition and dietary resource materials at the library to help you devise a healthy vegetarian diet and a healthy meat diet for an average teenager.

- Plan two diets. One should be for a no animal meat vegetarian, and one should be for a meat-eating person.
- Devise a seven-day menu for each diet, listing all nutrition facts such as calories, fat, cholesterol, sodium, carbohydrates, proteins, and vitamins.
- Can a healthy diet be maintained without animal products? Is an increase in fruit and vegetable consumption healthy? Explain your reasoning.
- Draw some conclusions about individual diets and food production from your research. Share your findings with the class.

1950 Luis Buñuel, Spanish filmmaker, directs his Mexican film *Los Olvidados,* "The Forgotten."

1980 Gae Veit founds Shingobee Construction in Minnesota, a successful business that hires mainly other American Indian workers.

1930 Ruth Wakefield invents a famous chocolate chip cookie.

1991 Carolyn Napoli co-invented the technology that can be applied to block genes in plants to reduce sugar and oil content.

2–1 Integers and the Number Line

***What* YOU'LL LEARN**

- To state the coordinate of a point on a number line,
- to graph integers on a number line, and
- to add integers by using a number line.

***Why* IT'S IMPORTANT**

You can use number lines to add and subtract integers and to display data.

APPLICATION

Entertainment

Do you like to play board games? In order to play one popular board game, you must know how to move playing pieces around the board. To do this, you add the numbers rolled on the dice and then move your playing piece the corresponding number of spaces forward. You also need to know how to move your playing piece *backward* when directed to do so. Understanding how to add and subtract integers can help you to play.

Nidi, Lynn, Michael, and Domingo are playing the game described above. The chart below shows a turn for each player. How can you represent Nidi's moves using numerals?

Player	Turn 1
Nidi	Rolls 2; lands on Chance — go back 3 spaces.
Lynn	Rolls double 3s; rolls 7.
Michael	Rolls 6 — go directly to jail (back 20).
Domingo	Rolls 9; lands on Community Chest — advance to next utility (forward 11).

You can solve problems like the one above by using a **number line.** A number line is drawn by choosing a starting position, usually 0, and marking off equal distances from that point. The set of **whole numbers** is often represented on a number line. This set can be written {0, 1, 2, 3, ...}, where "..." means that the set continues indefinitely.

Although only a portion of the number line is shown, the arrowhead indicates that the line and the set of numbers continue.

We can use the expression 2 − 3 to represent Nidi's moves.

goes forward 2 spaces → 2 − 3 ← *goes back 3 spaces*

$$2 - 3$$

The number line below shows that the value of $2 - 3$ should be 1 less than 0. However, there is no whole number that corresponds to 1 less than 0. You can write the number 1 *less than* 0 as -1. This is an example of a **negative number.**

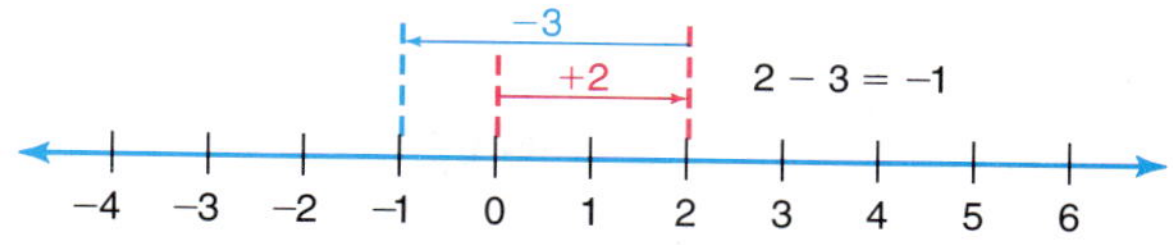

Any nonzero number written without a sign is understood to be positive.

To include negative numbers on the number line, extend the number line to the left of zero and mark off equal distances. The points to the right of zero are named using the *positive sign* (+). The points to the left of zero are named using the *negative sign* (−). Zero is neither positive nor negative.

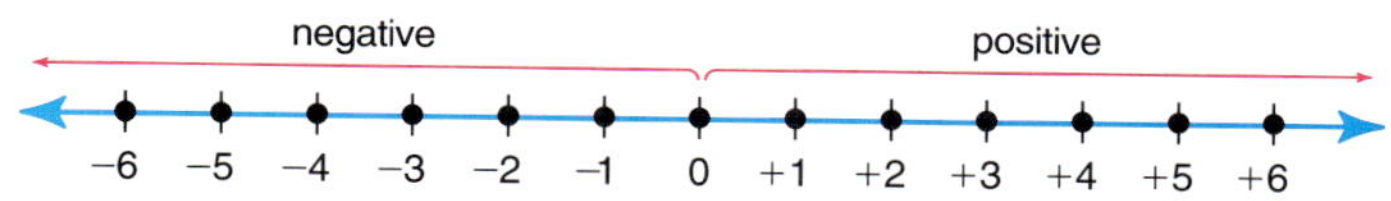

Read "−5" as *negative* 5. Read "+5" as *positive* 5.

The set of numbers used on the number line above is called the set of **integers.** This set can be written {..., −6, −5, −4, −3, −2, −1, 0, 1, 2, 3, 4, 5, 6, ...}.

Venn diagrams are figures often used to represent sets of numbers.

Sets	Examples
Natural numbers	1, 2, 3, 4, 5, ...
Whole numbers	0, 1, 2, 3, 4, ...
Integers	..., −2, −1, 0, 1, 2, ...

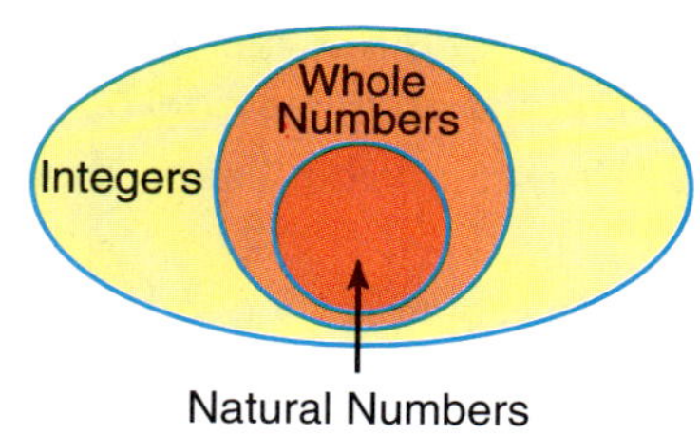

GLOBAL CONNECTIONS

Some of the most popular board games around the world are:

Pachisi—India
Go—Japan
Mancala—Africa
Alquerque—Spain
Senet—Egypt
Backgammon—Middle East
Checkers—England
Dominoes—Korea

Notice that the natural numbers are a subset of the whole numbers and the whole numbers are a subset of the integers.

To **graph** a set of numbers means to draw, or plot, the points named by those numbers on a number line. The number that corresponds to a point on a number line is called the **coordinate** of that point.

Example 1 **Name the set of numbers graphed.**

a.

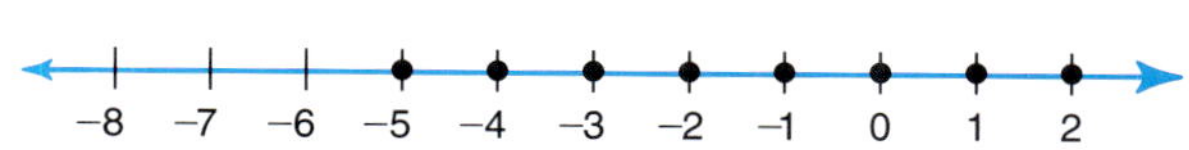

The bold arrow means that the graph continues indefinitely in that direction.

The set is {−5, −4, −3, −2, −1, 0, 1, 2, ...}.

b.

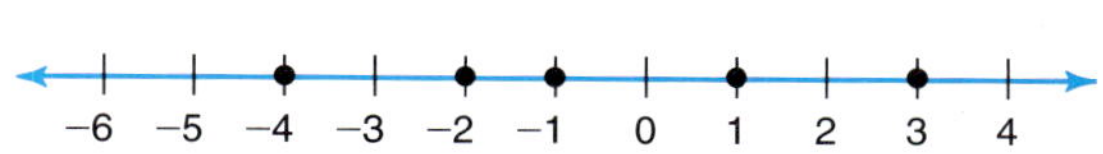

The set is {−4, −2, −1, 1, 3}.

You can use a number line to add integers.

MODELING MATHEMATICS — Adding Integers

To find the sum of -7 and -5, follow the steps below.

Step 1
Draw an arrow starting at 0 to -7, the first addend.

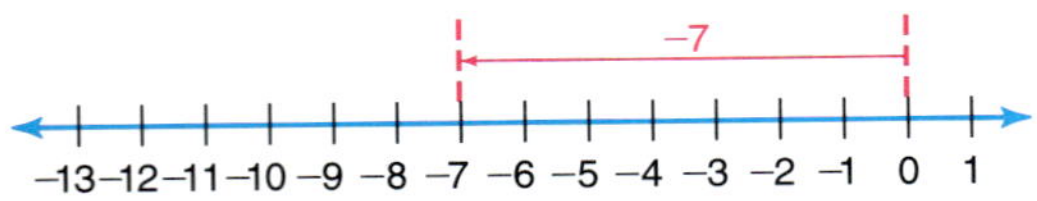

Step 2
Starting at -7, draw an arrow and go to the left 5 units long. This represents the second addend, -5.

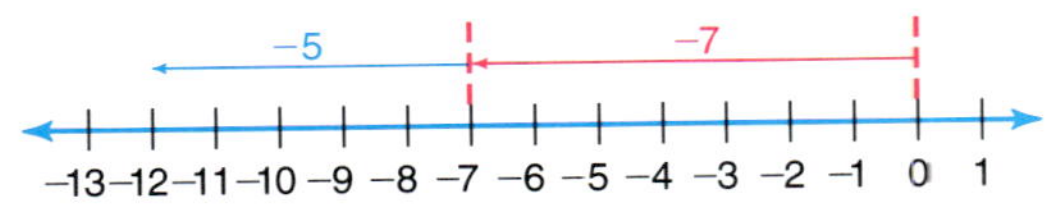

Step 3
The arrow ends at the sum, -12.

So, $-7 + (-5) = -12$.

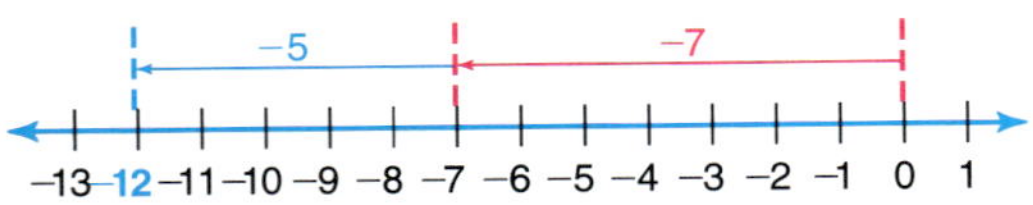

Notice that parentheses are used in the equation so that the sign of the number is not confused with a subtraction sign.

Your Turn

a. What addition sentence is modeled on the number line shown at the right?

b. Draw a number line to show the addition sentence $-3 + (-2) = -5$.

c. Use a number line to find $-4 + 5$.

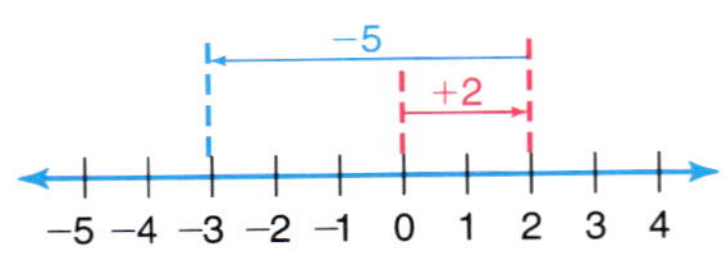

Example 2

APPLICATION — Meteorology

At 4:08 A.M., the temperature in Casper, Wyoming, was −10°F. By 1:30 P.M., the temperature had risen 17° to the daytime high. What was the high temperature?

Draw and label a number line. Draw an arrow from 0 to -10. Then draw an arrow to the right 17 units long.

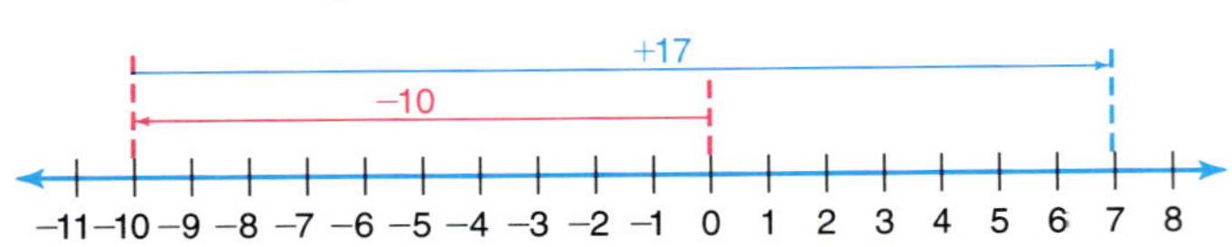

The high temperature of the day was 7°F.

CHECK FOR UNDERSTANDING

Communicating Mathematics

Study the lesson. Then complete the following.

1. **Explain** how you would find the sum $-4 + 6$ on a number line.
2. **Draw** a number line to show that $-17 < 0$, $-3 < 1$, and $-5 > -10$.
3. Refer to the application at the beginning of the lesson. Draw number lines to show the first moves for Lynn, Michael, and Domingo.
4. **Research** instances where integers are used in real-life situations by collecting newspaper clippings that show integers.

MODELING MATHEMATICS

5. Use a number line to find 5 + (−6).

Guided Practice

Name the set of numbers graphed.

6. 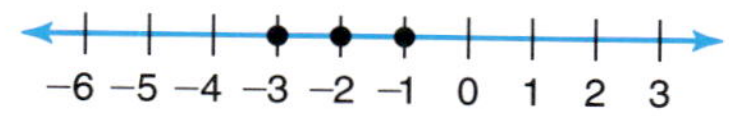

7. 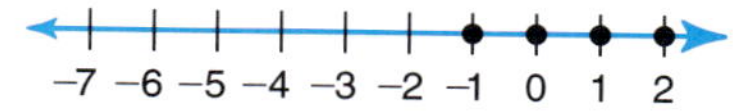

Graph each set of numbers on a number line.

8. {0, 2, 4, 6}

9. {−1, 0, 1, 2, 3,...}

10. {integers greater than −3}

Write a corresponding addition sentence for each diagram.

11. 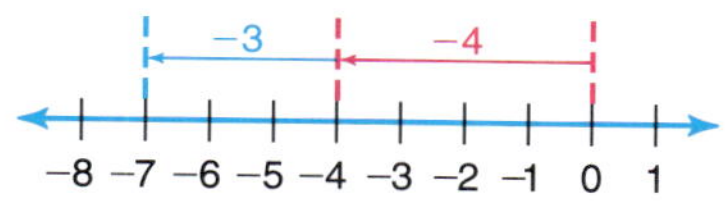

12. 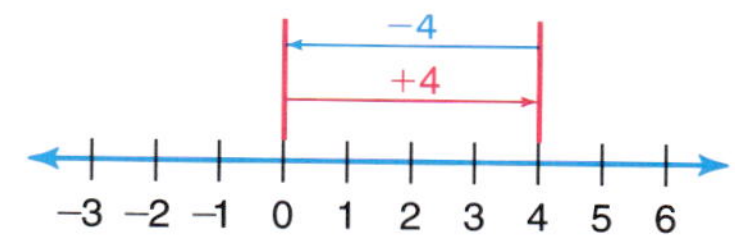

Find each sum. If necessary, use a number line.

13. −8 + 3

14. −7 + (−15)

15. **Football** The Barnesville Bruins' offense lined up on their 20-yard line. They gained 5 yards on the first down, lost 3 yards on the second down, gained 7 yards on the third down, and punted on the fourth down. What was the net gain or loss after the third down?

EXERCISES

Practice

Name the set of numbers graphed.

16. 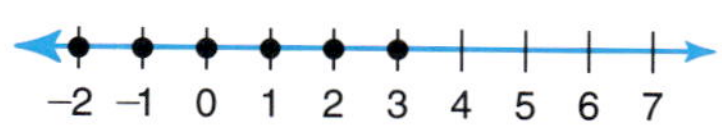

17. 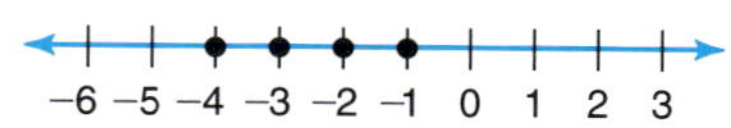

18. 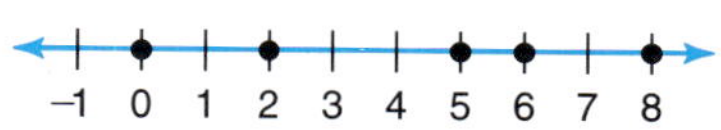

19. 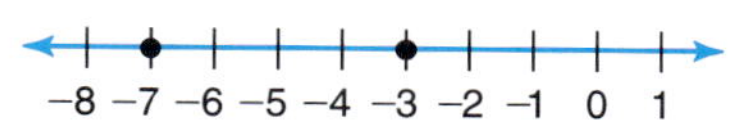

20. 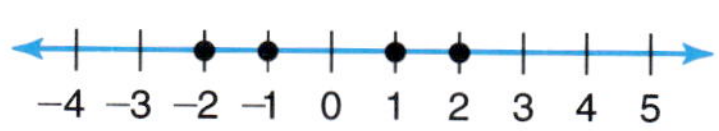

21. 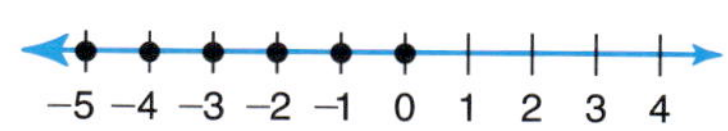

Graph each set of numbers on a number line.

22. {−4, −3, −1, 3}

23. {..., −2, −1, 0, 1}

24. {integers between −6 and 10}

25. {integers less than 0}

26. {integers between −2 and 5}

27. {integers less than −3 +(−1)}

28. {whole numbers greater than −4 + 4}

29. {integers less than 0 but greater than −6}

30. {integers less than or equal to −3 and greater than or equal to −10}

Find each sum. If necessary, use a number line.

31. 8 + 5

32. −6 + (−7)

33. 7 + (−12)

34. −4 + (−9)

35. 0 + (−12)

36. 5 + (−3)

37. −3 + 9

38. −13 + 13

39. −14 + (−9)

Critical Thinking

40. Write three different equations using integers that have a sum of -14.

Applications and Problem Solving

For Exercises 41–42, write an open sentence using addition. Then solve each problem.

41. **Meteorology** On February 10, the low temperature in Houlton, Maine, and Fort Yukon, Alaska, was $-17°$. On the same date, the high temperature in Lajitas, Texas, was 82° higher. What was the temperature in Lajitas, Texas, on February 10?

42. **Geography** Use the map below to determine what time it is in each city if it is 10:00 A.M. in New York City.

 a. Hong Kong
 b. Los Angeles
 c. Rio de Janeiro
 d. Bombay

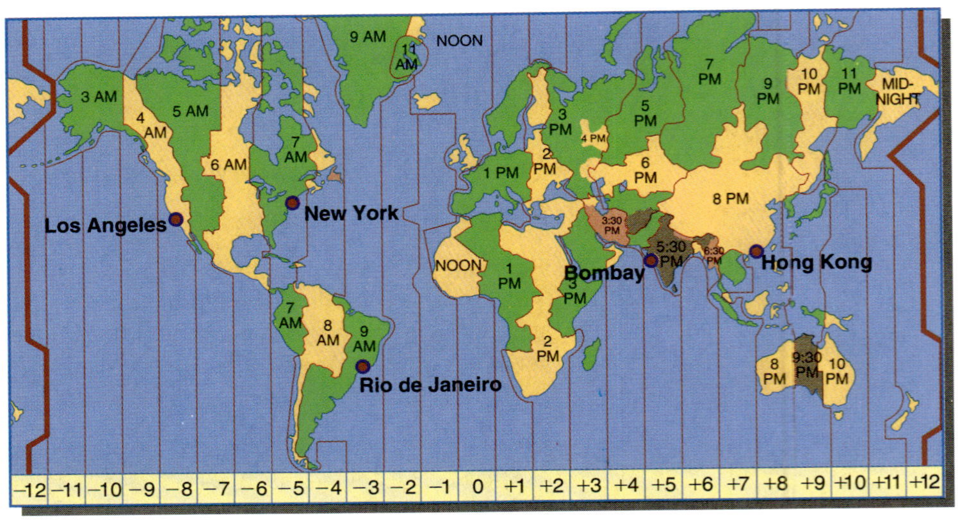

43. **Meteorology** *Windchill factor* is an estimate of the cooling effect the wind has on a person in cold weather. Meteorologists use a chart like the one below to predict the windchill factor. Use the chart below to find each windchill factor.

 a. 20°F, 10 mph
 b. 0°F, 15 mph
 c. -10°F, 5 mph
 d. 30°F, 15 mph

Wind speed (mph)	Actual temperature (°Fahrenheit)						
	30	20	10	0	−10	−20	−30
	Equivalent temperature (°Fahrenheit)						
0	30	20	10	0	−10	−20	−30
5	27	16	6	−5	−15	−26	−36
10	16	4	−9	−21	−33	−46	−58
15	9	−4	−18	−31	−45	−58	−72

44. **Baseball** Sometimes baseball team owners develop incentive clauses for hitters in an effort to win more games. Suppose an owner decided to pay each hitter \$500 for each run scored, \$400 for each hit, and \$500 for each run batted in. Look in the sports section of a newspaper. Choose a team's box score and calculate the value of the incentive clause for the first five hitters in a game.

Mixed Review

45. Entertainment Juanita has the volume on her stereo turned up because her parents are not home. Suddenly, she sees her father's car pull into the driveway. She runs to her room to turn down the volume. Juanita's father comes in, grabs an umbrella, and leaves, so Juanita returns the volume to its previous level. Sketch a reasonable graph to show the volume of Juanita's stereo during this time. (Lesson 1–9)

46. Physical Fitness Mitchell likes to exercise regularly. On Mondays, he likes to walk two miles, run three miles, sprint one-half of a mile, and then walk for another mile. Identify the graph that best represents Mitchell's heart rate as a function of time. (Lesson 1–9)

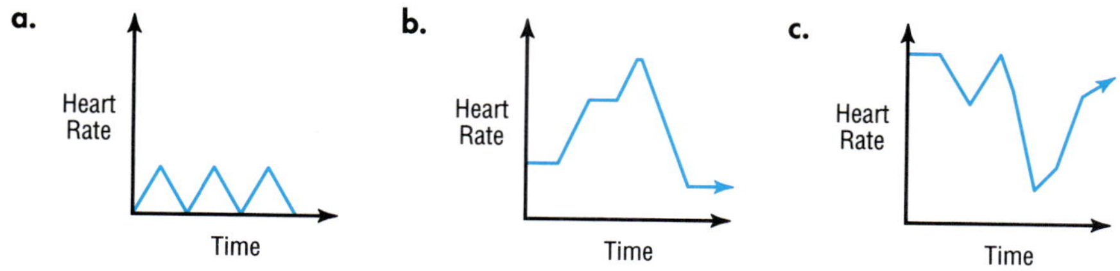

47. Name the property illustrated by $8(2 \cdot 6) = (2 \cdot 6)8$. (Lesson 1–8)

48. Simplify $16a + 21a + 30b - 7b$. (Lesson 1–7)

49. Name the property illustrated by $(12 - 9)(4) = 3(4)$. (Lesson 1–6)

50. Solve $5(7) + 6 = x$. (Lesson 1–5)

51. Evaluate $9(0.4 + 1.2) - 0.5$. (Lesson 1–3)

52. Patterns Find the next three numbers in the pattern 5, 6.5, 8, 9.5, ... (Lesson 1–2)

Mathematics and SOCIETY

Mayan Mathematics

The excerpt below is from an article that appeared in *The Columbus Dispatch* on January 15, 1995. It describes the number system developed by the Mayan Indians, an ancient civilization that lived in southern Mexico and Central America until the 16th century.

> THE MAYAS USED A COUNTING SYSTEM based on 20. And while we add digits to the left of numbers to show their increased size, the Mayas piled them upwards. In our decimal system, as you look at a number from right to left, each digit tells us how much value it has, based on the number 10. The number 326, for instance, is really 3 hundreds, 2 tens and 6 ones....The Mayas used the same principle, but used the vigesimal system (based on 20). Units were represented by dots. Five dots were represented by a horizontal line. ■

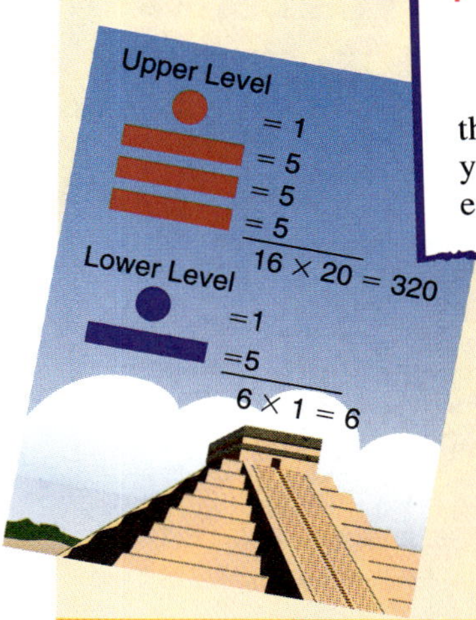

1. What combinations of dots and horizontal lines (bars) are needed to write the number 252 using the Mayan system? (*Hint:* Two levels are required.)
2. What uses would the Mayas and other ancient civilizations have had for the number systems they developed?
3. Would a number system based on a number other than 10 be as accurate as the decimal system? Would it be as easy to use? Explain your answers.

2-2 Integration: Statistics
Line Plots

What YOU'LL LEARN

- To interpret numerical data from a table, and
- to display and interpret statistical data on a line plot.

Why IT'S IMPORTANT

Line plots are a useful way to display data.

APPLICATION
Television

Are you a fan of sitcoms? Media ratings are used to determine which shows are popular and which shows are not. They are also used to determine which shows should be continued or canceled. The chart at the right shows the media ratings for Monday, February 6, 1995.

Media Ratings

Monday, February 6, 1995

TIME	PROGRAM	VIEWERS (rounded to nearest million)
8:00	Show A	22
	Show B	19
	Show C	14
	Show D	15
	Show E	14
8:30	Show F	21
	Show G	19
	Show H	16
9:00	Show I	22
	Show J	19
	Show K	10
	Show L	5
9:30	Show M	19
	Show N	4
10:00	Show O	19

In some cases, data can be presented on a number line. Numerical data displayed on a number line is called a **line plot.** The data in the table above can be presented in a line plot as follows.

Step 1 Draw and label a number line. You can see that the data in the table ranges from 4 million to 22 million viewers. In order to represent the data on a number line, a *scale* must be used that includes this range of values. You can use a scale from 0 to 25 with *intervals* of five.

Step 2 Draw the line plot. Write a "v" for each TV show above its share of viewers. A completed line plot for the media ratings is shown below.

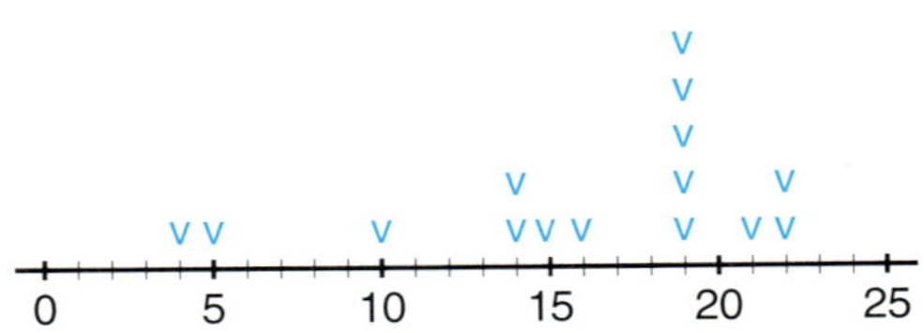

Notice that some data values are located between marked intervals on the number line.

Example

APPLICATION
Basketball

In 1994 and 1995, Houston won back-to-back professional basketball championships. The table at the right shows the standings for each of the 27 teams for the 1994–1995 season on April 28, 1995.

a. Make a line plot to show the number of wins by each playoff team.

Final Regular-Season Standings

EASTERN CONFERENCE

ATLANTIC	W	L
y-Orlando	57	25
x-New York	55	27
x-Boston	35	47
Miami	32	50
New Jersey	30	52
Philadelphia	24	58
Washington	21	61
CENTRAL	**W**	**L**
z-Indiana	52	30
x-Charlotte	50	32
x-Chicago	47	35
x-Cleveland	43	39
x-Atlanta	42	40
Milwaukee	34	48
Detroit	28	54

WESTERN CONFERENCE

MIDWEST	W	L
y-San Antonio	62	20
x-Utah	60	22
x-Houston	47	35
x-Denver	41	41
Dallas	36	46
Minnesota	21	61
PACIFIC	**W**	**L**
z-Phoenix	59	23
x-Seattle	57	25
x-L.A. Lakers	48	34
x-Portland	44	38
Sacramento	39	43
Golden State	26	56
L.A. Clippers	17	65

x–clinched playoff berth; y–clinched conference; z–clinched division

Source: *USA Today*, 4-28-95

The scale ranges from 35 to 65 with intervals of 5.

The teams with an x, y, or z next to their names made the playoffs. The number of wins by the playoff teams ranges from 35 to 62. You can use a "w" to represent the number of each team's wins.

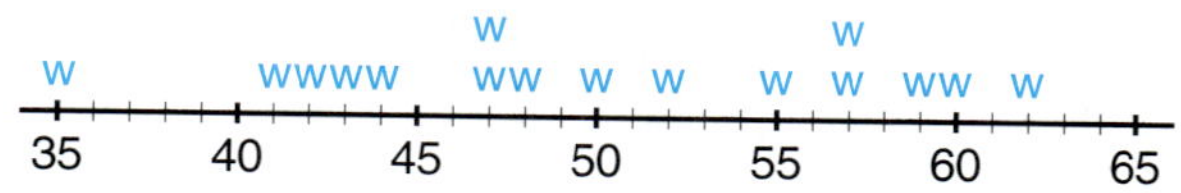

b. How many playoff teams won fewer than 50 games?
From the line plot, you can see that 8 teams won fewer than 50 games. These teams were Boston, Chicago, Cleveland, Atlanta, Houston, Denver, L.A. Lakers, and Portland.

c. Which playoff team had the best record? the worst record?
San Antonio had the best record and Boston had the worst record of the playoff teams.

d. How many teams made the playoffs?
Count the number of w's on the line plot. Sixteen teams made the playoffs.

The data in the application at the beginning of the lesson was the result of an actual survey. The data in the example was collected by checking NBA records. Data can be collected by taking actual measurements, by conducting surveys or polls, by using questionnaires, by simulation, or by consulting reference materials.

It is important that you know how the data were obtained. For example, would you want to draw conclusions about changing the name of your school mascot based on a result of a survey of seniors only? Why or why not?

MODELING MATHEMATICS

Line Plots

Materials: small packages of plain colored candy

In 1994 and 1995, a candy company conducted surveys to determine whether a new color should be added. The choices were blue, pink, purple, or leave them as they are. The color blue was chosen.

Your Turn

a. Open a package of candy. Separate the candies by color. Find the total number of each color.

b. Make a line plot to show the number of each color. Use b for brown, r for red, y for yellow, o for orange, g for green, and bl for blue.

c. Do the colors cluster around any number?

d. Make a class line plot of your data. Are the data in the class line plot different or the same as yours? Explain.

e. Make a class line plot showing the total number of candies in each of your packages. Do the packages have the same number in them?

CHECK FOR UNDERSTANDING

Communicating Mathematics

Study the lesson. Then complete the following.

1. **Describe** a situation in which it would be valuable to obtain data in order to make a decision.
2. **Compare and contrast** line plots and tables as a means of reporting data. What are the advantages and disadvantages of each?
3. **Develop** a survey and collect data on the Monday night television viewing habits of your classmates. Make a line plot of the data. Compare your class findings to those of another class and to a media ratings chart from a magazine or newspaper. What conclusions can you draw?

MODELING MATHEMATICS

Guided Practice

State the scale you would use to make a line plot for the following data. Then draw the line plot.

4. 50, 50, 30, 30, 20, 10, 60, 40
5. 52, 43, 67, 69, 37, 76
6. **Retail Sales** The advertisement below lists the cars for sale at California Motors.

'93 Mars Excellence	$9995	'92 Neptune Niagra	$8995	'90 Neptune Beret	$3995
'93 Venus Wagon	6995	'92 Cadet Ellipsis	9650	'89 Zebra Cellex	1950
'93 Venus Gazelle LG	7988	'92 Venus Gazelle	6995	'89 Pluto 535	7995
'93 Venus Carnival	4995	'92 Venus Aquarius	8995	'88 Cheetah 259	3495
'93 Jupiter Ruby	7988	'92 Mars Conv.	10,495	'88 Venus Aquarius	3995
'93 Venus Superior	11,475	'92 Cadet Precise	5875	'87 Jupiter Wagon	3988
'93 Venus Coupe	7995	'91 Mars Moonbeam EL	5995	'86 Venus Gazelle	1995
'92 Pluto Prize	7988	'90 Jupiter Tiger SL	8988	'84 Tiara Victory	3270

a. Make a line plot to show how many cars from each year are in stock.
b. What is the price range for the used cars?
c. Make a line plot to show the costs of the cars. Round each price to the nearest thousand dollars. Let each number on the number line represent thousands of dollars.

EXERCISES

Applications and Problem Solving

7. **Animals** The speeds of 20 of the fastest animals in miles per hour according the *The World Almanac*, 1995, are listed below.

40	61	50	50	32	70	35	30	50	45
43	40	30	30	35	45	42	32	40	30

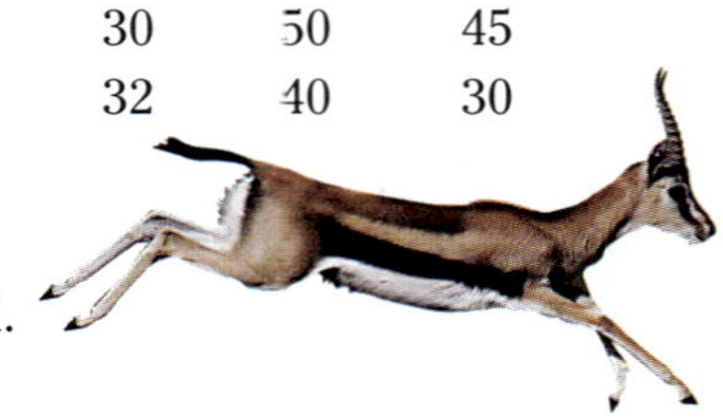

a. Make a line plot of the data.
b. What is the fastest speed of any animal? Research to find the name of the fastest animal.
c. What is the slowest speed of the 20 animals?
d. Which speed occurred most frequently?
e. How many animals had a speed of at least 40 mph?
f. How many animals had speeds greater than 30 and less than 40 mph?

8. History The table below lists the fifty United States and the years they entered the Union.

Years States Entered the Union

State	Year	State	Year	State	Year	State	Year
AL	1819	IN	1816	NE	1867	SC	1788
AK	1959	IA	1846	NV	1864	SD	1889
AZ	1912	KS	1861	NH	1788	TN	1796
AR	1836	KY	1792	NJ	1787	TX	1845
CA	1850	LA	1812	NM	1912	UT	1896
CO	1876	ME	1820	NY	1788	VT	1791
CT	1788	MD	1788	NC	1789	VA	1788
DE	1787	MA	1788	ND	1889	WA	1889
FL	1845	MI	1837	OH	1803	WV	1863
GA	1788	MN	1858	OK	1907	WI	1848
HI	1959	MS	1817	OR	1859	WY	1890
ID	1890	MO	1821	PA	1787		
IL	1818	MT	1889	RI	1790		

Source: *The World Almanac,* 1995

a. What is the range of years for states entering the Union?

b. Make a line plot that shows the year each state joined the Union.

c. Do the years cluster around a certain number? If so, which years are those? What would explain this?

9. Weather The average rainfall per year, rounded to the nearest inch, for ten cities around the world is shown on the map below.

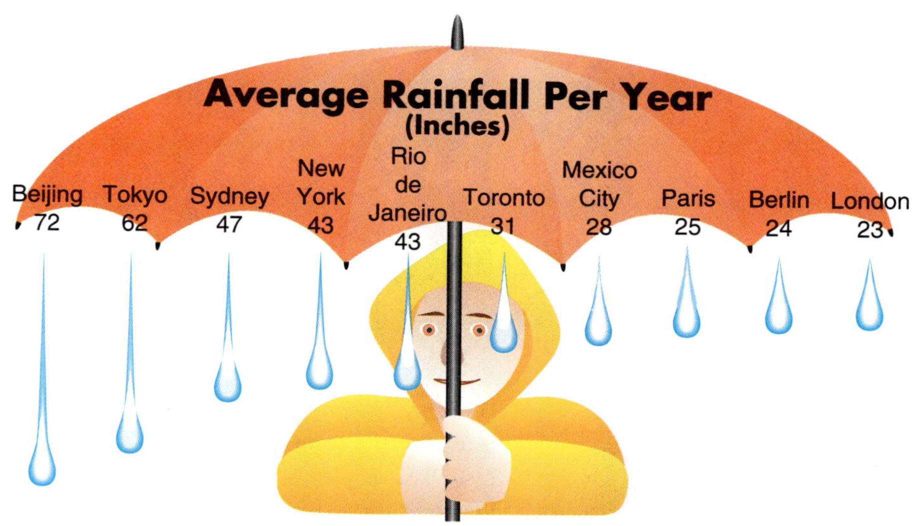

a. Make a line plot of the data. What scale did you use?

b. Do the average amounts of rain cluster about a certain number?

c. Do you think that the average rainfall for your community is close to that of any of the cities above? Why or why not?

d. Look up the average rainfall for your community. How does it compare to the average rainfall for London? for Tokyo?

10. Tornadoes A tornado is a powerful, twisting windstorm. The winds of a tornado are the most dangerous winds that occur on Earth, with speeds of more than 200 miles per hour. The table below lists the average number of tornadoes that occurred per year in each state for a 30-year period.

TORNADO OCCURRENCE BY STATE, 1962–1991

STATE	AVG.	STATE	AVG.	STATE	AVG.	STATE	AVG.
AL	22	IN	20	NE	37	SC	10
AK	0	IA	36	NV	1	SD	29
AZ	4	KS	40	NH	2	TN	12
AR	20	KY	10	NJ	3	TX	139
CA	5	LA	28	NM	9	UT	2
CO	26	ME	2	NY	6	VT	1
CT	1	MD	3	NC	15	VA	6
DE	1	MA	3	ND	21	WA	2
FL	53	MI	19	OH	15	WV	2
GA	21	MN	20	OK	47	WI	21
HI	1	MS	26	OR	1	WY	12
ID	3	MO	26	PA	10		
IL	27	MT	6	RI	0		

Source: National Severe Storm Forecast Center

a. Make a line plot of the average number of tornado occurrences.

b. Do any of the numbers appear clustered? If so, which ones?

c. Which state had the highest average? Why do you think it had the most tornadoes?

11. School Mr. Thomas and Ms. Martinez each asked 10 students from their algebra classes how many hours they spent talking on the telephone last week. The results are shown in the line plot below. Use this plot to answer each question.

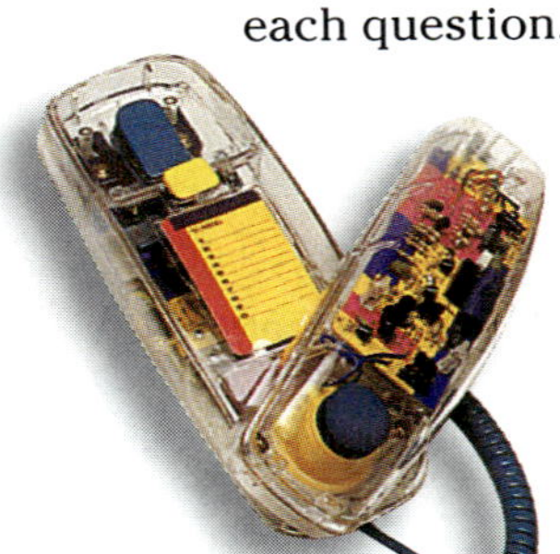

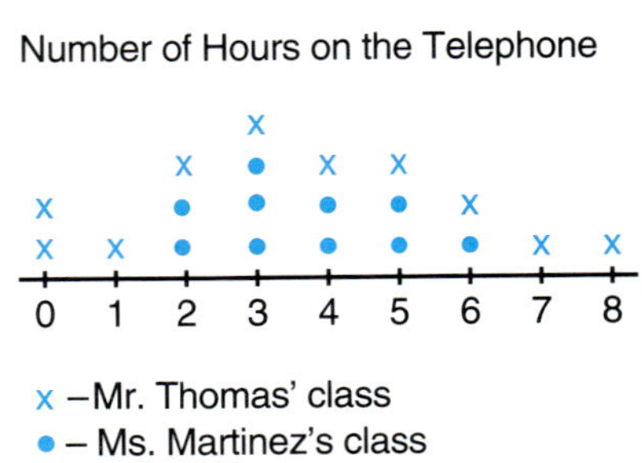

a. Which group of 10 students talked on the telephone the most?

b. Does the pattern for the number of hours spent talking on the telephone appear to be the same for both groups? Explain.

12. Winter Olympics The table below lists the medal standings for the 1994 Winter Olympics.

Winter Olympics, Medal Standings

Nation	Gold	Silver	Bronze	Total
Norway	10	11	5	26
Germany	9	7	8	24
Russia	11	8	4	23
Italy	7	5	8	20
United States	6	5	2	13
Canada	3	6	4	13
Switzerland	3	4	2	9
Austria	2	3	4	9
South Korea	4	1	1	6
Finland	0	1	5	6

a. Make a line plot that shows the number of gold medals won by the countries.

b. Write three questions that can be answered using the line plot.

Critical Thinking

13. Use the line plot in Exercise 11. Find the average number of hours that the students in Mr. Thomas and Ms. Martinez's classes spent on the telephone. Do the values support your answer to Exercise 11b? Explain.

Mixed Review

14. Graph $\{..., -5, -4, -3\}$ on a number line. (Lesson 2–1)

15. Name the property illustrated by $6(jk) = (6j)k$. (Lesson 1–8)

16. Use the distributive property to find 15(124). (Lesson 1–7)

17. Solve $m = \frac{22 - 8}{7}$. (Lesson 1–5)

18. Evaluate $np + st$ when $n = 7$, $p = 6$, $s = 4$, and $t = 5$. (Lesson 1–3)

WORKING ON THE

In•ves•ti•ga•tion

Refer to the Investigation on pages 68–69.

the Greenhouse Effect

1 Examine the data from the control experiment. Look for patterns and relationships in the data. Analyze how the change in temperature is a function of the distance. Describe your analysis in writing. Be sure to explain any patterns you see in the data.

2 Examine the data from the greenhouse experiment. Look for patterns and relationships in the data. Analyze how the change in temperature is a function of the distance. Describe your analysis in writing. Use the terms *function, independent, dependent, domain,* and *range*.

3 Compare the two experiments. List the similarities and differences in the data and explain the factors that might cause them.

4 Think about the design of the two experiments. How were they different? Why do you think they were designed the way they were? How do they relate to the greenhouse effect?

Add the results of your work to your Investigation Folder.

MODELING MATHEMATICS

A Preview of Lesson 2–3

2–3A Adding and Subtracting Integers

Materials: counters, integer mat

You can use counters to help you understand addition and subtraction of integers. In these activities, yellow counters represent positive integers, and red counters represent negative integers.

Rules for Integer Models	
A zero pair is formed by pairing one positive counter with one negative counter.	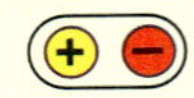
You can remove or add zero pairs to a set because removing or adding zero does not change the value of the set.	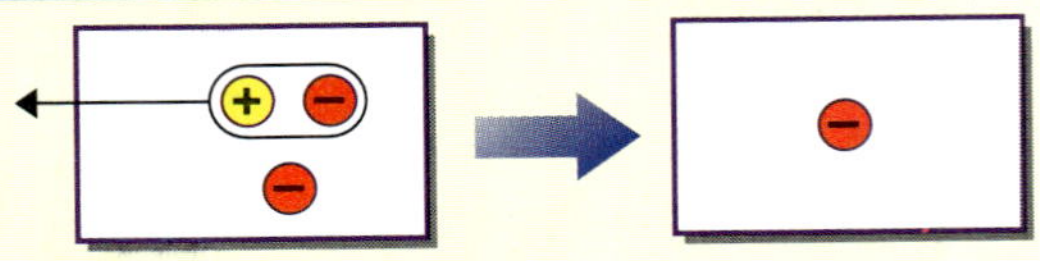

Activity 1 Use counters to find the sum −2 + 3.

Step 1 Place 2 negative counters and 3 positive counters on the mat.

Step 2 Remove the 2 zero pairs. Since 1 positive counter remains, the sum is 1. Therefore, −2 + 3 = 1.

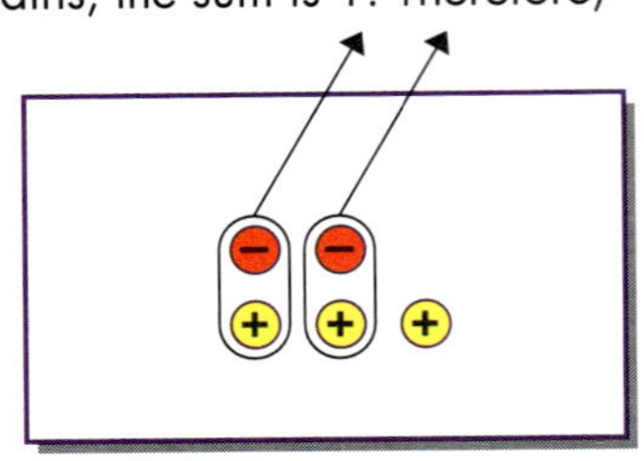

Activity 2 Use counters to find the difference 3 − (−2).

Step 1 Place 3 positive counters on the mat. There are no negative counters, so you cannot remove 2 negatives. Add 2 zero pairs to the mat. Adding zero pairs does not change the value of the set.

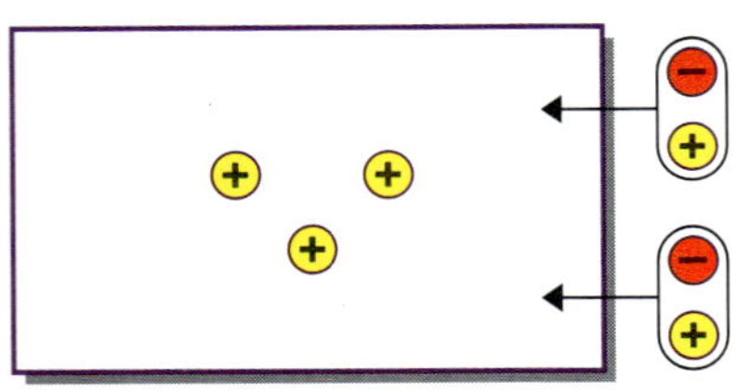

Step 2 Now remove 2 negative counters. Since 5 positive counters remain, the difference is 5. Therefore, 3 − (−2) = 5.

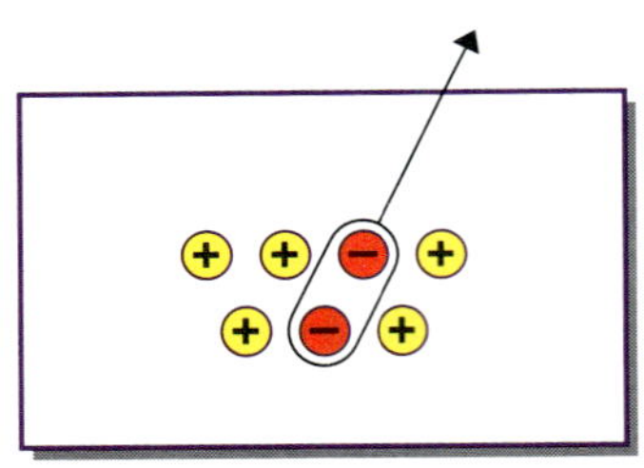

Model **Find each sum or difference by using counters.**

1. 4 + 2
2. 4 + (−2)
3. −4 + 2
4. −4 + (−2)
5. 4 − 2
6. −4 − (−2)
7. 4 − (−2)
8. −4 − 2

Draw **Tell whether each statement is *true* or *false*. Justify your answer with a drawing.**

9. 5 − (−2) = 3
10. −5 + 7 = 2
11. 2 − 3 = −1
12. −1 − 1 = 0

Write

13. Write a paragraph explaining how to find the sum of two integers without using counters. Be sure to include all possibilities.

2-3 Adding and Subtracting Integers

What YOU'LL LEARN

- To find the absolute value of a number, and
- to add and subtract integers.

Why IT'S IMPORTANT

You can add and subtract integers to help you solve problems involving weather, business, and golf.

APPLICATION

Space Science

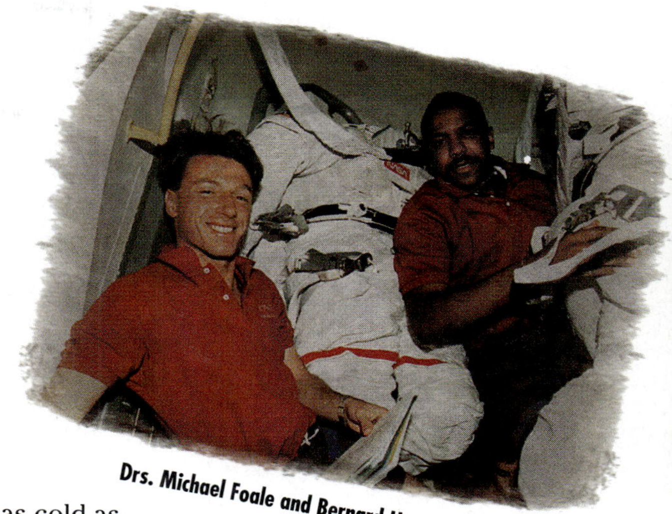

Drs. Michael Foale and Bernard Harris in space

On February 10, 1995, Dr. Bernard A. Harris, Jr. became the first African-American to walk in space. During the walk, he and Dr. Michael Foale, a British-born astronaut who is a U.S. citizen, were exposed to temperatures as cold as −125°F. The scheduled five-hour spacewalk to test thermal improvements to NASA spacesuits was cut short by 30 minutes because the astronauts experienced icy fingers.

Usually, spacewalkers spend some of their time basking in the sun's rays where temperatures can be as high as 200°F. But throughout the spacewalk, Drs. Harris and Foale remained in the shadow of the shuttle Discovery and Earth, the coldest possible spot.

As you can see, spacewalkers must be able to survive in extreme temperatures. You can use a number line to determine the range of the temperature extremes. −125 and 200 are graphed on the number line below. Notice that −125°F is 125 units from 0 and 200°F is 200 units from 0. So, the total number of units from −125 to 200 is 125 + 200 or 325.

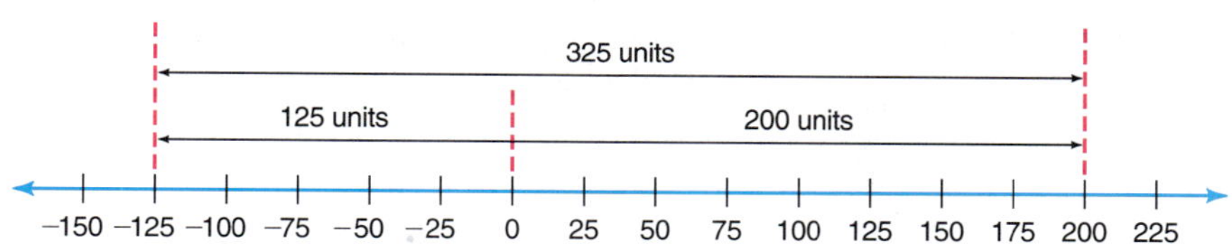

The temperature range from −125°F to 200°F is 325°F.

You used the idea of **absolute value** to find the range from −125°F to 200°F.

Definition of Absolute Value	**The absolute value of a number is its distance from zero on a number line.**

Since distance cannot be less than zero, absolute values are always greater than or equal to zero.

The symbol for the absolute value of a number is two vertical bars around the number.

Note that the absolute value bars can serve as grouping symbols.

$|-125| = 125$ is read *The absolute value of −125 equals 125.*

$|200| = 200$ is read *The absolute value of 200 equals 200.*

$|-7 + 6| = 1$ is read *The absolute value of the quantity −7 + 6 equals 1.*

You can evaluate expressions involving absolute value.

Example 1 **Evaluate $-|x + 6|$ if $x = -10$.**

$$
\begin{aligned}
-|x+6| &= -|-10+6| && \textit{Substitution property of equality}\\
&= -|-4| \\
&= -(4) && \textit{The absolute value of } -4 \textit{ is } 4.\\
&= -4
\end{aligned}
$$

You can use absolute value to add integers.

Same Signs

a. $4 + 3 = 7$ — *Notice that the sign of each addend is positive. The sum is positive.*

b. $-4 + (-3) = -7$ — *Notice that the sign of each addend is negative. The sum is negative.*

Different Signs

c. $6 + (-8) = -2$ — *Notice that $8 - 6 = 2$. Since the integer -8 has the greater absolute value, the sign of the sum is also negative.*

d. $-6 + 8 = 2$ — *Notice that $8 - 6 = 2$. Since the integer 8 has the greater absolute value, the sign of the sum is also positive.*

These examples suggest the following rules.

Adding Integers	**To add integers with the *same sign,* add their absolute values. Give the result the same sign as the integers.** **To add integers with *different signs,* subtract the lesser absolute value from the greater absolute value. Give the result the same sign as the integer with the greater absolute value.**

Example 2 **Find each sum.**

a. $\mathbf{-10 + (-17)}$

$$
\begin{aligned}
-10 + (-17) &= -(|-10| + |-17|) && \textit{Both numbers are negative,}\\
&= -(10 + 17) && \textit{so the sum is negative.}\\
&= -27
\end{aligned}
$$

b. $\mathbf{39 + (-22)}$

$$
\begin{aligned}
39 + (-22) &= +(|39| - |-22|) && \textit{Subtract the absolute values. Since the}\\
&= +(39 - 22) && \textit{number with the greater absolute value,}\\
&= 17 && \textit{39, is positive, the sum is positive.}
\end{aligned}
$$

c. $\mathbf{-28 + 16}$

$$
\begin{aligned}
-28 + 16 &= -(|-28| - |16|) && \textit{Subtract the absolute values. Since the}\\
&= -(28 - 16) && \textit{number with the greater absolute value,}\\
&= -12 && \textit{28, is negative, the sum is negative.}
\end{aligned}
$$

Notice that both +2 and −2 are 2 units away from 0. That is, −2 and 2 have the same absolute value.

Every positive integer can be paired with a negative integer. These pairs are called **opposites.** For example, the opposite of +2 is −2.

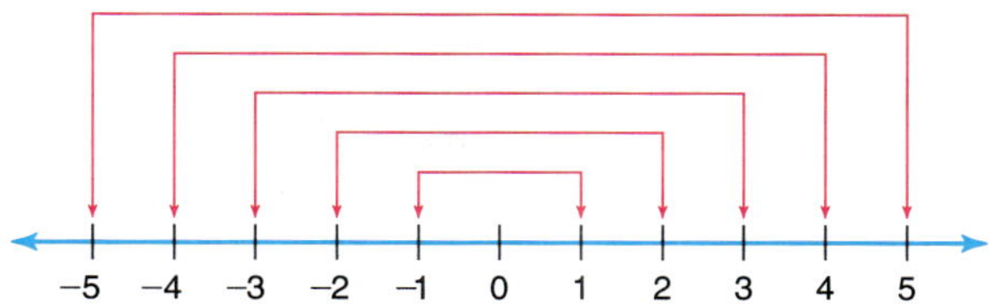

A number and its opposite are called **additive inverses** of each other. Look at the sum of each number and its additive inverse below. What pattern do you notice?

$$2 + (-2) = 0 \qquad -67 + 67 = 0 \qquad 409 + (-409) = 0$$

These examples suggest the following rule.

Additive Inverse Property	**For every number a, $a + (-a) = 0$.**

Additive inverses can be used when you subtract numbers.

Subtraction	**Addition**
$6 - 2 = 4$	$6 + (-2) = 4$

additive inverses (2 and −2)

same result (4 and 4)

It appears that subtracting a number is equivalent to adding its additive inverse.

Subtracting Integers	**To subtract a number, add its additive inverse.** **For any numbers a and b, $a - b = a + (-b)$.**

Example 3

Find each difference.

a. 6 − 14

Method 1

Use the rule.

To subtract 14, add −14.

$$6 - 14 = 6 + (-14)$$
$$= -8$$

Method 2

Use models.

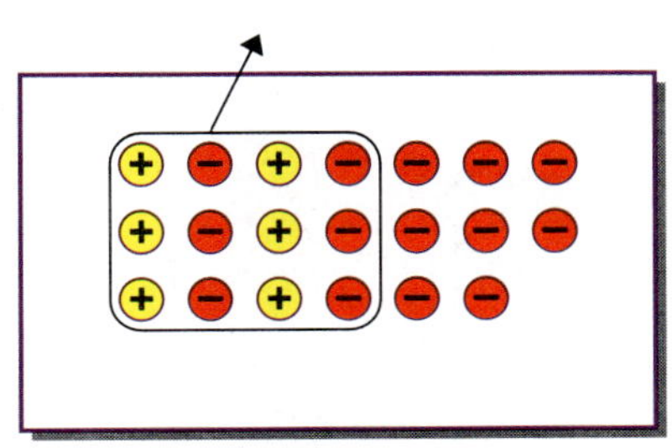

Place 6 positive counters on the mat. Add 14 negative counters. Form and remove six zero pairs.

$$6 - 14 = -8$$

TECHNOLOGY Tip

On a TI-83, enter the following keystrokes.

[(−)] 12 [−] [(−)] 8 [ENTER] −4

b. $-12 - (-8)$

Method 1

Use the rule.

To subtract −8, add its inverse, +8.

$$-12 - (-8) = -12 + (+8)$$
$$= -4$$

Method 2

Use a scientific calculator.

The [+/−] key on a scientific calculator, called the *change-sign key,* changes the sign of the number on the display. You can find $-12 - (-8)$ by using this key.

Enter: 12 [+/−] [−] 8 [+/−] [=] −4

c. $43 - (-26)$

$$43 - (-26) = 43 + 26$$
$$= 69$$

Check by using a calculator.

Enter: 43 [−] 26 [+/−] [=] 69 ✓

The plural of matrix is matrices.

A **matrix** is a rectangular arrangement of elements in rows and columns. Although matrices are sometimes used as a problem-solving tool, their importance extends to another branch of mathematics called **discrete mathematics.** Discrete mathematics deals with finite or discontinuous quantities. The distinction between continuous and discrete quantities is one that you have encountered throughout your life. Think of a staircase. You can slide your hand up the banister, but you have to climb the stairs one by one. The banister represents a continuous quantity, like the graph of {all numbers greater than 3}. However, each step represents a discrete quantity, like an element in a matrix, or a point in the graph of {2, 4, 7, 12}.

When entries in corresponding positions of two matrices are equal, the matrices are equal.

$$\begin{bmatrix} 4 & 2 \\ -2 & 5 \end{bmatrix} = \begin{bmatrix} 4 & 2 \\ -2 & 5 \end{bmatrix} \qquad \begin{bmatrix} 4 & 2 \\ -2 & 5 \end{bmatrix} \neq \begin{bmatrix} 2 & 4 \\ -2 & 1 \end{bmatrix}$$

You can add or subtract matrices only if they have the same number of rows and columns. You add and subtract matrices by adding or subtracting corresponding entries.

Example 4

APPLICATION

Business

The Paw Print at Gahanna Lincoln High School in Gahanna, Ohio, is a school store run by seniors in a yearlong marketing education class. The store is stocked with school items such as sweatshirts, T-shirts, school supplies, and snacks. The sales, cost of goods, and expenses for each semester in 1994 and 1995, rounded to the nearest dollar, are shown below.

Semester 1	Sales	Cost of Goods	Expenses
1994	$47,981	$32,627	$12,999
1995	$70,018	$49,013	$12,705

Semester 2	Sales	Cost of Goods	Expenses
1994	$31,988	$21,752	$8666
1995	$30,008	$21,005	$5445

FYI

When the Paw Print opened in 1976, sales totaled $7800. In 1995, sales hit $100,000. The profits are used to buy new equipment and merchandise. Donations are also made to charities.

a. Find the total sales, cost of goods, and expenses for each year at The Paw Print.

To find the total sales, cost of goods, and expenses for each year, add the matrices for semester 1 and semester 2.

$$\begin{bmatrix} \$47{,}981 + \$31{,}988 & \$32{,}627 + \$21{,}752 & \$12{,}999 + \$8666 \\ \$70{,}018 + \$30{,}008 & \$49{,}013 + \$21{,}005 & \$12{,}705 + \$5445 \end{bmatrix}$$

$$= \begin{bmatrix} \$79{,}969 & \$54{,}379 & \$21{,}665 \\ \$100{,}026 & \$70{,}018 & \$18{,}150 \end{bmatrix}$$

b. Find the store's gross income, or profit, by year. The gross income is the difference between the sales and the sum of the cost of goods and expenses.

$$\text{Profit for 1994} = \$79{,}969 - (54{,}379 + 21{,}665) = \$3925$$

$$\text{Profit for 1995} = \$100{,}026 - (70{,}018 + 18{,}150) = \$11{,}858$$

The rule for subtracting integers and the distributive property can be used to combine like terms.

Example 5 **Simplify $2x - 5x$.**

$2x - 5x = 2x + (-5x)$ *To subtract 5x, add its additive inverse, −5x.*

$= [2 + (-5)]x$ *Use the distributive property.*

$= -3x$

CHECK FOR UNDERSTANDING

Communicating Mathematics

Study the lesson. Then complete the following.

1. **Explain** how a zero pair of counters illustrates the additive inverse property.
2. **Write** an integer on a piece of paper. Have a friend explain how to find its absolute value without a number line and without knowing the integer.
3. **Explain** to a friend how you would find each sum or difference below.
   a. $-3 + (-1)$ **b.** $5 + (-7)$ **c.** $4 - 9$ **d.** $6 - (-5)$
4. **a.** Find a value for x if $x = -x$.
   b. Find a value for x if $|x| = -|x|$.

MODELING MATHEMATICS

5. Write a statement that represents the model shown below.

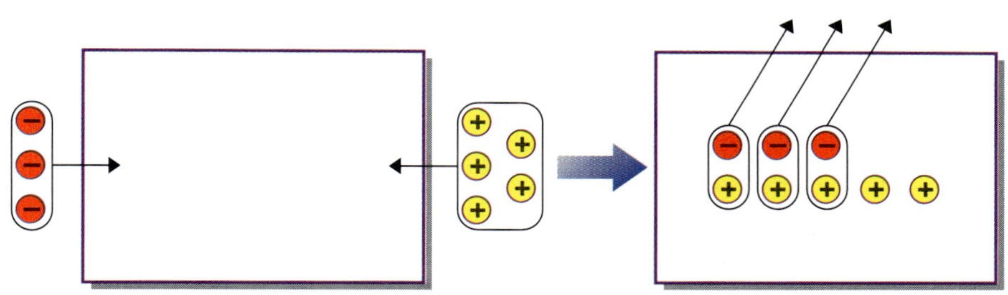

6. Find $-9 - (-4)$ by using counters.

Guided Practice

State the additive inverse and absolute value of each integer.

7. $+7$
8. -20
9. 0

Find each sum or difference.

10. $-12 + (-8)$
11. $-11 - (-7)$
12. $-36 + 15$
13. $18 - 29$
14. $|-6 - 4|$
15. $-|5 - 5|$

Simplify each expression.

16. $-16y - 5y$
17. $32c - (-8c)$
18. $-9d + (-6d)$

Evaluate each expression if $x = -5$, $y = 3$, and $z = -6$.

19. $y - 7$
20. $16 + z$
21. $|8 + x|$

Let $A = \begin{bmatrix} 3 & 2 \\ 5 & 0 \end{bmatrix}$ and $B = \begin{bmatrix} 4 & -2 \\ -1 & 6 \end{bmatrix}$.

22. Find $A + B$.
23. Find $A - B$.
24. **Space Science** Refer to the application at the beginning of the lesson. The Discovery astronauts were working in temperatures ranging from $-125°F$ to $200°F$.
    a. Which is colder, $-125°F$ or $200°F$?
    b. Write an equation that uses addition or subtraction to show how much colder one temperature is than the other.

EXERCISES

Practice

State the additive inverse and absolute value of each integer.

25. $+12$
26. -45
27. -302

Find each sum or difference.

28. $18 + (-16)$
29. $47 + (-47)$
30. $-9 + 32$
31. $0 - 32$
32. $16 - (-23)$
33. $-5 + (-11)$
34. $-104 + 16$
35. $-9 + (-61)$
36. $-18 - 4$
37. $9 - 24$
38. $-21 - (-24)$
39. $-13 - (-8)$

Simplify each expression.

40. $29t - 17t$
41. $17b - (-23b)$
42. $-6w + (-13w)$
43. $6p + (-35p)$
44. $54y - 47y$
45. $-5d + 31d$

Evaluate each expression if $b = -4$, $d = 2$, and $p = -5$.

46. $b + 14$
47. $d - 6$
48. $15 + p$
49. $d + (-17)$
50. $d + 7$
51. $|p|$
52. $|6 + b|$
53. $|p - 3|$
54. $-|-22 + p|$

Find each sum or difference.

55. $|-58 + (-41)|$
56. $|-93| - (-43)$
57. $-|-345 - (-286)|$

INTEGRATION **Discrete Mathematics**

58. $\begin{bmatrix} 3 & 2 \\ 4 & -1 \end{bmatrix} + \begin{bmatrix} 0 & 5 \\ -3 & -4 \end{bmatrix}$
59. $\begin{bmatrix} 2 & 4 \\ -1 & 0 \end{bmatrix} + \begin{bmatrix} -2 & -1 \\ 3 & 2 \end{bmatrix}$
60. $\begin{bmatrix} 1 & 6 \\ -4 & -5 \end{bmatrix} - \begin{bmatrix} -3 & -6 \\ 2 & -4 \end{bmatrix}$
61. $\begin{bmatrix} 2 & 3 \\ 4 & 2 \\ 5 & -5 \end{bmatrix} - \begin{bmatrix} 6 & 8 \\ 8 & 7 \\ -5 & -2 \end{bmatrix}$

Critical Thinking

62. Geometry Use the number line below to find the length of segment QS if segment RT has a length of 15 units.

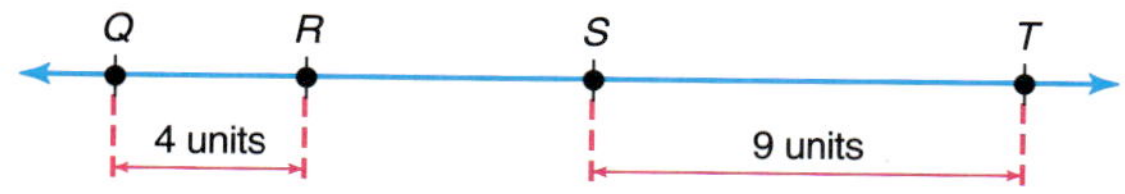

Applications and Problem Solving

Yokohama Landmark Tower

63. Elevators The 70-floor Yokohama Landmark Tower houses the world's fastest passenger elevators. Passengers travel from the second floor to the 69th floor in 40 seconds at an average speed of 28 miles per hour. If an employee rode the elevator up to his office on the 67th floor, then came down 43 floors to deliver a report, which floor is he on now?

64. Puzzles The sum of the numbers in each row, column, and diagonal of a magic square is the same. In the magic square at the right, the sum is 0. New magic squares can be formed by adding the same number to each entry. Complete each magic square.

1	2	−3
−4	0	4
3	−2	−1

a.

3	4	−1

b.

−2		
	−3	
		−4

c.

	−7	

65. Business The manager of The Best Bagel Shop keeps a record of each type of bagel sold each day at their two stores. Two days of sales are shown below.

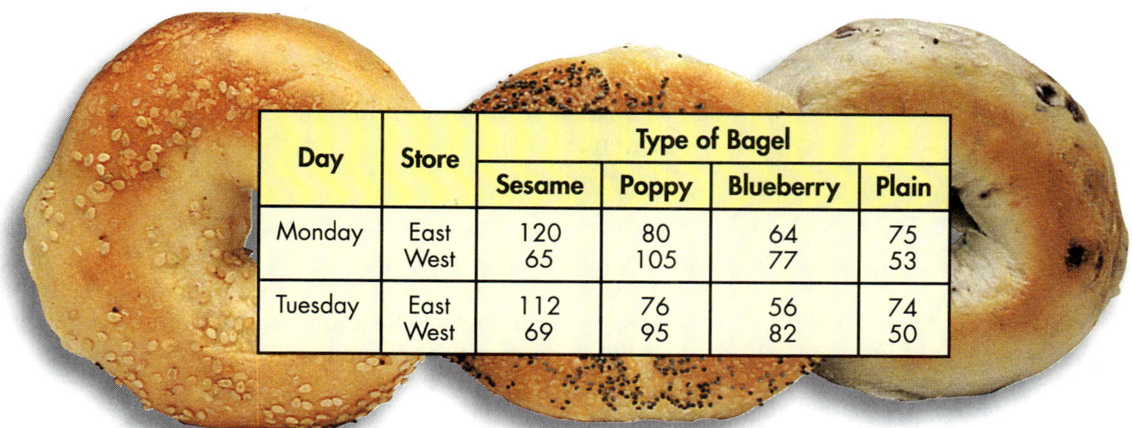

Day	Store	Type of Bagel			
		Sesame	Poppy	Blueberry	Plain
Monday	East West	120 65	80 105	64 77	75 53
Tuesday	East West	112 69	76 95	56 82	74 50

a. Write a matrix for each day's sales.

b. Find the sum of the two days' sales using matrix addition.

c. Subtract Tuesday's sales from Monday's sales by using matrix subtraction. What does this matrix represent?

66. Golf In golf, scores are based on *par.* Par 72 means that a golfer should hit the ball 72 times to complete 18 holes of golf. A score of 68, or 4 under par, is written as −4. A score of 2 over par is written as +2. At the Oldsmobile Classic LPGA tournament in June 1995, at a par-72 course in Michigan, Helen Alfredsson shot 65, 74, 69, and 71 during four rounds of golf.

a. Use integers to write Ms. Alfredsson's score for each round as over or under par.

b. Add the integers to find Ms. Alfredsson's overall score.

c. Was Ms. Alfredsson's score under or over par? Would you want to have her score? Explain.

Mixed Review

67. Trees The table below lists twenty different species of American trees and their highest recorded height in feet. (Lesson 2–2)

American Trees

Type	Height (feet)	Type	Height (feet)	Type	Height (feet)
American Beech	130	Bitter Cherry	104	Mockernut Hickory	125
American Chestnut	110	Black Maple	118	Pecan	143
American Elm	100	Black Walnut	105	Shellback Hickory	105
American Sweetgum	136	Cherrybark Oak	124	Siberian Elm	146
Arizona Sycamore	114	Common Hackberry	111	Virginia Pine	120
Balsam Poplar	138	Digger Pine	114	Weeping Willow	114
Bishop Pine	112	Honeylocust	115		

Source: *The World Almanac,* 1995

a. What is the range of heights for the trees?

b. Make a line plot showing the height of the trees.

c. Do the heights cluster around a certain number?

d. Which tree is the tallest? the shortest?

68. Write a corresponding addition sentence for the diagram at the right. (Lesson 2–1)

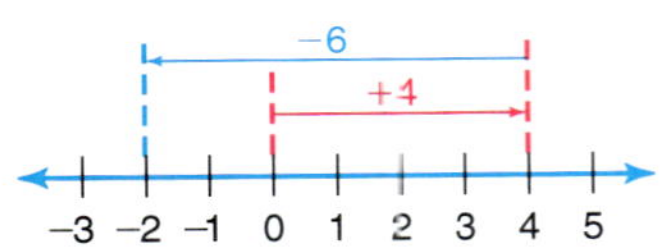

69. Sketch a reasonable graph for the following situation.
The water level in Craig Pond is extremely high at the beginning of the summer. Throughout the summer, the water level lowers steadily. By the end of the summer, the pond is almost dry. (Lesson 1–9)

70. Name the property illustrated by $3 + 4 = 4 + 3$. (Lesson 1–8)

71. Simplify $23y^2 + 32y^2$. (Lesson 1–7)

Name the property illustrated by each statement. (Lesson 1–6)

72. $3abc \cdot 0 = 0$

73. If $12xy - 3 = 4$, then $4 = 12xy - 3$.

74. Solve $p = 6\frac{1}{4} + \frac{1}{2}$. (Lesson 1–5)

75. Statistics Write the stems that would be used for a plot of the following data: 29.1, 34.7, 20.05, 74.9, 64, 14.2, 84.9, 38.26, 20.9, 34, 59.42, 37.107, and 43.676. (Lesson 1–4)

76. Evaluate $19 + 5 \cdot 4$. (Lesson 1–3)

77. Patterns Find the sixth term in the sequence 4, 8, 12, 16, ... (Lesson 1–2)

78. Write an algebraic expression for the sum of n and 33. (Lesson 1–1)

2–4 Rational Numbers

What YOU'LL LEARN

- To compare and order rational numbers, and
- to find a number between two rational numbers.

Why IT'S IMPORTANT

You need to know the values of rational numbers to solve problems involving consumerism and archaeology.

APPLICATION

Recycling

Many people all over the world recycle their aluminum cans in order to help our environment. The graph below shows the fraction of aluminum cans that have been recycled over the years.

Source: The Aluminum Association

The numbers shown in the graph are examples of **rational numbers.**

Definition of a Rational Number	A rational number is a number that can be expressed in the form $\frac{a}{b}$, where a and b are integers and b is not equal to 0.

Examples of rational numbers expressed in the form $\frac{a}{b}$ are shown below.

Notice that all integers are rational numbers.

Rational Numbers	4	$-3\frac{3}{4}$	0.250	0	$0.33\overline{3}$
Form $\frac{a}{b}$	$\frac{4}{1}$	$-\frac{15}{4}$	$\frac{1}{4}$	$\frac{0}{1}$	$\frac{1}{3}$

Rational numbers can be graphed on a number line in the same manner as integers. The number line below is separated into fourths to show the graphs of some common fractions and decimals.

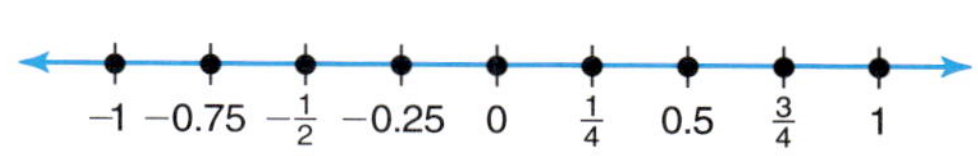

You can compare rational numbers by graphing them on a number line. Recall that a mathematical sentence that uses < and > to compare two expressions is called an *inequality*.

The following statements can be made about the graphs of -5, -2, $1\frac{1}{2}$ and 3.5 shown on the number line below.

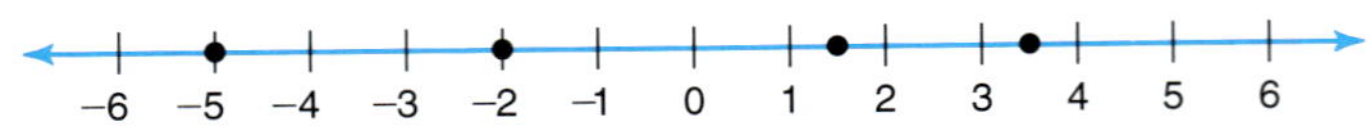

a. The graph of -2 is to the left of the graph of 3.5. $-2 < 3.5$

b. The graph of $1\frac{1}{2}$ is to the right of the graph of -5. $1\frac{1}{2} > -5$

These examples suggest the following rule.

Comparing Numbers on the Number Line	**If *a* and *b* represent any numbers and the graph of *a* is to the left of the graph of *b*, then $a < b$. If the graph of *a* is to the right of the graph of *b*, then $a > b$.**

If $<$, $>$, and $=$ are used to compare two numbers, then the following property applies.

Comparison Property	**For any two numbers *a* and *b*, exactly one of the following sentences is true.** $a < b$ $\quad a = b \quad$ $a > b$

The symbols $\neq$, $\leq$, and $\geq$ can also be used to compare numbers. The chart below shows several inequality symbols and their meanings.

Symbol	Meaning
$<$	is less than
$>$	is greater than
$\neq$	is not equal to
$\leq$	is less than or equal to
$\geq$	is greater than or equal to

Example 1 **Replace each __?__ with $<$, $>$, or $=$ to make each sentence true.**

a. -75 __?__ 13

Since any negative number is less than any positive number, the true sentence is $-75 < 13$.

Note that the closed ends of $<$ and $>$ always point to the lesser number.

b. -14 __?__ $-22 + 9$

-14 __?__ $-22 + 9$

-14 __?__ -13 *Simplify.*

Since -14 is less than -13, the true sentence is $-14 < -22 + 9$.

c. $\frac{3}{8}$ __?__ $-\frac{7}{8}$

Since 3 is greater than -7, the true sentence is $\frac{3}{8} > -\frac{7}{8}$.

You can use **cross products** to compare two fractions with different denominators. When two fractions are compared, the cross products are the products of the terms on the diagonals.

Comparison Property for Rational Numbers	For any rational numbers $\frac{a}{b}$ and $\frac{c}{d}$, with $b > 0$ and $d > 0$: 1. if $\frac{a}{b} < \frac{c}{d}$, then $ad < bc$, and 2. if $ad < bc$, then $\frac{a}{b} < \frac{c}{d}$.

This property also holds if $<$ is replaced by $>$, $\leq$, $\geq$, or $=$.

Example 2 **Replace each __?__ with <, >, or = to make each sentence true.**

a. $\frac{7}{13}$ __?__ $\frac{4}{15}$

$7(15)$ __?__ $13(4)$

$105 > 52$

The true sentence is $\frac{7}{13} > \frac{4}{15}$.

b. $\frac{7}{8}$ __?__ $\frac{8}{9}$

$7(9)$ __?__ $8(8)$

$63 < 64$

The true sentence is $\frac{7}{8} < \frac{8}{9}$.

fabulous FIRSTS

Alberto Salazar (1958–)

Alberto Salazar won the first marathon he entered, the 1980 New York Marathon. His track career included a world record and six U.S. records.

Every rational number can be expressed as a terminating or repeating decimal. You can use a calculator to write rational numbers as decimals.

Example 3 **Use a calculator to write the fractions $\frac{3}{8}$, $\frac{4}{5}$, and $\frac{1}{6}$ as decimals. Then write the fractions in order from least to greatest.**

It is helpful to know these commonly used fraction-decimal equivalencies by memory.

$\frac{1}{2} = 0.5$, $\frac{1}{3} = 0.\overline{3}$,

$\frac{1}{4} = 0.25$, $\frac{1}{5} = 0.2$,

$\frac{1}{8} = 0.125$

$\frac{3}{8} = 0.375$ This is a terminating decimal.

$\frac{4}{5} = 0.8$ This is also a terminating decimal.

$\frac{1}{6} = 0.16666\ldots$ or $0.1\overline{6}$ This is a repeating decimal.

In order from least to greatest, the decimals are $0.1\overline{6}$, 0.375, 0.8. So, the fractions in order from least to greatest are $\frac{1}{6}$, $\frac{3}{8}$, $\frac{4}{5}$.

You can use a calculator to compare the cost per unit, or **unit cost,** of two similar items. Many people comparison shop to find the best buys at the grocery store. The item that has the lesser unit cost is the better buy.

unit cost = total cost ÷ number of units

Example 4 **APPLICATION Consumerism**

Erica and Gabriella are running in a 5-kilometer race to raise money for The Multiple Sclerosis Foundation. They want to buy a sports beverage to drink after they finish the race. Which is the better buy?

Use a calculator to find the unit cost of each brand. In each case, the unit cost is expressed in cents per ounce.

unit cost of 20-ounce bottle: 1.09 [÷] 20 [=] 0.0545

unit cost of 32-ounce bottle: 1.69 [÷] 32 [=] 0.0528

Since $0.053 < 0.055$, the 32-ounce drink is the better buy.

Can you always find another rational number between two rational numbers? One point that lies between any two points is their midpoint. Consider $\frac{1}{3}$ and $\frac{1}{2}$.

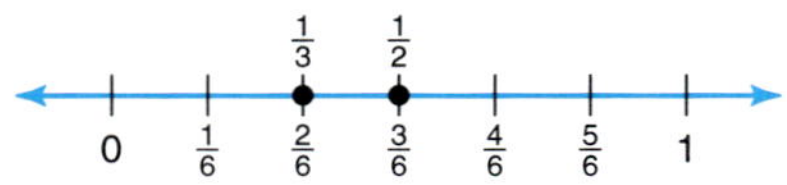

To find the average of two numbers, add the numbers and then divide by 2.

Multiplying by $\frac{1}{2}$ is the same as dividing by 2.

To find the coordinate of the midpoint for $\frac{1}{3}$ and $\frac{1}{2}$, find the average, or mean, of the two numbers.

average: $\frac{1}{2}\left(\frac{1}{3} + \frac{1}{2}\right) = \frac{1}{2}\left(\frac{5}{6}\right)$ or $\frac{5}{12}$

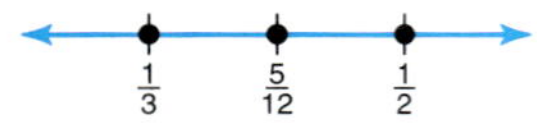

This process can be continued indefinitely. The pattern suggests the **density property.**

Density Property for Rational Numbers	**Between every pair of distinct rational numbers, there are infinitely many rational numbers.**

Example 5 **Find a rational number between $-\frac{2}{5}$ and $-\frac{3}{8}$.**

Find the average of the two rational numbers.

Method 1

Use a pencil and paper.

$$\frac{1}{2}\left[-\frac{2}{5} + \left(-\frac{3}{8}\right)\right] = \frac{1}{2}\left[-\frac{16}{40} + \left(-\frac{15}{40}\right)\right]$$
$$= \frac{1}{2}\left(-\frac{31}{40}\right)$$
$$= -\frac{31}{80}$$

Method 2

Use a scientific calculator.

Enter: (2 ÷ 5 +/− + 3 ÷ 8 +/−) ÷ 2 = *−0.3875*

A rational number between $-\frac{2}{5}$ and $-\frac{3}{8}$ is $-\frac{31}{80}$ or -0.3875.

CHECK FOR UNDERSTANDING

Communicating Mathematics

Study the lesson. Then complete the following.

1. **Write** three examples of rational numbers.
2. **State** any assumptions you can make about y and z if $x < y$ and $x < z$.
3. **Show** two ways to find three rational numbers between $\frac{1}{5}$ and $\frac{1}{4}$.
4. **Explain** why the definition of a rational number states that b cannot be zero.
5. **You Decide** To find a number between $\frac{3}{4}$ and $\frac{6}{7}$, John added as follows.

   $\frac{3+6}{4+7} = \frac{9}{11}$; $\frac{9}{11}$ is between $\frac{3}{4}$ and $\frac{6}{7}$.

   He claimed that this method will always work. Do you agree? Explain.

MATH JOURNAL

6. **Assess Yourself** Describe two situations in which you would prefer to use decimals instead of fractions.

Guided Practice

Replace each $\underline{\ ?\ }$ with <, >, or = to make each sentence true.

7. $-4 \underline{\ ?\ } 8$
8. $-5 \underline{\ ?\ } 0 - 3$
9. $\frac{5}{14} \underline{\ ?\ } \frac{25}{70}$

Write the numbers in each set in order from least to greatest.

10. $\frac{2}{3}, \frac{1}{6}, \frac{1}{2}$
11. $2.5, \frac{3}{4}, -0.5, \frac{7}{8}$

12. Which is a better buy: a 6-ounce can of tuna for $1.59 or a package of 3 three-ounce cans for $2.19?
13. Find a number between $\frac{1}{2}$ and $\frac{5}{7}$.

EXERCISES

Practice

Replace each $\underline{\ ?\ }$ with <, >, or = to make each sentence true.

14. $-3 \underline{\ ?\ } 5$
15. $-1 \underline{\ ?\ } -4$
16. $-6 - 3 \underline{\ ?\ } -9$
17. $5 \underline{\ ?\ } 8.4 - 1.5$
18. $4 \underline{\ ?\ } \frac{16}{3}$
19. $\frac{8}{15} \underline{\ ?\ } \frac{9}{16}$
20. $\frac{14}{5} \underline{\ ?\ } \frac{25}{13}$
21. $\frac{4}{3}(6) \underline{\ ?\ } 4\left(\frac{3}{2}\right)$
22. $\frac{0.4}{3} \underline{\ ?\ } \frac{1.2}{8}$

Write the numbers in each set in order from least to greatest.

23. $\frac{6}{7}, \frac{2}{3}, \frac{3}{8}$
24. $-\frac{4}{15}, -\frac{6}{17}, -\frac{3}{16}$
25. $\frac{4}{14}, \frac{3}{23}, \frac{8}{42}$
26. $6.7, -\frac{5}{7}, \frac{6}{13}$
27. $0.2, -\frac{2}{5}, -0.2$
28. $\frac{4}{5}, \frac{9}{10}, 0.7$

Which is the better buy?

29. a 16-ounce drink for $0.59 or a 20-ounce drink for $0.89
30. a 32-ounce bottle of shampoo for $3.59 or a 64-ounce bottle for $6.99
31. a package of 48 paper plates for $2.39 or a package of 75 paper plates for $3.29

Find a number between the given numbers.

32. $\frac{2}{5}$ and $\frac{7}{2}$
33. $\frac{19}{30}$ and $\frac{31}{45}$
34. $-\frac{2}{15}$ and $-\frac{6}{3}$

35. Name a fraction between $\frac{1}{4}$ and $\frac{1}{2}$ whose denominator is 20.
36. Name a fraction between $\frac{1}{3}$ and $\frac{5}{6}$ whose denominator is 12.
37. Name a fraction between -0.5 and $\frac{1}{3}$ whose denominator is 6.

Critical Thinking

38. Three numbers a, b, and c satisfy the following conditions: $b - c < 0$, $a - b > 0$, and $c - a < 0$. Which one is the greatest?

39. Find the coordinates of E, G, and H if the distances between the points are equal.

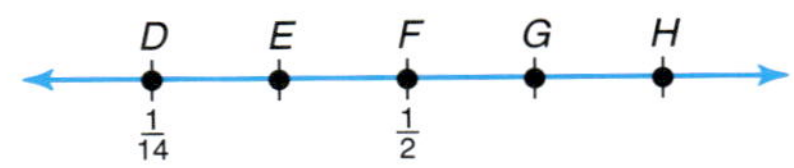

Applications and Problem Solving

40. Personal Computers Study the graph at the right. Write an inequality that compares the total number of PCs shipped for home use in 1995 to those shipped in 1996.

Sources: Dataquest, LINK

41. Aviation When building or servicing airplanes, an airplane mechanic sometimes needs to drill holes. Drill bit sizes are given in fractions, yet many blueprints list hole diameters in decimals. One blueprint calls for a hole of 0.391 inches. Find the fractional drill size required if the hole must be drilled $\frac{1}{64}$-inch undersize.

42. Archaeology To calculate a person's height, archaeologists measure the lengths of certain bones. The bones measured are the femur or thigh bone F, the tibia or leg bone T, the humerus or upper arm bone H, and the radius or lower arm bone R. When the length of one of these bones is known, scientists can use one of the formulas below to determine the person's height h in centimeters.

Males	Females
$h = 69.089 + 2.238F$	$h = 61.412 + 2.317F$
$h = 81.688 + 2.392T$	$h = 72.572 + 2.533T$
$h = 73.570 + 2.970H$	$h = 64.977 + 3.144H$
$h = 80.405 + 3.650R$	$h = 73.502 + 3.876R$

a. The femur of a 37-year old woman measured 47.9 cm. Use a calculator to find the height of the woman to the nearest tenth of a centimeter.

b. The humerus of a 49-year old man measured 35.7 cm. Use a calculator to find the height of the man to the nearest tenth of a centimeter.

Mixed Review

43. State the additive inverse and absolute value of +9. (Lesson 2–3)

44. **Statistics** State the scale you would use to make a line plot for the following data. Then draw the line plot. (Lesson 2–2)
145, 130, 135, 150, 145, 145, 140, 130, 145, 150, 130

45. Graph $\{-3, -2, 2, 3\}$ on a number line. (Lesson 2–1)

46. **Soccer** Bryce, Maria, and Holly are three offensive players for the Rocks soccer team. The graph at the right describes the players' offensive skills in their last season. (Lesson 1–9)
    a. Who scored the most goals?
    b. Who helped the team most with goals and assists overall?
    c. Another player, Ian, had the same number of goals as Maria and the same number of assists as Holly. Describe where on the graph a point should go that would show his offensive skills.

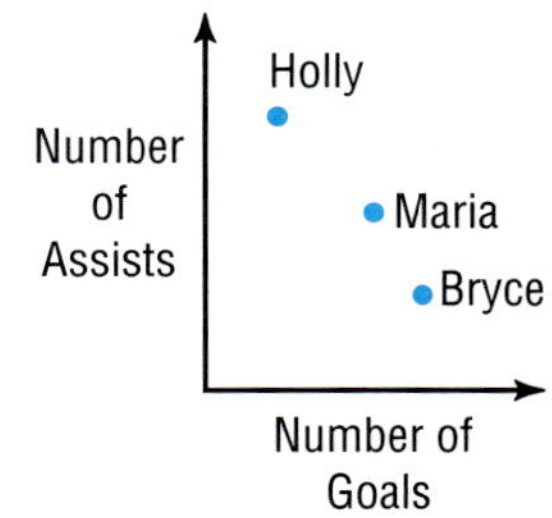

47. Simplify $\frac{2}{5}m + \frac{1}{5}(6n + 3m) + \frac{1}{10}(8n + 15)$. (Lesson 1–6)

48. **Patterns** Find the next three terms in the sequence 1, 3, 9, 27, ... (Lesson 1–2)

49. Write a verbal expression for $2x^2 + 6$. (Lesson 1–1)

SELF TEST

Graph each set of numbers on a number line. (Lesson 2–1)

1. $\{-3, 0, 2\}$
2. {numbers greater than -2}

Find each sum or difference. (Lesson 2–3)

3. $-9 + (-8)$
4. $6 + (-15)$
5. $23 - (-32)$
6. $-12 - 4$
7. **Mountain Bikes** The table at the right shows prices of several mountain bikes. (Lesson 2–2)
    a. Make a line plot of the data.
    b. Do the numbers cluster around any certain price?

Bike	Price
Kert 820	$325
Threshold	270
Yukon	370
Rincon	300
Timber Wolf	270
Clear Creek	320
Sidewinder	260
Hardrock	270
M40GS	290
Kert 800	240

Replace each ? with <, >, or = to make each sentence true. (Lesson 2–4)

8. $-7 - 5$? -11
9. $\frac{7}{16}$? $\frac{8}{15}$
10. $\frac{5}{4}(4)$? $8\left(\frac{1}{2}\right)$

2–5 Adding and Subtracting Rational Numbers

What **YOU'LL LEARN**

- To add and subtract rational numbers, and
- to simplify expressions that contain rational numbers.

Why **IT'S IMPORTANT**

You can add and subtract rational numbers to help you solve problems involving the stock market and track and field.

APPLICATION

Employment

In 1982, the average number of weekly overtime hours worked by a U.S. worker was $2\frac{1}{4}$ hours. This average increased $1\frac{1}{4}$ hours by 1989 and then decreased $\frac{1}{2}$ hour by 1991. What was the average number of weekly overtime hours worked in 1991?

To answer this question, you need to find the following sum.

1982 → $2\frac{1}{4}$; *increase by 1989* → $1\frac{1}{4}$; *increase by 1991* → $\left(-\frac{1}{2}\right)$

$$2\frac{1}{4} + 1\frac{1}{4} + \left(-\frac{1}{2}\right)$$

LOOK BACK

You can refer to Lesson 1-8 for information on the commutative and associative properties.

To add rational numbers such as these, use the same rules you used to add integers. When adding three or more rational numbers, you can use the commutative and associative properties to rearrange the addends.

Method 1: Use the rules.

$2\frac{1}{4} + 1\frac{1}{4} + \left(-\frac{1}{2}\right) = 3\frac{2}{4} + \left(-\frac{1}{2}\right)$ *Add the first two addends.*

$= 3\frac{1}{2} + \left(-\frac{1}{2}\right)$ *Simplify.*

$= +\left(\left|3\frac{1}{2}\right| - \left|-\frac{1}{2}\right|\right)$ *$3\frac{1}{2}$ has the greater absolute value,*

$= +\left(3\frac{1}{2} - \frac{1}{2}\right)$ *so the sign of the sum is positive.*

$= 3$

Method 2: Use a number line.

As with integers, you can also add rational numbers by using a number line.

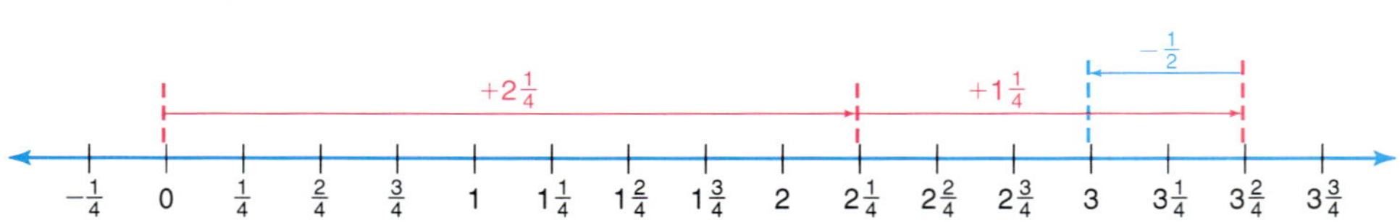

The average number of weekly overtime hours worked in 1991 was 3.

Example 1 **Find each sum.**

a. $4\frac{1}{8} + \left(-1\frac{1}{2}\right)$ *Estimate:* $4 + (-2) = 2$

$$4\frac{1}{8} + \left(-1\frac{1}{2}\right) = 4\frac{1}{8} + \left(-1\frac{4}{8}\right)$$ *The LCD is 8. Replace $-1\frac{1}{2}$ with $-1\frac{4}{8}$.*

$$= +\left(\left|4\frac{1}{8}\right| - \left|-1\frac{4}{8}\right|\right)$$ *The sum is positive. Why?*

$$= +\left(4\frac{1}{8} - 1\frac{4}{8}\right)$$

$$= +\left(3\frac{9}{8} - 1\frac{4}{8}\right)$$ *Replace $4\frac{1}{8}$ with $3\frac{9}{8}$.*

$$= 2\frac{5}{8}$$ *Compare to the estimate.*

b. $-1.34 + (-0.458)$ *Estimate:* $-1 + (-0.5) = -1.5$

$$-1.34 + (-0.458) = -(|-1.34| + |-0.458|)$$
$$= -(1.34 + 0.458)$$
$$= -1.798$$
The numbers have the same sign. Their sum is negative.

c. $-\frac{2}{5} + 1\frac{1}{2} + \left(-\frac{2}{3}\right)$ *Estimate:* $-\frac{1}{2} + 1\frac{1}{2} + \left(-\frac{1}{2}\right) = \frac{1}{2}$

$$-\frac{2}{5} + 1\frac{1}{2} + \left(-\frac{2}{3}\right) = \left[-\frac{2}{5} + \left(-\frac{2}{3}\right)\right] + 1\frac{1}{2}$$ *Group the negative numbers together.*

$$= \left[-\frac{12}{30} + \left(-\frac{20}{30}\right)\right] + \frac{45}{30}$$ *The LCD is 30.*

$$= -\frac{32}{30} + \frac{45}{30}$$

$$= \frac{13}{30}$$ *Compare to the estimate.*

To subtract rational numbers, use the same process you used to subtract integers.

Example 2 **Find each difference.**

a. $-\frac{3}{5} - \left(-\frac{4}{7}\right)$

$$-\frac{3}{5} - \left(-\frac{4}{7}\right) = -\frac{3}{5} + \frac{4}{7}$$ *To subtract $-\frac{4}{7}$, add its inverse, $+\frac{4}{7}$.*

$$= -\frac{21}{35} + \frac{20}{35}$$ *The LCD is 35.*

$$= -\frac{1}{35}$$

b. $-6.24 - 8.52$

$$-6.24 - 8.52 = -6.24 + (-8.52)$$
$$= -14.76$$

Example 3

APPLICATION

Stock Market

A corporation produces a high-speed processor for personal computers. In November of 1994, the corporation announced that there was a flaw in the processor that could cause errors in complex mathematical calculations. In one week, the corporation's stock dropped $2\frac{1}{4}$ points. By December 13, the stock had dropped another $2\frac{1}{8}$ points. How many points did the stock drop in this time period?

We can represent the drops in the price of the stock with negative numbers.

$$-2\frac{1}{4} - 2\frac{1}{8} = -2\frac{1}{4} + \left(-2\frac{1}{8}\right) \quad \textit{To subtract } 2\tfrac{1}{8}\textit{, add its additive inverse.}$$

$$= -2\frac{2}{8} + \left(-2\frac{1}{8}\right) \quad \textit{The LCD is 8.}$$

$$= -4\frac{3}{8}$$

The corporation's stock dropped $4\frac{3}{8}$ points during this time period.

FYI

In the 18th century, the U.S. dollar was equal to the Spanish silver dollar. This coin was often divided into eight parts, so when the stock market opened, the practice of quoting prices in eighths of a dollar began.

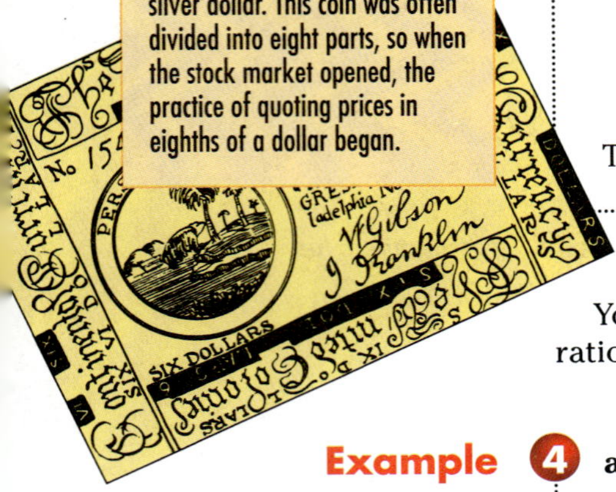

You can also evaluate expressions involving the addition and subtraction of rational numbers.

Example 4

a. Evaluate $p - 3.5$ if $p = 2.8$.

$$p - 3.5 = 2.8 - 3.5 \quad \textit{Replace p with 2.8.}$$

$$= -0.7$$

b. Evaluate $\frac{11}{4} - x$ if $x = \frac{27}{8}$.

$$\frac{11}{4} - x = \frac{11}{4} - \frac{27}{8} \quad \textit{Replace x with } \tfrac{27}{8}.$$

$$= \frac{22}{8} - \frac{27}{8} \quad \textit{The LCD is 8.}$$

$$= -\frac{5}{8}$$

CHECK FOR UNDERSTANDING

Communicating Mathematics

Study the lesson. Then complete the following.

1. **Describe** two ways to find $-2.4 + 5.87 + (-2.87) + 6.5$.
2. **Find** an example of addition or subtraction of rational numbers in a newspaper or magazine.

MODELING MATHEMATICS

3. **Draw** and use a number line to show the sum of $-\frac{4}{5}$ and $\frac{3}{5}$.
4. **Use** a number line to solve the problem in Example 3.

Guided Practice

Find each sum or difference.

5. $\frac{7}{9} - \frac{8}{9}$
6. $-\frac{7}{12} + \frac{5}{6}$
7. $-\frac{1}{8} + \left(-\frac{5}{2}\right)$
8. $-69.5 - 82.3$
9. $4.57 + (-3.69)$
10. $-\frac{2}{5} + \frac{3}{15} + \frac{3}{5}$

Evaluate each expression.

11. $a - (-5)$, if $a = 0.75$

12. $\frac{11}{2} - b$ if $b = -\frac{5}{2}$

13. **Business** For the week of July 22, 1995, the following day-to-day changes were recorded in the Dow Jones Industrial Average:

    Monday, $+2\frac{3}{8}$; Tuesday, $-\frac{1}{4}$; Wednesday, $-\frac{3}{8}$;

    Thursday, $+2\frac{1}{4}$; Friday, $-3\frac{1}{2}$.

    a. What was the net change for the week?

    b. Draw a number line that shows the change each day.

EXERCISES

Practice

Find each sum or difference.

14. $\frac{5}{8} + \left(-\frac{3}{8}\right)$

15. $-\frac{7}{8} - \left(-\frac{3}{16}\right)$

16. $-1.6 - 3.8$

17. $3.2 + (-4.5)$

18. $\frac{1}{2} + \left(-\frac{8}{16}\right)$

19. $\frac{2}{3} + \left(-\frac{2}{9}\right)$

20. $-38.9 + 24.2$

21. $-0.0007 + (-0.2)$

22. $-\frac{3}{7} + \frac{1}{4}$

23. $-5\frac{7}{8} - 2\frac{3}{4}$

24. $79.3 - (-14.1)$

25. $-0.0015 + 0.05$

26. $-9.16 - (-10.17)$

27. $-5.6 + (-9.45) + (-7.89)$

28. $\frac{1}{4} + 2 + \left(-\frac{3}{4}\right)$

29. $-0.87 + 3.5 + (-7.6) + 2.8$

30. $\frac{3}{4} + \left(-\frac{4}{5}\right) + \frac{2}{5}$

31. $-4\frac{1}{4} + 6\frac{1}{3} + 2\frac{2}{3} + \left(-3\frac{3}{4}\right)$

Evaluate each expression.

32. $-3\frac{1}{3} - b$, if $b = \frac{1}{2}$

33. $r - 2.7$, if $r = -0.8$

34. $n - 0.5$, if $n = -0.8$

35. $t - (-1.3)$, if $t = -18$

36. $\frac{4}{3} - p$, if $p = \frac{4}{5}$

37. $-\frac{12}{7} - s$, if $s = \frac{16}{21}$

INTEGRATION
Discrete Mathematics

Find each sum or difference.

38. $\begin{bmatrix} 3 & -2 \\ 5 & 6.2 \end{bmatrix} + \begin{bmatrix} 2.4 & 5 \\ -4 & 1 \end{bmatrix}$

39. $\begin{bmatrix} -1.3 & 4.2 \\ 0 & -3.4 \end{bmatrix} - \begin{bmatrix} 2.5 & 4.3 \\ -1.7 & -6.3 \end{bmatrix}$

40. $\begin{bmatrix} \frac{1}{2} & -2 \\ 7 & \frac{1}{4} \end{bmatrix} + \begin{bmatrix} 3 & -5 \\ \frac{2}{3} & 6 \end{bmatrix}$

41. $\begin{bmatrix} \frac{1}{2} & 6 \\ -1 & 5 \\ 4 & -7 \end{bmatrix} + \begin{bmatrix} -\frac{1}{4} & 5 \\ -4 & 3 \\ -3\frac{1}{2} & -5 \end{bmatrix}$

42. $\begin{bmatrix} 3.2 & 6.4 & -4.3 \\ 5 & -4 & 0.4 \end{bmatrix} - \begin{bmatrix} 1.4 & 3.7 & 5 \\ -1 & 5 & 0.4 \end{bmatrix}$

Critical Thinking

43. **Discrete Mathematics** Create four 2×2 matrices. Use the matrices to support or disprove the following statement: *Matrix addition is associative and commutative.*

Applications and Problem Solving

44. **Book Binding** A textbook like this one is made up of sets of 32 pages called *signatures*. A signature is made from one piece of large paper that is folded several times. Signatures are bound together to make a book. Suppose when this book was printed, there were $1\frac{1}{2}$ rolls of paper available in the warehouse. The printer had three jobs to do that utilized this type of paper. This textbook required $\frac{1}{4}$ roll, another book required $\frac{2}{5}$ roll, and the third book needed $\frac{1}{2}$ roll. Is there enough paper available for all three jobs? Explain.

45. **Discrete Mathematics** An arithmetic sequence is a sequence in which the difference between any two consecutive terms is the same.
    a. Write the next three terms in the arithmetic sequence 4.53, 5.65, 6.77, 7.89, ...
    b. What is the common difference?
    c. Write the first five terms of an arithmetic sequence in which the first term is -2 and the common difference is $\frac{3}{4}$. Find the sum of the first five terms.

46. **Track and Field** In 1995, Sheila Hudson-Strudwick set the U.S. women's triple jump record. Suppose her first jump was 46 feet 9 inches and her next jump was $1\frac{3}{4}$ inches longer. Her record-setting jump was 1 foot $2\frac{1}{2}$ inches longer than her second jump. What was the length of her record-setting jump?

Mixed Review

47. Replace __?__ with <, >, or = to make -3.833 __?__ -3.115 true. (Lesson 2–4)

48. Evaluate $-|-9 + 2x|$ when $x = 7$. (Lesson 2–3)

49. **Statistics** The points scored by the winning teams in the first 29 Super Bowls are listed below. (Lesson 2–2)

35	33	16	23	16	24	14	24
16	21	32	27	35	31	27	26
27	38	38	46	39	42	20	55
20	37	52	30	49			

    a. Make a line plot of the data.
    b. Do the numbers cluster around any number?

50. **Restaurant Sales** Rosa's Deli made 3 cheesecakes, each having 12 slices, on Sunday. On Monday, they sold 3 slices. On Tuesday, they sold one entire cheesecake and 2 additional slices. The baker made another cheesecake on Wednesday and sold nine slices. If Rosa's Deli sold 11 slices of cheesecake on Thursday, how many slices were left on Friday? (Lesson 2–1)

51. Name the property illustrated by $7(0) = 0$. (Lesson 1–6)

52. Evaluate $7[4^3 - 2(4 + 3)] \div 7 + 2$. (Lesson 1–3)

53. **Patterns** Find the next term in the sequence $\frac{1}{3}, \frac{3}{6}, \frac{5}{12}, \ldots$. (Lesson 1–2)

54. Evaluate 8^4. (Lesson 1–1)

MODELING MATHEMATICS

A Preview of Lesson 2–6

2–6A Multiplying Integers

Materials: counters, integer mat

You can use counters to model multiplication of integers. Remember that yellow counters represent positive integers and red counters represent negative integers. When multiplying whole numbers, 2×4 means *two sets of four items.* When multiplying integers with counters, $(+2)(+4)$ means *to put in two sets of four positive counters.* $(-2)(+4)$ means to take out two sets of four positive counters.

Activity 1 Use counters to find the product $(+2)(-4)$.

Step 1 Place, or *put in,* two sets of four negative counters on the mat.

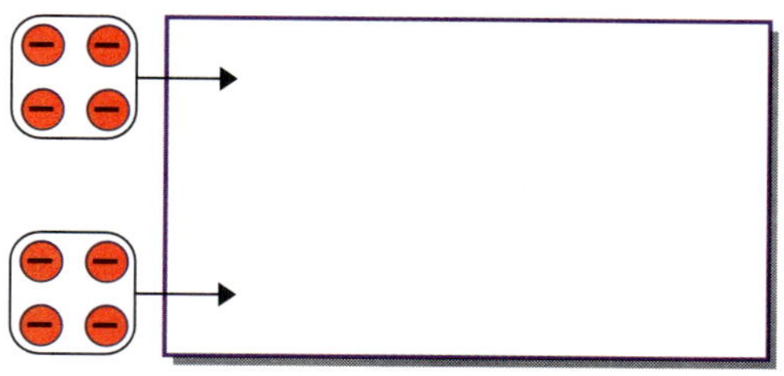

Step 2 Since there are eight negative counters on the mat, the product is -8. Thus, $(+2)(-4) = -8$.

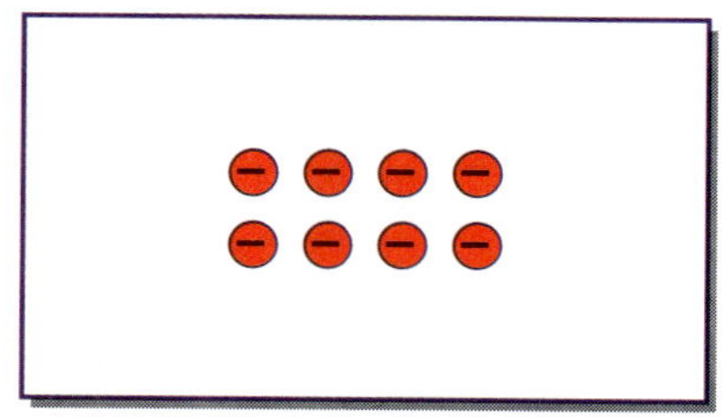

Activity 2 Use counters to find the product $(-2)(+4)$.

Step 1 Add enough zero pairs so that you can *take out* two sets of four positive counters.

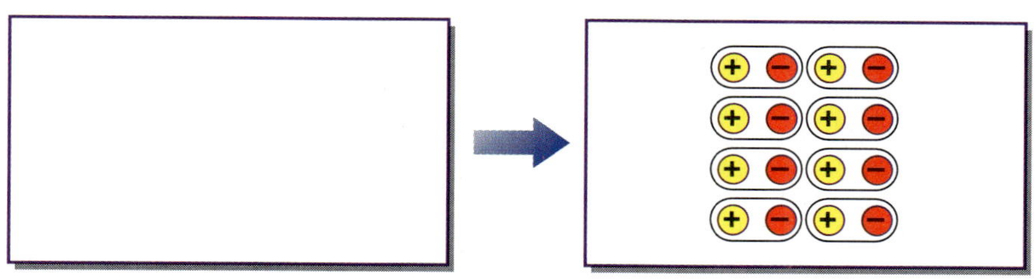

Step 2 Now take out two sets of four positive counters from the mat.

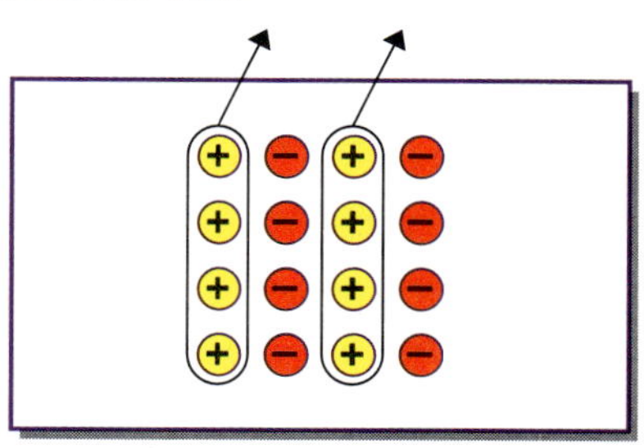

Step 3 Since there are eight negative counters on the mat, the product is -8. Thus, $-2(+4) = -8$.

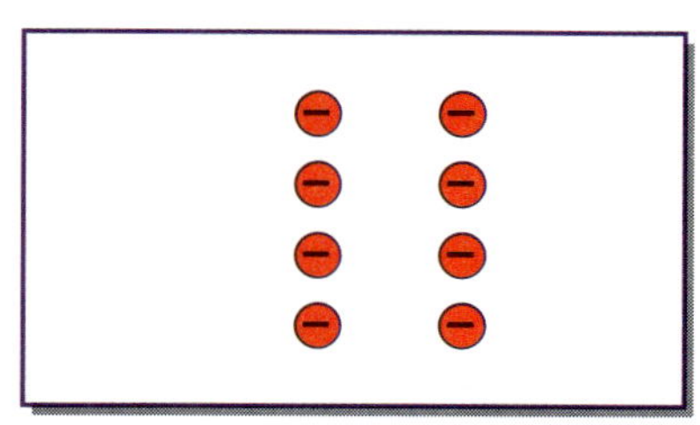

Write 1. Model $-2(-4)$. Write a short paragraph explaining what $(-2)(-4)$ means.

Model **Use counters to find each product.**

2. $2(-5)$
3. $-2(5)$
4. $-2(-5)$
5. $5(-2)$
6. $-5(2)$
7. $-5(-2)$

Write 8. How are the operations $-2(5)$ and $5(-2)$ the same? How do they differ?

2–6

Multiplying Rational Numbers

What YOU'LL LEARN

- To multiply rational numbers.

Why IT'S IMPORTANT

You can multiply rational numbers to help you solve problems involving geometry and business.

INTEGRATION

Geometry

Once called "the world's largest office building," the Pentagon, the five-story, five-sided defense building in Washington, D.C., was designed by G.E. Bergstrom to maximize space and efficiency. No two offices are more than a seven-minute walk from one another.

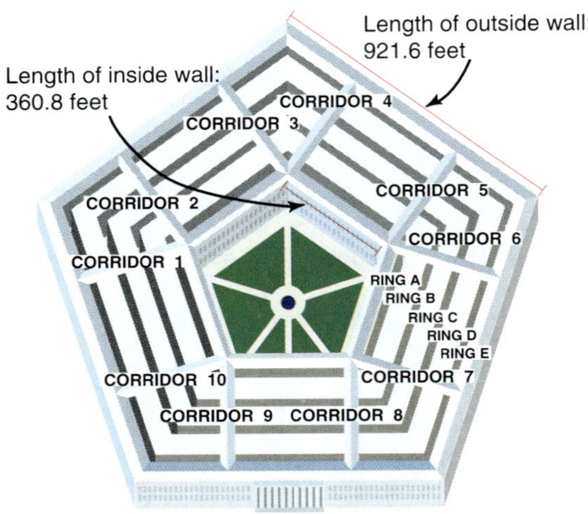

THE PENTAGON

The building is made up of 10 corridors and five rings. There are 230 restrooms, 150 stairways, and 7748 windows. Each outside wall of the building is 921.6 feet in length, slightly longer than three football fields. The inner walls, also in the shape of a pentagon, are each 360.8 feet in length. What is the outer perimeter of the Pentagon?

One way to solve this problem is to use repeated addition.

$$921.6 + 921.6 + 921.6 + 921.6 + 921.6 = 4608$$

An easier method would be to multiply 921.6 by 5.

$$5(921.6) = 4608$$

The perimeter of the Pentagon is 4608 feet.

Since this method would not work if you wanted to find the product of $\frac{2}{3}$ and $-\frac{2}{5}$ or the product of -5 and -0.3, you can use the following patterns to discover a rule for multiplying rational numbers.

$\frac{2}{3} \times \frac{2}{5} = \frac{4}{15}$ $\qquad -5 \cdot 0.3 = -1.5$

$\frac{2}{3} \times \frac{1}{5} = \frac{2}{15}$ $\qquad -5 \cdot 0.2 = -1.0$

$\frac{2}{3} \times \frac{0}{5} = \frac{0}{15}$ $\qquad -5 \cdot 0.1 = -0.5$

$\frac{2}{3} \times \left(-\frac{1}{5}\right) = -\frac{2}{15}$ $\qquad -5 \cdot 0 = 0$

$\frac{2}{3} \times \left(-\frac{2}{5}\right) = -\frac{4}{15}$ $\qquad -5 \cdot (-0.1) = 0.5$

$-5 \cdot (-0.2) = 1.0$

$-5 \cdot (-0.3) = 1.5$

The examples on the previous page suggest the following rules.

Multiplying Two Rational Numbers	**The product of two numbers having the *same sign* is positive. The product of two numbers having *different signs* is negative.**

Example 1 **Find each product.**

a. $(-9.8)4$

$(-9.8)4 = -39.2$

Estimate: $(-10)4 = -40$

Since the factors have different signs, the product is negative.

b. $\left(-\frac{3}{4}\right)\left(-\frac{2}{3}\right)$

Estimate: $(-1)\left(-\frac{1}{2}\right) = \frac{1}{2}$

$\left(-\frac{3}{4}\right)\left(-\frac{2}{3}\right) = \frac{6}{12}$ or $\frac{1}{2}$

Since the factors have the same sign, the product is positive.

Sometimes you need to evaluate expressions that contain rational numbers.

Example 2 **Evaluate $a\left(\frac{5}{6}\right)^2$ if $a = 2$.**

$a\left(\frac{5}{6}\right)^2 = 2\left(\frac{5}{6} \cdot \frac{5}{6}\right)$ *Replace a with 2.*

$= 2\left(\frac{25}{36}\right)$ *Multiply.*

$= \frac{\overset{1}{\cancel{2}}}{1}\left(\frac{25}{\underset{18}{\cancel{36}}}\right)$ or $\frac{25}{18}$

You may need to simplify expressions by multiplying rational numbers.

Example 3 **Simplify each expression.**

a. $(2b)(-3a)$

$(2b)(-3a) = 2(-3)ab$

$= -6ab$

Commutative and associative properties of multiplication

b. $3x(-3y) + (-6x)(-2y)$

$3x(-3y) + (-6x)(-2y) = -9xy + 12xy$ *Multiply.*

$= 3xy$ *Combine like terms.*

Notice that multiplying a number or expression by -1 results in the opposite of the number or expression.

$-1(4) = -4$ $(1.5)(-1) = -1.5$ $(-1)(-3m) = 3m$

Multiplicative Property of −1	**The product of any number and −1 is its additive inverse.** $-1(a) = -a$ **and** $a(-1) = -a$

To find the product of three or more numbers, you may want to first group the numbers in pairs.

Example 4 Find $\left(-\frac{3}{4}\right)\left(-4\frac{1}{3}\right)\left(3\frac{2}{5}\right)(4)(-1)$.

$$\left(-\frac{3}{4}\right)\left(-4\frac{1}{3}\right)\left(3\frac{2}{5}\right)(4)(-1) = \left[\left(-\frac{3}{4}\right)(4)\right]\left[\left(-4\frac{1}{3}\right)(-1)\right]\left(3\frac{2}{5}\right)$$ *Commutative and associative properties*

$$= (-3)\left(4\frac{1}{3}\right)\left(3\frac{2}{5}\right)$$

$$= \left(-\frac{\overset{1}{\cancel{3}}}{1}\right)\left(\frac{13}{\underset{1}{\cancel{3}}}\right)\left(\frac{17}{5}\right)$$

$$= -\frac{221}{5} \text{ or } -44\frac{1}{5}$$

You can multiply any matrix by a constant. This is called **scalar multiplication.** When scalar multiplication is performed, each element is multiplied by that constant and a new matrix is formed.

Scalar Multiplication of a Matrix

$$m\begin{bmatrix} a & b & c \\ d & e & f \end{bmatrix} = \begin{bmatrix} ma & mb & mc \\ md & me & mf \end{bmatrix}$$

Example 5

APPLICATION

Airlines

From July 3 through July 6, 1995, a major airline quoted round-trip coach fares, in dollars, to and from the selected cities below.

	Chicago	Dallas	Las Vegas
Atlanta	**$198.00**	**$198.00**	**$1214.00**
New York	**$246.00**	**$1224.00**	**$1342.00**

Suppose the other major airlines lower fares and begin an airfare war. To increase their air travel, the original airline decides to lower their fares by 30% or $\frac{3}{10}$. Find the new fares for travel to the cities above.

To find the new fares, you can use scalar multiplication. If fares are reduced by $\frac{3}{10}$, travelers will pay $1 - \frac{3}{10}$ or $\frac{7}{10}$ of the original price. Multiply to find the discount prices.

$$\frac{7}{10}\begin{bmatrix} 198.00 & 198.00 & 1214.00 \\ 246.00 & 1224.00 & 1342.00 \end{bmatrix} = \begin{bmatrix} 138.60 & 138.60 & 849.80 \\ 172.20 & 856.80 & 939.40 \end{bmatrix}$$

The new fares are shown below.

	Chicago	Dallas	Las Vegas
Atlanta	$138.60	$138.60	$849.80
New York	$172.20	$856.80	$939.40

CHECK FOR UNDERSTANDING

Communicating Mathematics

Study the lesson. Then complete the following.

1. **List** the conditions under which each statement is true. Then give an example that verifies your conditions.
   a. ab is positive. **b.** ab is negative. **c.** ab is equal to 0.
2. **Explain** what you can conclude about a if each statement is true.
   a. a^2 is positive. **b.** a^3 is positive. **c.** a^3 is negative.
3. If $a = -2$, which is greater, $a + a^2$ or -4?

MODELING MATHEMATICS

4. **Write** a multiplication sentence for the model at the right.

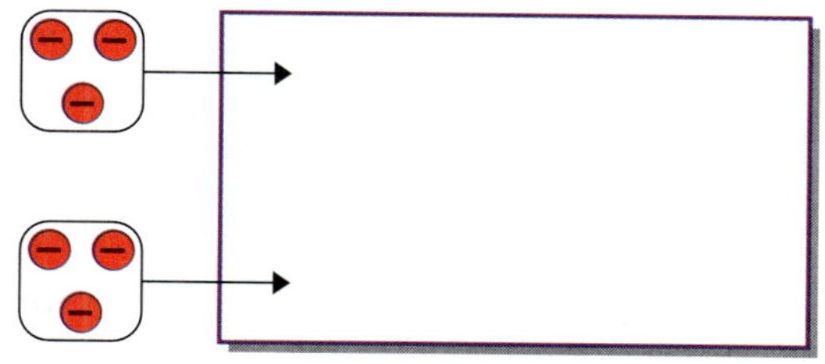

Guided Practice

Find each product.

5. $6(-3)$
6. $(-4)(-8)$
7. $(-4)(2)(-3)$
8. $\left(\frac{7}{3}\right)\left(\frac{7}{3}\right)$
9. $\left(-\frac{4}{5}\right)\left(-\frac{1}{5}\right)(-5)$
10. $\left(\frac{3}{5}\right)\left(-\frac{4}{7}\right)$

Evaluate each expression if $x = \frac{1}{2}$ and $y = -\frac{2}{3}$.

11. $3y - 4x$
12. x^2y

Simplify.

13. $5s(-6t) + 2s(-8t)$
14. $6x(-7y) + (-3x)(-5y)$

Find each product.

15. $3\begin{bmatrix} -2 & 4 \\ -1 & 5 \end{bmatrix}$
16. $-5\begin{bmatrix} -1 & 0 \\ 4.5 & 8 \\ 3.2 & -4 \end{bmatrix}$

17. **Business** Employees of a company are reimbursed for the "wear and tear" that occurs to their car while on company business. One employee's odometer read 19,438.6 at the beginning of the day and 19,534.1 at the end of the day. How much should the employee be reimbursed if the rate is \$0.30 per mile?

EXERCISES

Practice

Find each product.

18. $6(13)$
19. $(-5)(12)$
20. $(-7)(-6)$
21. $\left(-\frac{8}{9}\right)\left(\frac{9}{8}\right)$
22. $-\frac{5}{6}\left(-\frac{2}{5}\right)$
23. $(-5)\left(-\frac{2}{5}\right)$
24. $(-100)(-3.6)$
25. $(-2.93)(-0.003)$
26. $(-5)(3)(-4)$
27. $\left(\frac{2}{3}\right)\left(\frac{3}{5}\right)(-3)$
28. $\left(-\frac{7}{12}\right)\left(\frac{6}{7}\right)\left(-\frac{3}{4}\right)$
29. $\frac{6}{11}\left(-\frac{33}{34}\right)$
30. $(-0.075)(-5.5)$
31. $(-5.8)(-6.425)(2.3)$
32. $(-4)(0)(-2)(-3)$
33. $\frac{3}{5}(5)(-2)\left(-\frac{1}{2}\right)$
34. $(3)(-4)(-1)(-2)$
35. $\frac{2}{11}(-11)(-4)\left(-\frac{3}{4}\right)$

Evaluate each expression if $m = -\frac{2}{3}$, $n = \frac{1}{2}$, $p = -3\frac{3}{4}$, and $q = 2\frac{1}{6}$.

36. $6m$
37. nq
38. $2m - 3n$
39. $pq - m$
40. $m^2\left(-\frac{1}{4}\right)$
41. $n^2(q + 2)$

Simplify.

42. $-2a(-3c) + (-6y)(6r)$

43. $(5t)(-6r) - (-4s)$

44. $7m(-3n) + 3m(-4n)$

45. $5(2x - x) + 4(x + 3x)$

46. $(-6b)(-3c) - (-9a)(7b)$

47. $3.2(5x - y) - 0.3(-1.6x + 7y)$

INTEGRATION
Discrete Mathematics

Find each product.

48. $-7\begin{bmatrix} -1 & 8.2 & 0 \\ 4 & 5.6 & -1 \\ 3.2 & 7 & 7 \end{bmatrix}$

49. $\frac{1}{2}\begin{bmatrix} 4 & 12 & 6 \\ 5 & 10 & 2 \end{bmatrix}$

50. $4\begin{bmatrix} 1.3 & -2 & -4 \\ 0.5 & -0.3 & 5 \\ 6.6 & 2.1 & -8 \end{bmatrix}$

51. $-4\begin{bmatrix} 2.25 & -5.67 \\ 5.6 & 2.5 \\ -7.2 & -2.78 \end{bmatrix}$

52. $-8\begin{bmatrix} 0.2 & 4.5 \\ -1.4 & -3 \\ 3 & 2.4 \\ -7 & -3.2 \end{bmatrix}$

53. $\frac{2}{3}\begin{bmatrix} 9 & 27 & 6 \\ 0 & 3 & 4 \end{bmatrix}$

Critical Thinking

54. If a product has an even number of negative factors, what must be true of the product?

55. If a product has an odd number of negative factors, what must be true of the product?

Applications and Problem Solving

56. **Discrete Mathematics** A *geometric sequence* is a sequence in which the ratio of any term divided by the term before it is the same for any two terms.
    a. Write the next three terms in the geometric sequence 9, 3, 1, $\frac{1}{3}$, ...
    b. What is the common ratio?
    c. Write the first five terms in a geometric sequence in which the first term is -6 and the common ratio is 0.5. Then find the sum of the five terms.

57. **Construction** Ryduff Builders is building homes in a new residential development. The building code for the development states that lots must have a minimum of 1250 square feet and no dimension can be less than 20 feet.
    a. Determine whether a plot plan would be approved if it measured 32 feet by 38 feet. Explain your reasoning.
    b. Determine whether a plot plan would be approved if it measured 19 feet by 70 feet. Explain your reasoning.
    c. If one dimension of a plot plan was 42 feet, find another dimension that would satisfy the building code conditions.

58. **Civics** The length of a flag is called the *fly,* and the width is called the *hoist.* The blue rectangle in the United States flag is called the *union.* The length of the union is $\frac{2}{5}$ of the fly, and the width is $\frac{7}{13}$ of the hoist. If the fly of a United States flag is 3 feet, how long is the union?

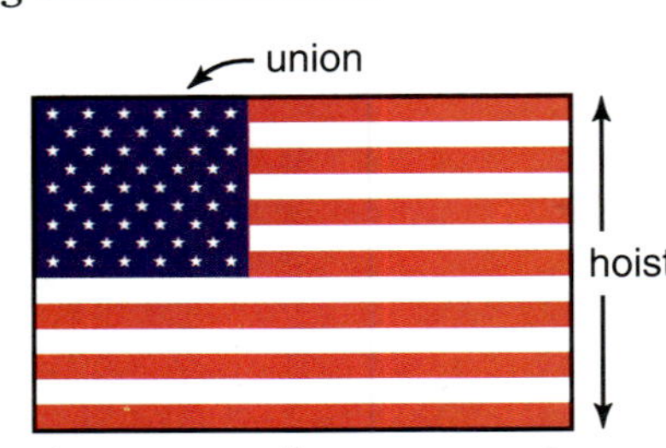

Mixed Review

59. Find $5.7 + (-7.9)$. (Lesson 2–5)

60. Replace _?_ with <, >, or = to make 12 _?_ 15 − 7 true. (Lesson 2–4)

61. Evaluate $a - 12$ if $a = -8$. (Lesson 2–3)

62. **Statistics** State the scale you would use to make a line plot for the following data. Then draw the line plot. (Lesson 2–2)

4, 9, 2, 2, 15, 7, 6, 6, 9, 12, 1, 3, 2, 11, 10, 2, 6, 4, 12, 13

63. Find $6 + (-13)$. If necessary, use a number line. (Lesson 2–1)

64. Write an algebraic expression for *five times the sum of x and y decreased by z.* (Lesson 1–8)

65. Find the solution set for $y + 3 > 8$ if the replacement set is {3, 4, 5, 6, 7}. (Lesson 1–5)

66. **Statistics** Suppose the number 27,878 is rounded to 27,900 and plotted using stem 27 and leaf 9. Write the stem and leaf for each number below if the numbers are part of the same set of data. (Lesson 1–4)
   a. 13,245 b. 35,684 c. 153,436

67. Evaluate $6(4^3 + 2^2)$. (Lesson 1–3)

68. **Geometry** Write an expression that represents the total number of small cubes in the large cube shown at the right. Then evaluate the expression. (Lesson 1–1)

WORKING ON THE

In•ves•ti•ga•tion

Refer to the Investigation on pages 68–69.

the Greenhouse Effect

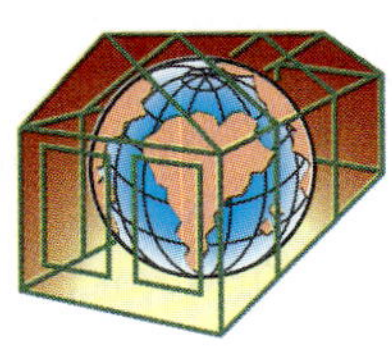

Without a heat-trapping blanket of naturally occurring CO_2, it is believed that Earth would have an average surface temperature of −17°C, instead of its current average, 15°C. There is evidence that Mars has little CO_2 in its atmosphere, and its temperature never exceeds −31°C. At the other extreme, Venus, with lots of CO_2, has an average temperature of 454°C.

1 What would the difference in temperature be between Earth with CO_2 and Earth without CO_2? Do you think life could exist on Earth without CO_2? Explain.

2 What is the difference in temperature between Mars and Earth without CO_2? Explain what other factors contribute to the difference in temperature.

3 What is the difference in temperature between Venus and Mars? Explain what other factors contribute to the difference in temperature.

4 Make a chart that shows the three planets and their temperatures with CO_2 in their atmospheres and with little or no CO_2. Assume that the differences in the temperatures for the other planets would be the same as the difference in Earth's temperatures with CO_2 and without CO_2. You will use this information later on as you work on the Investigation.

Add the results of your work to your Investigation Folder.

2–7 Dividing Rational Numbers

What **YOU'LL LEARN**

- To divide rational numbers.

Why **IT'S IMPORTANT**

You can divide rational numbers to help you solve problems involving drafting, nursing, and economics.

APPLICATION
Aviation

Vicki Van Meter had a lot to write in her report about her summer vacation of 1993. At 12 years old, inspired by Amelia Earhart, she became the youngest female to pilot a plane across the Atlantic Ocean. Vicki did all of the flying, navigation, and communication for her 3200-kilometer flight aboard a single-engine Cessna 210. She also had to be concerned about how supplies and fuel were loaded onto the plane.

Location	Weight (pounds)	Arm (inches)	Moment
Empty weight	2181	80	174,480
Front seats	340	85	28,900
Rear seats	125	117	14,625
Oil	30	−24	−720
Fuel	444	75	33,300
Total	3120		250,585

Before any small aircraft can take off, the pilot must be sure that the aircraft is loaded so that the center of gravity is within certain safe limits. If it is, the pilot is ready for takeoff. If not, the weight must be rebalanced.

You can use the table at the left to find the center of gravity for a particular aircraft. The safe limit for this aircraft is 82.1. For each location, the weight and the arm are multiplied to find the moment.

Now add the moments, divide by the total weight, and round to the nearest tenth to find the center of gravity.

Total Moments		*Total Weight*		*Center of Gravity*
250,585	÷	3120	≈	80.3

Since 80.3 is less than 82.1, the aircraft is safe and ready for takeoff.

You already know that the quotient of two positive numbers is positive. But how do you determine the sign of the quotient when negative numbers are involved? Since multiplication and division are inverse operations, the rule for finding the sign of the quotient of two numbers is similar to the rule for finding the sign of the product. Study these patterns.

$$-5 \cdot 8 = -40 \qquad -40 \div 8 = -5$$

$$-10 \cdot \left(-\frac{1}{2}\right) = 5 \qquad 5 \div \left(-\frac{1}{2}\right) = -10$$

These examples suggest the following rules.

Dividing Two *Rational Numbers*	**The quotient of two numbers having the *same sign* is positive.** **The quotient of two numbers having *different signs* is negative.**

Example 1 **Find each quotient.**

a. $-75 \div (-15)$

This division problem may also be written as $\frac{-75}{-15}$.

$\frac{-75}{-15} = 5$ *The fraction bar indicates division.*

Since the signs are the same, the quotient is positive.

b. $\frac{72}{-8}$

$\frac{72}{-8} = -9$ *Since the signs are different, the quotient is negative.*

Recall that you can change any division expression to an equivalent multiplication expression. To divide by any nonzero number, multiply by the reciprocal of that number.

Example 2 **Find each quotient.**

a. $\frac{1}{2} \div 5$

$\frac{1}{2} \div 5 = \frac{1}{2} \cdot \frac{1}{5}$ *Multiply by $\frac{1}{5}$, the reciprocal of 5.*

$= \frac{1}{10}$ *The signs are the same, so the product is positive.*

b. $-\frac{6}{7} \div 3$

$-\frac{6}{7} \div 3 = -\frac{6}{7} \cdot \frac{1}{3}$ *Multiply by $\frac{1}{3}$, the reciprocal of 3.*

$= -\frac{6}{21}$ or $-\frac{2}{7}$ *The signs are different, so the product is negative.*

Example 3

APPLICATION

Nursing

Three of the measurements nurses commonly use are cubic centimeters (cc), drops, and grains. Use this information to solve the following.

a. A doctor orders $\frac{1}{400}$ of a grain of medicine to be given to a patient. The nurse has a vial labeled $\frac{1}{200}$ grain per cc. How many cc of the medicine should the nurse give the patient?

b. The doctor also prescribes a 1000-cc intravenous (IV) pouch of fluid to be given to the patient over an 8-hour period. If there are 15 drops in 1 cc, for how many drops per minute should the nurse set the IV?

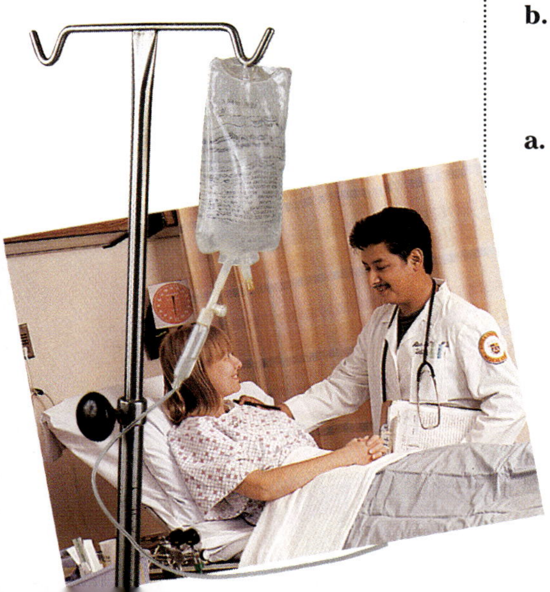

a. How many cc are in $\frac{1}{400}$ of a grain? Divide $\frac{1}{400}$ grain by $\frac{1}{200}$ grain/cc.

$$\frac{1}{400} \text{ grain} \div \frac{1}{200} \text{ grain/cc} = \frac{1 \text{ grain}}{400} \cdot \frac{200 \text{ cc}}{1 \text{ grain}}$$

$$= \frac{\overset{1}{\cancel{1 \text{ grain}}}}{\underset{2}{\cancel{400}}} \cdot \frac{\overset{1}{\cancel{200}} \text{ cc}}{\underset{1}{\cancel{1 \text{ grain}}}}$$

$$= \frac{1}{2} \text{ cc}$$

The nurse should give the patient $\frac{1}{2}$ cc of the medicine.

(continued on the next page)

b. $\dfrac{1000 \text{ cc}}{8 \text{ h}} = \left(\dfrac{\overset{125}{\cancel{1000} \text{ cc}}}{\underset{1}{\cancel{8 \text{ h}}}}\right)\left(\dfrac{\overset{1}{\cancel{15}} \text{ drops}}{1 \cancel{\text{cc}}}\right)\left(\dfrac{1 \cancel{\text{h}}}{\underset{4}{\cancel{60}} \text{ min}}\right)$ *There are 15 drops in 1 cc and 60 minutes in 1 hour.*

$= \dfrac{125 \text{ drops}}{4 \text{ min}}$

$= 31\frac{1}{4}$ drops/min

The nurse should set the IV for $31\frac{1}{4}$ drops per minute.

If a fraction has one or more fractions in the numerator or denominator, it is called a **complex fraction.** To simplify a complex fraction, rewrite it as a division sentence.

Example 4 **Write each fraction in simplest form.**

a. $\dfrac{\frac{2}{3}}{8}$

Rewrite the fraction as $\frac{2}{3} \div 8$, since fractions indicate division.

$\frac{2}{3} \div 8 = \frac{2}{3} \cdot \frac{1}{8}$ *Multiply by $\frac{1}{8}$, the reciprocal of 8.*

$= \frac{2}{24}$ or $\frac{1}{12}$

b. $\dfrac{-5}{\frac{3}{7}}$

Rewrite the fraction as $-5 \div \frac{3}{7}$.

$-5 \div \frac{3}{7} = -5 \times \frac{7}{3}$ *Multiply by $\frac{7}{3}$, the reciprocal of $\frac{3}{7}$.*

$= -\frac{35}{3}$ or $-11\frac{2}{3}$ *The signs are different, so the product is negative.*

You can use the distributive property to simplify fractional expressions.

Example 5 **Simplify $\dfrac{-3a + 16}{4}$.**

Method 1

$\dfrac{-3a + 16}{4} = (-3a + 16) \div 4$

$= (-3a + 16)\left(\frac{1}{4}\right)$ *To divide by 4, multiply by $\frac{1}{4}$.*

$= -3a\left(\frac{1}{4}\right) + 16\left(\frac{1}{4}\right)$ *Distributive property*

$= -\frac{3}{4}a + 4$

Method 2

$\dfrac{-3a + 16}{4} = -\dfrac{3a}{4} + \dfrac{16}{4}$

$= -\frac{3}{4}a + 4$

CHECK FOR UNDERSTANDING

Communicating Mathematics

Study the lesson. Then complete the following.

1. **Compare** multiplying rational numbers to dividing rational numbers. How are the two operations similar?
2. **Complete** the sentence: Dividing by any number, except zero, is the same as ___?___.
3. **Find** a value for x if $\frac{1}{x} > x$.
4. **You Decide** Simone says that $-\frac{4}{5}$ is equal to $\frac{-4}{-5}$. Miguel says that $-\frac{4}{5}$ is equal to $\frac{-4}{5}$ or $\frac{4}{-5}$. Which one is correct, and why?

Guided Practice

Simplify.

5. $\frac{32}{-8}$
6. $\frac{-77}{11}$
7. $-\frac{3}{4} \div 8$
8. $\frac{2}{3} \div 9$
9. $\frac{\frac{-5}{6}}{8}$
10. $\frac{54s}{6}$
11. $\frac{-300x}{50}$
12. $\frac{6b + 12}{6}$
13. **Money** On October 10, 1994, *USA Today* reported that the United States government spends about \$168 million per hour. Stanley Newberg, who came to the United States from Austria in 1906, died in 1994 at age 81 and left the government \$5.6 million. How long did it take the government to spend Mr. Newberg's money?

EXERCISES

Practice

Simplify.

14. $\frac{-36}{4}$
15. $\frac{-96}{-16}$
16. $-9 \div \left(-\frac{10}{17}\right)$
17. $-\frac{2}{3} \div 12$
18. $-64 \div (-8)$
19. $-\frac{3}{4} \div 12$
20. $-18 \div 9$
21. $78 \div (-13)$
22. $-108 \div (-9)$
23. $-\frac{2}{3} \div 8$
24. $\frac{-1}{3} \div (-4)$
25. $-9 \div \left(-\frac{10}{27}\right)$
26. $\frac{\frac{5}{6}}{-10}$
27. $-\frac{7}{\frac{3}{5}}$
28. $\frac{-5}{\frac{2}{7}}$
29. $\frac{-650m}{10}$
30. $\frac{81c}{-9}$
31. $\frac{8r + 24}{8}$
32. $\frac{6a + 24}{6}$
33. $\frac{40a + 50b}{-2}$
34. $\frac{-5x + (-10y)}{-5}$
35. $\frac{42c - 18d}{-3}$
36. $\frac{-8f + (-16g)}{8}$
37. $\frac{-4a + (-16b)}{4}$

Evaluate if $a = 5$, $b = -6$, and $c = -1.5$.

38. $\frac{b}{c}$
39. $b \div a$
40. $(a + b) \div c$
41. $(a + b + c) \div 3$
42. $\frac{c}{a}$
43. $\frac{ab}{ac}$

Critical Thinking

44. The $\boxed{1/x}$ key on a scientific calculator is called the *reciprocal key*. When this key is pressed, the calculator replaces the number on the display with its reciprocal.

a. Enter 0 and then press the reciprocal key. What happened? Explain.

b. Enter a number and then press the reciprocal key twice. What happened? Predict what will happen if you press the key n times.

c. Enter 6.435 $\boxed{1/x}$ $\boxed{\times}$ 6.435 $\boxed{=}$. What is the result? Why?

Applications and Problem Solving

45. Drafting Sofia Fernandez is making a dresser for her little sister's nursery. The dresser will be 30 inches high and will have a 4-inch-thick base and a $1\frac{1}{2}$-inch-thick top. Four equal-sized drawers are to fit in the remaining space, with $\frac{3}{4}$ inch between each drawer.

a. Sketch the dresser, labeling each part.

b. What is the height of each drawer?

46. Economics Kim Lee's shoe store has a buy one, get one half-price sale. You must pay full price for the more expensive pair of shoes in order to receive half off the second pair. If you buy a single pair of shoes, you get $\frac{1}{5}$ off. Together, Sharon and LaShondra find five pair of shoes that cost \$45.99, \$23.88, \$36.99, \$19.99, and \$14.99. How should they pay for the shoes in order to get the best buy?

47. Science *Precision* is the degree of exactness to which a measurement can be reproduced. It is determined by subtracting the least measurement from the greatest measurement, and dividing by 2. Suppose you conducted an experiment to determine the length of a piece of lumber. After measuring several times, you have recorded measurements ranging between 17.239 cm and 17.561 cm, inclusive.

a. Use the plus-or-minus symbol ($\pm$) to describe your measurements.

b. What was the precision of your measurement?

Mixed Review

48. Find $\left(-\frac{1}{5}\right)\left(\frac{3}{2}\right)(-2)$. (Lesson 2–6)

49. Evaluate $\frac{9}{4} + \frac{x}{6}$ if $x = -7$. (Lesson 2–5)

50. Name a fraction between $\frac{2}{3}$ and $\frac{7}{8}$ whose denominator is 24. (Lesson 2–4)

51. Let $A = \begin{bmatrix} 1 & 4 \\ 5 & 7 \end{bmatrix}$ and $B = \begin{bmatrix} -3 & 0 \\ -2 & 5 \end{bmatrix}$. (Lesson 2–3)

a. Find $A + B$. **b.** Find $A - B$.

52. Statistics The table below shows the mean scores for the mathematics portion of the Scholastic Assessment Test (SAT) by state for 1994. (Lesson 2–2)

SAT Mean Mathematics Scores, 1994

State	Score	State	Score	State	Score	State	Score	State	Score
AL	529	HI	480	MA	475	NM	528	SD	548
AK	477	ID	508	MI	537	NY	472	TN	535
AZ	496	IL	546	MN	562	NC	455	TX	474
AR	518	IN	466	MS	528	ND	559	UT	558
CA	482	IA	574	MO	532	OH	510	VT	472
CO	513	KS	550	MT	523	OK	537	VA	469
CT	472	KY	523	NE	543	OR	491	WA	488
DE	464	LA	530	NV	484	PA	462	WV	482
FL	466	ME	463	NH	486	RI	462	WI	557
GA	446	MD	479	NJ	475	SC	443	WY	521

Source: College Entrance Examination Board

a. What is the range of scores for the fifty states?

b. Make a line plot of the data.

c. Do the scores cluster around a certain number? If so, which ones?

53. Simplify $8b + 12(b + 2)$. (Lesson 1–7)

54. Name the multiplicative inverse of $\frac{4}{5}$. (Lesson 1–6)

55. Statistics The list below shows the prices of several 1995 models of sport utility vehicles, rounded to the nearest hundred dollars. (Lesson 1–4)

\$22,000	\$19,400	\$29,000	\$13,000	\$22,200	\$17,300
\$25,400	\$25,100	\$33,000	\$20,000	\$30,700	\$15,400
\$27,900	\$34,600	\$30,400	\$24,500	\$52,500	\$17,200

a. Make a stem-and-leaf plot of these data.

b. What was the least expensive price?

c. What was the most expensive price?

d. How many prices were over \$25,000?

MODELING MATHEMATICS

A Preview of Lesson 2–8

2–8A Estimating Square Roots

Materials: base-ten tiles

You can use base-ten tiles to model square roots. A **square root** is one of two identical factors of a number. For example, a square root of 144 is 12 since $12^2 = 144$.

Activity 1 Use base-ten tiles to find the square root of 121.

Step 1 Model 121 with base-ten tiles.

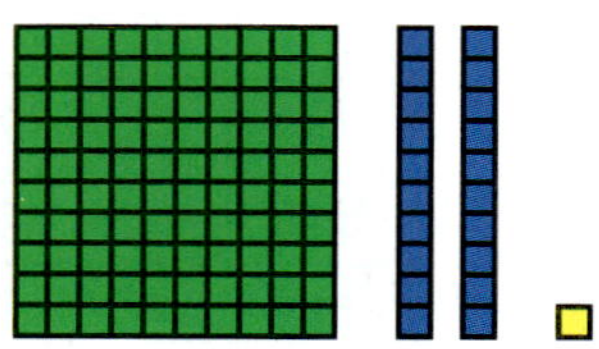

Step 2 Arrange the tiles into a square. The square root of 121 is 11 because $11^2 = 121$.

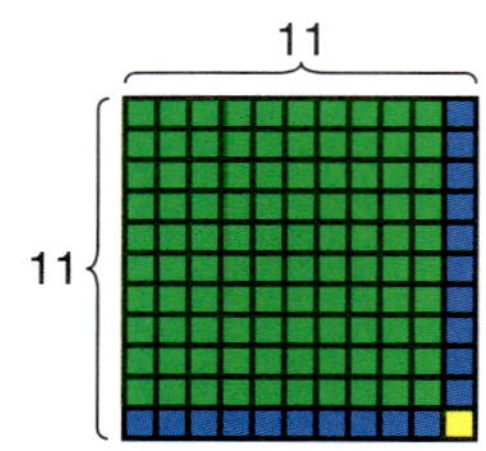

Activity 2 Use base-ten tiles to estimate the square root of 151.

Step 1 Model 151 with base-ten tiles.

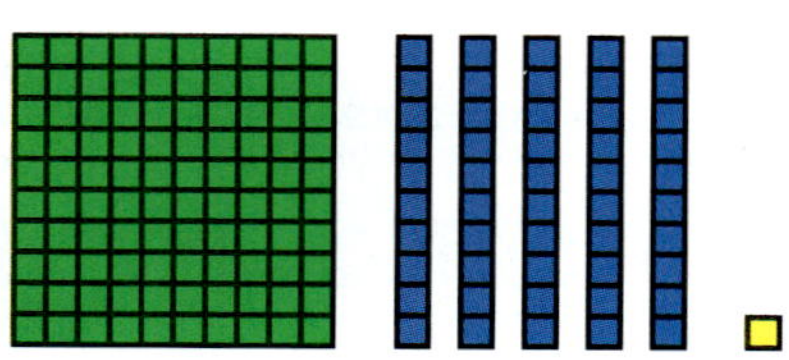

Step 2 Arrange the tiles into a square. The largest square possible has 144 tiles, with 7 tiles left over.

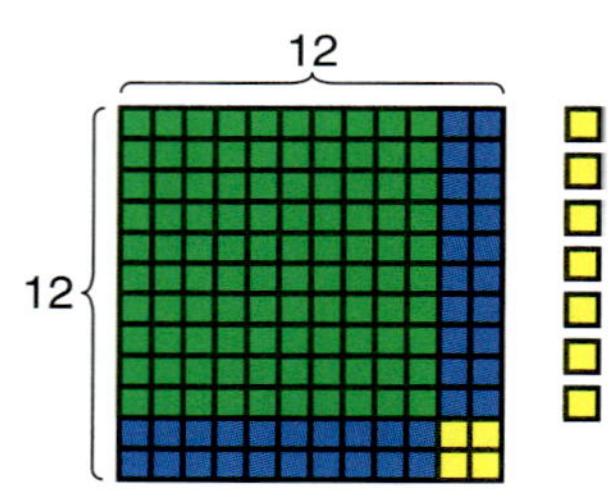

Trade a 10-tile for 10 1-tiles when necessary.

Step 3 Add tiles until you have the next larger square. You need to add 18 tiles. Since 151 is between 144 and 169, the square root of 151 is between 12 and 13.

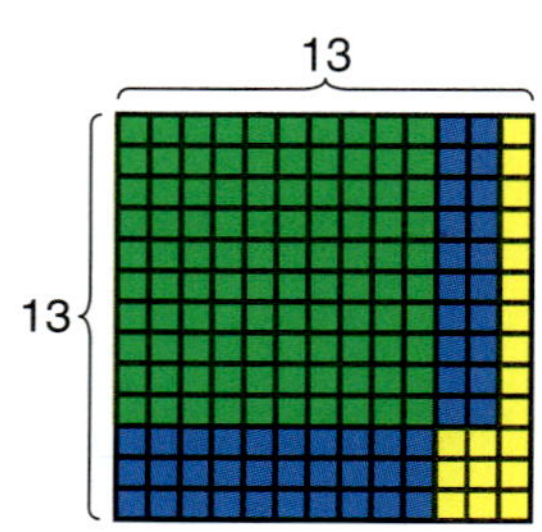

Model Use base-ten tiles to estimate the square root of each number.

1. 20 **2.** 450 **3.** 180 **4.** 200 **5.** 2

Write

6. If you list all of the factors of a number in numerical order, the square root of the number either is the middle number or lies between the two middle numbers. How can you use tiles to show this?

2-8 Square Roots and Real Numbers

What YOU'LL LEARN

- To find square roots,
- to classify numbers, and
- to graph solutions of inequalities on number lines.

Why IT'S IMPORTANT

You need to know the values of irrational numbers to solve problems involving traffic safety and flying.

CONNECTION

Biology

Swedish botanist Carolus Linnaeus (1707–1778) developed the system we use today to classify every kind of living thing according to common characteristics. For example, an African elephant is from the Mammalia Class and also from the Animalia Kingdom.

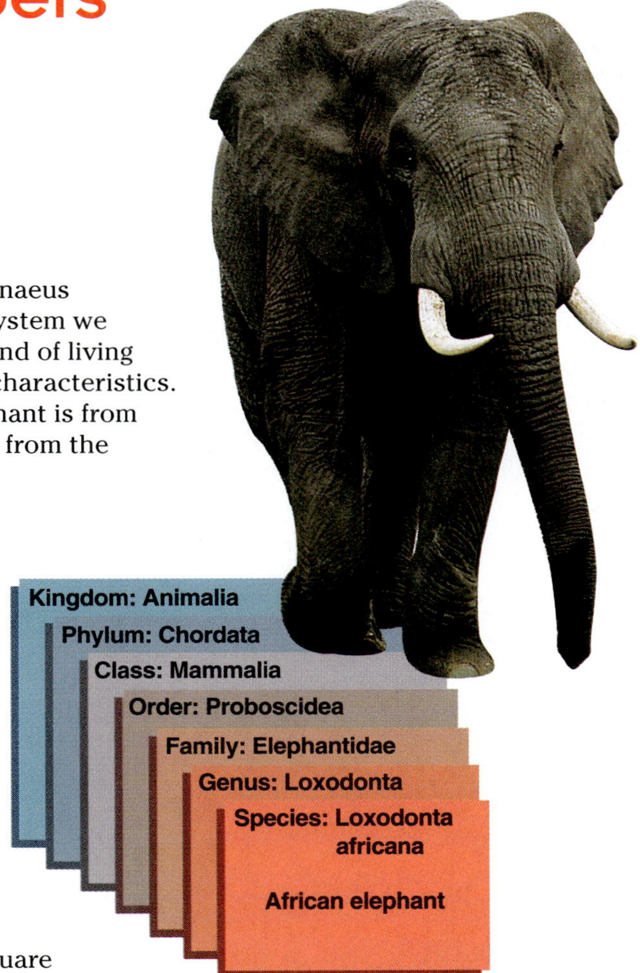

In mathematics, we classify numbers that have common characteristics. So far in this text, we have classified numbers as natural numbers, whole numbers, integers, and rational numbers.

Finding a square root of 81 is the same as finding a number whose square is 81.

The square roots of perfect squares are classified as rational numbers. A **square root** is one of two equal factors of a number. For example, one square root of 81 is 9 since $9 \cdot 9$ or 9^2 is 81. A rational number, like 81, whose square root is a rational number, is called a **perfect square**.

It is also true that $-9 \cdot (-9) = 81$. Therefore, -9 is another square root of 81.

$$9^2 = 9 \cdot 9$$
$$= 81$$

9^2 is read "nine squared" and means that 9 is used as a factor two times.

$$(-9)^2 = (-9)(-9)$$
$$= 81$$

-9 is used as a factor two times.

Definition of Square Root	If $x^2 = y$, then x is a square root of y.

The symbol $\sqrt{\ }$, called a **radical sign**, is used to indicate a nonnegative or **principal square root** of the expression under the radical sign.

$\sqrt{81} = 9$ — $\sqrt{81}$ indicates the *principal* square root of 81.

$-\sqrt{81} = -9$ — $\sqrt{-81}$ indicates the *negative* square root of 81.

$\pm\sqrt{81} = \pm 9$ — $\pm\sqrt{81}$ indicates *both* square roots of 81.

$\pm\sqrt{81}$ is read "plus or minus the square root of 81."

Example 1 **Find each square root.**

Some square roots can be found mentally.

a. $\sqrt{25}$

The symbol $\sqrt{25}$ represents the principal square root of 25.

Since $5^2 = 25$, you know that $\sqrt{25} = 5$.

b. $-\sqrt{144}$

The symbol $-\sqrt{144}$ represents the negative square root of 144.

Since $12^2 = 144$, you know that $-\sqrt{144} = -12$.

c. $\pm\sqrt{0.16}$

The symbol $\pm\sqrt{0.16}$ represents both square roots of 0.16.

Since $(0.4)^2 = 0.16$, you know that $\pm\sqrt{0.16} = \pm 0.4$.

Most scientific calculators have a *square root* key labeled [√] *or* [√x]. When you press this key, the number in the display is replaced by its principal square root.

Example 2 **Use a scientific calculator to evaluate each expression if $x = 2401$, $a = 147$, and $b = 78$.**

a. $\sqrt{x}$

$\sqrt{x} = \sqrt{2401}$ *Replace x with 2401.*

Enter: 2401 [2nd] [√x] 49

Therefore, $\sqrt{2401} = 49$.

b. $\pm\sqrt{a + b}$

$\pm\sqrt{a + b} = \pm\sqrt{147 + 78}$ *Replace a with 147 and b with 78.*

Enter: [(] 147 [+] 78 [)] [2nd] [√x] 15

Therefore, $\pm\sqrt{a + b}$ is $\pm$ 15.

Numbers such as $\sqrt{5}$ and $\sqrt{13}$ are the square roots of numbers that are *not* perfect squares. Notice what happens when you find these square roots with your calculator.

Enter: 5 [2nd] [√x] 2.236067978...

Enter: 13 [2nd] [√x] 3.605551275...

These numbers continue indefinitely without any pattern of repeating digits. These numbers are not rational numbers since they are not repeating or terminating decimals. Numbers like $\sqrt{5}$ and $\sqrt{13}$ are called **irrational numbers.**

Definition of an Irrational Number	**An irrational number is a number that *cannot* be expressed in the form $\frac{a}{b}$, where a and b are integers and $b \neq 0$.**

The set of rational numbers and the set of irrational numbers together form the set of **real numbers**. The Venn diagram at the right shows the relationships among natural numbers, whole numbers, integers, rational numbers, irrational numbers, and real numbers.

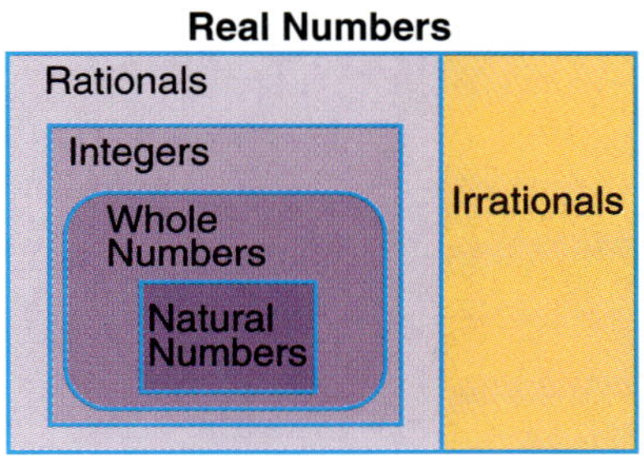

Example 3 **Name the set or sets of numbers to which each real number belongs.**

a. 0.8333333... This repeating decimal is a rational number since it is equivalent to $\frac{5}{6}$. *This number can also be expressed as $0.8\overline{3}$.*

b. $-\sqrt{16}$ Since $-\sqrt{16} = -4$, this number is an integer and a rational number.

c. $\frac{14}{2}$ Since $\frac{14}{2} = 7$, this number is an integer, a natural number, a whole number, and a rational number.

d. $\sqrt{120}$ Since $\sqrt{120} = 10.95445115...$, which is not a repeating or terminating decimal, this number is irrational.

The solutions to many real-world problems are irrational numbers.

Example 4

INTEGRATION
Geometry

The area of a square is 325 square inches. Find its perimeter to the nearest hundredth.

First find the length of each side. Since the area of a square is the length of the side squared, find the square root of 325.

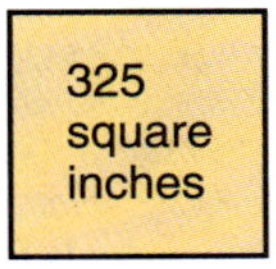

Enter: 325 [2nd] [$\sqrt{x}$] 18.02775638

The length of each side is about 18.02775638 inches. Use the formula $P = 4s$ to find the perimeter.

$P = 4s$
$= 4 \cdot 18.02775638$ *Replace s with 18.02775638.*

Enter: 18.02775638 [×] 4 [=] 72.11102655I

The perimeter is about 72.11 inches.

You have graphed rational numbers on number lines. Yet, if you graphed all of the rational numbers, the number line would still not be complete. The irrational numbers complete the number line. The graph of all real numbers is the entire number line. This is illustrated by the **completeness property.**

Completeness Property for Points on the Number Line	**Each real number corresponds to exactly one point on the number line. Each point on the number line corresponds to exactly one real number.**

Recall that equations like $x - 5 = 11$ are open sentences. Inequalities like $x < 6$ are also considered to be open sentences. To solve $x < 6$, determine what replacements for x make $x < 6$ true. All numbers less than 6 make the inequality true. This can be shown by the solution set {real numbers less than 6}. Not only does this include integers like 3, 0, and -4, but it also includes all rational numbers less than 6 such as $\frac{1}{2}$, $-5\frac{3}{8}$, and -3 and all irrational numbers less than 6 such as $\sqrt{5}$, $\sqrt{3}$, and π.

Example 5 **Graph each solution set.**

a. $y \geq -7$

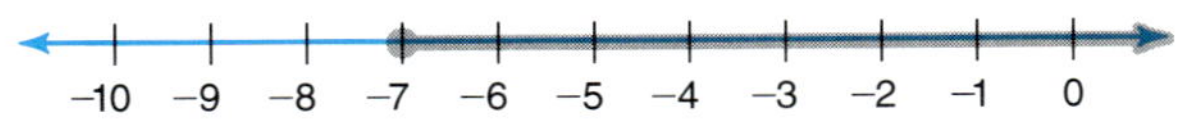

The heavy arrow indicates that all numbers to the right of -7 are included. The *dot* indicates that the point corresponding to -7 is included in the graph of the solution set.

b. $p \neq \frac{3}{4}$

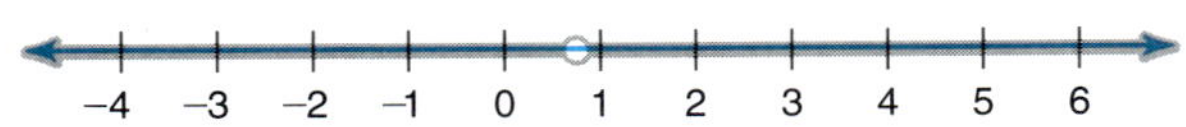

The heavy arrows indicate that all numbers to the left and to the right of $\frac{3}{4}$ are included in the graph of the solution set. The *circle* indicates that the point corresponding to $\frac{3}{4}$ is not included in the graph.

CHECK FOR UNDERSTANDING

Communicating Mathematics

Study the lesson. Then complete the following.

Deep down inside, Coach Knott had always wanted to be a math teacher.

1. You have studied the following sets of numbers: integers, irrational, natural, rational, real, and whole numbers. Draw a number line and label at least one number from each set of numbers. Indicate which number is from each set.

2. Study the comic at the left. Explain why it is humorous.

3. **Determine** whether 36 is a perfect square. If it is, to what set of numbers does $\sqrt{36}$ belong?

4. **Explain** why 3 and -3 are both square roots of 9.

5. **Write** an inequality for the graph below.

MATH JOURNAL

6. **Write** a paragraph explaining the difference between rational and irrational numbers to a classmate.

Guided Practice

Find each square root. Use a calculator if necessary. Round to the nearest hundredth if the result is not a whole number.

7. $\sqrt{64}$
8. $-\sqrt{36}$
9. $\sqrt{122}$
10. $\pm\sqrt{0.08}$

Evaluate each expression. Use a calculator if necessary. Round to the nearest hundredth if the result is not a whole number.

11. $\sqrt{x}$, if $x = 256$
12. $\sqrt{y}$, if $y = 151$

Name the set or sets of numbers to which each real number belongs. Use N for natural numbers, W for whole numbers, Z for integers, Q for rational numbers, and I for irrational numbers.

13. $-\frac{3}{4}$
14. $\frac{8}{4}$
15. 0.6666...
16. $\sqrt{13}$

Graph the solution set of each inequality on a number line.

17. $p < 7$
18. $r \geq -3$
19. $x \neq 2$

20. **Discrete Mathematics** In the geometric sequence 5, 15, __?__, 135, 405, the missing number is called the *geometric mean* of 15 and 135. It can be found by evaluating $\sqrt{ab}$, where a and b are the numbers on either side of the geometric mean. Find the missing number.

EXERCISES

Practice

Find each square root. Use a calculator if necessary. Round to the nearest hundredth if the result is not a whole number or simple fraction.

21. $\sqrt{169}$
22. $\sqrt{0.0049}$
23. $\sqrt{\frac{4}{9}}$
24. $-\sqrt{289}$
25. $\sqrt{420}$
26. $\sqrt{\frac{25}{64}}$
27. $\sqrt{225}$
28. $\pm\sqrt{1158}$
29. $-\sqrt{625}$
30. $\sqrt{1.96}$
31. $\sqrt{\frac{9}{25}}$
32. $-\sqrt{5.80}$

Evaluate each expression. Use a calculator if necessary. Round to the nearest hundredth if the result is not a whole number.

33. $\sqrt{x}$, if $x = 87$
34. $\pm\sqrt{t}$, if $t = 529$
35. $-\sqrt{m}$, if $m = 2209$
36. $\sqrt{c + d}$, if $c = 23$ and $d = 56$
37. $-\sqrt{np}$, if $n = 16$ and $p = 25$
38. $\pm\sqrt{\frac{a}{b}}$, if $a = 64$ and $b = 4$

Name the set or sets of numbers to which each real number belongs. Use N for natural numbers, W for whole numbers, Z for integers, Q for rational numbers, and I for irrational numbers.

39. $-\sqrt{49}$
40. 0
41. 0.4583
42. $0.\overline{3}$
43. $-\frac{1}{2}$
44. $\sqrt{49}$
45. 0.6666
46. $\frac{10}{5}$
47. $\sqrt{37}$
48. 3.14
49. $\frac{3}{5}$
50. 5

Graph the solution set of each inequality on a number line.

51. $y > -2$ **52.** $x < 1$ **53.** $p \geq -4$

54. $n \neq 6$ **55.** $c > -12$ **56.** $r \leq 4.5$

57. $b \geq -5.2$ **58.** $y \neq \frac{3}{4}$ **59.** $s \leq 5\frac{1}{2}$

60. Geometry The volume of a rectangular solid is 100 cm^3. Its height is the product of its length and width. The base of the solid is a square.

a. Draw the solid from two different perspectives.

b. Find the dimensions of the solid. Use a calculator as needed and round decimal answers to the nearest hundredth.

Critical Thinking

61. Determine whether $\sqrt{733}$ is an irrational number. If it is, name two consecutive integers between which its graph lies on the number line.

62. Find all numbers of the form $\sqrt{n}$ such that n is a natural number and the graph of $\sqrt{n}$ lies between each pair of numbers on the number line.

a. 3 and 4 **b.** 5.25 and 5.5

Applications and Problem Solving

63. Military The formula to determine the distance d in miles that an object can be seen on a clear day on the surface of the ocean is $d = 1.4\sqrt{h}$, where h is the height in feet the viewer's eyes are above the surface of the water. About how many miles can the pilot of a U.S. Coast Guard plane see if he is flying at 1275 feet?

a. Write an equation to represent the distance. Then approximate the distance mentally.

b. Use a calculator to find the exact distance.

64. Traffic Safety When investigating a traffic accident, police officers often need to estimate how fast a car was traveling by measuring the length of its skid marks. The formula $s = \sqrt{24d}$ can be used to estimate the speed on a dry, concrete road. In the formula, s is the speed in miles per hour, and d is the distance in feet the car skidded after its brakes were applied. What was the approximate speed of a car that left skid marks 40 feet long?

a. Write an equation to represent the speed. Then approximate the speed mentally.

b. Use a calculator to find the exact speed.

65. Math History One of the great mathematical challenges in early mathematics was to find an exact value for π. Today, 3.14 and $\frac{22}{7}$ are two frequently used approximations for π. In the third century, Chinese mathematician Liu Hui used the number $3\frac{7}{50}$ as an approximation of π. The Italian mathematician Leonardo Fibonacci used $\frac{864}{275}$ as an approximation of π. Which mathematician's approximation was closer to the generally-accepted approximation of π, 3.141592654...?

66. Business The Spanish Club at Alexander Manor High School is selling chocolate bars to raise money for a trip to Mexico. The bars are sold only by the case, with 24 bars per case. Each bar costs \$1.00. The club's goal is to raise at least \$2450 in gross sales.

a. How many cases of chocolate bars must the club sell in order to reach or exceed their goal?

b. Graph the solution set.

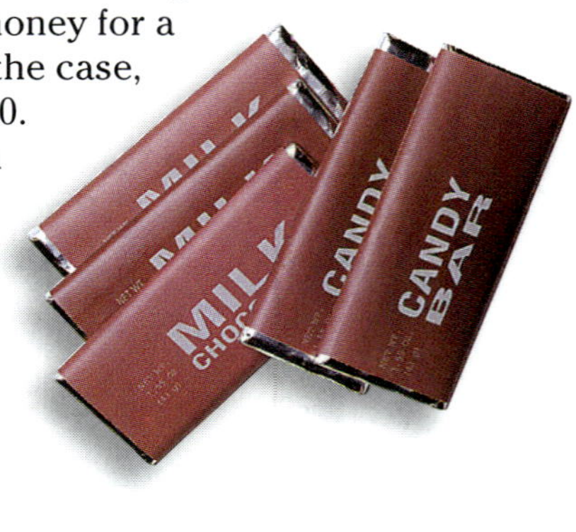

Mixed Review

67. Evaluate $(-3a)(4)\left(\frac{2}{3}\right)\left(\frac{1}{6}a\right)$ if $a = 3$. (Lesson 2–6)

68. Find $-\frac{5}{12} + \frac{3}{8}$. (Lesson 2–5)

69. Which is the better buy, a 1-pound package of lunch meat for \$1.95 or a 12-ounce package for \$1.80? (Lesson 2–4)

70. Find $-5 - (-6)$. (Lesson 2-3)

71. Statistics State the scale you would use to make a line plot for the following data: 504, 509, 520, 500, 513, 517, 517, 508, 502, 518, 509, 520, 504, 509, 517, 511, 520. Then draw the line plot. (Lesson 2–2)

72. Graph {0, 2, 6} on a number line. (Lesson 2–1)

73. Suppose a basketball was dropped from a tall building onto a sidewalk. Identify the graph below that best represents this situation. (Lesson 1–9)

a.

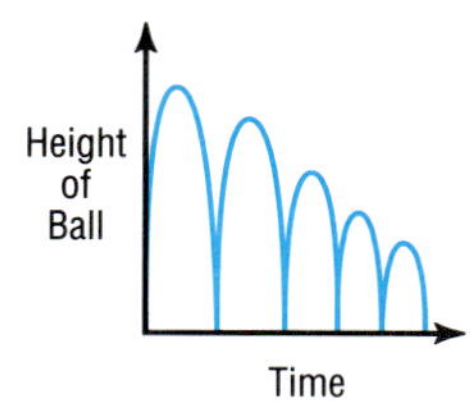

b.

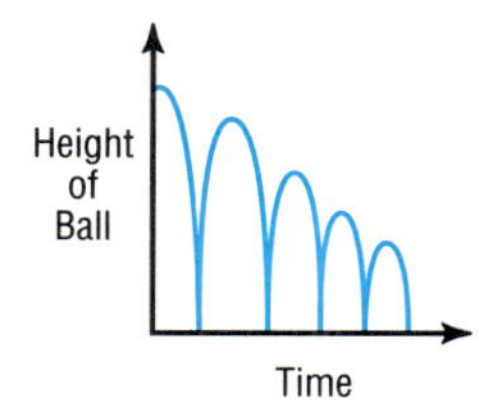

c.

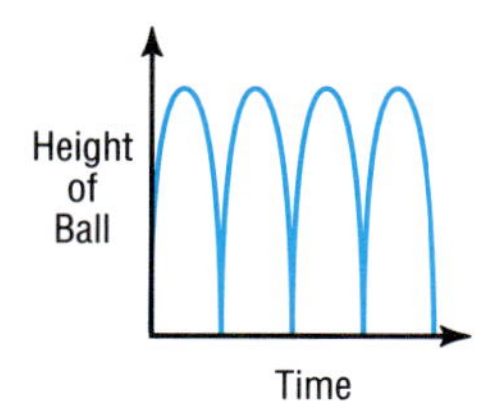

74. Name the property illustrated by $a + (2b + 5c) = (a + 2b) + 5c$. (Lesson 1–8)

Laura Davies studies her putt.

75. Golf The stem-and-leaf plot below shows the earnings of the top 25 U.S. women professional golfers for 1994 according to the *Sports Almanac*. (Lesson 1–4)

Stem	Leaf
6	6 9
5	0
4	0 1 2 3 7
3	2 3 4 5 9
2	0 0 1 1 3 4 4 5 6 7 7 8

4|3 = \$430,000

a. How have these numbers been rounded?

b. How many of these golfers made between \$300,000 and \$490,000?

c. Laura Davies had the highest earnings of all women golfers in 1994. How much money did she earn?

76. Evaluate $12(19 - 15) - 3 \cdot 8$. (Lesson 1–3)

77. Find the next two terms in the sequence 2, 8, 14, 20,... (Lesson 1–2)

78. Write an algebraic expression for p to the sixth power. (Lesson 1–1)

2-9 Problem Solving
Write Equations and Formulas

What YOU'LL LEARN
- To explore problem situations, and
- to translate verbal sentences and problems into equations or formulas and vice versa.

Why IT'S IMPORTANT

In the world of work, exploring problems and translating them into formulas that can be solved are valuable skills.

CONNECTION
Biology

Bugs, bugs, everywhere! That could be the slogan for James Fujita, an avid bug collector. Fujita has been fascinated with bugs since he was bitten by a cricket at the age of three. His collection includes hundreds of bugs—beetles, spiders, millipedes, scorpions, just to name a few—both living and dead.

Fujita has studied bugs as far away as Japan and Costa Rica, as well as in his own backyard in Oxnard, California. He has given bug presentations and workshops, donated some of his bugs to museums and zoos, and even appeared on a television talk show with some of his larger bugs. Fujita is a big believer in reading and exploring all you can about bug collecting—if you get the itch!

You can explore problems by asking and answering questions. In this text, we will use a four-step plan to solve problems. All of the steps are listed below.

Problem-Solving Plan

1. **Explore the problem.**
2. **Plan the solution.**
3. **Solve the problem.**
4. **Examine the solution.**

CAREER CHOICES

An **entomologist** is a scientist who studies the origin, development, anatomy, and distribution of insects and their effects on humans.

An inquistive mind, and a knowledge of biology, chemistry, and mathematics are necessary and are required for this career.

For more information, contact:

The Entomological Society of America
9301 Annapolis Road
Lanham, MD 20706

The first step in solving a problem is to read and explore it until you completely understand the relationships in the given information.

Step 1: Explore the Problem
To solve a verbal problem, first read the problem carefully and explore what the problem is about.

- Identify what information is given.
- Identify what you are asked to find.

Questions	Answers
a. How old was James when he became interested in bugs?	**a.** 3 years old
b. In what countries other than the U.S. has James studied bugs?	**b.** Japan and Costa Rica
c. If James is n years old now, for how many years has he been a collector of bugs?	**c.** $n - 3$
d. If James has b bugs and finds 14 new bugs, how many bugs are in his collection now?	**d.** $b + 14$

Other strategies are:
- *look for a pattern*
- *solve a simpler problem*
- *act it out*
- *guess and check*
- *draw a diagram*
- *make a table or chart*
- *work backward*

Step 2: Plan the Solution
One strategy you can use to solve a problem is to write an equation. Choose a variable to represent one of the unspecified numbers in the problem. This is called **defining the variable.** Then use the variable to write expressions for the other unspecified numbers in the problem.

Step 3: Solve the Problem
Use the strategy you chose in Step 2 to solve the problem.

Step 4: Examine the Solution
Check your answer within the context of the original problem. Does your answer make sense? Does it fit the information in the problem?

Example 1

APPLICATION
Computers

Gregory Arakelian of Herndon, Virginia, set a speed record for typing the most words per minute, with no errors, on a personal computer in the KeyTronic World Invitational Type-Off on September 24, 1991. Suppose his closest competitor typed 10 fewer words per minute than Arakelian. If his closest competitor typed 148 words per minute, how many words did Arakelian type per minute?

Explore
- How many words can Arakelian type in relation to his closest competitor? 10 more words
- How many words per minute did his competitor type? 148 words

Plan Write an equation to represent the situation. Let w represent the words per minute that Arakelian typed.

$$\underbrace{w}_{\text{words Arakelian typed}} - 10 = \underbrace{148}_{\text{words competitor typed}}$$

Solve

$$w - 10 = 148 \quad \textit{Solve mentally by asking,}$$
$$w = 158 \quad \textit{“What number minus 10 is 148?”}$$

Arakelian typed 158 words per minute.

Examine The problem asks how many words Arakelian typed per minute. His competitor typed 10 fewer words per minute. Since $158 - 10 = 148$, the answer makes sense.

Gregory Arakelian

In Lesson 2–4, you studied meanings for the symbols $<, >, \neq, \leq$, and $\geq$.

When solving problems, many sentences can be written as equations. Use variables to represent the unspecified numbers or measures referred to in the sentence or problem. Then write the verbal expressions as algebraic expressions. Some verbal expressions that suggest the *equals sign* are listed below.

- is
- equals
- is equal to
- is the same as
- is as much as
- is identical to

Example 2 Translate each sentence into an algebraic sentence.

a. ***Six times a number x is equal to 7 times the sum of z and y.***

Six times | a number x | is equal to | 7 times | the sum of z and y.

$6 \quad \times \quad x \quad = \quad 7\times \quad (z + y)$

The algebraic sentence is $6x = 7(z + y)$.

b. ***A number is less than or equal to 5.***

A number | is less than or equal to | 5.

$n \quad \leq \quad 5$

The algebraic sentence is $n \leq 5$.

Another strategy you can use to solve a problem is to write a formula. A **formula** is an equation that states a rule for the relationship between certain quantities. Sometimes you can develop a formula by making a model.

MODELING MATHEMATICS

Surface Area

Materials: rectangular box, scissors

You need to find the surface area of a rectangular box.

- Cut up a box like the one shown at the right.
- Find the area of each face.

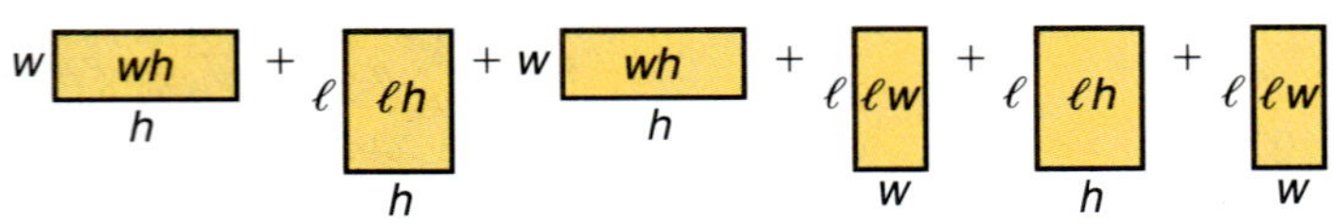

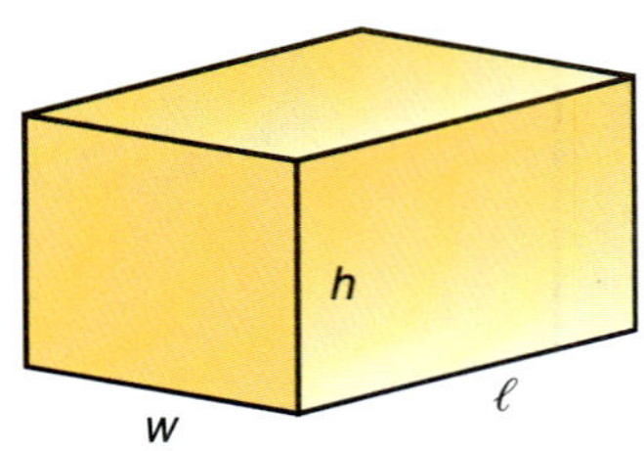

- Write the formula by adding the areas.

$S = wh + wh + \ell h + \ell h + \ell w + \ell w$

$= 2wh + 2\ell h + 2\ell w$

$= 2(wh + \ell h + \ell w)$

Your Turn

a. Find a box that is the shape of a cube. Take the box apart. Draw and label each side. Then write a formula for finding the surface area of the cube.

b. How are the box (rectangular prism) and cube the same? How are they different?

c. Find a formula for the surface area of the triangular prism below. Use S, h, w, and ℓ in your formula.

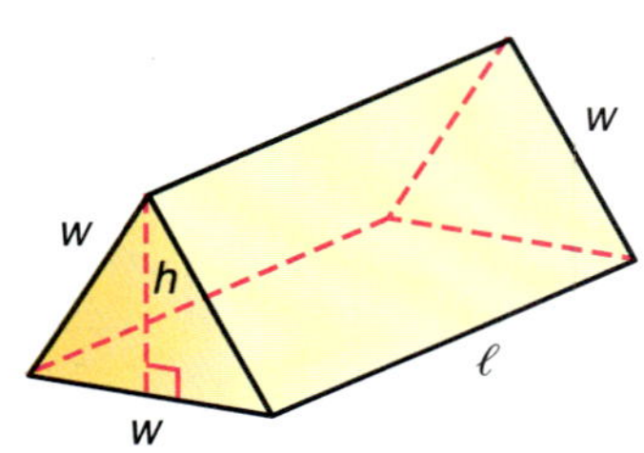

Example 3 **INTEGRATION Geometry**

Translate the sentence into a formula.

The area of a circle equals the product of π and the square of the radius r.

The area of a circle *equals* *π* *times* *the square of the radius r.*

$$A \quad = \quad \pi \quad \times \quad r^2$$

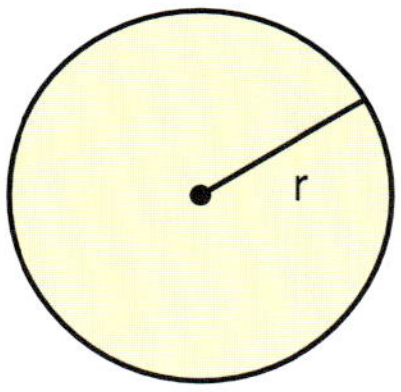

The formula is $A = \pi r^2$.

You can also translate equations into verbal sentences or make up your own verbal problem if you are given an equation or two.

Example 4 **Translate $x^2 + 6 = 39$ into a verbal sentence.**

$$x^2 \quad + \quad 6 \quad = \quad 39$$

The sum of the square of a number and six equals 39.

Example 5 **Write a problem based on the given information.**

ℓ = Lawana's height in inches
$\ell + 5$ = Tatewin's height in inches
$2\ell + (\ell + 5) = 194$

Here's a sample problem.

Tatewin is 5 inches taller than Lawana. The sum of Tatewin's height and twice Lawana's is 194 inches. How tall is Lawana?

CHECK FOR UNDERSTANDING

Communicating Mathematics

Study the lesson. Then complete the following.

1. **Write** three questions you would ask yourself in order to understand the problem below.
   Consuelo's target heart rate is 140 beats per minute. Her normal heart rate is 60 beats per minute. After running for 10 minutes, her heart rate rises by 65 beats. It drops by 32 beats after a 5-minute rest period and then rises by 50 beats after another 15-minute run. Did she reach her target heart rate?
2. **Explain** whether an equation is a type of formula or a formula is a type of equation.
3. **Write** a problem that uses the formula for the area of a rectangle, $A = \ell w$.

MODELING MATHEMATICS

4. **Find** any gift box. Measure each side. Use the formula $S = 2(wh + \ell h + \ell w)$ to find its surface area, including the lid.

Guided Practice

5. Answer the related questions for the verbal problem below.
Each question in the computation section of a mathematics test is worth 4 points. Each question in the problem-solving section is worth 6 points. Madison needs to answer 15 questions correctly to have a total of 86 points and get a B on the test. How many problem-solving questions must she answer correctly?
   a. How many points are the computation questions worth?
   b. How many questions does Madison need to answer correctly?
   c. What score does Madison need to make on the test?
   d. How many points are the problem-solving questions worth?
   e. If n represents the number of correct computation questions, how many problem-solving questions does she need to answer correctly?
   f. If n represents the number of correct answers in the computation section of the test, how does Madison compute the number of points in this section of the test?

Translate each sentence into an equation, inequality, or formula.

6. The sum of twice x and three times y is equal to thirteen.
7. The sum of a number and 5 is at least 48.
8. The perimeter P of a parallelogram is twice the sum of the lengths of two adjacent sides, a and b.

Define a variable, and then write an equation for each problem. Do *not* try to solve.

9. Olivia drove 189 miles from her home in Fort Worth, Texas, to Austin in three hours. What was her average speed?
10. Shane has 4 more dimes than quarters and 7 fewer nickels than dimes. He has 28 coins in all. How many quarters does Shane have?
11. Translate $a(y + 1) = b$ into a verbal sentence.
12. Write a problem based on the given information.
Let h = the number of hours you can work during the summer.
$5h - 8$

EXERCISES

Practice

13. Answer the related questions for the verbal problem below.
The Johnson Sisters' Construction Company is planning to build a playground for a housing development. The blueprints allow an area of 20,000 square feet for the playground. The width of the rectangular playground is 80 feet less than its length, and its perimeter is 640 feet. Is there enough space to build the playground as designed?
   a. What is the perimeter of the playground?
   b. If y represents the length of the playground, what is its width?
   c. What is the formula for the perimeter of a rectangular shape?
   d. What is the length of the playground?
   e. What is the area of the playground?
   f. What does the problem ask?

Translate each sentence into an equation, inequality, or formula.

14. The volume V of a pyramid is equal to one third the product of the area of the base b and its height h.
15. The sum of the square of a and the cube of b is equal to twenty-five.
16. The quotient of x and y is at least 18 more than five times the sum of x and y.
17. The quantity x is less than the square of the difference of a and 4.
18. The circumference C of a circle is the product of 2, π, and the radius r.
19. Seven-eighths of the sum of a, b, and the square of c is the same as 48.

Define a variable, and then write an equation for each problem. Do *not* try to solve.

20. Nicole has 26 CDs and tapes altogether. When she tries to pair them up, she has 4 CDs left over. How many tapes does Nicole have?
21. One number is 25 more than a second number. The sum of these two numbers is 106. Find the numbers.
22. Anna is twice as old as her brother Dennis, who is 4 years older than their brother Curtis. The sum of their ages is 32. How old is Anna?
23. Hector works for a lawn care service. He gets paid twice a month and saves \$50 of each pay. After 7 months, how much will he have saved?

Translate each equation or formula below into a verbal sentence.

24. $(mn)^2 = p$
25. $V = \frac{ah}{3}$
26. $\frac{(a + 2)}{5} > 10$

Write a problem based on the given information.

27. x = the number of miles from home to school
    $3x = 36$
28. p = the cost of a suit
    $p - 25 = 150$
29. d = the number of appointments a doctor has scheduled
    $6d + 5 = 47$

Write a formula for each shaded area.

30.

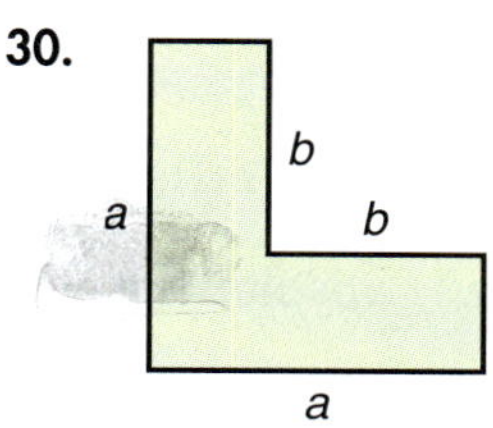

31.

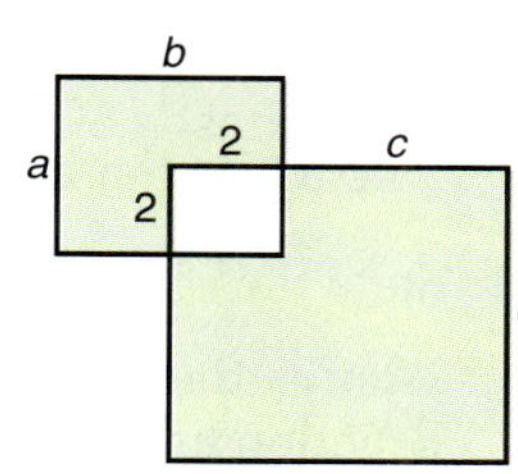

32.

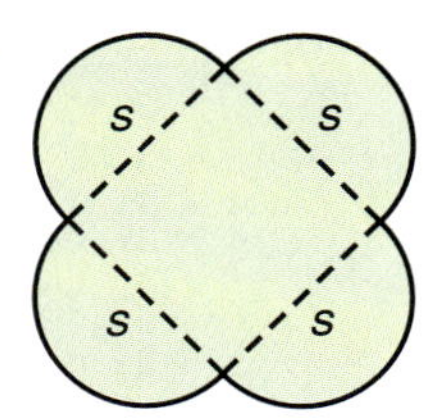

Critical Thinking

33. **Geometry** The two line segments below are the same length.

Write an equation that describes this situation. Then, use guess and check or any other strategy to find x.

Applications and Problem Solving

34. **Food** Aaron and Ellie went out for pizza. After looking at the menu, they couldn't decide whether to order two 7-inch round pizzas or one 12-inch round pizza because the cost was the same. Which is the better buy?

   a. What questions do you need to answer?
   b. Draw and label diagrams that describe the situation.
   c. Write the formulas or equations needed to solve the problem, then solve.
   d. Ellie's favorite part of a pizza is the crust. Explain how knowing this might affect your answer.

35. **Geometry** The area of a trapezoid equals one half the product of its height and the sum of the lengths of its two bases.
   a. Write a formula for the area of a trapezoid. Let A represent the area, let a and b represent the bases, and let h represent the height.
   b. Find the area for a trapezoid with a base of 20 feet, another base of 11 feet, and a height of 7 feet.

36. **Geometry** Study the diagram at the right.
   a. Based on the dimensions given, label the remaining sides. Assume that all angles are right angles.
   b. Write a formula to represent the perimeter.
   c. Write a formula to represent the area.
   d. If x is 5.5 cm and y is 4 cm, find the perimeter and area.

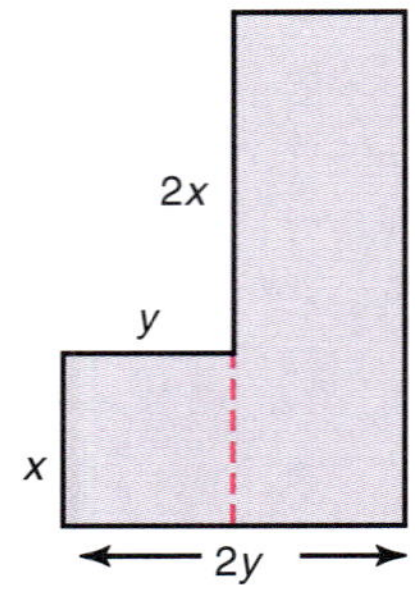

Mixed Review

37. Find $-\sqrt{64}$. (Lesson 2–8)

38. Simplify $-72 \div (-6)$. (Lesson 2–7)

39. Find $-4\begin{bmatrix} -2 & 0.4 \\ -3 & 5 \end{bmatrix}$. (Lesson 2–6)

40. Find a fraction between $\frac{1}{3}$ and $\frac{4}{7}$ whose denominator is 42. (Lesson 2–4)

41. State the additive inverse and absolute value of +25. (Lesson 2–3)

42. Identify the graph below that best represents the following situation. Brandon has a deflated balloon. He slowly fills the balloon up with air. Without tying the balloon, he lets it go. (Lesson 1–9)

a.
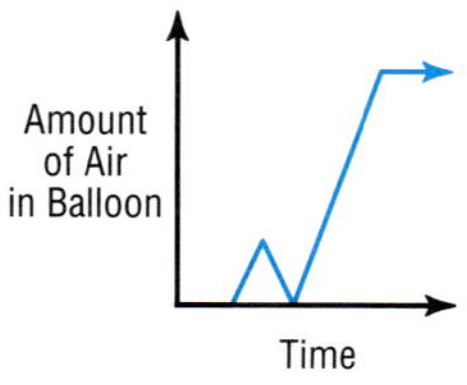

b.
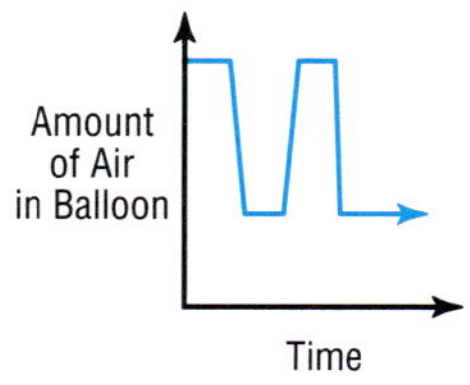

c.
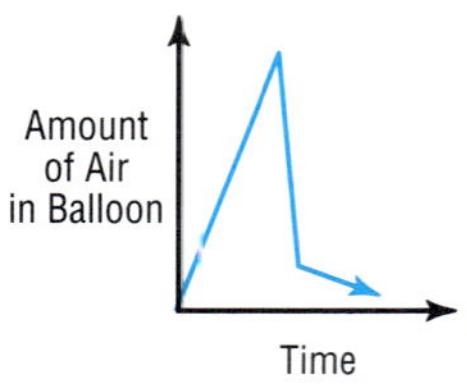

43. Find the solution set for the inequality $4y + 2 > 9$ if the replacement set is $\{1, 2, 3, 4, 5\}$. (Lesson 1–5)

CHAPTER 2 HIGHLIGHTS

VOCABULARY

After completing this chapter, you should be able to define each term, property, or phrase and give an example or two of each.

Algebra

absolute value (p. 85)
adding integers (p. 86)
additive inverses (p. 87)
additive inverse property (p. 87)
comparison property (p. 94)
completeness property (p. 121)
complex fraction (p. 114)
cross products (p. 94)
defining the variable (p. 127)
density property (p. 96)
dividing rational numbers (p. 112)
formula (p. 128)
integer (p. 73)
irrational number (p. 120)
multiplicative property of -1 (p. 107)
multiplying rational numbers (p. 107)
negative number (p. 73)
number line (p. 72)
opposites (p. 87)
perfect square (p. 119)
principal square root (p. 119)
radical sign (p. 119)
rational number (p. 93)
real number (p. 121)
square root (pp. 118, 119)
subtracting integers (p. 87)
unit cost (p. 95)
Venn diagram (p. 73)
whole number (p. 72)

Geometry

coordinate (p. 73)
graph (p. 73)

Statistics

line plot (p. 78)

Problem Solving

problem-solving plan (p. 126)

Discrete Mathematics (p. 88)

matrix (p. 88)
scalar multiplication (p. 108)

UNDERSTANDING AND USING THE VOCABULARY

State whether each sentence is *true* or *false*. If false, replace the underlined word or number to make a true sentence.

1. The absolute value of -26 is 26.
2. The multiplicative inverse of 2 is -2.
3. Terminating decimals are rational numbers.
4. The square root of 144 is 12.
5. $2\frac{1}{2}$ is a complex fraction.
6. $-\sqrt{576}$ is an irrational number.
7. 225 is a perfect square.
8. -3.1 is an integer.
9. $0.66\overline{6}$ is a repeating decimal.
10. $\frac{10}{5}$ is a whole number.

CHAPTER 2 STUDY GUIDE AND ASSESSMENT

SKILLS AND CONCEPTS

OBJECTIVES AND EXAMPLES

Upon completing this chapter, you should be able to:

- graph integers on a number line (Lesson 2–1)

Graph $\{\ldots, -5, -4, -3\}$.

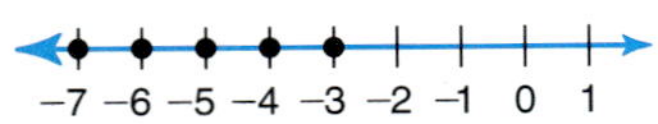

REVIEW EXERCISES

Use these exercises to review and prepare for the chapter test.

Graph each set of numbers on a number line.

11. $\{5, 3, -1, -3\}$

12. {integers greater than -3}

13. {integers less than 4 and greater than or equal to -2}

- add integers by using a number line (Lesson 2–1)

$4 + (-3) = 1$

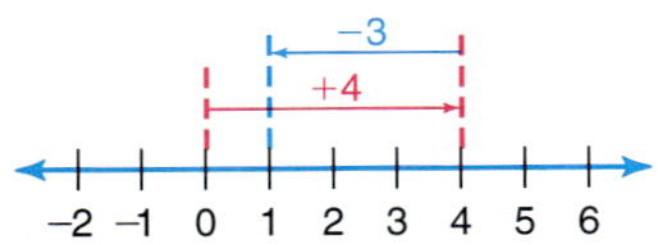

Find each sum. If necessary, use a number line.

14. $4 + (-4)$

15. $2 + (-7)$

16. $-8 + (-12)$

17. $-9 + 5$

18. $-14 + (-8)$

19. $6 + (-11)$

- display and interpret statistical data on a line plot (Lesson 2–2)

Make a line plot for the set of data.

78, 74, 86, 88, 99, 63, 85, 85, 85

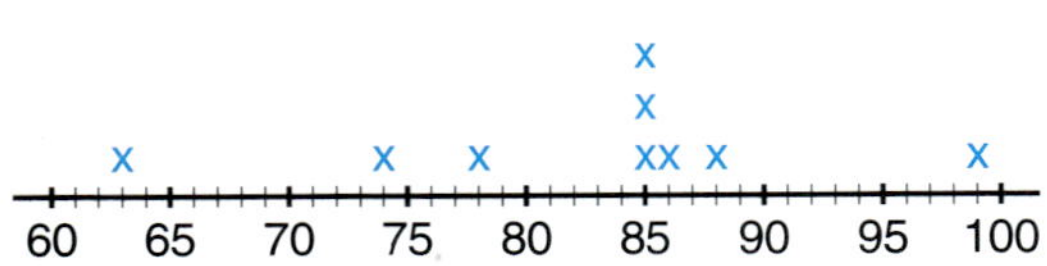

The following table lists the percent of 18-year-olds with high school diplomas for each of 9 years.

Year	'50	'55	'60	'65	'70	'75	'80	'85	'90
%	56	65	72	71	77	74	72	74	72

20. Make a line plot of the data.

21. What was the lowest percent of 18-year-olds with high school diplomas?

22. In how many years was the percent with diplomas between 70 and 75%?

- add and subtract integers (Lesson 2–3)

$$-14 + (-9) = -(|-14| + |-9|)$$
$$= -(14 + 9)$$
$$= -23$$

$7 - 9 = 7 + (-9)$ *To subtract 9, add −9.*

$= -2$

Find each sum and difference.

23. $17 + (-9)$

24. $14 - 36$

25. $-10 + 8$

26. $18 - (-5)$

27. $-7 - (-11)$

28. $-17 + (-31)$

29. $-12 + 7$

30. $-54 - (-34)$

OBJECTIVES AND EXAMPLES

- compare and order rational numbers (Lesson 2–4)

$\frac{5}{9}$ __?__ $\frac{3}{5}$

$5 \cdot 5$ __?__ $9 \cdot 3$ *Find the cross products.*

$25 < 27$

$\frac{5}{9} < \frac{3}{5}$

REVIEW EXERCISES

Replace each __?__ with <, >, or = to make each sentence true.

31. -8 __?__ -14
32. $\frac{3}{8}$ __?__ $\frac{4}{11}$
33. -5.6 __?__ -4.5
34. $\frac{-3.6}{0.6}$ __?__ -7

Find a number between the given numbers.

35. $-\frac{3}{5}$ and $\frac{7}{12}$
36. $-\frac{2}{9}$ and $-\frac{5}{8}$

- add and subtract rational numbers (Lesson 2–5)

$$-0.37 + 0.812 = +(|0.812| - |0.37|)$$
$$= 0.442$$

$$7\frac{3}{10} - \left(-4\frac{1}{5}\right) = 7\frac{3}{10} + 4\frac{1}{5}$$
$$= 7\frac{3}{10} + 4\frac{2}{10}$$
$$= 11\frac{5}{10} \text{ or } 11\frac{1}{2}$$

Find each sum or difference.

37. $\frac{6}{7} + \left(-\frac{13}{7}\right)$
38. $-0.0045 + 0.034$
39. $3.72 - (-8.65)$
40. $-\frac{4}{3} + \frac{5}{6} + \left(-\frac{7}{3}\right)$
41. $-4.57 - 8.69$
42. $-4.5 - 8.1$

- multiply rational numbers (Lesson 2–6)

$$-4(-2) + 6(-3) = 8 + (-18)$$
$$= -10$$

$$-2\frac{1}{7}\left(3\frac{2}{3}\right) + \left(-5\frac{5}{7}\right) = \left(-\frac{15}{7}\right)\left(\frac{11}{3}\right) + \left(-\frac{40}{7}\right)$$
$$= -\frac{55}{7} + \left(-\frac{40}{7}\right)$$
$$= -\frac{95}{7}$$

Find each product.

43. $(-11)(9)$
44. $(-7)(12)(-3)$
45. $\left(\frac{3}{5}\right)\left(-\frac{5}{7}\right)$
46. $(-5.733)(-2.43)(-3.6)$
47. $-2(45)$
48. $-4\left(\frac{7}{12}\right)$

- divide rational numbers (Lesson 2–7)

$$\frac{-12}{-\frac{2}{3}} = -12 \div \left(-\frac{2}{3}\right)$$
$$= -12\left(-\frac{3}{2}\right)$$
$$= 18$$

Simplify.

49. $\frac{-54}{6}$
50. $-15 \div \left(\frac{3}{4}\right)$
51. $\frac{\frac{4}{5}}{-7}$
52. $\frac{-575x}{5}$
53. $218 \div (-2)$
54. $-78 \div (-6)$

OBJECTIVES AND EXAMPLES

- find square roots (Lesson 2–8)

Evaluate $\sqrt{a+b}$ if $a = 489$ and $b = 295$.

$$\sqrt{489 + 295} = \sqrt{784}$$
$$= 28$$

REVIEW EXERCISES

Evaluate each expression. Use a calculator if necessary. Round to the nearest hundredth if the result is not a whole number.

55. $\sqrt{y}$, if $y = 196$

56. $\pm\sqrt{t}$, if $t = 112$

57. $-\sqrt{ab}$, if $a = 36$ and $b = 25$

58. $\pm\sqrt{\frac{c}{d}}$, if $c = 169$ and $d = 16$

APPLICATIONS AND PROBLEM SOLVING

59. Consumerism The cost per cup, in cents, of 28 different liquid laundry detergents are listed below. (Lesson 2–2)

28	17	16	18
19	21	26	15
19	19	16	14
21	12	26	17
30	17	13	18
14	22	20	12
19	9	15	12

a. Make a line plot of the data.

b. How many detergents cost at most 17¢ per cup?

60. Aquatics A submarine descended to a depth of 432 meters and then rose 189 meters. How far below the surface of the water is the submarine now? (Lesson 2–3)

61. Consumerism Which is the better buy: 0.75 liter of soda for 89¢ or 1.25 liters of soda for \$1.31? (Lesson 2–4)

62. Electricity A circuit is designed with two resistance settings R, 4.6 ohms and 5.2 ohms, and two power settings P, 1200 watts and 1500 watts. Which settings can be used so that the voltage of the circuit is between 75 volts and 85 volts? Use $V = \sqrt{PR}$. (Lesson 2–8)

63. Stock The changes in two separate stocks for one week are listed below. (Lesson 2–5)

	M	T	W	TH	F
CompNet	$+\frac{3}{8}$	$+\frac{1}{8}$	0	$-\frac{3}{4}$	$+\frac{1}{2}$
AccuFirm	$-\frac{1}{4}$	$+\frac{1}{8}$	$+\frac{1}{8}$	$-\frac{1}{4}$	$+\frac{1}{2}$

a. Which stock saw the largest gain for the week?

b. Which stock had the greatest change from one day to the next?

c. What was the change and on what days?

Define a variable, and then write an equation for each problem. Do not try to solve. (Lesson 2–9)

64. Minal weighs 8 pounds less than Claudia. Together they weigh 182 pounds. How much does Minal weigh?

65. Three times a number decreased by 21 is 57. Find the number.

66. Four years ago, three times Cecile's age was 42, her father's age now. How old is Cecile now?

A practice test for Chapter 2 is provided on page 788.

ALTERNATIVE ASSESSMENT

COOPERATIVE LEARNING PROJECT

Cooking In this project, you are hosting a party for the cast members of the school play. You must prepare enough chili and peanut butter brownies to serve 100 individuals. (Recipes are given below.) You will also need bowls, napkins, and spoons. You start out with \$50 in your checking account. You write a check to a party goods store for the bowls, napkins, and spoons. You then go to the grocery and buy everything except the ground beef because you decide to buy the ground beef at the local meat market.

Follow these steps to prepare a grocery list and a checkbook register.

- Determine the amount of each ingredient needed for the chili and the peanut butter brownies.
- Write a grocery list including the total amount of ingredients needed.
- Go to the grocery and record the size of the package you would need to buy for each item, the quantity you would need to buy, and the price of the package.
- Keep a running total with entries for your checkbook register.
- Write several paragraphs incorporating your data and your money situation for a report to be given to the school play director.

Every time you run a negative balance in your checking account your bank deducts \$10. Did you ever run a negative balance? If so, when would have been a good time to deposit more money? How much more money should you have deposited in order to cover all your checks?

THINKING CRITICALLY

- Write a sentence explaining why terminating and repeating decimals are rational numbers.
- A number is both multiplied and divided by the same rational number n, where $0 < n < 1$. Which is greater, the product or the quotient? Explain your reasoning.

PORTFOLIO

Make a grocery list containing ten items. Go to a grocery store and record the price of two different size containers for each of these items. Be sure to also include the brand names and the different sizes in your record. Make a chart of this data.

When you have completed the chart, calculate the unit cost and include it in your chart. Write a new grocery list of the ten items containing the exact brand name and size of container that should be bought in order to insure the best buy. Place these items in your portfolio.

SELF EVALUATION

Comparing numbers is often useful when solving a problem. It can be beneficial when estimating and in decision-making. When comparing numbers or items, be sure to consider other factors.

Assess yourself. When do you use comparison? Do you evaluate new situations based on comparing that situation to another situation that was similar? Describe two ways in which you have used or could use comparison to solve a problem or situation in mathematics and in your daily life.

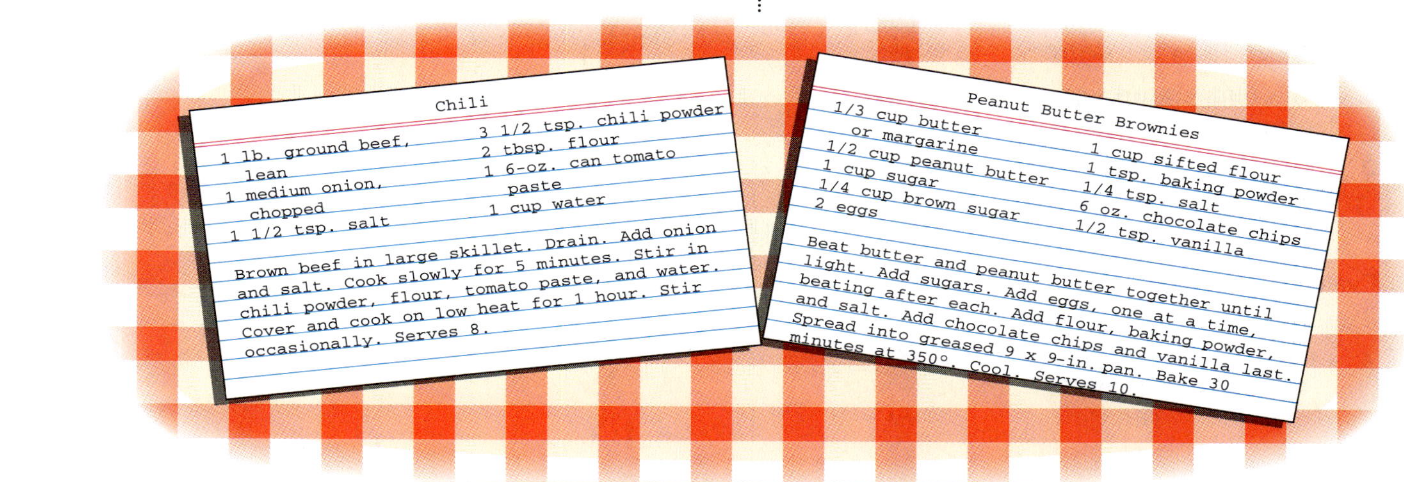
Chili

1 lb. ground beef, lean
1 medium onion, chopped
1 1/2 tsp. salt
3 1/2 tsp. chili powder
2 tbsp. flour
1 6-oz. can tomato paste
1 cup water

Brown beef in large skillet. Drain. Add onion and salt. Cook slowly for 5 minutes. Stir in chili powder, flour, tomato paste, and water. Cover and cook on low heat for 1 hour. Stir occasionally. Serves 8.

Peanut Butter Brownies

1/3 cup butter or margarine
1/2 cup peanut butter
1 cup sugar
1/4 cup brown sugar
2 eggs
1 cup sifted flour
1 tsp. baking powder
1/4 tsp. salt
6 oz. chocolate chips
1/2 tsp. vanilla

Beat butter and peanut butter together until light. Add sugars. Add eggs, one at a time, beating after each. Add flour, baking powder, and salt. Add chocolate chips and vanilla last. Spread into greased 9 x 9-in. pan. Bake 30 minutes at 350°. Cool. Serves 10.

CUMULATIVE REVIEW

CHAPTERS 1–2

SECTION ONE: MULTIPLE CHOICE

There are eight multiple-choice questions in this section. After working each problem, write the letter of the correct answer on your paper.

1. **Patterns** Find the sixth term in the sequence $-6, -3\frac{1}{2}, -1, \ldots$.

   A. 0
   B. $2\frac{1}{2}$
   C. 4
   D. $6\frac{1}{2}$

2. **Travel** Travel agencies often give information on a state's temperature during the year in order to prepare their customers for their vacation. The stem-and-leaf plot shows daily high temperatures recorded for April in Ohio. Which statement best describes the data in order to prepare travelers for their visit to Ohio in April?

Stem	Leaf
8	0 2 2 5
7	0 3 3 4 5 7 7 7 8 9 9
6	1 2 3 5 5 6 7 8 8 9
5	4 7 8 8
4	9 $\quad$ 5|7 = 57

   A. April temperatures can range from 49 to 85 degrees.
   B. April is mild, with temperatures usually between 60 and 80 degrees.
   C. April's temperatures can soar as high as 85 degrees.
   D. April is a cold month with temperatures as low as 49 degrees.

3. Evaluate $3t^2 - g(w - t)$ if $t = 3$, $g = 5$, and $w = -2$.

   A. -110
   B. 20
   C. 43
   D. 52

4. Tyrone is 3 years older than Bill. In 5 years, twice the sum of their ages will equal 5 times Bill's age now. Choose the equation that should be used to solve this problem.

   A. $b + (b + 3) = 5b$
   B. $2b + (b + 3) + 5 = 5b$
   C. $2[(b + 5) + (b + 3 + 5)] = 5b$
   D. $2[(b + 3) + (b - 3 + 5)] = 5b$

5. Quan is working as a mailroom clerk in a busy downtown office building for the summer. His morning route takes him from the mailroom up two floors to the payroll office, up four more floors to the attorney's office, down three floors to the cafeteria, up seven floors to the executive offices, and down twelve floors to the security desk on the first floor. On what floor is the mailroom?

   A. second floor
   B. third floor
   C. sixth floor
   D. top floor

6. Stephen bought a 5-foot-long submarine sandwich to serve at his Super Bowl party. How many pieces would he have to serve if he cut the sub into $1\frac{1}{2}$-inch pieces?

   A. 3 pieces
   B. 8 pieces
   C. 30 pieces
   D. 40 pieces

7. Simplify $10a^3 + 7 - 2(2a^3 + a) + 3$.

   A. $-2a^4 + 10a^3 + 10$
   B. $8a^3 + 2a + 10$
   C. $6a^3 - 2a + 10$
   D. $6a^3 + a + 10$

8. Choose the expression that has a value of 28.

   A. $4 + 3 \cdot 4$
   B. $\frac{75}{3} - 2$
   C. $8 \cdot 4 - 8$
   D. $(5 + 3) \cdot 7 \div 2$

SECTION TWO: FREE RESPONSE

This section contains seven questions for which you will provide short answers. Write your answer on your paper.

9. Rewrite the expression $7 + 15 \div 2 + 4 - 2$ using grouping symbols so that the value of the expression is $6\frac{1}{2}$.

10. Three integers x, y, and z satisfy the following conditions:

    $y - z < 0$, $x - y > 0$, and $z - x < 0$.

    Arrange the integers in order from least to greatest.

11. Graph the solution set of $k \neq 1$ on a number line.

12. **Geometry** Find the perimeter of the figure below if $x = 7$, $y = 3$, and $z = 1\frac{1}{2}$.

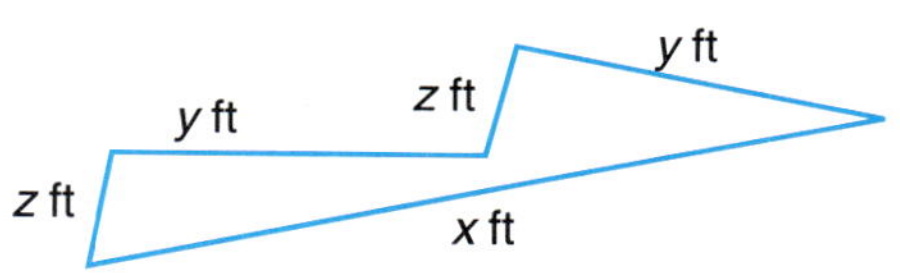

13. **School** The students in Miss Stickler's algebra class scored the following points on their last test: 88, 89, 85, 92, 91, 86, 90, 95, 91, 86, 90, 92, 91, 89, 91, and 90. Make a line plot of the scores and write a sentence to describe the data shown.

14. The average hourly rate of a teenage baby-sitter on a Saturday night is \$5 in Los Angeles and \$2 in Pittsburgh. Corey, who lives in Pittsburgh, baby-sits his little brother every Saturday night for 5 hours. Ella lives in Los Angeles and baby-sits her cousin for 3 hours every other Saturday night. How many Saturday nights will each have to baby-sit to earn the same amount of money?

15. What is the absolute value of a if $-a > a$?

16. Write an algebraic expression to represent *nine decreased by the product of y and 3.*

17. **Patterns** Find the next five terms of the sequence 3, 4.5, 6, ...

18. Replace __?__ with >, <, or = to make a true statement.

    $-2 - 1$ __?__ $-2(-1)$

SECTION THREE: OPEN-ENDED

This section contains two open-ended problems. Demonstrate your knowledge by giving a clear, concise solution to each problem. Your score on these problems will depend on how well you do the following.

- Explain your reasoning.
- Show your understanding of the mathematics in an organized manner.
- Use charts, graphs, and diagrams in your explanation.
- Show the solution in more than one way or relate it to other situations.
- Investigate beyond the requirements of the problem.

19. Latisha and Joia are planning to purchase a CD player for their dorm room. Latisha works at the campus book store and earns \$5.35 per hour. Joia has a job off campus as a waitress and earns \$2.00 per hour, plus tips. Each student works 20 hours per week.

    A. How long will they have to work to earn enough money to buy a CD player worth \$350?

    B. What other factors may affect when they can buy the CD player?

20. If $2(b + c) = 2b + 2c$, does $2 + (b \cdot c) = (2 + b)(2 + c)$? Use values for b and c to justify your answer.

CHAPTER 3

Solving Linear Equations

Objectives

In this chapter, you will:

- solve equations using one or more operations,
- solve problems that can be represented by equations,
- work backward to solve problems,
- define and study angles and triangles, and
- find measures of central tendency.

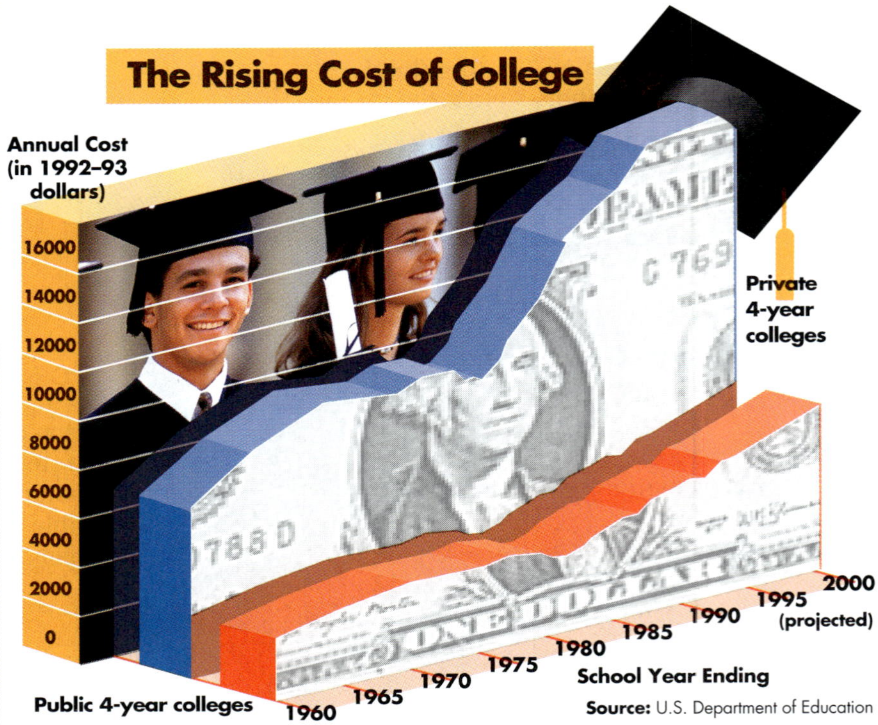

TIME*Line*

Over the last thirty years, tuition at public 4-year colleges has increased by about 50%, and tuition at private 4-year colleges has increased by a whopping 110%! How do you and your family intend to fund your college experience?

A.D. 240 In *Arithmetica,* Diophantus obtains negative numbers as solutions to equations, but dismisses them as "absurd."

575 B.C. Early standard coins, Lydia, Turkey

PEOPLE IN THE NEWS

When **Marianne Ragins** was a high-school student in her hometown of Macon, Georgia, she applied for scholarship funds from several sources so she could go to college. By the time Marianne was a freshman at Florida A & M University, she had won more than $400,000 in scholarship offers.

When she graduates from college, Marianne will have used $120,000 of those scholarships for her college expenses. Marianne, who is now 21, is the author of *Winning Scholarships for College,* and she now conducts The Scholarship Workshop across the country.

Chapter Project

Juan Ramirez has been offered two college scholarships. Under the terms of the first scholarship, University A will pick up one-half of all his college expenses. Under the terms of the second scholarship, University B will pick up $30,000 of his college expenses. There is $27,500 in the college fund his parents set up for him when he was born.

- Suppose college fees for one year at University A, a state university, are $9500 per year and fees for one year at University B, a private university, are $19,000.
- Write an equation to represent the cost for Juan to attend University A for four years. Write another equation to represent the cost for Juan to attend University B for four years.
- Which school should Juan attend, and why? Be sure to completely explain your reasoning.

780 Muhammed ibn Musa Al-Khowarizmi, Arabian mathematician, born; from his name we get the word *algebra.*

1848 Maria Mitchell is the first woman elected to the American Academy of Science.

1158 The University of Bologna, Italy, is founded.

1989 Ileana Ros-Lehtinen becomes the first Latina ever elected to Congress.

MODELING MATHEMATICS

A Preview of Lesson 3–1

3–1A Solving One-Step Equations

Materials: cups & counters   equation mat

You can use cups and counters as a model for solving equations. After you model the equation, the goal is to get the cup by itself on one side of the mat by using the rules stated below.

Rules for Equation Models	
You can remove or add the same number of identical counters to each side of the equation mat without changing the equation.	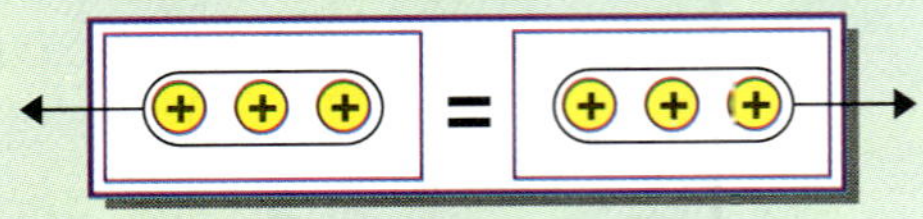
You can remove or add zero pairs to either side of the equation mat without changing the equation.	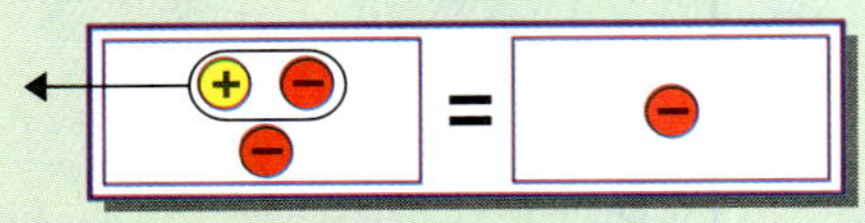

Activity 1 Use an equation model to solve $x + (-3) = -5$.

Step 1 Model the equation $x + (-3) = -5$ by placing 1 cup and 3 negative counters on one side of the mat. Place 5 negative counters on the other side of the mat. The two sides of the mat represent equal quantities.

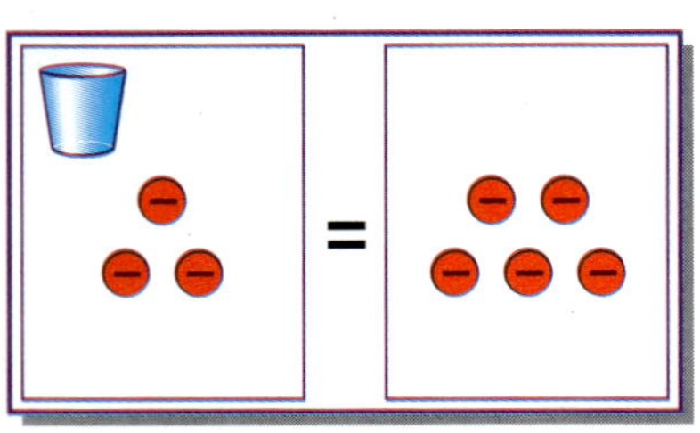

$x + (-3) = -5$

Step 2 Remove 3 negative counters from each side to get the cup by itself.

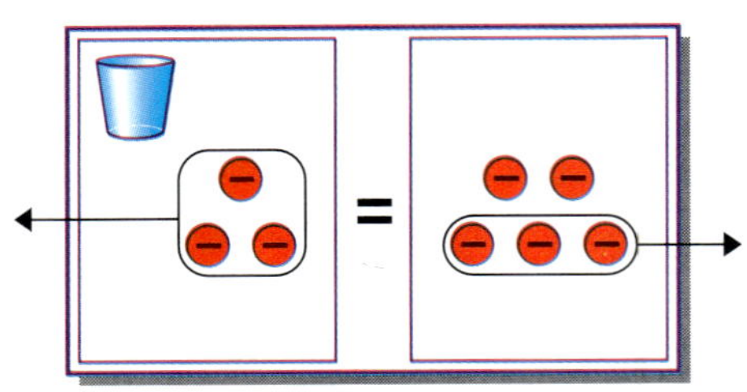

$x + (-3) - (-3) = -5 - (-3)$

Step 3 The cup on the left side of the mat is matched with 2 negative counters. Therefore, $x = -2$.

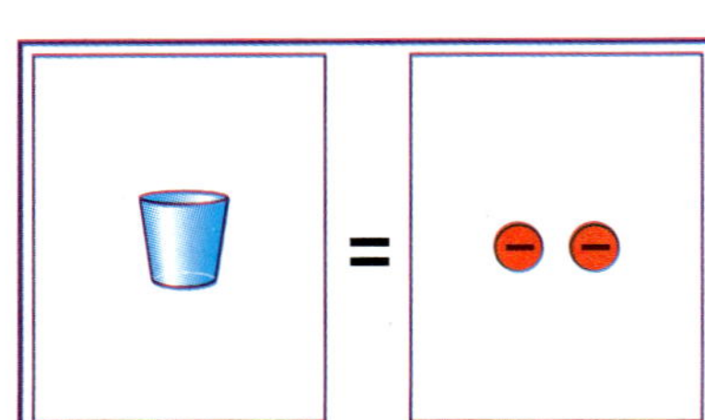

$x = -2$

Activity 2 Use an equation model to solve $2p = -6$.

Step 1 Model the equation $2p = -6$ by placing 2 cups on one side of the mat. Place 6 negative counters on the other side of the mat.

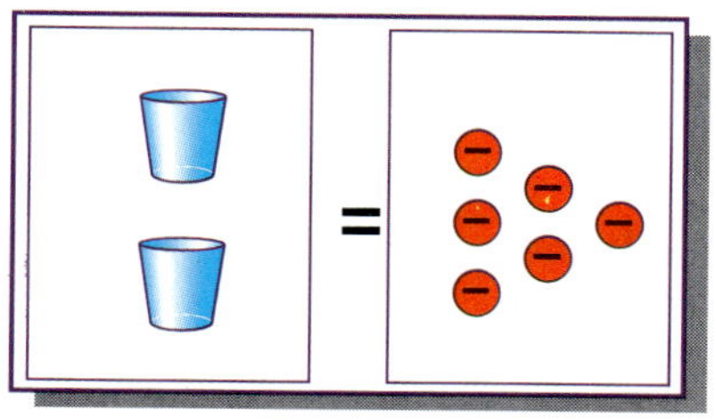

$2p = -6$

Step 2 Separate the counters into 2 equal groups to correspond to the 2 cups. Each cup on the left is matched with 3 negative counters. Therefore, $p = -3$.

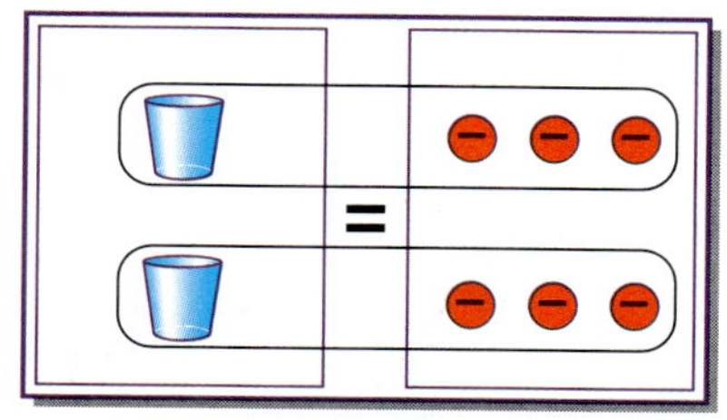

$p = -3$

Activity 3 Use an equation model to solve $r - 2 = 3$.

Step 1 Write the equation in the form $r + (-2) = 3$. Place 1 cup and 2 negative counters on one side of the mat. Place 3 positive counters on the other side of the mat. Notice that it is not possible to remove the same kind of counters from each side. Add 2 positive counters to each side.

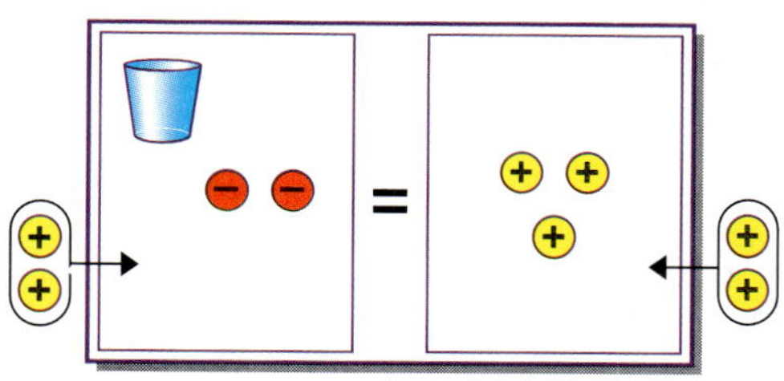

$r + (-2) = 3$

Step 2 Group the counters to form zero pairs. Then remove all the zero pairs. The cup on the left is matched with 5 positive counters. Therefore, $r = 5$.

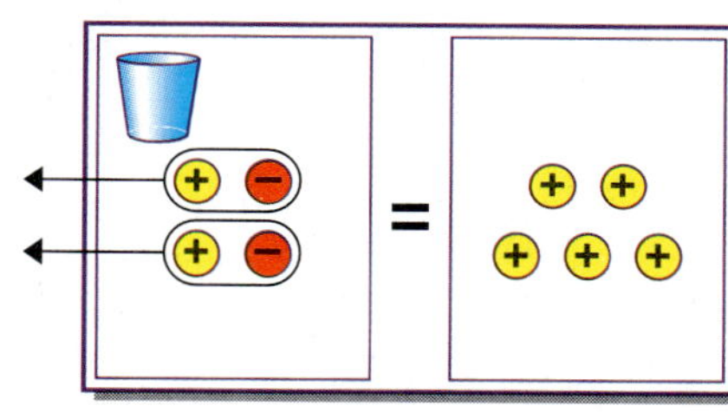

$r = 5$

Model **Use equation models to solve each equation.**

1. $x + 4 = 5$
2. $y + (-3) = -1$
3. $y + 7 = -4$
4. $3z = -9$
5. $m - 6 = 2$
6. $-2 = x + 6$
7. $8 = 2a$
8. $w - (-2) = 2$

Draw **Tell whether each number is a solution of the given equation. Justify your answer with a drawing.**

9. -3; $x + 5 = -2$
10. -1; $5b = -5$
11. -4; $y - 4 = -8$

Write

12. Write a paragraph explaining how you use zero pairs to solve an equation like $m + 5 = -8$.

3-1 Solving Equations with Addition and Subtraction

What YOU'LL LEARN

- To solve equations by using addition and subtraction.

Why IT'S IMPORTANT

You can use equations to solve problems involving sports, telecommunications, and economics.

APPLICATION
Football

According to the graph below, the Oakland Raiders and the Dallas Cowboys have each appeared on television on Monday night a total of 41 times through the 1992–1993 season.

Most Appearances on Monday Night

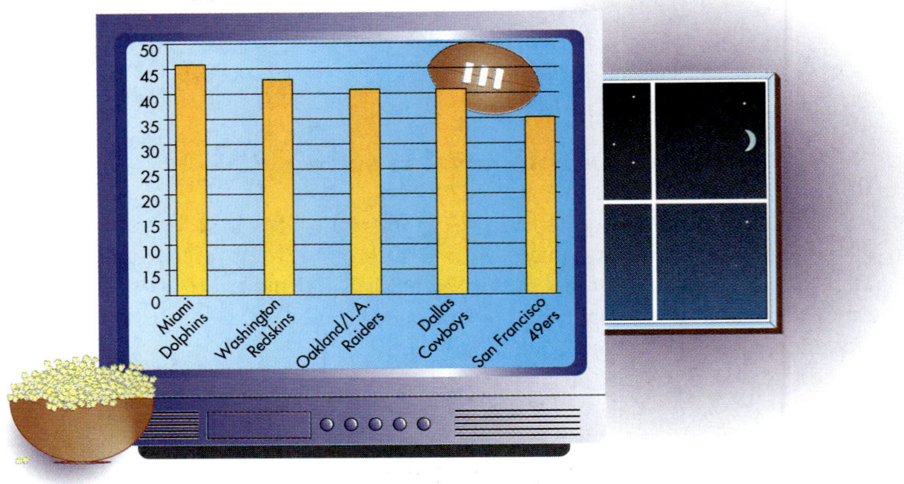

If during the next five seasons, each team appears an average of two times per season, the two teams would still have an equal number of appearances on television on Monday nights.

$$41 = 41$$

$$41 + 5(2) = 41 + 5(2)$$ *Two appearances per season for five seasons can be represented as 5(2).*

This example illustrates the **addition property of equality.**

Addition Property of Equality	**For any numbers a, b, and c, if $a = b$, then $a + c = b + c$.**

Note that c can be positive, negative, or 0. In the equation on the left below, $c = 5$. In the equation on the right, $c = -5$.

$$18 + 5 = 18 + 5 \qquad\qquad 18 + (-5) = 18 + (-5)$$

If the same number is added to each side of an equation, then the result is an **equivalent equation.** Equivalent equations are equations that have the same solution.

$y + 7 = 13$ *The solution to this equation is 6.*

$y + 7 + 3 = 13 + 3$ *Using the addition property of equality, add 3 to each side.*

$y + 10 = 16$ *The solution to this equation is also 6.*

Recall that an equation mat is a model of an equation. The sides of the mat represent the sides of an equation. When you add counters to each side, the result is an equivalent equation, as shown below.

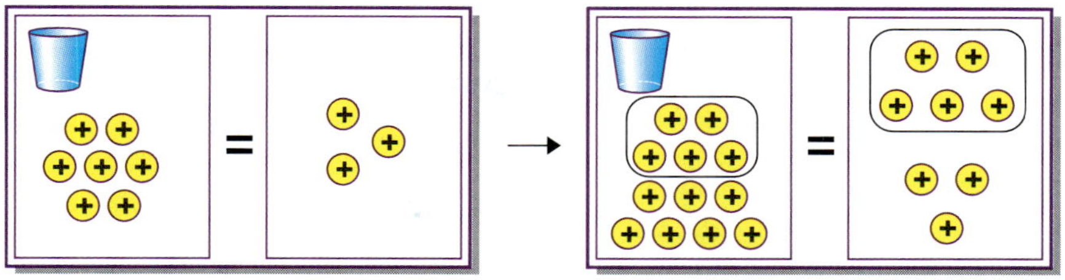

$y + 7 = 3$ $\qquad$ $y + 7 + 5 = 3 + 5$

Remember, x means 1 · x. The coefficient of x is 1.

To **solve an equation** means to isolate the variable having a coefficient of 1 on one side of the equation. You can do this by using the addition property of equality.

Example 1 **Solve 23 + t = −16.**

$$23 + t = -16$$
$$23 + t + (-23) = -16 + (-23) \quad \textit{Add } -23 \textit{ to each side.}$$
$$t + 0 = -39 \quad \textit{The sum of 23 and } -23 \textit{ is } 0.$$
$$t = -39$$

To check that −39 is the solution, substitute −39 for t in the original equation.

Check:
$$23 + t = -16$$
$$23 + (-39) \stackrel{?}{=} -16$$
$$-16 = -16 \checkmark$$

The solution is −39.

You can and will use equations to solve many real-world problems.

Example 2

Football

Refer to the application at the beginning of the lesson. San Francisco appeared fewer times than Washington through the 1992–1993 season. How many more times did Washington appear?

Explore Read the problem to find out what is asked. Then define a variable.

The problem asks how many more times Washington appeared on television on Monday night than San Francisco through the 1992–1993 season. From the chart, we can see that Washington appeared 43 times.

Let n = the difference in the number of times each team appeared. Then $43 - n$ = the number of times the 49ers appeared.

Plan Write an equation.

You know that $43 - n$ represents the number of times San Francisco appeared. From the chart, we can see that San Francisco appeared 35 times. Thus, $43 - n = 35$.

LOOK BACK

You can refer to Lesson 2-10 for information on solving problems by writing and solving equations.

(continued on the next page)

Solve Solve the equation and answer the problem.

$$43 - n = 35$$

$$43 + (-43) - n = 35 + (-43)$$ *Add −43 to each side.*

$$-n = -8$$ *The opposite of n is negative 8.*

$$n = 8$$ *Therefore, n is positive 8.*

Thus, Washington appeared 8 times more than San Francisco.

Examine Check to see if the answer makes sense.

If Washington appeared 43 times and San Francisco appeared 35 times, then the difference is $43 - 35$ or 8 times.

In addition to the addition property of equality, there is a **subtraction property of equality** that may also be used to solve equations.

Subtraction Property of Equality	**For any numbers a, b, and c, if $a = b$, then $a - c = b - c$.**

Example 3 Solve $190 - x = 215$.

$$190 - x = 215$$

$$190 - x - 190 = 215 - 190$$ *Subtract 190 from each side.*

$$-x = 25$$ *The opposite of x is 25.*

$$x = -25$$

Check:

$$190 - x = 215$$

$$190 - (-25) \stackrel{?}{=} 215$$

$$190 + 25 \stackrel{?}{=} 215$$

$$215 = 215 \checkmark$$

The solution is −25.

Most equations can be solved in two ways. Remember that subtracting a number is the same as adding its inverse.

Example 4 Solve $a + 3 = -9$ in two ways.

Method 1: Use the subtraction property of equality.

$$a + 3 = -9$$

$$a + 3 - 3 = -9 - 3$$ *Subtract 3 from each side.*

$$a = -12$$

Check:

$$a + 3 = -9$$

$$-12 + 3 \stackrel{?}{=} -9$$

$$-9 = -9 \checkmark$$

Method 2: Use the addition property of equality.

$$a + 3 = -9$$
$$a + 3 + (-3) = -9 + (-3) \quad \textit{Add } -3 \textit{ to each side.}$$
$$a = -12 \quad \textit{The answers are the same.}$$

The solution is -12.

Sometimes equations can be solved more easily if they are first rewritten in a different form.

Example 5

Solve $y - \left(-\frac{3}{7}\right) = -\frac{4}{7}$.

This equation is equivalent to $y + \frac{3}{7} = -\frac{4}{7}$. *Why?*

$$y + \frac{3}{7} = -\frac{4}{7}$$
$$y + \frac{3}{7} - \frac{3}{7} = -\frac{4}{7} - \frac{3}{7} \quad \textit{Subtract } \tfrac{3}{7} \textit{ from each side.}$$
$$y = -\frac{7}{7} \text{ or } -1$$

Check:
$$y - \left(-\frac{3}{7}\right) = -\frac{4}{7}$$
$$-\frac{7}{7} - \left(-\frac{3}{7}\right) \stackrel{?}{=} -\frac{4}{7}$$
$$-\frac{7}{7} + \frac{3}{7} \stackrel{?}{=} -\frac{4}{7}$$
$$-\frac{4}{7} = -\frac{4}{7} \ ✔$$

The solution is -1.

EXPLORATION — CALCULATORS

You can use a scientific or graphing calculator to solve equations that involve decimals.

[+/–] If you're using a scientific calculator like the TI-34, you can use the *plus/minus* key to input negative numbers or to change the sign of any number.

[(–)] If you're using a graphing calculator like the TI-82 or TI-83, you can use the *negative* key to input negative numbers.

[–] On all calculators, use the *subtraction* key to subtract two numbers.

Your Turn

a. Take some time to work through the examples in this lesson using your calculator.

b. Describe the difference between the key you use to indicate a negative number on your calculator and the subtraction key.

c. Does the order in which you use these keys matter? Why or why not?

d. How would you use your calculator to solve $x + (-9.016) = 5.14$?

Example 6 **Solve $b + (-7.2) = -12.5$.**

This equation is equivalent to $b - 7.2 = -12.5$. *Why?*

$$b - 7.2 = -12.5$$
$$b - 7.2 + 7.2 = -12.5 + 7.2 \quad \textit{Add 7.2 to each side.}$$
$$b = -5.3$$

Check:

Method 1

$$b + (-7.2) = -12.5$$
$$-5.3 + (-7.2) \stackrel{?}{=} -12.5$$
$$-12.5 = -12.5 \checkmark$$

Method 2

Use a calculator.

5.3 [+/−] [+] 7.2 [+/−] [=] −12.5 ✓

The solution is -5.3.

CHECK FOR UNDERSTANDING

Communicating Mathematics

Study the lesson. Then complete the following.

1. Choose the equation that is equivalent to $2.3 - w = 7.8$.
   a. $w - 2.3 = 7.8$ b. $w - 2.3 = -7.8$ c. $-w = -5.5$
2. **Write** three equivalent equations.
3. **Explain** how you can prove that 4.5 is the solution of $x - 1.2 = 3.3$.
4. **Complete:** If $x - 6 = 21$, then $x + 7 =$ __?__ . Explain your reasoning.

MODELING MATHEMATICS

5. Write an equation for the model at the right. Then use cups and counters to solve the equation.

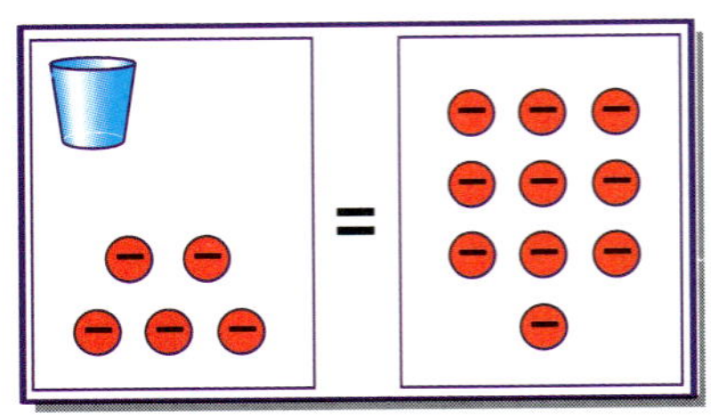

Guided Practice

Solve each equation. Then check your solution.

6. $m + 10 = 7$
7. $a - 15 = -32$
8. $5.7 + a = -14.2$
9. $y + (-7) = -19$
10. $\frac{1}{6} - n = \frac{2}{3}$
11. $d - (-27) = 13$

Define a variable, write an equation, and solve each problem. Then check your solution.

12. Thirteen subtracted from a number is -5. Find the number.
13. A number increased by -56 is -82. Find the number.

EXERCISES

Practice

Solve each equation. Then check your solution.

14. $k + 11 = -21$
15. $41 = 32 - r$
16. $-12 + z = -36$
17. $2.4 = m + 3.7$
18. $-7 = -16 - k$
19. $0 = t + (-1.4)$
20. $r + (-8) = 7$
21. $h - 26 = -29$
22. $-23 = -19 + n$
23. $-11 = k + (-5)$
24. $r - 6.5 = -9.3$
25. $t - (-16) = 9$
26. $-1.43 + w = 0.89$
27. $m - (-13) = 37$
28. $-4.1 = m + (-0.5)$
29. $-\frac{5}{8} + w = \frac{5}{8}$
30. $x - \left(-\frac{5}{6}\right) = \frac{2}{3}$
31. $g + \left(-\frac{1}{5}\right) = -\frac{3}{10}$

Define a variable, write an equation, and solve each problem. Then check your solution.

32. Twenty-three minus a number is 42. Find the number.
33. A number increased by 5 is equal to 34. Find the number.
34. What number decreased by 45 is -78?
35. The difference of a number and -23 is 35. Find the number.
36. A number increased by -45 is 77. Find the number.
37. The sum of a number and -35 is 98. Find the number.

Critical Thinking

38. Suppose a solution of an equation is a number n. Is it possible for $-n$ to also be a solution of this equation? If not, explain why not. If so, give an example of such an equation and its solutions n and $-n$.

Applications and Problem Solving

Write two different equations to represent each situation. Then solve the problem.

39. **Telecommunications** The graph at the right shows the growth in the number of people who own and use cellular telephones.
    a. How many more cellular phone subscribers were there in 1994 than there were in 1985?
    b. Predict how many cellular phone subscribers there will be in the year 2000. Write a justification for your prediction.

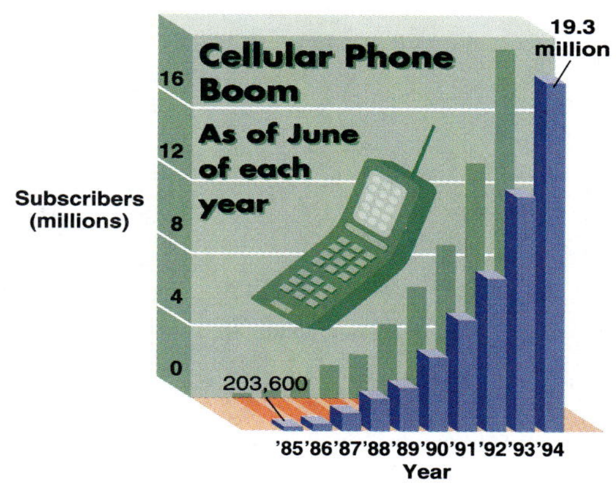

Source: Cellular Telecommunications Industry Association

40. **Consumerism** According to Runzheimer International, in 1994, a tube of lipstick cost \$5.94 in Los Angeles, California. The same tube cost \$4.89 more than that in London, England. In Sao Paulo, Brazil, the lipstick cost \$26.54.
    a. How much did the lipstick cost in London?
    b. How much more did the lipstick cost in Sao Paulo than in Los Angeles?

Mixed Review

41. Alejandra Salazar said, "I am 24 years younger than my mom and the sum of our ages is 68 years." (Lesson 2–9)
    a. How old was Mrs. Salazar when Alejandra was born?
    b. How much older than Alejandra is Mrs. Salazar now?
    c. What will be the sum of their ages in 5 years?
    d. How old was Mrs. Salazar when Alejandra was 10 years old?
    e. In ten years, how much younger than Mrs. Salazar will Alejandra be?
42. Find the principal square root of 256. (Lesson 2–8)
43. Simplify $65 \div (-13)$. (Lesson 2–7)
44. **Statistics** Odina's algebra average dropped three fourths of a point for each of eight consecutive months. If her average was originally 82, what was her average at the end of eight months? (Lesson 2–6)
45. Find the sum. $-0.23x + (-0.5x)$ (Lesson 2–5)
46. Simplify $6(5a + 3b - 2b)$. (Lesson 1–7)
47. Evaluate $12 \div 4 + 15 \cdot 3$. (Lesson 1–3)

3–2 Solving Equations with Multiplication and Division

What YOU'LL LEARN

- To solve equations by using multiplication and division.

Why IT'S IMPORTANT

You can use equations to solve problems involving construction, sociology, and demographics.

APPLICATION

Construction

In 1990, Congress passed into law the Americans with Disabilities Act. One of the provisions of that law has to do with ramps installed on buildings to give people with disabilities access to those buildings. The law states that for a *rise* of 1″, there should be at least 12″ of *run*. The maximum rise is 30″.

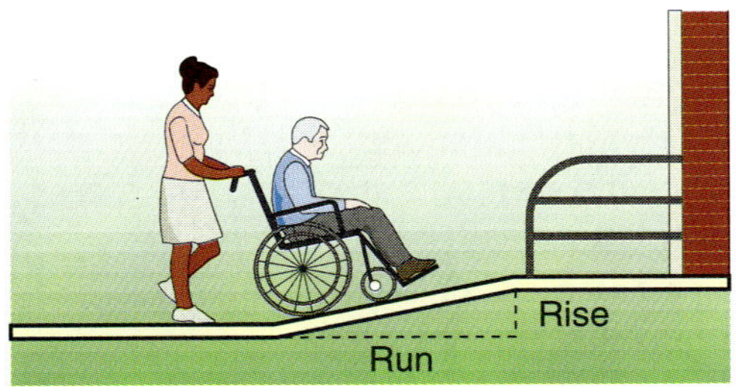

Rick Hansen, wheelchair athlete

If a contractor wants to build a ramp that has a 180-inch run, what is the greatest rise that the ramp can have?

Since run is dependent on rise, run is a function of rise. Rise is the independent quantity, and run is the dependent quantity. Only positive values for rise and run make sense.

In the table at the right, the pattern suggests that the run is always 12 times the rise. Let x represent the number of inches in the rise. Then $12x$ represents the number of inches in the run. Write an equation to represent the situation.

Rise	Run
1	12
2	24
3	36
4	48
x	$12x$

$12x = 180$ *This equation will be solved in Example 3.*

To solve equations with multiplication and division, you will need new tools. Equations of the form $ax = b$, where a and/or b are fractions, are generally solved by using the **multiplication property of equality**.

Multiplication Property of Equality	For any numbers a, b, and c, if $a = b$, then $ac = bc$.

Example 1 Solve $\frac{g}{24} = \frac{5}{12}$.

$$\frac{g}{24} = \frac{5}{12}$$

$$24\left(\frac{g}{24}\right) = 24\left(\frac{5}{12}\right) \quad \textit{Multiply each side by 24.}$$

$$g = 2(5) \text{ or } 10$$

Check:

$$\frac{g}{24} = \frac{5}{12}$$

$$\frac{10}{24} \stackrel{?}{=} \frac{5}{12} \quad \textit{Replace g with 10.}$$

$$\frac{5}{12} = \frac{5}{12} \checkmark$$

The solution is 10.

Example 2 Solve each equation.

a. $\left(3\frac{1}{4}\right)p = 2\frac{1}{2}$

$$\left(3\frac{1}{4}\right)p = 2\frac{1}{2}$$

$$\frac{13}{4}p = \frac{5}{2} \quad \textit{Rewrite the mixed numbers as improper fractions.}$$

$$\frac{4}{13}\left(\frac{13}{4}\right)p = \frac{4}{13}\left(\frac{5}{2}\right) \quad \textit{Multiply each side by } \tfrac{4}{13}\textit{, the reciprocal of } \tfrac{13}{4}.$$

$$p = \frac{20}{26} \text{ or } \frac{10}{13} \quad \textit{Check this result.}$$

The solution is $\frac{10}{13}$.

b. $40 = -5d$

$$40 = -5d$$

$$-\frac{1}{5}(40) = -\frac{1}{5}(-5d) \quad \textit{Multiply each side by } -\tfrac{1}{5}.$$

$$-8 = d \quad \textit{Check this result.}$$

The solution is -8.

GLOBAL CONNECTIONS

From 1985 to 1987, Rick Hansen, a wheelchair athlete, went around the world in a wheelchair. He covered 34 countries on four continents, logging 24,000 miles and raising money for wheelchair sports and research on spinal cord injuries.

The equation in Example 2b, $40 = -5d$, was solved by multiplying each side by $-\frac{1}{5}$. The same result could have been obtained by dividing each side by -5. This method uses the **division property of equality**. It is often easier to use than the multiplication property of equality.

Division Property of Equality	For any numbers a, b, and c, with $c \neq 0$, if $a = b$, then $\frac{a}{c} = \frac{b}{c}$.

Example 3

APPLICATION
Construction

Refer to the application at the beginning of the lesson. Solve $12x = 180$.

$$12x = 180$$

$$\frac{12x}{12} = \frac{180}{12} \quad \textit{Divide each side by 12.}$$

$$x = 15$$

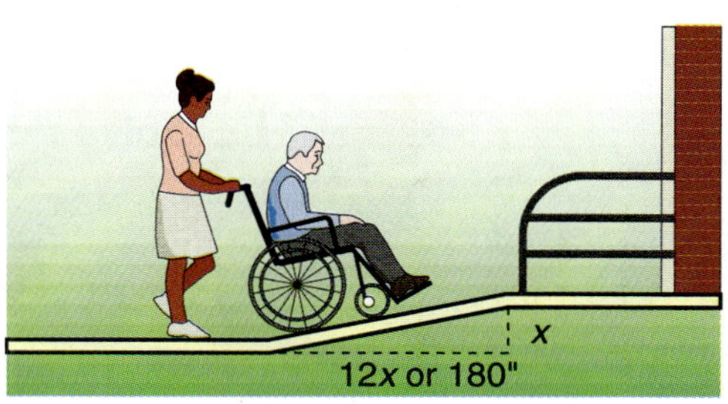

Check:

$$12x = 180$$

$$12(15) \stackrel{?}{=} 180$$

$$180 = 180 \ \checkmark$$

The rise of the ramp could be at most 15 inches.

Example **4** **Solve $3x = -9$.**

$$3x = -9$$

$$\frac{3x}{3} = \frac{-9}{3} \quad \textit{Divide each side by 3.}$$

$$x = -3$$

Recall that an equation mat is a model of an equation. You can group each cup on the left side of the mat with the same number of counters on the right side of the mat.

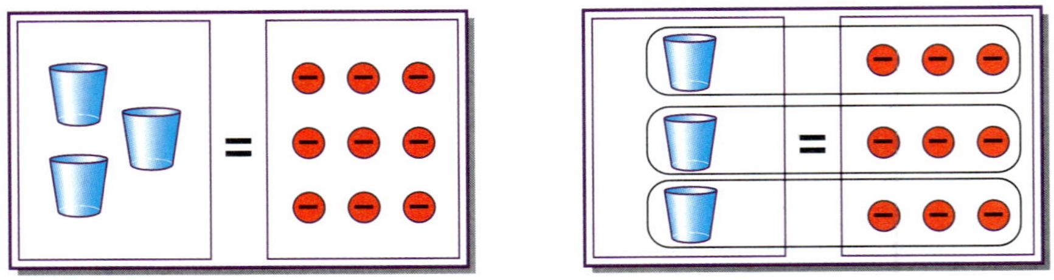

$3x = -9$ $\qquad$ $x = -3$

The solution is -3.

CHECK FOR UNDERSTANDING

Communicating Mathematics

Study the lesson. Then complete the following.

1. **You Decide** Kezia says that the equation $0x = 8$ has a solution. Doralina says it doesn't. Which one is correct, and why?
2. **Define** the terms *rise* and *run* in your own words.
3. **Refer** to the application at the beginning of the lesson. If the maximum rise is 30″, what is the maximum run?
4. **Draw** a model and explain how to find the width of a rectangle if its area is 51 m^2 and its length is 17 m.

MODELING MATHEMATICS

5. Use cups and counters to model $4x = 16$. Then solve the equation.

Guided Practice

Solve each equation. Then check your solution.

6. $-8t = 56$
7. $-5s = -85$
8. $42.51x = 8$
9. $\frac{k}{8} = 6$
10. $-10 = \frac{b}{-7}$
11. $-5x = -3\frac{2}{3}$

Define a variable, write an equation, and solve the problem. Then check your solution.

12. Eight times a number is 216. What is the number?
13. The product of -7 and a number is 1.477. What is the number?

EXERCISES

Practice

Solve each equation. Then check your solution.

14. $-4r = -28$	**15.** $5x = -45$	**16.** $9x = 40$
17. $-3y = 52$	**18.** $3w = -11$	**19.** $434 = -31y$
20. $1.7b = -39.1$	**21.** $0.49x = 6.277$	**22.** $-5.73c = 97.41$
23. $-0.63y = -378$	**24.** $11 = \frac{x}{5}$	**25.** $\frac{h}{11} = -25$
26. $\frac{c}{-8} = -14$	**27.** $\frac{2}{5}t = -10$	**28.** $-\frac{11}{8}x = 42$
29. $-\frac{13}{5}y = -22$	**30.** $3x = 4\frac{2}{3}$	**31.** $\left(-4\frac{1}{2}\right)x = 36$

Define a variable, write an equation, and solve each problem. Then check your solution.

32. Six times a number is -96. Find the number.

33. Negative twelve times a number is -156. What is the number?

34. One fourth of a number is -16.325. What is the number?

35. Four thirds of a number is 4.82. What is the number?

36. Seven eighths of a number is 14. What is the number?

Complete.

37. If $3x = 15$, then $9x =$ __?__ .

38. If $10y = 46$, then $5y =$ __?__ .

39. If $2a = -10$, then $-6a =$ __?__ .

40. If $12b = -1$, then $4b =$ __?__ .

41. If $7k - 5 = 4$, then $21k - 15 =$ __?__ .

Critical Thinking

42. If $-x$ and $-1 \cdot x$ always represent the same number, does $-x$ always stand for a negative number? Explain your reasoning.

Applications and Problem Solving

Write an equation to represent each situation. Then solve the problem.

43. Sociology Research conducted by a daily U.S. newspaper has shown that about 1 in 7 people in the world are left-handed.

a. About how many left-handed people are there in a group of 350 people? 583 people?

b. If there are 65 left-handed people in a group, about how many people are in that group?

44. Demographics In the year 2000, there will be about $1\frac{1}{2}$ times the number of 15- to 19-year-olds in the U.S than there were in 1960. If the U.S. Census Bureau projects that there will be 19,819,000 15- to 19-year-olds in the year 2000, about how many were there in 1960?

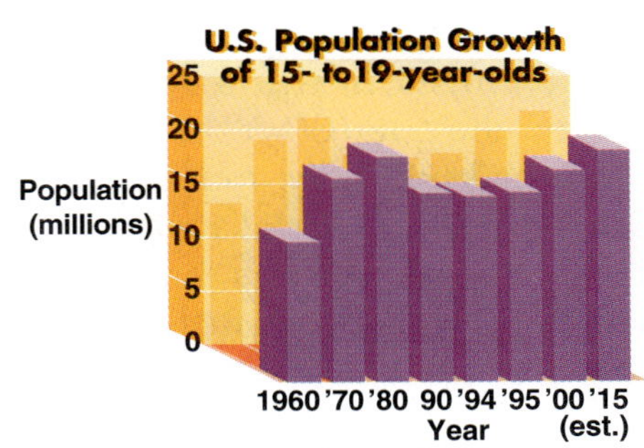

Source: U.S.Census Bureau

45. Telecommunications In 1995, a long-distance company introduced a plan in which long-distance calls placed on weekends cost only \$0.10 per minute.

a. How long could you talk for \$2.30?

b. What would be the cost of an 18-minute call?

Mixed Review

46. Solve $-11 = a + 8$. Then check your solution. (Lesson 3–1)

47. Define a variable, then write an equation for the problem below. (Lesson 2–9)
Ponderosa pines grow about $1\frac{1}{2}$ feet each year. If a pine tree is now 17 feet tall, about how long will it take for the tree to become $33\frac{1}{2}$ feet tall?

48. **World Records** The longest loaf of bread ever baked was 2132 feet $2\frac{1}{2}$ inches. If this loaf were cut into $\frac{1}{2}$-inch slices, how many slices of bread would there have been? (Lesson 2–7)

49. Find a number between $\frac{1}{2}$ and $\frac{6}{7}$. (Lesson 2–4)

50. Graph $\{-1, 1, 3, 5\}$ on a number line. (Lesson 2–1)

51. The graph at the right shows the number of bags of potato chips in the snack machine at Lee High School two times during an average day. (Lesson 1–9)
   a. What can you learn from looking at the graph?
   b. What do you think happened between the times indicated by the dots?
   c. If lunch at Lee is between 11:45 A.M. and 1:15 P.M., estimate the number of bags you think would be in the machine at 1:30 P.M. Justify your estimate.

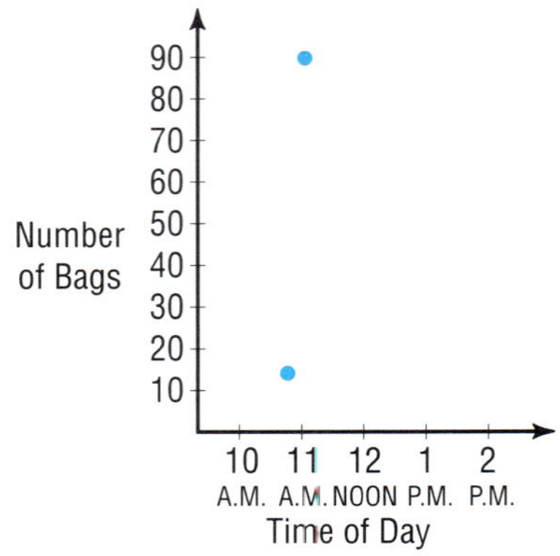

52. Simplify $5(3x + 2y - 4y)$. (Lesson 1–7)

53. Evaluate $a + b^2 + c^2$ if $a = 6$, $b = 4$, and $c = 3$. (Lesson 1–1)

WORKING ON THE In·ves·ti·ga·tion

Refer to the Investigation on pages 68–69.

the Greenhouse Effect

The changes in the levels of carbon dioxide (CO_2) on Earth happened naturally until nearly 200 years ago. During the Industrial Revolution of the early 1800s, a new factor was thrown into the equation. When wood and fossil fuels like coal, oil, and natural gas are burned, CO_2 is released in large quantities. Oceans and vegetation absorb the gas. But due to the widespread cutting of trees to produce goods in the 1900s, few remained to soak up excess CO_2. In 1920, atmospheric CO_2 stood at about 280 parts per million (ppm). By 1996, it had risen to 356 ppm.

1. Make a chart that shows the changes in the levels of CO_2 in our atmosphere. Assume that the levels of CO_2 grow at a constant rate over the years. Use the headings *Year, Amount of CO_2 (ppm),* and *Change.* Start the chart with 1920, and end with the present year.
2. Write a paragraph about the patterns you see in your chart. Use the terms *function, independent, dependent, domain,* and *range.*
3. Based on the relationships you found in the previous question, determine how much CO_2 was in the atmosphere in 1800 and 1950. Explain how you found those amounts.
4. Predict the amounts of CO_2 that will be in the atmosphere in the years 2000, 2020, 2050, and 3000. Explain how you made your predictions.

Add the results of your work to your Investigation Folder.

MODELING MATHEMATICS

A Preview of Lesson 3–3

3–3A Solving Multi-Step Equations

Materials: cups & counters; equation mat

You can use an equation model to solve equations with more than one operation or equations with a variable on each side.

Activity 1 Use an equation model to solve $2x + 2 = -4$.

Step 1 Model the equation by placing 2 cups and 2 positive counters on one side of the mat. Place 4 negative counters on the other side of the mat. Add 2 negative counters to each side to form zero pairs on the left.

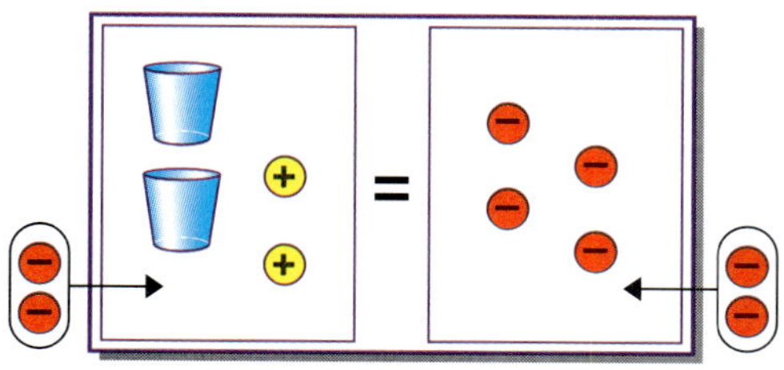

$2x + 2 = -4$

Step 2 Group the counters to form zero pairs and remove the zero pairs. Separate the remaining counters into 2 equal groups to match the 2 cups. Each cup is paired with 3 negative counters. Therefore, $x = -3$.

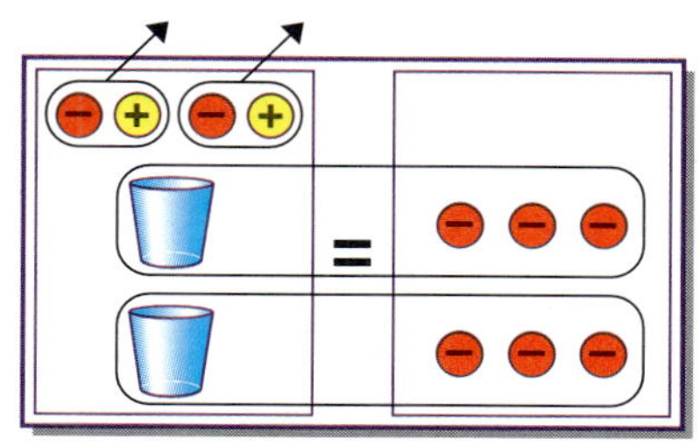

$x = -3$

Activity 2 Use an equation model to solve $w - 3 = 2w - 1$.

Step 1 Model the equation by placing 1 cup and 3 negative counters on one side of the mat. Place 2 cups and 1 negative counter on the other side of the mat. Remove 1 negative counter from each side of the mat.

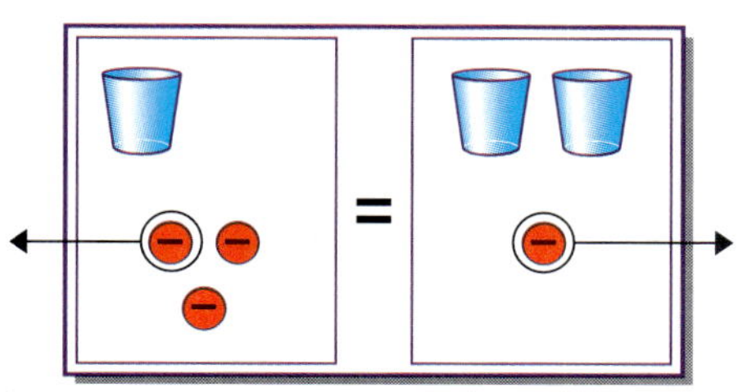

$w - 3 = 2w - 1$

Step 2 You can remove the same number of cups from each side of the mat. In this case, remove 1 cup from each side. The cup on the right is matched with 2 negative counters. Therefore, $w = -2$.

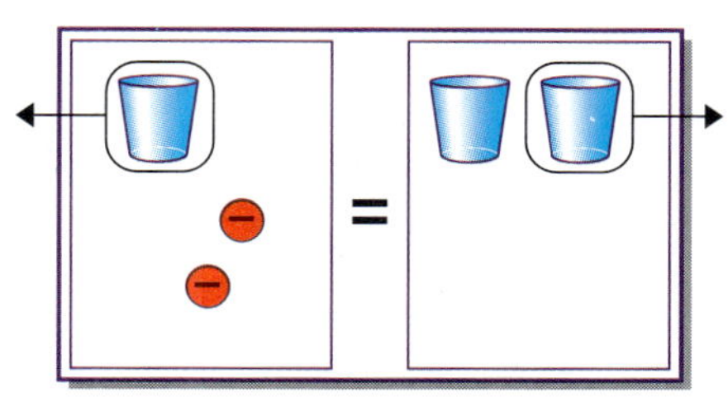

$w = -2$

Model Use equation models to solve each equation.

1. $2x + 3 = 13$

2. $2y - 2 = -4$

3. $-4 = 3a + 2$

4. $3m - 2 = 4$

5. $3x + 2 = x + 6$

6. $3x + 7 = x + 1$

7. $3x - 2 = x + 6$

8. $y + 1 = 3y - 7$

9. $2b + 3 = b + 1$

3-3 Solving Multi-Step Equations

What YOU'LL LEARN

- To solve equations involving more than one operation, and
- to solve problems by working backward.

Why IT'S IMPORTANT

You can use equations to solve problems involving home repair, health, and world cultures.

F Y I

The *kimono* has been worn by Japanese men and women since the 7th Century A.D. It is an ankle-length gown with long wide sleeves and is secured by a sash called an *obi.*

APPLICATION
World Cultures

On June 9, 1993, Japan's Crown Prince Naruhito wed former diplomat Masako Owada. It took Ms. Owada about $2\frac{1}{2}$ hours to put on her wedding kimono, a 12-layered silk garment that weighed about 30 pounds. The prince wore a kimono of bright orange—the "sunrise color"—that can only be worn by the heir to the throne.

After the wedding, the crown prince changed into a tuxedo and the princess into a bridal gown to formally announce their marriage to the Emperor and Empress. To change into the bridal gown, Princess Masako and her attendants had to remove the wedding kimono, a process that was similar to putting on the garment, only in reverse order. You will solve certain kinds of problems by working in reverse order, or **working backward.** Work backward is one of many *problem-solving strategies* that you can use to solve problems. Here are some other problem-solving strategies.

Problem-Solving Strategies	
draw a diagram	solve a simpler (or a similar) problem
make a table or chart	eliminate the possibilities
make a model	look for a pattern
guess and check	act it out
check for hidden assumptions	list the possibilities
use a graph	identify subgoals

Example 1 **Due to melting, an ice sculpture loses one-half its weight every hour. After 8 hours, it weighs $\frac{5}{16}$ of a pound. How much did it weigh in the beginning?**

Make a table to show weight as a function of time. Work backward to find the original weight.

Recall that the sculpture loses one-half its weight every hour. Multiply the current weight of the sculpture by 2 to find its weight an hour before. Continue multiplying until you reach the original weight.

The original weight of the sculpture was 80 pounds.

Hour	Weight
8	$\frac{5}{16}$
7	$2\left(\frac{5}{16}\right) = \frac{5}{8}$
6	$2\left(\frac{5}{8}\right) = \frac{5}{4}$
5	$2\left(\frac{5}{4}\right) = \frac{5}{2}$
4	$2\left(\frac{5}{2}\right) = 5$
3	$2(5) = 10$
2	$2(10) = 20$
1	$2(20) = 40$
0	$2(40) = 80$

To solve equations with more than one operation, often called **multi-step equations,** you will undo the operations by working backward.

Example 2

APPLICATION
Home Repair

Mrs. Guzman needs a repairperson to fix her washing machine. Since her machine is pretty old, she doesn't want to spend more than \$100 for repairs. The owner of Albie's Appliances told her that a service call would cost \$35 and the labor would be an additional \$20 per hour. What is the maximum number of hours that the repairperson can work and keep the total cost at \$100?

Explore Read the problem and define the variable.
Let h represent the maximum number of hours the repair can take.

Plan Write an equation.

\$35 plus \$20 per hour for h hours equals \$100.

$$35 + 20h = 100$$

Solve Work backward to solve the equation.

$$35 + 20h = 100$$
$$35 - 35 + 20h = 100 - 35$$
Undo the addition first. Use the subtraction property of equality.

$$20h = 65$$
$$\frac{20h}{20} = \frac{65}{20}$$
Then undo the multiplication. Use the division property of equality.

$$h = \frac{13}{4} \text{ or } 3\frac{1}{4}$$

The repairperson has up to $3\frac{1}{4}$ hours to fix the washing machine.

Examine Check to see if the answer makes sense.

$3\frac{1}{4} \times \$20 = \$65$ $\quad$ $\$35 + \$65 = \$100$

EXPLORATION — GRAPHING CALCULATORS

You can use a graphing calculator to solve multi-step equations. The *solve(* function will solve an equation if it is rewritten as an expression that equals zero, or most commonly, in the form $ax + b - c = 0$. This function also requires that you include a guess about the solution to the equation. The format is as follows.

solve(*expression,variable,guess*)

To solve the equation $3x - 4 = 2$, access the math function by pressing the MATH key. Then choose 0, for solve. Enter the expression $3x - 4 - 2$, the variable x, and a guess about its solution. If we guess -1, then this appears on the calculator screen: solve(3X-4-2,X,-1). When you press ENTER, the solution, 2, appears on the screen.

Your Turn

a. Work through the examples in this lesson by using a graphing calculator.

b. Describe the process of using a graphing calculator to solve equations in your own words.

c. Why did we input the equation $3x - 4 = 2$ as $3x - 4 - 2$?

d. How would you use a graphing calculator to solve the equation $3x - 4 = -2x + 6$?

You have seen a multi-step equation in which the first, or *leading,* coefficient is an integer. You can use the same steps if the leading coefficient is a fraction.

Example 3 **Solve each equation.**

a. $\frac{y}{5} + 9 = 6$

$\frac{y}{5} + 9 = 6$ *The leading coefficient is $\frac{1}{5}$.*

$\frac{y}{5} + 9 - 9 = 6 - 9$ *First, subtract 9 from each side. Why?*

$\frac{y}{5} = -3$

$5\left(\frac{y}{5}\right) = 5(-3)$ *Then, multiply each side by 5.*

$y = -15$

Check: $\frac{y}{5} + 9 = 6$

$\frac{-15}{5} + 9 \stackrel{?}{=} 6$

$-3 + 9 \stackrel{?}{=} 6$

$6 = 6$ ✔

The solution is -15.

b. $\frac{d-2}{3} = 7$

$\frac{d-2}{3} = 7$

$3\left(\frac{d-2}{3}\right) = 3(7)$ *Multiply each side by 3. Why?*

$d - 2 = 21$

$d - 2 + 2 = 21 + 2$ *Add 2 to each side.*

$d = 23$

Check: $\frac{d-2}{3} = 7$

$\frac{23-2}{3} \stackrel{?}{=} 7$

$\frac{21}{3} \stackrel{?}{=} 7$

$7 = 7$ ✔

The solution is 23.

Consecutive integers are integers in counting order, such as 3, 4, 5. Beginning with an even integer and counting by two will result in *consecutive even integers.* For example, -6, -4, -2, 0, and 2 are consecutive even integers. Beginning with an odd integer and counting by two will result in *consecutive odd integers.* For example, -1, 1, 3, and 5 are consecutive odd integers.

The study of numbers and the relationships between them is called **number theory.** Number theory involves the study of odd and even numbers.

Example 4 INTEGRATION Number Theory

Find three consecutive odd integers whose sum is −15.

Let n = the least odd integer.
Then $n + 2$ = the next greater odd integer,
and $n + 4$ = the greatest of the three odd integers.

$$n + (n + 2) + (n + 4) = -15$$
$$3n + 6 = -15 \quad \textit{Simplify.}$$
$$3n + 6 - 6 = -15 - 6 \quad \textit{Subtract 6 from each side.}$$
$$3n = -21$$
$$\frac{3n}{3} = \frac{-21}{3} \quad \textit{Divide each side by 3.}$$
$$n = -7$$

$n + 2 = -7 + 2$ $\qquad$ $n + 4 = -7 + 4$
$n + 2 = -5$ $\qquad$ $n + 4 = -3$

The consecutive odd integers are −7, −5, and −3.

CHECK FOR UNDERSTANDING

Communicating Mathematics

Study the lesson. Then complete the following.

1. a. **Explain** how you would solve $2p + 10 = 42$ if you had to undo the multiplication first.
   b. **Explain** why undoing the multiplication first would be inconvenient for solving the equation $7x - 4 = 24$.
2. **Determine** if the following statement is *sometimes, always,* or *never* true. Explain your thinking. The sum of two consecutive even numbers equals the sum of two consecutive odd numbers.
3. If n is an even integer, explain how to find the even integer just before it.
4. **Explain** why −2 is not the solution of the equation $4x + 3x - 5 = 27$.
5. **List** three consecutive even integers if the greatest one is −18.
6. If $2x + 1 = 5$, then $3x - 4$ is *sometimes, always,* or *never* 2? Explain your reasoning.

MODELING MATHEMATICS

7. Write an equation for the model at the right. Then use cups and counters to solve the equation.

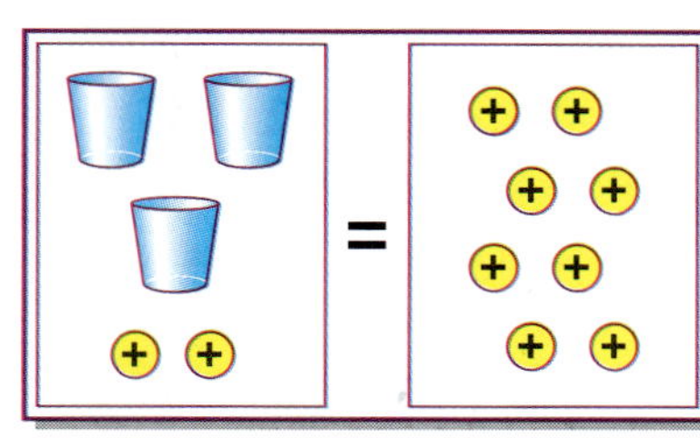

Guided Practice

Explain how to solve each equation. Then solve.

8. $4a - 5 = 15$
9. $7 + 3c = -11$
10. $\frac{2}{9}v - 6 = 14$
11. $3 - \frac{a}{7} = -2$
12. $\frac{x - 3}{7} = -2$
13. $\frac{p - (-5)}{-2} = 6$

Define a variable, write an equation, and solve each problem. Then check your solution.

14. Find two consecutive integers whose sum is −31.
15. Find three consecutive odd integers whose sum is 21.
16. Twenty-nine is 13 added to 4 times a number. Find the number.

EXERCISES

Practice

Solve each equation. Then check your solution.

17. $3x - 2 = -5$ **18.** $-4 = 5n + 6$ **19.** $5 - 9w = 23$

20. $17 = 7 + 8y$ **21.** $-2.5d - 32.7 = 74.1$ **22.** $0.2n + 3 = 8.6$

23. $\frac{3}{2}a - 8 = 11$ **24.** $5 = -9 - \frac{p}{4}$ **25.** $7 = \frac{c}{-3} + 5$

26. $\frac{m}{-5} + 6 = 31$ **27.** $\frac{g}{8} - 6 = -12$ **28.** $6 = -12 + \frac{h}{-7}$

29. $\frac{b+4}{-2} = -17$ **30.** $\frac{z-7}{5} = -3$ **31.** $-10 = \frac{17-s}{4}$

32. $\frac{4t-5}{-9} = 7$ **33.** $\frac{7n+(-1)}{6} = 5$ **34.** $\frac{-3j-(-4)}{-6} = 12$

INTEGRATION
Number Theory

Define a variable, write an equation, and solve each problem. Then check your solution.

35. Twelve decreased by twice a number is -7.

36. Find three consecutive integers whose sum is -33.

37. Find four consecutive integers whose sum is 86.

38. Find two consecutive odd integers whose sum is 196.

INTEGRATION
Geometry

Make a diagram to represent each situation. Then define a variable, write an equation, and solve each problem. Check your solution.

39. The lengths of the sides of a triangle are consecutive odd integers. The perimeter is 39 meters. What are the lengths of the sides?

40. The lengths of the sides of a quadrilateral are consecutive even integers. Twice the length of the shortest side plus the length of the longest side is 120 inches. Find the lengths of the four sides.

Graphing Calculator

Solve each equation. Then use a graphing calculator to verify your solution.

41. $0.2x + 3 = 8.6$ **42.** $4.91 + 7.2x = 39.4201$

43. $\frac{3+x}{7} = -5$ **44.** $\frac{-3n-(-4)}{-6} = -9$

Critical Thinking

45. Write an expression for the sum of three consecutive even integers if $3n - 1$ is the least integer.

Applications and Problem Solving

For Exercises 46–47, write an equation to represent each situation. Then solve the problem.

46. Health According to the American Medical Association, the average birth weight of a baby in the United States is 7.5 pounds. After birth, most babies lose an average of 1 ounce a day for the first 5 days and then gain an average of 1 ounce a day for the next 13 weeks.

a. Suppose a baby weighs 7.5 pounds at birth. After how many days will the baby weigh 12 pounds?

b. Draw a graph that shows the expected weight of a 7.5-pound baby for each of its first 13 weeks of life.

47. World Cultures Hawaii became our 50th state in 1959. It's the only state that is not on the North American continent. The English alphabet contains 2 more than twice as many letters as the Hawaiian alphabet. How many letters are there in the Hawaiian alphabet?

48. **Work Backward** Four families went to a baseball game. A vendor selling bags of popcorn came by. The Wilson family bought half of the bags of popcorn plus one. The Martinez family bought half of the remaining bags of popcorn plus one. The Brightfeather family bought half of the remaining bags of popcorn plus one. The Wimberly family bought half of the remaining bags of popcorn plus one, leaving the vendor with no bags of popcorn. If the Wimberlys bought 2 bags of popcorn, how many bags did each of the four families buy?

Mixed Review

49. **Health** One way to calculate your suggested daily intake of fat grams is to multiply your ideal weight in pounds times 0.454. (Lesson 3–2)
   a. Write an equation to represent your suggested daily intake.
   b. What is your suggested daily intake of fat grams?

50. Complete: If $x + 4 = 15$, then $x - 2 = \underline{\ ?\ }$. (Lesson 3–1)

51. Name the set or sets of numbers to which $\sqrt{11}$ belongs. Use N for natural numbers, W for whole numbers, Z for integers, Q for rational numbers, or I for irrational numbers. (Lesson 2–8)

52. Simplify $\frac{-200x}{50}$. (Lesson 2–7)

53. Simplify $4(7) - 3(11)$. (Lesson 2–6)

54. Name the property illustrated by $9 + (2 + 10) = 9 + 12$. (Lesson 1–6)

55. Solve $a = \frac{12 + 8}{4}$. (Lesson 1–5)

56. Evaluate $\frac{3}{4}(6) + \frac{1}{3}(12)$. (Lesson 1–3)

SELF TEST

Solve each equation. (Lessons 3–1, 3–2, and 3–3)

1. $-10 + k = 34$
2. $y - 13 = 45$
3. $20.4 = 3.4y$
4. $-65 = \frac{f}{29}$
5. $-3x - 7 = 18$
6. $5 = \frac{m - 5}{4}$

Write an equation and solve. Then check your solution.

7. Twenty-three minus a number is 42. Find the number. (Lesson 3–1)
8. **Geometry** The length of one side of a rectangle is 34 cm. The area of the rectangle is 68 cm^2. Find the width of the rectangle. (Lesson 3–2)
9. **Number Theory** Find two consecutive even integers whose sum is 126. (Lesson 3–3)
10. **Economics** According to the *Baltimore Sun,* if inflation continues at the current rate, the price of a movie ticket in 40 years will be $3.50 less than 10 times the current average price of $5.05. What will be the price of a movie ticket in 40 years? (Lesson 3–3)

3–4 Integration: Geometry
Angles and Triangles

What YOU'LL LEARN

- To find the complement and supplement of an angle, and
- to find the measure of the third angle of a triangle given the measures of the other two angles.

Why IT'S IMPORTANT

A knowledge of angles and triangles will help you further your study of geometry and trigonometry.

APPLICATION
Football

On fourth down in a football game, the team with the ball usually *punts.* A punt is a kick in which the ball is dropped by the kicker and is kicked before it hits the ground.

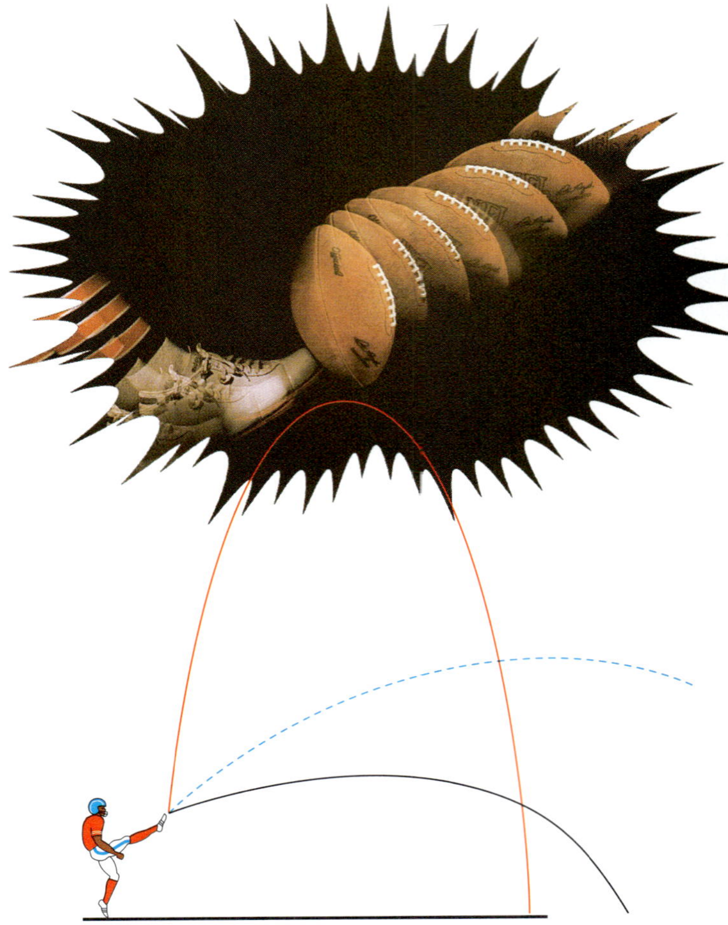

The longest punt ever kicked in a college football game was kicked by Pat Brady of the University of Nevada-Reno in their 1950 game against Loyola University. The punt was 99 yards long—just 1 yard short of spanning the entire length of the football field.

How far a football will travel once it is punted depends not only on the strength of the punter, but also on the angle at which the ball is kicked. If the angle is too small, the ball will travel close to the ground, then drop; if the angle is too large, the ball will travel high, but not very far. What do you think would be the best angle at which to kick the ball?

The symbol for angle is $\angle$.

You can use a *protractor* to measure angles, as shown below.

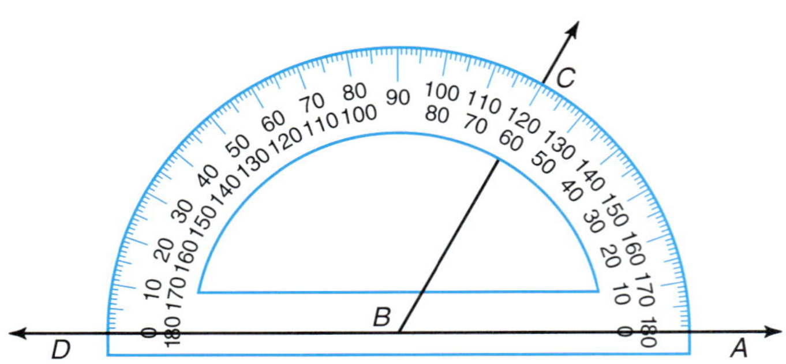

Angle ABC (denoted $\angle ABC$) measures 60°. However, where ray BC (denoted $\overrightarrow{BC}$) intersects the curve of the protractor, there are two readings, 60° and 120°. The measure of $\angle DBC$ is 120°. What is the sum of the measures of $\angle ABC$ and $\angle DBC$?

Supplementary Angles	**Two angles are supplementary if the sum of their measures is 180°.**

Example 1 **The measure of an angle is three times the measure of its supplement. Find the measure of each angle.**

Let x = the lesser measure. Then $3x$ = the greater measure.

$x + 3x = 180$ *The angles are supplementary.*

$4x = 180$ *Add like terms.*

$\frac{4x}{4} = \frac{180}{4}$ *Divide each side by 4.*

$x = 45$

The measures are 45° and $3 \cdot 45°$ or 135°. *Check this result.*

Complementary Angles — **Two angles are complementary if the sum of their measures is 90°.**

Example 2

APPLICATION

Golf

Top Five List

Lowest winning scores in the U.S. Masters Tournament

1. 271, Raymond Floyd, 1976
1. 271, Jack Nicklaus, 1965
3. 274, Ben Hogan, 1953
4. 275, Severiano Ballesteros, 1980
4. 275, Fred Couples, 1992

The backward slant of the face of a golf club head is called the *loft*. It is designed to drive the ball in a high arc. Assuming that the angle made by the ground and the face of the club is 79°, what is the measure of the loft?

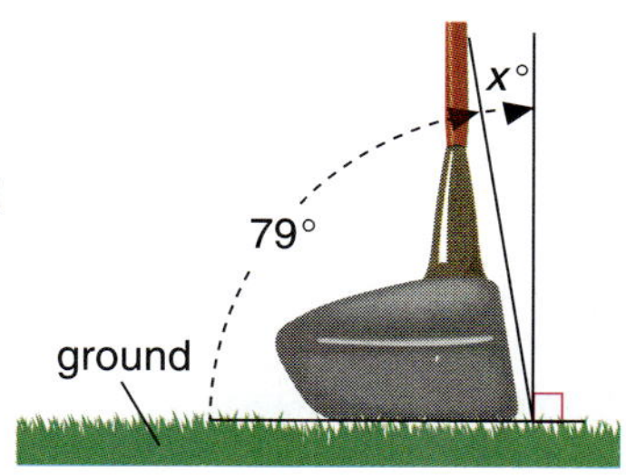

Let x = the measure of the loft.

$79° + x = 90°$ *The angles are complementary.*

$79° - 79° + x = 90° - 79°$ *Subtract 79° from each side.*

$x = 11°$

The club has an 11° loft.

Example 3 **The measure of an angle is 34° greater than its complement. Find the measure of each angle.**

Let x = the lesser measure. Then $x + 34$ = the greater measure.

$x + (x + 34) = 90$ *The angles are complementary.*

$2x + 34 = 90$

$2x + 34 - 34 = 90 - 34$ *Subtract 34 from each side.*

$2x = 56$

$\frac{2x}{2} = \frac{56}{2}$ *Divide each side by 2.*

$x = 28$

The measures are 28° and 28° + 34° or 62°. *Check this result.*

A **triangle** is a polygon with three sides and three angles. What is the sum of the measures of the three angles of a triangle?

MODELING MATHEMATICS

Angles of a Triangle

Materials: 3 sheets of construction paper, protractor, scissors

Copy each triangle below onto a sheet of construction paper. If possible, you may want to enlarge the triangles on a photocopier.

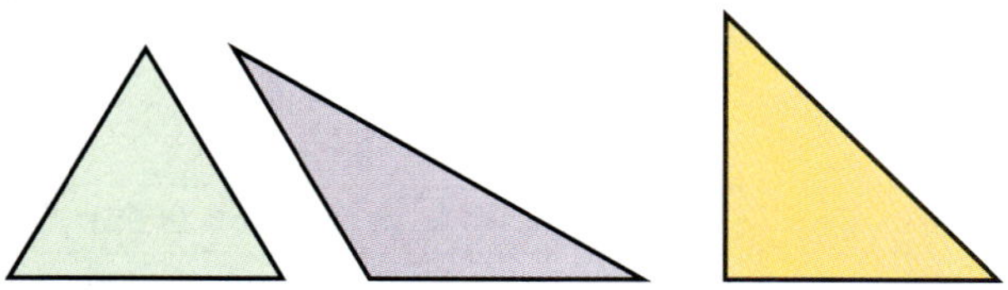

Your Turn

a. Use a protractor to measure the angles of each triangle above. What is the sum of the measures of the three angles of each triangle?

b. Cut out one of the triangles. Label the angles *A*, *B*, and *C*. Tear off the angles and arrange as shown.

c. When the angles were put together, what was the measure of the new angle they formed?

d. Try this activity with another triangle. What do you think is true about the measures of the angles of any triangle?

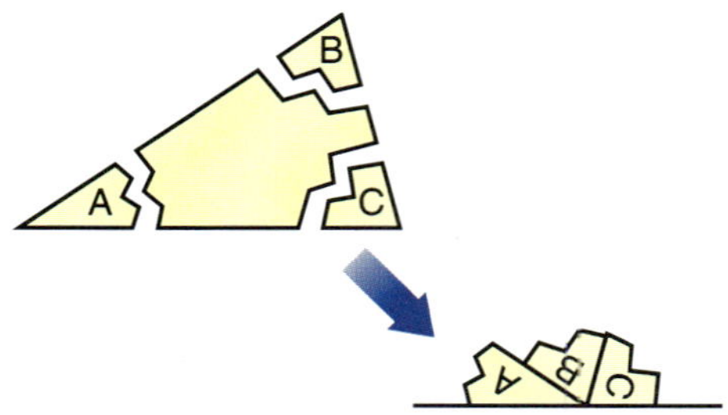

Sum of the Angles of a Triangle	The sum of the measures of the angles in any triangle is 180°.

In an **equilateral triangle,** each angle has the same measure. We say that the angles are **congruent.** The sides of an equilateral triangle are also congruent. What is the measure of each angle of an equilateral triangle?

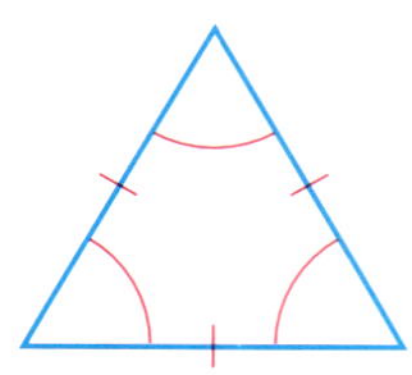

Let x = the measure of each angle.

$x + x + x = 180$

$3x = 180$ *Add like terms.*

$\frac{3x}{3} = \frac{180}{3}$ *Divide each side by 3.*

$x = 60$ Each angle measures 60°.

In an **isosceles triangle,** at least two angles have the same measure. Generally, the two congruent angles are the base angles.

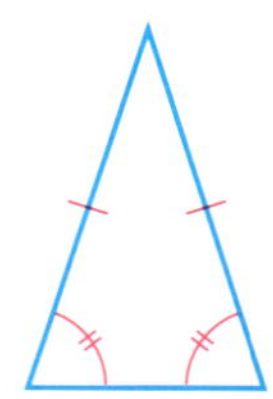

Example 4 **What are the measures of the base angles of an isosceles triangle in which the vertex angle measures 45°?**

Let x = the measure of each base angle.

$x + x + 45 = 180$

$2x + 45 = 180$ *Add like terms.*

$2x + 45 - 45 = 180 - 45$ *Subtract 45 from each side.*

$2x = 135$

$\frac{2x}{2} = \frac{135}{2}$ *Divide each side by 2.*

$x = \frac{135}{2}$ or $67\frac{1}{2}$ The base angles each measure $67\frac{1}{2}°$.

Triangles are often classified in one of three ways. A **right triangle** has one angle that measures 90°. An **obtuse triangle** has one angle with measure greater than 90°. In an **acute triangle,** all of the angles measure less than 90°.

Example 5 **The measures of the angles of a triangle are given as $x°$, $2x°$, and $3x°$.**

a. What are the measures of each angle?
b. Classify the triangle.

a. The sum of the measures of the angles of a triangle is 180°.

$$x + 2x + 3x = 180$$
$$6x = 180 \quad \textit{Add like terms.}$$
$$\frac{6x}{6} = \frac{180}{6} \quad \textit{Divide each side by 6.}$$
$$x = 30$$

The measures are 30°, 2(30°) or 60°, and 3(30°) or 90°.

b. Since the triangle has one angle that measures 90°, it is a right triangle.

CHECK FOR UNDERSTANDING

Communicating Mathematics

Study the lesson. Then complete the following.

1. The words *complement* and *compliment* sound very much alike.
   a. What are their meanings?
   b. Which word has the mathematical meaning?
2. **Compare and contrast** the standard definition and the mathematical meaning of the word *supplement.*
3. **Classify** each of the three triangles in the Modeling Mathematics activity on page 164 as right, obtuse, or acute. Justify your classifications.
4. **Make up a problem** in which you must use an equation to find the measures of the angles of a triangle. Then solve the problem, explaining each step.

MODELING MATHEMATICS

5. Draw a right triangle on a separate piece of paper and cut it out. Cut or tear off the two acute angles and arrange as shown. What seems to be true about the two acute angles?

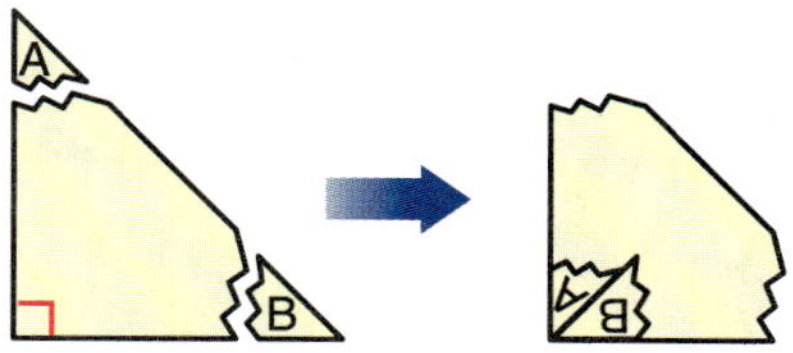

Guided Practice

Find both the complement and the supplement of each angle measure.

6. 130°
7. 11°
8. 24°
9. $3x°$
10. $(2x + 40)°$
11. $(x - 20)°$

Find the measure of the third angle of each triangle in which the measures of two angles of the triangle are given.

12. 16°, 42°
13. 50°, 45°
14. $x°$, $(x + 20)°$

Make a diagram to represent each situation. Then define a variable, write an equation, and solve each problem. Check your solution.

15. An angle measures 38° less than its complement. Find the measures of the two angles.
16. The measures of the angles of a triangle are given as $x°$, $(x + 5)°$, and $(2x + 3)°$. What are the measures of each angle?

EXERCISES

Practice

Find both the complement and the supplement of each angle measure.

17. 42°	**18.** 87°	**19.** 125°
20. 90°	**21.** 21°	**22.** 174°
23. 99°	**24.** $y°$	**25.** $3a°$
26. $(x + 30)°$	**27.** $(b - 38)°$	**28.** $(90 - z°)$

The measures of two angles of a triangle are given. Find the measure of the third angle.

29. 40°, 70°	**30.** 90°, 30°	**31.** 63°, 12°
32. 43°, 118°	**33.** 4°, 38°	**34.** $x°$, $y°$
35. $p°$, $(p - 10)°$	**36.** $c°$, $(2c + 1)°$	**37.** $y°$, $(135 - y)°$

Draw a diagram to represent each situation. Then define a variable, write an equation, and solve each problem. Check your solution.

38. One of the congruent angles of an isosceles triangle measures 37°. Find the measures of the other angles.
39. Find the measure of an angle that is 30° less than its supplement.
40. One of the angles of a triangle measures 53°. Another angle measures 37°. What is the measure of the third angle?
41. One of two complementary angles measures 30° more than three times the other. Find the measure of each angle.
42. Find the measure of an angle that is one-half the measure of its supplement.
43. The measures of the angles of a triangle are given as $x°$, $(3x)°$, and $(4x)°$. What are the measures of each angle?

Critical Thinking

44. Draw a diagram that shows the relationships among right, isosceles, equilateral, acute, scalene, and obtuse triangles.

Applications and Problem Solving

45. **Carpentry** A *stringer* is a triangular piece of wood on which staircases are based. If the stringer makes a 30° angle with the floor, what is the measure of the angle that the stringer makes with the vertical?

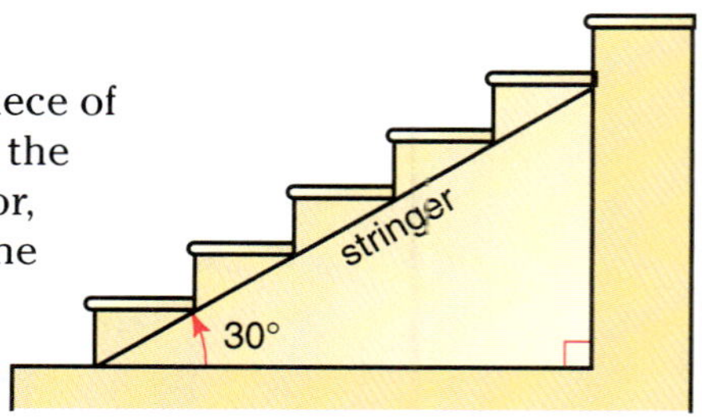

46. **Aeronautics** One of the newer space shuttles is *Endeavour.* Its first flight left Earth on May 7, 1992. The oldest shuttle is *Columbia,* which flew its first flight on April 12, 1981. A space shuttle lands at an angle six times as great as that of the average commercial jet.

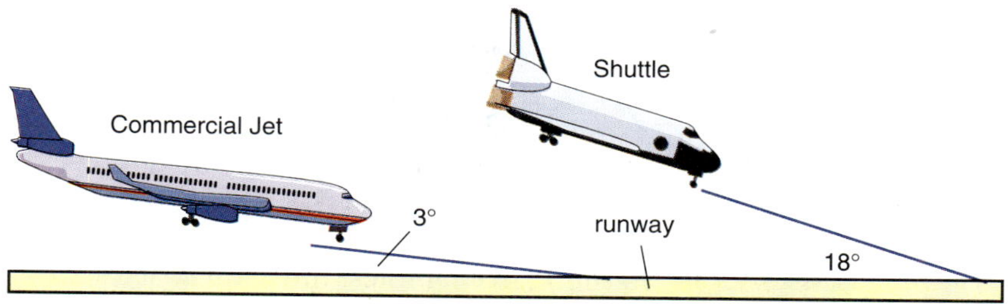

a. What is the measure of the angle the path of the jet makes with the vertical?

b. What is the measure of the angle the path of the shuttle makes with the vertical?

c. Which craft lands at a steeper angle?

47. **Mountain Climbing** *Rapelling* is a technique used by climbers to make a difficult descent. Climbers back to the edge and then spring off. To avoid slipping, the climber's legs should remain at a 90° angle with the side of the ledge. The ledge at the right is 50° off the vertical. What is the measure of the climber's angle with the vertical?

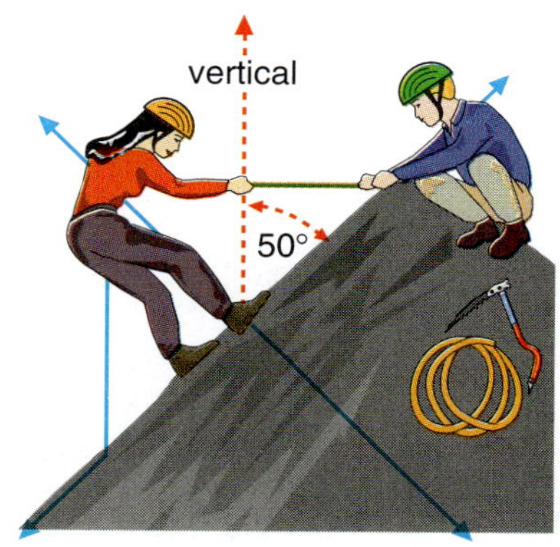

Mixed Review

48. Solve $4 + 7x = 39$. (Lesson 3–3)

49. **Consumerism** When stores go out of business, there is generally a period when all of the items in the store can be purchased for a fraction of the original price. When Central Hardware went out of business, all of the items in the store began at $\frac{1}{4}$ off. (Lesson 3–2)

a. What was the original price of a circular saw if you save $20.00 during the sale?

b. How much would you save on patio furniture that originally cost $299.00?

50. Solve $h + (-13) = -5$. (Lesson 3–1)

51. Simplify $5(3t - 2t) + 2(4t - 3t)$. (Lesson 2–6)

52. Find the sum $5y + (-12y) + (-21y)$. (Lesson 2–5)

53. **American History** Each number below represents the age of a U.S. president on his first inauguration. (Lesson 2–2)

57 61 57 57 58 57 61 54 68 51 49 64 50 48
65 52 56 46 54 49 50 47 55 55 54 42 51 56
55 51 54 51 60 62 43 55 56 61 62 69 64 46

a. Make a number line plot of the ages of the presidents.

b. Do any of the ages appear to be clustered? If so, which ones?

54. Name the property illustrated by $5a + 2b = 2b + 5a$. (Lesson 1–8)

55. **Statistics** Make a stem-and-leaf plot of the data in Exercise 53. (Lesson 1–4)

3-5 Solving Equations with the Variable on Both Sides

What YOU'LL LEARN

- To solve equations with the variable on both sides, and
- to solve equations containing grouping symbols.

Why IT'S IMPORTANT

You can use equations to solve problems involving track and field, business, and geometry.

APPLICATION
Track and Field

In the 1928 Olympics, the winner of the men's 800-meter run, Douglas Lowe of Great Britain, won the race in 1 minute 51.8 seconds, or 111.8 seconds. In that same year, the winner of the women's 800-meter run, Lina Radke of Germany, won the race in 2 minutes 16.8 seconds, or 136.8 seconds. Over the next 64 years, the men's winning times decreased an average of 0.127 seconds per year, and the women's winning times decreased an average of 0.332 seconds per year. Suppose the times continued to decrease at these rates. When will men and women have the same winning times in the 800-meter run?

fabulous FIRSTS

Wilma Rudolph (1940–1994)

Wilma Rudolph was the first woman to win three gold medals at a single Olympic games. She won the 100-meter sprint, the 200-meter dash, and the 4×100-meter relay at the 1960 Olympic Games.

After x years, the men's winning times can be represented by $111.8 - 0.127x$. After x years, the women's winning times can be represented by $136.8 - 0.332x$. The times would be the same when the two expressions are equal.

$$111.8 - 0.127x = 136.8 - 0.332x$$

Many equations contain variables on each side. To solve these types of equations, first use the addition or subtraction property of equality to write an equivalent equation that has all of the variables on one side. Then solve the equation.

Method 1

$$111.8 - 0.127x = 136.8 - 0.332x \quad \text{Use a calculator.}$$

$$111.8 - 0.127x + 0.332x = 136.8 - 0.332x + 0.332x \quad \text{Add } 0.332x \text{ to each side.}$$

$$111.8 + 0.205x = 136.8$$

$$111.8 - 111.8 + 0.205x = 136.8 - 111.8 \quad \text{Subtract 111.8 from each side.}$$

$$0.205x = 25$$

$$\frac{0.205x}{0.205} = \frac{25}{0.205} \quad \text{Divide each side by 0.205.}$$

$$x \approx 122$$

At these rates, the men's and women's winning times will be equal about 122 years after 1928, or in the year 2050.

Method 2

Since two of the decimals involve thousandths, another way to solve the equation would be to multiply each side by 1000 to clear the decimals.

$$111.8 - 0.127x = 136.8 - 0.332x$$

Multiply each side by 1000. $$1000(111.8) - 1000(0.127x) = 1000(136.8) - 1000(0.332x)$$

$$111{,}800 - 127x = 136{,}800 - 332x$$

Add 332x to each side. $$111{,}800 + 205x = 136{,}800$$

Subtract 111,800 from each side. $$205x = 25{,}000$$

Divide each side by 205. $$x \approx 122$$

Example 1 **Solve $\frac{3}{8} - \frac{1}{4}x = \frac{1}{2}x - \frac{3}{4}$.**

$\frac{3}{8} - \frac{1}{4}x = \frac{1}{2}x - \frac{3}{4}$ *The least common denominator is 8.*

$8\left(\frac{3}{8} - \frac{1}{4}x\right) = 8\left(\frac{1}{2}x - \frac{3}{4}\right)$ *Multiply each side by 8.*

$8\left(\frac{3}{8}\right) - 8\left(\frac{1}{4}x\right) = 8\left(\frac{1}{2}x\right) - 8\left(\frac{3}{4}\right)$ *Use the distributive property.*

$3 - 2x = 4x - 6$ *The fractions are eliminated.*

$3 = 6x - 6$ *Add 2x to each side.*

$9 = 6x$ *Add 6 to each side.*

$\frac{3}{2} = x$ *Divide each side by 6.*

The solution is $\frac{3}{2}$. *Check this result.*

TECHNOLOGY Tip

Look back to Lesson 3–3 to see how you would solve an equation with the variable on both sides by using a graphing calculator.

When solving equations that contain grouping symbols, first use the distributive property to remove the grouping symbols.

Example 2 **INTEGRATION Geometry**

One angle of a triangle measures 10° more than the second. The measure of the third angle is twice the sum of the first two angles. Find the measure of each angle.

Make a drawing. Let y = the measure of one angle. Let $y + 10$ = the measure of another angle. Then $2[y + (y + 10)]$ = the measure of the third angle. Recall that the sum of the measures of the angles in any triangle is 180°.

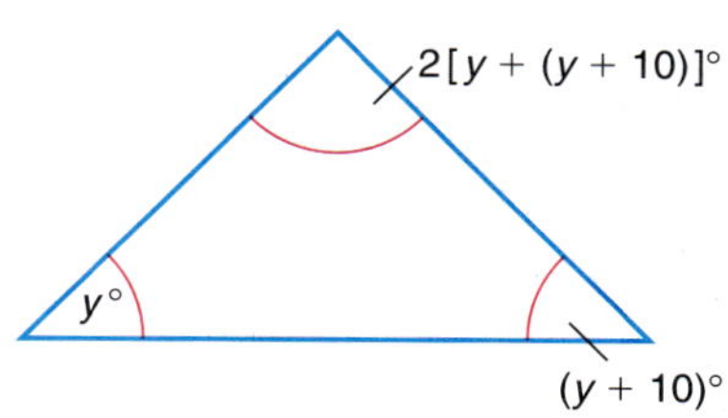

$y + (y + 10) + 2[y + (y + 10)] = 180$

$2y + 10 + 2(2y + 10) = 180$ *Simplify.*

$2y + 10 + 4y + 20 = 180$ *Use the distributive property.*

$6y + 30 = 180$ *Simplify.*

$6y + 30 - 30 = 180 - 30$ *Subtract 30 from each side.*

$6y = 150$

$y = 25$ *Divide each side by 6.*

The measures of the three angles are 25°, (25 + 10)° or 35°, and 2(25 + 35)° or 120°. *Check this result.*

Some equations with the variable on both sides may have no solution. That is, there is no value of the variable that will result in a true equation.

Example 3 **Solve $5n + 4 = 7(n + 1) - 2n$.**

$5n + 4 = 7(n + 1) - 2n$

$5n + 4 = 7n + 7 - 2n$ *Distributive property*

$5n + 4 = 5n + 7$

$4 = 7$ Since $4 = 7$ is a false statement, this equation has no solution.

An equation that is true for every value of the variable is called an **identity.**

Example 4 **Solve $7 + 2(x + 1) = 2x + 9$.**

$7 + 2(x + 1) = 2x + 9$

$7 + 2x + 2 = 2x + 9$ *Distributive property*

$2x + 9 = 2x + 9$ *Reflexive property of equality*

Since the expressions on each side of the equation are the same, this equation is an identity. The statement $7 + 2(x + 1) = 2x + 9$ is true for all values of x.

CHECK FOR UNDERSTANDING

Communicating Mathematics

Study the lesson. Then complete the following.

1. a. **Explain** why you think winning times in the 800-meter run for men and women are growing closer.
   b. **Use a table** to show how women's winning times in the 800-meter run could catch up to men's winning times in the same race.
   c. Do you think the times will ever be the same? Why or why not?
2. **Describe** the difference between an identity and an equation with no solution.
3. **You Decide** Lauren says that to solve the equation $2[x + 3(x - 1)] = 18$, the first step should be to multiply 2 by $[x + 3(x - 1)]$. Carmen says the first step should be to multiply 3 by $(x - 1)$. Which one is correct, and why?

MATH JOURNAL

4. **Assess Yourself** Describe your favorite sport and explain how math is used in it.

Guided Practice

Explain how to solve each equation. Then solve each equation and check your solution.

5. $3 - 4x = 10x + 10$
6. $8y - 10 = -3y + 2$
7. $\frac{3}{5}x + 3 = \frac{1}{5}x - 7$
8. $5.4y + 8.2 = 9.8y - 2.8$
9. $5x - 7 = 5(x - 2) + 3$
10. $4(2x - 1) = -10(x - 5)$

Define a variable, write an equation, and solve each problem. Then check your solution.

11. Twice the greater of two consecutive odd integers is 13 less than three times the lesser. Find the integers.
12. **Geometry** The measures of the angles of a triangle are given as $6x°$, $(x - 3)°$, and $(3x + 7)°$. What are the measures of each angle?
13. One half of a number increased by 16 is four less than two thirds of the number. Find the number.

EXERCISES

Practice

Solve each equation. Then check your solution.

14. $6x + 7 = 8x - 13$

15. $17 + 2n = 21 + 2n$

16. $\frac{3n - 2}{5} = \frac{7}{10}$

17. $\frac{7 + 3t}{4} = -\frac{t}{8}$

18. $13.7b - 6.5 = -2.3b + 8.3$

19. $18 - 3.8x = 7.36 - 1.9x$

20. $\frac{3}{2}y - y = 4 + \frac{1}{2}y$

21. $\frac{3}{4}n + 16 = 2 - \frac{1}{8}n$

22. $-7(x - 3) = -4$

23. $4(x - 2) = 4x$

24. $28 - 2.2y = 11.6y + 262.6$

25. $1.03x - 4 = -2.15x + 8.72$

26. $7 - 3x = x - 4(2 + x)$

27. $6 = 3 + 5(y - 2)$

28. $6(y + 2) - 4 = -10$

29. $5 - \frac{1}{2}(b - 6) = 4$

30. $-8(4 + 9x) = 7(-2 - 11x)$

31. $2(x - 3) + 5 = 3(x - 1)$

32. $4(2a - 8) = \frac{1}{7}(49a + 70)$

33. $-3(2n - 5) = \frac{1}{2}(-12n + 30)$

Define a variable, write an equation, and solve each problem. Then check your solution.

34. Three times the greatest of three consecutive even integers exceeds twice the least by 38. Find the integers.

35. One fifth of a number plus five times that number is equal to seven times the number less 18. Find the number.

36. The difference of two numbers is 12. Two fifths of the greater number is six more than one third of the lesser number. Find both numbers.

INTEGRATION
Geometry

Make a diagram to represent each situation. Then define a variable, write an equation, and solve each problem. Check your solution.

37. The measures of the angles of a certain triangle are consecutive even integers. Find their measures.

38. One angle of a triangle measures 30° more than another angle. The measure of the third angle is three times the sum of the first two angles. Find the measure of each angle.

Programming

39. The graphing calculator program at the right can help you solve equations of the form $ax + b = cx + d$.

```
PROGRAM:SOLVE
: Disp "ENTER A,B,C,D"
: Prompt A: Prompt B: Prompt C:
  Prompt D
: If A - C≠0
: Goto 2
: If D - B≠0
: Goto 1
: Disp "THIS IS AN"
: Disp "IDENTITY"
: Goto 3
: Lbl 1
: Disp "NO SOLUTION"
: Goto 3
: Lbl 2
: Disp "X = ", (D - B)/(A - C)
: Lbl 3
```

Write each equation in the form $ax + b = cx + d$. Then run the program to find the solution.

a. $2(2x + 3) = 4x + 6$

b. $5x - 7 = x + 3$

c. $6 - 3x = 3x - 6$

d. $6.8 + 5.4x = 4.6x + 2.8$

e. $5x - 8 - 3x = 2(x - 3)$

Critical Thinking

40. Mathematics History Diophantus of Alexandria was one of the greatest mathematicians of the Greek civilization. Little is known of his life except for the following problem, which was first printed in a work called the *Greek Anthology*. Although the problem was not written by Diophantus, it is believed to accurately describe his life.

Diophantus passed one sixth of his life in childhood, one twelfth in youth, and one seventh more as a bachelor. Five years after his marriage, there was born a son who died four years before his father, at half his father's (final) age. How old was Diophantus when he died?

Applications and Problem Solving

For Exercises 41–42, assume that the rates of change continue indefinitely.

41. Sales According to the Association of Home Appliance Manufacturers, sales of room air conditioners were 4.6 million units in 1988, and sales of window fans were 0.975 million units in 1988. Since 1988, sales of room air conditioners have decreased about 0.425 million units per year, and sales of window fans have increased about 0.106 million units per year.

a. If the trend continues, after how many years will sales of room air conditioners and window fans be equal?

b. How would you explain these trends?

42. Pet Ownership According to the American Veterinary Medical Association, in 1987, 34.7 million households owned a dog, and 27.7 million households owned a cat. Since 1987, dog ownership has decreased by about 0.025 million households per year, and cat ownership has increased by about 0.375 million households per year. If the trend continues, after how many years will the number of households that own dogs and cats be equal?

Mixed Review

43. Find the supplement of a 32° angle. (Lesson 3–4)

44. Work Backward A number is decreased by 35, then multiplied by 6, then added to 87, then divided by 3. The result is 67. What is the number? (Lesson 3–3)

45. Solve $x + 4.2 = 1.5$. Check your solution. (Lesson 3–1)

46. Define a variable, then write an equation for the following problem. (Lesson 2–9)

Karen is 10, and she has always admired her 15-year-old sister Kristy. Karen wants to be exactly like Kristy. She knows that she will never catch up with Kristy in age, but she has heard that when one person is 0.9 times as old as another, you can't really tell them apart. How long will it be before Karen is 0.9 times as old as Kristy?

47. Which is greater, $\frac{11}{9}$ *or* $\frac{12}{10}$? (Lesson 2–4)

48. Explain what the graph at the right tells you about test scores as a function of hours spent watching television. (Lesson 1–9)

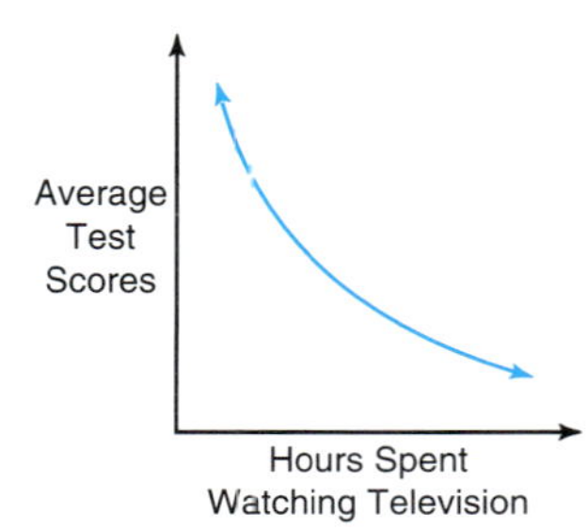

49. Solve $14.8 - 3.75 = t$. (Lesson 1–5)

3-6 Solving Equations and Formulas

***What* YOU'LL LEARN**

- To solve equations and formulas for a specified variable.

***Why* IT'S IMPORTANT**

You can use equations and formulas to solve problems involving physics and geometry.

INTEGRATION

Geometry

Some equations contain more than one variable. At times you will need to solve these equations for one of the variables. For example, suppose the variables x, y, and z were all in the same equation. To *solve for x* would mean to get x by itself on one side of the equation, with no x's on the other side. In the same way, to *solve for y* would mean to get y by itself on one side of the equation, with no y's on the other side.

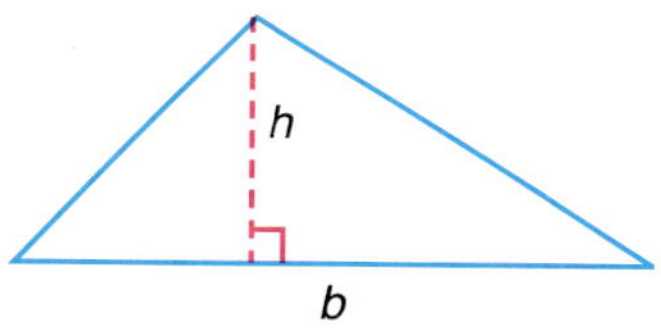

The formula for the area of a triangle is $A = \frac{1}{2}bh$ where b represents the length of the base and h represents the height of the triangle. Suppose you know the areas and the lengths of the bases of several triangles and you want to find the height of each triangle. Rather than solve the formula over and over for different values of A and b, it would be easier to solve the formula for h before substituting the values for the other variables.

$$A = \frac{1}{2}bh$$

$$2A = 2\left[\frac{1}{2}bh\right] \quad \text{Multiply each side by 2.}$$

$$2A = bh$$

$$\frac{2A}{b} = \frac{bh}{b} \quad \text{Divide each side by } b.$$

$$\frac{2A}{b} = h$$

When you divide by a variable in an equation, remember that division by 0 is undefined. For example, in the formula above, b cannot equal zero.

LOOK BACK

You can refer to Lesson 2-9 for information on writing equations and formulas.

Example 1 **Solve the equation $-5x + y = -56$**

a. for y, and

b. for x.

a.

$$-5x + y = -56$$

$$-5x + 5x + y = -56 + 5x \quad \text{Add } 5x \text{ to each side.}$$

$$y = -56 + 5x$$

b.

$$-5x + y = -56$$

$$-5x + y - y = -56 - y \quad \text{Subtract } y \text{ from each side.}$$

$$-5x = -56 - y$$

$$\frac{-5x}{-5} = \frac{-56 - y}{-5} \quad \text{Divide each side by } -5.$$

$$x = \frac{-56 - y}{-5} \text{ or } \frac{56 + y}{5}$$

Example 2 Solve for y in $3y + z = am - 4y$.

$$3y + z = am - 4y$$
$$3y + z - z = am - 4y - z \quad \textit{Subtract z from each side.}$$
$$3y = am - 4y - z$$
$$3y + 4y = am + 4y - 4y - z \quad \textit{Add 4y to each side.}$$
$$3y + 4y = am - z$$
$$(3 + 4)\,y = am - z \quad \textit{Use the distributive property.}$$
$$7y = am - z$$
$$\frac{7y}{7} = \frac{am - z}{7} \quad \textit{Divide each side by 7.}$$
$$y = \frac{am - z}{7}$$

CAREER CHOICES

A **computer programmer** writes a detailed plan for solving a problem with an ordered sequence of instructions, often including equations or formulas.

Programming requires a degree in computer science with a working knowledge of computer languages and mathematics.

For more information, contact:

Association for Computing Machinery
11 W. 42nd St.
3rd Floor
New York, NY 10036

Many real-world problems require the use of formulas. When using formulas, you may need to use **dimensional analysis.** This is the process of carrying units throughout a computation. You may also be asked to solve the formula for a specific variable. This may make it easier to use certain formulas.

Example 3 **The formula $P = \frac{1.2W}{H^2}$ represents the amount of pressure exerted on the floor by the heel of a shoe. In this formula, P represents the pressure in pounds per square inch (lb/in^2), W represents the weight of the person wearing the shoe in pounds, and H is the width of the heel of the shoe in inches.**

a. Find the amount of pressure exerted if a 130-pound person wore shoes with heels $\frac{1}{2}$ inch wide.

b. Solve the formula for W.

c. Find the weight of the person if the heel is 3 inches wide and the pressure exerted is 40 lb/in^2.

a. $P = \frac{1.2W}{H^2}$

$$= \frac{1.2(130\text{ lb})}{\left(\frac{1}{2}\text{ in}\right)^2} \quad \textit{W = 130 lb, H = }\tfrac{1}{2}\textit{ in.}$$
$$= \frac{156\text{ lb}}{\frac{1}{4}\text{ in}^2}$$
$$= 624\text{ lb/in}^2$$

624 lb/in^2 of pressure are exerted.

b. $P = \frac{1.2W}{H^2}$

$$H^2P = H^2\left(\frac{1.2W}{H^2}\right) \quad \textit{Multiply each side by } H^2.$$
$$H^2P = 1.2W$$
$$\frac{H^2P}{1.2} = \frac{1.2W}{1.2} \quad \textit{Divide each side by 1.2.}$$
$$\frac{H^2P}{1.2} = W$$

c. $\dfrac{H^2P}{1.2} = W$

$\dfrac{(3\text{ in.})^2(40\text{ lb/in}^2)}{1.2} = W$ *Estimate:* $[(3)^2 - 40] \div 1 = 360$ *Will the actual answer be greater or less? Why?*

$\dfrac{360\text{ lb}}{1.2} = W$ $(9\ \cancel{\text{in}^2})(40\text{ lb}/\cancel{\text{in}^2}) = 360\text{ lb}$

$300\text{ lb} = W$ The person weighs 300 pounds.

CHECK FOR UNDERSTANDING

Communicating Mathematics

Study the lesson. Then complete the following.

1. **Show** how you would solve the equation in Example 2 for m.
2. **Compare and contrast** the amount of pressure being exerted in the case of the two people described in Example 3.

MATH JOURNAL

3. Find a formula in a newspaper or magazine. Define all of the variables and explain what the purpose of the formula is.

Guided Practice

Solve each equation or formula for the variable specified.

4. $3x - 4y = 7$, for x
5. $3x - 4y = 7$, for y
6. $a(y + 1) = b$, for y
7. $4x + b = 2x + c$, for x
8. $F = G\left(\dfrac{Mm}{d^2}\right)$, for M
9. $S = \dfrac{n}{2}(A + t)$, for A

Write an equation and solve for the variable specified.

10. Twice a number x and 12 is 31 less than three times another number y. Solve for y.

EXERCISES

Practice

Solve each equation or formula for the variable specified.

11. $-3x + b = 6x$, for x
12. $ex - 2y = 3z$, for x
13. $\dfrac{y + a}{3} = c$, for y
14. $\dfrac{3}{5}y + a = b$, for y
15. $v = r + at$, for a
16. $y = mx + b$, for m
17. $I = prt$, for r
18. $\dfrac{by + 2}{3} = c$, for y
19. $H = (0.24)I^2Rt$, for R
20. $P = \dfrac{E^2}{R}$, for R
21. $4b - 5 = -t$, for b
22. $km + 5x = 6y$, for m
23. $c = \dfrac{3}{4}y + b$, for y
24. $p(t + 1) = -2$, for t
25. $\dfrac{5x + y}{a} = 2$, for a
26. $\dfrac{3ax - n}{5} = -4$, for x

Write an equation and solve for the variable specified.

27. Twice a number x increased by 12 is 31 less than three times another number y. Solve for x.

28. Five eighths of a number x is three more than one half of another number y. Solve for y.

29. Five more than two thirds of a number x is the same as three less than one half of another number y. Solve for x.

Critical Thinking

30. **Weather** Here's a conversation between a mother and her teenage daughter, adapted from the pages of *Games* magazine.

> Mrs. Weatherby: "This thermometer's no good. It's in Celsius, and I want to know the temperature in Fahrenheit."
>
> Mercuria: "You're so old-fashioned, Mother. Just use the formula $\frac{9}{5}C + 32 = F$, where C is the temperature in Celsius and F is the temperature in Fahrenheit. If that's too hard for you, then just double the number on the thermometer and add 30. Of course, you won't get a precise answer."

The two women each computed the temperature in degrees Fahrenheit, Mercuria with her formula and Mrs. Weatherby by the approximation. Surprisingly, they got exactly the same answer. Just how hot was it? Justify your reasoning.

Applications and Problem Solving

31. **Business** The formula in Exercise 17 is the formula for computing simple interest, where I is the interest, p is the principal or amount invested, r is the interest rate, and t is the time in years. Find the amount of interest earned if you were to invest \$5000 at 6% interest (use 0.06), for 3 years.

32. **Physics** The formula $d = vt + \frac{1}{2}at^2$ is the formula for distance d, given the initial velocity v, the time t, and the acceleration a. Suppose a biker going 4.5 meters per second (m/s) passes a lamppost at the top of a hill and then accelerates down the hill at a constant rate of 0.4 m/s^2 for 12 seconds. How far does she go down the hill during this time?

33. **Work** The formula $s = \frac{w - 10e}{m}$ is often used by placement services to find keyboarding speeds. In the formula, w represents the number of words typed, e represents the number of errors, m represents the number of minutes typed, and s represents the speed in words per minute.

    a. On a 10-minute keyboarding test, Sally typed 420 words with 6 errors. Find Sally's speed in words per minute.

    b. Who has the greater speed on a 5-minute test: Isabel, who types 500 words with 14 errors, or Clarence, who types 410 words with 4 errors?

Mixed Review

34. Solve $2(x - 2) = 3x - (4x - 5)$. (Lesson 3–5)

35. Find the complement of an 85° angle. (Lesson 3–4)

36. Work Backward Greta Moore's plane is scheduled to leave for Dallas at 9:30 A.M. She is to pick up her tickets at the boarding gate thirty minutes before departure. It takes Ms. Moore fifty minutes to drive to the airport, ten minutes to park her car in the overnight lot, and ten more minutes to get to the gate. On her way to the airport, Ms. Moore needs to pick up some materials from her office. This detour will take about fifteen minutes. If it takes her an hour to get dressed and out the door, for what time should Ms. Moore set her alarm? (Lesson 3–3)

37. Write an inequality for the graph shown below. (Lesson 2–4)

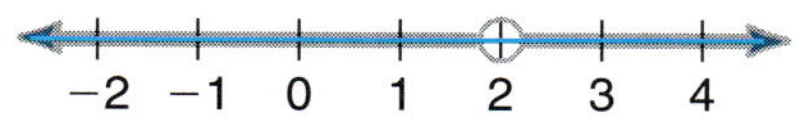

38. Use a number line to find the sum of 9 and −5. (Lesson 2–1)

39. Find the solution set for $x - 3 > \frac{x + 1}{2}$ if the replacement set is $\{4, 5, 6, 7, 8\}$. (Lesson 1–5)

40. Health Your optimum exercise heart rate per minute is given by the expression $0.7(220 - a)$, where a represents your age. Find your optimum exercise heart rate. (Lesson 1–1)

WORKING ON THE In·ves·ti·ga·tion

Refer to the Investigation on pages 68–69.

the Greenhouse Effect

Two scales are used to measure temperature. The Celsius scale, part of the metric system, was invented in 1741 by Swedish astronomer Anders Celsius (1701–1744). The Celsius scale has the freezing point of water at 0°C and the boiling point of water at 100° C. The scale most frequently used in the United States is the Fahrenheit scale, invented in 1714 by German physicist Gabriel Daniel Fahrenheit (1686–1736). On the Fahrenheit scale, the boiling point of water is 212°F, and the freezing point is 32°F.

To convert Celsius temperatures to Fahrenheit, use the formula $F = \frac{9}{5}C + 32$.

1. Using the formula, convert the average temperatures of Mars, Earth, and Venus from Celsius to Fahrenheit. How do the temperatures compare?
2. The greenhouse effect may raise the average temperature of Earth 8°F by the year 2050. What will be the average temperature of Earth in degrees Celsius at that time?
3. Change the formula for converting Celsius to Fahrenheit to a formula for converting Fahrenheit to Celsius.

Add the results of your work to your Investigation Folder.

3–7 Integration: Statistics
Measures of Central Tendency

What **YOU'LL LEARN**

- To find and interpret the mean, median, and mode of a set of data.

Why **IT'S IMPORTANT**

Measures of central tendency can help you easily describe a set of data.

APPLICATION
Charities

The table at the right shows the top 10 charities in amount of contributions for 1993.

When analyzing data, it is helpful to have one number that describes the entire set of data. Numbers known as **measures of central tendency** are often used to describe sets of data because they represent a centralized, or *middle,* value. Three of the most commonly used measures of central tendency are the **mean, median,** and **mode.**

Charity	Millions of Dollars
Salvation Army	$726
Catholic Charities USA	411
United Jewish Appeal	407
Second Harvest	407
American Red Cross	395
American Cancer Society	355
YMCA	317
American Heart Association	235
YWCA	218
Boy Scouts of America	211

Source: *The Chronicle of Philanthropy,* Nov., 1993

Definition of Mean	**The mean of a set of data is the sum of the numbers in the set divided by the number of numbers in the set.**

FYI

Until 1994, the Cardwell sisters of Sweetwater, Texas, were the oldest living set of triplets. However, on October 2, 1994, the firstborn triplet, Faith, died at the age of 95. She was survived by her sisters Hope and Charity.

To find the mean of the charity data, find the sum of the dollar values and divide by 10, the number of numbers in the set. ***Estimate:*** *Is an answer of $500 reasonable?*

$$\text{mean} = \frac{726 + 411 + 407 + 407 + 395 + 355 + 317 + 235 + 218 + 211}{10}$$
$$= \frac{3682}{10}$$
$$= 368.2$$

The mean is $368.2 million. Notice that the amount collected by the Salvation Army, $726 million, is far greater than the amounts collected by the other charities. Because the mean is an average of several numbers, a single number that is so much greater than the others can affect the mean a great deal. In extreme cases, the mean becomes less representative of the values in a set of data.

The median is another measure of central tendency.

Definition of Median	**The median of a set of data is the middle number when the numbers in the set are arranged in numerical order.**

To find the median of the charity data, arrange the dollar values in order.

726 411 407 407 395 355 317 235 218 211

If there were an odd number of dollar values, the middle one would be the median. However, since there is an even number of dollar values, the median is the average of the two middle values, 395 and 355.

$$\begin{aligned} \text{median} &= \frac{395 + 355}{2} \\ &= \frac{750}{2} \\ &= 375 \end{aligned}$$

The median is $375 million. Notice that the number of values that are greater than the median is the same as the number of values that are less than the median.

A third measure of central tendency is the mode.

Definition of Mode	**The mode of a set of data is the number that occurs most often in the set.**

To find the mode of the charity data, look for the number that occurs most often.

726 411 407 407 395 355 317 235 218 211

In this set, 407 appears twice. Thus, $407 million is the mode of the data.

It is possible for a set of data to have more than one mode. For example, the set of data {2, 3, 3, 4, 6, 6} has two modes, 3 and 6.

Based on our results, the charity data has mean $368.2 million, median $375 million, and mode $407 million. As you can see, the mean, median, and mode are rarely the same value.

Example 1

CONNECTION History

When the Declaration of Independence was signed in 1776, George III was king of Great Britain. After George III, Great Britain had seven monarchs before Queen Elizabeth II was crowned queen in 1952. The table at the right shows the number of years that each monarch reigned. Find the mean, median, and mode of the data.

Monarch	Reign (years)
George III	59
George IV	10
William IV	7
Victoria	63
Edward VII	9
George V	25
Edward VIII	1
George VI	15

$$\begin{aligned} \textbf{mean} &= \frac{59 + 10 + 7 + 63 + 9 + 25 + 1 + 15}{8} \\ &= \frac{189}{8} \\ &= 23.625 \end{aligned}$$

The mean is 23.625 years.

(continued on the next page)

median 1 7 9 10 15 25 59 63

The median is $\frac{10 + 15}{2}$ or $12\frac{1}{2}$ years. Why do you think the mean and median are so different? Which value, mean or median, do you think is more representative of the data?

mode Since each number appears exactly once, there is no mode.

You can also determine the mean, median, and mode of a set of data by examining stem-and-leaf plots.

Example 2

APPLICATION
Demographics

Since it would be inconvenient to list every stem, we have used dots to indicate that some stems are missing.

The stem-and-leaf plot at the right shows population data for the 20 largest cities in the United States to the nearest ten thousand. Find the mean, median, and mode of the data.

Stem	Leaf
73	2
⋮	⋮
34	9
⋮	⋮
27	8
⋮	⋮
16	9 3
⋮	⋮
10	3 1
⋮	⋮
8	8
7	9 9 4 3
6	8 4 4 3 3 3 1
5	7

8|8 = 880,000 people

mean Add the 20 values and then divide by 20. Since the sum of the 20 values is 2791, the mean is $\frac{2791}{20}$ or 139.55. This represents a mean population of 1,395,500.

median Since there are 20 values, the median is the average of the 10th and 11th values. Counting from the top down, you will find that the 10th and the 11th values are 79 and 74. The average of 79 and 74 is $\frac{79 + 74}{2}$ or 76.5. Thus, the median population is 765,000.

mode There are three entries for 63. Thus, the mode is 630,000.

EXPLORATION GRAPHING CALCULATORS

You can use a graphing calculator and the MEAN and MEDIAN functions to find the mean and median of a list of numbers. The format is as follows.

mean({*a*,*b*,*c*,*d*,...*z*}) median({*a*,*b*,*c*,*d*,...*z*})

To find the mean of the data in Example 2, access the LIST MATH function by pressing [2nd] [LIST] [▶]. Then choose 3, for mean or 4, for median. Enter the list of numbers, beginning with a left brace ([2nd] [{]) and ending with a right brace ([2nd] [}]) and a right parenthesis. When you press [ENTER], the mean or median appears on the screen.

Your Turn

Take time to work through the examples in this lesson using a graphing calculator.

CHECK FOR UNDERSTANDING

Communicating Mathematics

Study the lesson. Then complete the following.

1. **Explain** why you think the mean, median, and mode are rarely the same value.
2. **Discuss** which of the measures of central tendency you would use to describe the data in Example 2. Explain your reasoning.
3. **Describe** the steps you would take to find the mean, median, and mode of the data represented by the line plot shown at the right.

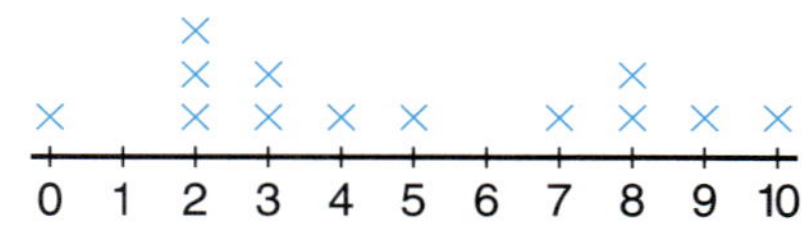

4. Suppose you conducted a survey in which you asked your classmates, "What's your favorite rock group?" Which measure of central tendency could you use to analyze the data, and why?

MATH JOURNAL

5. Find some data that interests you in a newspaper or magazine. Find the mean, median, and mode and discuss which of these measures you think best describes the data.

Complete.

6. Measures of central tendency represent __?__ values of a set of data.
7. If the numbers in a set of data are arranged in numerical order, then the __?__ of the set is the middle number.
8. Extremely high or low values affect the __?__ of a set of data.
9. If all the numbers in a set of data occur the same number of times, then the set has no __?__ .

Guided Practice

Find the mean, median, and mode for each set of data.

10. 4, 6, 12, 5, 8
11. 8, 8, 8, 8, 9
12.

Stem	Leaf
7	3 5
8	2 2 4
9	0 4 7 9
10	5 8
11	4 6

9|4 = 94

List six numbers that satisfy each set of conditions.

13. The mean is 50, the median is 40, and the mode is 20.
14. The mean is 70, the median is 70, and the modes are 65 and 70.
15. **Basketball** The table at the right shows the names of players most often named most valuable player of the NBA.
    a. Find the mean, median, and mode of the data.
    b. Which measure of central tendency best represents these data, and why?

Player	MVP Wins
Kareem Abdul-Jabbar	6
Bill Russell	5
Wilt Chamberlain	4
Larry Bird	3
Magic Johnson	3
Moses Malone	3
Michael Jordan	3

Source: *World Almanac,* 1995

EXERCISES

Practice

Find the mean, median, and mode for each set of data.

16. 2, 4, 7, 9, 12, 15

17. 300, 34, 40, 50, 60

18. 23, 23, 23, 12, 12, 12

19. 10, 3, 17, 1, 8, 6, 12, 15

20. 7, 19, 9, 4, 7, 2

21. 2.1, 7.4, 13.9, 1.6, 5.21, 3.901

22.

Stem	Leaf
5	3 6 8
6	5 8
7	0 3 7 7 9
8	1 4 8 8 9
9	9

$6|8 = 68$

23.

Stem	Leaf
19	3 5 5
20	2 2 5 8
21	5 8 8 9 9 9
22	0 1 7 8 9

$21|5 = 215$

24. List ten numbers that satisfy each set of conditions.

a. The mean is less than all but one of the numbers.

b. The mean is greater than all but one of the numbers.

c. The mean is greater than all of the numbers.

d. Would you be able to complete parts a, b, and c if the word *mean* were replaced by the word *median*? Why or why not?

25. The mean of a set of ten numbers is 5. When the greatest number in the set is eliminated, the mean of the new set of numbers is 4. What number was eliminated from the original set of numbers?

26. The first of three consecutive odd integers is $2n + 1$.

a. What is the mean of the three integers?

b. What is the median?

Critical Thinking

27. This paragraph appeared in the *San Diego Union-Tribune* on August 8, 1993.

> Lawyers at the top of their profession earn more than \$1 million a year, while the typical attorney makes almost \$67,000—far more than the average American. . . . According to census figures, lawyers and judges earned a median pay of \$66,784 in 1991, which means that half of them made more than that amount and half made less. . . . However R. Wilson Montjoy II of Jackson, Mississippi, said, "We have lots more people at or below the median than above it."

a. To which measure of central tendency do you think the word *average* refers?

b. Has *median* been defined correctly in this passage? Why or why not?

c. In the statement by R. Wilson Montjoy II, did he use the term *median* correctly? If not, which term should he have used? Justify your answer.

Applications and Problem Solving

28. Demographics The table at the right shows population data for 10 South American countries, according to the 1990 Census.

Country	Population (millions)
Argentina	32
Bolivia	7
Brazil	150
Chile	13
Colombia	33
Ecuador	10
Paraguay	5
Peru	22
Uruguay	3
Venezuela	19

a. Find the mean, median, and mode of the data.

b. If you were reporting these data in a newspaper article, which measure would you use, and why?

29. **Geography** The areas of each of the South American countries listed in the table on the previous page are as follows (in millions of square miles): 1085, 139, 7778, 670, 3166, 1068, 177, 1135, 154, and 1234, respectively. Find the mean, median, and mode area of the countries.

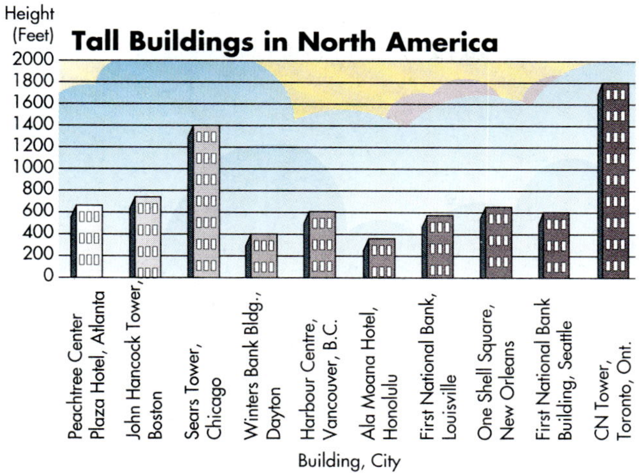

30. **American Landmarks** The graph at the left shows the height in feet of several tall buildings in North America. Find the mean and median height of the buildings.

31. **Commuting** On her way home from work, Luisa drives 10 miles through the city at about 30 mph and then 10 miles on the highway at about 50 mph. What is her average speed? Use $d = rt$. (*Hint:* The answer is *not* 40 mph.)

Mixed Review

32. Solve $\frac{a+5}{3} = 7x$ for x. (Lesson 3–6)

33. Solve $\frac{3}{4}n - 3 = 9$. Then check your solution. (Lesson 3–3)

34. Evaluate $|k| + |m|$ if $k = 3$ and $m = -6$. (Lesson 2–3)

35. Use a number line to add $-6 + (-14)$. (Lesson 2–1)

36. Evaluate $\left(13 + \frac{2}{5} \cdot 5\right)(3^2 - 2^3)$. Indicate the property used in each step. (Lesson 1–8)

37. Simplify $5 + 7(ac + 2b) + 2ac$. (Lesson 1–7)

Mathematics and SOCIETY

Teen Talk Dolls

The article below appeared in a magazine on August 30, 1993.

Some time ago, [a toy company] recalled any [talking fashion dolls] programmed to say "Math class is tough" because some women's groups complained the comment perpetuated the view that girls are bad at mathematics. According to a news piece in a December issue of [an Atlanta newspaper], only five [doll] buyers in the United States turned in their dolls because of [the company's] offer. While some talking [dolls] may have found math tough, the consumer/collectors who own the doll won't have trouble adding up the profits. ... Savvy collectors were tearing open [doll] boxes trying to find a [doll] who talked about math. Mike Huen, a professional toy collector, estimates the doll, which sold for $35, will be worth several hundred dollars now. ■

Source: *Antique Week*

1. Why do you think some women's groups objected to what the dolls say? Do you think that what the dolls say has any influence on the girls who play with them? Why or why not?
2. Why do you think only five doll buyers have returned their dolls? Explain.
3. Do you think it is right for people to make money on this doll? Justify your reasoning.

CLOSING THE

In•ves•ti•ga•tion

the Greenhouse Effect

Refer to the Investigation on pages 68–69.

For more than a decade, scientists have warned that cars and factories spew so many gases into the atmosphere that Earth could soon be affected by disastrous climatic changes. The loss of rain forests is reducing the number of trees to offset the large increases in carbon dioxide in our atmosphere. The possible consequences are so frightening that it makes sense to slow the buildup of CO_2 through preventive measures, such as encouraging energy conservation, developing alternatives to fossil fuels, and preventing the destruction of the rain forests.

Analyze

You have conducted experiments and done research on this important problem. It is now time to analyze your findings and state your conclusions.

> **PORTFOLIO ASSESSMENT**
>
> You may want to keep your work on this Investigation in your portfolio.

1. Create a graph of the data from your experiments. Let the vertical axis represent the changes in temperature. Let the horizontal axis represent the distances between the lamp and the thermometer. Use different colors to indicate the control experiment and the greenhouse experiment.
2. Use the data from your experiments to draw a conclusion about the relationship between the temperature and the distance between the thermometer and the lamp. Describe this relationship as a function, and justify your reasoning.
3. Use the data from Working on the Investigation in Lesson 2–6 to make a chart. Use the headings *Planet, Temperature Without CO_2, Temperature With CO_2,* and *Distance from the Sun.*
4. Draw a conclusion about the relationship between the distance from the sun and the temperature of Venus and Earth with CO_2. Describe this relationship as a function, and justify your reasoning.
5. Draw a conclusion about the relationship between the distance from the sun and the temperature of Mars and Earth with CO_2. Describe this relationship as a function, and justify your reasoning.
6. How does your experiment explore the temperatures of the planets? How are the relationships similar and different?
7. Predict what the temperature of Mars would be if it had the same amount of CO_2 that Earth has. Explain your calculations.

Write

Some scientists predict that by the year 2050, Earth's atmosphere will contain between 500 and 700 ppm of CO_2. Write a one-page paper explaining the situation to a group of concerned citizens. Consider some of the following questions to address in your paper.

8. What factors will cause this increase in CO_2?
9. How different is this estimate from the amount of CO_2 calculated earlier?
10. In your opinion, what will the approximate average temperature on Earth be at that time?
11. What might occur if the temperature reaches that point? What are some of the dangers involved?

CHAPTER 3

HIGHLIGHTS

VOCABULARY

After completing this chapter, you should be able to define each term, property, or phrase and give an example or two of each.

Algebra

addition property of equality (p. 144)
consecutive integers (p. 158)
dimensional analysis (p. 174)
division property of equality (p. 151)
equivalent equation (p. 144)
identity (p. 170)
multi-step equations (p. 157)
multiplication property of equality (p. 150)
number theory (p. 158)
solve an equation (p. 145)
subtraction property of equality (p. 146)

Statistics

mean (p. 178)
measures of central tendency (p. 178)
median (p. 178)
mode (p. 178)

Geometry

acute triangle (p. 165)
complementary angles (p. 163)
congruent (p. 164)
equilateral triangle (p. 164)
isosceles triangle (p. 164)
obtuse triangle (p. 165)
right triangle (p. 165)
supplementary angles (p. 162)
triangle (p. 163)

Problem Solving

work backward (p. 156)

UNDERSTANDING AND USING THE VOCABULARY

Choose the letter of the term that best matches each statement or phrase.

1. If $a = b$, then $a + c = b + c$.
2. If $a = b$, then $a - c = b - c$.
3. If $a = b$, then $ac = bc$.
4. If $a = b$ and $c \neq 0$, then $\frac{a}{c} = \frac{b}{c}$.
5. a triangle in which each angle has the same measure
6. a triangle in which two angles have the same measure
7. a triangle in which one angle measures 90°
8. a triangle in which one angle measures more than 90°
9. a triangle in which all of the angles measure less than 90°
10. the sum of the numbers divided by the number of numbers
11. the middle number when data is in numerical order
12. the number that occurs most often in a set of data

a. acute triangle
b. addition property of equality
c. division property of equality
d. equilateral triangle
e. isosceles triangle
f. mean
g. median
h. mode
i. multiplication property of equality
j. obtuse triangle
k. right triangle
l. subtraction property of equality

CHAPTER 3 STUDY GUIDE AND ASSESSMENT

SKILLS AND CONCEPTS

OBJECTIVES AND EXAMPLES

Upon completing this chapter, you should be able to:

- solve equations by using addition or subtraction (Lesson 3–1)

$$x - 13 = 45$$
$$x - 13 + 13 = 45 + 13$$
$$x = 58$$

$$y - (-33) = 14$$
$$y + 33 = 14$$
$$y + 33 - 33 = 14 - 33$$
$$y = -19$$

REVIEW EXERCISES

Use these exercises to review and prepare for the chapter test.

Solve each equation. Then check your solution.

13. $r - 21 = -37$

14. $14 + c = -5$

15. $-27 = -6 - p$

16. $b + (-14) = 6$

17. $r + (-11) = -21$

18. $d - (-1.2) = -7.3$

19. A number decreased by 14 is −46. Find the number.

20. The sum of two numbers is −23. One of the numbers is 9. What is the other number?

21. Eighty-two increased by some number is −34. Find the number.

- solve equations by using multiplication or division (Lesson 3–2)

$$\frac{4}{9}t = -72$$
$$\frac{9}{4}\left(\frac{4}{9}t\right) = \frac{9}{4}(-72)$$
$$t = -162$$

$$-5c = -8$$
$$\frac{-5c}{-5} = \frac{-8}{-5}$$
$$c = \frac{8}{5}$$

Solve each equation. Then check your solution.

22. $6x = -42$

23. $-7w = -49$

24. $\frac{3}{4}n = 30$

25. $-\frac{3}{5}y = -50$

26. $\frac{5}{2}x = -25$

27. $\frac{5}{12} = \frac{r}{24}$

28. Negative seven times a number is −56. Find the number.

29. Three fourths of a number is −12. What is the number?

30. One and two thirds of a number equals one and a half. What is the number?

- solve equations involving more than one operation (Lesson 3–3)

$$34 = 8 - 2t$$
$$34 - 8 = 8 - 8 - 2t$$
$$26 = -2t$$
$$\frac{26}{-2} = \frac{-2t}{-2}$$
$$-13 = t$$

$$\frac{d+5}{3} = -9$$
$$3\left(\frac{d+5}{3}\right) = 3(-9)$$
$$d + 5 = -27$$
$$d = -32$$

Solve each equation. Then check your solution.

31. $4t - 7 = 5$

32. $6 = 4n + 2$

33. $\frac{y}{3} + 6 = -45$

34. $\frac{c}{-4} - 8 = -42$

35. $\frac{4d+5}{7} = 7$

36. $\frac{7n + (-1)}{8} = 8$

37. Four times a number decreased by twice the number is 100. What is the number?

38. Find four consecutive integers whose sum is 130.

39. Find two consecutive integers such that twice the lesser integer increased by the greater integer is 49.

OBJECTIVES AND EXAMPLES

- find the complement and supplement of an angle (Lesson 3–4)

Find the complement and supplement of an angle with measure 70°.

complement: 90° − 70° or 20°

supplement: 180° − 70° or 110°

REVIEW EXERCISES

Find both the complement and supplement of each angle measure.

40. 28°
41. 69°
42. $5x°$
43. $(y + 20)°$

44. Find the measure of an angle that is 10° more than its supplement.

45. Find the measure of an angle that is one-half the measure of its complement.

- find the measure of the third angle of a triangle given the measures of the other two angles (Lesson 3–4)

The measures of two angles of a triangle are 89° and 90°. The measure of the third angle is 180° − (89° + 90°) or 1°.

Find the measure of the third angle of each triangle in which the measures of two angles of the triangle are given.

46. 16°, 47°

47. 45°, 120°

48. $y°$, $x°$

49. $(z - 30)°$, $z°$

- solve equations with the variable on both sides and solve equations containing grouping symbols (Lesson 3–5)

$$-3(x + 5) = 3(x - 1)$$
$$-3x - 15 = 3x - 3$$
$$-3x - 15 + 15 = 3x - 3 + 15$$
$$-3x = 3x + 12$$
$$-3x - 3x = 3x - 3x + 12$$
$$\frac{-6x}{-6} = \frac{12}{-6}$$
$$x = -2$$

Solve each equation. Then check your solution.

50. $4(3 + 5w) = -11$

51. $\frac{2}{3}n + 8 = \frac{1}{3}n - 2$

52. $3x - 2(x + 3) = x$

53. $\frac{4 - x}{5} = \frac{1}{5}x$

54. The sum of two numbers is 25. Twelve less than four times one of the numbers is 16 more than twice the other number. Find both numbers.

- solve equations and formulas for a specified variable (Lesson 3–6)

Solve $\frac{x + y}{b} = c$ for x.

$$b\left(\frac{x + y}{b}\right) = b(c)$$
$$x + y = bc$$
$$x = bc - y$$

Solve each equation for the variable specified.

55. $5x = y$, for x

56. $ay - b = c$, for y

57. $yx - a = cx$, for x

58. $\frac{2y - a}{3} = \frac{a + 3b}{4}$, for y

OBJECTIVES AND EXAMPLES

- find and interpret the mean, median, and mode of a set of data (Lesson 3–7)

Find the mean, median, and mode of 1.5, 3.4, 5.4, 5.6, 5.7, 6.2, 6.8, 7.1, 7.1, 8.4, and 9.9.

mean: The sum of the 11 values is 67.1.

$$\frac{67.1}{11} = 6.1$$

median: The 6th value is 6.2.

mode: 7.1

REVIEW EXERCISES

59. School Marisa's scores on the 25-point quizzes in her English class are 20, 21, 18, 21, 22, 22, 24, 21, 20, 19, and 23. Find the mean, median, and mode of her scores.

60. Business Of the 42 employees at Pirate Printing, sixteen make \$4.75 an hour, four make \$5.50 an hour, three make \$6.85 an hour, six make \$4.85 an hour, and thirteen make \$5.25 an hour. Find the mean, median, and mode of the hourly wages.

APPLICATIONS AND PROBLEM SOLVING

61. Food and Nutrition According to the National Eating Trends Service, in 1984, the average person ate 71 meals in a restaurant and purchased 20 meals to go. The number of meals eaten in a restaurant decreased 0.7 meals per year, and the number of meals purchased to go increased 1.3 meals per year. (Lesson 3–5)

a. After how many years will people eat the same number of meals in restaurants as they order to go and eat at home?

b. How would you explain these trends?

62. Health You can estimate your ideal weight with the following formulas.

Male	Female
$w = 100 + 6(h - 60)$	$w = 100 + 5(h - 60)$

In each formula, w is your ideal weight in pounds and h represents your height in inches. (Lesson 3–6)

a. Find your ideal weight.

b. Solve each formula for h.

c. How tall is a man that is at his ideal weight of 170 pounds?

63. Home Economics According to a newspaper, the average refrigerator lasts $2\frac{1}{4}$ years less than twice as long as the average color television. The average color television lasts for 8 years. How long does the average refrigerator last? (Lesson 3–3)

Source: *Dallas Morning News*

64. Postal Service The graph below shows the cost of mailing a first-class letter in several countries in 1994. (Lesson 3–7)

a. Find the mean, median, and mode cost.

b. Round each cost to the nearest cent. Then find the mean, median, and mode cost and compare your two answers.

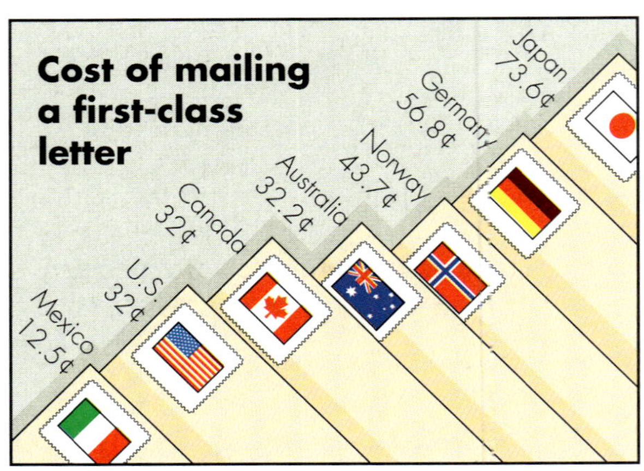

A practice test for Chapter 3 is provided on page 789.

ALTERNATIVE ASSESSMENT

COOPERATIVE LEARNING PROJECT

Balances and Solving Equations In this chapter, you learned the addition, subtraction, multiplication, and division properties of equality. Each definition begins with an equation in *balance*, $a = b$, and states that if something is done to one side of the equation, the equation can be kept in balance by doing the same thing to the other side.

A basic principle is that two quantities in balance will remain in balance until something is done to only one of the quantities. To bring the quantities back into balance, you must do the same thing to the other quantity or undo what was done to the first quantity.

In this project, you will construct a device to demonstrate the principle of balance and how it relates to solving equations. All balances have certain features in common. A horizontal bar is balanced on a vertical support. Pans are suspended from the ends of the bar. A pointer attached to the bar moves along a scale on the support, indicating when the pans are balanced.

Follow these steps to design and build your balance.

- Outline a plan you can follow.
- Use materials you can easily find. The precision of your balance depends more on the care and accuracy with which you build it than it does on the materials you use.
- Carry out your plan.
- Determine how you might use your balance to represent equations. Include ways to solve equations by using the balance.
- Write several paragraphs describing how you can solve equations using the balance. Be sure to give examples of equations and their solutions.

THINKING CRITICALLY

- Write an equation that has no solution. Explain why there is no solution.
- Write an equation that has an infinite number of solutions. Explain why.

PORTFOLIO

Select one of the assignments from this chapter that you found especially challenging. Revise your work if necessary and place it in your portfolio. Explain why you found it to be a challenge.

SELF EVALUATION

One characteristic of a good problem solver is persistence. If you don't succeed the first time you attempt something, you should learn from your mistakes and try again.

Assess yourself. How persistent are you? How do you react when you fail at something? List two or three ways that you can make a conscious effort to be more persistent in solving problems both in your mathematics studies and in your daily life.

LONG-TERM PROJECT

In·ves·ti·ga·tion

Go Fish!

MATERIALS NEEDED

- paper lunch bag
- 2 bags of dry beans, each a different color
- 5-oz. paper cup

Imagine that you are asked to determine the number of fish in a nearby pond. To count the fish one by one, you could remove the fish from the pond and stack them to one side, or mark each fish so you would not count them over and over again. Counting like this could be hazardous to a fish's health!

To determine the number of animals in a population, scientists often use the *capture-recapture* method. A number of animals are captured, carefully tagged, and returned to their native habitat. Then a second group of animals is captured and counted, and the number of tagged animals is noted. Scientists then use proportions to estimate the number in the entire population.

In this Investigation, you will work in pairs to model the process used by scientists to estimate the number of fish in a large lake. The lunch bag will represent the lake, the beans will represent fish, and the paper cup will represent a net.

Make an Investigation Folder in which you can store all of your work on this Investigation for future use.

CASTING	A Total Number of Tagged Fish	B Total Number of Fish in Sample	C Number of Tagged Fish in Sample	D Estimate
1				
2				
3				
4				
5				

CAPTURE

1 Begin by copying the chart above onto a sheet of paper.

2 Write your name on the paper bag. Empty one bag of beans into the bag.

3 Use your net to remove a sample of fish. Count the number of fish you netted. Since this number will remain constant for all casts, you can record this number in each row of column A.

4 Replace all of the beans you counted with beans of a different color. Put these "tagged fish" back into the lake and gently shake your bag to mix the fish.

RECAPTURE

5 For your first casting, use your net to remove a sample of fish. Count the total number of fish in your sample and record this number in column B. Then count the number of tagged fish in this sample and record this number in column C of your chart. Return these fish to the lake and gently shake your bag to mix the fish.

6 Cast your net a second time and record your findings. Continue casting and recording until you have counted five samples.

You will continue working on this Investigation throughout Chapters 4 and 5.

Be sure to keep your chart and materials in your Investigation Folder.

Go Fish! Investigation

Working on the Investigation Lesson 4–1, p. 200

Working on the Investigation Lesson 4–5, p. 227

Working on the Investigation Lesson 5–2, p. 269

Working on the Investigation Lesson 5–6, p. 302

Closing the Investigation End of Chapter 5, p.314

CHAPTER 4

Using Proportional Reasoning

Objectives

In this chapter, you will:

- solve proportions,
- find the unknown measures of the sides of two similar triangles,
- use trigonometric ratios to solve right triangles,
- solve percent problems,
- find the probability and odds of a simple event, and
- solve problems involving direct and inverse variation.

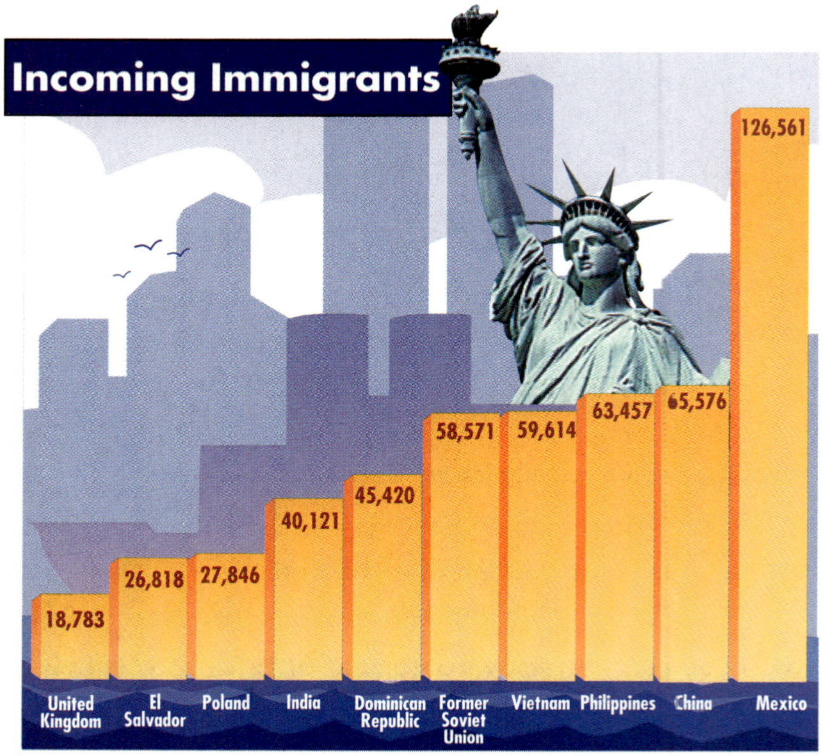

Source: U.S. Immigration and Naturalization Service

Some people blame immigrants, both legal and illegal, for many of the economic and social problems in the United States. Others believe immigrants bring vitality, diversity, and economic strength to the United States. What effect does immigration have on American society? Do you have any personal experiences with new immigrants?

TIME Line

280 B.C. The Colossus of Rhodes, standing 110 feet tall, is built on the Greek island of Rhodes.

1893 Poet Paul Laurence Dunbar writes *Oak and Ivy*.

400 B.C. | 300 | 200 | 100 | 0 | A.D. 100 | 1500 | 1600 | 1700 | 1880 | 1885 | 1890 | 1895

A.D. 1662 Englishman John of Gaunt publishes the first book of statistics.

PEOPLE IN THE NEWS

Ayrris Layug Aunario won the grand prize in *Filipinas* magazine's 1994 National Essay Contest with an essay describing what it means to be Filipino-American. The 16-year-old from Waukegan, Illinois, is a student at the Illinois Mathematics and Science Academy, a public school for gifted students in science and mathematics.

Ayrris' essay explains what it was like to be a 10-year-old immigrant to the U.S., arriving in Chicago and learning to live with people of many different cultures and beliefs. He had to master English quickly and soon learned the American virtues of independence, self-reliance, and assertiveness. Ayrris plans to attend college in the field of physics.

Chapter Project

Work in cooperative groups to take a heritage survey of students in your school.

- Determine the geographic birthplace of each student and the birthplace of their parents or guardians. If possible, gather information about the birthplace of each student's grandparents and great-grandparents.
- Use a world map to pinpoint each geographic location. Connect the generations of each student using colored yarn.
- Draw some conclusions about the birthplaces of the students you surveyed. Share your findings with the class.

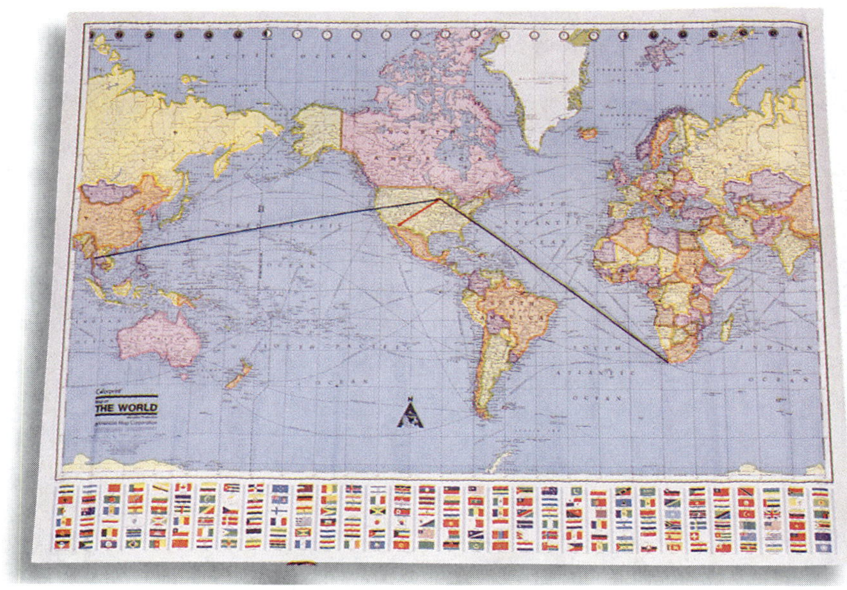

1903 Marie Sklodowska Curie becomes the first woman to win a Nobel Prize in science.

1954 Ellis Island in New York Bay closes after 62 years and the processing of 20 million immigrants.

1971 Romana Acosta Bañuelos becomes the first Latina to hold high government office, as U.S. Treasurer.

1992 Physicists in Germany fuse two isotopes of bismuth and iron to make Element 109, the heaviest known element in the universe.

00 | 1905 | 1910 | 1915 | 1920 | 1925 | 1940 | 1950 | 1960 | 1970 | 1980 | 1990 | 2000

MODELING MATHEMATICS

A Preview of Lesson 4–1

4–1A Ratios

Materials: tape measure

You can collect data to determine whether there is a relationship between the length of an individual's head and an individual's body.

Activity 1 Use a tape measure to find the length of your head.

Step 1 Measure your head from the top of your skull to the bottom of your chin. Since the top of your head is round, hold something flat, such as a piece of cardboard, across the top of your head to get an accurate measurement.

Step 2 Make a measuring "stick" with the length of your head as one unit to find the following measurements.

- total height
- chin to waist
- waist to hip
- knee to ankle
- ankle to bottom of bare heel
- underarm to elbow
- elbow to wrist
- wrist to tip of finger
- shoulder to tip of finger

Step 3 Make a table to record the relationship, or *ratio,* of each measurement to the measurement of your head.

Body Proportions of an Average Adult

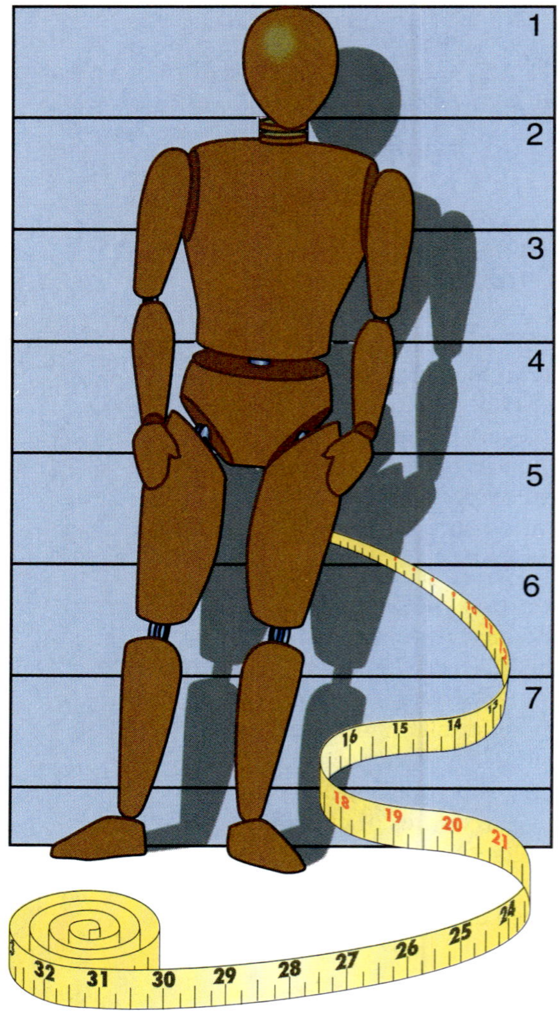

Draw 1. The average adult is seven and one-half heads tall. Use the information in your table to draw an outline of the proportions of your body. How does your drawing compare to the one above?

Write 2. Compare your ratios to those of your classmates. Find the number of heads tall of a random student in your class. Write a paragraph explaining how you compare to this average.

4–1 Ratios and Proportions

***What* YOU'LL LEARN**

- To solve proportions.

***Why* IT'S IMPORTANT**

You can use proportions to solve problems involving food and entertainment.

APPLICATION

Food

How would you like to eat chocolate for a living? That's exactly what Carl Wong does every day as associate director of product development for a chocolate company. His job is to create new candy bars as well as taste test existing candy bars in order to improve them.

The chocolate company keeps their candy recipes confidential, but the basic ingredients found in a batch of chocolate bars are sugar, cocoa beans, milk, and flavorings. The ingredients for a batch of candy are shown in the table below.

Ingredient	Parts Per Batch
Sugar	10
Cocoa Beans	5
Milk	4
Flavorings	1

A **ratio** is a comparison of two numbers by division. The ratio of x to y can be expressed in the following ways.

x to y $\qquad$ $x{:}y$ $\qquad$ $\frac{x}{y}$

Ratios are often expressed as fractions in simplest form. A ratio that is equivalent to a whole number is written with a denominator of 1.

In the application at the beginning of the lesson, the table shows that for every 10 parts sugar in a batch of chocolate bars, there are 5 parts cocoa beans. The ratio of sugar to cocoa beans is $\frac{10}{5}$. Suppose the company uses 30 pounds of sugar and 15 pounds of cocoa beans in a batch of chocolate bars. This ratio is $\frac{30}{15}$. Is this ratio different than the first ratio of $\frac{10}{5}$? When simplified, both ratios are equivalent to $\frac{2}{1}$.

$$\frac{10 \div 5}{5 \div 5} = \frac{2}{1} \qquad \frac{30 \div 15}{15 \div 15} = \frac{2}{1}$$

FYI

Almost 500 new candy and chocolate products were introduced in the first four months of 1995.

An equation stating that two ratios are equal is called a **proportion**. So, $\frac{10}{5} = \frac{30}{15}$ is a proportion.

To solve a proportion, cross multiply.

One way to determine if two ratios form a proportion is to check their cross products. In the proportion at the right, the cross products are $10 \cdot 15$ and $5 \cdot 30$. In this proportion, 10 and 15 are called the **extremes,** and 5 and 30 are called the **means.**

$$\frac{10}{5} = \frac{30}{15}$$

$$10(15) = 5(30)$$

extremes = means

$$150 = 150$$

The cross products of a proportion are equal.

Means-Extremes Property of Proportions	**In a proportion, the product of the extremes is equal to the product of the means.** **If $\frac{a}{b} = \frac{c}{d}$, then $ad = bc$.**

Example 1

Use cross products to determine whether each pair of ratios forms a proportion.

a. $\frac{2}{3}, \frac{12}{18}$

$$2 \cdot 18 \stackrel{?}{=} 3 \cdot 12$$

$$36 = 36$$

So, $\frac{2}{3} = \frac{12}{18}$.

This is a proportion.

b. $\frac{2.5}{6}, \frac{3.4}{5.2}$

Enter: 2.5 [×] 5.2 [=] 13

Enter: 6 [×] 3.4 [=] 20.4

Since $13 \neq 20.4$, $\frac{2.5}{6} \neq \frac{3.4}{5.2}$.

This is not a proportion.

GLOBAL CONNECTIONS

Chocolate is made from the seeds, or cacao beans, of a tree called the *cacao*. The word cacao comes from two Maya Indian words meaning bitter juice. Because of a mistake in spelling by English importers, these beans became known as cocoa beans.

You can write proportions that involve a variable and then use cross products to solve the proportion.

Example 2

APPLICATION

Food

Refer to the application at the beginning of the lesson. Suppose the chocolate company makes a batch of chocolate with 75 pounds of cocoa beans. How many gallons of milk will they use?

You know that the ratio of cocoa beans to milk is 5:4. Let m represent the gallons of milk.

$$\frac{\text{5 parts cocoa beans}}{\text{4 parts milk}} = \frac{\text{75 pounds of cocoa beans}}{m \text{ gallons of milk}}$$

$$\frac{5}{4} = \frac{75}{m}$$

$5m = 4(75)$ *Find the cross products.*

$$5m = 300$$

$$m = 60$$

In a batch of chocolate with 75 pounds of cocoa beans, the company needs to use 60 gallons of milk.

A ratio called a **scale** is used when making a model to represent something that is too large or too small to be conveniently drawn at actual size. The scale compares the size of the model to the actual size of the object being modeled.

Example 3 APPLICATION Entertainment

In a recent movie about dinosaurs, the dinosaurs were scale models and so was the sport utility vehicle that the T-Rex overturned. The vehicle was made to the scale of 1 inch to 8 inches. The actual vehicle was about 14 feet long. What was the length of the model sport utility vehicle?

First, change 14 feet to 168 inches. Then let ℓ represent the length of the model vehicle.

$$\begin{matrix}\textit{scale} \rightarrow \\ \textit{actual} \rightarrow\end{matrix} \frac{1}{8} = \frac{\ell}{168}$$

$168 = 8\ell$ *Find the cross products.*

$21 = \ell$

The model sport utility vehicle was 21 inches long.

You can solve proportions by using a calculator.

Example 4 **Solve each proportion.**

a. $\frac{5}{4.25} = \frac{11.32}{m}$

Method 1
Use paper and a pencil.

$\frac{5}{4.25} = \frac{11.32}{m}$

$5m = 4.25(11.32)$

$5m = 48.11$

$m = 9.622$

Method 2
Use a calculator.

By the means-extremes property, $5m = 4.25(11.32)$. Multiply the means. Then divide by 5.

Enter: 4.25 [×] 11.32 [÷] 5 [=] 9.622

Rounded to the nearest hundredth, the solution is 9.62.

b. $\frac{x}{3} = \frac{x + 5}{15}$

$\frac{x}{3} = \frac{x + 5}{15}$

$15x = 3(x + 5)$ *Means-extremes property*

$15x = 3x + 15$ *Distributive property*

$12x = 15$

$x = \frac{5}{4}$ *Check this result.*

The solution is $\frac{5}{4}$.

The ratio of two measurements having different units of measure is called a **rate.** For example, 30 miles per gallon is a rate. Proportions are often used to solve problems involving rates.

Example 5

APPLICATION
State Fair

In the first 30 minutes of the opening day of the Texas State Fair, 1252 people entered the gates. If this attendance rate continued, how many people visited the fair during the operating hours of 8:00 A.M. and 12:00 midnight the first day?

Explore Let p represent the number of people attending the fair on opening day.

Plan Write a proportion for the problem.

$$\frac{1252}{0.5} = \frac{p}{16}$$ *Notice that both ratios compare the number of people per hour.*

Solve
$$\frac{1252}{0.5} = \frac{p}{16}$$
$$1252(16) = 0.5p$$
$$40{,}064 = p$$

If the attendance rate continued, 40,064 people visited the fair on opening day.

Examine Use estimation to check your answer. About 1250 people entered the fair every 30 minutes. This means that about 2500 people entered every hour. The fair was open for 16 hours each day. Therefore, about 16 × 2.5 thousand or 40,000 people entered, and the answer is reasonable.

CHECK FOR UNDERSTANDING

Communicating Mathematics

Study the lesson. Then complete the following.

1. **Explain** how to determine whether two ratios are equivalent.
2. **Explain** how to use a calculator to solve a proportion.
3. **Find** three examples of ratios in a newspaper or magazine.

MODELING MATHEMATICS

4. **Draw** an outline of an infant's body if the average infant is three heads long.

Guided Practice

Use cross products to determine whether each pair of ratios forms a proportion.

5. $\frac{3}{2}, \frac{21}{14}$
6. $\frac{2.3}{3.4}, \frac{0.3}{3.6}$

Solve each proportion.

7. $\frac{2}{3} = \frac{8}{x}$
8. $\frac{4}{w} = \frac{2}{10}$
9. $\frac{3}{15} = \frac{1}{y}$
10. $\frac{5.22}{13.92} = \frac{b}{48}$
11. $\frac{1.1}{0.6} = \frac{8.47}{n}$
12. $\frac{x}{1.5} = \frac{2.4}{1.6}$
13. **Travel** A 96-mile trip requires 6 gallons of gasoline. At that rate, how many gallons would be required for a 152-mile trip?

EXERCISES

Practice

Use cross products to determine whether each pair of ratios forms a proportion.

14. $\frac{6}{8}, \frac{22}{28}$ **15.** $\frac{4}{5}, \frac{16}{20}$ **16.** $\frac{4}{11}, \frac{12}{33}$

17. $\frac{8}{9}, \frac{16}{17}$ **18.** $\frac{2.1}{3.6}, \frac{5}{7}$ **19.** $\frac{0.4}{0.8}, \frac{0.7}{1.4}$

Solve each proportion.

20. $\frac{3}{4} = \frac{x}{8}$ **21.** $\frac{a}{45} = \frac{3}{15}$ **22.** $\frac{y}{9} = \frac{-7}{16}$

23. $\frac{3}{5} = \frac{x+2}{6}$ **24.** $\frac{w+2}{5} = \frac{7}{5}$ **25.** $\frac{x}{8} = \frac{0.21}{2}$

26. $\frac{5+y}{y-3} = \frac{14}{10}$ **27.** $\frac{m+9}{5} = \frac{m-10}{11}$ **28.** $\frac{r+7}{-4} = \frac{r-12}{6}$

29. $\frac{85.8}{t} = \frac{70.2}{9}$ **30.** $\frac{z}{33} = \frac{11.75}{35.25}$ **31.** $\frac{0.19}{2} = \frac{0.5x}{12}$

32. $\frac{2.405}{3.67} = \frac{g}{1.88}$ **33.** $\frac{x}{4.085} = \frac{5}{16.33}$ **34.** $\frac{3t}{9.65} = \frac{21}{1.066}$

Critical Thinking

35. Mariah is exactly eight years older than her cousin Louis.

a. Copy and complete the table below.

Louis' age	1	2	3	6	10	20	30
Mariah's age	9						

b. Find the ratio in decimal form of Mariah's age to Louis' age for each pair of ages listed in the table.

c. Write a formula for the ratio of Mariah's age to Louis' age when Louis is y years old.

d. As Mariah and Louis grow older, explain what happens to the ratio of their ages.

e. Explain whether the ratio of their ages will ever equal 1.

Applications and Problem Solving

36. Biology A flea, usually less than an eighth of an inch long, can long jump about thirteen inches and high jump about eight inches. If humans could jump in proportion to the flea, it would take only nine leaps to go one mile! At this rate, how many leaps would it take a human to travel 693 miles from Louisville, Kentucky to Norfolk, Virginia?

37. Movies When rating movies in 1994, critic Gene Siskel gave four thumbs up to every five thumbs up given by his partner Roger Ebert. If Mr. Siskel gave thumbs up to 68 movies, how many movies did Mr. Ebert rate favorably?

38. Recycling When a pair of blue jeans is made, the leftover denim scraps can be recycled to make stationery, pencils, and more denim. One pound of denim is left after making every five pairs of jeans. How many pounds of denim would be left from 250 pairs of jeans?

Mixed Review

39. **Statistics** Find the mean, median, and mode for the following set of data. (Lesson 3–7)

    19, 21, 18, 22, 46, 18, 17

40. Solve $a = \frac{v}{t}$ for t. (Lesson 3–6)

41. Define a variable, write an equation, and then solve the following problem. (Lesson 3–2)
    Four times a number decreased by twice the number is 100. What is the number?

42. Solve $-15 + d = 13$. (Lesson 3–1)

43. **Sales** Tanya is a sales representative for Unlimited Universe. A CD and tape player manufacturer is having a sales competition. Anyone who sells more than 40 CD players in one day wins a trip to Hawaii. Tanya sold 93 CD and tape players in one day for a total of \$9695. The CD players sold for \$135 and the tape players for \$80. (Lesson 2–9)
    a. How many CD and tape players were sold?
    b. What was the total amount of Tanya's CD and tape player sales?
    c. How many CD players does Tanya need to sell for her trip award?
    d. If p represents the number of CD players sold, what was the number of tape players sold?
    e. Will Tanya win the trip to Hawaii?

44. **Golf** In four rounds of a recent golf tournament, Heather shot 3 under par, 2 over par, 4 under par, and 1 under par. What was her score for the tournament? (Lesson 2–5)

45. Evaluate $|m - 4|$ if $m = -6$. (Lesson 2–3)

46. Simplify $x^2 + \frac{7}{8}x - \frac{x}{8}$. (Lesson 1–7)

WORKING ON THE In·ves·ti·ga·tion

Refer to the Investigation on pages 190–191.

Since it is impossible to count all the fish in the lake, you can use your samples to estimate the population in the lake.

1. Write a proportion that relates the numbers in your chart and the estimated number of fish in the lake.
2. Imagine that the only information you had was the data you recorded after your first casting. What would have been your estimate of the number of fish in the lake? Justify your reasoning. Record your estimate in the last column of your chart.
3. Make estimates for each of your castings and record them in the last column of your chart.
4. Taking all of your castings into consideration, if you had to give an official estimate of the number of fish in the lake, what would it be? Justify your reasoning.

Add the results of your work to your Investigation Folder.

4–2

Integration: Geometry
Similar Triangles

What YOU'LL LEARN

- To find the unknown measures of the sides of two similar triangles.

Why IT'S IMPORTANT

You can use similar triangles to solve problems involving tennis, architecture, and billiards.

APPLICATION
Architecture

"Rock n' roll is here to stay," is what you might hear after visiting the Rock and Roll Hall of Fame and Museum in Cleveland, Ohio. Memorabilia from musicians such as the Beatles, U2, and Carlos Santana cover the walls inside. The automatic teller machines in the building are even shaped like jukeboxes.

The building itself, designed by architect I.M. Pei, is made up of several geometric forms—a triangle, a cylinder, a rectangle, and a trapezoid. The triangular section of the building is similar to the one Pei designed for the Louvre in Paris, France. Both are made up of similar triangles.

Two figures are **similar** if they have the same shape, but not necessarily the same size.

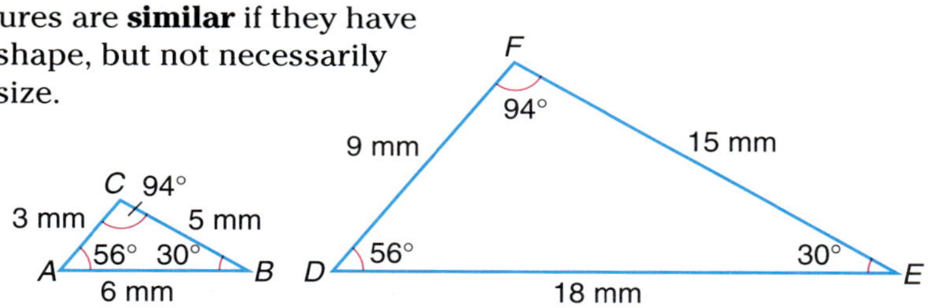

If **corresponding angles** of two triangles have equal measures, the triangles are similar. The two triangles above are similar. We write this as $\Delta ABC \sim \Delta DEF$. The order of the letters indicates the angles that correspond.

corresponding angles	corresponding sides
$\angle A$ and $\angle D$	$\overline{AB}$ and $\overline{DE}$
$\angle B$ and $\angle E$	$\overline{BC}$ and $\overline{EF}$
$\angle C$ and $\angle F$	$\overline{AC}$ and $\overline{DF}$

The sides opposite corresponding angles are called **corresponding sides**. Compare the measures of the corresponding sides. Note that AC means the measure of $\overline{AC}$, DF means the measure of $\overline{DF}$ and so on.

$$\frac{AB}{DE} = \frac{6}{18} = \frac{1}{3} \qquad \frac{BC}{EF} = \frac{5}{15} = \frac{1}{3} \qquad \frac{AC}{DF} = \frac{3}{9} = \frac{1}{3}$$

When the measures of the corresponding sides form equal ratios, the measures are said to be *proportional*.

***fabulous* FIRSTS**

Maya Ying Lin
(1959–)

Maya Lin became the first woman and the first student to design a major Washington, D.C., monument. In 1981, as a 21-year-old Yale architecture student, Lin won the design competition for the Vietnam Veterans Memorial. The black granite wall rising from Earth is the most visited site in the capital.

Similar Triangles	**If two triangles are similar, the measures of their corresponding sides are proportional, and the measures of their corresponding angles are equal.**

Proportions can be used to find the measures of the sides of similar triangles when some measurements are known.

Example 1

APPLICATION

Surveying

Surveyors normally use instruments to measure objects that are too large or too far away to measure by hand. They also can use the shadows that objects cast to find the height of the objects without measuring them directly. How can a surveyor use a telephone pole that is 25 feet tall and casts a shadow 20 feet long to find the height of a building that casts a shadow 52 feet long?

ΔNOP is similar to ΔMRQ.

$\frac{RQ}{OP} = \frac{QM}{PN}$ *Corresponding sides of similar triangles are proportional.*

$\frac{25}{x} = \frac{20}{52}$

$20x = 25(52)$ *Find the cross products.*

$20x = 1300$

$x = 65$

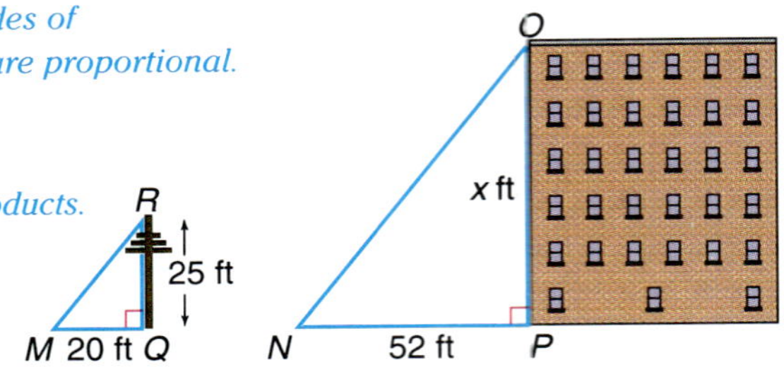

The building is 65 feet high.

Similar triangles may be positioned so that the corresponding parts are not obvious.

Example 2

Find the missing measures of the sides if each pair of triangles below are similar.

Remember that the sum of the measures of the angles in a triangle is 180°.

a. The measure of $\angle Q$ is $180° - (117° + 27°)$ or 36°.

The measure of $\angle T$ is $180° - (117° + 36°)$ or 27°.

Since the corresponding angles have equal measures, $\Delta QRS \sim \Delta VUT$. This means that the lengths of the corresponding sides are proportional.

$\frac{SQ}{TV} = \frac{QR}{VU}$ $\frac{SQ}{TV} = \frac{SR}{TU}$

$\frac{33}{12} = \frac{x}{6}$ $\frac{33}{12} = \frac{y}{8}$

$12x = 33(6)$ $12y = 33(8)$

$12x = 198$ $12y = 264$

$x = 16.5$ $y = 22$

The missing measures are 16.5 and 22.

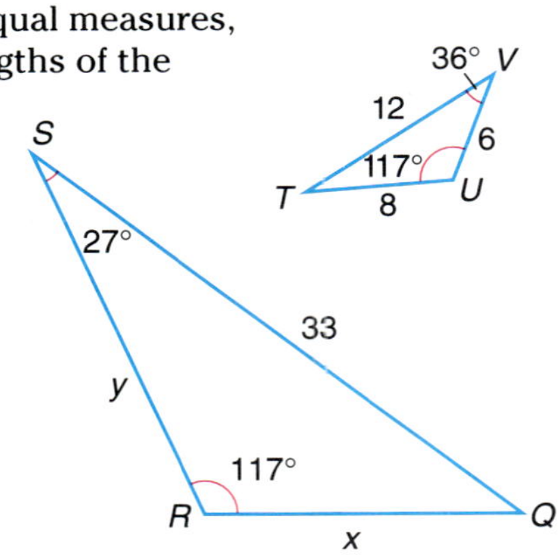

b. ΔNRT is similar to ΔMST.

$\frac{RN}{SM} = \frac{NT}{MT}$

$\frac{9}{x} = \frac{12}{28}$

$12x = 9(28)$ *Find the cross products.*

$12x = 252$

$x = 21$

The measure of $\overline{SM}$ is 21 meters.

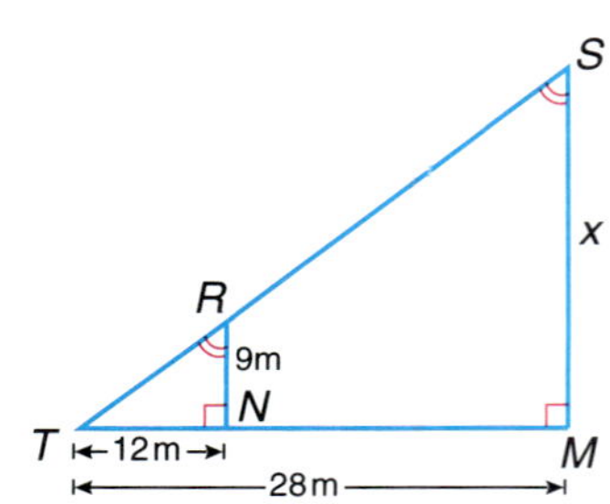

CAREER CHOICES

Land Surveyors use technical expertise to determine official land, space, and water boundaries. They plan field work, research legal records, record survey results, and prepare maps and reports. High school students should take courses in algebra, geometry, trigonometry, and drafting. Many colleges offer 4-year programs leading to a B.S. degree in surveying.

For more information, contact:

American Congress on Surveying and Mapping
5410 Grosvenor Lane
Bethesda, MD 20814–2122

CHECK FOR UNDERSTANDING

Communicating Mathematics

Study the lesson. Then complete the following.

1. **Name** the pairs of corresponding angles in Example 2a.
2. **List** what you know about the angles and sides of two triangles that are similar.
3. **List** the corresponding angles and corresponding sides if $\Delta RED \sim \Delta SOX$. Then write three proportions that correspond to these triangles.

MODELING MATHEMATICS

4. **Model** a triangle using toothpicks or straws. Then make a similar triangle using more toothpicks or straws. Write a proportion to show that the two triangles are similar.

Guided Practice

5. For the pair of similar triangles at the right, name the triangle that is similar to ΔXYZ. Make sure you have the letters in the correct order.

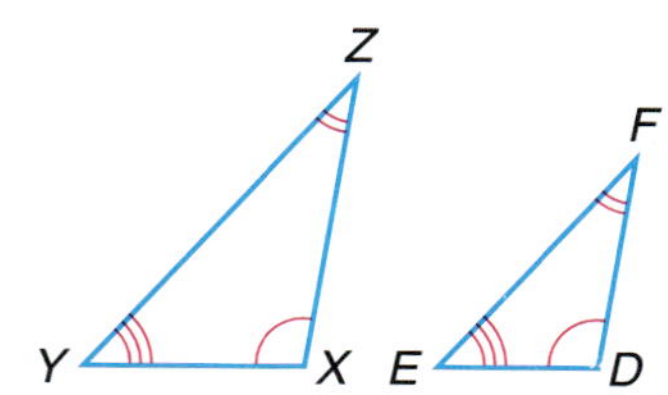

Determine whether each pair of triangles is similar. Justify your answer.

6\.

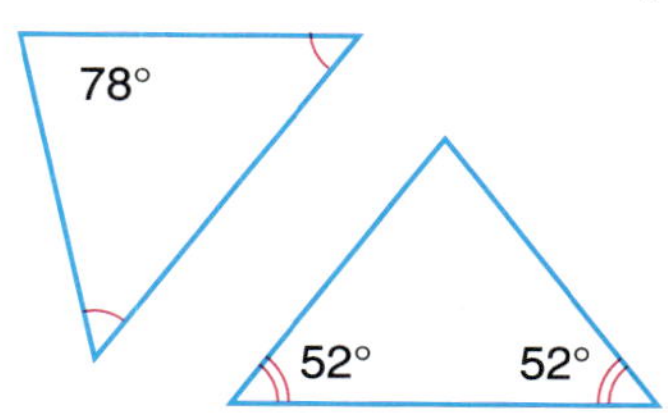

7\.

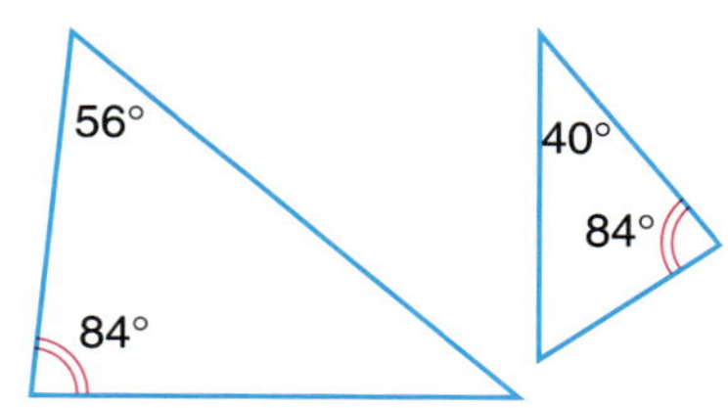

ΔKLM and ΔNOP are similar. For each set of measures given, find the measures of the remaining sides.

8. $k = 24, \ell = 30, m = 15, n = 16$
9. $k = 9, n = 6, o = 8, p = 4$
10. $n = 6, p = 2.5, \ell = 4, m = 1.25$

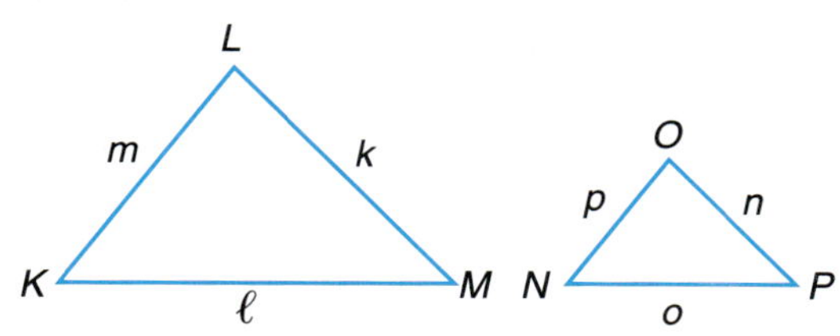

11. If a tree 6 feet tall casts a shadow 4 feet long, how high is a flagpole that casts a shadow 18 feet long at the same time of day?

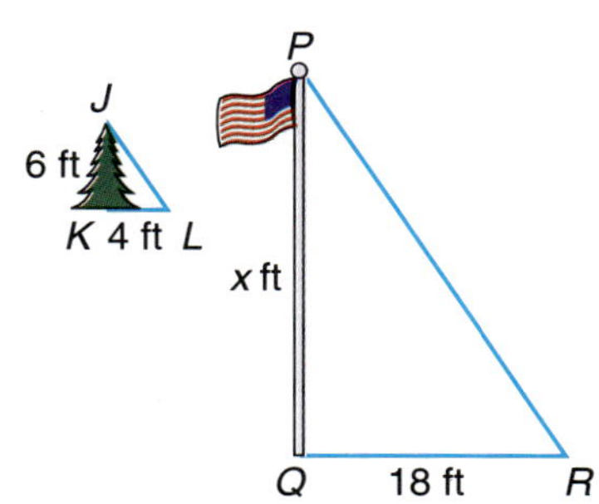

EXERCISES

Practice

For each pair of similar triangles, name the triangle that is similar to ΔWXY.

12. 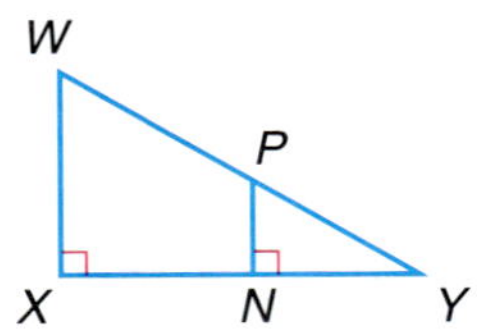

13. 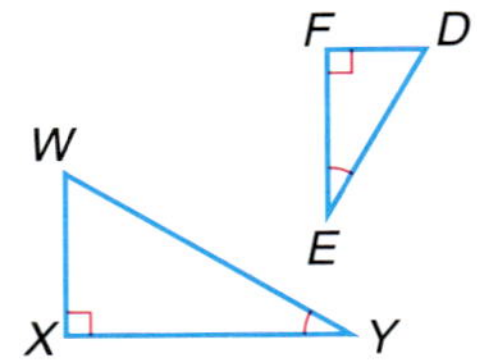

14. 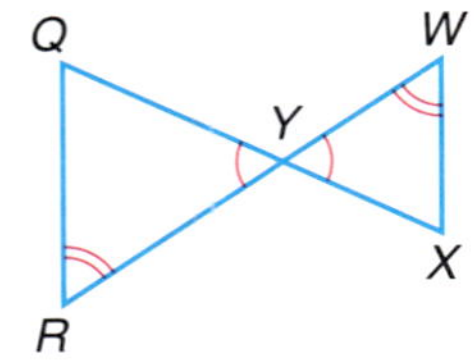

Determine whether each pair of triangles is similar. Justify your answer.

15. 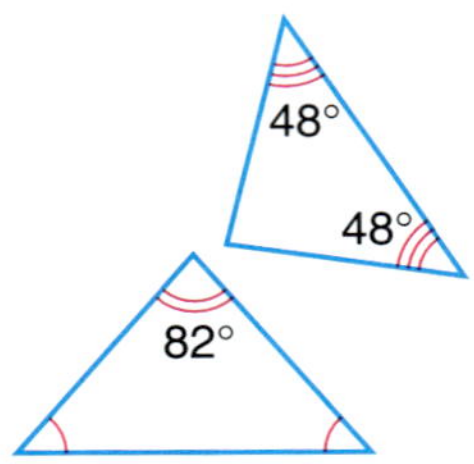

16. 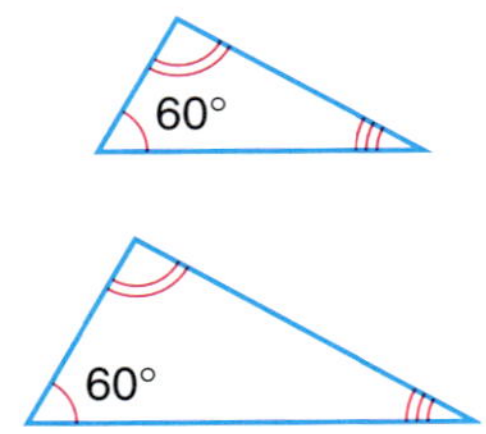

17. 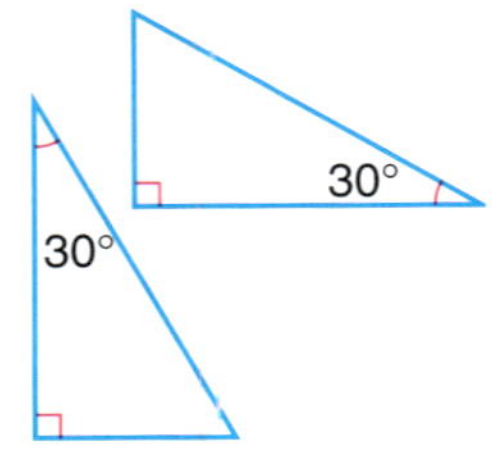

18. 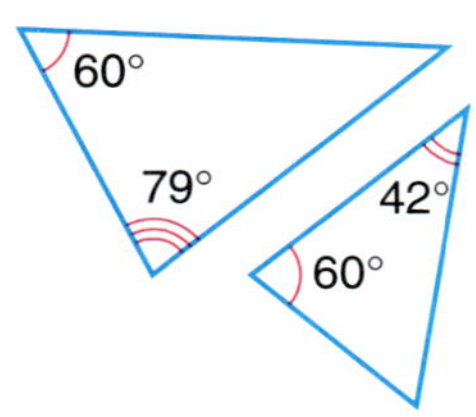

19. 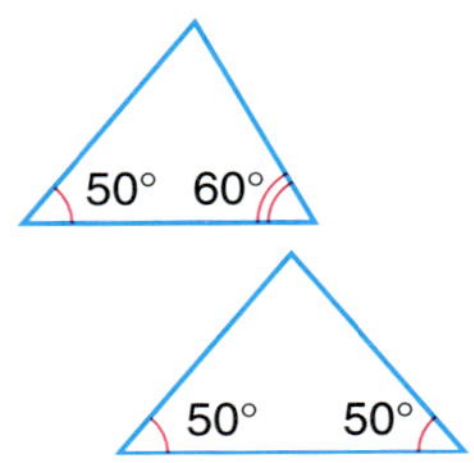

20. 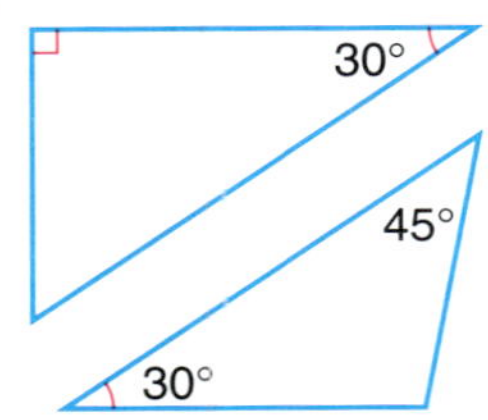

ΔABC and ΔDEF are similar. For each set of measures given, find the measures of the remaining sides.

21. $c = 11, f = 6, d = 5, e = 4$
22. $a = 5, d = 7, f = 6, e = 5$
23. $a = 17, b = 15, c = 10, f = 6$
24. $a = 16, e = 7, b = 13, c = 12$
25. $d = 2.1, b = 4.5, f = 3.2, e = 3.4$
26. $f = 12, d = 18, c = 18, e = 16$
27. $c = 5, a = 12.6, e = 8.1, f = 2.5$
28. $f = 5, a = 10.5, b = 15, c = 7.5$
29. $a = 4\frac{1}{4}, b = 5\frac{1}{2}, e = 2\frac{3}{4}, f = 1\frac{3}{4}$

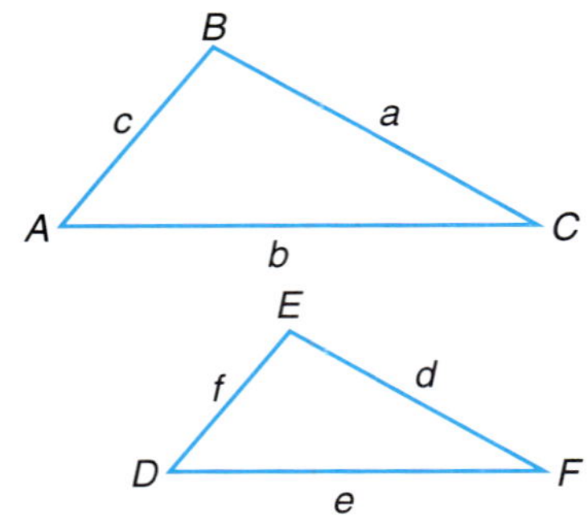

Critical Thinking

30. ΔABC and ΔDEF are similar. If the ratio of AC to DF is 2 to 3, what is the ratio of the area of ΔABC to the area of ΔDEF?

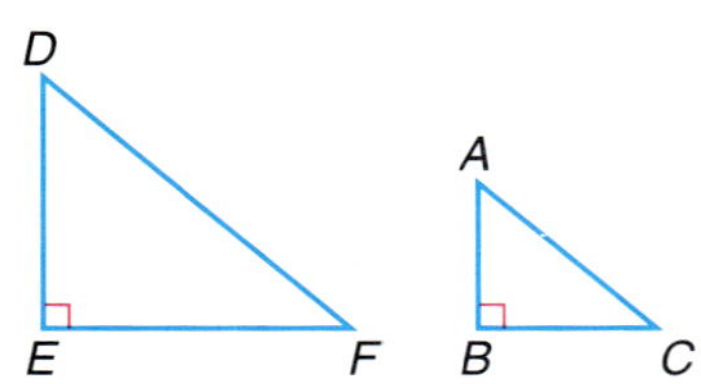

31. Draw an equilateral triangle. Try to cut it into three similar parts with no two parts that are congruent. Describe the process you used.

Applications and Problem Solving

32. Billiards Meda is playing billiards on a table like the one show at the right. If she can make her next shot, she figures she will have no trouble winning. She wants to strike the cue ball at D, bank it at C, and hit another ball at the mouth of pocket A. Use similar triangles to find where Meda's cue ball should strike the rail.

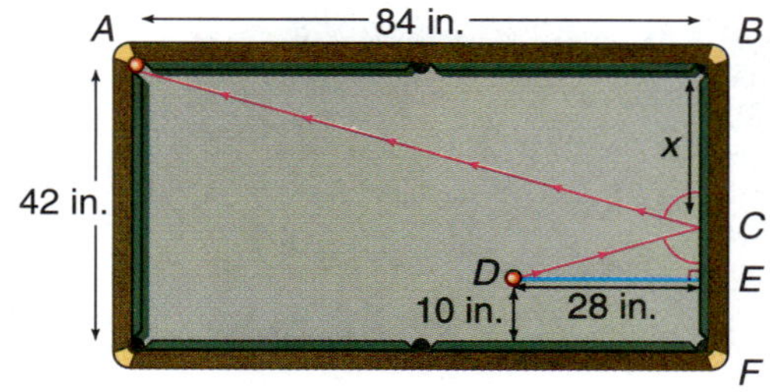

33. Tennis When serving in tennis, a player hits the ball standing at point E as shown in the figure at the right. To be a good serve, the ball must go over the net and land in the shaded area. Assume that all serves travel in a straight line and that all serves just clear the net. The figure below shows the view from the sideline.

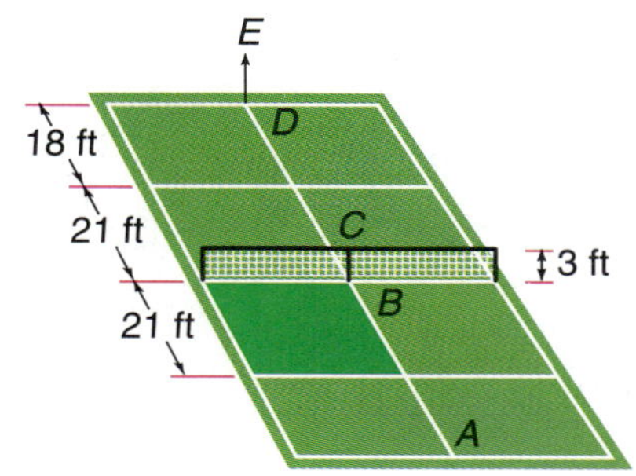

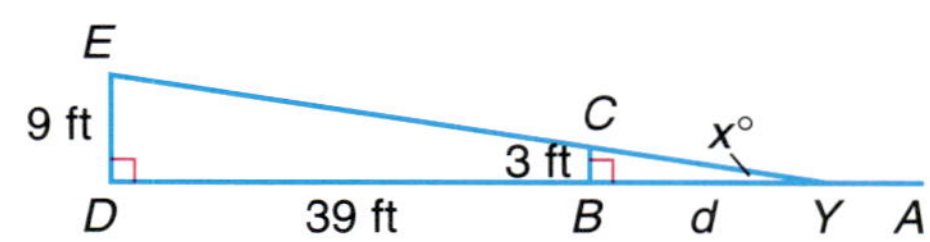

Let $\overline{EY}$ represent the flight of the ball.

a. Suppose you hit the ball when it is 9 feet above the ground. Write a proportion and solve for d to determine whether the serve is good.

b. Repeat the calculation of the distance d if the ball is hit from 8 feet above the ground and from 10 feet above the ground. Use the results to help you determine which players have an easier time hitting a good serve, tall players or short players. Explain.

Mark Clark Expressway

34. Bridges Haylee is making a model of the Mark Clark Expressway, a continuous truss bridge that spans the Cooper River in Charleston, South Carolina. Parts of the trusses are made up of triangles. Haylee plans to make the model bridge to the following scale: 1 inch to 12 feet. If the height of the triangle on the actual bridge is 40 feet, what will the height be on the model?

Mixed Review

35. Drafting The scale on the blueprint for a house is 1 inch to 3 feet. If the living room on the blueprint is $5\frac{1}{2}$ inches by 7 inches, what are the dimensions of the actual room? (Lesson 4–1)

36. Solve $7 = 3 - \frac{n}{3}$. (Lesson 3–3)

37. Table Tennis Each table tennis ball weighs about $\frac{1}{10}$ of an ounce. How many table tennis balls weigh 1 pound altogether? (Lesson 3–2)

38. Solve $x + (-8) = -31$. (Lesson 3–1)

39. Ecology Americans use about 2.5 million plastic bottles every hour. How many do they use in one day? How many in one week? (Lesson 2–6)

40. Replace __?__ with <, >, or = to make $\frac{8}{15}$ __?__ $\frac{9}{16}$ true. (Lesson 2–4)

41. Evaluate $(19 - 12) \div 7 \cdot 23$. Name the property used in each step. (Lesson 1–6)

4-3 Integration: Trigonometry
Trigonometric Ratios

***What* YOU'LL LEARN**

- To use trigonometric ratios to solve right triangles.

***Why* IT'S IMPORTANT**

You can use the trigonometric ratios to solve problems involving architecture and archaeology.

APPLICATION

Architecture

The Leaning Tower of Pisa, a bell tower in Pisa, Italy, currently leans 16.5 feet off center. The tower was closed in 1990 in order for workers to attempt to stabilize the tower's foundation to prevent it from eventually collapsing. By 1994, the tower's lean had decreased about $\frac{2}{5}$ of an inch. No date has been scheduled for reopening the tower.

If you were to draw a line from the top of the tower to the ground, a right triangle would be formed with the ground. If enough is known about a right triangle, certain ratios can be used to find the measures of the remaining parts of the triangle. These ratios are called **trigonometric ratios.** *Trigonometry is an area of mathematics that studies angles and triangles.*

A typical right triangle is shown at the right.

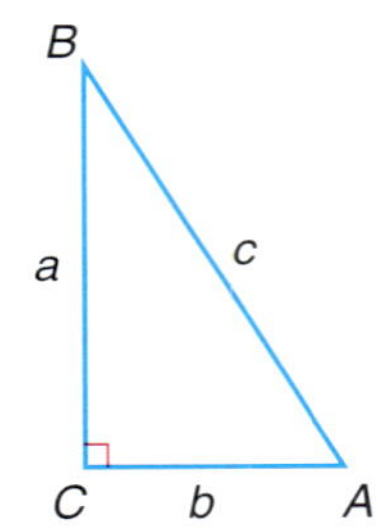

a is the measure of the side *opposite* $\angle A$, $\overline{BC}$.

b is the measure of the side *opposite* $\angle B$, $\overline{AC}$.

c is the measure of the side *opposite* $\angle C$, $\overline{AB}$.

a is *adjacent* to $\angle B$ and $\angle C$.

b is *adjacent* to $\angle A$ and $\angle C$.

c is *adjacent* to $\angle A$ and $\angle B$.

The side opposite $\angle C$, the right angle, is called the **hypotenuse.** The other two sides are called **legs.**

Three common trigonometric ratios are defined as follows.

Definition of Trigonometric Ratios

$$\text{sine of } \angle A = \frac{\text{measure of leg opposite } \angle A}{\text{measure of hypotenuse}}$$

$$\sin A = \frac{a}{c}$$

$$\text{cosine of } \angle A = \frac{\text{measure of leg adjacent to } \angle A}{\text{measure of hypotenuse}}$$

$$\cos A = \frac{b}{c}$$

$$\text{tangent of } \angle A = \frac{\text{measure of leg opposite } \angle A}{\text{measure of leg adjacent to } \angle A}$$

$$\tan A = \frac{a}{b}$$

Notice that sine, cosine, and tangent are abbreviated as sin, cos, and tan, respectively.

Example 1

Find the sine, cosine, and tangent of each acute angle. Round your answers to the nearest thousandth.

$\sin J = \dfrac{\text{opposite leg}}{\text{hypotenuse}}$

$= \dfrac{7}{25}$ or 0.280

$\cos J = \dfrac{\text{adjacent leg}}{\text{hypotenuse}}$

$= \dfrac{24}{25}$ or 0.960

$\tan J = \dfrac{\text{opposite leg}}{\text{adjacent leg}}$

$= \dfrac{7}{24}$ or about 0.292

$\sin L = \dfrac{\text{opposite leg}}{\text{hypotenuse}}$

$= \dfrac{24}{25}$ or 0.960

$\cos L = \dfrac{\text{adjacent leg}}{\text{hypotenuse}}$

$= \dfrac{7}{25}$ or 0.280

$\tan L = \dfrac{\text{opposite leg}}{\text{adjacent leg}}$

$= \dfrac{24}{7}$ or about 3.429

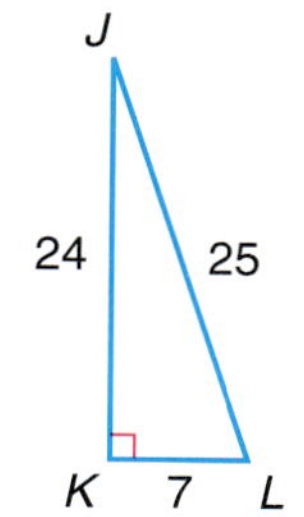

Consider triangles QTV and MSO. Since corresponding angles have the same measure, $\Delta QTV \sim \Delta MSO$. Recall that in similar triangles, the corresponding sides are proportional.

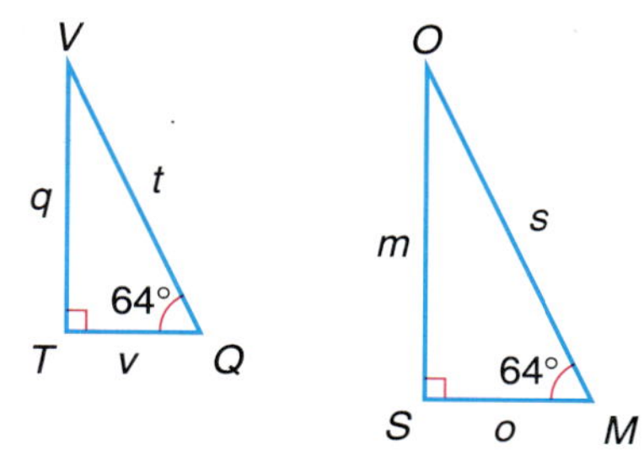

$\dfrac{m}{q} = \dfrac{s}{t}$

$\dfrac{q}{s} \cdot \dfrac{m}{q} = \dfrac{q}{s} \cdot \dfrac{s}{t}$ *Multiply each side by* $\frac{q}{s}$.

$\dfrac{m}{s} = \dfrac{q}{t}$

$\sin M = \sin Q$

In general, the sine of a 64° angle of a right triangle will be the same number no matter how large or small the triangle is. A similar result holds for cosine and tangent.

You can use a calculator to find the values of trigonometric functions or to find the measure of an angle.

Example 2

Find the value of sin 64° to the nearest ten thousandth.

Use a scientific calculator.

Enter: 64 [SIN] 0.898794046 *The calculator must be in degree mode.*

Rounded to the nearest ten thousandth, $\sin 64° \approx 0.8988$.

Example 3

Find the measure of $\angle P$ to the nearest degree.

Since the length of the opposite and adjacent sides are known, use the tangent ratio.

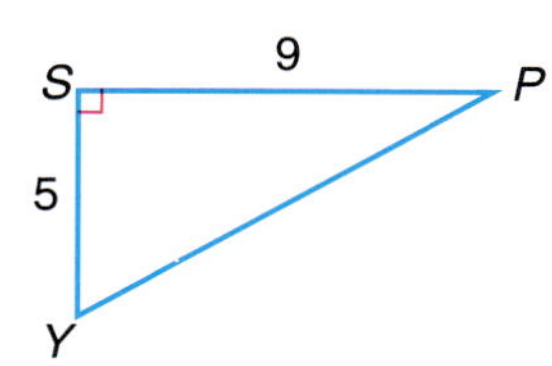

$\tan P = \dfrac{\text{opposite leg}}{\text{adjacent leg}}$

$= \dfrac{5}{9}$

Use a scientific calculator to find the angle measure with a tangent of $\frac{5}{9}$.

Enter: 5 [÷] 9 [=] [2nd] [TAN⁻¹] 29.0546041 *The TAN^{-1} key "undoes" the original function.*

To the nearest degree, the measure of $\angle P$ is 29°.

Many real-world applications involve trigonometry.

Example 4 APPLICATION **Architecture**

Refer to the application at the beginning of the lesson. Engineers working to correct the lean of the Leaning Tower of Pisa could check the angle the Tower makes with the ground to find any increase in the lean. Use the measurements to find the angle to the nearest degree that the Tower made with the ground.

Since the length of adjacent side and hypotenuse are known, use the cosine.

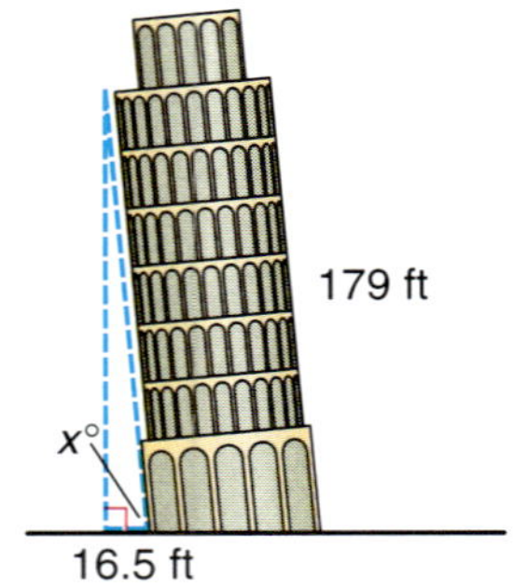

$\cos x = \frac{\text{adjacent leg}}{\text{hypotenuse}}$

$\cos x = \frac{16.5}{179}$

$\cos x = 0.09217877$ *Use a calculator to find x.*

$x \approx 85°$

To the nearest degree, the measure of the angle is 85°.

You can find the missing measures of a right triangle if you know the measure of two sides of the triangle or the measure of one side and one acute angle. Finding all of the measures of the sides and the angles in a right triangle is called **solving the triangle**.

Example 5 **Solve ΔABC.**

The measure of $\angle C$ is $90° - 42°$ or $48°$.

$\sin 42° = \frac{x}{22}$

$0.6691 \approx \frac{x}{22}$

$14.7 \approx x$

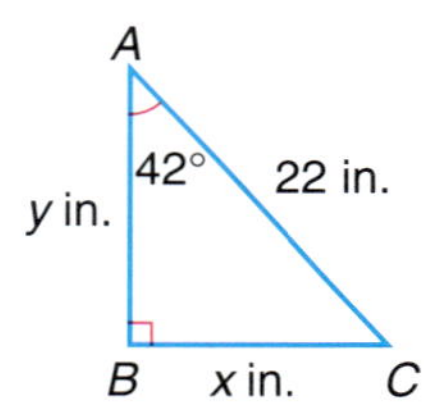

Thus, $\overline{BC}$ is about 14.7 inches long.

$\cos 42° = \frac{y}{22}$

$0.7431 \approx \frac{y}{22}$

$16.3 \approx y$

Thus, $\overline{AB}$ is about 16.3 inches long.

In the real world, trigonometric ratios are often used to find distances or lengths that cannot be measured directly. In these applications, you will sometimes use an angle of elevation or an angle of depression. An **angle of elevation** is formed by a horizontal line of sight and a line of sight above it. An **angle of depression** is formed by a horizontal line of sight and a line of sight below it.

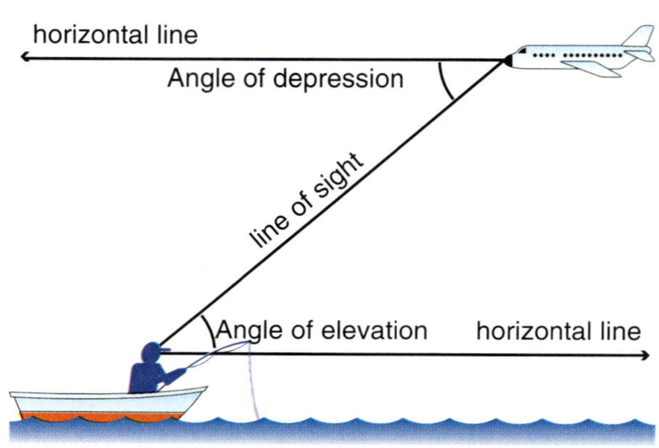

MODELING MATHEMATICS

Make a Hypsometer

Materials: protractor, straw, tape, paper clip, string

You can make a hypsometer to find the angle of elevation of an object that is too tall to measure.

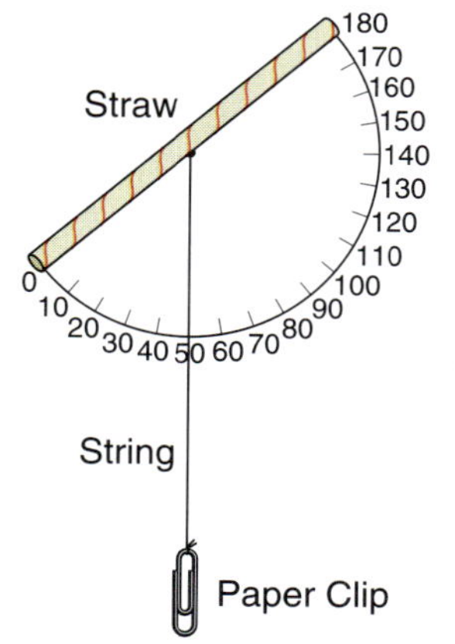

Your Turn

a. Tie one end of a piece of string to the middle of a straw. Tie the other end of string to a paper clip.

b. Tape a protractor to the side of the straw. Make sure that the string hangs freely to create a vertical or plumb line.

c. Find an object outside that is too tall to measure directly, such as a basketball hoop, a flagpole, or the school building.

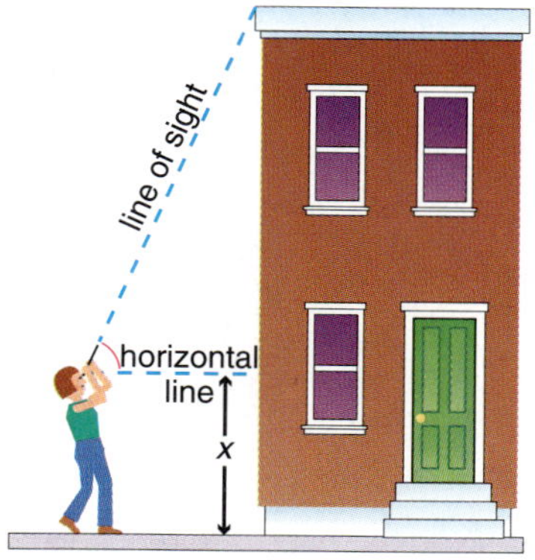

d. Look through the straw to the top of the object you are measuring. Find a horizontal line of sight as shown above. Find the measurement where the string and protractor intersect. Determine the angle of elevation by subtracting this measurement from 90°.

e. Use the equation tan (angle sighted) = $\frac{\text{height of object} - x}{\text{distance of object}}$, where x represents the distance from the ground to your eye level, to find the height of the object.

f. Compare your answer with someone who measured the same object. Did your heights agree? Why or why not?

Example 6

APPLICATION
Balloons

What would the Macy's Thanksgiving Day Parade be without balloons? In 1994, Dr. Suess' The Cat in the Hat made its first appearance. It took 36 people to maneuver the cat along the parade route. Suppose you were watching the parade. You noticed that two of the handling lines formed a right triangle with the ground. You estimated the angle of elevation to the bottom of the balloon to be 60°, and the handlers to be about 35 feet away from each other. Find the altitude of the bottom of the balloon to the nearest foot.

Explore You know the distance from one handler to another and the approximate angle of elevation. You need to find the height from the handlers to the bottom of the balloon.

(continued on the next page)

Plan Let h represent the distance to the bottom of the balloon in feet. Use the tangent ratio to solve this problem.

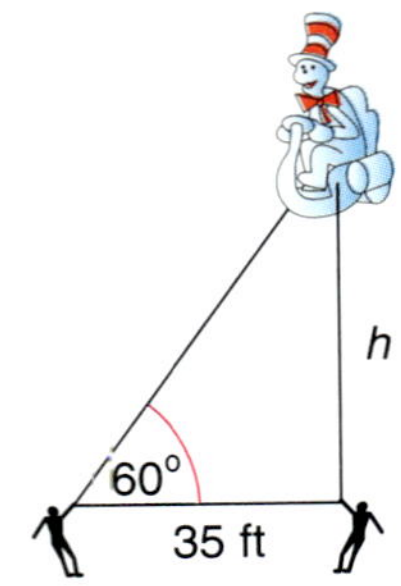

Solve

$$\tan 60^\circ = \frac{\text{opposite leg}}{\text{adjacent}}$$

$$\tan 60^\circ = \frac{h}{35}$$

$$1.7321 \approx \frac{h}{35}$$

$$1.7321(35) \approx h$$

$$60.6235 \approx h$$

The altitude of the bottom of the balloon is about 61 feet above the handlers.

Examine You can examine the solution by determining the angle of elevation in the equation $\tan x = \frac{61}{35}$. Since $x = 60.15^\circ$, the solution is reasonable.

CHECK FOR UNDERSTANDING

Communicating Mathematics

Study the lesson. Then complete the following.

1. **Use** the figure at the right to answer the following questions.
   a. What is the measure of the leg adjacent to $\angle C$?
   b. What is the measure of the leg opposite $\angle C$?

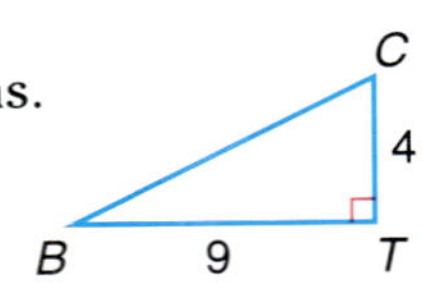

2. **List** the trigonometric ratio or ratios that involve the measure of the hypotenuse.

3. **Explain** how to determine which trigonometric ratio to use when solving for an unknown measure of a right triangle.

4. **Name** the angles of elevation and depression in the drawing at the right.

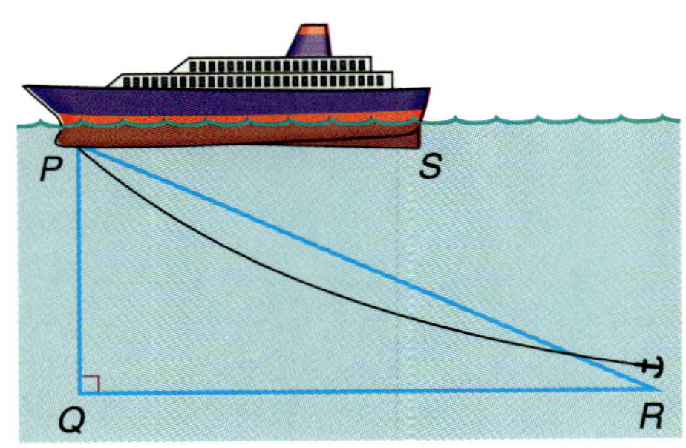

5. State which trigonometric ratio you could use to find x.

a.

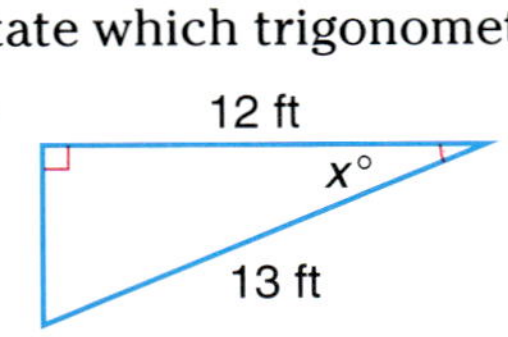

b.

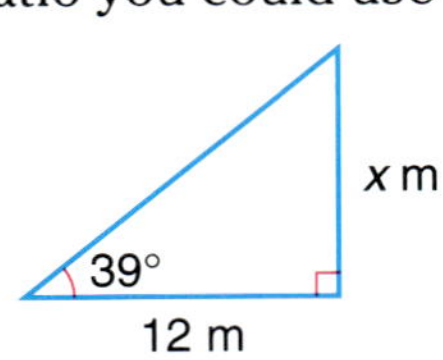

c.

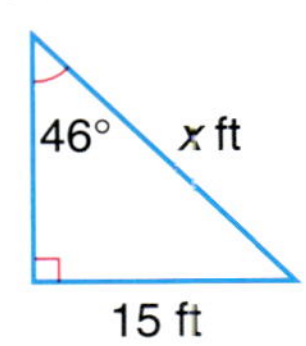

MODELING MATHEMATICS

6. **Use** a hypsometer to find the height of a tree in your community. Then write a paragraph explaining how you found the height.

Guided Practice

For each triangle, find sin *Y*, cos *Y*, and tan *Y* to the nearest thousandth.

7. 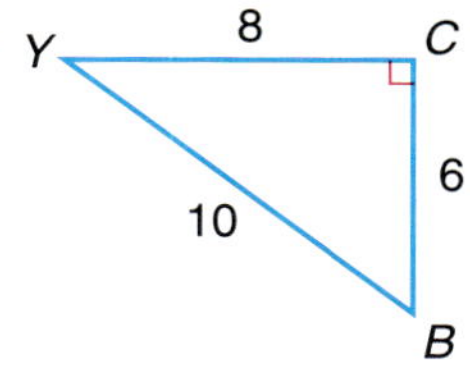

8. 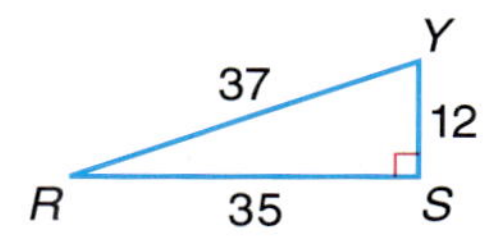

Use a calculator to find the value of each trigonometric ratio to the nearest ten thousandth.

9. $\cos 35°$ **10.** $\sin 63°$ **11.** $\tan 7°$

Use a calculator to find the measure of each angle to the nearest degree.

12. $\cos C = 0.9613$ **13.** $\sin X = 0.7193$ **14.** $\tan W = 2.4752$

For each triangle, find the measure of the marked acute angle to the nearest degree.

15. 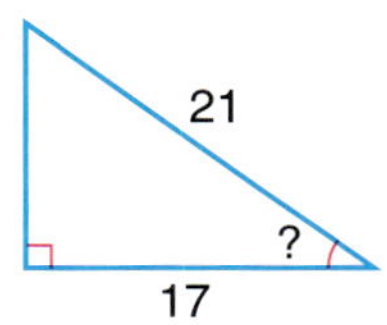

16. 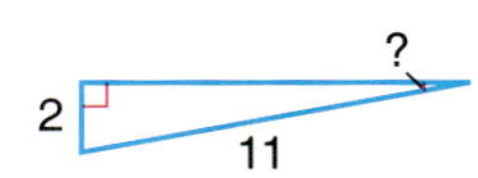

Solve each right triangle. State the side lengths to the nearest tenth and the angle measures to the nearest degree.

17. 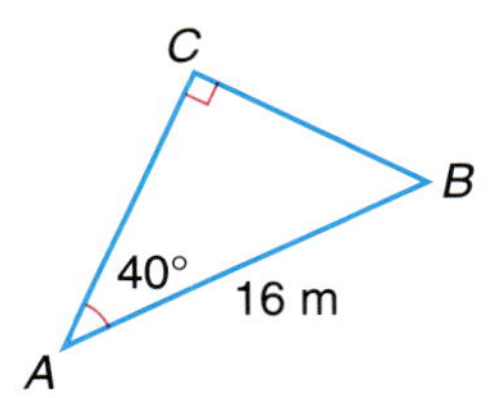

18. 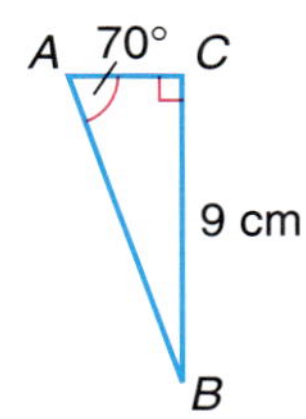

19. 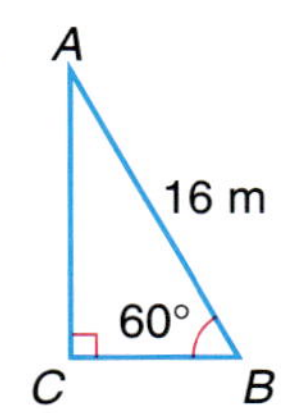

20. Transportation Find the angle of elevation of a train track if a train in the mountains rises 15 feet for every 250 feet it moves along the track.

EXERCISES

Practice

For each triangle, find sin *G*, cos *G*, and tan *G* to the nearest thousandth.

21. 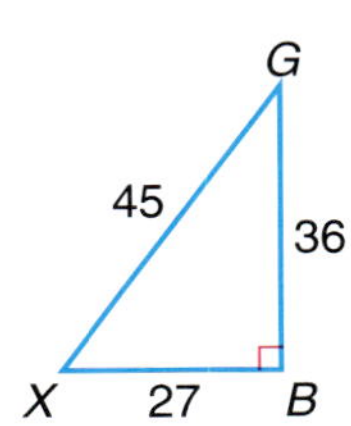

22. 

23. 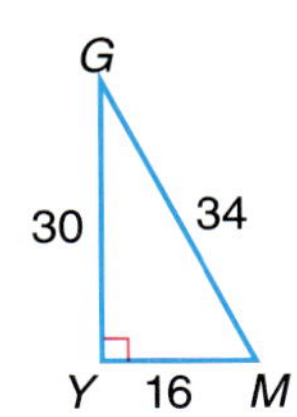

For each triangle, find sin *G*, cos *G*, and tan *G* to the nearest thousandth.

24. 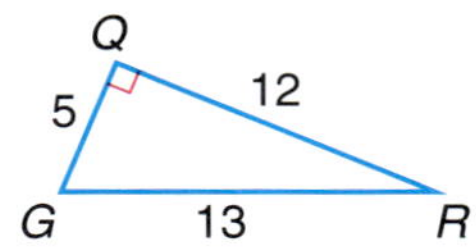

25. 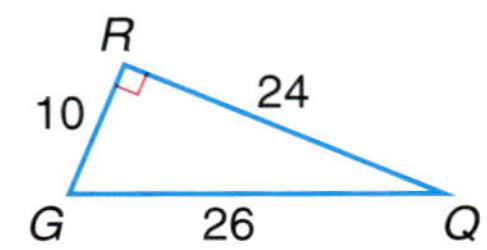

26. 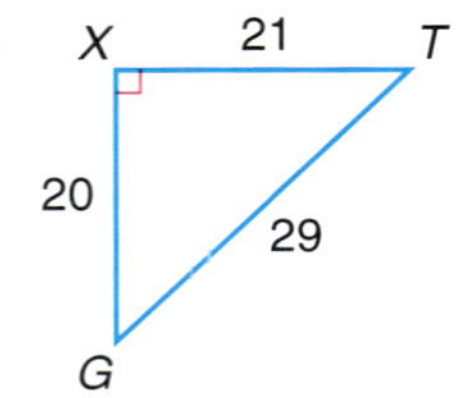

Use a calculator to find the value of each trigonometric ratio to the nearest ten thousandth.

27. $\sin 21°$
28. $\cos 15°$
29. $\sin 76°$
30. $\tan 56°$
31. $\cos 68°$
32. $\tan 30°$

Use a calculator to find the measure of each angle to the nearest degree.

33. $\tan A = 0.6473$
34. $\cos B = 0.7658$
35. $\sin F = 0.3823$
36. $\cos Q = 0.2993$
37. $\sin R = 0.8827$
38. $\tan J = 8.8988$

For each triangle, find the measure of the marked acute angle to the nearest degree.

39. 

40. 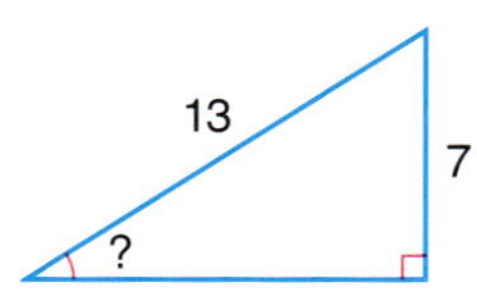

41. 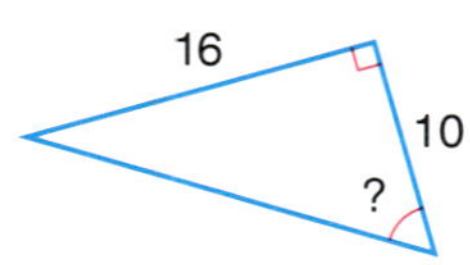

42. 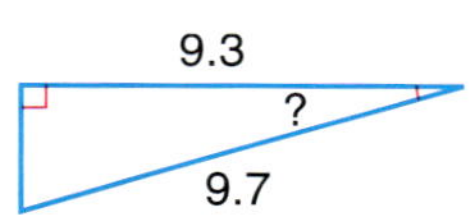

43. 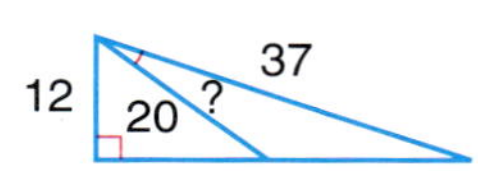

44. 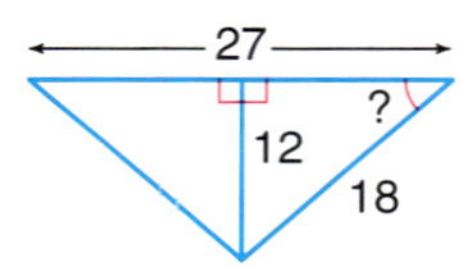

Solve each right triangle. State the side lengths to the nearest tenth and the angle measures to the nearest degree.

45. 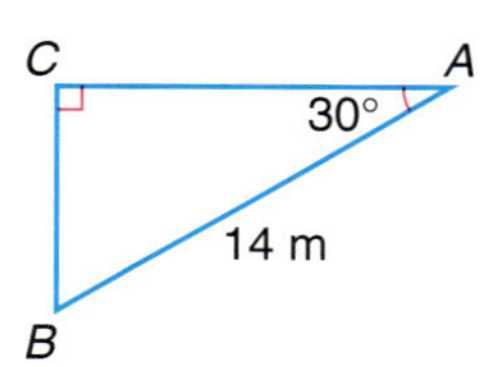

46. 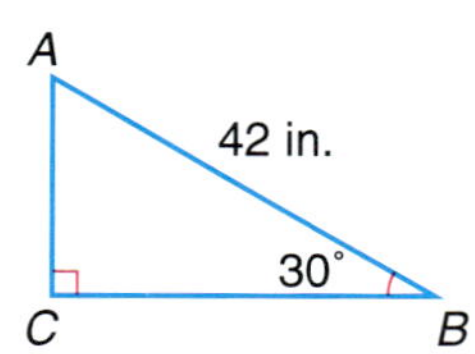

47. 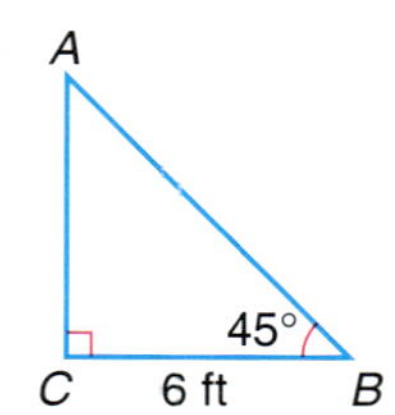

48. 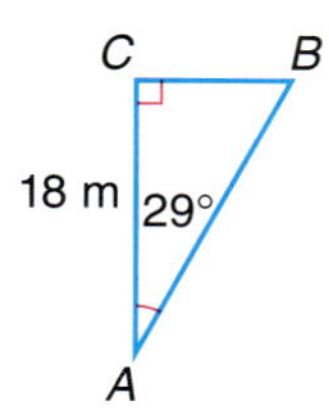

49. 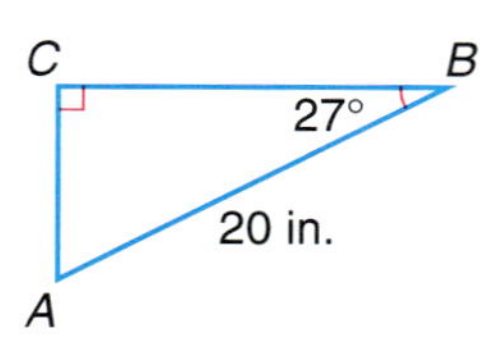

50. 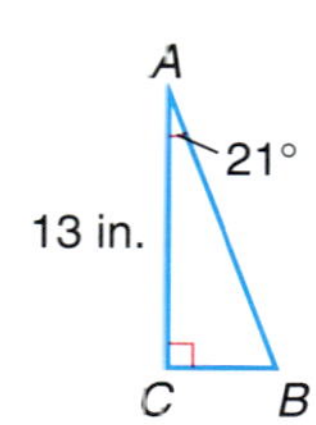

51. 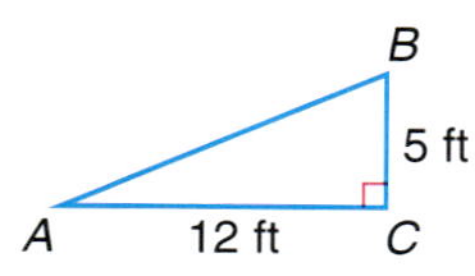

52. 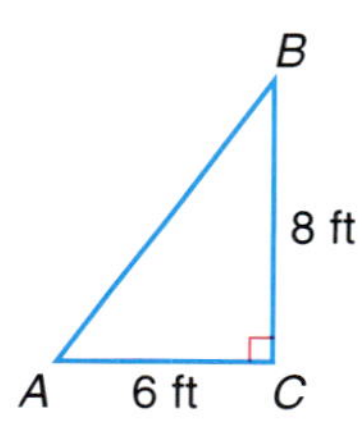

53. 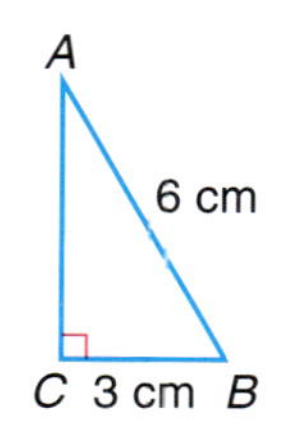

Programming

To run the program repeatedly, press ENTER *after each run is completed and the prompt will appear again for new values of a and b.*

54. Suppose $\angle ABC$ has a right angle C, and the measures of its legs are a and b. The graphing calculator program at the right asks you to enter the lengths of the legs of the triangle. It then calculates the measure of the hypotenuse c, the measures of the acute angles, and the trigonometric ratios for each acute angle. The PAUSE commands in the program stop the calculator's computations and allow you to record the information shown on the screen. Press ENTER to continue the program. Make sure your calculator is in degree mode before running the program.

```
PROGRAM: LEGS
: Disp "ENTER LENGTHS OF",
  "LEGS A AND B"
: Prompt A,B
: √(A² + B²)→C
: Disp "SIDE C =",C
: Disp "ANGLE A =", tan⁻¹ (A/B)
: Disp "ANGLE B =", tan⁻¹ (B/A)
: Pause
: Disp "sin (A)=",A/C
: Disp "sin (B)=",B/C
: Disp "cos (A)=",B/C
: Pause
: Disp "cos (B)=",A/C
: Disp "tan (A)=",A/B
: Disp "tan (B)=",B/A
```

Use the program for each pair of values for *a* and *b*.

a. 3, 4 **b.** 5, 12
c. 20, 40 **d.** 125, 100

Critical Thinking

55. Use the triangle below to determine which of the following statements are true. Justify your answers.

a. $\sin C = \cos B$

b. $\cos B = \dfrac{1}{\sin B}$

c. $\tan C = \dfrac{\cos C}{\sin C}$

d. $\tan C = \dfrac{\sin C}{\cos C}$

e. $\sin B = (\tan B)(\cos B)$

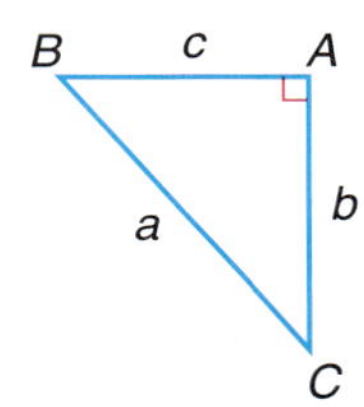

Applications and Problem Solving

56. Archaeology The largest of the pyramids of Egypt has a square base with sides 755 feet long. $\angle PQR$ has a measure of 52°. The top of the pyramid is no longer there. What was the pyramid's original height ($\overline{RP}$) to the nearest foot?

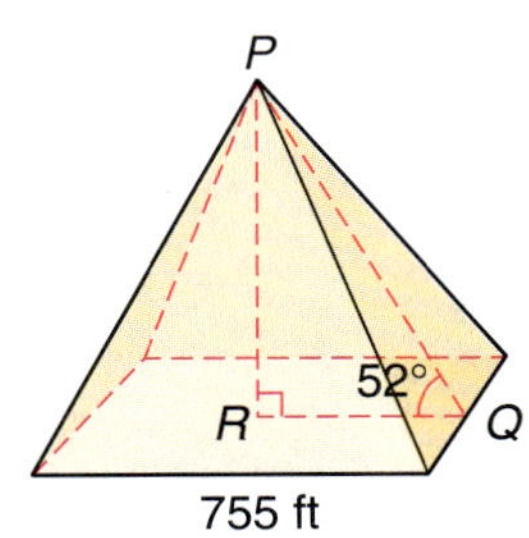

57. Make a Drawing On September 30, 1995, the Ohio State Buckeyes defeated the Notre Dame Fighting Irish in football as a blimp relayed aerial views from above. Suppose the blimp was directly over the 50-yard line. A photographer on the ground estimated the angle of elevation to be 85° when she was 65 yards away from the point on the ground directly under the blimp. How high is the blimp? Round your answer to the nearest foot.

Mixed Review

58. **Civil Engineering** The city of Mansfield plans to build a bridge across Spring Lake. Use the information in the diagram at the right to find the distance across Spring Lake. (Lesson 4–2)

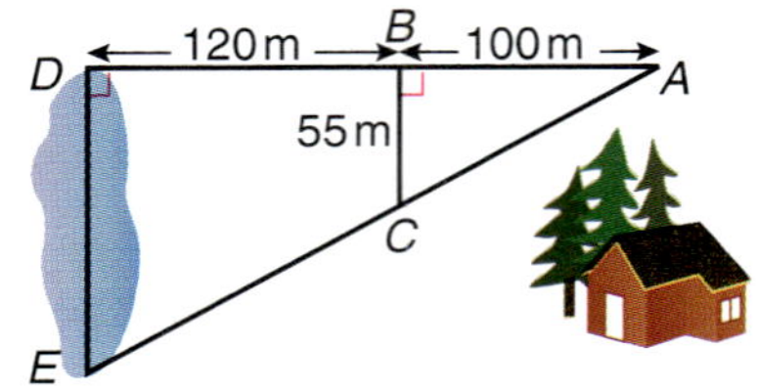

59. Solve $\frac{x}{5} = \frac{x+3}{10}$. (Lesson 4–1)

60. **Baseball** The batting averages for 10 players on a baseball team are 0.234, 0.253, 0.312, 0.333, 0.286, 0.240, 0.183, 0.222, 0.297, and 0.275. Find the median batting average for these players. (Lesson 3–7)

61. Solve $\frac{2}{5}y + \frac{y}{2} = 9$. (Lesson 3–3)

62. Write an equation to represent the situation below. Then solve the problem. (Lesson 3–2)

    Joyce Conners paid \$47.50 for five football tickets. What was the cost per ticket?

63. Name the sets of numbers to which $\sqrt{36}$ belongs. Use N for natural numbers, W for whole numbers, Z for integers, Q for rational numbers, and I for irrational numbers. (Lesson 2–8)

64. Simplify $\frac{3a+9}{3}$. (Lesson 2–7)

65. Find $\left(-\frac{2}{3}\right)\left(-\frac{1}{5}\right)$. (Lesson 2–6)

66. Find $-13 + (-8)$. (Lesson 2–3)

67. Simplify $8x + 2y + x$. (Lesson 1–8)

68. Evaluate $(9 - 2 \cdot 3)^3 - 27 + 9 \cdot 2$. (Lesson 1–6)

69. Evaluate 5^3. (Lesson 1–1)

Mathematics and SOCIETY

Morgan's Conjecture

The excerpt below appeared in an article in *The Columbus Dispatch* on December 21, 1994.

RYAN MORGAN WOULD HAVE GOTTEN an "A" in geometry even if he hadn't unearthed a mathematical treasure. But the persistent Baltimore high school sophomore pushed a hunch into a theory. He calls it "Morgan's Conjecture" and is hoping it will soon be "Morgan's Theorem." In geometric circles, developing a theorem is a big deal—especially if you're only 15....What did Ryan see?...When the sides of a triangle are divided by an odd number larger than one, and when lines are drawn from the division points on the sides of the triangle to the vertices, there always will be a hexagon in the interior of the triangle. And the area of that hexagon always will be a predictable fraction of the area of the larger triangle. The fraction is determined by a complex formula that Ryan worked out. ■

1. In talking about his work, the student said, "It's mostly just luck in playing around with it." What other factors besides luck might have been involved?
2. Are you surprised to learn that students can discover theorems? Why or why not?
3. Is there an area of mathematics that interests you that you would like to explore further? How would you do it?

4–4 Percents

***What* YOU'LL LEARN**

- To solve percent problems, and
- to solve problems involving simple interest.

***Why* IT'S IMPORTANT**

You can use percents to solve problems involving finance, nutrition, and statistics.

APPLICATION

Cosmetics

According to a magazine, 3 out of 5 teenage girls wear mascara. What is the rate of teenage girls wearing mascara per 100 girls? **Source:** *Good Housekeeping*

You can solve this problem by using a proportion. The ratio of teenage girls who wear mascara to the total number of teenage girls is $\frac{3}{5}$. Write a proportion that sets $\frac{3}{5}$ equal to a ratio with a denominator of 100.

$$\frac{3}{5} = \frac{n}{100}$$

$$60 = n$$

Teenage girls wear mascara at a rate of 60 per 100, or 60 percent. A **percent** is a ratio that compares a number to 100. Percent also means *per hundred*, or *hundredths*. Percents can be expressed with a percent symbol (%), as fractions, or as decimals.

$$60\% = \frac{60}{100} = 0.60$$

Example 1 **Write $\frac{3}{4}$ as a percent.**

Method 1

Use a proportion.

$$\frac{3}{4} = \frac{n}{100}$$

$$300 = 4n$$

$$75 = n$$

Thus, $\frac{3}{4}$ is equal to $\frac{75}{100}$ or 75%.

Method 2

Use a calculator.

$$\frac{3}{4} = \frac{n}{100}$$

$$100\left(\frac{3}{4}\right) = n$$

Enter: 100 [×] 3 [÷] 4 [=] 75

FYI

Sixty percent of teenage girls wear lipstick and lip gloss, 72% wear nail polish, 55% wear eye shadow, and 50% wear blush.

Proportions are often used to solve percent problems. One of the ratios in these proportions is always a comparison of two numbers called the **percentage** and the **base**. The other ratio, called the **rate**, is a fraction with a denominator of 100.

$$\begin{matrix}\textit{percentage} \rightarrow \\ \textit{base} \rightarrow\end{matrix} \quad \left.\frac{3}{4} = \frac{75}{100}\right\} \leftarrow \textit{Rate}$$

Percent Proportion

$$\frac{\textbf{Percentage}}{\textbf{Base}} = \textbf{Rate} \quad \textbf{or} \quad \frac{\textbf{Percentage}}{\textbf{Base}} = \frac{r}{100}$$

The $\frac{\textit{percentage}}{\textit{base}}$ represents $\frac{\textit{part}}{\textit{whole}}$.

Example 2

a. 30 is what percent of 50?

Use the percent proportion.

$$\frac{\text{Percentage}}{\text{Base}} = \frac{r}{100}$$

The percentage is 30.
The base is 50.

$$\frac{30}{50} = \frac{r}{100}$$

$$3000 = 50r$$

$$60 = r$$

Thus, 30 is 60% of 50.

b. 20 is what percent of 30?

Use a calculator.

$$\frac{\text{Percentage}}{\text{Base}} = \frac{r}{100}$$

$$\frac{20}{30} = \frac{r}{100}$$

Enter: 20 [÷] 30 [×] 100 [=] 66.66666667

Thus, 20 is $66.\overline{6}\%$ of 30. This can also be written as $66\frac{2}{3}\%$.

You can also write equations to solve problems with percents.

Example 3

TECHNOLOGY Tip

Most calculators have a key labeled [%]. To find 28% of 58.4 on a scientific calculator, enter:

28 [2nd] [%] [×] 58.4 [=] 16.352.

a. 60% of what number is 54?

60% of what number is 54?

$$\frac{60}{100} \cdot x = 54$$

$$0.6x = 54$$

$$x = 90$$

Thus, 60% of 90 is 54.

b. What number is 40% of 37.5?

What number is 40% of 37.5?

$$x = \frac{40}{100} \cdot 37.5$$

$$x = 15$$

Thus, 15 is 40% of 37.5.

MODELING MATHEMATICS

Making Circle Graphs

Materials: compass, protractor

You can use a circle graph to compare parts of a whole. Follow the steps to display the data below in a circle graph.

Where's the Remote?	
Number of Times TV Remote Misplaced Per Week	**Number of People Responding**
Never	220
1–5	190
5 or more	85
Don't Know	5

Your Turn

a. Find the total number of people surveyed.

b. Find the ratio that compares the number of people that responded for each category to the total number of people that responded.

c. Since there are 360° in a circle, multiply each ratio by 360 to find the number of degrees for each section of the graph. Round to the nearest degree.

d. Use a compass to draw a circle and a radius as shown at the right.

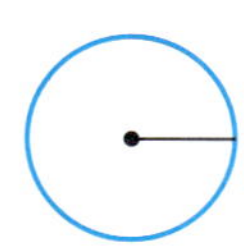

e. Use a protractor to draw angles. Start with the least number of degrees. Repeat for the remaining sections. Label each section and give the graph a title.

f. What is the sum of the percents in your graph?

Percents are also used in simple interest problems. **Simple interest** is the amount paid or earned for the use of money. The formula $I = prt$ is used to solve problems involving simple interest. In the formula, I represents the interest, p represents the amount of money invested, called the *principal*, r represents the annual interest rate, and t represents time in years.

Example 4 APPLICATION **Finance**

a. Luis Hernandez has some money he has saved over the summer from mowing lawns. He wants to put some of it in a 6-month certificate of deposit (CD) account that would pay 6% annual interest. He doesn't want to put all of his money in the CD because he wants some spending money. He is hoping to earn $45 in interest to buy a new video game. How much money should Luis put in the CD?

Explore Let p = the amount of money Luis should deposit.

Plan

$I = prt$

$45 = p(0.06)(0.5)$ *Write 6% as 0.06 and 6 months as 0.5 years.*

Solve

$45 = 0.03p$ *Multiply 0.06 by 0.5.*

$1500 = p$ *Divide each side by 0.03.*

Examine When p is 1500, $I = (1500)(0.06)(0.5)$ or \$45. Luis should deposit \$1500.

b. Whitney Williamson has $30,000 she would like to invest. She has a choice of two interest-paying bonds, one offering a 6% annual interest and the other paying 7.5% annual interest. She would like to earn $2100 in interest in one year. If she earns any more than $2100, she would need to pay a higher rate of income tax. How much money should she invest in each bond?

Explore Let n = the amount of money invested at 6%. Then $30{,}000 - n$ = the amount of money invested at 7.5%.

Plan

interest on 6% investment

$n(0.06)(1)$ or $0.06n$

interest on 7.5% investment

$(30{,}000 - n)(0.075)(1)$ or $2250 - 0.075n$

Solve

interest at 6% + *interest at 7.5%* = *total interest*

$$0.06n + (2250 - 0.075n) = 2100$$

$$-0.015n + 2250 = 2100$$ *Add 0.06n and −0.075n.*

$$-0.015n = -150$$

$$n = 10{,}000$$

Whitney should invest \$10,000 at 6% and \$30,000 − \$10,000 or \$20,000 at 7.5%.

Examine $(10{,}000)(0.06)(1) + (20{,}000)(0.075)(1) = 2100$

The answer checks.

CHECK FOR UNDERSTANDING

Communicating Mathematics

Study the lesson. Then complete the following.

1. **Compare** $\frac{r}{100}$ in the percent proportion and r in the simple interest formula. How are they the same? How are they different?
2. **Explain** how to find 57% of 42 using a scientific calculator.
3. **Explain** why an investor might invest a greater amount of money in a lower rate of interest instead of a higher rate.
4. **Read** the following excerpt from an article about the America's Cup yacht race in a magazine. Explain what is incorrect in this excerpt and why.

> With a Ph.D. from MIT, (Dr. Koch) takes a scientific view of things, and quantifies the effort involved in winning the Cup as 55 percent boat speed, 20 percent tactics, 20 percent crew work, 5 percent luck, and less than 5 percent physical strength.

Source: *Motor Boating & Sailing* magazine

MODELING MATHEMATICS

5. **Draw** a circle graph to represent the number of students in your school by grade level.

Guided Practice

Write each ratio as a percent and then as a decimal.

6. $\frac{3}{4}$ 7. $\frac{43}{100}$ 8. $\frac{2}{25}$

Use a proportion to answer each question.

9. Eleven is what percent of 20? 10. What percent of 80 is 45?

Use an equation to answer each question.

11. What number is 30% of 50? 12. What percent of 75 is 16?

Use $I = prt$ to find the missing quantity.

13. Find I if $p = \$1500$, $r = 7\%$, and $t = 6$ months.
14. Find p if $I = \$196$, $r = 10\%$, and $t = 7$ years.
15. **Finance** Kaylee Richardson invested \$7200 for one year, part at 10% annual interest and the rest at 14% annual interest. Her total interest for the year was \$960. How much money did she invest at each rate?

EXERCISES

Practice

Write each ratio as a percent and then as a decimal.

16. $\frac{67}{100}$ 17. $\frac{6}{20}$ 18. $\frac{5}{8}$
19. $\frac{7}{10}$ 20. $\frac{5}{6}$ 21. $\frac{9}{5}$
22. $\frac{2}{3}$ 23. $\frac{25}{40}$ 24. $\frac{20}{8}$

Use a proportion to answer each question.

25. Thirty-five is what percent of 70?
26. What percent of 60 is 18?
27. Eight is what percent of 64?
28. Six is what percent of 15?
29. What percent of 2 is 8?
30. What percent of 14 is 4.34?

Use an equation to answer each question.

31. What percent of 160 is 4?
32. What number is 25% of 56?
33. Twelve is 16.6% of what number?
34. Thirty-two is what percent of 80?
35. 17.56 is 2.5% of what number?
36. What percent of 75 is 30?

Solve.

37. \$64.93 is what percent of \$231.90?
38. Find 112% of \$500.
39. Find 81% of 32.

Use $I = prt$ to find the missing quantity.

40. Find r if $I = \$5920$, $p = \$4000$, and $t = 3$ years.
41. Find r if $I = \$780$, $p = \$6500$, and $t = 1$ year.
42. Find I if $p = \$3200$, $r = 9\%$, and $t = 18$ months.
43. Find I if $p = \$5000$, $r = 12\frac{1}{2}\%$, and $t = 5$ years.
44. Find t if $I = \$2160$, $p = \$6000$, and $r = 8\%$.
45. Find p if $I = \$756$, $r = 9\%$, and $t = 3\frac{1}{2}$ years.

Critical Thinking

46. If x is 225% of y, then y is what percent of x?

Applications and Problem Solving

47. **Health** Physicians in the United States treated 4.1 million broken bones in 1992. The chart at the right shows the fractures by age. Find the percentage of fractures by age.

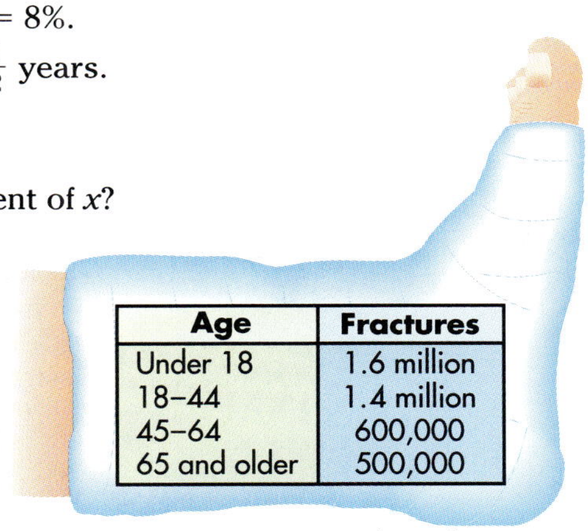

Age	Fractures
Under 18	1.6 million
18–44	1.4 million
45–64	600,000
65 and older	500,000

Source: American Academy of Orthopedic Surgeons

48. **Finance** Melanie Morgan invested \$5000 for one year, part at 9% annual interest and the rest at 12% annual interest. The interest from the investment at 9% was \$198 more than the interest from the investment at 12%. How much money did she invest at 9%?

49. **Finance** Juan and Rosita Diaz have invested \$2500 at 10% annual interest. They have \$6000 more to invest. At what rate must they invest the \$6000 to have a total of \$9440 at the end of the year?

50. **Statistics** According to The Alden Group, desserts in the home are not always eaten in the kitchen or dining room. In fact, only 30% of desserts are eaten in the kitchen and 14% in the dining room. Eighteen percent are most often eaten in the living room, 10% in the den, and an amazing 28% are eaten in the bedroom. Make a circle graph showing these data.

51. **Consumerism** Luke's father used his credit card to purchase a $330 television. The bank that issued the credit card charges an annual interest rate of 19.8%. Each month they charge interest on the unpaid balance of the account. If Luke's father does not make any more purchases and makes no payments, how much interest will he be charged next month?

52. **Nutrition** The table at the right lists the number of calories and grams of fat in eight popular pizza toppings. The estimates are based on two slices of a 14-inch pizza. To find the percentage of calories from fat, multiply the fat grams by 9 and divide the result by the number of calories. Which of the toppings gets the highest percentage of its calories from fat?

Topping	Calories	Fat Grams
Extra Cheese	168	8
Sausage	97	8
Pepperoni	80	7
Black Olives	56	5
Ham	41	2
Onion	11	<1
Green Pepper	5	0
Mushrooms	5	0

53. **Data Analysis** A survey was taken recently to determine what Americans would serve President Clinton and his family for dinner. The survey results are shown at the right.

   a. Suppose 258 people were surveyed. How many people said they would serve chicken marsala? How many said pizza?

   b. The sum of the percentages in the survey is not 100%. Why do you think this is the case?

What Would You Serve?	
steak and potatoes	39%
lasagna	25%
chicken marsala	21%
poached salmon	18%
hamburgers or hot dogs	15%
spaghetti and meatballs	14%
pasta primavera	13%
chef salad	10%
pizza	9%
spaghetti with tomato sauce	8%
soup and sandwiches	5%

Source: The Ragu Corporation

54. **Money** The number of coins minted in 1994 is shown in the table at the right. Make a circle graph of the data.

U.S. Coins Minted in 1994	
Pennies	14,120,000,000
Nickels	1,480,000,000
Dimes	2,600,000,000
Quarters	1,760,000,000
Half-Dollars	40,000,000

Mixed Review

General Sherman

55. **Trees** While visiting the Sequoia National Park in California, Tyler stops near a tree called the "General Sherman." The guide tells him it is the world's largest tree according to its volume of wood. Tyler is standing about 160 feet from the tree. If he is looking at the top of the tree at a 60° angle, about how tall is the tree? (Lesson 4–3)

56. **Geometry** ΔABC and ΔRQP are similar. If $a = 10$, $r = 5$, $q = 3$, and $p = 4$, find the measures of the remaining sides. (Lesson 4–2)

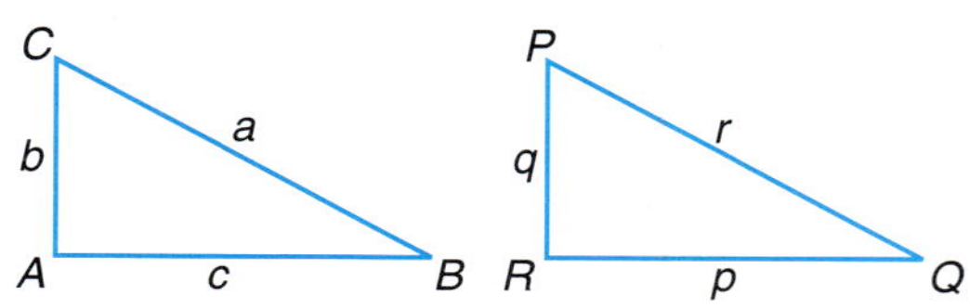

57. Solve $\frac{9}{x-8} = \frac{4}{5}$. (Lesson 4–1)

58. Statistics In a girl's basketball game between East High School and Monroe High School, the East players' individual scores were 12, 4, 5, 3, 11, 23, 4, 6, 7, and 8. Find the mean, median, and mode of the individual points. (Lesson 3–7)

59. Solve $y + (-7.5) = -12.2$. (Lesson 3-1)

60. Diving Greg Louganis of the United States has won a record of five world titles in diving. He won the highboard title in 1978, the highboard and springboard in 1982 and 1986, and four Olympic gold medals in 1984 and 1988. The total score for a dive is the sum of the scores of each dive times the degree of difficulty of the dive. His final dive in 1988 had a degree of difficulty of 3.4. If his scores were 9, 8, and 8.5, find his total score for the dive. (Lesson 2–6)

61. Find $5y + (-12y) + (-21y)$. (Lesson 2–5)

62. Statistics Mr. Crable asked his students how many hours of sleep they got on the average each night for a week. He labeled the data with G for girls and B for boys. Use Gs and Bs to make a line plot of these data. (Lesson 2–2)

10-G	7.5-B	9-B	9-G	8-G	8.5-G	9.5-B	8.5-B	8.5-G
9.5-B	8-G	8-B	10-B	10-G	9.5-G	7.5-G	9-G	8.5-B

63. Solve $\frac{21-3}{12-3} = x$. (Lesson 1–5)

64. Patterns Find the next three terms in the sequence 3, 8.5, 14, 19.5.... (Lesson 1–2)

SELF TEST

Solve each proportion. (Lesson 4–1)

1. $\frac{2}{10} = \frac{1}{a}$ **2.** $\frac{3}{5} = \frac{24}{x}$ **3.** $\frac{y}{4} = \frac{y+5}{8}$

4. ΔWYQ and ΔMVT shown at the right are similar. Find the measures of the missing sides. (Lesson 4–2)

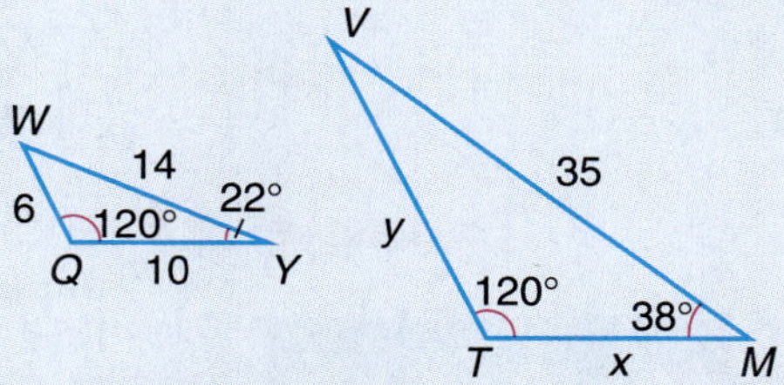

Solve each right triangle. State the side lengths to the nearest tenth and the angle measures to the nearest degree. (Lesson 4–3)

5.

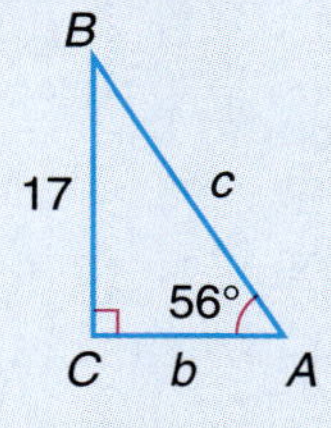

6.

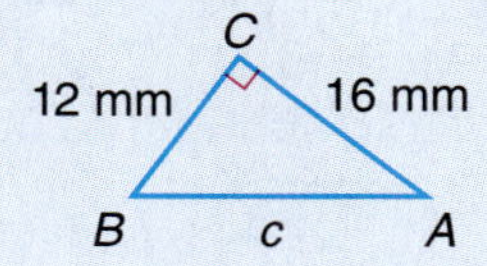

7. Refer to the triangles in Exercises 5 and 6. Determine whether the triangles are similar. (Lesson 4–2)

8. Thirty-six is 45% of what number? (Lesson 4–4)

9. Fifty-five is what percent of 88? (Lesson 4–4)

10. Research Suppose 6% of 8000 people polled regarding an election expressed no opinion. How many people had an opinion? (Lesson 4–4)

4–5 Percent of Change

mallow plant

What YOU'LL LEARN

- To solve problems involving percent of increase or decrease, and
- to solve problems involving discounts or sales tax.

Why IT'S IMPORTANT

You can use percents to solve problems involving sales, health, and shopping.

APPLICATION
Food

If you've ever bought a package of marshmallows, you've mostly bought air. That's right, marshmallows are 80% air! Today, marshmallows come in a variety of flavors such as vanilla, chocolate, toasted coconut, and fruit flavors like laser lime and astroberry. The marshmallow was invented in ancient Egypt and made with honey and the sap of the mallow plant that grows in swamps, or marshes. Since then, the marshmallow has gone through many changes.

Today, marshmallows are mass produced and made from cornstarch and gelatin. In 1955, the height of marshmallow making in the United States, there were 30 marshmallow companies. Today there are only a handful.

Let's say there are only six marshmallow companies today. You can write a ratio that compares the amount of decrease in marshmallow companies to the original number of companies in 1955. This ratio can be written as a percent. First, subtract to find the amount of change: $30 - 6 = 24$. Then divide by the original number of companies.

$$\frac{\text{amount of decrease} \rightarrow}{\text{original amount} \rightarrow} = \frac{r}{100}$$

$$24 \cdot 100 = 30 \cdot r \quad \textit{Find the cross products.}$$

$$80 = r \quad \textit{Solve for r.}$$

The amount of decrease is $\frac{80}{100}$ or 80% of the original number of companies. So, we can say that the **percent of decrease** is 80%.

The **percent of increase** can be found in a similar way.

Example 1

CONNECTION
Biology

FYI

In 1982, the California Condor Recovery Program, made up of a team of specialists and zoos, was formed to assist in the capturing, breeding, and freeing of the condors into the wild.

In 1982, the California condor was on the verge of extinction. The population had dwindled to a total of 21, making the condor the rarest bird in North America. According to the Refuge Department of the U.S. Fish and Wildlife Service, however, there were 64 condors in existence in 1992 and 103 as of October 1995. Find the percent of increase in the population of California condors from 1992 to 1995.

Method 1

First, subtract to find the amount of change.

$103 - 64 = 39$

$$\frac{\text{amount of increase}}{\text{original number}} = \frac{39}{64}$$

$$\frac{39}{64} = \frac{r}{100}$$

$$60.9375 = r$$

The percent of increase is about 61%.

Method 2

Divide the new amount by the original amount.

$103 \div 64 = 1.609375$

Subtract 1 from the result and write the decimal as a percent.

$1.609375 - 1 = 0.609375$ or 60.9%

The percent of increase is about 61%.

Sometimes an increase or decrease is given as a percent, rather than an amount. Two applications of percent of change are discounts and sales tax.

Example 2

APPLICATION

Sales

A discount of 20% means that the price is decreased by 20%.

Ayita received a coupon in the mail offering her a 20% discount on the price of a pair of jeans at Jean Express. Ayita visited the store and found a pair of jeans she wants to buy that cost \$48. What will be the discounted price?

Explore The original price is \$48.00, and the discount is 20%.

Plan You want to find the amount of discount, then subtract that amount from \$48.00. The result is the discounted price.

Estimate: *20% of \$48 → 2(10% of \$50) = 2(\$5) or \$10.*

Solve 20% of \$48.00 = 0.20(48.00) *Note that 20% = $\frac{20}{100}$ = 0.20.*

= 9.60

Subtract this amount from the original price.

\$48.00 − \$9.60 = \$38.40

The discounted price will be \$38.40.

Examine Solve the problem another way. The discount was 20%, so the discounted price will be 80% of the original price. *100% − 20% = 80%*

Find 80% of \$48.00. 0.80(48.00) = 38.40

This method produces the same discounted price, \$38.40.

How does this compare to the estimate?

Example 3

APPLICATION

Sales

Sales tax of $5\frac{3}{4}$% means that the price is increased by $5\frac{3}{4}$%.

Karen Danko, a sophomore at Westerville North High School, is ordering a class ring. The ring she has chosen costs \$169.99. She also needs to pay a sales tax of $5\frac{3}{4}$%. What is the total price?

Explore The price is \$169.99 and the tax rate is $5\frac{3}{4}$%.

Plan First find $5\frac{3}{4}$% of \$169.99. Then add the result to \$169.99.

Estimate: *$5\frac{3}{4}$% of \$169.99 → $\frac{1}{2}$(10% of 170) = $\frac{1}{2}$(\$17) or \$8.50. The total will be about \$170 + \$8.50 or \$178.50.*

Solve $5\frac{3}{4}$% of \$169.99 = 0.0575(169.99) *Note that $5\frac{3}{4}$% = 0.0575.*

= 9.774425 *Round 9.774425 to 9.78, since tax is always rounded up.*

Add this amount to the original price.

\$169.99 + \$9.78 = \$179.77

The total price is \$179.77.

Examine The tax rate is $5\frac{3}{4}$%, so the total price was 100% + $5\frac{3}{4}$% or 105.75% of the purchase price. Find 105.75% of \$169.99.

(1.0575)(169.99) = 179.76442

Thus, the total price of \$179.77 is correct.

How does this compare to the estimate?

EXPLORATION — PROGRAMMING

Suppose a newspaper ad states that a discount store's microwave ovens are discounted 20% from the manufacturer's suggested retail price (MSRP). The store is running a special sale that says all kitchen appliances have been discounted an additional 15%. What is the final sale price of a microwave oven whose MSRP is $250?

There are two ways you might interpret the ad in the paper.

- The discounts can be successive. That is, 20% is taken off the MSRP and then 15% is taken off the resulting price.
- The discounts can be combined. So the price is 35% off the MSRP.

The graphing calculator program at the right finds the cost of an item for each interpretation of the ad. You must enter the original price and each discount amount (as a decimal) when prompted.

```
PROGRAM:DISCOUNT
: Disp "ORIG. PRICE"
: Input P
: Disp "1ST DISCOUNT?"
: Input A
: Disp "2ND DISCOUNT?"
: Input B
: P(1-A)(1-B)→C
: P(1-(A+B))→D
: Disp "SUCCESSIVE",
  "DISCOUNT",C
: Disp "COMBINED",
  "DISCOUNT",D
```

Your Turn

Copy the following table and use the program to complete it.

	Price	First Discount	Second Discount	Sale Price Successive Discount	Sale Price Combined Discount
a.	$49.00	20%	10%		
b.	$185.00	25%	10%		
c.	$12.50	30%	12.5%		
d.	$156.95	30%	15%		

e. What is the relationship between the sale price using successive discounts and the sale price using combined discounts? Which one is usually used in stores?

CHECK FOR UNDERSTANDING

Communicating Mathematics

Study the lesson. Then complete the following.

1. **Explain** how to find a percent of increase.
2. **Explain** how to find the sales tax if you know the rate of tax.
3. **Write** the equation you would use to find the percent of increase on a car that cost $17,972 in 1995 and $19,705 in 1996.

MATH JOURNAL

4. **Assess Yourself** Find an advertisement or article in the newspaper that shows a percent of change. Determine whether it is a percent of increase or decrease. Explain your reasoning.

Guided Practice

State whether each percent of change is a percent of increase or a percent of decrease. Then find the percent of increase or decrease.

5. original: $50
   new: $70
6. original: $200
   new: $172
7. original: 72 ounces
   new: 36 ounces

Find the final price of each item. When there is a discount and sales tax, first compute the discount price and then compute the sales tax and final price.

8. CD player: $149
   discount: 15%
9. athletic shoes: $89.99
   discount: 10%
   sales tax: 6%
10. sweater: $45
    sales tax: 6.5%
11. **Sales** Kevin Mason paid $205.80 for his senior class photographs. This included 5% sales tax. What was the cost of the pictures before taxes?

EXERCISES

Practice

State whether each percent of change is a percent of increase or a percent of decrease. Then find the percent of increase or decrease. Round to the nearest whole percent.

12. original: $100
    new: $59
13. original: 324 people
    new: 549 people
14. original: 58 homes
    new: 152 homes
15. original: 66 dimes
    new: 30 dimes
16. original: $53
    new: $75
17. original: 15.6 liters
    new: 11.4 liters
18. original: $3.78
    new: $2.50
19. original: 231.2 mph
    new: 236.4 mph
20. original: 124 tons
    new: 137 tons

Find the final price of each item. When there is a discount and sales tax, first compute the discount price and then compute the sales tax and final price.

21. VCR: $219
    sales tax: 6.5%
22. jeans: $39.99
    discount: 15%
    sales tax: 4%
23. book: $19.95
    discount: 5%
    sales tax: 5%
24. concert tickets: $52.50
    sales tax: 7%
25. in-line skates: $99.99
    discount: 20%
    sales tax: 6.75%
26. hiking boots: $59
    discount: 10%
    sales tax: 5.5%
27. compact disc: $15.88
    sales tax: 4.5%
28. amusement park tickets: $37.50
    sales tax: 6%
29. software: $29.99
    discount: 6%
    sales tax: 6.75%

Graphing Calculator

30. Use a graphing calculator to find the sale price of each item using successive discounts and then one combined discount.
    a. price, $89; discounts, 25% and 10%
    b. price, $254; discounts 30% and 14.5%

Critical Thinking

31. An amount is increased by 15%. The result is decreased by 15%. Is the final result equal to the original amount? Explain your reasoning with an example.

32. **Sales** The advertisement below was used by a local optician's office in Walkersville, Maryland.

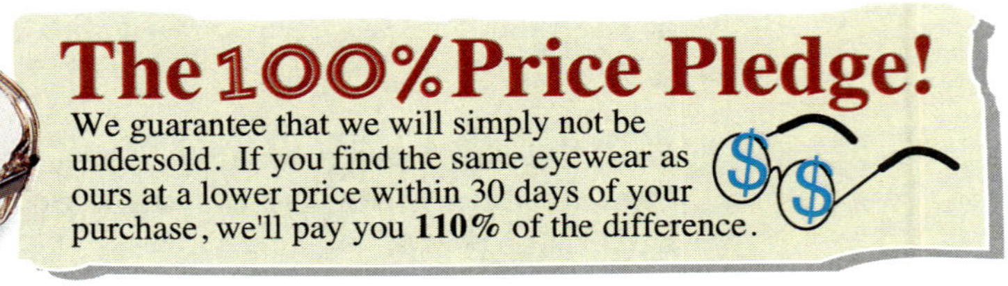

Suppose you bought a pair of glasses from this optician for \$150. You then found the same glasses from a competitor for \$125. What should the optician do to honor the pledge?

Applications and Problem Solving

33. **Predictions** The World Future Society predicts that by the year 2020, airplanes will be able to carry 1400 passengers. Today's biggest jets can carry 600 people. What will be the percent of increase of airplane passengers?

34. **Computers** In 1995, an internet supplier had about 3,000,000 users. Over the next decade, users are expected to increase from a few million to the tens of millions. Suppose the number of users increases by 150% by the year 2000. How many users will there be in the year 2000?

35. **Taxes** As the saying goes, time is money. The graph at the right shows a function of how much time it takes out of each eight-hour day to earn enough money to pay a day's worth of taxes. What was the percent of increase from 1970 to 1994?

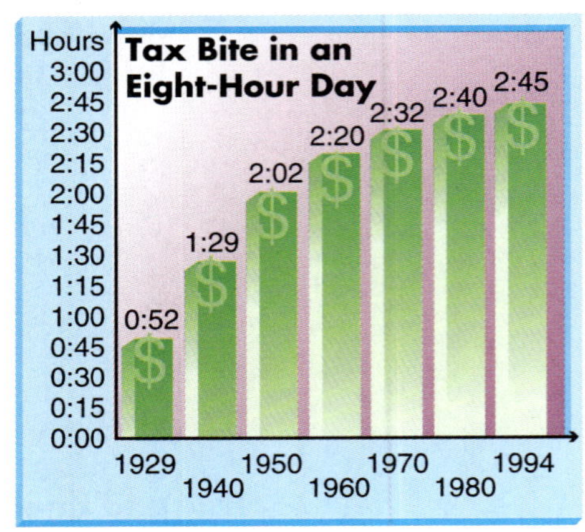

Source: *The Universal Almanac,* 1995

36. **Sales** Music Systems, Inc. allows a 10% discount if a purchase is paid for within 30 days. An additional 5% discount is given if the purchase is paid for within 15 days. Brent Goodson buys a sound system that originally cost \$360. If he pays the entire amount at the time of purchase, how much does he pay for his system after the successive discounts?

37. **Health** The excerpt below is from the March 1994 issue of a magazine for runners.

When you first get up in the morning, your muscles and soft tissues are tight. In fact, at that time your muscles are generally about 10 percent shorter than their normal resting length. As you move around, they stretch to their normal length. Then when you start to exercise, your muscles stretch even more, to about 10 percent longer than resting length. This means you have a 20 percent change in muscle length from the time you get out of bed until your muscles are well warmed up.

According to the basic laws of physics, muscles work more efficiently when they are longer; they can exert more force with less effort. This means, too, that longer muscles are much less prone to injury.

Source: *Runner's World* magazine

What is the percent change in muscle length from the time a runner gets up in the morning until after he or she has exercised for a while?

38. **Consumer Awareness** A windsuit that costs $75 is discounted 25%. The sales tax is 6%.
   a. Would it be better for the customer to have the discount taken off before adding the sales tax or after the sales tax has been added? Explain your reasoning.
   b. Do you think stores have a choice in which order to calculate discounts and sales tax? Explain your reasoning.

39. **Automobiles** As soon as a new car is purchased and driven away from the dealership, it begins to lose its value, or depreciate. Alonso bought a 1994 compact car for $9559. One year later, the value of the car was $8500. What is the percent of decrease of the value of the car?

Mixed Review

40. **Entertainment** A theater was filled to 75% capacity. How many of the 720 seats were filled? (Lesson 4–4)

41. **Geometry** A chimney casts a shadow 75 feet long when the angle of elevation of the sun is 41°. How tall is the chimney? (Lesson 4–3)

42. **Construction** To paint his house, Lonnie needs to purchase an extension ladder that reaches at least 24 feet off the ground. Ladder manufacturers recommend the angle formed by the ladder and the ground be no more than 75°. What is the shortest ladder he could buy to reach 24 feet safely? (Lesson 4–3)

43. Solve $0.2x + 1.7 = 3.9$. (Lesson 3–6)

44. **Geometry** The measures of two angles of a triangle are 38° and 41°. Find the measure of the third angle. (Lesson 3–4)

45. **Dietetics** A hospitalized diabetic is on a carefully controlled 2000-calorie diet distributed over five feedings a day. There are two heavy feedings consisting each of $\frac{2}{7}$ of the total calories. There are also three light feedings consisting each of $\frac{1}{7}$ of the total calories. Determine the number of calories for a heavy feeding and for a light feeding. (Lesson 2–6)

46. **Statistics** State the scale you would use to make a line plot for the following data. Then draw the line plot. 4.2, 5.3, 7.6, 9.6, 7.3, 6.7 (Lesson 2–2)

WORKING ON THE In·ves·ti·ga·tion

Refer to the Investigation on pages 190–191.

1 Count all of the fish in your lake. Record the actual population and your estimates on a class chart.

2 How close were your estimates? How would you account for the difference between your estimates and the actual number of fish in the lake?

3 What percent of the fish in the lake was tagged? What percent of the fish in your samples was tagged?

4 Suppose you went fishing at that lake and caught one fish. What is the probability, or chance, that the fish you caught would be tagged? Justify your reasoning.

5 Write a paragraph or two that relates proportions, percents, and probability in this situation. *You will learn more about probability in the next lesson.*

Add the results of your work to your Investigation Folder.

4-6

Integration: Probability
Probability and Odds

What YOU'LL LEARN

- To find the probability of a simple event, and
- to find the odds of a simple event.

Why IT'S IMPORTANT

You can use probability to calculate the chances that something will happen. This is especially helpful in sports.

APPLICATION
Contests

Have you ever heard anyone say that one man's trash is another man's treasure? For garbage truck driver Craig Randall of East Bridgewater, Massachusetts, the treasure was a hamburger chain's soft-drink cup. By peeling off a contest sticker on the discarded cup, Randall won the grand prize of $200,000 toward the purchase of a home! Since there was only one grand prize available and 24,059,900 cups were distributed, the probability of winning the grand prize was $\frac{1}{24{,}059{,}900}$.

You can calculate the chance, or **probability,** that a certain event, such as winning a particular prize, will happen. The **probability of an event** is a ratio of the number of ways a certain event can occur to the number of possible outcomes. The numerator is the number of favorable outcomes, and the denominator is the total number of possible outcomes. *The probability of an event may be written as a percent, a fraction, or a decimal.*

For example, suppose you want to know the probability of getting a 2 on one roll of a die. When you roll a die, there are six possible outcomes. Of these outcomes, only one is favorable, a 2. Therefore, the probability is $\frac{1}{6}$. We write $P(2)$ to represent *the probability of getting a 2 on one roll of a die.*

Definition of Probability	$P(\text{event}) = \frac{\text{number of favorable outcomes}}{\text{total number of possible outcomes}}$

Example 1

APPLICATION
Games

Top Five List

Letters of Alphabet with Most Entries in *Oxford English Dictionary*

1. S
2. C
3. P
4. M
5. A

Lauren Slocum is representing her sophomore class in a word board game tournament. She is the first player to select her seven tiles out of the 100 available tiles. The distribution of tiles is shown at the right. Find the probability of each selection below.

Letters	Number of Tiles
J, K, Q, X, Z	1
B, C, F, H, M, P, V, W, Y, blank	2
G	3
D, L, S, U	4
N, R, T	6
O	8
A, I	9
E	12

a. an O on the very first selection

There are eight O tiles and 100 tiles in all. $P(\text{selecting an O}) = \frac{8}{100}$ or $\frac{2}{25}$

The probability that Lauren selects an O is $\frac{2}{25}$ or 8%.

b. an E if 5 tiles have been selected and 2 of them were Es

There are 12 E tiles. If 2 have been chosen, 10 remain. There are $100 - 5$ or 95 tiles from which to select.

$P(\text{choosing an E}) = \frac{10}{95}$ or $\frac{2}{19}$

The probability of selecting an E is $\frac{2}{19}$ or about 10%.

The probability that an event will occur is somewhere between 0 and 1.

- A probability of 0 means that it is impossible for an event to occur.
- A probability of 1 means that an event is certain to occur.
- A probability between 0 and 1 means that an event is neither impossible nor certain.

Based on the situations above, the probability of any event can be expressed as $0 \leq P(\text{event}) \leq 1$.

Some outcomes have an equal chance of occurring. We say that such outcomes are **equally likely.** When an outcome is chosen without any preference, we say that the outcome occurs at **random.**

MODELING MATHEMATICS — Probability

Materials: grid paper

What are the chances that two of the Oscar-winning actors or actresses from 1983 to 1993 share the same birthday? Considering that there are only 24 people in this group, you would probably say the chances are slim.

You may be surprised that in a group of only 24 people, the likelihood that two of them have the same birthday is just about 50%, or one out of two.

For example, in this group of Academy Award winners, Holly Hunter and William Hurt were both born on March 20.

Your Turn

a. Survey a group of 24 people in your school. Tally the results.

b. Does your group contain a shared birthday? Display your findings in a chart or graph.

c. Combine your results with those of your classmates. Does your class graph differ from your individual graph? Explain.

d. Use the graph below to find the likelihood of birthdays shared by the Presidents of the United States. Research to find any shared Presidential birthdays. Compare your findings. Do you agree or disagree with the percentages? Explain your reasoning.

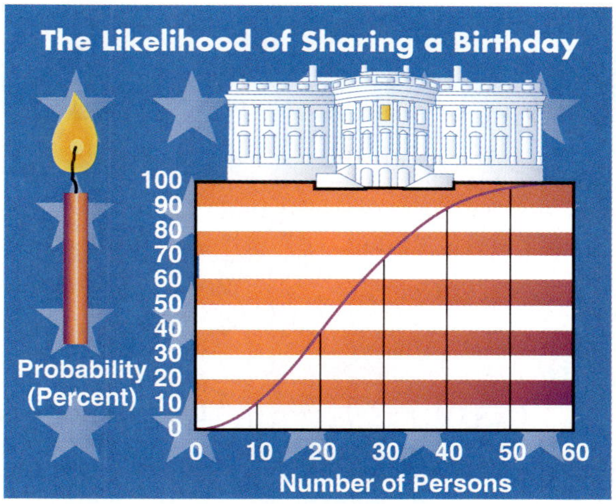

Another way to express the chance of an event's occurring is with **odds.** The odds of an event is the ratio that compares the number of ways an event can occur to the number of ways it *cannot* occur.

Definition of Odds	**The odds of an event occurring is the ratio of the number of ways the event can occur (successes) to the number of ways the event cannot occur (failures).**

Odds = number of successes: number of failures

Example 2

Mike's Submarine Shop has a business card drawing for a free lunch every Tuesday. Four coworkers from Invo Accounting put their business cards in the bowl for the drawing. If 80 cards were in the bowl, what are the odds that one of the coworkers will win a free lunch?

The coworkers have 4 of the 80 business cards. Thus, there are 80 − 4 or 76 business cards that will not be winning cards for the coworkers.

Odds of winning = number of chances of drawing winning card : number of chances of drawing other cards
= 4:76 or 1:19 *1:19 is read "1 to 19".*

Example 3

Do you have a better chance of winning a prize or not winning a prize?

Refer to the application at the beginning of the lesson. The probability of winning any prize or food discount in the peel-off sticker contest was 20% or $\frac{1}{5}$. Find the odds of winning a prize or discount.

If the probability of winning a prize or discount is $\frac{1}{5}$, then the number of successes (prize) is 1, while the total number of outcomes is 5. This means that the number of failures (no prize) must be 5 − 1 or 4.

Odds of prize = number of successes : number of failures
= 1:4 *This is read "1 to 4."*

CHECK FOR UNDERSTANDING

Communicating Mathematics

Study the lesson. Then complete the following.

1. **Refer** to Example 1. Find the probability of selecting a Z if 25 tiles have been selected and one of them was a Z.
2. **Give** examples of an impossible event and a certain event when rolling a die.
3. **Tell** what the odds would be for an event not occurring if the odds for the event occurring are 3:5.
4. **Write** a problem in which the answer will be a probability of $\frac{3}{4}$.

MODELING MATHEMATICS

5. Choose another group of 24 people to survey. Record their birthdays. Does your group contain a shared birthday?

Guided Practice

Determine the probability of each event.

6. This is an algebra book.
7. A coin will land tails up.

Find the probability of each outcome if a die is rolled.

8. a 6
9. a number greater than 2

Find the odds of each outcome if a die is rolled.

10. a number greater than 2
11. not a 3
12. If the probability that an event will occur is $\frac{3}{7}$, what are the odds that the event will *not* occur?

EXERCISES

Practice

Determine the probability of each event.

13. A coin will land heads up.
14. There is a January 1 this year.
15. A baby will be a boy.
16. Pigs will fly.
17. You will roll a multiple of 2 on a die.
18. A person's birthday is in June.

Find the probability of each outcome if a computer randomly chooses a letter in the word "probability."

19. the letter b
20. $P(not\ \mathrm{i})$
21. the letter e
22. $P(\text{vowel})$
23. *not b* or *y*
24. the letters *a* or *t*

Find the odds of each outcome if you randomly select a coin from a jar containing 80 pennies, 100 nickels, 70 dimes, and 50 quarters.

25. selecting a quarter
26. selecting a nickel
27. selecting a penny
28. *not* selecting a nickel
29. *not* selecting a dime
30. selecting a penny or dime

A card is selected at random from a standard deck of 52 cards.

31. What is the probability of selecting a red card?
32. What is the probability of selecting a queen?
33. What are the odds of selecting a heart?
34. What are the odds of *not* selecting a black 6?
35. If the odds that an event will occur are 8:5, what is the probability that the event will occur?
36. If the probability that an event will occur is $\frac{2}{3}$, what are the odds that the event will occur?

Critical Thinking

37. **Geometry** If a point inside the figure at the right is chosen at random, what is the probability that it will be in the shaded region?

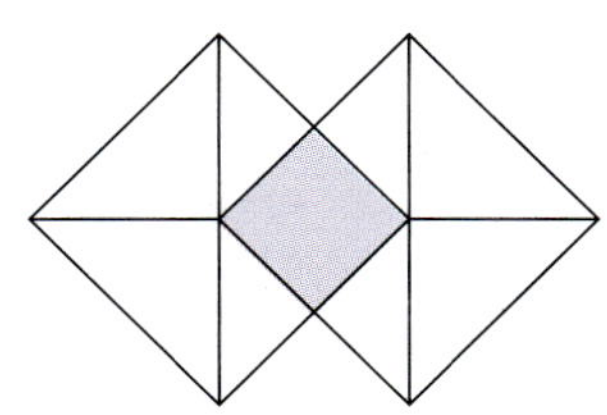

38. **Geometry** If a point inside the figure at the right is chosen at random, what is the probability that it will *not* be in the shaded region?

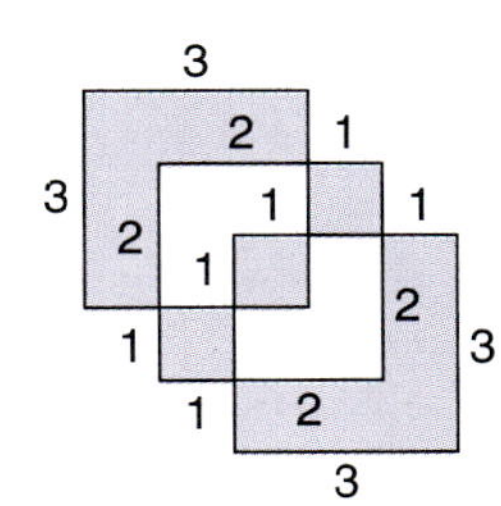

Applications and Problem Solving

39. **Games** A game board is divided into 30 squares. There are six categories with five questions in each category. In the Double round, 2 Double squares are hidden among the 30 squares.
    a. What are the odds of choosing a Double square on the first selection?
    b. If you are making the fourth selection of the Double round, what is the probability of choosing a Double square if one has been chosen?

40. **School** Have you ever had to make an oral presentation before your classmates? Did the teacher tell everyone to be prepared and then choose the first day's presenters at random?
    a. If there are 35 students in your class, and four students will be chosen to give a presentation each day until everyone has made a presentation, what is the probability that you will be chosen to make your presentation the first day?
    b. If you have not been chosen by the fourth day, what is the probability that you will be chosen on the fourth day?

41. **Statistics** The stem-and-leaf plot at the right shows the total points earned by each of the 26 teams in the professional hockey league for the 1993–1994 season.
    a. What is the probability that a team earned 97 points?
    b. What is the probability that a team earned less than 80 points?
    c. What are the odds in favor of a team scoring more than 100 points?

Stem	Leaf
11	2
10	0 1 6
9	1 5 6 7 7 7 8
8	0 2 3 4 5 7 8
7	1 1 6
6	3 4 6
5	7
4	
3	7 $9\|1 = 91$

Mixed Review

42. **Chocolate** Illinois is the number one candy-producing state. A chocolate shop in Sterling, Illinois, is known for its pecan dumplings. The owners used to make nine pounds of pecan dumplings at one time. Now they make 300 pounds in the same amount of time! Find the percent of change. (Lesson 4–5)

43. **Geometry** In a parking garage, there are 20 feet between each level. Each ramp to a level is 130 feet long. Find the measure of the angle of elevation of each ramp. (Lesson 4–3)

44. Solve $\frac{5}{8}x + \frac{3}{5} = x$. (Lesson 3–5)

45. **Work Backward** Kristen spent one fifth of her money for gasoline. Then she spent half of what was left for a haircut. She bought lunch for \$7. When she got home, she had \$13 left. How much did Kristen have originally? (Lesson 3–3)

46. Simplify $\pm\sqrt{1764}$. (Lesson 2–8)

47. Find $\frac{17}{21} + \left(-\frac{13}{21}\right)$. (Lesson 2–5)

48. **School** Each number below represents the age of a student in Ms. Wallace's evening calculus class at DeSantis Community College. (Lesson 1–4)

    22 17 25 24 19 27 33 16 35 26 20 18 24 33 18 19 48
    36 19 23 55 18 18 19 27 18 19 25 17 32 19 45 19 20 30

    a. Make a stem-and-leaf plot of the data.
    b. How many people attend Ms. Wallace's class?
    c. What is the difference in ages between the oldest and youngest person in class?
    d. What is the most common age for a student in the class?
    e. Which age group is most widely represented in the class?

49. Evaluate $8(a - c)^2 + 3$ if $a = 6$, $b = 4$, and $c = 3$. (Lesson 1–3)

4–7 Weighted Averages

What YOU'LL LEARN

- To solve mixture problems, and
- to solve problems involving uniform motion.

Why IT'S IMPORTANT

You can use weighted averages to solve problems involving travel, transportation, and chemistry.

APPLICATION

School

In Mr. Calloway's American History class, semester grades are based on five unit exams, one semester exam, and a long-term project. Each unit exam is worth 15% of the grade, the semester exam is worth 20% of the grade, and the project is worth 5% of the grade.

Parker's scores for the semester are given in the table at the right. If 100% is a perfect score for each item, find Parker's average for the semester.

Semester Grades

Item	Score
Unit Exam A	79%
Unit Exam B	83
Unit Exam C	96
Unit Exam D	91
Unit Exam E	89
Semester Exam	90
Project	95

In order to find Parker's average for the semester, you may want to add the percentages and then divide by the number of items, 7. But this assumes that each has the same weight. So, you need to find the **weighted average** of the scores.

Definition of Weighted Average	The weighted average *M* of a set of data is the sum of the product of each number in the set and its weight divided by the sum of all the weights.

You can find the weighted average for the application above by multiplying each score by the percentage of the semester grade that it represents and then dividing by the sum of the weights, or 100. *5(15) + 1(20) + 1(5) = 100*

$$M = \frac{15(79 + 83 + 96 + 91 + 89) + 20(90) + 5(95)}{100}$$

$$= \frac{8845}{100} \text{ or } 88.45$$

So, Parker's average for the semester is about 88%.

Mixture problems involve weighted averages. In a mixture problem, the weight is usually a price or a percentage of something.

Example 1

PROBLEM SOLVING

Make a Chart

Suppose the Central Perk coffee shop sells a cup of espresso for \$2.00 and a cup of cappuccino for \$2.50. On Friday, Rachel sold 30 more cups of cappuccino than espresso, and she sold \$178.50 worth of espresso and cappuccino. How many cups of each were sold?

Explore Let e represent the number of cups of espresso sold. Then $e + 30$ represents the number of cups of cappuccino sold.

(continued on the next page)

Plan Make a chart of the information.

	Number of Cups	Price Per Cup	Total Price
espresso	e	\$2.00	$2e$
cappuccino	$e + 30$	\$2.50	$2.5(e + 30)$

Solve $\underbrace{\text{total sales of espresso}}_{2e} + \underbrace{\text{total sales of cappuccino}}_{2.5(e+30)} = \underbrace{\text{total sales}}_{178.50}$

$$2e + 2.5e + 75 = 178.50$$
$$4.5e + 75 = 178.50$$
$$4.5e = 103.50$$
$$e = 23$$

There were 23 cups of espresso sold. There were 23 + 30, or 53 cups of cappuccino sold.

Examine If 23 cups of espresso were sold, the total sales of those cups of coffee would be 23(\$2.00) or \$46.00. If 53 cups of cappuccino were sold, the total sales of those cups of coffee would be 53(\$2.50) or \$132.50.

Since \$46.00 + \$132.50 = \$178.50, the solution is correct.

Sometimes mixture problems are expressed in terms of percents.

Example 2

APPLICATION
Food Preparation

An advertisement for an orange drink claims that the drink contains 10% orange juice. Jamel needs 6 quarts of the drink to serve at a party and he wants the drink to contain 40% orange juice. How much of the 10% drink and pure orange juice should Jamel mix to obtain 6 quarts of a mixture that contains 40% orange juice?

Explore Let p represent the amount of pure juice to be added.

Plan Make a chart of the information.

	Quarts	Amount of Orange Juice
10% juice	$6 - p$	$0.10(6 - p)$
Pure juice	p	$1.00p$
40% juice	6	$0.40(6)$

Solve $\underbrace{\text{amount of orange juice in 10\% juice}}_{0.10(6-p)} + \underbrace{\text{amount of orange juice in pure juice}}_{1.00p} = \underbrace{\text{amount of orange juice in 40\% juice}}_{0.40(6)}$

$$0.6 - 0.1p + 1.00p = 2.4$$
$$0.9p = 1.8$$
$$p = 2$$

Jamel needs to combine 2 quarts of pure orange juice with 6 − 2 or 4 quarts of 10% juice to obtain a 6-quart mixture that is 40% orange juice. *Examine this solution.*

Motion problems are another application of weighted averages. When an object moves at a constant speed, or rate, it is said to be in **uniform motion**. The formula $d = rt$ is used to solve uniform motion problems. In the formula, d represents distance, r represents rate, and t represents time. You can also use equations and charts when solving motion problems.

Example 3

APPLICATION

Travel

On Friday, Shenae and her brother Rafiel went to visit their grandparents for the weekend. Luckily, traffic was light and they were able to make the 50-mile trip in exactly one hour. On Sunday, they weren't so lucky. The trip home took exactly two hours. What was their average speed for the round trip?

To find the average speed for each leg of the trip, rewrite $d = rt$ as $r = \frac{d}{t}$.

Going

$$r = \frac{d}{t}$$
$$= \frac{50 \text{ miles}}{1 \text{ hour}} \text{ or 50 miles per hour}$$

Returning

$$r = \frac{d}{t}$$
$$= \frac{50 \text{ miles}}{2 \text{ hours}} \text{ or 25 miles per hour}$$

You may think that the average speed of the trip would be $\frac{50 + 25}{2}$ or 37.5 miles per hour. However, Shenae did not drive at these speeds for equal amounts of time. You can find the weighted average for their trip.

Round Trip

$$M = \frac{50(1) + 25(2)}{3}$$
$$= \frac{100}{3} \text{ or } 33\frac{1}{3}$$

Their average speed was $33\frac{1}{3}$ miles per hour.

Example 4

APPLICATION

Transportation

Two city buses leave their station at the same time, one heading east and the other heading west. The eastbound bus travels at 35 miles per hour, and the westbound bus travels at 45 miles per hour. In how many hours will they be 60 miles apart?

Explore Draw a diagram to help analyze the problem.

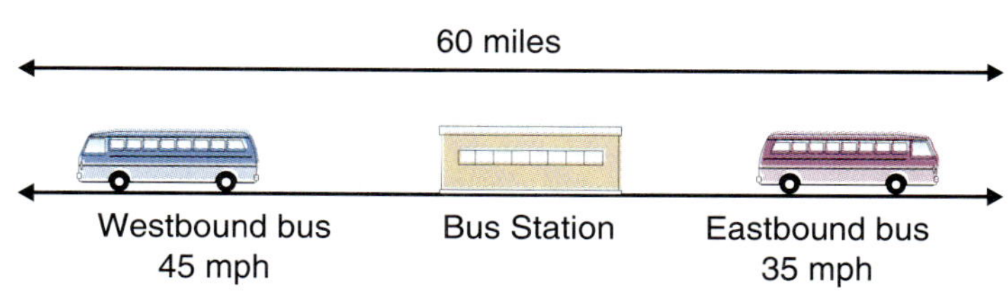

Plan Organize the information in a chart. Let t represent the number of hours until they are 60 miles apart. Remember that $rt = d$.

Bus	r	t	d
Eastbound	35	t	35t
Westbound	45	t	45t

The eastbound bus travels 35t miles.
The westbound bus travels 45t miles.

eastbound distance + *westbound distance* = *total distance*

$$35t + 45t = 60$$

(continued on the next page)

Solve

$$35t + 45t = 60$$
$$80t = 60$$
$$t = \frac{3}{4}$$

In $\frac{3}{4}$ hour, or 45 minutes, the buses will be 60 miles apart.

Examine To check the answer, find the distance each bus could travel in $\frac{3}{4}$ hour and see if it totals 60 miles.

$$\left(\frac{3}{4}\text{h}\right)(35 \text{ mph}) + \left(\frac{3}{4}\text{h}\right)(45 \text{ mph}) \stackrel{?}{=} 60 \text{ mi}$$
$$26\frac{1}{4} \text{ mi} + 33\frac{3}{4} \text{ mi} \stackrel{?}{=} 60 \text{ mi}$$
$$60 \text{ mi} = 60 \text{ mi} \checkmark$$

CHECK FOR UNDERSTANDING

Communicating Mathematics

Study the lesson. Then complete the following.

1. **Tell** what the d, r, and t represent in the formula $d = rt$.
2. **Explain** why it is sometimes helpful to use charts and diagrams.

MATH JOURNAL

3. **Describe** your favorite mode of transportation. Then write a problem using the formula $d = rt$ and your favorite mode.

Guided Practice

4. **Chemistry** Joshua is doing a chemistry experiment that calls for a 30% solution of copper sulfate. He has 40 mL of 25% solution. How many milliliters of 60% solution should Joshua add to obtain the required 30% solution?

	Amount of Solution (mL)	Amount of Copper Sulfate
25% solution	40	
60% solution	x	
30% solution		

5. **Sales** The Cookie Crumbles Company sells two kinds of cookies daily: peanut butter at $6.50 per dozen and chocolate chip at $9.00 per dozen. Yesterday, Cookie Crumbles sold 85 dozen more peanut butter than chocolate chip cookies. The total sales for both were $4055.50. How many dozen of each were sold?
6. **Air Travel** An airplane flies 1000 miles due east in 2 hours and 1000 miles due south in 3 hours. What is the average speed of the airplane?
7. **Boating** *The Yankee Clipper* leaves the pier at 9:00 A.M. at 8 knots (nautical miles per hour). A half hour later, *The Riverboat Rover* leaves the same pier in the same direction traveling at 10 knots. At what time will *The Riverboat Rover* overtake *The Yankee Clipper*?

EXERCISES

Applications and Problem Solving

8. **Sales** The Madison Local High School marching band sold gift wrap to earn money for a band trip to Orlando, Florida. The gift wrap in solid colors sold for $4.00 per roll, and the print gift wrap sold for $6.00 per roll. The total number of rolls sold was 480, and the total amount of money collected was $2340. How many rolls of each kind of gift wrap were sold?

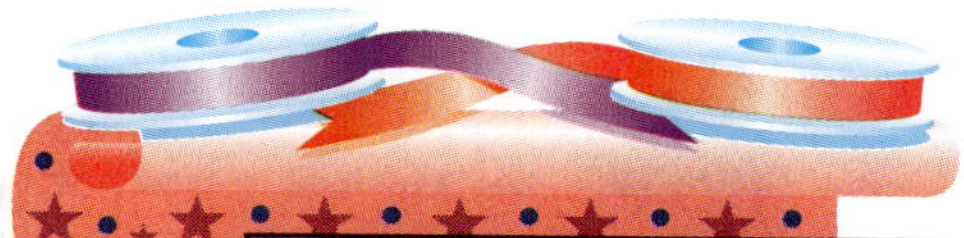

	Number of Rolls	Price Per Roll	Total Price
Solid	r	$4	$4r$
Print	$480 - r$	$6	$6(480 - r)$

9. **Money** Rochelle has $2.55 in dimes and quarters. She has eight more dimes than quarters. How many quarters does she have?

10. **Sales** The Nut House sells walnuts for $4.00 a pound and cashews for $7.00 a pound. How many pounds of cashews should be mixed with 10 pounds of walnuts to obtain a mixture that sells for $5.50 a pound?

11. **Travel** Ryan and Jessica Wilson leave their home at the same time, traveling in opposite directions. Ryan travels at 57 miles per hour and Jessica travels at 65 miles per hour. In how many hours will they be 366 miles apart?

12. **Travel** At 7:00 A.M., Brooke leaves home to go on a business trip driving 35 miles per hour. Fifteen minutes later, Bart discovers that Brooke forgot her presentation materials. He drives 50 miles per hour to catch up with her. If Bart is delayed 30 minutes with a flat tire, when will he catch up with Brooke?

13. **Cycling** Two cyclists begin traveling in the same direction on the same bike path. One travels at 20 miles per hour, and the other at 14 miles per hour. After how many hours will they be 15 miles apart?

14. **Entertainment** A local radio station is having a drawing to win tickets to see En Vogue in concert. The winners will be driven to the concert in a limousine that holds eight passengers. Concert tickets cost $22 for adults and $19 for students. After renting the limousine, the radio station has $167 left in their giveaway budget to buy the eight tickets. How many adult tickets and student tickets can the station buy?

15. **Travel** Pablo is driving 40 miles per hour. After he has driven 30 miles, his brother Ricardo starts driving in the same direction. At what rate must Ricardo drive to catch up with Pablo in 5 hours?

16. **Automotives** A car radiator has a capacity of 16 quarts and is filled with a 25% antifreeze solution. How much must be drained off and replaced with pure antifreeze to obtain a 40% antifreeze solution?

17. **Law Enforcement** A state patrol officer is chasing a car he believes is speeding. The officer is traveling 70 miles per hour to try to catch up with the car. But he can't say later that the other car was going 70 mph because the driver could ask, "If we were going the same speed, how did you catch up? Obviously I was going slower than you. I wasn't speeding." The officer sees the driver pass a mile marker, one-fourth of a mile ahead. From the marker, it takes the officer five minutes $\left(\frac{1}{12} \text{ of an hour}\right)$ to catch up. How fast was the driver going?

18. **Travel** An express train travels 80 kilometers per hour from Ironton to Wildwood. A local train, traveling at 48 kilometers per hour, takes 2 hours longer for the same trip. How far apart are Ironton and Wildwood?

19. **Colleges** Emilio is trying to decide what college he would like to attend. He has determined his five most important factors in choosing a school. A score of 1 is the lowest and 4 is the highest. The table at the right shows his ratings for one school he is considering.

	Importance Factor (1 to 4)	Rating (1 to 4)	Total
Distance from home	4	4	16
Academic reputation	3	2	6
Social climate	3	1	3
Quality of dorms	1	4	4
Community	2	3	6

a. Find the weighted average of his ratings for this school.

b. What is the highest rating that one of Emilio's schools can receive?

20. **School** Many schools base a student's grade point average, or GPA, on the grade a student receives as well as on the number of credits received for the class. Mercedes' grades for this semester are listed in the table at the right. Find Mercedes' GPA if a grade of A equals 4 and a B equals 3.

Grade Card

Class	Credits Rating	Grade
Honors Algebra	1	A
Biology	1	B
English 1	1	A
Spanish 2	1	B
Phys. Ed.	$\frac{1}{2}$	A

Critical Thinking

21. Write a mixture problem for the equation $1.00x + 0.20(40 - x) = 0.28(40)$.

22. Monica Morrison drove to work on Monday at 40 miles per hour and arrived one minute late. She left at the same time on Tuesday, drove at 45 miles per hour, and arrived one minute early. How far does Monica drive to work?

Mixed Review

23. **Probability** Find the probability of getting a number less than 1 if a die is rolled. (Lesson 4–6)

24. **Baseball** In 1994, DeMarini Sports Inc. sold 7500 aluminum softball bats to softball enthusiasts. In 1995, the company expected to increase sales by 60%. How many bats did the company expect to sell in 1995? (Lesson 4–5)

25. **Finance** Selena Cruz wants to invest a portion of her \$16,000 savings at 8% annual interest and the balance at a safer 5% annual interest. She hopes to earn \$1130 in the next year to pay for a Caribbean cruise. How much money should she invest at 8%? (Lesson 4–4)

26. **Model Trains** Model trains are scaled-down replicas of real trains that come in a variety of sizes, called scales. One of the most popular-sized models is called the HO. Every dimension of the HO model measures $\frac{1}{87}$ that of a real engine. The HO model of a modern diesel locomotive is about 8 inches long. About how many feet long is the real locomotive? (Lesson 4–1)

27. Solve $5.3 - 0.3x = -9.4$. (Lesson 3–3)

28. Solve $24 = -2a$. (Lesson 3–2)

29. Name the property illustrated in $(a + 3b) + 2c = a + (3b + 2c)$. (Lesson 1–8)

4–8 Direct and Inverse Variation

What YOU'LL LEARN

- To solve problems involving direct and inverse variation.

Why IT'S IMPORTANT

You can use direct and inverse variation to solve problems involving work and music.

FYI

A low-flow shower head uses only 2.5 gallons of water per minute.

APPLICATION

Water Usage

Do you find yourself singing in the shower? If you are like the average American, you have enough time to sing several songs. The national average for time spent in the shower is 12.2 minutes. A standard shower head uses about 6 gallons of water per minute. That means, you use 73.2 gallons of water for each shower you take. Taking one shower per day for one year would use 26,718 gallons of water!

The number of gallons of water used depends *directly* on the amount of time spent in the shower. The table below shows the number of gallons of water used y as a function of time in the shower x.

x (minutes)	3	6	9	12	15
y (gallons)	18	36	54	72	90

The relationship between the number of minutes in the shower and the gallons of water used is shown by the equation $y = 6x$. This type of equation is called a **direct variation.** We say that *y varies directly as x* or *y is directly proportional to x.* This means that as x increases in value, y increases in value, or as x decreases in value, y decreases in value.

Definition of Direct Variation	**A direct variation is described by an equation of the form $y = kx$, where $k \neq 0$.**

In the equation $y = kx$, k is called the **constant of variation**. To find the constant of variation, divide each side by x.

$$\frac{y}{x} = k$$

Example 1

APPLICATION

Employment

In this situation, Julio's pay is the dependent quantity and the number of hours Julio works is the independent quantity.

Julio's wages vary directly as the number of hours that he works. If his wages for 5 hours are \$29.75, how much will they be for 30 hours?

First, find Julio's hourly pay. Let x = number of hours Julio works, and let y = Julio's pay. Find the value of k in the equation $y = kx$. The value of k is the amount of money Julio is paid per hour.

$k = \frac{y}{x}$

$k = \frac{29.75}{5}$

$k = 5.95$

Julio is paid \$5.95 per hour.

(continued on the next page)

Next find out how much Julio's wages will be for 30 hours.

$y = kx$

$y = 5.95(30)$

$y = 178.50$

Thus, Julio's wages will be \$178.50 for 30 hours of work.

Using the table in the application at the beginning of the lesson, many proportions can be formed. Two examples are shown below.

number of minutes ↓ ↓

$$\frac{3}{18} = \frac{9}{54}$$

↑ ↑ gallons of water

number of minutes $\frac{3}{9} = \frac{18}{54}$ gallons of water

x_1 is read "x sub 1."

Two general forms for proportions like these can be derived from the equation $y = kx$. Let (x_1, y_1) be a solution for $y = kx$. Let a second solution be (x_2, y_2). Then $y_1 = kx_1$ and $y_2 = kx_2$.

$y_1 = kx_1$ This equation describes a direct variation.

$\frac{y_1}{y_2} = \frac{kx_1}{kx_2}$ Use the division property of equality. Since y_2 and kx_2 are equivalent, you can divide the left side by y_2 and the right side by kx_2.

$\frac{y_1}{y_2} = \frac{x_1}{x_2}$ Simplify.

Another proportion can be derived from this proportion.

$x_2y_1 = x_1y_2$ Find the cross products of the proportion above.

$\frac{x_2y_1}{y_1y_2} = \frac{x_1y_2}{y_1y_2}$ Divide each side by y_1y_2.

$\frac{x_2}{y_2} = \frac{x_1}{y_1}$ Simplify.

You can use either of these forms to solve problems involving direct proportion.

Example 2 **If y varies directly as x, and $y = 28$ when $x = 7$, find x when $y = 52$.**

Use $\frac{y_1}{y_2} = \frac{x_1}{x_2}$ to solve the problem.

$\frac{28}{52} = \frac{7}{x_2}$ Let $y_1 = 28$, $x_1 = 7$, and $y_2 = 52$.

$28x_2 = 52(7)$ Find the cross products.

$28x_2 = 364$

$x_2 = 13$

Thus, $x = 13$ when $y = 52$.

The reverse of direct variation is **inverse variation**. We say that *y varies inversely as x*. This means that as x increases in value, y decreases in value, or as y decreases in value, x increases in value. For example, the more miles you drive, the less gasoline you have in the tank.

Definition of Inverse Variation	An inverse variation is described by an equation of the form $xy = k$, where $k \neq 0$.

Sometimes inverse variations are written in the form $y = \frac{k}{x}$.

Example 3

APPLICATION

Music

The length of a violin string varies inversely as the frequency of its vibrations. A violin string 10 inches long vibrates at a frequency of 512 cycles per second. Find the frequency of an 8-inch string.

Let ℓ represent the length in inches and f represent the frequency in cycles per second. Find the value of k.

$$\ell f = k$$

$(10)(512) = k$ *Substitute 10 for ℓ and 512 for f.*

$5120 = k$ *The constant of variation is 5120.*

Next, find the frequency, in cycles per second, of the 8-inch string.

$\ell f = k$ *Use the same inverse variation equation.*

$8 \cdot f = 5120$ *Replace ℓ with 8 and k with 5120.*

$f = \frac{5120}{8}$ *Divide each side by 8.*

$f = 640$

The frequency of an 8-inch string is 640 cycles per second.

FYI

Midori, a classical violinist, got her first violin when she was 4. At age 10, she gave a solo performance with the New York Philharmonic. She now performs internationally.

Let (x_1, y_1) be a solution of an inverse variation, $xy = k$. Let (x_2, y_2) be a second solution. Then $x_1y_1 = k$ and $x_2y_2 = k$.

$x_1y_1 = k$

$x_1y_1 = x_2y_2$ *You can substitute x_2y_2 for k because $x_2y_2 = k$.*

The equation $x_1y_1 = x_2y_2$ is called the product rule for inverse variations. Study how it can be used to form a proportion.

$x_1y_1 = x_2y_2$

$\frac{x_1y_1}{x_2y_1} = \frac{x_2y_2}{x_2y_1}$ *Divide each side by x_2y_1.*

$\frac{x_1}{x_2} = \frac{y_2}{y_1}$ *Notice that this proportion is different from the proportion for direct variation.*

You can use either the product rule or the proportion rule to solve problems involving inverse variation.

Example 4 **If y varies inversely as x, and $y = 5$ when $x = 15$, find x when $y = 3$.**

Let $x_1 = 15$, $y_1 = 5$, and $y_2 = 3$. Solve for x_2.

Method 1

Use the product rule.

$$x_1 y_1 = x_2 y_2$$
$$15 \cdot 5 = x_2 \cdot 3$$
$$\frac{75}{3} = x_2$$
$$25 = x_2$$

Method 2

Use the proportion.

$$\frac{x_1}{x_2} = \frac{y_2}{y_1}$$
$$\frac{15}{x_2} = \frac{3}{5}$$
$$75 = 3x_2$$
$$25 = x_2$$

Thus, $x = 25$ when $y = 3$.

If you have observed people on a seesaw, you may have noticed that the heavier person must sit closer to the fulcrum (pivot point) to balance the seesaw. A seesaw is a type of *lever,* and all lever problems involve inverse variation.

Suppose weights w_1 and w_2 are placed on a lever at distances d_1 and d_2, respectively, from the fulcrum. The lever is balanced when $w_1 d_1 = w_2 d_2$. This property of levers is illustrated at the right.

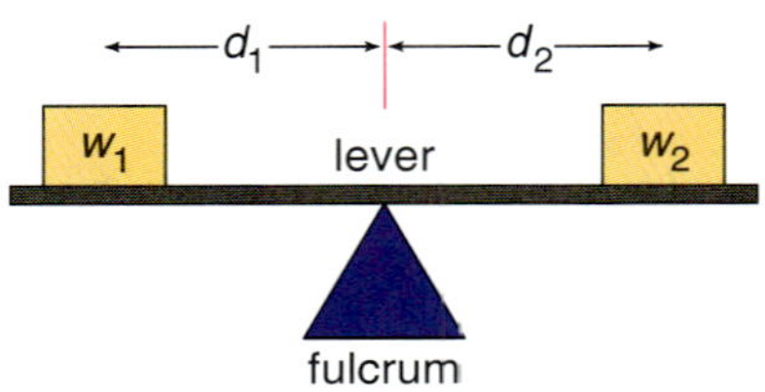

Example 5

APPLICATION

Physics

The fulcrum is placed in the middle of a 20-foot seesaw. Cholena, who weighs 120 pounds, is seated 9 feet from the fulcrum. How far from the fulcrum should Antonio sit if he weighs 135 pounds?

Let $w_1 = 120$, $d_1 = 9$, and $w_2 = 135$. Solve for d_2.

$$w_1 d_1 = w_2 d_2$$
$$120 \cdot 9 = 135 \cdot d_2$$
$$1080 = 135 d_2$$
$$d_2 = 8$$

Antonio should sit 8 feet from the fulcrum.

CHECK FOR UNDERSTANDING

Communicating Mathematics

Study the lesson. Then complete the following.

1. **Tell** whether an equation of the form $xy = k$, where $k \neq 0$, represents a direct or inverse variation.
2. Refer to the application at the beginning of the lesson. Describe a reasonable domain and range.
3. **Explain** how you find the constant of variation in a direct variation.
4. **You Decide** Morgan says that a person's height varies directly as his or her age. Do you agree? Explain.

Guided Practice

Determine which equations represent inverse variations and which represent direct variations. Then find the constant of variation.

5. $mn = 5$
6. $a = -3b$

Solve. Assume that y varies directly as x.

7. If $y = 27$, when $x = 6$, find x when $y = 45$.
8. If $y = -7$ when $x = -14$, find y when $x = 20$.

Solve. Assume that y varies inversely as x.

9. If $y = 99$ when $x = 11$, find x when $y = 11$.
10. If $y = -6$ when $x = -2$, find y when $x = 5$.
11. **Physics** An 8-ounce weight is placed at one end of a yardstick. A 10-ounce weight is placed at the other end. Where should the fulcrum be placed to balance the yardstick?

EXERCISES

Practice

Determine which equations represent inverse variations and which represent direct variations. Then find the constant of variation.

12. $c = 3.14d$
13. $15 = rs$
14. $\frac{35}{p} = q$
15. $s = \frac{9}{t}$
16. $\frac{1}{3}x = z$
17. $4a = b$

Solve. Assume that y varies directly as x.

18. If $y = -8$ when $x = -3$, find x when $y = 6$.
19. If $y = 12$ when $x = 15$, find x when $y = 21$.
20. If $y = 2.5$ when $x = 0.5$, find y when $x = 20$.
21. If $y = 4$ when $x = 12$, find y when $x = -24$.
22. If $y = -6$ when $x = 9$, find y when $x = 6$.
23. If $y = 2\frac{2}{3}$ when $x = \frac{1}{4}$, find y when $x = 1\frac{1}{8}$.

Solve. Assume that y varies inversely as x.

24. If $y = 9$ when $x = 8$, find y when $x = 6$.
25. If $x = 2.7$ when $y = 8.1$, find y when $x = 3.6$.
26. If $y = 24$ when $x = -8$, find y when $x = 4$.
27. If $x = 6.1$ when $y = 4.4$, find x when $y = 3.2$
28. If $y = 7$ when $x = \frac{2}{3}$, find y when $x = 7$.
29. If $x = \frac{1}{2}$ when $y = 16$, find x when $y = 32$.

Critical Thinking

30. Assume that y varies inversely as x.
    a. If the value of x is doubled, what happens to the value of y?
    b. If the value of y is tripled, what happens to the value of x?

Applications and Problem Solving

31. **Space** The weight of an object on the moon varies directly as its weight on Earth. With all of his gear on, Neil Armstrong weighed 360 pounds on Earth. When he became the first person to step on the moon on July 20, 1969, he weighed 60 pounds. Tara weighs 108 pounds on Earth. What would she weigh on the moon?

32. **Physics** Pam and Adam are seated on the same side of a seesaw. Pam is 6 feet from the fulcrum and weighs 115 pounds. Adam is 8 feet from the fulcrum and weighs 120 pounds. Kam is seated on the other side of the seesaw, 10 feet from the fulcrum. If the seesaw is balanced, how much does Kam weigh?

33. **Music** The pitch of a musical tone varies inversely as its wavelength. If one tone has a pitch of 440 vibrations per second and a wavelength of 2.4 feet, find the wavelength of a tone that has a pitch of 660 vibrations per second.

Neil Armstrong on the moon

Mixed Review

34. **Travel** At 8:00 A.M., Alma drove west at 35 miles per hour. At 9:00 A.M., Reiko drove east from the same point at 42 miles per hour. At what time will they be 266 miles apart? (Lesson 4–7)

35. **Probability** If the probability that an event will occur is $\frac{2}{3}$, what are the odds that the event will occur? (Lesson 4–6)

36. **Retail Sales** A department store buys clothing at wholesale prices and then marks the clothing up 25% to sell at retail price to customers. If the retail price of a jacket is \$79, what was the wholesale price? (Lesson 4–5)

37. **Finance** Hiroko invested \$11,700, part at 5% interest and the balance at 7% interest. If her annual earnings from both investments is \$733, how much is invested at each rate? (Lesson 4–4)

38. Solve $\frac{2x}{5} + \frac{x}{4} = \frac{26}{5}$ for x. (Lesson 3–6)

39. Solve $\frac{x}{4} + 9 = 6$. (Lesson 3–3)

40. Simplify $\frac{4a + 32}{4}$. (Lesson 2–7)

CHAPTER 4 HIGHLIGHTS

VOCABULARY

After completing this chapter, you should be able to define each term, property, or phrase and give an example or two of each.

Algebra

base (p. 215)
constant of variation (p. 239)
direct variation (p. 239)
extremes (p. 196)
inverse variation (p. 241)
means (p. 196)
odds (p. 229)
percent (p. 215)
percentage (p. 215)
percent of decrease (p. 222)
percent of increase (p. 222)
percent proportion (p. 215)
proportion (p. 195)
rate (pp. 197, 215)
ratio (p. 195)
scale (p. 197)
simple interest (p. 217)
uniform motion (p. 235)
weighted average (p. 233)

Geometry

angle of depression (p. 208)
angle of elevation (p. 208)
corresponding angles (p. 201)
corresponding sides (p. 201)
hypotenuse (p. 206)
legs (p. 206)
similar (p. 201)
similar triangles (p. 201)
trigonometric ratios (p. 206)

Probability

equally likely (p. 229)
probability (p. 228)
probability of an event (p. 228)
random (p. 229)

Trigonometry

cosine (p. 206)
sine (p. 206)
solving the triangle (p. 208)
tangent (p. 206)

UNDERSTANDING AND USING THE VOCABULARY

Choose the correct term to complete each sentence.

1. The angle formed by a person in a radio tower looking up at an airplane in flight is called the (*angle of depression, angle of elevation*).
2. The equation $\frac{3}{5} = \frac{9}{15}$ is a (*proportion, ratio*).
3. If $\Delta ABC \sim \Delta DEF$, then their corresponding angles are (*equal, proportional*), and their corresponding sides are (*equal, proportional*).
4. A ratio (*can, cannot*) be expressed in the following ways: $\frac{4}{5}$, 4:5, and 4 to 5.
5. In a right triangle, the sides that form the right angle are called the (*hypotenuse, legs*) .
6. In $\frac{2}{x} = \frac{3}{9}$, 3 and x are called the (*extremes, means*).
7. The (*odds, probability*) that a certain event will occur is the ratio of the number of ways it can occur to the number of ways it cannot occur.
8. In the ratio $\frac{5}{28}$, 5 is the (*base, percentage*), and 28 is the (*base, percentage*).
9. A(n) (*direct variation, inverse variation*) is described by an equation of the form $xy = k$, where $k \neq 0$.
10. The tangent of an angle is defined as the measure of the (*adjacent, opposite*) leg divided by the measure of the (*adjacent leg, hypotenuse*).

STUDY GUIDE AND ASSESSMENT

SKILLS AND CONCEPTS

OBJECTIVES AND EXAMPLES	REVIEW EXERCISES

OBJECTIVES AND EXAMPLES

Upon completing this chapter, you should be able to:

- solve proportions (Lesson 4–1)

$\frac{x}{3} = \frac{x+1}{2}$

$2(x) = 3(x + 1)$ *Find the cross products.*

$2x = 3x + 3$

$-3 = x$

REVIEW EXERCISES

Use these exercises to review and prepare for the chapter test.

Use cross products to determine whether each pair of ratios forms a proportion.

11. $\frac{10}{3}, \frac{150}{45}$

12. $\frac{8}{7}, \frac{2}{1.75}$

13. $\frac{30}{12}, \frac{5}{4}$

14. $\frac{2.7}{3.1}, \frac{8.1}{9.3}$

Solve each proportion.

15. $\frac{6}{15} = \frac{n}{45}$

16. $\frac{x}{11} = \frac{35}{55}$

17. $\frac{y+4}{y-1} = \frac{4}{3}$

18. $\frac{z-7}{6} = \frac{z+3}{7}$

- find the unknown measures of the sides of two similar triangles (Lesson 4–2)

$\frac{10}{5} = \frac{6}{a}$

$10a = 5(6)$

$10a = 30$

$a = 3$

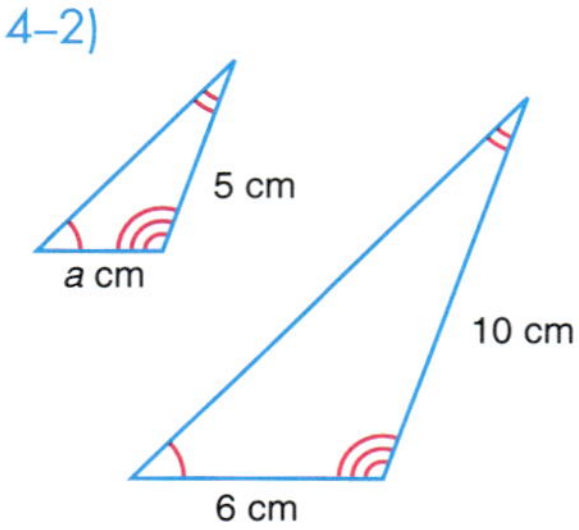

ΔABC and ΔDEF are similar. For each set of measures given, find the measures of the remaining sides.

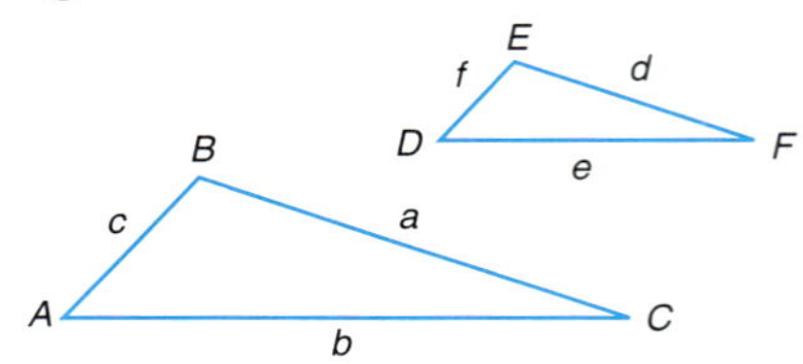

19. $c = 16, b = 12, a = 10, f = 9$

20. $a = 8, c = 10, b = 6, f = 12$

21. $c = 12, f = 9, a = 8, e = 11$

22. $b = 20, d = 7, f = 6, c = 15$

- use trigonometric ratios to solve right triangles (Lesson 4–3)

$\sin A = \frac{\text{measure of leg opposite } \angle A}{\text{measure of hypotenuse}}$

$\cos A = \frac{\text{measure of leg adjacent } \angle A}{\text{measure of hypotenuse}}$

$\tan A = \frac{\text{measure of leg opposite } \angle A}{\text{measure of leg adjacent } \angle A}$

For ΔABC, find each value to the nearest thousandth.

23. $\cos B$

24. $\tan A$

25. $\sin B$

26. $\cos A$

27. $\tan B$

28. $\sin A$

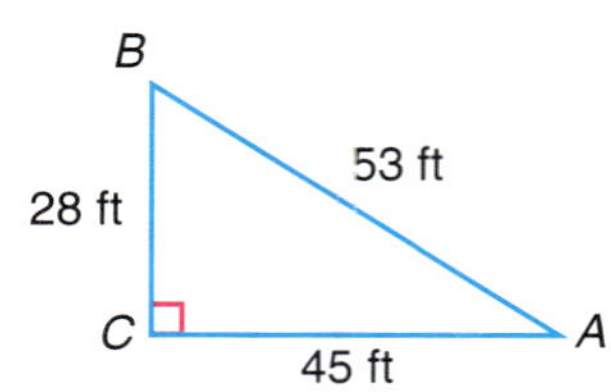

- use trigonometric ratios to solve right triangles (Lesson 4–3)

$\cos M = 0.3245$

Enter: 0.3245 [2nd] [COS^{-1}] 71.064715

The measure of $\angle M$ is about 71°.

Use a calculator to find the measure of each angle to the nearest degree.

29. $\tan M = 0.8043$

30. $\sin T = 0.1212$

31. $\tan Q = 5.9080$

32. $\cos F = 0.7443$

OBJECTIVES AND EXAMPLES

- use trigonometric ratios to solve right triangles (Lesson 4–3)

Solve right ΔABC *if* $m\angle B = 40°$ and $c = 6$.

$m\angle A = 180° - (90° + 40°)$ or $50°$

$\cos 40° = \frac{a}{6}$	$\sin 40° = \frac{b}{6}$
$0.7660 \approx \frac{a}{6}$	$0.6428 \approx \frac{b}{6}$
$0.7660(6) \approx a$	$0.6428(6) \approx b$
$4.596 \approx a$	$3.857 \approx b$

REVIEW EXERCISES

Solve each right triangle. State the side lengths to the nearest tenth and the angle measures to the nearest degree.

33.

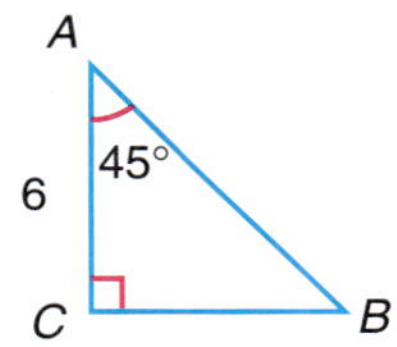

34.

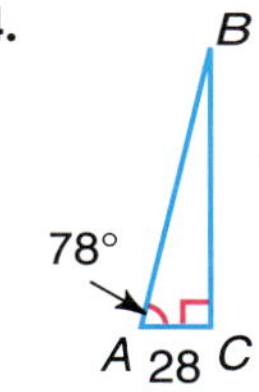

35.

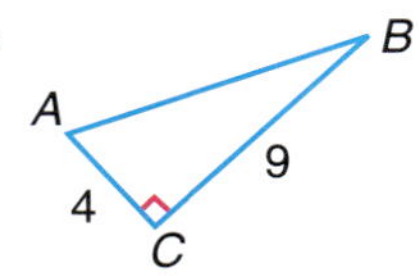

36.

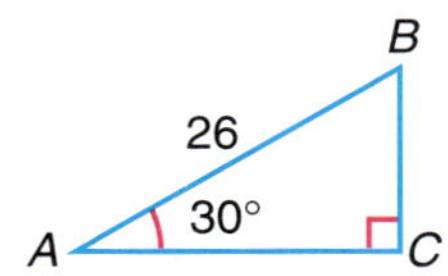

- solve percent problems (Lesson 4–4)

Nine is what percent of 15?

$\frac{9}{15} = \frac{r}{100}$ *Use a proportion.*

$9(100) = 15r$ *Find the cross products.*

$900 = 15r$

$60 = r$

Solve.

37. What number is 60% of 80?

38. Twenty-one is 35% of what number?

39. Eighty-four is what percent of 96?

40. What percent of 17 is 34?

41. What number is 0.3% of 62.7?

42. Find 0.12% of $5200.

- solve problems involving percent of increase or decrease (Lesson 4–5)

original: $120 new: $114

amount of decrease: $120 − $114 = $6

$$\frac{\text{amount of decrease}}{\text{original}} = \frac{r}{100}$$

$$\frac{6}{120} = \frac{r}{100}$$

$$5 = r$$

The percent of decrease is 5%.

State whether each percent of change is a percent of increase or a percent of decrease. Then find the percent of increase or decrease. Round to the nearest whole percent.

43. original: $40
new: $35

44. original: 97 cases
new: 115 cases

45. original: $35
new: $37.10

46. original: $50
new: $88

47. original: 1500 employees
new: 1350 employees

48. original: 12,500 students
new: 11,800 students

- solve problems involving discounts or sales tax (Lesson 4–5)

running shoes: $74; discount: 15%; sales tax: 6%

15% of $74 = (0.15)(74) or $11.10

$74 − $11.10 = $62.90 ← *sale price*

6% of $62.90 = (0.06)(62.90) or $3.77

$62.90 + $3.77 = $66.67 ← *price with tax*

The total price is $66.67 for the shoes.

Find the final price of each item. When there is a discount and sales tax, compute the discount price first.

49. calculator: $81
sales tax: 5.75%

50. gasoline: $21.50
discount: 2%

51. used car: $8,690
sales tax: 6.7%

52. dress: $89
discount: 25%
sales tax: 7%

OBJECTIVES AND EXAMPLES

- find the probability of a simple event and find the odds of a simple event (Lesson 4–6)

Find the probability of a computer randomly choosing the letter I in the word MISSISSIPPI.

$$\frac{\text{number of favorable outcomes}}{\text{number of possible outcomes}} = \frac{4}{11}$$

Find the odds that you will randomly *not* select the letter S in the word MISSISSIPPI.

number of successes:number of failures = 7:4

REVIEW EXERCISES

Find the probability of each outcome if a computer randomly chooses a letter in the word REPRESENTING.

53. the letter S
54. the letter E
55. P(not N)
56. the letters R or P

Find the odds of each outcome if you randomly select a coin from a jar containing 90 pennies, 75 nickels, 50 dimes, and 30 quarters.

57. selecting a dime
58. selecting a penny
59. *not* selecting a nickel
60. selecting a nickel or a dime

OBJECTIVES AND EXAMPLES

- solve problems involving direct and inverse variation (Lesson 4–8)

If x varies directly as y and $x = 15$ when $y = 1.5$, find x when $y = 9$.

$$\frac{1.5}{9} = \frac{15}{x}$$

$1.5x = 9(15)$

$1.5x = 135$

$x = 90$

If y varies inversely as x and $y = 24$ when $x = 30$, find x when $y = 10$.

$$\frac{30}{x} = \frac{10}{24}$$

$(30)(24) = 10x$

$720 = 10x$

$72 = x$

REVIEW EXERCISES

Solve. Assume that y varies directly as x.

61. If $y = 15$ when $x = 5$, find y when $x = 7$.
62. If $y = 35$ when $x = 175$, find y when $x = 75$.
63. If $y = 10$ when $x = 0.75$, find x when $y = 80$.
64. If $y = 3$ when $x = 99.9$, find y when $x = 522.81$.

Solve. Assume that y varies inversely as x.

65. If $y = 28$ when $x = 42$, find y when $x = 56$.
66. If $y = 15$ when $x = 5$, find y when $x = 3$.
67. If $y = 18$ when $x = 8$, find x when $y = 3$.
68. If $y = 35$ when $x = 175$, find y when $x = 75$.

APPLICATIONS AND PROBLEM SOLVING

69. Travel Two airplanes leave Dallas at the same time and fly in opposite directions. One airplane travels 80 miles per hour faster than the other. After three hours, they are 2940 miles apart. What is the rate of each airplane? (Lesson 4–7)

70. Coffee Anne Leibowitz owns "The Coffee Pot," a specialty coffee store. She wants to create a special mix using two coffees, one priced at \$8.40 per pound and the other at \$7.28 per pound. How many pounds of the \$7.28 coffee should she mix with 9 pounds of the \$8.40 coffee to sell the mixture for \$7.95 per pound? (Lesson 4–7)

A practice test for Chapter 4 is provided on page 790.

ALTERNATIVE ASSESSMENT

COOPERATIVE LEARNING PROJECT

Letter Occurrence In this project, you will determine percentages, percent of change, and probability and odds.

There is an uneven distribution of letters which occur in words. Christofer Sholes, the inventor of the typewriter, may not have been aware of this unevenness. He gave the left hand 56 percent of all the strokes, and the two most agile fingers on the right hand hit two of the least often used letters of the alphabet, j and k.

The table below shows the percentages of the occurrence of letters in large samples.

E	12.3%	R	6.0%	F	2.3%	K	1.5%
T	9.6%	H	5.1%	M	2.2%	Q	0.2%
A	8.1%	L	4.0%	W	2.0%	X	0.2%
O	7.9%	D	3.7%	Y	1.9%	J	0.1%
N	7.2%	C	3.2%	B	1.6%	Z	0.1%
I	7.2%	U	3.1%	G	1.6%		
S	6.6%	P	2.3%	V	0.9%		

Use the second paragraph on this page to count the number of times that e, s, c, w, and k occur and compute their percentages. Compare your answers with the table. What is the probability that a letter picked at random from the paragraph is a vowel? Are the odds better that a vowel or a consonant was used in the above paragraph? What are these odds?

Write a paragraph describing similar triangles. Then determine the percentages of the occurrence of the above mentioned letters in your paragraph. Do they coincide with the percentages in the table? Determine the percent of change for the above letters in the paragraph above and the paragraph you wrote.

Follow these guidelines.

- Determine what type of data you will need in order to calculate your answers.
- Devise a chart that will be helpful in organizing the data you will need.
- Write a paragraph describing what your answers mean.
- Using the percentages from the above table, draw your idea of where the letters should be on a typewriter and explain why.

THINKING CRITICALLY

- Use an example to describe the difference between odds and probability. Explain why some events are described in terms of odds and others in terms of probability.
- Use the definitions of the trigonometric ratios to explain why, in any right ΔABC with right angle C, $\sin A = \cos B$, and $\cos A = \sin B$.

PORTFOLIO

Even after working through a chapter of material, you can get to the end and still feel uncertain about a concept or a certain type of problem. Find a problem that you still cannot solve or that you are worried you might not be able to solve on a test. Write out the question and as much of the solution as you can until you get to the hard part. Then explain what it is that keeps you from solving the problem. Be clear and precise. Place this in your portfolio.

SELF EVALUATION

Theme learning occurs when the subject matter being studied is all related to the same theme, such as water, animals, and so on. When the course material is presented, it is all applied to that theme.

Assess yourself. Are you a person who would enjoy theme learning? Would you like to relate all your course work to one area or do you prefer having a variety of application themes? Describe a theme that would be of interest to you and tell how you would use that theme to introduce and apply the contents of a specific math subject.

CUMULATIVE REVIEW

CHAPTERS 1–4

SECTION ONE: MULTIPLE CHOICE

There are nine multiple-choice questions in this section. After working each problem, write the letter of the correct answer on your paper.

1. Solve the equation $7(3b + x) = 5a$ for x.

A. $5a - 21b = x$ **B.** $\frac{5a}{7} - 21b = x$

C. $\frac{5a - 3b}{7} = x$ **D.** $\frac{5a - 21b}{7} = x$

2. **Sales** A Tampa Bay Buccaneers sweatshirt decreased in price from \$40 to \$35 during a clearance sale. Find the percent of decrease.

A. 5% **B.** 12.5%

C. 14.3% **D.** 114.3%

3. A caterpillar was trying to crawl out of a bucket into which it had fallen. It crawled up $1\frac{1}{4}$ feet before sliding down $\frac{3}{8}$ feet. It then crawled up $\frac{5}{6}$ feet before resting. How much farther must the caterpillar crawl to reach the top of the 2-foot bucket?

A. $\frac{7}{24}$ feet **B.** $\frac{7}{8}$ feet

C. $1\frac{1}{8}$ feet **D.** $1\frac{17}{24}$ feet

4. **Geometry** Choose the correct proportion to find the distance across the lake (AB) given ΔABC is similar to ΔEDC.

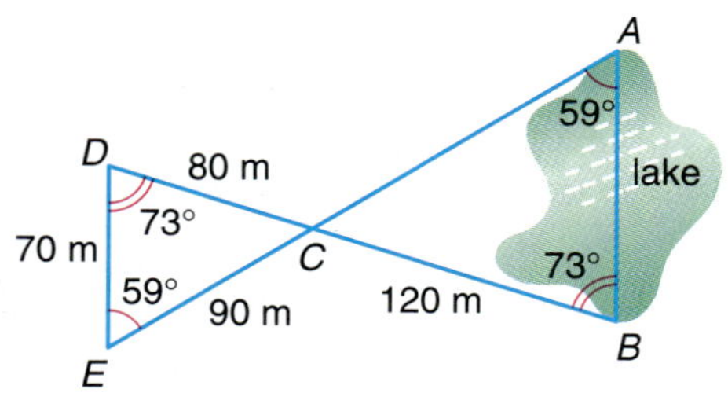

A. $\frac{70}{AB} = \frac{90}{120}$ **B.** $\frac{80}{70} = \frac{AB}{120}$

C. $\frac{70}{AB} = \frac{80}{120}$ **D.** $\frac{80}{90} = \frac{120}{AB}$

5. Kassim read 36 pages of a novel in 2 hours. At the same rate, find the number of hours it will take him to read the remaining 135 pages.

A. $3\frac{3}{4}$ **B.** $7\frac{1}{2}$

C. $9\frac{1}{2}$ **D.** $10\frac{1}{2}$

6. Choose an equivalent equation to represent "h is the product of g and the difference of the square of b and t".

A. $h - t = gb^2$

B. $h = g(b^2 - t)$

C. $h = g(b - t)^2$

D. $h + t = gb^2$

7. **Probability** The freshman class of Perry High School is planning an end-of-the-year dance. The dance committee decides to award door prizes. They want the odds of winning a prize to be 1:5. If they plan for 180 tickets to be sold for the dance, how many prizes will be needed?

A. 6 prizes **B.** 36 prizes

C. 30 prizes **D.** 150 prizes

8. **Sales** Raven sold her concert ticket to Sandra for 75% of the original ticket price. If Sandra paid \$26.25 for the ticket, choose the proportion that could be used to find the ticket's original price.

A. $\frac{75}{100} = \frac{26.25}{x}$ **B.** $\frac{x}{26.25} = \frac{75}{100}$

C. $\frac{x}{100} = \frac{75}{26.25}$ **D.** $\frac{x}{75} = \frac{26.25}{100}$

9. **Statistics** Carita's bowling scores for the first four games of a five-game series are $b + 2$, $b + 3$, $b - 2$, and $b - 1$. What must her score be for the last game to have an average of $b + 2$?

A. $b - 2$ **B.** $b + 2$

C. $b - 8$ **D.** $b + 8$

SECTION TWO: FREE RESPONSE

This section contains nine questions for which you will provide short answers. Write your answer on your paper.

10. Describe the steps required to solve the equation $4t - 5 = 7t - 23$.

11. Geometry Find the dimensions of a rectangle whose width is 5 inches less than its length and has a perimeter of 70 inches.

12. Finance In the beginning of the month, the balance in Marisa Fuente's checking account was \$428.79. After writing checks totaling \$1097.31, depositing 2 checks of \$691.53 each, and withdrawing \$100 from a bank machine, what was the new balance in Marisa's account?

13. Finance Maria Cruz wants to invest part of her \$8000 savings in a bond paying 12% annual interest, and the rest of it in a savings account paying 8%. If she wants to earn a total of \$760, how much money should Maria invest at each rate?

14. Weather The time t in hours, that a storm will last is given by the formula $t = \sqrt{\frac{d^3}{216}}$, where d is the diameter of the storm in miles. Suppose the umpires in a baseball game declared rain delay at 4:00 P.M. The storm causing the rain delay has a diameter of 12 miles. After the rain has stopped, can the game be restarted before 6:00 P.M.?

15. Statistics Find the mean, median, and mode of the data represented in the line plot below to the nearest tenth.

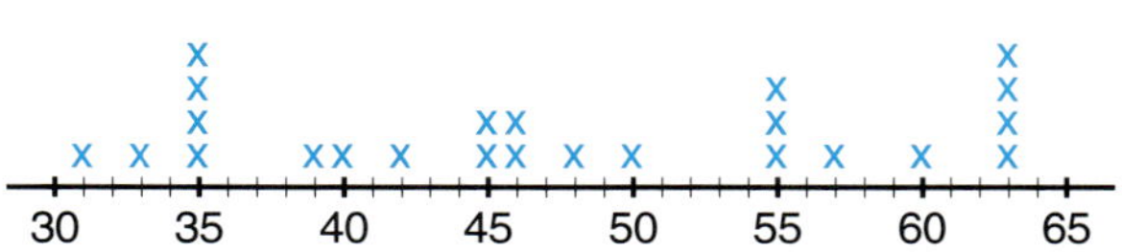

16. Running Raul ran a distance of 385 yards in $1\frac{3}{4}$ minutes. His younger sister, Luisa, estimated it would take her $3\frac{1}{2}$ minutes to run the same distance. If Luisa ran at a rate of 94 yards per minute, was her estimation correct? Verify your answer.

17. Government The term of office for a United States Senator is 150% as long as the term of office for the President. How long is the term of office for a United States Senator?

18. Physics Shannon weighs 126 pounds and Minal weighs 154 pounds. They are seated at opposite ends of a seesaw. Shannon and Minal are 16 feet apart, and the seesaw is balanced. How far is Shannon from the fulcrum?

SECTION THREE: OPEN-ENDED

This section contains two open-ended problems. Demonstrate your knowledge by giving a clear, concise solution to each problem. Your score on these problems will depend on how well you do the following.

- Explain your reasoning.
- Show your understanding of the mathematics in an organized manner.
- Use charts, graphs, and diagrams in your explanation.
- Show the solution in more than one way or relate it to other situations.
- Investigate beyond the requirements of the problem.

19. Geometry One angle of a triangle measures 15° more than the second. The measure of the third angle is the sum of the first two angles tripled. Find the measure of each angle.

20. Biology An adult African elephant can weigh up to 12,000 pounds. An adult blue whale can weigh as much as 37 adult African elephants. A newborn blue whale weighs one-third of an adult African elephant's weight. The newborn whale will gain 200 pounds per day until it reaches its adult weight. How many days will it take for the newborn to reach adult weight?

CHAPTER

5

Graphing Relations and Functions

Objectives

In this chapter, you will:

- graph ordered pairs, relations, and equations,
- solve problems by making a table,
- identify the domain, range, and inverse of a relation,
- determine if a relation is a function,
- write an equation to represent a relation, and
- calculate and interpret the range, quartiles, and interquartile range of a set of data.

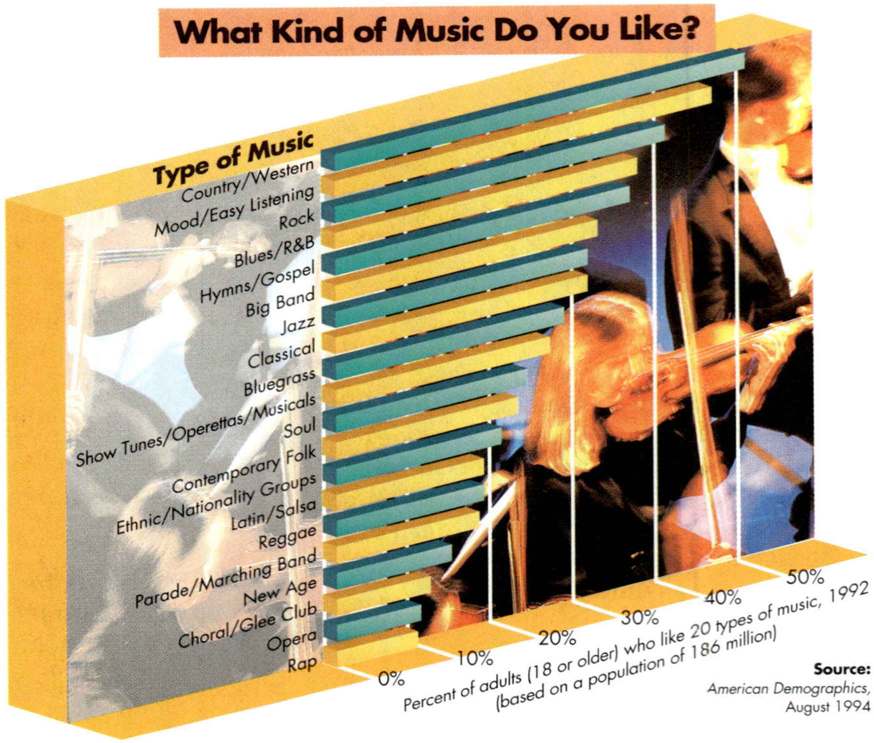

What kinds of music do you listen to most often? Most teenagers have predictable tastes in music—listening to and buying popular rock and country/western favorites. As you become an adult, you may learn to enjoy listening to many other types of music. Who knows, you may become a fan of 12th century Gregorian chants, or perhaps even Zydeco!

TIME Line

2400 B.C. Place value is used in the Sumerian number system in Mesopotamia.

1591 François Viète's *Isagoge in Artem Analyticam* (Introduction to the Analytic Art) is the first work in mathematics to use letters for variables and constants.

A.D. 1434 Jan van Eyck, a painter in the Netherlands, creates the brilliant double portrait *"The Anrolfini Marriage."*

PEOPLE IN THE NEWS

By the young age of 10, **Jamie Knight** was already an accomplished jazz singer. She has even performed at New York City's Carnegie Hall, following in the footsteps of Ella Fitzgerald and Mel Torme. Jamie is from Philadelphia, Pennsylvania, and has been performing since the age of 6. She has appeared at jazz festivals and on *Good Morning America.* She also has her own CD.

Chapter Project

Work in groups of three to conduct your own music survey.

- Each person in the group should survey 20 people of varying ages to determine their musical tastes. Use the graph on the previous page for ideas.
- Combine your results and compare them to the graph. Does your survey match the national results?
- Create a bar graph to show your results for each type of music. Also create bar graphs for the five most popular types of music you surveyed showing the age distribution for each type of music. Then create a line graph comparing male and female musical tastes in relation to age groups.
- Compare your graphs, make some conclusions, and report your findings.
- Do you think certain types of music are associated with different cultures? You may want to include your thoughts on this in your report.

1846 Adolphe Sax, attempting to improve on the bass clarinet, invents a new instrument, the saxophone.

1938 Ynes Mexia, who collects more than 137,600 botanical specimens for classification, dies.

1750 The great Chinese work of fiction *The Dream of the Red Chamber* is written by Tsao Hsueh Chin.

1882 African American Lewis H. Latimer patents the first cost-efficient method for producing electric lights.

1994 For her work as conservator of American Indian language and culture, Vi Hilbert is honored by the National Endowment for the Arts.

5–1 The Coordinate Plane

What YOU'LL LEARN

- To graph ordered pairs on a coordinate plane, and
- to solve problems by making a table.

Why IT'S IMPORTANT

You can use graphing to solve problems involving geography and cartography.

APPLICATION
Landmarks

In 1988, as part of Cincinnati's 200th birthday celebration, the city's Bicentennial Commission created parks along the Ohio River. They sold over 33,800 personalized bricks that were placed in the pathways in the parks. However, people had difficulty finding their bricks. So, in 1989, Mr. Frank Albi of Business Information Storage (BIS) developed a master directory, in which each patron's name was listed along with the section of the park and the column in which his or her brick was laid. BIS then added locator bricks to identify the columns in each section.

Perpendicular lines are lines that meet to form 90° angles.

Unless otherwise designated, you can assume that each division on the axes represents 1 unit.

The system used in Cincinnati helped to locate the specific site of each brick. In mathematics, points are located in reference to two perpendicular number lines called **axes.** The axes intersect at their zero points, a point called the **origin.** The horizontal number line, called the ***x*-axis,** and the vertical number line, called the ***y*-axis,** divide the plane into four **quadrants.** The quadrants are numbered as shown at the right. Notice that neither the axes nor any point on the axes are located in any quadrant. The plane containing the x- and y-axes is called the **coordinate plane.**

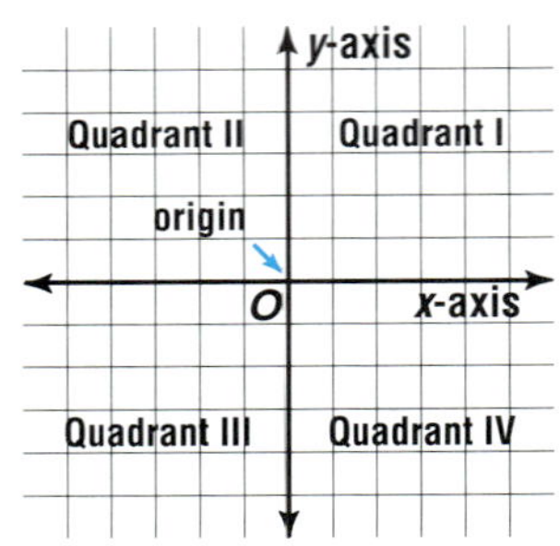

Points in the coordinate plane are named by *ordered pairs* of the form (x, y). The first number, or ***x*-coordinate,** corresponds to the numbers on the x-axis. The second number, or ***y*-coordinate,** corresponds to the numbers on the y-axis. The ordered pair for the origin is $(0, 0)$.

A point can be referred to by just a capital letter. Thus, Z can be used to mean point Z.

To find the ordered pair for point Z, shown at the right, first follow along a vertical line through Z to find the x-coordinate on the x-axis and along a horizontal line through Z to find the y-coordinate on the y-axis. The number on the x-axis that corresponds to Z is 4. The number on the y-axis that corresponds to Z is -6. Thus, the ordered pair for point Z is $(4, -6)$. This ordered pair can also be written as $Z(4, -6)$. The x-coordinate of Z is 4, and the y-coordinate of Z is -6. Point Z is located in Quadrant IV.

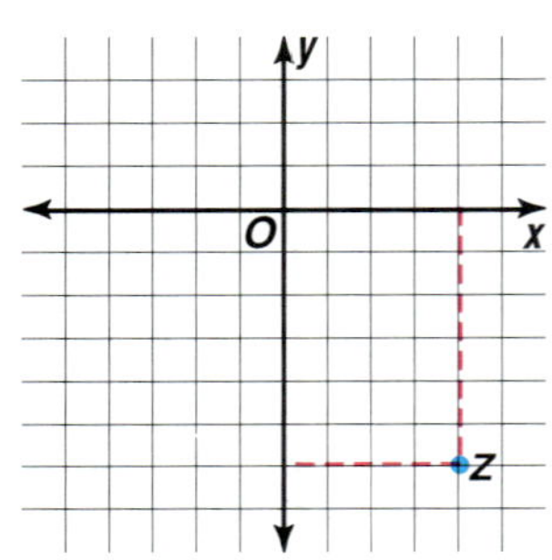

A table is often used when working with ordered pairs. It is a helpful organizational tool in problem solving.

Example 1 Write ordered pairs for points *E, F, G,* and *H* shown at the right. Name the quadrant in which each point is located.

PROBLEM SOLVING
Use a Table

Use a table to help find the coordinates of each point.

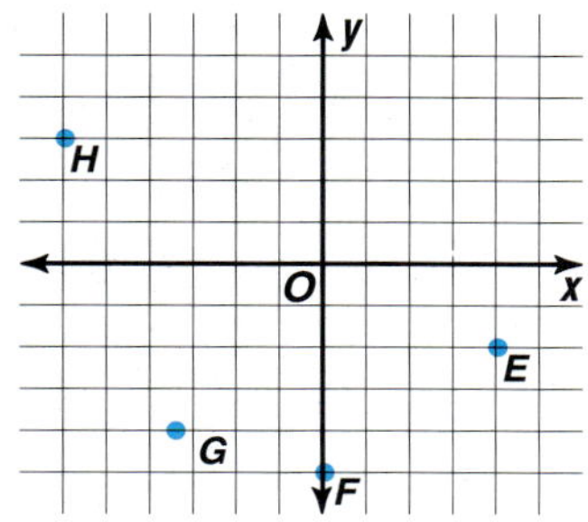

LOOK BACK You can review more about using tables in Lesson 4-7.

Point	*x*-coordinate	*y*-coordinate	Ordered Pair	Quadrant
E	4	–2	(4, –2)	IV
F	0	–5	(0, –5)	none
G	–3.5	–4	(–3.5, –4)	III
H	–6	3	(–6, 3)	II

To **graph** an ordered pair means to draw a dot at the point on the coordinate plane that corresponds to the ordered pair. This is sometimes called *plotting a point.* When graphing an ordered pair, start at the origin. The *x*-coordinate indicates how many units to move right (positive) or left (negative). The *y*-coordinate indicates how many units to move up (positive) or down (negative).

Example 2 Plot the following points on a coordinate plane.

a. $N(-3, -5)$

Start at the origin, *O.* Move left 3 units since the *x*-coordinate is −3. Then move down 5 units since the *y*-coordinate is −5. Draw a dot and label it *N.*

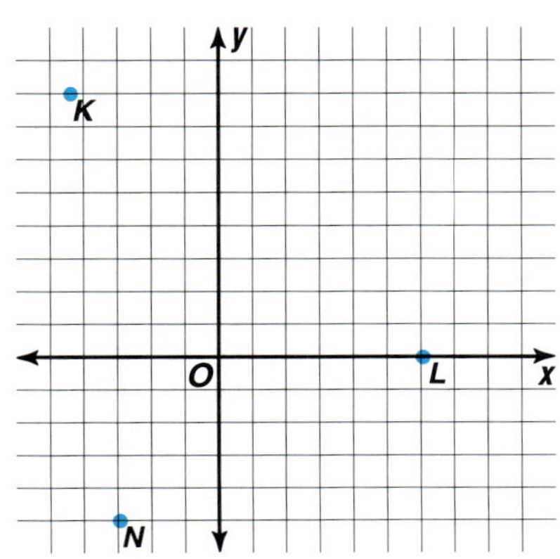

b. $K(-4.5, 8)$

Start at the origin, *O.* Move left 4.5 units and up 8 units. Draw a dot and label it *K.*

c. $L(6, 0)$

Start at the origin, *O.* Move right 6 units. Since the *y*-coordinate is 0, the point will be located on the *x*-axis. Draw the dot and label it *L.*

Each point in the coordinate plane can be named by exactly one ordered pair, and each ordered pair names exactly one point in the plane. Thus, there is a one-to-one correspondence between points and ordered pairs.

Completeness Property for Points in the Plane	**1. Exactly one point in the plane is named by a given ordered pair of numbers.** **2. Exactly one ordered pair of numbers names a given point in the plane.**

On city and state maps, letters and numbers are usually used to locate landmarks on the map. The number representing the horizontal coordinate is usually listed first followed by the letter representing the vertical coordinate. However, unlike the coordinate plane where a specific point is denoted by the ordered pair, the coordinates on a map define a region or sector in which the landmark is located.

FYI

César-François Cassini, who was born in Thury, France, in 1714, was the first cartographer to create a map according to modern principles. In 1744, he directed the first National Geographic survey, the triangulation of France.

Example 3 APPLICATION **Cartography**

Use ordered pairs to name all of the sectors that Interstate Highway 35 passes through on the map of San Antonio, Texas, shown below.

I-35 begins in the southwest corner and extends through San Antonio to the northeast corner. Part of it shares the same path as I-410.

I-35 goes through $(1, D)$, continuing through $(2, D)$, across the southeast corner of $(2, C)$, turning upward through $(3, C)$, across the southern portion of $(3, B)$, sharing the path with I-410 through $(4, B)$, and exiting the map at the eastern edge of $(4, A)$.

CHECK FOR UNDERSTANDING

Communicating Mathematics

Study the lesson. Then complete the following.

1. **Draw** a coordinate plane. Label the origin, *x*-axis, *y*-axis, and the quadrants.
2. **Explain** how you can tell which quadrant a point is in by just looking at the signs of its coordinates.

MODELING MATHEMATICS

3. **Copy or sketch** a map of the major thoroughfares in your community. Using a different color, draw a coordinate system on the map, making your home the origin. Find the coordinates of your school, a library, a shopping center or department store, and your favorite restaurant.

Guided Practice

Write the ordered pair for each point shown at the right. Name the quadrant in which the point is located.

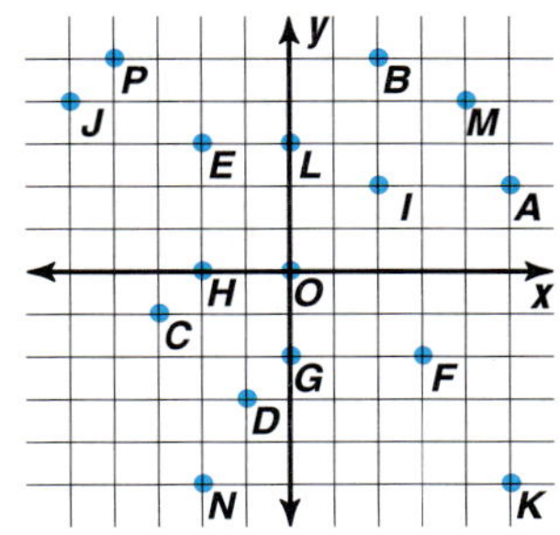

4. A
5. C
6. E
7. G

Graph each point.

8. $W(-5, 0)$
9. $X(-3, -4)$
10. $Y(3, -5)$
11. $Z(0, 4)$
12. Write the ordered pair that describes a point 15 units up from and 13 units to the left of the origin.

EXERCISES

Practice

Refer to the coordinate plane for Exercises 4–7. Write the ordered pair for each point. Name the quadrant in which the point is located.

13. D
14. H
15. L
16. P
17. O
18. K
19. F
20. B
21. I
22. M
23. J
24. N

Graph each point.

25. $A(2, -1)$
26. $B(-3, -3)$
27. $C(0, 3.5)$
28. $D(5, -2)$
29. $E(-3, 0)$
30. $F(3, 5)$
31. $G(-3, -4)$
32. $H(-5, -2)$
33. $I(0, -2)$
34. $J(-\frac{1}{2}, 1)$
35. $K(4, 0)$
36. $L(4, 2)$

Graph each point. Then connect the points in alphabetical order and identify the figure.

37. $A(2, 0)$, $B(2, 3)$, $C(1, 3)$, $D(-0.5, -1)$, $E(-2, 3)$, $F(-3, 3)$, $G(-3, -3)$, $H(-2, -3)$, $I(-2, 0)$, $J(-0.5, -3)$, $K(1, 0)$, $L(1, -3)$, $M(2, -3)$, $N(2, 0)$
38. $A(9, 0.5)$, $B(5, 1)$, $C(2, 1)$, $D(-1, 5)$, $E(-2, 5)$, $F(-1, 1)$, $G(-4, 1)$, $H(-5, 3)$, $I(-6, 3)$, $J(-5.5, 1)$, $K(-5.5, 0)$, $L(-6, -2)$, $M(-5, -2)$, $N(-4, 0)$, $P(-1, 0)$, $Q(-2, -4)$, $R(-1, -4)$, $S(2, 0)$, $T(5, 0)$, $U(9, 0.5)$

Programming

39. The graphing calculator program at the right will plot a group of points on the same coordinate plane. You will need to set an appropriate window so that you will be able to see all of the points. After each point is plotted, press [ENTER] to plot another point. To end the program, press [2nd] [QUIT] while you are at the home screen. Use this program to check the points you plotted in Exercises 37 and 38.

```
PROGRAM:PLOTPTS
:ClrDraw
:Lbl 1
:Prompt X,Y
:Pt-On(X,Y)
:Pause
:Goto 1
```

Critical Thinking

40. Describe the possible locations, in terms of quadrants or axes, for the graph of (x, y) if x and y satisfy the given conditions.

a. $xy > 0$ **b.** $xy < 0$ **c.** $xy = 0$

Applications and Problem Solving

41. **Geography** On a map of the United States, degrees of longitude and latitude can be used to form ordered pairs that name points on the map. Longitude lines run north and south and should be the first coordinates of the ordered pairs. Latitude lines run east and west and should be the second coordinates of the ordered pairs. (On this map, the numbers showing degrees of longitude are listed along the horizontal axis, and those showing degrees of latitude are listed along the vertical axis.)

a. Name the city at $(90°, 30°)$.

b. Name the state in which $(120°, 45°)$ is located.

c. Estimate the latitude and longitude of our nation's capital to the nearest 5°.

d. What state capital has its location at $(157°, 21°)$?

e. What is the approximate latitude and longitude of your community?

f. Look at the longitude and latitude lines on a globe and compare them to the ones shown on this map. What do you find?

42. Tourism Diana works for a travel agency and has been asked to highlight key landmarks on a map of the Miami area for a customer. Use the map of Miami at the left to answer the following questions.

a. What causeway is in sector (3, M)?

b. In what sector is the city of Coral Gables?

c. Which interstate goes from sector (2, L) to (2, O)?

d. Name all of the sectors through which Highway 826 passes.

43. Draw a Diagram Make a seating chart of the desks in your mathematics classroom. Create a coordinate plane on your diagram so that each desk corresponds to an ordered pair in the plane.

a. What are the coordinates of your desk in the room?

b. Name another student in your class. What is the coordinate of this person's desk?

Mixed Review

44. If y varies directly as x, and $y = 3$ when $x = 15$, find y when $x = -25$. (Lesson 4–8)

45. Two trains leave York at the same time, one traveling north, the other south. The first train travels at 40 miles per hour and the second at 30 miles per hour. In how many hours will the trains be 245 miles apart? (Lesson 4–7)

46. Use a calculator to find the measure of $\angle A$ to the nearest degree if $\sin A = 0.2756$. (Lesson 4–3)

47. Find the mean, median, and mode for $\{5, 9, 1, 2, 3\}$. (Lesson 3–7)

Simplify each expression.

48. $\sqrt{\frac{16}{25}}$ (Lesson 2–8)

49. $\frac{7a + 35}{-7}$ (Lesson 2–7)

50. Agriculture Agribusiness technicians assist in the organization and management of farms. They may prepare graphs of weather data for a given region. For example, the graph at the right displays normal maximum, minimum, and mean temperatures for the region around Des Moines, Iowa. (Lesson 1–9)

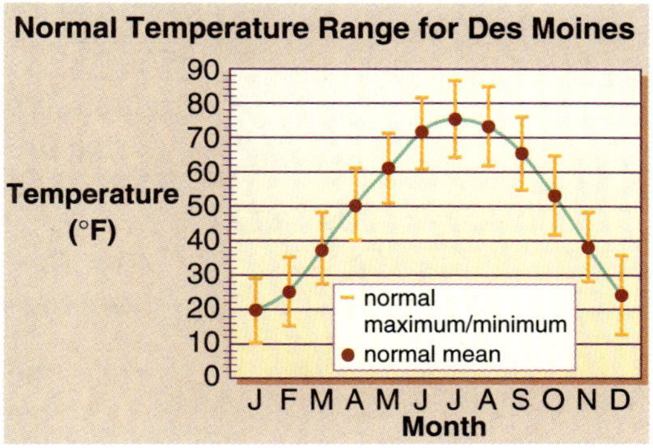

a. What is the normal maximum temperature for October?

b. What is the normal range of temperatures for May?

51. Simplify $7(5a + 3b) - 4a$. (Lesson 1–8)

5–2A Graphing Technology
Relations

A Preview of Lesson 5–2

A **relation** is a set of ordered pairs. You can graph a relation using a graphing calculator. Points can be plotted on the coordinate plane using the DRAW menu.

If you press 2nd DRAW ▶ *1 before pressing* GRAPH *, the prompt Pt-On(appears. To plot a point from this prompt, enter the coordinates of the point, a closing parenthesis, and* ENTER *. Then proceed with the cursor for the other points.*

Example 1 **Plot the following points on a coordinate plane: $M(4, 7)$, $A(-10, 25)$, $T(-17, -17)$, and $H(23, -11)$.**

Begin with a viewing window of $[-47, 47]$ by $[-31, 31]$ using a scale of 10 for each axis. This can be done quickly by entering ZOOM 6 ZOOM 8 ENTER. *This sets the scale to integer values.*

Clear the coordinate plane by turning off all stat plots and clearing the Y= list.

- To plot the first point, enter GRAPH 2nd DRAW ▶ 1. *The cursor appears at the origin and X = 0 and Y = 0 appears at the bottom of the screen.*
- Now use the arrow keys to move the cursor to the coordinates of the point you wish to graph. *The coordinates of each position of the cursor appear at the bottom of the viewing screen.*
- Press ENTER to put a dot at that point.

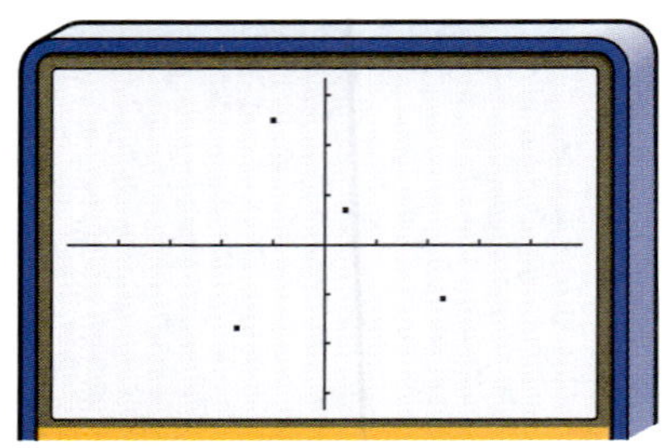

- Continue to move the cursor and press ENTER to graph the other three points.
- When finished, you can clear the screen by pressing 2nd DRAW 1.

If you do not need a range as great as the one you get by pressing ZOOM 8, you can set the WINDOW values in the usual manner or press ZOOM 6. Once you set your new window and try the method shown in Example 1, you will find that you cannot plot points at exact integer values by using the cursor. However, there is another way to plot exact points.

Example 2 **Plot $G(-4, 5)$, $R(1, 6)$, $A(-3, -6)$, $P(5, -8)$, and $H(0, 7)$ in the standard viewing window.**

- Set the standard viewing window. **Enter:** ZOOM 6
- Return to the home screen by pressing 2nd QUIT.
- You can graph all of the points by linking commands into a series using a colon.

Enter: 2nd DRAW ▶ 1 *Pt-On(appears on the screen.*

(–) 4 [,] 5 [)] [2nd] [:]

This enters the first point. Now repeat the steps without pressing ENTER to enter all the other points. Finally, press [ENTER] to graph the points.

Enter: [2nd] [DRAW] [▶] 1 1 [,] 6 [)] [2nd] [:] [2nd] [DRAW] [▶] 1 [(–)] 3 [,] [(–)] 6 [)] [2nd] [:] [2nd] [DRAW] [▶] 1 5 [,] [(–)] 8 [)] [2nd] [:] [2nd] [DRAW] [▶] 1 0 [,] 7 [)] [ENTER]

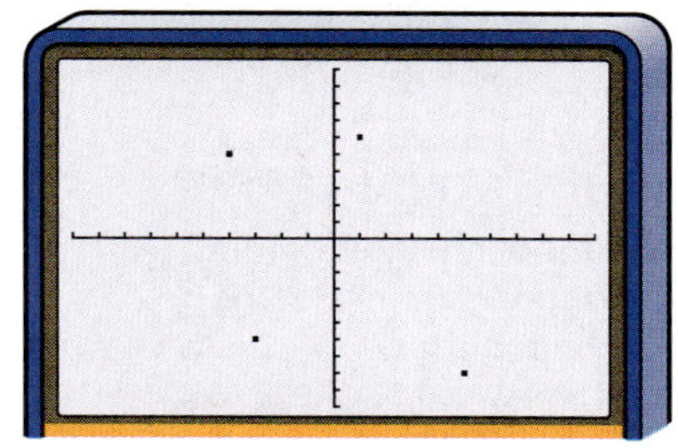

You can also use the Line(feature on the DRAW menu to connect the points. This can help you analyze the points in a relation. You must first clear the screen by pressing [2nd] [DRAW] 1 [ENTER] before beginning a new graph.

Example 3 **Determine if the graphs of (3, 5), (−3, −5), and (0, 7) are on the same line.**

If you connect the points and only a segment appears, the three points are probably on the same line.

Enter: [2nd] [DRAW] 2 3 [,] 5 [,] [(–)] 3 [,] [(–)] 5 [)] [2nd] [:] [2nd] [DRAW] 2 [(–)] 3 [,] [(–)] 5 [,] 0 [,] 7 [)] [2nd] [:] [2nd] [DRAW] 2 3 [,] 5 [,] 0 [,] 7 [)] [ENTER]

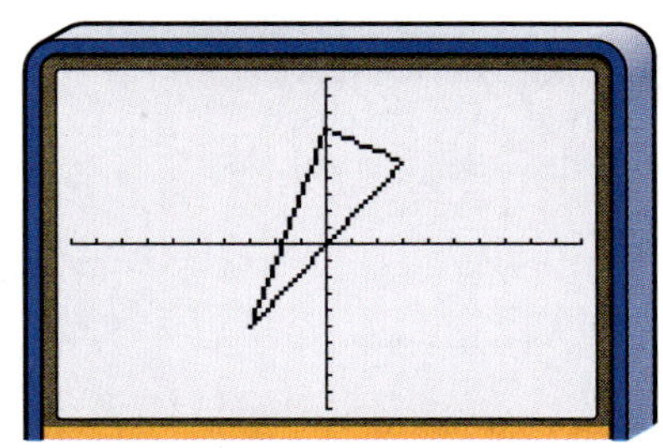

Because the resulting figure is a triangle, the three points are not on the same line.

EXERCISES

Use a graphing calculator to plot each point in the viewing window [−47, 47] by [−31, 31].

1. $X(10, 10)$
2. $Y(0, -6)$
3. $Z(-26, 11)$
4. $Q(-17, -19)$
5. $T(-21, 4)$
6. $P(-20, 0)$
7. Explain why, when you graph the points in Exercises 2 and 6, you do not see them on the screen.
8. a. Plot $H(9, 9)$ and $J(29, 9)$.
   b. Find two additional points E and F so that these four points form the vertices of a square. Are there other possible coordinates of E and F?
   c. Plot E and F to complete the square.

TECHNOLOGY Tip

To make your graph look like a square, press [ZOOM] 5 after setting the window and before using DRAW.

5–2 Relations

What **YOU'LL LEARN**

- To identify the domain, range, and inverse of a relation, and
- to show relations as sets of ordered pairs, tables, mappings, and graphs.

Why **IT'S IMPORTANT**

You can use relations to solve problems involving economics and probability.

CONNECTION

Biology

There are 1.4 million classified species of microorganisms, invertebrates, plants, fish, birds, reptiles, amphibians, and mammals. Currently, 930 species worldwide have been listed as *endangered.* A species becomes endangered when its numbers are so low that the species is in danger of extinction.

In the United States, the manatee, an aquatic mammal, is considered to be endangered. Although manatees were once common throughout the coastal areas of North America, they now live mainly in Florida. In the table below, you will find the number of manatees that have been found dead since 1976.

FYI

The U.S. Congress passed the Rare and Endangered Species Act in 1966, setting up rules by which the Fish and Wildlife Service can list and protect species in danger of extinction.

What is the trend over time?

Manatee Mortality In Florida

Year	1976	1977	1978	1979	1980	1981	1982	1983	1984
Number of Manatees	62	114	84	77	63	116	114	81	128
Year	**1985**	**1986**	**1987**	**1988**	**1989**	**1990**	**1991**	**1992**	**1993**
Number of Manatees	119	122	114	133	168	206	174	163	145

Source: Florida Marine Research Institute

The manatee data could also be represented by a set of ordered pairs, as shown in the list below. Each first coordinate is the year, and the second coordinate is the number of manatees. Each ordered pair can then be graphed.

{(1976, 62), (1977, 114), (1978, 84), (1979, 77), (1980, 63), (1981, 116), (1982, 114), (1983, 81), (1984, 128), (1985, 119), (1986, 122), (1987, 114), (1988, 133), (1989, 168), (1990, 206), (1991, 174), (1992, 163), (1993, 145)}

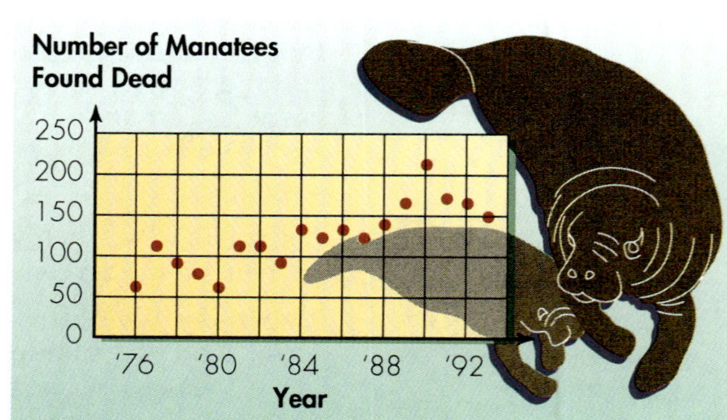

Recall that a *relation* is a set of ordered pairs, like the one shown on the previous page. The set of first coordinates of the ordered pairs is called the *domain* of the relation. The domain usually contains the x-coordinates. The set of second coordinates is called the *range* of the relation. It usually contains the y-coordinates.

Definition of the Domain and Range of a Relation

The domain of a relation is the set of all first coordinates from the ordered pairs in the relation. The range of the relation is the set of all second coordinates from the ordered pairs.

For the relation representing the manatee data, the domain and range are as follows.

Domain = {1976, 1977, 1978, 1979, 1980, 1981, 1982, 1983, 1984, 1985, 1986, 1987, 1988, 1989, 1990, 1991, 1992, 1993}

Range = {62, 114, 84, 77, 63, 116, 81, 128, 119, 122, 133, 168, 206, 174, 163, 145}

An element is a member of a set.

In addition to ordered pairs, tables, and graphs, a relation can be represented by a **mapping.** A mapping illustrates how each element of the domain is paired with an element in the range. For example, the relation {(3, 3), (−1, 4), (0, −4)} can be modeled in each of the following ways.

Ordered Pairs

(3, 3)
(−1, 4)
(0, −4)

Table

x	y
3	3
−1	4
0	−4

Graph

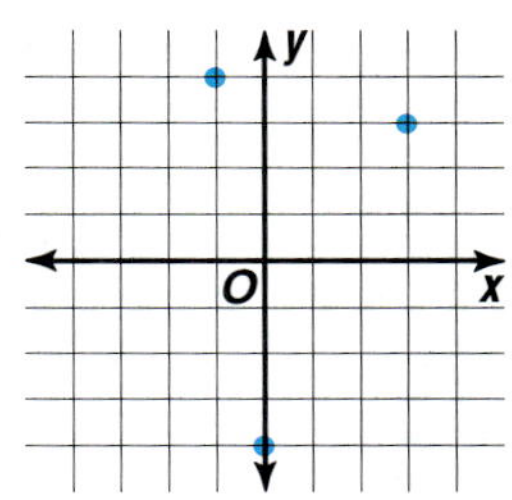

Mapping

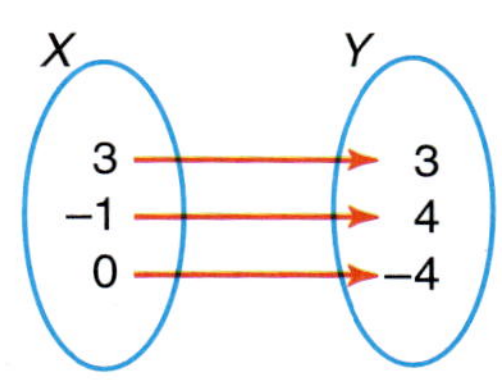

Example 1

Represent the relation shown in the graph at the right as

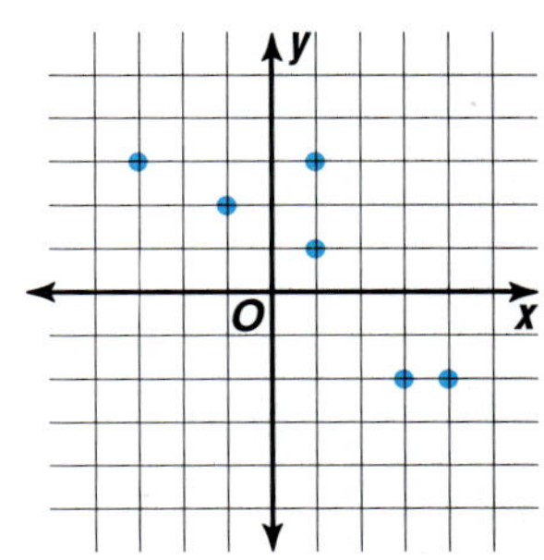

a. a set of ordered pairs,

b. a table, and

c. a mapping.

d. Then determine the domain and range.

a. The set of ordered pairs for the relation is
{(−3, 3), (−1, 2), (1, 1), (1, 3), (3, −2), (4, −2)}.

b.

x	y
−3	3
−1	2
1	1
1	3
3	−2
4	−2

c.

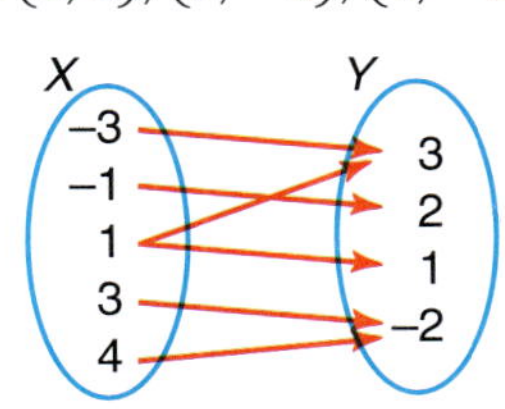

When giving the domain and range, if a value is repeated, you list it only once.

d. The domain for this relation is {−3, −1, 1, 3, 4}, and the range is {−2, 1, 2, 3}.

In real-life situations, you may need to select a range of values for the x- or y-axis that does not begin with 0 and does not have units of 1.

Example 2

CONNECTION

Biology

In order to protect endangered species, there is a limit to the number of animals that can be exported to other countries. The table below shows yearly quotas for the number of wild crocodiles that can be exported from Indonesia.

a. Determine the domain and range of the relation.

b. Graph the data.

c. What conclusions might you make from the graph of the data?

Maximum Exportation of Crocodiles from Indonesia									
Year	1986	1987	1988	1989	1990	1991	1992	1993	1994
Number of Crocodiles	2000	2000	4000	4000	3000	3000	2700	1500	1500

Source: *Traffic USA,* World Wildlife Fund, August 1992

a. The domain is {1986, 1987, 1988, 1989, 1990, 1991, 1992, 1993, 1994}. The range is {1500, 2000, 2700, 3000, 4000}.

Values are usually listed in numerical order.

b. The values for the x-axis need to go from 1986 to 1994. It is not efficient to begin the scale at 0. The values on the y-axis need to include values from 1500 to 4000. You can include 0 and use units of 500.

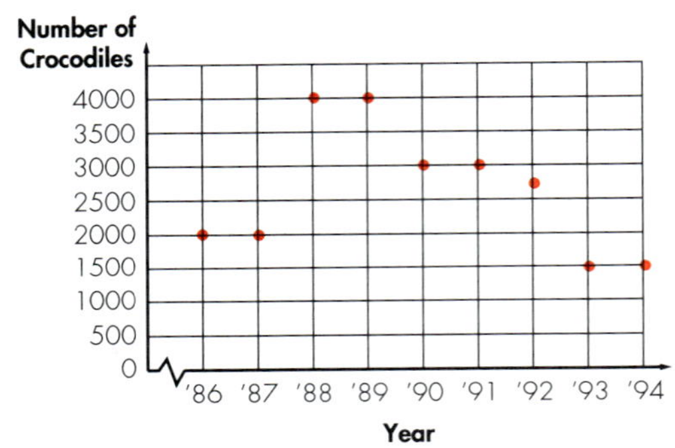

A jagged line is used to represent the values prior to 1986 that have been omitted.

c. While the number of crocodiles that could be exported rose in 1988, it has decreased since 1991. This may indicate that crocodiles in Indonesia are even more endangered.

CAREER CHOICES

A **zoologist** studies animals, their origin, life process, behavior, and diseases. They are usually identified by the animal group in which they specialize, for example herpetology (reptiles), ornithology (birds), and ichthyology (fish).

Zoology requires a minimum of a bachelor's degree. Many college positions in this field require a Ph.D. degree.

For more information, contact:

Occupational Outlook Handbook, 1994–95, U.S. Department of Labor.

The **inverse** of any relation is obtained by switching the coordinates in each ordered pair.

Relation	Inverse
(1, 4)	(4, 1)
(−3, 2)	(2, −3)
(7, −9)	(−9, 7)

Notice that the domain of the relation becomes the range of the inverse. Similarly, the range of the relation becomes the domain of the inverse.

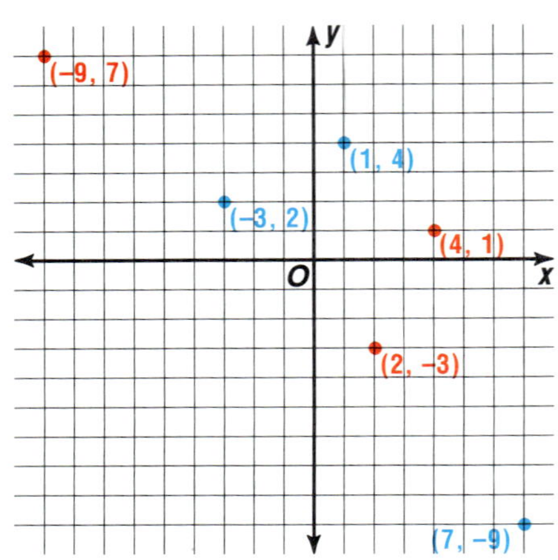

Definition of the Inverse of a Relation	Relation Q is the inverse of relation S if and only if for every ordered pair (a, b) in S, there is an ordered pair (b, a) in Q.

Example 3 **Express the relation shown in the mapping as a set of ordered pairs. Write the inverse of the relation and draw a mapping to model the inverse.**

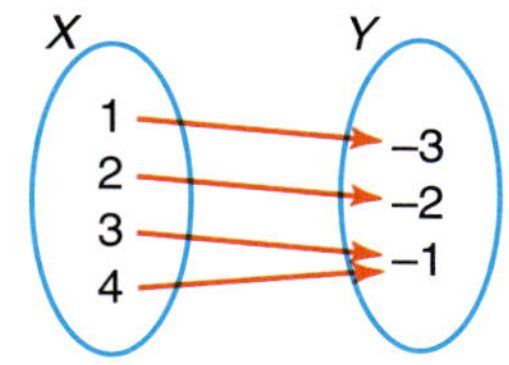

The mapping shows the relation $\{(1, -3), (2, -2), (3, -1), (4, -1)\}$.

The inverse of the relation is $\{(-3, 1), (-2, 2), (-1, 3), (-1, 4)\}$.

The mapping at the right shows the inverse.

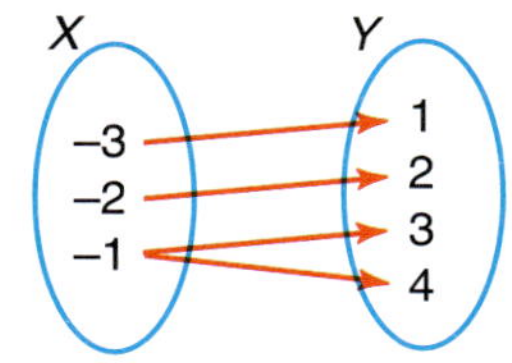

Relations and their inverses display some interesting characteristics, as you will discover below.

MODELING MATHEMATICS: Relations and Inverses

Materials: grid paper, straightedge, colored pencils

There is a special relationship between a relation and its inverse, which you can discover by paper folding.

Step 1 Graph the relation $\{(4, 5), (-3, 6), (-5, -3), (4, -7), (5, 0), (0, -3)\}$ on a coordinate plane using one color of pencil.

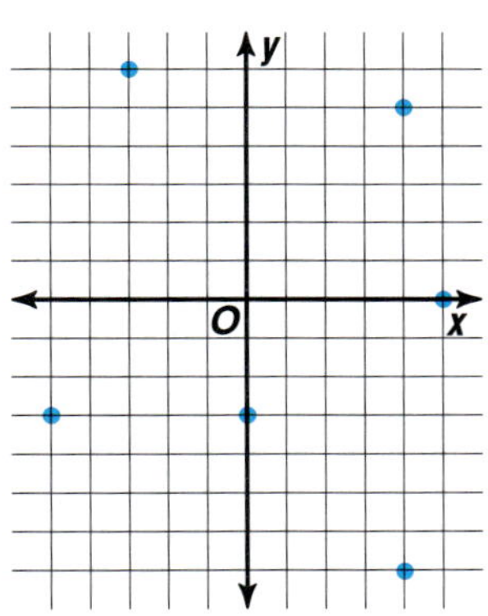

Connect the points in order using the same color pencil.

Step 2 Use a different color pencil to graph the inverse of the relation, connecting its points in order.

Step 3 Fold the graph paper through the origin so that the positive y-axis lies on top of the positive x-axis. Hold the paper up to a light so that you can see all of the points you graphed.

Your Turn

a. What do you notice about the location of the points you graphed when you looked at the folded paper?

b. Unfold the paper. Describe the pattern formed by the lines connecting the points in the relation and its inverse.

c. What do you think are the ordered pairs that represent the points on the fold line? Describe these in terms of x and y.

d. How could you graph the inverse of a function without writing ordered pairs first?

CHECK FOR UNDERSTANDING

Communicating Mathematics

Study the lesson. Then complete the following.

1. **Explain** why it is important to identify the domain and range values of a relation when graphing the relation.
2. Refer to the application at the beginning of the lesson. Explain what the manatee graph suggests about patterns in the rate of manatee deaths.
3. **State** the relationship between the domain and range of a relation and the domain and range of its inverse.

MODELING MATHEMATICS

4. Graph the relation $\{(0, 5), (2, 3), (1, -4), (-3, 3), (-1, -2)\}$. Draw a line that goes through the points $(-3, -3)$ and $(3, 3)$. Use this line to graph the inverse of the relation without writing the ordered pairs of the inverse.

Guided Practice

State the domain and range of each relation.

5. $\{(0, 2), (1, -2), (2, 4)\}$

6. $\{(-4, 2), (-2, 0), (0, 2), (2, 4)\}$

Express the relation shown in each table, mapping, or graph as a set of ordered pairs. Then state the domain, range, and inverse of the relation.

7.

x	y
1	3
2	4
3	5
5	7

8.

x	y
1	4
3	−2
4	4
6	−2

9.

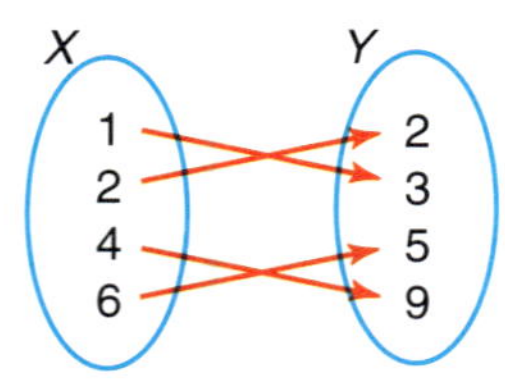

10.

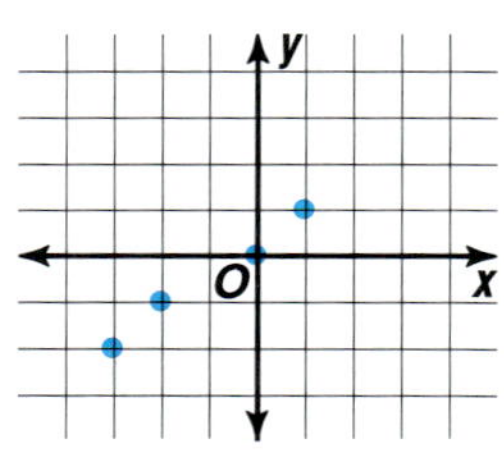

11.

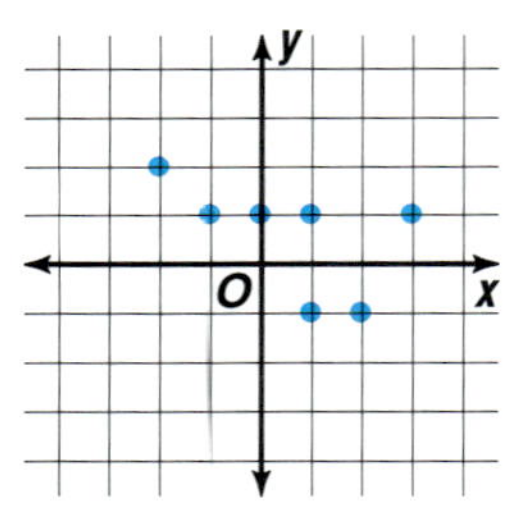

12–14. Graph the relations shown in Exercises 7–9.

15. **Economics** The graph at the right shows the unemployment rate in the United States from January 1992 to December 1994.
    a. Name three ordered pairs shown by the graph.
    b. Estimate the least value in the range.
    c. What conclusions might you make from the graph?

U.S. Unemployment Rate 1992–1994

EXERCISES

Practice

State the domain and range of each relation.

16. $\{(1, 3), (2, 5), (1, -7), (2, 9), (3, 3)\}$

17. $\{(1, 7), (-2, 7), (3, 7), (-5, 7)\}$

18. $\{3.1, -1), (-4.7, 3.9), (2.4, -3.6), (-9, 2)\}$

19. $\left\{\left(\frac{1}{2}, \frac{1}{4}\right), \left(1\frac{1}{2}, -\frac{2}{3}\right), \left(-3, \frac{2}{5}\right), \left(-5\frac{1}{4}, -6\frac{2}{7}\right)\right\}$

Express the relation shown in each table, mapping, or graph as a set of ordered pairs. Then state the domain, range, and inverse of the relation.

20.

x	y
0	4
1	5
2	6
3	6

21.

x	y
6	4
4	−2
3	4
1	−2

22.

x	y
−4	2
−2	0
0	2
2	4

23.

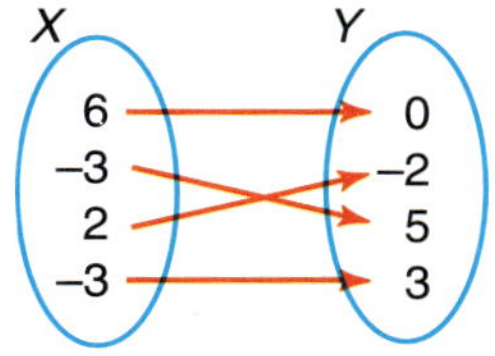

24.

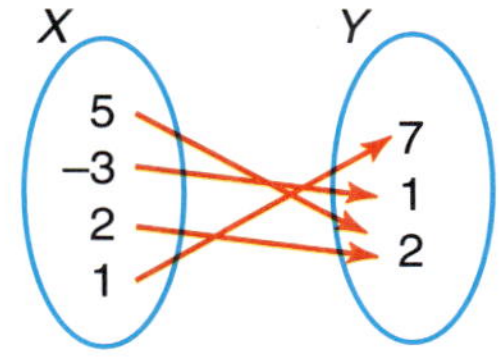

25.

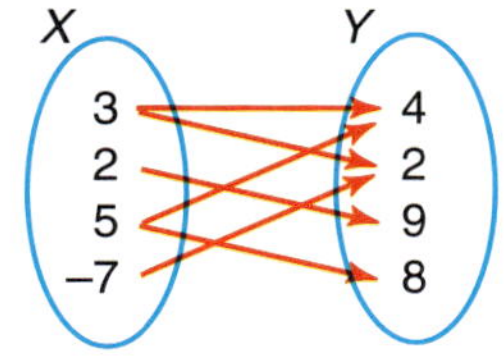

26. temperature of boiled water as it cools

time (minutes)	0	5	10	15	20	25	30
temperature (°C)	100	90	81	73	66	60	55

27. cost of car repairs

time (hours)	0	1	2	3
cost (dollars)	25	50	75	100

28. distance traveled at a rate of 55 mph

time (hours)	1.25	3.75	4.5	5.5	6
distance (miles)	68.75	206.25	247.5	302.5	330

29.

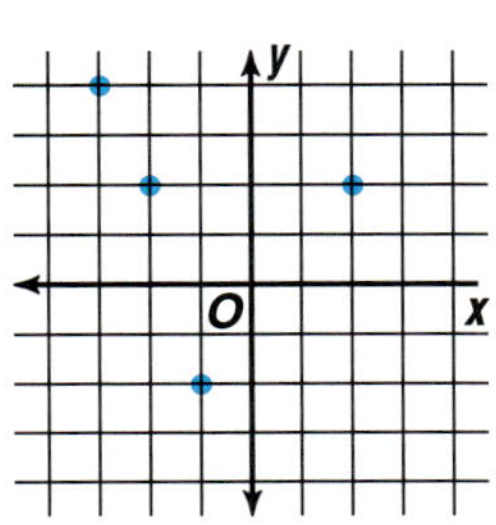

30.

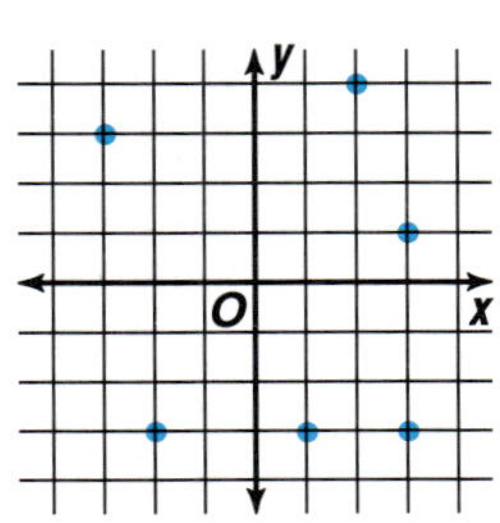

31.

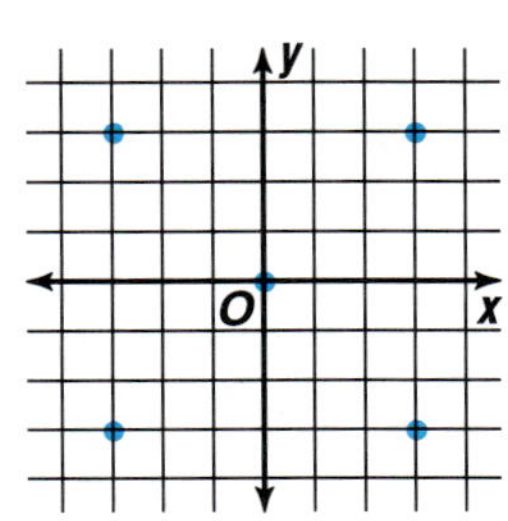

32.

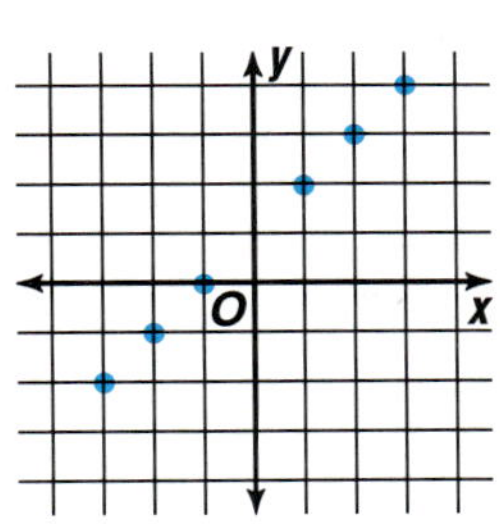

33.

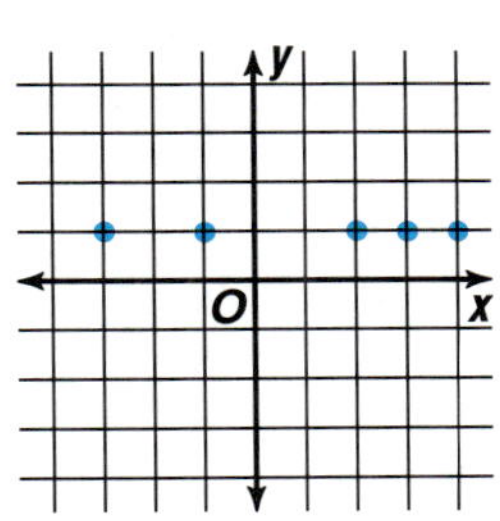

34.

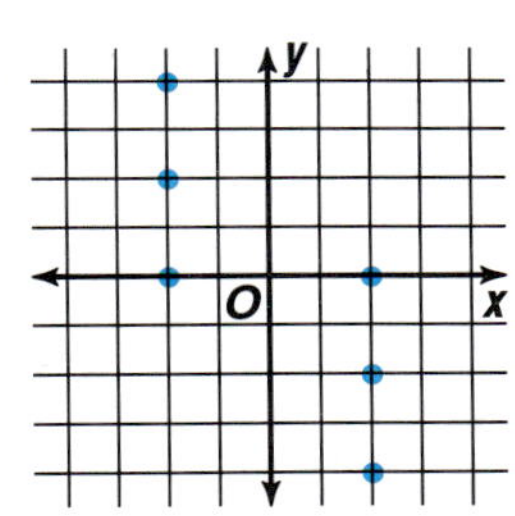

Draw a mapping and a graph for each relation.

35. $\{(8, 2), (4, 2), (8, -9), (7, 5), (-3, 2)\}$

36. $\{(3, 3), (2, 7), (-3, 3), (1, 3), (4, 1)\}$

37. $\{(6, 0), (6, -4), (4, -3), (5, -3)\}$

Graphing Calculator

Graph each relation on a graphing calculator.

a. **State the WINDOW settings that you used.**

b. **Write the coordinates of the inverse. Then graph the inverse.**

c. **Name the quadrants in which each point of the relation and its inverse lies.**

38.

x	y
1992	77
1993	200
1994	550
1995	880

39.

x	y
0	10
2	−8
6	6
9	−4

40.

x	y
−1	18
−2	23
−3	28
−4	33

41. Review your answers to part c of Exercises 38–40. What conclusions can you draw about the quadrant in which the inverse of a point will lie?

Critical Thinking

42. Write a relation with five ordered pairs such that the relation is its own inverse. Then describe the graph of the relation and its inverse.

Applications and Problem Solving

43. **Retail Sales** The graph at the right shows U.S. retail sales in billions of dollars. The amounts for each month have been adjusted to account for seasonal increases in sales.

a. Approximate the least and greatest values in the range.

b. In your own words, describe what the pattern formed by the points represents.

c. Compare this graph with the one in Exercise 15. How do you think unemployment rates might be compared with retail spending trends? Explain.

U.S. Retail Sales 1992–1994 (billions of dollars)

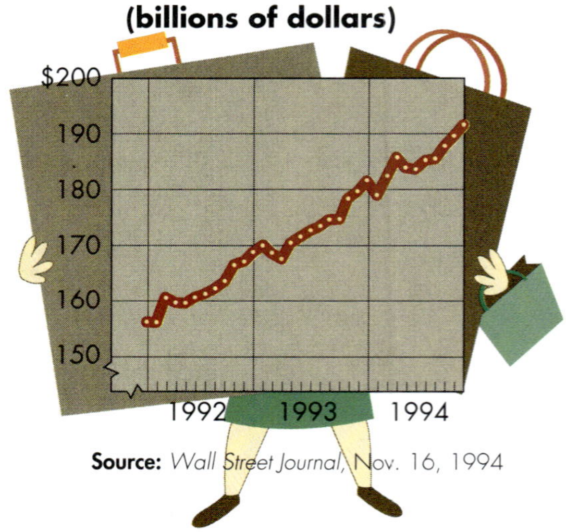

Source: *Wall Street Journal*, Nov. 16, 1994

44. **Make a Table** Mandy Chin is saving money to pay for the first year of her car insurance, which will cost about \$1200. She already has \$500 in her savings account. She gets a job working at a fast-food restaurant and plans to save \$45 per week.

a. Make a table to show the number of weeks and how much money Mandy will have in her account after each week. For example, on Week 1, she will have \$545. Graph the results.

b. When will she have enough money to pay her insurance premium?

45. **Probability** There are 36 different possible outcomes when you roll two dice. The outcomes can be expressed as ordered pairs, such as (4, 3).
   a. Graph all 36 possible outcomes. What is the domain and range?
   b. What is the domain and range of the inverse? What do you notice about the relation and its inverse?
   c. How many different sums are possible when two dice are rolled? Draw a line plot showing how many ways each sum can be rolled. Describe your line plot.
   d. Graph the outcomes that have a sum of 7.
   e. What is the probability of rolling a sum of 7? Explain.

Mixed Review

46. Graph $A(6, 2)$, $B(-3, 6)$, and $C(-5, -4)$ on the same coordinate plane. (Lesson 5–1)

47. If y varies inversely as x, and $y = 8$ when $x = 24$, find y when $x = 6$. (Lesson 4–8)

48. **Entertainment** At Backintime Cinema, tickets for adults cost \$5.75 and tickets for children cost \$3.75. How many of each kind of ticket were purchased if 16 tickets were bought for \$68? (Lesson 4–7)

49. Use $I = prt$ to find I if $p = \$8000$, $r = 6\%$, and $t = 1$ year. (Lesson 4–4)

50. Solve $E = mc^2$ for m. (Lesson 3–6)

51. **Space Science** Halley's Comet flashes through the sky every 76.3 years. It last appeared in 1986. In what year of the 23rd century is Halley's Comet expected to reappear? (Lesson 2–6)

52. **Agriculture** Refer to the graph in Exercise 50 on page 259. (Lesson 1–9)
   a. What is the normal minimum temperature for March?
   b. What happens to the temperature after July?

53. Simplify $4[1 + 4(5x + 2y)]$. (Lesson 1–8)

WORKING ON THE In·ves·ti·ga·tion

Refer to the Investigation on pages 190–191.

In tracking populations of fish, the Department of Natural Resources and Wildlife often chart their findings in a graph. They use these graphs to monitor the populations of the different types of fish. In this way they track which species are on the increase and which are in decline. This can be especially important in monitoring species that are rare or in danger of extinction.

1. Use the information in your chart to make a table of ordered pairs (x, y) such that x represents the number of the casting and y represents your estimate for the number of fish in the lake.
2. Draw a mapping for this relation.
3. Graph the ordered pairs on a coordinate grid. Describe the graph.

Add the results of your work to your Investigation Folder.

5–3A Graphing Technology
Equations

A Preview of Lesson 5–3

Ordered pairs can be used to represent solutions to equations in two variables. Thus, the solution set of an equation for a defined domain is a relation. We can use a graphing calculator to investigate the relation and determine the range when the domain is given.

Example **Solve $y = 2.5x + 4$ if the domain is $\{-8, -6, -4, -2, 0, 2, 4, 6, 8\}$.**

Method 1

Store the elements of the domain as a list of values in L1.

Enter: [2nd] [{] [(–)] 8 [,] [(–)] 6 [,] [(–)] 4 [,] [(–)] 2 [,] 0 [,] 2 [,] 4 [,] 6 [,] 8 [2nd] [}] [STO▸] [2nd] [L1] [ENTER]   {-8 -6 -4 -2 0 ...

To calculate the range values, compute the right-hand side of the equation, substituting L1 for x.

Enter: 2.5 [2nd] [L1] [+] 4 [ENTER]   {-16 -11 -6 -1 ...

Press the arrow keys to scroll right or left through the display to see all the values in the range.

The solution set is $\{(-8, -16), (-6, -11), (-4, -6), (-2, -1), (0, 4), (2, 9), (4, 14), (6, 19), (8, 24)\}$.

Method 2

Store the equation in the Y= menu of the calculator and view the table of values it creates.

Enter: [Y=] 2.5 [X,T,θ,n] [+] 4 [2nd] [TblSet] [(–)] 8 [ENTER] 2 [2nd] [TABLE]

ΔTbl means the increments in which the x values will appear in the table.

A table with columns X and Y_1 appears on the screen. The values in the Y_1 column represent the corresponding range values for each x value in the domain. This table helps you find the ordered pairs that are solutions for the equation. The solution set is $\{(-8, -16), (-6, -11), (-4, -6), (-2, -1), (0, 4), (2, 9), (4, 14), (6, 19), (8, 24)\}$, which agrees with the list in Method 1.

EXERCISES

Use a graphing calculator to solve each equation if the domain is $\{-3, -2, -1, 0, 1, 2, 3\}$.

1. $y = 4x - 7$ **2.** $y = x^2 + 11$ **3.** $1.2x - y = 6.8$ **4.** $6x + 2y = 12$

5–3 Equations as Relations

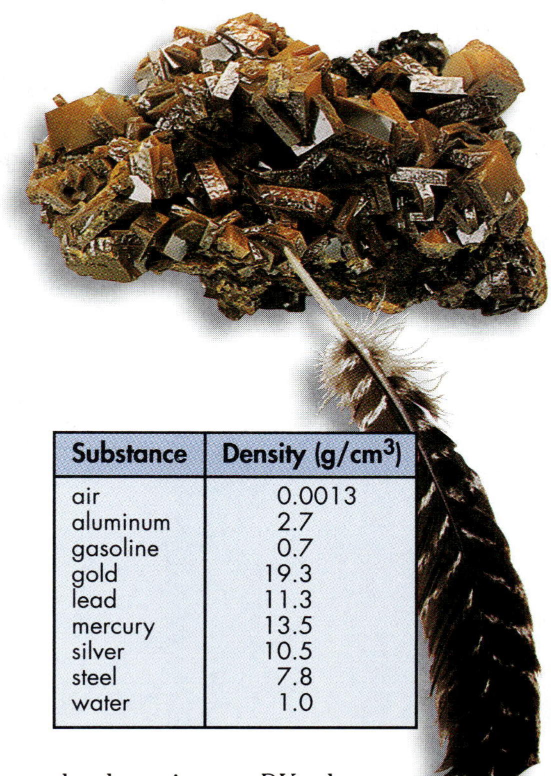

What YOU'LL LEARN

- To determine the range for a given domain, and
- to graph the solution set for the given domain.

Why IT'S IMPORTANT

You can use equations to explore the relations in physical science and anatomy.

CONNECTION

Physical Science

Are you as "light" as a feather or as "heavy" as a rock? The *density* of an object is the measure of its "lightness" or "heaviness." Density is defined as the mass per unit of volume. The chart at the right shows the densities of some common substances.

Substance	Density (g/cm^3)
air	0.0013
aluminum	2.7
gasoline	0.7
gold	19.3
lead	11.3
mercury	13.5
silver	10.5
steel	7.8
water	1.0

FYI

Water has a density of 1.0. Any substance with a density less than 1.0 will float in water. Any substance with a density greater than 1.0 will sink in water.

An equation relating density, mass, and volume is $m = DV$, where m is the mass of a substance, D is the density, and V is the volume. For example, the equation for gold is $m = 19.3V$ because the density of gold is 19.3 g/cm^3. This equation is called an **equation in two variables,** m and V.

No one knows exactly when gold was first discovered. However, there have been gold artifacts dug up in Ur in Mesopotamia (modern day Iraq) that date as early as 3500 B.C. Suppose we wanted to know the mass of four gold artifacts with volumes of 10 cm^3, 50 cm^3, 100 cm^3, and 150 cm^3. We can use a table to find ordered pairs (V, m) that satisfy the equation.

V	$D \cdot V$	m	Ordered Pair
10	19.3(10)	193	(10, 193)
50	19.3(50)	965	(50, 965)
100	19.3(100)	1930	(100, 1930)
150	19.3(150)	2895	(150, 2895)

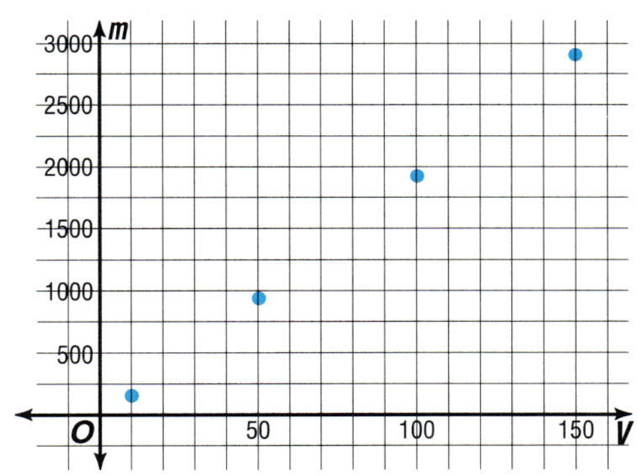

These four ordered pairs are graphed at the right. Since each ordered pair satisfies the equation, each ordered pair is a solution of the equation.

Definition of the Solution of an Equation in Two Variables	If a true statement results when the numbers in an ordered pair are substituted into an equation in two variables, then the ordered pair is a solution of the equation.

Since the solutions of an equation in two variables are ordered pairs, such an equation describes a relation. In an equation involving x and y, the set of x values is the domain of the relation. The set of corresponding y values is the range of the relation.

Example 1 Solve each equation for the given domain values. Graph the solution set.

a. $y = 4x$ **if the domain is** $\{-3, -2, 0, 1, 2\}$

Make a table. The values of x come from the domain. Substitute each value of x into the equation to determine the corresponding values of y.

Domain x	$4x$	Range y	Ordered Pair (x, y)
−3	4(−3)	−12	(−3, −12)
−2	4(−2)	−8	(−2, −8)
0	4(0)	0	(0, 0)
1	4(1)	4	(1, 4)
2	4(2)	8	(2, 8)

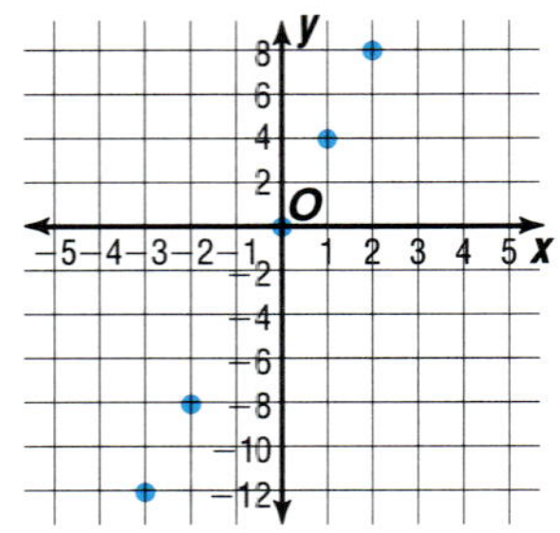

Then graph the solution set $\{(-3, -12), (-2, -8), (0, 0), (1, 4), (2, 8)\}$.

b. $y = x + 6$ **if the domain is** $\{-4, -3, -1, 2, 4\}$

Make a table. Find the values of y in the range by substituting the values of x from the domain into the equation.

x	$x + 6$	y	(x, y)
−4	−4 + 6	2	(−4, 2)
−3	−3 + 6	3	(−3, 3)
−1	−1 + 6	5	(−1, 5)
2	2 + 6	8	(2, 8)
4	4 + 6	10	(4, 10)

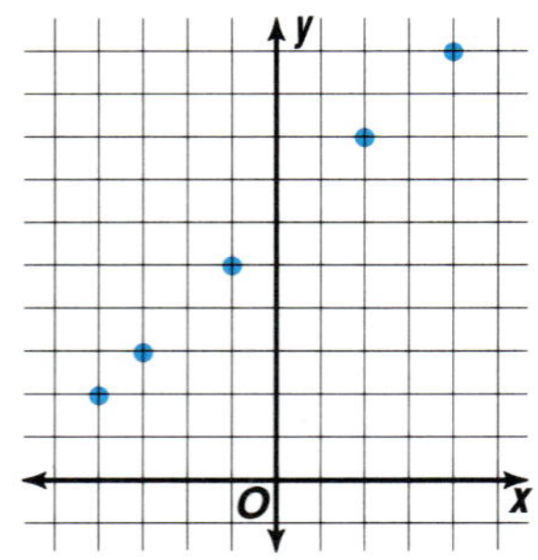

Then graph the solution set $\{(-4, 2), (-3, 3), (-1, 5), (2, 8), (4, 10)\}$.

It is often helpful to solve an equation for y before substituting each domain value into the equation. This makes creating a table of values easier.

Example 2 Solve $8x + 4y = 24$ if the domain is $\{-2, 0, 5, 8\}$.

First solve the equation for y in terms of x.

$$8x + 4y = 24$$

$$4y = 24 - 8x \quad \textit{Subtract 8x from each side.}$$

$$y = 6 - 2x \quad \textit{Divide each side by 4.}$$

Now substitute each value of x from the domain to determine the corresponding values of y in the range.

x	$6 - 2x$	y	(x, y)
−2	6 − 2(−2)	10	(−2, 10)
0	6 − 2(0)	6	(0, 6)
5	6 − 2(5)	−4	(5, −4)
8	6 − 2(8)	−10	(8, −10)

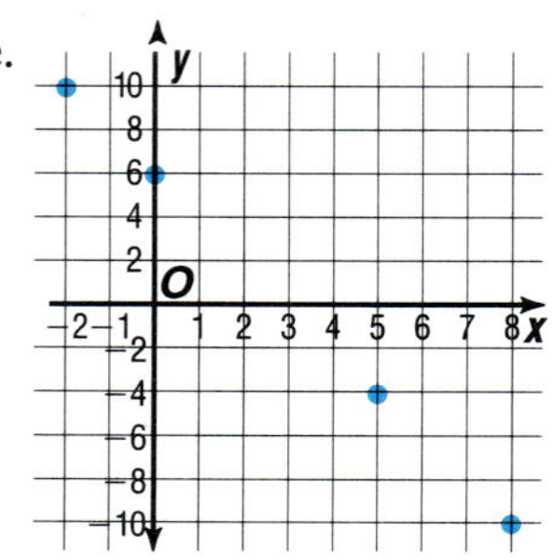

Then graph the solution set $\{(-2, 10), (0, 6), (5, -4), (8, -10)\}$.

EXPLORATION — GRAPHING CALCULATORS

You can enter selected x values in the TABLE feature of the graphing calculator, and it will calculate the corresponding y values for a given equation.

- Solve the equation for y and enter the equation into the Y= list.
- Press [2nd] [TblSet] and use the arrow keys to go to Indpnt:. Highlight Ask.
- Press [2nd] [TABLE]. Scroll up to the top of the X list. Enter the first value of the domain and press [ENTER]. The corresponding Y value appears in the second column. Enter the other values of the domain and record the range values.

Your Turn

a. Use a graphing calculator to find the corresponding y values for $y = -5x + 12$ if $x = \{-4, -2, 0, 1, 3, 5\}$. Write the solutions as ordered pairs.

b. Why do you think the Ask feature on the TABLE menu is helpful in finding the ordered pairs that are solutions for equations?

LOOK BACK

You can look back to Lesson 1-9 to review independent and dependent variables.

Variables other than x and y are often used in equations representing real situations. The domain contains values represented by the *independent variable*. Graph the domain values on the horizontal axis. The range contains the corresponding values represented by the *dependent variable*, determined by the given equation. Graph the range values on the vertical axis.

When you solve an equation for a given variable, that variable becomes the dependent variable. That is, its value depends upon the domain values chosen for the other variable.

Example 3 INTEGRATION Geometry

The equation for the perimeter of a rectangle is $2w + 2\ell = P$. Suppose the perimeter of a rectangle is 24 centimeters.

a. Solve the equation for ℓ.

b. State the independent and dependent variables and determine the domain and range values for which this equation makes sense.

c. Choose five values for w and find the corresponding values of ℓ.

a. First substitute 24 for P in the equation. Then solve for ℓ.

$$2w + 2\ell = P$$
$$2w + 2\ell = 24$$
$$2\ell = 24 - 2w \quad \textit{Subtract } 2w \textit{ from each side.}$$
$$\frac{2\ell}{2} = \frac{24 - 2w}{2} \quad \textit{Divide each side by } 2.$$
$$\ell = 12 - w$$

b. Since the value of ℓ depends on the value of w, ℓ is the dependent variable and w is the independent variable. Since distance can only be positive, the values in the domain and range must both be greater than zero.

(continued on the next page)

c. When choosing values for w, you can choose any number greater than zero. Suppose we choose the domain {1, 2, 3, 4, 5}. Make a table of values.

w	12 − w	ℓ	(ℓ, w)
1	12 − 1	11	(1, 11)
2	12 − 2	10	(2, 10)
3	12 − 3	9	(3, 9)
4	12 − 4	8	(4, 8)
5	12 − 5	7	(5, 7)

The solution set for the domain we chose is {(1, 11), (2, 10), (3, 9), (4, 8), (5, 7)}. *Check to see if each solution satisfies the equation $2w + 2\ell = 24$.*

CHECK FOR UNDERSTANDING

Communicating Mathematics

Study the lesson. Then complete the following.

1. Refer to the connection at the beginning of the lesson.
   a. Which of the substances listed will float on water? on mercury?
   b. State the domain and range of the graphed relation.
2. **Show** why $(1, -1)$ is or is not a solution of $x + 2y = 3$.
3. **Determine** which of the points shown in the graph at the right represent ordered pairs that are solutions for $y = 2x + 1$.

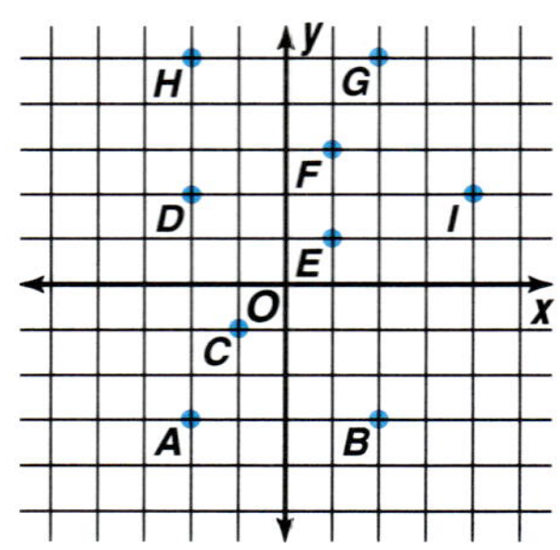

4. **Explain** why, in Example 3, you only consider values greater than zero.
5. Why should you solve for y before finding ordered pairs that are solutions for an equation?

MATH JOURNAL

6. In your own words, explain the difference between an independent variable and a dependent variable and how you know on which axis to graph each of them.

Guided Practice

Solve each equation for the domain given in the table.

7. $y = 2x + 3$

x	y	(x, y)
−2		
−1		
0		
1		
2		
3		

8. $a = \frac{3b - 5}{2}$

b	a	(b, a)
−5		
−2		
0		
2		
5		

Which ordered pairs are solutions of each equation?

9.	$1 + 5y = 2x$	**a.** $(-7, -3)$	**b.** $(7, 3)$	**c.** $(2, 1)$	**d.** $(-2, -1)$
10.	$11 - 2y = 3x$	**a.** $(1, 3)$	**b.** $(3, 1)$	**c.** $(5, -2)$	**d.** $(-1, 4)$

11. Find the solution set for $x + 2y = 14$ if the domain is $\{-2, -1, 0, 1, 2\}$. Then graph the solution set.

12. Geometry The formula for the area of a rectangle is $A = \ell w$. Suppose the area of a rectangle is 36 square meters.

a. Solve the equation for ℓ.

b. Choose five values for w and find the corresponding values of ℓ.

EXERCISES

Practice

Which ordered pairs are solutions of each equation?

13.	$3a + b = 8$	**a.** $(4, -4)$	**b.** $(8, 0)$	**c.** $(2, 2)$	**d.** $(3, 1)$
14.	$y = 3x$	**a.** $(6, 2)$	**b.** $(-2, -6)$	**c.** $(0, 0)$	**d.** $(-15, -5)$
15.	$3a - 8b = -4$	**a.** $(0, 0.5)$	**b.** $(4, 2)$	**c.** $(2, 0.75)$	**d.** $(2, 4)$
16.	$x = 3y - 7$	**a.** $(2, -1)$	**b.** $(2, 4)$	**c.** $(-1, 2)$	**d.** $(2, 3)$
17.	$2y + 4x = 8$	**a.** $(0, 2)$	**b.** $(-3, 0.5)$	**c.** $(2, 0)$	**d.** $(-2, 1)$
18.	$3x + 3y = 0$	**a.** $(1, -1)$	**b.** $(2, -2)$	**c.** $(-1, 1)$	**d.** $(-2, 2)$

Solve each equation if the domain is {−3, −2, 0, 3, 6}.

19. $y = 4x$	**20.** $y = 3x - 1$	**21.** $2x + 2y = 14$
22. $x = 4 + y$	**23.** $3x = 13 - 2y$	**24.** $y = 4 - 5x$
25. $5x + 3 = y$	**26.** $5x - 10y = 40$	**27.** $2x + 5y = 3$

Make a table and graph the solution set for each equation and domain.

28. $y = 3x$ for $x = \{-3, -2, -1, 0, 1, 2, 3\}$

29. $y = 2x + 1$ for $x = \{-5, -3, 0, 1, 3\ 6\}$

30. $3x - 2y = 5$ for $x = \{-3, -1, 2, 4, 7\}$

31. $5x = 8 - 4y$ for $x = \{-2, -1, 0, 1, 3, 4, 5\}$

32. Geometry A regular pentagon has five angles that have equal measures. Suppose the measure of one angle is $(a + b)°$. The sum of the measures of the angles of any pentagon is 540°.

a. Write an equation for the sum of the angle measures of a regular pentagon.

b. Solve the equation for a.

c. Choose five values for b and find the corresponding values of a.

33. Geometry Two angles that are supplementary have measures whose sum is 180°. Suppose the measures of two supplementary angles are $(x + y)°$ and $(2x + 3y)°$.

a. Write an equation for the sum of the measures of these two angles.

b. Solve the equation for y.

c. Choose five values for y and find the corresponding values of x.

Find the domain for each equation if the range is {−2, −1, 0, 2, 3}.

34. $y = x + 7$	**35.** $y = 3x$
36. $6x - y = -3$	**37.** $5y = 8 - 4x$

Make a table and graph the solution set for each equation.

38. $y = x^2 - 3x - 10$ if the domain is $\{-3, -1, 0, 1, 3, 5\}$

39. $y = x^3$ if the domain is $\{-2, -1, 0, 1, 2\}$

40. $y = 3^x$ if the domain is $\{1, 2, 3, 4\}$

Graphing Calculator

Use a graphing calculator to find the solution set for each domain.

41. $y = 1.4x - 0.76$ for $x = \{-2.5, -1.75, 0, 1.25, 3.33\}$

42. $y = 3.5x + 12$ for $x = \{-125, -37, -6, 12, 57, 150\}$

43. $3.6y + 12x = 60$ for $x = \{-100, -30, 0, 120, 360, 720\}$

44. $75y + 25x = 100$ for $x = \{-10, -5, 0, 5, 10, 15\}$

Critical Thinking

45. Find the domain values of each relation if the range is $\{0, 16, 36\}$.

a. $y = x^2$ **b.** $y = |4x| - 16$ **c.** $y = |4x - 16|$

46. Compare the graphs you drew in Exercises 38–40 with the other graphs in this lesson.

a. What is different about the pattern of the points for these relations?

b. Study the equations associated with the graphs. How do you think you could predict the pattern of the points by looking at the equation?

Applications and Problem Solving

47. Physical Science Refer to the connection at the beginning of the lesson. Suppose you have an unknown substance with a mass of 378 grams and a volume of 36 cm^3 and a second unknown substance with a mass of 87.5 grams and a volume of 125 cm^3.

a. Solve the formula $m = DV$ for D.

b. Identify the unknown substances.

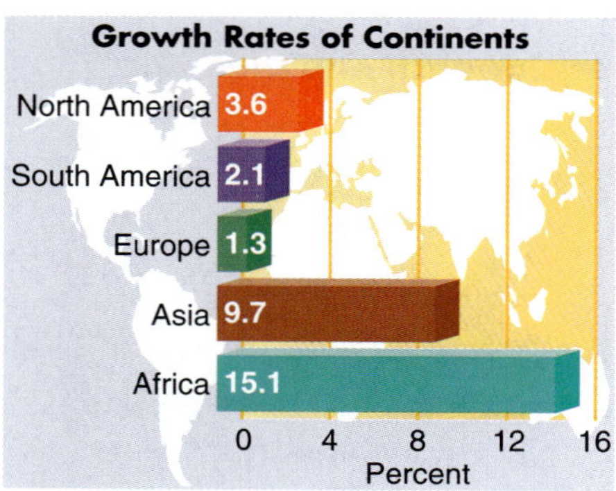

48. Demographics The time T (in years) needed for a population to double is calculated using the formula $T = \frac{70}{R}$, where R represents the percent growth rate of the population.

a. Determine the domain and range values for which this equation makes sense.

b. Use the formula to approximate the doubling time to the nearest year for the continents shown in the graph at the left.

c. The population of the United States in 1990 was 248,709,873. If the U.S. maintains the same growth rate as North America, what will be the population of the U.S. in the year 2000? in 2010? in 2020?

49. Anatomy The formula for relating the shoe size S and the length of a woman's foot in inches L is $S = 3L - 22$. The formula for relating a man's shoe size with his foot length is $S = 3L - 26$. Copy and complete each table below to determine shoe sizes given lengths of feet.

Women

L	S	(L, S)
$9\frac{1}{3}$		
$9\frac{5}{6}$		
$10\frac{1}{6}$		
$10\frac{2}{3}$		

Men

L	S	(L, S)
$11\frac{1}{3}$		
$11\frac{5}{6}$		
$12\frac{1}{3}$		
$12\frac{5}{6}$		

50. Make a Table Winona Brownsman is doing small jobs for her rich aunt. Her aunt has asked Winona how she wishes to be paid for her services. Winona has two choices.

- *Plan A:* Winona can be paid one dollar the first day of the month and an additional dollar for each day for a month. For example, she will be paid \$1 on Day 1, \$2 on Day 2, \$3 on Day 3, and so on.
- *Plan B:* Winona will be paid one cent on the first day and for each succeeding day, double the amount of the previous day. For example she will be paid 1¢ on Day 1, 2¢ on Day 2, 4¢ on Day 3, 8¢ on Day 4, and so on.

a. Use two tables to determine which plan would be more profitable.

b. On which day will the better plan become greater than the other?

Mixed Review

51. Basketball The table at the right shows the number of years that specific professional basketball players have been playing and the average number of points each player made during the 1993–1994 season. (Lesson 5–2)

Player	Years	Points
Charles Barkley	10	21.6
Glen Rice	5	21.1
Chris Mullin	9	16.8
Jamal Mashburn	1	19.2
Scottie Pippen	7	22.0
Dominique Wilkins	12	26.0

Source: *Hawes Fantasy Basketball Guide,* 1994–1995

a. Plot the points and describe the graph.

b. What do you think the graph suggests about the relationship of the number of years played and the point average?

52. Graph each point below. Then connect the points in alphabetical order and identify the figure. (Lesson 5–1)

$$A(0, 5), B(4, -3), C(-5, 2), D(5, 2), E(-4, -3), F(0, 5)$$

53. Employment Hugo's wages vary directly with the time he works. If his wages for 4 days are \$110, how much will they be for 17 days? (Lesson 4–8)

54. What number decreased by 80% is 14? (Lesson 4–5)

55. Finance If Li Fong had earned one fourth of a percent more in annual interest on an investment, the interest for one year would have been \$45 greater. How much did he invest at the beginning of the year? (Lesson 4–4)

56. Solve $\frac{1}{3}a - 2b = -9c$ for a. (Lesson 3–6)

57. Geometry The perimeter of a rectangle is 148 inches.

a. Write an equation to represent this situation.

b. Find its dimensions if the length is 17 inches greater than three times the width. (Lesson 3–3)

58. Find a number between $-\frac{8}{17}$ and $\frac{1}{9}$. (Lesson 2–4)

59. Evaluate $3x^3 - 2y$ if $x = 0.2$ and $y = 4$. (Lesson 1–3)

5–4A Graphing Technology
Linear Relations and Functions

A Preview of Lesson 5–4

The graphing calculator is a powerful tool that can be used to study a wide variety of graphs. In many cases, equations are graphed in the standard viewing window, $[-10, 10]$ by $[-10, 10]$. To set the standard viewing window, press ZOOM 6. You do not need to press GRAPH after using ZOOM 6.

The examples below illustrate how you can use the calculator to graph linear relations and functions.

Example 1 **Graph $2y - 6x = 8$ in the standard viewing window.**

First solve the equation for y.

$$2y - 6x = 8$$
$$2y = 6x + 8$$
$$y = 3x + 4$$

Then enter the equation into the calculator, set the standard viewing window, and graph.

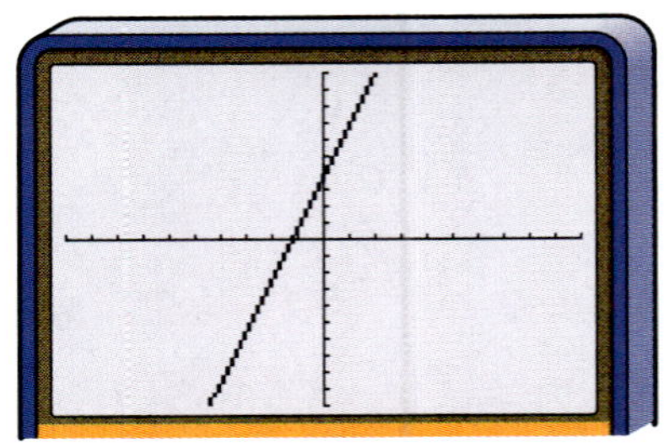

Note that the graph of this equation is a line.

Enter: Y= 3 X,T,θ,n + 4 *Enters the equation.*

ZOOM 6 *Sets the standard window.*

Example 2 **Graph $y = -x + 20$ in the standard viewing window.**

Enter: Y= (–) X,T,θ,n + 20

ZOOM 6

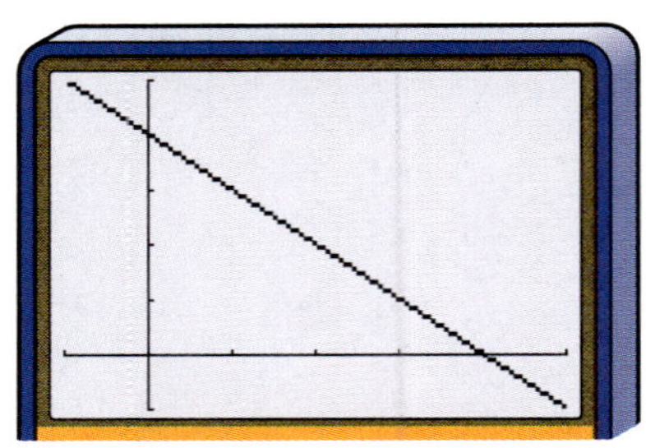

What happened? None of the graph is shown in the standard viewing window. Pressing the WINDOW key and changing the viewing window settings to $[-5, 25]$ by $[-5, 25]$ with scale settings of 5 for each axis will allow you to see where the graph crosses both the x- and y-axes.

An equation whose graph is a non-vertical line is called a ***linear function****.*

When the equation in Example 2 is graphed in the $[-5, 25]$ by $[-5, 25]$ viewing window, it is considered a **complete graph.** A complete graph shows all of the important characteristics of the graph on the screen. These include the origin and the points at which the graph crosses the x- and y-axes.

Example 3 **Use a graphing calculator to draw a graph that represents the solutions to this problem. Then list three of the solutions.**

A second number is two more than the opposite of the first.

Let x represent the first number, and let y represent the second number. The equation $y = -x + 2$ describes the relationship between the numbers for any first number x. Select the standard viewing window, enter the equation, and press GRAPH to view the graph of the equation. A complete graph is displayed.

You can find sample solutions for the equation in two ways.

Method 1

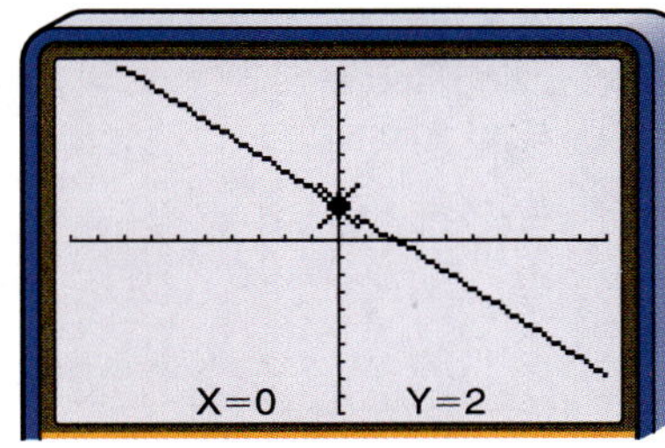

Press the TRACE key. The cursor appears as a flashing square and the approximate coordinates of the location of the cursor appears at the bottom of the screen. Use the right and left arrows to move the cursor along the line. New coordinates appear for each location of the cursor. These ordered pairs are approximate solutions for the equation. Sample solutions are (0, 2), (0.42553191, 1.5744681), and (−0.6382979, 2.6382979).

Method 2

You can obtain exact solutions by pressing 2nd TABLE. A table of x and y values for the equation appears.

X	Y1	
−3	5	
−2	4	
−1	3	
0	2	
1	1	
2	0	
3	−1	

X = 0

Use the up and down arrow keys to scroll through the list of values. Sample solutions are (−3, 5), (0, 2), and (3, −1).

EXERCISES

Use a graphing calculator to graph each equation in the standard viewing window. Sketch each graph on a sheet of paper.

1. $y = 3x - 6$
2. $y = 0.5x - 4$
3. $2x - 3y = 5$
4. $5x + y = 8$
5. $2y - 2x = 3$
6. $-10x - 2y = -14$

Graph each linear function.
a. Determine a viewing window that shows a complete graph.
b. Sketch the graph on a sheet of paper, noting the scale used for each axis.
c. Name three solutions for the equation.

7. $0.1x + y = 10$
8. $y = 3x + 17$
9. $y = 0.01x + 0.02$
10. $200x + y = 150$

5-4 Graphing Linear Equations

What YOU'LL LEARN

- To graph linear equations.

Why IT'S IMPORTANT

You can graph equations to solve problems involving health and physical science.

FYI

In science, a calorie is defined as the quantity of heat needed to raise the temperature of 1 gram of water 1°C. The word *calorie* that we use when referring to food actually refers to kilocalories (1000 calories). These are referred to as Calories (C) to differentiate them from the thermal unit.

CONNECTION

Health

The manner in which you burn Calories depends on your weight and the activity you are doing. The chart at the right shows the number of Calories burned per minute per kilogram (C/min/kg).

Activity	C/min/kg
Basketball	0.138
Cycling (leisure)	0.064
Cycling (racing)	0.169
Dancing (aerobic)	0.135
Dancing (normal)	0.075
Drawing	0.036
Eating	0.023
Football	0.132
Free weights	0.086
Golf	0.085
Gymnastics	0.066
Jumping rope	0.162
Playing drums	0.066
Playing flute	0.035
Playing horn	0.029
Playing piano	0.040
Playing trumpet	0.031
Weight training	0.092
Running (7.2 min/km)	0.135
Running (5.0 min/km)	0.208
Running (3.7 min/km)	0.252
Sitting Quietly	0.021
Swimming	0.156
Walking	0.080
Writing	0.029
Word processing	0.027

Manuel weighs 70 kilograms and wants to know how many Calories he burns playing football. The formula $C = wtr$, where w is his weight in kilograms, t is the time in minutes, and r is C/min/kg, can be used to determine how many Calories he burns.

$$C = wtr$$
$$C = 70 \cdot t \cdot 0.132$$
$$C = 9.24t$$

The number of Calories burned is dependent upon how long he exercises. So, t is the independent variable and C is the dependent variable.

t	$9.24t$	C	(t, C)
0	9.24(0)	0	(0, 0)
10	9.24(10)	92.4	(10, 92.4)
20	9.24(20)	184.8	(20, 184.8)
30	9.24(30)	277.2	(30, 277.2)
40	9.24(40)	369.6	(40, 369.6)

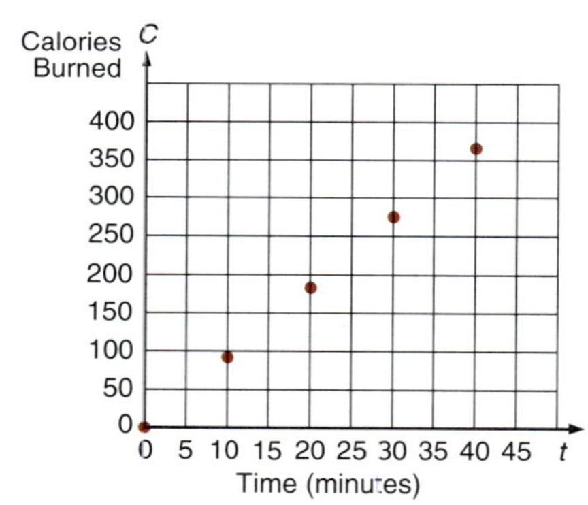

When you graph the ordered pairs, a pattern begins to form. The points seem to lie in a line.

What is the range for this relation?

Suppose the domain of $C = 9.24t$ is the set of positive real numbers. There would be an infinite number of ordered pairs that are solutions for the equation. If you graphed all the solutions, they would form a line. The line shown in the graph at the right represents all the solutions for $C = 9.24t$.

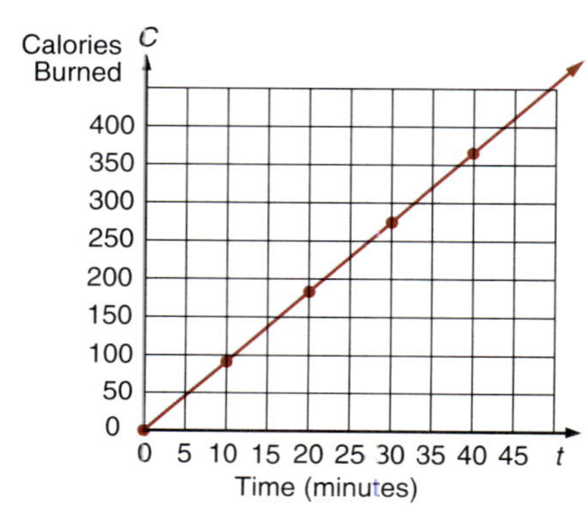

Since the graph of $C = 9.24t$ is a line, $C = 9.24t$ is called a **linear equation.**

Linear equations may contain one or two variables with no variable having an exponent other than 1.

Definition of a Linear Equation in Standard Form	**A linear equation is an equation that can be written in the form $Ax + By = C$, where A, B, and C are any real numbers, and A and B are not both zero.**

Example 1

Determine whether each equation is a linear equation. If so, identify A, B, and C.

a. $4x = 7 + 2y$

First, rewrite the equation so that both variables are on the same side of the equation.

$$4x = 7 + 2y$$

$4x - 2y = 7$ *Subtract 2y from each side.*

The equation is now in the form $Ax + By = C$, where $A = 4$, $B = -2$, and $C = 7$. This is a linear equation.

b. $2x^2 - y = 7$

The exponents of the variables in a linear equation must be 1. Since the exponent of x is 2, this is not a linear equation.

c. $x = 12$

This equation can be rewritten as $x + 0y = 12$. Therefore, it is a linear equation in the form $Ax + By = C$, where $A = 1$, $B = 0$, and $C = 12$.

To graph a linear equation, it is often helpful to make a table of ordered pairs that satisfy the equation. Then graph the ordered pairs and connect the points with a line.

Example 2

Graph each equation.

a. $y = 8x - 4$

Select five values for the domain and make a table. Then graph the ordered pairs and connect them to draw the line.

x	8x − 4	y	(x, y)
−2	8(−2) − 4	−20	(−2, −20)
−1	8(−1) − 4	−12	(−1, −12)
0	8(0) − 4	−4	(0, −4)
1	8(1) − 4	4	(1, 4)
2	8(2) − 4	12	(2, 12)

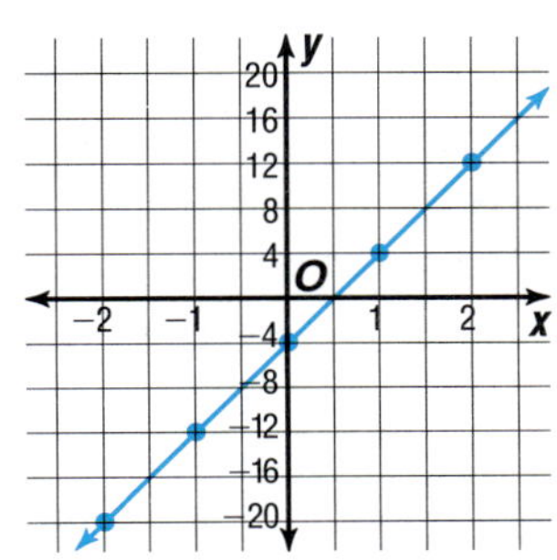

From the graph, you can find other ordered pairs that are solutions; for example, (2.5, 16).

The range of this relation is the set of real numbers.

(continued on the next page)

b. $2x + 5y = 10$

In order to find values for y more easily, solve the equation for y.

$$2x + 5y = 10$$

$$5y = 10 - 2x \quad \textit{Subtract 2x from each side.}$$

$$y = \frac{10 - 2x}{5} \quad \textit{Divide each side by 5.}$$

Now make a table and draw the graph.

x	$\frac{10 - 2x}{5}$	y	(x, y)
-10	$\frac{10 - 2(-10)}{5}$	6	$(-10, 6)$
-5	$\frac{10 - 2(-5)}{5}$	4	$(-5, 4)$
0	$\frac{10 - 2(0)}{5}$	2	$(0, 2)$
5	$\frac{10 - 2(5)}{5}$	0	$(5, 0)$
10	$\frac{10 - 2(10)}{5}$	-2	$(10, -2)$

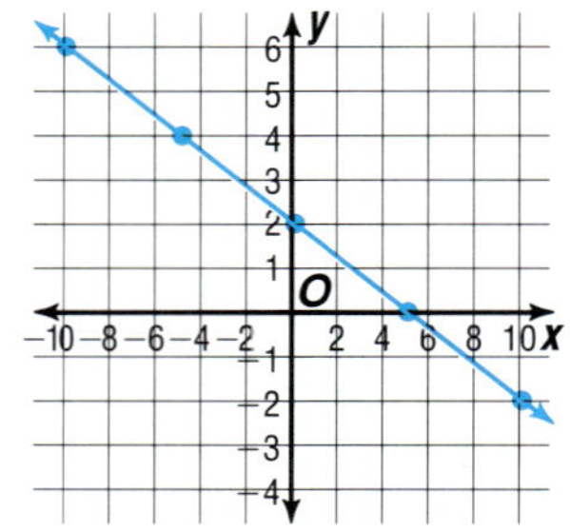

Using graphs is a good way to make comparisons in real-life situations.

Example 3

CONNECTION Health

Refer to the connection at the beginning of the lesson. Carmen Delgado is running in a cross-country meet at the rate of 5 min/km. Her weight is 50 kg. How does the number of Calories she is burning compare to those that she would be burning if she were at home word processing her research paper or if she were playing golf with her dad?

Explore Look up the Calories burned for each of the three types of activities in the chart on page 280.

Plan Write the equation for each activity using the formula $C = wtr$ and 50 for w.

Running	$C = 50(0.208)t$ or $C = 10.4t$
Word processing	$C = 50(0.027)t$ or $C = 1.35t$
Golfing	$C = 50(0.085)t$ or $C = 4.25t$

Solve Use a graphing calculator to graph all three equations. Enter the equations as Y_1, Y_2, and Y_3. Let x represent the t in each equation. Make a sketch of each graph and label each with its activity.

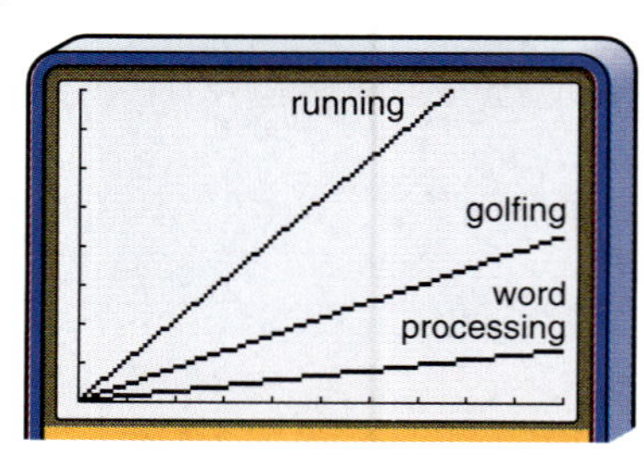

TECHNOLOGY Tip

Graphing calculators are helpful when comparing equations that are not easily graphed with pencil and paper.

For each value of t, Carmen burns many more Calories running than she does golfing or word processing. Carmen would burn more Calories golfing than she would word processing.

Examine Think about the physical movement required for each activity and how much energy that would take. Does the result make sense?

CHECK FOR UNDERSTANDING

Communicating Mathematics

Study the lesson. Then complete the following.

1. **Explain** why the ordered pair $(-1, 3)$ is a solution of $y = -2x + 1$.
2. **Describe** the graph of a linear equation in the form $Ax + By = C$ for which
   a. $A = 0$ **b.** $B = 0$ **c.** $C = 0$
3. **Show** how the graph of $y = 2x + 1$ for the domain $\{-1, 0, 2, 3\}$ differs from the graph of $y = 2x + 1$ for the domain of all real numbers.
4. **Explain** why the x and y values used to set the viewing window in Example 3 do not include negative numbers.

MATH JOURNAL

5. **Assess Yourself** During the next 48 hours, record three activities that you perform and the length of each activity. Determine how many Calories you burned in each activity. In which activity did you burn the most Calories? Explain why you think this activity burned the most Calories.

Guided Practice

Determine whether each equation is a linear equation. If an equation is linear, rewrite it in the form $Ax + By = C$.

6. $3x - 5y = 0$
7. $2x = 6 - y$
8. $3x^2 + 3y = 4$
9. $3x = 7 - 2y$

Graph each equation.

10. $3x + y = 4$
11. $4x + 3y = 12$
12. $\frac{1}{2}x = 8 - y$
13. $x = 6$
14. $y = -5$
15. $x - y = 0$

EXERCISES

Practice

Determine whether each equation is a linear equation. If an equation is linear, rewrite it in the form $Ax + By = C$.

16. $\frac{3}{x} + \frac{4}{y} = 2$
17. $\frac{3}{5}x - \frac{2}{3}y = 5$
18. $x + y^2 = 25$
19. $x + \frac{1}{y} = 7$
20. $3y + 2 = 0$
21. $2y = 3x - 8$
22. $5x - 7 = 0$
23. $2x + 5x = 7y$
24. $4x^2 - 3x = y$
25. $3m = 2n$
26. $\frac{x}{2} = 10 + \frac{2y}{3}$
27. $8a - 7b = 2a - 5$

Graph each equation.

28. $x + 6 = -5$
29. $y = 3x + 1$
30. $6x + 7 = -14y$
31. $2x + 7y = 9$
32. $y + 3 = 4$
33. $x - 6 = -\frac{1}{3}y$
34. $8x - y = 16$
35. $3x + 3y = 12$
36. $6x = 24 - 6y$
37. $x - \frac{7}{2} = 0$
38. $3x - 4y = 60$
39. $4x - \frac{3}{8}y = 1$
40. $2.5x + 5y = 7.5$
41. $x + 5y = 16$
42. $y + 0.25 = 2$
43. $\frac{4x}{3} = \frac{3y}{4} + 1$
44. $y + \frac{1}{3} = \frac{1}{4}x - 3$
45. $\frac{3x}{4} + \frac{y}{2} = 6$

Each table below represents points on a linear graph. Copy and complete each table.

46.

x	y
0	?
1	5
2	6
3	7
4	8
5	?

47.

x	y
10	?
5	−2.5
0	0
−5	2.5
−10	5
−15	?

48.

x	y
0	0
3	6
6	12
9	?
12	?
15	?

49.

x	y
−6	5
−4	?
−2	7
0	8
2	?
4	?

Graphing Calculator

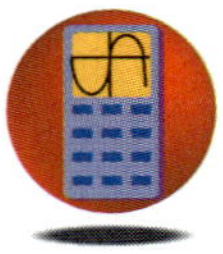

Graph each equation using a graphing calculator. Determine a WINDOW setting to use so that a complete graph is shown. Make a sketch of each graph, noting the scale used on each axis.

50. $y = 2x + 4$
51. $4x - 9y = 45$
52. $27x + 75y = 100$
53. $17y = 22$
54. $0.2x - 9.7y = 8.9$
55. $\frac{1}{2}x - \frac{2}{3}y = 10$

56. Clear the screen. Press [2nd] [DRAW] 4 3 [ENTER]. Describe the graph. Explain how you could use this approach to graph $x = -25$.

Critical Thinking

57. The graphs of each group of equations form a family of graphs. Graph each family on the same coordinate plane. Then write an explanation of the similarities and differences that exist in the graphs of each family.
   a. $y = 2x$ $y = 2x + 5$ $y = 2x - 9$ $y = 2x + 14$
   b. $y = -3x$ $y = -3x + 4$ $y = -3x - 10$ $y = -3x + 7$

Applications and Problem Solving

58. **Science** As a thunderstorm approaches, you see lightning as it occurs, but you hear the accompanying sound of the thunder a short time afterward. The distance y, in miles, that sound travels in t seconds is given by the equation $y = 0.21t$.
   a. Determine the domain and range values for which this equation makes sense.
   b. Graph the equation.
   c. Use the graph to estimate how long it will take you to hear the thunder from a storm that is 3 miles away.

59. **Employment** Elva Duran works as a sales representative for Brown's Electronics. She receives a salary of \$1800 per month plus a 6% commission on monthly sales over her target. Her sales in July will be \$800, \$1300, or \$2000 over target, depending on when her orders are filled by the company's distribution center.

   a. Graph ordered pairs that represent each of her possible incomes y for the three sales figures x.

   b. Will her total income for July be more than \$1850 if the equation that represents her income is $y = 1800 + 0.06x$? Explain.

60. **Weight Training** Hector Farentez, who weighs 68.2 kilograms, wanted to increase his body size by beginning a weight-training program. A local fitness club suggests that he begin his program using special equipment before he attempts the free weights. After several weeks of training, Hector has expanded his workout time from 30 minutes to 1 hour.

   a. Use the information in the table at the beginning of the lesson to determine a formula for determining how many Calories Hector is burning. Graph the equation showing each 5-minute interval.

   b. Later in his training at a weight of 72.3 kilograms, Hector plans to spend one-half hour on the special equipment and one-half hour on free weights. Will he use more or fewer Calories in this type of workout than an hour on the special equipment? Explain.

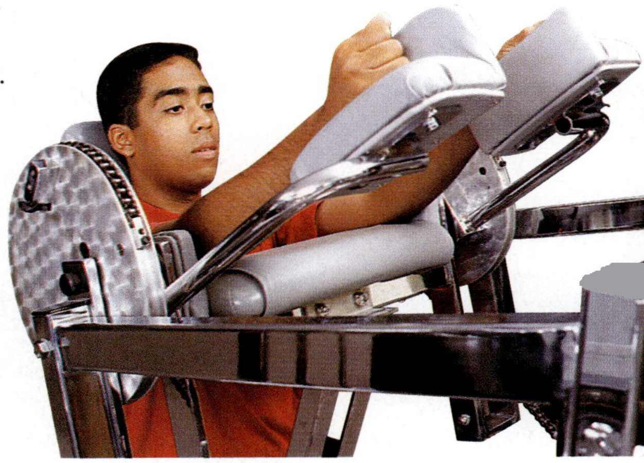

Mixed Review

61. Solve $8x + 2y = 6$ for y. (Lesson 5–3)

62. Draw a mapping for the relation $\{(2, 7), (-3, 7), (2, 4)\}$. (Lesson 5–2)

63. **Geometry** (Lesson 5–1)

   a. Graph (3, 2), (6, 2), and (6, 5).

   b. If these three points represent the vertices of a square, what would be the coordinates of the fourth point?

   c. Assume that each unit on each axis represents one inch. What is the perimeter of the square?

64. **Probability** A gumball machine has 24 cherry gumballs, 5 apple gumballs, 18 grape gumballs, 14 orange gumballs, and 9 licorice gumballs. What is the probability of getting an orange gumball? (Lesson 4–6)

65. Jimmy got a discount of \$4.50 on a new radio. The discounted price was \$24.65. What was the percent of discount to the nearest percent? (Lesson 4–5)

66. **Running** In cross-country meets, the team score is determined by totaling the finish numbers of the five runners on the team. One member of a cross-country team placed fourth, which means a score of 4 points for the team. The next four finishers on the team placed in consecutive order, but farther behind. The team score was 70. In what places did the other members finish? (Lesson 3–5)

67. **Miniature Golf** In miniature golf, balls bounce off the walls of the course at the same angle at which they hit. If a ball strikes the wall at 30°, what is the measure of the angle between the two paths of the ball? (Lesson 3–4)

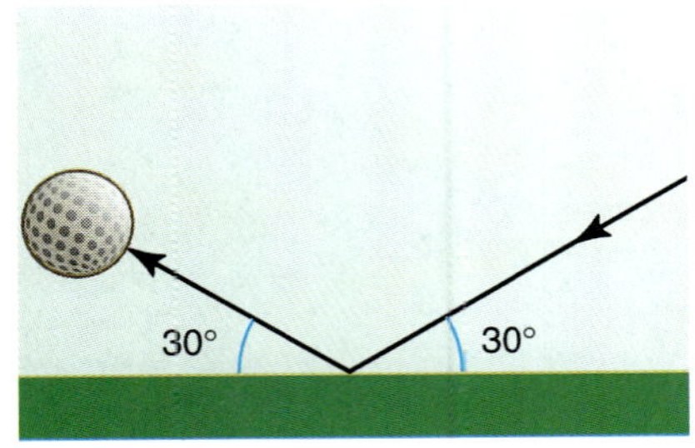

68. Two meters of copper tubing weigh 0.25 kilograms. How much do 50 meters of the same tubing weigh? (Lesson 3–3)

69. Simplify $\frac{\frac{-3}{4}}{-36}$. (Lesson 2–7)

70. Find $-21 + 52$. (Lesson 2–3)

SELF TEST

1. Graph $A(-6, 6)$, $B(3, -5)$, $C(0, 2)$, and $D(-3, -1)$. (Lesson 5–1)

Express each relation as a set of ordered pairs. Then state the domain, the range, and the inverse of the relation. (Lesson 5–2)

2.

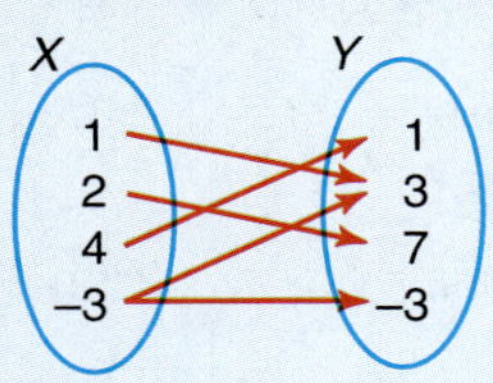

3.

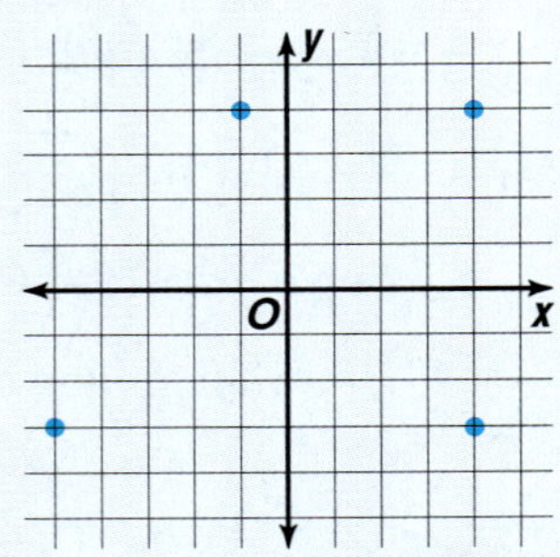

Solve each equation if the domain is {−2, −1, 0, 1, 3}. Then graph the solution set. (Lesson 5–3)

4. $3y + 6x = 12$ for y

5. $2a + 3b = 9$ for b

6. $5r = 8 - 4s$ for s

Graph each equation. (Lesson 5–4)

7. $y = x - 1$

8. $y = 2x - 1$

9. $3x + 2y = 4$

10. **Geometry** The formula for the area of a trapezoid is $A = \frac{1}{2}h(b_1 + b_2)$, where b_1 and b_2 are the lengths of the bases and h is the height. Find the height of the trapezoid shown at the right if its area is 40 m^2. (Lesson 5–3)

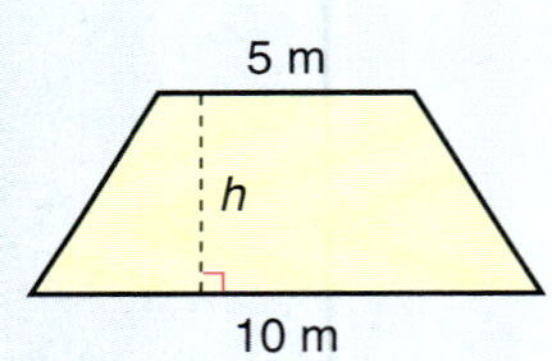

5-5 Functions

What YOU'LL LEARN

- To determine whether a given relation is a function, and
- to find the value of a function for a given element of the domain.

Why IT'S IMPORTANT

You can use functions to solve problems involving accounting, Earth science, and health.

APPLICATION

Air Travel

During certain times of the year, airlines offer lower rates to fly to selected cities. The advertisement below shows discount ticket fares. The mileage between the cities is also listed for those people who are enrolled in frequent flier programs.

Plan Your Vacation Now!

From	To	Regular Fare	Discount Fare	Mileage
Atlanta	New York	$ 89	$ 79	892
Baltimore	Houston	149	129	1454
Boston	Greensboro	109	79	786
Cleveland	Philadelphia	94	79	441
Dayton	Houston	109	99	1178
Greensboro	Miami	84	79	814
Houston	Jacksonville	104	99	875
Houston	Miami	109	99	1231
Los Angeles	San Antonio	139	129	1277

Sample sale prices. Coach class each way. Round-trip purchase required. Seats are limited and may not be available on all flights/days.

Suppose we let r represent the regular fare, d the discount fair, and m the mileage. The relation whose ordered pairs are of the form (r, d) is graphed below on the left. The relation whose ordered pairs are of the form (m, d) is graphed below on the right.

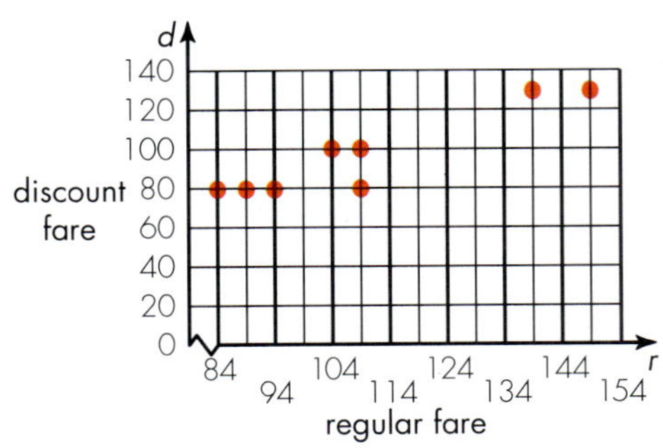

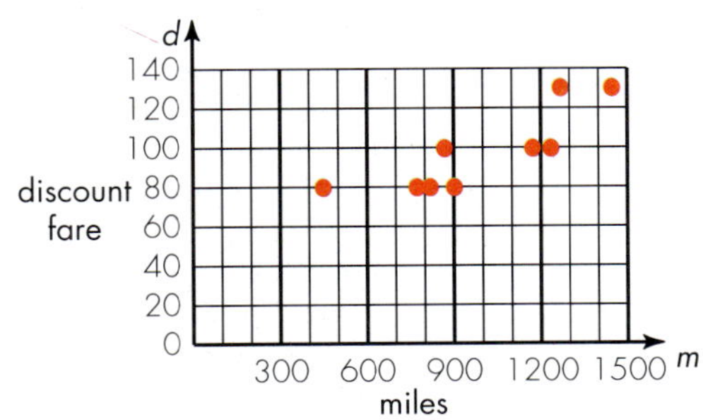

Notice that in the graph on the left, when $r = 109$, there is more than one value of d, 79 and 99. However, in the other graph, there is exactly one value of d for each value of m. Relations with this characteristic are called **functions.**

Definition of Function	**A function is a relation in which each element of the domain is paired with *exactly* one element of the range.**

Example 1 Determine whether each relation is a function. Explain your answer.

a. **{(2, 3), (3, 0), (5, 2), (−1, −2), (4, 1)}**

Since each element of the domain is paired with exactly one element of the range, this relation is a function.

b.

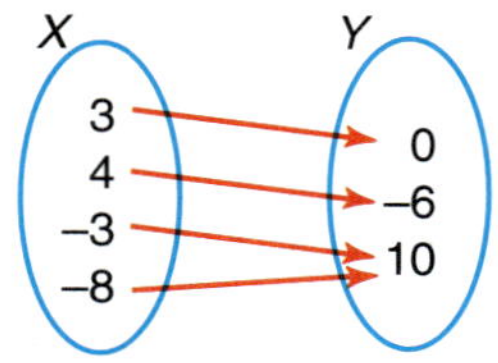

This mapping represents a function since, for each element of the domain, there is *only one* corresponding element in the range.

It does not matter if two elements of the domain are paired with the same element in the range.

c.

x	y
4	−1
5	2
5	3
6	6
−1	1

This table represents a relation that is not a function. The element 5, in the domain, is paired with both 2 and 3 in the range.

There are several ways to determine whether an equation represents a function.

Example 2 Determine whether $x - 4y = 12$ is a function.

Method 1: Make a table of solutions.

First solve for y.

$$x - 4y = 12$$

$$-4y = -x + 12 \quad \textit{Subtract x from each side.}$$

$$y = \frac{1}{4}x - 3 \quad \textit{Divide each side by } -4.$$

x	y
−8	−5
−4	−4
−2	−3.5
0	−3
2	−2.5
4	−2
8	−1

Next make a table of values like the one at the right.

It appears that for any given value of x, there is only one value for y that will satisfy the equation. Therefore, the equation $x - 4y = 12$ is a function.

Method 2: Graph the equation.

Since the equation is in the form $Ax + By = C$, the graph of the equation will be a line. Graph the ordered pairs from Method 1 and connect them with a line.

Now place your pencil at the left of the graph to represent a vertical line. Slowly move the pencil to the right across the graph.

For each value of x, this vertical line passes through no more than one point on the graph. Thus, the line represents a function.

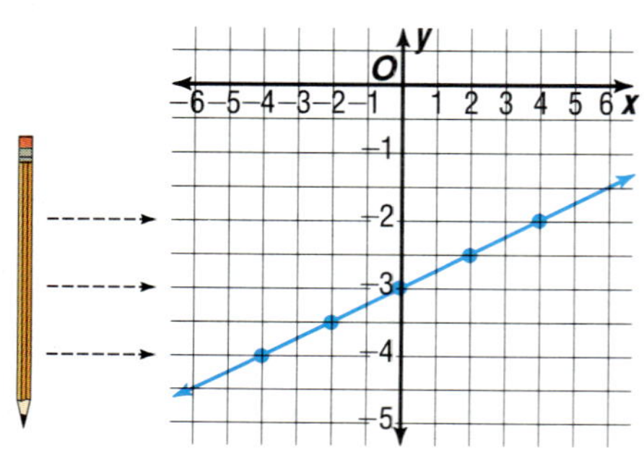

Using a pencil to see if a graph represents a function is one way to perform the **vertical line test.**

Vertical Line Test for a Function	**If any vertical line passes through no more than one point of the graph of a relation, then the relation is a function.**

Example 3 **Use the vertical line test to determine if each relation is a function.**

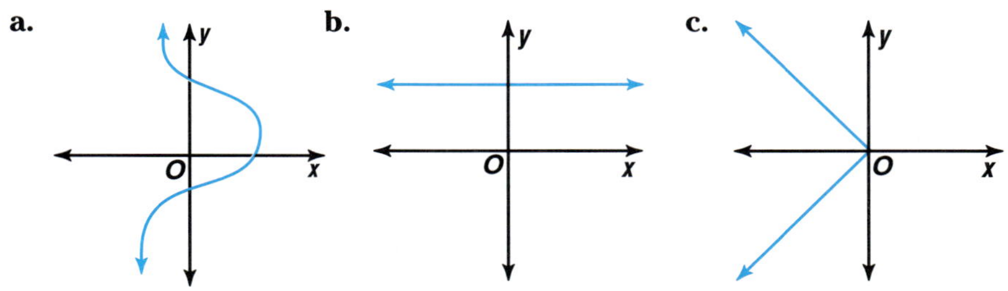

Graph b is the only relation to pass the vertical line test. Thus, it is the only function. With graphs a and c, a vertical line intersects the graph in more than one point. Thus, they are *not* functions.

Letters other than f are also used for names of functions. For example, g(x) and h(x) are sometimes used.

The ordered pair (4, f(4)) is a solution of the function f.

Equations that are functions can be written in a form called **functional notation.** For example, consider the equation $y = 3x - 7$.

equation	**functional notation**
$y = 3x - 7$	$f(x) = 3x - 7$
	The symbol f(x) is read "f of x."

In a function, x represents the elements of the domain and $f(x)$ represents the elements of the range. Suppose you want to find the value in the range that corresponds to the element 4 in the domain. This is written $f(4)$ and is read "f of 4." The value of $f(4)$ is found by substituting 4 for x in the equation. So, $f(4) = 3(4) - 7$ or 5.

Example 4 **If $f(x) = 2x - 9$, find each value.**

a. $f(6)$

$$f(6) = 2(6) - 9$$
$$= 12 - 9$$
$$= 3$$

b. $f(-2)$

$$f(-2) = 2(-2) - 9$$
$$= -4 - 9$$
$$= -13$$

c. $f(k + 1)$

$$f(k + 1) = 2(k + 1) - 9$$
$$= 2k + 2 - 9$$
$$= 2k - 7$$

The functions we have studied thus far have been linear functions. Many functions are not linear. However, you can find values of functions in the same way.

Example 5 **If $h(z) = z^2 - 4z + 9$, find each value.**

a. $h(-3)$

$$h(-3) = (-3)^2 - 4(-3) + 9$$
$$= 9 + 12 + 9 \text{ or } 30$$

(continued on the next page)

b. $h(5c)$

$h(5c) = (5c)^2 - 4(5c) + 9$ *Substitute 5c for z.*

$= 5 \cdot 5 \cdot c \cdot c - 4 \cdot 5 \cdot c + 9$

$= 25c^2 - 20c + 9$

c. $5[h(c)]$

$5[h(c)] = 5[(c)^2 - 4(c) + 9]$ *5[h(c)] means 5 times the value of h(c).*

$= 5 \cdot c^2 - 5 \cdot 4c + 5 \cdot 9$ *Distributive property*

$= 5c^2 - 20c + 45$

Notice that when comparing parts b and c, $5[h(c)] \neq h(5c)$.

Functions are often used in solving real-life problems.

Example 6 CONNECTION Health

The normal systolic blood pressure S is a function of the age a of the individual. That is, a person's normal blood pressure depends on how old the person is. To determine the normal systolic blood pressure of an individual, you can use the equation $S = 0.5a + 110$, where a represents age in years.

a. Write the equation in functional notation.

b. Find $S(10)$, $S(30)$, $S(50)$, and $S(70)$.

c. Graph the function. Name the independent and dependent quantities.

d. Use the graph of the function to estimate whether blood pressure increases or decreases with age. Then estimate the blood pressure of an 80-year-old person.

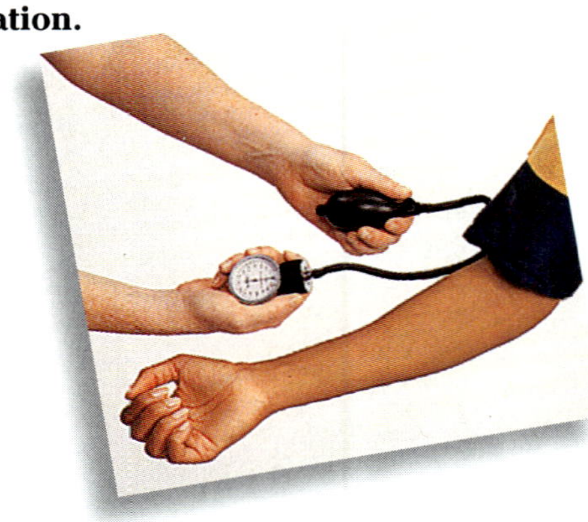

a. Let $S(a)$ represent the function. The equation becomes $S(a) = 0.5a + 110$.

b. Make a table with 10, 30, 50, and 70 as values of a.

a	$S(a) = 0.5a + 110$	$S(a)$	$(a, S(a))$
10	$S(10) = 0.5(10) + 110$	115	(10, 115)
30	$S(30) = 0.5(30) + 110$	125	(30, 125)
50	$S(50) = 0.5(50) + 110$	135	(50, 135)
70	$S(70) = 0.5(70) + 110$	145	(70, 145)

c. Use the ordered pairs from the table to graph the function. Age is the independent quantity, and systolic blood pressure is the dependent quantity.

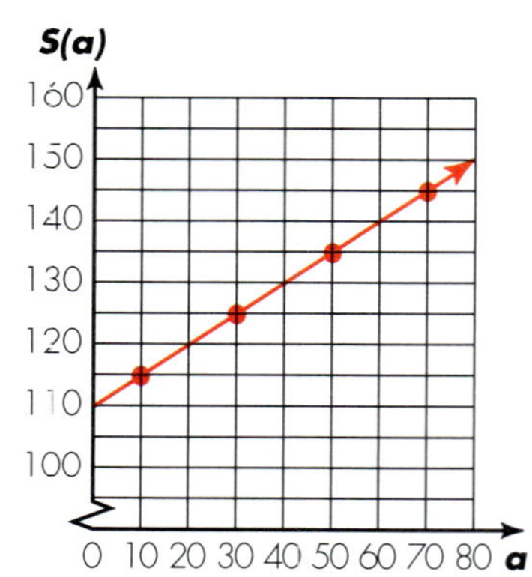

d. The graph indicates that as you age, your blood pressure is expected to rise. An 80-year-old person would expect to have a systolic pressure of about 150.

CHECK FOR UNDERSTANDING

Communicating Mathematics

Study the lesson. Then complete the following.

1. **Explain** any differences between a relation and a function.
2. **Describe** how the phrase "is a function of" relates to the mathematical definition of function. For example, the diameter of a tree is a function of its age.
3. **Write** how you would find $g(1)$ if $g(x) = 3x + 12$.
4. **You Decide** Is the statement "All linear equations are functions" true? Support your answer with examples or counterexamples.

MATH JOURNAL

5. In your own words, explain how and why the vertical line test works.

Guided Practice

Determine whether each relation is a function.

6. 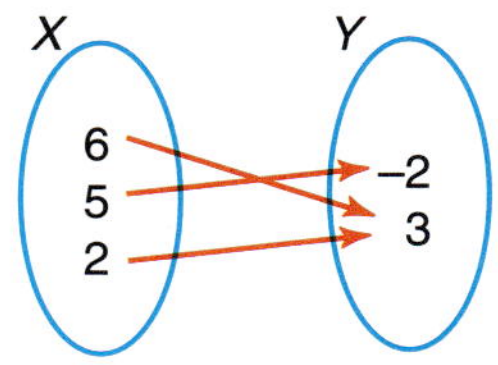

7.

x	y
−2	3
5	3
5	4
4	0

8. 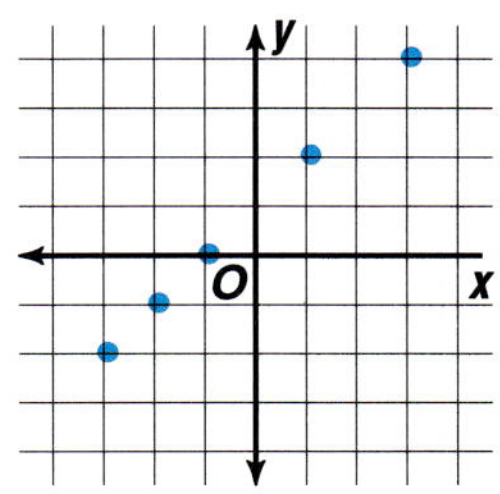

9. $\{(-3, 1), (-1, 3), (1, -2), (3, 2)\}$
10. $\{(3, 1), (-2, 2), (1, -1), (1, 2), (-3, 1), (-2, 5)\}$
11. $y + 5 = 7x$
12. $2x^2 + 3y^2 = 36$
13. The graph of $y^2 = x + 4$ is shown at the right. Use the vertical line test to determine if this relation is a function.

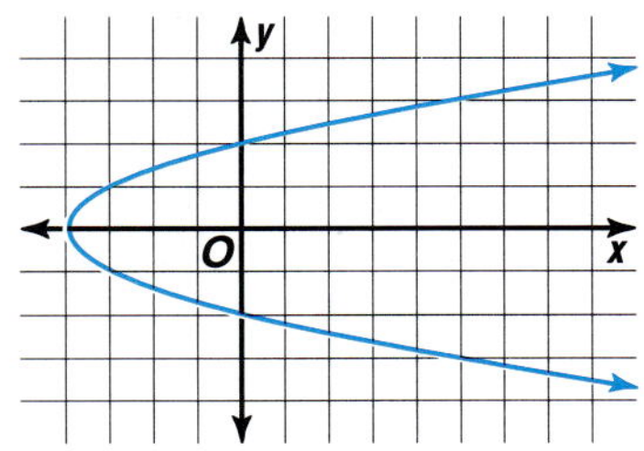

14. Which of the following graphs represent a function?

a. $y = |x - 1|$

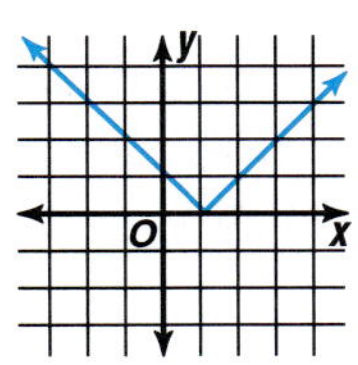

b. $x = |y| + 1$

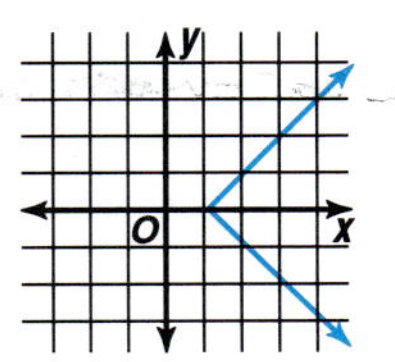

c. $y = |x| + 1$

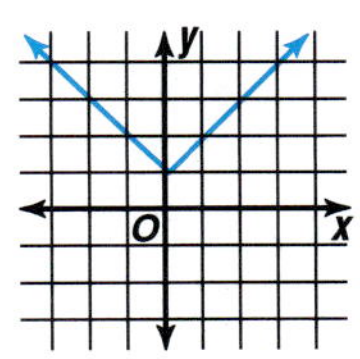

d. $x = 1 - |y|$

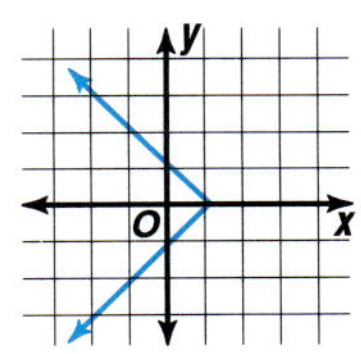

LOOK BACK
You can refer to Lesson 2-3 for more information on absolute value, $|x|$.

If $h(x) = 3x + 2$, find each value.

15. $h(-4)$
16. $h(2)$
17. $h(w)$
18. $h(r - 6)$

EXERCISES

Practice **Determine whether each relation is a function.**

19.

a	*b*
−3	3
−2	3
0	4
2	4
4	4

20.

r	*s*
−4	3
−4	2
−4	1
4	0
4	−1
4	−2

21.

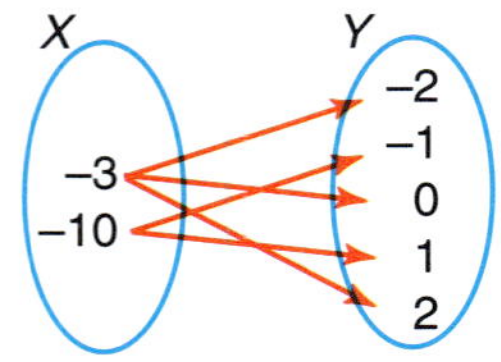

22.

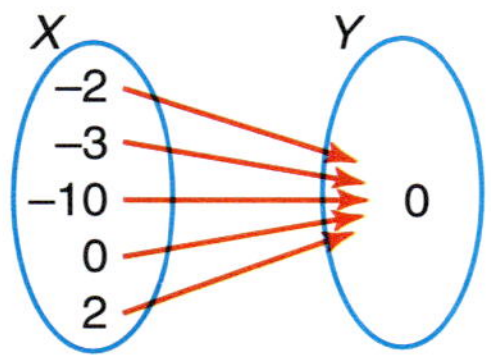

23.

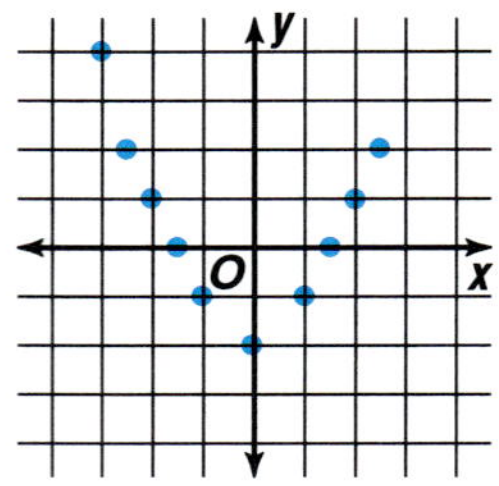

24.

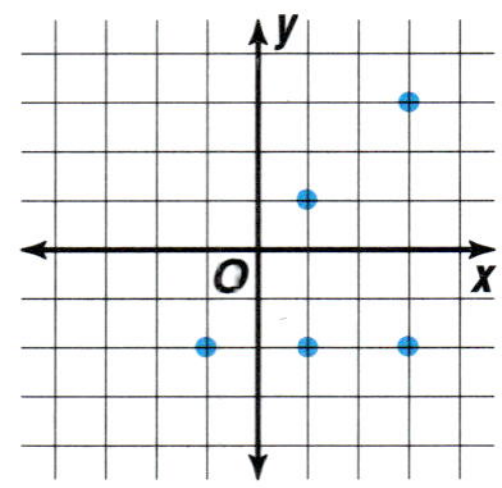

25. $\{(6, 3), (5, -2), (2, 3), (12, -12)\}$

26. $\{(4, 5), (3, -2), (-2, 5), (4, 7)\}$

27. $\{(5, -1), (6, -1), (-8, -1), (0, -1)\}$

28. $\{(4, -2), (-4, -2), (9, -2), (0, -2)\}$

29. $y = -15$

30. $x = 13$

31. $y = 3x - y$

32. $y = |x|$

33. $x = |y|$

34. $yx = 36$

If $f(x) = 4x + 2$ and $g(x) = x^2 - 2x$, find each value.

35. $f(-4)$

36. $g(4)$

37. $g\left(\frac{1}{5}\right)$

38. $f\left(\frac{3}{4}\right)$

39. $g(3.5)$

40. $f(6.2)$

41. $3[f(-2)]$

42. $-6[g(0.4)]$

43. $g(3b)$

44. $f(2y)$

45. $-3[g(1)]$

46. $3[g(2w)]$

47. $5[g(a^2)]$

48. $f(c + 3)$

49. $6[f(p - 2)]$

50. $-3[f(5w + 2)]$

51. **a.** Create and graph a relation that is a function and has an inverse that is also a function.

b. Create and graph a relation that is a function and has an inverse that is not a function.

Choose the graph that best represents the information given. Explain your choice. Determine whether the graph represents a function.

52. Communication A call to London, England costs \$1.78 for the first minute and \$1.00 for each additional minute. Fractions of a minute are charged as an entire minute.

a.

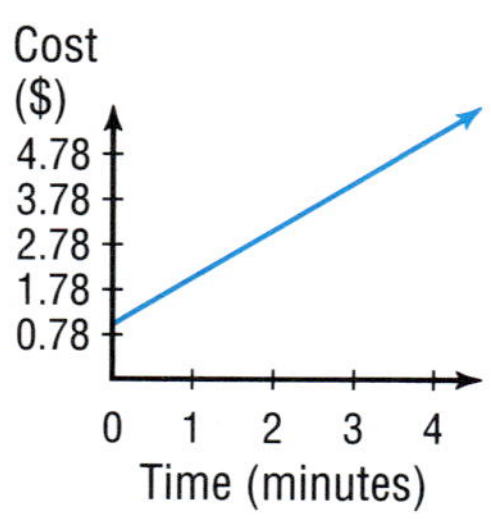

b.

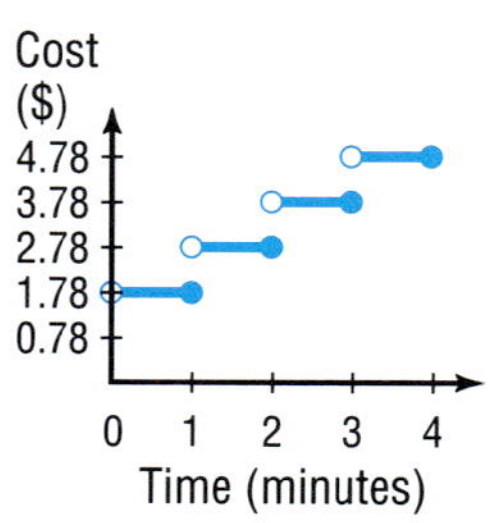

c.

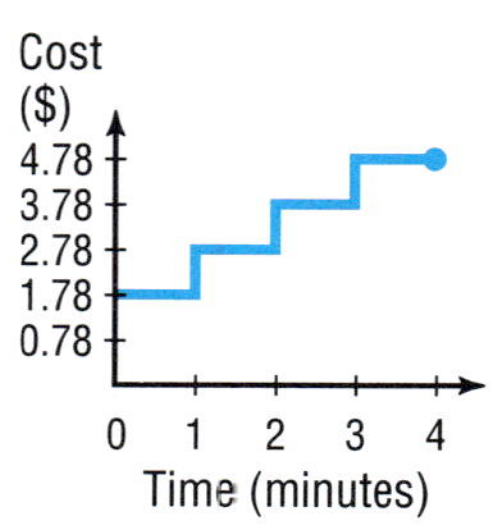

53. **Manufacturing** A company charges \$9.95 for each custom-printed T-shirt. If you order 8 or more, but less than 15, the charge is \$8.25 each. If you order 15 or more, the charge is \$6.50 each.

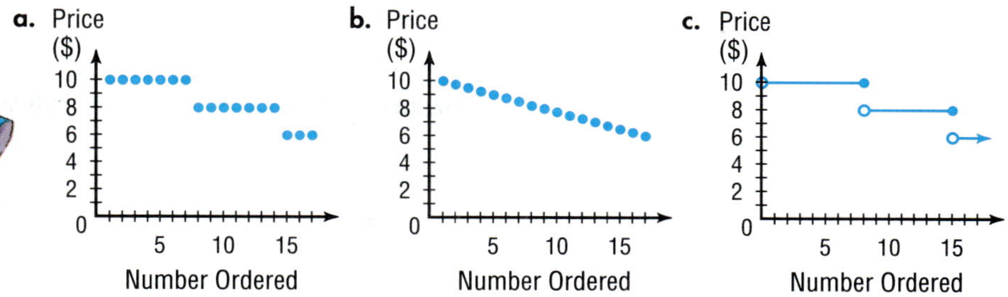

Critical Thinking

54. Let the domain of $f(x) = x^2 + 3x + 2$ be $\{-5, -4, -3, -2, -1, 0, 1, 2\}$.
   a. Graph the function, the ordered pairs that make up the inverse of the function, and the line $y = x$ on the same coordinate plane.
   b. Is the inverse of this function a function?
   c. How are the graphs of the function and its inverse related to the line $y = x$?

Applications and Problem Solving

55. **Metallurgy** Since pure gold is very soft, other metals are often added to gold to make an alloy that is stronger and more durable. The relative amount of gold in a piece of jewelry is measured in karats. The formula for the relationship is $g = \frac{25k}{6}$, where k represents the number of karats and g is the percent of gold in the piece.
   a. Determine the domain and range values for which this function makes sense.
   b. Graph the function and describe the graph.
   c. How many karats are in a ring made of pure gold?

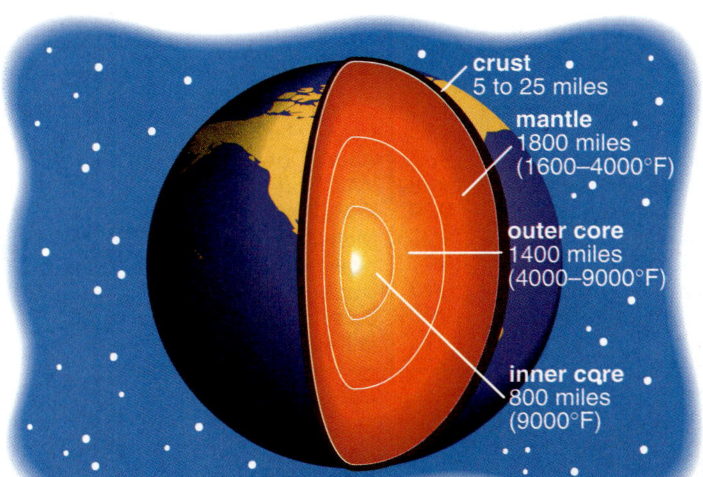

56. **Earth Science** Earth's interior is composed of four levels: the crust, the mantle, the outer core, and the inner core. The inner core is believed to be solid while the outer core is molten. The temperature in the first 62 miles below Earth's surface can be approximated with the formula $T = 35d + S$, where T is the temperature in degrees Fahrenheit, d is the distance in miles, and S is the temperature (°F) on the surface.
   a. Suppose the temperature at the surface is 75°F. Find the temperature at the lower edge of the crust if the crust is 30 miles deep at that point.
   b. Russian scientists are credited with drilling the deepest hole ever on the Kola Peninsula, which is located near the Arctic Circle in northwest Russia about 250 miles from Finland. Drilling began in 1970, but is only 7 miles deep thus far. What is the temperature at the bottom of this hole if the outside temperature is 0°F?
   c. Why do you think that there is a range of values given for the depth of the crust?

57. **Accounting** The following is adapted from an article by Gail A. Eisner, CPA (certified public accountant), in *The Mathematics Teacher.*

> Early in my accounting career, the partner who was directly supervising me, a very bright, young CPA, called me into his office and asked how a person could possibly calculate a bonus if the company's formula required that the bonus be 15 percent of the net profits *after* the bonus has been deducted? I showed him the linear equation $B = 0.15(P - B)$, where B is the bonus, and P (a known quantity) represents the profits before subtracting the bonus.

a. Suppose the profits are \$2000. Determine the amount of the bonus.

b. Solve the equation for B and graph the resulting equation.

Mixed Review

58. Graph $y - x = -5$. (Lesson 5–4)

59. Solve $3a - b = 7$ if the domain is $\{-3, -2, 4, 6\}$. (Lesson 5–3)

60. State the inverse of the relation $\{(-1, 1), (-5, 9), (4, 6)\}$. (Lesson 5–2)

61. **Probability** A card is selected at random from a deck of 52 cards. What is the probability of selecting a jack, queen, or king? (Lesson 4–6)

62. 44 is what percent of 89? (Lesson 4–4)

63. For what angle are the sine and cosine equal? (Lesson 4–3)

64. **Trigonometry** Find the measure of the third angle of a triangle if the other angles have measures 167° and 4°. (Lesson 3–4)

65. Solve $\frac{z}{-4} - 9 = 3$. (Lesson 3–3)

66. **Budgeting** The total of Jon Young's gas and electric bills was \$210.87. His electric bill was \$95.25. How much was his gas bill? (Lesson 3–2)

67. **Sports** The players with the most runs batted in (RBI) for the National League are listed below. (Lesson 2–2)

Year	Name	RBI	Year	Name	RBI
1971	Joe Torre	137	1983	Dale Murphy	121
1972	Johnny Bench	125	1984	Mike Schmidt	106
1973	Willie Stargell	119		Gary Carter	
1974	Johnny Bench	129	1985	Dave Parker	125
1975	Greg Luzinski	120	1986	Mike Schmidt	119
1976	George Foster	121	1987	Andre Dawson	137
1977	George Foster	149	1988	Will Clark	109
1978	George Foster	120	1989	Kevin Mitchell	125
1979	Dave Winfield	118	1990	Matt Williams	122
1980	Mike Schmidt	121	1991	Howard Johnson	117
1981	Mike Schmidt	91	1992	Darren Daulton	109
1982	Dale Murphy	109	1993	Barry Bonds	123
	Al Oliver		1994	Jeff Bagwell	116

Source: *The World Almanac,* 1995

a. Make a line plot of the data.

b. What was the greatest number of RBIs during one season?

c. What was the least number of RBIs during one season?

d. What was the most frequently-occurring number of RBIs during one season?

e. How many of the players had from 119 to 129 RBIs?

Writing Equations from Patterns

What YOU'LL LEARN

- To write equations to represent relations, given some of the solutions for the equations.

Why IT'S IMPORTANT

You can write equations to represent relations in scuba diving and aquatics.

APPLICATION

Scuba Diving

As scuba divers descend, the pressure of the water increases. Scuba divers can determine their depth by the pressure. Pressure can be expressed in atmospheres. An atmosphere is equivalent to 14.7 psi (pounds per square inch) of pressure. The table below shows the relationship between atmospheres of pressure and ocean depth.

Pressure (atmospheres)	1	2	3	4	5
Depth of Ocean (feet)	0	33	66	99	132

Suppose we let p represent the atmospheres of pressure, and let d represent the ocean depth. The relation shown in the table can also be represented by a graph. Graph the points and observe the pattern.

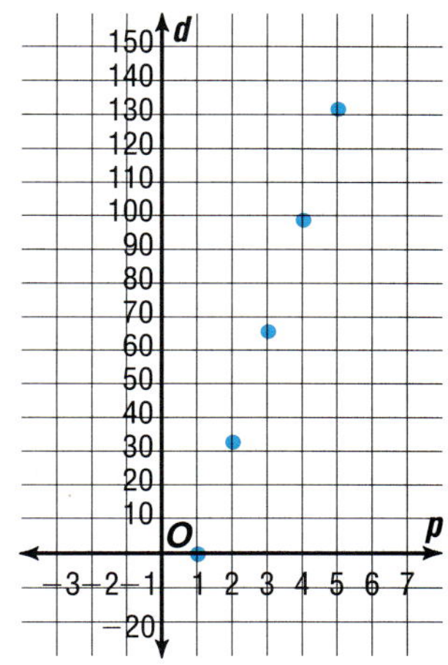

Notice that when the ordered pairs are graphed, they form a linear pattern. You can use a straightedge to draw the line through these points. Points that lie in a linear pattern can be described by an equation. Look at the relationship between the domain and range to find a pattern that can be described by an equation.

FYI

In 1943, Jacques-Yves Cousteau and E. Gagnon developed an apparatus to free divers from hoses connected to air sources on the surface. It is called *scuba* gear, which is an acronym for ***s**elf-**c**ontained **u**nderwater **b**reathing **a**pparatus.*

+1 +1 +1 +1

p	1	2	3	4	5
d	0	33	66	99	132

+33 +33 +33 +33

$$\frac{\text{range differences}}{\text{domain differences}} = \frac{33}{1}$$

Notice that the differences in the d values are 33 times the differences of the corresponding p values. It seems that this relationship can be described by the equation $d = 33p$. Check to see if this equation is correct by substituting values of p into the equation.

p	1	2	3	4	5
$33p$	33	66	99	132	165

These values do not match those in the first chart. However, note that each corresponding value for d using the equation is 33 more than the d in the relation. Thus, we need to adjust our equation to compensate for this difference. The equation that describes this relation is $d = 33p - 33$. Since this relation is also a function, we can write this equation as $d(p) = 33p - 33$.

Example 1 **Plot the points in the relation shown in the table. Then write an equation in functional notation for the relation.**

x	−4	−8	−12	−16	−20
y	1	2	3	4	5

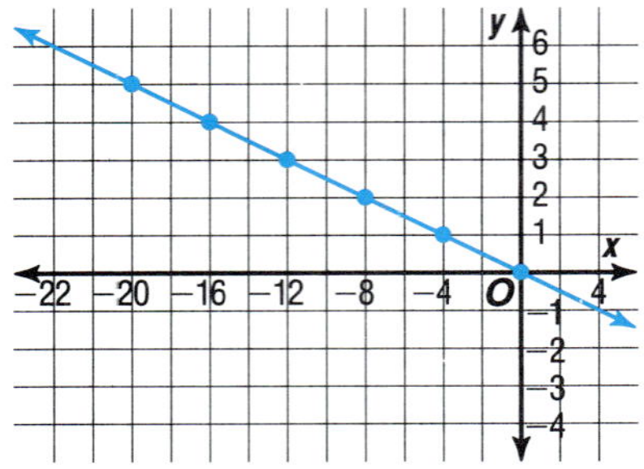

Since the points form a linear pattern, we know that there is a linear equation that describes this relation.

Differences in x: −4, −4, −4, −4

x	−4	−8	−12	−16	−20
y	1	2	3	4	5

Differences in y: +1, +1, +1, +1

$$\frac{\text{range differences}}{\text{domain differences}} = \frac{1}{-4}$$

The differences in the y values are one-fourth the differences in the x values. This pattern implies that the equation $y = -\frac{1}{4}x$ may describe the relation. Check the equation for the domain values in the relation.

Check: If $x = -4$, then $y = -\frac{1}{4}(-4)$ or 1. ✔

If $x = -8$, then $y = -\frac{1}{4}(-8)$ or 2. ✔

The equation that represents the relation is $y = -\frac{1}{4}x$. Since this relation is also a function, we can write this equation in functional notation as $f(x) = -\frac{1}{4}x$.

Sometimes you may need to find the equation for a graph.

Example 2 **Write an equation in functional notation for the relation graphed at the right.**

First make a table of ordered pairs for several points on the graph.

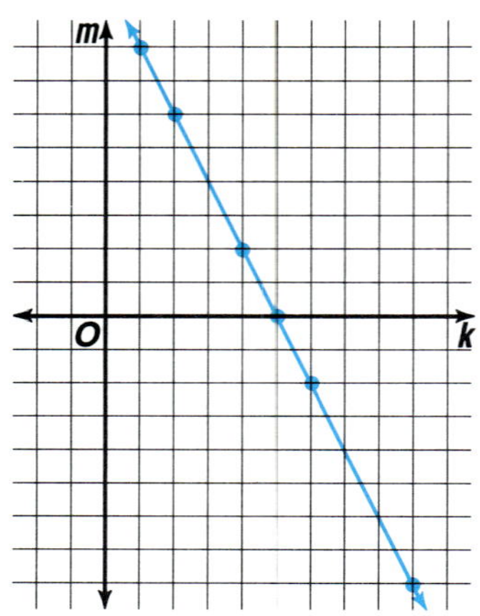

k	1	2	4	5	6	9
m	8	6	2	0	−2	−8

Now find the common differences of the domain and range.

Differences in k: +1, +2, +1, +1, +3

k	1	2	4	5	6	9
m	8	6	2	0	−2	−8

Differences in m: −2, −4, −2, −2, −6

Notice that there is not a consistent change in the domain and range values. However, you can still find the ratio of the range difference to the domain difference for each ordered pair. There are three possible ratios.

range differences / *domain differences* $\quad \frac{-2}{1} = -2 \quad \frac{-4}{2} = -2 \quad \frac{-6}{3} = -2$

Since all of the ratios are the same, it appears that the differences in the m values are -2 times that of the k values. This pattern suggests that $m = -2k$. Check the equation to see if it is correct.

Check: If $k = 2$, then $m = -2(2)$ or -4. But the range value for $k = 2$ is 6, a difference of 10. Try some other values in the domain to see if the same difference occurs.

k	1	4	5	6	9
$-2k$	-2	-8	-10	-12	-18
m	8	2	0	-2	-8

m is 10 more than −2k.

This pattern suggests that 10 should be added to one side of the equation in order to correctly describe the relation. Thus, the equation for this relation is $m = -2k + 10$. Check this equation.

Check: If $k = 2$, then $m = -2(2) + 10$ or 6. ✓
If $k = 9$, then $m = -2(9) + 10$ or -8. ✓

Therefore, $m = -2k + 10$ describes this relation. Since this relation is also a function, we can write this equation in functional notation as $f(k) = -2k + 10$.

Many times you can generalize the relationships among data you have collected with an equation.

EXPLORATION — SPREADSHEETS

In the relation $\{(-2, 2), (-1, 5), (0, 8), (1, 11), (2, 14)\}$, the range difference is 3 when the domain difference is 1. You might suggest that the equation of the relation is $y = 3x$. Let's use spreadsheet software to check this equation.

- Each cell of a spreadsheet is named by a letter and number. The letter refers to the column and the number of the row. Enter each x value into cells A1 through A5. Enter the y values into cells B1 through B5.
- In cell C1, enter the formula A1*3. This formula means take the value in cell A1 and multiply it by 3. Copy this formula to cells C2 through C5. The spreadsheet will automatically change the formula so that the appropriate cell in column A will be used.
- In cell D1, enter the formula B1 − C1. This formula will subtract the range value of the equation from the range value of the relation. Copy this formula to cells D2 through D5.

Column D tells what number to add to the equation so that it is correct. In this case, the entries in column D are 8s. The correct equation should be $y = 3x + 8$.

Your Turn

a. What formula would you use in cell C1 to test the first formula found in Example 2? Use a spreadsheet to check all the values in the relation.

b. What number would you expect to appear in column D if the equation you found is correct for a given relation?

Example 3

APPLICATION

Hardware

***Pennies* are units for measuring the lengths of nails. Nails measured in pennies can range from 2-penny nails to 60-penny nails. The graph at the right illustrates the lengths of several penny nails.**

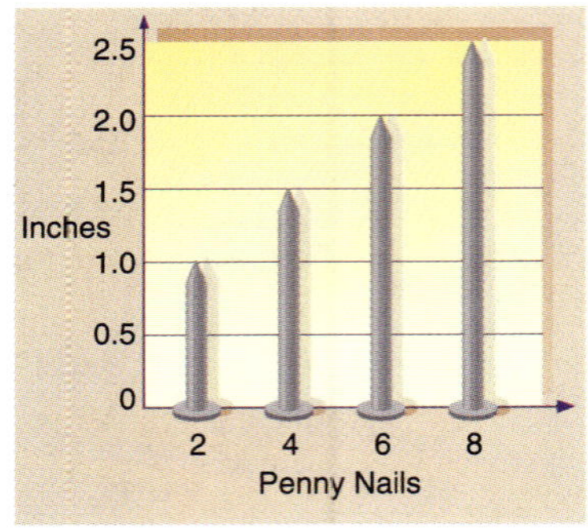

a. The length of a nail as a function of its penny status can be modeled by a linear function for 2- through 10-penny nails. Write an equation in functional notation for this relationship.

b. Find the lengths of a 3-penny nail, a 5-penny nail, and a 10-penny nail.

> **FYI**
>
> This pattern for nails does not hold for all penny sizes. For example, a 60-penny nail is only 6 inches long.

a. We can see from the graph that the points form a linear pattern. Thus, there is a linear equation that describes the relation for 2- through 10-penny nails.

+2 +2 +2

x	2	4	6	8
y	1	1.5	2	2.5

+0.5 +0.5 +0.5

$\frac{\text{range differences}}{\text{domain differences}} = \frac{0.5}{2}$ or 0.25

This pattern suggests that the equation $f(x) = 0.25x$ might model this situation. However, if you check the domain values with this equation, you will find that the values of $f(x)$ are off by 0.5. The correct equation is $f(x) = 0.25x + 0.5$.

b.

3-penny nail	*5-penny nail*	*10-penny nail*
$f(3) = 0.25(3) + 0.5$	$f(5) = 0.25(5) + 0.5$	$f(10) = 0.25(10) + 0.5$
$= 1.25$	$= 1.75$	$= 3$

A 3-penny nail is 1.25 inches long, a 5-penny nail is 1.75 inches long, and a 10-penny nail is 3 inches long.

CHECK FOR UNDERSTANDING

Communicating Mathematics

Study the lesson. Then complete the following.

1. **Analyze** the graphs in Examples 1 and 2 along with the ratios of the range differences to the domain differences. Then complete these sentences.
   a. If the ratio is positive, then the line slants __?__.
   b. If the ratio is negative, then the line slants __?__.
2. **Explain** how you can determine if an equation correctly represents a relation given as a table.
3. **You Decide** When the teacher was explaining Example 2, Narissa said she had another way to find the equation without calculating three ratios. She said she found other points that lie on the line so the differences were common. Is Narissa's method valid? Explain.
4. **Write** a linear equation in functional notation that has both (1, 1) and (0, 3) as solutions. Is this the only linear equation that has these two solutions? Explain.

Guided Practice

Write an equation in functional notation for each relation.

5.

x	3	4	5	6	7
f(x)	12	14	16	18	20

6.

x	2	4	6	8	10
f(x)	−4	−3	−2	−1	0

TECHNOLOGY Tip

You can use a spreadsheet to check all of your equations in this exercise set.

Write an equation for each graphed relation.

7. 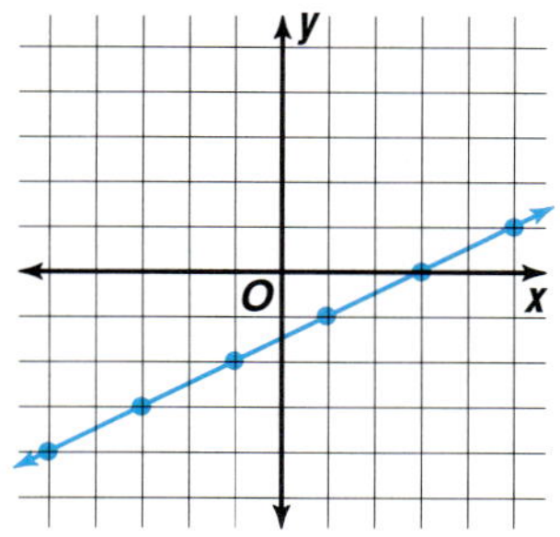

8. 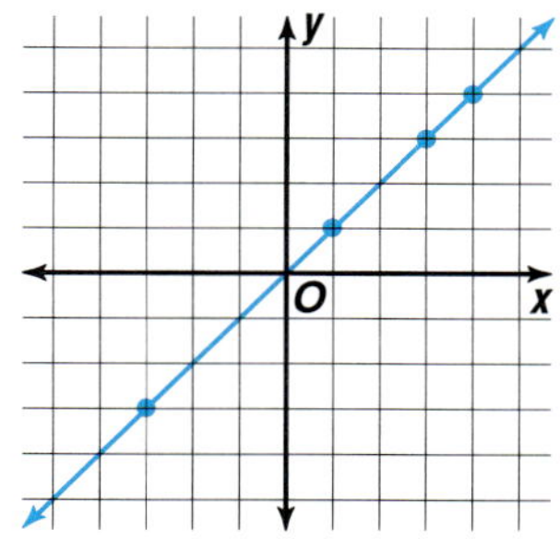

9. The table below represents values for the function $N(m)$. Copy and complete the table. Explain how you determined the missing value.

m	8	4	2	0
N(m)	−10	−8	−7	?

10. **Chemistry** Most substances contract when they freeze. However, water expands in volume when it freezes. Eleven cubic feet of water becomes 12 cubic feet of ice, 33 cubic feet of water becomes 36 cubic feet of ice, and 66 cubic feet of water becomes 72 cubic feet of ice.
   a. Make a graph of these data.
   b. Write a functional equation for the relationship between the volume of water and the corresponding volume of ice.

EXERCISES

Practice

Copy and complete the table for each function.

11.

x	1	2	3	4	5
f(x)	12	24	36		

12.

x	−4	−2	0	2	4
g(x)	−2	−1			2

13.

x	−3	−1	1	2	4
h(x)	18			−7	−17

14.

x	−2	0	2	4	6
p(x)			2	3	4

Write an equation for each relation.

15.

x	1	2	3	4	5
$f(x)$	5	10	15	20	25

16.

n	1	2	3	4	5
$f(n)$	1	4	7	10	13

17.

x	−2	−1	1	2	4
$g(x)$	13	12	10	9	7

18.

n	−4	−2	0	2	4
$m(n)$	−11	−3	5	13	21

19.

x	0	6	12	18	24
$h(x)$	−2	0	2	4	6

20.

n	−4	0	4	6	8
$m(n)$	26	18	10	6	2

21.
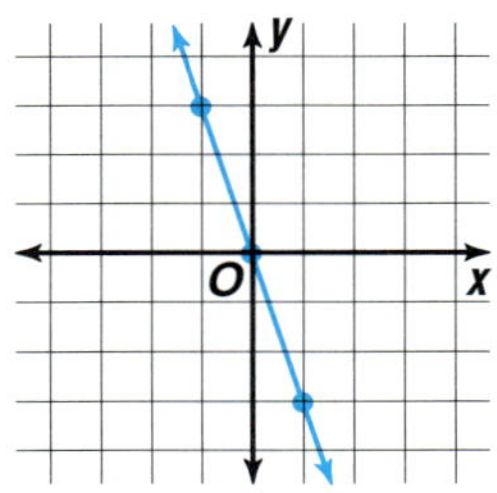

22.
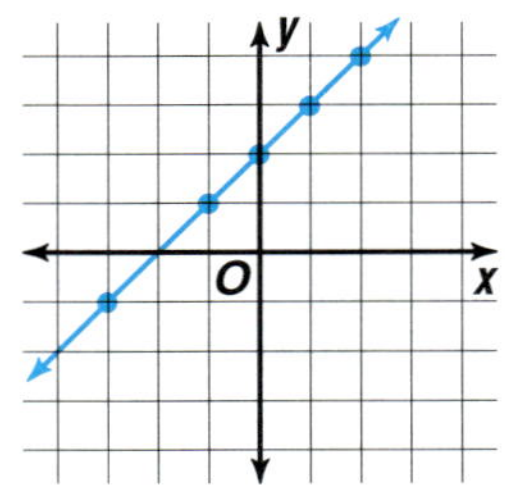

23.
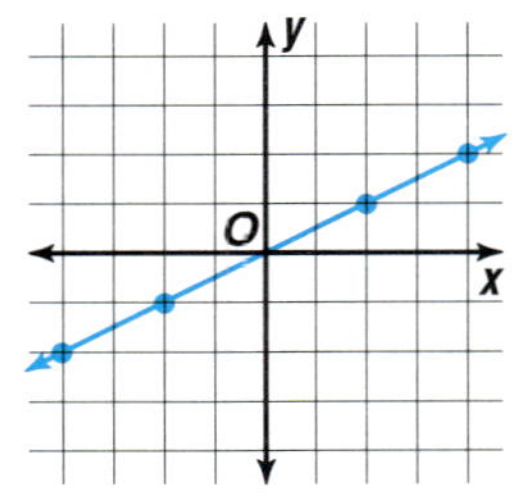

24.
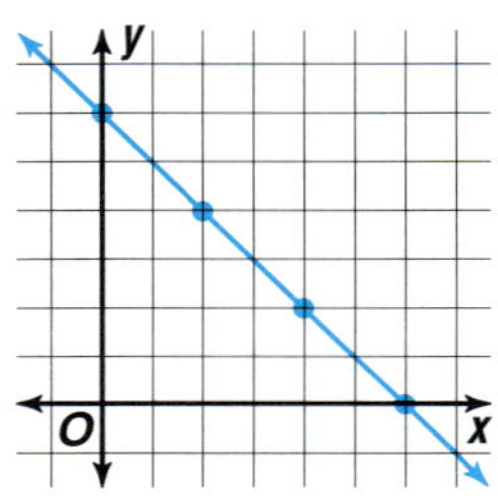

25.
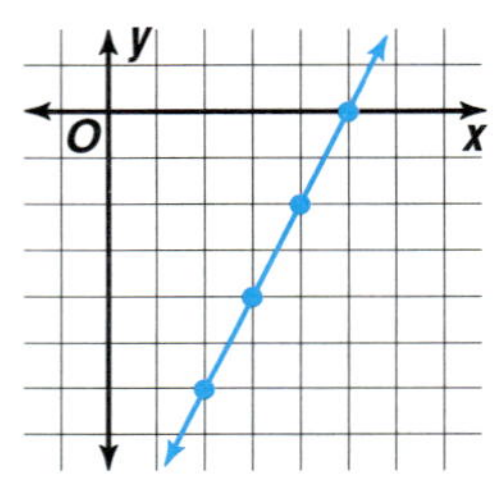

26.
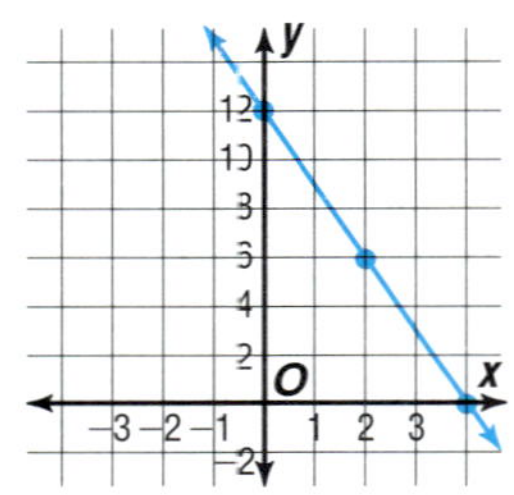

27. $\{(6, -4), (2, -12), (1, -24), (-3, 8), (-6, 4)\}$

28. $\{(-3, 10), (-2, 5), (-1, 2), (0, 1), (1, 2), (2, 5), (3, 10)\}$

29. $\{(-3, -27), (-1, -1), (2, 8), (3, 27), (10, 1000)\}$

30. $\{2, 12), (1, 48), (-1, 48), (-2, 12), (-4, 3)\}$

Critical Thinking

31. The y- and x-intercepts are those points at which a graph intersects the y- and x-axes, respectively. Use functional notation to describe these points.

32. Suppose the ratio of range differences to domain differences in a linear function $g(x)$ is $\frac{2}{3}$ and the graph of $g(x)$ goes through the point $(-3, 2)$. Draw the graph of $g(x)$ and explain why you drew it the way you did.

Applications and Problem Solving

33. **Aquatics** The table below illustrates the relationship between atmospheres of pressure and the depth of fresh water.

Pressure (atmospheres)	1	2	3	4	5
Depth of Fresh Water (ft)	0	34	68	102	136

a. Write an equation in functional notation for the relation.

b. Refer to the application at the beginning of the lesson. How does the pressure in fresh water compare to the pressure in ocean water?

34. **Archaeology** Archaeologists sometimes use lengths of heavy-duty wire to hold together the bones that compose the spinal columns of various vertebrates. Suppose a 70-foot length of wire weighs 23 pounds.

a. If this sample of wire is representative of all lengths of this wire, draw a graph showing the weight of the wire as a function of its length.

b. Use your graph to estimate the weight of 50 feet of wire to the nearest pound.

c. Write an equation to describe the relationship between the length of a wire and its weight.

d. Evaluate the equation in part c for $\ell = 50$. How does this result compare with your estimate in part b?

35. **Health** Alex Knockelmann is concerned about the number of Calories that she needs to intake during the basketball season so she will not lose weight. She wants to eat as many Calories before practice as she will use during practice. The table below shows some fast foods from restaurants near her school and their Calories.

Fast Food	Calories
Ham and Cheese	380
Roast Beef	350
Cheeseburger	577
Double Cheeseburger	797
Fries	327
Chocolate Shake	390
Cola (20 oz)	241
Lemon-Lime (20 oz)	219

a. Before practice, Alex ate a double cheeseburger, fries, and a chocolate shake. What was her Calorie intake for this meal?

b. In Lesson 5–4, you learned that playing basketball burns 0.138 C/min/kg. At Alex's weight of 80 kg, determine how many Calories she would burn each minute.

c. Make a table to show the number of Calories that Alex burns each minute for the first 10 minutes of practice. Graph the points.

d. Let C represent the number of Calories burned and t represent the number of minutes. Write a functional equation to represent the relation. Is it a linear function?

e. Use the graph and your equation to predict the number of Calories Alex would use during two hours of practice. Did she eat enough food so that she had Calories remaining at the end of practice?

Mixed Review

36. **Biology** The function $f(t) = \frac{t}{0.2} - 32$ shows that the number of times a cricket chirps in an hour is a function of the temperature in degrees Celsius. (Lesson 5–5)
    a. If it is 12°C outside, how many times will a cricket chirp in an hour?
    b. If a cricket chirps 54 times in 3 hours, what is the outside temperature?
37. State the domain and range of {(1, 6), (3, 4), (5, 2)}. (Lesson 5–2)
38. What number is 16% of 50? (Lesson 4–4)

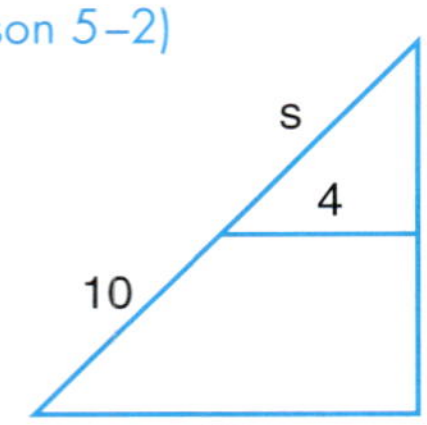

39. **Trigonometry** Given the similar triangles at the right, find *s*. (Lesson 4–2)
40. Solve $x + (-7) = 36$. (Lesson 3–1)
41. Graph {0, 3, 7} on a number line. (Lesson 2–1)
42. **Personal Finance** Many credit cards offer a protection plan so you can pay off your balance if you lose your job or have an accident and cannot work. The table below shows the monthly premium (in cents per $100 outstanding balance) for the plan on a credit card in the United States and its territories. Round each amount to the nearest cent and make a stem-and-leaf plot of these fees. (Lesson 1–4)

Area	Fee	Area	Fee	Area	Fee	Area	Fee	Area	Fee	Area	Fee
AK	68.2	FL	75	LA	74	NC	64.6	OK	75	UT	68.9
AL	66	GA	75	MA	63.5	ND	64.8	OR	69.8	VA	59.3
AR	66	HI	57.5	MD	75	NE	68	PA	22.5	VI	66
AZ	73.7	IA	58.8	ME	62	NH	46.9	PR	74	VT	56.7
CA	75	ID	60	MI	66	NJ	64.2	RI	67	WA	60
CO	68.1	IL	75	MN	32.3	NM	74	SC	71.9	WI	59
CT	53.2	IN	62.1	MO	75	NV	74	SD	66	WV	74
DC	66	KS	68.3	MS	74	NY	45.3	TN	75	WY	73.1
DE	66	KY	75	MT	74	OH	75	TX	42.7		

WORKING ON THE In·ves·ti·ga·tion

Refer to the Investigation on pages 190–191.

Many of the prcedures from one area of science can be applied to other areas of science. Estimating populations is not reserved just for fish. Conservationists also keep track of species of birds, insects, plants, and other wildlife in a similar way.

1 Design a different experiment that illustrates the capture-recapture method. Complete your experiment a few times to see if it is as accurate as the one you have completed.

2 What was the range of your estimates using the method described in the Investigation? What was the range of your estimates using your method? Which do you think is the most reliable method?

Add the results of your work to your Investigation Folder.

5–7A Graphing Technology
Measures of Variation

A Preview of Lesson 5–7

The graphing calculator is a powerful tool for observing patterns and analyzing data that come from research or experimentation. Many of the measures of variation you will learn about in Lesson 5–7 can be calculated by using a graphing calculator.

Before analyzing any data, you must know how to enter it into a list.

Example 1 **The Glencoe Publishing Golf Tournament is held every September to raise money for a scholarship fund. The list below includes the scores for the employees of the manufacturing department. Enter the data and find the range of these scores.**

139, 99, 105, 115, 88, 91, 105, 80, 102, 101, 103, 95, 99, 77, 112

LOOK BACK
You can review another method for using the graphing calculator to find the median of a set of data in Lesson 3-7.

First enter the data.

Method 1 Assign the data to List 1 (L1) from the home screen.

Enter: [2nd] [{] 139 [,] 99 [,] 105 [,] 115 [,] 88 [,] 91 [,] 105 [,] 80 [,] 102 [,] 101 [,] 103 [,] 95 [,] 99 [,] 77 [,] 112 [2nd] [}] [STO▸] [2nd] [L1] [ENTER]

You can use the calculator to sort the data from least to greatest by pressing [STAT] *2* [2nd] [L1] [ENTER]. *You can view the list by pressing* [STAT] [ENTER].

Method 2 Enter the data directly into the list display.

Before entering your data, you must clear the L1 list of previously entered data.

Enter: [STAT] 4 [2nd] [L1] [ENTER]

Enter each score into the L1 list.

Enter: [STAT] 1

The cursor appears in the L1 list. Enter the data one by one pressing [ENTER] after each entry, including the last one.

Then find the range.

The range of the scores is the difference of the maximum and minimum values in the list.

Enter: [2nd] [QUIT] [2nd] [LIST] [▶] 2 [2nd] [L1] [)] [–] [2nd] [LIST] [▶] 1 [2nd] [L1] [)] [ENTER] 62

If you do not use [2nd] [QUIT] *to leave the LIST menu, the range will be added to L1, which alters your data.*

The range of the data is 62.

The data can be arranged into four groups that have approximately the same number of data in each group. The points separating these groups are called **quartiles** and are symbolized by Q_1, Q_2, and Q_3. The median of the set is Q_2. The **interquartile range** is $Q_3 - Q_1$. Half of the data lie in this range. You can use a graphing calculator to help you find each of these measures.

Example 2 **Find the quartiles and the interquartile range of the golf data in Example 1.**

Before finding the measures you want, you must first make sure the calculator is set to refer to the correct set of data. Our data is in L_1.

Enter: STAT ▶ 3 and highlight L_1 under 1-Var Stats. Make sure that the frequency is 1.

Enter: STAT ▶ 1 ENTER

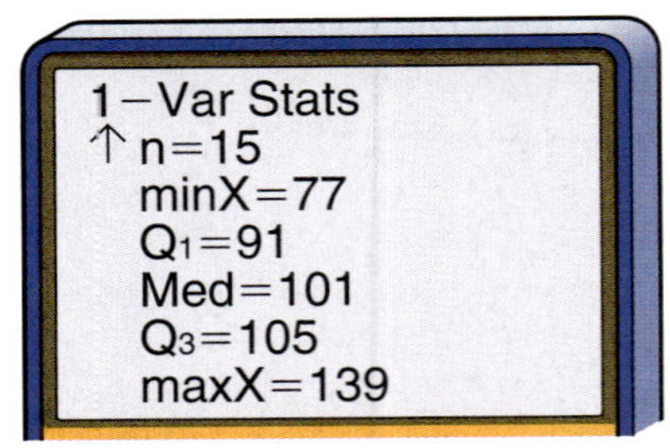

Use the down arrow key to scroll to the end of the statistics. Your screen should look like the one at the right. This tells you there are 15 items of data, the least value (minX) is 77, the greatest value (maxX) is 139, the lower quartile (Q_1) is 91, the median is 101, and the upper quartile (Q_3) is 105.

Use Q_3 and Q_1 to find the interquartile range: $Q_3 - Q_1 = 105 - 91$ or 14.

EXERCISES

Remember to change the Setup when calculating the measures for each set of data.

Enter each set of data into the list given. Then find the lower quartile, median, upper quartile, range, and interquartile range of the data.

1. 12, 17, 16, 23, 18 in L_1

2. 56, 45, 37, 43, 10, 34 in L_2

3. 77, 78, 68, 96, 99, 84, 65 in L_3

4. 30, 90, 40, 70, 50, 100, 80, 60 in L_4

5. 3, 3.2, 6, 45, 7, 26, 1, 3.4, 4, 5.3, 5, 78, 8, 21, 5 in L_5

6. 85, 77, 58, 69, 62, 73, 55, 82, 67, 77, 59, 92, 75, 69, 76 in L_6

7. Look at the range and the interquartile range of each set of data. What do you think it means if the range is great but the interquartile range is small?

8. Suppose you entered a set of data and the interquartile range was 0. What does that mean?

5–7 Integration: Statistics Measures of Variation

What YOU'LL LEARN

- To calculate and interpret the range, quartiles, and interquartile range of sets of data.

Why IT'S IMPORTANT

Measures of variation can help you easily describe the spread of a set of data.

LOOK BACK

You can review finding the mean and median of a set of data in Lesson 3-7.

APPLICATION

Climate

Justin Williams has been promoted and has the option of relocating either to Columbus, Ohio, or San Francisco, California. The Williams family lives in Tampa, Florida, where the average temperature is about 72°F and it is usually warm all year long. His family's wardrobe includes basically all lightweight apparel. He wondered if moving would mean they would have to get lots of new clothes. He looked up the average high temperature for the two cities and found the following information in a table of average high temperatures of U.S. cities.

Mr. Williams calculated the mean and median of the temperatures of each city. The mean high temperature for Columbus was 63.5°, and for San Francisco, it was 62.4°. The median high temperature for Columbus was 63.5°, and for San Francisco, it was 63°. He figured that meant the climate in the two cities was just about the same. But then he decided to take another look at the temperatures and find another way to analyze them.

The months and temperatures for each city form a relation. Mr. Williams decided to graph the relation for each city. He used different colors for each city.

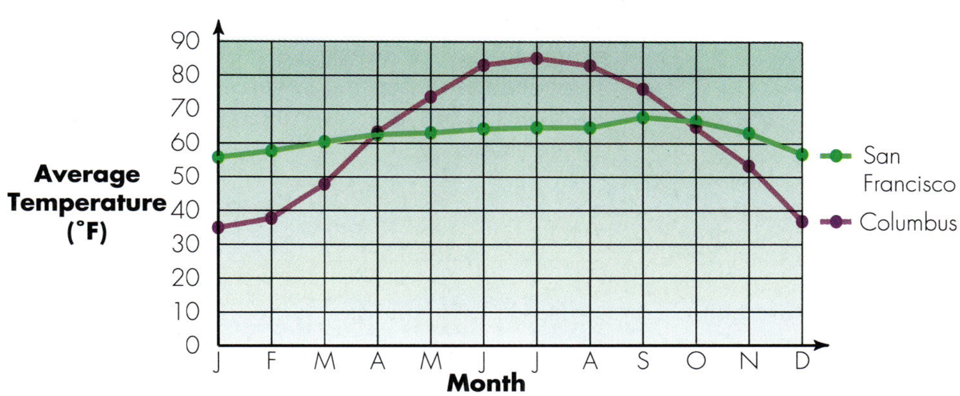

He noticed that the pattern in the temperatures was very different. This case shows that measures of central tendency may not give an accurate enough description of the data. Often **measures of variation** are also used to describe the distribution of the data.

One of the most common measures of variation is the **range.** Unlike the other definition of range in this chapter, the range of a set of data is a measure of the spread of the data.

Definition of Range	**The range of a set of data is the difference between the greatest and the least values of the set.**

GLOBAL CONNECTIONS

If you lived in Managua, Nicaragua, you would experience hot, humid weather averaging 80°F all year. In Largeau, Chad, daytime temperatures can reach 115°F. In Punta Arenas, Chile, it is constantly cold and windy because it is so close to Antarctica. Life in Reykjavik, Iceland, is not all snow and ice. It has long mild winters averaging 32°F and cool, short summers.

Let's find the range for each set of temperatures. Make a table to help organize the data.

City	Greatest Temperature	Least Temperature	Range
Columbus	84°	35°	84° − 35° or 49°
San Francisco	69°	56°	69° − 56° or 13°

The range of temperatures for Columbus is greater than that for San Francisco. This means that temperatures in Columbus vary more than temperatures in San Francisco. If his family moves to Columbus, he will definitely need some new clothes for their colder winters.

Another commonly used measure of variation is called the **interquartile range.** In a set of data, the **quartiles** are values that divide the data into four equal parts. Statisticians often use Q1, Q2, and Q3 to represent the three quartiles. Remember that the median separates the data into two equal parts. Q2 is the median. Q1 is the **lower quartile.** It divides the lower half of the data into two equal parts. Likewise, Q3 is the **upper quartile.** It divides the upper half of the data into two equal parts. The difference between the upper and lower quartiles is the interquartile range (IQR).

The abbreviations LQ and UQ are often used to represent the lower quartile and upper quartile.

Definition of Interquartile Range	**The difference between the upper quartile and the lower quartile of a set of data is called the interquartile range. It represents the middle half, or 50%, of the data in the set.**

Example 1

APPLICATION

Football

The table below shows the heights and weights of 13 veteran players on the 1994 Dallas Cowboys football team. Find the median, upper and lower quartiles, and the interquartile range for the weights of the players.

Player	Height	Weight (lb)
Aikman	6'4"	228
Daniel	5'11"	192
Gaines	5'11"	228
Harper	6'3"	208
Holmes	5'10"	181
Irvin	6'2"	205
Jones	6'2"	237
Marlon	5'11"	189
Newton	6'3"	325
Price	6'3"	247
Smith	5'11"	180
Tolbert	6'6"	263
Williams	5'9"	192

Source: *Gridiron 1994 Pro Football Yearbook*

Order the 13 weights from least to greatest. Then find the median.

180 181 189 192 192 205 208 228 228 237 247 263 325

↑ median (208)

Remember that the median is the middle number when the data are arranged in numerical order.

The lower quartile is the median of the lower half of the data, and the upper quartile is the median of the upper half of the data. If the median is an item in the set of data, it is not included in either half.

180 181 189 ↑ 192 192 205 208 228 228 237 ↑ 247 263 325

$Q_1 = 190.5$ $\qquad Q_2 = \text{median}$ $\qquad Q_3 = 242$

The interquartile range is 242 − 190.5 or 51.5. Therefore, the middle half, or 50% of the weights of the football players, varies within 51.5 pounds.

In Example 1, one weight, 325 pounds, is much greater than the others. In a set of data, a value that is much greater or much less than the rest of the data can be called an **outlier.** An outlier is defined as any element of a set of data that is at least 1.5 interquartile ranges greater than the upper quartile or less than the lower quartile.

An outlier will not affect the quartiles, but it will affect the mean.

The interquartile range of the football data is 51.5. So 1.5(51.5) is 77.25.

113.25 ← −77.25 | 180 181 189 | 192 192 205 208 228 228 237 | 247 263 | 325 +77.25 → 319.25

$Q_1 = 190.5$ $\qquad Q_2 = \text{median}$ $\qquad Q_3 = 242$

From the diagram above, you can see that the only item of data occurring beyond the dashed lines is 325. So, this is the only outlier.

Example 2

APPLICATION

Commerce

LOOK BACK

You can review stem-and-leaf plots in Lesson 1-4.

The double stem-and-leaf plot below represents the tonnage of domestic and foreign imports being delivered at the top 19 busiest ports in the United States during 1992.

Domestic	Stem	Foreign
[5	10	
	9	[5
	8	
5	7	3
5	6	
	5	
8 0	4	1 4
8 1	3	6 6
8 5] 3 [1	2	0 0 3 4 5 5] 5 [5 9 9
9 9 7 5 2 0	1	8 8
5 | 2 = 25,000,000 tons 9 8]	0	8] 7 | 3 = 73,000,000 tons

Source: Army Corps of Engineers, U.S. Dept. of Defense

a. The brackets group the values in the lower half and the values in the upper half. What do the triangles contain? What do the boxes contain?

b. Find the interquartile ranges of the domestic and the foreign tonnage.

c. Which type of imports had a more consistent tonnage—the domestic or the foreign?

d. Find any outliers.

a. The triangles contain the medians.
The boxes contain the lower and upper quartiles.

b. Domestic

Q1 is 15 and Q3 is 40.

IQR = Q3 − Q1

= 40 − 15 or 25

Foreign

Q1 is 20 and Q3 is 36.

IQR = Q3 − Q1

= 36 − 20 or 16

c. The foreign imports had more consistent tonnage because it had the smaller interquartile range.

d. Outliers are those values that lie 1.5 IQRs above Q3 or below Q1.

Domestic

1.5(IQR) + Q3 = 1.5(25) + 40 or 77.5

Q1 − 1.5 (IQR) = 15 − 1.5(25) or −22.5

Since 105 > 77.5, 105 is an outlier. There are no outliers below −22.5.

Foreign

1.5(IQR) + Q3 = (1.5)(16) + 36 or 60

Q1 − 1.5 (IQR) = 20 −(1.5)(16) or −4

Since 95 > 60 and 73 > 60, 95 and 73 are outliers.

There are no outliers below −4.

CHECK FOR UNDERSTANDING

Communicating Mathematics

Study the lesson. Then complete the following.

1. Refer to the application at the beginning of the lesson. Compare the interquartile ranges of the temperatures in San Francisco and Columbus.
2. **Describe** how the mean is affected by an outlier.
3. **Predict** the following.
   a. If you were to measure the height of all of the students in your school, in which group of students might you find outliers?
   b. If you were to measure the weight of all of the students in your school, in which group of students might you find outliers?
4. **Explain** the difference between range as defined in Lesson 5–2 and range as defined in this lesson.

MODELING MATHEMATICS

5. Along with your classmates, line up according to your heights.
   a. "Fold" the line in half by having the shortest person meet the tallest person. What is the median height?
   b. Do the same with each half of the line. What is lower quartile and upper quartile of the heights of the students in your classroom?

Guided Practice

Find the range, median, upper quartile, lower quartile, and interquartile range of each set of data. Identify any outliers.

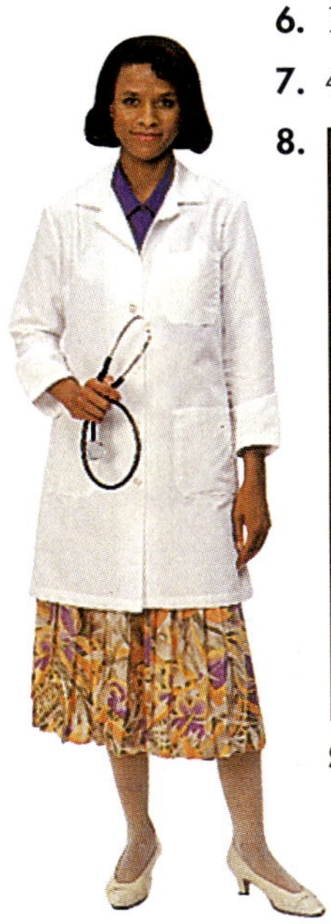

6. 16, 24, 11, 17, 19
7. 43, 45, 56, 37, 11, 34
8.

Top 10 Jobs of the Future

Job	Average Salary
Civil engineer	$55,800
Computer system analyst	42,700
Electrical engineer	59,100
Geologist	50,800
High school teacher	32,500
Pharmacist	47,500
Physical therapist	37,200
Physician	148,000
Psychologist	53,000
School principal	57,300

Source: *American Careers,* Fall 1994

9.

Stem	Leaf
0	0 2 3
1	1 7 9
2	2 3 5 6
3	3 4 4 5 9
4	0 7 8 8

$2|2 = 22$

10. **Football** Refer to the data in Example 1. Find the median, upper and lower quartiles, and the interquartile range for the heights of the players.

EXERCISES

Practice

Find the range, median, upper quartile, lower quartile, and interquartile range for each set of data.

11. 77, 78, 68, 96, 99, 84, 65

12. 17°, 46°, 18°, 22°, 18°, 21°, 19°

13. 2, 4, 6, 8, 2, 4, 6, 8, 10, 0

14. 89, 56, 75, 82, 64, 73, 87, 92

15. 30.8, 29.9, 30.0, 31.0, 30.1, 30.5, 30.7, 31.0

16. 78, 2, 3.4, 4, 45, 7, 5.3, 5, 3, 1, 3.2, 6, 26, 8, 5

17. 1050, 1175, 835, 1075, 1025, 1145, 1100, 1125, 975, 1005, 1125, 1095, 1075, 1055

18.

Stem	Leaf
5	3 6 8
6	5 8
7	0 3 7 7 9
8	1 4 8 8 9
9	9

9|9 = 9900

19.

Stem	Leaf
19	3 5 5
20	2 2 5 8
21	5 8 8 9 9 9
22	0 1 7 8 9
23	2

19|3 = $193

20.

Stem	Leaf
5	0 3 7 9
6	1 3 4 5 5 6
7	1 5 6 6 9
8	1 2 3 5 8
9	2 5 6 9

5|0 = 5.0 cm

Graphing Calculator

21. a. Use a graphing calculator to find the median, upper and lower quartiles, range, and interquartile range of the number of books given in the table below.

Selected Libraries Around the World

Library	Location	Year Founded	Number of Books
Bibliothèque Nationale	Paris, France	1480	9,000,000
British Library	London, UK	1753	18,000,000
Library of Congress	Washington, DC	1800	28,000,000
Russian State Library	Moscow, Russia	1862	11,750,000
Biblioteca Academiei Romane	Bucharest, Romania	1867	9,397,260
Chicago Public Library	Chicago, IL	1872	11,500,000
Denver Public Library	Denver, CO	1889	4,000,000
Brooklyn Public Library	Brooklyn, NY	1896	5,700,000
University of California, LA	Los Angeles, CA	1919	5,400,000
Columbia University	New York, NY	1961	6,100,000

Source: *The Top 10 of Everything Else*, Russell Ash

b. Would it make sense to find these values for the years in which these libraries were founded? Why or why not?

Critical Thinking

22. a. Write an example of a set of 19 numbers that has a range of 60, a median of 40, an interquartile range of 16, and one outlier.

b. Write an example of a set of 19 numbers that has a range of 20, a median of 40, an interquartile range of 11, and no outliers.

Applications and Problem Solving

Find the range, median, upper quartile, lower quartile, and interquartile range for each set of data.

23. **Entertainment**

Long-Running Broadway Plays	
Play	**Performances**
A	3,486
B	2,377
C	4,917
D	6,137
E	3,242
F	3,388
G	2,844
H	3,005
I	3,224
J	2,717
K	5,959
L	2,717
M	3,182

24. **Transportation**

Popular Passenger Cars	
Name of Car	**Number Sold**
Venus Gazelle	273,617
Venus Carnival	219,683
Mars Excellence	269,034
Mars Moonbeam	360,448
Mars Aquarius	217,644
Jupiter Ruby	330,030
Jupiter Tiger	255,579
Cadet Superior	214,761
Pluto	229,356
Cheetah Cellex	299,737

25. **Education**

Enrollment at Selected Colleges in the U.S. (1993–1994)	
College	**Enrollment**
Baylor University	12,194
Brown University	7,655
California Institute of Technology	1,977
Columbia University	3,441
Dartmouth College	5,475
Georgia State University	23,651
Howard University	10,736
Massachusetts Institute of Technology	9,790
Princeton University	6,444
Stanford University	14,002
Yale University	10,844

Source: *Peterson's Guides,* © 1994

26. **Nutrition**

Calories in Foods, per serving	
Food	**Calories**
Apple	100
Banana	130
Bread	60
Cupcake	200
Donut	120
Ice cream	185
Orange juice	85
Peach	50
Peanut butter	190
Potato	100
Soft taco	225
Whole milk	133

Source: U.S. Dept. of Agriculture

27. Sports The double stem-and-leaf plot below represents the ages of the top 20 male and female golfers for the 1994 season, according to *Golfer's Almanac,* 1995.

Male	Stem	Female
8	1	
9 9 8 8 5	2	3 4 5 5 9 9
8 8 7 6 6 5	3	1 2 2 2 4 4 5 8 9 9 9
6 2 0 0	4	0 4 6
4|5 = 54 years old 4 3 1 0	5	*4|6 = 46 years old*

a. Find the ranges, quartiles, and interquartile ranges of the average golfer's age for male and female golfers.

b. Identify any outliers.

c. Compare the ranges and interquartile ranges for male and female golfers. What can you conclude from these statistics?

28. Entertainment The total sales of movie rentals as of April 1994 for selected Academy Award winners are listed below.

Video	Total Rental Sales ($ million)	Video	Total Rental Sales ($ million)
A	38.7	L	23.1
B	59.8	M	60.0
C	81.5	N	27.5
D	50.5	O	19.0
E	86.8	P	56.5
F	70.0	Q	60.0
G	43.5	R	30.6
H	23.0	S	78.2
I	50.25	T	86.3
J	25.0	U	80.0
K	30.6		

a. Find the range, median, upper and lower quartiles, and interquartile range for the total rental sales.

b. Identify any outliers.

c. The least value on the list of all-time top 20 movie rentals as of April, 1994, is $96.3 million. What can you conclude about Academy Award winners in relation to this data?

29. a. List the grades you have made during this grading period in mathematics. Determine the range, the quartiles, and the interquartile range of the scores.

b. List the grades you have made during this grading period in English. Determine the range, the quartiles, and the interquartile range of the scores.

c. In which of the two courses are your grades more consistent? Why do you think this is the case?

Mixed Review

30. Geology The underground temperature of rocks varies with their depth below the surface. The temperature at the surface is about 20°C. At a depth of 2 km, the temperature is about 90°C, and at a depth of 10 km, the temperature is about 370°C. (Lesson 5–6)

a. Write an equation to describe this relationship.

b. Use the equation to predict the temperature at a depth of 13 km.

31. Which ordered pairs are solutions to $5 - 1.5x = 2y$? (Lesson 5–3)

a. (0, 1) **b.** (8, 2) **c.** $\left(4, -\frac{1}{2}\right)$ **d.** (2, 1)

32. **Ecology** For every 20 grams of smog produced by a typical automobile in an hour, gasoline-powered lawn mowers produce 50 grams. If it takes Jodi 1.5 hours to mow her lawn, how long would she be able to drive her car and produce the same amount of smog? (Lesson 4–1)

33. **Sports** The table at the right shows how many millions of people participated in in-line skating and mountain biking in 1991 and 1992. Write an equation to represent each situation. Then solve. (Lesson 3–1)

Year	1991	1992
In-Line Skating	6.2	9.4
Mountain Biking	6.0	6.9

Source: *Men's Fitness*

a. How many more people were participating in in-line skating in 1992 than in 1991?

b. How many more people were mountain biking in 1992 than in 1991?

34. Simplify $3(-4) + 2(-7)$. (Lesson 2–6)

Mathematics and SOCIETY

Record Cold Temperatures

The excerpt below appeared in an article in *Mother Earth News* in January, 1995. All of the temperatures are given in °F.

HOW COLD DOES IT GET IN ALASKA? The all-time low temperature is −80 degrees at Prospect Creek Camp on January 23, 1971. Think of it: that temperature is to 0 degrees what 0 degrees is to a typical summer afternoon. Still, you might say, Alaska is up there near the North Pole. Surely, down here in the "lower 48," we never approach such levels of incredible frigidity. Yes we do. On January 20, 1954, the temperature in Rogers Pass, Montana, nudged −70 degrees.... Is there anywhere that temperatures can get colder than in Alaska? Siberia can get a little colder. But there is one place on Earth that is much more frigid: Antarctica. Earth's all-time record low was set at Vostok Station in Antarctica in 1983: −128 degrees. ■

Antarctica

1. How much colder is Earth's record low temperature than a temperature of 80°F in summer?
2. The wind-chill factor is a measure of how cold we feel when we experience wind along with a low temperature. Do you think that the wind-chill factor also applies to nonliving objects such as bicycles and cars? Why or why not?
3. The hottest temperature recorded on Earth was 136°F at Azizia, Tripolitaina, in northern Africa, on September 13, 1922. If every country's record high and low temperatures for the 20th century were entered in a computer, what would be the range of the data?
4. If the interquartile range of temperatures in a country is very small, what does that tell you about the climate of that country?

CLOSING THE Investigation

Go Fish!

Refer to the Investigation on pages 190–191.

Sampling is a research method frequently used in many fields. Manufacturers use sampling to determine the quality of their products. Surveys are a way of sampling the opinions of the public about items they encounter in everyday life such as what television programs they watch or what food is their favorite. Capture-recapture is only one of many methods used in sampling a population.

Analyze

You have conducted experiments and organized your data in various ways. It is now time to analyze your findings and state your conclusions.

PORTFOLIO ASSESSMENT

You may want to keep your work on this Investigation in your portfolio.

1. What are the strengths and weaknesses of the capture-recapture method of sampling?
2. How many samples do you think give the best results? Why?
3. Write a one-page report on how the capture-recapture method is used in real life. Be sure to include references for your report.

Write

Imagine that the fish population in Moonlit Lake had been estimated each year for nine years and that these estimates are reflected in the following graph.

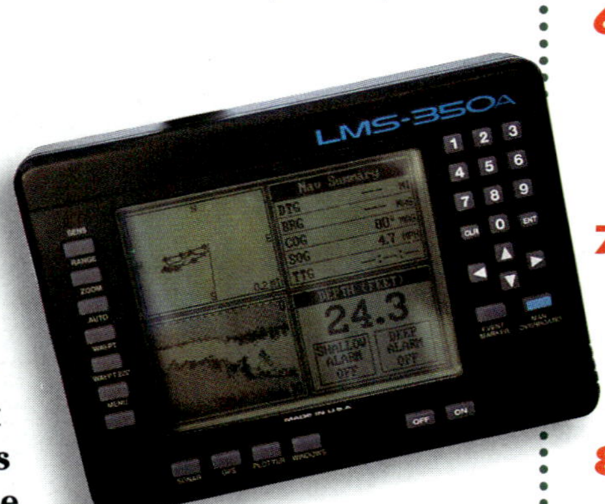

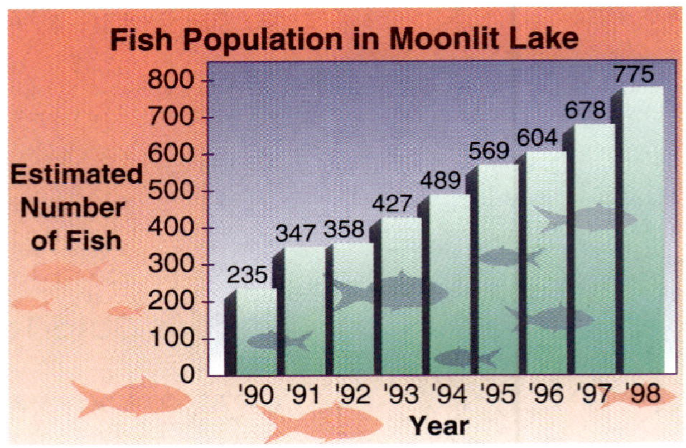

Notice that the fish population is increasing over time. Suppose city council member Aubrey Howard wanted to show other members of the city council that the growth in the fish population has been rapid. Mr. Howard might choose to find a best-fit line for the graph.

4. Plot the information from the graph as ordered pairs on a coordinate plane.
5. Use two vertical lines to separate the data into three sets of equal size.
6. Locate a point in each set whose x- and y-coordinates represent the medians of the x- and y-coordinates of all the points in that set. In other words, locate the middle point of the three sets.
7. Now take a straightedge and align it with the outer two median points. Then slide it one third of the distance to the median point of the center set of points. Then draw the line. This is a *best-fit line*.
8. What might Mr. Howard's argument be? Write a one-page speech for the council member, using the graph as evidence for your opinion.

CHAPTER 5 HIGHLIGHTS

VOCABULARY

After completing this chapter, you should be able to define each term, property, or phrase and give an example or two of each.

Algebra

axes (p. 254)
complete graph (p. 278)
completeness property for points in the plane (p. 256)
coordinate plane (p. 254)
domain (p. 263)
equation in two variables (p. 271)
function (p. 287)
functional notation (p. 289)
graph (p. 255)
inverse of a relation (p. 264)
linear equation (p. 280)
linear equation in standard form (p. 281)
linear function (p. 278)
mapping (p. 263)
origin (p. 254)
quadrants (p. 254)
range (p. 263)
relation (pp. 260, 263)
solution of an equation in two variables (p. 271)
vertical line test (p. 289)
x-axis (p. 254)
x-coordinate (p. 254)
y-axis (p. 254)
y-coordinate (p. 254)

Statistics

interquartile range (pp. 304, 306)
lower quartile (p. 306)
measures of variation (p. 306)
outlier (p. 307)
quartiles (pp. 304, 306)
range (p. 306)
upper quartile (p. 306)

Problem Solving

use a table (p. 255)

UNDERSTANDING AND USING THE VOCABULARY

Choose the letter of the term that best matches each statement or phrase.

1. In the coordinate plane, the axes intersect at the __?__.
2. A __?__ is a set of ordered pairs.
3. __?__ are graphed on a coordinate plane.
4. In a coordinate system, the __?__ is a horizontal line.
5. In the ordered pair, A(2, 7), 7 is the __?__.
6. The coordinate axes separate a plane into four __?__.
7. An equation whose graph is a non-vertical straight line is called a __?__.
8. In the relation $\{(4, -2), (0, 5), (6, 2), (-1, 8)\}$, the __?__ is the set $\{-1, 0, 4, 6\}$.
9. The domain contains values represented by the __?__.

a. domain
b. independent variable
c. linear function
d. ordered pairs
e. origin
f. quadrants
g. relation
h. *x*-axis
i. *y*-axis
j. *y*-coordinate

STUDY GUIDE AND ASSESSMENT

SKILLS AND CONCEPTS

OBJECTIVES AND EXAMPLES

Upon completing this chapter, you should be able to:

- graph ordered pairs on a coordinate plane (Lesson 5–1)

Graph $T(3, -2)$ and state the quadrant in which the point is located.

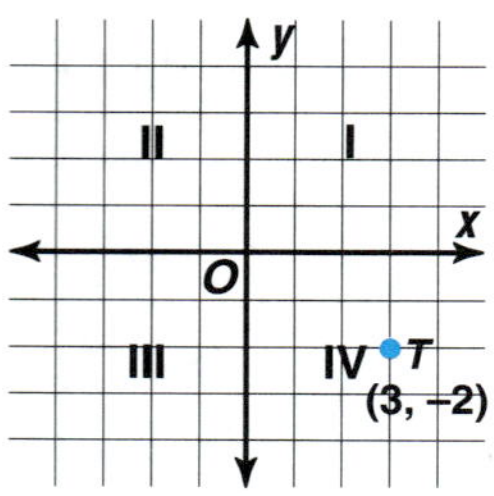

$T(3, -2)$ is located in Quadrant IV.

REVIEW EXERCISES

Use these exercises to review and prepare for the chapter test.

Graph each point.

10. $A(4, 2)$
11. $B(-1, 3)$
12. $C(0, -5)$
13. $D(-3, -2)$

Write the ordered pair for each point shown at the right. State the quadrant in which the point is located.

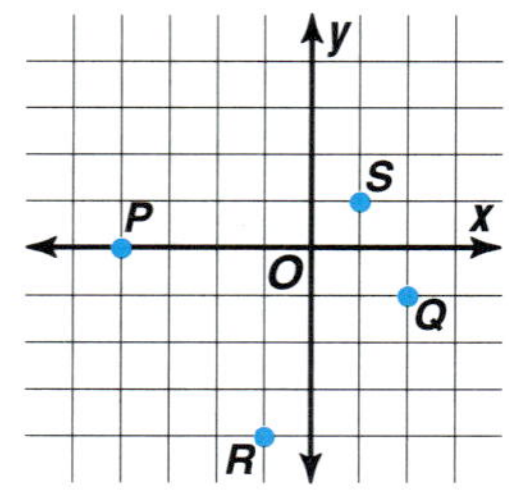

14. P
15. Q
16. R
17. S

- identify the domain, range, and inverse of a relation (Lesson 5–2)

Determine the domain, range, and inverse of $\{(6, 6), (4, -3), (6, 0)\}$.

The domain is $\{4, 6\}$.

The range is $\{-3, 0, 6\}$.

The inverse is $\{(6, 6), (-3, 4), (0, 6)\}$.

State the domain and range of each relation.

18. $\{(4, 1), (4, 6), (4, -1)\}$
19. $\{(-3, 5), (-3, 6), (4, 5), (4, 6)\}$
20. $\{(-2, 1), (-5, 1), (-7, 1)\}$
21. $\{(-3, 1), (-2, 0), (-1, 1), (0, 2)\}$

Draw a mapping and a graph for each relation. State the inverse of each relation.

22. $\{(4, 4), (-3, 5), (4, -1), (0, 3)\}$
23. $\{(0, 2), (3, -1), (2, 2), (-2, -1)\}$

- determine the range for a given domain (Lesson 5–3)

Solve $2x + y = 8$ if the domain is $\{3, 2, 1\}$.

Solve for y.

$2x + y = 8$
$y = 8 - 2x$

x	8 − 2x	y	(x, y)
3	8 − 2(3)	2	(3, 2)
2	8 − 2(2)	4	(2, 4)
1	8 − 2(1)	6	(1, 6)

Solve each equation if the domain is $\{-4, -2, 0, 2, 4\}$.

24. $y = 4x + 5$
25. $x - y = 9$
26. $3x + 2y = 9$
27. $4x - 3y = 0$

Make a table and graph the solution set for each equation and domain.

28. $y = 7 - 3x$ for $x = \{-3, -2, -1, 0, 1, 2, 3\}$
29. $5x - y = -3$ for $x = \{-2, 0, 2, 4, 6\}$

OBJECTIVES AND EXAMPLES

- graph linear equations (Lesson 5–4)

Graph $y = 3x - 4$.

x	$3x - 4$	y	(x, y)
0	$3(0) - 4$	-4	$(0, -4)$
1	$3(1) - 4$	-1	$(1, -1)$
2	$3(2) - 4$	2	$(2, 2)$

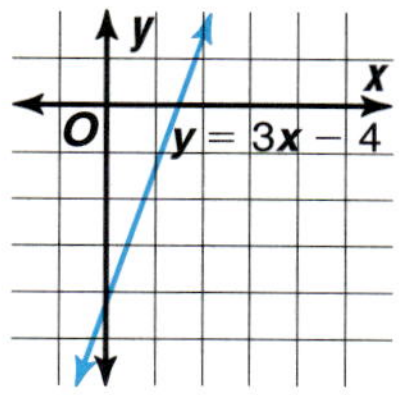

REVIEW EXERCISES

Graph each equation.

30. $y = -x + 2$
31. $x + 5y = 4$
32. $2x - 3y = 6$
33. $5x + 2y = 10$
34. $\frac{1}{2}x + \frac{1}{3}y = 3$
35. $y - \frac{1}{3} = \frac{1}{3}x + \frac{2}{3}$

- determine whether a given relation is a function (Lesson 5–5)

Is $\{(3, 2), (5, 3), (4, 3), (5, 2)\}$ a function?

Because there are two values of y for one value of x, 5, the relation is *not* a function.

Determine whether each relation is a function.

36.

a	b
-2	6
3	-2
3	0
4	6

37.

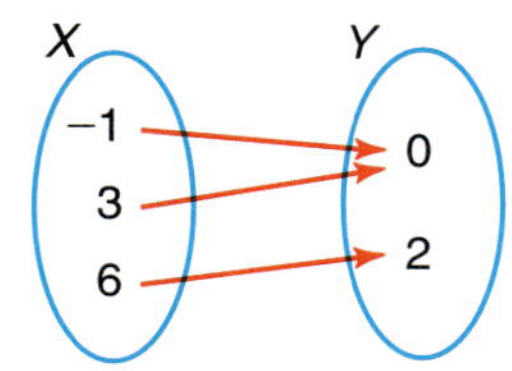

38. $\{(3, 8), (9, 3), (-3, 8), (5, 3)\}$
39. $x - y^2 = 4$
40. $xy = 6$
41. $3x - 4y = 7$

- find the value of a function for a given element of the domain (Lesson 5–5)

Given $g(x) = 2x - 1$, find $g(-6)$.

$$g(-6) = 2(-6) - 1$$
$$= -12 - 1$$
$$= -13$$

If $g(x) = x^2 - x + 1$, find each value.

42. $g(2)$
43. $g(-1)$
44. $g\left(\frac{1}{2}\right)$
45. $g(a + 1)$
46. $g(-2a)$
47. $2g(a - 3)$

- write an equation to represent a relation, given some of the solutions for the equation (Lesson 5–6)

Write an equation for the relation given in the chart below.

+1 +1 +1 +1

a	-2	-1	0	1	2
b	20	17	14	11	8

−3 −3 −3 −3

The equation is $b = 14 - 3a$.

Write an equation for each relation.

48.

x	0	1	2	3	4
y	5	8	11	14	17

49.

x	2	4	5	7	10
y	-2	0	1	3	6

50.

x	3	6	9	12	15
y	-1	-3	-5	-7	-9

OBJECTIVES AND EXAMPLES

- calculate and interpret the range, quartiles, and interquartile range of sets of data (Lesson 5–7)

Find the range, median, upper quartile, lower quartile, and interquartile range for the set of data below.

25, 20, 30, 24, 22, 26, 28, 29, 19

Order the set of data from least to greatest.

19 20 22 24 25 26 28 29 30

The range is $30 - 19 = 11$.

The median is the middle number, 25.

The lower quartile is $\frac{20 + 22}{2}$ or 21.

The upper quartile is $\frac{28 + 29}{2}$ or 28.5.

The interquartile range is $28.5 - 21$ or 7.5.

REVIEW EXERCISES

Find the range, median, upper quartile, lower quartile, and interquartile range for each set of data.

51. 30, 90, 40, 70, 50, 100, 80, 60

52. 3, 3.2, 45, 7, 2, 1, 3.4, 4, 5.3, 5, 78, 8, 21, 5

53. 85, 77, 58, 69, 62, 73, 55, 82, 67, 77, 59, 92, 75, 69, 76

54. The average annual snowfall, in inches, for each of 12 northeastern cities is listed below.

111.5	70.7	59.8	68.6	63.8	254.8
64.3	82.3	91.7	88.9	110.5	77.1

APPLICATIONS AND PROBLEM SOLVING

55. Finance To save for a new bicycle, Ralph begins a savings plan. Ralph's savings are described by the equation $s = 5w + 56$, where s represents his total savings in dollars and w represents the number of weeks since the start of the savings plan. (Lesson 5–4)

a. Draw a graph of this equation.

b. Use the graph to determine how much money Ralph had already saved when the plan started.

56. Car Rental The cost of a one-day car rental from A-1 Car Rental is \$41 if you drive 100 miles, \$51.80 if you drive 160 miles, and \$63.50 if you drive 225 miles. (Lesson 5–6)

a. Write an equation to describe this relationship.

b. Use the equation to determine the per-mile charge.

57. Entertainment The ratings of the top 20 favorite syndicated television programs for 1993–94 are listed below. (Lesson 5–7)

Program	Rating
A	6.1
B	6.5
C	5.7
D	6.6
E	5.1
F	8.4
G	5.9
H	6.7
I	7.3
J	12.6
K	6.9
L	7.5
M	9.7
N	7.9
O	5.2
P	10.8
Q	8.2
R	14.7
S	7.2
T	5.7

a. Find the range, quartiles, and interquartile range for the ratings.

b. Identify any outliers.

A practice test for Chapter 5 is provided on page 791.

ALTERNATIVE ASSESSMENT

COOPERATIVE LEARNING PROJECT

Graphs and Business In this chapter, you learned how to graph relations and determine whether the relation is a linear equation. Once a relation has been graphed, the process of analyzing it to determine more applicable information is necessary in order to completely understand the problem or situation.

In this project, imagine that your family owns a catering business and you want to look at the amount that you charge for banquets. You have been asked to present a report to the other members of your family that shows recommended charges and how they will affect your profit. After some research, you find that the initial basic charge for a banquet should be $250 plus $4 per person. Your food costs per person are $2.50, and your other costs such as labor, time, etc. total $1.00 per person.

Graph the various charges determined by the number of persons. Graph the various costs determined by the number of persons.

Follow these steps to organize your presentation.

- Determine the charges for various banquet sizes.
- Determine the costs for various banquet sizes.
- Determine how to plot and display your graphs appropriately.
- Write an algebraic model that describes the total charge for a banquet.
- Write an algebraic model that describes the total cost for a banquet.
- Write several paragraphs for your presentation and incorporate your algebraic models and graphs to help your presentation.

THINKING CRITICALLY

- Use one set of data to construct two graphs in which each represents the data, but portrays different meanings.
- Create a relation that is a function and one that is not a function. Compare and contrast the two relations.

PORTFOLIO

You have been asked to show another student how to graph an equation, but it must be completely written and nonverbal. Select one of the graphing assignments from this chapter and list the steps involved in graphing this equation. Be sure to include your steps in the appropriate order.

When you have completed this paper, give it to another student in your class and have him or her read it and follow the written steps to graph a different equation. Collect his or her graph and check for accuracy. Place both of these in your portfolio.

SELF EVALUATION

Graphs can be used to analyze functions or data. To *analyze* means to separate or distinguish all the parts of something in order to discover more information about the complex whole element.

Assess yourself. How analytical are you? Do you delve deeper into a problem and look for smaller components that will help you understand the larger problem, or do you look at the big picture and attempt to solve the problem within the larger view of things? Describe two or three ways in which you could divide a complex problem or situation in mathematics and/or in your daily life in order to analyze it.

LONG-TERM PROJECT

In·ves·ti·ga·tion

Smoke Gets In Your Eyes

MATERIALS NEEDED

- stopwatch
- grid paper
- balloons
- tape measure
- string

In the 1950s and '60s, scientists piled up a mountain of evidence on the life-threatening health consequences of smoking. Recently there have been studies done on the effects of secondhand smoke. Secondhand smoke is the smoke others breathe when they are close to a person who is smoking. In 1993, the Environmental Protection Agency (EPA) estimated that secondhand smoke is responsible for several thousands of cases of lung cancer among nonsmokers each year in the U.S. Passive smoke joins a select company of only about a dozen other environmental pollutants in this risk category.

As an aware citizen and health-conscious teenager, you understand this problem and want to start a campaign to limit the effects of secondhand smoke. In this Investigation, you will gather evidence about how much air is inhaled when you breathe and compare that to smoke in the room. You will also examine the financial and health aspects of this problem. Work in groups of three. Make an Investigation Folder in which you can store all of your work on this Investigation for future use.

Adult Cigarette Use in the United States

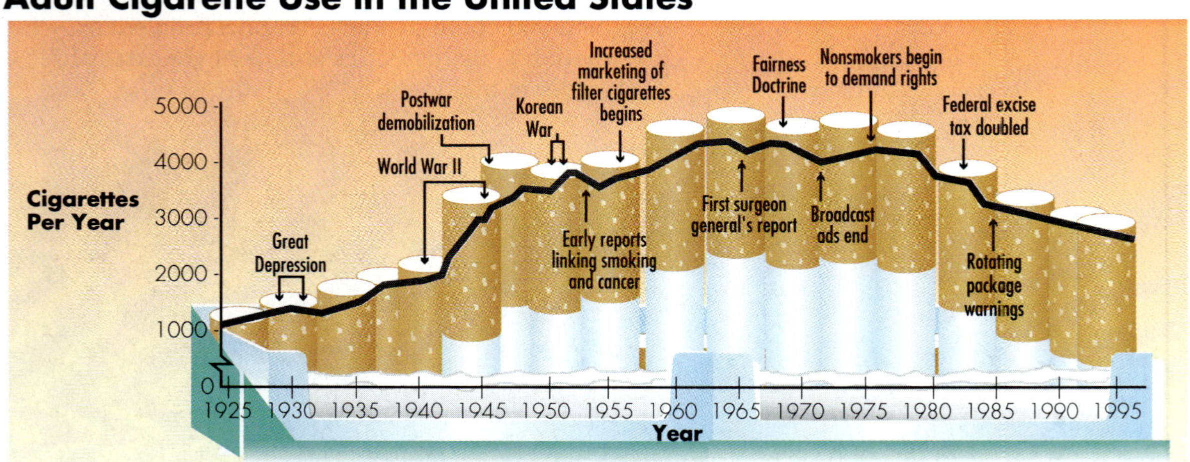

Source: U.S. Department of Health and Human Resources

GROUP MEMBER	1	2	3
Number of breaths			
Circumference of balloon			
Radius of balloon			
Volume of balloon			
Volume of each breath			

COLLECT THE DATA

1. Begin by copying the chart above onto a sheet of paper.
2. Stretch each balloon. Have each member of the group blow up at least three round balloons to full size and let the air out.
3. Give each team member time to rest.
4. Cut a piece of string that is approximately 30 inches long. Tie the string so that it can form a circle that is approximately 8 inches in diameter when laid on a flat surface.
5. One member of the group should hold the string hoop around the balloon and another member should blow the balloon up again. The remaining group member should count and record the number of puffs it takes to blow up each balloon to the size of the hoop. Each group member should blow up one balloon.
6. Measure each inflated balloon to estimate its circumference at the fullest part. Find the approximate radius of the balloon by using the formula $r = \frac{C}{2\pi}$. Record the radius.

ANALYZE THE DATA

7. Display your data on a graph.
8. Calculate the average number of breaths it takes to fill a balloon.
9. The volume of the spherical balloon can be estimated by the formula $V = \frac{4}{3}\pi r^3$. Compute the volume of each balloon. Then estimate the volume of each breath.

You will continue working on this Investigation throughout Chapters 6 and 7.

Be sure to keep your chart and materials in your Investigation Folder.

Smoke Gets In Your Eyes Investigation

Working on the Investigation
Lesson 6–2, p. 338

Working on the Investigation
Lesson 6–5, p. 361

Working on the Investigation
Lesson 7–2, p. 398

Working on the Investigation
Lesson 7–6, p. 426

Closing the Investigation
End of Chapter 7, p. 442

CHAPTER 6

Analyzing Linear Equations

Objectives

In this chapter, you will:

- find the slope of a line, given the coordinates of two of its points,
- write linear equations in point-slope, standard, and slope-intercept forms,
- draw a scatter plot and find the equation of a best-fit line for the data,
- solve problems by using models,
- graph linear equations, and
- use slope to determine if two lines are parallel or perpendicular.

Immigration on the Rise

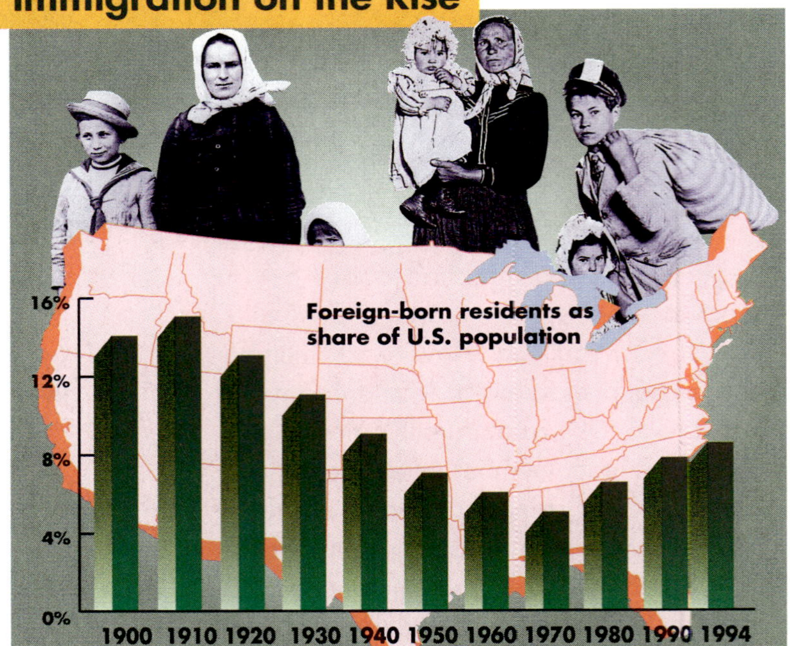

Source: *U.S. News and World Report*, September 25, 1995

Almost $20 billion a year is spent on bilingual programs in U.S. schools. These programs were launched in 1968 to help immigrant children learn English. The percentage of foreign-born Americans is rising. More than 22 states have enacted laws proclaiming English as the official language. What are your views on making English the official language of the U.S.?

TIME Line

435 B.C. The statue of Zeus is built at Olympia, Greece, by Pheidias.

A.D. 1321 French mathematician Levi ben Gerson is the first to use mathematical induction in a proof.

1790 French artist Marie-Louise-Elisabeth Vigee-Lebrun paints her *Self-portrait.*

PEOPLE IN THE NEWS

One student from Webster, Texas, **Jorge Arturo Pineda Aguilar,** is a member of the new immigrant minority. He and his family are from Monterrey, Mexico, and recently moved to Texas. At age 13, Jorge is one of the recent winners of the 1995 Youth Honor Awards presented by *Skipping Stones,* a multicultural children's magazine. His 1995 winning essay, written in both Spanish and English, deals with racial and ethnic prejudice.

Jorge regrets that so many people have ill-feelings about someone who doesn't speak English. He writes, "All of us are human beings and the color or nationality of a person should not be an issue. What should matter are the feelings of each person. We have to be together—work together for a common well being."

Chapter Project

The table below shows the per capita income and the total non-English speaking population (ages 5 years or older) in 15 selected states.

State	1993 Per Capita Income ($)	Non-English Speaking Population
AL	17,234	107,866
AR	16,143	60,781
FL	20,857	2,098,315
IL	22,582	1,499,112
IN	19,203	245,826
KY	17,173	86,482
LA	16,667	391,994
NC	17,488	240,866
NM	16,297	493,999
NY	24,623	3,908,720
OK	17,020	145,798
TN	17,666	131,550
TX	19,189	3,970,304
VA	21,634	418,521
WV	16,209	44,203

The population is given according to the 1990 U.S. Census.

Round the data to the nearest thousand. Graph the data for each state by plotting the per capita income data along the horizontal axis and the non-English-speaking population data along the vertical axis.

- What pattern, if any, do you notice?
- Can a best-fit line be drawn? If so, what might be the equation of this line?
- Can a valid relationship exist between these data? Why or why not?

1968 The U.S. Postal Service issues a stamp honoring the life of Chief Joseph of the Nez Perce Nation.

1973 Marion Wright Edelman founds the Children's Defense Fund.

1926 Mexican artist Diego Rivera paints *The Tortilla Maker.*

1995 Twins Chris and Courtney Salthouse from Chamblee, Georgia *both* score a perfect 1600 on their SATs.

MODELING MATHEMATICS

A Preview of Lesson 6–1

6–1A Slope

Materials: geoboard rubber bands

The **slope** of a line segment is the ratio of the change in the vertical distance between the endpoints of the segment to the change in the horizontal distance. You can use a geoboard to model a line segment and calculate its slope.

Activity **Model line segment *AB* whose endpoints are *A*(1, 2) and *B*(3, 5). Then find the slope of segment *AB*.**

Step 1 Suppose the pegs of the geoboard represent ordered pairs on a coordinate plane. Let's define the lower left peg as the point representing the ordered pair (1, 1). Locate the pegs that represent (1, 2) and (3, 5). Place a rubber band around these pegs to model segment *AB*.

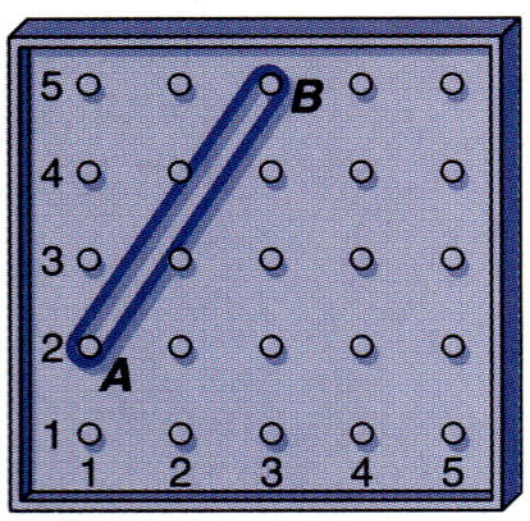

Step 2 Use a different color rubber band to show the horizontal distance from the *x* value of *A* to the *x* value of *B*. Use another color rubber band to show the vertical distance from the *y* value of *A* to the *y* value of *B*.

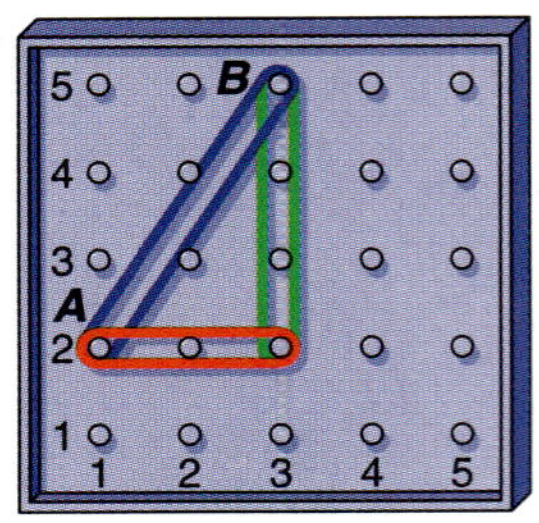

Step 3 As you move from point *A* to point *B*, you can go right and then up. These are positive directions on the coordinate plane. So, the red rubber band represents 2 units. The green rubber band represents 3 units. The slope of segment *AB* is the ratio of the *y* distance to the *x* distance or $\frac{3}{2}$.

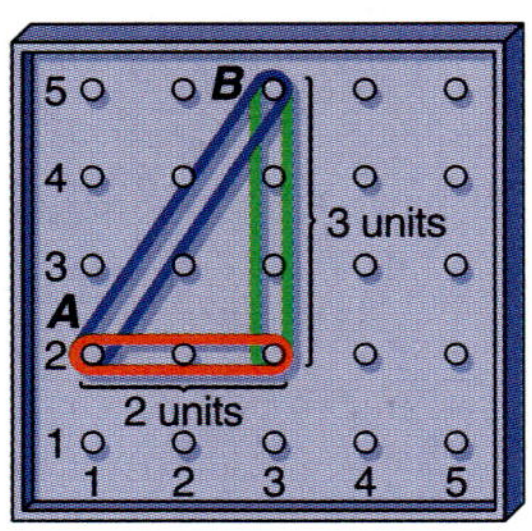

Model

1. Use a geoboard to find the slope of a segment whose endpoints are at (5, 2) and (1, 4).

Write

2. For the activity above and Exercise 1, write ratios that compare the differences in the *y* values of the ordered pairs to the differences in the *x* values of the ordered pairs. How do these compare with the slopes of the respective segments?
3. What value could you assign to the lower left peg if you were modeling segment *CD* with endpoints *C*(3, 5) and *D*(6, 7)?
4. Write a rule for finding the slope of any line segment shown on a coordinate plane.
5. Do you think the rule applies to ordered pairs that involve negative numbers? Explain your answer and give examples.

6–1 Slope

***What* YOU'LL LEARN**

- To find the slope of a line, given the coordinates of two points on the line.

***Why* IT'S IMPORTANT**

You can use slope to describe lines and solve problems involving construction and architecture.

CAREER CHOICES

Construction **contractors** plan, budget, and direct residential and commercial construction projects. They use computers to graphically implement a building plan. A bachelors degree in construction science is helpful.

For more information, contact:

American Institute of Constructors
9887 N. Gandy Blvd.
Suite 104
St. Petersburg, FL 33702

APPLICATION

Construction

Alan and Mabel Wong bought a lot in San Francisco on which to build a house. The lot is located on a street having an 11% grade. The length of the sidewalk along the lot is 43 feet. City ordinances state that there must be a 5-foot clearance on each side of the house to the property line. The house they would like to build is 32 feet wide. Will they be able to build their house on the lot they bought? *This problem will be solved in Example 4.*

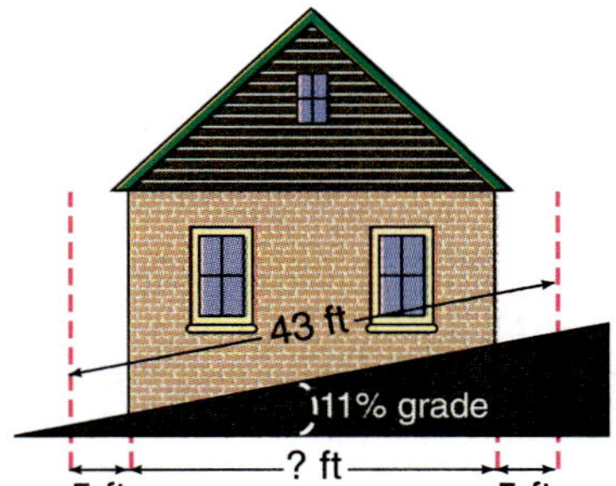

What do you think of when you hear the word *slope*? You might think of how something slants either uphill or downhill. Suppose you placed a ladder against a wall. Then you moved the base of the ladder out about a foot. What happens to the slant of the ladder? Suppose you move it again. What happens? Observe the pattern in the diagram below.

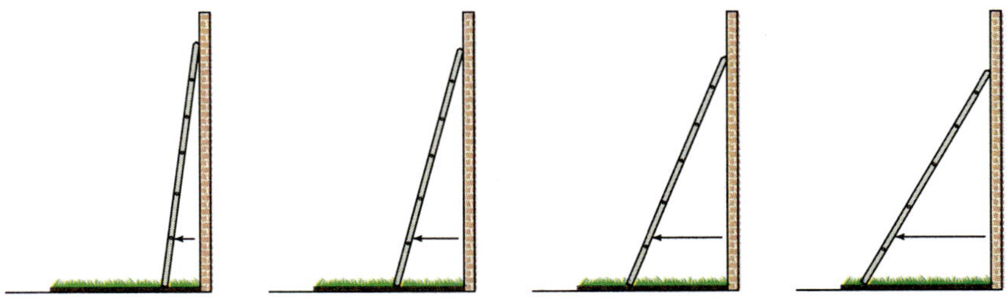

Notice that the top of the ladder moves down the wall when the bottom of the ladder moves out. As the top moves down the wall, the slant, or slope, becomes less steep. If you continued to move the ladder out, eventually it would lie flat on the ground, and there would be no slant at all.

The steepness of the line representing the ladder is called the **slope** of the line. It is defined as the ratio of the **rise,** or vertical change, to the **run,** or horizontal change, as you move from one point on the line to another. The graph at the right shows a line that passes through the origin and the point at (5, 4).

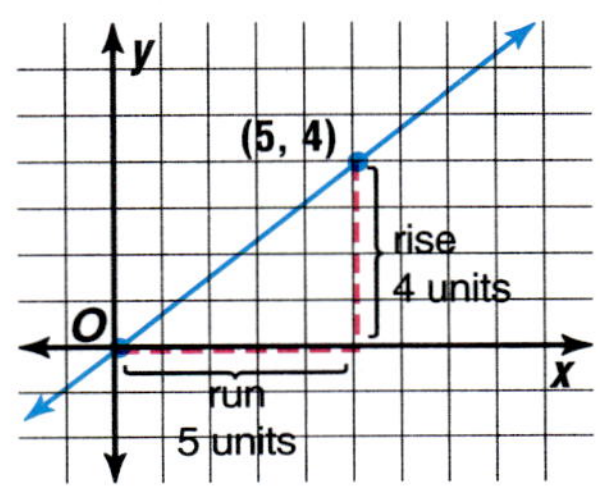

$$\text{slope} = \frac{\text{change in } y \text{ (rise)}}{\text{change in } x \text{ (run)}}$$

$$= \frac{4}{5}$$

So, the slope of this line is $\frac{4}{5}$.

Definition of Slope — **The slope m of a line is the ratio of the change in the y-coordinates to the corresponding change in the x-coordinates.**

For simplicity, we will refer to the change in the y-coordinates as the y change and the corresponding change in the x-coordinates as the x change.

Example 1

Determine the slope of each line.

a.

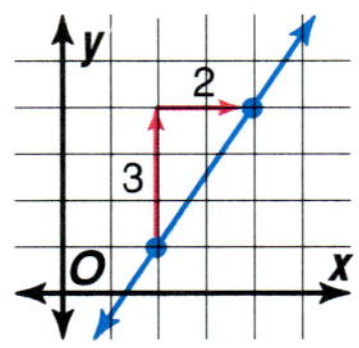

$\frac{y \text{ change}}{x \text{ change}} = \frac{3}{2}$

$m = \frac{3}{2}$

b.

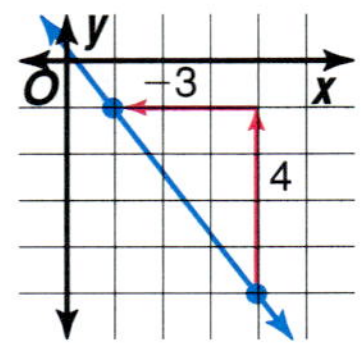

$\frac{y \text{ change}}{x \text{ change}} = \frac{4}{-3}$

$m = \frac{4}{-3}$

c.

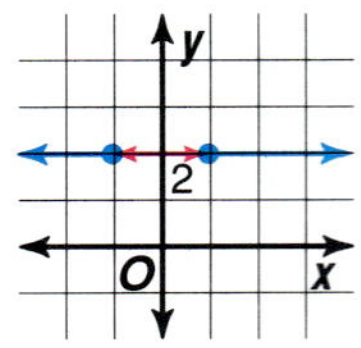

$\frac{y \text{ change}}{x \text{ change}} = \frac{0}{2}$

$m = 0$

d.

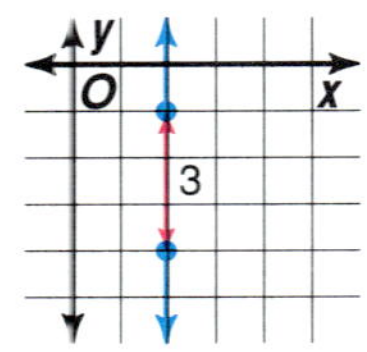

$\frac{y \text{ change}}{x \text{ change}} = \frac{3}{0}$

Since division by 0 is undefined, the slope is undefined.

Let's analyze the slopes of the graphs in Example 1.

- Graph a slopes upward from left to right and has a positive slope.
- Graph b slopes downward from left to right and has a negative slope.
- Graph c is a horizontal line and has a slope of 0.
- Graph d is a vertical line and its slope is undefined.

These observations are true of other lines that have the same characteristics.

Since a line is made up of an infinite number of points, you can use any two points on that line to find the slope of the line. So, we can generalize the definition of slope for any two points on the line.

Determining Slope Given Two Points — **Given the coordinates of two points, (x_1, y_1) and (x_2, y_2), on a line, the slope m can be found as follows:**

$$m = \frac{y_2 - y_1}{x_2 - x_1}, \text{ where } x_1 \neq x_2.$$

y_2 is read "y sub 2." The 2 is called a subscript.

Example 2

Determine the slope of the line that passes through (2, −5) and (7, −10).

Method 1

Let $(2, -5) = (x_1, y_1)$ and $(7, -10) = (x_2, y_2)$.

$$m = \frac{y_2 - y_1}{x_2 - x_1}$$

$$= \frac{-10 - (-5)}{7 - 2}$$

$$= \frac{-5}{5} \text{ or } -1$$

Method 2

Let $(7, -10) = (x_1, y_1)$ and $(2, -5) = (x_2, y_2)$.

$$m = \frac{y_2 - y_1}{x_2 - x_1}$$

$$= \frac{-5 - (-10)}{2 - 7}$$

$$= \frac{5}{-5} \text{ or } -1$$

The slope of the line is −1.

As you can see in Example 2, it does not matter which ordered pair is selected as (x_1, y_1).

You can use a spreadsheet to calculate the slopes of several lines very quickly.

EXPLORATION — SPREADSHEETS

A spreadsheet is a table of cells that can contain text (labels) or numbers and formulas. Each cell is named by the column and row in which it is located. In the spreadsheet below, cells A1, B1, C1, D1, E1, and F1 contain labels.

a. Enter the formula (E2–C2)/(D2–B2) into cell F2.

b. Copy the formula to all of the cells in the F column. When you do, the spreadsheet automatically changes the formula to correspond to the values in that row. That is, for F3 the formula becomes (E3–C3)/(D3–B3), for F4 it becomes (E4–C4)/(D4–B4), and so on.

	A	B	C	D	E	F
1	LINE	X1	Y1	X2	Y2	SLOPE
2	A	2	3	4	6	1.5
3						
4						
5						

Your Turn

a. Enter the following ordered pairs from each line in the spreadsheet.

line a (5, 5), (11, 11)
line b (4, −4), (3, 5)
line c (6, −1), (4, −1)
line d (11, 3), (1, 1)
line e (−1, 5), (6, 3)
line f (5, 3), (4, 0)
line g (2, 3), (11, 14)
line h (10, −5), (10, 3)

b. Use the calculate command to have the spreadsheet compute the slope.

c. Use the ordered pairs to graph each line on grid paper. Label each line.

d. From the results of your spreadsheet, make lists of lines with positive slope, negative slope, and 0 slope.

e. Compare the lists with the graphs of the lines. Write a statement to summarize your observations.

If you know the slope of a line and the coordinates of one of the points on a line, you can find the coordinates of other points on that line.

Example 3 **Determine the value of r so the line through $(r, 6)$ and $(10, -3)$ has a slope of $-\frac{3}{2}$.**

$$m = \frac{y_2 - y_1}{x_2 - x_1}$$

$$-\frac{3}{2} = \frac{-3 - 6}{10 - r} \quad (x_1, y_1) = (r, 6),\ (x_2, y_2) = (10, -3)$$

$$-\frac{3}{2} = \frac{-9}{10 - r}$$

$$-3(10 - r) = -9(2) \quad \textit{Find the cross products.}$$

$$-30 + 3r = -18 \quad \textit{Solve for r.}$$

$$3r = 12$$

$$r = 4$$

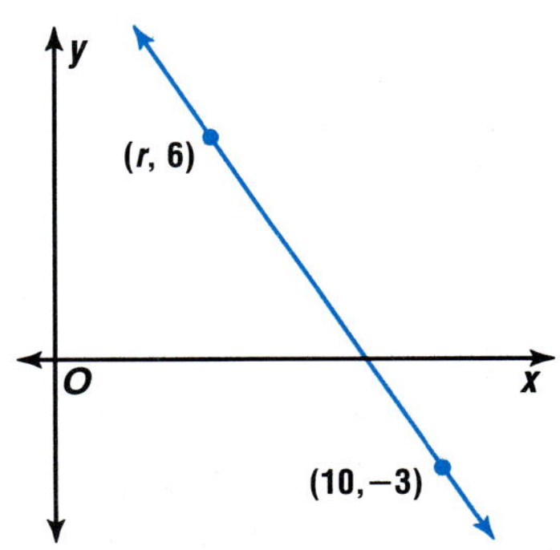

You can use slope with other mathematical skills to solve real-world problems like the one presented at the beginning of this lesson.

Example 4

APPLICATION
Construction

Refer to the application at the beginning of the lesson. Will the Wongs be able to build their house on their lot?

The width of the house and the two 5-foot clearances equal $32 + 2(5)$ or 42 feet. Thus, the horizontal measure between the property lines must be at least 42 feet.

LOOK BACK

You can refer to Lesson 4-3 for more information on trigonometric functions.

We can use trigonometric ratios to determine if there is adequate room for the house. A grade of 11 percent means that the rise is 11 feet while the run is 100 feet. We can use this information to find the measure of $\angle A$.

$\tan A = \frac{11}{100}$ ← *opposite* ← *adjacent*

$\tan A = 0.11$

$A \approx 6.3°$ *Use a calculator.*

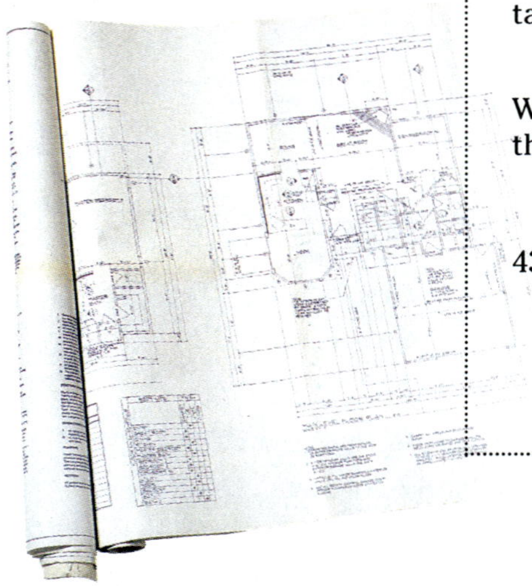

We can use the measure of $\angle A$ to find the horizontal measure x of the property.

$\cos A = \frac{x}{43}$ ← *adjacent* ← *hypotenuse*

$43(\cos 6.3°) = x$ *Multiply each side by 43.*

$42.74 = x$ *Use a calculator.*

The lot is 42.74 feet wide. The house and clearances will fit the 43-foot lot. So, the Wongs can build their house on the lot they bought.

CHECK FOR UNDERSTANDING

Communicating Mathematics

Study the lesson. Then complete the following.

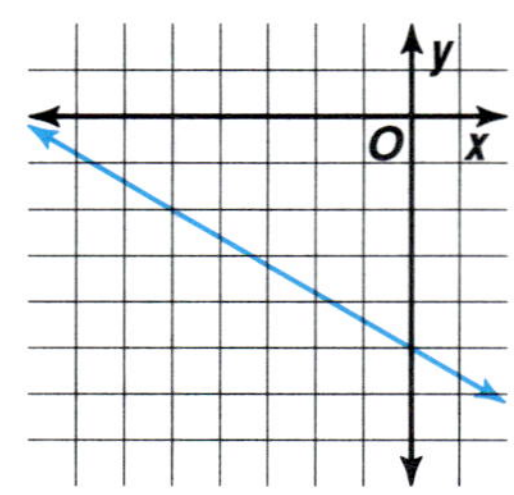

1. **Explain** how you would find the slope of the line in the graph at the right.
2. **Describe** what it means if a road has an 8% grade.
3. Would it matter if you subtracted the x-coordinates in the opposite order from the way you subtracted the y-coordinates?
4. **Draw** the graph of a line having each slope.
   a. a positive slope
   b. a negative slope
   c. a slope of 0
   d. undefined slope
5. **Explain** why the formula for determining the slope using two points does not apply to vertical lines.

MODELING MATHEMATICS

6. Use a geoboard to model line segments with each slope. Make a sketch of your model.
   a. 4
   b. $\frac{3}{4}$
   c. 0
   d. undefined
   e. $-\frac{3}{2}$

Guided Practice

Determine the slope of each line.

7. 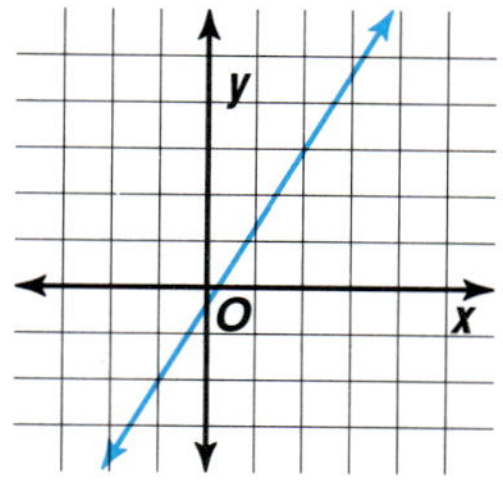

8. 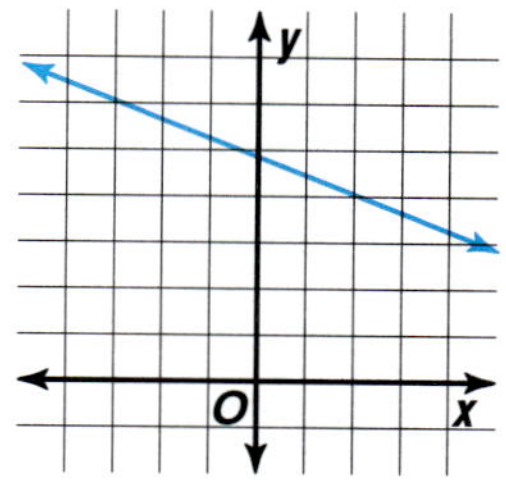

Determine the slope of the line that passes through each pair of points.

9. $(7, -4), (9, -1)$
10. $(5, 7), (-2, -3)$
11. $(0.75, 1), (0.75, -1)$

Determine the value of *r* so the line that passes through each pair of points has the given slope.

12. $(6, -2), (r, -6), m = -4$
13. $(9, r), (6, 3), m = -\frac{1}{3}$

14. **Architecture** The slope of the roof line of a building is often referred to as the *pitch* of the roof.
    a. Use a millimeter ruler to find the rise and run of the roof of the tower on the horse barn in Versailles, Kentucky, shown at the right.
    b. Then write the pitch as a decimal.

EXERCISES

Practice

Determine the slope of each line.

15. a
16. b
17. c
18. d
19. e
20. f

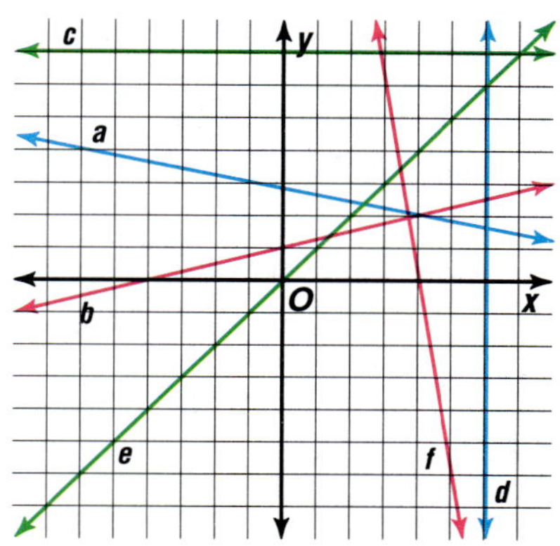

Determine the slope of the line that passes through each pair of points.

21. $(2, 3), (9, 7)$
22. $(-3, -4), (5, -1)$
23. $(2, -1), (5, -3)$
24. $(2, 6), (-1, 3)$
25. $(-5, 4), (-5, -1)$
26. $(-2, 3), (8, 3)$
27. $(4, -5), (4, 2)$
28. $\left(2\frac{1}{2}, -1\frac{1}{2}\right), \left(-\frac{1}{2}, \frac{1}{2}\right)$
29. $\left(\frac{3}{4}, 1\frac{1}{4}\right), \left(-\frac{1}{2}, -1\right)$

Determine the value of *r* so the line that passes through each pair of points has the given slope.

30. $(5, r), (2, -3), m = \frac{4}{3}$

31. $(-2, 7), (r, 3), m = \frac{4}{3}$

32. $(4, -5), (3, r), m = 8$

33. $(6, 2), (9, r), m = -1$

34. $(4, r), (r, 2), m = -\frac{5}{3}$

35. $(r, 5), (-2, r), m = -\frac{2}{9}$

Draw a line through the given point that has the given slope.

36. $(3, -1), m = \frac{1}{3}$

37. $(-2, -3), m = \frac{4}{3}$

38. $(4, -2), m = -\frac{2}{5}$

39. The points $A(12, -4)$ and $B(6, 8)$ lie on a line. Find the coordinates of a third point that lies on line AB. Describe how you determined the coordinates of this point.

Critical Thinking

40. Carpentry A carpenter was a member of a crew building a roof that is 30 feet long at the base. The roof had a pitch of 4 inches for every foot of length along the base. His task on the crew was to put in vertical supports every 16 inches along the base. He would climb up the ladder, measure 16 inches horizontally, and then measure the vertical height to the roof. He then climbed down the ladder, sawed the piece he needed, and went back up the ladder to put it in place. He wondered if there wasn't some way he could figure out how long each support would be ahead of time so he wouldn't have to climb the ladder so many times. Explain how you can use what you have learned in this chapter to help him out.

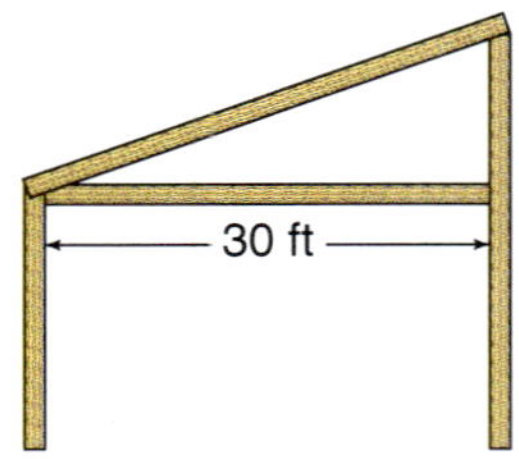

Applications and Problem Solving

41. Road Construction The Castaic Grade in Southern California has a grade of 5%. The length of the roadway is 5.6 miles. What is the change in elevation from the top of the grade to the bottom of the grade in feet?

42. Carpentry Julio Mendez is a carpenter. He is building a staircase between the first and second floors of a house, a height of 9 feet. The *tread*, or depth of each step, must be 10 inches. The slope of the staircase cannot exceed $\frac{3}{4}$.

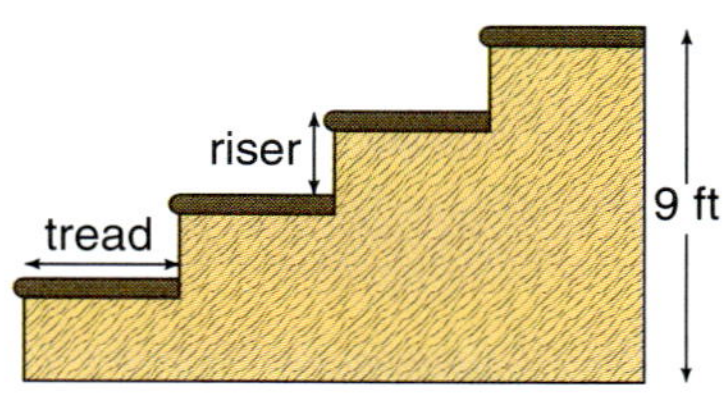

a. How many steps should he plan?

b. What is the measure of the riser, or height of each step?

43. Driving The Eisenhower Tunnel in Colorado was completed in 1973 and is the fourth longest road tunnel in the United States. The eastern entrance of the Eisenhower Tunnel is at an elevation of 11,080 feet. The tunnel is 8941 feet long and has an upgrade of 0.895% toward the western end. What is the elevation of the western end of the tunnel?

Top Five List

Longest Road Tunnels in the World

Tunnel	Length (miles)
1. St. Gotthard (Switzerland)	10.14
2. Arlberg (Austria)	8.69
3. Fréjus (France/Italy)	8.02
4. Mont-Blanc (France/Italy)	7.21
5. Gudvangen (Norway)	7.08

44. **Architecture** Use a millimeter ruler to estimate the pitch, or slope, of each object.

a. 

Uro Indian huts of Peru

b. 

S. Miniato, Florence, Italy

c. 

Great Pyramid at Giza, Egypt

Mixed Review

45. **Statistics** Find the range, median, upper and lower quartiles, and interquartile range for the set of data. (Lesson 5–7)
3, 3.2, 6, 45, 7, 26, 2, 3.4, 4, 5.3, 5, 78, 8, 1, 5

46. **Patterns** Copy and complete the table below. (Lesson 5–5)

n	1	2	3	4	5
$f(n)$			12	11	10

47. Use the formula $I = prt$ to find r if $I = \$2430$, $p = \$9000$, and $t = 2$ years 3 months. (Lesson 4–4)

48. Solve $\frac{6}{14} = \frac{7}{x-3}$. (Lesson 4–1)

Solve each equation. Check your solution.

49. $\frac{2}{3}x + 5 = \frac{1}{2}x + 4$ (Lesson 3–5)

50. $3x - 8 = 22$ (Lesson 3–3)

51. **Animals** The average lifespans of 20 different animals are listed below. (Lesson 2–2)

Animal	Lifespan (years)	Animal	Lifespan (years)
Baboon	20	Mouse	3
Camel	12	Opossum	1
Cow	15	Pig	10
Elephant	40	Rabbit	5
Fox	7	Sea Lion	12
Gorilla	20	Sheep	12
Hippopotamus	25	Squirrel	10
Kangaroo	7	Tiger	16
Lion	15	Wolf	5
Monkey	15	Zebra	15

a. How many animals live between 7 and 16 years, inclusive?
b. Make a line plot of the average lifespans of the animals from part a.
c. Which number occurred most frequently?
d. How many animals have an average lifespan of at least 20 years?

52. Evaluate $29 - 3(9 - 4)$. (Lesson 1–3)

6-2 Writing Linear Equations in Point-Slope and Standard Forms

***What* YOU'LL LEARN**

- To write linear equations in point-slope form, and
- to write linear equations in standard form.

***Why* IT'S IMPORTANT**

You can write linear equations to solve problems involving geometry.

CONNECTION

Geography

If you lived in Miami, Florida, and moved to Denver, Colorado, what adjustments do you think you might have to make? Obviously, the weather is different, but did you know you would also have to adjust to living at a higher altitude? As the altitude increases, the oxygen in the air decreases. This can affect your breathing and cause dizziness, headache, insomnia, and loss of appetite.

Over time, people who move to higher elevations experience acclimatization, or the process of getting accustomed to the new climate. Their bodies develop more red blood cells to carry oxygen to the muscles. Generally, long-term acclimatization to an altitude of 7000 feet takes about 2 weeks. After that, it takes 1 week for each additional 2000 feet of altitude. The graph at the right shows the acclimatization for altitudes greater than 7000 feet.

What are the independent and dependent variables of this relation?

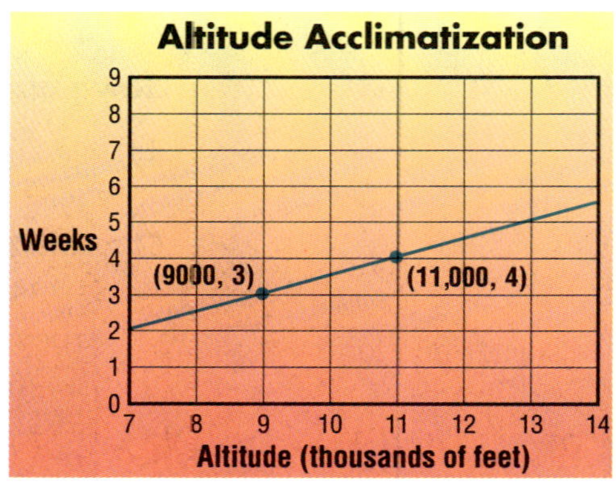

We can use any two points on the graph to find the slope of the line. For example, let (9000, 3) and (11,000, 4) represent (x_1, y_1) and (x_2, y_2), respectively.

$$m = \frac{y_2 - y_1}{x_2 - x_1}$$

$$= \frac{4 - 3}{11{,}000 - 9000} \text{ or } \frac{1}{2000}$$

Suppose we let (x, y) represent any other point on the line. We can use the slope and one of the given ordered pairs to write an equation for the line.

$$m = \frac{y_2 - y_1}{x_2 - x_1}$$

$$\frac{1}{2000} = \frac{y - 3}{x - 9000} \quad m = \frac{1}{2000}, (x_1, y_1) = (9000, 3), (x_2, y_2) = (x, y)$$

$$\frac{1}{2000}(x - 9000) = y - 3 \quad \textit{Multiply each side by } (x - 9000).$$

$$y - 3 = \frac{1}{2000}(x - 9000) \quad \textit{Reflexive property } (=)$$

Since this form of the equation was generated using the coordinates of a known point and the slope of the line, it is called the **point-slope form.**

Point-Slope Form of a Linear Equation	**For a given point (x_1, y_1) on a nonvertical line having slope m, the point-slope form of a linear equation is as follows.** $$y - y_1 = m(x - x_1)$$

You can write an equation in point-slope form for the graph of any nonvertical line if you know the slope of the line and the coordinates of one point on that line.

FYI

Tibet has one of the highest altitudes in the world. Nomads in Tibet tend their yaks for 5 months at altitudes of 14,000–17,000 feet above sea level. Then they return to their permanent homes, which are located 12,000 to 14,000 feet above sea level.

Example 1

Write the point-slope form of an equation for each line.

a. a line that passes through (−3, 5) and has a slope of $-\frac{3}{4}$

$$y - y_1 = m(x - x_1)$$
$$y - 5 = -\frac{3}{4}[x - (-3)] \quad \textit{Replace } x_1 \textit{ with } -3, \ y_1 \textit{ with 5, and } m \textit{ with } -\frac{3}{4}.$$
$$y - 5 = -\frac{3}{4}(x + 3)$$

An equation of the line is $y - 5 = -\frac{3}{4}(x + 3)$.

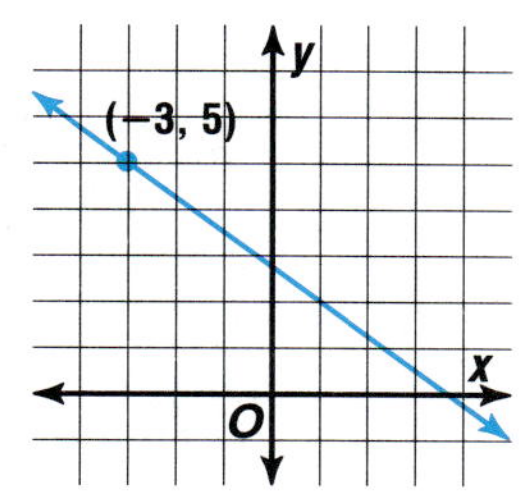

b. a horizontal line that passes through (−6, 2)

Horizontal lines have a slope of 0.

$$y - y_1 = m(x - x_1)$$
$$y - 2 = 0[x - (-6)]$$
$$y - 2 = 0$$
$$y = 2$$

An equation of the line is $y = 2$.

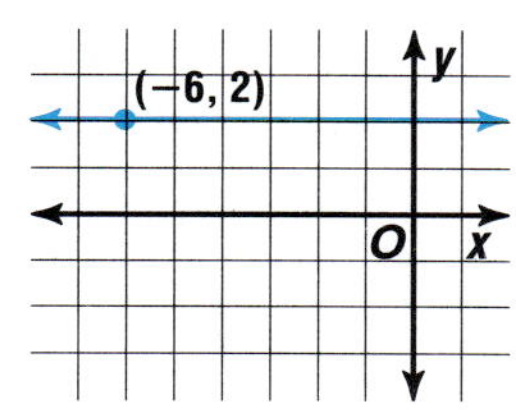

You can also write the equations of horizontal lines by using the y-coordinate as in Example 1b.

A vertical line has a slope that is undefined, so you cannot use the point-slope form of an equation. However, you can write the equation of a vertical line by using the coordinates of the points through which it passes. Suppose the line passes through (3, 5) and (3, −2). The equation of the line is $x = 3$, since the x-coordinate of every point on the line is 3.

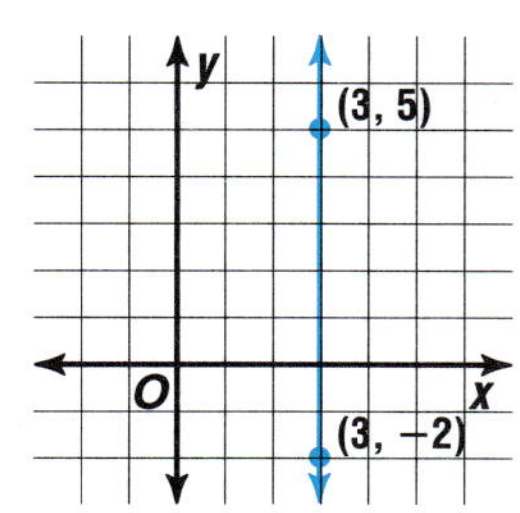

Any linear equation can also be expressed in the form $Ax + By = C$, where A, B, and C are integers and A and B are not both zero. This is called the **standard form** of a linear equation. *Usually, $A > 0$.*

Standard Form of a Linear Equation	**The standard form of a linear equation is $Ax + By = C$, where A, B, and C are integers, $A \geq 0$, and A and B are not both zero.**

Linear equations that are written in point-slope form can be rewritten in standard form.

Example 2 **Write $y + 5 = -\frac{5}{4}(x - 2)$ in standard form.**

$$y + 5 = -\frac{5}{4}(x - 2)$$

$$4(y + 5) = 4 \cdot \left(-\frac{5}{4}\right)(x - 2)$$ *Multiply each side by 4 to eliminate the fraction.*

$$4y + 20 = -5x + 10$$ *Distributive property*

$$4y = -5x - 10$$ *Subtract 20 from each side.*

$$5x + 4y = -10$$ *Add 5x to each side.*

The standard form of the equation is $5x + 4y = -10$.

You can write an equation of a line if you know the coordinates of two points on that line.

Example 3 **Write the point-slope form and the standard form of an equation of the line that passes through (−8, 3) and (4, 5).**

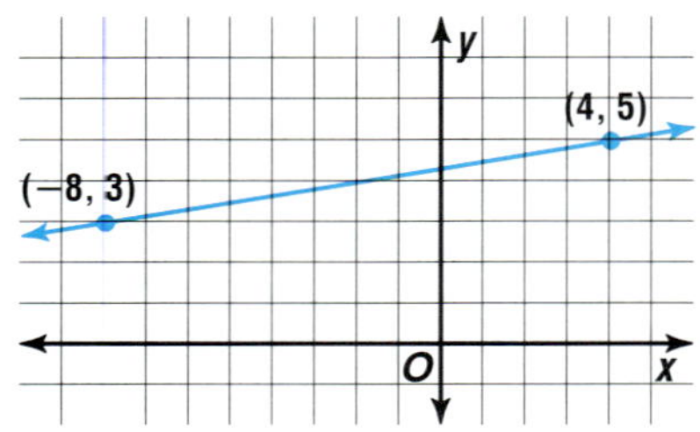

First determine the slope of the line.

$$m = \frac{5 - 3}{4 - (-8)} \text{ or } \frac{1}{6}$$

You can use either point for (x_1, y_1) in the point-slope form.

Method 1: Use (−8, 3).

$$y - 3 = \frac{1}{6}(x - (-8))$$

$$y - 3 = \frac{1}{6}(x + 8)$$

Method 2: Use (4, 5).

$$y - 5 = \frac{1}{6}(x - 4)$$

Both $y - 3 = \frac{1}{6}(x + 8)$ and $y - 5 = \frac{1}{6}(x - 4)$ are valid equations for the point-slope form of an equation for the line passing through (−8, 3) and (4, 5). Now let's find the standard form of each equation.

Method 1

$$y - 3 = \frac{1}{6}(x + 8)$$

$$6(y - 3) = 6 \cdot \frac{1}{6}(x + 8)$$ *Multiply each side by 6.*

$$6y - 18 = x + 8$$

$$6y = x + 26$$ *Add 18 to each side.*

$$-x + 6y = 26$$ *Subtract x from each side.*

$$x - 6y = -26$$ *Multiply by −1.*

Method 2

$$y - 5 = \frac{1}{6}(x - 4)$$

$$6(y - 5) = 6 \cdot \frac{1}{6}(x - 4)$$ *Multiply each side by 6.*

$$6y - 30 = x - 4$$

$$6y = x + 26$$ *Add 30 to each side.*

$$-x + 6y = 26$$ *Subtract x from each side.*

$$x - 6y = -26$$ *Multiply by −1.*

Regardless of which point was used to find the point-slope form, the standard form of the equation, when all common factors are removed, always results in the same equation.

Example 4 **INTEGRATION** **Geometry**

Write the equations of the lines containing the sides of parallelogram $ABCD$ in point-slope and standard forms.

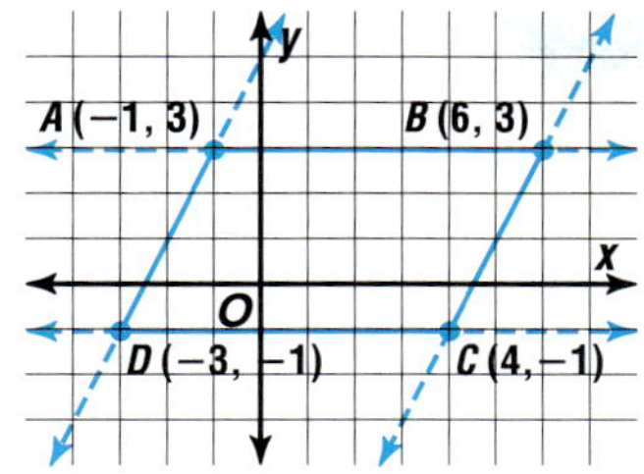

Since the lines containing segments AB and CD are horizontal, the slope of each line is 0.

The equation of $\overleftrightarrow{AB}$ is $y = 3$.

The equation of $\overleftrightarrow{CD}$ is $y = -1$.

Now use the coordinates of the points to find the slopes and equations of the lines containing the other two sides.

Use $A(-1, 3)$ and $D(-3, -1)$ to find the slope of $\overline{AD}$.

$$m = \frac{3 - (-1)}{-1 - (-3)}$$

$$= \frac{4}{2} \text{ or } 2$$

Let's use $A(-1, 3)$ for (x_1, y_1) in the point-slope form.

$$y - y_1 = m(x - x_1)$$
$$y - 3 = 2[x - (-1)]$$
$$y - 3 = 2(x + 1)$$

Now find the standard form of this equation.

$$y - 3 = 2(x + 1)$$
$$y - 3 = 2x + 2$$
$$y = 2x + 5$$
$$2x - y = -5$$

Use $B(6, 3)$ and $C(4, -1)$ to find the slope of $\overline{BC}$.

$$m = \frac{3-(-1)}{6-4}$$

$$= \frac{4}{2} \text{ or } 2$$

Let's use $B(6, 3)$ for (x_1, y_1) in the point-slope form.

$$y - y_1 = m(x - x_1)$$
$$y - 3 = 2(x - 6)$$

Now find the standard form of this equation.

$$y - 3 = 2(x - 6)$$
$$y - 3 = 2x - 12$$
$$y = 2x - 9$$
$$2x - y = 9$$

The equations of the lines containing the sides of the parallelogram $ABCD$ are $y = 3$, $y = -1$, $2x - y = -5$, and $2x - y = 9$.

CHECK FOR UNDERSTANDING

Communicating Mathematics

Study the lesson. Then complete the following.

1. **Explain** what x_1 and y_1 in the slope-intercept form of an equation represent.
2. **Compare and contrast** the graphs of $x = 6$ and $y = 6$.
3. **Explain** why A and B in the standard form of a linear equation cannot both be zero.
4. **You Decide** A line contains the points $P(-3, 2)$ and $Q(2, 5)$. Elena thinks that $R(12, 12)$ is also on the line. Use the point-slope form to determine if she is correct.

Guided Practice

State the slope and the coordinates of a point through which the line represented by each equation passes.

5. $y + 3 = 4(x - 2)$
6. $y - (-6) = -\frac{2}{3}(x + 5)$
7. $3(x + 7) = y - 1$

Write the point-slope form of an equation of the line that passes through the given point and has the given slope.

8. $(9, 1), m = \frac{2}{3}$ **9.** $(-2, 4), m = -3$ **10.** $(-3, 6), m = 0$

Write each equation in standard form.

11. $y + 3 = -\frac{3}{4}(x - 1)$ **12.** $y - \frac{1}{2} = \frac{5}{6}(x + 2)$ **13.** $y - 3 = 2(x + 1.5)$

Write the point-slope form and the standard form of an equation of the line that passes through each pair of points.

14. $(-6, 1), (-8, 2)$ **15.** $(-1, -2), (-8, 2)$ **16.** $(4, 8), (-2.5, 8)$

17. Geometry Write the standard form of the equation of the line containing the hypotenuse of the right triangle shown at the right.

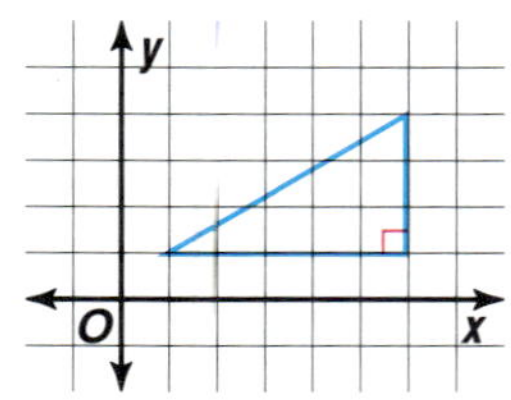

EXERCISES

Practice

Write the point-slope form of an equation of the line that passes through the given point and has the given slope.

18. $(3, 8), m = 2$ **19.** $(4, 5), m = 3$ **20.** $(-4, -3), m = 1$

21. $(-6, 1), m = -4$ **22.** $(0, 5), m = 0$ **23.** $(1, 3), m = -2$

24. $(3, 5), m = \frac{2}{3}$ **25.** $(8, -3), m = \frac{3}{4}$ **26.** $(-6, 3), m = -\frac{2}{3}$

Write the standard form of an equation of the line that passes through the given point and has the given slope.

27. $(2, 13), m = 4$ **28.** $(-5, -3), m = 4$

29. $(-4, 6), m = \frac{3}{2}$ **30.** $(-2, -7), m = 0$

31. $(8, 2), m = -\frac{2}{5}$ **32.** $(-5, 5), m =$ undefined

Write the point-slope form of an equation of the line that passes through each pair of points.

33. $(-5, 2), (4, -1)$ **34.** $(6, 1), (7, -4)$

35. $(-8, -1), (6, 5)$ **36.** $(2, 3), (5, 1)$

37. $(4, -2), (8, -2)$ **38.** $(2.5, 3), (-0.5, -4.5)$

Write the standard form of an equation of the line that passes through each pair of points.

39. (6, 5), (12, −3)

40. (−2, −7), (1, 2)

41. (−5, 9), (3, −2)

42. (0.7, −1.3), (−0.4, 3.1)

43. $\left(-\frac{2}{3}, -\frac{5}{6}\right), \left(\frac{3}{4}, -\frac{1}{3}\right)$

44. $\left(-2, 7\frac{2}{3}\right), \left(-2, \frac{16}{5}\right)$

Critical Thinking

45. A line contains the points at (9, 1) and (5, 5). Write a valid argument that the same line intersects the *x*-axis at (10, 0).

Applications and Problem Solving

46. Geometry Three lines intersect to form triangle *ABC,* as shown at the right.

a. Write the equation for each line in point-slope form.

b. Write the equation for each line in standard form.

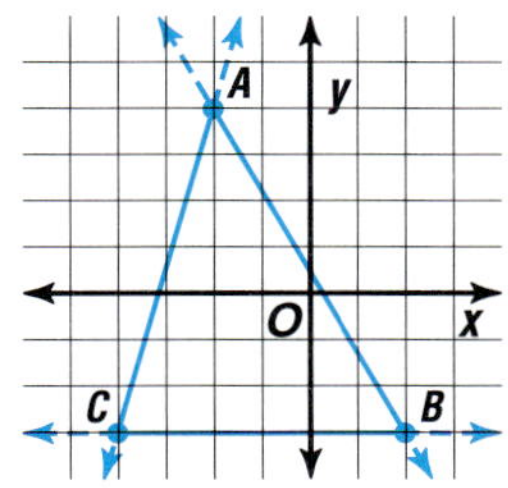

47. Draw a Diagram The Americans with Disabilities Act (ADA) of 1990 states that ramps should have at least a 12-inch run for each rise of 1 inch, with a maximum rise of 30 inches. The post office in Meyersville is changing one of its entrances to accommodate a wheelchair ramp. The distance from the street to the building is 18 feet. The current sidewalk has steps up to the entrance. The entranceway is 30 inches above ground level.

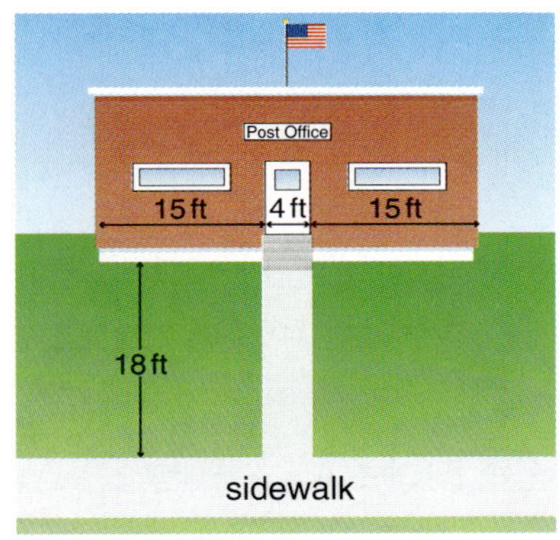

a. Determine if a wheelchair ramp that meets ADA standards can be placed over the existing sidewalk. Explain why or why not.

b. Draw a diagram of an alternative plan for the ramp.

Mixed Review

48. Aviation An airplane flying over Albuquerque at an elevation of 33,000 feet begins its descent to land at Santa Fe, 50 miles away. If the elevation of Santa Fe is 7000 feet, what should be the approximate slope of descent, expressed as a percent? (Lesson 6–1)

49. Statistics The stem-and-leaf plot at the right represents the cost per cup of various brands of coffee. (Lesson 5–7)

a. Find the range and interquartile range for the costs.

b. Identify any outliers.

Stem	Leaf
0	6 6 6 6 8 9 9 9 9
1	0 2 3 4 5 7 7 8 8
2	4 8 9
3	0 2 $1 \mid 2 = \$0.12$

50. Draw a mapping for {(−6, 0), (−1, 2), (−3, 4)}. (Lesson 5–2)

51. If $y = 12$ when $x = 3$, find y when $x = 7$. Assume that y varies directly as x. (Lesson 4–8)

52. **Motion** At 1:30 P.M., an airplane leaves Tucson for Baltimore, a distance of 2240 miles. The plane flies at 280 miles per hour. A second airplane leaves Tucson at 2:15 P.M., and is scheduled to land in Baltimore 15 minutes before the first airplane. At what rate must the second airplane travel to arrive on schedule? (Lesson 4–7)

53. **Work Backward** In Lupita's garden, all of the flowers are either pink, yellow, or white. Given any three of the flowers, at least one of them is pink. Given any three of the flowers, at least one of them is white. Can you say that given any three of the flowers, at least one of them must be yellow? Why? (Lesson 3–3)

54. **Printing** A customer orders a job requiring 2500 sheets of paper. He has a choice of ordering a full carton of 3000 sheets at \$27.50 per thousand or "breaking" a carton (ordering exactly the number of sheets required) and paying \$38.40 per thousand. Which would be least expensive in this case? (Lesson 2–6)

55. Name the property illustrated by $(a + 3b) + 2c = a + (3b + 2c)$. (Lesson 1–8)

WORKING ON THE In·ves·ti·ga·tion

Refer to the Investigation on pages 320–321.

Smoke Gets In Your Eyes

The amount of smoke exhaled into a room on each puff of a cigarette is comparable to the amount of air you exhale in a deep breath. The average smoker takes 10 puffs per cigarette.

1 Suppose that each breath into a balloon approximates the smoke from each exhale during smoking. How many cigarettes are represented by the air in the balloon?

2 Make a graph showing the number of breaths and the cumulative smoke in the air from smoking a cigarette. Describe the graph, and write a function that fits the data graphed.

3 Graph the relationship between the radius of the balloon and the circumference of the balloon. Write an equation to represent this relationship.

4 Find the volume of each balloon in milliliters if $1 \text{ in}^3 \approx 16.4$ milliliters. The average at-rest exhale is approximately 500 milliliters. How does the volume of the balloon compare with the volume of air you would expect from the number of breaths it took to inflate the balloon? What accounts for the difference?

Add the results of your work to your Investigation Folder.

6-3 Integration: Statistics

Scatter Plots and Best-Fit Lines

What YOU'LL LEARN

- To graph and interpret points on a scatter plot,
- to draw and write equations for best-fit lines and make predictions by using those equations, and
- to solve problems by using models.

Why IT'S IMPORTANT

You can use scatter plots to display data, examine trends, and make predictions.

APPLICATION

Education

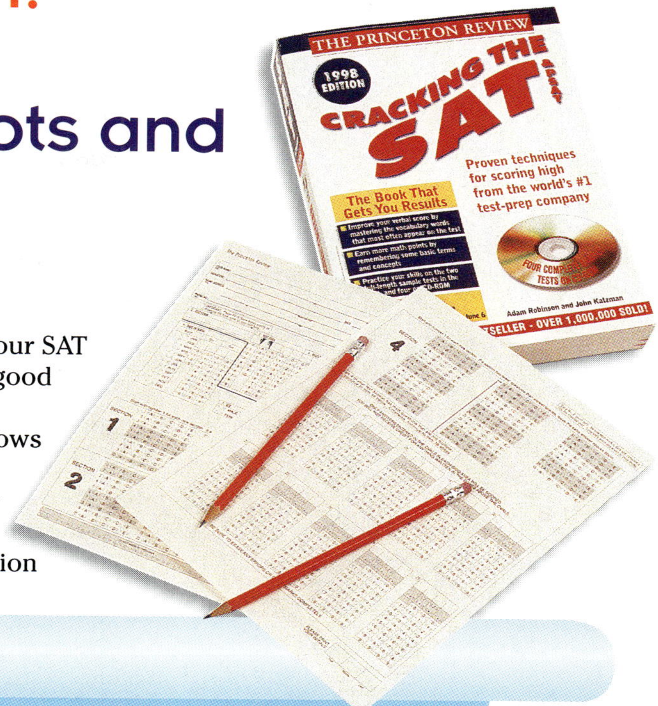

If you get a good score on your SAT does that mean you have a good chance of graduating from college? The table below shows the average SAT (Scholastic Assessment Test) scores for freshmen at selected universities and the graduation rate of those students.

School (State)	Average SAT	Graduation Rate
Baylor University (TX)	1045	69%
Brandeis University (MA)	1215	81%
Case Western Reserve University (OH)	1235	65%
College of William and Mary (VA)	1240	90%
Colorado School of Mines (CO)	1200	78%
Georgia Institute of Technology (GA)	1240	68%
Lehigh University (PA)	1140	88%
New York University (NY)	1145	69%
Penn State University, Main Campus (PA)	1096	61%
Pepperdine University (CA)	1070	64%
Rensselaer Polytechnic Institute (NY)	1190	68%
Rutgers at New Brunswick (NJ)	1110	74%
Tulane University (LA)	1168	71%
University of Florida (FL)	1135	64%
University of North Carolina at Chapel Hill (NC)	1045	81%
University of Texas at Austin (TX)	1135	62%
Wake Forest University (NC)	1250	86%

Source: *America's Best Colleges*, June, 1995

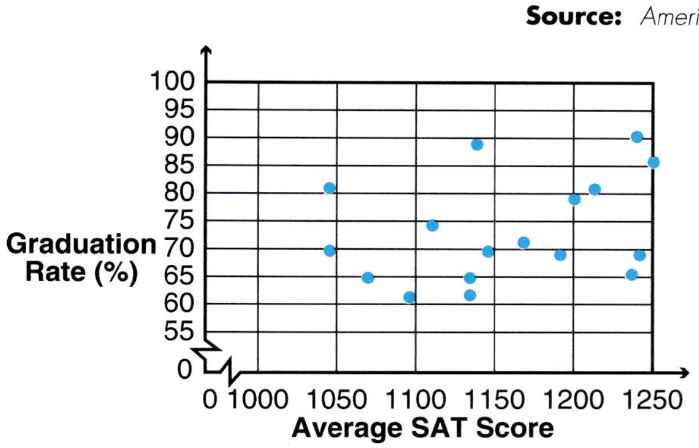

To determine if there is a relationship between SAT scores and graduation rates, we can display the data points in a graph called a **scatter plot.** In a scatter plot, the two sets of data are plotted as ordered pairs in the coordinate plane. In this example, the independent variable is the average SAT score, and the dependent variable is the graduation rate. The scatter plot is shown at the left. The graph indicates that higher SAT scores do not necessarily result in higher graduation rates.

One way to solve real-world problems is to **use a model.** Scatter plots are an excellent way to model real-life data to observe patterns and trends.

Look for a relationship between x and y in the graphs below.

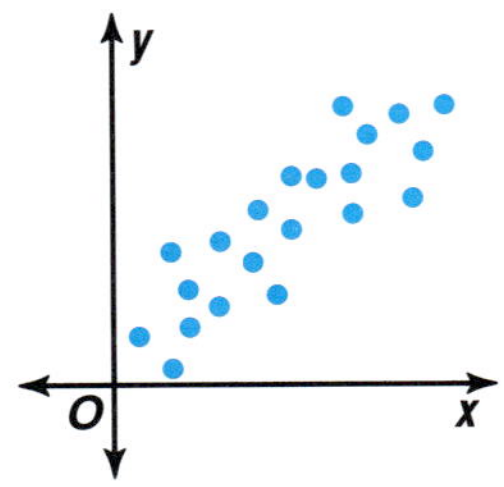

In this graph, x and y have a **positive correlation**. That is, the values are related in the same way. As x increases, y increases.

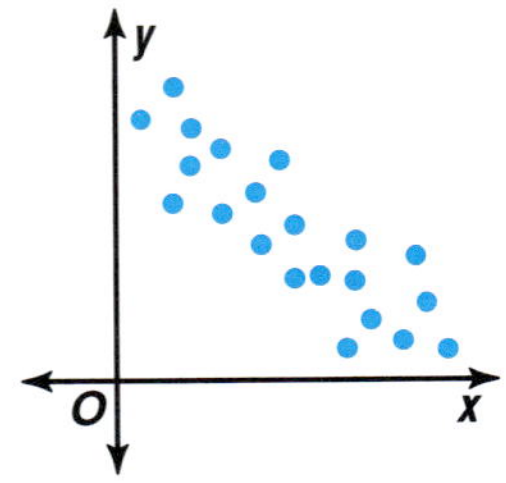

In this graph, x and y have a **negative correlation**. That is, the values are related in opposite ways. As x increases, y decreases.

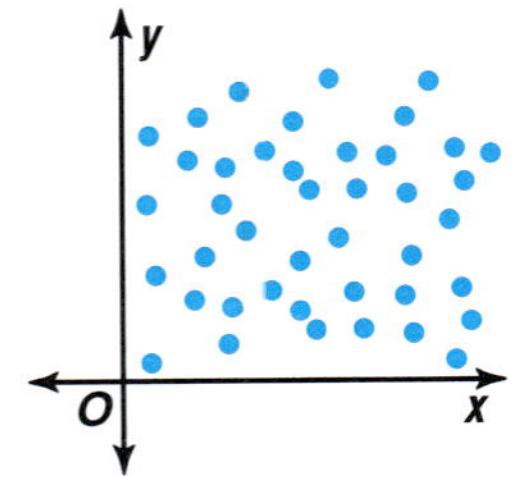

In this graph, x and y have *no correlation*. In this case, x and y are not related and are said to be *independent*.

Example 1 **The table below shows 13 of the fastest-growing cities in the United States and their latitude and longitude.**

PROBLEM SOLVING

Use a Model

Fastest-Growing Cities	Ranking	North Latitude	West Longitude
Austin, TX	9	30°	98°
Bakersfield, CA	1	35°	119°
Colorado Springs, CO	13	39°	105°
Durham, NC	8	36°	79°
Fresno, CA	2	37°	120°
Laredo, TX	10	28°	100°
Las Vegas, NV	3	36°	115°
Raleigh, NC	6	36°	79°
Reno, NV	12	40°	120°
Sacramento, CA	11	39°	121°
San Bernardino, CA	7	34°	117°
Stockton, CA	5	38°	121°
Tallahassee, FL	4	30°	84°

Source: Bureau of the Census, National Oceanic and Atmospheric Administration

a. Draw one scatter plot to represent the correlation between the rankings and each city's latitude, and another to represent the correlation between the rankings and each city's longitude.

b. Is there a correlation between the cities' locations and their popularity?

a. The scatter plots are shown below.

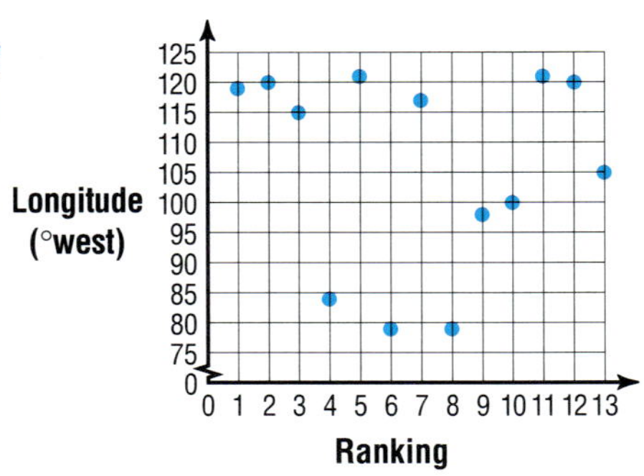

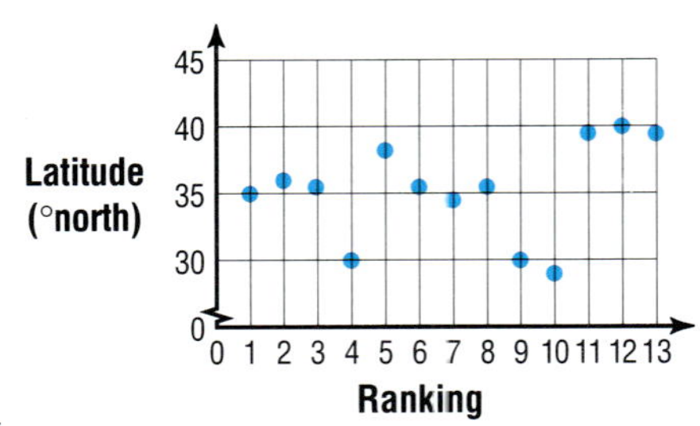

b. Both of the correlations are fairly weak. However, the correlation between the rankings and latitude is stronger than the correlation between the rankings and longitude because the data approximate a line a little more. It is impossible to tell whether either correlation is positive or negative. Thus, we could say that there is a weak correlation between the cities' location and popularity.

The best-fit line may not pass through any of the data points.

You can use a scatter plot to make predictions. To help you do this, you can draw a line, called a **best-fit line**, that passes close to most of the data points. Use a ruler to draw a line that is close to most or all of the points. Then use the ordered pairs representing points on the line to make predictions.

A best-fit line shows if the correlation between two variables is *strong* or *weak*. The correlation is strong if the data points come close to, or lie on, the best-fit line. The correlation is weak if the data points do not come close to the line.

Example 2

APPLICATION

Animals

Dogs age differently than humans do. You may have heard someone say that a dog ages 1 year for every 7 human years. However, that is not the case. The table at the right shows the relationship between dog years and human years.

Dog Years	Human Years
1	15
2	24
3	28
4	32
5	37
6	42
7	47

Source: *National Geographic World*, January, 1995

a. Draw a scatter plot to model the data and determine what relationship, if any, exists in the data.

b. Draw a best-fit line for the scatter plot.

c. Find an equation for the best-fit line.

d. Use the equation to determine how many human years are comparable to 13 dog years.

FYI

Almost 40% of U.S. households have at least one dog kept as a pet, accounting for over 50 million dogs. According to the American Kennel Club, the most popular dogs in America are Labrador retrievers.

a. Let the independent variable d be dog years, and let the dependent variable h be human years. The scatter plot is shown below.

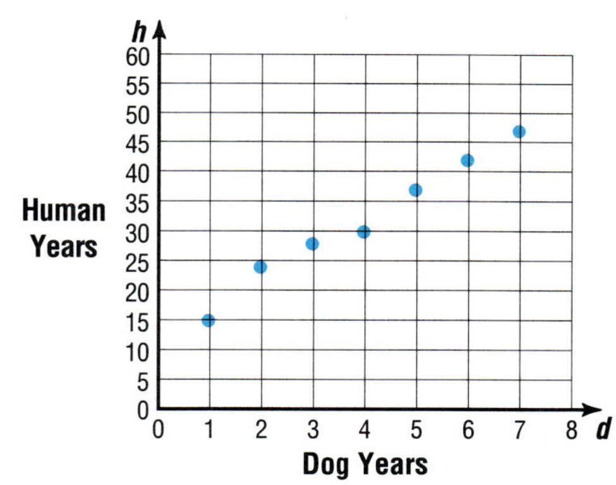

The plot seems to indicate that there is nearly a linear relationship between dog years and human years.

There also appears to be a positive correlation between the two variables. As x increases, y increases.

b. No line will pass through all of the data points. However, the best-fit line describes the trend of the data. Draw a line that seems to represent the data.

The best-fit line drawn in this example is arbitrary. You may draw another best-fit line that is equally as valid.

The slope of the best-fit line is positive. Thus, the correlation between the two variables is also positive.

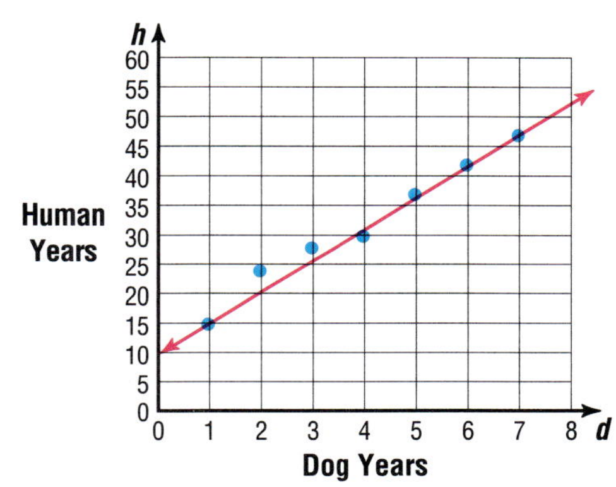

c. As you can see, the best-fit line we drew passes through three of the data points: (4, 32), (5, 37), and (6, 42). Use two of these points to write the equation of the line.

(continued on the next page)

First, find the slope.

$\frac{y_2 - y_1}{x_2 - x_1} = \frac{37 - 32}{5 - 4}$ or 5 $\quad (x_1, y_1) = (4, 32)$ and $(x_2, y_2) = (5, 37)$

Then, use the point-slope form.

$h - y_1 = m(d - x_1)$

$h - 32 = 5(d - 4)$ *Let (4, 32) represent* (x_1, y_1).

$h - 32 = 5d - 20$ *Distributive property*

$5d - h = -12$

d. To determine how many human years are comparable to 13 dog years, let $d = 13$ and solve for h.

$5d - h = -12$

$5(13) - h = -12$

$h = 77$

A dog that is 13 years old is comparable to a human that is 77 years old.

A **regression line** is the most accurate best-fit line for a set of data, and can be determined with a graphing calculator or computer. A graphing calculator assigns each regression line an r value. This value $(-1 \leq r \leq 1)$ measures how closely the data are related. -1 indicates a strong negative correlation and 1 indicates a strong positive correlation.

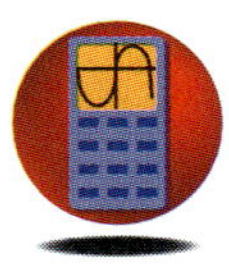

EXPLORATION — GRAPHING CALCULATORS

LOOK BACK

Refer to Lesson 5-7A for more information on entering data into lists on a graphing calculator.

The table at the right shows the years of rate increases and the fares charged to ride the subway in New York City.

Year	Fare
1953	$0.15
1966	0.20
1970	0.30
1972	0.35
1975	0.50
1981	0.75
1984	0.90
1986	1.00
1990	1.15
1992	1.25

Source: *New York Times*, July 25, 1993

a. Use the Edit option on the STAT menu to enter the year data in L1 and the fare data into L2.

b. Use the window [1950, 1995] with a scale factor of 5 and [0, 1.5] with a scale factor of 0.25. Make sure any equations are deleted from the Y= list. Then press [2nd] [STAT PLOT] 1. Make sure the following items are highlighted: On, the first type of graph (scatter plot), L1 as the Xlist, and L2 as the Ylist. Press [GRAPH], and describe the graph.

c. Then find an equation for the regression line.

Enter: [STAT] [▶] 5 [2nd] [L1] [,] [2nd] [L2] [ENTER].

The screen displays the equation $y = ax + b$ and gives values for a, b, and r. Record these values on your paper.

d. Now graph the best-fit line.

Enter: [Y=] [VARS] 5 [▶] [▶] 7 [GRAPH]

Your Turn

a. How well do you feel the graph of the equation fits the data? Justify your answer.

b. Do any of the data points lie on the best-fit line? If so, name them.

c. Remove the ordered pair (1953, $0.15) from the set of data and repeat the process. What impact has removing this ordered pair had on the fit of the line to the data? (*Hint:* Compare the r values.)

d. Use the equation and graph to predict the fares for the year 2000.

CHECK FOR UNDERSTANDING

Communicating Mathematics

Study the lesson. Then complete the following.

1. **Explain** how to determine whether a scatter plot has a positive or negative correlation.
2. **Draw** sketches of scatter plots that have each type of correlation.
   a. very strong positive b. very strong negative c. no correlation
3. **Describe** a situation that illustrates each type of plot in Exercise 2.
4. What does the *r* value on a graphing calculator tell you? Give examples.

MATH JOURNAL

5. What situations in your own life would present a negative correlation?

Guided Practice

Explain whether a scatter plot for each pair of variables would probably show a *positive, negative,* or *no* correlation between the variables.

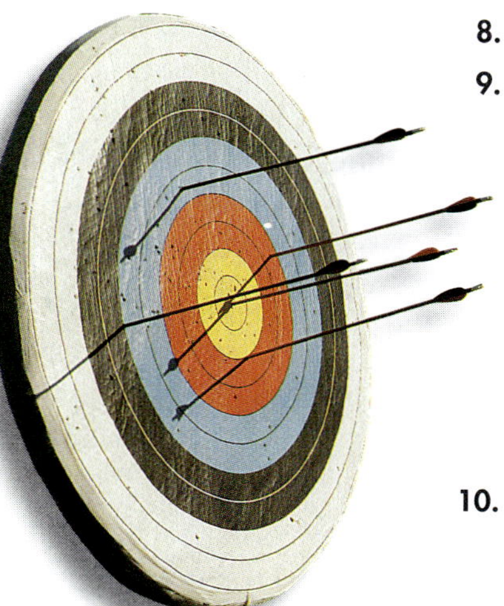

6. money earned by a restaurant worker and time spent on the job
7. heights of fathers and sons
8. grades in school and how many times you miss class
9. **Archery** The graph at the right shows the results when three student archers shot at a target nine times each.
   a. As the archers take more and more shots, what happens to the accuracy of the shots?
   b. Is there a correlation between the variables? Is it positive or negative?
   c. Which data points seem to be extremes from the rest of the data?

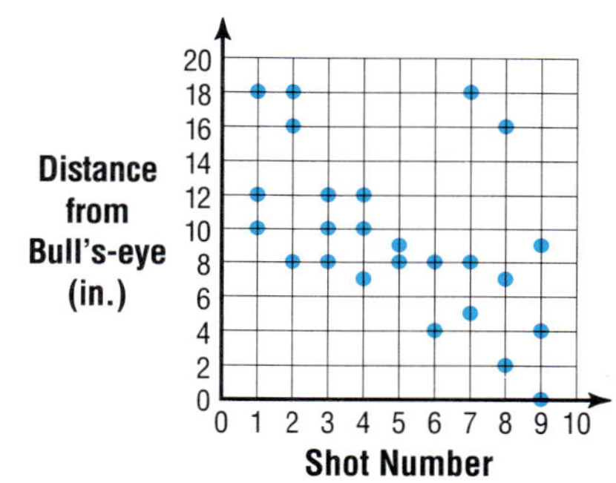

10. **Biology** The table below shows the average body temperature of 14 insects at a given air temperature.

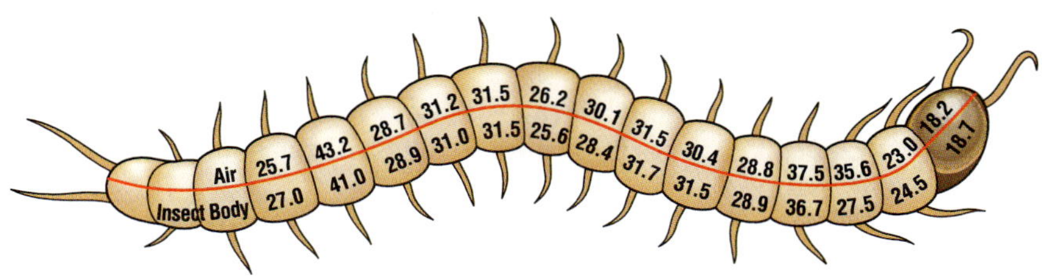

   a. Draw a scatter plot and a best-fit line for these data.
   b. Write an equation for the best-fit line.
   c. What conclusion might you draw from these data?

EXERCISES

Practice

Explain whether a scatter plot for each pair of variables would probably show a *positive, negative,* or *no* correlation between the variables.

11. your age and weight from ages 1 to 20
12. temperature of a cup of coffee and the time it sits on a table
13. the amount a mail carrier earns each day and the weight of the mail delivered each day

Explain whether a scatter plot for each pair of variables would probably show a *positive, negative,* or *no* correlation between the variables.

14. the distance traveled and the time driving
15. a person's height and their birth month
16. the amount of snow on the ground and the daily temperature
17. the amount of time you exercise and the amount of calories you burn
18. the time water boils and the amount of water in the pot
19. the number of files stored on a disk and the amount of memory left on the disk

Determine whether a best-fit line should be drawn for each set of data graphed below. Explain your reasoning.

20. 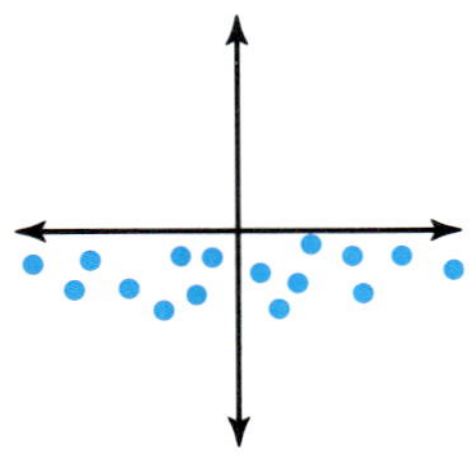

21. 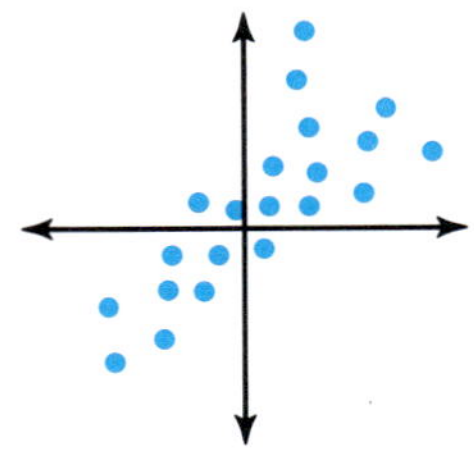

22. 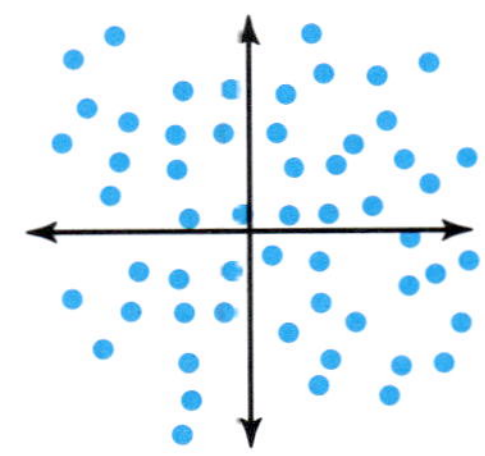

23. A test contains 20 true-false questions. Which scatter plot below best illustrates all the possible combinations of the numbers of correct and incorrect answers if the horizontal axis represents the number of responses that are correct and the vertical axis represents the number that are incorrect? Explain your choice.

a. 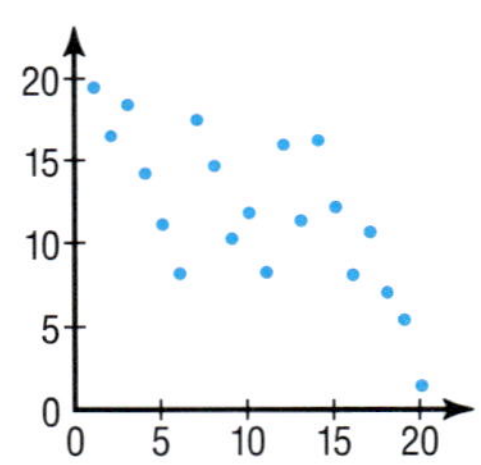

b. 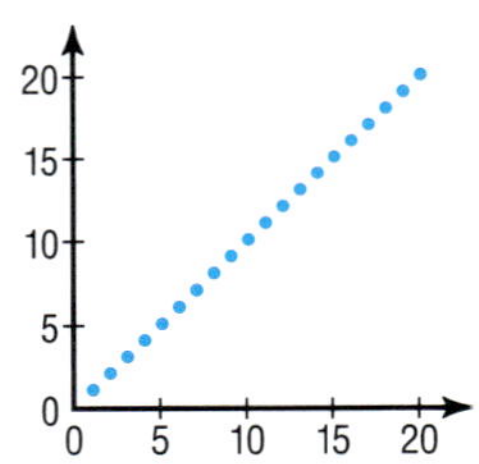

c. 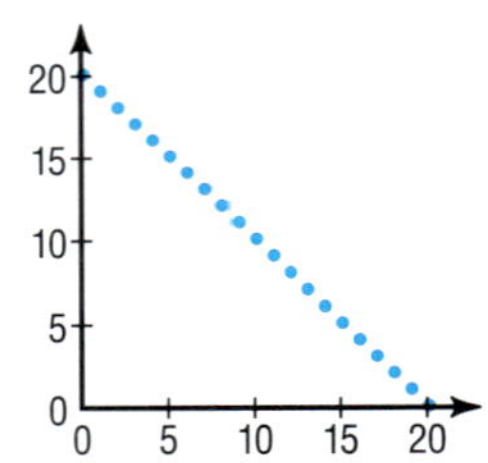

Graphing Calculator

24. The average January and July temperatures (°F) for 14 cities in various parts of the United States are listed below.

Jan.	21	35	42	32	51	7	30	21	20	40	28	45	56	39
July	71	79	79	77	82	70	73	73	70	86	81	90	69	82

a. Use a graphing calculator to enter the January temperatures as L1 and the July temperatures as L2 and create a scatter plot.
b. Describe the pattern of the points in the scatter plot.
c. Record the equation of the regression line and the *r* value.
d. Write a sentence that generally describes the relationship between the January temperature in a city and its July temperature.

Critical Thinking

25. Different correlation values are acceptable for different situations. Give an example for each situation. Explain your reasoning.
   a. When is a strongly positive correlation a bad thing?
   b. When is a mildly positive correlation an acceptable outcome?
   c. When would a strongly negative correlation be the desired outcome?
   d. When would no correlation be acceptable?

26. Many verbal expressions can be translated into algebraic expressions or equations. How do you think you could illustrate the expression "The bigger they are, the harder they fall" as a scatter plot?

Applications and Problem Solving

27. **Education** Refer to the application at the beginning of the lesson.
   a. Describe the correlation of the SAT scores to the graduation rate.
   b. Copy the graph and draw a best-fit line. What is the equation of the best-fit line you drew?

28. **Biology** Scientists use samples to generalize relationships they observe in nature. The table at the right shows the length and weight of several humpback whales. A long ton is about 2240 pounds.

Length (feet)	Weight (long tons)
40	25
42	29
45	34
46	35
50	43
52	45
55	51

   a. Make a scatter plot of these data. Does a relationship exist? If so, what is the relationship?
   b. Use your scatter plot as a model to predict what you think a humpback whale 51 feet long might weigh.
   c. How long might a whale that weighs between 30 long tons and 35 long tons be?
   d. A 46-foot long humpback whale weighing 36 long tons was observed. Does this alter your conclusion about the correlation of the data? Explain.

29. **Test Scores** The scores received on the first two tests of the grading period for 30 students in algebra class are listed below as ordered pairs.

30, 43	58, 57	55, 61	4, 71	32, 27	68, 59
54, 47	38, 27	56, 47	72, 63	50, 23	70, 67
60, 53	73, 79	55, 68	19, 58	38, 41	71, 59
68, 75	74, 83	58, 67	66, 73	72, 67	42, 57
71, 69	70, 89	94, 59	8, 84	84, 71	82, 73

   a. Make a scatter plot of the data.
   b. What correlation, if any, do you observe in the data?
   c. Draw a best-fit line and write the equation of the line.

30. **Use a Model** Collect 10 round objects around your home. Treat each of them as a circle and measure the diameter and circumference in millimeters.
   a. Use a scatter plot as a model to relate the diameter and circumference of each object.
   b. Write an equation for the best-fit line.
   c. The actual formula that relates the circumference and diameter of a circle is $C = \pi d$. How does this formula compare with your equation?

Mixed Review

31. **Air Travel** A Boeing 747 takes off from the runway, and 20 minutes after liftoff, the plane is 30,000 feet from the ground. At 22 minutes after liftoff, the plane is 45,000 feet from the ground. (Lesson 6–2)
   a. Write an equation in standard form to represent the flight of the plane during this time, with x = time in minutes, and y = altitude in feet.
   b. Use the equation to find the plane's altitude 18 minutes after takeoff.
   c. Can this equation be used to determine the height of the plane at any time during the flight? If so, explain how.

32. Solve $6b - a = 32$ if the domain is $\{-2, -1, 0, 2, 5\}$. (Lesson 5–3)

33. **Trigonometry** Use a calculator to solve $\cos W = 0.2598$. (Lesson 4–3)

34. Simplify $1.2(4x - 5y) - 0.2(-1.5x + 8y)$. (Lesson 2–6)

35. Solve $8.2 - 6.75 = m$. (Lesson 1–5)

6–4 Writing Linear Equations in Slope-Intercept Form

What YOU'LL LEARN

- To determine the x- and y-intercepts of linear graphs from their equations,
- to write equations in slope-intercept form, and
- to write and solve direct variation equations.

Why IT'S IMPORTANT

You can write linear equations to solve problems involving swimming and banking.

APPLICATION

Banking

Have you seen advertisements like the one at the right in the newspaper? The bank is offering free checking. However, in the fine print of this ad, you will find that the free checking only occurs if you maintain a minimum daily balance of at least \$2000.

Suppose this bank charges a monthly service fee of \$3 plus 10¢ for each check or withdrawal transaction if you fail to maintain a minimum balance of \$2000. The graph at the right shows the line that represents this situation. *You will write an equation for this line in Exercise 57.*

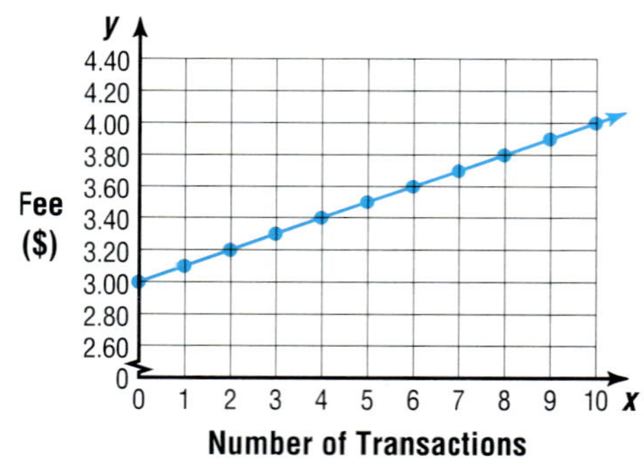

The coordinates at which a graph intersects the axes are known as the **y-intercept** and the **x-intercept**. Since this graph intersects the y-axis at (0, 3), the y-intercept is 3. If you were to extend the graph to the left, you would find that it crosses the x-axis at (−30, 0), so the x-intercept is −30.

Notice that the x-coordinate of the ordered pair for the y-intercept and the y-coordinate of the ordered pair for the x-intercept are both 0.

Example 1 **Find the x- and y-intercepts of the graph of $3x + 4y = 6$.**

Remember that the x-intercept is the point at which $y = 0$.

$$3x + 4y = 6$$
$$3x + 4(0) = 6 \quad \textit{Let } y = 0.$$
$$3x = 6$$
$$x = \frac{6}{3} \text{ or } 2 \quad \textit{Divide each side by 3.}$$

Now let $x = 0$ to find the y-intercept.

$$3x + 4y = 6$$
$$3(0) + 4y = 6 \quad \textit{Let } x = 0.$$
$$4y = 6$$
$$y = \frac{6}{4} \text{ or } \frac{3}{2} \quad \textit{Divide each side by 4.}$$

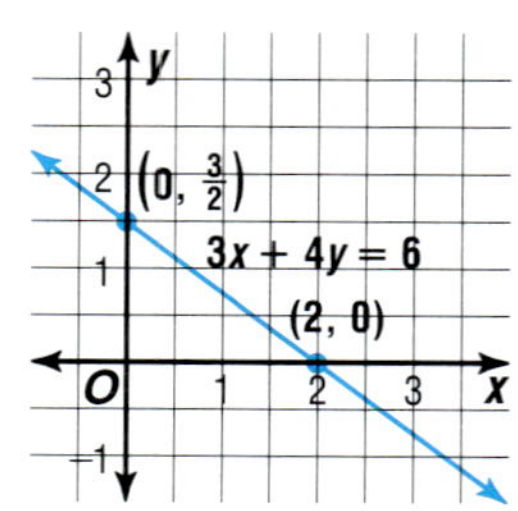

The x-intercept is 2, and the y-intercept is $\frac{3}{2}$. This means that the graph crosses the x-axis at (2, 0) and the y-axis at $\left(0, \frac{3}{2}\right)$. You can use these points to graph the equation $3x + 4y = 6$.

Consider the graph at the right. The line crosses the y-axis at $(0, b)$, so its y-intercept is b. Write the point-slope form of an equation for this line using $(0, b)$ as (x_1, y_1).

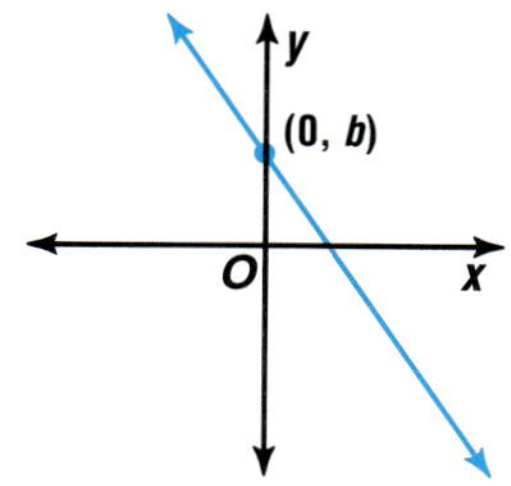

$y - y_1 = m(x - x_1)$ *Point-slope form*

$y - b = m(x - 0)$ *Replace (x_1, y_1) with $(0, b)$.*

$y - b = mx$

$y = mx + b$ *Add b to each side.*

This form of an equation is called the **slope-intercept form** of a linear equation, because in this form the slope and y-intercept are easily identified.

$$y = mx + b$$

↑ *slope* ↖ *y-intercept*

Slope-Intercept Form of a Linear Equation	**Given the slope m and the y-intercept b of a line, the slope-intercept form of an equation of the line is $y = mx + b$.**

If you know the slope and y-intercept of a line, you can write an equation of the line in slope-intercept form. This equation can also be written in standard form.

Example 2 **Write an equation of a line in slope-intercept form if the line has a slope of $\frac{2}{3}$ and a y-intercept of 6. Then write the equation in standard form.**

$y = mx + b$

$y = \frac{2}{3}x + 6$ *$b = 6$, $m = \frac{2}{3}$*

Now rewrite the equation in standard form.

$y = \frac{2}{3}x + 6$

$3y = 2x + 18$ *Multiply by 3 to eliminate the fraction.*

$-2x + 3y = 18$ *Subtract 2x from each side.*

or

$2x - 3y = -18$ *Multiply by −1 so that A is positive.*

Let's compare the slope-intercept form with the standard form of a linear equation. First solve $Ax + By = C$ for y.

$Ax + By = C$

$Ax - Ax + By = C - Ax$ *Subtract Ax from each side.*

$By = -Ax + C$ *Commutative property of addition*

$y = -\frac{A}{B}x + \frac{C}{B}$ *Divide each side by B.*

↑ *slope* ↑ *y-intercept*

Thus, you can identify the slope and y-intercept from an equation written in standard form by using $m = -\frac{A}{B}$ and $b = \frac{C}{B}$.

Example 3 **Find the slope and *y*-intercept of the graph of $5x - 3y = 6$.**

Method 1

In $5x - 3y = 6$, which is in standard form, $A = 5$, $B = -3$, and $C = 6$.

Find the slope.

$$m = -\frac{A}{B}$$
$$= -\frac{5}{-3} \text{ or } \frac{5}{3}$$

Find the *y*-intercept.

$$b = \frac{C}{B}$$
$$= \frac{6}{-3} \text{ or } -2$$

Method 2

Solve for *y* to find the slope-intercept form.

$$5x - 3y = 6$$
$$5x - 5x - 3y = 6 - 5x$$
$$-3y = -5x + 6$$
$$\frac{-3y}{-3} = \frac{-5x}{-3} + \frac{6}{-3}$$
$$y = \frac{5}{3}x + (-2)$$
$$m = \frac{5}{3},\ b = -2$$

In Lesson 6–2, you learned how to use the point-slope form to find an equation of a line passing through two given points. Now you have another tool that you can use for the same situation.

Example 4 **Write the slope-intercept and standard forms of the equation for a line that passes through $(-3, -1)$ and $(6, -4)$.**

First find the slope.

$$m = \frac{y_2 - y_1}{x_2 - x_1}$$
$$= \frac{-4 - (-1)}{6 - (-3)} \quad (x_1, y_1) = (-3, -1) \text{ and } (x_2, y_2) = (6, -4)$$
$$= \frac{-3}{9} \text{ or } -\frac{1}{3}$$

Method 1

In $Ax + By = C$, the slope is $-\frac{A}{B}$.

If $-\frac{A}{B} = -\frac{1}{3}$, then $A = 1$ and $B = 3$.

So $Ax + By = C$ becomes $1x + 3y = C$.

To find the value of C, substitute either ordered pair into the equation. For example, choose $(6, -4)$.

$$x + 3y = C$$
$$6 + 3(-4) = C \quad (x, y) = (6, -4)$$
$$-6 = C$$

An equation in standard form for the line is $x + 3y = -6$.

Solve the equation for *y* to find the slope-intercept form.

$$x + 3y = -6$$
$$3y = -x - 6$$
$$y = -\frac{1}{3}x - \frac{6}{3}$$
$$y = -\frac{1}{3}x - 2$$

Method 2

Use one of the points in the slope-intercept form to find *b*.

$$y = mx + b$$
$$-4 = -\frac{1}{3}(6) + b \quad (x, y) = (6, -4)$$
$$-4 = -2 + b$$
$$-2 = b$$

An equation in slope-intercept form for the line is $y = -\frac{1}{3}x - 2$.

Now write the equation in standard form.

$$y = -\frac{1}{3}x - 2$$
$$3y = 3\left(-\frac{1}{3}x - 2\right)$$
$$3y = -x - 6$$
$$x + 3y = -6$$

Check: Make sure that both points satisfy the equation.

$$x + 3y = -6$$
$$-3 + 3(-1) \stackrel{?}{=} -6 \quad (x, y) = (-3, -1)$$
$$-6 = -6 \ ✔$$

$$x + 3y = -6$$
$$6 + 3(-4) \stackrel{?}{=} -6 \quad (x, y) = (6, -4)$$
$$-6 = -6 \ ✔$$

A special case of the slope-intercept form occurs when the y-intercept is 0. When $m = k$ and $b = 0$, $y = mx + b$ becomes $y = kx$. You may recognize this as the equation for *direct variation*. Another way to write this equation is $\frac{y}{x} = k$.

Example 5 APPLICATION **Swimming**

Penny Dean holds the record for the fastest time swimming the English Channel. The 23-year-old Californian swam the 21-mile distance in $7\frac{2}{3}$ hours on July 29, 1978. At the same rate, how long would it take her to swim the Catalina Channel, a 26-mile distance near Los Angeles?

Explore Make a table to relate the information given in the problem.

Channel	Distance	Time
English	21 miles	$7\frac{2}{3}$ hours
Catalina	26 miles	? hours

Plan The formula that relates time t and distance d is $d = rt$, where r is the rate at which she travels. This formula is an example of direct variation. Use the information from the English Channel swim to find her rate. Then apply that rate to the Catalina Channel swim.

Solve For her English Channel swim, $d = 21$ miles, and $t = 7\frac{2}{3}$ or $\frac{23}{3}$ hours. Find the rate r.

$$d = rt$$

$$21 = r\left(\frac{23}{3}\right) \quad d = 21,\ r = \frac{23}{3}$$

$$\frac{3}{23}(21) = \left(\frac{23}{3}\right)\left(\frac{3}{23}\right)r$$

$$\frac{63}{23} = r$$

Now use the same formula and the rate r to find the time for the Catalina Channel swim.

$$d = rt$$

$$26 = \frac{63}{23}t$$

$$\frac{23}{63}(26) = \frac{23}{63}\left(\frac{63}{23}\right)t$$

$$9.5 \approx t \quad \textit{Use a calculator.}$$

At the same rate that she swam the English Channel, Ms. Dean could swim the Catalina Channel in 9.5 hours.

Examine You can also use a proportion to solve this problem since the rate r will be the same in each situation. If $d = rt$, then $r = \frac{d}{t}$, a form of the direct variation equation.

$$\frac{d_1}{d_2} = \frac{t_1}{t_2}$$

$$\frac{21}{26} = \frac{\frac{23}{3}}{t}$$

$$21t = \frac{23}{3}(26) \quad \textit{Find the cross products.}$$

$$t = \frac{23 \cdot 26}{3 \cdot 21} \quad \textit{Divide each side by 21.}$$

$$t \approx 9.5 \quad \textit{Use a calculator.}$$

The answer checks.

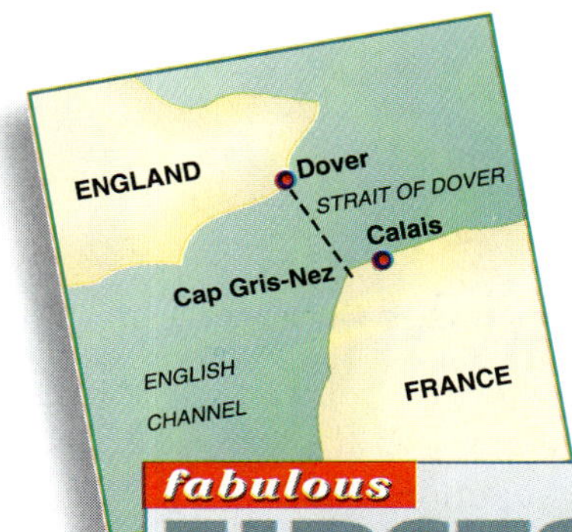

fabulous FIRSTS

Gertrude Ederle (1907–)

The first woman to swim the English Channel was an American, Gertrude Ederle. She was only 19 years old and made the swim in 14 hours, 39 minutes on August 6, 1926.

CHECK FOR UNDERSTANDING

Communicating Mathematics

Study the lesson. Then complete the following.

1. **Explain** how to find the intercepts of a line given its equation. Then find the intercepts of the standard form $Ax + By = C$.
2. **Write** a sentence to explain how direct variation and the slope-intercept form of a linear equation are related.
3. **Describe** two ways in which a direct variation problem may be solved.

4. Why can't you write the equation of a vertical line in slope-intercept form?

5. **You Decide** Taka wrote $y = 3.5x - 8$ as an equation of a line having a slope of 3.5 and a y-intercept of -8. Chuma wrote $7x - 2y = 16$ as an equation of the same line. Who is correct, and why?

MATH JOURNAL

6. List all the types of information you can use to write an equation of a line. Be sure to include examples of each.

Guided Practice

7. For the line shown in the graph at the right:
   a. state the slope,
   b. state the x- and y-intercepts, and
   c. write an equation in slope-intercept form.

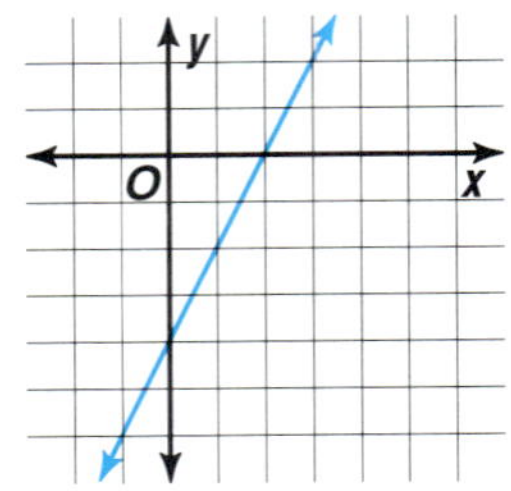

Find the x- and y-intercepts of the graph of each equation.

8. $3x + 4y = 24$

9. $\frac{3}{4}x - 2y + 7 = 0$

Write an equation in slope-intercept form of a line with the given slope and y-intercept. Then write the equation in standard form.

10. $m = -4, b = 5$

11. $m = \frac{2}{3}, b = -10$

Find the slope and y-intercept of the graph of each equation.

12. $y = -3x + 7$

13. $2x + y = -4$

14. $x = 3y - 2$

Write an equation in standard form for a line that passes through each pair of points.

15. $(8, 1), (-2, 3)$

16. $(5, 7), (1, 9)$

17. Write a direct variation equation that has $(3, 11)$ as a solution. Then find y when $x = 12$.

18. **Construction** The roof line of a house starts 12 feet above the ground and has a slope of $\frac{1}{4}$.
   a. If the outer wall of the house represents the y-axis and the floor represents the x-axis, find the equation, in slope-intercept form, of the line that represents the roof.
   b. If you are standing inside the house 6 feet from the wall, how high is the roof at that point?

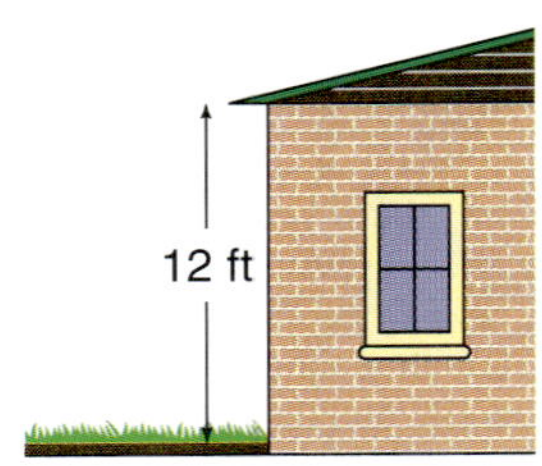

EXERCISES

Practice

For each line graphed at the right:
a. state the slope,
b. state the x- and y-intercepts, and
c. write an equation in slope-intercept form.

19. p

20. q

21. r

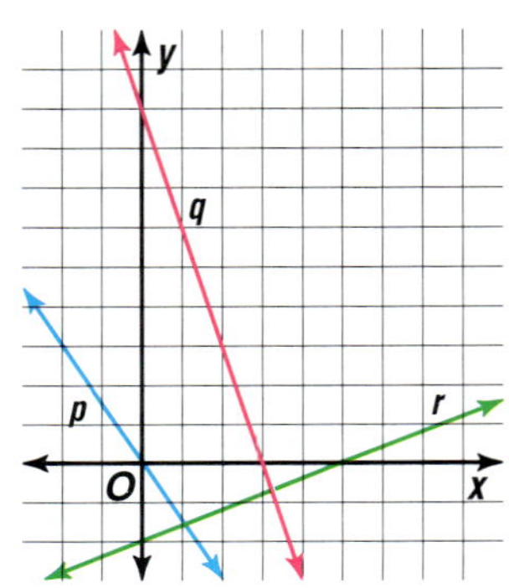

Find the x- and y-intercepts of the graph of each equation.

22. $5x - 3y = -12$ **23.** $4x + 7y = 8$ **24.** $5y - 2 = 2x$

25. $y - 6x = 5$ **26.** $4y - x = 3$ **27.** $3y = 18$

Write an equation in slope-intercept form of a line with the given slope and y-intercept. Then write the equation in standard form.

28. $m = 3, b = 5$ **29.** $m = 7, b = -2$ **30.** $m = -6, b = 0$

31. $m = -1.5, b = 3.75$ **32.** $m = \frac{1}{4}, b = -10$ **33.** $m = 0, b = -7$

Find the slope and y-intercept of the graph of each equation.

34. $3y = 2x - 9$ **35.** $5x + 4y = 10$

36. $4x - \frac{1}{3}y = -2$ **37.** $\frac{2}{3}x + \frac{1}{6}y = 2$

38. $5(x - 3y) = 2(x + 3)$ **39.** $4(3x + 9) - 3(5y + 7) = 11$

Write an equation in standard form for a line that passes through each pair of points.

40. $(-3, -5), (4, 5)$ **41.** $(7, -2), (-4, -2)$ **42.** $(-6, 1), (4, -2)$

43. $(3, 5), (3, -6)$ **44.** $(7, 4), (-5, 9)$ **45.** $(2, 9), (-5, 9)$

Write a direct variation equation that has each ordered pair as a solution. Then find the missing value.

46. $(-5, 8), (?, 11)$ **47.** $(24, 11), (36, ?)$ **48.** $(-17, 3), (?, 15)$

49. Write an equation in slope-intercept form of a line with slope $\frac{2}{3}$ and an x-intercept of 4.

50. Find the coordinates of a point on the graph of $5x - 3y = 10$ in which the x-coordinate is 5 greater than the y-coordinate.

51. Find the coordinates of a point on the graph of $3x + 7y = -16$ in which the x-coordinate is 3 times the y-coordinate.

52. Write the equation in standard form of the line with an x-intercept of 7 and a y-intercept of -2.

Programming

TECHNOLOGY Tip

The DrawF, Text(, and Vertical commands are located in the DRAW menu.

53. The program below finds the slope of a line, given the coordinates of two of the points through which it passes. Then it displays the graph of the line and gives the equation of the line in slope-intercept form.

```
PROGRAM:SLOPE
: ClrDraw
: Input "X1=",Q
: Input "Y1=",R
: Input "X2=",S
: Input "Y2=",T
: If Q-S≠0
: Then
: (R-T)/(Q-S)→A
: R-AQ→B
: DrawF AX+B
: Text(2,5,"EQUATION IS"
: Text(8,5,"Y=",A,"X+",B)
: Else
: ClrHome
: Text(2,5,"SLOPE UNDEFINED")
: Text(8,5,"EQUATION OF LINE")
: Text(15,5,"X=",Q)
: Vertical Q
```

a. Use the program to write an equation of a line that passes through $(8.57, -3.82)$ and $(11.09, 1.31)$. Round numbers to the nearest hundredth.

b. Use the program to check your equations in Exercises 40–45.

Critical Thinking

54. The x-intercept of a line is p, and the y-intercept is q. Write an equation of the line.

Applications and Problem Solving

55. **Chemistry** Charles' Law states that when the pressure is constant, the volume of a gas is directly proportional to the temperature on the Kelvin scale. Write an equation for each situation and solve.
   a. If the volume of a gas is 35 ft^3 at 290 K, what is the volume at 350 K?
   b. If the volume of a gas is 200 ft^3 at 300 K, at what temperature is the volume 180 ft^3?

56. **Life Expectancy** The life expectancies at birth of the average male and female born between 1970 and 2000 (estimated) are shown in the table at the right.
   a. Write an equation for the line that passes through (1970, 67.1) and (2000, 73.2).
   b. Write an equation for the line that passes through (1970, 74.7) and (2000, 80.2).
   c. Graph the ordered pairs for male life expectancy and the equation from part a.
   d. On the same graph, use a different color pencil to graph the ordered pairs for female life expectancy and the equation from part b.
   e. Write a paragraph to describe the relationship between the points and lines you graphed.
   f. Use the data to predict the life expectancy for males and females in the year 2100.

Life Expectancy

Year Born	Males (years)	Females (years)
1970	67.1	74.7
1975	68.8	76.6
1980	70.4	77.8
1985	71.1	78.2
1990	71.8	78.8
1995	72.8	79.7
2000 (est.)	73.2	80.2

57. **Banking** Refer to the application at the beginning of the lesson.
   a. Write an equation to represent the line that shows the service fees charged by the bank for an account that maintains a daily balance that is less than $2000.
   b. Suppose you are not able to maintain $2000 in an account and you write about 25 checks each month. Use the equation from part a to determine whether you should open an account at this bank or go to the bank across the street that charges a flat $5 each month.

Mixed Review

58. **Statistics** The table below shows the keyboarding speeds of 12 students in words per minute (wpm) and their weeks of experience. (Lesson 6–3)

Experience (weeks)	4	7	8	1	6	3	5	2	9	6	7	10
Keyboarding Speed (wpm)	33	45	46	20	40	30	38	22	52	44	42	55

   a. Make a scatter plot of these data.
   b. Draw a best-fit line for the data. Find the equation of the line.
   c. Use the equation to predict the keyboarding speed of a student after a 12-week course.
   d. Why can't this equation be used to predict the speed for any number of weeks of experience?

59. Determine the slope of the line that passes through (14, 3) and (−11, 3). (Lesson 6–1)

60. Write an equation for the function shown in the chart below. (Lesson 5–6)

m	1	2	4	5	6	9
n	9	6	0	−3	−6	−15

61. Graph $A(5, -2)$ on a coordinate plane. (Lesson 5–1)

62. **Probability** A card is selected at random from a deck of 52 cards. What is the probability of selecting a black card? (Lesson 4–6)

63. **Construction** When building a roof, a 5-foot support is to be placed at point B as shown on the diagram at the right. Find the length of the support that is to be placed at point A. (Lesson 4–2)

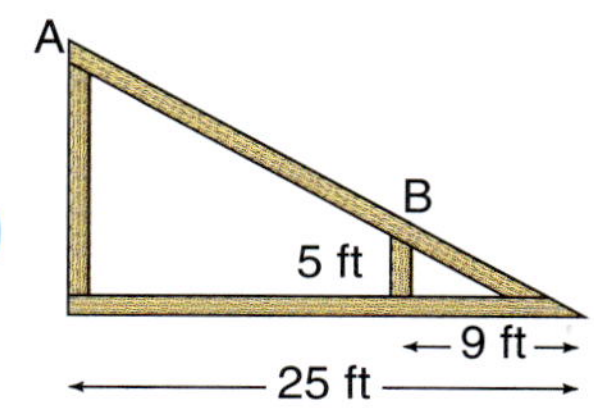

64. Solve $8x + 2y = 6$ for y. (Lesson 3–6)

65. Solve $-36 = 4z$. (Lesson 3–2)

66. Evaluate $|a + k|$ if $a = -5$ and $k = 3$. (Lesson 2–3)

67. Simplify $4(3x + 2) + 2(x + 3)$. (Lesson 1–7)

SELF TEST

Determine the slope of the line that passes through each pair of points. (Lesson 6–1)

1. (−7, 10) and (−2, 5)
2. (−6, 3) and (−12, 3)
3. (−5, 7) and (−5, −15)
4. Determine the value of r so the line through $(r, 3)$ and $(6, -2)$ has a slope of $-\frac{5}{2}$. (Lesson 6–1)

Write the point-slope form of an equation of the line that passes through the given point and has the given slope. (Lesson 6–2)

5. $(-6, 4)$, $m = \frac{1}{2}$
6. $(-12, 12)$, $m = 0$
7. Write the standard form of an equation of the line that passes through (−3, 4) and (2, 3). (Lesson 6–2)
8. **Computers** A newspaper article stated that with advancements in technology, computers would become cheaper and cheaper. Is this true? The table at the right shows the average cost of a computer system for each year from 1991 to 1994. (Lesson 6–3)
   a. Make a scatter plot of these data.
   b. Draw a best-fit line and write an equation that describes it.
   c. Does the scatter plot show a positive, negative, or no correlation between the variables?
   d. Write what this correlation means in words.
   e. With each year, computer systems become faster at handling more and more data. How can you use this fact to substantiate the newspaper article claim?

Year	Average Cost ($)
1991	1100
1992	1143
1993	1183
1994	1219

Source: *Vitality*, 1995

9. Find the x- and y-intercepts of the graph of $7x + 3y = -42$. (Lesson 6–4)
10. Write the slope-intercept form of an equation for the line that passes through (0, −3) and (6, 0). (Lesson 6–4)

6–5A Graphing Technology
Parent and Family Graphs

A Preview of Lesson 6–5

What is a family? Generally, a family is a group of people that are related either by birth, marriage, or adoption. Graphs can also form families. A **family of graphs** includes graphs and equations of graphs that have at least one characteristic in common. That characteristic differentiates the group of graphs from other groups.

Families of linear graphs often fall into two categories—those with the same slope or those with the same intercept. The **parent graph** is the simplest of the graphs in a family. For many linear functions, the parent graph is of the form $y = mx$, where m is any number.

A graphing calculator is a useful tool in studying a group of graphs to determine if they form a family.

Example 1 **Graph $y = x$, $y = 2x$, and $y = 4x$ in the standard viewing window. Describe any similarities and differences among the graphs. Write a description of the family.**

Clear the Y= list of all other equations.

Enter: [Y=] [X,T,θ,n] [ENTER] 2 [X,T,θ,n] [ENTER] 4 [X,T,θ,n] [ENTER] [ZOOM] 6

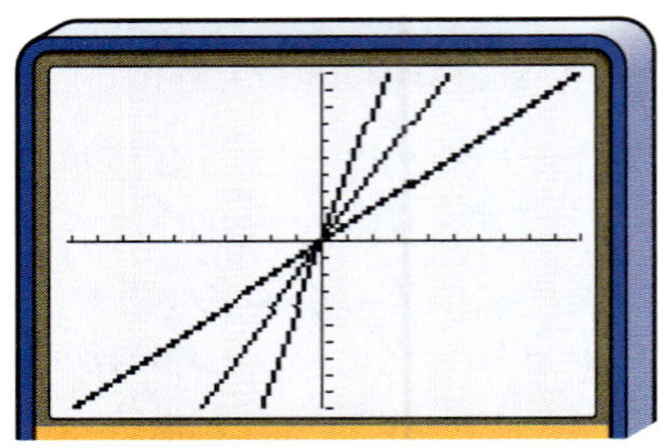

These three graphs form a family in which the slope of each graph is positive and each graph goes through the origin. However, each graph has a different slope. The parent graph is the graph of $y = x$. The graph of $y = 4x$ is the steepest, and the graph of $y = x$ is the least steep.

You might describe this family of graphs as lines that pass through the origin. Another description might be lines that have 0 as their y-intercept.

You can use braces to enter equations that have a common characteristic. Since all of the equations in Example 1 are of the form $y = mx$, you can use braces to enter the different values of m using one step as follows.

Enter: [Y=] [2nd] [{] 1 [,] 2 [,] 4 [2nd] [}] [X,T,θ,n] [GRAPH]

This tells the calculator to graphs equations for which the coefficients of x are 1, 2, and 4 and the y-intercept is 0.

Example 2 **Graph $y = x$, $y = x + 3$, and $y = x - 3$ in the standard viewing window. Describe any similarities and differences among the graphs. Write a description of the family.**

You can enter each of the graphs into the Y= list as you did in Example 1 or use braces to enter the equations in one step. Notice that all three equations can be written in the form $y = x + b$. The braces can be used to enter the different values of b.

Enter: [Y=] [X,T,θ,n] [+] [2nd] [{] 0 [,] 3 [,] [(–)] 3 [2nd] [}] 6 [ZOOM]

The parent graph in this example is the graph of $y = x$.

The slope of each graph is positive. However, each graph has a different y-intercept.

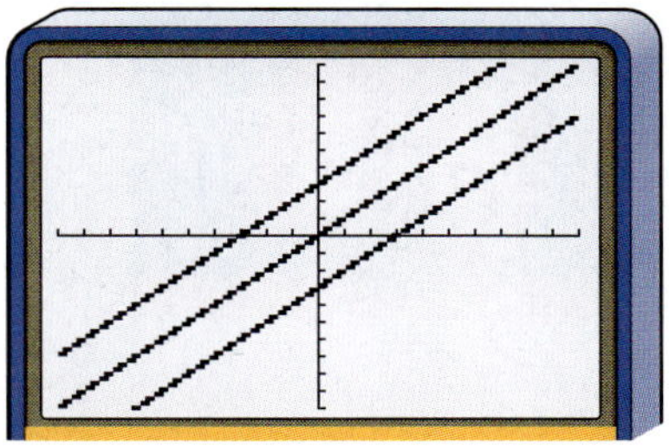

The graph of $y = x$ has a y-intercept of 0.
The graph of $y = x + 3$ has a y-intercept of 3.
The graph of $y = x - 3$ has a y-intercept of -3.

Since the slope of each line is 1, we can describe this family as linear graphs whose slope is 1.

A function that is closely related to linear functions is the **absolute value function.**

Example 3 **Graph $y = |x|$, $y = |x + 2|$, and $y = |x| + 4$ on the same screen. Describe any similarities and differences among the graphs.**

Enter: [Y=] [2nd] [ABS] [X,T,θ,n]
[ENTER] [2nd] [ABS] [(]
[X,T,θ,n] [+] 2 [)] [ENTER]
[2nd] [ABS] [X,T,θ,n] [+] 4
[ZOOM] 6

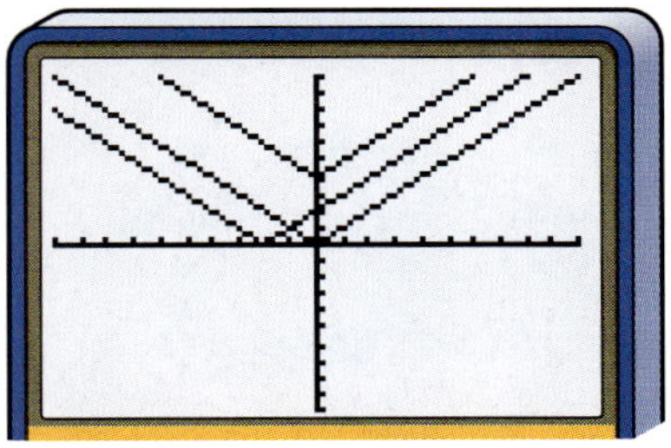

The parent graph in this example is the graph of $y = |x|$.

Each graph is shaped like the letter v. The graph of $y = |x + 2|$ is shaped like the graph of $y = |x|$, but is shifted 2 units to the left. The graph of $y = |x| + 4$ is shaped like the graph of $y = |x|$, but is shifted 4 units up.

EXERCISES

Graph each set of equations on the same screen. Describe any similarities or differences among the graphs. State what the graphs have in common.

1. $y = -x$
$y = -2x$
$y = -4x$

2. $y = |x|$
$y = 2|x|$
$y = 0.5|x|$

3. $y = -x$
$y = -x + 2$
$y = -x - 3$

4. Write a sentence comparing the graphs of equations with a positive coefficient of x and graphs with a negative coefficient of x.

Sketch a graph on paper to represent how you think the graph of each equation will appear. Describe any similarities to the graphs in Examples 1 and 2 and Exercises 1–3. Then use a graphing calculator to confirm your prediction and describe how accurate your sketch was.

5. $y = x - 5$ **6.** $y = -|x| + 6$ **7.** $y = 0.1x$ **8.** $y = \frac{1}{3}x + 4$

9. Write an equation of a line whose graph lies between the graphs of $y = -x + 2$ and $y = -x + 3$.

10. Write a paragraph explaining how the values of m and b in the slope-intercept form affect the graph of the equation. Include several graphs with your paragraph.

6–5 Graphing Linear Equations

What YOU'LL LEARN
- To graph a line given any linear equation.

Why IT'S IMPORTANT

You can graph linear equations to show trends in fields like health and physical science.

CONNECTION
Earth Science

Solome was flying from New York to Spain to be an exchange student for the spring quarter. After climbing to cruising level, the pilot announced that they were at an altitude of 13,700 meters and the outside temperature was about −76°C. You may think that since you get closer to the sun as you get farther from Earth, you might get warmer as altitude increases. However, as altitude increases, the air gets thinner and colder.

The air temperature above Earth on a day when the temperature at ground level is 15°C can be calculated using the formula $a + 150t = 2250$, where a is the altitude in meters and t is the temperature in degrees Celsius.

Suppose you wanted to graph $a + 150t = 2250$. In Chapter 5, you learned that you could graph a linear equation by finding and then graphing several ordered pairs that satisfy the equation.

Using the x- and y-intercepts is a convenient way to find ordered pairs to graph a linear equation. In $a + 150t = 2250$, these can be called the a-intercept and the t-intercept.

Find the a-intercept.

$$a + 150t = 2250$$
$$a + 150(0) = 2250 \quad \textit{Let } t = 0.$$
$$a = 2250$$

Find the t-intercept.

$$a + 150t = 2250$$
$$0 + 150t = 2250 \quad \textit{Let } a = 0.$$
$$t = 15$$

Now graph (2250, 0) and (0, 15), the ordered pairs for the intercepts. Draw the line representing the equation by connecting the points. Thus, you can graph a line if you know two points on that line.

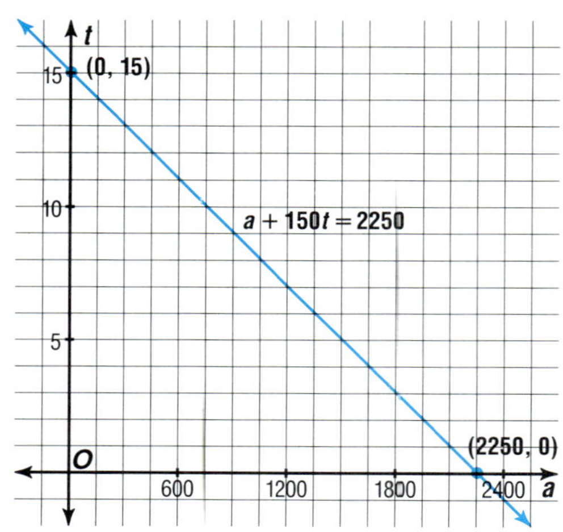

Use the equation to confirm the pilot's announcement that the temperature was −76°C at 13,700 meters altitude.

$$a + 150t = 2250$$
$$13{,}700 + 150t = 2250$$
$$150t = -11{,}450$$
$$t \approx -76.33$$

So, the pilot was correct in saying that the outside temperature was about −76°C.

You can also graph a line if you know its slope and a point on the line. The forms of linear equations you have learned in this chapter can help you find the slope and a point on the line.

Example 1 Graph $y - 1 = 3(x + 2)$.

This equation is in point-slope form. The slope is 3, and a point on the line is $(-2, 1)$.

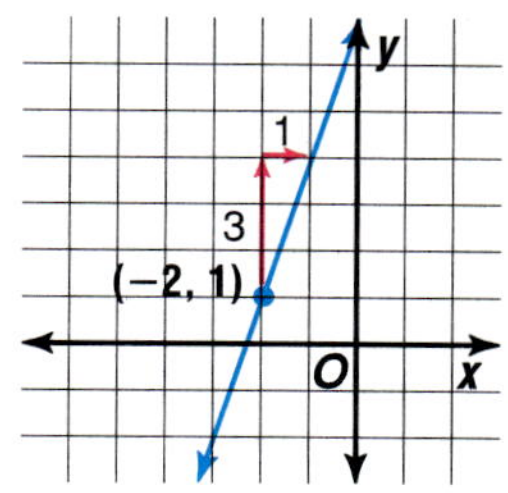

Graph the point $(-2, 1)$. Remember that the slope represents the change in y and x.

$$\frac{3}{1} = \frac{\text{change in } y}{\text{change in } x}$$

Thus, from the point $(-2, 1)$, you can move up 3 and right 1. Draw a dot. You can repeat this process to find another point on the graph. Draw a line connecting the points. This line is the graph of $y - 1 = 3(x + 2)$.

Check: Check $(-1, 4)$ to make sure that it satisfies the equation.

$$y - 1 = 3(x + 2)$$
$$4 - 1 \stackrel{?}{=} 3(-1 + 2)$$
$$3 = 3 \checkmark$$

You can also use the slope-intercept form to help you graph an equation.

Example 2 Graph $\frac{3}{4}x + \frac{1}{2}y = 4$.

Solve the equation for y to find the slope-intercept form.

$$\frac{3}{4}x + \frac{1}{2}y = 4$$

$$\frac{1}{2}y = -\frac{3}{4}x + 4 \quad \textit{Subtract } \tfrac{3}{4}x \textit{ from each side.}$$

$$y = -\frac{3}{2}x + 8 \quad \textit{Multiply each side by 2.}$$

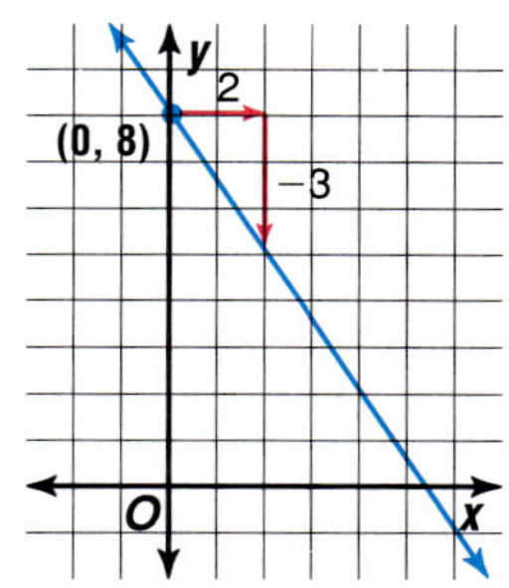

The slope-intercept form of this equation tells us that the slope is $-\frac{3}{2}$ and the y-intercept is 8. Graph the y-intercept, and then use the slope to find another point on the line. Draw the line.

Be sure to check your second point to make sure it satisfies the *original* equation.

You frequently need to rewrite equations before you can determine the best way to graph them.

Example 3 Graph $\frac{4}{5}(2x - y) = 6x + \frac{2}{5}y - 10$.

First, simplify the equation.

$$\frac{4}{5}(2x - y) = 6x + \frac{2}{5}y - 10$$

$4(2x - y) = 30x + 2y - 50$	*Multiply each side by 5 to eliminate the fractions.*
$8x - 4y = 30x + 2y - 50$	
$0 = 22x + 6y - 50$	*Add $-8x$ and $4y$ to each side.*
$50 = 22x + 6y$	*Add 50 to each side.*
$25 = 11x + 3y$	*Divide each side by 2.*
$11x + 3y = 25$	*Standard form*

(continued on the next page)

The equation is now in standard form. You can choose one of several methods to graph this equation.

ordered pairs

If $x = 2$, $y = 1$.

If $x = -1$, $y = 12$.

Graph (2, 1) and (−1, 12).

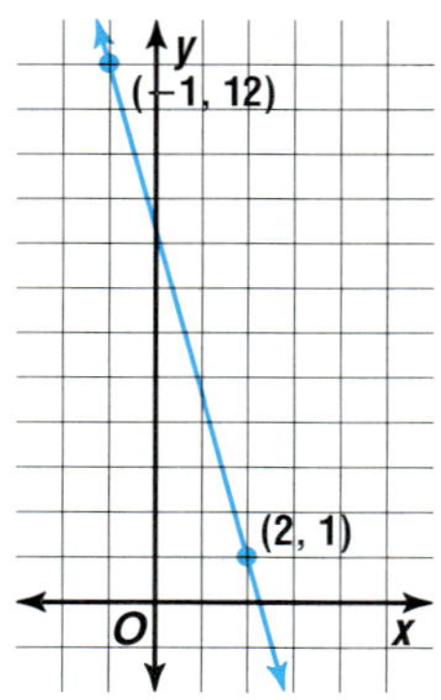

intercepts

If $x = 0$, $y = \frac{25}{3}$.

If $y = 0$, $x = \frac{25}{11}$.

Graph $\left(0, \frac{25}{3}\right)$ and $\left(\frac{25}{11}, 0\right)$.

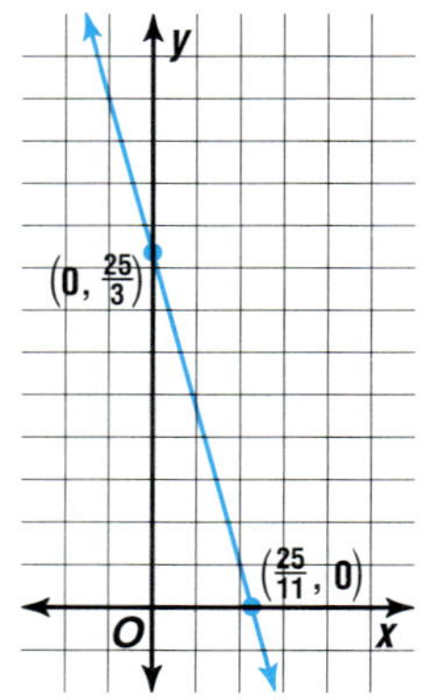

slope-intercept form

$$11x + 3y = 25$$
$$3y = -11x + 25$$
$$y = -\frac{11}{3}x + \frac{25}{3}$$

The y-intercept is $\frac{25}{3}$, and the slope is $-\frac{11}{3}$.

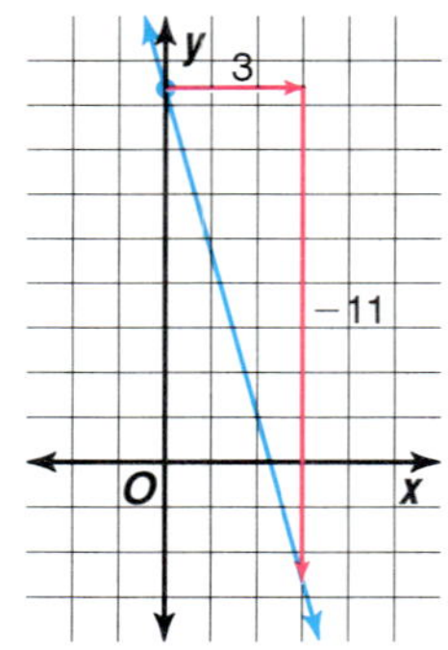

Notice that the result is the same regardless of the method you choose. Choose the method that is easiest for you.

It is often helpful to make a sketch of the graph of an equation when you are trying to observe patterns and make predictions.

Example 4

CONNECTION

Biology

FYI

The bitterbrush plant can grow as high as 10 feet. However, a plant this tall is very rare since it is often the sole source of food in many areas in the winter. Its growth is constantly stunted by grazing animals.

The mule deer likes to feed upon the bitterbrush plant, which is native to the dry regions of western North America. The diameter of each bitterbrush twig is related to the length of the twig by the function $\ell = 1.25 + 8.983d$, where ℓ is the length (inches) of the twig, d is its diameter in inches, and $d \geq 0.1$.

a. Graph the function. Name the independent and dependent variables.

b. Describe the relationship between a twig's diameter and length.

c. What would be the length of a twig if its diameter is 0.5 inch?

a. In this equation, d is the independent variable, and ℓ is the dependent variable. Since d must be a nonnegative value, it may be easier to choose two values of d and find the corresponding value of ℓ to graph. A calculator may be helpful.

Let $d = 0.1$

$\ell = 1.25 + 8.983(0.1)$
$= 2.1483$

Let $d = 1$.

$\ell = 1.25 + 8.983(1)$
$= 10.233$

Graph (0.1, 2.148) and (1, 10. 233). Connect them with a line.

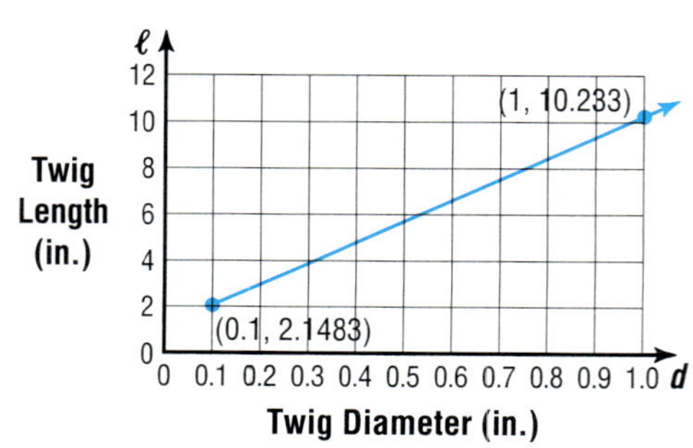

b. As the diameter of the twig increases, the length of the twig increases.

c. Let $d = 0.5$ and evaluate the equation.

$\ell = 1.25 + 8.983(0.5)$

$= 5.7415$

A 0.5-inch diameter twig is about 5.74 inches long.

Check to see if this point is on the graph.

CHECK FOR UNDERSTANDING

Communicating Mathematics

Study the lesson. Then complete the following.

1. **Write** a counterexample to the statement "You must always know two points that satisfy an equation in order to graph the equation."
2. **Explain** why the value of d cannot be zero in Example 4.
3. **Illustrate** how you graph a line if you know a point on the line and its slope.
4. **Describe** two ways in which you can interpret the slope $-\frac{3}{4}$ when using it to find another point on the graph of a line.

MATH JOURNAL

5. **Assess Yourself** List all the possible ways you know to graph the equation of a line. Which of these methods do you prefer and why?

Guided Practice

6. Graph $3x - 8y = 12$ by using the x- and y-intercepts.
7. Graph $y + 5 = -2(x + 1)$ by using the slope and a point on the line.
8. Graph $\frac{2}{3}x + \frac{1}{2}y = 3$ by using the slope and y-intercept.

Graph each equation.

9. $y = 2x - 3$ **10.** $y = \frac{2}{5}x - 4$ **11.** $6y + 12 = 18$ **12.** $5x = 9$

13. **Health** Did you know that your fingernails grow twice as fast as your toenails? Your fingernails grow about $\frac{1}{8}$ inch each month. Suppose the nail on your index finger is $\frac{1}{4}$ inch long.
    - **a.** Graph the line representing your fingernail's growth for a year.
    - **b.** How long would your nail be at the end of one year?
    - **c.** How much do your toenails grow each month?
    - **d.** Graph the line representing your toenail's growth for one year.
    - **e.** What does the slope of each line represent?

EXERCISES

Practice

Graph each equation by using the x- and y-intercepts.

14. $y = 5x - 10$ **15.** $6x - y = 9$ **16.** $\frac{1}{2}x - \frac{2}{3}y = -6$

Graph each equation by using the slope and a point on the line.

17. $y - 2 = 3(x - 5)$
18. $y + 6 = -\frac{3}{2}(x + 5)$
19. $2(x - 3) = y + \frac{3}{2}$

Graph each equation by using the slope and *y*-intercept.

20. $y = -\frac{3}{4}x + 4$
21. $2x - 3y = -7$
22. $5y + 3 = -5$

Graph each equation.

23. $y = 3x - 5$
24. $6y + 5 = 5y + 3$
25. $3(y + 4) = -2x$
26. $y = \frac{2}{3}x + 1$
27. $5x + 2y = 20$
28. $\frac{2}{3}x - y = 4$
29. $6x - y = 8$
30. $15x - 29y = 429$
31. $y = 0.17x + 1.75$
32. $y - 3 = \frac{2}{3}(x - 6)$
33. $y + 1 = -2(x + 3)$

Graphing Calculator

Graph each group of equations on the same screen. Describe the graphs in terms of a family of graphs.

34. $y = 2x + 4$
    $2x - 3y = -12$
    $y + 5 = 3(x + 3)$
35. $12x - 3y = 15$
    $y = 4x - 11$
    $y + x = 5x$

Critical Thinking

36. An equation belongs to the same family of graphs as $y = 3x + 5$, but it has a *y*-intercept of 7. How could you graph the equation without finding the equation first?

Applications and Problem Solving

37. **Health** In cardiopulmonary resuscitation (CPR) on an adult, you initially give two breaths before you begin a cycle of one breath for every five pumps on the heart per minute. Each pump of the heart takes about a second. Thus, in a minute (60 seconds), you give about 60 ÷ 5 or 12 breaths. The number of breaths can be described by the equation $B = 2 + 12t$, where t represents the amount of time in minutes and B is the total number of breaths after pumping starts.
    a. Graph the equation.
    b. It is recommended that CPR be sustained until an emergency squad can get to the patient. If the squad takes 10 minutes to get to the patients, how many breaths should the patient have received?

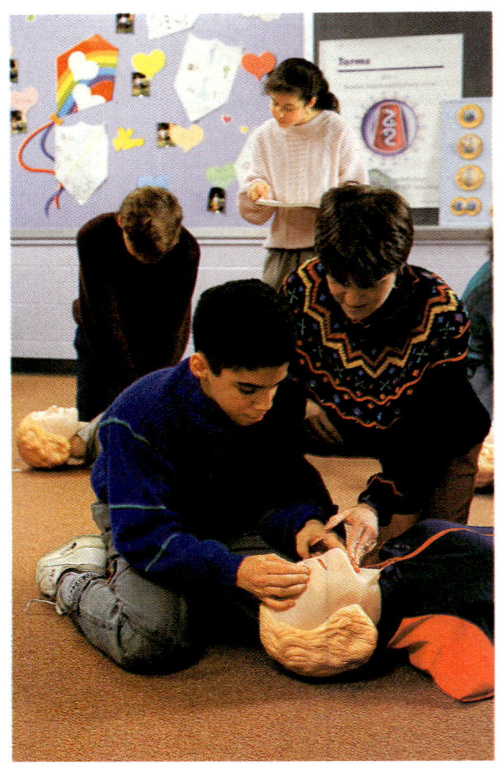

38. **Physical Science** The length of an object's shadow depends on its height. At a certain time of day on a particular day of the year, the lengths of shadows can be calculated by the formula $S = 1.5h$, where h is the height and S is the length of the shadow.

a. Graph the equation.

b. At the time of day for which the formula is valid, the oak tree in your back yard is casting a 30-foot shadow. What is the height of the tree?

Mixed Review

39. Write an equation in slope-intercept form of the line with y-intercept 12 and slope the same as the line whose equation is $2x - 5y - 10 = 0$. (Lesson 6–4)

40. Draw a mapping for the relation $\{(1, 3), (2, 3), (2, 1), (3, 2)\}$. (Lesson 5–2)

41. **Travel** Art leaves home at 10:00 A.M., driving at 50 miles per hour. At 11:30 A.M., Jennifer leaves home, going in the same direction, at 45 miles per hour. When will they be 100 miles apart? (Lesson 4–7)

42. **Geometry** Find the supplement of 87°. (Lesson 3–4)

43. Find the square root of 3.24. (Lesson 2–8)

44. Find $-13 + (-9)$. (Lesson 2–1)

45. Write a verbal expression for $m - 1$. (Lesson 1–1)

WORKING ON THE In•ves•ti•ga•tion

Refer to the Investigation on pages 320–321.

Smoke Gets In Your Eyes

Which of your group members was closest to the average in number of breaths it took to blow up a balloon? Use that group member to conduct another experiment. For this activity, assume that each breath into a balloon approximates the exhaled smoke from one puff of a cigarette.

1. Have that member simulate the amount of smoke from each exhale during smoking by blowing into a balloon. Use a tape measure to determine the circumference of the balloon after each breath. Record each measurement.
2. Calculate the volume after each breath. Graph the relationship of the volume to each breath. Describe the graph. Does the graph represent a function? If so, describe the domain and range.
3. There are 20 cigarettes in each pack. If a smoker smokes an entire pack of cigarettes, how many balloons would be filled? What would be the volume of smoke-filled air?
4. Graph the data relating the cumulative smoke in the air for each cigarette smoked in a pack of cigarettes.
5. If a smoker smokes an entire carton of cigarettes (10 packs/carton), how many balloons would be filled? What would be the volume of smoke-filled air?

Add the results of your work to your Investigation Folder.

6–6 Integration: Geometry
Parallel and Perpendicular Lines

What YOU'LL LEARN

- To determine if two lines are parallel or perpendicular by their slopes, and
- to write equations of lines that pass through a given point, parallel or perpendicular to the graph of a given equation.

Why IT'S IMPORTANT

You can use parallel and perpendicular lines to solve problems involving health and construction.

APPLICATION

World Cultures

Kite-making has been a national sport in some Far East countries since ancient times. In September, Chinese families celebrate the Ninth Day of the Ninth Moon as Kites' Day. Entire families go outside and fly kites. These kites may be simple diamond shapes or more complex shapes like fish, birds, dragons, and colorfully-dressed people.

The outline of a simple kite is shown on the coordinate plane at the right. The ordered pairs for the tips of the kite are labeled. We know that the two slats that support that kite meet at right angles. Lines that intersect at right angles are called **perpendicular lines.** *You will learn more about these lines later in the lesson.*

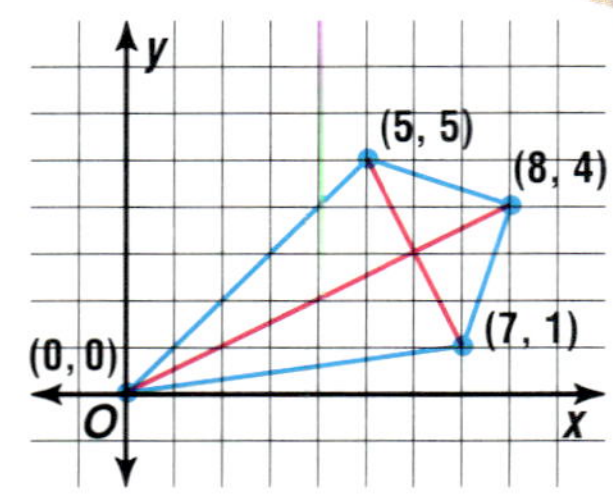

Lines in the same plane that never intersect are called **parallel lines.** Parallel lines can form families of graphs. In Lesson 6–5A, you learned that families of graphs can either have the same slope or the same intercept. The graph at the right shows a family of graphs represented by the following equations.

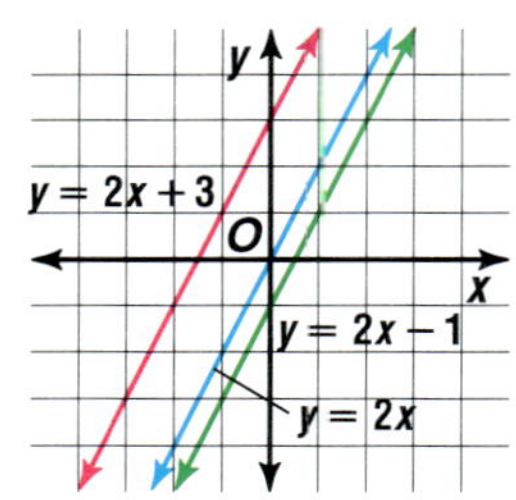

$y = 2x$ *The parent graph is the graph of $y = 2x$.*

$y = 2x + 3$

$y = 2x - 1$

The slope of each line is 2. Notice that the lines seem to be parallel. In fact, they are parallel.

Definition of Parallel Lines in a Coordinate Plane	**If two nonvertical lines have the same slope, then they are parallel. All vertical lines are parallel.**

A **parallelogram** is a quadrilateral in which opposite sides are parallel. We can use slope to determine if quadrilaterals graphed on a coordinate plane are parallelograms. *The slope of a segment is the same as the slope of the line containing that segment.*

Example 1 **Determine whether quadrilateral *ABCD* is a parallelogram if its vertices are $A(-5, -3)$, $B(5, 3)$, $C(7, 9)$, and $D(-3, 3)$.**

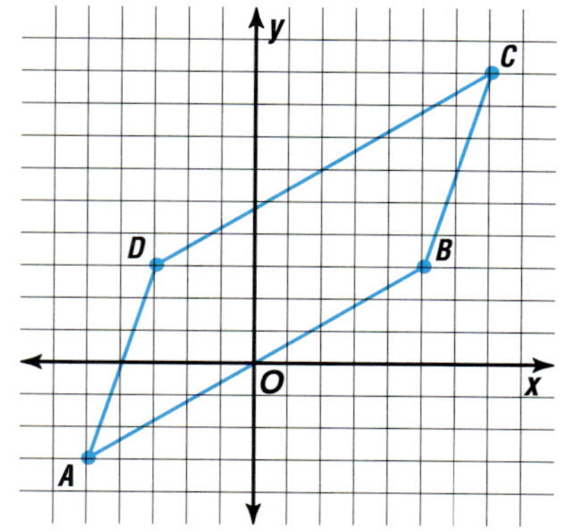

Explore Graph the four vertices. Connect the vertices to form the quadrilateral.

Plan Use each pair of vertices to find the slope of each segment.

Use $m = \frac{y_2 - y_1}{x_2 - x_1}$.

$\overline{AB}$ means a line segment whose endpoints are A and B.

Solve

$\overline{AB}$: $m = \frac{3-(-3)}{5-(-5)} = \frac{6}{10}$ or $\frac{3}{5}$

$\overline{BC}$: $m = \frac{9-3}{7-5} = \frac{6}{2}$ or 3

$\overline{CD}$: $m = \frac{3-9}{-3-7} = \frac{-6}{-10}$ or $\frac{3}{5}$

$\overline{AD}$: $m = \frac{3-(-3)}{-3-(-5)} = \frac{6}{2}$ or 3

$\overline{AB}$ and $\overline{CD}$ have the same slope, $\frac{3}{5}$. $\overline{BC}$ and $\overline{AD}$ have the same slope, 3. Both pairs of opposite sides are parallel. Thus, *ABCD* is a parallelogram.

Examine Another definition of a parallelogram is that its opposite sides are congruent, or equal in length. Use a millimeter ruler to measure each side. $\overline{AB}$ and $\overline{CD}$ are approximately 37 millimeters long. $\overline{BC}$ and $\overline{AD}$ are approximately 20 millimeters long. The figure is probably a parallelogram.

You can write the equation of a line parallel to another line if you know a point on the line and the equation of the other line.

Example 2 **Write an equation in slope-intercept form of the line that passes through (4, 0) and is parallel to the graph of $4x - 3y = 2$.**

First find the slope by rewriting the equation in slope-intercept form.

$$4x - 3y = 2$$
$$-3y = -4x + 2$$
$$y = \frac{4}{3}x - \frac{2}{3}$$

The slope is $\frac{4}{3}$.

GLOBAL CONNECTIONS

The largest kite ever flown was flown by a Dutch team at Scheveningen, Netherlands in 1991. The kite had a surface area of 5952 ft^2. A team at Sakvrajima, Kagoshima, Japan, set a world record by flying 11,284 kites on a single line.

Method 1

Use point-slope form.

$$y - y_1 = m(x - x_1)$$
$$y - 0 = \frac{4}{3}(x - 4) \quad m = \frac{4}{3}, x_1 = 4, \text{ and } y_1 = 0$$
$$y = \frac{4}{3}x - \frac{16}{3}$$

This equation is in slope-intercept form.

An equation for the line is $y = \frac{4}{3}x - \frac{16}{3}$.

Method 2

Use the slope-intercept form.

$$y = mx + b$$
$$0 = \frac{4}{3}(4) + b$$
$$0 = \frac{16}{3} + b$$
$$-\frac{16}{3} = b$$

Now substitute the values for *m* and *b* into the slope-intercept form.

$y = \frac{4}{3}x - \frac{16}{3}$

Sometimes graphs can be drawn in a way that leads you to the wrong conclusion. Mathematics can help you determine if a graph is misleading.

Example 3 CONNECTION **Health**

The American Heart Association recommends that men keep their weight within a certain "healthy weight band" as shown in the graph at the right. Are the lines parallel as they appear in the graph?

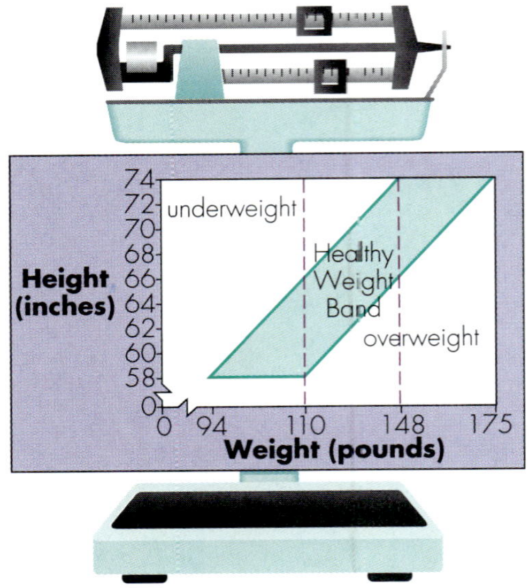

From the graph, we can determine that the endpoints of the minimum edge are (94, 58) and (148, 74). The endpoints of the maximum edge are (110, 58) and (175, 74). Find the slopes of each segment.

$$m_1 = \frac{74 - 58}{148 - 94} = \frac{16}{54} \text{ or about } 0.30$$

$$m_2 = \frac{74 - 58}{175 - 110} = \frac{16}{65} \text{ or about } 0.25$$

The segments do not have the same slope. Therefore, they are not parallel as they appear in this graph.

We have seen that the slopes of parallel lines are equal. What is the relationship of the slopes of perpendicular lines?

Example 4 APPLICATION **Kite-Making**

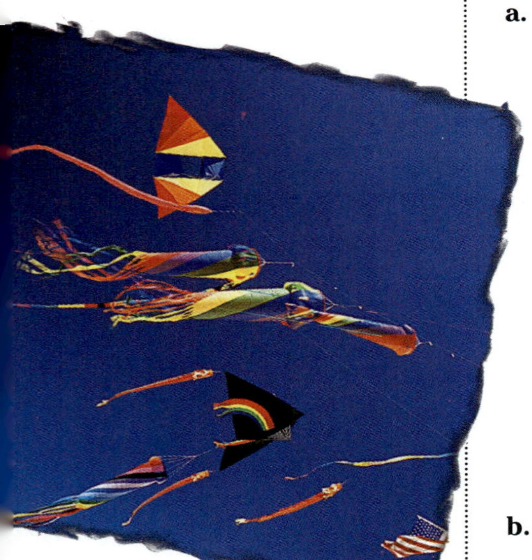

Refer to the application at the beginning of the lesson.

a. Write equations of the lines containing the slats of the kite in slope-intercept form.

b. Determine the relationship between the slopes of perpendicular lines.

a. The endpoints of the longer slat are (0, 0) and (8, 4). The endpoints of the shorter slat are (5, 5) and (7, 1). Find the slope of each slat and then use the point-slope form to find an equation for each slat.

long slat

$m = \frac{4 - 0}{8 - 0} = \frac{4}{8} \text{ or } \frac{1}{2}$

Let $(x_1, y_1) = (0, 0)$.

$y - y_1 = m(x - x_1)$

$y - 0 = \frac{1}{2}(x - 0)$

$y = \frac{1}{2}x$

short slat

$m = \frac{1 - 5}{7 - 5} = \frac{-4}{2} \text{ or } -2$

Let $(x_1, y_1) = (5, 5)$.

$y - y_1 = m(x - x_1)$

$y - 5 = -2(x - 5)$

$y - 5 = -2x + 10$

$y = -2x + 15$

Equations of the slats are $y = \frac{1}{2}x$ and $y = -2x + 15$.

b. The slats of the kite are perpendicular. The slopes of the slats are $\frac{1}{2}$ and -2. The two slopes are negative reciprocals of each other. Note that their product is $\frac{1}{2}(-2)$ or -1.

These results suggest the following definition.

Definition of Perpendicular Lines in a Coordinate Plane	**If the product of the slopes of two lines is −1, then the lines are perpendicular. In a plane, vertical lines and horizontal lines are perpendicular.**

The slopes of perpendicular lines are negative reciprocals of each other.

You can use a right triangle and a coordinate grid to model the slopes of perpendicular lines.

MODELING MATHEMATICS

Perpendicular Lines on a Coordinate Plane

Materials: grid paper scissors

a. A scalene triangle is one in which no two sides are equal. Cut out a scalene right triangle ABC so that $\angle C$ is the right angle. Label the vertices and the sides as shown at the right.

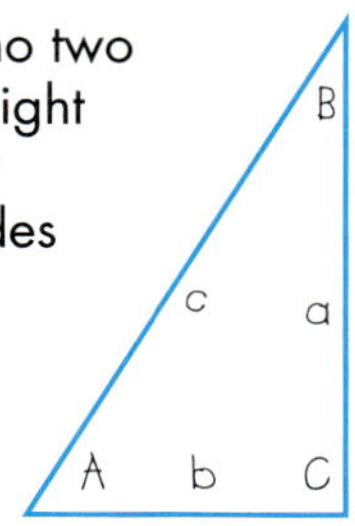

b. Draw a coordinate plane on the grid paper. Place ΔABC on the coordinate plane so that A is at the origin and side b lies along the positive x-axis.

c. Name the coordinates of B.

d. What is the slope of side c?

Your Turn

a. Rotate the triangle 90° counterclockwise so that A is still at the origin and side b is along the positive y-axis.

b. Name the coordinates of B.

c. What is the slope of c?

d. What is the relationship between the first position of c and the second?

e. What is the relationship between the slopes of c in each position?

You can use your knowledge of perpendicular lines to write equations of lines perpendicular to a given line.

Example 5

Write the slope-intercept form of an equation that passes through (8, −2) and is perpendicular to the graph of $5x - 3y = 7$.

First find the slope of the given line.

$$5x - 3y = 7$$
$$-3y = -5x + 7$$
$$y = \frac{5}{3}x - \frac{7}{3}$$

The slope of the line is $\frac{5}{3}$. The slope of the line perpendicular to this line is the negative reciprocal of $\frac{5}{3}$, or $-\frac{3}{5}$.

Use the point-slope form to find the equation.

$$y - y_1 = m(x - x_1)$$
$$y - (-2) = -\frac{3}{5}(x - 8) \quad m = -\frac{3}{5}, (x_1, y_1) = (8, -2)$$
$$y + 2 = -\frac{3}{5}x + \frac{24}{5} \quad \textit{Distributive property}$$
$$y = -\frac{3}{5}x + \frac{14}{5} \quad \textit{Subtract 2 or } \frac{10}{5} \textit{ from each side.}$$

An equation for the line is $y = -\frac{3}{5}x + \frac{14}{5}$.

CHECK FOR UNDERSTANDING

Communicating Mathematics

Study the lesson. Then complete the following.

1. **Describe** the relationship between the slopes of each of the following.
   a. two parallel lines
   b. two perpendicular lines
2. **Explain** what negative reciprocals are. Give an example.
3. **Check** the results of Examples 2 and 5 by graphing the original equation and the answer equation for each example on the same coordinate plane. Describe what happens.

MODELING MATHEMATICS

4. Refer to the Modeling Mathematics activity. Why do you think the right triangle should be scalene?
5. Repeat the activity with a different size right triangle.
   a. Are the results different?
   b. What do you think would happen if you used a triangle that was not a right triangle?

Guided Practice

State the slopes of the lines parallel to and perpendicular to the graph of each equation.

6. $6x - 5y = 11$
7. $y = \frac{2}{3}x - \frac{4}{5}$
8. $3x = 10y - 3$

Determine whether the graphs of each pair of equations are *parallel, perpendicular,* or *neither.*

9. $3x - 7y = 1,\ 7x + 3y = 4$
10. $5x - 2y = 6,\ 4y - 10x = -48$

Write an equation in slope-intercept form of the line that passes through the given point and is parallel to the graph of each equation.

11. $(9, -3),\ 5x - 6y = 2$
12. $(0, 4),\ 2y = 5x - 7$
13. $(7, -2),\ x - y = 0$

Write an equation in slope-intercept form of the line that passes through the given point and is perpendicular to the graph of each equation.

14. $(8, 5),\ 7x + 4y = 23$
15. $(0, 0),\ 9y = 3 - 5x$
16. $(-2, 7),\ 2x - 5y = 3$

17. **Geometry** The diagonals of a square are segments that connect the opposite vertices. Use what you've learned in this lesson to determine the relationship between the diagonals $\overline{AC}$ and $\overline{BD}$ of the square graphed at the right.

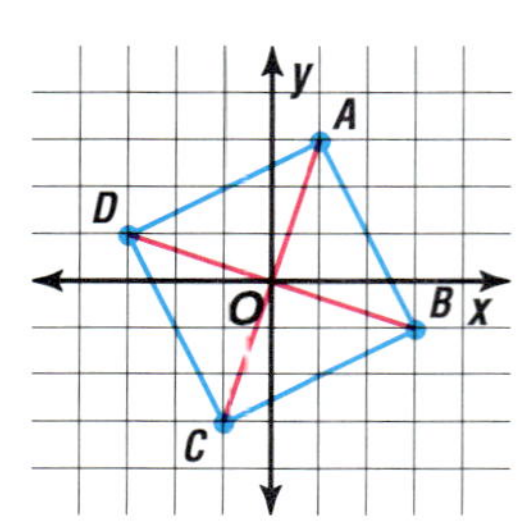

EXERCISES

Practice

Determine whether the graphs of each pair of equations are *parallel, perpendicular,* or *neither.*

18. $y = -2x + 11$
$y + 2x = 23$

19. $3y = 2x + 14$
$2x - 3y = 2$

20. $y = -5x$
$y = 5x - 18$

21. $y = 0.6x + 7$
$3y = -5x + 30$

22. $y = 3x + 5$
$y = 5x + 3$

23. $y + 6 = -5$
$y + x = y + 7$

Write an equation in slope-intercept form of the line that passes through the given point and is parallel to the graph of each equation.

24. $(2, -7), y = x - 2$

25. $(2, 3), y = x + 5$

26. $(-5, -4), 2x + 3y = -1$

27. $(5, 6), 8x - 7y = 23$

28. $(1, -2), y = -2x + 7$

29. $(0, -5), 5x - 2y = -7$

30. $(5, -4), x - 3y = 8$

31. $(-3, 2), 2x - 3y = 6$

32. $(2, -1), y = -0.5x + 2$

Write an equation in slope-intercept form of the line that passes through the given point and is perpendicular to the graph of each equation.

33. $(6, -13), 2x - 9y = 5$

34. $(-3, 1), y = \frac{1}{3}x + 2$

35. $(6, -1), 3y + x = 3$

36. $(6, -2), y = \frac{3}{5}x - 4$

37. $(0, -1), 5x - y = 3$

38. $(8, -2), 5x - 7 = 3y$

39. $(4, -3), 2x - 7y = 12$

40. $(3, 7), y = \frac{3}{4}x - 1$

41. $(3, -3), 3x + 7 = 2x$

Write an equation of the line having the following properties.

42. passes through $(-5, 3)$ and is perpendicular to the x-axis

43. is parallel to the graph of $y = \frac{5}{4}x - 3$ and passes through the origin.

44. has an x-intercept of 3 and is perpendicular to the graph of $5x - 3y = 2$

45. has a y-intercept of -6 and is parallel to the graph of $x - 3y = 8$

Critical Thinking

46. Lines a, b, and c lie on the same coordinate plane. Line a is perpendicular to line b and intersects it at $(3, 6)$. Line b is perpendicular to line c, which is the graph of $y = 2x + 3$.

a. Write the equation of lines a and b.

b. Graph the three lines.

c. What is the relationship of lines a and c?

Applications and Problem Solving

47. Geometry A rhombus is a parallelogram that has perpendicular diagonals. Determine if quadrilateral $ABCD$ with $A(-2, 1)$, $B(3, 3)$, $C(5, 7)$, and $D(0, 5)$ is a rhombus. Explain.

48. **Construction** A large roller is being used to flatten new asphalt on a hill that has a slope of $-\frac{1}{10}$. The steering mechanism for the front roller is perpendicular to the hill.

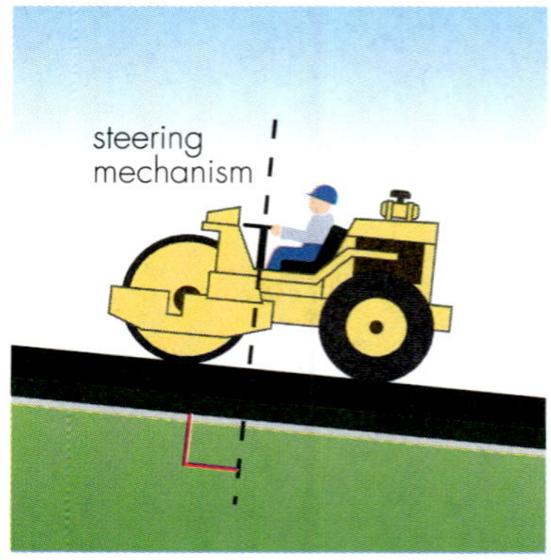

a. What is the slope of the steering mechanism?

b. If the bottom of the hill has coordinates (9, 3) and the point directly below the steering mechanism is at (−1, 4), write the equations of the lines representing the hill and the steering mechanism.

49. **Geometry** An angle inscribed in a circle is one in which the vertex of the angle lies on the circle and the two sides intersect the circle, as shown at the right.

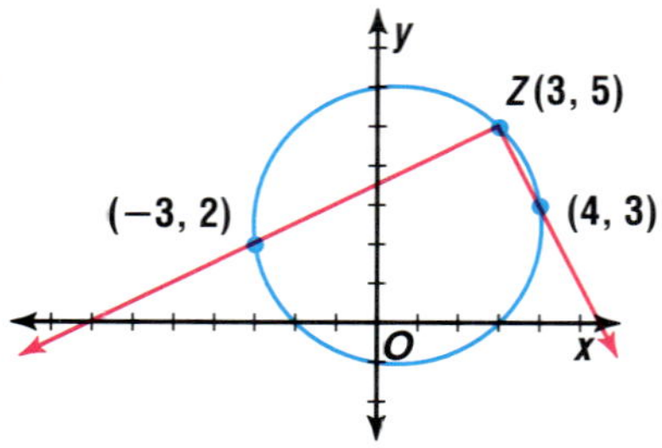

a. Find the equations of the lines that contain the sides of $\angle Z$.

b. What type of angle is $\angle Z$?

Mixed Review

50. Graph $7x - 2y = -7$ by using the x- and y-intercepts. (Lesson 6–5)

51. **Statistics** Make a scatter plot of the data below. (Lesson 6–3)

Miles Driven	200	322	250	290	310	135	60	150	180	70	315	175
Fuel Used (gallons)	7.5	14	11	10	10	5	2.3	5	6.2	3	11	6.5

52. **Patterns** Copy and complete the table below. (Lesson 5–4)

x	−1	2	5	8	11	14
$f(x)$		−1	−7		−19	

53. Find 4% of \$6070. (Lesson 4–4)

54. Solve $16 = \frac{s-8}{-7}$. Check your solution. (Lesson 3–3)

55. **Metallurgy** The gold content of jewelry is given in karats. For example, 24-karat gold is pure gold, and 18-karat gold is $\frac{18}{24}$ or 0.75 gold. (Lesson 2–7)

a. What fraction of 10-karat gold is pure gold? What fraction is *not* gold?

b. If a piece of jewelry is $\frac{2}{3}$ gold, how would you describe it using karats?

56. Find $-0.0005 + (-0.3)$. (Lesson 2–5)

57. Name the property illustrated by $1(87) = 87$. (Lesson 1–6)

58. Solve $x = 6 + 0.28$. (Lesson 1–5)

6-7 Integration: Geometry
Midpoint of a Line Segment

What **YOU'LL LEARN**

- To find the coordinates of the midpoint of a line segment in the coordinate plane.

Why **IT'S IMPORTANT**

You can find the midpoint of a line segment to solve problems involving geometry.

APPLICATION
Woodworking

Maria Hernandez made a frame for one of her watercolor paintings in a class offered at the community college. Because her canvas was heavy and the wooden frame was light, her instructor suggested that she stabilize her frame by adding crossbars connecting the consecutive sides. One of the books she used as a reference showed the crossbars inserted so that the bars are placed on the sides of the frame at the **midpoint** of each side. The midpoint of a line segment is the point that is halfway between the endpoints of the segment.

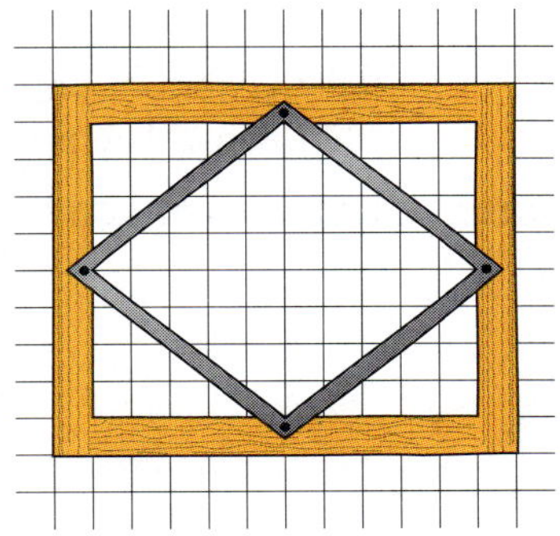

Maria decided to use some grid paper to model her frame and the crossbars she is going to insert. Each square of the paper represented 2 inches of her frame. To find the midpoint of the interior vertical edge, she counted how many units it was from one corner to the next and divided by 2. The inside of the frame is 16 inches high, so the midpoint is 8 inches from the corner. She counted 4 units on the grid and placed a bullet on her drawing. She used a similar method to find the midpoint of the interior horizontal edge. The inside is 20 inches wide, so the midpoint is 10 inches from the end.

Suppose we place Maria's frame drawing on a coordinate plane. Let's list the coordinates of the corners of the frame and the midpoints of the sides. What pattern do you notice?

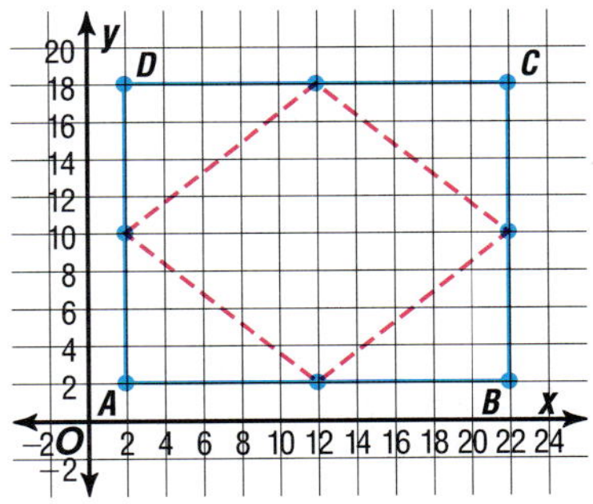

$A(2, 2)$
$B(22, 2)$
$C(22, 18)$
$D(2, 18)$

Midpoint of $\overline{AB}$: (12, 2)
Midpoint of $\overline{BC}$: (22, 10)
Midpoint of $\overline{CD}$: (12, 18)
Midpoint of $\overline{AD}$: (2, 10)

Notice that the coordinates of the midpoint of $\overline{AB}$ are the mean of the corresponding coordinates of A and B.

Midpoint of $\overline{AB}$: (12, 2)

mean of x-coordinates of A(2, 2) and B(22, 2)

$$\frac{2 + 22}{2} = 12$$

mean of y-coordinates of A(2, 2) and B(22, 2)

$$\frac{2 + 2}{2} = 2$$

The woodworking example uses the midpoints of horizontal and vertical line segments. The Modeling Mathematics activity on the next page applies to any line segment.

MODELING MATHEMATICS

Midpoint of a Line Segment

Materials: grid paper, ruler, colored pencils

- Create a coordinate plane on your grid paper.
- Use a ruler to draw any line segment on the coordinate plane. The segment should not be vertical or horizontal. Label the endpoints of the segment *A* and *B* with their coordinates.
- Hold the paper up to the light and fold it so that *A* and *B* coincide. Crease the paper at the fold.
- Unfold the paper. Label the point *M* at which the crease meets the segment and write the coordinates of *M*.
- Use a different color pencil to draw a vertical line through the lower endpoint of your segment. Then draw a horizontal line through the upper endpoint of your segment. Label the point of intersection *P*.
- Write the coordinates of the midpoints of $\overline{AP}$ and $\overline{BP}$.
- How do the *x*-coordinate of the vertical segment and the *y*-coordinate of the horizontal segment compare with the coordinates of *M*?

Your Turn

a. Create another coordinate plane and draw a segment with a different slope from the first one you drew.

b. Repeat the activity with this segment. What are your results?

c. Write a general rule for finding the midpoint of any segment.

This activity suggests the following rule for finding the midpoint of any segment, given the coordinates of its endpoints.

Midpoint of a Line Segment on a Coordinate Plane	**The coordinates of the midpoint of a line segment whose endpoints are at (x_1, y_1) and (x_2, y_2) are given by $\left(\frac{x_1 + x_2}{2}, \frac{y_1 + y_2}{2}\right)$.**

Example 1 **If the vertices of parallelogram *WXYZ* are *W*(3, 0), *X*(9, 3), *Y*(7, 10), and *Z*(1, 7), prove that the diagonals bisect each other. That is, prove that they intersect at their midpoints.**

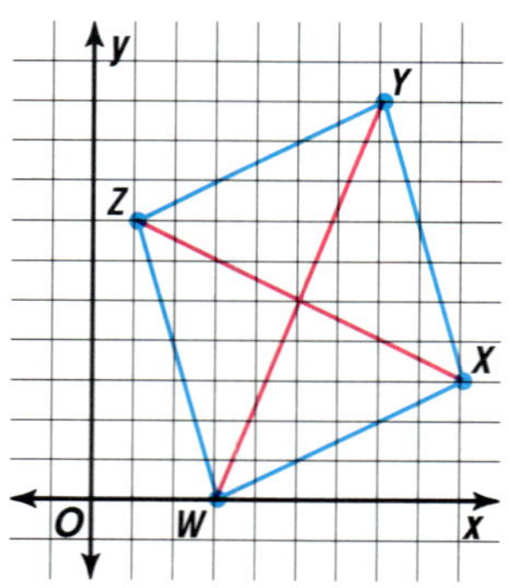

Explore Graph the vertices and draw the parallelogram and its diagonals.

Plan Find the coordinates of the midpoints of the diagonals to see if they are the same point.

Solve Find the midpoints of $\overline{WY}$ and $\overline{XZ}$.

$W(x_1, y_1) = W(3, 0)$
$Y(x_2, y_2) = Y(7, 10)$

$$\text{midpoint of } \overline{WY} = \left(\frac{3+7}{2}, \frac{0+10}{2}\right) = \left(\frac{10}{2}, \frac{10}{2}\right) = (5, 5)$$

$X(x_1, y_1) = X(9, 3)$
$Z(x_2, y_2) = Z(1, 7)$

$$\text{midpoint of } \overline{XZ} = \left(\frac{9+1}{2}, \frac{3+7}{2}\right) = \left(\frac{10}{2}, \frac{10}{2}\right) = (5, 5)$$

Examine Since the midpoint of $\overline{XZ}$ has the same coordinates as the midpoint of $\overline{WY}$, the diagonals bisect each other.

If you know the midpoint and one endpoint of a segment, you can find the other endpoint.

Example 2 **The center of a circle is $M(0, 2)$, and the endpoint of one of its radii is $A(-6, -4)$. If $\overline{AB}$ is a diameter of the circle, what are the coordinates of B?**

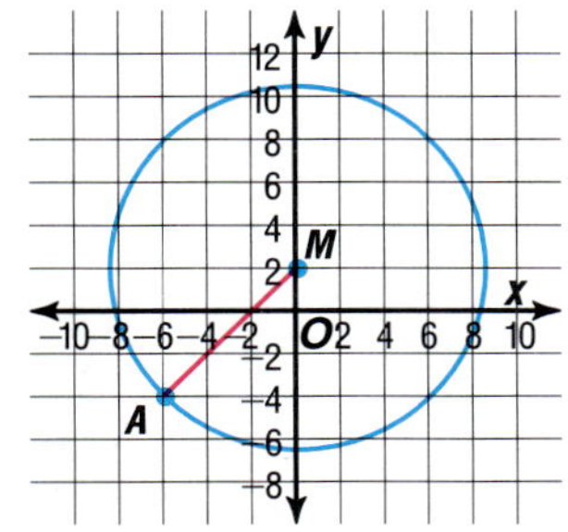

Use the midpoint formula and substitute the values you know.

$$(x, y) = \left(\frac{x_1 + x_2}{2}, \frac{y_1 + y_2}{2}\right)$$

$$(0, 2) = \left(\frac{-6 + x_2}{2}, \frac{-4 + y_2}{2}\right) \quad (x, y) = (0, 2),\ (x_1, y_1) = (-6, -4)$$

The x- and y-coordinates of the ordered pairs are equal since the ordered pairs are equal. So, two equations can be formed.

Find the x-coordinate.

$$0 = \frac{-6 + x_2}{2}$$

$$0 = -6 + x_2$$

$$6 = x_2$$

Find the y-coordinate.

$$2 = \frac{-4 + y_2}{2}$$

$$4 = -4 + y_2$$

$$8 = y_2$$

The coordinates of endpoint $B(x_2, y_2)$ are $(6, 8)$.

Check: Copy the graph of the circle and points A and M. Extend the radius through M to intersect the circle. This segment is the diameter of the circle. The intersection point is at $(6, 8)$, which are the coordinates of point B.

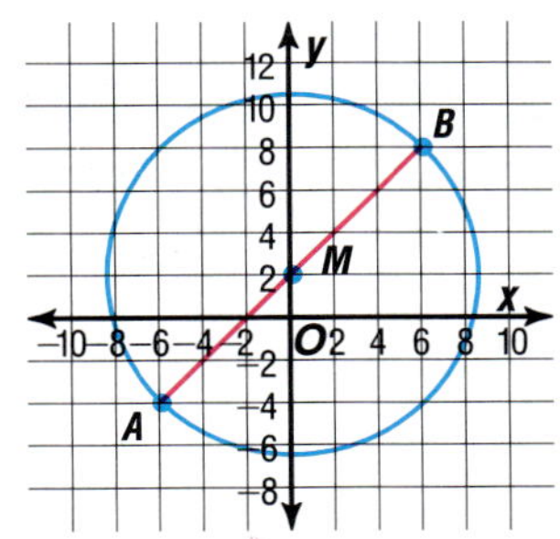

CHECK FOR UNDERSTANDING

Communicating Mathematics

Study the lesson. Then complete the following.

1. **Explain** how you can use the midpoint formula to find the midpoint of each of the following.
   a. a vertical line segment
   b. a horizontal line segment

2. **Demonstrate** how to find the coordinates of vertex C of rectangle $ABCD$ if its two diagonals meet at $M(-3, 4)$ and the coordinates of A are $(0, -1)$.

MODELING MATHEMATICS

3. Draw a rectangle on a coordinate plane.
   a. Find the midpoint of each side of the rectangle.
   b. Find the midpoint of the diagonals.
   c. How do the coordinates of the midpoint of the diagonal relate to the coordinates of the midpoints of the sides?

Guided Practice

Find the coordinates of the midpoint of a segment with each pair of endpoints.

4. $A(5, -2), B(5, 8)$
5. $C(-5, 6), D(8, 6)$
6. $E(6, 5), F(14, 7)$
7. $G(-9, -6), H(-3, 8)$

Find the coordinates of the other endpoint of a segment given one endpoint and the midpoint *M*.

8. $A(3, 6), M(-1.5, 5)$
9. $B(-3, 7), M(-7, 7)$
10. $C(8, 11), M\left(5, \frac{17}{2}\right)$
11. $D(8, 4.5), M(8, 7.15)$

12. **Archery** The target for archery competition is composed of 10 rings and 5 colored circles. Hitting the bull's-eye is worth ten points, and hitting the outer ring is worth one point. A target is shown on a coordinate plane at the right. The two labeled points are the endpoints of a diameter of the target. Find the coordinates of the center of the bull's-eye.

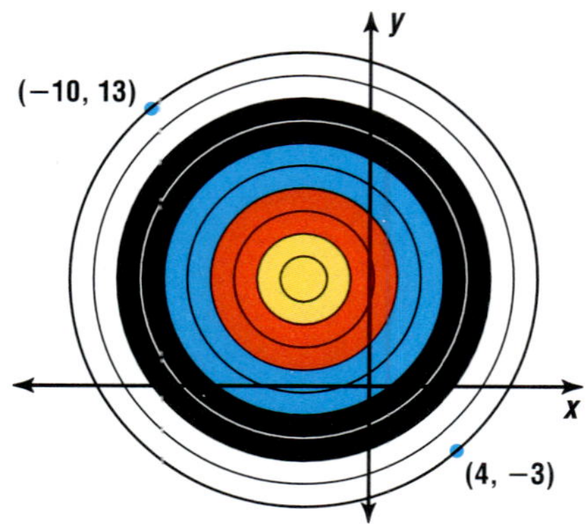

EXERCISES

Practice

Find the coordinates of the midpoint of a segment with each pair of endpoints.

13. $J(6, 6), K(19, 6)$
14. $L(5, 9), M(-7, 3)$
15. $P(-5, 9), Q(7, 1)$
16. $R(7, 4), S(11, -10)$
17. $T(8, -7), U(-2, 11)$
18. $V(-8, 1.2), W(-8, 7.4)$
19. $X(-3, 9), Y(4, -7)$
20. $B(9, -4), C(2, 7)$
21. $D(4.7, -2.9), E(-3.1, 8.3)$
22. $F(a, b), G(c, d)$
23. $Y(6x, 14y), Z(2x, 4y)$
24. $M(-2w, -7v), N(6w, 2v)$

Find the coordinates of the other endpoint of a segment given one endpoint and the midpoint *M*.

25. $E(-7, 8), M(-7, 4)$
26. $F(4, 2), M(2, 1)$
27. $G(3, -6), M(12, -6)$
28. $H(5, 3), M(6, 4)$
29. $L(-8, 4), M\left(\frac{1}{2}, 7\right)$
30. $N(5, -9), M(8, -7.5)$
31. $R\left(\frac{1}{6}, \frac{1}{3}\right), M\left(\frac{1}{2}, \frac{1}{3}\right)$
32. $S(a, b), M\left(\frac{x+a}{2}, \frac{y+b}{2}\right)$

If *P* is the midpoint of segment *AB*, find the coordinates of the missing point.

33. $A(6.5, -8.2), P(4.4, -0.7)$
34. $P(1.2, 4.5), B(5.3, 1.9)$
35. $A(9.7, -5.4), B(3.6, 1.7)$
36. $A(-5.9, 7.2), P(-1.05, 5.85)$

37. The coordinates of the endpoints of a diameter of a circle are (5, 8) and (−7, 2). Find the coordinates of the center.

38. Find the coordinates of the point on $\overline{AB}$ that is one-fourth the distance from A to B for $A(8, 3)$ and $B(10, -5)$.

39. The endpoints of $\overline{AB}$ are $A(-2, 7)$ and $B(6, -5)$. Find the coordinates of P if P lies on $\overline{AB}$ and is $\frac{3}{8}$ the distance from A to B.

Critical Thinking

40. Points W, X, Y, and Z are the midpoints of the sides of quadrilateral $QUAD$. Write a convincing argument that quadrilateral $WXYZ$ is a parallelogram.

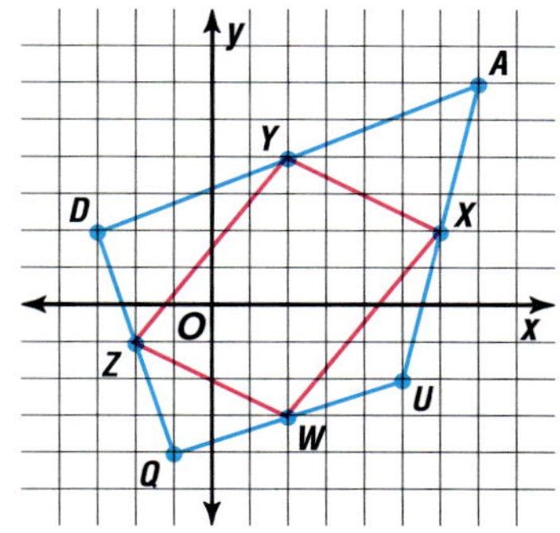

Applications and Problem Solving

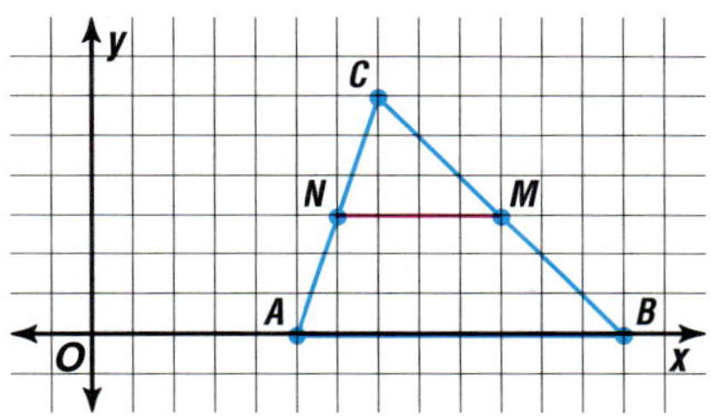

41. **Geometry** N is the midpoint of $\overline{AC}$ in the triangle shown at the left. M is the midpoint of $\overline{BC}$.
   a. Write the coordinates of M and N.
   b. Compare $\overline{MN}$ and $\overline{AB}$. Verify your findings.

42. **Technology** The screen of a graphing calculator is composed of tiny dots called *pixels* that are turned on or off during a display. Each pixel is named by the row and column in which it lies.

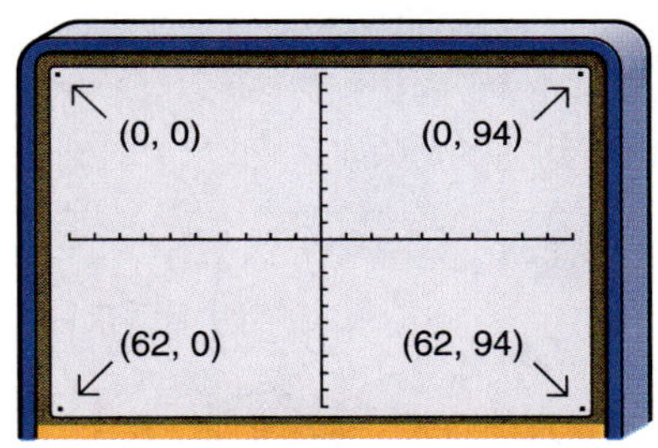

   a. If a segment drawn on the screen has one endpoint at pixel (20, 43) and its midpoint is at pixel (30, 60), what is the pixel name for the other endpoint of the segment?
   b. What is the pixel name of the origin?
   c. How does this coordinate system differ from the coordinate system we usually use for graphing?

43. **Geometry** S and T are the midpoints of their respective sides in the triangle shown at the right.
   a. Find the coordinates of P and Q.
   b. If the area of triangle RST is 15.5 square units, what is the area of triangle RPQ? Explain how you arrived at your answer.

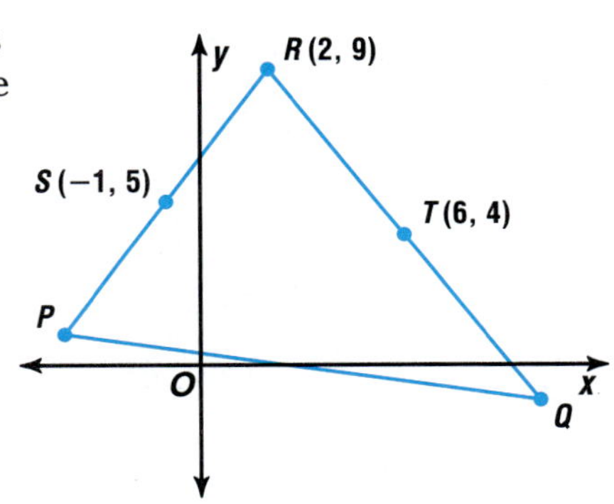

Mixed Review

44. Write an equation in slope-intercept form of the line that passes through $(8, -2)$ and is perpendicular to the graph of $5x - 3y = 7$. (Lesson 6–6)

45. Write an equation in slope-intercept form of the line that passes through $(-6, 2)$ and $(3, -5)$. (Lesson 6–4)

46. Given $g(x) = x^2 - x$, find $g(4b)$. (Lesson 5–5)

47. Determine whether $9x + (-7) = 6y$ is a linear equation. If it is, rewrite it in standard form. (Lesson 5–4)

48. **Trigonometry** If $\sin N = 0.6124$, use a calculator to find the measure of angle N to the nearest degree. (Lesson 4–3)

49. Solve $-27 - b = -7$. (Lesson 3–1)

50. In Mr. Tucker's algebra class, students can get extra points for finding the correct solution to the "Riddle of the Week." One week, Mr. Tucker posed this riddle. *Josh is 10 years older than his brother. Next year, he will be three times as old as his brother.* Answer the following questions. (Lesson 2–9)
    a. How old was Josh when his brother was born?
    b. If his brother's age is represented by a, what is Josh's age?
    c. India says that Josh is 12 years old and his brother is 4. Does India get the extra points for her answer? Why or why not?

51. Simplify $0.2(3x + 0.2) + 0.5(5x + 3)$. (Lesson 1–8)

Mathematics and SOCIETY

People Around the World

This excerpt is from an article in *The Amicus Journal*, Winter 1994.

THE LAST FORTY YEARS SAW THE FASTEST rise in human numbers in all previous history, from only 2.5 billion people in 1950 to 5.6 billion today....The second half of the 1990s will add an additional 94 million people per year. That is equivalent to a new United States every thirty-three months, another Britain every seven months, a Washington (DC) every six days. A whole Earth of 1800 was added in just one decade, according to United Nations Population Division statistics. After 2000, annual additions will slow, but by 2050 the United Nations expects the human race to total just over 10 billion—an extra Earth of 1980 on top of today's. ■

1. What effect does rapid population growth have on Earth's natural resources? Be specific.
2. What changes would you expect to see if the community in which you live doubles in population during your lifetime?
3. A village is deserted, but its buildings are intact and there are ample resources. Suppose 1000 refugees per day flock to this village.
    a. At this rate, how long would it take to reach the midpoint to a population of five million?
    b. Is the proposition of a village growing at this rate realistic? Why or why not?

CHAPTER 6 HIGHLIGHTS

VOCABULARY

After completing this chapter, you should be able to define each term, property, or phrase and give an example or two of each.

Algebra

family of graphs (p. 354)
parent graph (p. 354)
point-slope form (p. 333)
rise (p. 325)
run (p. 325)
slope (pp. 324, 325)
slope-intercept form (p. 347)
standard form (p. 333)
x-intercept (p. 346)
y-intercept (p. 346)

Problem Solving

use a model (p. 339)

Geometry

midpoint (p. 369)
parallel lines (p. 362)
parallelogram (p. 362)
perpendicular lines (p. 362)

Statistics

best-fit line (p. 341)
negative correlation (p. 340)
positive correlation (p. 340)
regression line (p. 342)
scatter plot (p. 339)

UNDERSTANDING AND USING THE VOCABULARY

Choose the correct term to complete each sentence.

1. The lines with equations $y = -2x + 7$ and $y = -2x - 6$ are (*parallel, perpendicular*) lines.
2. The equation $y - 2 = -3(x - 1)$ is written in (*point-slope, slope-intercept*) form.
3. If the endpoints of $\overline{AB}$ are $A(6, -3)$ and $B(2, 4)$, then the (*midpoint, slope*) of $\overline{AB}$ is at $\left(4, \frac{1}{2}\right)$.
4. The (*x-intercept, y-intercept*) of the equation $2x + 3y = -1$ is $-\frac{1}{2}$.
5. The lines with equations $y = \frac{1}{3}x + 1$ and $y = -3x - 5$ are (*parallel, perpendicular*) lines.
6. The slope of a line is defined as the ratio of the (*rise, run*), or vertical change, to the (*rise, run*), or horizontal change, as you move from one point on the line to another.
7. The equation $y = -\frac{1}{2}x + 3$ is written in (*slope-intercept, standard*) form.
8. The (*x-intercept, y-intercept*) of the equation $-x - 4y = 2$ is $-\frac{1}{2}$.
9. The (*midpoint, slope*) of the line with equation $-3y = 2x + 3$ is $-\frac{2}{3}$.
10. The equation $3x - 4y = -5$ is written in (*point-slope, standard*) form.

SKILLS AND CONCEPTS

OBJECTIVES AND EXAMPLES

Upon completing this chapter, you should be able to:

- find the slope of a line, given the coordinates of two points on the line (Lesson 6–1)

Determine the slope of the line that passes through (−6, 5) and (3, −2).

$$m = \frac{y_2 - y_1}{x_2 - x_1}$$
$$= \frac{-2 - 5}{3 - (-6)}$$
$$= -\frac{7}{9}$$

The slope is $-\frac{7}{9}$.

REVIEW EXERCISES

Use these exercises to review and prepare for the chapter test.

Determine the slope of the line that passes through each pair of points.

11. (8, 3), (2, 5)
12. (−2, 5), (−2, 9)
13. (−3, 6), (−8, 4)
14. (4, 3), (−5, 3)

Determine the value of *r* so the line that passes through each pair of points has the given slope.

15. $(r, 4), (7, 3), m = \frac{3}{4}$
16. $(4, -7), (-2, r), m = \frac{8}{3}$

- write linear equations in point-slope form (Lesson 6–2)

Write the point-slope form of an equation of the line that passes through the points at (−4, 7) and (−2, 3).

$$m = \frac{3 - 7}{-2 - (-4)} \text{ or } -2$$
$$y - y_1 = m(x - x_1)$$
$$y - 7 = -2[x - (-4)]$$
$$y - 7 = -2(x + 4)$$

An equation of the line is $y - 7 = -2(x + 4)$.

Write the point-slope form of an equation of the line that passes through the given point and has the given slope.

17. $(4, -3), m = -2$
18. $(8, 5), m = 5$
19. $(-5, 7), m = 0$
20. $(6, 2), m = \frac{1}{2}$

Write the point-slope form of an equation of the line that passes through each pair of points.

21. (0, 3), (−5, 0)
22. (5, 4), (6, 3)
23. (4, 1), (−3, 7)
24. (2, −5), (0, 4)

- write linear equations in standard form (Lesson 6–2)

Write the standard form of an equation of the line that passes through the points at (6, −4) and (−1, 5).

$$m = \frac{5 - (-4)}{-1 - 6} \text{ or } -\frac{9}{7}$$
$$y - y_1 = m(x - x_1)$$
$$y - (-4) = -\frac{9}{7}(x - 6)$$
$$y + 4 = -\frac{9}{7}(x - 6)$$

$$y + 4 = -\frac{9}{7}(x - 6)$$
$$7(y + 4) = 7 \cdot -\frac{9}{7}(x - 6)$$
$$7y + 28 = -9(x - 6)$$
$$7y + 28 = -9x + 54$$
$$9x + 7y = 26$$

An equation of the line is $9x + 7y = 26$.

Write the standard form of an equation of the line that passes through the given point and has the given slope.

25. $(4, -6), m = 3$
26. $(1, 5), m = 0$
27. $(6, -1), m = \frac{3}{4}$
28. $(8, 3), m =$ undefined

Write the standard form of an equation of the line that passes through each pair of points.

29. (−2, 5), (9, 5)
30. (0, 5), (−2, 0)
31. $\left(-2, \frac{2}{3}\right), \left(-2, \frac{2}{7}\right)$
32. $(-5, 7), \left(0, \frac{1}{2}\right)$

OBJECTIVES AND EXAMPLES

- graph and interpret points on a scatter plot; draw and write equations for best-fit lines and make predictions by using those equations (Lesson 6–3)

The scatter plot below shows a negative relationship since the line suggested by the points would have a negative slope.

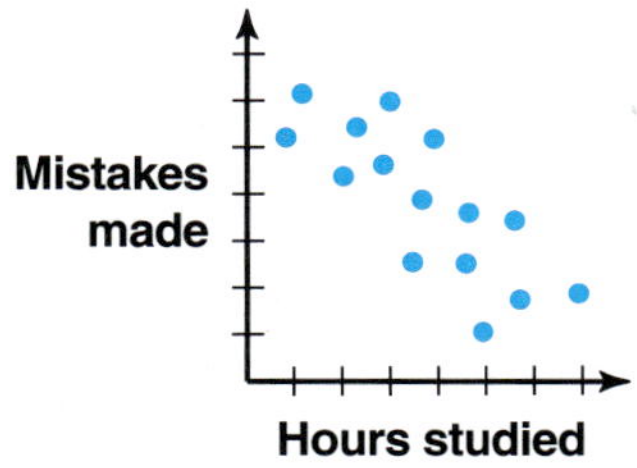

REVIEW EXERCISES

33. Draw a scatter plot of the data below. Let the independent variable be height.

Buildings in Oklahoma City	Height (feet)	Number of Stories
Liberty Tower	500	36
First National Center	493	28
City Place	440	33
First Oklahoma Tower	425	31
Kerr-McGee Center	393	30
Mid-America Tower	362	29

a. Does a relationship exist? If so, what is the relationship?

b. Use your scatter plot as a model to predict how many stories you might think a building 475 feet high would be.

c. Draw a best-fit line and write the equation of the line.

- determine the x- and y-intercepts of linear graphs from their equations and write equations in slope-intercept form (Lesson 6–4)

Determine the slope and x- and y-intercepts of the graph of $3x - 2y = 7$.

Solve for y to find the slope and y-intercept.

$$3x - 2y = 7$$
$$-2y = -3x + 7$$
$$y = \frac{3}{2}x - \frac{7}{2}$$

Let $y = 0$ to find the x-intercept.

$$3x - 2(0) = 7$$
$$3x = 7$$
$$x = \frac{7}{3}$$

The slope is $\frac{3}{2}$, the y-intercept is $-\frac{7}{2}$, and the x-intercept is $\frac{7}{3}$.

Write an equation in slope-intercept form of a line with the given slope and y-intercept.

34. $m = 2, b = 4$

35. $m = -3, b = 0$

36. $m = -\frac{1}{2}, b = -9$

37. $m = 0, b = 5.5$

Find the slope and y-intercept of the graph of each equation.

38. $x = 2y - 7$

39. $8x + y = 4$

40. $y = \frac{1}{4}x + 3$

41. $\frac{1}{2}x + \frac{1}{4}y = 3$

- graph a line given any linear equation (Lesson 6–5)

Graph $-2x - y = 5$.

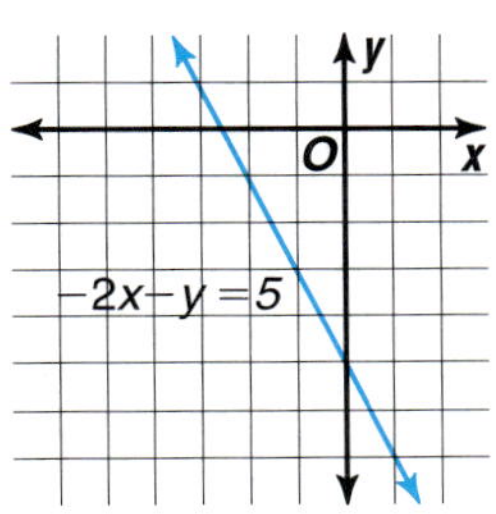

Graph each equation.

42. $3x - y = 9$

43. $5x + 2y = 12$

44. $y = \frac{2}{3}x + 4$

45. $y = -\frac{3}{2}x - 6$

46. $3x + 4y = 6$

47. $5x - \frac{1}{2}y = 2$

48. $y - 4 = -2(x + 1)$

49. $y + 5 = -\frac{3}{4}(x - 6)$

OBJECTIVES AND EXAMPLES	REVIEW EXERCISES

- write equations of lines that pass through a given point, parallel or perpendicular to the graph of a given equation (Lesson 6–6)

Write an equation of the line that is perpendicular to the graph of $2x + y = 6$ and passes through (2, 3).

$2x + y = 6$

$y = -2x + 6$

The slope of this line is -2. Therefore, the slope of the line perpendicular to it is $\frac{1}{2}$.

$y - 3 = \frac{1}{2}(x - 2)$ $\quad m = \frac{1}{2}, (x_1, y_1) = (2, 3)$

$y = \frac{1}{2}x + 2$

Write an equation of the line having the following properties

50. parallel to $4x - y = 7$ and passes through $(2, -1)$
51. perpendicular to $2x - 7y = 1$ and passes through $(-4, 0)$
52. parallel to $3x + 9y = 1$ and passes through $(3, 0)$
53. perpendicular to $8x - 3y = 7$ and passes through $(4, 5)$
54. parallel to $-y = -2x + 4$ and passes through $(5, -6)$
55. perpendicular to $5y = -x + 1$ and passes through $(2, -5)$

- find the coordinates of the midpoint of a line segment in the coordinate plane (Lesson 6–7)

The endpoints of a segment are at (11, 4) and (9, 2). Find its midpoint.

$(x, y) = \left(\frac{x_1 + x_2}{2}, \frac{y_1 + y_2}{2}\right)$

$= \left(\frac{11+9}{2}, \frac{4+2}{2}\right)$

$= (10, 3)$

Find the coordinates of the midpoint of a segment with each pair of endpoints.

56. $A(3, 5), B(9, -3)$
57. $A(-6, 6), B(8, -11)$
58. $A(14, 4), B(2, 0)$
59. $A(2, 7), B(8, 4)$
60. $A(2, 5), B(4, -1)$
61. $A(10, 4), B(-3, -7)$

Find the coordinates of the other endpoint of a segment given one endpoint and the midpoint *M*.

62. $A(3, 5), M(11, 7)$
63. $A(5, 3), M(9, 7)$
64. $A(4, -11), M(5, -9)$
65. $A(11, -4), M(3, 8)$

APPLICATIONS AND PROBLEM SOLVING

66. **Skiing** A course for cross-country skiing is regulated so that the slope of any hill cannot be greater than 0.33. Suppose a hill rises 60 meters over a horizontal distance of 250 meters.
    a. What is the slope of the hill?
    b. Does the hill meet the requirements? (Lesson 6–1)

67. **Travel** Jon Erlanger is taking a long trip. In the first two hours, he drives 80 miles. After that, he averages 45 miles per hour. Write an equation in slope-intercept form relating distance traveled and time. (Lesson 6–4)

68. **Entertainment** Carolyn Parks owns stock in Star Gazer Motion Picture Company. Every other week, she graphs the closing value of a share of the stock. What is the midpoint between the highest and lowest values of the stock? (Lesson 6–7)

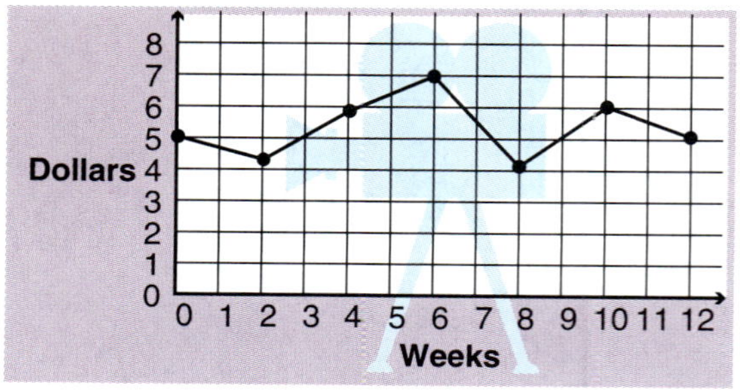

A practice test for Chapter 6 is provided on page 792.

ALTERNATIVE ASSESSMENT

COOPERATIVE LEARNING PROJECT

Video Rental In this chapter, you investigated graphing linear equations. You used slope and data points to graph equations. These graphs represented information that could be analyzed and extended in order to interpret further information than what was given.

In this project, you will analyze two video-store rental policies. There are two stores in Joe's neighborhood where he can rent videos: Video World and Mega Video. At one of the two stores, you have to buy a membership card first. The other one does not have these cards; you simply pay per video. Both have a daily charge (rate per day). Mega Video has a membership card that costs \$15 per year and then each video that is rented costs \$2 per day. Video World simply rents each video for \$3.25 per day.

Which is the most economical video store for Joe to use? If he rarely rents videos, which store should he use? If he often rents videos, which store should he use?

Follow these steps to determine the store he should use.

- Determine a way to graph this information.
- Develop a linear equation for each store that describes the amount of money it costs to rent a video.
- Determine whether the graphs should be drawn separately or on the same grid.
- Investigate the graphs and determine what each graph represents.
- What factors other than price might Joe want to consider before he chooses a store?
- Write a paragraph describing various situations for Joe and the appropriate solutions.

THINKING CRITICALLY

- Give an example of an equation of a line that has the same x- and y-intercepts. What is the slope of the line?
- Give an example of an equation of a line whose x- and y-intercepts are opposites. What is the slope of the line?
- Make a conjecture about the slopes of lines whose x- and y-intercepts are equal or opposites.
- The x-intercept of a line is s, and the y-intercept is t. Write the equation of the line.

PORTFOLIO

In mathematics, there is often more than one way to solve a problem. In order to graph a line for example, various information can be used. Sometimes you use two points, sometimes you use a point and a slope, and sometimes you use x- and y-intercepts. Find an equation from your work in this chapter and describe at least three ways in which to graph it. Place this in your portfolio.

SELF EVALUATION

Checking your answer is the final step in solving a problem. This step is the most critical, but it is also the step that is most often forgotten. When an answer is finally reached, it should be checked to see whether it makes sense and also whether it can be verified.

Assess yourself. Do you use all four steps when you solve a problem? Do you reach an answer, assume that it is the correct answer, and then move on without checking it? Do you ask yourself questions about your answer to verify that it is correct and that it makes sense? Can you think of an example of a problem in your daily life in which you didn't ask yourself questions about your solution to the problem and later you discovered that the solution didn't work?

CUMULATIVE REVIEW

CHAPTERS 1–6

SECTION ONE: MULTIPLE CHOICE

There are eight multiple-choice questions in this section. After working each problem, write the letter of the correct answer on your paper.

1. Name the quadrant in which point $P(x, y)$ is located if it satisfies the condition $x < 0$ and $y = -3$.

   A. I
   B. II
   C. III
   D. IV

2. Raini made a map of his neighborhood using a coordinate grid. His school has coordinates (3, 8), where 3 is the number of blocks east he must walk and 8 is the number of blocks north. From school, he walks 4 blocks east and 2 blocks south to get to his friend's house. Find the coordinates of the midpoint of the line segment that could be drawn to connect his school and his friend's house.

   A. (5, 7)
   B. (8, −2)
   C. (7, 6)
   D. (5, −6)

3. Determine the slope of the line that passes through the points at (−3, 6) and (−5, 9).

   A. $\frac{3}{2}$　　**B.** $\frac{2}{3}$
   C. $-\frac{3}{2}$　　**D.** none of these

4. **Probability** A shipment of 100 CDs was just received at Tunes R Us. There is a 4% probability that one of the CDs was damaged during shipment, even though the package may not be cracked. If Craig buys a CD from this shipment, what are the odds that he is buying a damaged CD?

   A. 1:25
   B. $\frac{4}{100}$
   C. 96:4
   D. 1:24

5. Choose the graph that represents a function.

   A.
   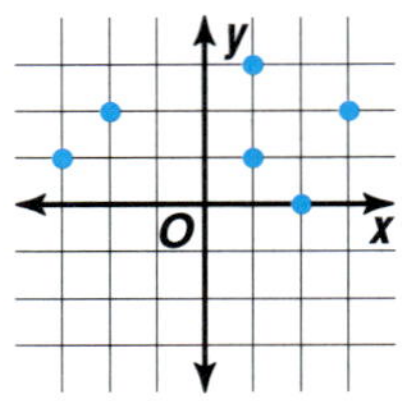

   B.
   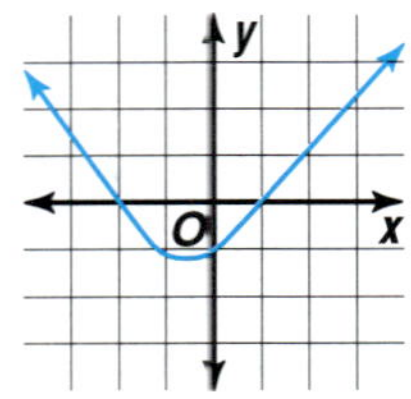

   C.
   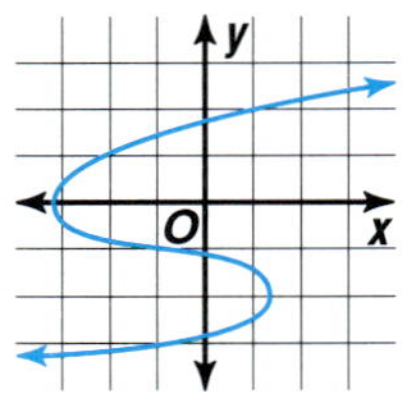

   D.
   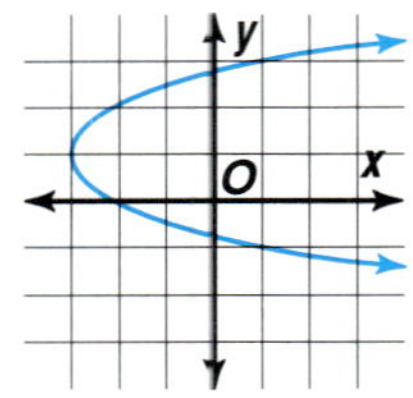

6. Choose the property illustrated by the statement *The quantity g plus h times b equals g times b plus h times b.*

   A. distributive property
   B. commutative property of multiplication
   C. multiplicative identity property
   D. associative property of addition

7. Choose the line that represents the graph of the equation $y = -\frac{2}{3}x + 2$.

   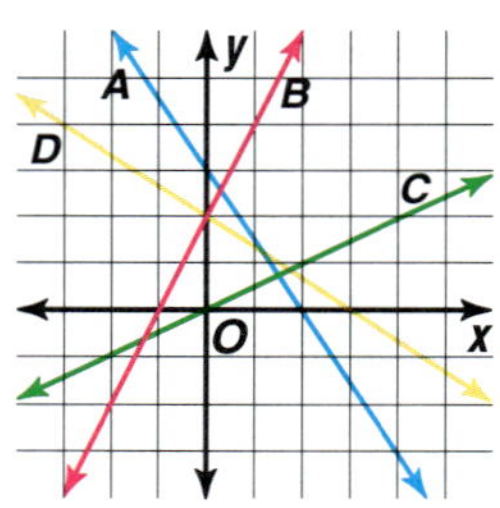

   A. line A
   B. line B
   C. line C
   D. line D

8. **Geometry** The formula Area $= \frac{1}{2}bc \sin A$ can be used to find the area of any triangle ABC. Find the area of the triangle shown below to the nearest tenth of a square centimeter if $b = 16$, $c = 9$, and $\angle A$ is a 36° angle.

   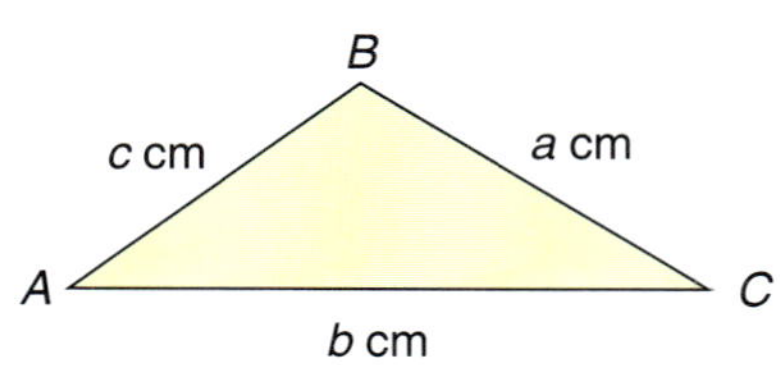

   A. 72 cm^2　　**B.** 42.3 cm^2
   C. 84.6 cm^2　　**D.** 144 cm^2

SECTION TWO: SHORT ANSWER

This section contains seven questions for which you will provide short answers. Write your answer on your paper.

9. Express the relation shown in the graph as a set of ordered pairs. Then draw a mapping of the relation.

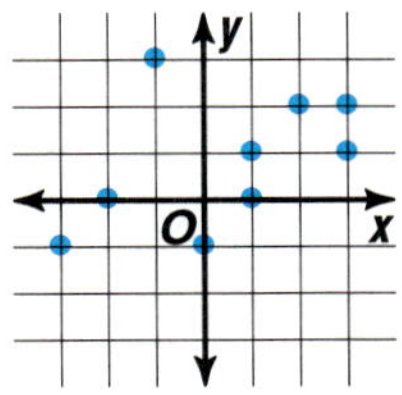

10. Write an equation of the line that passes through the point at $(2, -1)$ and is perpendicular to $4x - y = 7$.

11. The average person can live for eleven days without water, assuming a mean temperature of 60° F. Determine if survival is possible given daily high temperatures of 59°, 70°, 49°, 62°, 46°, 63°, 71°, 64°, 55°, 68°, and 54° F. Verify your answer.

12. Write the solution set for $5x + y = 4$, if the domain is $\{-2, -1, 0, 2, 5\}$.

13. Peanuts sell for \$3.00 per pound. Cashews sell for \$6.00 per pound. How many pounds of cashews should be mixed with 12 pounds of peanuts to obtain a mixture that sells for \$4.20 per pound?

14. At Videoville, Eshe earns a weekly salary of \$150 plus \$0.30 for each video over 100 that she sells each week. If Eshe sells v videos in a week, then her total weekly salary is $C(v) = 150 + 0.30(v - 100)$ for $v > 100$. If she wants to earn \$225 each week to save up for a stereo system, how many videos must she sell each week?

15. Graph the solution set {integers greater than or equal to -4} on a number line.

SECTION THREE: OPEN ENDED

This section contains two open-ended problems. Demonstrate your knowledge by giving a clear, concise solution to each problem. Your score on these problems will depend on how well you do the following.

- Explain your reasoning.
- Show your understanding of the mathematics in an organized manner.
- Use charts, graphs, and diagrams in your explanation.
- Show the solution in more than one way or relate it to other situations.
- Investigate beyond the requirements of the problem.

16. For long-distance phone calls, a telephone company charges \$1.72 for a 4-minute call, \$2.40 for a 6-minute call, and \$5.46 for a 15-minute call. Determine the charge for a 1-minute call.

17. The table below shows the annual income and the number of years of college education for eleven people.

Income (thousands)	College Education (years)
\$23	3.0
20	2.0
25	4.0
47	6.0
19	2.5
48	7.5
35	6.5
10	1.0
39	5.5
26	4.5
36	4.0

a. Make a scatter plot of the data.

b. Based on this plot, how does the number of years of college affect income?

CHAPTER

7 Solving Linear Inequalities

Objectives

In this chapter, you will:

- solve inequalities,
- graph solutions of inequalities,
- graph solutions of open sentences that involve absolute value,
- solve problems by drawing a diagram, and
- use box-and-whisker plots to display and analyze data.

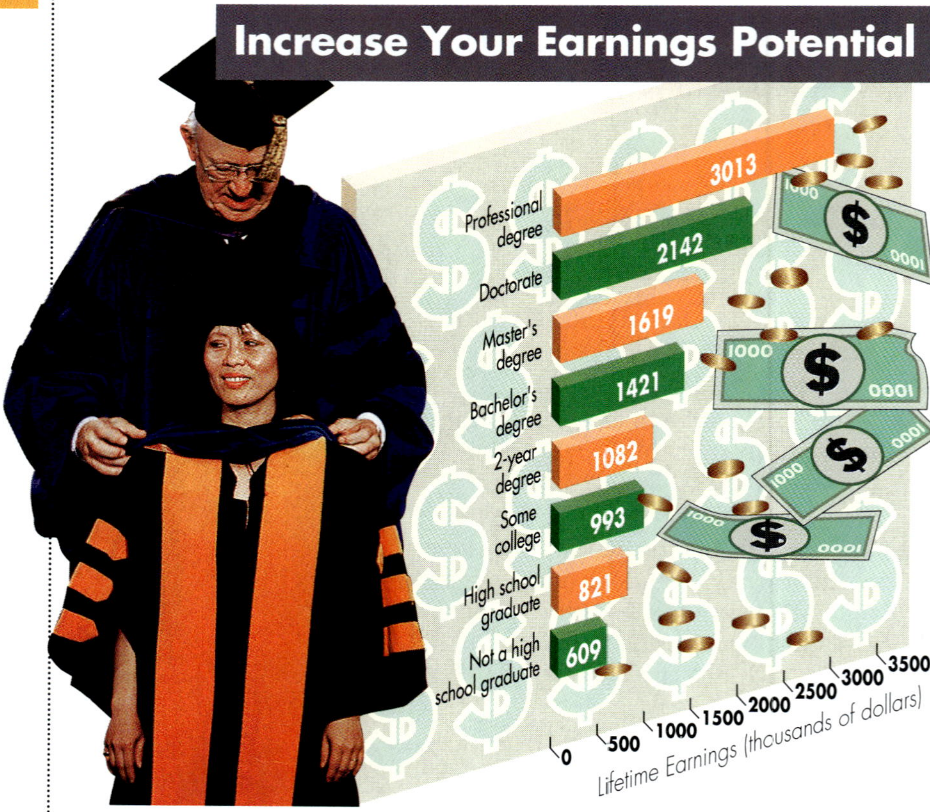

Source: *Chicago Tribune,* 1995

TIME *Line*

There is a direct relationship between lifetime earnings and educational attainment. College graduation and advanced degrees really do make a difference. Set your sights on a career and aim to be the best you can be.

A.D. 1142 Adelard of Bath translates Euclid's *Elements* from the Arabic.

1598 Spanish missionaries introduce theater to the residents of what is now New Mexico.

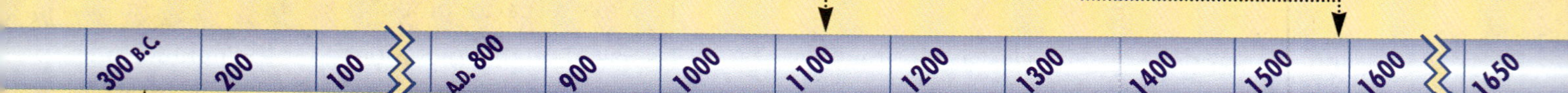

260 B.C. Archimedes develops a mathematical description of the lever and other simple machines.

1514 Dutch mathematician Vander Hoecke is the first to use plus and minus signs as we do today in algebra.

PEOPLE IN THE NEWS

Shakema Hodge is aiming for an advanced degree in microbiology. The young scientist from St. Thomas, Virgin Islands, earned her bachelor's degree in biology at the University of the Virgin Islands. Now she is enrolled in a 5-year Ph.D. program in molecular microbiology at the University of Rochester in New York. She would love to teach high school students, believing that "to capture a young person's mind, you have to expose them to the sciences at an early age."

Chapter Project

Kimana plans to study either botany, genetics, or microbiology at a nearby university. She hasn't ruled out teaching as a possible career choice, but is interested in finding other businesses in which she can apply the science she will be studying.

- Visit the public library or local college to investigate careers that relate to Kimana's interests.
- Which careers might offer Kimana an opportunity to earn an amount greater than that presented in the graph for a bachelor's degree?
- Which careers require a degree for which the years studied are greater than those for a bachelor's degree? Choose a career. Write an inequality that might express the time needed to study and train for that career.

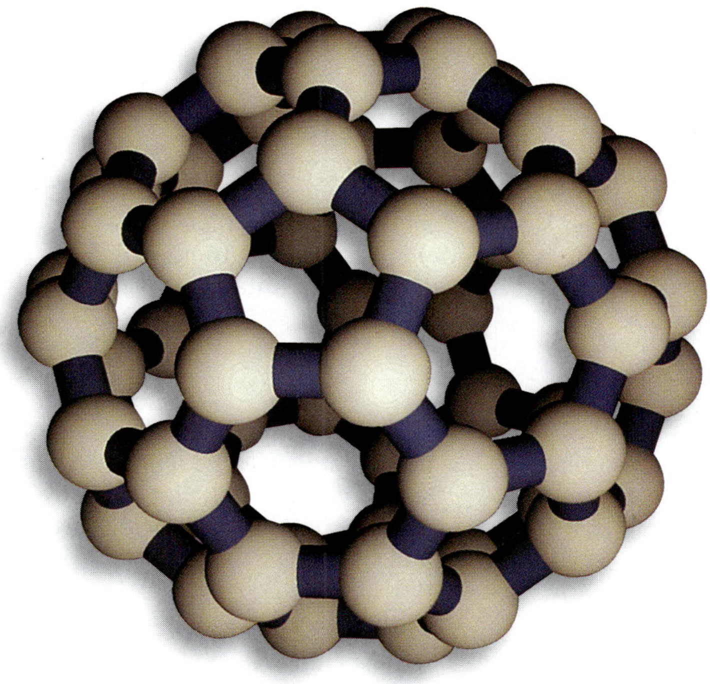

1891 Juan Vucetich develops a system for classifying fingerprints.

1995 Juliet Garcia, president of the University of Texas at Brownsville, becomes the first Latina to be named the president of a major U.S. university.

1909 Matthew Henson plants the U.S. flag at the North Pole after traveling with Robert Peary.

1996 Shirl Pinto receives the Crime Victim Service Award from U.S. Attorney General Janet Reno.

7–1 Solving Inequalities by Using Addition and Subtraction

What YOU'LL LEARN

- To solve inequalities by using addition and subtraction.

Why IT'S IMPORTANT

You can use inequalities to solve problems involving nutrition and personal finance.

CAREER CHOICES

Nutritionists plan dietary programs and supervise the preparation and serving of meals for hospitals, nursing homes, health maintenance organizations, and individuals. A bachelor's degree in dietetics, foods, or nutrition is required that includes studies in biology, physiology, mathematics, and chemistry.

For more information, contact:

The American Dietetic Association
216 West Jackson Blvd.
Chicago, IL 60606

APPLICATION

Nutrition

In 1990, the U.S. Department of Agriculture issued new dietary guidelines. These guidelines recommend that people greatly reduce their fat intake. Your recommended calorie intake depends on your height, desired weight, and physical activity. The average 14-year-old is 5 feet 2 inches tall and weighs 107 pounds. Boys should consume about 2434 calories per day and girls 2208 calories per day to maintain this weight.

Snack	Quantity	Fat (grams)
Cheese/peanut butter crackers	9 crackers	15
Whole roasted almonds	10 almonds	8
Candy bars	2 bars	4
Apples	2 medium	2

Oliana learned in health class that no more than 30% of her calorie intake should come from fat. For her 2030-calorie-a-day diet, that means no more than 68 grams of fat. She keeps track of her snacks for one day and records their fat content, as shown in the table above. How many grams of fat can Oliana have in the other foods she eats that day and stay within the guidelines?

Let's write an inequality to represent the problem. Let g represent the remaining grams of fat that Oliana can eat that day.

grams of fat in snacks	plus	grams of fat remaining	is less than or equal to	total grams
$15 + 8 + 4 + 2$	$+$	g	$\leq$	68

That is, $29 + g \leq 68$.

The symbol $\leq$ indicates *less than or equal to.* It is used in this situation because the total number of grams of fat in Oliana's daily diet should be no greater than 68. If this were an equation, we would subtract 29 from (or add -29 to) each side. Can the same procedure be used in an inequality? *This problem will be solved in Example 1.*

Let's explore what happens if inequalities are solved in the same manner as equations. We know that $7 > 2$. What happens when you add or subtract the same quantity to each side of the inequality? We can use number lines to model the situation.

Add 3 to each side.

$$7 > 2$$
$$7 + 3 \overset{?}{>} 2 + 3$$
$$10 > 5$$

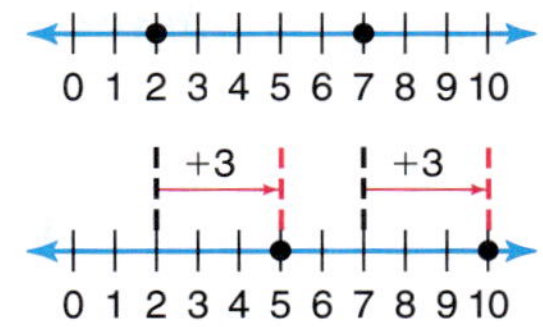

Subtract 4 from each side.

$$7 > 2$$
$$7 - 4 \overset{?}{>} 2 - 4$$
$$3 > -2$$

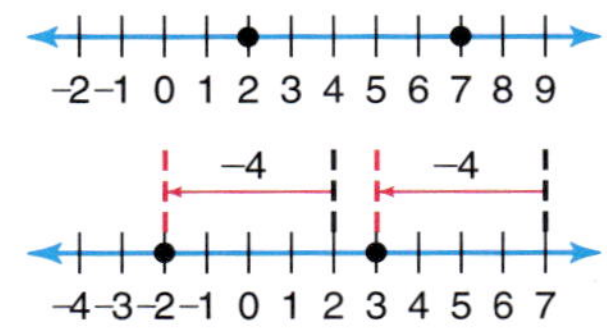

In each case, the inequality holds true. These examples illustrate two properties of inequalities.

Addition and Subtraction Properties for Inequalities	**For all numbers *a*, *b*, and *c*, the following are true.** **1. If $a > b$, then $a + c > b + c$ and $a - c > b - c$.** **2. If $a < b$, then $a + c < b + c$ and $a - c < b - c$.**

These properties are also true when $>$ and $<$ are replaced by $\geq$ and $\leq$. So, we can use these properties to obtain a solution to the application at the beginning of the lesson.

Example 1

APPLICATION

Nutrition

Refer to the application at the beginning of the lesson. Solve $29 + g \leq 68$.

$29 + g \leq 68$

$29 - 29 + g \leq 68 - 29$ *Subtract 29 from each side.*

$g \leq 39$ *This means all numbers less than or equal to 39.*

The solution set can be written as {all numbers less than or equal to 39}.

Check: To check this solution, substitute 39, a number less than 39, and a number greater than 39 into the inequality.

Let $g = 39$.	Let $g = 20$.	Let $g = 40$.
$29 + g \leq 68$	$29 + g \leq 68$	$29 + g \leq 68$
$29 + 39 \overset{?}{\leq} 68$	$29 + 20 \overset{?}{\leq} 68$	$29 + 40 \overset{?}{\leq} 68$
$68 \leq 68$ true	$49 \leq 68$ true	$69 \leq 68$ false

So, Oliana can have 39 or fewer grams of fat in other foods that day and stay within the dietary guidelines.

Top Five List

Preferred snack foods and % of calories from fat

1. potato chips	58%
2. tortilla chips	47%
3. popcorn	45%
4. pretzels	8%
5. mixed nuts	80%

The solution to the inequality in Example 1 was expressed as a set. A more concise way of writing a solution set is to use **set-builder notation**. The solution in set-builder notation is $\{g \mid g \leq 39\}$. This is read *the set of all numbers g such that g is less than or equal to 39.*

LOOK BACK

You can refer to Lesson 1-5 for information on solution sets.

In Lesson 2–4, you learned that you can show the solution to an inequality on a graph. The solution to Example 1 is shown on the number line below.

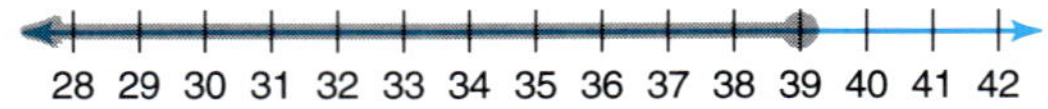

The closed circle at 39 tells us that 39 is included in the inequality. The heavy arrow pointing to the left shows that it also includes all numbers less than 39. *If the inequality was <, the circle would be open.*

Example 2 **Solve $13 + 2z < 3z - 39$. Then graph the solution.**

$$13 + 2z < 3z - 39$$
$$13 + 2z - 2z < 3z - 2z - 39 \quad \textit{Subtract 2z from each side.}$$
$$13 < z - 39$$
$$13 + 39 < z - 39 + 39 \quad \textit{Add 39 to each side.}$$
$$52 < z$$

Since $52 < z$ is the same as $z > 52$, the solution set is $\{z \mid z > 52\}$.

The graph of the solution contains an open circle at 52 since 52 is not included in the solution, and the arrow points to the right.

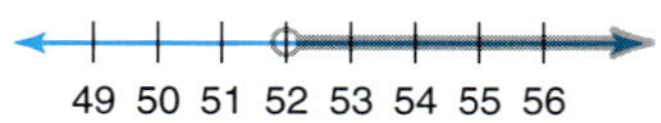

Verbal problems containing phrases like *greater than* or *less than* can often be solved by using inequalities. The following chart shows some other phrases that indicate inequalities.

Inequalities			
<	>	≤	≥
• less than • fewer than	• greater than • more than	• at most • no more than • less than or equal to	• at least • no less than • greater than or equal to

Example 3

APPLICATION
Budgeting

Alvaro, Chip, and Solomon have earned \$500 to buy equipment for their band. They have already spent \$275 on a used guitar and a drum set. They are now considering buying a \$125 amplifier. What is the most they can spend on promotional materials and T-shirts for the band if they buy the amplifier?

Explore *At most* means that they cannot go over what is left of their budget of \$500. They have spent \$275, so they have \$225 left. Let m = the amount of money for promotional materials and T-shirts.

Plan	*Total to spend*	*is at most*	*$225.*
	$125 + m$	$\leq$	225

Solve

$$125 + m \leq 225$$

$$125 - 125 + m \leq 225 - 125 \quad \textit{Subtract 125 from each side.}$$

$$m \leq 100$$

The members of the band can spend $100 or less on promotional materials and T-shirts.

Examine Since $275 + $125 + $100 = $500, Alvaro, Chip, and Solomon can spend $100 or less on promotional materials and T-shirts.

When solving problems involving equations, it is often necessary to write an equation that represents the words in the problem. This is also true of inequalities.

Example 4 **Write an inequality for the sentence below. Then solve the inequality and check the solution.**

Three times a number is more than the difference of twice that number and three.

Three times a number	*is more than*	*twice the number*	*minus*	*three*
$3x$	$>$	$2x$	$-$	3

$$3x > 2x - 3$$

$$3x - 2x > 2x - 2x - 3 \quad \textit{Subtract 2x from each side.}$$

$$x > -3$$

The solution set is $\{x \mid x > -3\}$.

CHECK FOR UNDERSTANDING

Communicating Mathematics

Study the lesson. Then complete the following.

1. **Write** three inequalities that are equivalent to $x < -10$.
2. **Explain** what $\{w \mid w > -3\}$ means.
3. **Explain** the difference between the solution sets for $x + 24 < 17$ and $x + 24 \leq 17$.
4. **Describe** how you would graph the solution to an inequality. Include examples and graphs in your explanation.
5. Is it possible for the solution set of an inequality to be the empty set? If so, give an example.

MATH JOURNAL

6. Sometimes statements we make can be translated into inequalities. For example, *In some states, you have to be at least 16 years old to have a driver's license* can be expressed as $a \geq 16$, and *Tomás cannot lift more than 72 pounds* can be translated into $w \leq 72$. Following these examples, write three statements that deal with your everyday life. Then translate each into a corresponding inequality.

Guided Practice

Match each inequality with the graph of its solution.

7. $b - 18 > -3$
8. $10 \geq -3 + x$
9. $x + 11 < 6$
10. $4c - 3 \leq 5c$

a. 

b. 

c. 

d. 

Solve each inequality. Then check your solution.

11. $x + 7 > 2$
12. $10 \geq x + 8$
13. $y - 7 < -12$
14. $-81 + q > 16 + 2q$

Define a variable, write an inequality, and solve each problem. Then check your solution.

15. A number decreased by 17 is less than -13.
16. A number increased by 4 is at least 3.

EXERCISES

Practice

Solve each inequality. Then check your solution, and graph it on a number line.

17. $a - 12 < 6$
18. $m - 3 < -17$
19. $2x \leq x + 1$
20. $-9 + d > 9$
21. $x + \frac{1}{3} > 4$
22. $-0.11 \leq n - (-0.04)$
23. $2x + 3 > x + 5$
24. $7h - 1 \leq 6h$

Solve each inequality. Then check your solution.

25. $x + \frac{1}{8} < \frac{1}{2}$
26. $3x + \frac{4}{5} \leq 4x + \frac{3}{5}$
27. $3x - 9 \leq 2x + 6$
28. $6w + 4 \geq 5w + 4$
29. $-0.17x - 0.23 < 0.75 - 1.17x$
30. $0.8x + 5 \geq 6 - 0.2x$
31. $3(r - 2) < 2r + 4$
32. $-x - 11 \geq 23$

Define a variable, write an inequality, and solve each problem. Then check your solution.

33. A number decreased by -4 is at least 9.

34. The sum of a number and 5 is at least 17.

35. Three times a number is less than twice the number added to 8.

36. Twenty-one is no less than the sum of a number and -2.

37. The sum of two numbers is less than 53. One number is 20. What is the other number?

38. The sum of four times a number and 7 is less than 3 times that number.

39. Twice a number is more than the difference of that number and 6.

40. The sum of two numbers is 100. One number is at least 16 more than the other number. What are the two numbers?

If $3x \geq 2x + 5$, then complete each inequality.

41. $3x + 7 \geq 2x + \underline{\ ?\ }$

42. $3x - 10 \geq 2x - \underline{\ ?\ }$

43. $3x + \underline{\ ?\ } \geq 2x + 3$

44. $\underline{\ ?\ } \leq x$

Programming

45. **Geometry** For three line segments to form a triangle, the sum of the lengths of any two sides must exceed the length of the third side. Let the lengths of the possible sides be a, b, and c. Then these three inequalities must be true: $a + b > c$, $a + c > b$, and $b + c > a$. The graphing calculator program at the right uses these inequalities to determine if the three lengths can be measures of the sides of a triangle.

```
PROGRAM: TRIANGLE
: Disp "ENTER THREE LENGTHS"
: Prompt A, B, C
: If C≥A+B
: Then
: Goto 1
: End
: If B≥A+C
: Then
: Goto 1
: End
: If A≥B+C
: Then
: Goto 1
: End
: Disp "THIS IS A TRIANGLE."
: Stop
: Lbl 1
: Disp "NOT A TRIANGLE"
```

Use the program to determine whether segments with the given lengths can form a triangle.

Tip: To run the program again after trying one set of numbers, press ENTER.

a. 10 in., 12 in., 27 in.

b. 3 ft, 4 ft, 5 ft

c. 125 cm, 140 cm, 150 cm

d. 1.5 m, 2.0 m, 2.5 m

Critical Thinking

46. Using an example, show that even though $x > y$ and $t > w$, $x - t > y - w$ may be false.

47. What does the sentence $-2.4 < x < 3.6$ mean?

Applications and Problem Solving

Define a variable, write an inequality, and solve each problem.

48. **Academics** Josie must have at least 320 points in her math class to get a B. She needs a B or better to maintain her grade-point average so she can play on the basketball team. The grade is based on four 50-point tests, three 20-point quizzes, two 20-point projects, and a final exam worth 100 points. Josie's record of her grades are shown in the table below.

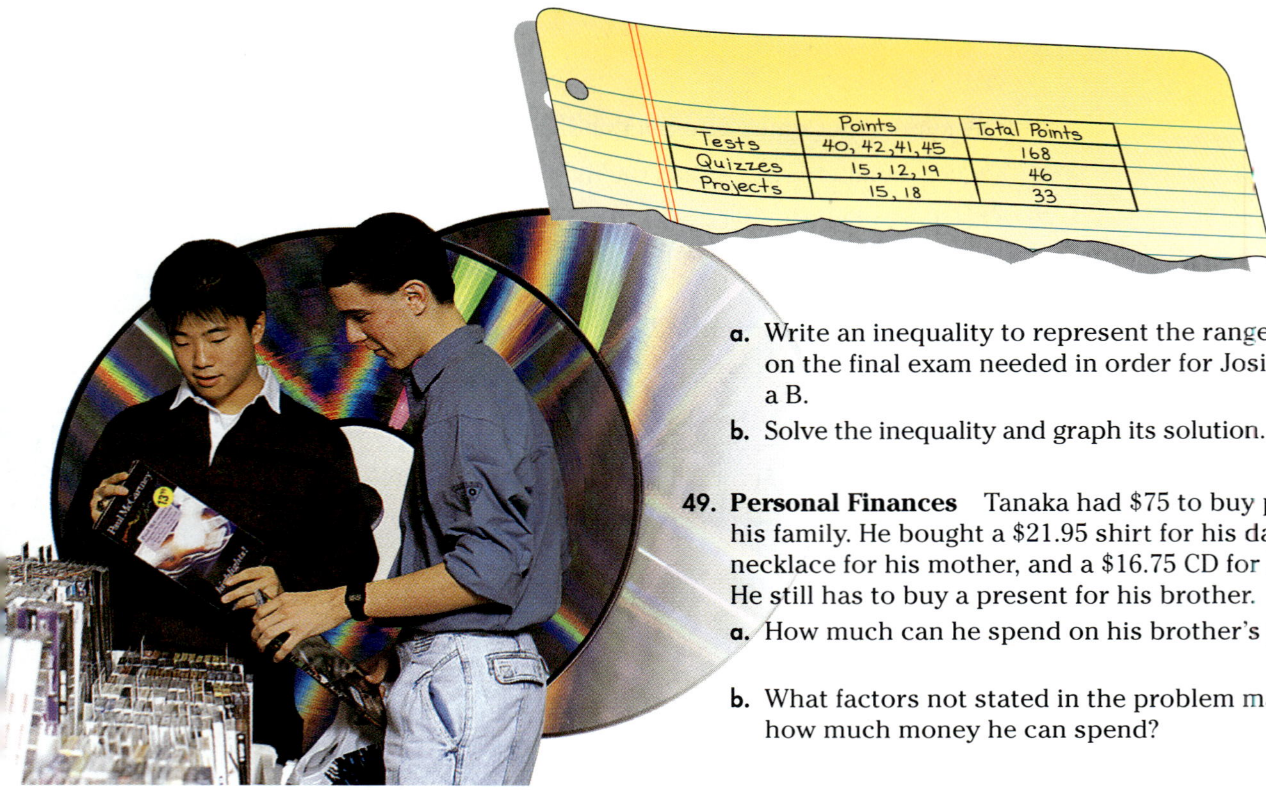

	Points	Total Points
Tests	40, 42, 41, 45	168
Quizzes	15, 12, 19	46
Projects	15, 18	33

a. Write an inequality to represent the range of scores on the final exam needed in order for Josie to make a B.

b. Solve the inequality and graph its solution.

49. **Personal Finances** Tanaka had \$75 to buy presents for his family. He bought a \$21.95 shirt for his dad, a \$23.42 necklace for his mother, and a \$16.75 CD for his sister. He still has to buy a present for his brother.

a. How much can he spend on his brother's present?

b. What factors not stated in the problem may affect how much money he can spend?

Mixed Review

50. Find the midpoint of the line segment whose endpoints are at $(-1, 9)$ and $(-5, 5)$. (Lesson 6–7)

Write an equation in slope-intercept form for a line that satisfies each condition. (Lesson 6–6)

51. perpendicular to $x + 7 = 3y$ that passes through $(1, 0)$

52. parallel to $\frac{1}{5}y - 3x = 2$ that passes through $(0, -3)$

53. **Statistics** Find the range, quartiles, and interquartile range for the set of data at the right. (Lesson 5–7)

Stem	Leaf
12	4 6 7 7
13	1 1 6 9
14	0 5 7
15	0 3 9 9 9
16	5 6 6

14 | 0 = \$140

54. Solve $4x + 3y = 16$ if the domain is $\{-2, -1, 0, 2, 5\}$. (Lesson 5–3)

55. If y varies inversely as x and $y = 32$ when $x = 3$, find y when $x = 8$. (Lesson 4–8)

56. Solve $y - \frac{7}{16} = -\frac{5}{8}$ (Lesson 3–1)

57. Replace the __?__ with <, >, or = to make $\frac{6}{13}$ __?__ $\frac{1}{2}$ true. (Lesson 2–4)

58. **Look for a Pattern** How many triangles are shown at the right? Count only the triangles pointing upward. (Lesson 1–2)

MODELING MATHEMATICS

7–2A Solving Inequalities

Materials: equation mat, cups and counters, self-adhesive note

A Preview of Lesson 7–2

You can use an equation model to solve inequalities.

Activity Model the solution for $-2x < 4$.

Step 1 Use the note to cover the equals sign on the equation mat. Then write a $<$ symbol on the note. Label 2 cups with a negative sign, and place them on the left side. Place 4 positive counters on the right.

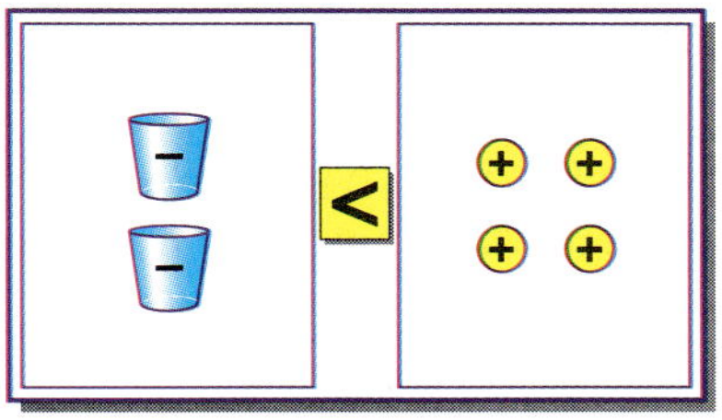

$-2x < 4$

Step 2 Since we cannot solve for a negative cup, we must eliminate the negative cups by adding 2 positive cups to each side. Remove the zero pairs.

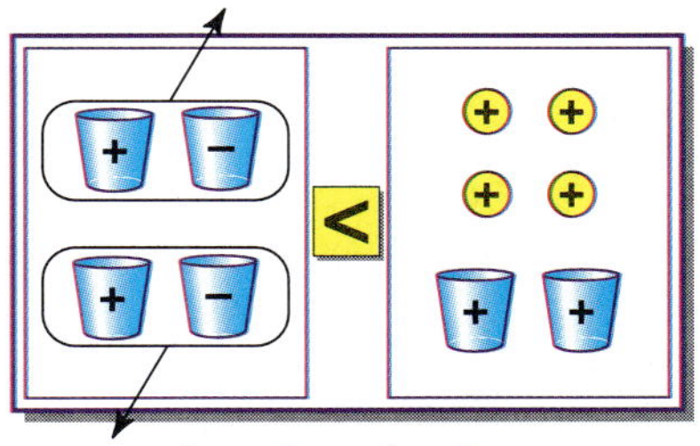

$-2x + 2x < 4 + 2x$

Step 3 Add 4 negative counters to each side to isolate the cups. Remove the zero pairs.

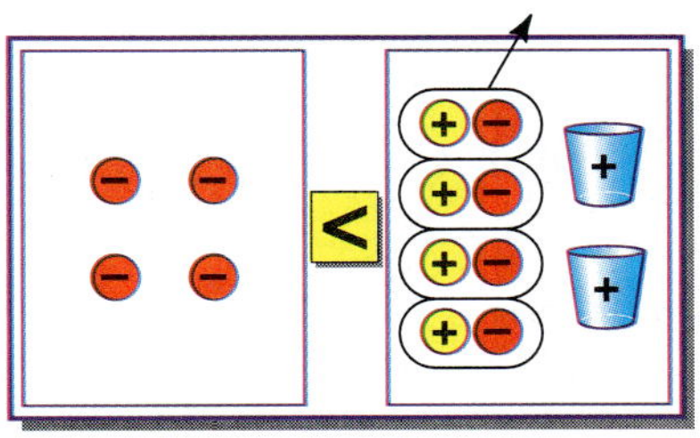

$-4 < 2x$

Step 4 Separate the counters into 2 groups.

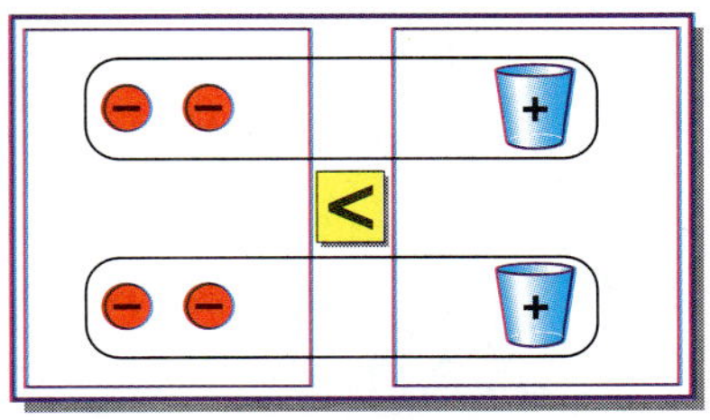

$-2 < x$ or $x > -2$

Model

1. Compare the symbol and location of the variable in the original problem with those in the solution. What do you find?
2. Model the solution for $3x > 12$. What do you find? How is this different from solving $-2x < 4$?

Write

3. Write a rule for solving inequalities involving multiplication.
4. Do you think the rule applies to inequalities involving division? *Remember that dividing by a number is the same as multiplying by its reciprocal.*

7–2 Solving Inequalities by Using Multiplication and Division

What YOU'LL LEARN

- To solve inequalities by using multiplication and division.

Why IT'S IMPORTANT

You can use inequalities to solve problems involving the physical and political sciences.

GLOBAL CONNECTIONS

About 15,000 years ago, an important application of the lever appeared as hunters used an *atlatl,* the Aztec word for spear-thrower. This simple device was a handle that provided extra mechanical advantage by adding length to the hunter's arm. This enabled the hunter to use less motion to get greater results when hunting.

CONNECTION

Physical Science

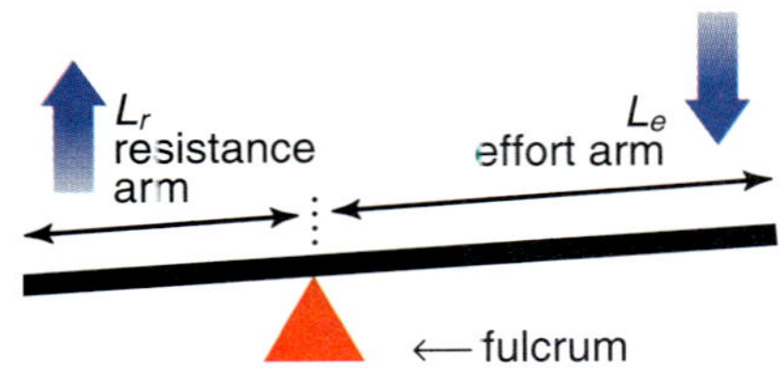

A lever can be used to multiply the effort force you exert when trying to move something. The fixed point or *fulcrum* of a lever separates the length of the lever into two sections—the *effort arm* on which the effort force is applied and the *resistance arm* that exerts the resistance force. The *mechanical advantage* of a lever is the number of times a lever multiplies that effort force.

The formula for determining the mechanical advantage *MA* of a lever can be expressed as $MA = \frac{L_e}{L_r}$, where L_e represents the length of the effort arm and L_r represents the length of the resistance arm.

Suppose a group of volunteers is clearing hiking trails at Yosemite National Park. They need to position a lever so that a mechanical advantage of at least 7 is achieved in order to remove a boulder blocking the trail. The volunteers place the lever on a rock so they can use the rock as a fulcrum. They will need the resistance arm to be 1.5 ft long so that it is long enough to get under the boulder. What should be the length of the lever in order to move the boulder?

We need to find the length of the effort arm to find the total length. Let L_e represent the length of the effort arm. We know that 1.5 feet is the length of the resistance arm L_r. Since the mechanical advantage must be at least 7, we can write an inequality using the formula.

$$MA \geq 7$$

$$\frac{L_e}{L_r} \geq 7 \quad \text{Replace } MA \text{ with } \frac{L_e}{L_r}.$$

$$\frac{L_e}{1.5} \geq 7 \quad \text{Replace } L_r \text{ with 1.5.}$$

You will solve this problem in Example 1.

If you were solving the equation $\frac{L_e}{1.5} = 7$, you would multiply each side by 1.5. Will this method work when solving inequalities? Before answering this question, let's explore how multiplying (or dividing) an inequality by a positive or negative number affects the inequality. Consider the inequality $10 < 15$, which we know is true.

Multiply by 2.

$$10 < 15$$
$$10(2) < 15(2)$$
$$20 < 30 \quad \text{true}$$

Multiply by −2.

$$10 < 15$$
$$10(-2) < 15(-2) \quad \text{false}$$
$$-20 < -30 \quad \text{false}$$
$$-20 > -30 \quad \text{true}$$

Divide by 5.

$$10 < 15$$
$$\frac{10}{5} < \frac{15}{5}$$
$$2 < 3 \quad \text{true}$$

Divide by −5.

$$10 < 15$$
$$\frac{10}{-5} < \frac{15}{-5} \quad \text{false}$$
$$-2 < -3 \quad \text{false}$$
$$-2 > -3 \quad \text{true}$$

These results suggest the following.

- If each side of a true inequality is multiplied or divided by the same positive number, the resulting inequality is also true.
- If each side of a true inequality is multiplied or divided by the same negative number, the direction of the inequality symbol must be *reversed* so that the resulting inequality is also true.

Multiplication and Division Properties for Inequalities

For all numbers, *a*, *b*, and *c*, the following are true.

1. **If *c* is positive and $a < b$, then $ac < bc$ and $\frac{a}{c} < \frac{b}{c}$, and if *c* is positive and $a > b$, then $ac > bc$ and $\frac{a}{c} > \frac{b}{c}$.**
2. **If *c* is negative and $a < b$, then $ac > bc$ and $\frac{a}{c} > \frac{b}{c}$, and if *c* is negative and $a > b$, then $ac < bc$ and $\frac{a}{c} < \frac{b}{c}$.**

These properties also hold for inequalities involving ≤ and ≥.

Example 1

CONNECTION Physical Science

Refer to the connection at the beginning of the lesson. What should the minimum length of the lever be?

$$\frac{L_e}{1.5} \geq 7$$
$$1.5 \cdot \frac{L_e}{1.5} \geq 1.5(7) \quad \textit{Multiply each side by 1.5.}$$
$$L_e \geq 10.5$$

The effort arm must be at least 10.5 feet long.

In order to find the length of the lever, add the lengths of the effort arm and the resistance arm. The lever should be at least 10.5 + 1.5 or 12 feet long.

Example 2 **Solve $\frac{x}{12} \le \frac{3}{2}$.**

$$\frac{x}{12} \le \frac{3}{2}$$

$$12 \cdot \frac{x}{12} \le 12 \cdot \frac{3}{2}$$ *Multiply each side by 12.*

$$x \le 18$$ *Since we multiplied by a positive number, the inequality symbol stays the same.*

The solution set is $\{x \mid x \le 18\}$.

Since dividing is the same as multiplying by the reciprocal, there can be two methods to solve an inequality that involves multiplication.

Example 3 **Solve $-3w > 27$.**

Method 1

$$-3w > 27$$

$$\frac{-3w}{-3} < \frac{27}{-3}$$ *Divide each side by −3 and change > to <.*

$$w < -9$$

Method 2

$$-3w > 27$$

$$\left(-\frac{1}{3}\right)(-3w) < \left(-\frac{1}{3}\right)(27)$$ *Multiply each side by $-\frac{1}{3}$ and change > to <.*

$$w < -9$$

Check: Let w be any number less than -9.

$$-3w > 27$$

$$-3(-10) \overset{?}{>} 27$$ *Suppose we select −10.*

$$30 > 27$$ true

Numbers less than -9 compose the solution set. The solution set is $\{w \mid w < -9\}$.

Example 4

APPLICATION

Business

Angelica Moreno is a sales representative for an appliance distributor. She needs at least \$5000 in weekly sales of a particular TV model to qualify for a sales competition to win a trip to the Bahamas. If the TVs sell for \$250 each, how many TVs will Ms. Moreno have to sell to qualify?

Explore Let t represent the number of TVs to be sold. At least \$5000 means greater than or equal to \$5000.

Plan The price of one TV times the number of sets sold must be greater than or equal to the total amount of sales needed.

The price of one TV	*times*	*the number of TVs sold*	*is at least*	*\$5000.*
\$250	$\times$	t	$\ge$	\$5000

Solve

$$250t \ge 5000$$

$$\frac{250t}{250} \ge \frac{5000}{250}$$ *Divide each side by 250.*

$$t \ge 20$$

Examine Ms. Moreno must sell a minimum of 20 TVs to qualify for the contest. The amount of money from the sale of 20 TVs is \$250(20) or \$5000.

Example 5 INTEGRATION Geometry

Triangle XYZ is not an acute triangle. The greatest angle in the triangle has a measure of $(6d)°$. What are the possible values of d?

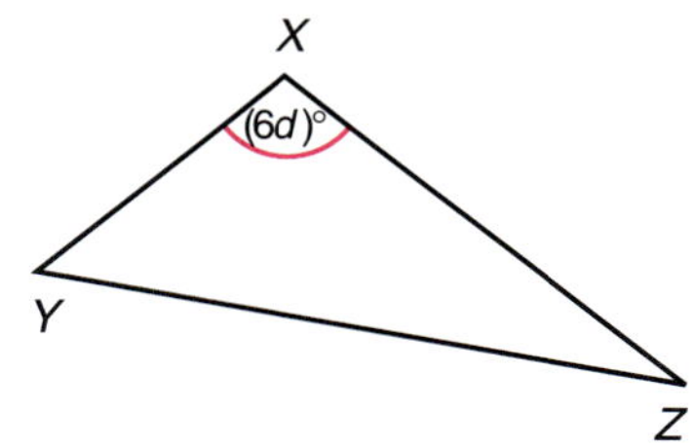

Since ΔXYZ is not acute, the measure of the greatest angle must be 90° or larger, but less than 180°. Thus, $6d \geq 90$ and $6d < 180$.

$$6d \geq 90$$
$$\frac{6d}{6} \geq \frac{90}{6} \quad \textit{Divide each side by 6.}$$
$$d \geq 15$$

$$6d < 180$$
$$\frac{6d}{6} < \frac{180}{6} \quad \textit{Divide each side by 6.}$$
$$d < 30$$

The value of d must be greater than or equal to 15 but less than 30.

CHECK FOR UNDERSTANDING

Communicating Mathematics

Study the lesson. Then complete the following.

1. **Classify** each statement as *true* or *false*. If false, explain how to change the inequality to make it true.
   a. If $x > 9$, then $-3x > -27$.
   b. If $x < 4$, then $3x < 12$.
2. **Complete** each statement.
   a. If each side of an inequality is multiplied by the same __?__ number, the direction of the inequality symbol must be reversed so that the resulting inequality is true.
   b. Multiplying by __?__ is the same as dividing by -6.
   c. An acute triangle has angles whose measures are all less than __?__.
3. **You Decide** Utina and Paige are discussing the rules for changes in the direction of the inequality symbol when solving inequalities. Paige says the rule is "Whenever you have a negative sign in the problem, the direction of the inequality symbol will change." Utina says that is not always true. Decide who is correct and give examples to support your answer.

MODELING MATHEMATICS

Use models to solve each inequality. Write the answer in set-builder notation.

4. $3x < 15$
5. $-6x < 18$
6. $2x + 6 > x - 7$
7. $-4x + 8 \geq 14$
8. Use models to determine the appropriate symbol (>, <, or =) to complete each comparison.
   a. $x + 5$ __?__ $x - 7$
   b. $x + 3 + (x - 6)$ __?__ $(2x + 7) - 4$
   c. $2x + 8$ __?__ $2x + 6 - x$

Guided Practice

State the number by which you multiply or divide to solve each inequality. Indicate whether the direction of the inequality symbol reverses. Then solve.

9. $-6y \geq -24$
10. $10x > 20$
11. $\frac{x}{4} < -5$
12. $-\frac{2}{7}z \geq -12$

Solve each inequality. Then check your solution.

13. $\frac{4}{5}x < 24$
14. $-\frac{v}{3} \geq 4$
15. $-0.1t \geq 3$
16. $5y > -25$

Define a variable, write an inequality, and solve each problem. Then check your solution.

17. One fifth of a number is at most 4.025.
18. The opposite of six times a number is less than 216.
19. **Geometry** Determine the value of s so that the area of the square is at least 144 square feet.

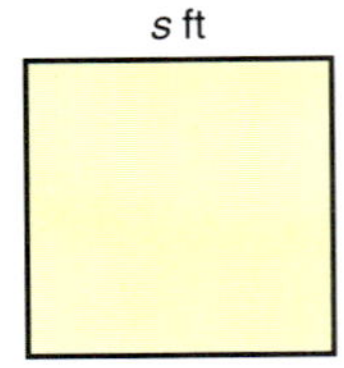

EXERCISES

Practice

Solve each inequality. Then check your solution.

20. $7a \leq 49$
21. $12b > -144$
22. $-5w > -125$
23. $-x \leq 44$
24. $4 < -x$
25. $-102 > 17r$
26. $\frac{b}{-12} \leq 3$
27. $\frac{t}{13} < 13$
28. $\frac{2}{3}w > -22$
29. $6 \leq 0.8g$
30. $-15b < -28$
31. $-0.049 \leq 0.07x$
32. $\frac{3}{7}h < \frac{3}{49}$
33. $\frac{12r}{-4} > \frac{3}{20}$
34. $\frac{3b}{4} \leq \frac{2}{3}$
35. $-\frac{1}{3}x > 9$
36. $\frac{y}{6} \geq \frac{1}{2}$
37. $\frac{-3m}{4} \leq 18$

Define a variable, write an inequality, and solve each problem. Then check your solution.

38. Four times a number is at most 36.
39. Thirty-six is at least one half of a number.
40. The opposite of three times a number is more than 48.
41. Three fourths of a number is at most -24.
42. Eighty percent of a number is less than 24.
43. The product of two numbers is no greater than 144. One of the numbers is -8. What is the other number?

44. **Geometry** Determine the value of x so that the area of the rectangle at the right is at least 918 square feet.

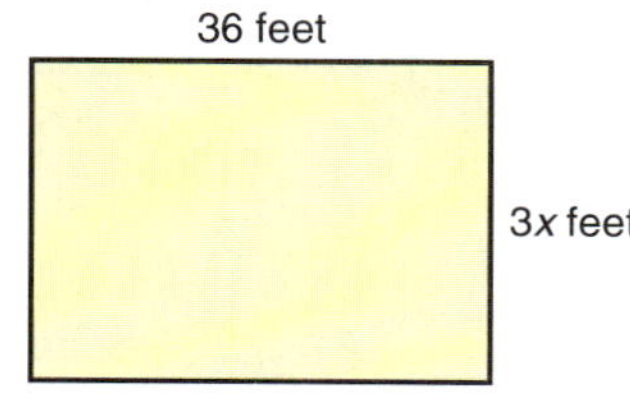

45. **Geometry** Determine the value of y so that the perimeter of the triangle at the right is less than 100 meters.

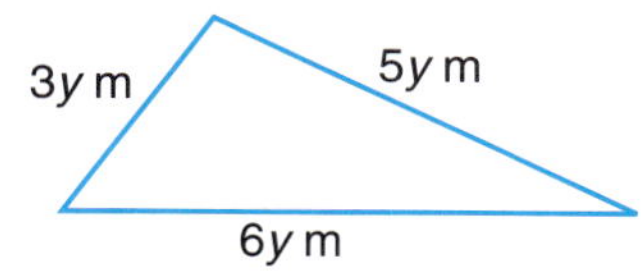

Complete.

46. If $24m \geq 16$, then $\underline{\ ?\ } \geq 12$.

47. If $-9 \leq 15b$, then $25b \underline{\ ?\ } -15$.

48. If $5y < -12$, then $20y < \underline{\ ?\ }$.

49. If $-10a > 21$, then $30a \underline{\ ?\ } -63$.

Critical Thinking

50. Use an example to show that if $x > y$, then $x^2 > y^2$ is not necessarily true.

Applications and Problem Solving

Define a variable, write an inequality, and solve each problem.

51. **Travel** The charge per mile for a compact rental car at 4-D Rentals is \$0.12. Mrs. Rodriguez is on a business trip and must rent a car to attend various meetings. She has a budget of \$50 per rental for mileage charges. What is the greatest number of miles Mrs. Rodriguez can travel without going over her budget?

52. **Physics** Refer to the application at the beginning of the lesson. A city worker needs to raise a utility access cover. She has an iron bar to use as a lever. When using a lever, the resistance force is equal to the effort force multiplied by the mechanical advantage, or $F_r = MA \cdot F_e$. The worker weighs 120 pounds, so she can supply that much effort force. All utility covers in the city weigh at least 360 pounds. What mechanical advantage does she need to lift the cover?

fabulous **FIRSTS**

Patsy Takemoto Mink (1927–)

In 1964, Patsy Takemoto Mink, a Democrat from Hawaii, became the first Asian-American woman elected to Congress. She served until 1977 and then was reelected in 1990.

53. **Political Science** A candidate needs 5000 signatures on a petition before she can run for a township office. Experience shows that 15% of the signatures on petitions are not valid. What is the smallest number of signatures the candidate should get to end up with 5000 valid signatures?

Mixed Review

54. Define a variable, write an inequality, and solve the following problem. The difference of five times a number less four times that number plus seven is at most 34. (Lesson 7–1)

55. **Geometry** Three vertices of a square are at $(-5, -3)$, $(-5, 5)$, and $(3, -3)$. Suppose you were to inscribe a circle in this square. What would the coordinates of the center of the circle be? (Lesson 6–7)

56. **Geometry** Determine the slopes of the lines parallel and perpendicular to the graph of $3x - 6 = -y$. (Lesson 6–6)

57. Determine the slope of the line that passes through $(4, -9)$ and $(-2, 3)$. (Lesson 6–1)

58. Write an equation in functional notation for the relation at the right. (Lesson 5–6)

a	−2	0	2	4	6	8	10
b	−5	−3	−1	1	3	5	7

59. **Budgeting** JoAnne Paulsen's take-home pay is \$1782 per month. She spends \$325 on rent, \$120 on groceries, and \$40 on gas. She allows herself 12% of the remaining amount for entertainment. How much can she spend on entertainment each month? (Lesson 4–4)

60. What number is 47% of 27? (Lesson 4–4)

61. **Soccer** A soccer field is 75 yards shorter than 3 times its width. Its perimeter is 370 yards. Find its dimensions. (Lesson 3–5)

62. Evaluate $5y + 3$ if $y = 1.3$. (Lesson 1–3)

WORKING ON THE

In•ves•ti•ga•tion

Refer to the Investigation on pages 320–321.

Smoke Gets In Your Eyes

Currently, about 50 million Americans smoke, and each smoker averages about 30 cigarettes a day. Consider the amount of smoke produced by a single cigarette. Make some projections on the volume of cigarette smoke generated by all 50 million smoking Americans.

1 Find the volume of smoke produced by the average smoker.

2 Project the amount of smoke generated by 50 million smokers in a year.

3 Estimate the volume of air in your room at home. Write an inequality that would estimate the number of puffs p it would take to fill your room. Solve the inequality.

4 Suppose a smoker was locked in your room with several cartons of cigarettes. Would it be possible for the smoker to fill the room completely with smoke in the same concentration as the smoke exhaled? Explain your answer.

Add the results of your work to your Investigation Folder.

7-3 Solving Multi-Step Inequalities

What YOU'LL LEARN

- To solve linear inequalities involving more than one operation, and
- to find the solution set for a linear inequality when replacement values are given for the variables.

Why IT'S IMPORTANT

You can use inequalities to solve problems involving engineering and real estate.

APPLICATION

Engineering

Rosa Whitehair is a partner in an engineering consulting firm. Her fee for consulting on large construction projects is \$1000 plus 10% of the design fee that the company charges its clients. Ms. Whitehair is considering two construction projects: a 50-story office building and the design of an airport terminal. She is interested in both projects, but decides to choose the one for which her fee is higher. The company that is designing the office building has agreed to pay Ms. Whitehair a flat fee of \$5000. How much does the design company's fee need to be for her to choose the terminal?

Let x represent the design fee for the airport terminal.

The flat fee	*plus*	*10% of the design fee*	*is more than*	*the flat fee for the office building.*
1000	+	$0.10x$	>	5000

LOOK BACK

You can review solving multi-step equations in Lesson 3-3.

This inequality involves more than one operation. It can be solved by undoing the operations in reverse of the order of operations in the same way you would solve an equation with more than one operation.

$$1000 + 0.10x > 5000$$

$$1000 - 1000 + 0.10x > 5000 - 1000 \quad \textit{Subtract 1000 from each side.}$$

$$0.10x > 4000$$

$$\frac{0.10x}{0.10} > \frac{4000}{0.10} \quad \textit{Divide each side by 0.10.}$$

$$x > 40{,}000$$

If the company charges design fees higher than \$40,000 for the terminal, Ms. Whitehair will choose them since her consulting fee is higher.

Example 1 **Determine the value of x so that $\angle A$ is acute.**

INTEGRATION
Geometry

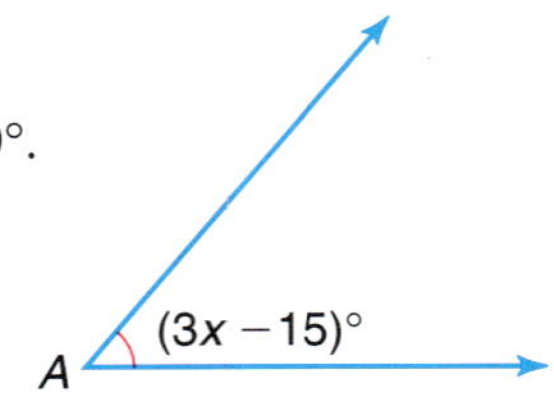

Assume that x is positive.

For $\angle A$ to be acute, its measure must be less than 90°.

Thus, $3x - 15 < 90$.

$$3x - 15 < 90$$

$$3x - 15 + 15 < 90 + 15 \quad \textit{Add 15 to each side.}$$

$$3x < 105$$

$$\frac{3x}{3} < \frac{105}{3} \quad \textit{Divide each side by 3.}$$

$$x < 35$$

For $\angle A$ to be acute, x must be less than 35.

Sometimes inequalities, like equations, involve variables on each side of the inequality.

Example 2 **Solve $-4w + 9 \leq w - 21$.**

$$-4w + 9 \leq w - 21$$

$$-w - 4w + 9 \leq w - 21 - w \quad \textit{Subtract } w \textit{ from each side.}$$

$$-5w + 9 \leq -21$$

$$-5w + 9 - 9 \leq -21 - 9 \quad \textit{Subtract 9 from each side.}$$

$$-5w \leq -30$$

$$\frac{-5w}{-5} \geq \frac{-30}{-5} \quad \textit{Divide each side by } -5 \textit{ and change} \leq \textit{to} \geq.$$

$$w \geq 6$$

The solution set is $\{w \mid w \geq 6\}$.

When we solve an inequality, the solution set usually includes all numbers for a certain criteria, such as $\{x \mid x > 4\}$. Sometimes a replacement set is given from which the solution set can be chosen.

Example 3 **Determine the solution set for $3x + 6 > 12$ if the replacement set for x is $\{-2, -1, 0, 1, 2, 3, 4, 5\}$.**

Method 1

Substitute values into the inequality to find the values that satisfy the inequality. Try -2.

$$3x + 6 > 12$$

$$3(-2) + 6 > 12$$

$$0 > 12 \quad \text{false}$$

From this trial, we can estimate that the value of x must be much greater than -2 to make the inequality true. Try 2.

$$3x + 6 > 12$$

$$3(2) + 6 > 12$$

$$12 > 12 \quad \text{false}$$

From this trial, we see that values greater than 2 must be in the solution set. Try 3.

$$3x + 6 > 12$$
$$3(3) + 6 > 12$$
$$15 > 12 \quad \text{true} \qquad \text{The solution set is } \{3, 4, 5\}.$$

Method 2

Solve the inequality for all values of x. Then determine which values from the replacement set belong to the solution set.

$$3x + 6 > 12$$
$$3x + 6 - 6 > 12 - 6$$
$$3x > 6$$
$$\frac{3x}{3} > \frac{6}{3}$$
$$x > 2$$

The solution set is those numbers from the replacement set that are greater than 2. Thus, the solution set is $\{3, 4, 5\}$.

EXPLORATION — GRAPHING CALCULATORS

You can use the inequality symbols in the TEST menu on a graphing calculator to find the solution to an inequality in one variable.

Your Turn

a. Clear the [Y=] list. Enter $3x + 6 > 4x + 9$ as Y1. (The symbol $>$ is item 3 on the TEST menu.) Press [GRAPH]. Describe what you see.

b. Use the TRACE function to scan the values along the graph. What do you notice about the values of y on the graph?

c. Solve the inequality algebraically. How does your solution compare to the pattern you noticed in part **b**?

When solving some inequalities that contain grouping symbols, remember to first use the distributive property to remove the grouping symbols.

Example 4 **Solve $5(k + 4) - 2(k + 6) \geq 5(k + 1) - 1$. Then graph the solution.**

$$5(k + 4) - 2(k + 6) \geq 5(k + 1) - 1$$
$$5k + 20 - 2k - 12 \geq 5k + 5 - 1 \qquad \textit{Distributive property.}$$
$$3k + 8 \geq 5k + 4 \qquad \textit{Combine like terms.}$$
$$3k - 5k + 8 \geq 5k - 5k + 4 \qquad \textit{Subtract 5k from each side.}$$
$$-2k + 8 \geq 4$$
$$-2k + 8 - 8 \geq 4 - 8 \qquad \textit{Subtract 8 from each side.}$$
$$-2k \geq -4$$
$$\frac{-2k}{-2} \leq \frac{-4}{-2} \qquad \textit{Divide each side by } -2 \textit{ and change } \geq \textit{ to } \leq.$$
$$k \leq 2$$

The solution set is $\{k \mid k \leq 2\}$.
The graph of $k \leq 2$ is shown at the right.

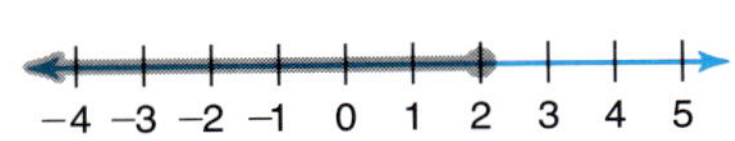

CHECK FOR UNDERSTANDING

Communicating Mathematics

Study the lesson. Then complete the following.

1. **Explain** each step in solving $-3x + 7 < 4x - 5$.
2. **Write** an inequality that expresses the fact that when you add 3 feet to the perimeter of a square of sides with length s, the resulting perimeter does not exceed 50 feet.
3. **Write** an inequality that has no solution.
4. **Describe** how you would solve $16 - 5w > 29$ without dividing by -5 or multiplying by $-\frac{1}{5}$.
5. Refer to Example 3. Which of the two methods seems more efficient in solving the inequality for the given replacement set? Explain your selection.

MODELING MATHEMATICS

6. Use the method shown in Lesson 7–2A to model the solutions for each inequality.
   a. $3 - 4x \geq 15$
   b. $6x - 1 < 5 + 3x$

Guided Practice

Choose the correct solution for each inequality.

7. Solve $2m + 5 \leq 4m - 1$.
   a. $m > -3$ b. $m < 3$ c. $m \geq 3$ d. $m \leq -3$
8. Solve $13r - 11 \geq 7r + 37$.
   a. $r < 8$ b. $r \geq 8$ c. $r \leq -8$ d. $r > -8$

Solve each inequality. Then check your solution.

9. $9x + 2 > 20$
10. $-4h + 7 > 15$
11. $-2 - \frac{d}{5} < 23$
12. $6a + 9 < -4a + 29$

Find the solution set of each inequality given the replacement set.

13. $3x - 1 > 4$, $\{-1, 0, 1, 2, 3\}$
14. $-7a + 6 \leq 48$, $\{-10, -9, -8, -7, -6, -5, -4, -3\}$
15. **Number Theory** Consider the sentence *The sum of two consecutive even integers is greater than 75.*
    a. Write an inequality for this statement.
    b. Solve the inequality.
    c. Name two consecutive even integers that meet the requirements of the statement.

EXERCISES

Practice

Find the solution set of each inequality if the replacement set for each variable is {−10, −9, −8, ..., 8, 9, 10}.

16. $n - 3 \geq \frac{n + 1}{2}$
17. $\frac{2(x + 2)}{3} < 4$
18. $1.3y - 12 < 0.9y + 4$
19. $-20 \geq 8 + 7k$

Solve each inequality. Then check your solution.

20. $2m + 7 > 17$

21. $-3 > -3t + 6$

22. $-2 - 3x \geq 2$

23. $\frac{2}{3}w - 3 \leq 7$

24. $7x - 1 < 29 - 2x$

25. $8n + 2 - 10n < 20$

26. $2x + 5 < 3x - 7$

27. $5 - 4m + 8 + 2m > -17$

28. $\frac{2x - 3}{5} < 7$

29. $x < \frac{2x - 15}{3}$

30. $9r + 15 \geq 24 + 10r$

31. $6p - 2 \leq 3p + 12$

32. $4y + 2 < 8y - (6y - 10)$

33. $3(x - 2) - 8x < 44$

34. $3.1q - 1.4 > 1.3q + 6.7$

35. $-5(k + 4) \geq 3(k - 4)$

36. $5(2h - 6) - 7(h + 7) > 4h$

37. $7 + 3y > 2(y + 3) - 2(-1 - y)$

Define a variable, write an inequality, and solve each problem. Then check your solution.

38. Two thirds of a number decreased by 27 is at least 9.

39. Three times the sum of a number and 7 is greater than 5 times the number less 13.

INTEGRATION
Number Theory

40. The sum of two consecutive odd integers is at most 123. Find the pair with the greatest sum.

41. Find all sets of two consecutive positive odd integers whose sum is no greater than 18.

42. Find all sets of three consecutive positive even integers whose sum is less than 40.

Solve each inequality. Then check your solution.

43. $3x + 4 > 2(x + 3) + x$

44. $3 - 3(y - 2) < 13 - 3(y - 6)$

Graphing Calculator

45. Use the methods presented in the Exploration to solve each inequality. Use the viewing window $[-9.4, 9.4]$ by $[-5, 5]$ with scale factors of 1.
   a. $-5 - 8x \geq 59$
   b. $13x - 11 > 7x + 37$
   c. $8x - (x - 5) > x + 17$
   d. $-5(x + 4) \geq 3(x - 4)$

Critical Thinking

46. We can write the expression *the numbers between −3 and 4* as $-3 < x < 4$. What does the algebraic sentence $-3 < x + 2 < 4$ represent?

Applications and Problem Solving

Define a variable, write an inequality, and solve each problem.

47. **Personal Finances** A couple does not want to have a charge of more than \$50 for dinner at a restaurant. A sales tax of 4% is added to the bill, and they plan to tip 15% after the tax has been added. What can the couple spend on the meal?

48. **Recreation** The admission fee to a video game arcade is \$1.25 per person, and it costs \$0.50 for each game played. Latoya and Donnetta have a total of \$10.00 to spend. What is the greatest number of games they will be able to play?

49. **Fund-raising** A university is running a drive to raise money. A corporation has promised to match 40% of whatever the university can raise from other sources. How much must the school raise from other sources to have a total of at least \$800,000 after the corporation's donation?

50. **Real Estate** A homeowner is selling her house. She must pay 7% of the selling price to her real estate agent after the house is sold. To the nearest dollar, what must be the selling price of her house to have at least \$90,000 after the agent is paid?

51. **Labor** A union worker is currently making \$400 per week. His union is seeking a one-year contract. If there is a strike, the new contract will provide for a 6% raise; if there is no strike, the worker expects no increase in salary.
    a. Assuming the worker will not be paid during the strike, how many weeks could he go on strike and still make at least as much for the year as he would have made without a strike?
    b. How would your answer change if the worker was currently making \$575 per week?
    c. How would your answer to part a change if the worker's union provided him with \$120 per week during the strike?

Mixed Review

Solve each inequality.

52. $2r - 2.1 < -8.7 + r$ (Lesson 7–2) 53. $7 - 2y < -y - 3$ (Lesson 7–1)

54. Write the slope-intercept form of an equation for the line that passes through $(-12, 12)$ and $(-2, 7)$. (Lesson 6–4)

55. Write the standard form of an equation of the line that passes through $(2, 4)$ with slope $-\frac{3}{2}$. (Lesson 6–2)

56. **Business** The owner of No Spots City Car Wash found that if c cars were washed in a day, the average daily profit $P(c)$ was given by the formula $P(c) = -0.027c^2 + 8c - 280$. Find the values of $P(c)$ for various values of c to determine the least number of cars that must be washed each day for No Spots City to make a profit. (Lesson 5–5)

57. Find the domain for $3y - 2 = x$ if the range is $\left\{-1, 6, 0, -\frac{1}{3}, 2\right\}$. (Lesson 5–3)

58. **Advertising** For many years, the slogan of a popular toothpaste has been "Four out of five dentists recommend that their patients use our toothpaste." What are the odds that your dentist will *not* recommend you use this toothpaste? (Lesson 4–6)

59. Jason scored the following points for his basketball team during the past ten games: 18, 32, 20, 21, 34, 9, 33, 37, 22, 25. Find the mean, median, and mode of his total points. (Lesson 3–7)

60. Find $18 - (-34)$. (Lesson 2–3)

7–4 Solving Compound Inequalities

What YOU'LL LEARN

- To solve problems by making a diagram,
- to solve compound inequalities and graph their solution sets, and
- to solve problems that involve compound inequalities.

Why IT'S IMPORTANT

You can use inequalities to solve problems involving chemistry and physics.

CONNECTION

Chemistry

The largest fish that spends its whole life in fresh water is the rare Pla beuk, found in the Mekong River in China, Laos, Cambodia, and Thailand. The largest specimen was reportedly 9 feet $10\frac{1}{4}$ inches long and weighed 533.5 pounds.

Such rare fish are sometimes displayed in aquariums. Aquariums can house freshwater or marine life and must be closely monitored to maintain the correct temperature and pH for the animals to survive. pH is a measure of acidity. To determine pH, a scale with values from 0 to 14 is used. One such scale is shown in the diagram below.

pH SCALE

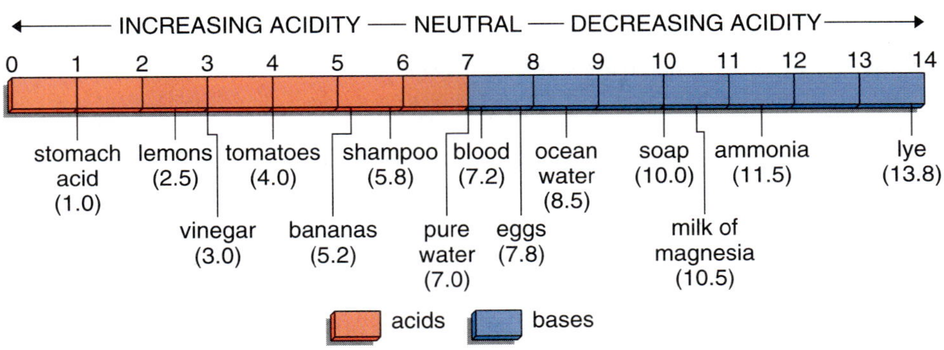

FYI

The largest fish ever caught is a whale shark. Caught near Karachi, Pakistan in 1949, it was 41.5 feet long and weighed 16.5 tons. The smallest fish is a dwarf goby found in the Indian Ocean. Males of this species are only 0.34 inches long.

whale shark

dwarf goby

If we let p represent the value of the pH scale, we can express the different pH levels by using inequalities. For example, an acid solution will have a pH level of $p \geq 0$ and $p < 7$. When considered together, these two inequalities form a **compound inequality.** This compound inequality can also be written without using *and* in two ways.

$$0 \leq p < 7 \quad \text{or} \quad 7 > p \geq 0$$

The statement $0 \leq p < 7$ can be read *0 is less than or equal to p, which is less than 7.* The statement $7 > p \geq 0$ can be read *7 is greater than p, which is greater than or equal to 0.*

The pH levels of bases could be written as follows.

$$p > 7 \text{ and } p \leq 14 \quad \text{or} \quad 7 < p \leq 14 \quad \text{or} \quad 14 \geq p > 7$$

You will graph this inequality in Exercise 6.

You can **draw a diagram** to help solve many problems. Sometimes a picture will help you decide how to work the problem. Other times the picture will show you the answer to the problem.

Example 1

PROBLEM SOLVING

Draw a Diagram

On May 6, 1994, President Francois Mitterrand of France and Queen Elizabeth II of England officially opened the Channel Tunnel connecting England and France. After the ceremonies, a group of 36 English and French government officials had dinner at a restaurant in Calais, France, to celebrate the occasion. Suppose the restaurant staff used small tables that seat four people each, placed end to end, to form one long table. How many tables were needed to seat everyone?

Draw a diagram to represent the tables placed end to end. Use Xs to indicate where the people are sitting. Let's start with a guess, say 10 tables.

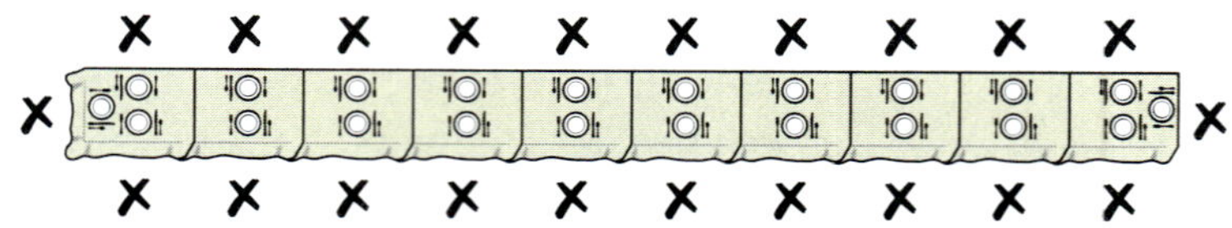

Ten tables will seat 22 people. If we use an extra table, we can seat 2 more people. Now, let's look for a pattern.

Number of tables	10	11	12	13	14	15	16	17
Number of people seated	22	24	26	28	30	32	34	36

This pattern shows that the restaurant needed 17 tables to seat all 36 officials.

The logic symbol for *<u>and</u>* *is* $\wedge$*. You can write* $x > 7$ *and* $x < 10$ *as* $(x > 7) \wedge (x < 10)$*.*

A compound inequality containing *and* is true only if *both* inequalities are true. Thus, the graphs of a compound inequality containing *and* is the **intersection** of the graphs of the two inequalities. The intersection can be found by graphing the two inequalities and then determining where these graphs overlap. In other words, draw a diagram to solve the inequality.

Example 2

Graph the solution set of $x \geq -2$ and $x < 5$.

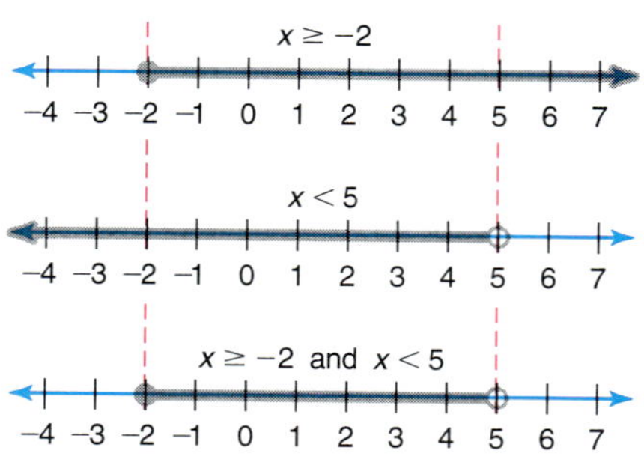

The solution set, shown in the bottom graph, is $\{x \mid -2 \leq x < 5\}$. Note that the graph of $x \geq -2$ includes the point -2. The graph of $x < 5$ does not include 5.

Example 3

Solve $-1 < x + 3 < 5$. Then graph the solution set.

First express $-1 < x + 3 < 5$ using *and.* Then solve each inequality.

$$
\begin{array}{rcl}
-1 < x + 3 & \text{and} & x + 3 < 5 \\
-1 - 3 < x + 3 - 3 & & x + 3 - 3 < 5 - 3 \\
-4 < x & & x < 2
\end{array}
$$

Now graph each solution and find the intersection of the solutions.

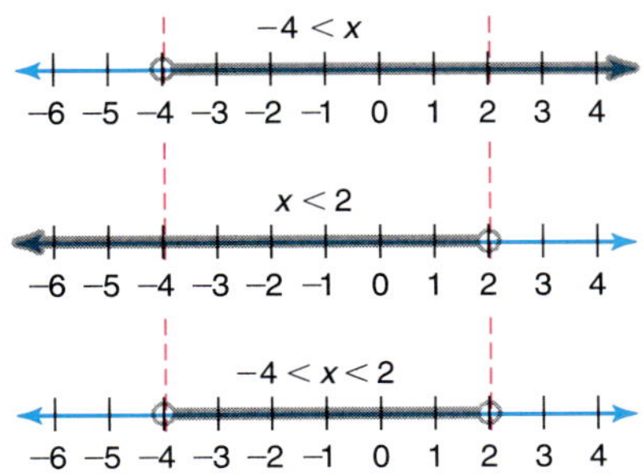

The solution set is $\{x \mid -4 < x < 2\}$.

The following example shows how you can solve a problem by using geometry, a diagram, and a compound inequality.

Example 4

PROBLEM SOLVING

Draw a Diagram

Mai and Luis hope someday to compete in the Olympics in pairs ice skating. Each day they travel from their homes to an ice rink to practice before going to school. Luis lives 17 miles from the rink, and Mai lives 20 miles from it. If this were all the information you were given, determine how far apart Mai and Luis live.

Explore Mai lives 20 miles from the rink and Luis lives 17 miles from the rink. We do not know the relative positions of Mai's and Luis's homes in relation to the rink.

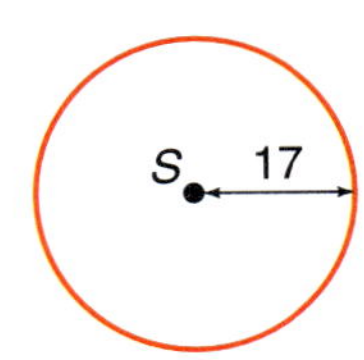

Plan Draw a diagram of the situation. Let S be the location of the skating rink. Since Luis lives 17 miles from the rink, we can draw a circle with a radius of 17. Luis will live somewhere on that circle. Likewise, we can draw another circle with radius of 20 for the location of Mai's home.

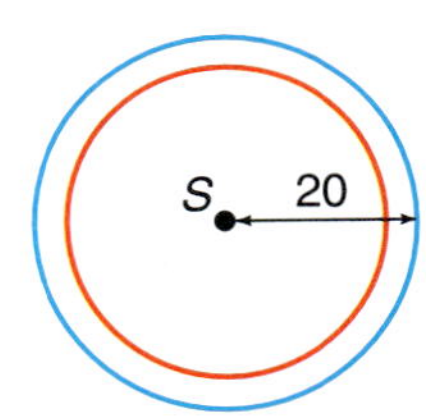

(continued on the next page)

Solve Let's examine three possibilities for the locations of Mai's and Luis's homes.

(1) Mai and Luis live along the same radius from the skating rink.
(2) Mai and Luis live on opposite radii from the skating rink.
(3) Mai and Luis live somewhere other than the locations described in (1) and (2).

Let L and M represent where Luis and Mai live, respectively.

LOOK BACK

You can find more information about the triangle inequality theorem in Exercise 45 (Programming) of Lesson 7–1.

(1) the same radius

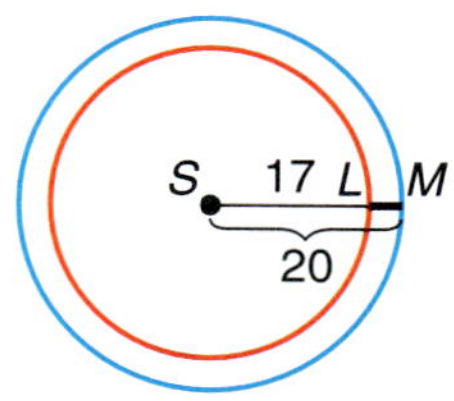

The distance is $20 - 17$ or 3 miles.

(2) opposite radii

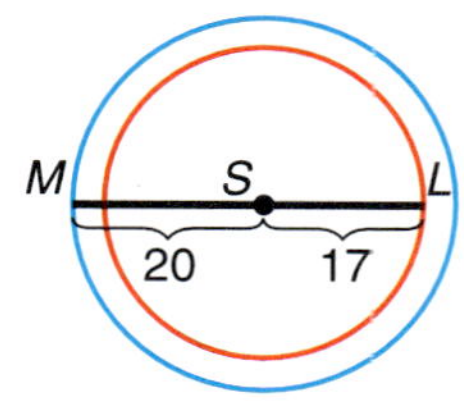

The distance is $20 + 17$ or 37 miles.

(3) somewhere other than (1) or (2)

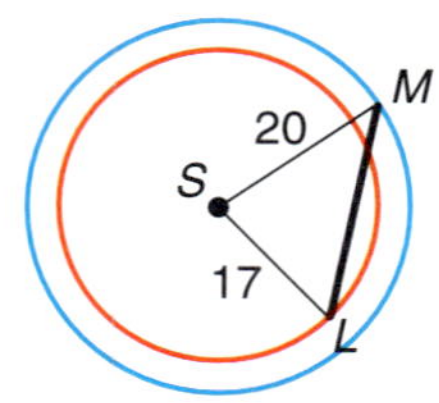

By the triangle inequality theorem, the distance must be less than 37 miles and greater than 3 miles.

The distance d can be described by the inequality $3 \leq d \leq 37$.

Examine Diagrams (1) and (2) show the least and greatest possiblities. To convince yourself that the statement with diagram (3) is always true, you may want to sketch a different triangle.

Another type of compound inequality contains the word *or* instead of *and.* A compound inequality containing *or* is true if one or more of the inequalities is true. The graph of a compound inequality containing *or* is the **union** of the graphs of the two inequalities.

Example 5 **Graph the solution set of $x \geq -1$ or $x < -4$.**

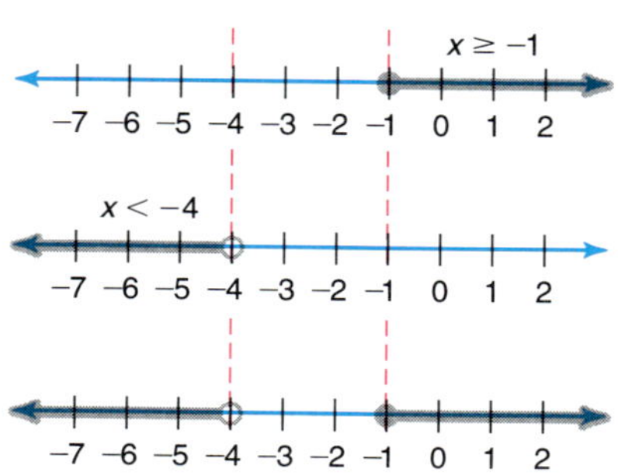

The last graph shows the solution set, $\{x \mid x \geq -1 \text{ or } x < -4\}$.

Example 6 **Solve $3w + 8 < 2$ or $w + 12 > 2 - w$. Graph the solution set.**

$$3w + 8 < 2 \qquad \text{or} \qquad w + 12 > 2 - w$$
$$3w + 8 - 8 < 2 - 8 \qquad\qquad w + w + 12 > 2 - w + w$$
$$3w < -6 \qquad\qquad 2w + 12 > 2$$
$$\frac{3w}{3} < \frac{-6}{3} \qquad\qquad 2w + 12 - 12 > 2 - 12$$
$$w < -2 \qquad\qquad 2w > -10$$
$$\frac{2w}{2} > \frac{-10}{2}$$
$$w > -5$$

Now graph each solution and find the union of the two.

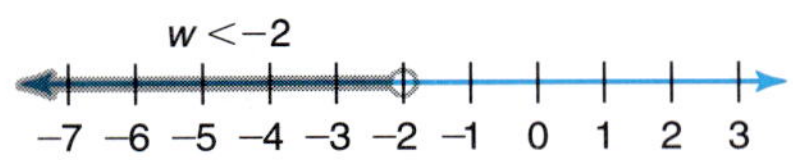

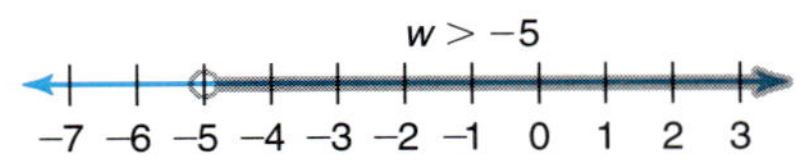

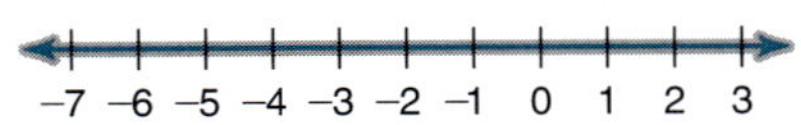

Find the union.

The last graph shows the solution set, $\{x \mid x \text{ is a real number}\}$.

CHECK FOR UNDERSTANDING

Communicating Mathematics

Study the lesson. Then complete the following.

1. **Write** a statement that could be represented by $\$7.50 < p \leq \$18.50$.
2. **Write** a compound inequality that describes the graph below.

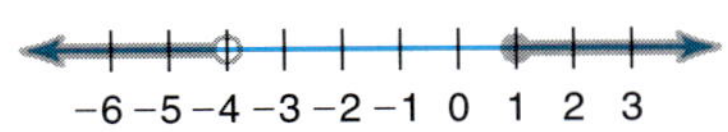

3. **List** two problem-solving strategies used in Example 1. Describe how each strategy helped in the solution of the problem.
4. **Describe** the difference between a compound inequality containing *and* and a compound inequality containing *or*.
5. **Name** two ways in which a picture or diagram can help you solve a problem more easily.
6. **Refer** to the connection at the beginning of the lesson. Graph the inequality that represents the pH levels of bases.

Guided Practice

Write each compound inequality without using *and*. Then graph the solution set.

7. $x < 9$ and $0 \leq x$
8. $x > -2$ and $x < 3$

Write a compound inequality for each solution set shown below.

9. 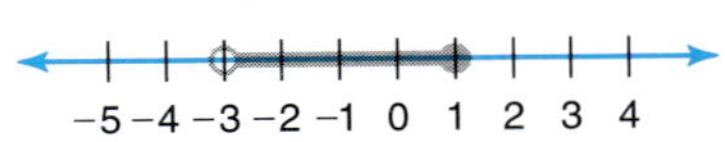

10. 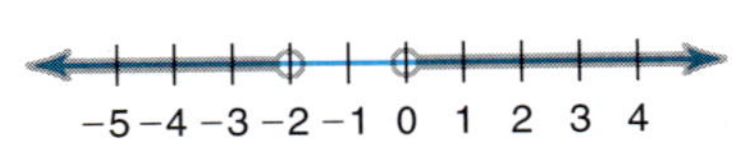

11. Graph the solution set of $y > 5$ and $y < -3$. Describe what the solution set means.

Solve each compound inequality. Then graph the solution set.

12. $2 \leq y + 6$ and $y + 6 < 8$

13. $4 + h \leq -3$ or $4 + h \geq 5$

14. $b + 5 > 10$ or $b \geq 0$

15. $2 + w > 2w + 1 \geq -4 + w$

16. Write a compound inequality without using *and* for the following situation. Solve the inequality and then check the solution.
It costs the same to register mail containing articles with values from \$0 to \$100.

17. **Draw a Diagram** You can cut a pizza into seven pieces with only three straight cuts as shown at the right. Draw a diagram to show the greatest number of pieces you can make with five straight cuts.

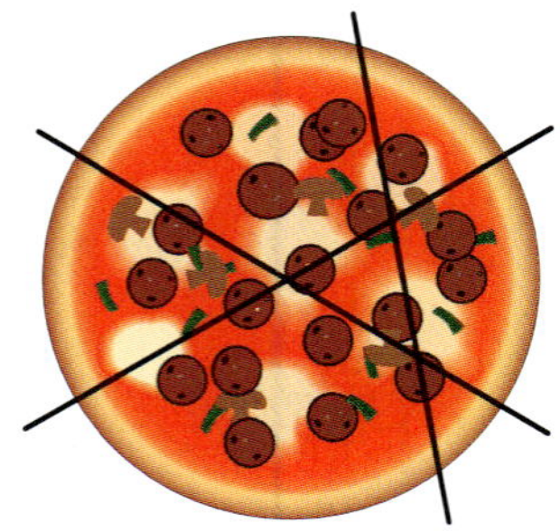

EXERCISES

Practice

Graph the solution set of each compound inequality.

18. $m \geq -5$ and $m < 3$

19. $p < -8$ and $p > 4$

20. $s < 3$ or $s \geq 1$

21. $n \leq -5$ or $n \geq -1$

22. $w > -3$ and $w < 1$

23. $x < -7$ or $x \geq 0$

Write a compound inequality for each solution set shown below.

24. 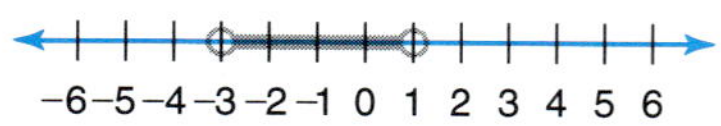

25. 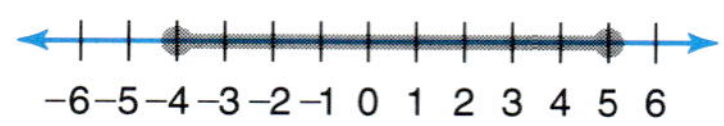

26. 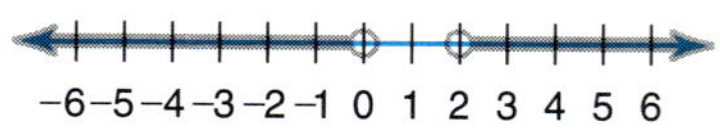

27. 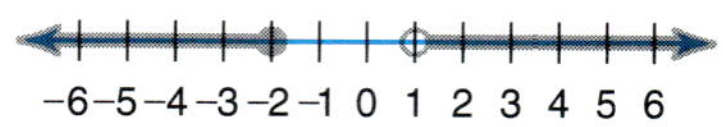

Solve each compound inequality. Then graph the solution set.

28. $4m - 5 > 7$ or $4m - 5 < -9$

29. $x - 4 < 1$ and $x + 2 > 1$

30. $y + 6 > -1$ and $y - 2 < 4$

31. $x + 4 < 2$ or $x - 2 > 1$

32. $10 - 2p > 12$ and $7p < 4p + 9$

33. $6 - c > c$ or $3c - 1 < c + 13$

34. $4 < 2x - 2 < 10$

35. $14 < 3h + 2 < 2$

36. $8 > 5 - 3q$ and $5 - 3q > -13$

37. $-1 + x \leq 3$ or $-x \leq -4$

38. $3n + 11 \leq 13$ or $2n \geq 5n - 12$

39. $3y + 1 > 10$ and $y \neq 6$

40. $4z + 8 \geq z + 6$ or $7z - 14 \geq 2z - 4$

41. $5x + 7 > 2x + 4$ or $3x + 3 < 24 - 4x$

42. $2 - 5(2y - 3) > 2$ or $3y < 2(y - 8)$

43. $5w > 4(2w - 3)$ and $5(w - 3) + 2 < 7$

Write a compound inequality for each solution set shown below.

44. 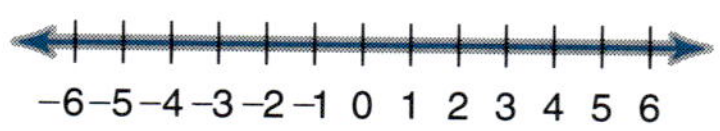

45. 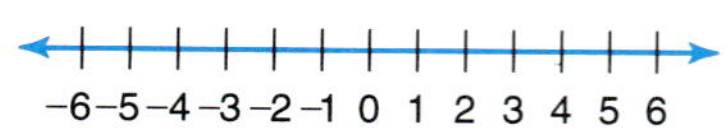

Define a variable, write a compound inequality, and solve each problem. Then check your solution.

46. When three times the distance to the finish line is increased by 5 km, the total kilometers covered in the race will be between 50 and 89 km.

47. The sum of a number and 2 is no more than 6 or no less than 10.

48. The sum of twice a number and 5 lies between 7 and 11.

49. Five less than 6 times a number is at most 37 and at least 31.

Solve each inequality. Then graph the solution set.

50. $3 + y > 2y > -3 - y$ **51.** $m > 2m - 1 > m - 5$ **52.** $\frac{5}{x} + 3 > 0$

Graphing Calculator

53. In Lesson 7–3, you learned how to use a graphing calculator to find graphically which values of x make a given inequality true. You can also use this method to test compound inequalities. The words *and* and *or* can be found in the LOGIC submenu of the TEST menu. Use this method to solve each of the following using your graphing calculator.

a. $3 + x < -4$ or $3 + x > 4$ **b.** $-2 \leq x + 3$ and $x + 3 < 4$

Critical Thinking

54. For what values of a does the compound inequality $-a < x <$ a have no solution?

55. Write a compound inequality for the solution set shown below.

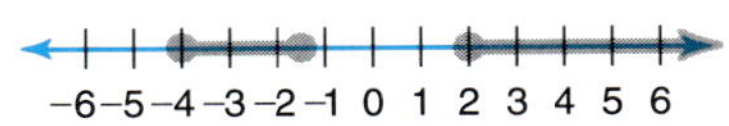

Applications and Problem Solving

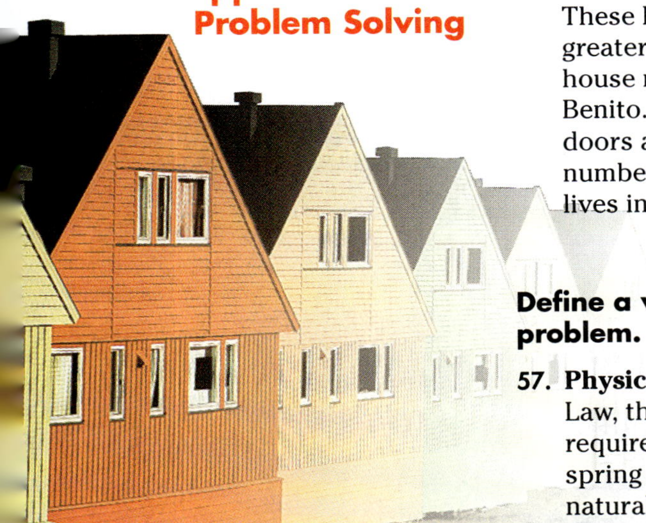

56. Draw a Diagram There are eight houses on McArthur Street, all in a row. These houses are numbered from 1 to 8. Allison, whose house number is greater than 2, lives next door to her best friend, Adrienne. Belinda, whose house number is greater than 5, lives two doors away from her boyfriend, Benito. Cheri, whose house number is greater than Benito's, lives three doors away from her piano teacher, Mr. Crawford. Darryl, whose house number is less than 4, lives four doors away from his teammate, Don. Who lives in each house?

Define a variable, write a compound inequality, and solve each problem.

57. Physics According to Hooke's Law, the force F (in pounds) required to stretch a certain spring x inches beyond its natural length is given by $F = 4.5x$. If forces between 20 and 30 pounds, inclusive, are applied to the spring, what will be the range of the increased lengths of the stretched spring?

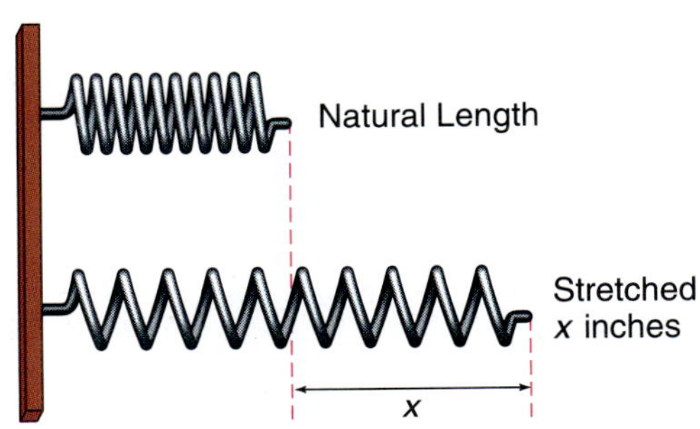

58. Statistics Clarissa must have an average of 92, 93, or 94 points to receive a grade of A– in social studies. She earned 92, 96, and 88 on the first three tests of the grading period. What range of scores on the fourth test will give her an A–?

Mixed Review

Define a variable, write an inequality, and solve each problem.

59. Three fourths of a number decreased by 8 is at least 3. (Lesson 7–3)

60. A number added to 23 is at most 5. (Lesson 7–1)

61. If $7x - 2 \leq 9x + 3$, then $2x \geq$ __?__ . (Lesson 7–1)

62. Geometry Line a is perpendicular to a line that is perpendicular to a line whose equation is $3x - 7y = -3$. If all lines are in the same plane, what is the slope of line a? (Lesson 6–6)

63. Graph $x = 2y - 4$ using the x- and y-intercepts. (Lesson 6–5)

64. Write an equation in functional notation for the relation graphed at the right. (Lesson 5–6)

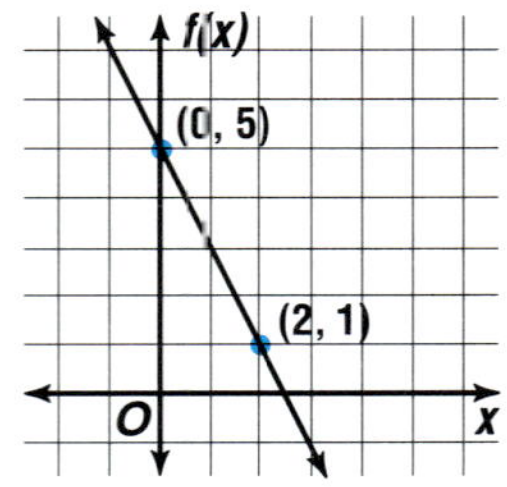

65. Sarah is visiting a friend about two miles away from her house. She sees a hot-air balloon directly above her house. Sara estimates that the angle of elevation formed by the hot-air balloon is about 15°. About how high is the hot-air balloon? (Lesson 4–3)

66. Solve $\frac{4m - 3}{-2} = 12$. (Lesson 3–3)

67. Simplify $-17px + 22bg + 35px + (-37bg)$. (Lesson 2–5)

68. Evaluate $3ab - c^2$ if $a = 6$, $b = 4$, and $c = 3$. (Lesson 1–3)

SELF TEST

Solve each inequality. Then check your solution. (Lessons 7–1, 7–2, and 7–3)

1. $y + 15 \geq -2$

2. $-102 > 17r$

3. $5 - 6n > -19$

4. $\frac{11 - 6w}{5} > 10$

5. $7(g + 8) < 3(g + 12)$

6. $0.1y - 2 \leq 0.3y - 5$

7. Choose an equivalent statement for $4 \geq x - 1 \geq -3$. (Lesson 7–4)

a. $5 \geq x \geq -4$ **b.** $3 \geq x \geq -4$ **c.** $5 \geq x \geq -2$ **d.** $3 \geq x \geq -2$

8. Solve $8 + 3t < 2$ or $-12 < 11t - 1$. Then graph the solution set. (Lesson 7–4)

9. Sports Jennifer has scored 18, 15, and 30 points in her last three starts on the junior varsity girls basketball team. How many points must she score in her next start so that her four-game average is greater than 20 points? (Lesson 7–3)

10. Draw a Diagram Suppose you roll a die two times. (Lesson 7–4)

a. Draw a diagram to show the possibilities of rolling an even number the first time and an odd number the second time.

b. How many of the possibilities have a sum of 7?

7-5 Integration: Probability
Compound Events

What YOU'LL LEARN

- To find the probability of a compound event.

Why IT'S IMPORTANT

You can use tree diagrams to solve problems involving business, sports, and games.

APPLICATION
Archaeology

A group of college students are planning a trip to visit Virgin Islands National Park, where they will study the Carib Indian relics and the remnants of the forts built by the Danes. The Carib Indians were the original occupants of the islands, but had died or left by the early 1600s. The Danes formally claimed the islands in 1666, and they remained under Danish control until 1917.

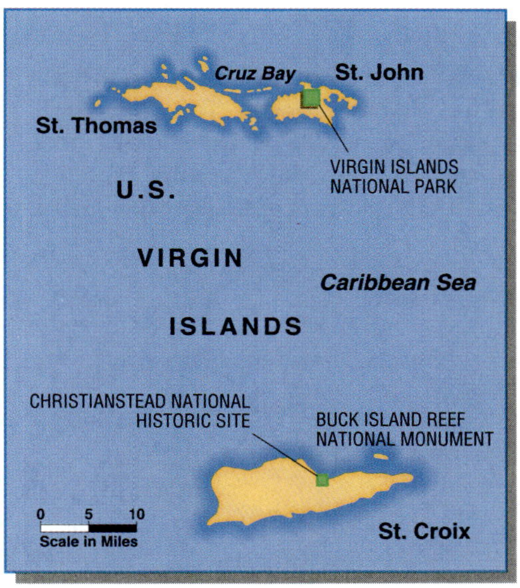

The group's advisor must plan how the group will get to the Virgin Islands. From their college, they will travel to Miami, Florida, by car, bus, train, or plane. Then to travel to St. Thomas in the Virgin Islands, they could take a plane or a ship. Suppose the advisor picks a mode of transportation at random. What is the probability that they will travel by car first and then fly?

To calculate this probability, you need to know all of the possible ways to get to St. Thomas. One method for finding this out is to draw a **tree diagram.** The tree diagram below shows how to get from the college to Miami and then to St. Thomas. The last column details all the possible combinations or **outcomes** of transportation.

Note that the number of outcomes is the product of the number of ways to Miami (4) and the number of ways to the Virgin Islands (2).

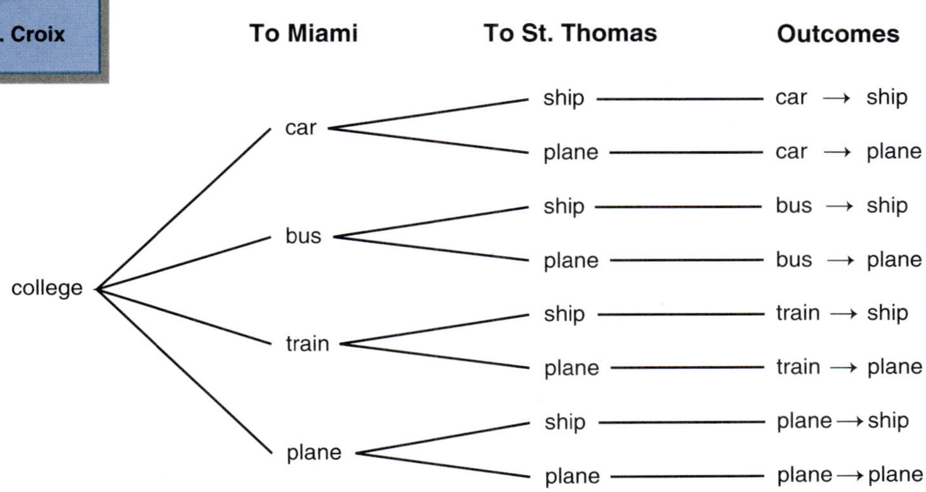

Since the mode of transportation is chosen at random, you can assume that all combinations of travel are equally likely. Since there are 8 outcomes, the probability of traveling by car first and then flying is $\frac{1}{8}$ or 0.125.

How is a compound event similar to a compound inequality?

This problem is an example of finding the probability of a **compound event.** A compound event consists of two or more **simple events.** Choosing a car, plane, train, or bus for the first part of the trip is a simple event. Then, selecting a plane or ship for the second stage of the trip is another simple event. The selection of a mode of transportation for each part of the trip is a compound event.

Example 1 **Use the tree diagram for the application at the beginning of the lesson to answer each question.**

a. What is the probability that the group will take a ship to get to St. Thomas?

b. What is the probability that the group will travel by plane for both parts of the trip?

LOOK BACK

You can find more information on probability in Lesson 4-6.

a. Since 4 of the 8 outcomes involve taking a ship, the probability is $\frac{4}{8}$ or 0.5.

b. Since only 1 outcome out of 8 involves taking a plane for both parts of the trip, the probability is $\frac{1}{8}$ or 0.125.

Refer to the application at the beginning of the lesson. Because one choice *does not affect* the others, we say that these are **independent events.** If the outcome of an event *does affect* the outcome of another event, we say that these are **dependent events.**

Example 2 **Booker T. Washington High School is having its annual Spring Carnival. The ninth grade class has decided to have a game booth. To win a small stuffed animal, a player will have to draw 2 marbles of the same color from a box containing 3 marbles—1 red, 1 white, and 1 yellow. First a marble is drawn, put back in the box, and then a second marble is drawn.**

a. What are the possible outcomes?

b. What is the probability of winning the game?

a. First, let's draw a tree diagram to see the possibilities of drawing 2 marbles of the same color.

Since the first marble is replaced, the outcome of the first selection does not affect the outcome of the second selection. Thus, they are independent events.

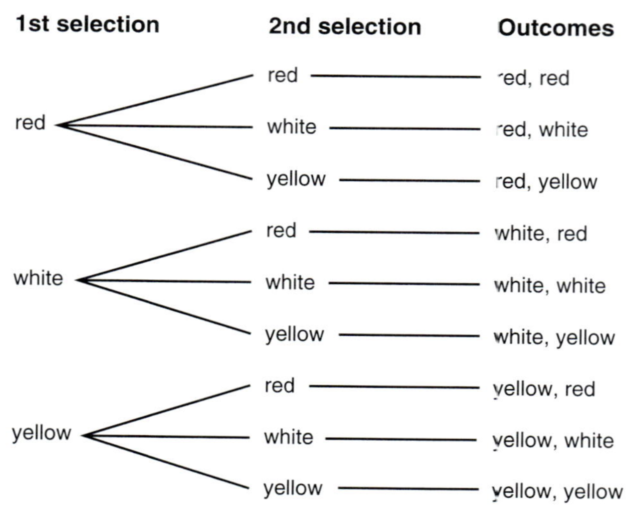

There are 9 outcomes.

b. There are 3 ways out of 9 to draw the same color twice. The probability for each draw is equally likely, so the probability is $\frac{3}{9}$ or $0.\overline{3}$.

Probability can also play an important role in determining the possible outcomes of a sporting event.

Example 3

APPLICATION

Basketball

The Rockets and the Knicks are going to play a best two out of three exhibition game series.

a. What are the possible outcomes of the series?

b. Assuming that the teams are equally matched, what is the probability that the the series will end in two games?

a. The tree diagram below shows the possible outcomes of the first two games.

1st game winner	2nd game winner	Outcomes
Rockets	Rockets	Rockets win in two games.
	Knicks	3rd game is required.
Knicks	Rockets	3rd game is required.
	Knicks	Knicks win in two games.

There are 4 possible outcomes

b. The series can end in two games in two ways. The probability is $\frac{2}{4}$ or 0.5.

CHECK FOR UNDERSTANDING

Communicating Mathematics

Study the lesson. Then complete the following.

1. **Draw** a tree diagram to represent the outcomes of tossing a coin twice.
2. **Describe** a compound event that involves three stages. Draw a tree diagram for such an event.
3. **Explain** the difference between a simple event and a compound event.
4. **Compare and contrast** the tree diagram used in Example 2 and the one used in Example 3.

MATH JOURNAL

5. Write a paragraph describing how probabilities are used in real life. Give specific examples.

Guided Practice

6. **Games** In one turn in a game, there are 13 different categories you try to complete by rolling five dice. On the first try of your turn, you roll all five dice. Then you may pick up any or all of the dice and roll again on a second and third try. To complete one of the 13 categories, you must have the same number appearing on all five dice. What is the probability that you will complete this category on the first try of a turn?

7. **Dining** For lunch at the 66 Diner, you can select one item from each of the following categories for express service guaranteed in 15 minutes.

Entree	Side Dish	Beverage
Burger	Soup	Lemonade
Sandwich	Salad	Soft Drink
Taco	French Fries	
Pizza		

a. Draw a tree diagram showing all of the meal combinations.

b. What is the probability that a customer will have soup with the meal?

c. What is the probability of selecting a burger with French fries?

d. What is the probability of having pizza with a salad and a soft drink?

EXERCISES

Applications and Problem Solving

8. **Video Games** In a computer video game, you have a choice of five roads to collect an important clue to solve a mystery. At the end of each road, there are two doors. The clue can only be found behind one door.

a. Draw a tree diagram to show the possibilities you have to find the clue.

b. What is the probability that you will find the clue?

9. **Travel** Three different airlines fly from Bowling Green to Lexington. Those same three airlines and two other airlines fly from Lexington to Louisville. There are no direct flights from Bowling Green to Louisville.

a. How many ways can a traveler book flights from Bowling Green to Louisville?

b. What is the probability that flights booked at random from Bowling Green to Louisville use the same airline?

10. **Business** On Wednesday, Ralph and Linda were talking about what they were going to wear on Friday since their company had declared it T-Shirt Day. Ralph said he only had three T-shirts he could wear to work. One was a solid color, one was an Earth Day shirt, and the other was a shirt with the company name and logo on it. He also said he would either wear tan pants or jeans. Linda is going to wear jeans and her company T-shirt. If Ralph selects a pair of pants and a T-shirt at random, what is the probability that he, too, will be wearing jeans and the company T-shirt?

11. **Food** Kita and Jason are working on the school newspaper's final layout for October. They decide that after they finish, they will go get pizza. They have a coupon for a large pizza with three toppings for $8.99. In discussing what the three toppings should be, they find they have four favorite toppings, and choosing three that both agreed upon was going to be difficult. After some discussion, they decided that pepperoni was the one topping they both agreed upon and they would put the names of the other three toppings in a bag and choose two at random. If the other three toppings are mushrooms, olives, and sausage, what is the probability they will get a pizza with mushrooms?

12. **Games** A popular floor game has a mat with four rows, each having six circles of the same color. One person uses a spinner and calls out *hand* or *foot, right* or *left,* and a color (*blue, red, green,* or *yellow*). Each player must then place that particular body part on a circle of that color. The caller continues to call out body parts and colors with the players moving in the appropriate manner. If a player falls down in the process, he or she is disqualified. The winner is the last player still in position.
   a. Draw a tree diagram to show the possibilities for body parts and colors.
   b. What is the probability that the caller will spin and say *"right hand yellow?"*

13. **Playing Cards** The deck for a card game has 57 cards. There are four suits (red, yellow, black, and green), each containing the numbers 1 to 14, and a card with a bird. Suppose there are two piles of five cards each with the cards turned face down. This first pile contains a red 3, a black 3, a red 5, a red 14, and a yellow 10. The second pile contains a green 5, a red 10, a black 10, a green 1, and a yellow 14. You are asked to draw a card from each pile.
   a. List all the possibilities of drawing two cards.
   b. What is the probability that both cards are red?
   c. What is the probability that both cards are 10s?
   d. What is the probability that both cards are green?
   e. What is the probability that the sum of the cards is at least 15?

14. **Testing** Marty is taking his final exam in algebra. He takes too long answering the calculation part of the exam to properly evaluate the last five questions, which are true-false. To keep from getting points off for not answering these questions at all, he guesses at them just as the bell rings.
   a. Draw a tree diagram to show the possible answer outcomes.
   b. What is the probability that he got at least two of the questions correct if the answers were T, F, F, T, F?
   c. Suppose Marty answered all the questions as true. Is this a good strategy to try to get the most correct without reading the question? Explain.

15. **Babies** According to the National Center for Health Statistics, each time a baby is born, the probability that it is a boy is always 51.3% and a girl is 48.7%, regardless of the sex of any previous births in the family. Suppose a couple has four children.
    a. What is the probability they are all girls?
    b. What is the probability there are one girl and three boys?
    c. How many children are there in your family? Find the probability of your family situation.

16. **Computers** The results of a survey in which students were asked how they used their computers are shown in the Venn diagram at the right. Based on these findings, what is the probability that a student, chosen at random, will use a computer only for word processing, and a second student will use it only for games?

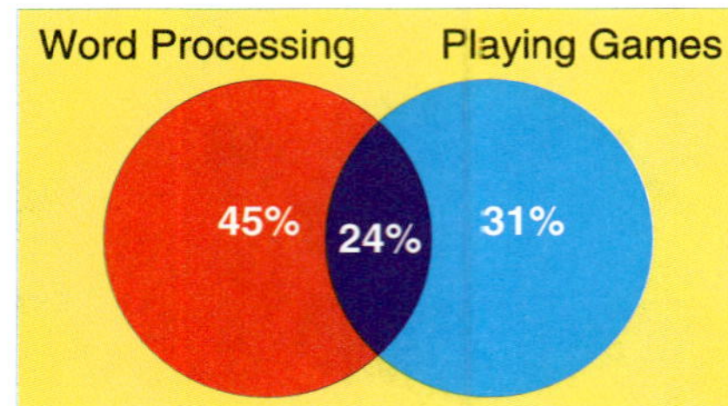

Critical Thinking

17. Every working day Adrianna either bicycles or drives to work. If she oversleeps, she drives to work 80% of the time. If she does not oversleep, she bicycles 80% of the time. She oversleeps 20% of the time. What is the probability that she will drive to work on any particular day?

18. A bag of marbles contains 2 yellow marbles, 1 blue marble, and 3 red marbles. Suppose you select one marble at random and *do not* put it back in the bag. Then you select another marble.
    a. Draw a tree diagram to model this situation. How many possible outcomes are there?
    b. What is the probability of selecting a red marble first and then a yellow one?

Mixed Review

19. **Statistics** Amy's scores on the first three of four 100-point biology tests were 88, 90, and 91. To get an A− in the class, her average must be between 88 and 92, inclusive, on all tests. What score must she receive on the fourth test to get an A− in biology? (Lesson 7–4)

20. Define a variable, write an inequality, and solve the following. Two thirds of a number is more than 99. (Lesson 7–2)

21. Determine the slope and y-intercept of the graph of $3x - y = 9$. (Lesson 6–4)

22. Solve $8r - 7t + 2 = 5(r + 2t) - 9$ for r. (Lesson 5–3)

23. Optics Peripheral vision is the ability to see around you when you keep your head and eyes pointed straight ahead. The average person with good peripheral vision can see about 180° when they are still. For a person in a moving vehicle, peripheral vision decreases as speed increases, as shown in the illustration below. (Lesson 3–4)

a. If Seth Lytle is driving at 65 mph, approximately how large is his angle of vision?

b. About how large an angle is he not seeing compared to his stationary angle of vision?

c. If there were a deer standing 50° to the right of Seth's center view and he was driving at 45 mph, would he be able to see the deer?

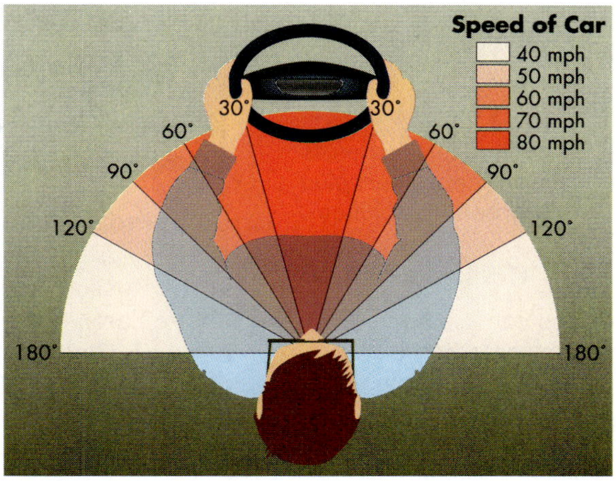

Mathematics and SOCIETY

Computers and Chess

The excerpt below appeared in an article in the January 1995 issue of *Discover* magazine.

HOW SMART HAVE COMPUTERS BECOME? Very smart, at least by one measure: this past August, a computer defeated the human world champion at chess for the first time. Russian grand master Garry Kasparov was outwitted by Genius 2, a computer program designed by an English physicist, Richard Lang, who calls himself a mediocre chess player.... Chess programs like Lang's work by focusing on what computers do best: long and intricate calculations. Before deciding on a move, the program examines each of the roughly 36 possibilities in an average game situation. For each of these 36 "branches," it looks 16 moves ahead, determining its opponent's possible countermoves, its own possible responses to each countermove, and so on. Sixteen moves ahead, the number of possible board configurations is huge. The genius of Genius 2 lies in the way it prunes the possibility tree, ruling out bad moves from the start. But the software also had help from the hardware; Lang's computer uses a speedy Intel Pentium microprocessor that can execute 166 million instructions per second. "We wouldn't have won (the computer world championship) had we not had this processor," Lang concedes. ■

1. Many chess-playing programs are written by people who are not top-level chess players. How then can these programs defeat very good players?
2. If you want to improve your chess game by practicing against a computer, would you choose a program that is below your playing level, at your level, a little above your level, or far above your level? Why?
3. Do you think it's fair to match human chess players against computers? Why or why not?
4. How might a computer use probability in determining the proper move to make?

7–6 Solving Open Sentences Involving Absolute Value

What YOU'LL LEARN

- To solve open sentences involving absolute value and graph the solutions.

Why IT'S IMPORTANT

You can use open sentences to solve problems involving space exploration, law enforcement, and entertainment.

fabulous FIRSTS

Sally Ride (1951–)

Sally Ride was the first American woman in space. She was a member of the *Challenger STS-7* crew that was launched June 18, 1983. She has a Ph.D. in physics from Stanford University.

APPLICATION

Space Exploration

On Tuesday, February 7, 1995, the space shuttle *Discovery* maneuvered within 37 feet of the Russian space station *Mir,* 245 miles above Earth. To accomplish this feat, *Discovery* had to be launched within 2.5 minutes of a designated time (12:45 A.M.). This time period is known as the *launch window.* If t represents the time elapsed since the launch countdown began and there are 300 minutes scheduled from the beginning of the countdown to blast-off, you can write the following inequality to represent the launch window.

$|300 - t| \leq 2.5$ *The difference between 300 minutes and the actual time elapsed since the countdown began must be less than or equal to 2.5 minutes.*

We use absolute value because $300 - t$ cannot be negative.

There are three types of open sentences that can involve absolute value. They are as follows, when n is nonnegative.

$|x| = n \qquad |x| < n \qquad |x| > n$

First let's consider the case of $|x| = n$.

If $|x| = 4$, this means that the difference from 0 to x is 4 units.

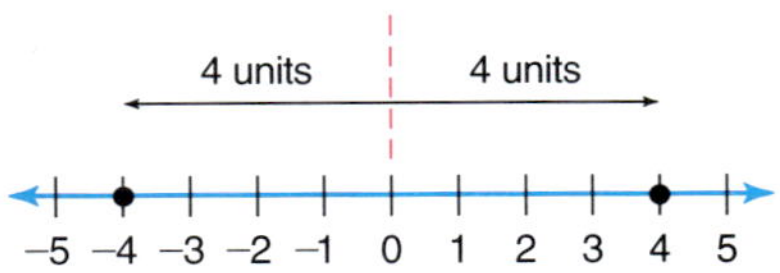

The solution set can also be written as $\{x \mid x = -4 \text{ or } x = 4\}$.

Therefore, if $|x| = 4$, then $x = -4$ or $x = 4$. The solution set is $\{-4, 4\}$. So, if $|x| = n$, then $x = -n$ or $x = n$.

Equations involving absolute value can be solved by graphing them on a number line or by writing them as a compound sentence and solving it.

Example 1 **Solve $|x - 3| = 5$.**

Method 1: Graphing

$|x - 3| = 5$ means the distance between x and 3 is 5 units. To find x on the number line, start at 3 and move 5 units in either direction.

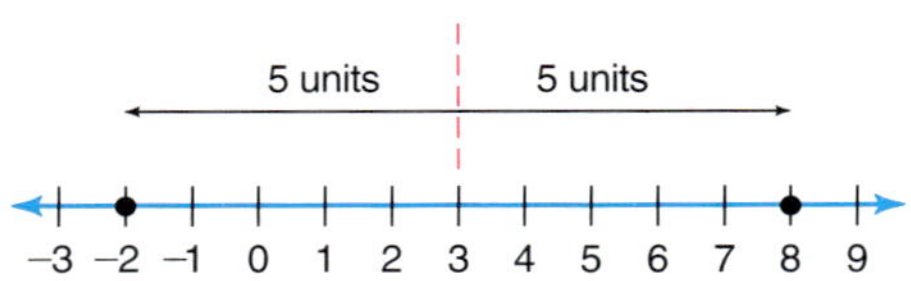

The solution set is $\{-2, 8\}$.

Method 2: Compound Sentence

$|x - 3| = 5$ also means $x - 3 = 5$ or $-(x - 3) = 5$.

$$x - 3 = 5 \quad \text{or} \quad -(x - 3) = 5$$
$$x - 3 + 3 = 5 + 3 \qquad x - 3 = -5 \quad \textit{Multiply each side by } -1.$$
$$x = 8 \qquad x - 3 + 3 = -5 + 3$$
$$x = -2$$

This verifies the solution set.

Now let's consider the case of $|x| < n$. Inequalities involving absolute value can also be represented on a number line or as compound inequalities. Let's examine $|x| < 4$.

$|x| < 4$ means that the distance from 0 to x is less than 4 units.

When the inequality is $<$ or $\leq$, the compound sentence uses *<u>and</u>*.

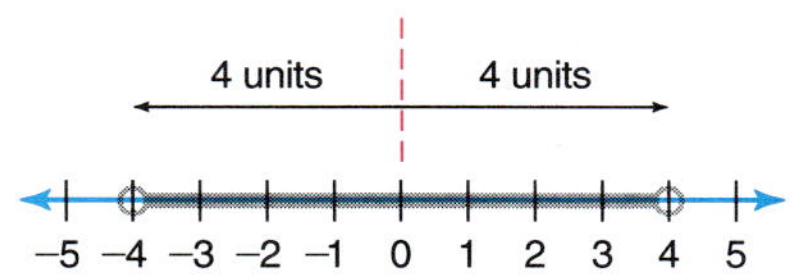

Therefore, $x > -4$ and $x < 4$. The solution set is $\{x \mid -4 < x < 4\}$. So, if $|x| < n$, then $x > -n$ and $x < n$.

Example 2 **Solve $|3 + 2x| < 11$ and graph the solution set.**

$|3 + 2x| < 11$ means $3 + 2x < 11$ and $3 + 2x > -11$.

$$3 + 2x < 11 \quad \text{and} \quad 3 + 2x > -11$$
$$3 - 3 + 2x < 11 - 3 \qquad 3 - 3 + 2x > -11 - 3$$
$$2x < 8 \qquad 2x > -14$$
$$\frac{2x}{2} < \frac{8}{2} \qquad \frac{2x}{2} > \frac{-14}{2}$$
$$x < 4 \qquad x > -7$$

The solution set is $\{x \mid x > -7 \text{ and } x < 4\}$, which can be written as $\{x \mid -7 < x < 4\}$.

Now graph the solution set.

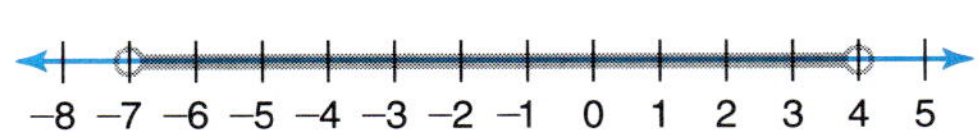

Finally let's examine $|x| > 4$. This means that the distance from 0 to x is greater than 4 units.

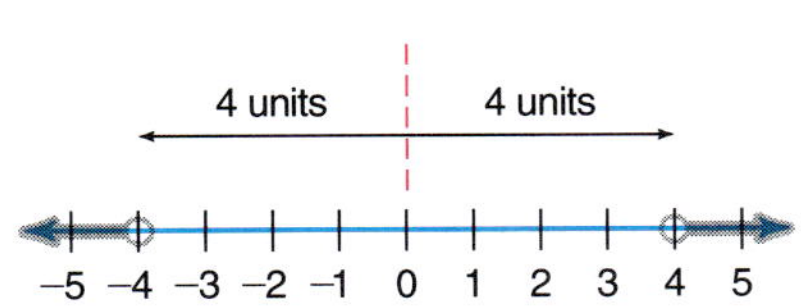

When the inequality is $>$ or $\geq$, the compound sentence uses *<u>or</u>*.

Therefore, $x < -4$ or $x > 4$. The solution set is $\{x \mid x < -4 \text{ or } x > 4\}$. So, if $|x| > n$, then $x < -n$ or $x > n$.

Example 3 Solve $|5 + 2y| \geq 3$ and graph the solution set.

$|5 + 2y| \geq 3$ means $5 + 2y \leq -3$ or $5 + 2y \geq 3$.

$$
\begin{aligned}
5 + 2y &\leq -3 & \text{or} \quad 5 + 2y &\geq 3 \\
5 - 5 + 2y &\leq -3 - 5 & 5 - 5 + 2y &\geq 3 - 5 \\
2y &\leq -8 & 2y &\geq -2 \\
\frac{2y}{2} &\leq \frac{-8}{2} & \frac{2y}{2} &\geq \frac{-2}{2} \\
y &\leq -4 & y &\geq -1
\end{aligned}
$$

The solution set is $\{y \mid y \leq -4 \text{ or } y \geq -1\}$.

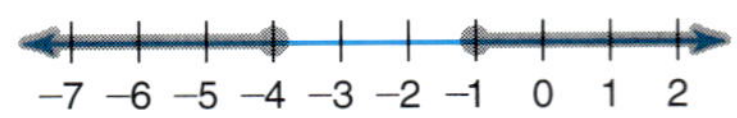

Organizations such as OSHA set standards for buildings to meet the needs of those using the building. Building code standards are often written as maximums or minimums that must be met. These standards can be written as inequalities.

Example 4

APPLICATION

Construction

There are a number of specifications in the building industry that address the needs of physically-challenged persons. For example, hallways in hospitals must have handrails. The handrails must be placed within a range of 2 inches from a height of 36 inches.

a. Write an open sentence that involves absolute value to represent the range of acceptable heights for hallway handrails.

b. Find and graph the corresponding compound sentence.

a. Let h be an acceptable height for the handrail. Then h can differ from 36 inches by no more than 2 inches. Write an open sentence that represents the range of acceptable heights.

h differs from 36	*by less than or equal to*	*2.*
$\lvert h - 36 \rvert$	$\leq$	2

Now, solve $|h - 36| \leq 2$ to find the compound sentence.

$$
\begin{aligned}
h - 36 &\geq -2 & \text{and} \quad h - 36 &\leq 2 \\
h - 36 + 36 &\geq -2 + 36 & h - 36 + 36 &\leq 2 + 36 \\
h &\geq 34 & h &\leq 38
\end{aligned}
$$

The compound sentence is $34 \leq h \leq 38$.

b. The graph of this sentence is shown below.

So, the handrail must be placed between 34 and 38, inclusive, inches from the floor.

CHECK FOR UNDERSTANDING

Communicating Mathematics

Study the lesson. Then complete the following.

1. **Describe** two ways you can solve an open sentence involving an absolute value.
2. **Explain** the difference in the solution for $|x + 7| > 4$ and the solution for $|x + 7| < 4$.
3. If $x < 0$ and $|x| = n$, describe n in terms of x.
4. **You Decide** Jamila's teacher said they should work out each problem and test points to determine whether their solutions are correct. Jamila thinks that she knows the solution for problems like $|w + 5| < 0$, where the absolute value quantity is always less than 0, without testing points. Is she correct? Why or why not?

Guided Practice

Choose the replacement set that makes each open sentence true.

5. $|x - 7| = 2$
   a. $\{9, -5\}$ **b.** $\{5, -9\}$ **c.** $\{5, 9\}$ **d.** $\varnothing$
6. $|x - 2| > 4$
   a. $\{x | -2 < x < 6\}$ **b.** $\{x | x = 6 \text{ or } x = 2\}$
   c. $\{x | x > 6 \text{ or } x > -2\}$ **d.** $\{x | x < -2 \text{ or } x > 6\}$

State which graph below matches each open sentence in Exercises 7–10.

7. $|y| = 3$
8. $|y| > 3$
9. $|y| < 3$
10. $|y| \leq 3$

a. 

b. 

c. 

d. 

Solve each open sentence. Then graph the solution set.

11. $|m| \geq 5$
12. $|n| < 6$
13. $|r + 3| < 6$
14. $|8 - t| \geq 3$

For each graph, write an open sentence involving absolute value.

15. 

16. 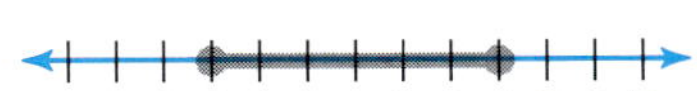

EXERCISES

Practice

Solve each open sentence. Then graph the solution set.

17. $|y - 2| = 4$

18. $|3 - 3x| = 0$

19. $|7x + 2| = -2$

20. $|w + 8| \geq 1$

21. $|2 - y| \leq 1$

22. $|t + 4| \geq 3$

23. $|4y - 8| < 0$

24. $|2x + 5| < 4$

25. $|3e - 7| < 2$

26. $|3x + 4| < 8$

27. $|1 - 3y| > -2$

28. $3 + |x| > 3$

29. $|8 - (w - 1)| \leq 9$

30. $|6 - (11 - b)| = -3$

31. $|2.2y - 1.1| = 5.5$

32. $|3r - 0.5| \geq 5.5$

33. $\left|\frac{2 - 3x}{5}\right| \geq 2$

34. $\left|\frac{1}{2} - 3p\right| < \frac{7}{2}$

Express each statement in terms of an inequality involving absolute value. Do *not* try to solve.

35. The diameter of the lead in a pencil p must be within 0.01 millimeters of 1 millimeter.

36. The cruise control of a car set at 55 mph should keep the speed s within 3 mph of 55 mph.

37. A liquid at 50°C will change to a gas or liquid if the temperature t increases or decreases more than 50°C.

For each graph, write an open sentence involving absolute value.

38.
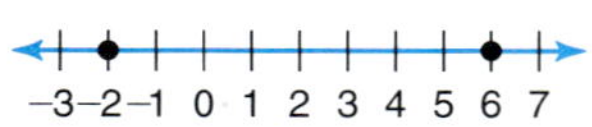

39.
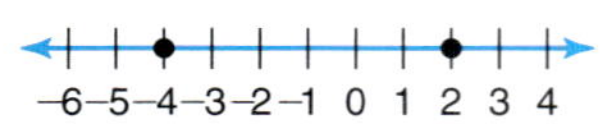

40.
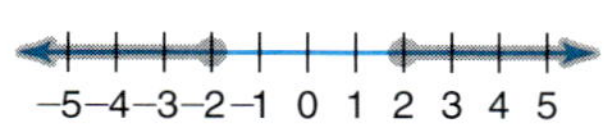

41.
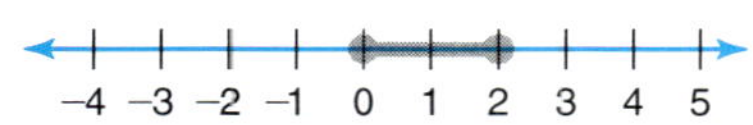

42.
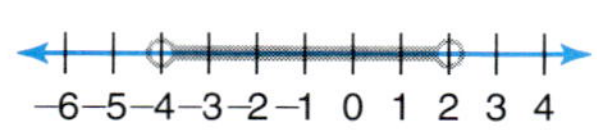

43.

44. Find all integer solutions of $|x| < 4$.

45. Find all integer solutions of $|x| \leq 2$.

46. If $a > 0$, how many integer solutions exist for $|x| < a$?

47. If $a > 0$, how many integer solutions exist for $|x| \leq a$?

Critical Thinking

48. Solve $|y - 3| = |2 + y|$.

49. For $a \neq 0$, is $-|a|$ *sometimes, always,* or *never* negative? positive? Explain.

50. Suppose $8 \leq x \leq 12$. Write an absolute value inequality that is equivalent to this compound inequality.

Applications and Problem Solving

51. Probability Suppose $|x| \leq 6$ and x is an integer. Find the probability of $|x|$ being a factor of 18.

52. Chemistry For hydrogen to be a liquid, its temperature must be within 2°C of −257°C. What is the range of temperatures for this substance to remain a liquid?

53. **Law Enforcement** A radar gun used to determine the speed of passing cars must be within 7 mph of the actual speed of a selected car. If a highway patrol officer reads a speed of 59 mph for a car, does he have irrefutable evidence that the car was speeding in a 55 mph zone? Explain your reasoning and include a graph.

54. **Space Exploration** Refer to the application at the beginning of the lesson. Find how much time can elapse from the beginning of the countdown to remain within the launch window.

55. **Entertainment** Luis Gomez is a contestant on a television game show. He must guess within \$1500 of the actual price of a car without going over in order to win the car. The actual price of the car is \$18,000. What is the range of guesses in which Luis can win the vehicle?

56. **Spending** The graph below shows the spending power of kids aged 3 to 17.

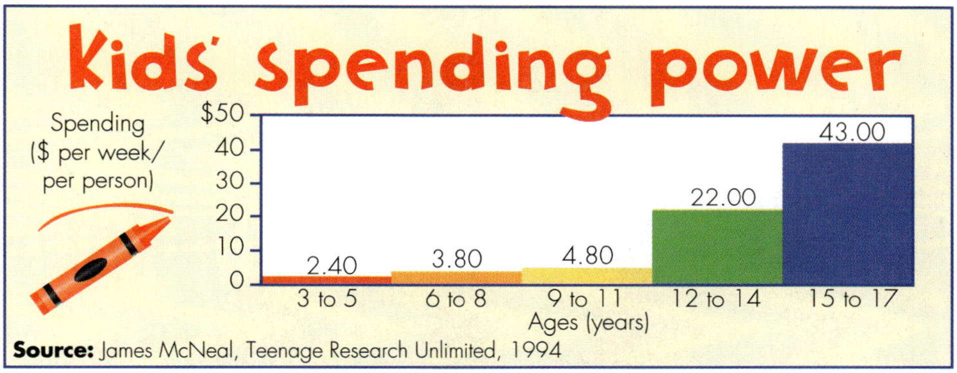

a. Write an inequality that represents the spending power of 3- to 17-year olds. Then write an absolute value inequality that describes their spending.

b. Write an inequality that represents the spending power of 12- to 17-year olds. Then write an absolute value inequality that describes their spending.

c. Keep a record of how much money you spend in a week. How does your spending compare with the data in this graph?

Mixed Review

57. **Draw a Diagram** The Sanchez family acts as a host family for foreign exchange students during each quarter of the year. Suppose it is equally likely that they get a boy or a girl each quarter. (Lesson 7–5)

a. Draw a tree diagram to represent the possible orders of boys (B) and girls (G) during the four quarters of the year. List the possible outcomes.

b. From the tree diagram, what is the probability that all of the students will be girls? boys?

c. From the tree diagram, what is the probability that they will host two boys and two girls?

58. Peter wants to buy Crystal an engagement ring. He wants to spend between \$1700 and \$2200. If he goes shopping during a 12%-off sale to celebrate the store's 12th anniversary, what would his price range be? (Lesson 7–4)

59. Solve $10x - 2 \geq 4(x - 2)$. (Lesson 7–3)

Solve each inequality.

60. $396 > -11t$ (Lesson 7–2)

61. $-11 \leq k - (-4)$ (Lesson 7–1)

62. Find the coordinates of the midpoint of the line segment whose endpoints are at $(-4, 1)$ and $(10, 3)$. (Lesson 6–7)

63. Graph $2x - 9 = 2y$. (Lesson 5–4)

64. **Architecture** Julie is making a model of a house for her drafting class. One part of the house has a triangle like the one below. She wants the base of the triangle to measure 2 inches. What will be the measures of the other two sides? (Lesson 4–2)

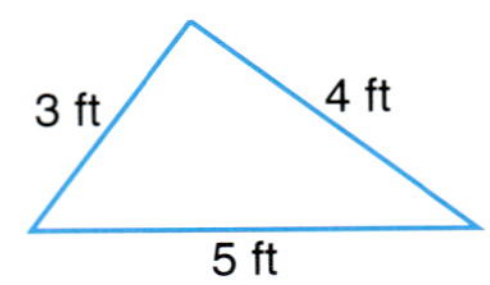

65. Solve $2m + \frac{3}{4}n = \frac{1}{2}m - 9$ for m. (Lesson 3–6)

66. Simplify $\frac{-42r + 18}{3}$. (Lesson 2–7)

WORKING ON THE In·ves·ti·ga·tion

Refer to the Investigation on pages 320–321.

Smoke Gets In Your Eyes

Smoking increases the chance of health problems. Constant exposure to secondhand smoke also puts the nonsmoker at risk. According to a statement from a tobacco company, a nonsmoker working among smoking coworkers inhales the smoke of 1.25 cigarettes per month. A restaurant worker in the smoking section breathes just 2 cigarettes per month. The Environmental Protection Agency (EPA) disagrees with these data.

1 Write an equation to express the equivalent number of cigarettes one would breathe if he/she worked in the smoking section of a restaurant for one year.

2 A lawsuit involving the tobacco industry and the EPA states that the EPA did not use the standard significance level of 5% in evaluating their data from various studies. A 5% level means that their numerical conclusions have a 5% margin of error. How does the margin of error relate to absolute value?

3 In January, 1995, the average price of a pack of cigarettes was \$2.06, of which 56¢ is federal and state excise tax. The price of cigarettes is on the rise. Write an inequality to represent how much is spent by the average smoker in a year. Solve the inequality.

4 How much tax revenue is generated by the sale of cigarettes to the estimated number of smokers in the United States?

Add the results of your work to your Investigation Folder.

7–7

Integration: Statistics
Box-and-Whisker Plots

What YOU'LL LEARN

- To display and interpret data on box-and-whisker plots.

Why IT'S IMPORTANT

Box-and-whisker plots are a useful way to display data. They allow you to see important characteristics of the data at a glance.

APPLICATION
Olympics

In 1992, the site of the Summer Games of the XXV Olympiad was Barcelona, Spain. More than 14,000 athletes from 172 nations competed for medals in 257 events. The table at the right shows the number of gold medals won by the top 16 medal-winning teams.

1992 SUMMER OLYMPICS Top 16 Medal Winners

Team	Number of Medals Won: Gold	Number of Medals Won: Total
Unified Team (formerly USSR)	45	112
USA	37	108
Germany	33	82
China	16	54
Cuba	14	31
Hungary	11	30
South Korea	12	29
France	8	29
Australia	7	27
Spain	13	22
Japan	3	22
Britain	5	20
Italy	6	19
Poland	3	19
Canada	6	18
Romania	4	18

Source: *The World Almanac, 1995*

We can describe these data using the mean, median, and mode. We can also use the median, along with the quartiles and interquartile range, to obtain a graphic representation of the data. A type of diagram, or graph, that shows quartiles and extreme values of data is called a **box-and-whisker plot.**

Box-and-whisker plots are sometimes called box plots.

Suppose we wanted to make a box-and-whisker plot of the numbers of gold medals won by each of the nations in the table. First, arrange the data in numerical order. Next, compute the median and quartiles. Also, identify the extreme values.

3 3 4 5 6 6 7 (8 ↑ 11) 12 13 14 16 33 37 45

median (Q2)

LOOK BACK

You can refer to Lesson 3-7 for information on measures of central tendency and Lesson 5-7 for measures of variation.

The median for this set of data is the average of the eighth and ninth values.

$$\text{median} = \frac{8 + 11}{2} \text{ or } 9.5$$

The median is not included in either half of the data.

Recall that the *lower quartile* (Q1) is the median of the lower half of the distribution of values. The *upper quartile* (Q3) is the median of the upper half of the data.

(3 3 4 5 ↑ 6 6 7 8) (11 12 13 14 ↑ 16 33 37 45)

Q1 Q3

$$Q1 = \frac{5 + 6}{2} \text{ or } 5.5 \qquad Q3 = \frac{14 + 16}{2} \text{ or } 15$$

The **extreme values** are the least value (LV), 3, and the greatest value (GV), 45.

Now we have the information we need to draw a box-and-whisker plot.

Step 1 Draw a number line. Assign a scale to the number line that includes the extreme values. Plot dots to represent the extreme values (LV and GV), the upper and lower quartile points (Q3 and Q1), and the median (Q2).

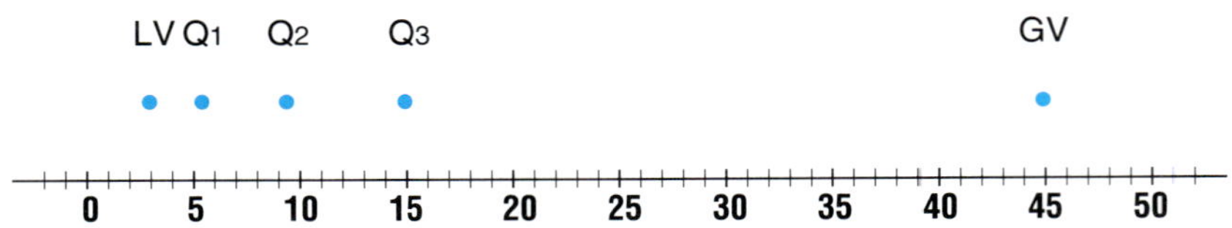

The median line will not always divide the box into equal parts.

Step 2 Draw a box to designate the data falling between the upper and lower quartiles. Draw a vertical line through the point representing the median. Draw a segment from the lower quartile to the least value and one from the upper quartile to the greatest value. These segments are the **whiskers** of the plot.

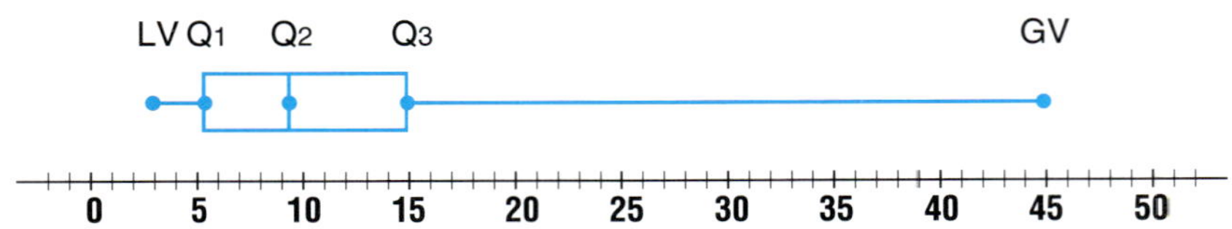

TECHNOLOGY *Tip*

You can use your graphing calculator to find the values you need to make a box-and-whisker plot. Refer to Lesson 5–7A for instructions on finding these values.

Even though the whiskers are different lengths, each whisker contains at least one fourth of the data while the box contains one half of the data. Compound inequalities can be used to describe the data in each fourth. Assume that the replacement set for x is the set of data.

1st fourth	$\{x \mid x < 5.5\}$
2nd fourth	$\{x \mid 5.5 < x < 9.5\}$
3rd fourth	$\{x \mid 9.5 < x < 15\}$
4th fourth	$\{x \mid x > 15\}$

Step 3 Before finishing the box-and-whisker plot, check for outliers. In Lesson 5–7, you learned that an outlier is any element of the set of data that is at least 1.5 interquartile ranges above the upper quartile or below the lower quartile. Recall that the *interquartile range* (IQR) is the difference between the upper and lower quartiles, or in this case, $15 - 5.5$ or 9.5.

$x \geq Q3 + 1.5(IQR)$	or	$x \leq Q1 - 1.5(IQR)$
$x \geq 15 + 1.5(9.5)$		$x \leq 5.5 - 1.5(9.5)$
$x \geq 15 + 14.25$		$x \leq 5.5 - 14.25$
$x \geq 29.25$		$x \leq -8.75$

Step 4 If x is an outlier in this set of data, then the outliers can be described as $\{x \mid x \leq -8.75 \text{ or } x \geq 29.5\}$. In this case, there are no data less than -8.75. However, 45, 37, and 33 are greater than 29.25, so they are outliers. We now need to revise the box-and-whisker plot. Outliers are plotted as isolated points, and the right whisker is shortened to stop at 16.

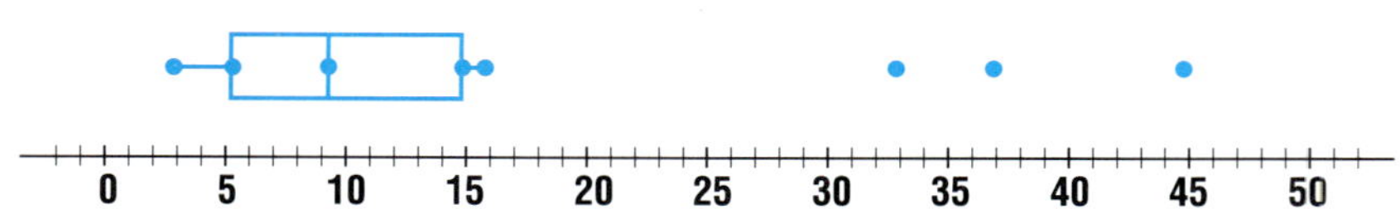

Example

Refer to the application at the beginning of the lesson. Use the box-and-whisker plot for the gold medals to answer each question.

a. What percent of the teams won between 6 and 15 gold medals?

b. What does the box-and-whisker plot tell us about the upper half of the data compared to the lower half?

a. The box in the plot indicates 50% of the values in the distribution. Since the box goes from 5.5 to 15, we know that 50% of the teams won between 6 and 15 gold medals.

b. The upper half of the data is spread out while the lower half is fairly clustered together.

CHECK FOR UNDERSTANDING

Communicating Mathematics

Study the lesson. Then complete the following.

1. **Explain** how to determine the scale of the number line in a box-and-whisker plot.
2. **Describe** which two points the two whiskers of a box-and-whisker plot connect.
3. What does Q2 represent?
4. Refer to the box-and-whisker plot at the right. Assume that LV, Q1, Q2, Q3, and GV are whole numbers.

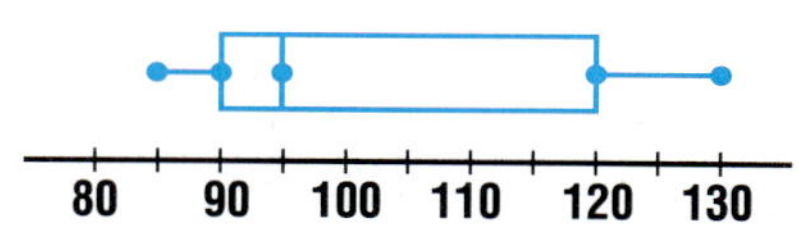

   a. What percent of the data is between 85 and 90?
   b. Between what two values does the middle 50% of the data lie?
   c. What outliers are represented in the box-and-whisker plot?
5. **Describe** what characteristics of a set of data you can gather from its box-and-whisker plot. What are some things you cannot gather from a box-and-whisker plot?

Guided Practice

6. The table at the right shows the birthrates for 15 selected countries.
   a. Find the median, upper quartile, lower quartile, and interquartile range for each year's data.
   b. Are there any outliers? If so, name them.
   c. Draw a box-and-whisker plot for each set of data on the same number line.
   d. Which set of data seems to be more clustered? Why?

Birth Rates for Selected Countries
(per 1000 population)

Country	1985	1992
Australia	15.7	15.1
Cuba	18.0	14.5
Denmark	10.6	13.1
France	13.9	12.9
Hong Kong	14.0	11.9
Israel	23.5	21.5
Italy	10.1	9.9
Japan	11.9	9.7
Netherlands	12.3	13.0
Panama	26.6	23.3
Poland	18.2	13.4
Portugal	12.8	11.4
Singapore	16.6	17.7
Switzerland	11.6	12.6
United States	15.7	15.7

Source: United Nations, *Monthly Bulletin of Statistics*, May 1994

7. Refer to box-and-whisker plots A and B.

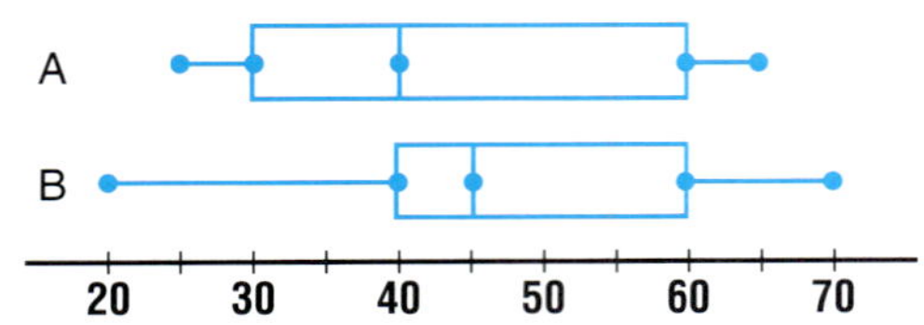

   a. Estimate the least value, greatest value, lower quartile, upper quartile, and median for each plot. Assume that these values are whole numbers.
   b. Which set of data contains the least value?
   c. Which plot has the greatest interquartile range?
   d. Which plot has the greatest range?

EXERCISES

Applications and Problem Solving

8. **Manufacturing** The box-and-whisker plots at the right show the results of testing the useful life of 10 light bulbs each from two manufacturers.

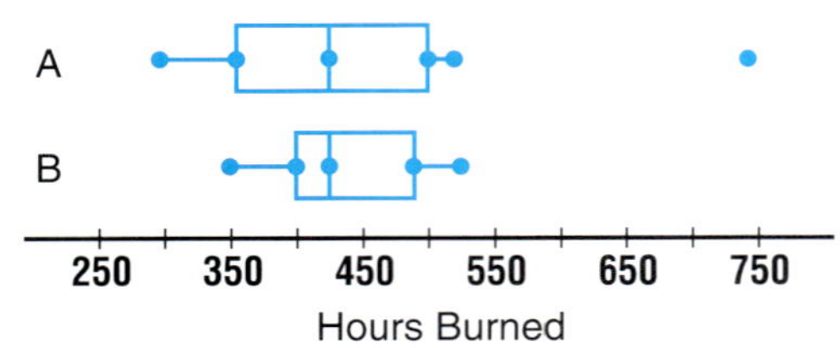

   a. Which test had the most varied results?
   b. Were there any outliers? If so, for which brand?
   c. How would you compare the medians of the tests?
   d. Based on this plot, from which manufacturer would you buy your light bulbs? Why?

9. **Meteorology** Meteorologists keep track of temperatures for four 90-day periods during the year to predict the trends in weather for future years. The following low temperatures were recorded during a 2-week cold snap in Indianapolis during 1993.

$$30°, 20°, 2°, 12°, 5°, 4°, 17°, 7°, 6°, 16°, 5°, 0°, 5°, 16°$$

   a. Find the median, upper quartile, lower quartile, and interquartile range.
   b. Are there any outliers? If so, name them.
   c. Draw a box-and-whisker plot of the data.

10. **Football** The table below shows the American Football Conference's leading quarterbacks in touchdowns for the 1993 season. Make a box-and-whisker plot for the data.

1993 AFC Individual Leaders in Passing

Player	Team	Touchdowns
Steve DeBerg	Miami	7
John Elway	Denver	25
Boomer Esiason	N.Y. Jets	16
John Friesz	San Diego	6
Jeff George	Indianapolis	8
Jeff Hostetler	L.A. Raiders	14
Jim Kelly	Buffalo	18
Scott Mitchell	Miami	12
Joe Montana	Kansas City	13
Warren Moon	Houston	21
Neil O'Donnell	Pittsburgh	14
Vinny Testaverde	Cleveland	14

Source: *The World Almanac, 1995*

11. **Demographics** According to the 1990 Census, the American Indian population in the United States is 1.959 million. Many American Indian people live on reservations or trust lands. The stem-and-leaf plot shows the number of reservations in the 34 states that have them.

Stem	Leaf
0	1 1 1 1 1 1 1 1 1 1 1 1 1 2
•	3 3 3 3 3 4 4 4 4 7 7 8 8 9
1	1 4 9
2	3 5 7
9	6 *9 | 6 = 96*

a. Make a box-and-whisker plot of these data.
b. Describe the distribution of the data.
c. Why do you think there are so many outliers?
d. The mean of these data is about 8.8. How does this compare with the median?

12. **Environment** The table below shows the number of hazardous waste sites in 25 states.

Hazardous Waste Sites in the United States (selected states)

State	No.	State	No.	State	No.	State	No.	State	No.
AL	13	FL	57	LA	13	OH	38	TN	17
AR	12	GA	13	MD	13	OK	11	TX	30
CA	96	IL	37	MI	77	OR	12	VA	25
CO	18	IN	33	NY	85	PA	101	WA	56
CT	16	KY	20	NC	22	SC	24	WV	6

Source: Environmental Protection Agency, May 1994

a. Make a box-and-whisker plot of the data.
b. What is the median number of waste sites for the states listed?
c. Which states, if any, are outliers?
d. Which half of the data is more widely dispersed?

13. **Education** The graph below shows the average American College Testing (ACT) Program mathematics scores for students from 1985–1993.

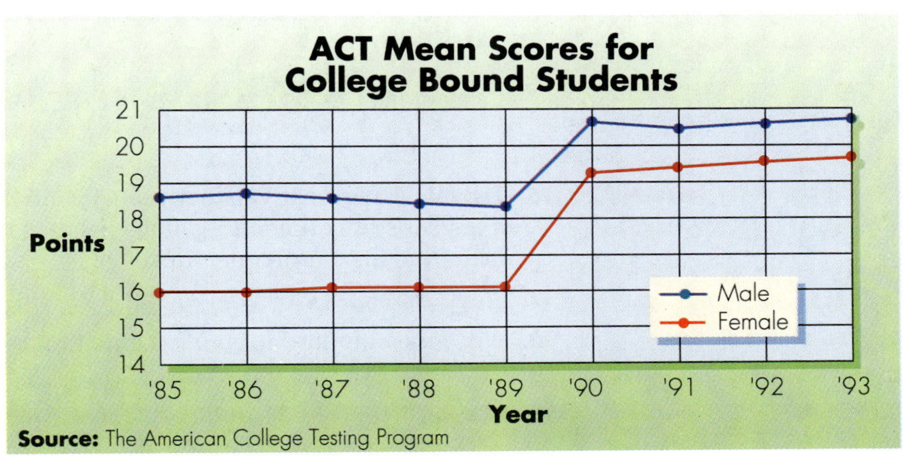

(continued on the next page)

a. Make a box-and-whisker plot of the scores for the male students and another for the female students using the same scale. Compare the plots.

b. In a particular year, an entirely new ACT Assessment was given that emphasized rhetorical skills, advanced mathematics items, and a new reading test. From the data on the graph, in which year do you think this occurred? Why?

14. **History** Did you know that there have been more U.S. vice-presidents than presidents? As of 1995, there have been 41 presidents and 45 vice-presidents. Some presidents had more than one vice-president, and some had none. The line plot below shows the ages of vice-presidents on their inauguration days.

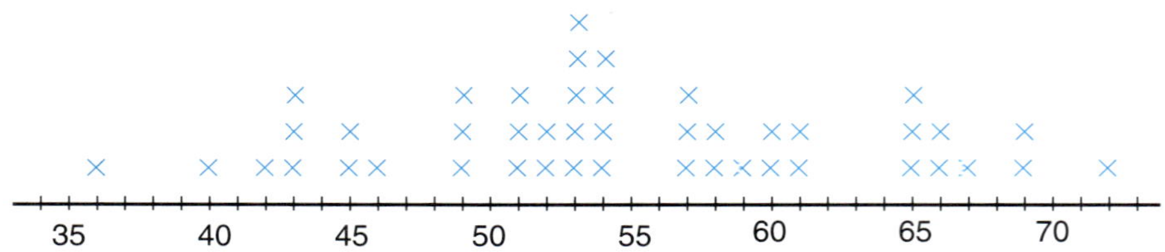

Source: *The World Almanac,* 1995

a. Make a box-and-whisker plot of these data.

b. The ages for presidents on their inauguration days have the following statistics: LV = 42, $Q_1 = 51$, $Q_2 = 55$, $Q_3 = 58$, GV = 68, and 69 is an outlier. Make a box-and-whisker plot to represent these ages.

c. Which set of data is more clustered? Explain your answer.

d. Fourteen vice-presidents went on to become presidents. Which ages of vice-presidents were definitely not those who went on to become president?

Critical Thinking

15. The box-and-whisker plots shown below picture the distribution of test scores in two algebra classes taught by two different teachers. If you could select one of the classes to be in, which one would it be, and why?

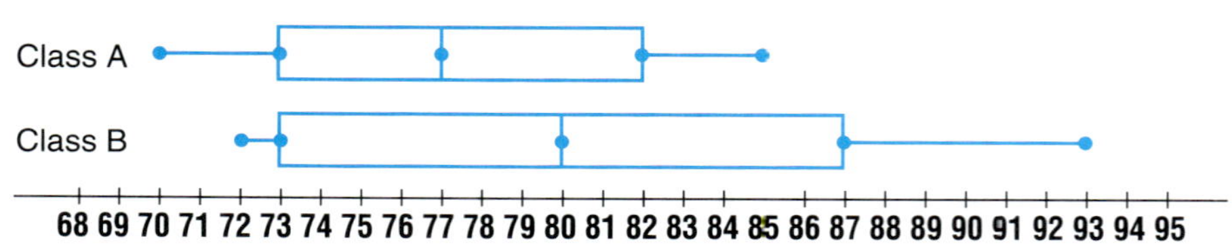

Mixed Review

16. **Travel** Greg's car gets between 18 and 21 miles per gallon of gasoline. If his car's tank holds 15 gallons, what is the range of distances that Greg can drive his car on one tank of gas? (Lesson 7–6)

17. Solve $2m - 3 > 7$ or $2m + 7 > 9$. (Lesson 7–4)

18. Write the standard form of an equation of the line that passes through (4, 7) and (1, −2). (Lesson 6–2)

19. Graph (0, 6), (8, −1), and (−3, 2). (Lesson 5–1)

20. Solve $\frac{6}{x-3} = \frac{3}{4}$. (Lesson 4–1)

7–7B Graphing Technology
Box-and-Whisker Plots

An Extension of Lesson 7–7

You can use a graphing calculator to compare two sets of data by using a double box-and-whisker plot. The plots that the calculator draws, however, do not account for outliers. If you want to use a graphing calculator to help you sketch a plot, it will be necessary for you to check for outliers and adjust the graph as needed.

In an experiment, the ability of boys and girls to identify objects held in their left hands versus those held in their right hands was tested. The left side of the body is controlled by the right side of the brain and vice versa. The results of the experiment found that the boys did not identify objects with their right hand as well as with their left. The girls could identify objects equally as well with either hand.

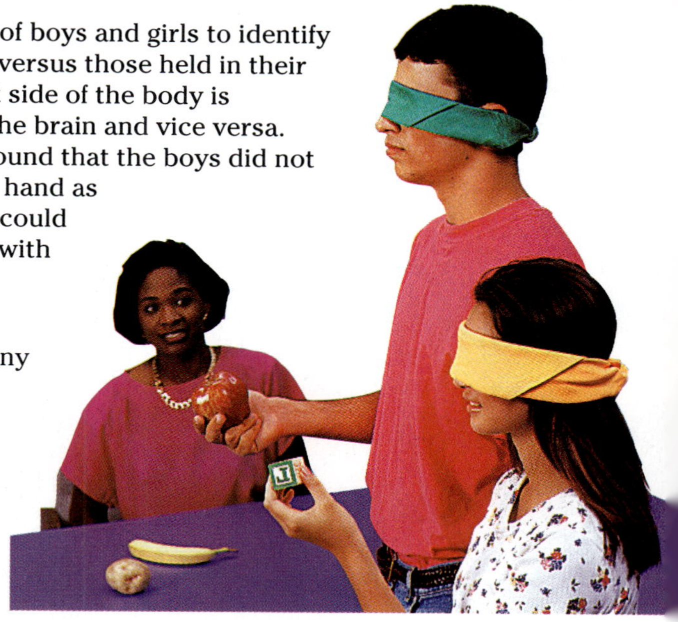

A graphing calculator company decided to test this premise by conducting the same tests with 12 male and 10 female employees, chosen at random. Thirty small objects were selected and separated into two groups—one for the right hand and one for the left hand. Blindfolded employees felt each of the objects with the prescribed hand and tried to identify them. The results are presented in the chart below.

LOOK BACK

For more information on entering data into lists on the graphing calculator, see Lesson 5-7A.

Each employee had a score for left and right hands.

Correct Responses			
Female Left Hand	Female Right Hand	Male Left Hand	Male Right Hand
8	4	7	12
9	3	8	6
12	7	7	12
11	12	5	12
10	11	7	7
8	11	8	11
12	13	11	12
7	12	4	8
9	11	10	12
11	12	14	11
		13	9
		5	9

Make a double box-and-whisker plot of the data to compare the results of Female Left Hand with Female Right Hand using a graphing calculator.

Step 1 Clear lists L1, L2, L3, and L4. Enter the data from each column of the table into lists L1, L2, L3, and L4, respectively.

Step 2 Select the box-and-whisker plot and define which list will be used.

Enter: [2nd] [STAT PLOT] 1 [ENTER] *Turns plot on.*

[▼] [▶] [▶] [ENTER] *Selects box-and-whisker plot.*

If L1 is not highlighted in the Xlist, use the down arrow and [ENTER] to highlight it and make sure the frequency is set for 1.

Repeat the process to assign Plot2 as a box-and-whisker plot using L2.

Step 3 Clear the Y= list. Set the WINDOW settings for Xscl = 1, Ymin = 0, and Yscl = 0. Ignore the other settings. Press [ZOOM] 9 to select ZoomStat. This sets the other settings and displays the box-and-whisker plots. It will only display those plots that you have turned on.

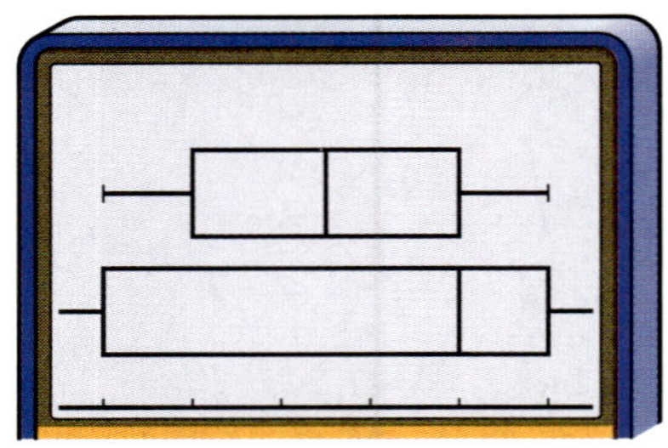

Step 4 Use [TRACE] to examine the minX (least value), Q1 (lower quartile), Med (median), Q3 (upper quartile), and maxX (greatest value).

EXERCISES

1. Which set of data does the upper plot represent?

2. Observe the two graphs. Does it appear that the females guessed correctly more often with the left hand or the right? How do you know?

3. Reset your calculator to define Plot1 as L3 and Plot 2 as L4 to examine the males' data. What do you observe in these plots?

4. Reset the calculator to compare the left-hand results of males and females. Were the males or females better at guessing with their left hands?

5. Reset the calculator to compare the right-hand results of males and females. Which group seemed more adept at identifying objects with their right hands?

6. How do the results of this experiment compare with the study of boys and girls mentioned at the beginning of this lesson? What reasons may account for any discrepancies?

7–8A Graphing Technology
Graphing Inequalities

A Preview of Lesson 7–8

Inequalities in two variables can be graphed on a graphing calculator using the "Shade(" command, which is option 7 on the DRAW menu. You must enter *two* functions to activate the shading since the calculator always shades between two specified functions. The first function entered defines the lower boundary of the region to be shaded. The second function defines the upper boundary of the region. The calculator graphs both functions and shades between the two.

Example 1 **Graph $y \geq 2x - 3$ in the standard viewing window.**

Before using the "Shade(" option, be sure to clear any equations stored in the Y= list, and press ZOOM 6 for the standard viewing window.

The inequality refers to points at which y is *greater than or equal to* $2x - 3$. This means we want to shade above the graph of $y = 2x - 3$. Since the calculator screen shows only part of the coordinate plane, we can use the top of the screen, Ymax or 10, as the upper boundary and $2x - 3$ as the lower boundary.

Enter: 2nd DRAW 7 2 X,T,θ,n – 3 , 10) ENTER

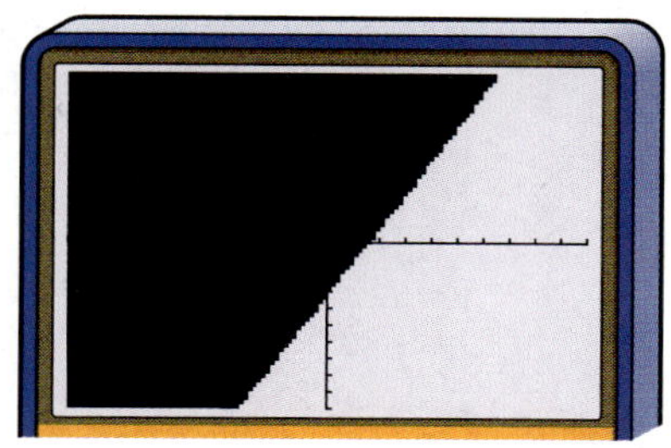

Since both the x- and y-intercepts of the graph and the origin are within the current viewing window, the graph of the inequality is complete.

When finished, press 2nd DRAW 1 to clear the screen.

Example 2 **Graph $y - x \leq 1$ in the standard viewing window.**

First solve the inequality for y: $y \leq x + 1$. This inequality refers to points where y is *less than or equal to* $x + 1$. This means we want to shade below the graph of $y = x + 1$. We can use the bottom of the screen, Ymin or -10, as the lower boundary and $x + 1$ as the upper boundary.

Enter: 2nd DRAW 7 (–) 10 , X,T,θ,n + 1) ENTER

Don't forget to clear the screen when finished.

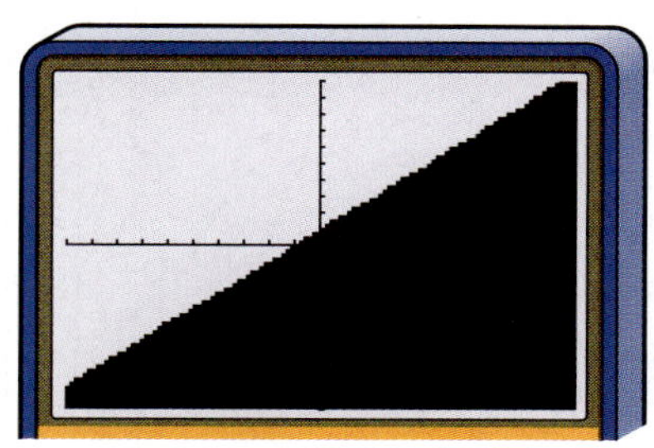

EXERCISES

Use a graphing calculator to graph each inequality. Sketch each graph on a sheet of paper.

1. $y \geq x + 2$ **2.** $y \leq -2x - 4$ **3.** $y + 1 \leq 0.5x$
4. $y \geq 4x$ **5.** $x + y \leq 0$ **6.** $2y + x \geq 4$
7. $3x + y \leq 18$ **8.** $y \geq 3$ **9.** $0.2x + 0.1y \leq 1$

7-8 Graphing Inequalities in Two Variables

What YOU'LL LEARN

- To graph inequalities in the coordinate plane.

Why IT'S IMPORTANT

You can graph inequalities to solve problems involving manufacturing and health.

APPLICATION
Manufacturing

Rapid Cycle, Inc. is a manufacturer and distributor of racing bicycles. It takes 3 hours to assemble a bicycle and 1 hour to road test a bicycle. Each technician in the company works no more than 45 hours a week. How many racing bikes can one technician assemble, and how many can he or she road test in one week?

Let x represent the number of bikes that are assembled in a week, and let y represent the number of bikes that are road-tested. Then the following inequality can be used to represent the solution.

Total time to assemble x bikes	plus	Total time to road test y bikes	is no more than	45 hours.
$3x$	$+$	y	$\leq$	45

There are an infinite number of ordered pairs that are solutions to this inequality. The easiest way to show all of these solutions is to draw a *graph* of the inequality. Before doing this, let's consider some simpler inequalities. *This problem will be solved in Example 3.*

Example 1 **From the set {(3, 4), (0, 1), (1, 4), (1, 1)}, which ordered pairs are part of the solution set for $4x + 2y < 8$?**

Let's use a table to substitute the x and y values of each ordered pair into the inequality.

x	y	4x + 2y < 8	True or False?
3	4	$4(3) + 2(4) < 8$ $20 < 8$	false
0	1	$4(0) + 2(1) < 8$ $2 < 8$	true
1	4	$4(1) + 2(4) < 8$ $12 < 8$	false
1	1	$4(1) + 2(1) < 8$ $6 < 8$	true

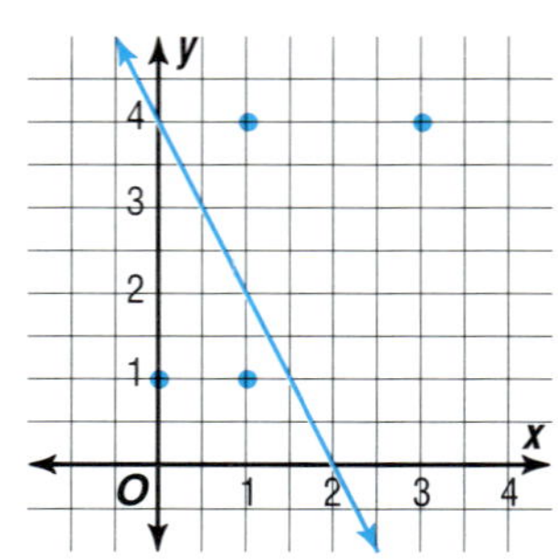

The ordered pairs {(0, 1), (1, 1)} are part of the solution set of $4x + 2y < 8$. The graph above shows the four ordered pairs of the replacement set and the equation $4x + 2y = 8$. Notice the location of the two ordered pairs that are solutions for $4x + 2y < 8$ in relation to the graph of the line.

EXPLORATION — PROGRAMMING

You can use the following graphing calculator program to find out if a given ordered pair (x, y) is a solution for the inequality $5x - 3y \geq 15$.

```
PROGRAM: XYTEST
: Disp "IS (X, Y) A ","SOLUTION?"
: Prompt X,Y
: If 5X−3Y≥15
: Then
: Disp "YES"
: Else
: Disp "NO"
```

To run the program for other ordered pairs, simply press ENTER and the program will begin again.

Your Turn

a. Try the program for ten ordered pairs (x, y). Keep a list of which ordered pairs you tried and which ones were solutions.

b. How do you think you could change this program to test the inequality $2x + y \geq 2y$?

c. Use your changed program to find the solution set if $x = \{-1, 0, 1\}$ and $y = \{-2, -1, 0, 1\}$.

The solution set for an inequality contains many ordered pairs when the domain and range are the set of real numbers. The graphs of all of these ordered pairs fill an area on the coordinate plane called a **half-plane.** An equation defines the **boundary** or edge for each half-plane. For example, suppose you wanted to graph the inequality $y > 5$ on the coordinate plane.

First determine the boundary by graphing $y = 5$.

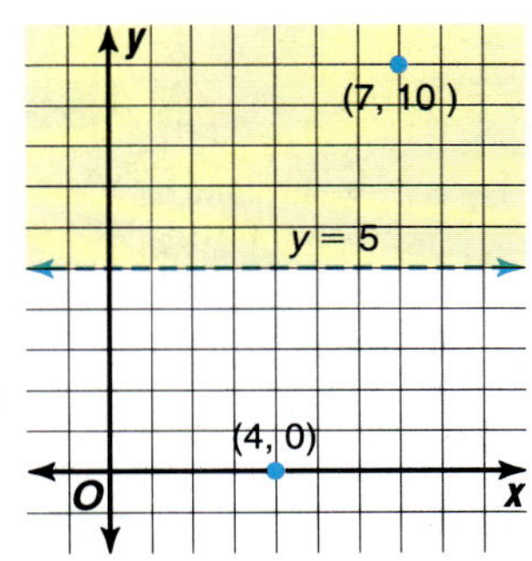

This graph is called an <u>*open half-plane*</u> *because the boundary is not part of the graph.*

Since the inequality involves only $>$, the line should be dashed. The boundary divides the coordinate plane into two half-planes.

If the inequality contains $\geq$ or $\leq$, the graph of the boundary equation would be drawn as a solid line.

To determine which half-plane contains the solution, choose a point from each half-plane and test it in the inequality.

Try (7, 10).		Try (4, 0).	
$y > 5$	*$y = 10$*	$y > 5$	*$y = 0$*
$10 > 5$	true	$0 > 5$	false

The half-plane that contains (7, 10) contains the solution. Shade that half-plane.

Example 2 **Graph $y + 2x \leq 3$.**

First solve for y in terms of x.

$$y + 2x \leq 3$$

$$y + 2x - 2x \leq 3 - 2x \quad \textit{Subtract 2x from each side.}$$

$$y \leq 3 - 2x$$

(continued on the next page)

Graph $y = 3 - 2x$. Since $y \leq 3 - 2x$ means $y < 3 - 2x$ or $y = 3 - 2x$, the boundary is included in the graph and should be drawn as a solid line.

Select a point in one of the half-planes and test it. For example, use the origin (0, 0).

$y \leq 3 - 2x$

The half-plane that contains the origin should be shaded.

Check: Test a point in the other half-plane, for example (3, 3).

Since the statement is false, the half-plane containing (3, 3) is not part of the solution.

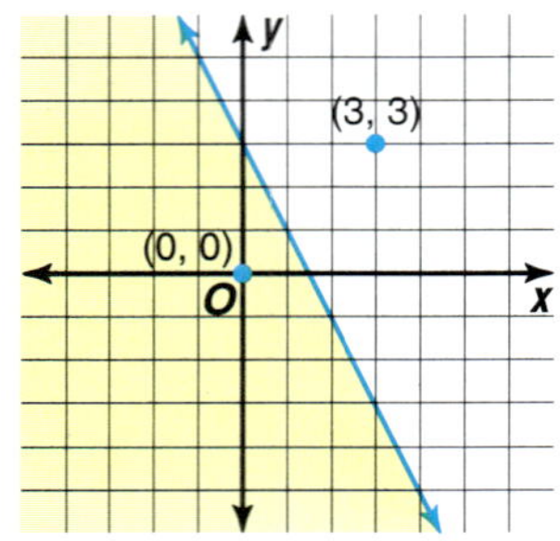

This graph is called a closed half-plane because the boundary line is included.

The origin is often used as a test point because the values are easy to substitute into the inequality.

When solving real-life inequalities, the domain and range of the inequality are often restricted to nonnegative numbers or whole numbers.

Example 3

APPLICATION Manufacturing

Refer to the application at the beginning of the lesson. How many racing bikes will the technician be able to assemble and road test?

First, solve for y in terms of x.

$3x + y \leq 45$

$3x - 3x + y \leq 45 - 3x$

$y \leq 45 - 3x$

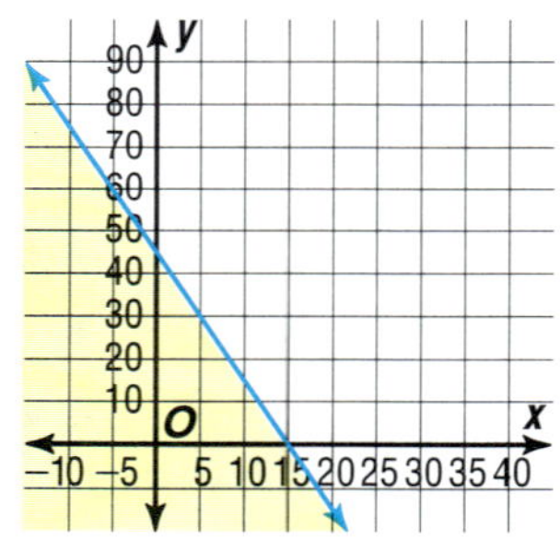

Since the open sentence includes the equation, graph $y = 45 - 3x$ as a solid line. Test a point in one of the half-planes, for example (0, 0). The half-plane containing (0, 0) represents the solution since $3(0) + 0 \leq 45$ is true.

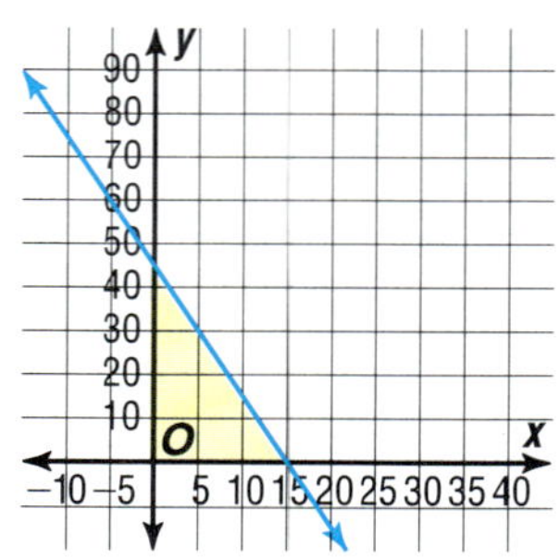

Let's examine what the solution means. The technician cannot complete negative numbers of racing bikes. So, any point in the half-plane whose x- and y-coordinates are whole numbers is a possible solution. That is, only the portion of the shading in the first quadrant is the solution for this problem. One solution is (5, 30). This represents 5 bicycles assembled and 30 road tested by the technician in a 45-hour week.

FYI

The world speed record for bicycles over a 200-meter course using a flying start is 65.484 mph by Fred Markham at Mono Lake, California, set in 1986.

CHECK FOR UNDERSTANDING

Communicating Mathematics

Study the lesson. Then complete the following.

1. a. **Graph** $y \geq x + 1$.
   b. **Identify** the boundary and indicate whether it is included or not.
   c. **Identify** the half-plane that is part of the graph.
   d. **Write** the coordinates of a point not on the boundary that satisfy the inequality.
2. **Explain** how you would check whether a point is part of the graph of an inequality.

MATH JOURNAL

3. **Assess Yourself** What do you think was the most challenging concept you learned in this chapter? Give an example of that concept and tell why you thought it was challenging.

Guided Practice

Match each inequality with its graph.

4. $y \geq \frac{1}{2}x - 2$
5. $y \leq 0.5x - 2$
6. $y \geq \frac{2}{3}x + 2$
7. $y \leq \frac{2}{3}x + 2$

a.
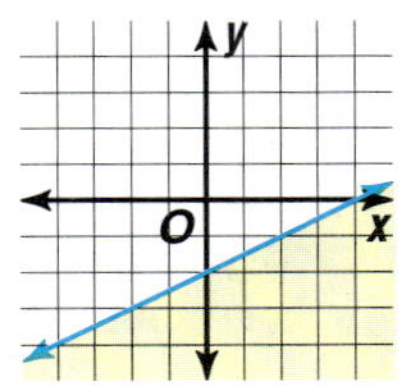

b.
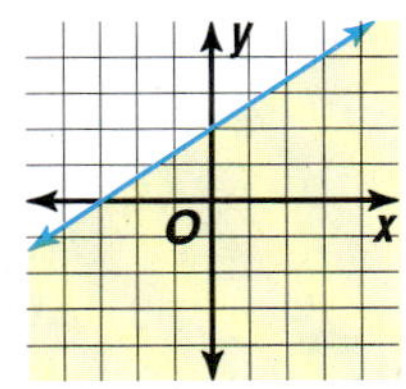

c.
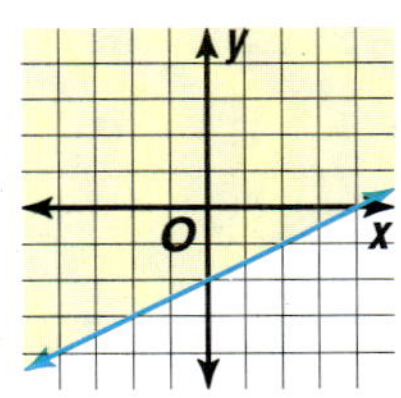

d.
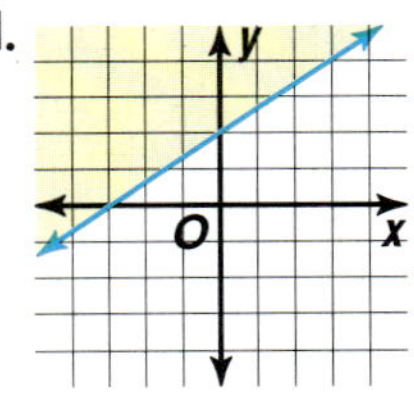

Determine which ordered pairs are solutions to the inequality. State whether the boundary is included in the graph.

8. $y \leq x$ a. $(-3, 2)$ b. $(1, -2)$ c. $(0, -1)$
9. $y > x - 1$ a. $(0, 0)$ b. $(2, 0)$ c. $(1, 3)$
10. Find which ordered pairs from the set $\{(-2, 2), (-2, 3), (2, 2), (2, 3)\}$ are part of the solution set for $a + b < 1$.

Graph each inequality.

11. $y > 3$
12. $x + y > 1$
13. $2x + 3y \geq -2$
14. $-x < -y$

EXERCISES

Practice

Copy each graph. Shade the appropriate half-plane to complete the graph of the inequality.

15. $x > 4$

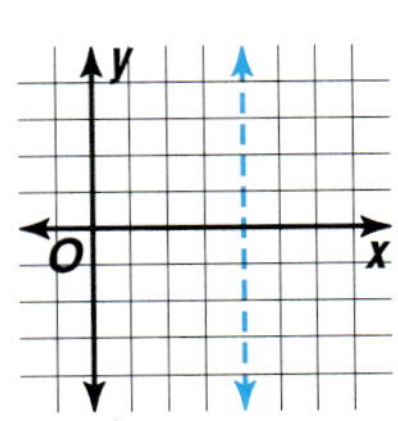

16. $3y < x$

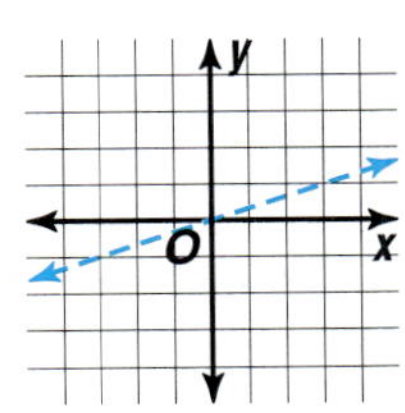

17. $3x + y > 4$

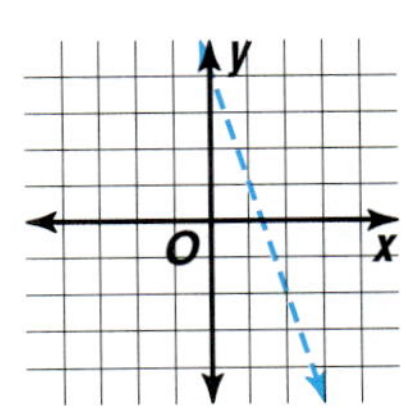

18. $2x - y \leq -2$

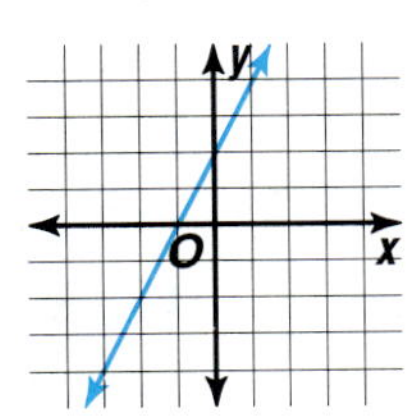

Find which ordered pairs from the given set are part of the solution set for each inequality.

19. $y < 3x$, $\{(-3, 1), (-3, 2), (1, 1), (1, 2)\}$

20. $y - x > 0$, $\{(1, 1), (1, 2), (4, 1), (4, 2)\}$

21. $2y + x \geq 4$, $\{(-1, -3), (-1, 0), (-2, -3), (-2, 0)\}$

Graph each inequality.

22. $x > -5$	**23.** $y < -3$	**24.** $3y + 6 > 0$
25. $4x + 8 < 0$	**26.** $y \leq x + 1$	**27.** $x + y > 2$
28. $x + y < -4$	**29.** $3x - 1 \geq y$	**30.** $3x + y < 1$
31. $x - y \geq -1$	**32.** $x < y$	**33.** $-y > x$
34. $2x - 5y \leq -10$	**35.** $8y + 3x < 16$	**36.** $\lvert y \rvert \geq 2$
37. $y > \lvert x + 2 \rvert$	**38.** $y > 2$ and $x < 3$	**39.** $y \leq -x$ and $x \geq -3$

Graphing Calculator

Use a graphing calculator to graph each inequality. Make a sketch of the graph.

40. $y > x - 1$ **41.** $4y + x < 16$ **42.** $x - 2y < 4$

Programming

Use the program in the Exploration to determine which pairs are solutions for each inequality.

43. $x + 2y \geq 3$	**a.** $(-2, 2)$	**b.** $(4, -1)$	**c.** $(3, 1)$	**d.** $(0, 0)$
44. $2x - 3y \leq 1$	**a.** $(2, 1)$	**b.** $(5, -1)$	**c.** $(1, 1)$	**d.** $(0, 0)$
45. $-2x < 8 - y$	**a.** $(5, 10)$	**b.** $(3, 6)$	**c.** $(-4, 0)$	**d.** $(0, 0)$

Critical Thinking

46. What compound inequality is described by the graph at the right? Find a simple inequality that also describes this graph.

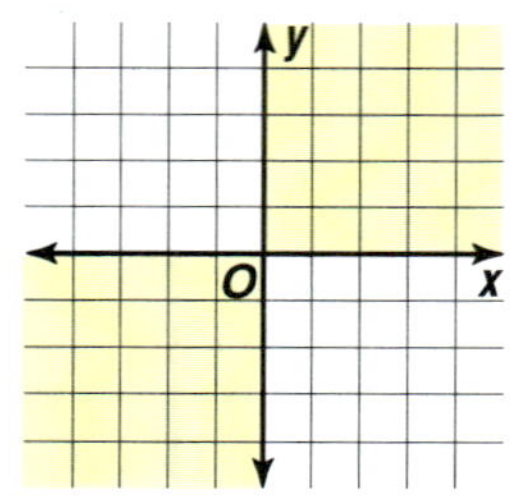

Applications and Problem Solving

47. Health The graph below shows the effective heart rate ranges for each type of exercise goal.

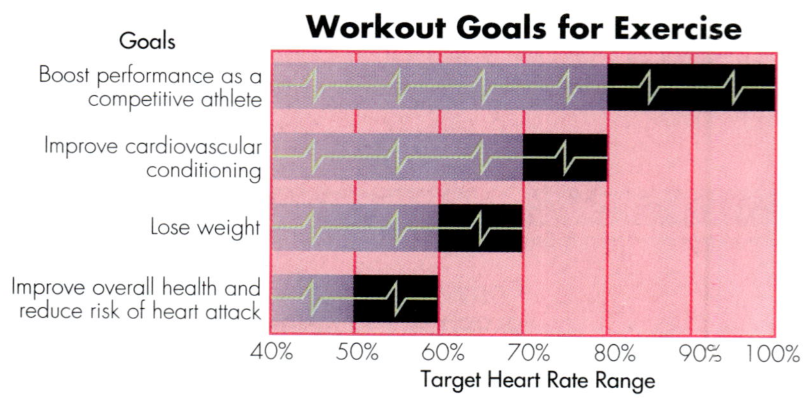

Source: *Vitality,* May 1994

Arrio is 35 years old and just beginning a bench-stepping aerobics class. In the orientation at the beginning of the first class, he learned that during exercise an effective minimum heart rate (beats/minute) should be 70% of the difference of 220 and his age. A maximum heart rate should be 80% of the difference of 220 and his age.

a. Write a compound inequality that expresses the effective rate zone for a person a years of age.

b. In class, the participants take a break and count their heart beats for 15 seconds. What should be Arrio's effective heart rate zone for that 15-second count?

c. According to the graph and the heart rate range given, what is the goal of the bench-stepping class?

48. Snowmobiling Although snowmobiling is an exhilarating sport, it can be very dangerous. The chart below shows the reported accidents in Minnesota involving snowmobiles.

Reported Snowmobile Accidents in Minnesota

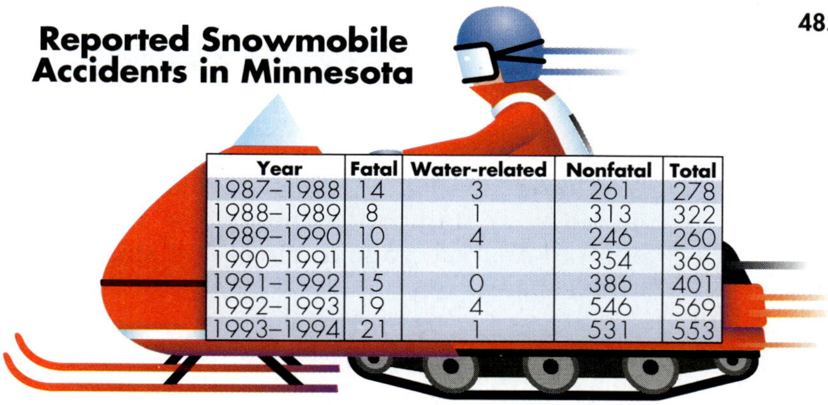

Year	Fatal	Water-related	Nonfatal	Total
1987–1988	14	3	261	278
1988–1989	8	1	313	322
1989–1990	10	4	246	260
1990–1991	11	1	354	366
1991–1992	15	0	386	401
1992–1993	19	4	546	569
1993–1994	21	1	531	553

Source: Minnesota Department of Natural Resources

a. A study suggests that the average number of nonfatal snowmobile accidents per year nationwide is about 350. Suppose x represents the total number of fatal snowmobile accidents in Minnesota and y represents the total number of snowmobile accidents in Minnesota. In what years is $x + 350 > y$?

b. Graph $x + 350 > y$.

c. The snowmobiling season in Minnesota goes from November to March. The lack of snow during the 1994–1995 season caused many to resort to riding their snowmobiles on icy lakes instead of on land. As of December 1, there had been 7 fatal accidents, 1 water-related fatal accident, and 81 nonfatal accidents. Do you think that the 1994–1995 season's accident count was greater or less than the 1993–1994 season? Explain your answer.

Mixed Review

49. Statistics Make a box-and-whisker plot of the total number of snowmobiling accidents shown in the chart for Exercise 48. (Lesson 7–7)

50. Solve $5 - |2x - 7| > 2$. (Lesson 7–6)

51. Write an equation in slope-intercept of the line that is parallel to the graph of $8x - 2y = 7$ and whose y-intercept is the same as the line whose equation is $2x - 9y = 18$. (Lesson 6–4)

52. Determine the value of r so that the line passing through $(r, 4)$ and $(-4, r)$ has a slope of 4. (Lesson 6–1)

53. Graph $-y + \frac{2}{7}x = 1$. (Lesson 5–4)

54. State the inverse of the relation $\{(4, -1), (3, 2), (-4, 0), (17, 9)\}$. (Lesson 5–2)

55. What is 98.5% of \$140.32? (Lesson 4–4)

56. Find three consecutive integers whose sum is 87. (Lesson 3–3)

CLOSING THE

In·ves·ti·ga·tion

Smoke Gets In Your Eyes

Refer to the Investigation on pages 320–321. Add the results of your work below to your Investigation Folder.

The EPA's most recent long-term study on the effects of secondhand smoke shows that nonsmokers married to smokers have a 19% increased risk of having lung cancer. Lung cancer is not the only danger of secondhand smoke. Twelve studies show that heart disease is another danger. Nonsmokers who are exposed to their spouses' smoke have a 30% increased chance of death from heart disease than do other nonsmokers. After reviewing a number of studies, the EPA's risk analysis has also concluded that secondhand smoke causes an extra 150,000 to 300,000 respiratory infections a year among the nations 5.5 million children under the age of 18 months.

Katharine Hammond, an environmental-health expert at the University of California, Berkeley, has also conducted a study on the *carcinogenic* components of secondhand smoke. The carcinogenic components are the parts of smoke that are known to cause cancer in humans. She found that "in the same room, at the same time, the nonsmoker is getting as much benzene (a chemical that is known to cause cancer in humans) as a smoker gets smoking six cigarettes."

James Repace and Alfred Lowery, two statistical researchers who study the effects of secondhand smoke, have concluded that a lifetime increase in lung-cancer risk of 1 in 1000 could be caused by long-term exposure to air containing more than 6.8 micrograms of nicotine per cubic meter of air.

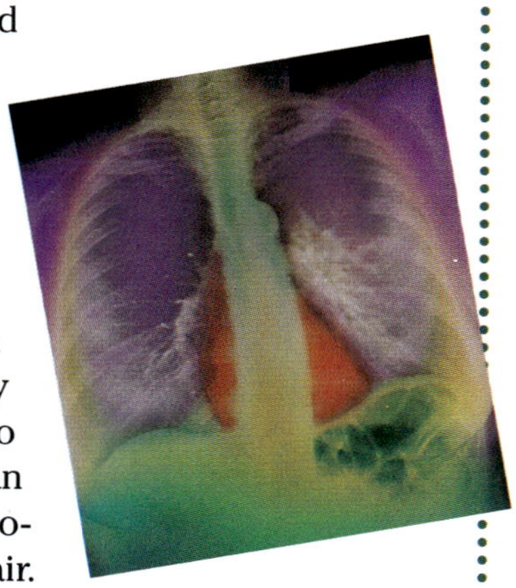

Analyze

You have conducted experiments and organized your data in various ways. It is now time to analyze your findings and state your conclusions.

PORTFOLIO ASSESSMENT

You may want to keep your work on this Investigation in your portfolio.

1 True secondhand smoke consists mostly of sidestream smoke. This is the smoke that comes from the smoldering cigarette. This smoke is much more toxic than inhaled smoke. How does this information affect your conclusions about the amount of smoke inhaled by nonsmokers in a room?

2 If you are a nonsmoker and live with a smoker, what are the cost factors involved? Explain your calculations.

3 Describe your personal experience with secondhand smoke.

Write

You want to inform people of the effects of secondhand smoke. You decide to write a letter to the editor of a local paper describing your investigation on the effects of secondhand smoke.

4 Use the information above and the results of your experiments and explorations to write a paper regarding the health risks of secondhand smoke.

5 You may want to do further research. The American Cancer Society and other agencies have information regarding the health risks of smoking and secondhand smoke.

6 Use data, charts, and graphs to justify your position. Use mathematics to help convince your readers of the conclusions you drew from this Investigation.

CHAPTER 7 HIGHLIGHTS

VOCABULARY

After completing this chapter, you should be able to define each term, property, or phrase and give an example or two of each.

Algebra

addition property for inequality (p. 385)
boundary (p. 437)
compound inequality (p. 405)
division property for inequality (p. 393)
half-plane (p. 437)
intersection (p. 406)
multiplication property for inequality (p. 393)
set-builder notation (p. 385)
subtraction property for inequality (p. 385)
union (p. 408)

Statistics

box-and-whisker plot (p. 427)
extreme values (p. 427)
whiskers (p. 428)

Probability

compound event (p. 414)
outcomes (p. 413)
simple events (p. 414)
tree diagram (p. 413)

Problem Solving

draw a diagram (p. 406)

UNDERSTANDING AND USING THE VOCABULARY

Choose the letter of the term that best matches each statement, algebraic expression, or algebraic sentence.

1. If $\frac{1}{2}x \leq -5$, then $x \leq -10$.
2. If $8 > 4$, then $8 + 5 > 4 + 5$.
3. $\{h \mid h > 43\}$
4. $x \geq -3$ or $x < -10$
5. $x \geq -4$ and $x < 2$
6. If $4x - 1 < 7$, then $4x - 4 < 4$.
7. If $-3x < 9$, then $x > -3$.
8. $>$
9. $<$
10. $7 > x > 1$
11. $|x + 6| > 12$ means $x + 6 > 12$ or $-(x + 6) > 12$.

a. absolute value inequality
b. addition property for inequality
c. compound inequality
d. division property for inequality
e. greater than
f. intersection
g. less than
h. multiplication property for inequality
i. set builder notation
j. subtraction property for inequality
k. union

CHAPTER 7 STUDY GUIDE AND ASSESSMENT

SKILLS AND CONCEPTS

OBJECTIVES AND EXAMPLES

Upon completing this chapter, you should be able to:

- solve inequalities by using addition and subtraction (Lesson 7–1)

$$56 > m + 16$$
$$56 - 16 > m + 16 - 16$$
$$40 > m$$
$$\{m \mid m < 40\}$$

REVIEW EXERCISES

Use these exercises to review and prepare for the chapter test.

Solve each inequality. Then check your solution.

12. $r + 7 > -5$

13. $-35 + 6n < 7n$

14. $2t - 0.3 \leq 5.7 + t$

15. $-14 + p \geq 4 - (-2p)$

Define a variable, write an inequality, and solve each problem. Then check your solution.

16. The difference of a number and 3 is at least 2.

17. Three times a number is greater than four times the number less eight.

- solve inequalities by using multiplication and division (Lesson 7–2)

$$\frac{-5}{6}m > 25$$
$$\frac{-6}{5}\left(\frac{-5}{6}m\right) > \frac{-6}{5}(25)$$
$$m < -30$$
$$\{m \mid m < -30\}$$

Solve each inequality. Then check your solution.

18. $7x \geq -56$

19. $90 \leq -6w$

20. $\frac{2}{3}k \geq \frac{2}{15}$

21. $9.6 < 0.3x$

Define a variable, write an inequality, and solve each problem. Then check your solution.

22. Six times a number is at most 32.4.

23. Negative three fourths of a number is no more than 30.

- solve linear inequalities involving more than one operation (Lesson 7–3)

$$15b - 12 > 7b + 60$$
$$15b - 7b - 12 > 7b - 7b + 60$$
$$8b - 12 > 60$$
$$8b - 12 + 12 > 60 + 12$$
$$8b > 72$$
$$\frac{8b}{8} > \frac{72}{8}$$
$$b > 9$$
$$\{b \mid b > 9\}$$

Find the solution set of each inequality if the replacement set for each variable is {−5, −4, −3, . . . 3, 4, 5}.

24. $\frac{x - 5}{3} > -3$

25. $3 \leq -4x + 7$

Solve each inequality. Then check your solution.

26. $2r - 3.1 > 0.5$

27. $4y - 11 \geq 8y + 7$

28. $-3(m - 2) > 12$

29. $-5x + 3 < 3x + 23$

30. $4(n - 1) < 7n + 8$

31. $0.3(z - 4) \leq 0.8(0.2z + 2)$

OBJECTIVES AND EXAMPLES

- solve compound inequalities and graph their solution sets (Lesson 7–4)

$$\begin{array}{lcl} 2a > a - 3 & \text{and} & 3a < a + 6 \\ 2a - a > a - a - 3 & & 3a - a < a - a + 6 \\ a > -3 & & 2a < 6 \\ & & \frac{2a}{2} < \frac{6}{2} \\ & & a < 3 \end{array}$$

$\{a \mid -3 < a < 3\}$

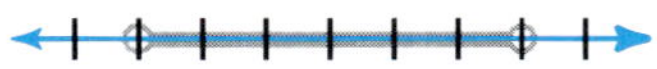

- find the probability of a compound event (Lesson 7–5)

Draw a tree diagram to show the possibilities for boys and girls in a family of 3 children. Assume that the probabilities for girls and boys being born are the same.

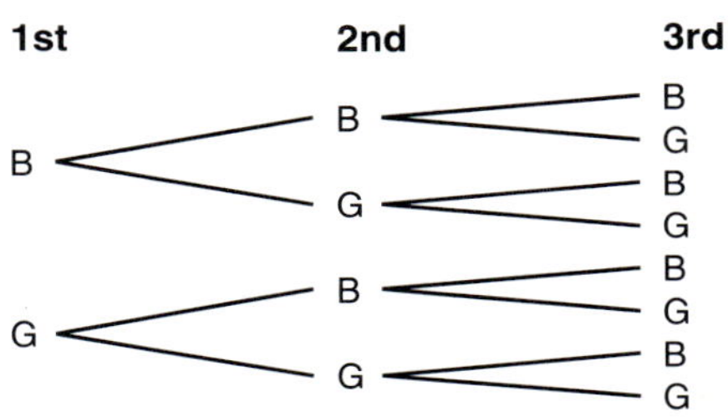

The probability that the family has exactly 3 girls is $\frac{1}{8}$ or 0.125, because there is 1 way out of 8 for this to happen. The probability that the family has exactly 2 boys and 1 girl is $\frac{3}{8}$ or 0.375, because there are 3 ways out of 8 for this to happen.

- solve open sentences involving absolute value and graph the solutions (Lesson 7–6)

$$|2x + 1| > 1$$

$$\begin{array}{lcl} 2x + 1 > 1 & \text{or} & 2x + 1 < -1 \\ 2x + 1 - 1 > 1 - 1 & & 2x + 1 - 1 < -1 - 1 \\ \frac{2x}{2} > \frac{0}{2} & & \frac{2x}{2} < \frac{-2}{2} \\ x > 0 & & x < -1 \end{array}$$

$\{x \mid x > 0 \text{ or } x < -1\}$

REVIEW EXERCISES

Solve each compound inequality. Then graph the solution set.

32. $x - 5 < -2$ and $x - 5 > 2$

33. $2a + 5 \leq 7$ or $2a \geq a - 3$

34. $4r \geq 3r + 7$ and $3r + 7 < r + 29$

35. $-2b - 4 \geq 7$ or $-5 + 3b \leq 10$

36. $a \neq 6$ and $3a + 1 > 10$

37. With each shrimp, salmon, or crab dinner at the Seafood Palace, you may have soup or salad. With shrimp, you may have broccoli or a baked potato. With salmon, you may have rice or broccoli. With crab, you may have rice, broccoli, or a potato. If all combinations are equally likely, find the probability of an order containing each item.

a. salmon **b.** soup

c. rice **d.** shrimp and rice

e. salad and broccoli

f. crab, soup, and rice

38. Matthew has 2 brown and 4 black socks in his dresser. While dressing one morning, he pulled out 2 socks without looking. What is the probability that he chose a matching pair?

Solve each open sentence. Then graph the solution set.

39. $|y + 5| > 0$

40. $|1 - n| \leq 5$

41. $|4k + 2| \leq 14$

42. $|3x - 12| < 12$

43. $|13 - 5y| \geq 8$

44. $\left|2p - \frac{1}{2}\right| > \frac{9}{2}$

OBJECTIVES AND EXAMPLES

- display and interpret data on box-and-whisker plots (Lesson 7–7)

The following high temperatures were recorded during a two-week cold spell in St. Louis. Make a box-and-whisker plot of the temperatures.

20° 2° 12° 5° 4° 16° 17°
7° 6° 16° 5° 0° 5° 30°

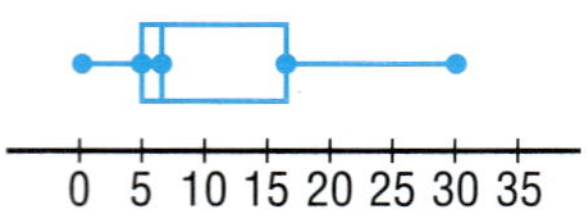

REVIEW EXERCISES

The number of calories in a serving of french fries at 13 restaurants are 250, 240, 220, 348, 199, 200, 125, 230, 274, 239, 212, 240, and 327.

45. Make a box-and-whisker plot of these data.

46. Are there any outliers? If so, name them.

- graph inequalities in the coordinate plane (Lesson 7–8)

Graph $2x + 3y < 9$.

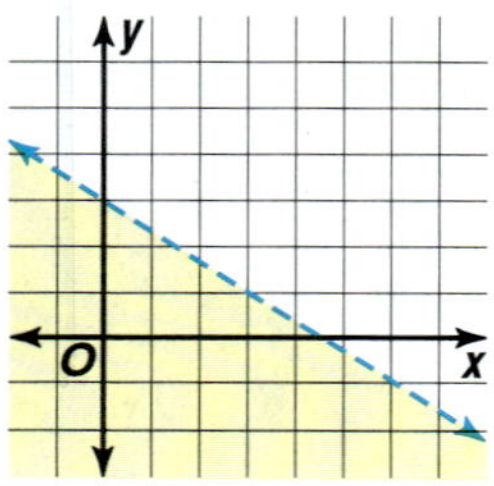

Find which ordered pairs from the given set are part of the solution set for each inequality.

47. $3x + 4y < 7$, $\{(1, 1), (2, -1), (-1, 1), (-2, 4)\}$

48. $4y - 8 \geq 0$, $\{(5, -1), (0, 2), (2, 5), (-2, 0)\}$

49. $-2x < 8 - y$, $\{(5, 10), (3, 6), (-4, 0), (-3, 6)\}$

Graph each inequality.

50. $x + 2y > 5$

51. $4x - y \leq 8$

52. $\frac{1}{2}y \geq x + 4$

53. $3x - 2y < 6$

APPLICATIONS AND PROBLEM SOLVING

54. Number Theory The sum of three consecutive integers is less than 100. Find the three integers with the greatest sum. (Lesson 7–3)

55. Shipping An empty book crate weighs 30 pounds. The weight of a book is 1.5 pounds. For shipping, the crate must weigh at least 55 pounds and no more than 60 pounds. What is the acceptable number of books that can be packed in the crate? (Lesson 7–4)

56. Automobiles An automobile dealer has cars available painted red or blue, with 4-cylinder or 6-cylinder engines, and with manual or automatic transmissions. (Lesson 7–5)

a. What is the probability of selecting a car with manual transmission?

b. What is the probability of selecting a car with a 4-cylinder engine and a manual transmission?

c. What is the probability of selecting a blue car with a 6-cylinder engine and an automatic transmission?

A practice test for Chapter 7 is provided on page 793.

ALTERNATIVE ASSESSMENT

COOPERATIVE LEARNING PROJECT

Statistics In this chapter, you learned how to make and interpret a box-and-whisker plot. Making a box-and-whisker plot and interpreting the data from a box-and-whisker plot are two different skills, however. One can go through the routine of drawing the plot but not be able to use the data portrayed by the plot to answer appropriate questions.

For this project, suppose there are two companies that manufacture window glass. They have each submitted a bid to a contractor who is building a library. Since glass that varies in thickness can cause distortions, the contractor has decided to measure the thickness of panes of glass from each factory, at several locations on each pane. The table below shows measurements for the two panes, one from each manufacturer.

Glass Thickness (mm)	
Company A	**Company B**
10.2	9.4
12.0	13.0
11.6	8.2
10.1	14.9
11.2	12.6
9.7	7.7
10.7	13.2
11.6	12.2
10.4	10.2
9.8	9.5
10.6	9.9
10.3	9.7
8.5	11.5
10.2	11.5
9.7	10.5
9.2	10.6
8.6	6.4
11.3	13.5

Prepare a stem-and-leaf plot and a box-and-whisker plot to organize and compare the two sets of data.

Follow these steps to organize your data.

- Determine how to set up the stem-and-leaf plot using decimals.
- Determine if using a common stem would be useful in comparing the two sets of data.
- Compare the ranges of the two sets of data.
- For which company is there "bunching" or "spreading out evenly" of the data?
- Compare the stem-and-leaf plot shape with the box-and-whisker plot shape.
- Compare the middle half of the data for each company.
- Write a comparative description of the sets of data and determine, with support, which company's glass should have less distortion.

THINKING CRITICALLY

- Why are multiplication and division the only two out of the four operations for which it is necessary to distinguish between positive and negative numbers when solving linear inequalities?
- Under what conditions will the compound sentence $x < a$ and $-a < x$ have no solutions?

PORTFOLIO

Select one of the assignments from this chapter for which you felt organization of the problem and reevaluation of the answer were important in order to get an accurate answer. Revise your work as necessary and place it in your portfolio. Explain why organization and reevaluation were important.

SELF EVALUATION

Do you look beyond the obvious in your math answers? Many times math students will work through a math problem rather routinely and not evaluate or check their answer. An answer must make sense and be accurate.

Assess yourself. Do you take the obvious solution as the whole answer or do you evaluate your answers for accuracy and rationalness? List two problems in mathematics and/or your daily life whereby the obvious answer was incorrect, so you needed to evaluate your solution for accuracy.

LONG-TERM PROJECT

In·ves·ti·ga·tion

Ready, Set, Drop!

MATERIALS NEEDED

- construction paper
- metric ruler
- paper clips
- scissors
- stopwatch
- tape
- tissue paper
- washers
- wire

Hang gliding became popular in the United States in the early 1970s. In most states, a hang gliding certification is required before you are allowed to participate in the sport. The U.S. Hang Gliding Association is located in Los Angeles and certifies instructors and safety officers to train would-be hang gliders.

A hang glider looks like a manned kite. It consists of a triangular sail of synthetic fabric attached to an aluminum frame. The pilot hangs from a harness and steers the glider with a control bar that adjusts as the pilot shifts his or her body weight.

Hang gliders can be launched in several ways. The pilot can hold the glider and run down a hill until the glider is airborne. In areas with high cliffs, the pilot can run and jump from the cliff's edge, using the air currents below to fly. In flatter landscapes, the glider is often launched by towing it with a rope from a truck or boat and releasing it at an altitude of 400–500 feet.

Imagine that you are an engineer for an aeronautical engineering firm. A group of people who are interested in hang gliding have asked your firm to design a hang glider that can be used for recreational purposes. Your task is to design a hang glider that is as compact as possible, yet is safe for flight and landings. You have no previous experience designing hang gliders. You don't know what size hang glider is needed or whether or not the size of a hang glider depends on the size of its load. (The people range in size.)

With so many unknowns, you decide to conduct some tests to understand the principles involved. In this Investigation, you will use mathematics to examine the relationship between the speed of descent and the size of a hang glider. As part of a three-member research team, you will use tissue-paper triangles to study hang gliders.

Make an Investigation Folder in which you can store all of your work on this Investigation for future use.

TRIANGLE TEST				
Test	5 cm	10 cm	20 cm	35 cm
perimeter				
surface area				
1				
2				
3				
4				
5				

THE EXPERIMENT

1. Begin by copying the chart above.
2. Cut out four equilateral triangles from tissue paper. The sides of the triangles should be 5, 10, 20, and 35 centimeters long, respectively. These triangles will serve as models of hang gliders. Find the perimeter and surface area of each of these triangles and record them in your chart.
3. Measure a height of five feet on a wall. Mark this height with a piece of masking tape.
4. Hold the smallest triangle parallel to the ground at a height of 5 feet. Have a second person ready to use a stopwatch to time how long it takes the triangle to reach the floor. A third person should give the verbal command, "Ready, set, drop." At the drop command, the person holding the tissue paper glider should let go of the paper. The timer starts the stopwatch at the verbal command and stops it when the glider hits the ground. Repeat this process until five drops have been made, recording your data after each drop.
5. Repeat Step 4 for the other three gliders, recording the data for each drop.
6. Review the data that you collected. What observations can you make? Are there any relationships that you can see from the data? Do the perimeter and surface area have a relationship with the time of the drop? Explain.

You will continue working on this Investigation throughout Chapters 8 and 9.

Be sure to keep your triangle models, charts, and other materials in your Investigation Folder.

Ready, Set, Drop! Investigation

Working on the Investigation
Lesson 8–1, p. 461

Working on the Investigation
Lesson 9–4, p. 519

Working on the Investigation
Lesson 9–7, p. 541

Closing the Investigation
End of Chapter 9, p. 548

CHAPTER

8

Solving Systems of Linear Equations and Inequalities

Objectives

In this chapter, you will:

- graph systems of equations,
- solve systems of equations using various methods,
- organize data to solve problems, and
- solve systems of inequalities by graphing.

Games People Play

Here are the 18 most popular participation sports.

Sport	Percent of Participants	Change from 1993
Exercise walking	70.8	9.8
Swimming	60.3	−1.8
Bicycle Riding	49.8	4.0
Fishing	45.7	−10.8
Exercise with equipment*	43.8	25.5
Camping	42.9	0.5
Bowling	37.4	−9.6
Billiards/pool	34.0	15.6
Basketball	28.2	−4.9
Boating (motor/power)	26.4	27.6
Hiking	25.3	30.0
Golf	24.5	8.5
Aerobic exercising	23.2	−6.6
Dart throwing	21.2	10.1
Running/jogging	20.6	1.8
In-line roller skating	19.5	57.2
Softball	18.1	1.1
Volleyball	17.4	−15.1

*20.2 million people indicated they "worked out at a club" in 1994, up from 19.7 million in 1993.

Source: National Sporting Goods Association, 1994

TIME *Line*

Do you dream of starring in the NBA or playing for the New York Yankees? Do you devote all your leisure time to mainly one sport? Maybe you should try something new in the world of sports. Lacrosse, in-line skating, or judo, anyone?

1750 B.C. The Moscow Papyrus shows that the Egyptians possess considerable knowledge of geometry.

A.D. 1637 Pierre de Fermat develops his famous "Last Theorem," which was finally proved in September, 1994.

300 B.C. Euclid's *Elements* summarizes and organizes the mathematical knowledge developed in Greece in the three preceding centuries.

PEOPLE IN THE NEWS

Short-track speed skaters **Julie Goskowicz**, 15, and **Tony Goskowicz**, 18, are a brother-and-sister team aiming for the 1998 Olympics. They started skating eight years ago in their hometown of New Berlin, Wisconsin, when their father gave them each a pair of skates. Although both finished last in their first race, they enjoyed the sport and continued to train. Hard work has earned them a place at the U.S. Olympic Education Center in Marquette, Michigan, where they study and train while participating in the racing circuit.

Chapter Project

In 1994, five-time Boston Marathon winner Jim Knaub tested his wheelchair's aerodynamics in the same wind tunnel that a major car manufacturer uses to test its car and truck designs. Knaub gained invaluable information concerning racing posture as well as helmet, wheel, and seat design. Earlier in the year, Knaub's Boston-Marathon-winning streak ended when he had to pull over twice during the race to make repairs. The winner was Heinz Frei of Switzerland.

- Suppose during a race, Frei's speed is 45 mph and Knaub is 264 feet ahead of him, racing at 36 mph.
- Write a system of equations to represent this situation. (*Hint:* Convert units from miles per hour to feet per second.)
- If their speeds remained constant, when would Frei catch up with Knaub? Explain how you know using graphing.

1875 The first catcher's mask, designed by Harvard student Fred W. Thayer, is used in baseball.

1894 Mary Cassatt paints her impressionist painting *The Boating Party.*

1903 Dr. Santiago Ramón y Kajal wins the Nobel Prize for Physiology and Medicine for his research on the nervous system.

1964 Dr. Chien Shiung Wu, nuclear physicist, becomes the first woman to receive the Comstock Prize from the National Academy of Sciences.

1988 Jackie Joyner-Kersee is the first U.S. woman to win the Olympic long jump.

1760 1780 1800 1820 1840 1860 1880 1900 1920 1940 1960 1980 2000

8–1A Graphing Technology
Systems of Equations

A Preview of Lesson 8–1

When solving systems of linear equations graphically, each equation is graphed on the same coordinate plane. The coordinates of the point at which the graphs intersect is the solution of the system. The graphing calculator permits us to graph several equations on the same coordinate plane and approximate the coordinates of the intersection point.

Example 1

Use a graphing calculator to solve the system of equations.

$$\mathbf{x + y = 9}$$
$$\mathbf{2x - y = 15}$$

Begin by rewriting each equation in an equivalent form by solving for *y*.

$$x + y = 9 \qquad\qquad 2x - y = 15$$
$$y = -x + 9 \qquad\qquad 2x - 15 = y$$

Graph each equation in the integer window [−47, 47] by [−31, 31]. Recall that the integer window can be obtained by entering [ZOOM] 6 [ZOOM] 8 [ENTER].

Enter: [Y=] [(−)] [X,T,θ,n] [+] 9 [ENTER] 2 [X,T,θ,n] [−] 15 [ZOOM] 6 [ZOOM] 8 [ENTER]

The graphs intersect in one point. The coordinates of this point are the solution to the system of equations. Press the [TRACE] key and use the arrow keys to move the cursor to the point of intersection. The coordinates of the point are (8, 1). Thus, the solution is (8, 1).

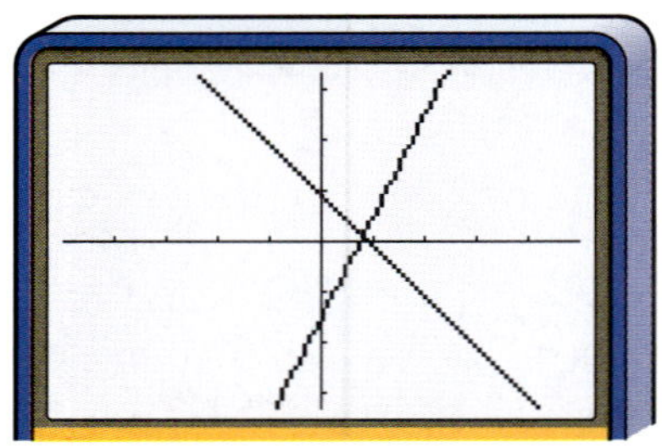

We can check this solution by using tables. Press [2nd] [TABLE]. On the screen you will see the coordinates of points on both lines. Use the arrow keys to scroll up or down and watch the trend of the coordinates. When you find a row at which $Y_1 = Y_2$, you have found the solution. *The solution checks.*

X	Y_1	Y_2
5	4	−5
6	3	−3
7	2	−1
8	1	1
9	0	3
10	−1	5
11	−2	7

X = 8

Sometimes solutions to systems of equations are not integers. Then you can use the ZOOM IN process to obtain an accurate approximate solution.

Example 2 **Use a graphing calculator to solve this system of equations to the nearest hundredth.**

$$y = 0.35x - 1.12$$
$$y = -2.25x - 4.05$$

Begin by graphing the equations in the standard viewing window.

Enter: [Y=] .35 [X,T,θ,n] [−] 1.12

[ENTER] [(−)] 2.25 [X,T,θ,n]

[−] 4.05 [ZOOM] 6

The graphs intersect at a point in the third quadrant. Use the TRACE function and the arrow keys to determine an approximation for the coordinates of the point of intersection. The ZOOM IN feature of the calculator is very useful for determining the coordinates of the intersection point with greater accuracy. Begin by placing the cursor on the intersection point and observing the coordinates, then press [ZOOM] 2 [ENTER]. Repeat this process as many times as necessary to get a more accurate answer.

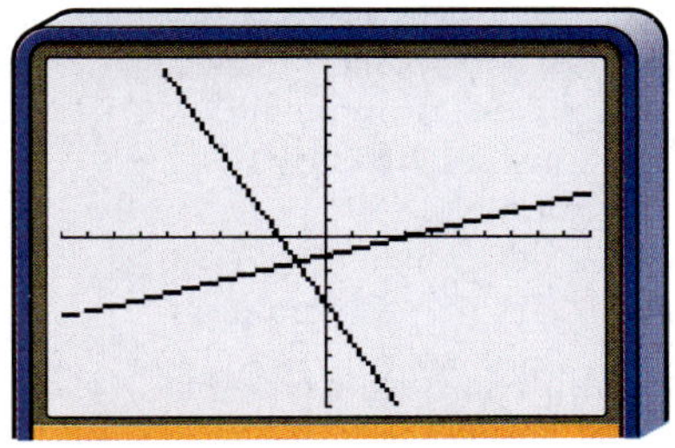

You may want to use the INTERSECT feature to find the coordinates of the point of intersection. Press [2nd] [CALC] 5 [ENTER] [ENTER] [ENTER].

The solution is $(-1.13, -1.51)$.

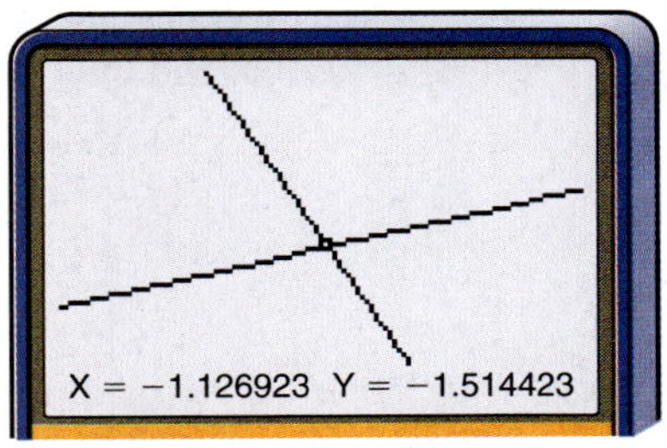

EXERCISES

Use a graphing calculator to solve each system of equations. State each decimal solution to the nearest hundredth.

1. $y = x + 7$
   $y = -x + 9$
2. $x + y = 27$
   $3x - y = 41$
3. $y = 3x - 4$
   $y = -0.5x + 6$
4. $x - y = 6$
   $y = 9$
5. $x + y = 5.35$
   $3x - y = 3.75$
6. $5x - 4y = 26$
   $4x + 2y = 53.3$
7. $2x + 3y = 11$
   $4x + y = -6$
8. $2.93x + y = 6.08$
   $8.32x - y = 4.11$
9. $125x - 200y = 800$
   $65x - 20y = 140$
10. $0.22x + 0.15y = 0.30$
    $-0.33x + y = 6.22$

8–1 Graphing Systems of Equations

What YOU'LL LEARN

- To solve systems of equations by graphing, and
- to determine whether a system of equations has one solution, no solution, or infinitely many solutions by graphing.

Why IT'S IMPORTANT

You can graph systems of equations to solve problems involving business and geometry.

APPLICATION
World Records

Cape Verde is a group of islands located off the westernmost point of Africa. In December, 1994, Frenchman Guy Delage set off from these islands for a 2400-mile swim across the Atlantic Ocean. He arrived at Barbados in the West Indies eight weeks later. Every day he would swim a while and then rest while floating with the current on a huge raft equipped with a fax machine, a computer, and a two-way radio.

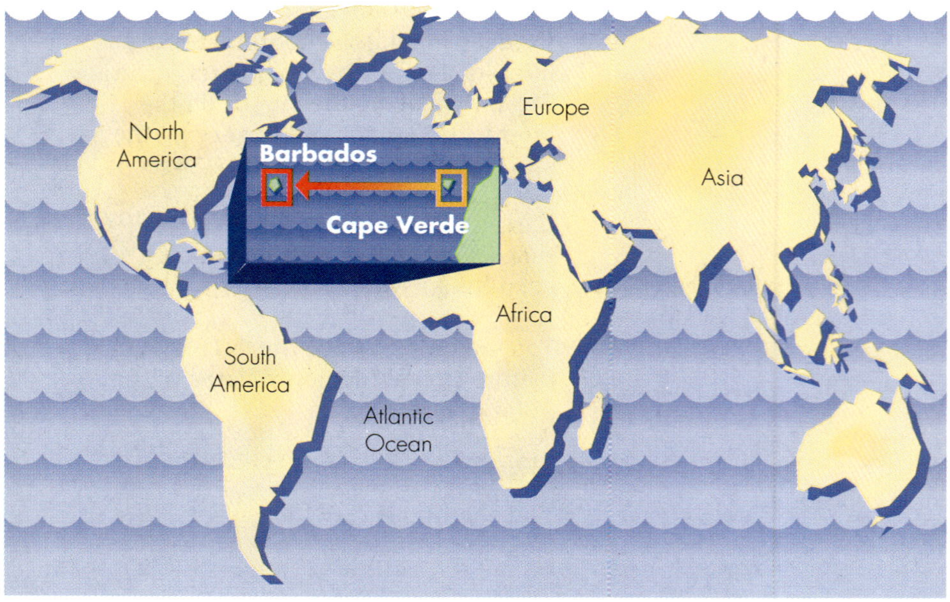

People are already considering trying to break Guy's record, but before a challenger makes the attempt, he or she should know what is required. Guy traveled approximately 44 miles per day. A good swimmer like Guy can swim about 3 miles per hour for an extended period, and the Atlantic currents will float a raft about 1 mile per hour. To match Guy's record, how many hours per day would one have to swim? How many hours would one be able to spend floating on the raft?

To solve this problem, let s represent the number of hours Guy swam, and let f represent the number of hours he floated. Then $3s$ represents the number of miles he traveled while swimming and $1f$ represents the number of miles he traveled while floating. You can write two equations to represent this situation.

number of hours swimming	*plus*	*number of hours floating*	*is*	*total number of hours in a day*
s	$+$	f	$=$	24

miles traveled while swimming	*plus*	*miles traveled while floating*	*is*	*total miles traveled in a day*
$3s$	$+$	$1f$	$=$	44

Top Five List

Fastest swimmers to cross the English Channel (hr:min)

1. Penny Lee Dean, 7:40
2. Philip Rush, 7:55
3. Richard Davey, 8:05
4. Irene van der Laan, 8:06
5. Paul Asmuth, 8:12

The equations $s + f = 24$ and $3s + f = 44$ together are called a **system of equations**. The solution to this problem is the ordered pair of numbers that satisfies both of these equations.

One method for solving a system of equations is to carefully graph the equations on the same coordinate plane. The coordinates of the point at which the graphs intersect is the solution of the system.

Guy Delage's raft

With most graphs of systems of equations, we can only estimate the solution. In this case, the graphs of $s + f = 24$ and $3s + f = 44$ appear to intersect at the point with coordinates (10, 14).

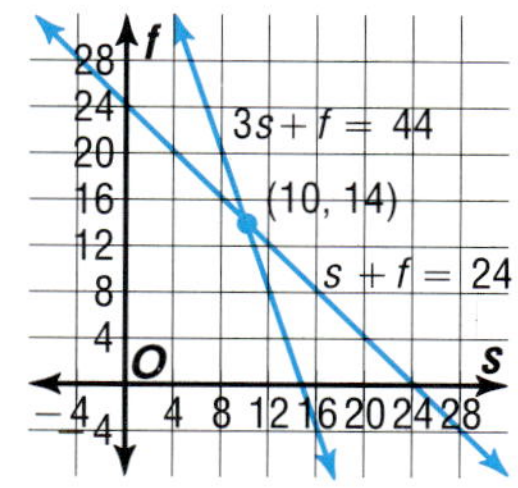

Check: In each equation, replace s with 10 and f with 14.

$$s + f = 24 \qquad 3s + f = 44$$
$$10 + 14 \stackrel{?}{=} 24 \qquad 3(10) + 14 \stackrel{?}{=} 44$$
$$24 = 24 \checkmark \qquad 44 = 44 \checkmark$$

The solution of the system of equations $s + f = 24$ and $3s + f = 44$ is (10, 14). The ordered pair (10, 14) means that a person trying to match Guy Delage's record would have to spend approximately 10 hours a day swimming and 14 hours floating.

Example 1 **Graph the system of equations to find the solution.**

$\mathbf{x + 2y = 1}$

$\mathbf{2x + y = 5}$

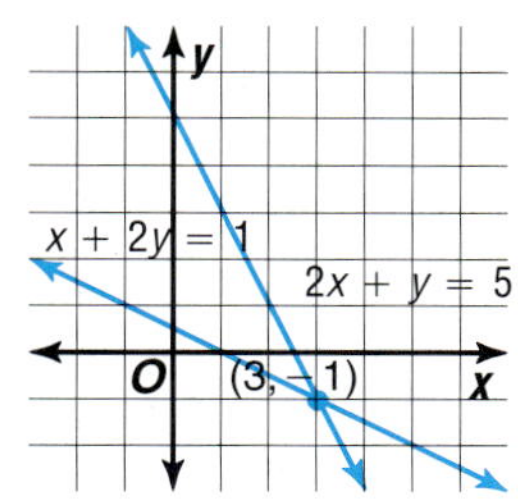

The graphs appear to intersect at the point with coordinates (3, −1). Check this estimate by replacing x with 3 and y with −1 in each equation.

Check: $x + 2y = 1 \qquad 2x + y = 5$

$$3 + 2(-1) \stackrel{?}{=} 1 \qquad 2(3) + (-1) \stackrel{?}{=} 5$$
$$1 = 1 \checkmark \qquad 5 = 5 \checkmark$$

The solution is (3, −1).

CAREER CHOICES

Graphing systems of equations often arises in the study of populations of groups, and is used by people with careers in biological science, such as **ecologists**. An ecologist uses graphs of systems to study populations of organisms and how they relate to their environment.

A career as an ecologist usually requires a Ph.D. in a biological science and several years of laboratory work.

For more information, contact:

Ecological Society of America
2010 Massachusetts Ave.
Suite 400
Washington, D.C. 20036

A system of two linear equations has exactly one ordered pair as its solution when the graphs of the equations intersect at exactly one point. If the graphs coincide, they are the same line and have infinitely many points in common. In either case, the system of equations is said to be **consistent**. That is, it has *at least* one ordered pair that satisfies both equations.

It is also possible for the two graphs to be *parallel*. In this case, the system of equations is **inconsistent** because there is *no* ordered pair that satisfies both equations.

Another way to classify a system is by the number of solutions it has.

- If a system has exactly one solution, it is **independent**.
- If a system has an infinite number of solutions, it is **dependent**.

Thus, the system in Example 1 is said to be *consistent and independent*.

The chart below summarizes the possible solutions to systems of linear equations.

Graphs of Equations	Number of Solutions	Terminology
intersecting lines	exactly one	consistent and independent
same line	infinitely many	consistent and dependent
parallel lines	none	inconsistent

Example 2 **Graph each system of equations to determine the number of solutions.**

a. $x + y = 4$
$x + y = 1$

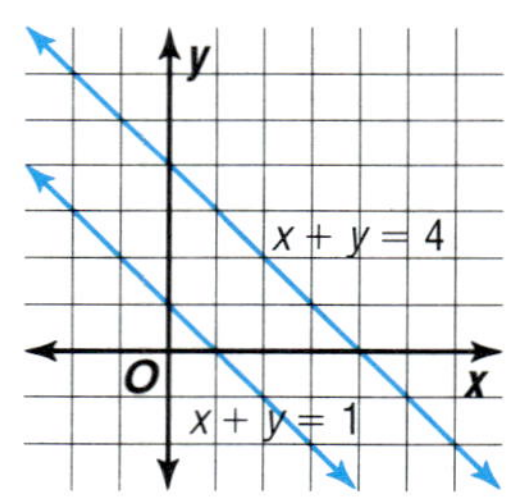

The graphs of the equations are parallel lines. Since they do not intersect, there is no solution to this system of equations. Notice that the two lines have the same slope but different y-intercepts.

Recall that a system of equations that has no solution is said to be inconsistent.

b. $x - y = 3$
$2x - 2y = 6$

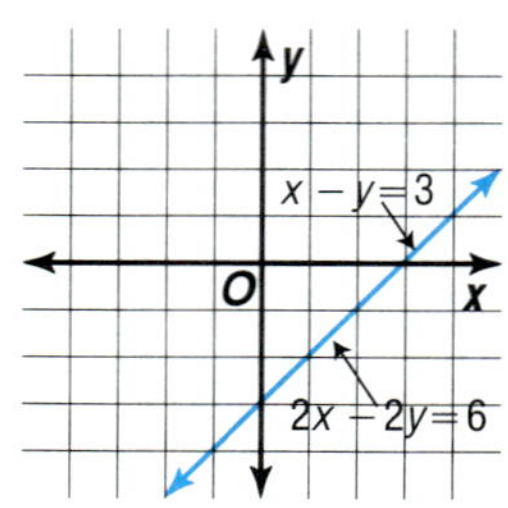

Each equation has the same graph. Any ordered pair on the graph will satisfy both equations. Therefore, there are infinitely many solutions of this system of equations. Notice that the graphs have the same slope and intercepts.

Recall that a system of equations that has infinitely many solutions is said to be consistent and dependent.

Check: Verify that the point at (4, 1) lies on both lines.

$x - y = 3$ $\quad\quad$ $2x - 2y = 6$

$4 - 1 \stackrel{?}{=} 3$ $\quad\quad$ $2(4) - 2(1) \stackrel{?}{=} 6$

$3 = 3$ ✔ $\quad\quad$ $6 = 6$ ✔

The methods you use to solve algebra problems are often useful in solving problems involving geometry.

Example 3 INTEGRATION Geometry

The points $A(-1, 6)$, $B(4, 8)$, $C(8, 3)$ and $D(-2, -1)$ are vertices of a quadrilateral.

a. Use a graph to determine the point of intersection of the diagonals of quadrilateral *ABCD*.

b. Find the equations of the lines containing the diagonals to verify the solution.

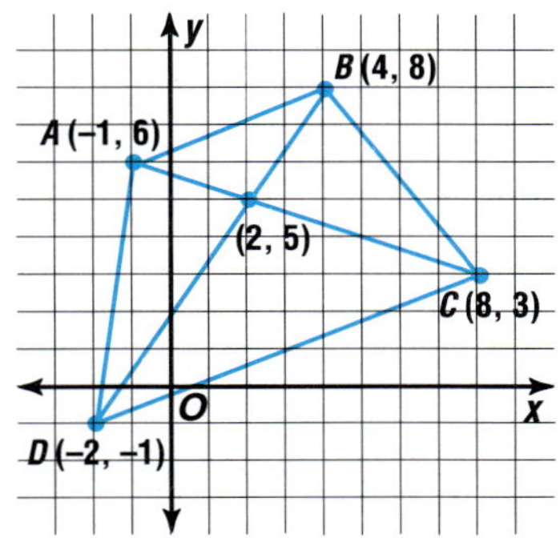

a. Draw quadrilateral *ABCD* with diagonals $\overline{AC}$ and $\overline{BD}$. The diagonals appear to intersect at the point (2, 5).

b. To check the solution, find the equations of lines *AC* and *BD* and then verify that (2, 5) is a solution of both equations. First, find the slope of each line using

$m = \frac{y_2 - y_1}{x_2 - x_1}$.

Slope of $\overleftrightarrow{AC}$

$$m = \frac{3 - 6}{8 - (-1)}$$
$$= \frac{-3}{9} \text{ or } -\frac{1}{3}$$

Slope of $\overleftrightarrow{BD}$

$$m = \frac{-1 - 8}{-2 - 4}$$
$$= \frac{-9}{-6} \text{ or } \frac{3}{2}$$

Then use the slope-intercept form, $y = mx + b$, to determine the equations.

Equation for $\overleftrightarrow{AC}$

$y = mx + b$

$6 = -\frac{1}{3}(-1) + b$ *Replace m with $-\frac{1}{3}$ and (x, y) with (−1, 6).*

$\frac{17}{3} = b$ The equation for $\overleftrightarrow{AC}$ is $y = -\frac{1}{3}x + \frac{17}{3}$.

Equation for $\overleftrightarrow{BD}$

$y = mx + b$

$8 = \frac{3}{2}(4) + b$ *Replace m with $\frac{3}{2}$ and (x, y) with (4, 8).*

$2 = b$ The equation for $\overleftrightarrow{BD}$ is $y = \frac{3}{2}x + 2$.

Check that (2, 5) is a solution to both equations.

$y = -\frac{1}{3}x + \frac{17}{3}$

$5 \stackrel{?}{=} -\frac{1}{3}(2) + \frac{17}{3}$ *(x, y) = (2, 5)*

$5 = 5$ ✓

$y = \frac{3}{2}x + 2$

$5 \stackrel{?}{=} \frac{3}{2}(2) + 2$ *(x, y) = (2, 5)*

$5 = 5$ ✓

The solution checks.

CHECK FOR UNDERSTANDING

Communicating Mathematics

Study the lesson. Then complete the following.

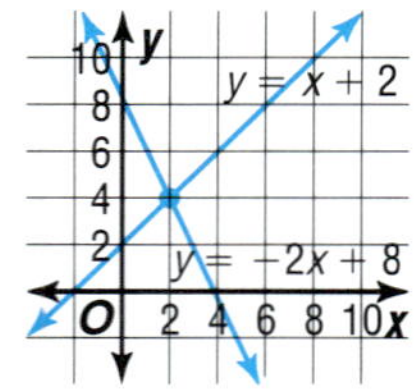

1. **State** the solution of the system of equations shown in the graph at the right. Justify your answer.
2. **Explain** what it means to *solve* a system of linear equations.
3. **Describe** the graph of a linear system that has infinitely many solutions.
4. **Name** two of the solutions for the system of equations in Example 2b. Verify your answers algebraically.
5. **Write** a system of linear equations that has $(-3, 5)$ as its only solution.
6. **Sketch** the graph of a linear system that has *no* solution.

MODELING MATHEMATICS

7. Use a geoboard and rubber bands to model a system of two equations that has the solution (3, 2). Let the lower left point on the geoboard represent the origin.

Guided Practice

Use the graphs at the right to determine whether each system has *one* solution, *no* solution, or *infinitely many* solutions. If the system has one solution, name it.

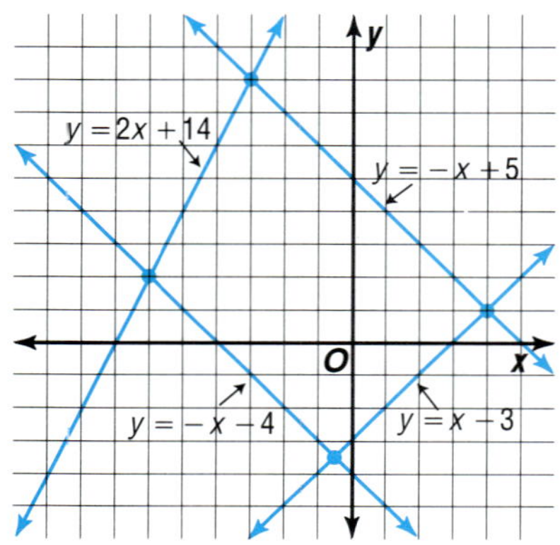

8. $y = -x + 5$
   $y = x - 3$
9. $y = -x - 4$
   $y = -x + 5$
10. $y = 2x + 14$
    $y = -x + 5$
11. $y = -x - 4$
    $y = 2x + 14$

State whether the given ordered pair is a solution to each system. Write *yes* or *no*.

12. $x - y = 6$
    $2x + y = 0$ $(-2, -4)$
13. $2x - y = 4$
    $3x + y = 1$ $(1, -2)$

Graph each system of equations. Then determine whether the system has *one* solution, *no* solution, or *infinitely many* solutions. If the system has one solution, name it.

14. $y = 3x - 4$
    $y = -3x - 4$
15. $y = -x + 8$
    $y = 4x - 7$
16. $x + 2y = 5$
    $2x + 4y = 2$
17. $y = -6$
    $4x + y = 2$
18. $2x + 3y = 4$
    $-4x - 6y = -8$
19. $2x + y = -4$
    $5x + 3y = -6$

20. a. Graph the line $y - x = 6$.
    b. Slide the entire line four units to the right and down one unit. Draw the new line.
    c. Describe this system of equations.

EXERCISES

Practice

Use the graphs below to determine whether each system has *one* solution, *no* solution, or *infinitely many* solutions. If the system has one solution, name it.

21. $y = x - 4$
$y = \frac{1}{3}x - 2$

22. $y = x - 4$
$y = -\frac{1}{3}x + 4$

23. $y = \frac{1}{3}x + 2$
$y = \frac{1}{3}x - 2$

24. $y = x - 4$
$y = \frac{1}{3}x + 2$

25. $y = -\frac{1}{3}x + 4$
$y = \frac{1}{3}x + 2$

26. $y = \frac{1}{3}x - 2$
$y = -\frac{1}{3}x + 4$

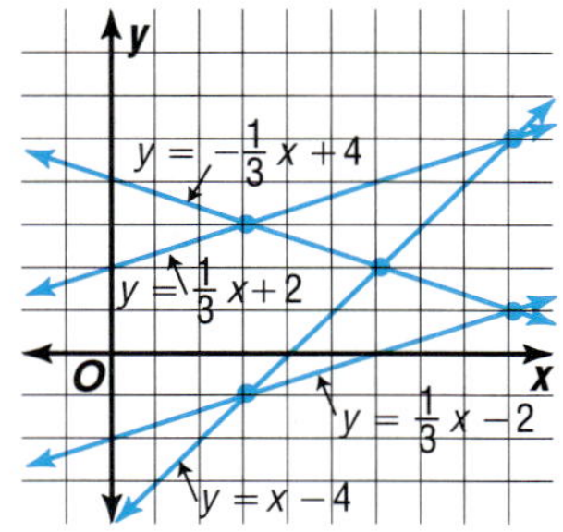

Graph each system of equations. Then determine whether the system has *one* solution, *no* solution, or *infinitely many* solutions. If the system has one solution, name it.

27. $y = -x$
$y = 2x - 6$

28. $y = 2x + 6$
$y = -x - 3$

29. $x + y = 2$
$y = 4x + 7$

30. $2x + y = 10$
$y = \frac{1}{2}x$

31. $x + y = 2$
$2y - x = 10$

32. $3x + 2y = 12$
$3x + 2y = 6$

33. $x - 2y = 2$
$3x + y = 6$

34. $x - y = 2$
$3y + 2x = 9$

35. $3x + y = 3$
$2y = -6x + 6$

36. $2x + 3y = -17$
$y = x - 4$

37. $y = \frac{2}{3}x - 5$
$3y = 2x$

38. $4x + 3y = 24$
$5x - 8y = -17$

39. $\frac{1}{2}x + \frac{1}{3}y = 6$
$y = \frac{1}{2}x + 2$

40. $6 - \frac{3}{8}y = x$
$\frac{2}{3}x + \frac{1}{4}y = 4$

41. $2x + 4y = 2$
$3x + 6y = 3$

INTEGRATION
Geometry

42. The graphs of the equations $-x + 2y = 6$, $7x + y = 3$, and $2x + y = 8$ contain the sides of a triangle. Find the coordinates of the vertices of the triangle.

43. Graph the system of equations below. Then find the area of the geometric figure.

$2x - 4 = 0$
$y = 8$
$x = 5$
$3y - 9 = 0$

Graphing Calculator

Use a graphing calculator to solve each system of equations. Approximate the coordinates of the point of intersection to the nearest hundredth.

44. $y = x + 2$
$y = -x - 1$

45. $y = \frac{1}{4}x - 3$
$y = -\frac{1}{3}x - 2$

46. $6x + y = 5$
$y = 9 + 3x$

47. $3 + y = x$
$2 + y = 5x$

Critical Thinking

48. If (0, 0) and (2, 2) are known to be solutions of a system of two linear equations, does the system have any other solutions? Justify your answers.

49. The solution to the system of equations $Ax + y = 5$ and $Ax + By = 7$ is $(-1, 2)$. What are the values of A and B?

Applications and Problem Solving

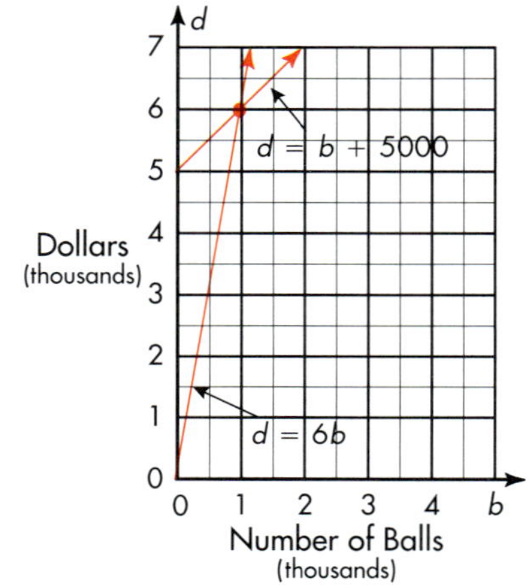

50. Business Mary Rodas is an 18-year-old toy specialist who tests and evaluates products at Catco, Inc., a company in New York City. She also helps design new toys, such as the Balzac Balloon Balls. Suppose the income from Balzac Balloon Balls is represented by the equation $d = 6b$ and the expenses are represented by the equation $d = b + 5000$. In both equations, b is the number of balls, and d is the number of dollars. Use the graph at the left to answer the following questions.

a. Find the solution to this system of equations. This solution is called the *break-even point.* What does this point represent?

b. A profit is made if income is greater than expenses. When is a profit made from the toys? How can you tell this from the graph?

c. Money is lost if expenses are greater than income. When is money lost from the Balzac Balloon Balls? How can you tell this from the graph?

FYI

Gupta doctors developed plastic surgery. Metallurgists made iron columns that are still free from rust after more than 1500 years. Gupta mathematicians developed a system of numbers that was later adopted by the Arabs.

51. World Cultures The Golden Age of India was during the expansion of the Gupta Empire, beginning in A.D. 320. India became a center of art, medicine, science, and mathematics. Suppose $P = \frac{1}{2}t + 22$ represents the percent of Indian people in the Gupta Empire, at time t. Let $P = -\frac{1}{2}t + 78$ represent the percent of Indian people that were not Guptas. Graph the system of equations and estimate the year in which the percent of Guptas equaled the percent of Indians that were not Gupta. (*Hint:* Let $t = 0$ correspond to A.D. 320.)

Mixed Review

52. Graph $y - 7 > 3x$. (Lesson 7–8)

53. Solve $|2m + 15| = 12$. (Lesson 7–6)

54. Solve $10p - 14 < 8p - 17$. (Lesson 7–3)

55. Write an equation for the line that passes through the point at $(2, -2)$ and is parallel to $y = -2x + 21$. (Lesson 6–6)

56. Statistics Find the range, median, upper and lower quartiles, and interquartile range of the data in the stem-and-leaf plot at the right. (Lesson 5–7)

Stem	Leaf
43	3 5 6 6 9
44	1 4 4 4 9 9
45	0 2 7 7 8
46	5 7 $44\|9 = 449$

57. Finance Patricia invested \$5000 for one year. Martin also invested \$5000 for one year. Martin's account earned interest at a rate of 10% per year. At the end of the year, Martin's account had earned \$125 more than Patricia's account. What was the annual interest rate on Patricia's account? (Lesson 4–4)

58. Solve $\frac{a-x}{-3} = \frac{-2}{b}$ for x. (Lesson 3–6)

59. Architecture Answer the related questions for the verbal problem below. A developer is designing a housing development. She proposes to have four times as many three-bedroom homes as four-bedroom homes. If the development is planned for 100 homes, how many three- and four-bedroom homes will be built? (Lesson 2–9)

a. What does the problem ask?

b. If h represents the number of four-bedroom homes that are planned, how many three-bedroom homes are planned?

c. If 20 four-bedroom homes are planned, how many three-bedroom homes should be built?

60. Evaluate $\frac{6ab}{3x+2y}$ if $a = 6$, $b = 4$, $x = 0.2$, and $y = 1.3$. (Lesson 1–3)

WORKING ON THE In·ves·ti·ga·tion

Refer to the Investigation on pages 448–449.

Ready, Set, Drop!

Your research team determines that hang gliders are not just dropped from a point as you did with your tissue paper triangles. They are always launched into forward motion before gliding. The team decides that scale models are needed in order to get a feel for the launching and landing aspects of a real hang glider.

1. Each team in your class will construct a hang glider model using tissue paper and wire. A table top will act as the top of the cliff from which the glider is to be launched.
2. Each team should discuss different types of methods for launching their hang glider models from the table top. They should present their ideas to the class, and the class should agree upon which method they prefer to use. Then each team tests their glider using the method that the class has chosen.
3. Launch the glider 10 times. For each trial, measure the horizontal distance (along the floor) from the table to the spot at which the glider lands. Record this measurement and the height of the launch site.
4. Use these data to write a linear equation that describes the path of your glider. What is the slope of the path for your glider?
5. Using the linear equations from each of the other teams' data, would your glider collide with any of the other teams' gliders if they were launched at the same time from cliffs that are opposite each other? Write a detailed report on your conclusions.

Add the results of your work to your Investigation Folder.

8-2 Substitution

What **YOU'LL LEARN**

- To solve systems of equations by using the substitution method, and
- to organize data to solve problems.

Why **IT'S IMPORTANT**

You can use systems of equations to solve problems involving geography and accounting.

CONNECTION

Geography

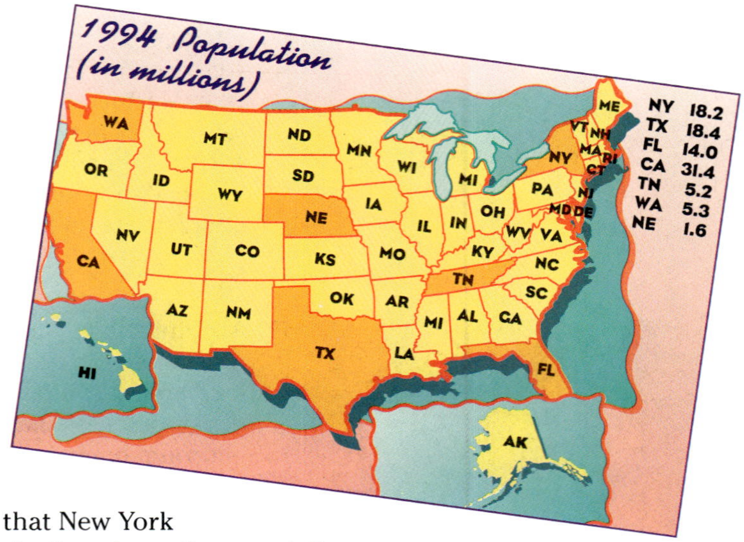

A recent article in a newspaper reported that New York lost its position as the second most populous state when Texas slipped into the No. 2 spot at the end of 1994. Census Bureau projections show that New York will likely be pushed even further down the population ladder when Florida catches up early in the 21st century.

FYI

California has 12% of the entire U.S. population.

Alaska, the largest state in the U.S., has the second smallest population.

If New York's population grows at a constant rate of 0.02 million people per year and Florida's population grows at a constant rate of 0.26 million people per year, when would Florida catch up to New York in population? What would their populations be then?

Let P represent the population in millions, and let t represent the amount of time in years. The information above can be described by the following system of equations.

$$P = 18.2 + 0.02t$$
$$P = 14 + 0.26t$$

You could try to solve this system of equations by graphing, as shown at the right. Notice that the *exact* coordinates of the point where the lines intersect cannot be easily determined from this graph. An estimate is (18, 18).

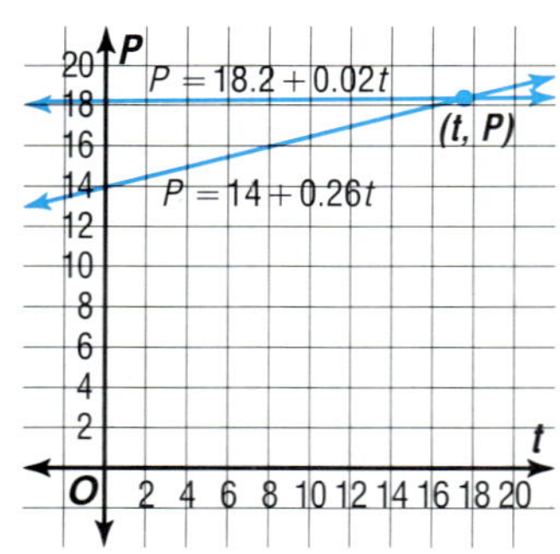

The exact solution of this system of equations can be found by using algebraic methods. One such method is called **substitution**.

From the first equation in the system, $P = 18.2 + 0.02t$, you know that P is equal to $18.2 + 0.02t$. Since P must have the same value in *both* equations, you can substitute $18.2 + 0.02t$ for P in the second equation $P = 14 + 0.26t$.

$$\begin{aligned} P &= 14 + 0.26t \\ 18.2 + 0.02t &= 14 + 0.26t \\ 0.02t &= -4.2 + 0.26t \\ -0.24t &= -4.2 \\ t &= 17.5 \end{aligned}$$

Substitute $18.2 + 0.02t$ for P so the equation will have only one variable.

Now find the value of P by substituting 17.5 for t in either equation.

$P = 18.2 + 0.02t$
$= 18.2 + 0.02(17.5)$ *You could also substitute 17.5 for t in P = 14 + 0.26t.*
$= 18.55$

Check: In each equation, replace t with 17.5 and P with 18.55.

$P = 18.2 + 0.02t$	$P = 14 + 0.26t$
$18.55 \stackrel{?}{=} 18.2 + 0.02(17.5)$	$18.55 \stackrel{?}{=} 14 + 0.26(17.5)$
$18.55 = 18.55$ ✔	$18.55 = 18.55$ ✔

The solution of the system of equations is (17.5, 18.55). Therefore after 17.5 years, or in 2011, the populations of New York and Florida would both be 18.55 million. *Compare this result to the estimate we obtained from the graph.*

You can use substitution to solve systems of equations even when the equations are more complex.

Example 1 **Use substitution to solve each system of equations.**

a. $\mathbf{x + 4y = 1}$
$\mathbf{2x - 3y = -9}$

Solve the first equation for x since the coefficient of x is 1.

$x + 4y = 1$
$x = 1 - 4y$

Next, find the value of y by substituting $1 - 4y$ for x in the second equation.

$2x - 3y = -9$
$2(1 - 4y) - 3y = -9$
$2 - 8y - 3y = -9$
$-11y = -11$
$y = 1$

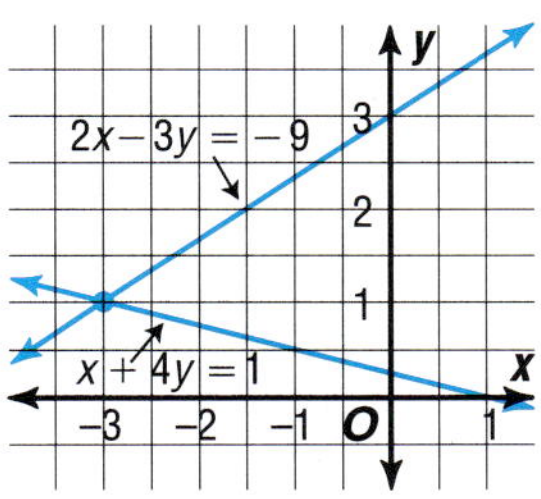

Then substitute 1 for y in either of the original equations and find the value of x. *Choose the equation that is easier for you to solve.*

$x + 4y = 1$
$x + 4(1) = 1$
$x + 4 = 1$
$x = -3$

The solution of this system is (−3, 1). *Use the graph at the left to verify this result.*

b. $\mathbf{\frac{5}{2}x + y = 4}$
$\mathbf{5x + 2y = 8}$

Solve the first equation for y since the coefficient of y is 1.

$\frac{5}{2}x + y = 4$
$y = 4 - \frac{5}{2}x$

Next, find the value of x by substituting $4 - \frac{5}{2}x$ for y in the second equation.

$5x + 2y = 8$
$5x + 2\left(4 - \frac{5}{2}x\right) = 8$
$5x + 8 - 5x = 8$
$8 = 8$

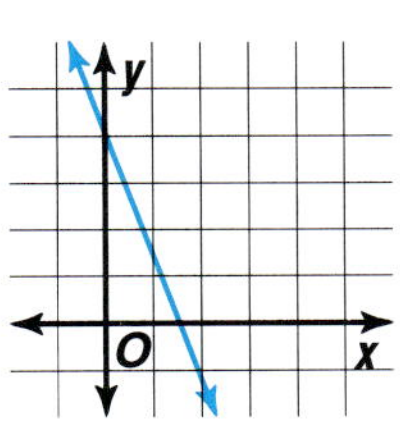

The statement $8 = 8$ is true. This means that there are infinitely many solutions to the system of equations. This is true because the slope intercept form of both equations is $y = 4 - \frac{5}{2}x$. That is, the equations are equivalent, and both have the same graph.

In general, if you solve a system of linear equations and the result is a true statement (an identity such as $8 = 8$), the system has an infinite number of solutions; if the result is a false statement (for example, $8 = 12$), the system has no solution.

MODELING MATHEMATICS

Systems of Equations

Materials: cups and counters, equation mat

Use a model to solve the system of equations.

$4x + 3y = 8$

$y = x - 2$

Your Turn

a. Let a cup represent the unknown value x. If $y = x - 2$, how can you represent y?

b. Represent $4x + 3y = 8$ on the equation mat. On one side of the mat, place four cups to represent $4x$ and three representations of y from step a. On the other side of the mat, place eight positive counters.

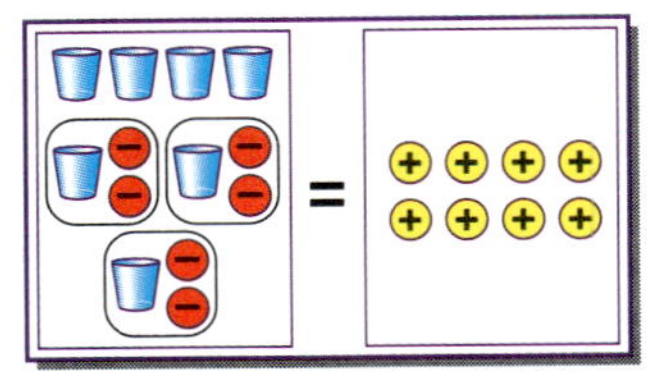

c. Use what you know about equation mats and zero pairs to solve the equation. What value of x is the solution of the system of equations?

d. Use the value of x from step c and the equation $y = x - 2$ to find the value of y.

e. What is the solution of the system of equations?

Sometimes it is helpful to **organize data** before solving a problem. Some ways to organize data are to use tables, charts, different types of graphs, or diagrams.

Example 2

PROBLEM SOLVING

Organize Data

EJH Labs needs to make 1000 gallons of a 34% acid solution. The only solutions available are 25% acid and 50% acid. How many gallons of each solution should be mixed to make the 34% solution?

Explore Let a represent the number of gallons of 25% acid.
Let b represent the number of gallons of 50% acid.

Make a table to organize the information in the problem.

	25% Acid	50% Acid	34% Acid
Total Gallons	a	b	1000
Gallons of Acid	$0.25a$	$0.50b$	0.34(1000)

Plan The system of equations is $a + b = 1000$ and $0.25a + 0.50b = 0.34(1000)$. Use substitution to solve this system.

Solve Since $a + b = 1000$, $a = 1000 - b$.

$$0.25a + 0.50b = 0.34(1000)$$
$$0.25(1000 - b) + 0.50b = 340 \quad \textit{Substitute } 1000 - b \textit{ for } a.$$
$$250 - 0.25b + 0.50b = 340 \quad \textit{Solve for } b.$$
$$0.25b = 90$$
$$b = 360$$

$$a + b = 1000$$
$$a + 360 = 1000 \quad \textit{Substitute 360 for } b.$$
$$a = 640 \quad \textit{Solve for } a.$$

Thus, 640 gallons of the 25% acid solution and 360 gallons of the 50% acid solution should be used.

Examine The 34% acid solution contains $0.25(640) + 0.50(360) = 160 + 180$ or 340 gallons of acid. Since $0.34(1000) = 340$, the answer checks.

Systems of equations can be useful in representing real-life situations and solving real-life problems.

Example 3

Entertainment

The Williams family is going to the Johnstown Summer Carnival. They have two ticket options, as shown in the table below.

Ticket Option	Admission Price	Price Per Ride
A	\$5	30¢
B	\$3	80¢

a. Write an equation that represents the cost per person for each option.

b. Graph the equations and estimate a solution. Explain what the solution means.

c. Solve the system using substitution.

d. Write a short paragraph advising the Williams family which option to choose.

a. Let r represent the number of rides. The total cost C for each person will be the cost of admission plus the cost of the rides.

Option A: $C = 5 + 0.30r$ *The cost of the rides is the price per*

Option B: $C = 3 + 0.80r$ *ride × number of rides, r.*

b. We can estimate from the graph that the solution is about (4, 6). This means that when the number of rides equals 4, both ticket options cost about \$6 per person.

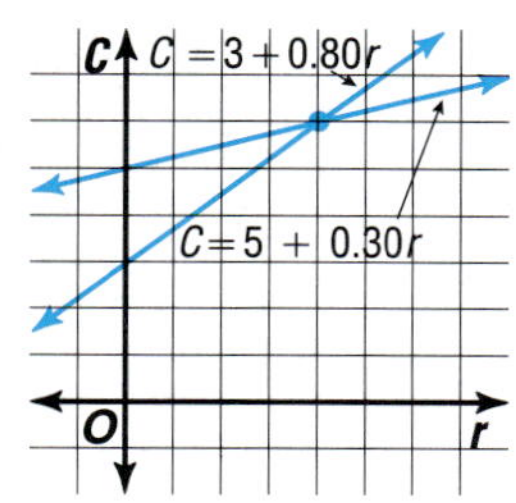

c. Use substitution to solve this system.

$$C = 5 + 0.30r$$

$$3 + 0.80r = 5 + 0.30r \quad \textit{Replace C with } 3 + 0.80r.$$

$$0.50r = 2 \quad \textit{Solve for r.}$$

$$r = 4$$

$$C = 5 + 0.30r$$

$$= 5 + 0.30(4) \quad \textit{Replace r with 4.}$$

$$= 6.2 \quad \textit{Solve for C.}$$

The solution is (4, 6.2). This means that if a person rides 4 rides, both options cost the same, \$6.20. From the graph, you can see that Option A tickets will cost less if a person rides more than 4 rides. Option B tickets will cost less if a person rides less than 4 rides.

d. You should advise the Williams family to purchase Option A tickets for those who plan to ride more than 4 rides and purchase Option B tickets for the rest of the family.

CHECK FOR UNDERSTANDING

Communicating Mathematics

Study the lesson. Then complete the following.

1. **Explain** why, when solving the system $y = 2x - 4$ and $4x - 2y = 0$, you can substitute $2x - 4$ for y in the second equation.
2. **State** what you would conclude if the solution to a system of linear equations yields the equation $8 = 0$.
3. **Describe** how you can tell just by looking at the equations $y = 9x + 2$ and $y = 9x - 5$ whether or not the system has a solution.
4. **Explain** why graphing a system of equations may not give you an exact solution.
5. Yolanda is walking across campus when she sees Adele walking about 30 feet ahead of her. In each graph, t represents time in seconds and d represents distance in feet. Describe what happens in each case and how it relates to the solution.

a. b. c.

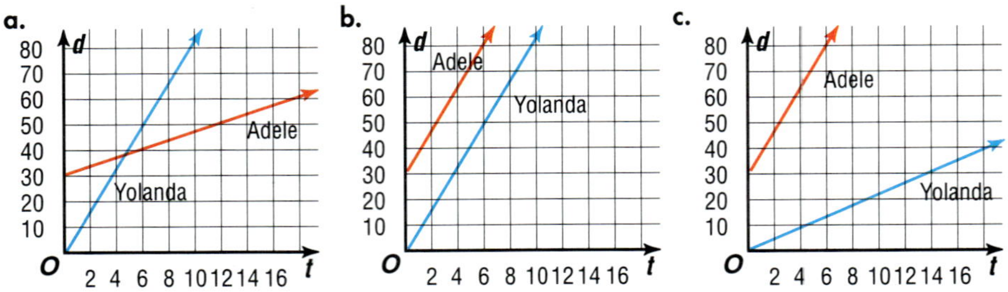

Modeling Mathematics

6. Use cups and counters to model and solve the system of equations.

   $y = 2x - 6$

   $3x + 2y = 9$

Guided Practice

Solve each equation for x. Then, solve each equation for y.

7. $x + 4y = 8$
8. $3x - 5y = 12$
9. $0.8x + 6 = -0.75y$

Use substitution to solve each system of equations. If the system *does not* have exactly one solution, state whether it has *no* solution or *infinitely many* solutions.

10. $y = 3x$
    $x + 2y = -21$
11. $x = 2y$
    $4x + 2y = 15$
12. $x + 5y = -3$
    $3x - 2y = 8$
13. $8x + 2y = 13$
    $4x + y = 11$
14. $2x - y = -4$
    $-3x + y = -9$
15. $6x - 2y = -4$
    $y = 3x + 2$

16. **Sales** Maria spent a long day working the cash register at Musicville during a sale on CDs. For this sale, all CDs in the store were marked either \$12 or \$10. Just when she thought she could go home, the store manager gave Maria the job of figuring out how many CDs they had sold at each price, so they could write the total in the store records. Maria doesn't want to sort through hundreds of sales slips, so she decided on an easier way. The counter at the exit of the store says that 500 people left with CDs (limit one per customer) during the sale, and the cash register contains \$5750 from the day's sales. Maria wrote a system of equations for the number of \$10 CDs and the number of \$12 CDs.
    a. What was the system of equations?
    b. How many CDs were sold at each price?

EXERCISES

Practice

Use substitution to solve each system of equations. If the system *does not* have exactly one solution, state whether it has *no* solution or *infinitely many* solutions.

17. $y = 3x - 8$
$y = 4 - x$

18. $2x + 7y = 3$
$x = 1 - 4y$

19. $x + y = 0$
$3x + y = -8$

20. $4c = 3d + 3$
$c = d - 1$

21. $4x + 5y = 11$
$y = 3x - 13$

22. $3x - 5y = 11$
$x - 3y = 1$

23. $c - 5d = 2$
$2c + d = 4$

24. $3x - 2y = 12$
$x + 2y = 6$

25. $x + 3y = 12$
$x - y = 8$

26. $x - 3y = 0$
$3x + y = 7$

27. $5r - s = 5$
$-4r + 5s = 17$

28. $2x + 3y = 1$
$-3x + y = 15$

29. $8x + 6y = 44$
$x - 8y = -12$

30. $0.5x - 2y = 17$
$2x + y = 104$

31. $-0.3x + y = 0.5$
$0.5x - 0.3y = 1.9$

32. $x = \frac{1}{2}y + 3$
$2x - y = 6$

33. $y = \frac{1}{2}x + 3$
$y = 2x - 1$

34. $y = \frac{3}{5}x$
$3x - 5y = 15$

Use substitution to solve each system of equations. Write each solution as an ordered triple of the form (*x, y, z*).

35. $x + y + z = -54$
$x = -6y$
$z = 14y$

36. $2x + 3y - z = 17$
$y = -3z - 7$
$2x = z + 2$

37. $12x - y + 7z = 99$
$x + 2z = 2$
$y + 3z = 9$

Critical Thinking

38. Number Theory If 36 is subtracted from certain two-digit positive integers, their digits are reversed. Find all integers for which this is true.

Applications and Problem Solving

39. Entertainment American songwriter Cole Porter completed his first professional score in 1916 at age 23. At Harding High, this year's spring musical is *Anything Goes,* which Porter completed in 1934. The production is going to be part of a dinner theater; each ticket includes dinner and the show. The total cost of producing the show (stage, costumes, and so on) is \$1000, and each dinner costs \$5 to prepare. The drama club is going to sell tickets for \$13 each.

a. Write a system of equations to represent the cost of and the income from the production.

b. How many tickets do they need to sell to break even?

40. Humor Refer to the cartoon below. Solve the problem that is sending Peppermint Patty into a frenzy. Find how much cream and milk must be mixed together to obtain 50 gallons of cream containing $12\frac{1}{2}\%$ butterfat.

Peanuts®

41. **Athletes** According to a magazine, top women athletes are narrowing the gap between their performances and those of their male counterparts. Speed skater Bonnie Blair's fastest time in the 500-meter would have won an Olympic gold medal in every men's 500-meter competition through 1976. The women's record time for the 500-meter in speed skating is 39.1 seconds, and the men's is 36.45 seconds. Suppose the women's record time decreases at an average rate of 0.20 second per year and the men's record time decreases at an average rate of 0.10 second per year. **Source:** *Health* magazine

a. When would the women's record time equal the men's?

b. What would the time be?

c. Do you think this could actually happen? Why or why not?

42. **Accounting** Sometimes accountants must figure out how many stock shares to transfer from one person to another to reach a certain proportion of ownership. Suppose Rebeca Avila owns \$3000 worth of stock in a new company that has no other stockholders. For tax purposes, the company is going to issue new stock to Muriel Eppick so that Ms. Avila owns 80%, rather than 100% of the total stock. Let S represent the new total value of company stock and let x represent the value of stock that Ms. Eppick is to receive. Use the equations below to find the value of stock to be issued to Ms. Eppick.

$S = 3000 + x$ *New total stock = Ms. Avila's share + Ms. Eppick's share.*

$3000 = 0.80S$ *Ms. Avila's share is 80% of new total stock.*

$x = 0.20S$ *Ms. Eppick's share is 20% of new total stock.*

43. **Organize Data** For thousands of years, gold has been considered one of Earth's most precious metals. When archaeologist Howard Carter discovered King Tutankhamun's tomb in 1922, he exclaimed that the tomb was filled with "strange animals, statues, and gold—everywhere the glint of gold." One hundred percent pure gold is 24-carat gold. If 18-carat gold is 75% gold and 12-carat gold is 50% gold, how much of each would be used to make a 14-carat gold bracelet weighing 300 grams? (*Hint:* 14-carat gold is about 58% gold.)

a. Make a table to organize the data.

b. Write a system of equations that represents this problem.

c. How much 18-carat gold and 12-carat gold would it take to make a 14-carat gold bracelet weighing 300 grams?

Mixed Review

44. Graph the system of equations below. Determine whether the system has *one* solution, *no* solutions, or *infinitely many* solutions. If the system has one solution, name it. (Lesson 8–1)

$y = 2x + 1$

$7y = 14x + 7$

45. **Finance** Michael uses at most 60% of his annual FlynnCo stock dividend to purchase more shares of FlynnCo stock. If his dividend last year was \$885 and FlynnCo stock is selling for \$14 per share, what is the greatest number of shares that he can purchase? (Lesson 7–2)

46. Graph $y = \frac{1}{5}x - 3$ using the slope and y-intercept. (Lesson 6–5)

47. Solve $3a - 4 = b$ if the domain is $\{-1, 4, 7, 13\}$. (Lesson 5–3)

48. What is 25% less than 94? (Lesson 4–5)

49. Solve $-8 - 12x = 28$. (Lesson 3–3)

50. Graph the solution set of $n \leq -2$ on a number line. (Lesson 2–8)

51. Write an algebraic expression for *twelve less than m*. (Lesson 1–1)

8-3 Elimination Using Addition and Subtraction

What YOU'LL LEARN

- To solve systems of equations by using the elimination method with addition or subtraction.

Why IT'S IMPORTANT

You can use systems of equations to solve problems involving entertainment and testing.

APPLICATION
Entertainment

Cartoons are animated using a computer process that makes the action flow smoothly and seem lifelike. On a Saturday afternoon, the Johnson and Olivera families decided to go see an animated movie together. The Johnson family, two adults and four children, can afford to spend \$30 from their entertainment budget this weekend for the movie tickets, while the Olivera family, two adults and two children, can afford to spend \$21.50. Different theaters around town charge different amounts for adult and child tickets. What price can the Johnsons and Oliveras afford to pay for each adult and each child?

fabulous FIRSTS

Elmer Simms Campbell (1906–1971)

Elmer Simms Campbell was the first African-American cartoonist to work for national publications. He contributed cartoons and other art work to several magazines, as well as syndicated features in 145 newspapers.

Let a represent the ticket price for one adult, and let c represent the ticket price for one child. Then the information in this problem can be represented by the following system of equations.

$$2a + 4c = 30$$
$$2a + 2c = 21.5$$

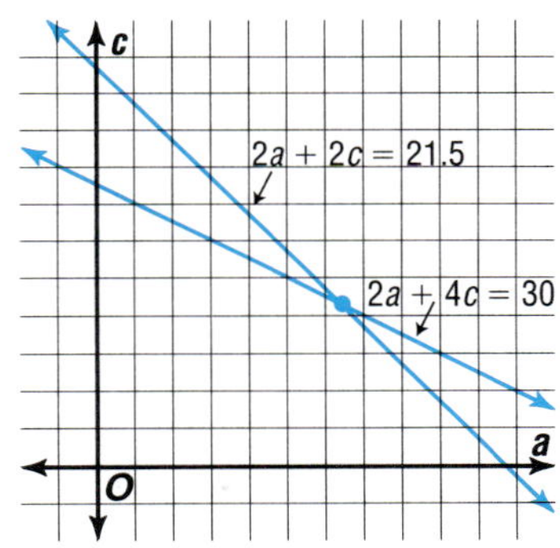

From the graph at the right, an estimated solution is (\$7, \$4). To get an exact solution, solve algebraically. You could solve this system by first solving either of the equations for a or c and then using substitution.

However, a simpler method of solution is to subtract one equation from the other since the coefficients of the variable a are the same. This method is called **elimination** because the subtraction eliminates one of the variables. First, write the equations in column form and subtract.

Recall that subtraction is the same as adding the opposite.

$$\begin{array}{r} 2a + 4c = 30 \\ \underline{(-)\ 2a + 2c = 21.5} \end{array} \quad \xrightarrow{\text{Multiply by } -1.} \quad \begin{array}{r} 2a + 4c = 30 \\ \underline{(+)\ -2a - 2c = -21.5} \\ 2c = 8.5 \\ c = 4.25 \end{array}$$

Then, substitute 4.25 for c in either equation and find the value of a.

$$\begin{aligned} 2a + 2c &= 21.5 \\ 2a + 2(4.25) &= 21.5 && \textit{Substitute 4.25 for c.} \\ 2a + 8.5 &= 21.5 \\ 2a &= 13 \\ a &= 6.5 && \text{Is } (6.5, 4.25) \text{ a solution of the system?} \end{aligned}$$

Check:

$$2a + 4c = 30 \qquad\qquad 2a + 2c = 21.5$$
$$2(6.5) + 4(4.25) \stackrel{?}{=} 30 \qquad\qquad 2(6.5) + 2(4.25) \stackrel{?}{=} 21.5$$
$$30 = 30 \checkmark \qquad\qquad 21.5 = 21.5 \checkmark$$

The solution of this system of equations is (6.5, 4.25). Thus, the Johnsons and Oliveras should look for a theater that charges \$6.50 for each adult and \$4.25 for each child.

In some systems of equations, the coefficients of terms containing the same variable are additive inverses. For these systems, the elimination method can be applied by adding the equations.

Example 1 **Use elimination to solve the system of equations.**

$\mathbf{3x - 2y = 4}$

$\mathbf{4x + 2y = 10}$

Since the coefficients of the y-terms, -2 and 2, are additive inverses, you can solve the system by adding the equations.

$$\begin{array}{rl} 3x - 2y = 4 & \\ (+)\ 4x + 2y = 10 & \\ \hline 7x \quad\quad = 14 & \\ x = 2 & \end{array}$$

Write the equations in column form and add.
Notice that the variable y is eliminated.

Now substitute 2 for x in either equation to find the value of y.

$$\begin{aligned} 3x - 2y &= 4 \\ 3(2) - 2y &= 4 \\ 6 - 2y &= 4 \\ -2y &= -2 \\ y &= 1 \end{aligned}$$

The solution of this system is (2, 1). *Check this result.*

Use subtraction to solve a system of two linear equations whenever one of the variables has the same coefficient in both equations.

Example 2

INTEGRATION
Number Theory

The sum of two numbers is 18. The sum of the greater number and twice the smaller number is 25. Find the numbers.

Let x = the greater number and let y = the lesser number. Since the sum of the numbers is 18, one equation is $x + y = 18$. Since the sum of the greater number and twice the smaller number is 25, the other equation is $x + 2y = 25$. Use elimination to solve this system.

$$\begin{array}{rl} x + \ \ y = 18 & \\ (-)\ x + 2y = 25 & \\ \hline -y = -7 & \\ y = 7 & \end{array}$$

Since the coefficients of the x terms are the same, use elimination by subtraction.

Find x by substituting 7 for y in one of the equations.

$x + y = 18$

$x + 7 = 18$ *Substitute 7 for y.*

$x = 11$ *Solve for x.*

The solution is (11, 7), which means that the numbers are 7 and 11. *Check this result.*

Several software packages can be used to help you solve systems of equations.

EXPLORATION — GRAPHING SOFTWARE

The *Mathematics Exploration Toolkit (MET)* can be used to graph and solve systems of equations. Use the following CALC commands.

CLEAR F (clr f)	Removes previous graphs from the graphing window.
GRAPH (gra)	Graphs the most recent equation in the expression window.
SCALE (sca)	Sets limits on the *x*- and *y*-axes.

To set up the graphing window, enter clr f. Then enter sca 10. This sets limits on the axes at -10 to 10 for x and y. Since only two points are needed to graph a line, use the command gra 2.

Your Turn

a. Check the solutions of the examples using *MET*.

b. Graph the system $3x + 2y = 7$ and $5x + 2y = 17$ and find the solution using *MET*.

c. Describe the difference between solving a system of equations using graphing software and using a graphing calculator. Which do you prefer, and why?

Example 3

APPLICATION

Testing

Lina is preparing to take the Scholastic Assessment Test (SAT). She has been taking practice tests for a year, and her scores are steadily improving. She always scores about 150 points higher on the math test than on the verbal test. She needs a combined score of 1270 to get into the college she has chosen. If she assumes she will still have that 150-point difference between the two tests, how high does she need to score on each part?

Let m represent Lina's math score. Let v represent Lina's verbal score. Since the sum of her scores is 1270, one equation is $m + v = 1270$. Since the difference of her scores is 150, another equation is $m - v = 150$. Use elimination to solve this system.

$$\begin{array}{rl} m + v &= 1270 \\ (+)\ m - v &= 150 \\ \hline 2m \quad &= 1420 \\ m &= 710 \end{array}$$

Since the coefficients of the v term are additive inverses, use elimination by addition.

Find v by substituting 710 for m in one of the equations.

$$\begin{aligned} m + v &= 1270 \\ 710 + v &= 1270 \quad \textit{Substitute 710 for m.} \\ v &= 560 \end{aligned}$$

The solution is (710, 560), which means that Lina must score 710 on the math portion and 560 on the verbal portion of the SAT.

CHECK FOR UNDERSTANDING

Communicating Mathematics

Study the lesson. Then complete the following.

1. **Explain** when it is easier to solve a system of equations in each way.
   a. by elimination using subtraction
   b. by elimination using addition

2. **a. State** the result when you add $3x - 8y = 29$ and $-3x + 8y = 16$. What does this result tell you about the system of equations?
   b. What does this result tell you about the graph of the system?

3. **You Decide** Maribela says that a system of equations has no solution if both variables are eliminated by addition or subtraction. Devin argues that there may be an infinite number of solutions. Who is correct? Explain your answer.

Guided Practice

4. Refer to the graph at the right.
   a. Estimate the solution of the system.
   b. Use elimination to find the exact solution.

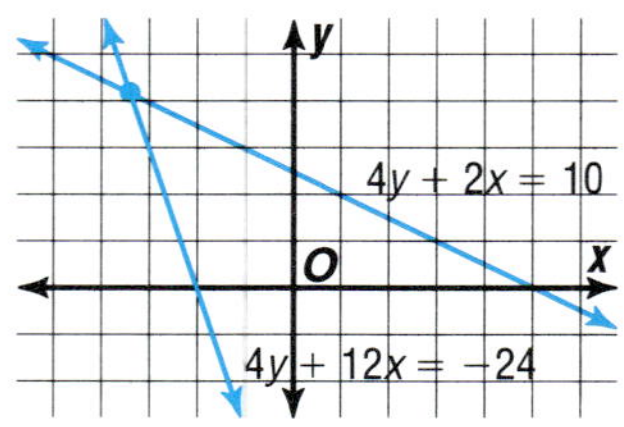

State whether addition, subtraction, or substitution would be most convenient to solve each system of equations. Then solve the system.

5. $3x - 5y = 3$
   $4x + 5y = 4$
6. $3x + 2y = 7$
   $y = 4x - 2$
7. $-4m + 2n = 6$
   $-4m + n = 8$
8. $8a + b = 1$
   $8a - 3b = 3$
9. $3x + y = 7$
   $2x + 5y = 22$
10. $2b + 4c = 8$
    $c - 2 = b$

11. **Statistics** The mean of two numbers is 28. Find the numbers if three times one of the numbers equals half the other number.

EXERCISES

Practice

For Exercises 12–14,
a. estimate the solution of each system of linear equations, and
b. use elimination to find the exact solution of each system.

12.
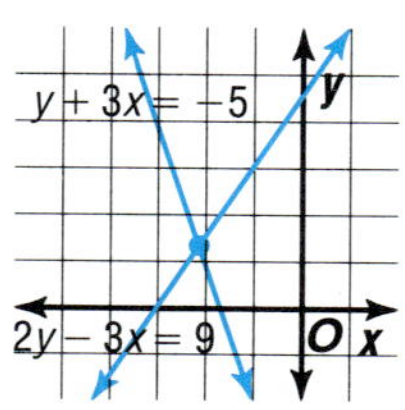

13.
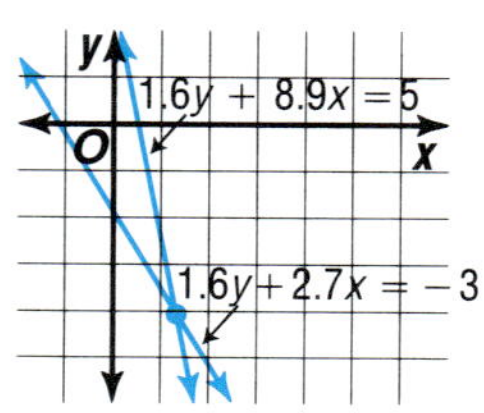

14.
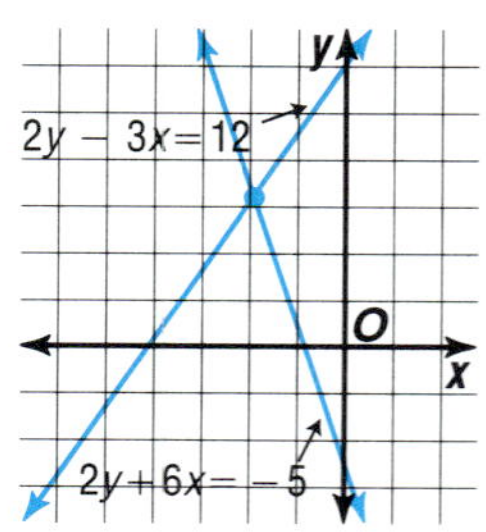

State whether addition, subtraction, or substitution would be most convenient to solve each system of equations. Then solve the system.

15. $x + y = 8$
$x - y = 4$

16. $2r + s = 5$
$r - s = 1$

17. $x - 3y = 7$
$x + 2y = 2$

18. $3x + y = 5$
$2x + y = 10$

19. $5s + 2t = 6$
$9s + 2t = 22$

20. $4x - 3y = 12$
$4x + 3y = 24$

21. $2x + 3y = 13$
$x - 3y = 2$

22. $2m - 5n = -6$
$2m - 7n = -14$

23. $x - 2y = 7$
$-3x + 6y = -21$

24. $3r - 5s = -35$
$2r - 5s = -30$

25. $13a + 5b = -11$
$13a + 11b = 7$

26. $a - 2b - 5 = 0$
$3a - 2b - 9 = 0$

27. $4x = 7 - 5y$
$8x = 9 - 5y$

28. $\frac{2}{3}x + y = 7$
$\frac{10}{3}x + 5y = 11$

29. $\frac{3}{5}c - \frac{1}{5}d = 9$
$\frac{7}{5}c + \frac{1}{5}d = 11$

30. $0.6m - 0.2n = 0.9$
$0.3m = 0.45 - 0.1n$

31. $1.44x - 3.24y = -5.58$
$1.08x + 3.24y = 9.99$

32. $7.2m + 4.5n = 129.06$
$7.2m + 6.7n = 136.54$

INTEGRATION
Number Theory

Use a system of equations and elimination to solve each problem.

33. Find two numbers whose sum is 64 and whose difference is 42.

34. Find two numbers whose sum is 18 and whose difference is 22.

35. Twice one number added to another number is 18. Four times the first number minus the other number is 12. Find the numbers.

36. If $x + y = 11$ and $x - y = 5$, what does xy equal?

Use elimination twice to solve each system of equations. Write the solution as an ordered triple of the form (*x*, *y*, *z*).

37. $x + y = 5$
$y + z = 10$
$x + z = 9$

38. $2x + y + z = 13$
$x - y + 2z = 8$
$4x - 3z = 7$

39. $x + 2z = 2$
$y + 3z = 9$
$12x - y + 7z = 99$

Critical Thinking

40. The graphs of $Ax + By = 7$ and $Ax - By = 9$ intersect at $(4, -1)$. Find A and B.

Applications and Problem Solving

41. On-Line Entertainment On June 27, 1994, Aerosmith became the first major rock band to release a song distributed exclusively in the U.S. through a computer on-line service. Users of the commercial service, CompuServe, were able to download the Aerosmith song *Head First* for free. However, it took a long time to download the song, which itself lasted only 3 minutes, 14 seconds, because of the high-fidelity sound. José and Ling share a personal computer, and one evening they each downloaded the song without realizing that the other had done it. Ling also wasted 18 minutes because he typed the wrong word and had to start over. At the end of the month, the bill from CompuServe said they had used a total of 2.6 hours of time that evening. How long did it take to download the song each time? (*Hint:* 18 minutes = 0.3 hour.)

> **FYI**
>
> The Great Pyramid of King Khufu, built around 2600 B.C., has only one entrance, which is nearly impossible to find. Centuries later, however, robbers stole everything from the pyramid, including the mummy of the king.

42. **World Cultures** The ancient Egyptians believed that the pharaohs lived forever after death in their houses of eternity, the pyramids. Suppose the side of the pyramid containing the entrance is represented by the line $13x + 10y = 9600$, the opposite side of the pyramid, by the line $13x - 10y = 0$, and the descending corridor leading to the entrance, by the line $3x - 10y = 1500$, where x is the distance in feet and y is the height in feet.
    a. Find the coordinates of the entrance.
    b. Find the height of the pyramid.

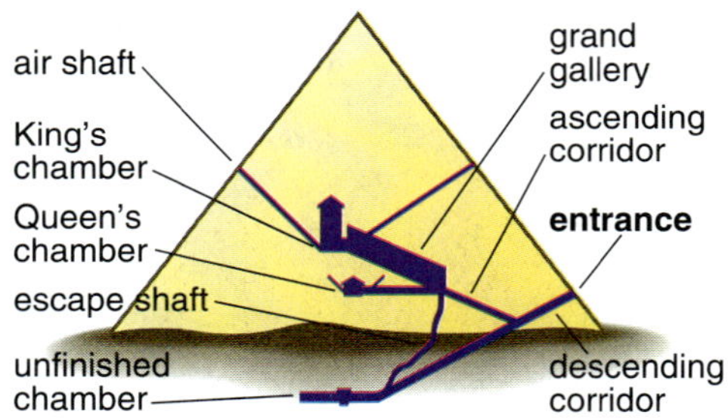

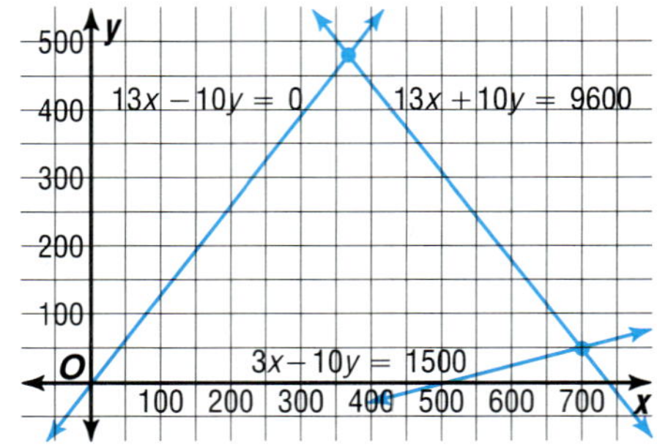

Mixed Review

43. **Chemistry** MX Labs needs to make 500 gallons of a 34% acid solution. The only solutions available are 25% acid and 50% acid. How many gallons of each solution should be mixed to make the 34% solution? Write and solve a system of equations by using substitution. (Lesson 8–2)
44. Solve $5 - 8h \leq 9$. (Lesson 7–3)
45. Determine the slope of the line that passes through the points at $(2, -9)$ and $(-1, 0)$. (Lesson 6–1)
46. Graph $6x - \frac{1}{2}y = -10$. (Lesson 5–4)
47. Solve $-2(3t + 1) = 5$. (Lesson 3–3)
48. Find an approximation to the nearest hundredth for $\sqrt{15}$. (Lesson 2–8)
49. Name the property illustrated by the following statement. (Lesson 1–6)
    If $6 = 2a$ *and* $a = 3$, *then* $6 = 2 \cdot 3$.

SELF TEST

Graph each system of equations. Then determine if the system has *one* solution, *no* solution, or *infinitely many* solutions. If the system has one solution, name it. (Lesson 8–1)

1. $x - y = 3$
   $3x + y = 1$
2. $2x - 3y = 7$
   $3y = 7 + 2x$
3. $4x + y = 12$
   $x = 3 - \frac{1}{4}y$

Use substitution to solve each system of equations. (Lesson 8–2)

4. $y = 5x$
   $x + 2y = 22$
5. $2y - x = -5$
   $y - 3x = 20$
6. $3x + 2y = 18$
   $x + \frac{8}{3}y = 12$

Use elimination to solve each system of equations. (Lesson 8–3)

7. $x - y = -5$
   $x + y = 25$
8. $3x + 5y = 14$
   $2x - 5y = 1$
9. $5x + 4y = 12$
   $3x + 4y = 4$

10. **Recreation** At a recreation and sports facility, 3 members and 3 nonmembers pay a total of \$180 to take an aerobics class. A group of 5 members and 3 nonmembers pay \$210 to take the same class. How much does it cost members and nonmembers to take an aerobics class? (Lesson 8–3)

8–4 Elimination Using Multiplication

What YOU'LL LEARN

- To solve systems of equations by using the elimination method with multiplication and addition, and
- to determine the best method for solving systems of equations.

Why IT'S IMPORTANT

You can use systems of equations to solve problems involving telecommunications and geography.

FYI

On January 14, 1876, Alexander Graham Bell beat Elisha Gray by only a few hours when filing a patent application for his telephone. Both men had invented workable prototypes simultaneously.

APPLICATION

Telecommunications

GBT Mobilnet provides monthly plans for cellular phone customers. Carla Ramos and Robert Johnson both selected Plan B for which monthly charges are based on per-minute rates of calls during peak and nonpeak hours. In one month, Carla made 75 minutes of peak calls and 30 minutes of nonpeak calls. Her bill was \$40.05. During the same period, Robert made 50 minutes of peak calls and 60 minutes of nonpeak calls. His bill was \$35.10. What is GBT Mobilnet's charge per minute for peak and nonpeak calls on Plan B?

Let p represent the rate per minute for peak calls, and let n represent the rate per minute for nonpeak calls. Then the information in this problem can be represented by the following system of equations.

$$75p + 30n = 40.05$$
$$50p + 60n = 35.10$$

So far, you have learned four methods for solving a system of two linear equations.

Method	The Best Time to Use
Graphing	if you want to estimate the solution, since graphing usually does not give an exact solution
Substitution	if one of the variables in either equation has a coefficient of 1 or −1
Addition	if one of the variables has opposite coefficients in the two equations
Subtraction	if one of the variables has the same coefficient in the two equations

The system above is not easily solved using any of these methods. However, there is an extension of the elimination method that can be used. Multiply one of the equations by some number so that adding or subtracting eliminates one of the variables.

For this system, multiply the first equation by −2 and add. Then the coefficient of n in both equations will be 60 or −60.

$$\begin{aligned} 75p + 30n &= 40.05 \\ 50p + 60n &= 35.10 \end{aligned} \quad \xrightarrow{\text{Multiply by } -2.} \quad \begin{aligned} -150p - 60n &= -80.10 \\ (+)\ 50p + 60n &= 35.10 \\ \hline -100p \qquad &= -45 \\ p &= 0.45 \end{aligned}$$

Now, solve for n by replacing p with 0.45.

$$\begin{aligned} 75p + 30n &= 40.05 \\ 75(0.45) + 30n &= 40.05 && \textit{Substitute 0.45 for p.} \\ 33.75 + 30n &= 40.05 && \textit{Solve for n.} \\ 30n &= 6.3 \\ n &= 0.21 && \text{Is } (0.45, 0.21) \text{ a solution?} \end{aligned}$$

Check: $75p + 30n = 40.05$ $\quad$ $50p + 60n = 35.10$

$75(0.45) + 30(0.21) \stackrel{?}{=} 40.05$ $\quad$ $50(0.45) + 60(0.21) \stackrel{?}{=} 35.10$

$40.05 = 40.05$ ✓ $\quad$ $35.10 = 35.10$ ✓

The solution of this system is (0.45, 0.21). Thus, the per-minute rate for peak-hour calls is 45¢, and the per-minute rate for nonpeak calls is 21¢ on this plan.

For some systems of equations, it is necessary to multiply *each* equation by a different number in order to solve the system by elimination. You can choose to eliminate either variable.

Example 1

Use elimination to solve the system of equations in two different ways.

$$\mathbf{2x + 3y = 5}$$
$$\mathbf{5x + 4y = 16}$$

Method 1

You can eliminate the variable x by multiplying the first equation by 5 and the second equation by -2 and then adding the resulting equations.

$2x + 3y = 5$ → Multiply by 5. → $10x + 15y = 25$

$5x + 4y = 16$ → Multiply by −2. → $(+)\ -10x - 8y = -32$

$$7y = -7$$
$$y = -1$$

Now find x using one of the original equations.

$2x + 3y = 5$

$2x + 3(-1) = 5$ *Substitute −1 for y.*

$2x - 3 = 5$ *Solve for x.*

$2x = 8$

$x = 4$

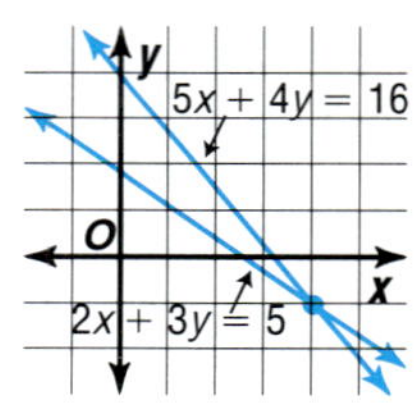

The solution of the system is $(4, -1)$.

Method 2

You can also solve this system by eliminating the variable y. Multiply the first equation by -4 and the second equation by 3. Then add.

$2x + 3y = 5$ → Multiply by −4. → $-8x - 12y = -20$

$5x + 4y = 16$ → Multiply by 3. → $(+)\ 15x + 12y = 48$

$$7x = 28$$
$$x = 4$$

Now find y.

$2x + 3y = 5$

$2(4) + 3y = 5$ *Substitute 4 for x.*

$8 + 3y = 5$ *Solve for y.*

$3y = -3$

$y = -1$

The solution is $(4, -1)$, which matches the result obtained with Method 1.

Example **2**

APPLICATION

Testing

Luis Diaz discovered while entering test scores into his computer that he had accidentally reversed the digits of a test and shorted a student 36 points. Mr. Diaz told the student that the sum of the digits was 14 and agreed to give the student his correct score plus extra credit if he could determine his actual score without looking at his test. What was his actual score on the test?

Explore Let t represent the tens digit of the score. Let u represent the units digit.

The actual score on the test can be represented by $10t + u$. The amount entered in the computer can be represented by $10u + t$. *Why?*

Plan Since the sum of the digits is 14, one equation is $t + u = 14$. Since the teacher accidentally shorted the student by 36 points, another equation is $(10t + u) - (10u + t) = 36$ or $9t - 9u = 36$.

Solve

$$t + u = 14 \quad \xrightarrow{\text{Multiply by 9.}} \quad 9t + 9u = 126$$

$$9t - 9u = 36 \qquad\qquad (+)\ 9t - 9u = 36$$

$$18t \qquad = 162$$

$$t = 9$$

Now find u using one of the original equations.

$t + u = 14$

$9 + u = 14$ *Substitute 9 for t.*

$u = 5$ *Solve for u.*

The solution is (9, 5), which means that the student's actual test score was $10(9) + 5$, or 95 points.

Examine The sum of the digits, $9 + 5$, is 14 and $95 - 59$ is 36.

You can use systems of equations to solve problems involving the distance formula, $rt = d$.

Example **3**

APPLICATION

Uniform Motion

FYI

The world's largest riverboat is the 418-ft *American Queen.* Passengers paid up tp $9400 to take its first cruise in June, 1995.

A riverboat on the Mississippi River travels 48 miles upstream in 4 hours. The return trip takes the riverboat only 3 hours. Find the rate of the current.

Explore Let r represent the rate of the riverboat in still water. Let c represent the rate of the current.

Then $r + c$ represents the rate of the riverboat traveling downstream *with* the current and $r - c$ represents the rate of the riverboat traveling upstream *against* the current.

(continued on the next page)

Plan Use the formula rate × time = distance, or $rt = d$, to write a system of equations. Then solve the system to find the value of c.

	r	t	d	$rt = d$
Downstream	$r + c$	3	48	$3r + 3c = 48$
Upstream	$r - c$	4	48	$4r - 4c = 48$

Solve

$3r + 3c = 48$ **Multiply by 4.** $12r + 12c = 192$

$4r - 4c = 48$ **Multiply by −3.** $(+)\ -12r + 12c = -144$

$$24c = 48$$
$$c = 2$$

The rate of the current is 2 miles per hour.

Examine Find the value of r for this system and then check the solution.

CHECK FOR UNDERSTANDING

Communicating Mathematics

Study the lesson. Then complete the following.

1. **Write** a problem about a real-life situation in which only an estimate of the solution is needed rather than the exact solution. The problem should involve a system of equations.
2. **Explain** why you might need to multiply each equation by a different number when using elimination to solve a system of equations.
3. **Write** a system of equations that could best be solved by using multiplication and then elimination using addition or subtraction.

Math Journal

4. **Assess Yourself** Describe the method you like to use best when solving systems of linear equations. Explain your reasons.

Guided Practice

Explain the steps you would follow to eliminate the variable x in each system of equations. Then solve the system.

5. $x + 5y = 4$, $3x - 7y = -10$
6. $2x - y = 6$, $3x + 4y = -2$
7. $-5x + 3y = 6$, $x - y = 4$

Explain the steps you would follow to eliminate the variable y in each system of equations. Then solve the system.

8. $4x + 7y = 6$, $6x + 5y = 20$
9. $3x - 8y = 13$, $4x - 5y = 6$
10. $2x - 3y = 2$, $5x + 4y = 28$

Match each system of equations with the method that could be most efficiently used to solve it. Then solve the system.

11. $3x - 7y = 6$, $2x + 7y = 4$
12. $y = 4x + 11$, $3x - 2y = -7$
13. $4x + 3y = 19$, $3x - 4y = 8$

a. substitution
b. elimination using addition or subtraction
c. elimination using multiplication

14. **Uniform Motion** A riverboat travels 36 miles downstream in 2 hours. The return trip takes 3 hours.
   a. Find the rate of the riverboat in still water.
   b. Find the rate of the current.

EXERCISES

Practice

Use elimination to solve each system of equations.

15. $2x + y = 5$
    $3x - 2y = 4$
16. $4x - 3y = 12$
    $x + 2y = 14$
17. $3x - 2y = 19$
    $5x + 4y = 17$
18. $9x = 5y - 2$
    $3x = 2y - 2$
19. $7x + 3y = -1$
    $4x + y = 3$
20. $6x - 5y = 27$
    $3x + 10y = -24$
21. $8x - 3y = -11$
    $2x - 5y = 27$
22. $11x - 5y = 80$
    $9x - 15y = 120$
23. $4x - 7y = 10$
    $3x + 2y = -7$
24. $3x - \frac{1}{2}y = 10$
    $5x + \frac{1}{4}y = 8$
25. $2x + \frac{2}{3}y = 4$
    $x - \frac{1}{2}y = 7$
26. $\frac{2x + y}{3} = 15$
    $\frac{3x - y}{5} = 1$
27. $7x + 2y = 3(x + 16)$
    $x + 16 = 5y + 3x$
28. $0.4x + 0.5y = 2.5$
    $1.2x - 3.5y = 2.5$
29. $1.8x - 0.3y = 14.4$
    $x - 0.6y = 2.8$

INTEGRATION
Number Theory

Use a system of equations and elimination to solve each problem.

30. The sum of the digits of a two-digit number is 14. If the digits are reversed, the new number is 18 less than the original number. Find the original number.
31. Three times one number equals twice a second number. Twice the first number is 3 more than the second number. Find the numbers.
32. The ratio of the tens digit to the units digit of a two-digit number is 1:4. If the digits are reversed, the sum of the new number and the original number is 110. Find the original number.

Determine the best method to solve each system of equations. Then solve the system.

33. $9x - 8y = 17$
    $4x + 8y = 9$
34. $3x - 4y = -10$
    $5x + 8y = -2$
35. $x + 2y = -1$
    $2x + 4y = -2$
36. $5x + 3y = 12$
    $4x - 5y = 17$
37. $\frac{2}{3}x - \frac{1}{2}y = 14$
    $\frac{5}{6}x - \frac{1}{2}y = 18$
38. $\frac{1}{2}x - \frac{2}{3}y = \frac{7}{3}$
    $\frac{3}{2}x + 2y = -25$

Use elimination to solve each system of equations.

39. $\frac{1}{x - 5} - \frac{3}{y + 6} = 0$
    $\frac{2}{x + 7} - \frac{1}{y - 3} = 0$
40. $\frac{2}{x} + \frac{3}{y} = 16$
    $\frac{1}{x} + \frac{1}{y} = 7$
41. $\frac{1}{x - y} = \frac{1}{y}$
    $\frac{1}{x + y} = 2$

Programming

42. The graphing calculator program at the right finds the solution of two linear equations written in standard form.

$ax + by = c$

$dx + ey = f$

The formulas for the solution of this system are as follows.

$$x = \frac{ce - bf}{ae - bd}, \quad y = \frac{af - cd}{ae - bd}$$

```
PROGRAM:SOLVE
: Disp "ENTER COEFFICIENTS"
: Prompt A,B,C,D,E,F
: If AE−BD =0
: Then
: Goto 1
: End
: (CE−BF)/(AE-BD)→X
: (AF−CD)/(AE-BD)→Y
: Disp "THE SOLUTION IS"
: Disp "X= ",X
: Disp "Y= ",Y
: Stop
: Lbl 1
: If CE−BF=0 or AF−CD=0
: Then
: Disp "INFINITELY","MANY"
: Else
: Disp "NO SOLUTION"
```

Use the program to solve each system.

a. $8x + 2y = 0$
$12x + 3y = 0$

b. $x - 2y = 5$
$3x - 5y = 8$

c. $5x + 5y = 16$
$2x + 2y = 5$

d. $7x - 3y = 5$
$14x - 6y = 10$

Critical Thinking

43. The graphs of the equations $5x + 4y = 18$, $2x + 9y = 59$, and $3x - 5y = -4$ contain the sides of a triangle. Determine the coordinates of the vertices of the triangle.

Applications and Problem Solving

44. Geography Benjamin Banneker, a self-taught mathematician and astronomer, was the first African-American to publish an almanac. He is most noted for being the assistant surveyor on the team that designed the ten-mile square of Washington, D.C. The White House is located in the center of the square, at the intersection of Pennsylvania Avenue and New York Avenue. Let $-5x + 7y = 0$ represent New York Avenue and let $3x + 8y = 305$ represent Pennsylvania Avenue. Find the coordinates for the White House.

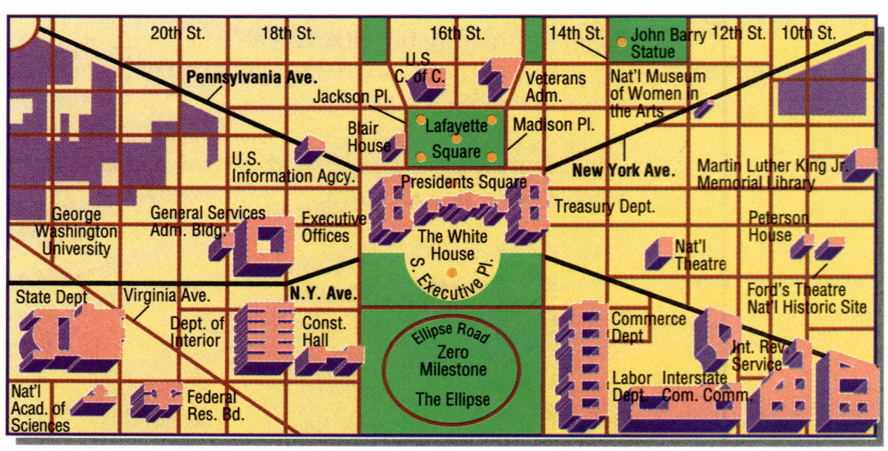

45. Organize Data At the new Cozy Inn Restaurant, which is still under construction, the owners have hired enough waiters and waitresses to handle 17 tables of customers. The fire marshall has looked at the plans for the restaurant and says he will approve it for a limit of 56 customers. The restaurant owners are now deciding how many two-seat tables and how many four-seat tables to buy for the restaurant. How many of each kind should they buy?

46. **Information Highway** The Mercury Center provides a reference and research service for on-line computer users based on peak and nonpeak usage. Miriam and Lesharo are both subscribers. The chart below displays the number of peak and nonpeak minutes each of them spent on-line in one month and how much it cost. Use the information to find the Mercury Center's rate per minute for its peak and nonpeak on-line research service.

User	Number of Peak Minutes	Number of Nonpeak Minutes	Cost
Lesharo	45	50	$27.75
Miriam	70	30	$36

Mixed Review

47. Use elimination to solve the system of equations. (Lesson 8–3)
$2x - y = 10$
$5x + 3y = 3$

48. **Statistics** What is the outlier in the box-and-whisker plot? (Lesson 7–7)

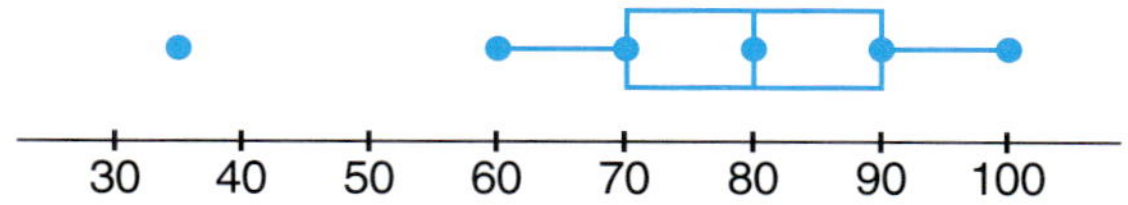

49. **Probability** If Bill, Raul, and Kenyatta each have an equal chance of winning a bicycle race, find the probability that Raul finishes last. (Lesson 7–5)

50. Find the coordinates of the midpoint of the line segment whose endpoints are at (1, 6) and (−3, 4). (Lesson 6–7)

51. **Track** Alfonso runs a 440-yard race in 55 seconds, and Marcus runs it in 88 seconds. To have Alfonso and Marcus finish at the same time, how much of a head start should Alfonso give Marcus? (Lesson 4–7)

52. If $12m = 4$, then $3m =$ __?__. (Lesson 3–2)

53. **Cooking** If there are four sticks in a pound of butter and each stick is $\frac{1}{2}$ cup, how many cups of butter are in a pound of butter? (Lesson 2–6)

54. Evaluate $288 \div [3(9 + 3)]$. (Lesson 1–3)

Mathematics and SOCIETY

High-Tech Checkout Lanes

The article below appeared in a publication for grocers in February, 1994.

[A MAJOR DISCOUNT DEPARTMENT STORE]...has installed a new technology in 48 stores that helps ensure that enough check-lanes are open to serve customers in a store. The system counts the number of adults and children who are in a store at any given moment. The system, called ShopperTrak...uses infrared technology on door-mounted units to give a continuous count of shoppers entering and exiting a store...The data is channeled to software in a PC called FastLane, which uses it to calculate how many checklanes should be open during the next 20 minutes so that no more than two to three people are in line at each lane. Managers read the data at monitors stationed at the checkout area. ■

Source: *Progressive Grocer*

1. How do you think the ShopperTrak system can count the number of children entering and leaving the store as well as the number of adults? Why might separate counts of children and adults be useful?
2. Do you think the average shopping times would differ between men and women, boys and girls, or senior citizens and young people? Why do you think the ShopperTrak system doesn't consider these factors?

8–5 Graphing Systems of Inequalities

What YOU'LL LEARN

- To solve systems of inequalities by graphing.

Why IT'S IMPORTANT

You can use systems of inequalities to solve problems involving travel and nutrition.

APPLICATION

Employment

Unita likes her job as a baby-sitter, but it pays only \$3 per hour. She has been offered a job as a tutor that pays \$6 per hour. Because of school, her parents only allow her to work a maximum of 15 hours per week. How many hours can Unita tutor *and* baby-sit and still make at least \$65 per week?

Let x represent the number of hours Unita can baby-sit each week. Let y represent the number of hours she can tutor each week. Since both x and y represent a number of hours, neither can be a negative number. Thus, $x \geq 0$ and $y \geq 0$. Then the following **system of inequalities** can be used to represent the conditions of this problem.

$$x \geq 0$$
$$y \geq 0$$
$$3x + 6y \geq 65 \quad \textit{She wants to earn at least \$65.}$$
$$x + y \leq 15 \quad \textit{She can work up to 15 hours.}$$

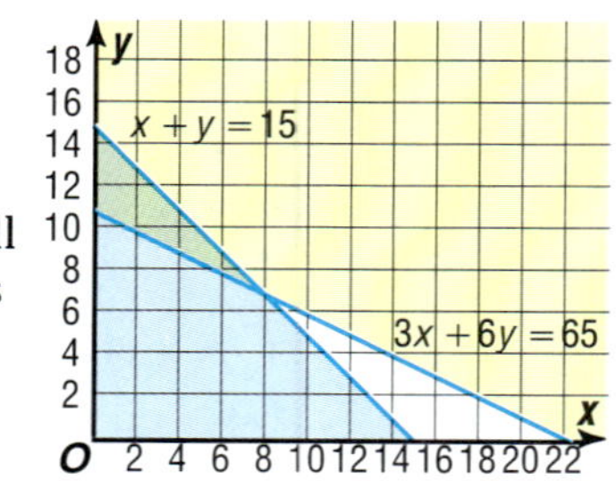

The solution of this system is the set of all ordered pairs that satisfies both inequalities and lies in the first quadrant. The solution can be determined by graphing each inequality on the same coordinate plane.

Recall that the graph of each inequality is called a *half-plane*. The intersection of the two half-planes represents the solution to the system of inequalities. This solution is a region that contains the graphs of an infinite number of ordered pairs. The boundary line of the half-plane is solid and is included in the graph if the inequality is $\leq$ or $\geq$. The boundary line of the half-plane is dashed and is not included in the graph if the inequality is $<$ or $>$.

LOOK BACK

You can refer to Lesson 7-8 for information on graphing inequalities in two variables.

The graphs of $3x + 6y = 65$ and $x + y = 15$ are the boundaries of the region and are included in the graph of this system. This region is shown in green above. Only the portion in the first quadrant is shaded since $x \geq 0$ and $y \geq 0$. Every point in this region is a possible solution to the system. For example, since the graph of (5, 9) is a point in the region, Unita could baby-sit for 5 hours and tutor for 9 hours. In this case, she would make \$3(5) + \$6(9) or \$69. *Does this meet her requirements of time and earnings?*

Example 1 **Solve each system of inequalities by graphing.**

a. $\boldsymbol{y < 2x + 1}$
$\boldsymbol{y \geq -x + 3}$

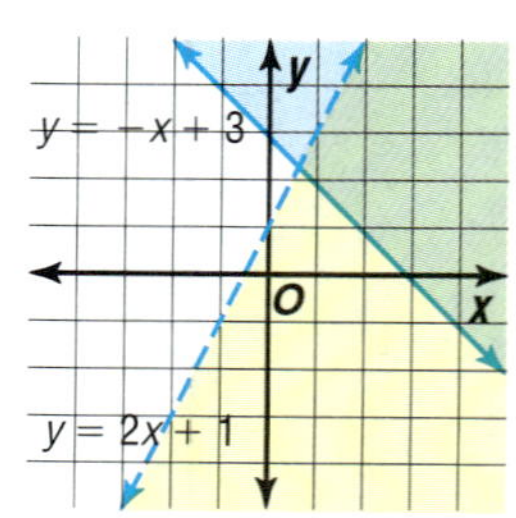

The solution includes the ordered pairs in the intersection of the graphs of $y < 2x + 1$ and $y \geq -x + 3$. This region is shaded in green at the right. The graphs of $y = 2x + 1$ and $y = -x + 3$ are the boundaries of this region. The graph of $y = 2x + 1$ is dashed and is *not* included in the graph of $y < 2x + 1$. The graph of $y = -x + 3$ is included in the graph of $y \geq -x + 3$.

b. $2x + y \geq 4$
$y \leq -2x - 1$

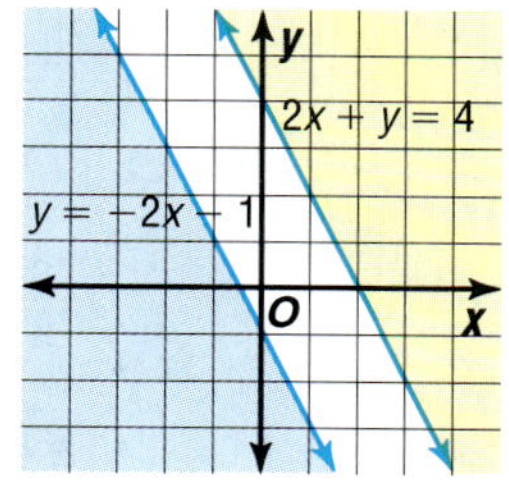

The graphs of $2x + y = 4$ and $y = -2x - 1$ are parallel lines. Because the two regions have no points in common, the system of inequalities has no solution.

Sometimes in real-life problems involving systems, only whole-number solutions make sense.

Example 2

APPLICATION

Vacations

Elena Ayala wants to spend no more than \$700 for hotels while vacationing in Hawaii. She wants to stay at the Highville Resort at least one night and at the Coral Hotel for the remainder of her stay. The Highville Resort costs \$130 per night, and the Coral Hotel costs \$85 per night.

a. If she wants to stay in Hawaii at least 6 nights, how many nights could she spend at each hotel and still stay within her budget?

b. What advice might you give Elena concerning her options?

> **GLOBAL CONNECTIONS**
>
> Polynesians from the Marquesas Islands settled in Hawaii in about A.D. 400. A second wave of immigration arrived from Tahiti approximately 400 to 500 years later.

a. Let c represent the number of nights she will stay at the Coral Hotel. Let h represent the number of nights she will stay at the Highville Resort.

Then the following system of inequalities can be used to represent the conditions of this problem.

$h + c \geq 6$	*Elena wants to stay at least 6 nights.*
$h \geq 1$	*She wants to stay at least 1 night at the Highville Resort.*
$130h + 85c \leq 700$	*She wants to spend no more than \$700.*

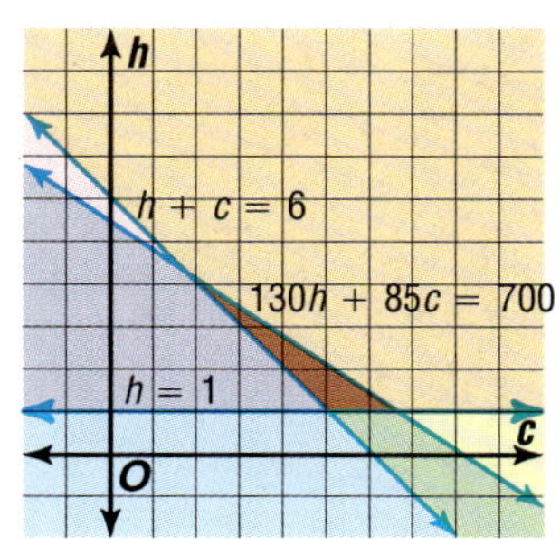

The solution is the set of all ordered pairs whose graphs are in the intersection of the graphs of these inequalities. This region is shown in brown at the right.

Any point in this region is a possible solution; however, only whole-number solutions make sense in this problem. *Why?* For example, since (3, 3) is a point in the region, Elena could stay 3 nights at each hotel. In this case, she would spend 3(\$130) or \$390 at the Highville Resort and 3(\$85) or \$255 at the Coral Hotel for a total of \$645. The other solutions are (5, 1), (6, 1), (4, 2), (5, 2) and (2, 4). *Check this result.*

b. You could advise Elena that she could stay in Hawaii a maximum of 7 nights if she stayed at the Highville Resort only 1 or 2 nights and stayed at the Coral Hotel for the remainder of her vacation.

A graphing calculator is a useful tool for graphing systems of inequalities. It is important to enter the functions in the correct order, since this determines the shading.

EXPLORATION — GRAPHING CALCULATORS

You can use a graphing calculator to solve systems of inequalities. It graphs functions and shades above the first function entered and below the second function entered. Select 7 on the DRAW menu to choose the SHADE feature. First, enter the function that is the lower boundary of the region to be shaded. (Note that inequalities that have $>$ or $\geq$ are lower boundaries and inequalities that have $<$ or $\leq$ are upper boundaries.) Press [,]. Then enter the function that is the upper boundary of the region. Press [ )] [ENTER].

Your Turn

a. Use a graphing calculator to graph the system of inequalities.

$y \geq 4x - 3$

$y \leq -2x + 9$

b. Use a graphing calculator to work through the examples in this lesson. List and explain any disadvantages that you discovered when using the graphing calculator to graph systems of inequalities.

c. Describe the process of using a graphing calculator to solve systems of linear inequalities in your own words.

CHECK FOR UNDERSTANDING

Communicating Mathematics

Study the lesson. Then complete the following.

1. **Explain** how to determine whether boundary lines should be included in the graph of a system of inequalities.

2. **You Decide** Joshua says that the intersection point of the boundary lines is always a solution of a system of inequalities. Rolanda says the point of intersection may not be part of the solution set. Explain who is correct and give an example to support your answer.

3. **Write** a system of inequalities that has no solutions. Describe the graph of your system.

4. **State** which points are solutions to the system of inequalities graphed at the right. Explain how you know.

   a. (0, 0) **b.** (−1, 4)

   c. (2, 5) **d.** (0.5, −1.7)

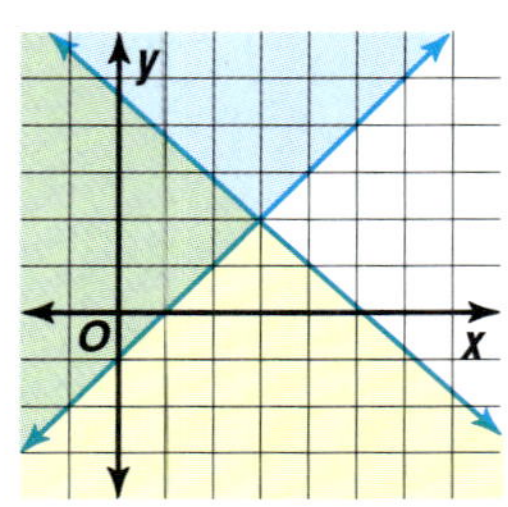

MATH JOURNAL

5. Describe a real-life situation that you can model using a system of linear inequalities.

Guided Practice

Solve each system of inequalities by graphing.

6. $x < 1$
   $x > -4$
7. $y \geq -2$
   $y - x < 1$
8. $y \geq 2x + 1$
   $y \leq -x + 1$
9. $y \geq 3x$
   $3y < 5x$
10. $y - x < 1$
    $y - x > 3$
11. $2x + y \leq 4$
    $3x - y \geq 6$

Write a system of inequalities for each graph.

12.

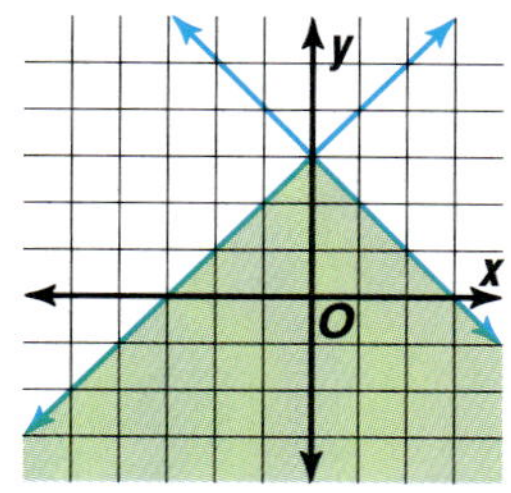

13.

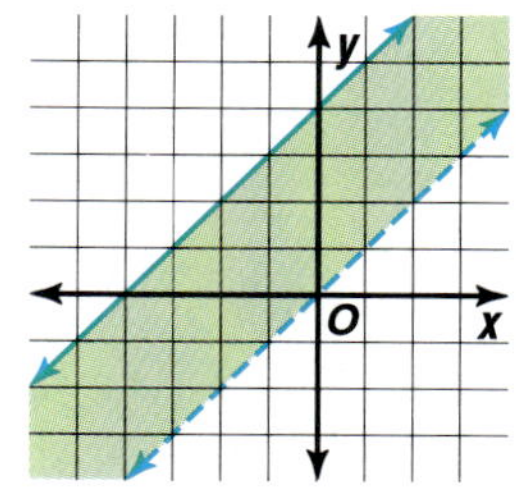

14. **Sales** Ms. Johnson's homeroom class can order up to \$90 of free pizzas from Angelino's Pizza as a reward for selling the most magazines during the magazine drive. They need to order at least 6 large pizzas in order to serve the entire class. If a pepperoni pizza costs \$9.95 and a supreme pizza costs \$12.95, how many of each type can they order? List three possible solutions.

EXERCISES

Practice

Solve each system of inequalities by graphing.

15. $x > 5$
    $y \leq 4$
16. $y < 0$
    $x \geq 0$
17. $y > 3$
    $y > -x + 4$
18. $x \leq 2$
    $y - 4 \geq 5$
19. $x \geq 2$
    $y + x \leq 5$
20. $y < -3$
    $x - y > 1$
21. $y \leq 2x + 3$
    $y < -x + 1$
22. $y - x < 3$
    $y - x \geq 2$
23. $y \geq 3x$
    $7y < 2x$
24. $x - y < -1$
    $x - y > 3$
25. $2y + x < 6$
    $3x - y > 4$
26. $3x - 4y < 1$
    $x + 2y \leq 7$
27. $y - 4 > x$
    $y + x < 4$
28. $5y \geq 3x + 10$
    $2y \leq 4x - 10$
29. $y + 2 \leq x$
    $2y - 3 > 2x$
30. $2x + y \geq -4$
    $-5x + 2y < 1$
31. $x + y > 4$
    $-2x + 3y < -12$
32. $-4x + 5y \leq 41$
    $x + y > -1$

Write a system of inequalities for each graph.

33.

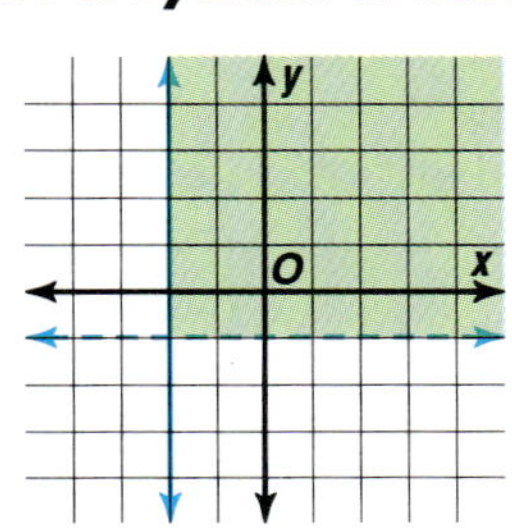

34.

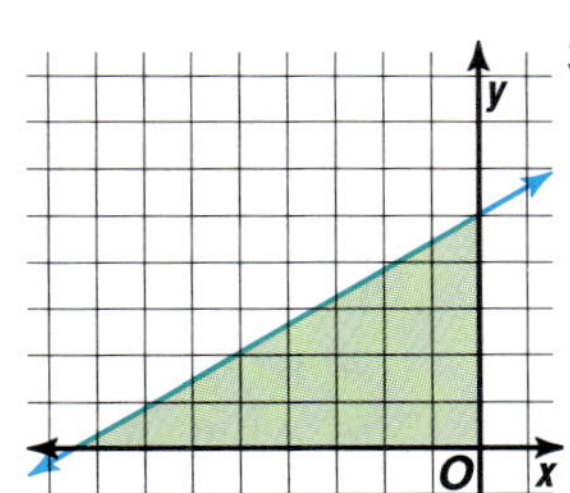

35.

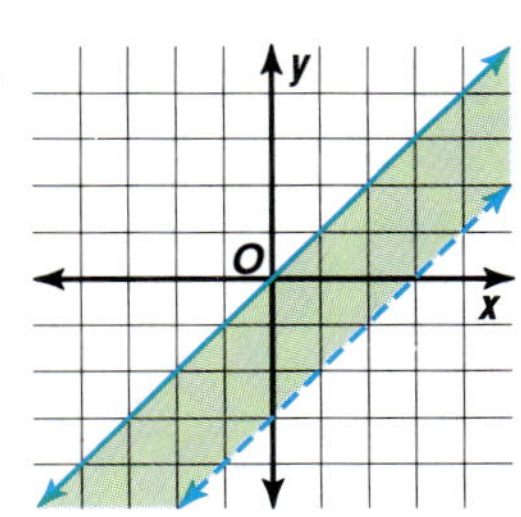

Write a system of inequalities for each graph.

36.

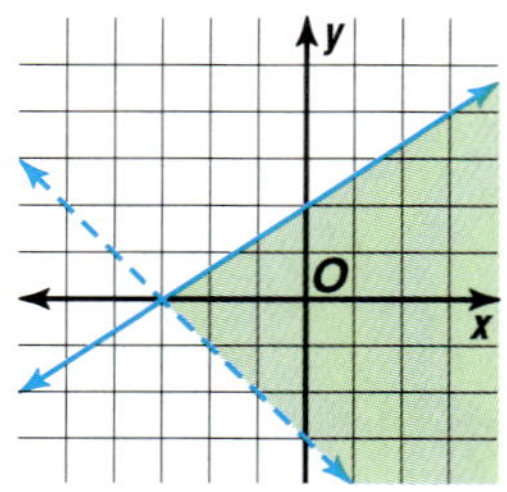

37.

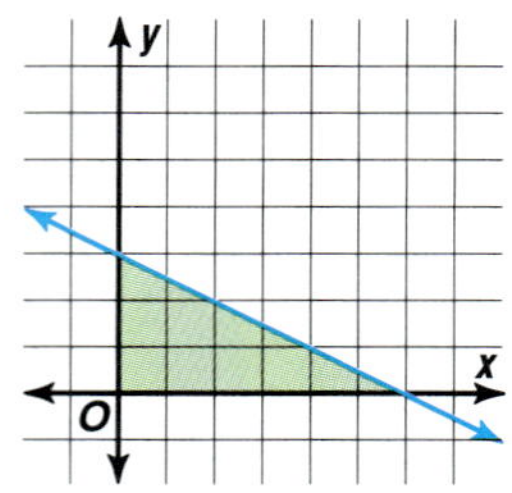

38.

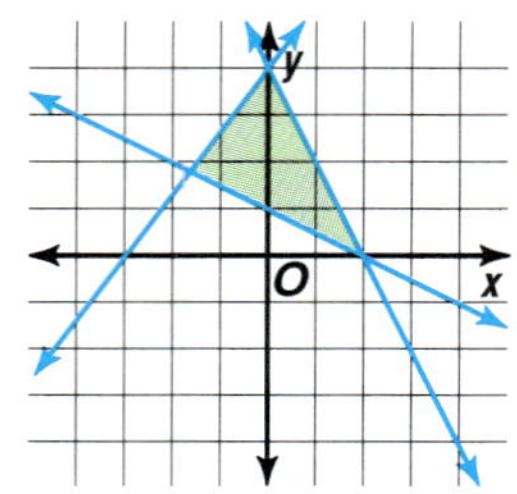

Solve each system of inequalities by graphing.

39. $x - 2y \le 2$
$3x + 4y \le 12$
$x \ge 0$

40. $x - y \le 5$
$5x + 3y \ge -6$
$y \le 3$

41. $x < 2$
$4y > x$
$2x - y < -9$
$x + 3y < 9$

Graphing Calculator

Use a graphing calculator to solve each system of inequalities.

42. $y \ge 3x - 6$
$y \le x + 1$

43. $y \le x + 9$
$y > -x - 4$

44. $y < 2x + 10$
$y \ge 7x + 15$

Critical Thinking

45. Solve the inequality $|y| \le 3$ by graphing. (*Hint:* Graph as a system of inequalities.)

Applications and Problem Solving

Graph a system of inequalities to solve each problem.

46. **Nutrition** Young people between the ages of 11 and 18 should get at least 1200 milligrams of calcium each day. One ounce of mozzarella cheese has 147 milligrams of calcium, and one ounce of Swiss cheese has 219 milligrams. If you wanted to eat no more than 8 ounces of cheese, how much of each type could you eat and still get your daily requirement of calcium? List three possible solutions.

47. **Organize Data** Kenny Choung likes to exercise every day by walking and jogging at least 3 miles. Kenny walks at a rate of 4 mph and jogs at a rate of 8 mph. If he has only a half hour to exercise, how much time can he spend walking and jogging and cover at least 3 miles? List 3 possible solutions.

Mixed Review

48. **Number Theory** If the digits of a two-digit positive integer are reversed, the result is 6 less than twice the original number. Find all such integers for which this is true. (Lesson 8–4)

49. **Organize Data** When Roberta cashed her check for \$180, the bank teller gave her 12 bills, each one worth either \$5 or \$20. How many of each bill did she receive? (Lesson 8–2)

50. Solve $4 > 4a + 12 > 24$ and graph the solution set. (Lesson 7–4)

51. Write an equation in slope-intercept form of a line that passes through the points at (3, 3) and (−1, 5). (Lesson 6–2)

52. Solve $y = -\frac{1}{2}x + 3$ if the domain is {2, 4, 6}. (Lesson 5–3)

53. What number increased by 40% equals 14? (Lesson 4–5)

54. **Travel** Paloma Rey drove to work on Wednesday at 40 miles per hour and arrived one minute late. She left home at the same time on Thursday, drove 45 miles per hour, and arrived one minute early. How far does Ms. Rey drive to work? (*Hint:* Convert hours to minutes.) (Lesson 3–5)

55. Define a variable, then write an equation for the following problem. Diego gained 134 yards running. This was 17 yards more than in the previous game. How many yards did he gain in both games? (Lesson 2–9)

56. Name the property illustrated by $(3 \cdot x) \cdot y = 3 \cdot (x \cdot y)$. (Lesson 1–8)

CHAPTER 8 HIGHLIGHTS

VOCABULARY

After completing this chapter, you should be able to define each term, property, or phrase and give an example or two of each.

Algebra

consistent (p. 455)
dependent (p. 456)
elimination (p. 469)
independent (p. 456)
inconsistent (p. 456)
substitution (p. 462)
system of equations (p. 455)
system of inequalities (p. 482)

Problem Solving

organize data (p. 464)

UNDERSTANDING AND USING THE VOCABULARY

Choose the correct term to complete each statement.

1. The method used in solving the following system of equations is (*elimination*, *substitution*).

$$\left.\begin{aligned} x &= 4y + 1 \\ x + y &= 6 \end{aligned}\right\} \rightarrow \quad \begin{aligned} (4y + 1) + y &= 6 \\ 5y + 1 &= 6 \\ 5y &= 5 \\ y &= 1 \end{aligned} \qquad \begin{aligned} x &= 4(1) + 1 \\ x &= 4 + 1 \\ x &= 5 \\ \text{solution: } & (5, 1) \end{aligned}$$

2. If a system of equations has exactly one solution, it is (*dependent, independent*).
3. If the graph of a system of equations is parallel lines, the system of equations is said to be (*consistent, inconsistent*).
4. A system of equations that has infinitely many solutions is (*dependent, independent*).
5. The method used in solving the following system of equations is (*elimination, substitution*).

$$\left.\begin{aligned} -2c + b &= 3 \\ -b - c &= -6 \end{aligned}\right\} \rightarrow \quad \begin{aligned} b - 2c &= 3 \\ (+)\ -b - c &= -6 \\ \hline -3c &= -3 \\ c &= 1 \end{aligned} \qquad \begin{aligned} -b - (1) &= -6 \\ -b - 1 &= -6 \\ -b &= -5 \\ b &= 5 \end{aligned} \quad \text{solution: } (5, 1)$$

6. If a system of equations has the same slope and different intercepts, the graph of the system is (*intersecting lines, parallel lines*).
7. If a system of equations has the same slope and intercepts, the system has (*exactly one, infinitely many*) solutions.
8. The solution to a system of equations is (3, −5); therefore, this system is (*consistent, inconsistent*).
9. The graph of a system of equations is shown at the right. This system has (*infinitely many, no*) solution.
10. The solution to a system of inequalities is the (*intersection, union*) of two half-planes.
11. A system of inequalities that includes $x < 0$ and $y > 0$ is in the (*second, fourth*) quadrant.

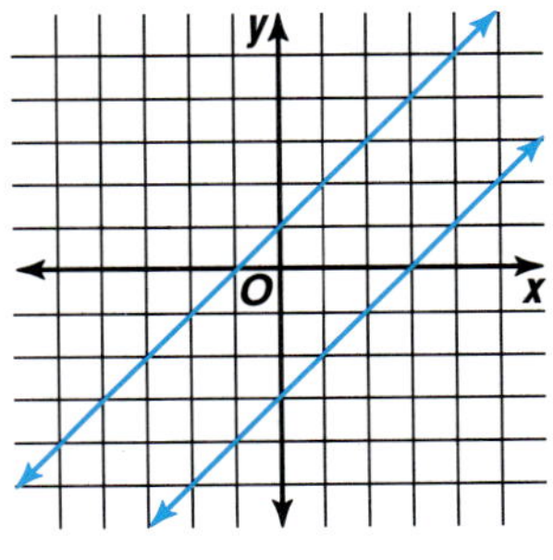

CHAPTER 8

STUDY GUIDE AND ASSESSMENT

SKILLS AND CONCEPTS

OBJECTIVES AND EXAMPLES

Upon completing this chapter, you should be able to:

- solve systems of equations by graphing (Lesson 8–1)

Graph $x + y = 6$ and $x - y = 2$. Then find the solution.

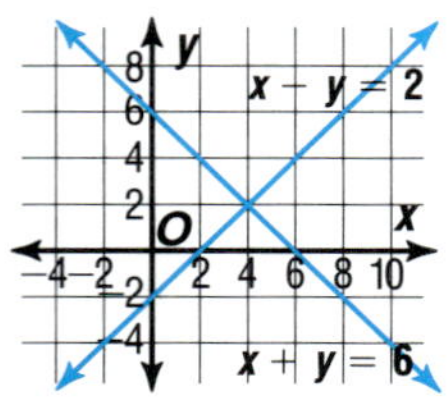

The solution is (4, 2).

REVIEW EXERCISES

Use these exercises to review and prepare for the chapter test.

Graph each system of equations to find the solution.

12. $y = 2x - 7$
$x + y = 11$

13. $x + 2y = 6$
$2y - 8 = -x$

14. $3x + y = -8$
$x + 6y = 3$

15. $5x - 3y = 11$
$2x + 3y = -25$

- determine whether a system of equations has one solution, no solution, or infinitely many solutions by graphing (Lesson 8–1)

Graph $3x + y = -4$ and $6x + 2y = -8$. Then determine the number of solutions.

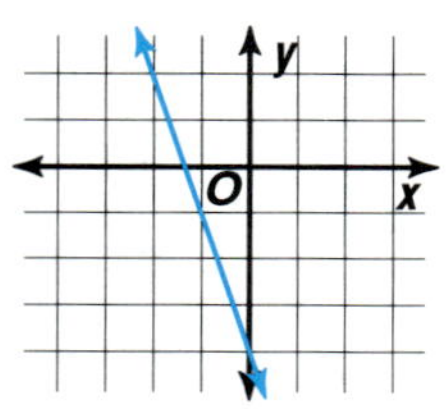

There are infinitely many solutions.

Graph each system of equations. Then determine whether the system of equations has *one* solution, *no* solution, or *infinitely many* solutions. If the system has one solution, name it.

16. $x - y = 9$
$x + y = 11$

17. $9x + 2 = 3y$
$y - 3x = 8$

18. $2x - 3y = 4$
$6y = 4x - 8$

19. $3x - y = 8$
$3x = 4 - y$

- solve systems of equations by using the substitution method (Lesson 8–2)

Use substitution to solve the system of equations.

$y = x - 1$
$4x - y = 19$

$$\begin{aligned} 4x - y &= 19 \\ 4x - (x - 1) &= 19 \\ 4x - x + 1 &= 19 \\ 3x + 1 &= 19 \\ 3x &= 18 \\ x &= 6 \end{aligned}$$

$$\begin{aligned} y &= x - 1 \\ y &= 6 - 1 \\ y &= 5 \end{aligned}$$

The solution is (6, 5).

Use substitution to solve each system of equations. If the system *does not* have exactly one solution, state whether it has *no* solution or *infinitely many* solutions.

20. $2m + n = 1$
$m - n = 8$

21. $3a - 2b = -4$
$3a + b = 2$

22. $x = 3 - 2y$
$2x + 4y = 6$

23. $3x - y = 1$
$2x + 4y = 3$

OBJECTIVES AND EXAMPLES

- solve systems of equations by using the elimination method with addition or subtraction (Lesson 8–3)

Use elimination to solve the system of equations.

$2m - n = 4$
$m + n = 2$

$$\begin{aligned} 2m - n &= 4 \\ (+)\ m + n &= 2 \\ \hline 3m &= 6 \\ m &= 2 \end{aligned} \qquad \begin{aligned} m + n &= 2 \\ 2 + n &= 2 \\ n &= 0 \end{aligned}$$

The solution is (2, 0).

REVIEW EXERCISES

Use elimination to solve each system of equations.

24. $x + 2y = 6$
    $x - 3y = -4$
25. $2m - n = 5$
    $2m + n = 3$
26. $3x - y = 11$
    $x + y = 5$
27. $3s + 6r = 33$
    $6r - 9s = 21$
28. $3x + 1 = -7y$
    $6x + 7y = 0$
29. $12x - 9y = 114$
    $7y + 12x = 82$

OBJECTIVES AND EXAMPLES

- solve systems of equations by using the elimination method with multiplication and addition (Lesson 8–4)

Use elimination to solve the system of equations.

$3x - 4y = 7$
$2x + y = 1$

$3x - 4y = 7 \qquad\qquad 3x - 4y = 7$
$2x + y = 1$ **Multiply by 4.** → $(+)\ 8x + 4y = 4$
$\qquad\qquad\qquad 11x = 11$
$\qquad\qquad\qquad x = 1$

$$\begin{aligned} 2x + y &= 1 \\ 2(1) + y &= 1 \\ y &= -1 \end{aligned}$$

The solution is (1, −1).

REVIEW EXERCISES

Use elimination to solve each system of equations.

30. $x - 5y = 0$
    $2x - 3y = 7$
31. $x - 2y = 5$
    $3x - 5y = 8$
32. $2x + 3y = 8$
    $x - y = 2$
33. $-5x + 8y = 21$
    $10x + 3y = 15$
34. $5m + 2n = -8$
    $4m + 3n = 2$
35. $6x + 7y = 5$
    $2x - 3y = 7$

OBJECTIVES AND EXAMPLES

- determine the best method for solving systems of equations (Lesson 8–4)

Use the best method to solve the system of equations.

$x + 2y = 8$
$3x + 2y = 6$

$$\begin{aligned} 3x + 2y &= 6 \\ (-)\ x + 2y &= 8 \\ \hline 2x \quad &= -2 \\ x &= -1 \end{aligned} \qquad \begin{aligned} x + 2y &= 8 \\ -1 + 2y &= 8 \\ 2y &= 9 \\ y &= \frac{9}{2} \end{aligned}$$

The solution is $\left(-1, \frac{9}{2}\right)$.

REVIEW EXERCISES

Determine the best method to solve each system of equations. Then solve the system.

36. $y = 2x$
    $x + 2y = 8$
37. $9x + 8y = 7$
    $18x - 15y = 14$
38. $2x - y = 36$
    $3x - 0.5y = 26$
39. $3x + 5y = 2x$
    $x + 3y = y$
40. $5x - 2y = 23$
    $5x + 2y = 17$
41. $2x + y = 3x - 15$
    $x + 5 = 4y + 2x$

OBJECTIVES AND EXAMPLES

- solve systems of inequalities by graphing (Lesson 8–5)

Solve the system of inequalities.

$x \geq -3$
$y \leq x + 2$

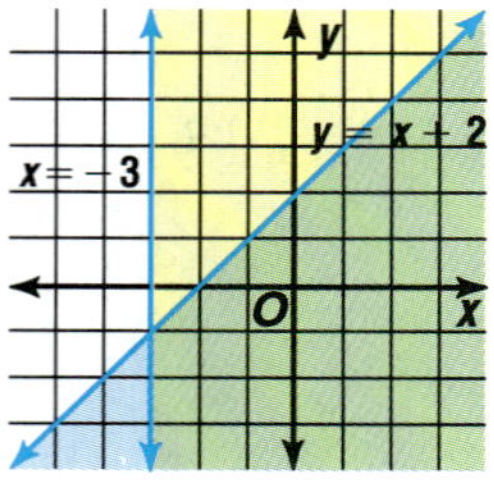

REVIEW EXERCISES

Solve each system of inequalities by graphing.

42. $y < 3x$
$x + 2y \geq -21$

43. $y > -x - 1$
$y \leq 2x + 1$

44. $2x + y < 9$
$x + 11y < -6$

45. $x \geq 1$
$y + x \leq 3$

46. $y \geq x - 3$
$y \geq -x - 1$

47. $x - 2y \leq -4$
$4y < 2x - 4$

APPLICATIONS AND PROBLEM SOLVING

48. Ballooning A hot-air balloon is 10 meters above the ground rising at a rate of 15 meters per minute. Another balloon is 150 meters above the ground descending at a rate of 20 meters per minute. (Lesson 8–1)

a. After how long will the balloons be at the same height?

b. What is that height?

49. Number Theory A two-digit number is 7 times its units digit. If 18 is added to the number, its digits are reversed. Find the original number. (Lesson 8–2)

50. Travel While driving to Fullerton, Mrs. Sumner travels at an average speed of 40 mph. On the return trip, she travels at an average speed of 56 mph and saves two hours of travel time. How far does Mrs. Sumner live from Fullerton? (Lesson 8–4)

51. Sales The Beach Resort is offering two weekend specials. One includes a 2-night stay with 3 meals and costs \$195. The other includes a 3-night stay with 5 meals and costs \$300. (Lesson 8–4)

a. What is the cost of a 1-night stay?

b. What is the cost per meal?

52. Organize Data Abby plans to spend at most \$24 to buy cashews and peanuts for her Fourth of July party. The Nut Shoppe sells peanuts for \$3 a pound and cashews for \$5 a pound. If Abby needs to have at least 5 pounds of nuts for the party, how many of each type can she buy? List three possible solutions. (Lesson 8–5)

A practice test for Chapter 8 is provided on page 794.

ALTERNATIVE ASSESSMENT

COOPERATIVE LEARNING PROJECT

Landscaping Gavin Royse needs a layout of his yard. He is doing some landscaping and needs to have a grid of his yard for the landscape workers to use when putting in his fence and the two new trees that he bought. His house sits on an angle on the lot, which measures 80 feet by 80 feet. The boundaries of his house are described by the four equations below.

$3x - 4y = 55$
$3x + 2y = 85$
$3x - 4y = -125$
$3x + 2y = 175$

The house faces southwest.

The fence will run from the farthest north corner of the house to (5, 80) and then run along the north lot line to the corner of the lot (80, 80). It will then head south on the lot line to (80, 30). From there it will angle toward the house to (55, 5) and then head to the farthest east corner of the house.

A shade tree will be placed at the intersection of $3x - 4y = 55$ and $x + 3y = 170$, while an ornamental tree will be placed 15 feet south of the west corner of the house.

Prepare a graph for the landscape workers to use as a guide. Follow these steps to organize your data.

- Determine how to set up the graph and its scale.
- Construct a colorful and detailed graph that Gavin could give to the landscape workers.
- Create the system of inequalities that describes Gavin's fenced area.
- Determine the vertices of the house.
- Determine the vertices of the two trees.

Write a detailed description for the workers of the work that needs to be done and the area where the work is to be done.

THINKING CRITICALLY

- How does the elimination or substitution method show that a system of equations is inconsistent or that a system of equations is consistent and dependent?
- Create a system of equations for which there are no solutions. What were your criteria for creating this system?

PORTFOLIO

Select one of the systems of equations from this chapter that could be solved by various methods. Use this system of equations and solve it using each of the methods introduced in this chapter: graphing, substitution, elimination using addition and subtraction, and elimination using multiplication and addition. Write an explanation involving the pros and cons of using each of these methods for this problem.

SELF EVALUATION

Are you a team player? Do you pull your end of the load? Do you pull too much of the load? Since you will often need to work in cooperative groups, you need to be responsible for your actions and understand how they affect the group. A person who is too dominant can stifle the learning process of other students. On the other end of the spectrum, a person who is too passive can get left out and not experience the whole learning process.

Assess yourself. What kind of a group worker are you? Do you take the initiative to enhance the whole group or do you look out only for your own learning? Think about a group that you were recently a part of, either in mathematics or your daily life. List two positive actions that you observed in the group that helped the group. Then list two negative actions that you observed in the group that hindered the group.

CUMULATIVE REVIEW

CHAPTERS 1–8

SECTION ONE: MULTIPLE CHOICE

There are eight multiple-choice questions in this section. After working each problem, write the letter of the correct answer on your paper.

1. Choose the statement that is true for a system of two linear equations.

   A. There are no solutions when the graphs of the equations are perpendicular lines.

   B. There is exactly one solution when the graphs of the equations are one line.

   C. A system can only be solved by graphing the equations.

   D. There are infinitely many solutions when the graphs of the equations have the same slope and intercepts.

2. The scale on a map is 2 centimeters to 5 kilometers. Doe Creek and Kent are 15.75 kilometers apart. How far apart are they on the map?

   A. 7.88 cm

   B. 39.38 cm

   C. 6.3 cm

   D. 31.5 cm

3. Choose the graph that represents $2x - y < 6$.

   A.

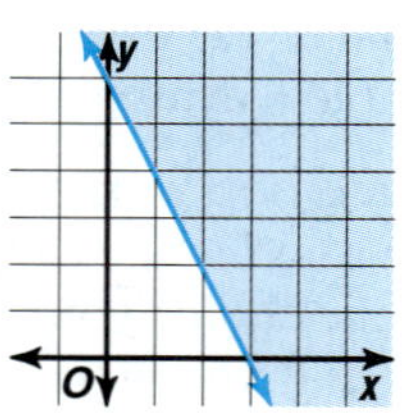

   B.

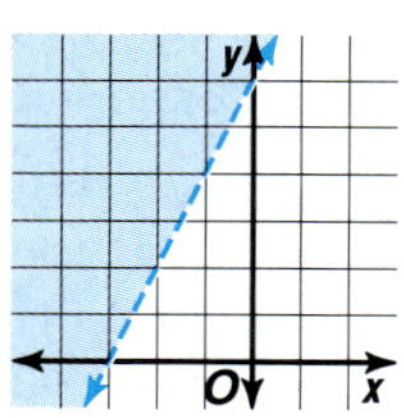

   C.

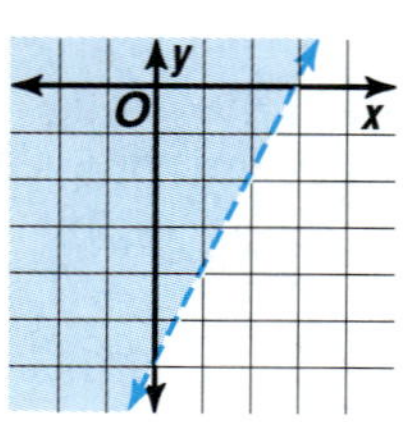

   D.

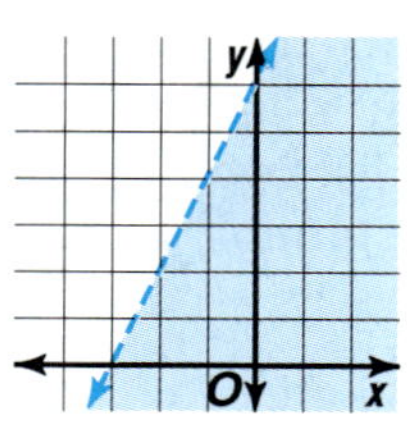

4. The units digit of a two-digit number exceeds twice the tens digit by 1. Find the number if the sum of its digits is 7.

   A. 25 B. 16

   C. 34 D. 61

5. State which region in the graph shown below is the solution of the system.

   $y \geq 2x + 2$

   $y \leq -x - 1$

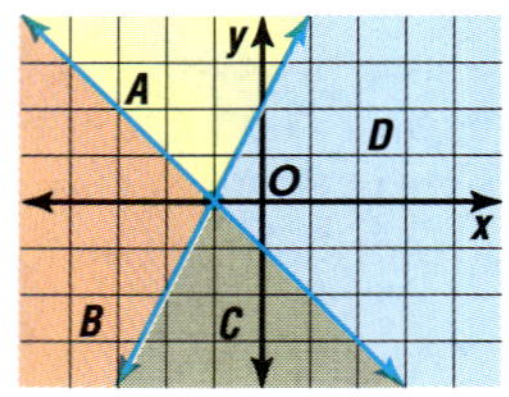

   A. Region A

   B. Region B

   C. Region C

   D. Region D

6. Abeytu's scores on the first four of five 100-point tests were 85, 89, 90, and 81. What score must she receive on the fifth test to have an average of at least 87 points for all of the tests?

   A. at least 86 points

   B. at least 90 points

   C. at least 69 points

   D. at least 87 points

7. The frequency of a vibrating violin string is inversely proportional to its length. If a 10-inch violin string vibrates at a frequency of 512 cycles per second, find the frequency of an 8-inch violin string.

   A. 284.4 cycles per second

   B. 409.6 cycles per second

   C. 514 cycles per second

   D. 640 cycles per second

8. Find the mean of $3\frac{1}{2}$, 5, $4\frac{1}{8}$, $7\frac{3}{4}$, 4, and $6\frac{5}{8}$.

   A. $5\frac{1}{6}$

   B. 6

   C. $6\frac{1}{5}$

   D. 31

SECTION TWO: SHORT ANSWER

This section contains seven questions for which you will provide short answers. Write your answer on your paper.

9. Eric is preparing to run in the Bay Marathon. One day, he ran and walked a total of 16 miles. He ran the first mile, and after that walked one mile for every two miles he ran. How many miles did he run, and how many did he walk?

10. The number of Calories in a serving of French fries at 13 restaurants are 250, 240, 220, 348, 199, 200, 125, 230, 274, 239, 212, 240, and 327. Make a box-and-whisker plot of these data.

11. Find three consecutive odd integers whose sum is 81.

12. The concession stand sells hot dogs and soda during Beck High School football games. John bought 6 hot dogs and 4 sodas and paid \$6.70. Jessica bought 4 hot dogs and 3 sodas and paid \$4.65. At what prices are the hot dogs and sodas sold?

13. Draw a tree diagram to show the possible meals that could be created from the following choices.

Meat: chicken, steak

Vegetable: broccoli, baked potato, tossed salad, carrots

Drink: milk, cola, juice

14. Patricia is going to purchase graduation gifts for her friends, Sarah and Isabel. She wants to spend at least \$5 more on Isabel's gift than on Sarah's. She can afford to spend at most a total of \$56. Draw a graph showing the possible amounts she can spend on each gift.

15. The cost of a one-day car rental from Rossi Rentals is given by the formula $C(m) = 31 + 0.13m$, where m is the number of miles that the car is driven, \$0.13 is the cost per mile driven, and $C(m)$ is the total cost. If Sheila drove a distance of 110 miles and back in one day, what is the cost of the car rental?

SECTION THREE: OPEN-ENDED

This section contains two open-ended problems. Demonstrate your knowledge by giving a clear, concise solution to each problem. Your score on these problems will depend on how well you do the following.

- Explain your reasoning.
- Show your understanding of the mathematics in an organized manner.
- Use charts, graphs, and diagrams in your explanation.
- Show the solution in more than one way or relate it to other situations.
- Investigate beyond the requirements of the problem.

16. Curtis has a coupon for 33% off any purchase of \$50 or more at First Place Sports Shop. His grandmother has given him \$75 for his birthday. Write a problem about how Curtis spends his money if he wants to buy several items, including a baseball hat for \$18.75, a pair of cleats for \$53.95, and a \$26.95 sweatshirt discounted 15%. Then solve the problem.

17. The graphs of the equations $y = x + 3$, $2x - 7y = 4$, and $2y + 3x = 6$ contain the sides of a triangle. Write a problem about these graphs that requires using systems of equations to solve. Then solve the problem.

CHAPTER

9 Exploring Polynomials

Objectives

In this chapter, you will:

- solve problems by looking for a pattern,
- multiply and divide monomials,
- express numbers in scientific notation, and
- add, subtract, and multiply polynomials.

Keeping Up With Technology

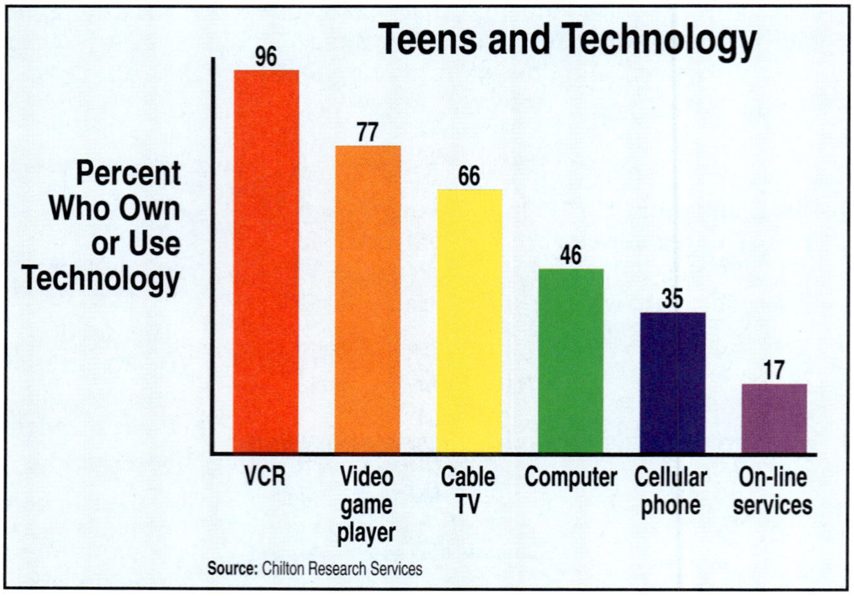

Source: Chilton Research Services

The graph shows what percent of all teenagers own or use technology. Do you use a computer to do your homework? What are the advantages and disadvantages of doing your homework this way?

TIME Line

239 B.C. Leap year introduced into the Egyptian calendar.

1149 Hildegard von Bingen, a female medical practitioner, is named a supervisor at St. Ruperts on the Rhine.

400 B.C. | 300 | 200 | A.D. 500 | 600 | 700 | 800 | 900 | 1000 | 1100 | 1200 | 1300 | 1400

A.D. 600 Zu Chong-zhi and his son Zu Geng-shi of China calculate π to be between 3.1415926 and 3.1415927.

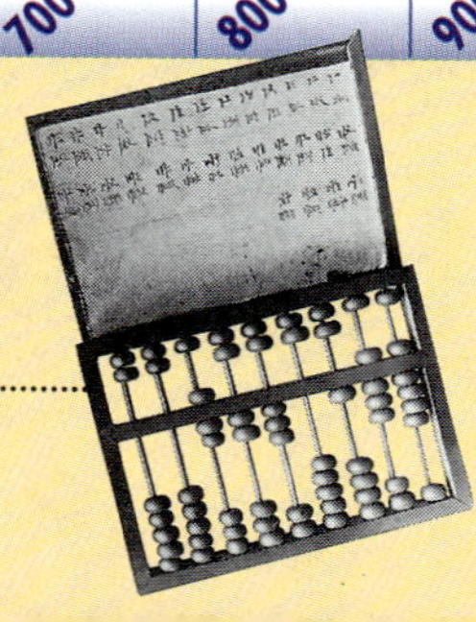

1364 Aztecs build their capital Tenochtitlan at the site of present-day Mexico City.

PEOPLE IN THE NEWS

Jenny **Slabaugh** and **Amy Gusfa** help produce a weekly video show created by students at Dearborn High School in Michigan. When they were only 15 years old, their expertise in electronics and video won each a $1000 scholarship to a technology institute in Hollywood. They were the first females to receive a scholarship from the institute, and they spent a week there studying theoretical and applied electronics.

Their interest in video production came from Dearborn High's nationally honored video program. They are combining their interests in science, math, electronics, music, and art to create video programs. They both think that more girls should investigate video technology, and they see themselves contributing to this field in the future.

Chapter Project

A byte is a single unit of information such as a number or a letter processed by a computer. A megabyte is 1.048576×10^6 bytes, which is just over 1 million bytes.

- Research three personal computers and three laptop computers. Find out the amount of RAM and hard drive memory in megabytes for each computer. Write each number in standard notation and in scientific notation.
- Use scientific notation to write the amount of memory in bytes for each computer.

- Find the mean of the memory in megabytes for the three personal computers. Find the mean of the memory in megabytes for the three laptop computers. Write the answers in scientific notation.
- Write the ratio of the mean memory for the personal computers to the mean memory for the laptop computers. Write the ratio as a decimal. Discuss the significance of this ratio.
- Investigate the size of the memory of computers that are being developed for the future. How many bytes are in a gigabyte? How many times larger is a gigabyte than a megabyte?

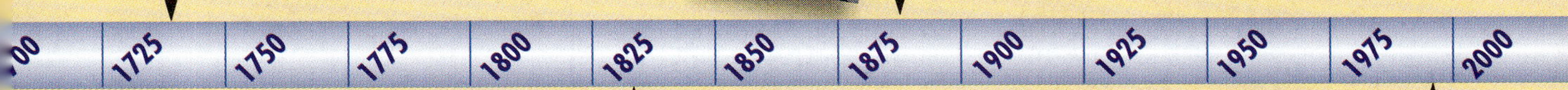

9–1 Multiplying Monomials

What YOU'LL LEARN

- To multiply monomials,
- to simplify expressions involving powers of monomials, and
- to solve problems by looking for a pattern.

Why IT'S IMPORTANT

You can use monomials to solve problems involving finance and geometry.

fabulous FIRSTS

Muriel Siebert (1932–)

The first woman to hold a seat on the New York Stock Exchange was Muriel ("Mickey") Siebert. She paid \$445,000 and was admitted as a full member on December 28, 1967.

APPLICATION

Finance

Since 1983, the Beardstown Business and Professional Women's Investment Club ("Beardstown Ladies") has been able to earn enough of a profit in the stock market to make any market expert envious. The club was started when each of 16 women from a small town in Illinois contributed \$100 to start an investment fund. Dividends and monthly dues of \$25 are also invested. The Beardstown Ladies have earned an average annual profit of 23% on their investments. How has each woman's initial investment of \$100 increased over the years?

At the end of the first year (1984), each initial investment would be worth $100(1 + 0.23)$, or \$123. By the end of the second year, the initial investment would have grown to $100(1 + 0.23)(1 + 0.23)$, which is the same as $100(1 + 0.23)^2$ or \$151.29. The table below shows the value of an initial investment of \$100 for each of the first 13 years.

Year	Yearly Calculation	Value
1984	$100(1 + 0.23)$	\$123.00
1985	$100(1 + 0.23)^2$	\$151.29
1986	$100(1 + 0.23)^3$	\$186.09
1987	$100(1 + 0.23)^4$	\$228.89
1988	$100(1 + 0.23)^5$	\$281.53
1989	$100(1 + 0.23)^6$	\$346.28
1990	$100(1 + 0.23)^7$	\$425.93
1991	$100(1 + 0.23)^8$	\$523.89
1992	$100(1 + 0.23)^9$	\$644.39
1993	$100(1 + 0.23)^{10}$	\$792.59
1994	$100(1 + 0.23)^{11}$	\$974.89
1995	$100(1 + 0.23)^{12}$	\$1199.12
1996	$100(1 + 0.23)^{13}$	\$1474.91

After 13 years, the initial \$100 investment was worth \$1474.91! If we let x equal the factor $(1 + 0.23)$, then the value of the initial investment after 13 years can be represented by $100x^{13}$.

An expression like $100x^{13}$ is called a **monomial.** A monomial is a number, a variable, or a product of a number and one or more variables. Monomials that are real numbers are called **constants.**

Monomials	Not Monomials
12	$a + b$
q	$\frac{a}{b}$
$4x^3$	$5 - 7d$
$11ab$	$\frac{5}{a^2}$
$\frac{1}{3}xyz^{12}$	$\frac{5a}{7b}$

Recall that an expression of the form x^n is a *power.* The base is x, and the exponent is n. A table of powers of 2 is shown below.

2^1	2^2	2^3	2^4	2^5	2^6	2^7	2^8	2^9	2^{10}
2	4	8	16	32	64	128	256	512	1024

In the following products, each number can be expressed as a power of 2. Study the pattern of the exponents.

Number	$8(32) = 256$	$8(64) = 512$	$4(16) = 64$	$16(32) = 512$
Power	$2^3(2^5) = 2^8$	$2^3(2^6) = 2^9$	$2^2(2^4) = 2^6$	$2^4(2^5) = 2^9$
Pattern of Exponents	$3 + 5 = 8$	$3 + 6 = 9$	$2 + 4 = 6$	$4 + 5 = 9$

These examples suggest that you can multiply powers with the same base by adding exponents.

Product of Powers

For any number *a*, and all integers *m* and *n*,
$a^m \cdot a^n = a^{m+n}$.

Example 1 **Simplify each expression.**

a. $(3a^6)(a^8)$

$$(3a^6)(a^8) = 3a^{6+8}$$
$$= 3a^{14}$$

b. $(8y^3)(-3x^2y^2)\left(\frac{3}{8}xy^4\right)$

$$(8y^3)(-3x^2y^2)\left(\frac{3}{8}xy^4\right)$$
$$= \left(8 \cdot (-3) \cdot \frac{3}{8}\right)(x^2 \cdot x)(y^3 \cdot y^2 \cdot y^4)$$
$$= -9x^{2+1}y^{3+2+4}$$
$$= -9x^3y^9$$

We looked for a pattern to discover the product of powers property. **Look for a pattern** is an important strategy in problem solving.

Example 2 **Solve by extending the pattern.**

PROBLEM SOLVING
Look for a Pattern

4 × 6 = 24
14 × 16 = 224
24 × 26 = 624
34 × 36 = 1224
124 × 126 = ?

Explore Look at the problem. You need to find a pattern to determine the product of 124 and 126.

Plan The last two digits of the product are always 24. To find the first digit(s) of the product, look at the tens place of each pair of factors. Notice that $0 \times 1 = 0$, $1 \times 2 = 2$, $2 \times 3 = 6$, and $3 \times 4 = 12$. Extend this pattern to find the product.

Solve $12 \times 13 = 156$

Therefore, $124 \times 126 = 15{,}624$

Examine Use a calculator to verify that the product is 15,624. The pattern remains true and the product is correct.

Study the examples below.

$$(8^3)^5 = (8^3)(8^3)(8^3)(8^3)(8^3) \qquad\qquad (y^7)^3 = (y^7)(y^7)(y^7)$$

$$= 8^{3+3+3+3+3} \longleftarrow \textit{Product of powers} \longrightarrow = y^{7+7+7}$$

$$= 8^{15} \qquad\qquad = y^{21}$$

Therefore, $(8^3)^5 = 8^{15}$ and $(y^7)^3 = y^{21}$. These examples suggest that you can find the power of a power by multiplying the exponents.

Power of a Power	**For any number *a*, and all integers *m* and *n*, $(a^m)^n = a^{mn}$.**

> **LOOK BACK**
>
> *You can refer to Lesson 1-1 for information on using a calculator to find a power of a number.*

Look for a pattern in the examples below.

$$(ab)^4 = (ab)(ab)(ab)(ab)$$
$$= (a \cdot a \cdot a \cdot a)(b \cdot b \cdot b \cdot b)$$
$$= a^4b^4$$

$$(5pq)^5 = (5pq)(5pq)(5pq)(5pq)(5pq)$$
$$= (5 \cdot 5 \cdot 5 \cdot 5 \cdot 5)(p \cdot p \cdot p \cdot p \cdot p)(q \cdot q \cdot q \cdot q \cdot q)$$
$$= 5^5p^5q^5 \text{ or } 3125p^5q^5$$

These examples suggest that the power of a product is the product of the powers.

Power of a Product	**For all numbers *a* and *b*, and any integer *m*, $(ab)^m = a^mb^m$.**

The power of a power property and the power of a product property can be combined into the following property.

Power of a Monomial	**For all numbers *a* and *b*, and all integers *m*, *n*, and *p*, $(a^mb^n)^p = a^{mp}b^{np}$.**

Example 3 **Simplify $(2a^4b)^3[(-2b)^3]^2$.**

$(2a^4b)^3[(-2b)^3]^2 = (2a^4b)^3(-2b)^6$	*Power of a power property*
$= 2^3(a^4)^3b^3(-2)^6b^6$	*Power of a product property*
$= 8a^{12}b^3(64)b^6$	*Power of a power property*
$= 512a^{12}b^9$	*Product of powers property*

To simplify an expression involving monomials, write an equivalent expression in which:

- there are no powers of powers,
- each base appears exactly once, and
- all fractions are in simplest form.

CHECK FOR UNDERSTANDING

Communicating Mathematics

Study the lesson. Then complete the following.

1. **Write** in your own words.
   a. the product of powers property
   b. the power of a power property
   c. the power of a product property
2. **Explain** why the product of powers property does not apply when the bases are different.
3. **You Decide** Luisa says $10^4 \times 10^5 = 100^9$, but Taryn says that $10^4 \times 10^5 = 10^9$. Who is correct? Explain your answer.

MATH JOURNAL

4. **Write** 64 in six different ways using exponents; for example, $64 = (2^2)^3$.

Guided Practice

Determine whether each pair of monomials is equivalent. Write *yes* or *no*.

5. $2d^3$ and $(2d)^3$
6. $(xy)^2$ and x^2y^2
7. $-x^2$ and $(-x)^2$
8. $5(y^2)^2$ and $25y^4$

Simplify.

9. $a^4(a^7)(a)$
10. $(xy^4)(x^2y^3)$
11. $[(3^2)^4]^2$
12. $(2a^2b)^2$
13. $(-27ay^3)\left(-\frac{1}{3}ay^3\right)$
14. $(2x^2)^2\left(\frac{1}{2}y^2\right)^2$
15. **Geometry** Find the measure of the area of the rectangle at the right.

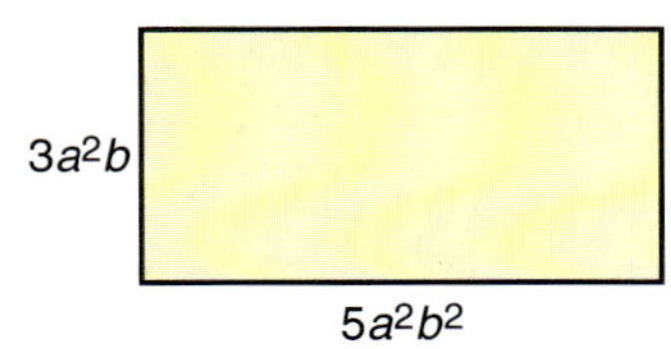

EXERCISES

Practice

Simplify.

16. $b^3(b)(b^5)$
17. $(m^3n)(mn^2)$
18. $(a^2b)(a^5b^4)$
19. $[(2^3)^2]^2$
20. $(3x^4y^3)(4x^4y)$
21. $(a^3x^2)^4$
22. $m^7(m^3b^2)$
23. $(3x^2y^2z)(2x^2y^2z^3)$
24. $(0.6d)^3$
25. $(ab)(ac)(bc)$
26. $-\frac{5}{6}c(12a^3)$
27. $\left(\frac{2}{5}d\right)^2$
28. $-3(ax^3y)^2$
29. $(0.3x^3y^2)^2$
30. $(-3ab)^3(2b^3)$
31. $\left(\frac{3}{10}y^2\right)^2(10y^2)^3$
32. $(3x^2)^2\left(\frac{1}{3}y^2\right)^2$
33. $\left(\frac{2}{5}a\right)^2(25a)(13b)\left(\frac{1}{13}b^4\right)$
34. $(3a^2)^3 + 2(a^3)^2$
35. $(-2x^3)^3 - (2x)^9$

Critical Thinking

36. Make a valid argument explaining why $(x + y)^z$ does not equal $x^z + y^z$.

37. Make a valid argument explaining why -2^4 does not equal $(-2)^4$.

Applications and Problem Solving

38. Investments Refer to the application at the beginning of the lesson. Each of the Beardstown Ladies added \$25 to the investments each month. This amounts to \$300 a year. Assume that each member invested the \$300 at the beginning of each year starting in 1984. You can use the formula $T = p\left[\frac{(1 + r)^t - 1}{r}\right]$ to determine how each member's money grew. T represents the total amount, p represents the regular payment, r represents the annual interest rate, and t represents the time in years.

a. How much money did each member make from their additional investments from 1984 to 1996?

b. What was the total value of each member's investment in 1996?

39. Look for a Pattern The symbol used for a U.S. dollar is a capital S with a vertical line through it. The line separates the S into 4 parts, as shown at the right. How many parts would there be if the S had 100 vertical lines through it?

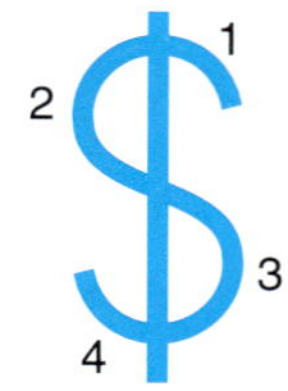

Mixed Review

40. Write a system of inequalities for the graph at the right. (Lesson 8–5)

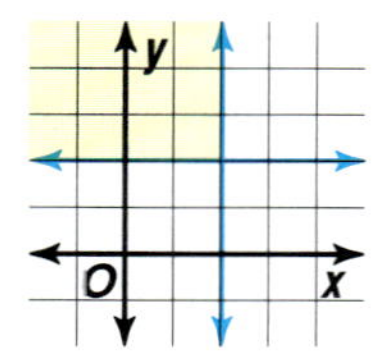

41. Graph the system of equations. Determine whether the system has *one* solution, *no* solution, or *infinitely many* solutions. If the system has one solution, name it. (Lesson 8–1)
$x + 2y = 0$
$y + 3 = -x$

42. Business Jorge Martinez has budgeted \$150 to have business cards printed. A card printer charges \$11 to set up each job and an additional \$6 per box of 100 cards printed. What is the greatest number of cards Mr. Martinez can have printed? (Lesson 7–3)

43. Write an equation from the relation shown in the chart below. Then copy and complete the chart. (Lesson 5–6)

m	−3	−2	−1	0	1
n	−5	−3	−1		

44. Travel Tiffany wants to reach Dallas at 10 A.M. If she drives at 36 miles per hour, she would reach Dallas at 11 A.M. But if she drives 54 miles per hour, she would arrive at 9 A.M. At what average speed should she drive to reach Dallas exactly at 10 A.M.? (Lesson 4–7)

45. Geometry Find the supplement of 44°. (Lesson 3–4)

46. Simplify $-16 \div 8$. (Lesson 2–7)

47. Simplify $0.3(0.2 + 3y) + 0.21y$. (Lesson 1–8)

9–2 Dividing by Monomials

What YOU'LL LEARN

- To simplify expressions involving quotients of monomials, and
- to simplify expressions containing negative exponents.

Why IT'S IMPORTANT

You can use monomials to solve problems involving finance and geometry.

INTEGRATION
Geometry

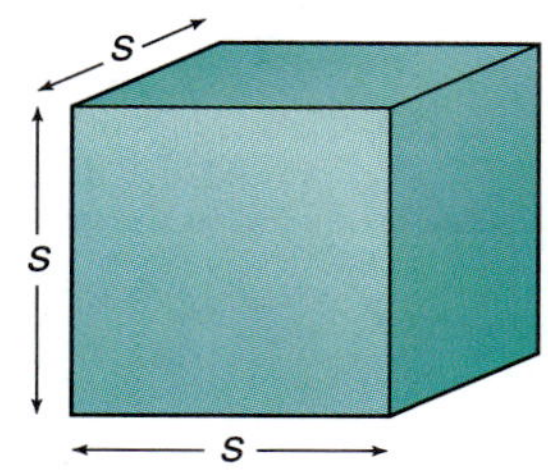

$V = s \cdot s \cdot s$ or s^3

The volume of a cube with each side s units long is s^3 cubic units. So, the ratio of the measure of the volume of a cube to the measure of the length of each side is $\frac{s^3}{s}$. How can you express this ratio in simplest form?

Just as we used a pattern to discover the product of powers property, we can use a pattern to discover a property for a quotient of powers such as $\frac{s^3}{s}$. In the following quotients, each number can be expressed as a power of 2. Study the pattern of exponents.

Number	$\frac{64}{32} = 2$	$\frac{32}{8} = 4$	$\frac{64}{8} = 8$	$\frac{32}{2} = 16$
Power	$\frac{2^6}{2^5} = 2^1$	$\frac{2^5}{2^3} = 2^2$	$\frac{2^6}{2^3} = 2^3$	$\frac{2^5}{2^1} = 2^4$
Pattern of Exponents	$6 - 5 = 1$	$5 - 3 = 2$	$6 - 3 = 3$	$5 - 1 = 4$

These examples suggest that you can divide powers with the same base by subtracting exponents.

Quotient of Powers	For all integers m and n, and any nonzero number a, $\frac{a^m}{a^n} = a^{m-n}$.

To write $\frac{s^3}{s}$ in simplest form, subtract the exponents.

$$\frac{s^3}{s} = s^{3-1} \quad \textit{Recall that } s = s^1\textit{, and apply the quotient of powers property.}$$
$$= s^2$$

In simplest form, $\frac{s^3}{s} = s^2$.

Example 1 Simplify $\frac{y^4z^3}{y^2z^2}$.

$$\frac{y^4z^3}{y^2z^2} = \left(\frac{y^4}{y^2}\right)\left(\frac{z^3}{z^2}\right) \quad \textit{Group the powers with the same base, } y^4 \textit{ with } y^2 \textit{ and } z^3 \textit{ with } z^2.$$
$$= (y^{4-2})(z^{3-2}) \quad \textit{Quotient of powers property.}$$
$$= y^2z$$

A calculator can be used to find the value of expressions with 0 as an exponent as well as expressions with negative exponents.

EXPLORATION — SCIENTIFIC CALCULATORS

You can use the $\boxed{y^x}$ key to find the value of expressions with exponents.

Your Turn

a. Copy the following table. Use a scientific calculator to complete the table.

Exponential Expression	2^4	2^3	2^2	2^1	2^0	2^{-1}	2^{-2}	2^{-3}	2^{-4}
Decimal Form									
Fraction Form									

b. According to your calculator display, what is the value of 2^0?

c. Compare the values of 2^2 and 2^{-2}.

d. Compare the values of 2^4 and 2^{-4}.

e. What happens when you evaluate 0^0?

Study the following methods used to simplify $\frac{b^4}{b^4}$ where $b \neq 0$.

Method 1
Definition of Powers or Expanded Form

$$\frac{b^4}{b^4} = \frac{\overset{1}{\cancel{(b)}}\,\overset{1}{\cancel{(b)}}\,\overset{1}{\cancel{(b)}}\,\overset{1}{\cancel{(b)}}}{\underset{1}{\cancel{(b)}}\,\underset{1}{\cancel{(b)}}\,\underset{1}{\cancel{(b)}}\,\underset{1}{\cancel{(b)}}}$$

$$= 1$$

Method 2
Quotient of Powers

$$\frac{b^4}{b^4} = b^{4-4}$$

$$= b^0$$

How does this value for b^0 compare with the value displayed on your calculator for 2^0?

Since $\frac{b^4}{b^4}$ cannot have two different values, we can conclude that $b^0 = 1$. This example and the Exploration suggest the following definition.

Zero Exponent	**For any nonzero number a, $a^0 = 1$.**

We can also simplify $\frac{r^3}{r^7}$ in two ways.

Method 1
Definition of Powers or Expanded Form

$$\frac{r^3}{r^7} = \frac{\overset{1}{\cancel{(r)}}\,\overset{1}{\cancel{(r)}}\,\overset{1}{\cancel{(r)}}}{\underset{1}{\cancel{(r)}}\,\underset{1}{\cancel{(r)}}\,\underset{1}{\cancel{(r)}}\,(r)\,(r)\,(r)\,(r)}$$

$$= \frac{1}{r^4}$$

Method 2
Quotient of Powers

$$\frac{r^3}{r^7} = r^{3-7} \quad \textit{Quotient of powers}$$

$$= r^{-4}$$

Did the display on your calculator for 2^{-4} equal $\frac{1}{2^4}$?

Since $\frac{r^3}{r^7}$ cannot have two values, we conclude that $\frac{1}{r^4} = r^{-4}$. This example and the Exploration suggest the following definition.

Negative Exponents	**For any nonzero number a and any integer n, $a^{-n} = \frac{1}{a^n}$.**

Example 2 Simplify each expression.

a. $\dfrac{-9m^3n^5}{27m^{-2}n^5y^{-4}}$

$$\begin{aligned}\frac{-9m^3n^5}{27m^{-2}n^5y^{-4}} &= \left(\frac{-9}{27}\right)\left(\frac{m^3}{m^{-2}}\right)\left(\frac{n^5}{n^5}\right)\left(\frac{1}{y^{-4}}\right)\\ &= \frac{-1}{3}m^{3-(-2)}n^{5-5}y^4 && \tfrac{1}{y^{-4}} = y^4\\ &= -\frac{1}{3}m^5n^0y^4 && \text{Subtract the exponents.}\\ &= -\frac{m^5y^4}{3} && n^0 = 1\end{aligned}$$

b. $\dfrac{(5p^{-2})^{-2}}{(2p^3)^2}$

$$\begin{aligned}\frac{(5p^{-2})^{-2}}{(2p^3)^2} &= \frac{5^{-2}p^4}{2^2p^6} && \text{Power of a monomial property}\\ &= \left(\frac{1}{2^2}\right)\left(\frac{1}{5^2}\right)\left(\frac{p^4}{p^6}\right)\\ &= \left(\frac{1}{4}\right)\left(\frac{1}{25}\right)p^{4-6} && \text{Quotient of powers property}\\ &= \frac{1}{100}p^{-2}\\ &= \frac{1}{100p^2} && \text{Definition of negative exponents}\end{aligned}$$

CHECK FOR UNDERSTANDING

Communicating Mathematics

Study the lesson. Then complete the following.

1. **Explain** why 0^0 is not defined. (*Hint:* Think of computing $\frac{0^m}{0^m}$.)
2. **Explain** why a cannot equal zero in the negative exponents property.
3. **Write** a convincing argument to show why $3^0 = 1$ using the following pattern.

   $3^5 = 243, 3^4 = 81, 3^3 = 27, 3^2 = 9, \ldots$

4. **Study** the pattern below.

5^5	5^4	5^3	5^2	5^1	5^0	5^{-1}	5^{-2}	5^{-3}	5^{-4}
3125	625	125	25	5	1				

   Copy the table and complete the pattern. Write an explanation of the pattern you used.

5. **You Decide** Taigi and Isabel each simplified $\left(\frac{x^{-2}y^3}{x}\right)^{-2}$ correctly as shown below.

Taigi

$$\left(\frac{x^{-2}y^3}{x}\right)^{-2} = \frac{x^4y^{-6}}{x^{-2}}$$
$$= x^{4-(-2)}y^{-6}$$
$$= x^6y^{-6}$$
$$= \frac{x^6}{y^6}$$

Isabel

$$\left(\frac{x^{-2}y^3}{x}\right)^{-2} = (x^{-2-1}y^3)^{-2}$$
$$= (x^{-3}y^3)^{-2}$$
$$= x^6y^{-6}$$
$$= \frac{x^6}{y^6}$$

Whose method do you prefer? Why?

MATH JOURNAL

6. **Assess Yourself** Which properties of monomials do you find easy to understand? Which properties do you need to study more?

Guided Practice

Simplify. Assume that no denominator is equal to zero.

7. 11^{-2}
8. $(6^{-2})^2$
9. $\left(\frac{1}{4} \cdot \frac{2}{3}\right)^{-2}$
10. $a^4(a^{-7})(a^0)$
11. $\frac{6r^3}{r^7}$
12. $\frac{(a^7b^2)^2}{(a^{-2}b)^{-2}}$

13. **Geometry** Write the ratio of the area of the circle to the area of the square in simplest form.

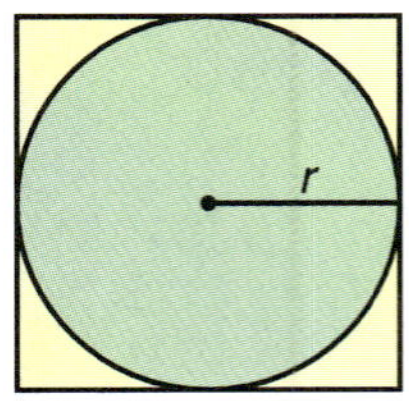

EXERCISES

Practice

Simplify. Assume that no denominator is equal to zero.

14. $a^0b^{-2}c^{-1}$
15. $\frac{a^0}{a^{-2}}$
16. $\frac{5n^5}{n^8}$
17. $\frac{m^2}{m^{-4}}$
18. $\frac{b^5d^2}{b^3d^8}$
19. $\frac{10m^4}{30m}$
20. $\frac{(-y)^5m^8}{y^3m^{-7}}$
21. $\frac{b^6c^5}{b^{14}c^2}$
22. $\frac{22a^2b^5c^7}{-11abc^2}$
23. $\frac{(a^{-2}b^3)^2}{(a^2b)^{-2}}$
24. $\frac{7x^3z^5}{4z^{15}}$
25. $\frac{(-r)^5s^8}{r^5s^2}$
26. $\frac{(r^{-4}k^2)^2}{(5k^2)^2}$
27. $\frac{16b^4}{-4bc^3}$
28. $\frac{27a^4b^6c^9}{15a^3c^{15}}$
29. $\frac{(4a^{-1})^{-2}}{(2a^4)^2}$
30. $\left(\frac{3m^2n^2}{6m^{-1}k}\right)^0$
31. $\frac{r^{-5}s^{-2}}{(r^2s^5)^{-1}}$
32. $\left(\frac{7m^{-1}n^3}{n^2r^{-1}}\right)^{-1}$
33. $\frac{(-b^{-1}c)^0}{4a^{-1}c^2}$
34. $\left(\frac{3xy^{-2}z}{4x^{-2}y}\right)^{-2}$

Critical Thinking

Simplify. Assume that no denominator is equal to zero.

35. $m^3(m^n)$

36. $y^{2c}(y^{5c})$

37. $(3^{2x+1})(3^{2x-7})$

38. $\frac{r^{y-2}}{r^{y+3}}$

39. $\frac{(q^{y-7})^2}{(q^{y+2})^2}$

40. $\frac{y^x}{y^{a-x}}$

Applications and Problem Solving

41. Finance You can use the formula $P = A\left[\frac{i}{1-(1+i)^{-n}}\right]$ to determine the monthly payment on a home. P represents the monthly payment, A represents the price of the home less the down payment, i represents the *monthly* interest rate (annual rate ÷ 12), and n is the total number of monthly payments. Find the monthly payment on a \$180,000 home with 10% down and an *annual* interest rate of 8.6% over 30 years.

42. Finance You can use the formula $B = P\left[\frac{1-(1+i)^{k-n}}{i}\right]$ to calculate the balance due on a car loan after a certain number of payments have been made. B represents the balance due (or payoff), P represents the current monthly payment, i represents the *monthly* interest rate (annual rate ÷ 12), k represents the total number of monthly payments already made, and n is the total number of monthly payments. Find the balance due on a 48-month loan for \$10,562 after 20 monthly payments of \$265.86 have been made at an *annual* interest rate of 9.6%.

Mixed Review

43. Simplify $(2a^3)(7ab^2)^2$. (Lesson 9–1)

44. Aviation Flying with the wind, a plane travels 300 miles in 40 minutes. Flying against the wind, it travels 300 miles in 45 minutes. Find the air speed of the plane. (Lesson 8–4)

45. Write an open sentence involving the absolute value for the graph at the right. (Lesson 7–6)

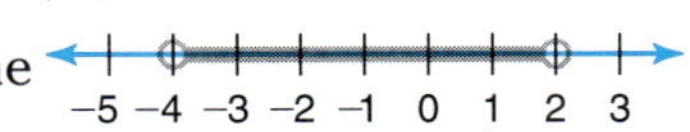

46. Solve $-\frac{2}{5} > \frac{4z}{7}$. (Lesson 7–2)

47. Geometry Find the coordinates of the midpoint of the line segment whose endpoints are $(5, -3)$ and $(1, -7)$. (Lesson 6–7)

48. Sales Latoya bought a new dress for \$32.86. This included 6% sales tax. What was the cost of the dress before tax? (Lesson 4–5)

49. Solve $\frac{4-x}{3+x} = \frac{16}{25}$. (Lesson 4–1)

50. Simplify $41y - (-41y)$. (Lesson 2–3)

9–3 Scientific Notation

What YOU'LL LEARN

- To express numbers in scientific and standard notation, and
- to find products and quotients of numbers expressed in scientific notation.

Why IT'S IMPORTANT

You can use scientific notation to express the solutions to many problems.

APPLICATION

Transportation

The numbers of passengers arriving at and departing from some major U. S. airports for 1993 are listed in the table below.

Airport	City	Number of Passengers Arriving and Departing (nearest million)
O'Hare International	Chicago	65,000,000
Dallas/Ft. Worth International	Dallas/Ft. Worth	50,000,000
Los Angeles International	Los Angeles	48,000,000
Hartsfield Atlanta International	Atlanta	48,000,000
San Francisco International	San Francisco	32,000,000
Miami International	Miami	29,000,000
J. F. Kennedy International	New York	27,000,000
Newark International	Newark	26,000,000
Detroit Metropolitan Wayne County	Detroit	24,000,000
Logan International	Boston	24,000,000

Source: Air Transport Association of America

When dealing with very large numbers, keeping track of place value can be difficult. For this reason, it is not always desirable to express numbers in standard notation as shown in the chart. Large numbers such as these may be expressed in **scientific notation.**

Definition of Scientific Notation	**A number is expressed in scientific notation when it is in the form $a \times 10^n$, where $1 \leq a < 10$ and n is an integer.**

For example, the number of passengers arriving at and departing from Miami International was about 29,000,000. To write this number in scientific notation, express it as a product of a number greater than or equal to 1, but less than 10, and a power of 10.

$$\begin{aligned} 29{,}000{,}000 &= 2.9 \times 10{,}000{,}000 \\ &= 2.9 \times 10^7 \end{aligned}$$

Scientific notation is also used to express very small numbers. When numbers between zero and one are written in scientific notation, the exponent of 10 is negative.

Example 1 Express each number in scientific notation.

a. 98,700,000,000

$$\begin{aligned} 98{,}700{,}000{,}000 &= 9.87 \times 10{,}000{,}000{,}000 \\ &= 9.87 \times 10^{10} \end{aligned}$$

b. 0.0000056

$$\begin{aligned} 0.0000056 &= 5.6 \times 0.000001 \\ &= 5.6 \times \frac{1}{1{,}000{,}000} \\ &= 5.6 \times \frac{1}{10^6} \\ &= 5.6 \times 10^{-6} \end{aligned}$$

Example 2 Express each number in standard notation.

a. 3.45×10^5

$$\begin{aligned} 3.45 \times 10^5 &= 3.45 \times 100{,}000 \\ &= 345{,}000 \end{aligned}$$

b. 9.72×10^{-4}

$$\begin{aligned} 9.72 \times 10^{-4} &= 9.72 \times \frac{1}{10^4} \\ &= 9.72 \times \frac{1}{10{,}000} \\ &= 9.72 \times 0.0001 \\ &= 0.000972 \end{aligned}$$

CAREER CHOICES

A **pilot** is a highly trained professional who flies planes and helicopters for the transportation of people and cargo, law enforcement, or emergency rescues.

Pilots are required to have a license, which is earned through extensive flight training and written examinations. A college degree is recommended for pilot candidates.

For more information, contact:

Future Aviation Professionals of America
4291J Memorial Dr.
Atlanta, GA 30032

You can use scientific notation to simplify computation with very large numbers and/or very small numbers.

EXPLORATION GRAPHING CALCULATORS

You can use a graphing calculator to solve problems using scientific notation. First, put your calculator in scientific mode. To enter 3.5×10^9, enter 3.5 [X] 10 [^] 9.

Your Turn

a. Use your calculator to find $(3.5 \times 10^9)(2.36 \times 10^{-3})$.
b. Explain how the calculator calculated the product in part a.
c. Write the product for part a in standard notation.
d. Use your calculator to find $(5.544 \times 10^3) \div (1.54 \times 10^7)$.
e. Explain how the calculator calculated the quotient in part d.
f. Write the quotient for part d in standard notation.

Example 3 Use scientific notation to evaluate each expression.

a. (610)(2,500,000,000) *Estimate: 2.5 billion × 600 = 1.5 trillion*

$$\begin{aligned} (610)(2{,}500{,}000{,}000) &= (6.1 \times 10^2)(2.5 \times 10^9) \\ &= (6.1 \times 2.5)(10^2 \times 10^9) \quad \textit{Associative property} \\ &= 15.25 \times 10^{11} \\ &= 1.525 \times 10^{12} \text{ or } 1{,}525{,}000{,}000{,}000 \end{aligned}$$

b. (0.000009)(3700) *Estimate: 0.00001 × 3700 = 0.037*

$$\begin{aligned} (0.000009)(3700) &= (9 \times 10^{-6})(3.7 \times 10^3) \\ &= (9 \times 3.7)(10^{-6} \times 10^3) \quad \textit{Associative property} \\ &= 33.3 \times 10^{-3} \\ &= 3.33 \times 10^{-2} \text{ or } 0.0333 \end{aligned}$$

c. $\dfrac{2.0286 \times 10^8}{3.15 \times 10^3}$ *Estimate:* $\dfrac{210{,}000{,}000}{3000} = 70{,}000$

$$\frac{2.0286 \times 10^8}{3.15 \times 10^3} = \left(\frac{2.0286}{3.15}\right)\left(\frac{10^8}{10^3}\right)$$
$$= 0.644 \times 10^5$$
$$= 6.44 \times 10^4 \text{ or } 64{,}400$$

Scientific notation is extensively used by scientists in fields such as physics and astronomy.

Example 4

APPLICATION

Astronomy

A black hole is a region in space where matter seems to disappear. A star becomes a black hole when the radius of the star reaches a certain critical value called the *Schwarzschild radius.* The value is given by the equation $R_s = \frac{2GM}{c^2}$, where R_s is the Schwarzschild radius in meters, G is the gravitational constant (6.7×10^{-11}), M is the mass in kilograms, and c is the speed of light (3×10^8 meters per second).

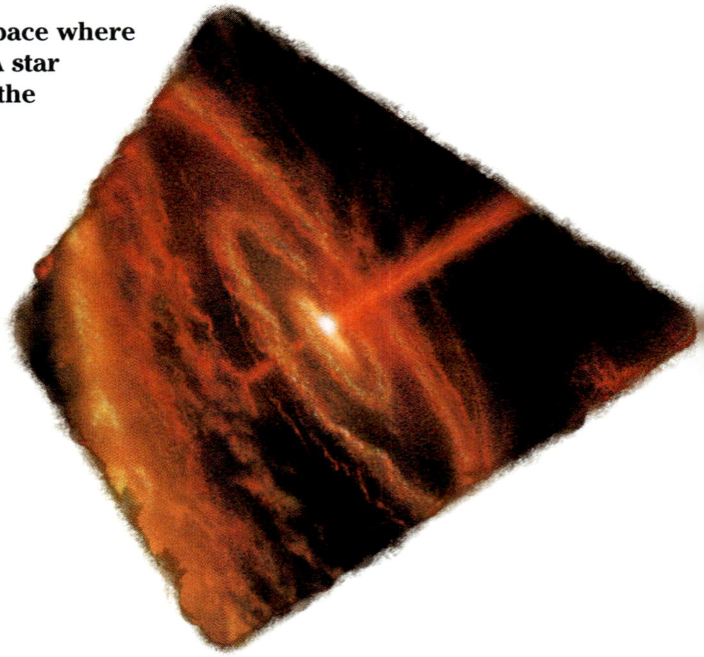

a. The mass of the sun is 2×10^{30} kilograms. Find the Schwarzschild radius of the sun.

b. The actual radius of the sun is 700,000 kilometers. Is it in danger of becoming a black hole in the near future?

FYI

Stephen W. Hawking is a theoretical physicist from Great Britain. Dr. Hawking has made many contributions to the field of science including extensive work dealing with black holes.

a. Use your knowledge of exponents and scientific notation to evaluate the expression for the sun's Schwarzschild radius.

$$R_s = \frac{2GM}{c^2}$$
$$= \frac{2(6.7 \times 10^{-11})(2 \times 10^{30})}{(3 \times 10^8)^2}$$
$$= \frac{2(6.7 \times 10^{-11})(2 \times 10^{30})}{3^2 \times 10^{16}} \quad \textit{Power of a monomial property}$$
$$= \left(\frac{2(6.7)(2)}{3^2}\right)\left(\frac{10^{-11}(10^{30})}{10^{16}}\right)$$
$$= \left(\frac{26.8}{9}\right)10^{-11+30-16} \quad \textit{Product and quotient of powers}$$
$$\approx 2.98 \times 10^3 \text{ or } 2980$$

The Schwarzschild radius for the sun is about 2980 meters.

b. Since the actual radius of the sun is 700,000 kilometers, it does not seem to be in danger of becoming a black hole in the near future.

CHECK FOR UNDERSTANDING

Communicating Mathematics

Study the lesson. Then complete the following.

1. When do you use positive exponents in scientific notation?
2. When do you use negative exponents in scientific notation?
3. **Explain** how you can find the product of (1.2×10^5) and (4×10^8) without using pencil and paper or a calculator.
4. **Explain** how you can find the quotient of (4.4×10^4) and (4×10^7) without using pencil and paper or a calculator.

Guided Practice

Express each number in the second column in standard notation. Express each number in the third column in scientific notation.

	Planet	Maximum Distance from Sun (miles)	Radius (miles)
5.	Mercury	4.34×10^7	1515
6.	Earth	9.46×10^7	3963
7.	Jupiter	5.07×10^8	44,419
8.	Uranus	1.8597×10^9	15,881
9.	Pluto	4.5514×10^9	714

Express each number in scientific notation.

10. **Chemistry** The wavelength of cadmium's green line is 0.0000509 centimeters.
11. **Physics** The mass of a proton is 0.000000000000000000001672 milligrams.
12. **Health** The length of the AIDS virus is 0.00011 millimeters.
13. **Biology** The diameter of an organism called the *Mycoplasma laidlawii* is 0.000004 inch.

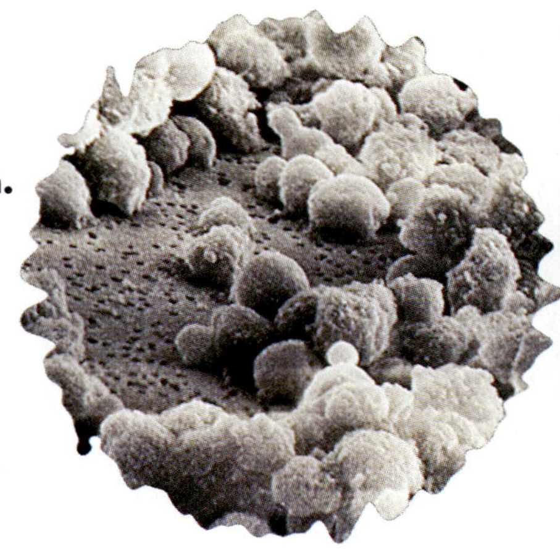

AIDS virus

Evaluate. Express each result in scientific and standard notation.

14. $(3.24 \times 10^3)(6.7 \times 10^4)$
15. $(0.2 \times 10^{-3})(31 \times 10^{-4})$
16. $\dfrac{8.1 \times 10^2}{2.7 \times 10^{-3}}$
17. $\dfrac{52{,}440{,}000{,}000}{(2.3 \times 10^6)(38 \times 10^{-5})}$

EXERCISES

Practice

Express each number in scientific notation.

18. 9500
19. 0.0095
20. 56.9
21. 87,600,000,000
22. 0.000000000761
23. 312,720,000
24. 0.00000008
25. 0.090909
26. 355×10^7
27. 78.6×10^3
28. 112×10^{-8}
29. 0.007×10^{-7}
30. 7830×10^{-2}
31. 0.99×10^{-5}

Evaluate. Express each result in scientific and standard notation.

32. $(6.4 \times 10^3)(7 \times 10^2)$

33. $(4 \times 10^2)(15 \times 10^{-6})$

34. $360(5.8 \times 10^7)$

35. $(5.62 \times 10^{-3})(16 \times 10^{-5})$

36. $\frac{6.4 \times 10^9}{1.6 \times 10^2}$

37. $\frac{9.2 \times 10^3}{2.3 \times 10^5}$

38. $\frac{1.035 \times 10^{-3}}{4.5 \times 10^2}$

39. $\frac{2.795 \times 10^{-7}}{4.3 \times 10^{-2}}$

40. $\frac{3.6 \times 10^2}{1.2 \times 10^7}$

41. $\frac{5.412 \times 10^{-2}}{8.2 \times 10^3}$

42. $\frac{(35{,}921{,}000)(62 \times 10^3)}{3.1 \times 10^5}$

43. $\frac{1.6464 \times 10^5}{(98{,}000)(14 \times 10^3)}$

Graphing Calculator

Use a graphing calculator to evaluate each expression. Express each answer in scientific notation.

44. $(4.8 \times 10^6)(5.73 \times 10^2)$

45. $(5.07 \times 10^{-4})(4.8 \times 10^2)$

46. $(9.1 \times 10^6) \div (2.6 \times 10^{10})$

47. $(9.66 \times 10^3) \div (3.45 \times 10^{-2})$

Programming

48. The graphing calculator program at the right evaluates the expression $(2ab^2)^3$ for the values you input. It expresses the result in scientific notation. If $a = 9$, $b = 10$, and $c = 0$, the result is 5.832E9.

```
PROGRAM:SCINOT
: Sci
: Prompt A,B,C
: Disp "(2AB^2)^3 =",
  (2AB^2)^3
```

Edit the program to evaluate each expression. Then evaluate for $a = 4$, $b = 6$, and $c = 8$.

a. $a^2b^3c^4$ b. $(-2a)^2(4b)^3$ c. $(4a^2b^4)^3$ d. $(ac)^3 + (3b)^2$

Critical Thinking

49. Use a calculator to multiply 3.7×10^{112} and 5.6×10^{10}.
   a. Describe what happens when you multiply these values.
   b. Describe how you could find the product.
   c. Write the product in scientific notation.

Applications and Problem Solving

50. **Biology** Seeds come in all sizes. The largest seed is the seed from the double coconut tree, which can have a mass as great as 23 kilograms. In contrast, the mass of the seed of an orchid is about 3.5×10^{-6} grams. Use a calculator to find how many times greater the mass of the seed of the double coconut tree is than the mass of the seed of the orchid. Express your answer in scientific notation.

Germination of wheat seedling

51. **Movies** In a recent movie, Albert Einstein, played by Walter Matthau, tries to start a romance between his niece Catherine Boyd, played by Meg Ryan, and an auto mechanic named Ed Walters, played by Tim Robbins. When Ed asks Catherine to estimate the number of stars in the sky, she answers "$10^{12} + 1$." Write this number in standard notation.

52. National Parks Each year, millions of people visit our national parks and recreational areas. The five most popular locations are listed at the right. Write the number of visitors to each location in scientific notation.

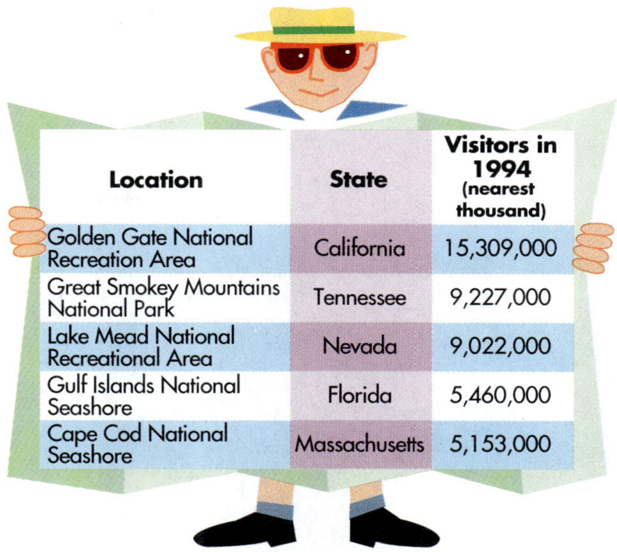

Location	State	Visitors in 1994 (nearest thousand)
Golden Gate National Recreation Area	California	15,309,000
Great Smokey Mountains National Park	Tennessee	9,227,000
Lake Mead National Recreational Area	Nevada	9,022,000
Gulf Islands National Seashore	Florida	5,460,000
Cape Cod National Seashore	Massachusetts	5,153,000

Source: *Good Housekeeping*, Sept., 1994

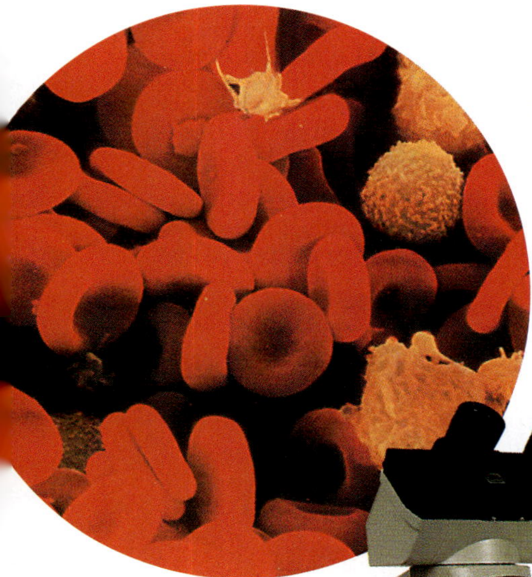

53. Biology There are an average of 25 billion red blood cells in the human body and about 270 million hemoglobin molecules in each red blood cell. Use a calculator to find the average number of hemoglobin molecules in the human body. Write your answer in scientific notation.

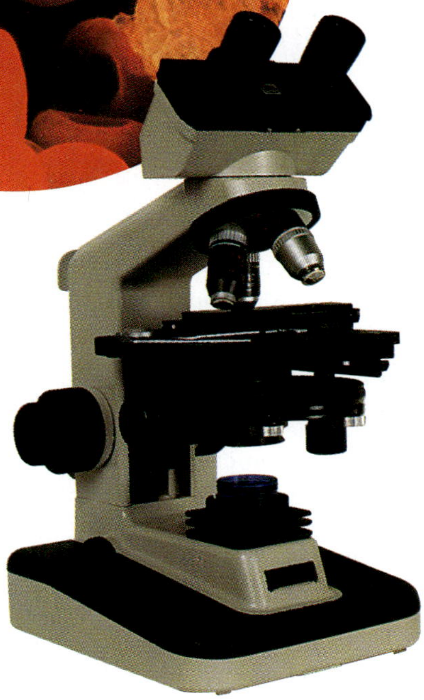

54. Health Laboratory technicians look at bacteria through microscopes. A microscope set on 1000× makes an organism appear to be 1000 times larger than its actual size. Most bacteria are between 3×10^{-4} and 2×10^{-3} millimeters in diameter.

a. How large would bacteria appear under a microscope set on 1000×?

b. Do you think a microscope set on 1000× would allow the technician to see all the bacteria? Explain your answer.

55. Economics Suppose you try to feed all of the people on Earth using the 4.325×10^{11} kilograms of food produced each year in the United States and Canada. You need to divide this food among the population of the world so that each person receives the same amount of food each day. The population of Earth is about 4.8×10^9.

a. How much food will each person have each day?

b. Do you think the amount in part a is enough to live on? Justify your answer.

Mixed Review

56. Simplify $\dfrac{24x^2y^7z^3}{-6x^2y^3z}$. (Lesson 9–2)

57. Graph the system of inequalities. (Lesson 8–5)

$y \leq -x$

$x \geq -3$

58. Use substitution to solve the system of equations. (Lesson 8–2)

$x = 2y - 12$

$x - 3y = 8$

59. Statistics What percent of the data represented at the right is between 15 and 25? (Lesson 7–7)

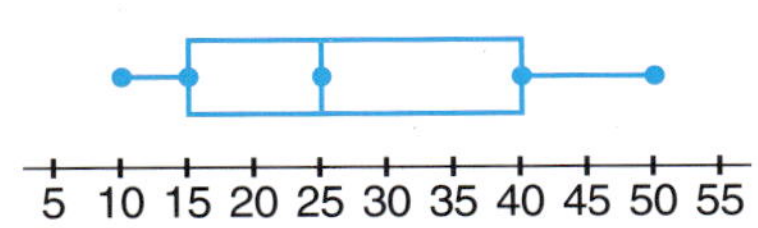

60. Graph the solution set of $x < -3$ or $x \geq 1$. (Lesson 7–4)

61. **Geometry** Write an equation of the line that is perpendicular to the line $5x + 5y = 35$ and passes through the point at $(-3, 2)$. (Lesson 6–6)

62. **Aviation** An airplane passing over Sacramento at an elevation of 37,000 feet begins its descent to land at Reno, 140 miles away. If the elevation of Reno is 4500 feet, what should be the approximate slope of descent? (Lesson 6–1)

63. Is $\{(3, 4), (5, 4), (7, 5), (9, 5)\}$ a function? (Lesson 5–5)

64. State the domain of $\{(4, 4), (0, 1), (21, 5), (13, 0), (3, 9)\}$. (Lesson 5–2)

65. **Geometry** Suppose $\sin K = 0.4563$. Find the measure of $\angle K$ to the nearest degree. (Lesson 4–3)

66. **Swimming** Rosalinda swims the 50-yard freestyle for the Wachung High School swim team. Her times in the last six meets were 26.89 seconds, 26.27 seconds, 25.18 seconds, 25.63 seconds, 27.16 seconds, and 27.18 seconds. Find the mean and median of her times. (Lesson 3–7)

67. Solve $x - 44 = -207$. (Lesson 3–1)

Mathematics and SOCIETY

Measurements Great and Small

The excerpt below appeared in an article in the *New York Times* on September 12, 1993.

ONCE UPON A TIME, WHEN THE WORLD was simpler, a foot was really as long as someone's foot, and a cubit the distance from someone's elbow to the end of the middle finger. Now we measure things that are much smaller than shoes and larger than arms, but there is still a desire to put them into a human context. Take the micron, for example, a unit so small—one millionth of a meter—that it seems hard to cast in a human context. But that doesn't stop newspapers from trying; they inevitably hitch it to something else: a human hair. Earlier this year, describing the one-micron width of a computer circuit, one newspaper article said a hair, by comparison, is 100 microns across. But another article, on cancer-causing soot particles smaller than 10 microns, said a human hair was 75 microns in diameter. Last year, in an article on fiber-optic beams, a human hair was 70 microns; in 1982, in one on coatings for cutting tools, the hair was down to 25 microns. . . . It can be hard to grope with the big, too. *Strategically Speaking*, a marketing newsletter, said recently that 1.8 billion slices of frozen pizza are sold each year—enough to cover 511,366 square miles. How big is that? The newsletter had the sense not to give the answer in microns: enough to cover New York, California, Texas, Maine, Delaware, and Rhode Island combined. ■

1. Based on the data above, what is the average size of one slice of frozen pizza? (State the answer in square feet.) Does this size seem reasonable to you? Explain.
2. Did you have any difficulty performing the calculations for Exercise 1? How is scientific notation useful in calculations with very large numbers?
3. When you can, do you check the numbers you see presented in newspapers or magazines to see if they are reasonable? Why or why not?

MODELING MATHEMATICS

A Preview of Lesson 9–4

9–4A Polynomials

Materials: algebra tiles

Algebra tiles can be used as a model for polynomials. A **polynomial** is a monomial or the sum of monomials. The diagram below shows the models.

Polynomial Models	
Polynomials are modeled using three types of tiles.	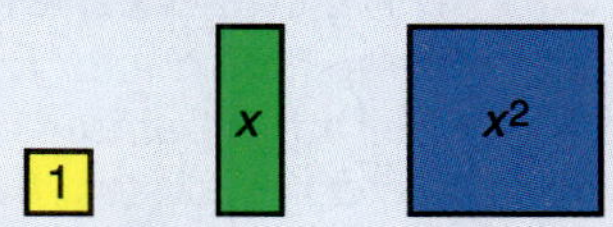
Each tile has an opposite.	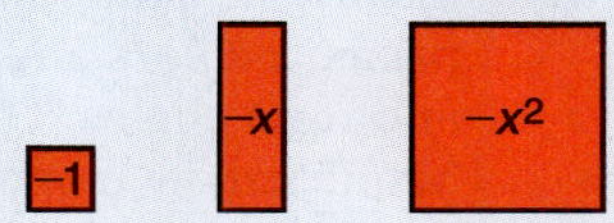

Activity **Use algebra tiles to model each polynomial.**

a. $2x^2$

To model this monomial, you will need 2 blue x^2-tiles.

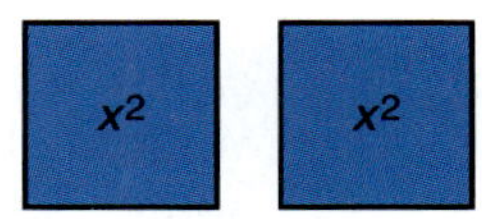

b. $x^2 - 3x$

To model this polynomial, you will need 1 blue x^2-tile and 3 red x-tiles.

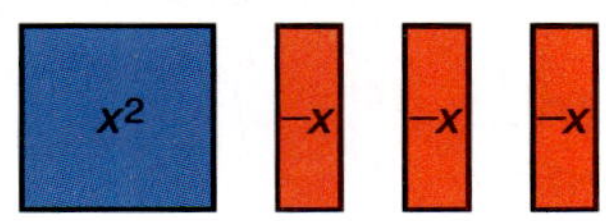

c. $x^2 + 2x - 3$

To model this polynomial, you will need 1 blue x^2-tile, 2 green x-tiles, and 3 red 1-tiles.

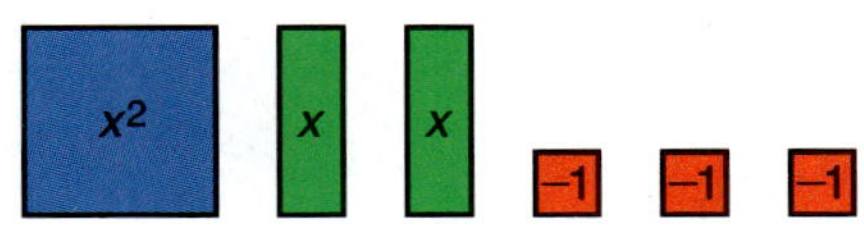

Model **Use algebra tiles to model each monomial or polynomial. Then draw a diagram of your model.**

1. $-3x^2$ **2.** $2x^2 - 3x + 5$ **3.** $2x^2 - 7$ **4.** $6x - 4$

Write **Write each model as an algebraic expression.**

5.

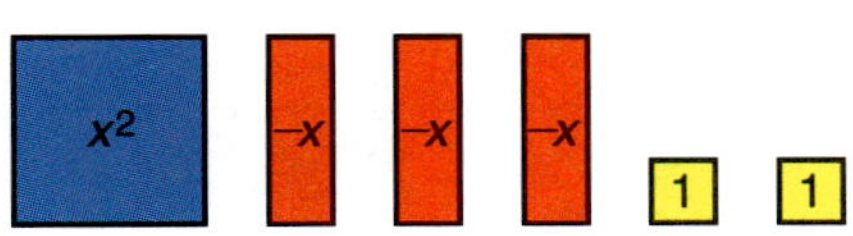

6.

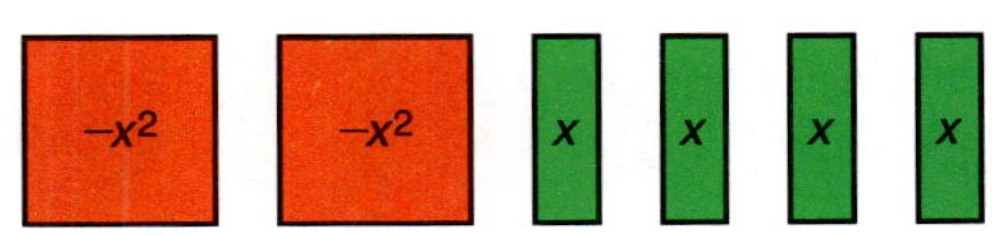

7.

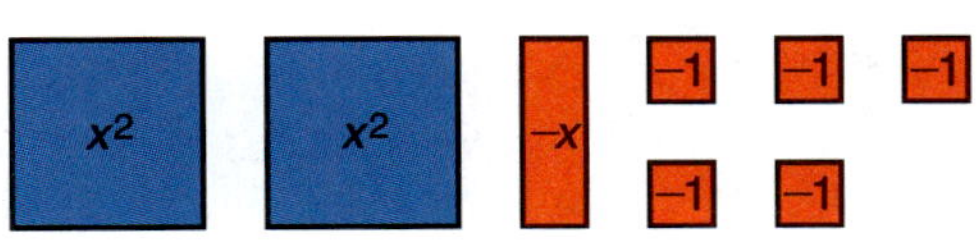

8.

9. Write a few sentences giving reasons why algebra tiles are sometimes called *area tiles.*

9–4 Polynomials

What YOU'LL LEARN

- To find the degree of a polynomial, and
- to arrange the terms of a polynomial so that the powers of a variable are in ascending or descending order.

Why IT'S IMPORTANT

You can use polynomials to solve problems involving agriculture and biology.

Top Five List

Selling Prices of Paintings

1. *Portrait du Dr. Gachet* by van Gogh, \$75,000,000
2. *Au Moulin de la Galette* by Renoir, \$71,000,000
3. *Les Noces de Pierrette* by Picasso, \$51,700,000
4. *Irises* by van Gogh, \$49,000,000
5. *Yo Picasso* by Picasso, \$43,500,000

CONNECTION Art

The picture at the right shows the painting *Composition with Red, Yellow, and Blue* by the Dutch painter Piet Mondrian. Mondrian preferred abstraction and simplification in his art. He liked to limit his palette to the primary colors and to use straight lines and right angles. The style of painting that Mondrian developed is called *neoplasticism,* and he is considered one of the most influential painters of the 20th century.

Consider a portion of the painting *Composition with Red, Yellow, and Blue.* The length of the sides and the area of each section are given.

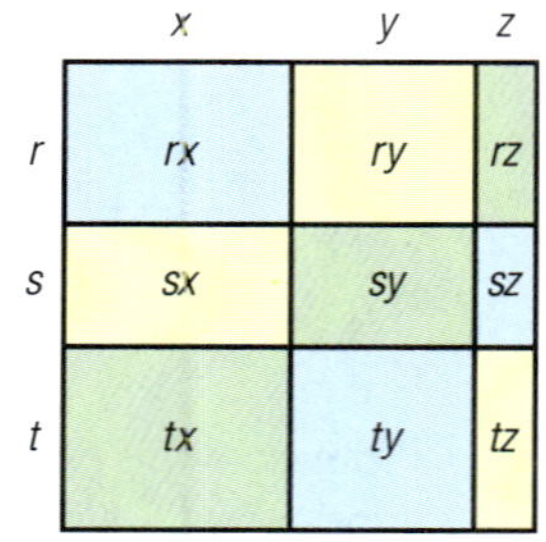

We can find the area of this portion of the painting by adding the areas of each section.

$$rx + ry + rz + sx + sy + sz + tx + ty + tz$$

The expression representing the area of this portion of the painting is called a **polynomial**. A polynomial is a monomial or a sum of monomials. Recall that a monomial is a number, a variable, or a product of numbers and variables. The exponents of the variables of a monomial must be positive. A **binomial** is the sum of two monomials. A **trinomial** is the sum of three monomials. Here are some examples of each. *Polynomials with more than three terms have no special names.*

Monomial	Binomial	Trinomial
$3y^2$	$4x - 7$	$a + 2b + 4c$
$2abc^2$	$2x + 9y$	$x^2 + 8x + 9$
-9	$3x^2 - 11xy$	$x^2 + 2xy + y^2$
$14m$	$2 + 13x$	$3a - 7b^2 - 4c$

Irises by van Gogh

Au Moulin de la Galette by Renoir

Example 1

State whether each expression is a polynomial. If it is a polynomial, identify it as either a *monomial, binomial,* or *trinomial.*

a. $3a - 7bc$

The expression $3a - 7bc$ can be written as $3a + (-7bc)$. Therefore, it is a polynomial. Since $3a - 7bc$ can be written as a sum of two monomials, $3a$ and $-7bc$, it is a binomial.

LOOK BACK

You can refer to Lesson 1-7 for information on simplifying expressions.

b. $3x^2 + 7a - 2 + a$

The expression $3x^2 + 7a - 2 + a$ can be written as $3x^2 + 8a + (-2)$. Therefore, it is a polynomial. Since it can be written as the sum of three monomials, $3x^2$, $8a$, and -2, it is a trinomial.

c. $\frac{7}{2r^2} + 6$

The expression $\frac{7}{2r^2} + 6$ is not a polynomial because $\frac{7}{2r^2}$ is not a monomial.

Polynomials can be used to represent savings accumulated over several years.

Example 2

APPLICATION

Finance

Each of the three summers before Li Chiang attends college, she plans to work as a lifeguard and save $2000 towards her college expenses. She plans to invest the money in a savings account at her local bank. The value of each year's savings can be found by the expression px^t where p represents the amount invested, x represents the sum of 1 and the annual interest rate, and t represents the time in years.

a. Write a polynomial that represents the total amount of money Li will have when she starts college.

b. Find the amount of money Li will have if the bank is paying 6% annually.

a. By the time Li goes to college, the money she makes the last summer will be worth $2000. The money she makes the second summer will be worth $2000x$, and money she makes the first summer will be worth $2000x^2$. Altogether, she will have $2000 + 2000x + 2000x^2$.

b. Replace x with 1.06 and calculate the total amount of money Li will have.

$$2000 + 2000(1.06) + 2000(1.06)^2 = 6367.20 \quad x = 1 + 6\% \text{ or } 1.06$$

Li will have $6367.20 for college.

The **degree** of a monomial is the sum of the exponents of its variables.

Monomial	Degree	
$8y^3$	3	
$4y^2ab$	$2 + 1 + 1 = 4$	*Remember that $a = a^1$ and $b = b^1$.*
-14	0	*Remember that $x^0 = 1$ and $-14 = -14x^0$.*
$42abc$	$1 + 1 + 1 = 3$	

To find the degree of a polynomial, you must find the degree of each term. The greatest degree of any term is the degree of the polynomial.

Polynomial	Terms	Degree of the Terms	Degree of the Polynomial
$3x^2 + 8a^2b - 4$	$3x^2, 8a^2b, -4$	2, 3, 0	3
$7x^4 - 9x^2y^7 + 4x$	$7x^4, -9x^2y^7, 4x$	4, 9, 1	9

Example 3 **Find the degree of each polynomial.**

a. $\mathbf{9xy + 2}$

The degree of $9xy$ is 2.

The degree of 2 is 0.

Thus, the degree of $9xy + 2$ is 2.

b. $\mathbf{18x^2 + 21xy^2 + 13x - 2abc}$

The degree of $18x^2$ is 2.

The degree of $21xy^2$ is 3.

The degree of $13x$ is 1.

The degree of $2abc$ is 3.

Thus, the degree of $18x^2 + 21xy^2 + 13x - 2abc$ is 3.

The terms of a polynomial are usually arranged so that the powers of one variable are in ascending or descending order. Later in this chapter, you will learn to add, subtract, and multiply polynomials. These operations are easier to perform if the polynomials are arranged in one of these orders.

Ascending Order	Descending Order
$4 + 5a - 6a^2 + 2a^3$	$2a^3 - 6a^2 + 5a + 4$
$-5 - 2x + 4x^5$	$4x^5 - 2x - 5$
(in x) $8xy - 3x^2y + x^5 - 2x^7y$	(in x) $-2x^7y + x^5 - 3x^2y + 8xy$
(in y) $2x^4 - 3x^3y + 2x^2y^2 - y^{12}$	(in y) $-y^{12} + 2x^2y^2 - 3x^3y + 2x^4$

CHECK FOR UNDERSTANDING

Communicating Mathematics

Study the lesson. Then complete the following.

1. **Explain** why the degree of an integer like -27 is 0.
2. **Explain** why $m + \frac{34}{n}$ is not a binomial.
3. In this lesson, you were introduced to the words *polynomial, monomial, binomial,* and *trinomial.* These words begin with the prefixes poly-, mono-, bi-, and tri- respectively. Find the meaning of each prefix. List two other words that begin with each prefix, and define each of these words.

MODELING MATHEMATICS

4. The model below represents a polynomial.

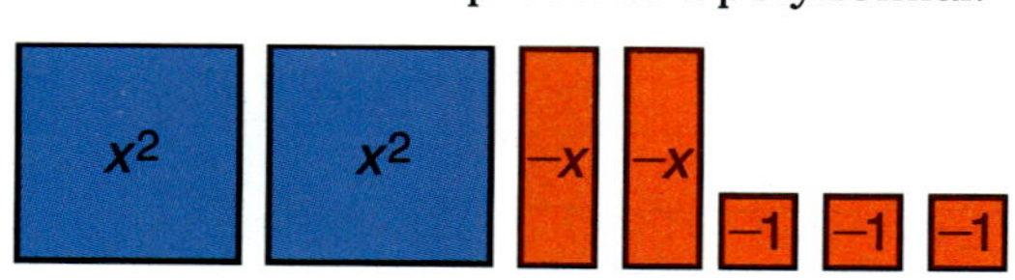

Write this polynomial in simplest form.

Guided Practice

State whether each expression is a polynomial. If the expression is a polynomial, identify it as a *monomial,* a *binomial,* or a *trinomial.*

5. $4x^3 - 11ab + 6$
6. $x^3 - \frac{7}{4}x + \frac{y}{x^2}$
7. $4c + ab - c$

Find the degree of each polynomial.

8. $11d$
9. 10
10. $42x^{12}y^3 - 23x^8y^6$
11. Arrange the terms of $-11x + 5x^3 - 12x^6 + x^8$ so that the powers of x are in descending order.
12. Arrange the terms of $y^4x + y^5x^3 - x^2 + yx^5$ so that the powers of x are in ascending order.
13. **Geometry** The area of a rectangle equals the length times the width. The area of a square equals the square of the length of a side. The area of a circle equals the number pi (π) times the square of the radius. The figure at the right consists of a rectangle, a circle, and a square.

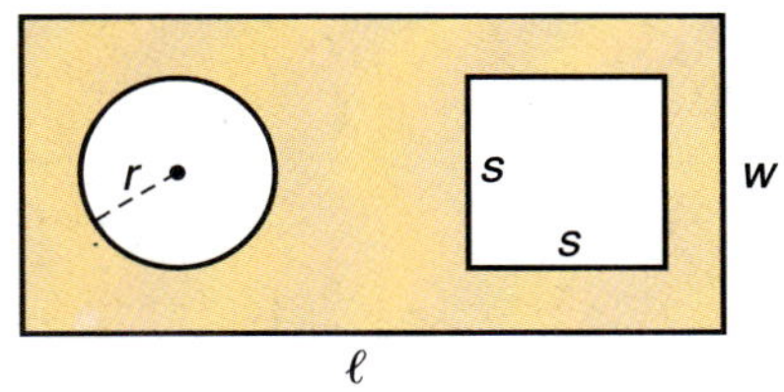

a. Write a polynomial expression that represents the area of the shaded region at the right.
b. Find the area of the shaded region if $w = 8$, $\ell = 15$, $r = 2$, and $s = 4$.

EXERCISES

Practice

State whether each expression is a polynomial. If the expression is a polynomial, identify it as a *monomial,* a *binomial,* or a *trinomial.*

14. $\frac{r^5}{26}$
15. $x^2 - \frac{1}{3}x + \frac{y}{234}$
16. $\frac{y^3}{12x}$
17. $5a - 6b - 3a$
18. $\frac{7}{t} + t^2$
19. $9ag^2 + 1.5g^2 - 0.7ag$

Find the degree of each polynomial.

20. $6a^2$
21. $15t^3y^2$
22. 24
23. $m^2 + n^3$
24. $x^2y^3z - 4x^3z$
25. $3x^2y^3z^4 - 18a^5f^3$
26. $8r - 7y + 5d - 6h$
27. $9 + t^2 - s^2t^2 + rs^2t$
28. $-4yzw^4 + 10x^4z^2w$

Arrange the terms of each polynomial so that the powers of x are in descending order.

29. $5 + x^5 + 3x^3$
30. $8x - 9x^2y + 5 - 2x^5$
31. $abx^2 - bcx + 34 - x^7$
32. $7a^3x + 9ax^2 - 14x^7 + \frac{12}{19}x^{12}$

Arrange the terms of each polynomial so that the powers of x are in ascending order.

33. $1 + x^3 + x^5 + x^2$
34. $4x^3y + 3xy^4 - x^2y^3 + y^4$
35. $7a^3x - 8a^3x^3 + \frac{1}{5}x^5 + \frac{2}{3}x^2$
36. $\frac{3}{4}x^3y - x^2 + 4 + \frac{2}{3}x$

INTEGRATION
Geometry

Write a polynomial to represent the area of each shaded region. Then find the area of each region if $a = 20$, $b = 6$, $c = 2$, $r = 5$, and $x = 1$.

37.

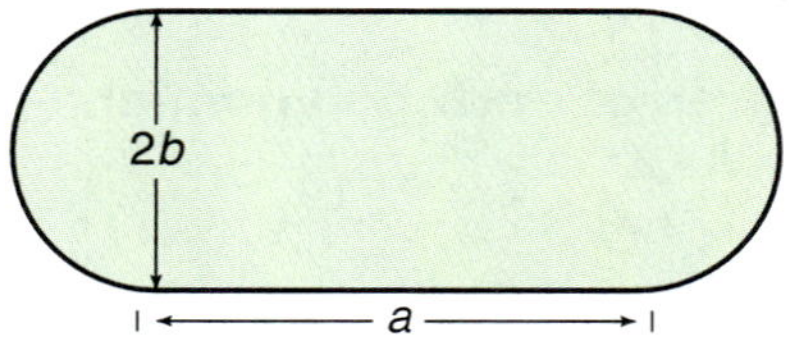

38.

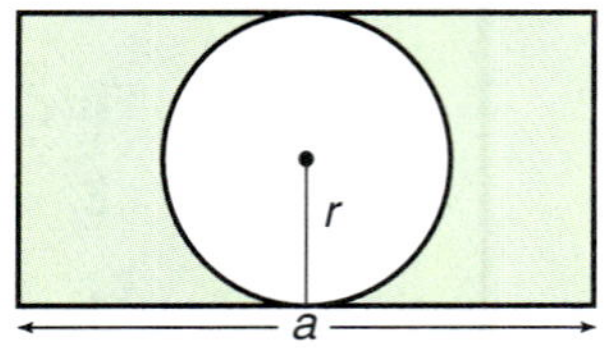

39.

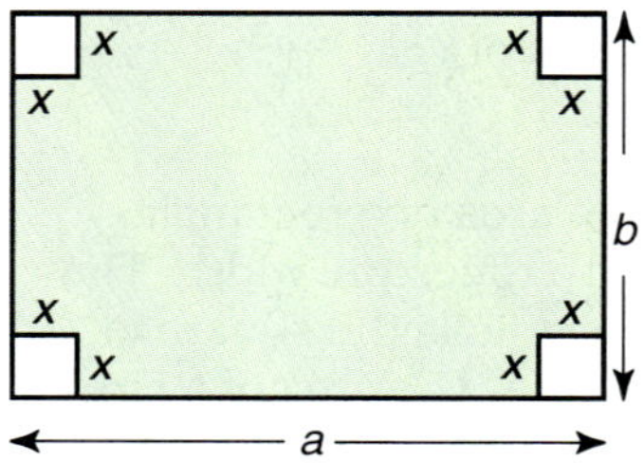

40.

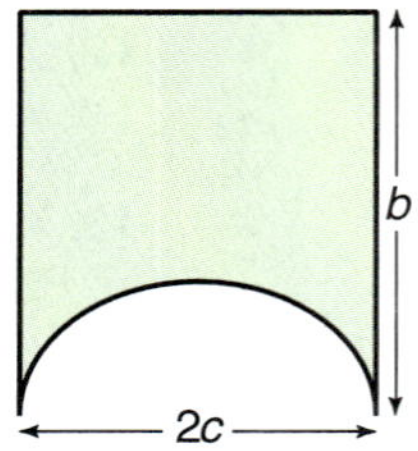

Critical Thinking

41. You can write a numeral in base 10 in polynomial form. For example, $3892 = 3(10)^3 + 8(10)^2 + 9(10)^1 + 2(10)^0$.

a. Write the year of your birth in polynomial form.

b. Suppose 89435 is a numeral in base a. Write 89435 in polynomial form.

Applications and Problem Solving

42. Banking Tawana Hodges inherited $25,000. She invested the money at an annual interest rate of 7.5%. Each year she added $2000 of her own money. Will her original investment of $25,000 double in 7 years? If not, how many years will it take to double the $25,000?

43. Biology The width of the abdomen of a certain type of female moth is useful in estimating the number of eggs that she can carry. The average number of eggs can be estimated by $14x^3 - 17x^2 - 16x + 34$, where x represents the width of the abdomen in millimeters. About how many eggs would you expect this type of moth to produce if her abdomen measures 2.75 millimeters?

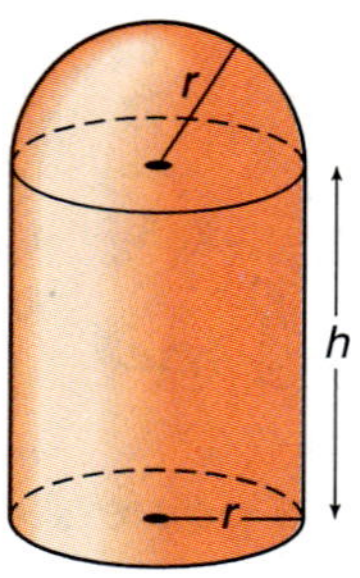

44. Agriculture A diagram of a silo is shown at the left. The volume of a cylinder is the product of π, the square of the radius, and the height. The volume of a sphere is the product of $\frac{4}{3}$, π, and the cube of the radius.

a. Write a polynomial that represents the volume of the silo.

b. If the height is 40 feet and the radius is 8 feet, find the volume of the silo.

Mixed Review

45. Express 42,350 in scientific notation. (Lesson 9–3)

46. Use elimination to solve the system of equations. (Lesson 8–3)

$$\frac{3}{2}x + \frac{1}{5}y = 5$$

$$\frac{3}{4}x - \frac{1}{5}y = -5$$

47. Number Theory If 6.5 times an integer is increased by 11, the result is between 55 and 75. What is the integer? List all possible answers. (Lesson 7–4)

48. **Manufacturing** During one month, Tanisha's Sporting Equipment manufactured a total of 3250 tennis racket covers. Assuming that the planned production of tennis racket covers can be represented by a straight line, determine how many covers will be manufactured by the end of the year. (Lesson 6–4)

49. Solve $4x + 3y = 12$ if the domain is $\{-3, 1, 3, 9\}$. (Lesson 5–3)

50. **Probability** Suppose you meet someone whose birthday is in March. What is the probability that the day of the person's birthday has a 3 in the numeral? (Lesson 4–6)

51. **Insurance** Insurance claims are usually paid based on the depreciated value of the item in question. An item stolen or destroyed with half its useful life remaining would bring a payment equal to half of its original cost. If a battery was stolen when it was 5 months old, find the depreciated value if the battery cost \$45 new and was guaranteed for 36 months. (Lesson 4–1)

52. Solve $ax - by = 2cz$ for y. (Lesson 3–6)

WORKING ON THE Investigation

Refer to the Investigation on pages 448–449.

Ready, Set, Drop!

You can determine an average drop time for each triangle and then use these data to predict glide times for triangles of different sizes.

1. Using either the mean, median, or mode, find an average glide time from the data for each of the four triangles. For each average, explain which measure you used and why you selected that measure to give you the best average or most typical time for the experiment. Are the average glide times best represented by scientific notation? Explain.
2. Describe a hypothetical case for which the mode would be the most appropriate average time, one for which the median would be the most appropriate average time, and one for which the mean would be most appropriate.
3. At this point, you have four average times—one for the typical glide time of each of the four triangles. Draw a scatter plot of the data. Let the independent variable be the perimeter, and let the dependent variable be the average glide time.
4. Describe the graph. Describe any mathematical relationships that you see. What is the relationship of the perimeter of a triangular piece of tissue paper to the speed of the glide?
5. Draw a best-fit line for your data. Write a linear equation to model this best fit line.
6. Draw a second scatter plot in which the horizontal axis represents the area of the triangles and the vertical axis represents the average glide time.
7. Use your scatter plots to predict the glide time for a triangle with a perimeter of 36 centimeters. Use that glide time and the second scatter plot to predict the surface area of that triangle. How does your prediction compare with the actual area of an equilateral triangle whose perimeter is 36 centimeters? Explain your results.

Add the results of your work to your Investigation Folder.

MODELING MATHEMATICS

A Preview of Lesson 9–5

9–5A Adding and Subtracting Polynomials

Materials: algebra tiles

Monomials such as $4x^2$ and $-7x^2$ are called *like terms* because they have the same variable to the same power. When you use algebra tiles, you can recognize like terms because the individual tiles have the same size and shape.

Polynomial Models	
Like terms are represented by tiles that are the same shape and size.	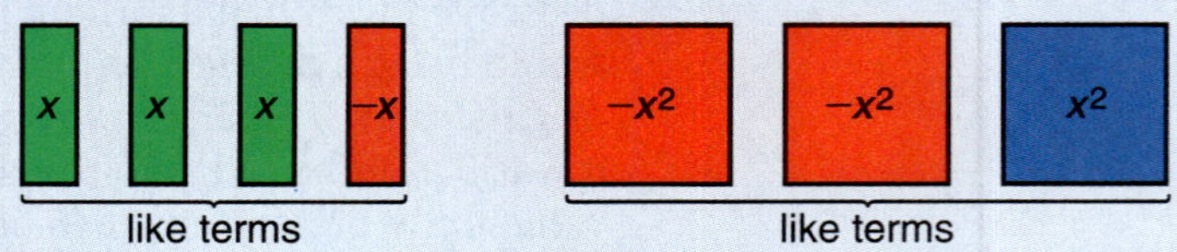
A zero pair may be formed by pairing one tile with its opposite. You can remove or add zero pairs without changing the polynomial.	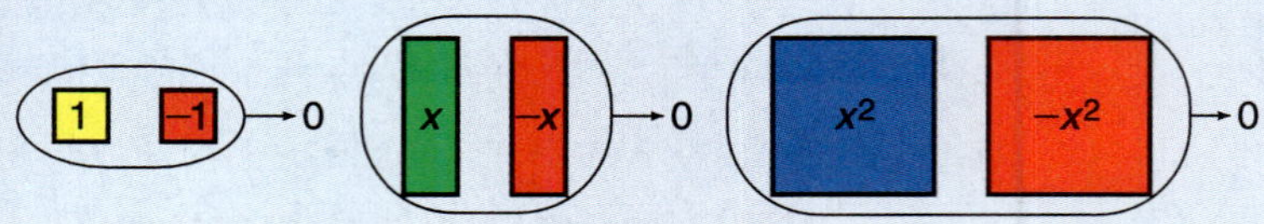

Activity 1 Use algebra tiles to find $(2x^2 + 3x + 2) + (x^2 - 5x - 5)$.

Step 1 Model each polynomial. You may want to arrange like terms in columns for convenience.

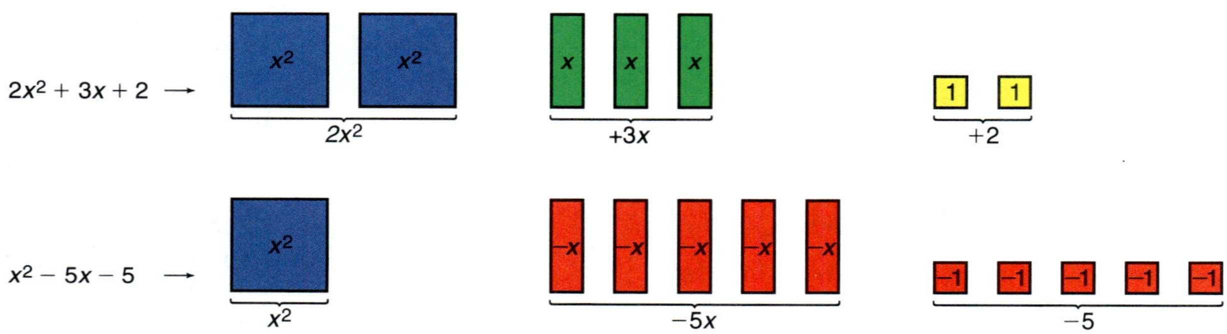

Step 2 Combine like terms and remove all zero pairs.

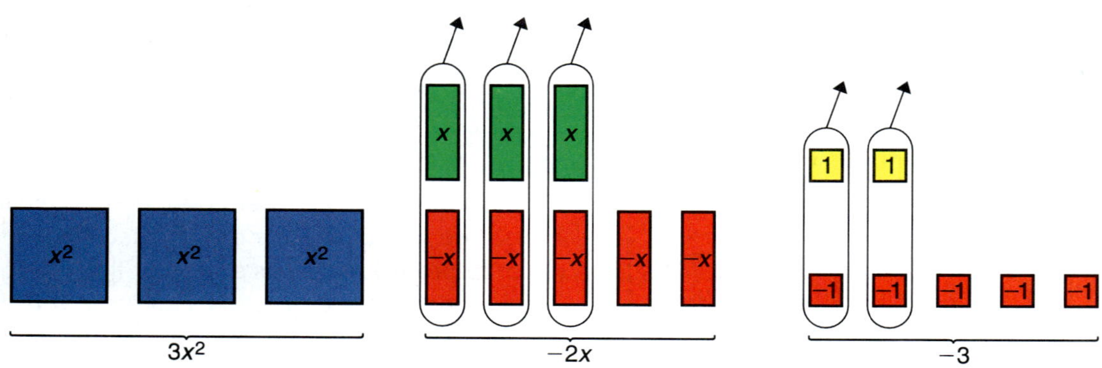

Step 3 Write the polynomial for the tiles that remain.
$(2x^2 + 3x + 2) + (x^2 - 5x - 5) = 3x^2 - 2x - 3$

Activity 2 **Use algebra tiles to find $(2x + 5) - (-3x + 2)$.**

Step 1 Model the polynomial $2x + 5$.

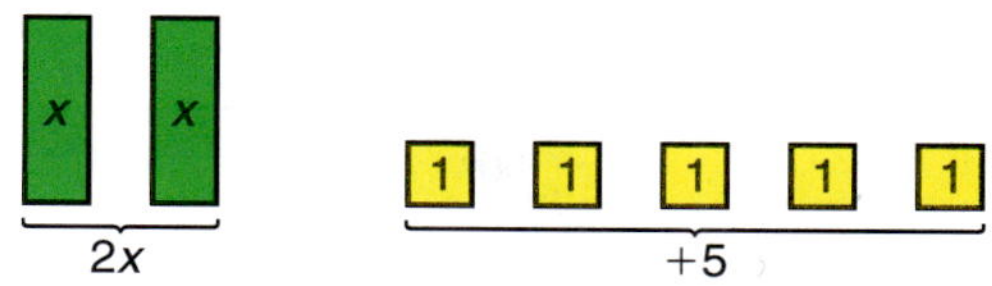

Step 2 To subtract $-3x + 2$, you must remove 3 red x-tiles and 2 yellow 1-tiles. You can remove the yellow 1-tiles, but there are no red x-tiles. Add 3 zero pairs of x-tiles. Then remove the 3 red x-tiles.

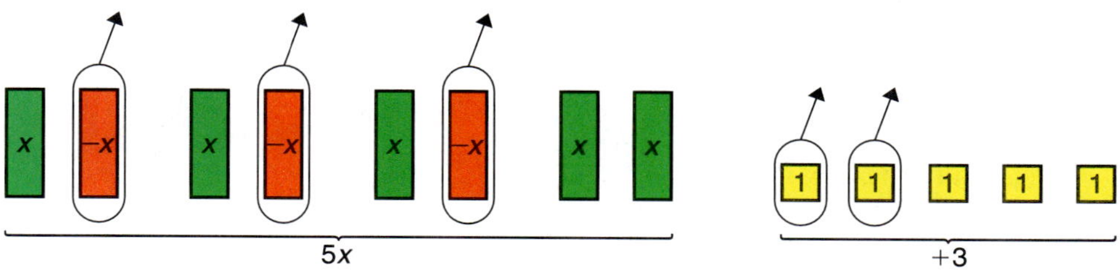

Remember that the value of a zero pair is 0.

Step 3 Write the polynomial for the tiles that remain.
$(2x + 5) - (-3x + 2) = 5x + 3$

Recall that you can subtract a number by adding its additive inverse or opposite. Similarly, you can subtract a polynomial by adding its opposite.

Activity 3 **Use algebra tiles and the additive inverse, or opposite, to find $(2x + 5) - (-3x + 2)$.**

Step 1 To find the difference of $2x + 5$ and $-3x + 2$, add $2x + 5$ and the opposite of $-3x + 2$.

$2x + 5 \rightarrow$

The opposite of $-3x + 2$ is $3x - 2$. $\rightarrow$

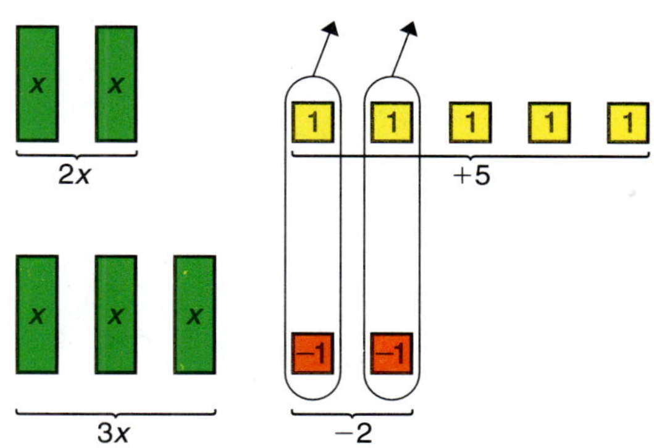

Step 2 Write the polynomial for the tiles that remain.
$(2x + 5) - (-3x + 2) = 5x + 3$ *This is the same answer as in Activity 2.*

Model **Use algebra tiles to find each sum or difference.**

1. $(2x^2 - 7x + 6) + (-3x^2 + 7x)$
2. $(-2x^2 + 3x) + (-7x - 2)$
3. $(x^2 - 4x) - (3x^2 + 2x)$
4. $(3x^2 - 5x - 2) - (x^2 - x + 1)$
5. $(x^2 + 2x) + (2x^2 - 3x + 4)$
6. $(2x^2 + 3x - 4) - (3x^2 - 4x + 1)$

Draw **Is each statement *true* or *false*? Justify your answer with a drawing.**

7. $(3x^2 + 2x - 4) + (-x^2 + 2x - 3) = 2x^2 + 4x - 7$
8. $(x^2 - 2x) - (-3x^2 + 4x - 3) = -2x^2 - 6x - 3$

Write

9. Find $(x^2 - 2x + 4) - (4x + 3)$ using each method from Activity 2 and Activity 3. Illustrate with drawings and explain in writing how zero pairs are used in each case.

9–5 Adding and Subtracting Polynomials

What YOU'LL LEARN

- To add and subtract polynomials.

Why IT'S IMPORTANT

You can use polynomials to solve problems involving architecture and geometry.

APPLICATION
Postal Service

The U.S. Postal Service has restrictions on the sizes of boxes that may be shipped by parcel post. The length plus the girth of the box must not exceed 108 inches. Girth is the shortest distance around the package. It is defined as follows.

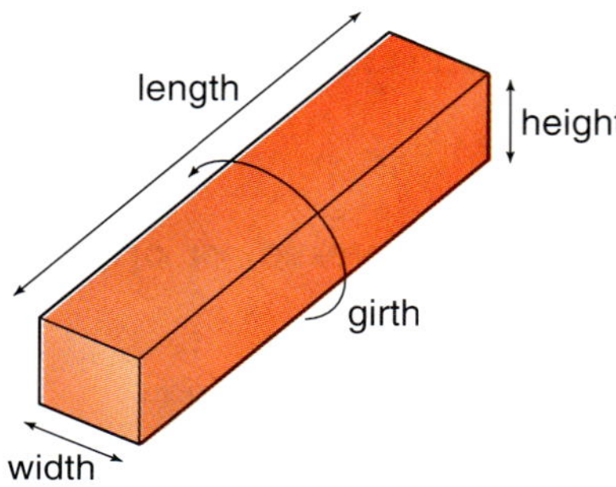

girth = twice the width + twice the height or $w + w + h + h$

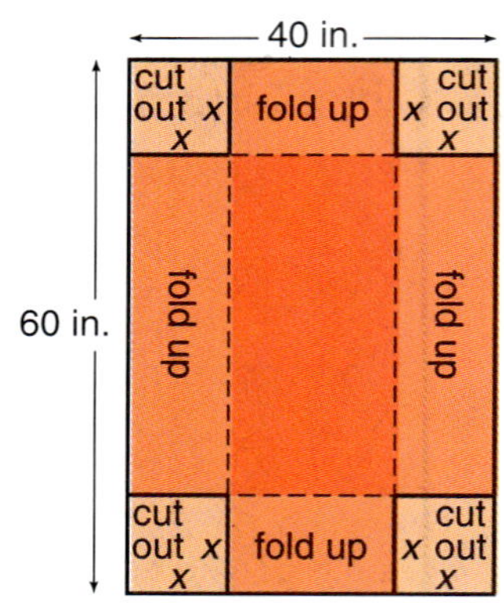

Mrs. Diaz wants to send a package to her daughter, who is a student at Auburn University. She can't find any cardboard boxes at home; all she has is a 60-by-40 inch rectangle of cardboard. She decides that she can make a box out of it by cutting squares out of each corner and folding up the flaps. Then she will use another rectangle of cardboard for the top of the box. She doesn't know how big the squares should be, though. For now, she is calling the side of each square x.

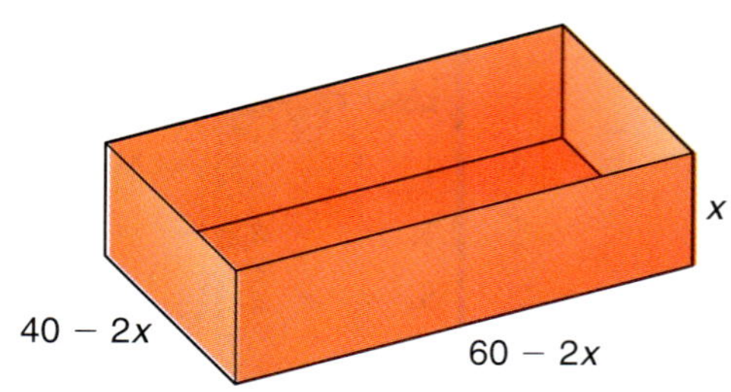

$$\begin{aligned}\text{Girth} &= w + w + h + h\\ &= (40 - 2x) + (40 - 2x) + x + x\end{aligned}$$

In order to mail this box, the length plus the girth must be at most 108 inches. That is, $(60 - 2x) + (40 - 2x) + (40 - 2x) + x + x \le 108$. *You will solve this problem in Exercise 42.*

To add polynomials, you can group like terms and then find the sum, or you can write them in column form and then add.

Example 1 **Find $(4a^2 + 7a - 12) + (-9a^2 - 6 + 2a)$.**

Method 1
Group the like terms together.

$(4a^2 + 7a - 12) + (-9a^2 - 6 + 2a)$
$= [4a^2 + (-9a^2)] + (7a + 2a) + [-12 + (-6)]$
$= [4 + (-9)]a^2 + (7 + 2)a + (-18)$ *Distributive property*
$= -5a^2 + 9a - 18$

Method 2
Arrange the like terms in column form and add.

$$\begin{array}{r} 4a^2 + 7a - 12 \\ (+)\ -9a^2 + 2a - \ \ 6 \\ \hline -5a^2 + 9a - 18 \end{array}$$

Notice that terms are in descending order and like terms are aligned.

Recall that you can subtract a rational number by adding its opposite or additive inverse. Similarly, you can subtract a polynomial by adding its additive inverse. To find the additive inverse of a polynomial, replace each term with its additive inverse or opposite.

Polynomial	Additive Inverse
$2a - 3b$	$-2a + 3b$
$4x^2 + 7x - 18$	$-4x^2 - 7x + 18$
$-9y + 4x - 2z$	$9y - 4x + 2z$
$7x^3 + 12x^2 + 21$	$-7x^3 - 12x^2 - 21$

Example 2 **Find $(6a^2 - 8a + 12b^3) - (-11a^2 + 6b^3)$.**

Method 1
Find the additive inverse of $-11a^2 + 6b^3$. Then group the like terms and add.

The additive inverse of $-11a^2 + 6b^3$ is $11a^2 - 6b^3$.

$(6a^2 - 8a + 12b^3) - (-11a^2 + 6b^3)$
$= (6a^2 - 8a + 12b^3) + (11a^2 - 6b^3)$
$= (6a^2 + 11a^2) + (-8a) + [12b^3 + (-6b^3)]$
$= (6 + 11)a^2 - 8a + [12 + (-6)]b^3$
$= 17a^2 - 8a + 6b^3$

Method 2
Arrange like terms in column form and then subtract by adding the additive inverse.

$$\begin{array}{r} 6a^2 - 8a + 12b^3 \\ (-)\ -11a^2 \qquad + \ \ 6b^3 \\ \hline \end{array} \quad \rightarrow \quad \begin{array}{r} 6a^2 - 8a + 12b^3 \\ (+)\ 11a^2 \qquad - \ \ 6b^3 \\ \hline 17a^2 - 8a + \ \ 6b^3 \end{array}$$

Polynomials can be used to represent measures of geometric figures.

Example 3 INTEGRATION Geometry

The measure of the perimeter of the triangle at the right is represented by $11x^2 - 29x + 10$. Find the polynomial that represents the measure of the third side of the triangle.

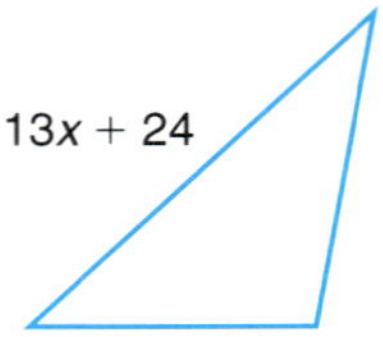

Explore Look at the problem. You know the perimeter of the triangle and the measures of two sides. You need to find the measure of the third side.

Plan The perimeter of a triangle is the sum of the measures of the three sides. To find the measure of the missing side, subtract the two given measures from the perimeter.

Solve

$$
\begin{aligned}
&(11x^2 - 29x + 10) - [(5x^2 - 13x + 24) + (x^2 + 7x + 9)]\\
&= (11x^2 - 29x + 10) - (5x^2 - 13x + 24) - (x^2 + 7x + 9)\\
&= (11x^2 - 29x + 10) + (-5x^2 + 13x - 24) + (-x^2 - 7x - 9)\\
&= [11x^2 + (-5x^2) + (-x^2)] + [-29x + 13x + (-7x)] +\\
&\quad [10 + (-24) + (-9)]\\
&= 5x^2 - 23x - 23
\end{aligned}
$$

The measure of the third side of the triangle is $5x^2 - 23x - 23$.

Examine The sum of the measures of the three sides should equal the perimeter.

$$
\begin{array}{r}
5x^2 - 13x + 24\\
x^2 + 7x + 9\\
(+)\ 5x^2 - 23x - 23\\
\hline
11x^2 - 29x + 10
\end{array}
$$

The sum of the measures of the three sides of the triangle equals the measure of the perimeter. The answer is correct.

CHECK FOR UNDERSTANDING

Communicating Mathematics

Study the lesson. Then complete the following.

1. **Describe** the first step you take when you add or subtract polynomials in column form.
2. **Write** three like terms containing powers of a and b. Find the sum of your three terms.
3. **Explain** how to check your answer when you subtract two polynomials.
4. **Write** a paragraph explaining how to subtract a polynomial.

MODELING MATHEMATICS

5. Use algebra tiles to find each sum or difference.
   a. $(3x^2 + 2x - 7) + (-2x^2 + 15)$ **b.** $(4x + 1) - (x^2 - 2x + 3)$

Guided Practice

Find the additive inverse of each polynomial.

6. $5y - 7z$
7. $-6a^2 + 3$
8. $7y^2 - 3x^2 + 2$
9. $-4x^2 - 3y^2 + 8y + 7x$

Name the like terms in each group.

10. $3m, 8n, 4mn, 5n, 6m$

11. $-8y^2, 2x, 3y^2, 4x, 2z$

12. $2x^3, 5xy, -x^2y, 14xy, 12xy$

13. $3p^3q, -2p, 10p^3q, 15pq, -p$

Find each sum or difference.

14.
$$\begin{array}{rrrr} & 5ax^2 + 3a^2x & & - 5x \\ (+) & 2ax^2 & - 5ax & + 7x \\ \hline \end{array}$$

15.
$$\begin{array}{rr} & 11m^2n^2 + 2mn - 11 \\ (-) & 5m^2n^2 - 6mn + 17 \\ \hline \end{array}$$

16. $(4x^2 + 5x) + (-7x^2 + x)$

17. $(3y^2 + 5y - 6) - (7y^2 - 9)$

18. $(5b - 7ab + 8a) - (5ab - 4a)$

19. $(6p^3 + 3p^2 - 7) + (p^3 - 6p^2 - 2p)$

20. **Geometry** The sum of the degree measures of the angles of a triangle is 180.

a. Write a polynomial to represent the measure of the third angle of the triangle at the right.

b. If $x = 15$, find the measures of the three angles of the triangle.

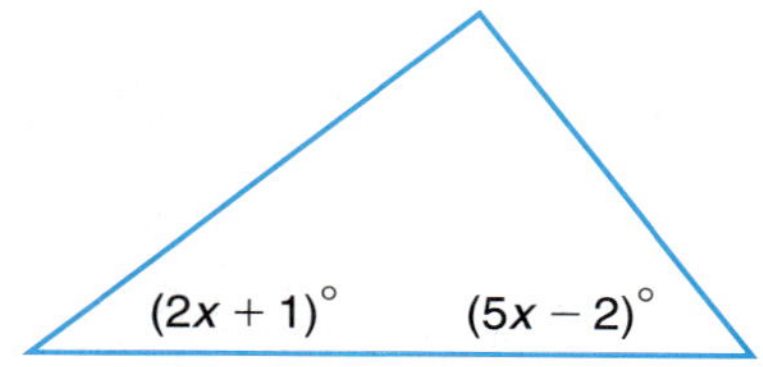

EXERCISES

Practice

Find each sum or difference.

21.
$$\begin{array}{rr} & 4x^2 + 5xy - 3y^2 \\ (+) & 6x^2 + 8xy + 3y^2 \\ \hline \end{array}$$

22.
$$\begin{array}{rr} & 6x^2y^2 - 3xy - 7 \\ (-) & 5x^2y^2 + 2xy + 3 \\ \hline \end{array}$$

23.
$$\begin{array}{rrrr} & a^3 & & - b^3 \\ (+) & 3a^3 + 2a^2b & - b^2 & + 2b^3 \\ \hline \end{array}$$

24.
$$\begin{array}{rrr} & 3a^2 & - 8 \\ (-) & 5a^2 + 2a & + 7 \\ \hline \end{array}$$

25.
$$\begin{array}{rr} & 3a + 2b - 7c \\ & -4a + 6b + 9c \\ (+) & -3a - 2b - 7c \\ \hline \end{array}$$

26.
$$\begin{array}{rrr} & 2x^2 - 5x & + 7 \\ & 5x^2 & - 3 \\ (+) & x^2 - x & + 11 \\ \hline \end{array}$$

27. $(5a - 6m) - (2a + 5m)$

28. $(3 + 2a + a^2) + (5 - 8a + a^2)$

29. $(n^2 + 5n + 13) + (-3n^2 + 2n - 8)$

30. $(5x^2 - 4) - (3x^2 + 8x + 4)$

31. $(13x + 9y) - 11y$

32. $(5ax^2 + 3ax) - (2ax^2 - 8ax + 4)$

33. $(3y^3 + 4y - 7) + (-4y^3 - y + 10)$

34. $(7p^2 - p - 7) - (p^2 + 11)$

35. $(4z^3 + 5z) + (-2z^2 - 4z)$

36. $(x^3 - 7x + 4x^2 - 2) - (2x^2 - 9x + 4)$

INTEGRATION
Geometry

The measures of two sides of a triangle are given. *P* represents the measure of the perimeter. Find the measure of the third side.

37. $P = 5x + 2y$

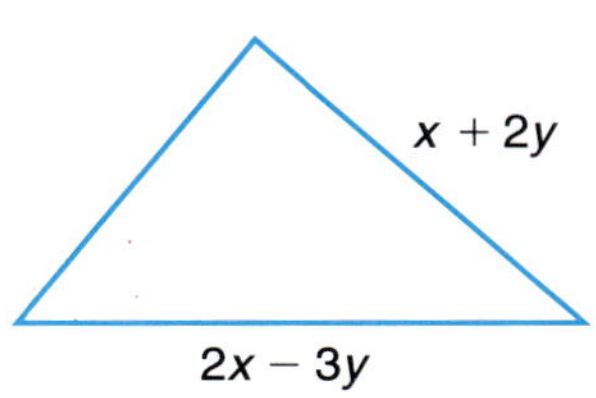

38. $P = 13x^2 - 14x + 12$

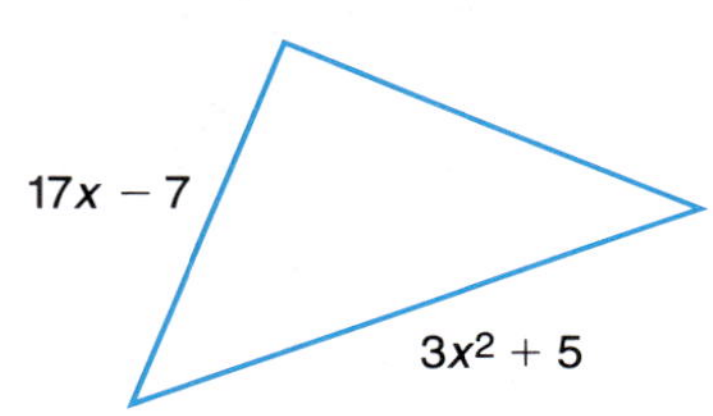

The sum of the degree measures of the angles of a quadrilateral is 360. Find the measure of the fourth angle of each quadrilateral given the degree measures of the other three angles.

39. $4x + 12, 8x - 10, 6x + 5$

40. $x^2 - 2, x^2 + 5x - 9, -8x - 42$

Critical Thinking

41. Your teacher gives you two polynomials. When the first polynomial is subtracted from the second polynomial, the difference is $2n^2 + n - 4$. What is the difference when the second polynomial is subtracted from the first?

Applications and Problem Solving

42. **Postal Service** Refer to the application at the beginning of the lesson.

a. Solve the inequality to find the possible values of x Mrs. Diaz could use in designing her package.

b. For reasons other than Postal Service regulations, what is the greatest integral value x could have?

c. Use a calculator to find the volume of the box when x is the minimum value and when x is the maximum value.

d. What can you conclude about the volume of this box at various heights?

43. **Architecture** The Sears Tower in Chicago is one of the tallest structures in the world. It is actually a building of varying heights as shown in the photo at the left. The diagram below indicates the height of each section in stories.

x	50 stories	89 stories	66 stories
x	110 stories	110 stories	89 stories
x	66 stories	89 stories	50 stories
	x	x	x

Use stories as a unit of measure. Assume that each section is x stories long and x stories wide. Write an expression for the volume of the Sears Tower.

44. **Look for a Pattern** At City Center Mall, there are 25 lockers numbered 1 through 25. Suppose a shopper opens every locker. Then a second shopper closes every second locker. Next a third shopper changes the state of every third locker. (If it's open, the shopper closes it. If it's closed, the shopper opens it.) Suppose this process continues until the 25th shopper changes the state of the 25th locker.

a. Which lockers will still be open?

b. Describe the numbers in your answer for part a.

c. Give the next three numbers for the pattern you found in part a.

d. If there were n lockers in this pattern, which lockers will be open?

Mixed Review

45. Arrange the terms of $-3x + 4x^5 - 2x^3$ so that the powers of x are in ascending order. (Lesson 9–4)

46. **Finance** The current balance on a car loan can be found by evaluating the expression $P\left[\frac{1-(1+r)^{k-n}}{r}\right]$, where P is the monthly payment, r is the monthly interest rate, k is the number of payments already made, and n is the total number of monthly payments. Find the current balance if $P = \$256$, $r = 0.01$, $k = 20$, and $n = 60$. (Lesson 9–2)

47. Solve the system of equations by graphing. Then state the solution of the system of equations. (Lesson 8–1)

$5x - 3y = 12$
$2x - 5y = 1$

48. **Statistics** What is the upper quartile of the data represented by the box-and-whisker plot at the right? (Lesson 7–7)

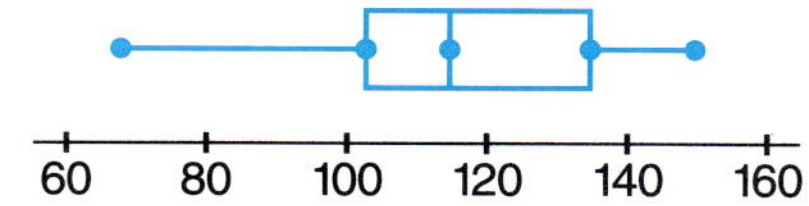

49. **Business** Janet's Garage charges \$83 for a two-hour repair job and \$185 for a five-hour repair job. Define the variables and write a linear equation that Janet can use to bill customers for repair jobs of any length of time. (Lesson 6–4)

50. **Finance** The selling price of \$145,000 for a home included a 6.5% commission for a real estate agent. How much money did the owners receive from the sale? (Lesson 4–5)

51. Solve $\frac{-3n - (-4)}{-6} = -9$. (Lesson 3–3)

52. **Tennis** The diameter of a circle is the distance across the circle. If the diameter of a tennis ball is $2\frac{1}{2}$ inches, how many tennis balls will fit in a can 12 inches high? (Lesson 2–7)

SELF TEST

Simplify. Assume that no denominator is equal to zero. (Lessons 9–1 and 9–2)

1. $(-2n^4y^3)(3ny^4)$
2. $(-3a^2b^5)^2$
3. $\frac{24a^3b^6}{-2a^2b^2}$
4. $\frac{(5r^{-1}s)^3}{(s^2)^3}$

Express each number in scientific notation. (Lesson 9–3)

5. 5,670,000
6. 0.86×10^{-4}
7. **Space Exploration** A space probe that is 2.85×10^9 miles away from Earth sends radio signals back to NASA. If the radio signals travel at the speed of light (186,000 miles per second), how long will it take the signals to reach NASA? (Lesson 9–3)
8. Find the degree of the polynomial $11x^2 + 7ax^3 - 3x + 2a$. Then write the polynomial so that the powers of x are in ascending order. (Lesson 9–4)

Find each sum or difference. (Lesson 9–5)

9. $(x^2 + 3x - 5) + (4x^2 - 7x - 9)$
10. $(2a - 7) - (2a^2 + 8a - 11)$

MODELING MATHEMATICS

9–6A Multiplying a Polynomial by a Monomial

A Preview of Lesson 9–6

Materials: algebra tiles, product mat

You have used rectangles to model multiplication. In this activity, you will use algebra tiles to model the product of simple polynomials. The width and length of a rectangle will represent a monomial and a polynomial, respectively. The area of the rectangle will represent the product of the monomial and the polynomial.

Activity 1 Use algebra tiles to find $x(x - 4)$.

The rectangle will have a width of x units and a length of $(x - 4)$ units. Use your algebra tiles to mark off the dimensions on a product mat. Then make the rectangle with algebra tiles.

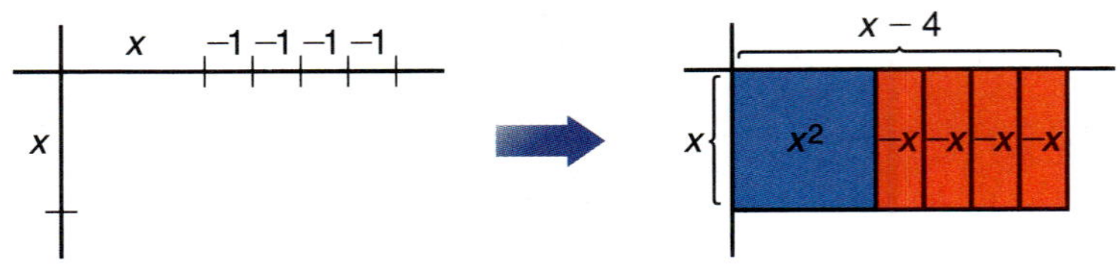

The rectangle consists of 1 blue x^2-tile and 4 red x-tiles.
The area of the rectangle is $x^2 - 4x$. Therefore, $x(x - 4) = x^2 - 4x$.

Activity 2 Use algebra tiles to find $2x(x + 2)$.

The rectangle will have a width of $2x$ units and a length of $(x + 2)$ units. Make the rectangle with algebra tiles.

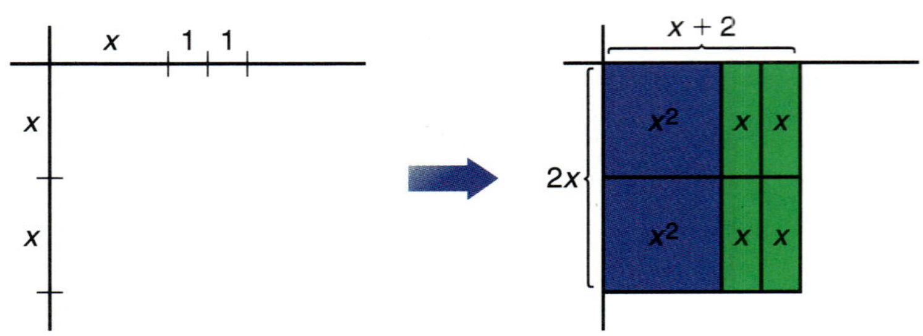

The rectangle consists of 2 blue x^2-tiles and 4 green x-tiles.
The area of the rectangle is $2x^2 + 4x$. Therefore, $2x(x + 2) = 2x^2 + 4x$.

Model **Use algebra tiles to find each product.**

1. $x(x + 2)$
2. $x(x - 3)$
3. $2x(x + 1)$
4. $2x(x - 3)$
5. $x(2x + 1)$
6. $3x(2x - 1)$

Draw **Is each statement *true* or *false*? Justify your answer with a drawing.**

7. $x(2x + 4) = 2x^2 + 4x$
8. $2x(3x - 4) = 6x^2 - 8$

Write

9. Suppose you have a square storage building that measures x feet on a side. You triple the length of the building and increase the width by 15 feet.
   a. What will be the dimensions of the new building?
   b. What is the area of the new building? Write your solution in paragraph form, complete with drawings.

9–6

Multiplying a Polynomial by a Monomial

What YOU'LL LEARN

- To multiply a polynomial by a monomial, and
- to simplify expressions involving polynomials.

Why IT'S IMPORTANT

You can use monomials and polynomials to solve problems involving travel and recreation.

APPLICATION

Recreation

Have you ever played the game of hopscotch? Children from all over the world like to play some form of this game. The following diagrams show versions from different countries.

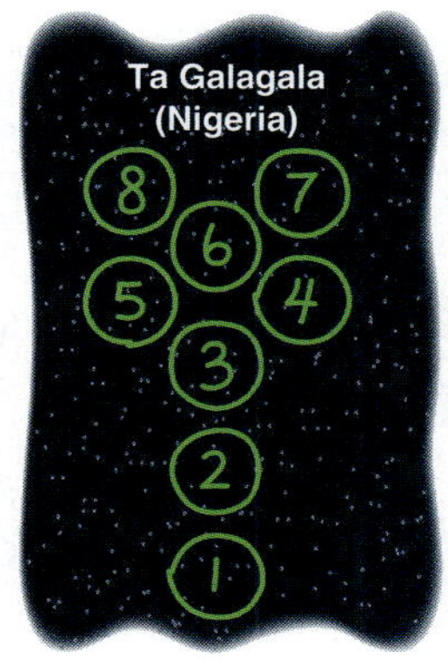

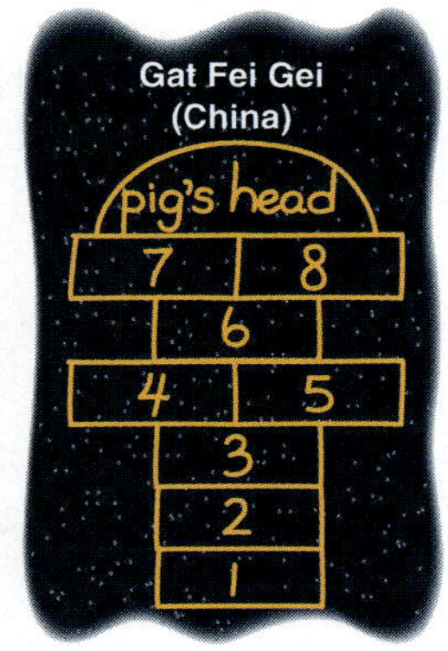

FYI

Tourists can still see the hopscotch pattern carved into the floor of the ancient Forum in Rome.

On the Caribbean island of Trinidad, the children play Jumby. The pattern for this game is shown at the right. Suppose the dimensions of each rectangle are x and $x + 14$. To find the area of each rectangle, you must multiply its length by its width.

This diagram of one of the rectangles shows that the area is $x(x + 14)$.

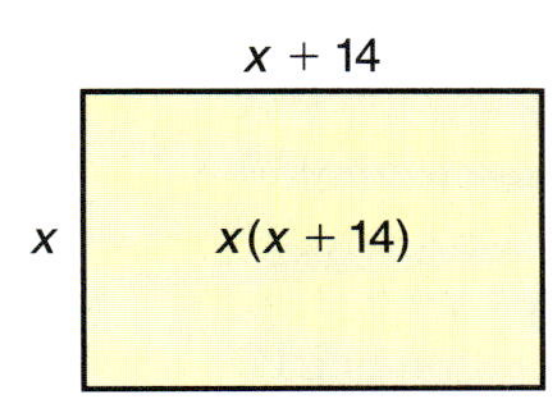

This diagram of the same rectangle shows that the area is $x^2 + 14x$.

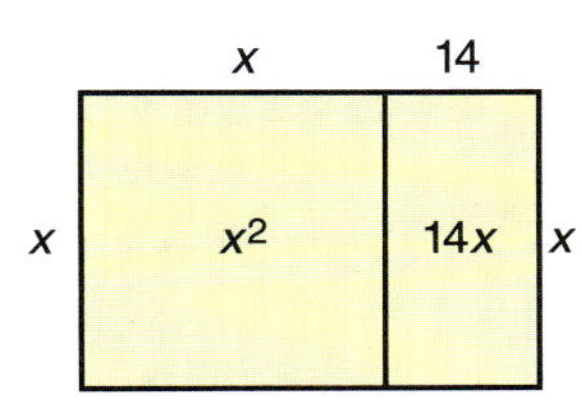

Since the areas are equal, $x(x + 14) = x^2 + 14x$.

The application above shows how the distributive property can be used to multiply a polynomial by a monomial.

Example 1 **Find each product.**

a. $\mathbf{7b(4b^2 - 18)}$

You can multiply horizontally or vertically.

Method 1: Horizontal

$$7b(4b^2 - 18) = 7b(4b^2) - 7b(18)$$
$$= 28b^3 - 126b$$

Method 2: Vertical

$$\begin{array}{r} 4b^2 - 18 \\ (\times) \quad\quad 7b \\ \hline 28b^3 - 126b \end{array}$$

b. $\mathbf{-3y^2(6y^2 - 8y + 12)}$

$$-3y^2(6y^2 - 8y + 12) = -3y^2(6y^2) - (-3y^2)(8y) + (-3y^2)(12)$$
$$= -18y^4 + 24y^3 - 36y^2$$

Some expressions may contain like terms. In these cases, you will need to simplify by combining like terms.

Example 2 **Find** $\mathbf{-3pq(p^2q + 2p - 3p^2q)}$**.**

Method 1

Multiply first and then simplify by combining like terms.

$$-3pq(p^2q + 2p - 3p^2q) = -3pq(p^2q) + (-3pq)(2p) - (-3pq)(3p^2q)$$
$$= -3p^3q^2 - 6p^2q + 9p^3q^2$$
$$= 6p^3q^2 - 6p^2q$$

Method 2

Simplify by combining like terms and then multiply.

$$-3pq(p^2q + 2p - 3p^2q) = -3pq(-2p^2q + 2p)$$
$$= -3pq(-2p^2q) + (-3pq)(2p)$$
$$= 6p^3q^2 - 6p^2q$$

p^2q and $-3p^2q$ are like terms.

Example 3

APPLICATION

Track

The runners in a 200-meter dash race around the curved part of a track. If the runners start and finish at the same line, the runner on the outside lane would run farther than the other runners. To compensate for this situation, the starting points of the runners are staggered. If the radius of the inside lane is $\mathbf{x}$ **and each lane is 2.5 feet wide, how far apart should the officials start the runners in the two inside lanes?**

The formula for the circumference C of a circle is $C = 2\pi r$, where r is the radius of the circle. The distance around half of a circle is πr. Use this information to find the distance around the curve for the two inside lanes and subtract the quantities to find the stagger distance.

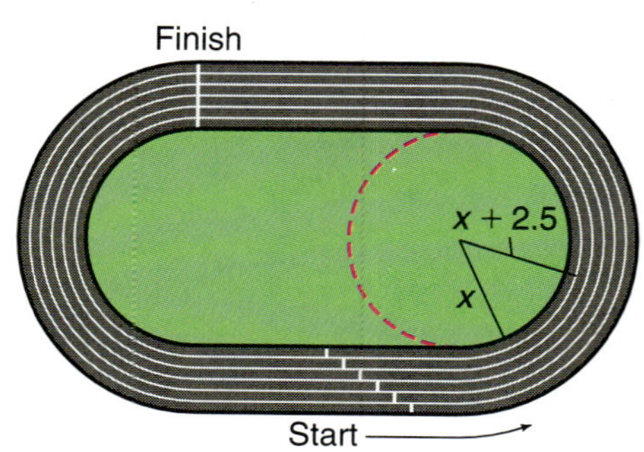

$$\underbrace{\pi(x+2.5)}_{\text{outside semicircle}} - \underbrace{\pi x}_{\text{inside semicircle}} = \pi x + 2.5\pi - \pi x \quad \textit{Distributive property}$$
$$= 2.5\pi \quad \textit{Combine like terms.}$$

The two runners should start 2.5π, or about 7.9, feet apart.

Many equations contain polynomials that must be added, subtracted, or multiplied before the equation can be solved. The distributive property is frequently used as at least one of the steps in solving equations.

Example 4 **Solve $x(x + 3) + 7x - 5 = x(8 + x) - 9x + 14$.**

$$\begin{aligned} x(x+3) + 7x - 5 &= x(8+x) - 9x + 14 \\ x^2 + 3x + 7x - 5 &= 8x + x^2 - 9x + 14 && \textit{Distributive property} \\ x^2 + 10x - 5 &= x^2 - x + 14 && \textit{Combine like terms.} \\ 10x - 5 &= -x + 14 && \textit{Subtract } x^2 \textit{ from each side.} \\ 11x - 5 &= 14 && \textit{Add } x \textit{ to each side.} \\ 11x &= 19 && \textit{Add 5 to each side.} \\ x &= \frac{19}{11} && \textit{Divide each side by 11.} \end{aligned}$$

The solution is $\frac{19}{11}$.

CHECK FOR UNDERSTANDING

Communicating Mathematics

Study the lesson. Then complete the following.

1. **Name** the property used to simplify $3a(5a^2 + 2b - 3c^2)$.
2. Refer to the application at the beginning of the lesson.
   a. **Describe** how you could find the area of the entire pattern used to play Jumby.
   b. **Write** an expression in simplest form for the area of this pattern.
   c. If x represents 8 inches, find the area of the pattern.
3. Refer to Example 4.
   a. **Explain** how you could check the solution to the equation.
   b. **Check** the solution.

MATH JOURNAL

4. A rectangular garden is $2x + 3$ units long and $3x$ units wide.
   a. Draw a model of the garden.
   b. Find the area of the garden.

Guided Practice

Find each product.

5. $-7b(9b^3c + 1)$
6. $4a^2(-8a^3c + c - 11)$
7. $\begin{array}{r} 5y - 13 \\ \underline{(\times)\ 2y} \end{array}$
8. $\begin{array}{r} 2ab - 5a \\ \underline{(\times)\ 11ab} \end{array}$

Simplify.

9. $w(3w - 5) + 3w$

10. $4y(2y^3 - 8y^2 + 2y + 9) - 3(y^2 + 8y)$

Solve each equation.

11. $12(b + 14) - 20b = 11b + 65$

12. $x(x - 4) + 2x = x(x + 12) - 7$

13. **Number Theory** Suppose a is an even integer.
   a. Write the product, in simplest form, of a and the next integer after it.
   b. Write the product, in simplest form, of a and the next even integer after it.

EXERCISES

Practice

Find each product.

14. $-7(2x + 9)$

15. $\frac{1}{3}x(x - 27)$

16. $3st(5s^2 + 2st)$

17. $-4m^3(5m^2 + 2m)$

18. $3d(4d^2 - 8d - 15)$

19. $5m^3(6m^2 - 8mn + 12n^3)$

20. $7x^2y(5x^2 - 3xy + y)$

21. $-4d(7d^2 - 4d + 3)$

22. $2m^2(5m^2 - 7m + 8)$

23. $-8rs(4rs + 7r - 14s^2)$

24. $-\frac{3}{4}ab^2\left(\frac{1}{3}abc + \frac{4}{9}a - 6\right)$

25. $\frac{4}{5}x^2(9xy + \frac{5}{4}x - 30y)$

Simplify.

26. $b(4b - 1) + 10b$

27. $3t(2t - 4) + 6(5t^2 + 2t - 7)$

28. $8m(-9m^2 + 2m - 6) + 11(2m^3 - 4m + 12)$

29. $8y(11y^2 - 2y + 13) - 9(3y^3 - 7y + 2)$

30. $\frac{3}{4}t(8t^3 + 12t - 4) + \frac{3}{2}(8t^2 - 9t)$

31. $6a^2(3a - 4) + 5a(7a^2 - 6a + 5) - 3(a^2 + 6a)$

Solve each equation.

32. $2(5w - 12) = 6(-2w + 3) + 2$

33. $7(x - 12) = 13 + 5(3x - 4)$

34. $\frac{1}{2}(2d - 34) = \frac{2}{3}(6d - 27)$

35. $p(p + 2) + 3p = p(p - 3)$

36. $y(y + 12) - 8y = 14 + y(y - 4)$

37. $x(x - 3) - x(x + 4) = 17x - 23$

38. $a(a + 8) - a(a + 3) - 23 = 3a + 11$

39. $t(t - 12) + t(t + 2) + 25 = 2t(t + 5) - 15$

INTEGRATION
Geometry

Find the measure of the area of each shaded region in simplest terms.

40.

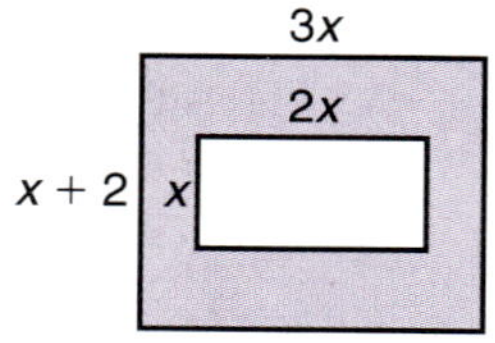

41.

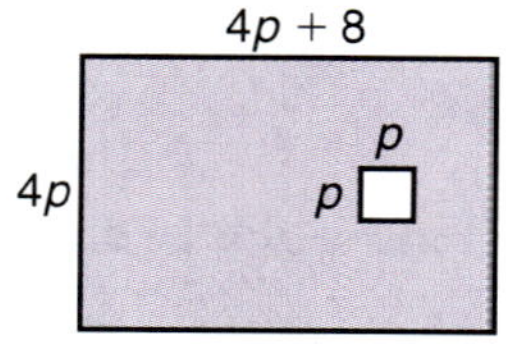

42.

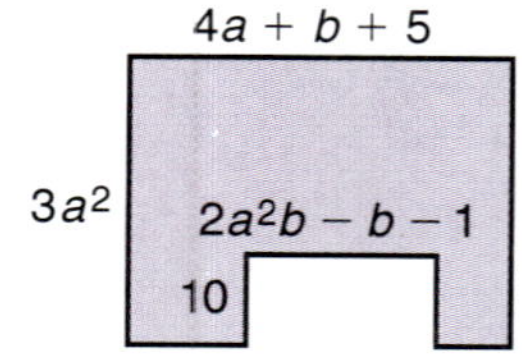

Critical Thinking

43. Write eight multiplication problems whose product is $8a^2b + 18ab$.

Applications and Problem Solving

44. **Recreation** In Honduras, children play a form of hopscotch called La Rayuela. The pattern for this game is shown at the right. Suppose that each rectangle is $2y + 1$ units long and y units wide.

    a. Write an expression in simplest form for the area of the pattern.

    b. If y represents 9 inches, find the area of the pattern.

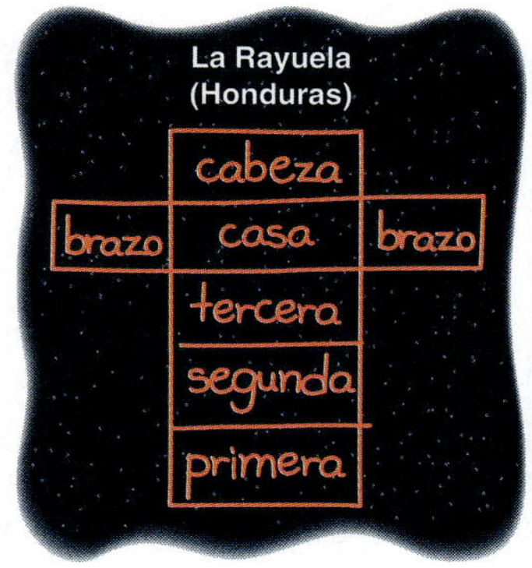

45. **Travel** The Drama Club of Lincoln High School is visiting New York City. They plan to take taxis from the World Trade Center to the Metropolitan Museum of Art. The fare for a taxi is \$2.75 for the first mile and \$1.25 for each additional mile. Suppose the distance between the two locations is m miles and t taxis are needed to transport the entire group. Write an expression in simplest form for the cost to transport the group to the Metropolitan Museum of Art excluding the tip.

46. **Construction** A landscaper is designing a rectangular garden for an office complex. There will be a concrete walkway on three sides of the garden, as shown at the right. The width of the garden will be 24 feet, and the length will be 42 feet. The width of the longer portion of the walkway will be 3 feet. The concrete will cost \$20 per square yard, and the builders have told the landscaper that she can spend \$820 on the concrete. How wide should the two remaining sides be?

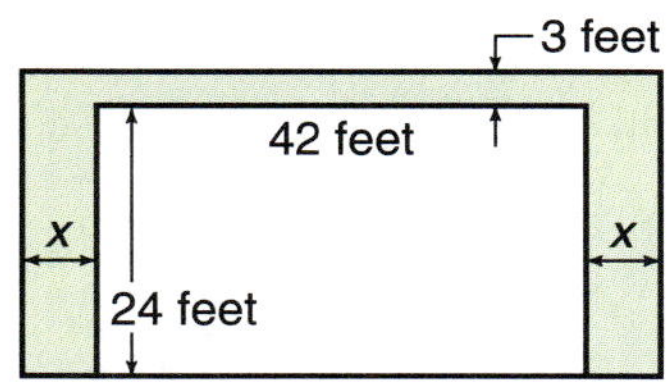

47. **Geometry** The number of diagonals that can be drawn for a polygon with n sides is represented by the expression $\frac{1}{2}n(n - 3)$.

    a. Draw polygons with 3, 4, 5, and 6 sides. Show that this expression is true for these polygons.

    b. Find the product of this expression.

    c. How many diagonals can be drawn for a polygon with 15 sides?

Mixed Review

48. Find $(3a - 4ab + 7b) - (7a - 3b)$. (Lesson 9–5)

49. **Chemistry** One solution is 50% glycol, and another is 30% glycol. How much of each solution should be mixed to make a 100-gallon solution that is 45% glycol? (Lesson 8–2)

50. Determine the slope of the line that passes through $A(1, 5)$ and $B(-3, 0)$. (Lesson 6–1)

51. If $g(x) = x^2 + 2x$, find $g(a - 1)$. (Lesson 5–5)

52. Draw the graph of $2x - y = 8$. (Lesson 5–4)

53. **Finance** Antonio earned \$340 in 4 days by mowing lawns and doing yard work. At this rate, how long will it take him to earn \$935? (Lesson 4–8)

54. **Geometry** Find the measure of an angle that is 44° less than its complement. (Lesson 3–4)

55. Evaluate $(15x)^3 - y$ if $x = 0.2$ and $y = 1.3$. (Lesson 1–3)

MODELING MATHEMATICS

9–7A Multiplying Polynomials

Materials: algebra tiles product mat

You can find the product of binomials by using algebra tiles.

A Preview of Lesson 9–7

Activity 1 Use algebra tiles to find $(x + 2)(x + 3)$.

The rectangle will have a width of $x + 2$ and a length of $x + 3$. Use your algebra tiles to mark off the dimensions on a product mat. Then make the rectangle with algebra tiles.

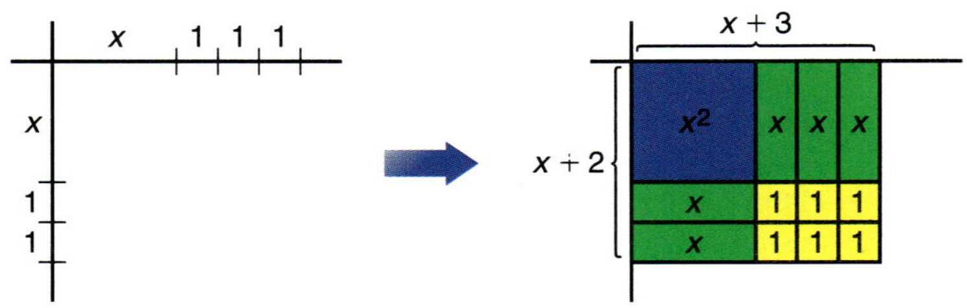

The rectangle consists of 1 blue x^2-tile, 5 green x-tiles, and 6 yellow 1-tiles. The area of the rectangle is $x^2 + 5x + 6$. Therefore, $(x + 2)(x + 3) = x^2 + 5x + 6$.

Activity 2 Use algebra tiles to find $(x - 1)(x - 3)$.

Step 1 The rectangle will have a width of $(x - 1)$ units and a length of $(x - 3)$ units. Use your algebra tiles to mark off the dimensions on a product mat. Then begin to make the rectangle with algebra tiles.

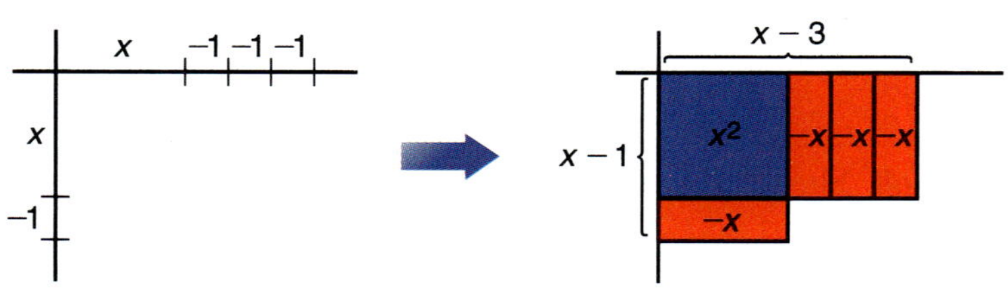

Step 2 Determine whether to use 3 yellow 1-tiles or 3 red 1-tiles to complete the rectangle. Remember that the numbers at the top and side give the dimensions of the tile needed. The area of each tile is the product of -1 and -1. This is represented by a yellow 1-tile. Fill in the space with 3 yellow 1-tiles to complete the rectangle.

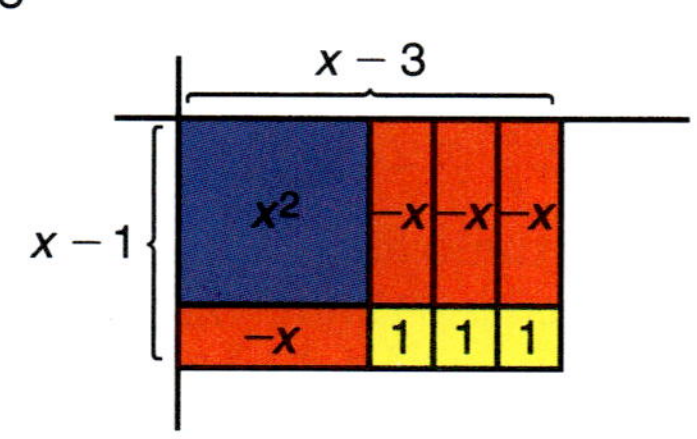

The rectangle consists of 1 blue x^2-tile, 4 red x-tiles, and 3 yellow 1-tiles. The area of the rectangle is $x^2 - 4x + 3$. Therefore, $(x - 1)(x - 3) = x^2 - 4x + 3$.

Activity 3 Use algebra tiles to find $(x + 1)(2x - 1)$.

Step 1 The rectangle will have a width of $(x + 1)$ units and a length of $(2x - 1)$. Use your algebra tiles to mark off the dimensions on a product mat. Then begin to make the rectangle with algebra tiles.

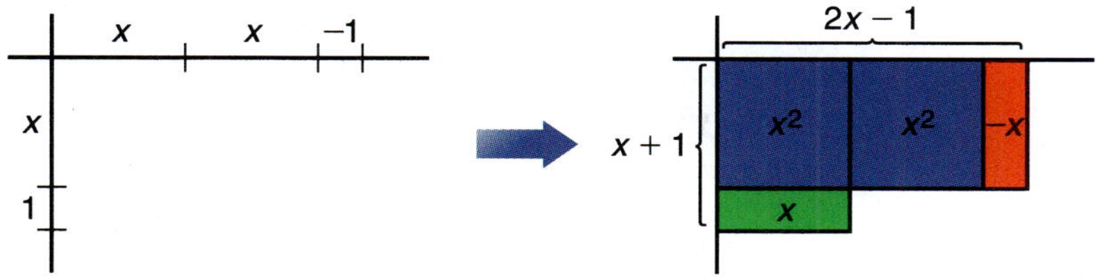

Step 2 Determine what color x-tile and what color 1-tile to use to complete the rectangle. The area of the x-tile is the product of x and 1. This is represented by a green x-tile. The area of the 1-tile is represented by the product of -1 and 1. This is represented by a red 1-tile.

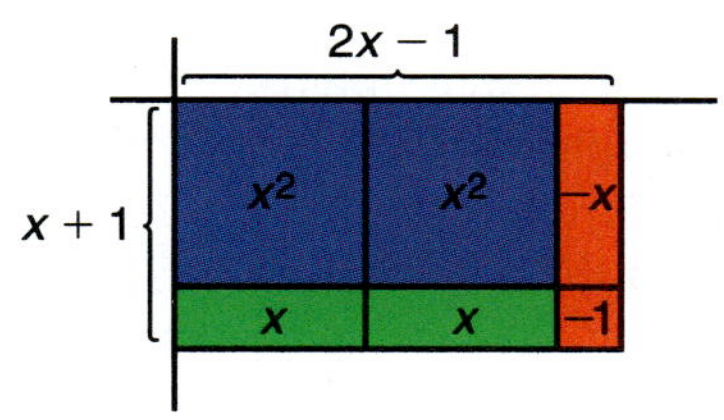

Step 3 Rearrange the tiles to simplify the polynomial you have formed. Notice that a zero pair is formed by the x-tiles.

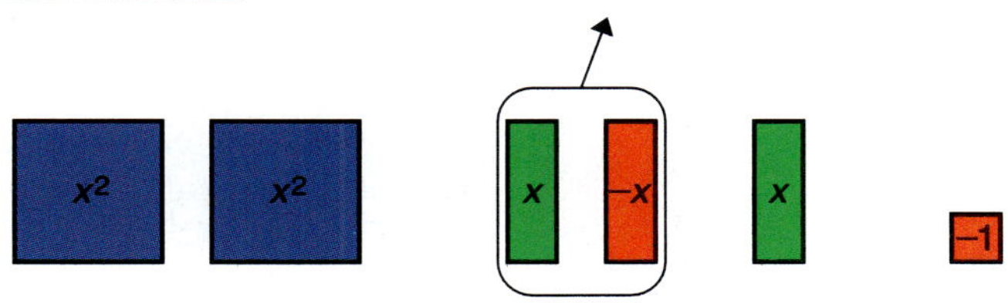

There are 2 blue x^2-tiles, 1 green x-tile, and 1 red 1-tile left. In simplest form, $(x + 1)(2x - 1) = 2x^2 + x - 1$.

Model Use algebra tiles to find each product.

1. $(x + 1)(x + 2)$ **2.** $(x + 1)(x - 3)$ **3.** $(x - 2)(x - 4)$

4. $(x + 1)(2x + 2)$ **5.** $(x - 1)(2x + 2)$ **6.** $(x - 3)(2x - 1)$

Draw Is each statement *true* or *false*? Justify your answer with a drawing.

7. $(x + 4)(x + 6) = x^2 + 24$ **8.** $(x + 3)(x - 2) = x^2 + x - 6$

9. $(x - 1)(x + 5) = x^2 - 4x - 5$ **10.** $(x - 2)(x - 3) = x^2 - 5x + 6$

Write

11. You can also use the distributive property to find the product of two binomials. The figure at the right shows the model for $(x + 3)(x + 2)$ separated into four parts. Write a paragraph explaining how this model shows the use of the distributive property.

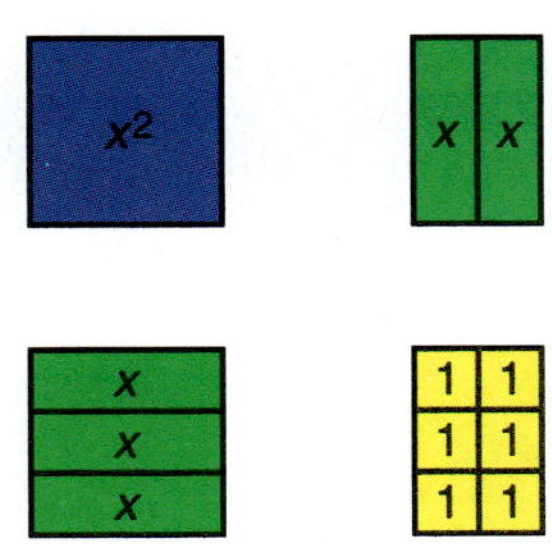

9–7 Multiplying Polynomials

What YOU'LL LEARN

- To use the FOIL method to multiply two binomials, and
- to multiply any two polynomials by using the distributive property.

Why IT'S IMPORTANT

You can use polynomials to solve problems involving art and business.

CONNECTION

Art

Have you ever flown over farm land and looked down? You probably saw various fields that gave the appearance of a patchwork quilt. However, if you had flown over a field designed by Stan Herd, you may have seen some sunflowers in a vase or a picture of Will Rogers. Since 1981, Stan Herd has been combining his interests in art and agriculture to form crop art. Most of Herd's work is harvested, and therefore is only visible for a short time.

In 1991, however, Herd created the picture above using native perennials. This picture is called *Little Girl in the Wind*. It depicts a Kickapoo Indian girl by the name of Carole Cadue. If you fly near Salina, Kansas, you may see this work of art.

GLOBAL CONNECTIONS

There is an historic work of art in Ohio that is best experienced from a bird's eye view. It is a mound built by the Adena Indians perhaps 30 centuries ago. The mound is in the shape of a snake and is about one-quarter mile long.

Suppose the measure of the length of the field used for *Little Girl in the Wind* can be represented by the polynomial $7x + 2$ units and the width can be represented by $5x + 1$. You know that the area of a rectangle is the product of its length and width. You can multiply $7x + 2$ and $5x + 1$ to find the area of the rectangle.

$$
\begin{aligned}
(7x + 2)(5x + 1) &= 7x(5x + 1) + 2(5x + 1) && \textit{Distributive property} \\
&= 7x(5x) + 7x(1) + 2(5x) + 2(1) && \textit{Distributive property} \\
&= 35x^2 + 7x + 10x + 2 && \textit{Substitution property} \\
&= 35x^2 + 17x + 2 && \textit{Combine like terms.}
\end{aligned}
$$

The area can also be determined by finding the sum of the areas of four smaller rectangles.

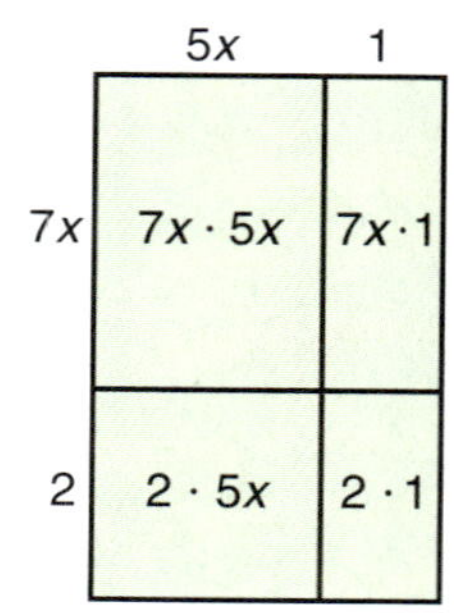

$$
\begin{aligned}
(7x + 2)(5x + 1) &= 7x \cdot 5x + 7x \cdot 1 + 2 \cdot 5x + 2 \cdot 1 && \textit{Find the sum of the four areas.} \\
&= 35x^2 + 7x + 10x + 2 && \textit{Substitution property} \\
&= 35x^2 + 17x + 2 && \textit{Combine like terms.}
\end{aligned}
$$

This example illustrates a shortcut of the distributive property called the **FOIL method**. You can use the FOIL method to multiply two binomials.

$$(7x + 2)(5x + 1) = \underset{F}{(7x)(5x)} + \underset{O}{(7x)(1)} + \underset{I}{(2)(5x)} + \underset{L}{(2)(1)}$$

$$= 35x^2 + 7x + 10x + 2$$

$$= 35x^2 + 17x + 2$$

FOIL Method for Multiplying Two Binomials	To multiply two binomials, find the sum of the products of **F** the *First* terms, **O** the *Outer* terms, **I** the *Inner* terms, and **L** the *Last* terms.

Example 1

Find each product.

a. $(x - 4)(x + 9)$

$$(x - 4)(x + 9) = \underset{F}{(x)(x)} + \underset{O}{(x)(9)} + \underset{I}{(-4)(x)} + \underset{L}{(-4)(9)}$$

$$= x^2 + 9x - 4x - 36$$

$$= x^2 + 5x - 36 \qquad \textit{Combine like terms.}$$

b. $(4x + 7)(3x - 8)$

$$(4x + 7)(3x - 8) = \underset{F}{(4x)(3x)} + \underset{O}{(4x)(-8)} + \underset{I}{(7)(3x)} + \underset{L}{(7)(-8)}$$

$$= 12x^2 - 32x + 21x - 56$$

$$= 12x^2 - 11x - 56 \qquad \textit{Combine like terms.}$$

The distributive property can be used to multiply any two polynomials.

Example 2

Find each product.

a. $(2y + 5)(3y^2 - 8y + 7)$

$(2y + 5)(3y^2 - 8y + 7)$

$= 2y(3y^2 - 8y + 7) + 5(3y^2 - 8y + 7)$ *Distributive property*

$= (6y^3 - 16y^2 + 14y) + (15y^2 - 40y + 35)$ *Distributive property*

$= 6y^3 - 16y^2 + 14y + 15y^2 - 40y + 35$

$= 6y^3 - y^2 - 26y + 35$ *Combine like terms.*

b. $(x^2 + 4x - 5)(3x^2 - 7x + 2)$

$(x^2 + 4x - 5)(3x^2 - 7x + 2)$

$= x^2(3x^2 - 7x + 2) + 4x(3x^2 - 7x + 2) - 5(3x^2 - 7x + 2)$

$= (3x^4 - 7x^3 + 2x^2) + (12x^3 - 28x^2 + 8x) - (15x^2 - 35x + 10)$

$= 3x^4 - 7x^3 + 2x^2 + 12x^3 - 28x^2 + 8x - 15x^2 + 35x - 10$

$= 3x^4 + 5x^3 - 41x^2 + 43x - 10$ *Combine like terms.*

Polynomials can also be multiplied in column form. Be careful to align the like terms.

Example 3 **Find $(x^3 - 8x^2 + 9)(3x + 4)$ using column form.**

Since there is no x term in $x^3 - 8x^2 + 9$, $0x$ is used as a placeholder.

$$\begin{array}{rrrrrl}
 & x^3 & -\ 8x^2 & +\ 0x & +\ 9 & \\
(\times) & & & 3x & +\ 4 & \\
\hline
 & 4x^3 & -\ 32x^2 & +\ 0x & +\ 36 & \leftarrow \textit{product of } x^3 - 8x^2 + 0x + 9 \textit{ and } 4 \\
3x^4 & -\ 24x^3 & +\ 0x^2 & +\ 27x & & \leftarrow \textit{product of } x^3 - 8x^2 + 0x + 9 \textit{ and } 3x \\
\hline
3x^4 & -\ 20x^3 & -\ 32x^2 & +\ 27x & +\ 36 & \leftarrow \textit{sum of the partial products}
\end{array}$$

Example 4 **INTEGRATION Geometry**

The volume V of a prism equals the area of the base B times the height h.

a. Write a polynomial expression that represents the volume of the prism shown at the right.

b. Find the volume if $a = 5$.

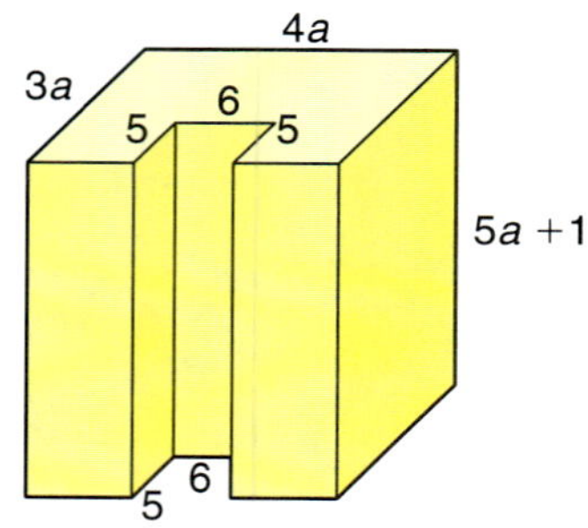

a. A diagram of the base is shown below.

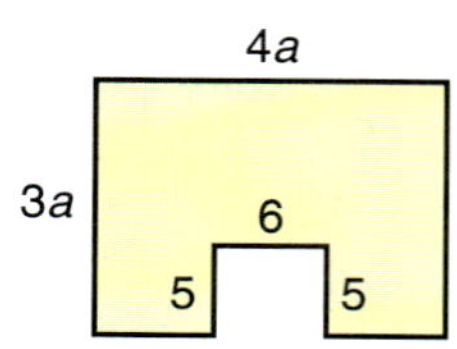

To find the area of the base, first find the area of a rectangle that is $3a$ by $4a$. Then subtract the area of a rectangle that is 6 by 5.

$B = 3a(4a) - 6(5)$

$= 12a^2 - 30$

The volume of this prism equals the product of the base and the height, $12a^2 - 30$ and $5a + 1$, respectively. Use FOIL to find the product.

$$(12a^2 - 30)(5a + 1) = \overset{F}{(12a^2)(5a)} + \overset{O}{(12a^2)(1)} + \overset{I}{(-30)(5a)} + \overset{L}{(-30)(1)}$$

$$= 60a^3 + 12a^2 - 150a - 30$$

The volume of the prism is $(60a^3 + 12a^2 - 150a - 30)$ cubic units.

b. Substitute 5 for a and evaluate the expression.

$60(5^3) + 12(5^2) - 150(5) - 30 = 7500 + 300 - 750 - 30$

$= 7020$

If $a = 5$, the volume of the prism is 7020 cubic units.

CHECK FOR UNDERSTANDING

Communicating Mathematics

Study the lesson. Then complete the following.

1. Use the FOIL method to evaluate each product.
   a. 42(27) (*Hint:* Rewrite as $(40 + 2)(20 + 7)$ or $(40 + 2)(30 - 3)$.)
   b. $4\frac{1}{2} \cdot 6\frac{3}{4}$

2. **You Decide** Adita and Delbert used the following methods to find the product of $(t^3 - t^2 + 5t)$ and $(6t^2 + 8t - 7)$.

Adita:

$$
\begin{aligned}
&(t^3 - t^2 + 5t)(6t^2 + 8t - 7)\\
&\quad = t^3(6t^2 + 8t - 7) - t^2(6t^2 + 8t - 7) + 5t(6t^2 + 8t - 7)\\
&\quad = 6t^5 + 8t^4 - 7t^3 - 6t^4 - 8t^3 + 7t^2 + 30t^3 + 40t^2 - 35t\\
&\quad = 6t^5 + 2t^4 + 15t^3 + 47t^2 - 35t
\end{aligned}
$$

Delbert:

$$
\begin{array}{rrrrrr}
 & & t^3 & - t^2 & + 5t & \\
 & (\times) & 6t^2 & + 8t & - 7 & \\
\hline
 & & -7t^3 & + 7t^2 & - 35t & \\
 & 8t^4 & - 8t^3 & + 40t^2 & & \\
6t^5 & - 6t^4 & + 30t^3 & & & \\
\hline
6t^5 & + 2t^4 & + 15t^3 & + 47t^2 & - 35t &
\end{array}
$$

Which method do you prefer? Why?

3. **Draw** a diagram to show how you would use algebra tiles to find the product of $(2x - 3)$ and $(x + 2)$.

MODELING MATHEMATICS

4. **Write** two binomials whose product is represented at the right.

$2ax$	$3a$
$2x^2$	$3x$

Guided Practice

Find each product.

5. $(d + 2)(d + 8)$
6. $(r - 5)(r - 11)$
7. $(y + 3)(y - 7)$
8. $(3p - 5)(5p + 2)$
9. $(2x - 1)(x + 5)$
10. $(2m + 5)(3m - 8)$
11. $(2a + 3b)(5a - 2b)$
12. $(2x - 5)(3x^2 - 5x + 4)$

13. a. **Number Theory** Find the product of three consecutive integers if the least integer is a.
    b. Choose an integer as the first of three consecutive integers. Find their product.
    c. Evaluate the polynomial in part a for these integers. Describe the result.

EXERCISES

Practice

Find each product.

14. $(y + 5)(y + 7)$
15. $(c - 3)(c - 7)$
16. $(x + 4)(x - 8)$
17. $(w + 3)(w - 9)$
18. $(2a - 1)(a + 8)$
19. $(5b - 3)(2b + 1)$
20. $(11y + 9)(12y + 6)$
21. $(13x - 3)(13x + 3)$
22. $(8x + 9y)(3x + 7y)$
23. $(0.3v - 7)(0.5v + 2)$
24. $\left(3x + \frac{1}{3}\right)\left(2x - \frac{1}{9}\right)$
25. $\left(a - \frac{2}{3}b\right)\left(\frac{2}{3}a + \frac{1}{2}b\right)$
26. $(2r + 0.1)(5r - 0.3)$
27. $(0.7p + 2q)(0.9p + 3q)$
28. $(x + 7)(x^2 + 5x - 9)$
29. $(3x - 5)(2x^2 + 7x - 11)$
30. $\begin{array}{r} a^2 - 3a + 11 \\ (\times)\ \ 5a + \ \ 2 \\ \hline \end{array}$
31. $\begin{array}{r} 3x^2 - 7x + 2 \\ (\times)\ \ \ 3x - 8 \\ \hline \end{array}$
32. $\begin{array}{r} 5x^2 + 8x - 11 \\ (\times)\ x^2 - 2x - \ \ 1 \\ \hline \end{array}$
33. $\begin{array}{r} 5d^2 - 6d + \ \ 9 \\ (\times)\ 4d^2 + 3d + 11 \\ \hline \end{array}$

Find each product.

34. $(x^2 - 8x - 1)(2x^2 - 4x + 9)$

35. $(5x^2 - x - 4)(2x^2 + x + 12)$

36. $(-7b^3 + 2b - 3)(5b^2 - 2b + 4)$

37. $(a^2 + 2a + 5)(a^2 - 3a - 7)$

INTEGRATION
Geometry

Find the measure of the volume of each prism.

38.

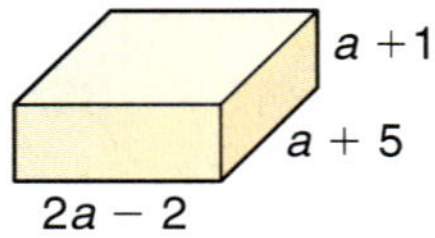

39.

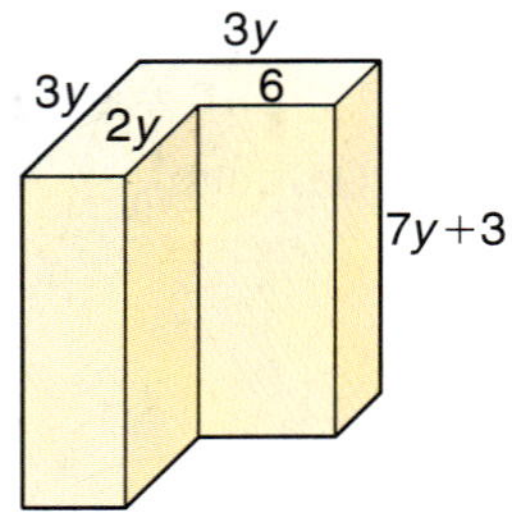

40.

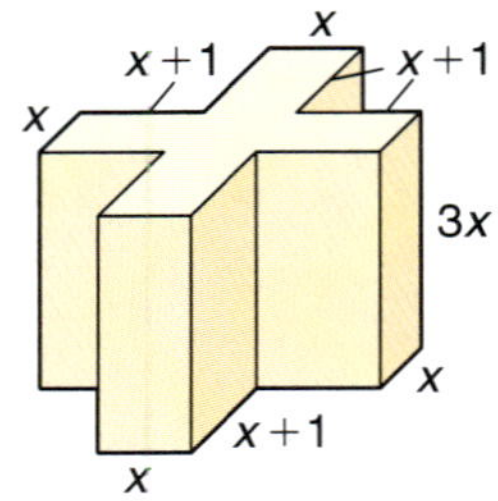

41. **Geometry** Refer to the prism in Exercise 38. Suppose a represents 15 centimeters.
   a. Find the length, width, and height of the prism.
   b. Use the values in part a to find the volume of the prism.
   c. Evaluate your answer for Exercise 38 if $a = 15$.
   d. How do your answers for parts b and c compare?

Critical Thinking

If $A = 3x + 4$, $B = x^2 + 2$, and $C = x^2 + 3x - 2$, find each of the following.

42. $AC + B$

43. $2B(3A - 4C)$

44. ABC

45. $(A + B)(B - C)$

Applications and Problem Solving

46. **Construction** A homeowner is considering installing a swimming pool in his backyard. He wants its length to be 5 yards longer than its width, to make room for a diving area at one end. Then he wants to surround it with a concrete walkway 4 yards wide. After finding out the price of concrete, he decides that he can afford 424 square yards of it for the walkway. What should the dimensions of the pool be?

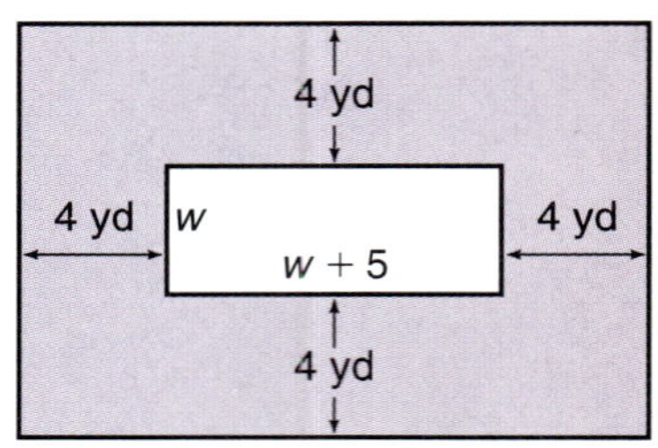

47. **Business** Raul Agosto works for a company that has modular offices. His office space is presently a square. A new floor plan calls for his office to become 2 feet shorter in one direction and 3 feet longer in the other.
   a. Write expressions that represent the new dimensions of Mr. Agosto's office.
   b. Find the area of his new office.
   c. Suppose his office is presently 8 feet by 8 feet. Will his new office be bigger or smaller than this office? by how much?

Mixed Review

48. Find $\frac{3}{4}a(6a + 12)$. (Lesson 9–6)

49. Solve $6 - 9y < -10y$. (Lesson 7–3)

50. **National Landmarks** At the Royal Gorge in Colorado, an inclined railway takes visitors down to the Arkansas River. Suppose the slope is 50% and the vertical drop is 1015 feet. What is the horizontal change of the railway? (Lesson 6–1)

51. Write an equation to represent the relation. (Lesson 5–6)
$\{(-1, -1), (0, 1), (1, 3), (2, 5), (3, 7)\}$

52. Determine the domain, range, and inverse of the relation. (Lesson 5–2)
$\{(8, 1), (4, 2), (6, -4), (5, -3), (6, 0)\}$

53. **Geometry** ΔABC and ΔXYZ are similar. Find the values of a and y. (Lesson 4–2)

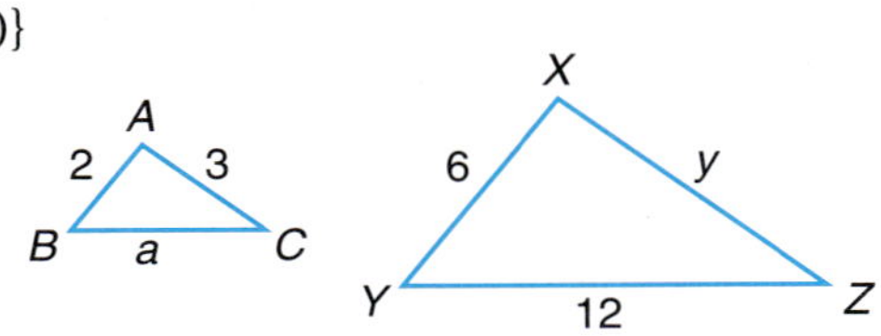

54. **Consumerism** The prices of six different models of printers in a computer store are $299, $369, $359, $228, $525, and $398. Find the mean and median prices for the printers. (Lesson 3–7)

55. **Temperature** The formula for finding the Celsius temperature C when you know the Fahrenheit temperature F is $C = \frac{5}{9}(F - 32)$. Find the Celsius temperature when the Fahrenheit temperature is 59°. (Lesson 2–9)

56. Replace the variable to make the sentence $\frac{3}{4}s = 6$ true. (Lesson 1–5)

WORKING ON THE In·ves·ti·ga·tion

Refer to the Investigation on pages 448–449.

You have experimented with various sizes of gliders to explore their flying abilities. You now need to investigate how the size of the glider and the weight of the load are related.

1 Cut out two equilateral triangles from construction paper so that the side of one is 6 centimeters long, and the side of the other is 12 centimeters long. What is the surface area and perimeter of each triangle?

2 Straighten two paper clips and bend them into the shape shown at the right. Punch the bent end of the paper clip through the center of the triangle, and tape it into place so that the hook-end hangs down under the other side of the triangle.

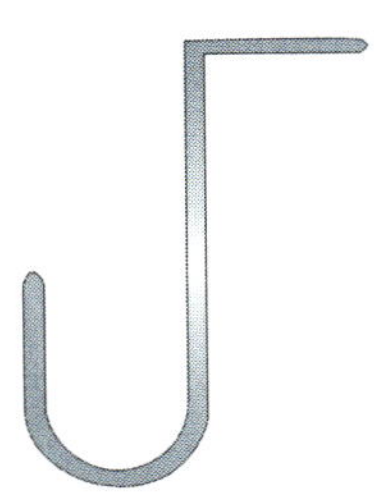

3 One at a time, drop each hang glider from the top of the bleachers or out of a second-floor window. (In order to get more accurate data, a greater height is needed than those used for previous experiments.) Record the glide time of each hang glider.

4 Add one washer onto the hook of each glider. Repeat the dropping procedure and record the times. How do those times compare with the first drop? Continue to add washers, one at a time, to each glider and record the glide times in a chart that compares the glide times with the number of washers carried by each glider.

5 Graph the relationship between the weight and the glide times. Let the independent variable be the weight, and let the dependent variable be the glide time. Analyze your findings.

6 Look at the weight, glide time, surface area, and perimeter in your data. Write a polynomial expression to relate some, if not all, of these measures.

Add the results of your work to your Investigation Folder.

9–8 Special Products

What YOU'LL LEARN

- To use patterns to find $(a + b)^2$, $(a - b)^2$, and $(a + b)(a - b)$.

Why IT'S IMPORTANT

You can use polynomials to solve problems involving biology and history.

FYI

Punnett squares are named after the English zoologist and geneticist Reginald Crundall Punnett (1875–1967). He held the first chair in genetics at Cambridge University and helped build the science of genetics in the 20th century.

CONNECTION

Biology

Punnett squares are diagrams that are used to show the possible ways that genes can combine at fertilization. In a Punnett square, *dominant* genes are shown with capital letters. Recessive genes are shown with lowercase letters. Letters representing the parents' genes are placed on two of the outer sides of the Punnett square. Letters inside the boxes of the square show the possible gene combinations of their offspring.

The Punnett square below represents a cross between tall pea plants and short pea plants. Let T represent the dominant gene for tallness. Let t represent the recessive gene for shortness. The parents are called *hybrids,* since they have one of each kind of gene.

Hybrid tall × Hybrid tall

Tall = T

Short = t

Offspring

$\frac{1}{4}$ or 25% pure tall (TT)

$\frac{2}{4}$ or 50% hybrid tall (Tt)

$\frac{1}{4}$ or 25% pure short (tt)

hybrid tall	T	t
T	TT	Tt
t	Tt	tt

Because the parent plants have both a dominant tall gene and a recessive short gene, biologists know that their offspring can be predicted by squaring the binomial $(0.5T + 0.5t)^2$. Therefore, the following must be true.

$$\begin{aligned}(0.5T + 0.5t)^2 &= (0.5T + 0.5t)(0.5T + 0.5t)\\ &= 0.5T(0.5T) + 0.5T(0.5t) + 0.5t(0.5T) + 0.5t(0.5t)\\ &= 0.25T^2 + 0.25Tt + 0.25Tt + 0.25t^2\\ &= 0.25T^2 + 0.50Tt + 0.25t^2\end{aligned}$$

T^2 and t^2 represent TT and tt, respectively.

You can use the diagram below to derive a general form for the expression $(a + b)^2$.

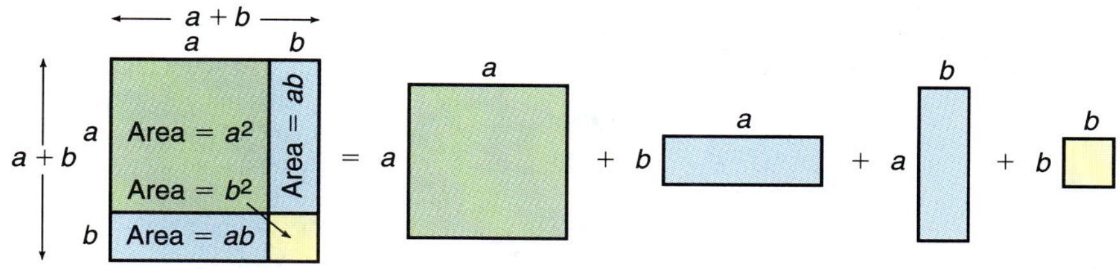

$$(a + b)^2 \quad = \quad a^2 \quad + \quad ab \quad + \quad ab \quad + \quad b^2$$
$$= a^2 + 2ab + b^2 \quad \textit{Check this result by using FOIL.}$$

In general, the square of a binomial that is a sum can be found by using the following rule.

Square of a Sum	$(a + b)^2 = (a + b)(a + b)$ $= a^2 + 2ab + b^2$

Example 1

Find each product.

a. $\mathbf{(y + 7)^2}$

Method 1

Use the square of a sum rule.

$(a + b)^2 = a^2 + 2ab + b^2$

$(y + 7)^2 = y^2 + 2(y)(7) + 7^2$

$= y^2 + 14y + 49$

Method 2

Use FOIL.

$(y + 7)^2 = (y + 7)(y + 7)$

$= y^2 + 7y + 7y + 49$

$= y^2 + 14y + 49$

b. $\mathbf{(6p + 11q)^2}$

$(a + b)^2 = a^2 + 2ab + b^2$

$(6p + 11q)^2 = (6p)^2 + 2(6p)(11q) + (11q)^2$ *$a = 6p$ and $b = 11q$*

$= 36p^2 + 132pq + 121q^2$

The square of a sum rule can be used with other rules to simplify products of polynomials.

Example 2

CONNECTION
History

Tourists to the southern part of England can visit the historic Gwennap Pit. In the 16th century, the pit of a tin mine was converted into an amphitheater. During the 18th century, John Wesley spoke to overflow crowds in this amphitheater. Gwennap Pit consists of a circular stage surrounded by circular levels used for seating. Each seating level is 1 meter wide. Suppose the radius of the stage is *s* meters. Find the area of the third seating level.

(continued on the next page)

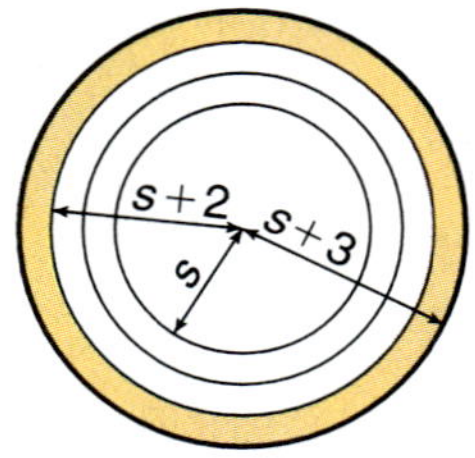

The area of a circle equals πr^2. The radius of the second seating level is $s + 2$ meters, and the radius of the third seating level is $s + 3$. The area of the third seating level can be found by subtracting the areas of two circles.

$$A = \underbrace{\pi(s+3)^2}_{\text{area of third level}} - \underbrace{\pi(s+2)^2}_{\text{area of second level}}$$

$$= \pi(s^2 + 6s + 9) - \pi(s^2 + 4s + 4) \quad \textit{Square of a sum rule}$$

$$= (\pi s^2 + 6\pi s + 9\pi) - (\pi s^2 + 4\pi s + 4\pi) \quad \textit{Distributive property}$$

$$= \pi s^2 + 6\pi s + 9\pi - \pi s^2 - 4\pi s - 4\pi$$

$$= 2\pi s + 5\pi \quad \textit{Combine like terms.}$$

The area of the third seating level is $2\pi s + 5\pi$, or about $6.3s + 15.7$ square meters.

To find $(a - b)^2$, write $(a - b)$ as $[a + (-b)]$ and square it.

$$(a - b)^2 = [a + (-b)]^2$$

$$= a^2 + 2(a)(-b) + (-b)^2$$

$$= a^2 - 2ab + b^2$$

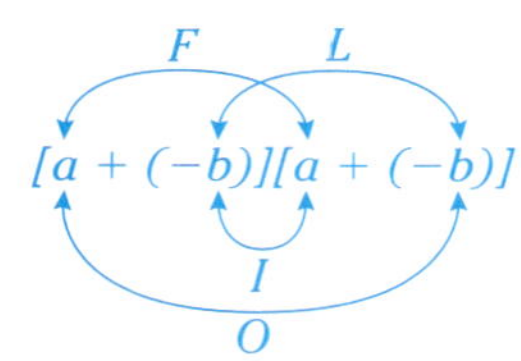

In general, the square of a binomial that is a difference can be found by using the following rule.

Square of a Difference

$$(a - b)^2 = (a - b)(a - b)$$
$$= a^2 - 2ab + b^2$$

Example 3 **Find each product.**

a. $(r - 6)^2$

Method 1

Use the square of a difference rule.

$$(a - b)^2 = a^2 - 2ab + b^2$$

$$(r - 6)^2 = r^2 - 2(r)(6) + 6^2$$

$$= r^2 - 12r + 36$$

Method 2

Use FOIL.

$$(r - 6)^2 = (r - 6)(r - 6)$$

$$= r^2 - 6r - 6r + 36$$

$$= r^2 - 12r + 36$$

b. $(4x^2 - 7t)^2$

$$(a - b)^2 = a^2 - 2ab + b^2$$

$$(4x^2 - 7t)^2 = (4x^2)^2 - 2(4x^2)(7t) + (7t)^2 \quad a = 4x^2 \text{ and } b = 7t$$

$$= 16x^4 - 56x^2t + 49t^2$$

MODELING MATHEMATICS

Product of a Sum and a Difference

Materials: algebra tiles, product mat

You have learned how to use algebra tiles to find the product of two binomials. In this activity, you will use algebra tiles to study a special situation.

Your Turn

a. Use algebra tiles to find each product.

$(x + 3)(x - 3)$ $\quad$ $(x + 5)(x - 5)$

$(x + 1)(x - 1)$ $\quad$ $(x + 2)(x - 2)$

$(x + 6)(x - 6)$ $\quad$ $(x + 4)(x - 4)$

b. What do you notice about the binomials used as factors in part a?

c. What pattern do the products in part a have?

You can use the FOIL method to find the product of a sum and a difference of the same two numbers.

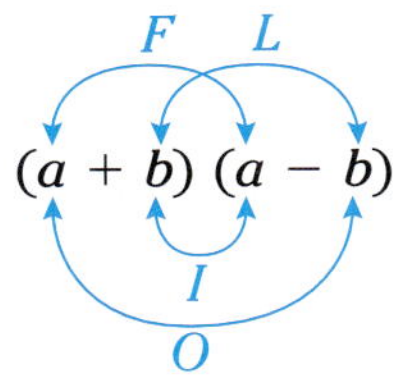

$$(a + b)(a - b) = a(a) + a(-b) + b(a) + b(-b)$$
$$= a^2 - ab + ab - b^2$$
$$= a^2 - b^2$$

The resulting product, $a^2 - b^2$, has a special name. It is called a **difference of squares.**

Difference of Squares	$(a + b)(a - b) = (a - b)(a + b) = a^2 - b^2$

Example 4 **Find each product.**

a. $(m - 2n)(m + 2n)$

$$(a - b)(a + b) = a^2 - b^2$$
$$(m - 2n)(m + 2n) = m^2 - (2n)^2 \quad a = m \text{ and } b = 2n$$
$$= m^2 - 4n^2$$

b. $(0.3t + 0.25w^2)(0.3t - 0.25w^2)$

$$(a + b)(a - b) = a^2 - b^2$$
$$(0.3t + 0.25w^2)(0.3t - 0.25w^2) = (0.3t)^2 - (0.25w^2)^2 \quad a = 0.3t \text{ and } b = 0.25w^2$$
$$= 0.09t^2 - 0.0625w^4$$

CHECK FOR UNDERSTANDING

Communicating Mathematics

Study the lesson. Then complete the following.

1. **Explain** how the square of a difference and the square of a sum are different.
2. **Compare and contrast** the square of a difference and the difference of two squares.
3. **Explain** how you could mentally multiply 29×31. (*Hint:* $29 = 30 - 1$ and $31 = 30 + 1$)

MODELING MATHEMATICS

4. Draw a diagram to represent each of the following.
   a. $(x + y)^2$
   b. $(x - y)^2$
5. What does the diagram at the right represent if the shading represents regions to be removed or subtracted?

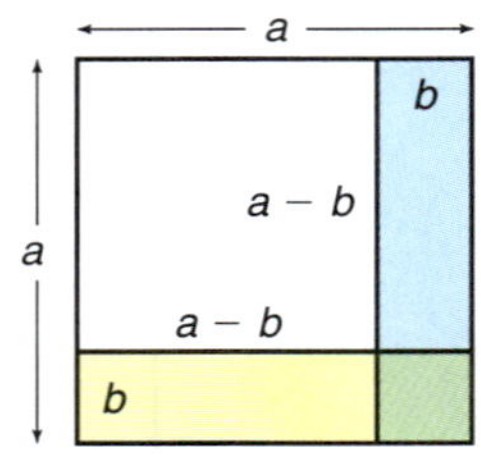

Guided Practice

Find each product.

6. $(2x + 3y)^2$
7. $(m - 3n)^2$
8. $(2a + 3)(2a - 3)$
9. $(m^2 + 4n)^2$
10. $(4y + 2z)(4y - 2z)$
11. $(5 - x)^2$
12. **Recreation** In India, children play a form of hopscotch called Chilly. One of the three possible patterns for this game is shown at the right. Suppose each side of the small squares is $2x + 5$ units long. Find the area of this Chilly pattern.

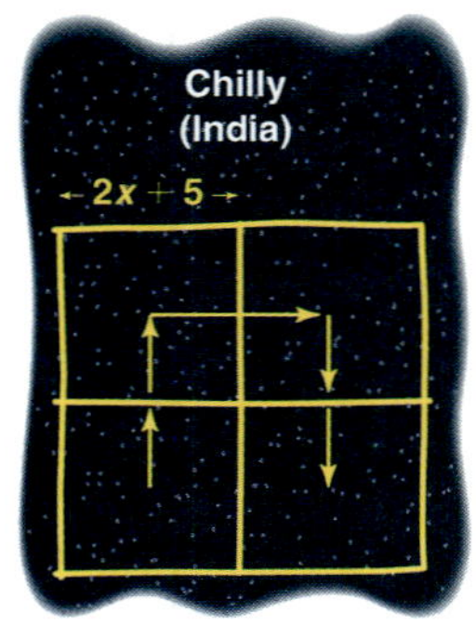

EXERCISES

Practice

Find each product.

13. $(x + 4y)^2$
14. $(m - 2n)^2$
15. $(3b - a)^2$
16. $(3x + 5)(3x - 5)$
17. $(9p - 2q)(9p + 2q)$
18. $(5s + 6t)^2$
19. $(5b - 12a)^2$
20. $(2a + 0.5y)^2$
21. $(x^3 + a^2)^2$
22. $\left(\frac{1}{2}b^2 - a^2\right)^2$
23. $(8x^2 - 3y)(8x^2 + 3y)$
24. $(7c^2 + d^3)(7c^2 - d^3)$
25. $(1.1g + h^5)^2$
26. $(9 - z^9)(9 + z^9)$
27. $\left(\frac{4}{3}x^2 - y\right)\left(\frac{4}{3}x^2 + y\right)$
28. $\left(\frac{1}{3}v^2 - \frac{1}{2}w^3\right)^2$
29. $(3x + 1)(3x - 1)(x - 5)$
30. $(x - 2)(x + 5)(x + 2)(x - 5)$
31. $(a + 3b)^3$
32. $(2m - n)^4$

Critical Thinking

33. Find $(x + y + z)^2$. Draw a diagram to show each term of the polynomial.

Applications and Problem Solving

34. Biology Refer to the application at the beginning of the lesson.

a. Make a Punnett square for pea plants if one parent is pure short (*tt*) and the other parent is hybrid tall (*Tt*).

b. What percent of the offspring will be pure short?

c. What percent of the offspring will be hybrid tall?

d. What percent of the offspring will be pure tall?

35. History Refer to Example 2.

a. Write an expression for the area of the fourth seating level in the Gwennap Pit.

b. The radius of the stage level of the Gwennap Pit is 3 meters. Find the area of the stage.

c. Find the area of the fourth seating level in the Gwennap Pit.

36. Photography Lenora cut off a 0.75-inch strip all around a square photograph so it would fit in an envelope she was mailing to her aunt. She decided to have the photo lab make a copy of the photo from the negative, but she forgot to measure how large the original photo was. All she had was the strips she cut off, whose area was 33.75 square inches. What were the original dimensions of the photograph?

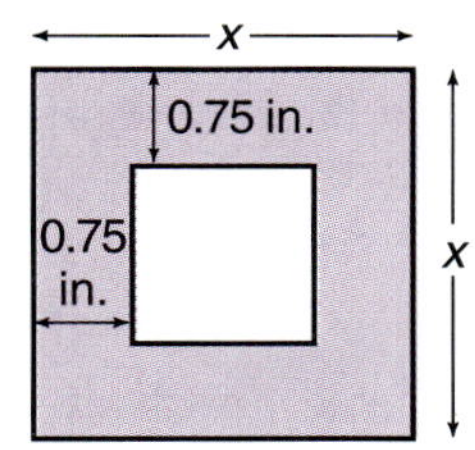

Mixed Review

37. Find $(3t - 3)(2t + 1)$. (Lesson 9–7)

38. Solve $-13z > -1.04$. (Lesson 7–2)

39. Statistics The table below shows the heights and weights of each of 12 players on a pro basketball team. (Lesson 6–3)

Height (in.)	75	82	75	74	80	80	75	79	80	78	76	81
Weight (lb)	180	235	184	185	230	205	185	230	221	195	205	215

a. Make a scatter plot of these data.

b. Describe the correlation between height and weight.

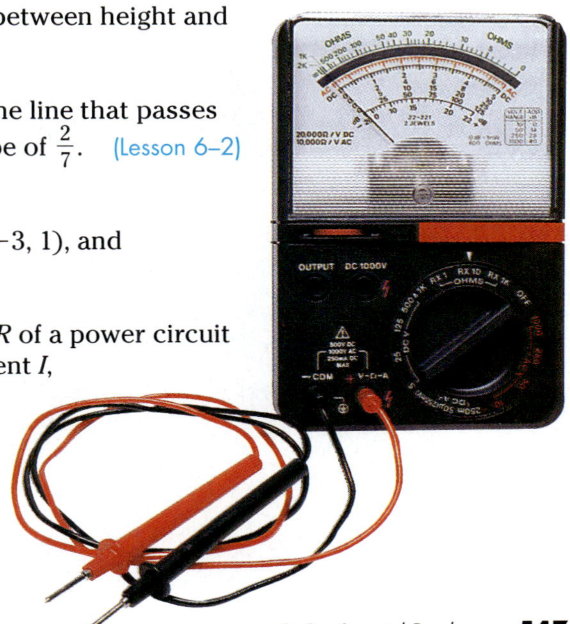

40. Write the standard form of the line that passes through (3, 1) and has a slope of $\frac{2}{7}$. (Lesson 6–2)

41. Graph the points $A(4, 2)$, $B(-3, 1)$, and $C(-2, -3)$. (Lesson 5–1)

42. Electricity The resistance R of a power circuit is 4.5 ohms. How much current I, in amperes, can the circuit generate if it can produce at most 1500 watts of power? Use $I^2R = P$. (Lesson 2–8)

43. Evaluate $5(9 \div 3^2)$. (Lesson 1–6)

CLOSING THE

In•ves•ti•ga•tion

Ready, Set, Drop!

Refer to the Investigation on pages 448–449.

Analyze

You have conducted several experiments and organized your data in various ways. It is now time to analyze your findings and state your conclusions.

PORTFOLIO ASSESSMENT

You may want to keep your work on this Investigation in your portfolio.

1 Look over your data and organize it in such a way that the various relationships are obvious.

2 Describe the relationships in the data. What does weight have to do with glide time? Does perimeter or surface area have an effect on glide time? What other factors need to be considered?

Write

The report to the people interested in hang gliding should explain your process for investigating these hang glider models and what you found from your investigations.

3 Begin the report by stating the process you used to investigate the matter. Explain all the experiments conducted. State the purpose and findings for each.

4 Show the data you collected in tables, charts, and graphs. Explain your analysis of the data and conclusions you found.

5 Make a recommendation to the group about the size of hang glider(s) that is most suited for them. Include the weight of the object that the hang glider(s) should carry to be most efficient.

6 While you were conducting experiments, one of your team members found that the frames for most hang gliders are 32 feet wide. Explain how this information affects your generalizations regarding the weight and size of hang gliders.

7 Summarize your findings in a concluding statement to the group.

CHAPTER 9 HIGHLIGHTS

VOCABULARY

After completing this chapter, you should be able to define each term, property, or phrase and give an example or two of each.

Algebra

binomial (p. 514)
constants (p. 496)
degree of monomial (p. 515)
degree of polynomial (p. 516)
difference of squares (p. 545)
FOIL method (p. 537)
monomial (p. 496)
negative exponent (p. 503)
polynomial (pp. 513, 514)
power of a monomial (p. 498)
power of a power (p. 498)
power of a product (p. 498)
product of powers (p. 497)
quotient of powers (p. 501)
scientific notation (p. 506)
square of a difference (p. 544)
square of a sum (p. 543)
trinomial (p. 514)
zero exponent (p. 502)

Problem Solving

look for a pattern (p. 497)

UNDERSTANDING AND USING THE VOCABULARY

Choose the letter of the term that best matches each example.

1. $4^{-3} = \frac{1}{4^3}$ or $\frac{1}{64}$
2. $(x + 2y)(x - 2y) = x^2 - 4y^2$
3. $\frac{4x^2y}{8xy^3} = \frac{x}{2y^2}$
4. $4x^2$
5. $x^2 - 3x + 1$
6. $2^0 = 1$
7. $x^4 - 3x^3 + 2x^2 - 1$
8. $(x + 3)(x - 4) = x^2 - 4x + 3x - 12$
9. $x^2 + 2$
10. $(a^3b)(2ab^2) = 2a^4b^3$

a. binomial
b. difference of squares
c. FOIL method
d. monomial
e. negative exponent
f. polynomial
g. product of powers
h. quotient of powers
i. trinomial
j. zero exponent

CHAPTER 9 STUDY GUIDE AND ASSESSMENT

SKILLS AND CONCEPTS

OBJECTIVES AND EXAMPLES

Upon completing this chapter, you should be able to:

- multiply monomials and simplify expressions involving powers of monomials (Lesson 9–1)

$$(2ab^2)(3a^2b^3) = (2 \cdot 3)(a \cdot a^2)(b^2 \cdot b^3) = 6a^3b^5$$

$$(2x^2y^3)^3 = 2^3(x^2)^3(y^3)^3 = 8x^6y^9$$

REVIEW EXERCISES

Use these exercises to review and prepare for the chapter test.

Simplify.

11. $y^3 \cdot y^3 \cdot y$
12. $(3ab)(-4a^2b^3)$
13. $(-4a^2x)(-5a^3x^4)$
14. $(4a^2b)^3$
15. $(-3xy)^2(4x)^3$
16. $(-2c^2d)^4(-3c^2)^3$
17. $-\frac{1}{2}(m^2n^4)^2$
18. $(5a^2)^3 + 7(a^6)$

- simplify expressions involving quotients of monomials and negative exponents (Lesson 9–2)

$$\frac{2x^6y}{8x^2y^2} = \frac{2}{8} \cdot \frac{x^6}{x^2} \cdot \frac{y}{y^2} = \frac{x^4}{4y}$$

$$\frac{3a^{-2}}{4a^6} = \frac{3}{4}(a^{-2-6}) = \frac{3}{4}(a^{-8}) \text{ or } \frac{3}{4a^8}$$

Simplify. Assume that no denominator is equal to zero.

19. $\frac{y^{10}}{y^6}$
20. $\frac{(3y)^0}{6a}$
21. $\frac{42b^7}{14b^4}$
22. $\frac{27b^{-2}}{14b^{-3}}$
23. $\frac{(3a^3bc^2)^2}{18a^2b^3c^4}$
24. $\frac{-16a^3b^2x^4y}{-48a^4bxy^3}$

- express numbers in scientific and decimal notation (Lesson 9–3)

$$3{,}600{,}000 = 3.6 \times 1{,}000{,}000 = 3.6 \times 10^6$$

$$0.0021 = 2.1 \times 0.001 = 2.1 \times 10^{-3}$$

Express each number in scientific notation.

25. 240,000
26. 0.000314
27. 4,880,000,000
28. 0.00000187
29. 796×10^3
30. 0.03434×10^{-2}

- find products and quotients of numbers expressed in scientific notation (Lesson 9–3)

$$(2 \times 10^2)(5.2 \times 10^6) = (2 \times 5.2)(10^2 \times 10^6) = 10.4 \times 10^8 = 1.04 \times 10^9$$

$$\frac{1.2 \times 10^{-2}}{0.6 \times 10^3} = \frac{1.2}{0.6} \times \frac{10^{-2}}{10^3} = 2 \times 10^{-5}$$

Evaluate. Express each result in scientific notation.

31. $(2 \times 10^5)(3 \times 10^6)$
32. $(3 \times 10^3)(1.5 \times 10^6)$
33. $\frac{5.4 \times 10^3}{0.9 \times 10^4}$
34. $\frac{8.4 \times 10^{-6}}{1.4 \times 10^{-9}}$
35. $(3 \times 10^2)(5.6 \times 10^{-4})$
36. $34(4.7 \times 10^5)$

OBJECTIVES AND EXAMPLES	REVIEW EXERCISES

- find the degree of a polynomial (Lesson 9–4)

Find the degree of $2xy^3 + x^2y$.

degree of $2xy^3$: 1 + 3 or 4

degree of x^2y: 2 + 1 or 3

degree of $2xy^3 + x^2y$: 4

Find the degree of each polynomial.

37. $n - 2p^2$
38. $29n^2 + 17n^2t^2$
39. $4xy + 9x^3z^2 + 17rs^3$
40. $-6x^5y - 2y^4 + 4 - 8y^2$
41. $3ab^3 - 5a^2b^2 + 4ab$
42. $19m^3n^4 + 21m^5n^2$

- arrange the terms of a polynomial so that the powers of a variable are in ascending or descending order (Lesson 9–4)

Arrange the terms of $4x^2 + 9x^3 - 2 - x$ in descending order.

$$9x^3 + 4x^2 - x - 2$$

Arrange the terms of each polynomial so that the powers of x are in descending order.

43. $3x^4 - x + x^2 - 5$
44. $-2x^2y^3 - 27 - 4x^4 + xy + 5x^3y^2$

- add and subtract polynomials (Lesson 9–5)

$$\begin{array}{r} 4x^2 - 3x + 7 \\ (+)\ 2x^2 + 4x \phantom{{}+7} \\ \hline 6x^2 + x + 7 \end{array}$$

$$\begin{aligned} (7r^2 + 9r) - (12r^2 - 4) &= 7r^2 + 9r - 12r^2 + 4 \\ &= (7r^2 - 12r^2) + 9r + 4 \\ &= -5r^2 + 9r + 4 \end{aligned}$$

Find each sum or difference.

45. $(2x^2 - 5x + 7) - (3x^3 + x^2 + 2)$
46. $(x^2 - 6xy + 7y^2) + (3x^2 + xy - y^2)$
47. $\begin{array}{r} 11m^2n^2 + 4mn - 6 \\ (+)\ 5m^2n^2 - 6mn + 17 \\ \hline \end{array}$
48. $\begin{array}{r} 7z^2 \phantom{{}+2z} + 4 \\ (-)\ 3z^2 + 2z - 6 \\ \hline \end{array}$
49. $\begin{array}{r} 13m^4 - 7m - 10 \\ (+)\ 8m^4 - 3m + 9 \\ \hline \end{array}$
50. $\begin{array}{r} -5p^2 + 3p + 49 \\ (-)\ 2p^2 + 5p + 24 \\ \hline \end{array}$

- multiply a polynomial by a monomial (Lesson 9–6)

$ab(-3a^2 + 4ab - 7b^3) = -3a^3b + 4a^2b^2 - 7ab^4$

Find each product.

51. $4ab\,(3a^2 - 7b^2)$
52. $7xy(x^2 + 4xy - 8y^2)$
53. $4x^2y(2x^3 - 3x^2y^2 + y^4)$
54. $5x^3(x^4 - 8x^2 + 16)$

- simplify expressions involving polynomials (Lesson 9–6)

$$\begin{aligned} x^2(x + 2) + 3(x^3 + 4x^2) &= x^3 + 2x^2 + 3x^3 + 12x^2 \\ &= 4x^3 + 14x^2 \end{aligned}$$

Simplify.

55. $2x(x - y^2 + 5) - 5y^2(3x - 2)$

56. $x(3x - 5) + 7(x^2 - 2x + 9)$

OBJECTIVES AND EXAMPLES

- use the FOIL method to multiply two binomials and multiply any two polynomials by using the distributive property (Lesson 9–7)

$$(3x+2)(x-2) = \overset{F}{(3x)(x)} + \overset{O}{(3x)(-2)} + \overset{I}{(2)(x)} + \overset{L}{(2)(-2)}$$
$$= 3x^2 - 6x + 2x - 4$$
$$= 3x^2 - 4x - 4$$

$$(4x-3)(3x^2 - x + 2)$$
$$= 4x(3x^2 - x + 2) - 3(3x^2 - x + 2)$$
$$= (12x^3 - 4x^2 + 8x) - (9x^2 - 3x + 6)$$
$$= 12x^3 - 4x^2 + 8x - 9x^2 + 3x - 6$$
$$= 12x^3 - 13x^2 + 11x - 6$$

REVIEW EXERCISES

Find each product.

57. $(r-3)(r+7)$
58. $(x+5)(3x-2)$
59. $(4x-3)(x+4)$
60. $(2x+5y)(3x-y)$
61. $(3x+0.25)(6x-0.5)$
62. $(5r-7s)(4r+3s)$
63. $\begin{array}{r} x^2 + 7x - 9 \\ (\times)\ \ 2x + 1 \\ \hline \end{array}$
64. $\begin{array}{r} a^2 - 17ab - 3b^2 \\ (\times)\qquad 2a + b \\ \hline \end{array}$

- use patterns to find $(a+b)^2$, $(a-b)^2$, and $(a+b)(a-b)$ (Lesson 9–8)

$$(x+4)^2 = x^2 + 2(4x) + 4^2$$
$$= x^2 + 8x + 16$$
$$(r-5)^2 = r^2 - 2(5r) + 5^2$$
$$= r^2 - 10r + 25$$
$$(b+9)(b-9) = b^2 - 9^2$$
$$= b^2 - 81$$

Find each product.

65. $(x-6)(x+6)$
66. $(7-2x)(7+2x)$
67. $(4x+7)^2$
68. $(8x-5)^2$
69. $(5x-3y)(5x+3y)$
70. $(a^2+b)^2$
71. $(6a-5b)^2$
72. $(3m+4n)^2$

APPLICATIONS AND PROBLEM SOLVING

73. **Finance** Find the current monthly payment on a 36-month car loan for $18,543. Twenty-five monthly payments have already been made at an annual interest rate of 8.7%. There is a balance due of $3216.27 at this time. Use the formula $B = P\left[\frac{1-(1+i)^{k-n}}{i}\right]$, where B represents the balance, P represents the current monthly payment, i represents the *monthly* interest rate (annual rate ÷ 12), k represents the total number of monthly payments already made, and n is the total number of monthly payments. (Lesson 9–2)

74. **Health** A radio station advertised the Columbus Marathon by saying that about 19,500,000 Calories would be burned in one day. If there were 6500 runners, about how many Calories did each runner burn? (Use scientific notation to solve.) (Lesson 9–3)

75. **Finance** Upon his graduation from college, Mark Price received $10,000 in a trust fund from his grandparents. If he invests this money in an account with an annual interest rate of 6% and adds $1000 of his own money to the account at the end of each year, will his money have doubled after 5 years? If not, when? (Lesson 9–4)

A practice test for Chapter 9 is provided on page 795.

ALTERNATIVE ASSESSMENT

COOPERATIVE LEARNING PROJECT

Saving for College In this chapter, you developed the concept of polynomials. You performed operations on polynomials, simplified polynomials, and solved polynomial equations. They were helpful in setting up a general formula to be used for inputting various data.

In this project, you will forecast a friend's finances. Jane has received \$75 from her grandparents on every birthday since she was one year old. She has been saving the money in an account that pays 5% interest. She is saving her money to help pay for her college education, which she will start this fall after her 18th birthday. She also has been receiving birthday checks from her other relatives, but these didn't start until she was 12 years old. The amounts of these checks from her 12th birthday until her 18th birthday are \$45, \$45, \$55, \$50, \$55, \$60, and \$65.

How much money will she have saved just from her birthdays by the time she starts college? Is this a reasonable amount to pay for a used car during her junior year in college? If she had invested her money in a different account that had earned 7% interest, how much more money would she have saved?

Follow these steps to accomplish your task.

- Construct a pattern for this situation.
- Develop a polynomial model to describe the amount of money she has each year.
- Determine the amount of money she received on birthdays 12 through 18.
- Determine what needs to be changed in your model when changing the interest rate.
- Write a paragraph describing the problem and your solution.

THINKING CRITICALLY

- Can $(-b)^2$ ever equal $-b^2$? Explain and give an example to support your answer.
- For all numbers a and b and any integer m, is $(a + b)^m = a^m + b^m$ a true sentence? Explain and give examples.

PORTFOLIO

Error analysis shows common mistakes that happen when performing an operation. Here is an example of an error when multiplying like bases.

$$4^3 \cdot 4^4 = 16^7$$

Actually, $4^3 \cdot 4^4 = 4^7$. The error of multiplying the bases while adding the exponents was incorrect. The base should stay the same while adding the exponent.

From the material in this chapter, find a problem that occurs often and write an error analysis for it. Describe the situation, give an example of the incorrect method, give the correct method for that example, and write a paragraph about it. Place this in your portfolio.

SELF EVALUATION

In this chapter, there are several words that have prefixes or suffixes that can be analyzed to determine what the word means. Do you break down words to find their meanings or do you just skip over those words and look for the meaning in the context of the sentence or paragraph? Maybe you go straight to the dictionary to get the meaning.

Assess yourself. How do you best learn new vocabulary words? After learning the meaning of the new word, do you then try to use that new word in your speaking and/or writing? Describe the plan that you use when learning a new word and how you accomplish it. Give an example of a new math-related word and a new word used in your daily life and explain how you found the meaning of each of these words.

LONG-TERM PROJECT

In·ves·ti·ga·tion

the BRICKYARD

MATERIALS NEEDED

- construction paper
- scissors
- ruler

You work for a construction company that specializes in brick patios. Your job is to create custom-designed patios. The company manufactures square and rectangular bricks. Recently, your manager sent your department the memo shown below.

In this Investigation, you must design brick patios that fit the specifications given in the memo. The design plans must be explicit and detailed, so that the construction crew can build them accordingly. Your design team consists of three people.

Make an Investigation Folder in which you can store all of your work on this Investigation for future use.

MEMO

To: Custom Design Department
From: Joanna Brown, Manager *JB*

We have a problem, and I need your help in solving it. We have an excess inventory of three types of bricks:

- small square bricks,
- large square bricks, and
- rectangular bricks that are as long as the large square brick and as wide as the small square brick.

We need to move this inventory, so I am asking you to investigate the possible patio design patterns using these three types of bricks.

I don't know if this is helpful, but the length of the larger brick is the same length as the diagonal of the smaller square brick.

Our other custom designs include using triangles, rectangles, and hexagons exclusively to create repeating patterns. However, for these surplus bricks, we need to concentrate on repeating rectangular patterns.

Please create several patio designs that will utilize these bricks. Submit at least three different plans, explaining the materials required for each patio. I am anxious to see the different ways in which these bricks can be arranged to form rectangular patios. Is there a general formula or pattern we can use to design these in the future? I look forward to your report on helping us solve our inventory problem.

PATIO SKETCH #____	DIMENSIONS	MATERIALS USED		
	small square: ___ × ___	bricks	number	total area
	large square: ___ × ___	sm. squares		
	rectangle: ___ × ___	lg. squares		
	design size: ___ × ___	rectangles		
		TOTAL		

CREATE MODELS

1 Copy the table above. You will use it, along with other tables, to record the data as you explore the designs that are possible.

2 Using the measurement requirements from Ms. Brown's memo, create a model of each of the three sizes of bricks.

3 After determining that your three models comply with the given specifications, use construction paper to make several copies of each model.

ANALYZE THE MODELS

4 Share the dimensions of your models with the other design teams in your class. Obviously the models of each design team will not be the same size, but each set of models must comply with the requirements Ms. Brown wrote in her memo.

5 Explain how the three sizes relate to each other. Make a chart listing the dimensions of each of the models from the other design teams. Do each set of dimensions relate in the same way that your dimensions do? Should they? Explain.

6 How do the lengths of the two square bricks relate? If you were to make one row of small squares and below it make one row of large squares, how many small squares would it take to match the exact length of the row of large squares? Explain your answer mathematically.

You will continue working on this Investigation throughout Chapters 10 and 11.

Be sure to keep your individual brick models, chart, and other materials in your Investigation Folder.

The Brickyard Investigation

Working on the Investigation
Lesson 10–4, p. 586

Working on the Investigation
Lesson 10–6, p. 600

Working on the Investigation
Lesson 11–1, p. 617

Working on the Investigation
Lesson 11–2, p. 627

Closing the Investigation
End of Chapter 11, p. 650

CHAPTER 10

Using Factoring

The Impact of the Media

Objectives

In this chapter, you will:

- find the prime factorization of integers,
- find the greatest common factors (GCF) for sets of monomials,
- factor polynomials,
- solve problems by using guess and check, and
- use the zero product property to solve equations.

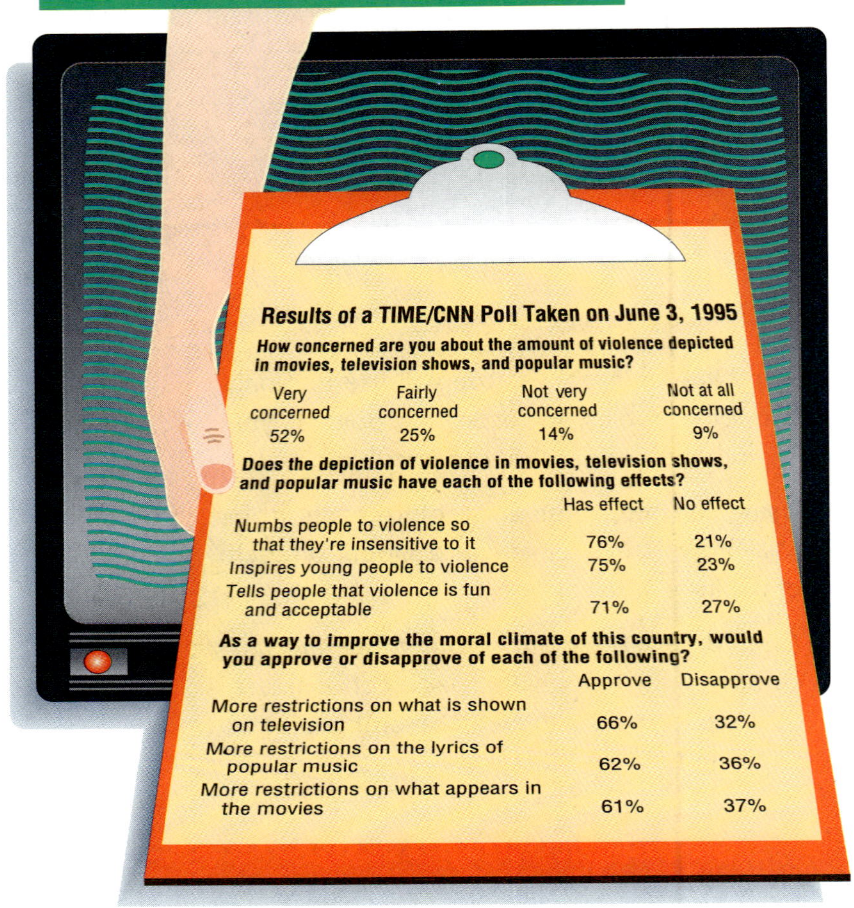

Results of a TIME/CNN Poll Taken on June 3, 1995

How concerned are you about the amount of violence depicted in movies, television shows, and popular music?

Very concerned	Fairly concerned	Not very concerned	Not at all concerned
52%	25%	14%	9%

Does the depiction of violence in movies, television shows, and popular music have each of the following effects?

	Has effect	No effect
Numbs people to violence so that they're insensitive to it	76%	21%
Inspires young people to violence	75%	23%
Tells people that violence is fun and acceptable	71%	27%

As a way to improve the moral climate of this country, would you approve or disapprove of each of the following?

	Approve	Disapprove
More restrictions on what is shown on television	66%	32%
More restrictions on the lyrics of popular music	62%	36%
More restrictions on what appears in the movies	61%	37%

Source: *Time Magazine,* June 12, 1995

TIME Line

Is American culture too violent? Do movies, television, magazines, and music reflect a true picture of America or do they contribute to the violence in our culture? What impact does the media have on American youth?

575 Ishtar Gate in Babylon is built.

A.D. 705 Ch'ang-an Pagoda in China is completed.

9000 B.C. | 8500 | 8000 | 7500 | 1000 | 500 | 0 | A.D. 500 | 1000 | 1500 | 1600 | 1650 | 1700

8000 B.C. People in Mesopotamia use clay tokens to record numbers of animals and amounts of grain.

1663 Isaac Newton discovers the binomial theorem.

PEOPLE IN THE NEWS

The title of **Robert Rodriquez's** new book is *Rebel Without a Crew: Or How a 23-Year-Old Filmmaker with $7,000 Became a Hollywood Player*. It is the story of how the University of Texas film student from Austin, Texas, made a feature film on a very small budget. He used friends as actors, wrote the script, directed the 14-day shoot, and handled the camera work as a one-man crew. The film, *El Mariachi*, went on to win the Audience Award at the Sundance Film Festival, was released by Columbia, and is now on video.

Robert's second film, a full budget production, was *Desperado*, released in 1995. He told Columbia that he would sign a contract if he could stay in Texas, near his family and his inspiration. His advice to future film makers, "Grab your camera and just do it."

Chapter Project

- Pick five of your favorite movies. List five hints for each movie that will help your classmates to guess the names of the movies.
- Exchange your list of hints with a classmate. Try to guess your classmate's favorite movies. Explain how each hint helped you to eliminate some movies and to concentrate on others. Did you guess your classmate's favorite movies correctly?
- Explain how guessing can help when factoring polynomials.
- List five polynomials for one of your classmates to factor. Make sure that one of your polynomials cannot be factored.
- Exchange your polynomials with a classmate and factor the polynomials on the list you receive.

1986 Franklin Chang-Diaz, plasmaphysicist, is a member of the crew of the space shuttle *Columbia*.

1939 Marian Anderson gives a concert for 75,000 at the Lincoln Memorial.

1975 The VHS format (Video Home System) is launched by the Japanese company JVC.

10–1 Factors and Greatest Common Factors

What YOU'LL LEARN

- To find prime factorizations of integers, and
- to find greatest common factors (GCF) for sets of monomials.

Why IT'S IMPORTANT

You can use factors to solve problems involving packaging and gardening.

INTEGRATION

Geometry

Suppose you were asked to use grid paper to draw all of the possible rectangles with whole number dimensions that have areas of 12 square units each. The figure at the right shows one possible drawing.

Rectangles A and B are both 3 by 4 and, therefore, can be considered the same. Likewise, Rectangles C and D and Rectangles E and F are considered the same.

Recall that when two or more numbers are multiplied to form a product, each number is a *factor* of the product. In the example above, 12 is expressed as the product of different pairs of whole numbers.

$12 = 3 \times 4 \qquad 12 = 2 \times 6 \qquad 12 = 12 \times 1$

$12 = 4 \times 3 \qquad 12 = 6 \times 2 \qquad 12 = 1 \times 12$

The whole numbers 1, 2, 3, 4, 6, and 12 are factors of 12.

Example 1 **Find the factors of 72.**

To find the factors of 72, list all the pairs of numbers whose product is 72.

$1 \times 72 \qquad 2 \times 36 \qquad 3 \times 24 \qquad 4 \times 18 \qquad 6 \times 12 \qquad 8 \times 9$

Therefore, the factors of 72, in increasing order, are 1, 2, 3, 4, 6, 8, 9, 12, 18, 24, 36, and 72.

Some whole numbers have exactly two factors, the number itself and 1. These numbers are called **prime numbers**. Whole numbers that have more than two factors are called **composite numbers**.

Definitions of Prime and Composite Numbers	**A prime number is a whole number, greater than 1, whose only factors are 1 and itself. A composite number is a whole number, greater than 1, that is not prime.**

0 and 1 are neither prime nor composite.

FYI

The greatest known prime number was discovered by computer scientists Paul Gage and David Slowinski in 1994, using a Cray supercomputer. The number has 258,716 digits and is expressed as $2^{859,433} - 1$.

The number 6 is a factor of 12, but not a *prime factor* of 12, since 6 is not a prime number. When a whole number is expressed as a product of factors that are all prime numbers, the expression is called the **prime factorization** of the number. Thus, the prime factorization of 12 is $2 \cdot 2 \cdot 3$ or $2^2 \cdot 3$.

The prime factorization of every number is unique except for the order in which the factors are written. For example, $2 \cdot 3 \cdot 2$ is also a prime factorization of 12, but it is the same as $2 \cdot 2 \cdot 3$. This property of numbers is called the **unique factorization theorem**.

Example 2 **Find the prime factorization of 140.**

Method 1

$140 = 2 \cdot 70$ — *The least prime factor of 140 is 2.*

$= 2 \cdot 2 \cdot 35$ — *The least prime factor of 70 is 2.*

$= 2 \cdot 2 \cdot 5 \cdot 7$ — *The least prime factor of 35 is 5.*

All the factors in the last row are prime. Thus, the prime factorization of 140 is $2 \cdot 2 \cdot 5 \cdot 7$ or $2^2 \cdot 5 \cdot 7$.

Method 2

Use a factor tree.

140

10 · 14 — *140 = 10 · 14*

2 · 5 · 2 · 7 — *10 = 2 · 5 and 14 = 2 · 7*

All of the factors in the last branch of the factor tree are prime. Thus, the prime factorization of 140 is $2 \cdot 2 \cdot 5 \cdot 7$ or $2^2 \cdot 5 \cdot 7$.

FYI

Computer scientists have been able to find the prime factors of a 155-digit number. This is particularly significant because some secret codes are based on the factors of large numbers.

A negative integer is factored completely when it is expressed as the product of -1 and prime numbers.

Example 3 **Factor -150 completely.**

$-150 = -1 \cdot 150$ — *Express −150 as −1 times 150.*

$= -1 \cdot 2 \cdot 75$ — *Find the prime factors of 150.*

$= -1 \cdot 2 \cdot 3 \cdot 25$

$= -1 \cdot 2 \cdot 3 \cdot 5 \cdot 5$ or $-1 \cdot 2 \cdot 3 \cdot 5^2$

A monomial is in **factored form** when it is expressed as the product of prime numbers and variables and no variable has an exponent greater than 1.

Example 4 **Factor $45x^3y^2$.**

$45x^3y^2 = 3 \cdot 15 \cdot x \cdot x \cdot x \cdot y \cdot y$

$= 3 \cdot 3 \cdot 5 \cdot x \cdot x \cdot x \cdot y \cdot y$

Two or more numbers may have some common factors. Consider the numbers 84 and 70, for example.

Factors of 84: 1, 2, 3, 4, 6, 7, 12, 14, 21, 28, 42, 84

Factors of 70: 1, 2, 5, 7, 10, 14, 35, 70

There are some factors that appear on both lists. The greatest of these numbers is 14, which is called the **greatest common factor (GCF)** of 84 and 70.

Definition of Greatest Common Factor

The greatest common factor of two or more integers is the greatest number that is a factor of all of the integers.

There is an easier way to find the GCF of numbers without having to find all of their factors. Look at the prime factorizations of the numbers, and multiply all the prime factors they have in common. *If there are no common prime factors, the GCF is 1.*

$$84 = \mathbf{2} \cdot 2 \cdot 3 \cdot \mathbf{7} \qquad 70 = \mathbf{2} \cdot 5 \cdot \mathbf{7}$$

The integers 84 and 70 have 2 and 7 as common prime factors. The product of these common prime factors is 14, the GCF of 84 and 70.

Example 5 **Find the GCF of 54, 63, and 180.**

$54 = 2 \cdot 3 \cdot (3) \cdot (3)$ *Factor each number.*

$63 = (3) \cdot (3) \cdot 7$ *Circle the common factors.*

$180 = 2 \cdot 2 \cdot (3) \cdot (3) \cdot 5$

The GCF of 54, 63, and 180 is $3 \cdot 3$ or 9.

Example 6

APPLICATION
Packaging

A bakery packages its fat-free cookies in two sizes of boxes. One box contains 18 cookies, and the other contains 24 cookies. In order to keep the cookies fresh, the bakery plans to wrap a smaller number of cookies in cellophane before they are placed in the boxes. To save money, the bakery wants to use the same size cellophane packages for each box and to place the greatest possible number of cookies in each cellophane package.

a. How many cookies should the bakery place in each cellophane package?

b. How many cellophane packages will go in each size of box?

a. Find the GCF of 18 and 24.

$18 = (2) \cdot 3 \cdot (3)$

$24 = (2) \cdot 2 \cdot 2 \cdot (3)$

The bakery should put $2 \cdot 3$ or 6 cookies in each inner cellophane package.

b. The box of 18 cookies will contain $18 \div 6$ or 3 cellophane packages. The box of 24 cookies will contain $24 \div 6$ or 4 cellophane packages.

CAREER CHOICES

Pastry chefs are professionals who prepare bread and pastry goods for restaurants, institutions, and retail bakery shops. They do most of their work by hand, taking pride in their creations.

Apprenticeship programs include studying food preparation, decoration techniques, purchasing, and business mathematics.

For more information, contact:

The Educational Foundation of the National Restaurant Association
250 South Wacker Dr.
Suite 1400
Chicago, IL 60606

The GCF of two or more monomials is the product of their common factors, when each monomial is expressed in factored form.

Example 7 **Find the GCF of $12a^2b$ and $90a^2b^2c$.**

$12a^2b = (2) \cdot 2 \cdot (3) \cdot (a) \cdot (a) \cdot (b)$ *Factor each monomial.*

$90a^2b^2c = (2) \cdot 3 \cdot (3) \cdot 5 \cdot (a) \cdot (a) \cdot (b) \cdot b \cdot c$ *Circle the common factors.*

The GCF of $12a^2b$ and $90a^2b^2c$ is $2 \cdot 3 \cdot a \cdot a \cdot b$ or $6a^2b$.

CHECK FOR UNDERSTANDING

Communicating Mathematics

Study this lesson. Then complete the following.

1. **Draw** and label as many rectangles as possible with whole number dimensions that have an area of 48 square inches.
2. Is $2 \cdot 3^2 \cdot 4$ the prime factorization of 72? Why or why not?
3. If the GCF of two numbers is 1, must the numbers be prime? Explain.

4. How many prime numbers do you believe there are? Write a statement to support your opinion.

Guided Practice

Find the factors of each number.

5. 4
6. 56

State whether each number is *prime* or *composite*. If the number is composite, find its prime factorization.

7. 89
8. 39

Factor each expression completely. Do not use exponents.

9. -30
10. $22m^2n$

Find the GCF of the given monomials.

11. 4, 12
12. 10, 15
13. $24d^2$, $30c^2d$
14. 18, 35
15. $-20gh$, $36g^2h^2$
16. $30a^2$, $42a^3$, $54a^3b$
17. **Geometry** Suppose Terrell cuts out a rectangle that has an area of 96 square inches. If the length and width are both whole numbers, what is the minimum perimeter of the rectangle? Explain how you found the answer.

EXERCISES

Practice

Find the factors of each number.

18. 25
19. 67
20. 36
21. 80
22. 400
23. 950

State whether each number is *prime* or *composite*. If the number is composite, find its prime factorization.

24. 17
25. 63
26. 91
27. 97
28. 304
29. 1540

Factor each expression completely. Do not use exponents.

30. -70
31. -117
32. $66z^2$
33. $4b^3d^2$
34. $-102x^3y$
35. $-98a^2b$

Find the GCF of the given monomials.

36. 18, 36
37. 18, 45
38. 84, 96
39. 28, 75
40. −34, 51
41. 95, −304
42. $17a$, $34a^2$
43. $21p^2q$, $35pq^2$
44. $12an^2$, $40a^4$
45. $-60r^2s^2t^2$, $45r^3t^3$
46. 18, 30, 54
47. 24, 84, 168
48. $14a^2b^3$, $20a^3b^2c$, $35ab^3c^2$
49. $18x^2$, $30x^3y^2$, $54y^3$
50. $14a^2b^2$, $18ab$, $2a^3b^3$
51. $32m^2n^3$, $8m^2n$, $56m^3n^2$

Find each missing factor.

52. $42a^2b^5c = 7a^2b^3(\underline{\ ?\ })$
53. $-48x^4y^2z^3 = 4xyz(\underline{\ ?\ })$
54. $48a^5b^5 = 2ab^2(4ab)(\underline{\ ?\ })$
55. $36m^5n^7 = 2m^3n(6n^5)(\underline{\ ?\ })$

56. **Geometry** The area of a rectangle is 116 square inches. What are its possible whole number dimensions?

57. **Geometry** The area of a rectangle is 1363 square centimeters. If the measures of the length and width are both prime numbers, what are the dimensions of the rectangle?

58. **Number Theory** Check to see if your house number is a prime number and if the last four digits in your telephone number form a prime number. Explain how you decided.

59. **Number Theory** *Twin primes* are two consecutive odd numbers that are prime, such as 11 and 13. List the twin primes where both primes are less than 100.

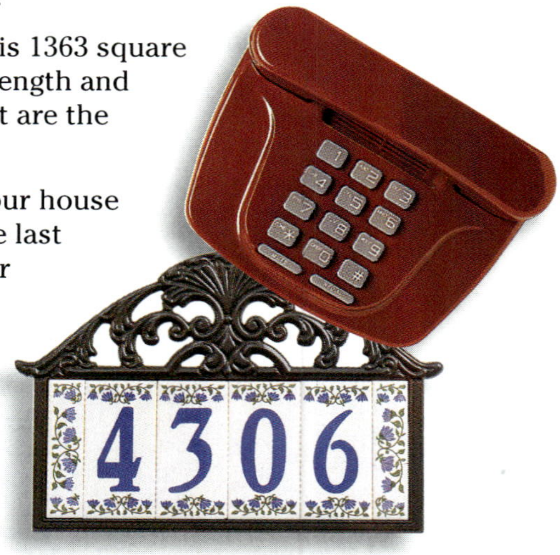

Programming

60. Use the graphing calculator program below to find the GCF of two numbers.

```
PROGRAM:GCF
: Input "INTEGER=",A      : Goto 4
: Input "INTEGER=",B      : A-B→A
: A→E                     : Goto R
: B→F                     : Lbl 4
: Lbl R                   : B-A→B
: If A=B                  : Goto R
: Goto 5                  : Lbl 5
: If A<B                  : Disp "GCF IS", A
```

Use the program to find the GCF of each pair of numbers.

a. 896, 700
b. 1015, 3132
c. 567, 416
d. 486, 432
e. 891, 1701
f. 1105, 1445

Critical Thinking

61. Suppose that 8 is a factor of ab, where a and b are natural numbers. Which of the following assertions is true? Make a valid argument to explain why an assertion is true or provide a counterexample to show that an assertion is false.
   a. 8 must be a factor of a or of b.
   b. 4 must be a factor of a or of b.
   c. 4 must be a factor of a and of b.

Applications and Problem Solving

62. **Gardening** Marisela is planning to have 100 tomato plants in her garden. In what ways can she arrange them so that she has the same number of plants in each row, at least 5 rows of plants, and at least 5 plants in each row?
63. **Sports** A new athletic field is being sodded at Beck High School using 2-yard-by-2-yard squares of sod. If the length of the field is 70 yards longer than the width and its area is 6000 square yards, how many squares of sod will be needed?

Mixed Review

64. Find $(1.1x + y)^2$. (Lesson 9–8)
65. Simplify $\frac{12b^5}{4b^4}$. (Lesson 9–2)
66. Solve the system of equations by graphing. (Lesson 8–1)
    $y = -x$
    $y = 2x$
67. Graph the compound inequality $y > 2$ or $y < 1$. (Lesson 7–4)
68. Solve $16x < 96$. Check your solution. (Lesson 7–2)
69. Write the standard form of an equation of the line that passes through $(4, -2)$ and $(4, 8)$. (Lesson 6–2)
70. Graph $8x - y = 16$. (Lesson 5–4)
71. **Physics** Weights of 50 pounds and 75 pounds are placed on a lever. The two weights are 16 feet apart, and the lever is balanced. How far from the fulcrum is the 50-pound weight? (Lesson 4–8)
72. **Waves** The highest wave ever sighted and recorded was 112 feet high. This wave was brought on by a wind of 74 mph. Using ratios, determine how high a wave brought on by a 25-mph wind could reach. (Lesson 4–1)
73. Solve $9 = x + 13$. (Lesson 3–1)
74. Write a verbal expression for $z^7 + 2$. (Lesson 1–1)

Mathematics and SOCIETY

Number Sieve

The article below appeared in *Science News* on October 1, 1994.

It looks like a cross between an antique music box and an old-fashioned, hand-cranked phonograph. But no music emanates from the contraption. Instead, this ingenious mechanical device operates as a number sieve. It automatically sifts through arrays of numbers to identify certain patterns. From these data, mathematicians can determine whether a given number is a prime or the product of two or more primes multiplied together. Constructed 75 years ago, it also represents the first known, successful attempt to automate the factoring of whole numbers. Until three researchers tracked down the machine recently, few people knew of its existence. Now, this unique device can take its proper place in the history of computational number theory. ■

1. After the death of the machine's French inventor Eugène Olivier Carissan in 1925, the machine was given to an astronomer who put it away for safekeeping. Why do you think a machine so far ahead of its time did not find a greater use?
2. One of the main uses of prime numbers today is in cryptography, the coding and decoding of data and messages. Why are more sophisticated codes needed today than they were in the 1920s?

MODELING MATHEMATICS

A Preview of Lesson 10–2

10–2A Factoring Using the Distributive Property

Materials: algebra tiles   product mat

When two or more numbers are multiplied, these numbers are factors of the product. Sometimes you know the product of binomials and are asked to find the factors. This is called **factoring.** You can use algebra tiles to factor binomials.

Activity 1 Use algebra tiles to factor $2x + 8$.

Step 1 Model the polynomial $2x + 8$.

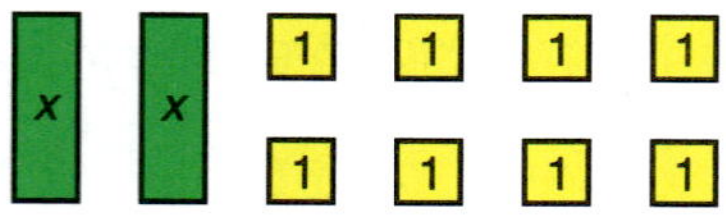

Step 2 Arrange the tiles into a rectangle. The total area of the tiles represents the product and its length and width represent the factors.

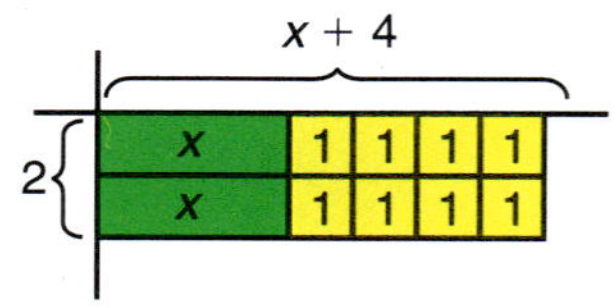

The rectangle has a width of 2 and a length of $x + 4$. Therefore, $2x + 8 = 2(x + 4)$.

Activity 2 Use algebra tiles to factor $x^2 - 3x$.

Step 1 Model the polynomial $x^2 - 3x$.

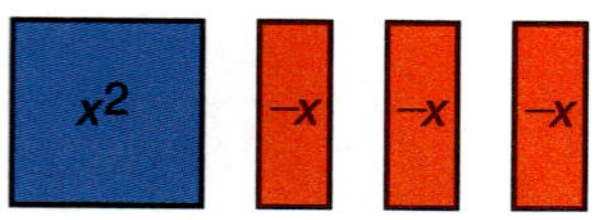

Step 2 Arrange the tiles into a rectangle.

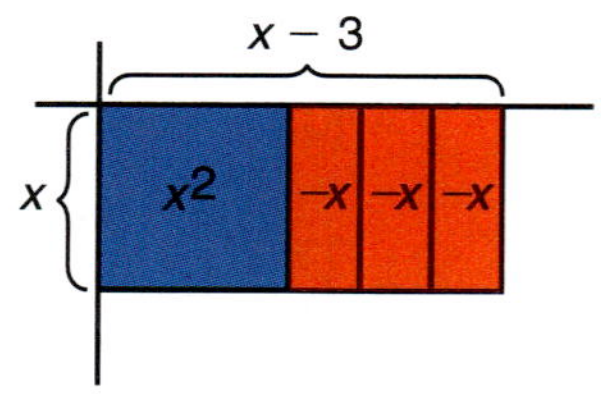

The rectangle has a width of x and a length of $x - 3$. Therefore, $x^2 - 3x = x(x - 3)$.

Model **Use algebra tiles to factor each binomial.**

1. $3x + 9$
2. $4x - 10$
3. $3x^2 + 4x$
4. $10 - 5x$

Draw **Tell whether each binomial can be factored. Justify your answer with a drawing.**

5. $2x + 3$
6. $3 - 9x$
7. $x^2 - 5x$
8. $3x^2 + 5$

Write

9. Write a paragraph that explains how you can determine whether a binomial can be factored. Include an example of one binomial that can be factored and one that cannot.

10-2 Factoring Using the Distributive Property

What YOU'LL LEARN

- To use the greatest common factor (GCF) and the distributive property to factor polynomials, and
- to use grouping techniques to factor polynomials with four or more terms.

Why IT'S IMPORTANT

You can use factoring to solve problems involving sports and construction.

APPLICATION

Sports

Rugby is a contact sport in which each of two teams tries to get an oval ball behind its opponent's goal line or kick it over its opponent's goal. It is similar to American football. However, the action in the game is almost nonstop, and the players wear little protective gear.

There are two versions of rugby—Rugby Union and Rugby League. Rugby Union is popular in Australia, Canada, England, France, Ireland, Japan, New Zealand, Scotland, South Africa, and Wales. It is played on a rectangular field.

LOOK BACK

You can refer to Lesson 1-7 for information on the distributive property.

If the width of this field is represented by x, its length can be represented by $x + 75$ and the area of the field by $x(x + 75)$, or $x^2 + 75x$. If $x(x + 75) = x^2 + 75x$, then $x^2 + 75x = x(x + 75)$. *Why?*

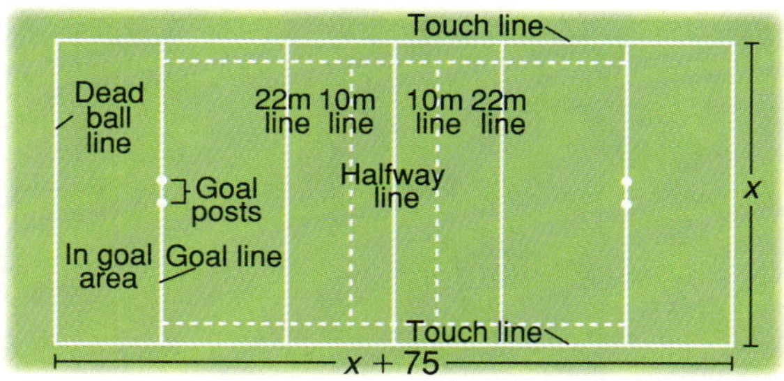

The expression $x(x + 75)$ is called the *factored form* of $x^2 + 75x$. A polynomial is in factored form, or **factored,** when it is expressed as the product of monomials and polynomials.

GLOBAL CONNECTIONS

Rugby is named for Rugby School in England where the game was first played in 1823. The game has spread throughout the British Empire and into Asia. The Rugby World Cup, the World Championship played in 1995, was won by the South African team.

In Chapter 9, you multiplied a polynomial by a monomial using the distributive property. You can also reverse this process and express a polynomial in factored form by using the distributive property.

Model	Multiplying Polynomials	Factoring Polynomials
width 3; lengths $2a$, b; areas $6a$, $3b$	$3(2a + b) = 6a + 3b$	$6a + 3b = 3(a + 2b)$
width $5x$; lengths $3x$, $-4y$; areas $15x^2$, $-20xy$	$5x(3x - 4y) = 15x^2 - 20xy$	$15x^2 - 20xy = 5x(3x - 4y)$
width 3; lengths x^2, $5x$; areas $3x^2$, $15x$	$3(x^2 + 5x) = 3x^2 + 15x$	$3x^2 + 15x = 3(x^2 + 5x)$

Factoring a polynomial or finding the factored form of a polynomial means to find its *completely* factored form. The expression $3(x^2 + 5x)$ above is not considered completely factored since the polynomial $x^2 + 5x$ can be factored as $x(x + 5)$. The completely factored form of $3x^2 + 15x$ is $3x(x + 5)$.

Example 1 **Use the distributive property to factor each polynomial.**

a. $\mathbf{12mn^2 - 18m^2n^2}$

First find the GCF for $12mn^2$ and $18m^2n^2$.

$$12mn^2 = 2 \cdot 2 \cdot 3 \cdot m \cdot n \cdot n$$
$$18m^2n^2 = 2 \cdot 3 \cdot 3 \cdot m \cdot m \cdot n \cdot n$$ *The GCF is $2 \cdot 3 \cdot m \cdot n \cdot n$ or $6mn^2$.*

Notice that $12mn^2 = 6mn^2(2)$ and $18m^2n^2 = 6mn^2(3m)$. Then use the distributive property to express the polynomial as the product of the GCF and the remaining factor of each term.

$$12mn^2 - 18m^2n^2 = 6mn^2(2) - 6mn^2(3m)$$
$$= 6mn^2(2 - 3m)$$ *Distributive property*

b. $\mathbf{20abc + 15a^2c - 5ac}$

$$20abc = 2 \cdot 2 \cdot 5 \cdot a \cdot b \cdot c$$
$$15a^2c = 3 \cdot 5 \cdot a \cdot a \cdot c$$
$$5ac = 5 \cdot a \cdot c$$ *The GCF is $5ac$.*

$$20abc + 15a^2c - 5ac = 5ac(4b) + 5ac(3a) - 5ac(1)$$
$$= 5ac(4b + 3a - 1)$$

Factoring a polynomial can simplify computations.

Example 2

APPLICATION
Construction

The Lopez family wants to build a swimming pool in the shape of the figure below. Although the family has not yet decided on the actual dimensions of the pool, they do know that they want to build a deck that is 4 feet wide around the pool.

a. Write an equation for the area of the deck.

b. If they decide to let a be 24 feet long, b be 6 feet long, and c be 10 feet, find the area of the deck.

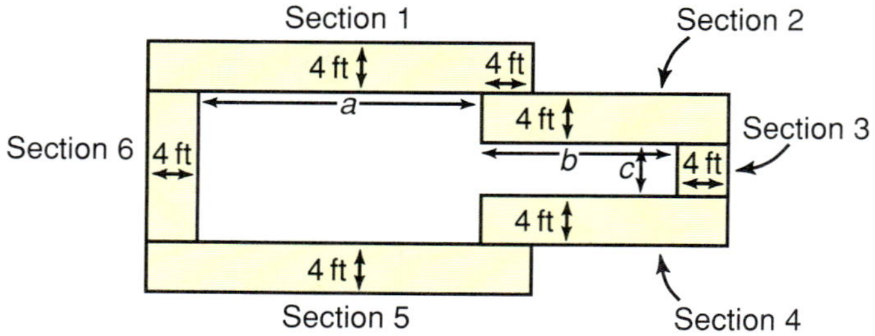

a. You can find the area of the deck by finding the sum of the areas of the 6 rectangular sections shown in the figure. The resulting expression can be simplified by first using the distributive property and then factoring.

Section 1, *Section 2*, *Section 3*, *Section 4*, *Section 5*, *Section 6*

$$A = 4(a + 4 + 4) + 4(b + 4) + 4c + 4(b + 4) + 4(a + 4 + 4) + 4(c + 4 + 4)$$
$$= 4a + 16 + 16 + 4b + 16 + 4c + 4b + 16 + 4a + 16 + 16 + 4c + 16 + 16$$
$$= 8a + 8b + 8c + 128 \quad \textit{Combine like terms.}$$
$$= 8(a + b + c + 16) \quad \textit{The GCF is 8.}$$

The area of the deck is $8(a + b + c + 16)$ square feet.
Would dividing the deck into different sections result in a different answer?

b. Replace a with 24, b with 6, and c with 10.

$$A = 8(24 + 6 + 10 + 16)$$
$$= 8(56) \text{ or } 448$$

The area of the deck would be 448 square feet.

Just as it is possible to use the distributive property to factor a polynomial into monomial and polynomial factors, it is possible to factor some polynomials containing four or more terms into the product of two polynomials. Consider $(3a + 2b)(4c + 7d) = 12ac + 21ad + 8bc + 14bd$. Here, the product of two binomials results in a polynomial with four terms. How can the process be reversed to factor the four-term polynomial into its two binomial factors?

Example 3 **Factor $12ac + 21ad + 8bc + 14bd$.**

$12ac + 21ad + 8bc + 14bd$

$= (12ac + 21ad) + (8bc + 14bd)$ *Apply the associative property, since a common factor of 3a appears in the first two terms and a common factor of 2b appears in the last two terms.*

$= 3a(4c + 7d) + 2b(4c + 7d)$ *Factor the first two terms and the last two terms.*

$= (3a + 2b)(4c + 7d)$ *4c + 7d is a common factor. Use the distributive property.*

Check by using FOIL.

$$(3a + 2b)(4c + 7d) = \overset{F}{(3a)(4c)} + \overset{O}{(3a)(7d)} + \overset{I}{(2b)(4c)} + \overset{L}{(2b)(7d)}$$
$$= 12ac + 21ad + 8bc + 14bd \ \checkmark$$

LOOK BACK

You can refer to Lesson 9-6 for information on FOIL.

This method is called **factoring by grouping**. It is necessary to group the terms and factor each group separately so that the remaining polynomial factors of each group are the same. This allows the distributive property to be applied a second time with a polynomial as the common factor.

Sometimes you can group the terms in more than one way when factoring a polynomial. For example, the polynomial in Example 3 could have been factored in the following way.

$$\begin{aligned} 12ac + 21ad + 8bc + 14bd &= (12ac + 8bc) + (21ad + 14bd) \\ &= 4c(3a + 2b) + 7d(3a + 2b) \\ &= (4c + 7d)(3a + 2b) \end{aligned}$$

The result is the same as in Example 3.

$-1(a - 3) = -a + 3$
$= 3 - a$

Recognizing binomials that are additive inverses is often helpful in factoring. For example, the binomials $3 - a$ and $a - 3$ are additive inverses since the sum of $3 - a$ and $a - 3$ is 0. Thus, $3 - a$ and $-a + 3$ are equivalent. What is the additive inverse of $5 - y$?

Example 4 **Factor $15x - 3xy + 4y - 20$.**

$$\begin{aligned} 15x - 3xy + 4y - 20 &= (15x - 3xy) + (4y - 20) \\ &= 3x(5 - y) + 4(y - 5) \\ &= 3x(-1)(y - 5) + 4(y - 5) \\ &= -3x(y - 5) + 4(y - 5) \\ &= (-3x + 4)(y - 5) \end{aligned}$$

$(5 - y)$ and $(y - 5)$ are additive inverses. $(5 - y) = (-1)(-5 + y)$ or $(-1)(y - 5)$

Check: $$\begin{aligned} (-3x + 4)(y - 5) &= (-3x)(y) + (-3x)(-5) + 4(y) + 4(-5) \\ &= -3xy + 15x + 4y - 20 \\ &= 15x - 3xy + 4y - 20 \quad ✓ \end{aligned}$$

In summary, a polynomial can be factored by grouping if all of the following situations exist.

- There are four or more terms.
- Terms with common factors can be grouped together.
- The two common factors are identical or differ by a factor of -1.

CHECK FOR UNDERSTANDING

Communicating Mathematics

Study the lesson. Then complete the following.

1. a. **Express** $8d^2 - 14d$ as a product of factors in three different ways.
   b. Which of the three answers in part a is the completely factored form of $8d^2 - 14d$? Explain.

2. a. **Express** the area of the rectangle at the right by adding the areas of the smaller rectangles.
   b. **Express** the area as the product of the length and the width.
   c. What is the relationship between the expressions in parts a and b?

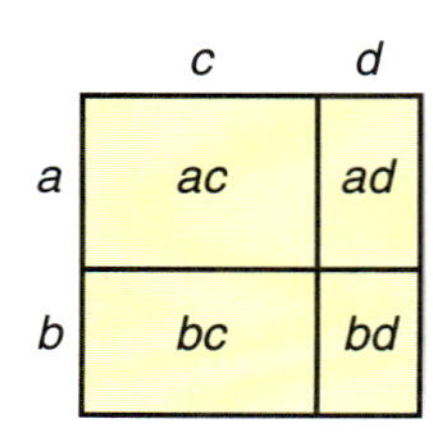

3. **List** the properties used to factor $4gh + 8h + 3g + 6$ by grouping.
4. **Group** the terms of $4gh + 8h + 3g + 6$ in pairs in two different ways so that the pairs of terms have a common monomial factor.
5. **Write** the additive inverse of $7p^2 - q$.

MODELING MATHEMATICS

6. Use algebra tiles to factor $2x^2 - x$.

Guided Practice

Find the GCF of the terms in each expression.

7. $3y^2 + 12$
8. $5n - n^2$
9. $5a + 3b$
10. $6mn + 15m^2$
11. $12x^2y^2 - 8xy^2$
12. $4x^2y - 6xy^2$

Express each polynomial in factored form.

13. $a(x + y) + b(x + y)$
14. $3m(a - 2b) + 5n(a - 2b)$
15. $x(3a + 4b) - y(3a + 4b)$
16. $x^2(a^2 + b^2) + (a^2 + b^2)$

Complete. In Exercise 18, both blanks represent the same expression.

17. $20s + 12t = 4(5s + \underline{\ ?\ })$
18. $(6x^2 - 10xy) + (9x - 15y) = 2x(\underline{\ ?\ }) + 3(\underline{\ ?\ })$

Factor each polynomial.

19. $29xy - 3x$
20. $x^5y - x$
21. $3c^2d - 6c^2d^2$
22. $ay - ab + cb - cy$
23. $rx + 2ry + kx + 2ky$
24. $5a - 10a^2 + 2b - 4ab$

25. **Volleyball** Peta is scheduling the games for a volleyball league. To find the number of games she needs to schedule, she can use the equation $g = \frac{1}{2}n^2 - \frac{1}{2}n$, where g represents the number of games needed for each team to play each other team exactly once and n represents the number of teams.
    a. Write this equation in factored form.
    b. How many games are needed for 14 teams to play each other exactly once?
    c. How many games are needed for 7 teams to play each other exactly 3 times?

EXERCISES

Practice

Complete. In exercises with two blanks, both blanks represent the same expression.

26. $10g - 15h = 5(\underline{\ ?\ } - 3h)$
27. $8rst + 8rs^2 = \underline{\ ?\ }(t + s)$
28. $11p - 55p^2q = \underline{\ ?\ }(1 - 5pq)$
29. $(6xy - 15x) + (-8y + 20) = 3x(\underline{\ ?\ }) - 4(\underline{\ ?\ })$
30. $(a^2 + 3ab) + (2ac + 6bc) = a(\underline{\ ?\ }) + 2c(\underline{\ ?\ })$
31. $(20k^2 - 28kp) + (7p^2 - 5kp) = 4k(\underline{\ ?\ }) - p(\underline{\ ?\ })$

Factor each polynomial.

32. $9t^2 + 36t$
33. $14xz - 18xz^2$
34. $15xy^3 + y^4$
35. $17a - 41a^2b$
36. $2ax + 6xc + ba + 3bc$
37. $2my + 7x + 7m + 2xy$
38. $3m^2 - 5m^2p + 3p^2 - 5p^3$
39. $3x^3y - 9xy^2 + 36xy$
40. $5a^2 - 4ab + 12b^3 - 15ab^2$
41. $2x^3 - 5xy^2 - 2x^2y + 5y^3$
42. $12ax + 20bx + 32cx$
43. $4ax - 14bx + 35by - 10ay$
44. $3my - ab + am - 3by$
45. $28a^2b^2c^2 + 21a^2bc^2 - 14abc$
46. $6a^2 - 6ab + 3bc - 3ca$
47. $12mx - 8m + 6rx - 4r$
48. $2ax + bx - 6ay - 3by - bz - 2az$
49. $7ax + 7bx + 3at + 3bt - 4a - 4b$

INTEGRATION
Geometry

Write an expression in factored form for the area of each shaded region.

50.
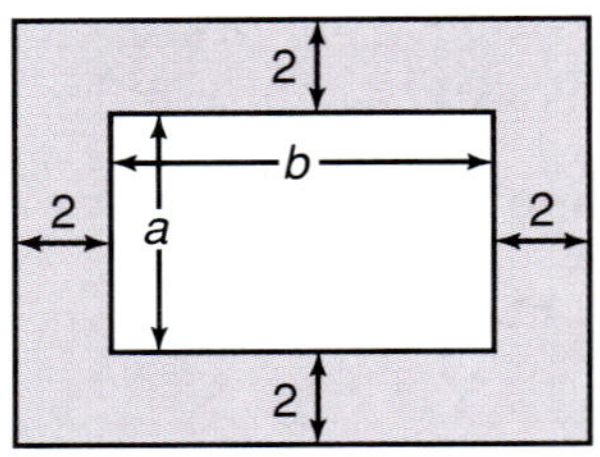

51.
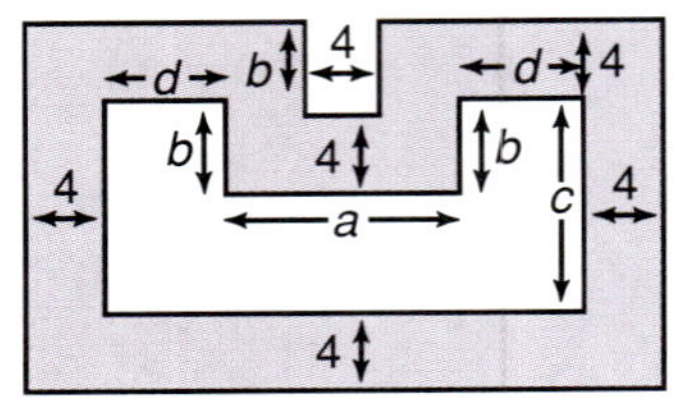

52.
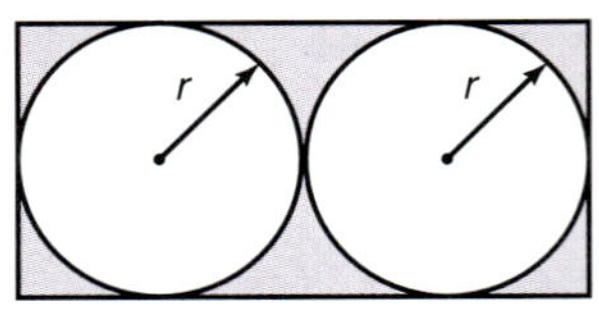

53.
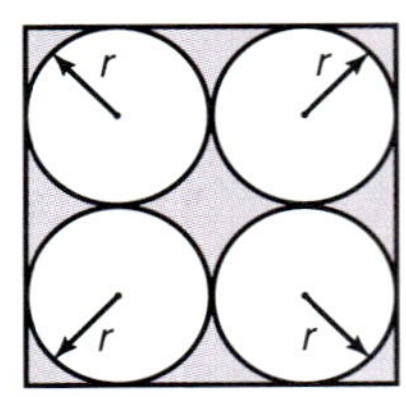

Find the dimensions of a rectangle having the given area if its dimensions can be represented by binomials with integral coefficients.

54. $(5xy + 15x - 6y - 18)$ cm^2
55. $(4z^2 - 24z - 18m + 3mz)$ cm^2

56. **Geometry** The perimeter of a square is $(12x + 20y)$ inches. Find the area of the square.

Critical Thinking

57. **Geometry** The perimeter of a rectangle is $(6a + 4b + 2ab + 12)$ centimeters. Find three possible expressions, in factored form, for the measure of its area.

Applications and Problem Solving

58. **Gardening** The length of Eduardo's garden is 5 feet more than twice its width w. This year, Eduardo decided to make the garden 4 feet longer and double its width. How much additional area did Eduardo add to his garden?

59. **Construction** A 4-foot wide stone path is to be built along each of the longer sides of a rectangular flower garden. The length of the longer side of the garden is 3 feet less than twice the length of the shorter side s. Write an expression, in factored form, to represent the measure of the total area of the garden and path.

60. **Rugby** Refer to the application at the beginning of the lesson.

a. The width of a Rugby Union field is 69 meters. What is the length of the field?

b. What is the area of a Rugby Union field?

c. The length of a Rugby League field is 52 meters longer than its width. Write an expression for the area of the field.

d. The width of a Rugby League field is 68 meters. Find the area of the field.

e. Which type of rugby field has a greater area?

Mixed Review

61. **Music** Two musical notes played at the same time produce harmony. The closest harmony is produced by frequencies with the greatest GCF. A, C, and C sharp have frequencies of 220, 264, and 275, respectively. Which pair of these notes produces the closest harmony? (Lesson 10–1)

62. **Government** In 1990, the population of the United States was 248,200,000. The area of the United States is 3,540,000 square miles. (Lesson 9–3)

a. If the population were equally spaced over the land, how many people would there be for each square mile?

b. In 1990, the federal budget deficit was $220,000,000,000. How much would each American have had to pay in 1990 to erase the deficit?

fabulous FIRSTS

Charles Curtis (1860–1936)

In 1929, Charles Curtis became the first American Indian to serve as vice president of the United States, under Herbert Hoover. Curtis was a member of the U.S. House of Representatives from 1893–1907 and then won a seat in the U.S. Senate (1907–1913, 1915–1929) before becoming vice president.

63. **Geometry** The graphs of $3x + 2y = 1$, $y = 2$, and $3x - 4y = -29$ contain the sides of a triangle. Find the measure of the area of the triangle. (Hint: Use the formula $A = \frac{1}{2}bh$.) (Lesson 8–2)

64. **Statistics** The ten highest-paying occupations in America are shown in the table at the right. (Lesson 7–7)

a. Make a box-and-whisker plot of the data.

b. Name any outliers.

Occupation	Median Salary
Physician	$148,000
Dentist	93,000
Lobbyist	91,300
Management Consultant	61,900
Lawyer	60,500
Electrical Engineer	59,100
School Principal	57,300
Aeronautical Engineer	56,700
Airline Pilot	56,500
Civil Engineer	55,800

Source: Bureau of Labor Statistics

65. Solve $17.42 - 7.029z \geq 15.766 - 8.029z$. (Lesson 7–1)

66. **Geometry** Find the coordinates of the midpoint of the line segment whose endpoints are $A(5, -2)$ and $B(7, 3)$. (Lesson 6–7)

67. Solve $3a + 2b = 11$ if the domain is $\{-3, 0, 1, 2, 5\}$. (Lesson 5–3)

68. Fourteen is 50% less than what number? (Lesson 4–5)

69. Solve $4x + 3y = 7$ for y. (Lesson 3–6)

70. Solve $\frac{5}{2}x = -25$. (Lesson 3–2)

71. Find the value of $(2^5 - 5^2) + (4^2 - 2^4)$. (Lesson 1–6)

MODELING MATHEMATICS

A Preview of Lesson 10–3

10–3A Factoring Trinomials

Materials: algebra tiles   product mat

You can use algebra tiles to factor trinomials. If a rectangle cannot be formed to represent the trinomial, then the trinomial is not factorable.

Activity 1 Use algebra tiles to factor $x^2 + 4x + 3$.

Step 1 Model the polynomial $x^2 + 4x + 3$.

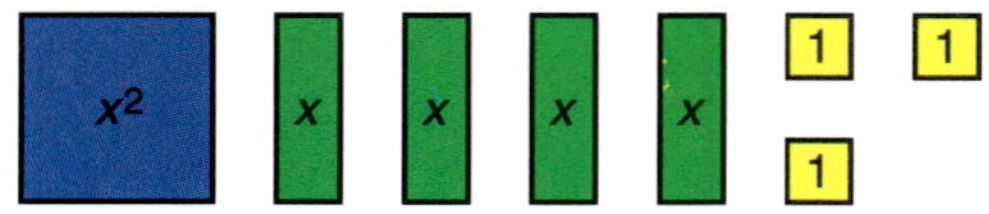

Step 2 Place the x^2-tile at the corner of the product mat. Arrange the 1-tiles into a 1-by-3 rectangular array as shown.

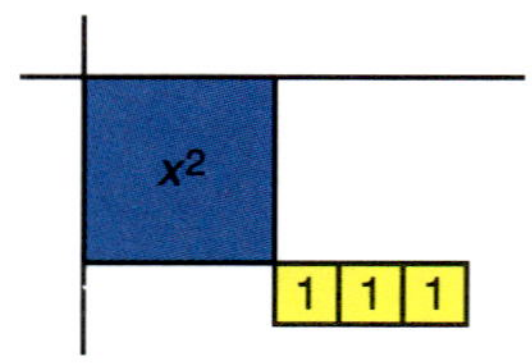

Step 3 Complete the rectangle with the x-tiles.

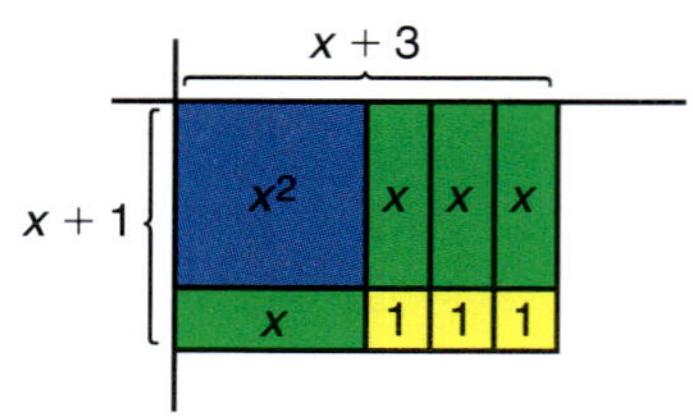

The rectangle has a width of $x + 1$ and a length of $x + 3$. Therefore, $x^2 + 4x + 3 = (x + 1)(x + 3)$.

You will need to use the guess-and-check strategy with many trinomials.

Activity 2 Use algebra tiles to factor $x^2 + 5x + 4$.

Step 1 Model the polynomial $x^2 + 5x + 4$.

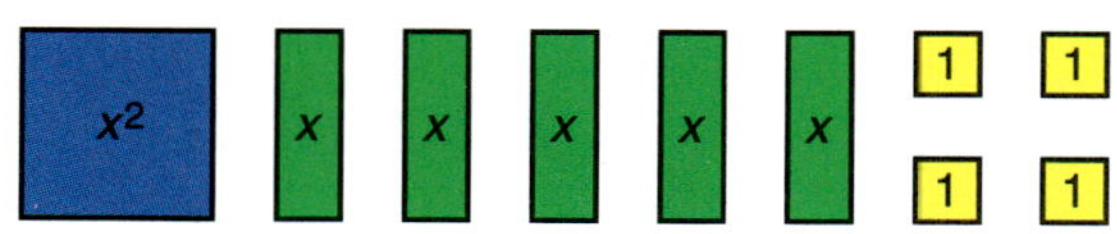

Step 2 Place the x^2 tile at the corner of the product mat. Arrange the 1-tiles into a 2-by-2 rectangular array as shown. Try to complete the rectangle. Notice that there is an extra x-tile.

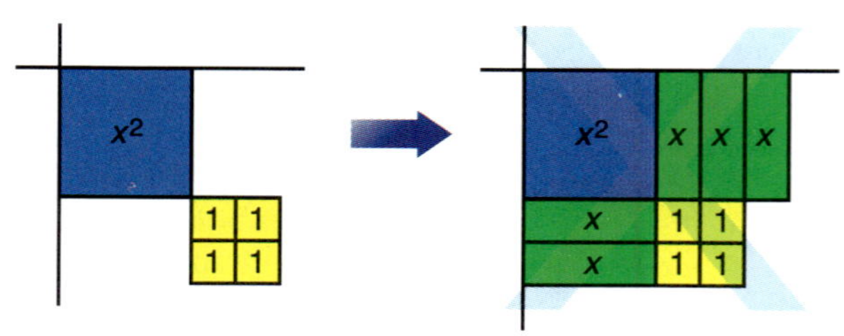

Step 3 Arrange the 1-tiles into a 1-by-4 rectangular array. This time you can complete the rectangle with the x-tiles.

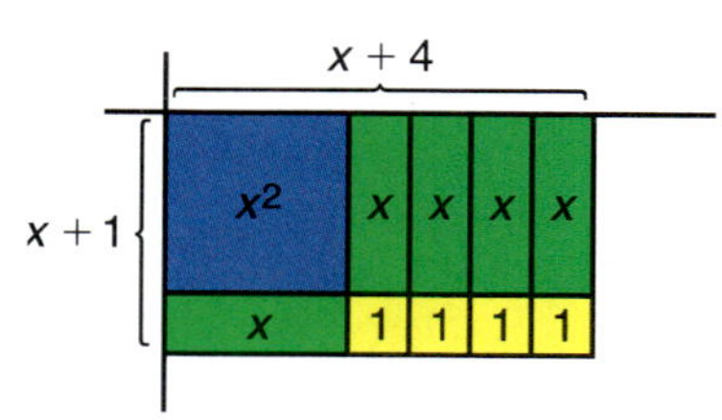

The rectangle has a width of $x + 1$ and a length of $x + 4$. Therefore, $x^2 + 5x + 4 = (x + 1)(x + 4)$.

Activity 3 Use algebra tiles to factor $x^2 - 4x + 4$.

Step 1 Model the polynomial $x^2 - 4x + 4$.

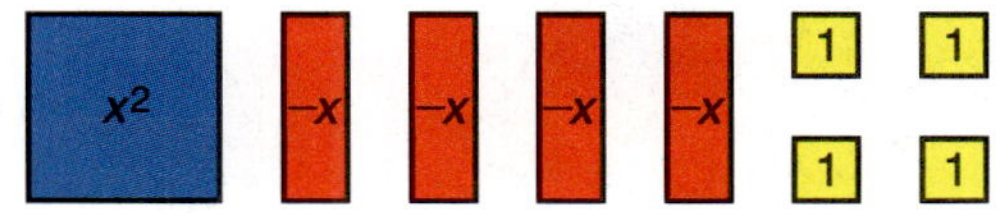

Step 2 Place the x^2-tile at the corner of the product mat. Arrange the 1-tiles into a 2-by-2 rectangular array as shown.

Step 3 Complete the rectangle with the x-tiles.

The rectangle has a width of $x - 2$ and a length of $x - 2$. Therefore, $x^2 - 4x + 4 = (x - 2)(x - 2)$.

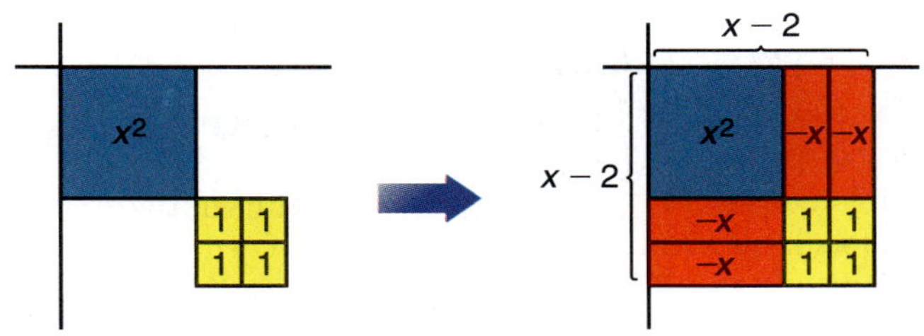

Activity 4 Use algebra tiles to factor $x^2 - x - 2$.

Step 1 Model the polynomial $x^2 - x - 2$.

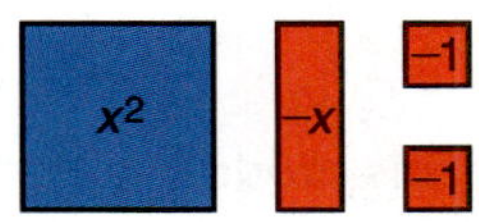

Step 2 Place the x^2-tile at the corner of the product mat. Arrange the 1-tiles into a 1-by-2 rectangular array as shown.

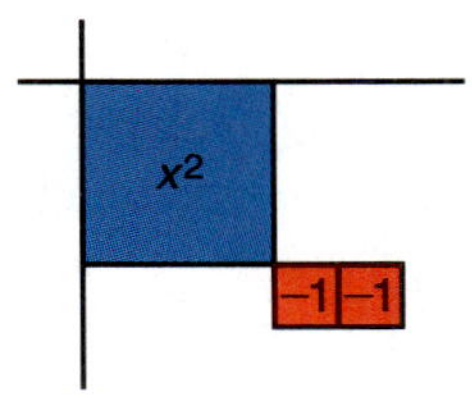

Step 3 Place the x-tile as shown. Recall that you can add zero-pairs without changing the value of the polynomial. In this case, add a zero pair of x-tiles.

The rectangle has a width of $x + 1$ and a length of $x - 2$. Therefore, $x^2 - x - 2 = (x + 1)(x - 2)$.

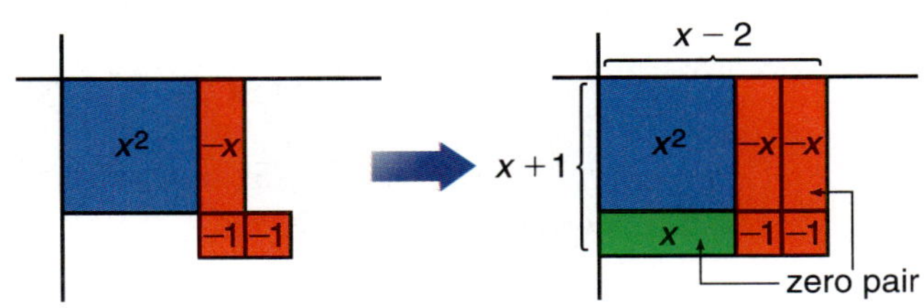

Model

Use algebra tiles to factor each trinomial.

1. $x^2 + 6x + 5$
2. $x^2 + 5x + 6$
3. $x^2 + 7x + 12$
4. $x^2 - 6x + 9$
5. $x^2 - 3x + 2$
6. $x^2 - 6x + 8$
7. $x^2 + 4x - 5$
8. $x^2 - x - 6$

Draw

Tell whether each trinomial can be factored. Justify your answer with a drawing.

9. $x^2 + 7x + 10$
10. $x^2 - 4x + 5$
11. $x^2 + 5x - 4$
12. $x^2 + 2x + 6$

Write

13. Write a paragraph that explains how you can determine whether a trinomial can be factored. Include an example of one trinomial that can be factored and one that cannot.

10-3 Factoring Trinomials

What YOU'LL LEARN

- To solve problems by using guess and check, and
- to factor quadratic trinomials.

Why IT'S IMPORTANT

You can use factoring to solve problems involving shipping and geometry.

INTEGRATION

Number Theory

The product of two consecutive odd integers is 3363. What are the numbers?

One way to find the two numbers is to use a problem-solving strategy called **guess and check**. To use this strategy, guess the answer to the problem, and then check whether the guess is correct. If the first guess is incorrect, guess and check again until you find the correct answer. Often, the results of one guess can help you make a better guess. Always keep an organized record of your guesses so you don't make the same guess twice.

Guess: Try 41 and 43.

Check: $41 \times 43 = 1763$
This product is considerably less than 3363.

Guess: Try two numbers greater than 41 and 43, such as 61 and 63.

Check: $61 \times 63 = 3843$
This product is greater than 3363.

Guess: Try 51 and 53.

Check: $51 \times 53 = 2703$
This product is less than 3363. Since the ones digit is not 0 or 5, do not use 55 as one of the numbers. *Why?*

Guess: Try 57 and 59.

Check: $57 \times 59 = 3363$

The two numbers are 57 and 59.

In Lesson 10–1, you learned that when two numbers are multiplied, each number is a factor of the product. Similarly, when two binomials are multiplied, each binomial is a factor of the product. You can use the guess-and-check strategy to find the factors of a trinomial. Consider the binomials $5x + 3$ and $2x + 7$. You can use the FOIL method to find their product.

$$\begin{aligned}(5x + 3)(2x + 7) &= \overset{F}{(5x)(2x)} + \overset{O}{(5x)(7)} + \overset{I}{(3)(2x)} + \overset{L}{(3)(7)} \\ &= 10x^2 + 35x + 6x + 21 \\ &= 10x^2 + (35 + 6)x + 21 \\ &= 10x^2 + 41x + 21\end{aligned}$$

Notice that $10 \cdot 21 = 210$ and $35 \cdot 6 = 210$.

The binomials $5x + 3$ and $2x + 7$ are factors of $10x^2 + 41x + 21$.

When using the FOIL method above, look at the product of the coefficients of the first and last terms, 10 and 21. Notice that this product, 210, is the same as the product of the coefficients of the two middle terms, 35 and 6. Their sum is the coefficient of the middle term of the final product.

You can use this pattern to factor quadratic trinomials, such as $3y^2 + 10y + 8$.

$3y^2 + 10y + 8$ The product of 3 and 8 is 24.

$3y^2 + (\underline{?} + \underline{?})y + 8$

You need to find two integers whose *product is 24* and whose *sum is 10.*

Use the guess-and-check strategy to find these numbers.

Factors of 24	Sum of Factors	
1, 24	$1 + 24 = 25$	*no*
2, 12	$2 + 12 = 14$	*no*
3, 8	$3 + 8 = 11$	*no*
4, 6	$4 + 6 = 10$	*yes*

$3y^2 + 10y + 8$

$= 3y^2 + (4 + 6)y + 8$ *Select the factors 4 and 6.*

$= 3y^2 + 4y + 6y + 8$

$= (3y^2 + 4y) + (6y + 8)$ *Group terms that have a common monomial factor.*

$= y(3y + 4) + 2(3y + 4)$ *Factor.*

$= (y + 2)(3y + 4)$ *Use the distributive property.*

Therefore, $3y^2 + 10y + 8 = (y + 2)(3y + 4)$. *Check by using FOIL.*

Example 1 **Factor $10x^2 - 27x + 18$.**

$10x^2 - 27x + 18$ The product of 10 and 18 is 180.

$10x^2 + (\underline{?} + \underline{?})x + 18$ Since the product is positive and the sum is negative, both factors of 180 must be negative. *Why?*

Factors of 180	Sum of Factors	
$-180, -1$	$-180 + (-1) = -181$	*no*
$-90, -2$	$-90 + (-2) = -92$	*no*
$-45, -4$	$-45 + (-4) = -49$	*no*
$-15, -12$	$-15 + (-12) = -27$	*yes*

You can stop listing factors when you find a pair that works.

$10x^2 - 27x + 18$

$= 10x^2 + [-15 + (-12)]x + 18$

$= 10x^2 - 15x - 12x + 18$

$= (10x^2 - 15x) + (-12x + 18)$

$= 5x(2x - 3) + (-6)(2x - 3)$ *Factor the GCF from each group.*

$= (5x - 6)(2x - 3)$ *Use the distributive property.*

Therefore, $10x^2 - 27x + 18 = (5x - 6)(2x - 3)$. *Check by using FOIL.*

Example 2

INTEGRATION
Geometry

The area of a rectangle is $(a^2 - 3a - 18)$ square inches. This area is increased by adding 5 inches to both the length and the width. If the dimensions of the original rectangle are represented by binomials with integral coefficients, find the area of the new rectangle.

To determine the area of the new rectangle, you must first find the dimensions of the original rectangle by factoring $a^2 - 3a - 18$. The coefficient of a^2 is 1. Thus, you must find two numbers whose product is $1 \cdot (-18)$ or -18 and whose sum is -3.

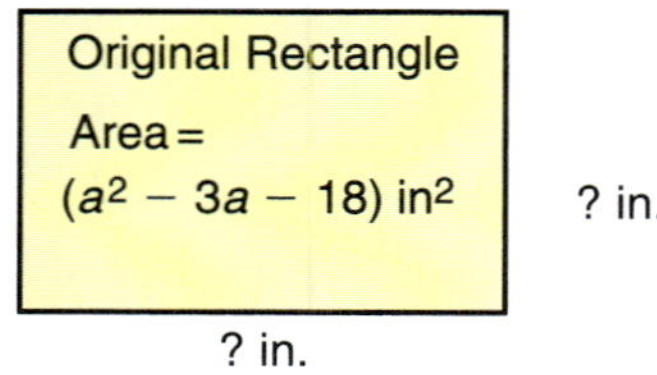

Factors of -18	Sum of Factors	
$-18, 1$	$-18 + 1 = -17$	*no*
$-9, 2$	$-9 + 2 = -7$	*no*
$-6, 3$	$-6 + 3 = -3$	*yes*

The factors of -18 should be chosen so that exactly one factor in each pair is negative and that factor has the greater absolute value. Why?

$$\begin{aligned} a^2 - 3a - 18 &= a^2 + [(-6) + 3]a - 18 \\ &= a^2 - 6a + 3a - 18 \\ &= (a^2 - 6a) + (3a - 18) \\ &= a(a - 6) + 3(a - 6) \\ &= (a + 3)(a - 6) \quad \textit{Check by using FOIL.} \end{aligned}$$

The dimensions of the original rectangle are $(a + 3)$ inches and $(a - 6)$ inches. Therefore, the dimensions of the new rectangle are $(a + 3) + 5$ or $(a + 8)$ inches and $(a - 6) + 5$ or $(a - 1)$ inches. Now, find an expression for the area of the new rectangle.

$$\begin{aligned} (a + 8)(a - 1) &= a^2 - a + 8a - 8 \\ &= a^2 + 7a - 8 \end{aligned}$$

The area of the new rectangle is $(a^2 + 7a - 8)$ square inches.

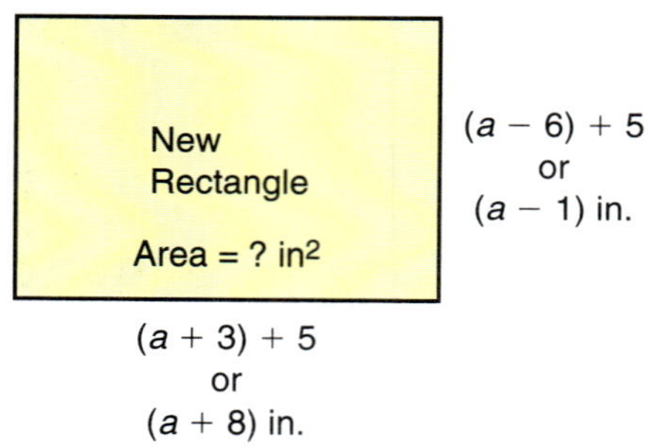

Let's study the factorization of $a^2 - 3a - 18$ from Example 2 more closely.

$$a^2 - 3a - 18 = (a + 3)(a - 6)$$

Notice that the sum of 3 and -6 is equal to -3, the coefficient of a in the trinomial. Also, the product of 3 and -6 is equal to -18, the constant term of the trinomial. This pattern holds for all trinomials whose quadratic term has a coefficient of 1.

Occasionally the terms of a trinomial will contain a common factor. In these cases, first use the distributive property to factor out the common factor, and then factor the trinomial.

Example 3 **Factor $14t - 36 + 2t^2$.**

First rewrite the trinomial so the terms are in descending order.

$$14t - 36 + 2t^2 = 2t^2 + 14t - 36$$
$$= 2(t^2 + 7t - 18)$$ *The GCF of the terms is 2. Use the distributive property.*

Now factor $t^2 + 7t - 18$. Since the coefficient of t^2 is 1, we need to find two factors of -18 whose sum is 7.

Factors of -18	Sum of Factors	
$18, -1$	$18 + (-1) = 17$	*no*
$9, -2$	$9 + (-2) = 7$	*yes*

The desired factors are 9 and -2 and $t^2 + 7t - 18 = (t + 9)(t - 2)$.
Therefore, $2t^2 + 14t - 36 = 2(t + 9)(t - 2)$.

A polynomial that cannot be written as a product of two polynomials with integral coefficients is called a **prime polynomial**.

Example 4 **Factor $2a^2 - 11a + 7$.**

You must find two numbers whose product is $2 \cdot 7$ or 14 and whose sum is -11. Since the sum has to be negative, both factors of 14 have to be negative.

Factors of 14	Sum of Factors	
$-1, -14$	$-1 + (-14) = -15$	*no*
$-2, -7$	$-2 + (-7) = -9$	*no*

There are no factors of 14 whose sum is -11.

Therefore, $2a^2 - 11a + 7$ cannot be factored using integers.
Thus, $2a^2 - 11a + 7$ is a prime polynomial.

You can use your knowledge of factoring to write polynomials that can be factored using integers.

Example 5 **Find all values of k so the trinomial $3x^2 + kx - 4$ can be factored using integers.**

For $3x^2 + kx - 4$ to be factorable, k must equal the sum of the factors of $3(-4)$ or -12.

Factors of -12	Sum of Factors (k)
$-12, 1$	$-12 + 1 = -11$
$12, -1$	$12 + (-1) = 11$
$-6, 2$	$-6 + 2 = -4$
$6, -2$	$6 + (-2) = 4$
$-4, 3$	$-4 + 3 = -1$
$4, -3$	$4 + (-3) = 1$

Therefore, the values of k are -11, 11, -4, 4, -1, and 1.

You can graph a polynomial and its factored form on the same axes to see if you have factored correctly. If the two graphs coincide, the factored form is probably correct.

EXPLORATION — GRAPHING CALCULATORS

Suppose $x^2 - x + 6$ has been factored as $(x + 2)(x - 3)$.

a. Press [Y=]. Enter $x^2 - x + 6$ for Y1 and $(x + 2)(x - 3)$ for Y2.

b. Press [ZOOM] 6. Notice that two different graphs appear. Therefore, $x^2 - x + 6 \neq (x + 2)(x - 3)$.

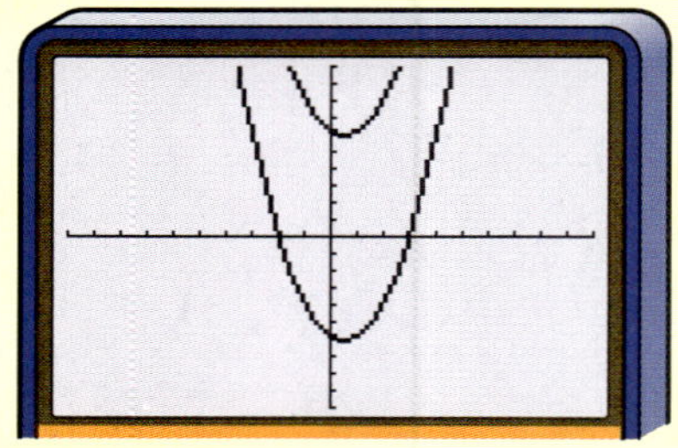

Your Turn

Determine whether each equation is a true statement. If it is not correct, state the correct factorization of the trinomial.

a. $x^2 - x - 2 = (x - 1)(x + 2)$

b. $x^2 - 2x - 3 = (x - 3)(x + 1)$

c. $x^2 - 5x + 4 = (x - 4)(x - 1)$

d. $2x^2 + 3x - 2 = (2x + 2)(x - 1)$

CHECK FOR UNDERSTANDING

Communicating Mathematics

Study this lesson. Then complete the following.

1. **Explain** why you should keep a record of your guesses when you are using the guess-and-check strategy.
2. **Write** an example of a prime polynomial.

MODELING MATHEMATICS

3. **Study** the model at the right.
   a. **Explain** how this model could help to factor $x^2 + 8x + 12$.
   b. **Factor** $x^2 + 8x + 12$.

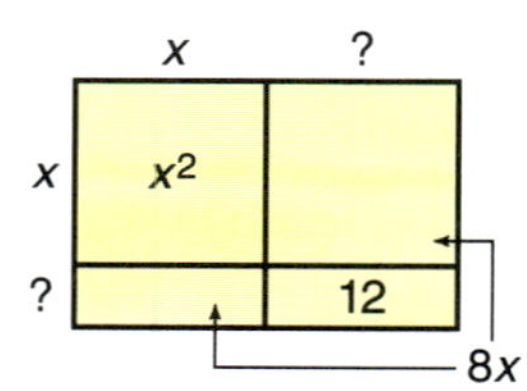

4. Use algebra tiles to factor $x^2 + 3x - 4$. Make a drawing of the algebra tiles.

Guided Practice

For each trinomial of the form $ax^2 + bx + c$, find two integers whose product is equal to ac and whose sum is equal to b.

5. $x^2 + 11x + 24$
6. $x^2 + 4x - 45$
7. $2x^2 + 13x + 20$
8. $3x^2 - 19x + 6$
9. $4x^2 - 8x + 3$
10. $5x^2 - 13x - 6$

Complete.

11. $r^2 - 5r - 14 = (r + 2)(r \underline{\ ?\ } 7)$
12. $2g^2 + 5g - 12 = (2g - 3)(g + \underline{\ ?\ })$

Factor each trinomial, if possible. If the trinomial cannot be factored using integers, write *prime*.

13. $t^2 + 7t + 12$
14. $c^2 - 13c + 36$
15. $2y^2 - 2y - 12$
16. $3d^2 - 12d + 9$
17. $2x^2 + 5x - 2$
18. $6p^2 + 15p - 9$

Find all values of k so each trinomial can be factored using integers.

19. $x^2 + kx + 14$
20. $2b^2 + kb - 3$

21. **Geometry** The area of a rectangle is $(3x^2 + 14x + 15)$ square meters. This area is reduced by decreasing both the length and width by 3 meters. If the dimensions of the original rectangle are represented by binomials with integral coefficients, find the area of the new rectangle.

EXERCISES

Practice

Complete.

22. $a^2 + a - 30 = (a - 5)(a \underline{\ ?\ } 6)$
23. $g^2 - 8g + 16 = (g - 4)(g \underline{\ ?\ } 4)$
24. $4y^2 - y - 3 = (\underline{\ ?\ } + 3)(y - 1)$
25. $6t^2 - 23t + 20 = (3t - 4)(2t - \underline{\ ?\ })$
26. $4x^2 + 4x - 3 = (2x - 1)(\underline{\ ?\ } + 3)$
27. $15g^2 + 34g + 15 = (5g + 3)(3g + \underline{\ ?\ })$

Factor each trinomial, if possible. If the trinomial cannot be factored using integers, write *prime*.

28. $b^2 + 7b + 12$
29. $m^2 - 14m + 40$
30. $z^2 - 5z - 24$
31. $t^2 - 2t + 35$
32. $s^2 + 3s - 180$
33. $2x^2 + x - 21$
34. $7a^2 + 22a + 3$
35. $2x^2 - 5x - 12$
36. $3c^2 - 3c - 5$
37. $4n^2 - 4n - 35$
38. $72 - 26y + 2y^2$
39. $10 + 19m + 6m^2$
40. $a^2 + 2ab - 3b^2$
41. $12r^2 - 11r + 3$
42. $15x^2 - 13xy + 2y^2$
43. $12x^3 + 2x^2 - 80x$
44. $5a^3b^2 + 11a^2b^2 - 36ab^2$
45. $20a^4b - 58a^3b^2 + 42a^2b^3$

Find all values of *k* so each trinomial can be factored using integers.

46. $r^2 + kr - 13$
47. $x^2 + kx + 10$
48. $2c^2 + kc + 12$
49. $3s^2 + ks - 14$
50. $x^2 + 8x + k, k > 0$
51. $n^2 - 5n + k, k > 0$

52. **Geometry** The area of a rectangle is $(6x^2 - 31x + 35)$ square inches. If the dimensions of the rectangle are all whole numbers, what is the minimum possible area of the rectangle?

53. **Geometry** The volume of a rectangular prism is $(15r^3 - 17r^2 - 42r)$ cubic centimeters. If the dimensions of the prism are represented by polynomials with integral coefficients, find the dimensions of the prism.

Graphing Calculator

Use a graphing calculator to determine whether each equation is a true statement. If it is not correct, state the correct factorization of the trinomial.

54. $x^2 - 2x - 15 = (x - 5)(x + 3)$
55. $2x^2 + x - 3 = (2x - 1)(x + 3)$
56. $3x^2 - 4x - 4 = (3x - 2)(x + 2)$
57. $x^2 - 6x + 9 = (x + 3)(x - 3)$

Critical Thinking

58. Complete each polynomial in three different ways so that the resulting polynomial can be factored. Then factor each polynomial.
 a. $x^2 + 8x + \underline{\ ?\ }$
 b. $x^2 + \underline{\ ?\ }x - 10$

Applications and Problem Solving

59. **Shipping** A shipping crate is to be built in the shape of a rectangular solid. The volume of the crate is $(45x^2 - 174x + 144)$ cubic feet where x is a positive integer. If the height of the crate is 3 feet, what is the minimum volume possible for this crate?

60. **Guess and Check** Place the digits 1, 2, 3, 4, 5, 6, 8, 9, 10, 12 on the dots at the right so that the sum of the integers on any line equals the sum on any other line.

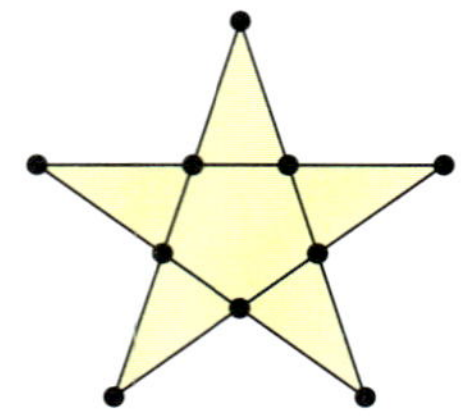

Mixed Review

61. **Finance** During the first hour of trading, John Sugarman sold x shares of stock that cost \$4 per share. During the next hour, he sold stock that cost \$8 per share. He sold 5 more shares during the first hour than the second hour. If he had sold only the stock that cost \$4 per share during the two hours, how many shares would he have needed to sell to have the same amount of total sales? (Lesson 10–2)

62. Find the degree of $7x^3 + 4xy + 3xz^3$. (Lesson 9–4)

63. Use elimination to solve the system of equations. (Lesson 8–3)
$2x = 4 - 3y$
$3y - x = -11$

64. Solve $|2y - 7| \geq -6$. (Lesson 7–6)

65. Write an equation of the line that is parallel to the graph of $2x + 3y = 1$ and passes through (4, 2). (Lesson 6–6)

66. Determine the slope of the line that passes through the points at $(-3, 6)$ and $(-5, 9)$. (Lesson 6–1)

67. State the domain and range of $\{(0, 2), (1, -2), (2, 4)\}$. (Lesson 5–2)

68. **Geography** There is three times as much water as land on Earth's surface. What percent of Earth is covered by water? (Lesson 4–4)

69. Find the supplement of 90°. (Lesson 3–4)

70. **Time** When it is noon in Richmond, Virginia, it is 2:00 A.M. the following morning in Kanagawa, Japan. Joel, who teaches English in Kanagawa, would like to call his mother in Richmond at 7:30 on the morning of her birthday, October 26. On what day and at what time would Joel have to call her? (Lesson 2–3)

71. Simplify $3(x + 2y) - 2y$. (Lesson 1–7)

SELF TEST

Find the GCF of the given monomials. (Lesson 10–1)

1. $50n^4, 40n^2p^2$
2. $15abc, 35a^2c, 105a$

Factor each polynomial, if possible. If the polynomial cannot be factored using integers, write *prime*. (Lessons 10–2 and 10–3)

3. $18xy^2 - 24x^2y$
4. $2ab + 2am - b - m$
5. $2q^2 - 9q - 18$
6. $t^2 + 5t - 20$
7. $3y^2 - 8y + 5$
8. $27m^2n^2 - 75mn$

9. **Guess and Check** Write an eight-digit number using the digits 1, 2, 3, and 4 each twice so that the 1s are separated by 1 digit, the 2s are separated by 2 digits, the 3s are separated by 3 digits, and the 4s are separated by 4 digits. (Lesson 10–3)

10. **Geometry** The area of a rectangle is $(x^2 - x - 6)$ square meters. The length and width are each increased by 9 meters. If the dimensions of the original rectangle are binomials with integral coefficients, find the area of the new rectangle. (Lesson 10–3)

10–4 Factoring Differences of Squares

What YOU'LL LEARN

- To identify and factor binomials that are the differences of squares.

INTEGRATION

Modeling

You have used algebra tiles to factor trinomials. You can also use algebra tiles to factor some binomials.

MODELING MATHEMATICS

Difference of Squares

Materials: algebra tiles product mat

Factor $x^2 - 9$.

Step 1

Model the polynomial $x^2 - 9$.

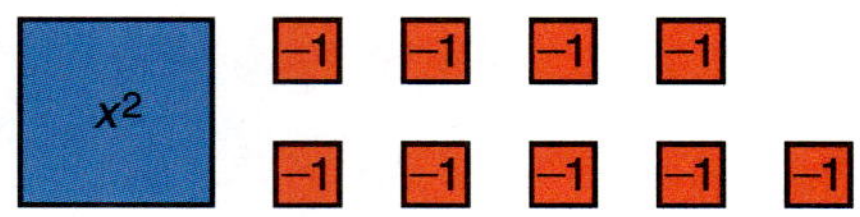

Step 2

Place the x^2-tile at the corner of the product mat. Arrange the 1-tiles into a 3-by-3 square.

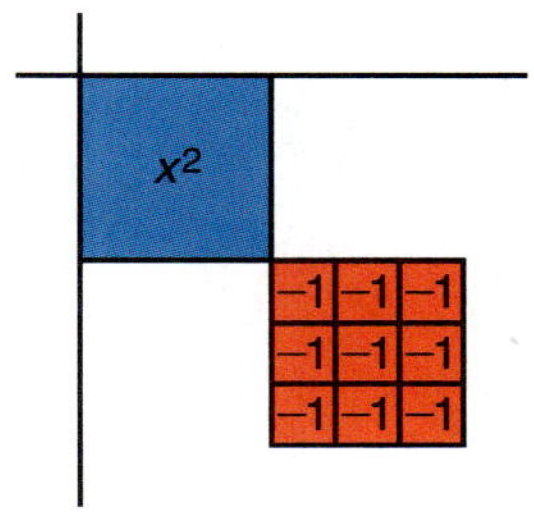

Step 3

Complete the rectangle using 3 zero pairs as shown.

The rectangle has a width of $x - 3$ and a length of $x + 3$. Therefore, $x^2 - 9 = (x - 3)(x + 3)$.

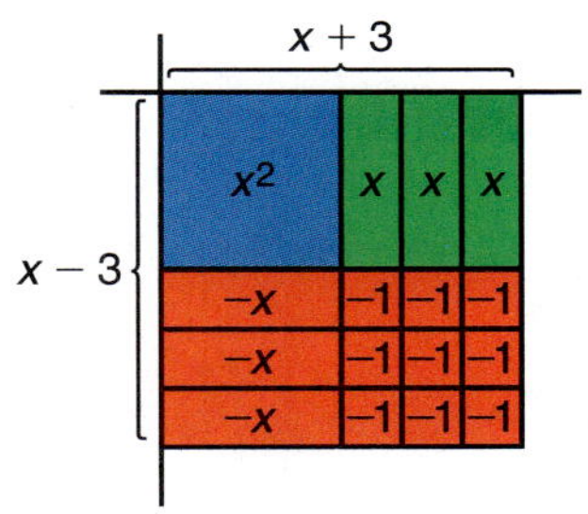

Your Turn

a. Use algebra tiles to factor each binomial.

$x^2 - 16$	$x^2 - 4$	$x^2 - 1$
$4x^2 - 9$	$9x^2 - 4$	$4x^2 - 1$

b. Binomials such as those in part a are called the *difference of squares*. Explain why you think this term applies to these binomials.

c. Study the factors of the binomials in part a. What do you notice about the signs of the factors? about the terms of the factors?

d. Use the pattern that you observe to factor $x^2 - 100$.

e. Use FOIL to check your answer in part d. Was your answer correct?

Why IT'S IMPORTANT

You can use factoring to solve problems involving geometry and number theory.

Recall that the product of the sum and difference of two binomials such as $n + 8$ and $n - 8$ is called the *difference of squares*.

$(n + 8)(n - 8) = n^2 - 8n + 8n - 64$ *Use FOIL.*

$= n^2 - 64$ *Note that this is the difference of two squares, n^2 and 64.*

The Modeling Mathematics activity suggests the following rule for factoring the difference of squares.

Difference of Squares $a^2 - b^2 = (a - b)(a + b) = (a + b)(a - b)$

You can use this rule to factor binomials that can be written in the form $a^2 - b^2$.

Example 1 **Factor each binomial.**

a. $m^2 - 81$

$$\begin{aligned} m^2 - 81 &= (m)^2 - (9)^2 && \textit{m} \cdot \textit{m} = \textit{m}^2 \textit{ and } 9 \cdot 9 = 81 \\ &= (m - 9)(m + 9) && \textit{Use the difference of squares.} \end{aligned}$$

b. $100s^2 - 25t^2$

$$\begin{aligned} 100s^2 - 25t^2 &= 25(4s^2 - t^2) && \textit{25 is the GCF.} \\ &= 25[(2s)^2 - t^2] && 2s \cdot 2s = 4s^2 \textit{ and } t \cdot t = t^2 \\ &= 25(2s - t)(2s + t) && \textit{Use the difference of squares.} \end{aligned}$$

c. $\frac{1}{9}x^2 - \frac{4}{25}y^2$

$$\begin{aligned} \frac{1}{9}x^2 - \frac{4}{25}y^2 &= \left(\frac{1}{3}x\right)^2 - \left(\frac{2}{5}y\right)^2 && \textit{Why?} \\ &= \left(\frac{1}{3}x - \frac{2}{5}y\right)\left(\frac{1}{3}x + \frac{2}{5}y\right) && \textit{Check this result by using FOIL.} \end{aligned}$$

Sometimes the terms of a binomial have common factors. If so, the GCF should always be factored out first. Occasionally, the difference of squares needs to be applied more than once or along with grouping in order to completely factor a polynomial.

Example 2 **Factor each polynomial.**

a. $20cd^2 - 125c^5$

$$\begin{aligned} 20cd^2 - 125c^5 &= 5c(4d^2 - 25c^4) && \textit{The GCF of } 20cd^2 \textit{ and } 125c^5 \textit{ is } 5c. \\ &= 5c(2d - 5c^2)(2d + 5c^2) && 2d \cdot 2d = 4d^2 \textit{ and } 5c^2 \cdot 5c^2 = 25c^4 \end{aligned}$$

b. $3k^4 - 48$

$$\begin{aligned} 3k^4 - 48 &= 3(k^4 - 16) && \textit{Why?} \\ &= 3(k^2 - 4)(k^2 + 4) && k^2 \cdot k^2 = k^4 \\ &= 3(k - 2)(k + 2)(k^2 + 4) && k^2 + 4 \textit{ cannot be factored. Why not?} \end{aligned}$$

c. $9x^5 + 11x^3y^2 - 100xy^4$

To factor the trinomial, we need two numbers whose product is −900 and whose sum is 11.

$$\begin{aligned} 9x^5 + 11x^3y^2 - 100xy^4 &= x(9x^4 + 11x^2y^2 - 100y^4) \\ &= x[(9x^4 - 25x^2y^2) + (36x^2y^2 - 100y^4)] \\ &= x[x^2(9x^2 - 25y^2) + 4y^2(9x^2 - 25y^2)] \\ &= x(x^2 + 4y^2)(9x^2 - 25y^2) \\ &= x(x^2 + 4y^2)(3x - 5y)(3x + 5y) \end{aligned}$$

The difference of squares can be used to multiply numbers mentally.

Example 3 **Show a method for finding the product of 37 and 43 mentally.**

Since $37 = 40 - 3$ and $43 = 40 + 3$, the product of (37)(43) can be expressed as $(40 - 3)(40 + 3)$.

$$\begin{aligned}(43)(37) &= (40 + 3)(40 - 3)\\ &= 40^2 - 3^2\\ &= 1600 - 9 \text{ or } 1591\end{aligned}$$

Pythagoras

According to the Pythagorean theorem, the sum of the squares of the measures of the legs of a right triangle equals the square of the measure of the hypotenuse.

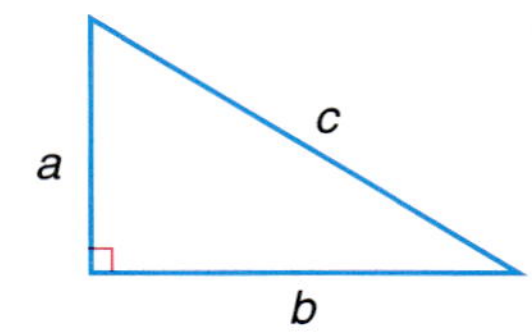

$$a^2 + b^2 = c^2$$

A **Pythagorean triple** is a group of three whole numbers that satisfy the equation $a^2 + b^2 = c^2$. For example, the numbers 3, 4, and 5 form a Pythagorean triple.

$$\begin{aligned}3^2 + 4^2 &\stackrel{?}{=} 5^2\\ 9 + 16 &\stackrel{?}{=} 25\\ 25 &= 25 \checkmark\end{aligned}$$

You can use the difference of squares to find Pythagorean triples.

Example 4 **Find a Pythagorean triple that includes 8 as one of its numbers.**

INTEGRATION Number Theory

First find the square of 8.	$8^2 = 64$
Factor 64 into two even factors or two odd factors.	$64 = (2)(32)$
Find the mean of the two factors.	$\frac{2 + 32}{2} = 17$

Complete the following statement.

$$\begin{aligned}(2)(32) &= (17 - \underline{?})(17 + \underline{?})\\ &= (17 - 15)(17 + 15)\\ &= 17^2 - 15^2\end{aligned}$$

Therefore, $8^2 = 17^2 - 15^2$ or $8^2 + 15^2 = 17^2$. The numbers 8, 15, and 17 form a Pythagorean triple.

FYI

Finding Pythagorean triples has interested mathematicians since ancient times. Some Pythagorean triples have been found on Babylonian cuneiform tablets.

CHECK FOR UNDERSTANDING

Communicating Mathematics

Study this lesson. Then complete the following.

1. **Describe** a binomial that is the difference of two squares.
2. **Write** a polynomial that is the difference of two squares. Factor your polynomial.
3. **Explain** how to factor a difference of squares by using the method for factoring trinomials presented in Lesson 10-3.
4. **You Decide** Patsy says that $28f^2 - 7g^2$ can be factored using the difference of squares. Sally says it cannot. Who is correct? Explain.
5. **Show** how to use the difference of squares to find $\frac{15}{16} \cdot \frac{17}{16}$.

MODELING MATHEMATICS

6. Use algebra tiles to factor $4 - x^2$.

Guided Practice

State whether each binomial can be factored as a difference of squares.

7. $p^2 - 49q^2$
8. $25a^2 - 81b^4$
9. $9x^2 + 16y^2$

Match each binomial with its factored form.

10. $4x^2 - 25$ a. $25(x - 1)(x + 1)$
11. $16x^2 - 4$ b. $(5x - 2)(5x + 2)$
12. $25x^2 - 4$ c. $(2x - 5)(2x + 5)$
13. $25x^2 - 25$ d. $4(2x - 1)(2x + 1)$

Factor each polynomial, if possible. If the polynomial cannot be factored, write *prime*.

14. $t^2 - 25$
15. $1 - 16g^2$
16. $2a^2 - 25$
17. $20m^2 - 45n^2$
18. $(a + b)^2 - c^2$
19. $x^4 - y^4$
20. Find the product of 17 and 23 mentally using difference of squares.
21. The difference of two numbers is 3. If the difference of their squares is 15, what is the sum of the numbers?

EXERCISES

Practice

Factor each polynomial, if possible. If the polynomial cannot be factored, write *prime*.

22. $w^2 - 81$
23. $4 - v^2$
24. $4q^2 - 9$
25. $100d^2 - 1$
26. $16a^2 - 25b^2$
27. $2z^2 - 98$
28. $9g^2 - 75$
29. $4t^2 - 27$
30. $8x^2 - 18$
31. $17 - 68k^2$
32. $25y^2 - 49z^4$
33. $36x^2 - 125y^2$
34. $-16 + 49h^2$
35. $16b^2c^4 + 25d^8$
36. $-9r^2 + 81$
37. $a^2x^2 - 0.64y^2$
38. $\frac{1}{16}x^2 - 25z^2$
39. $\frac{9}{2}a^2 - \frac{49}{2}b^2$
40. $(4p - 9q)^2 - 1$
41. $(a + b)^2 - (c + d)^2$
42. $25x^2 - (2y - 7z)^2$
43. $x^8 - 16y^4$
44. $a^6 - a^2b^4$
45. $a^4 + a^2b^2 - 20b^4$

Find each product mentally by using differences of squares.

46. 29×31
47. 24×26
48. 94×106

INTEGRATION
Geometry

Find the dimensions of a rectangle with the same area as the shaded region in each drawing. Assume that the dimensions of the rectangle must be represented by binomials with integral coefficients.

49.

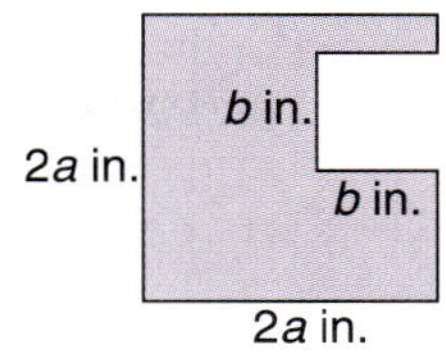

50.

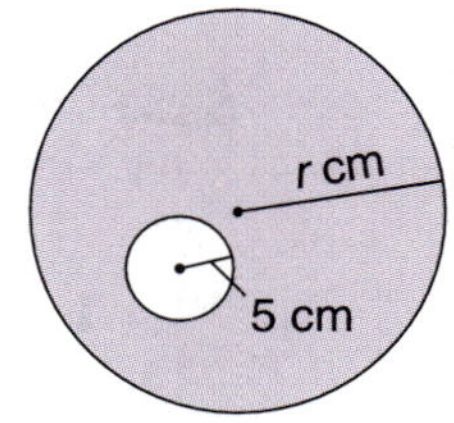

51.

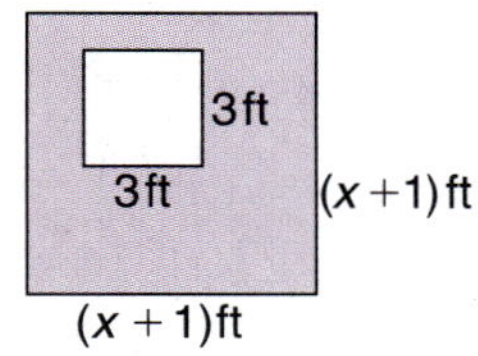

Find the dimensions of a rectangular solid having the given volume if each dimension can be written as a binomial with integral coefficients.

52. $(7mp^2 + 2np^2 - 7mr^2 - 2nr^2)$ cubic centimeters

53. $(5a^3 - 125ab^2 - 75b^3 + 3a^2b)$ cubic inches

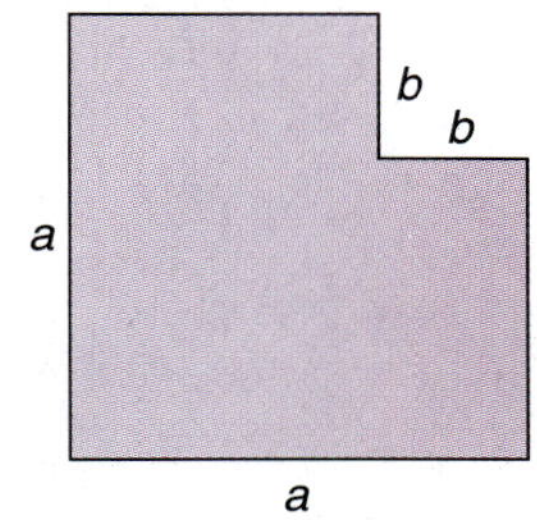

Critical Thinking

54. Show how to divide and rearrange the diagram at the right to show that $a^2 - b^2 = (a - b)(a + b)$. Make a diagram to show your reasoning.

Applications and Problem Solving

55. Geometry The side of a square is x centimeters long. The length of a rectangle is 5 centimeters longer than a side of the square, and the width of the rectangle is 5 centimeters shorter than the side of the square.

a. Which has the greater area, the square or the rectangle?

b. How much greater is that area?

56. Number Theory Find a Pythagorean triple that includes 7.

57. Number Theory Find a Pythagorean triple that includes 9.

58. Geometry Express the square of the length of the missing side of the triangle at the right as the product of two binomials.

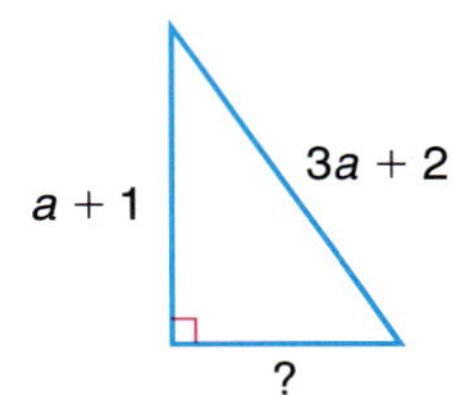

Mixed Review

59. Guess and Check Julie went to the corner store to buy four items. The clerk at the store had to use a calculator to add the four prices, since her cash register was broken. When the clerk figured Julie's bill, she mistakenly hit the multiplication key each time, instead of the plus key. Julie had already mentally computed her sum, so, realizing that the total was actually correct, she paid the clerk the amount of \$7.11. How much was each item that Julie bought? (Lesson 10–3)

60. Find $(n^2 + 5n + 3) + (2n^2 + 8n + 8)$. (Lesson 9–5)

61. Use elimination to solve the system of equations. (Lesson 8–4)

$x + y = 20$

$0.4x + 0.15y = 4$

62. Probability Use a tree diagram to find the probability of getting at least one tail when four fair coins are tossed. (Lesson 7–5)

63. Graph $6x - 3y = 6$. (Lesson 6–5)

64. Write an equation for the relation given in the chart below. (Lesson 5–6)

a	1	2	3	4	5	6
b	1	4	7	10	13	16

65. Graph $M(0, 3)$. (Lesson 5–1)

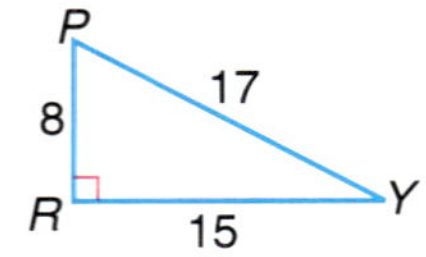

66. Trigonometry For the triangle at the right, find $\sin Y$, $\cos Y$, and $\tan Y$ to the nearest thousandth. (Lesson 4–3)

67. Statistics The populations in millions of the 50 states in 1993 are shown below. Find the mean, median, and mode population. (Lesson 3–7)

1.2	1.1	0.6	6.0	1.0	3.3	18.2	7.9	12.0
11.1	5.7	11.7	9.5	5.0	4.5	2.8	5.2	0.6
0.7	1.6	2.5	0.7	5.0	6.5	1.8	6.9	3.6
6.9	13.7	3.8	5.1	4.2	2.6	2.4	4.3	3.2
18.0	0.8	1.1	0.5	3.6	1.6	3.9	1.9	1.4
5.3	3.0	31.2	0.6	1.2				

68. In Mr. Tucker's algebra class, students can get extra points for finding the correct solution to the "Riddle of the Week." One week, Mr. Tucker posed this riddle. (Lesson 2–9)

Luis is 10 years older than his brother. Next year, he will be three times as old as his brother. How old is Luis now?

Josh's answer is: *Luis is 12 years old and his brother is 4.*

a. If the brother's age is represented by a, what is Luis' age?

b. What will be the brother's age next year?

c. Does Josh get the extra points for his answer? Why or why not?

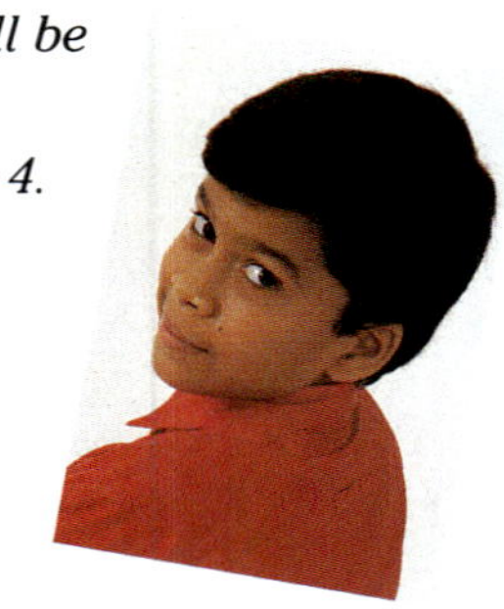

WORKING ON THE In·ves·ti·ga·tion

Refer to the Investigation on pages 554–555.

the BRICKYARD

Suppose your manager, Ms. Brown, also gave you certain specifications as to which bricks to use and how many of each kind to use.

1 Using one of each type of brick, is there a rectangular pattern you can make with just three bricks? Justify your answer.

2 Select two of one type of brick and one each of the other two types. Is there a way to arrange these bricks into a rectangular pattern? If so, is there more than one pattern? Sketch a drawing of the rectangular pattern(s) you found and label the size of each brick.

3 If there is not a way to arrange the bricks into a rectangular pattern, explain why not. Is there more than one possible choice of four bricks that will make a rectangular pattern?

4 Now, using at least one brick of each type, find all the different patterns (if any) there are to arrange the bricks into a rectangular pattern of five bricks.

5 Now try designs using at least one of each type for a pattern of six bricks, seven bricks, eight bricks, nine bricks, and ten bricks.

6 Draw a diagram of all of the possible patterns. Label the size of each brick. Describe how you developed a process for finding the patterns. Are there generalizations you can make about the number of bricks and rectangular arrangements? Justify any generalizations. Explain how you know you have all of the possible patterns.

Add the results of your work to your Investigation Folder.

10-5 Perfect Squares and Factoring

What YOU'LL LEARN

- To identify and factor perfect square trinomials.

Why IT'S IMPORTANT

You can use factoring to solve problems involving finance and construction.

INTEGRATION
Number Theory

Recall that the numbers 1, 4, 9, 16, and 25 are called *perfect square* numbers, since they can each be expressed as the square of an integer.

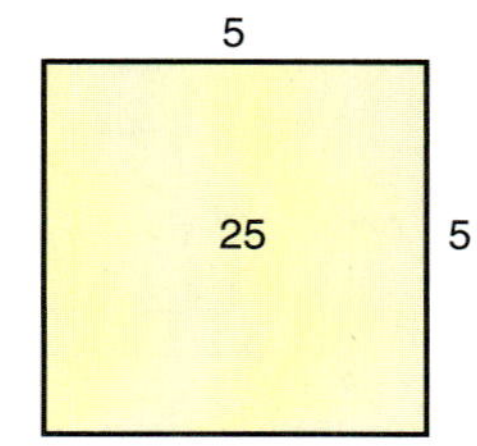

The equation $5^2 = 25$ can be modeled as the area of a square having a side of length 5 as shown at the right.

Suppose $(3 + 2)$ is substituted for 5. Then $(3 + 2)^2$ can be modeled by using a 5-by-5 square and divided it into four regions as shown at the right. The sum of the areas of the four regions equals the area of the square.

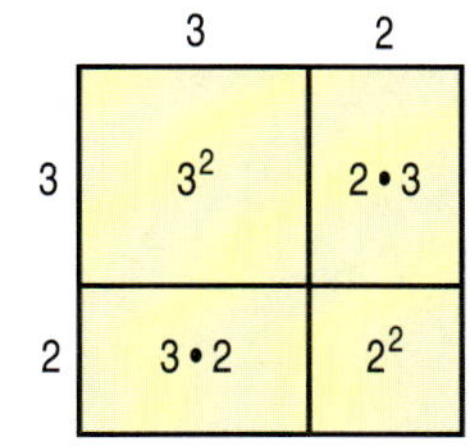

$$\begin{aligned}(3 + 2)^2 &= 3^2 + (2 \cdot 3) + (3 \cdot 2) + 2^2\\ &= 3^2 + (3 \cdot 2) + (3 \cdot 2) + 2^2\\ &= 3^2 + 2(3 \cdot 2) + 2^2\end{aligned}$$

The last line shows a very interesting relationship.

$$(3 + 2)^2 = \overbrace{3^2}^{\text{square}} + \underbrace{2(3 \cdot 2)}_{\text{twice the product of 3 and 2}} + \overbrace{2^2}^{\text{square}}$$

The square of this binomial is the sum of

- the square of the first term,
- twice the product of the first and second term, and
- the square of the second term.

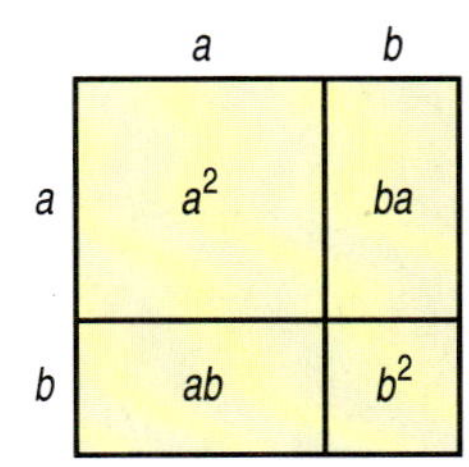

This observation is generalized by the model at the right.

$(a + b)^2 = a^2 + 2ab + b^2$

LOOK BACK

You can refer to Lesson 9-8 for information on squares of sums and squares of differences.

To square $(a - b)$, write the binomial as $[a + (-b)]$ and then square this binomial.

$$\begin{aligned}(a - b)^2 &= [a + (-b)]^2\\ &= a^2 + 2a(-b) + (-b)^2\\ &= a^2 - 2ab + b^2\end{aligned}$$

Products of the form $(a + b)^2$ and $(a - b)^2$ are called perfect squares, and their expansions are **perfect square trinomials.**

Perfect Square Trinomials	$(a + b)^2 = a^2 + 2ab + b^2$ $(a - b)^2 = a^2 - 2ab + b^2$

These patterns can be used to factor trinomials.

Model	Squaring a Binomial	Factoring a Perfect Square Trinomial
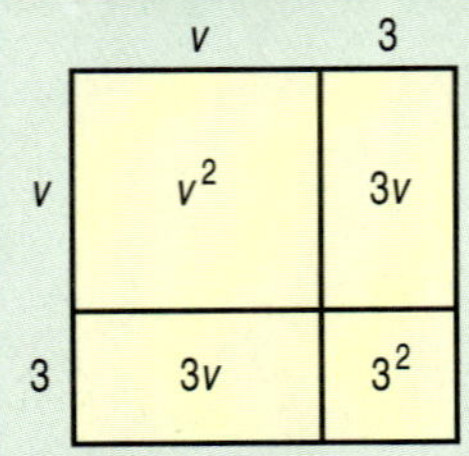	$(v+3)^2 = v^2 + 2(v)(3) + 3^2$ $= v^2 + 6v + 9$	$v^2 + 6v + 9 = (v)^2 + 2(v)(3) + (3)^2$ $= (v+3)^2$
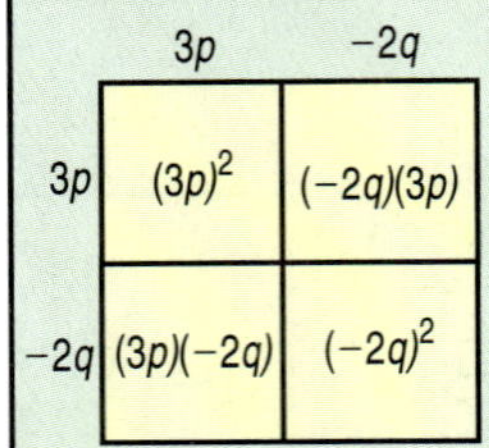	$(3p-2q)^2 = (3p)^2 + 2(3p)(-2q) + (-2q)^2$ $= 9p^2 - 12pq + 4q^2$	$9p^2 - 12pq + 4q^2 = (3p)^2 - 2(3p)(2q) + (2q)^2$ $= (3p-2q)^2$

To determine whether a trinomial can be factored using these patterns, you must decide if it is a perfect square trinomial. In other words, you must determine if it can be written in the form $a^2 + 2ab + b^2$ or in the form $a^2 - 2ab + b^2$. For a trinomial to be in one of these forms, the following must be satisfied.

- The first term is a perfect square.
- The third term is a perfect square.
- The middle term is either 2 or −2 times the product of the square root of the first term and the square root of the last term.

Example 1 **Determine whether each trinomial is a perfect square trinomial. If so, factor it.**

a. $4y^2 + 36yz + 81z^2$

To determine whether $4y^2 - 36yz + 81z^2$ is a perfect square trinomial, answer each question.

- Is the first term a perfect square? $4y^2 \stackrel{?}{=} (2y)^2$ *yes*
- Is the last term a perfect square? $81z^2 \stackrel{?}{=} (9z)^2$ *yes*
- Is the middle term twice the product of $2y$ and $9z$? $36yz \stackrel{?}{=} 2(2y)(9z)$ *yes*

$4y^2 + 36yz + 81z^2$ is a perfect square trinomial.

$$4y^2 + 36yz + 81z^2 = (2y)^2 + 2(2y)(9z) + (9z)^2$$
$$= (2y + 9z)^2$$

b. $9n^2 + 49 - 21n$

First arrange the terms of $9n^2 + 49 - 21n$ so that the powers of n are in descending order.

$9n^2 + 49 - 21n = 9n^2 - 21n + 49$

- Is the first term a perfect square? $9n^2 \stackrel{?}{=} (3n)^2$ *yes*
- Is the last term a perfect square? $49 \stackrel{?}{=} (7)^2$ *yes*
- Is the middle term the product of −2, $3n$, and 7? $-21n \stackrel{?}{=} -2(3n)(7)$ *no*

$9n^2 - 21n + 49$ is not a perfect square trinomial.

Example 2 Suppose the dimensions of a rectangle can be written as binomials with integral coefficients. Is the rectangle with the area of $(121x^2 - 198xy + 81y^2)$ square millimeters a square? If so, what is the measure of each side of the square?

INTEGRATION Geometry

Explore You know that the dimensions of the rectangle can be written as binomials with integral coefficients. The problem gives the area of a rectangle and asks whether it is a square. If it is a square, you need to find the dimension of each side.

Plan The rectangle is a square if $121x^2 - 198xy + 81y^2$ is a perfect square trinomial. You must answer three questions to determine if it is a perfect square trinomial. If it is a perfect square trinomial, you must factor it to find the measure of each side of the square.

Solve

- Is the first term a perfect square? $121x^2 \stackrel{?}{=} (11x)^2$ *yes*
- Is the last term a perfect square? $81y^2 \stackrel{?}{=} (9y)^2$ *yes*
- Is the middle term the product of -2, $11x$, and $9y$? $-198xy \stackrel{?}{=} -2(11x)(9y)$ *yes*

Since $121x^2 - 198xy + 81y^2$ is a perfect square trinomial, the rectangle is a square. To find the measure of each side, factor the trinomial.

$$\begin{aligned} 121x^2 - 198xy + 81y^2 &= (11x)^2 - 2(11x)(9y) + (9y)^2 \\ &= (11x - 9y)^2 \end{aligned}$$

The measure of each side is $(11x - 9y)$ millimeters.

Examine If each side of the square is $(11x - 9y)$ millimeters, then the area of the square is $(11x - 9y)^2$ square millimeters. Use FOIL to see if $(11x + 9y)^2$ equals $(121x^2 - 198xy + 81y^2)$.

$$\begin{aligned} (11x - 9y)^2 &= (11x - 9y)(11x - 9y) \\ &= (11x)(11x) + (11x)(-9y) + (-9y)(11x) + (-9y)(-9y) \\ &= 121x^2 - 99xy - 99xy + 81y^2 \\ &= 121x^2 - 198xy + 81y^2 \ \checkmark \end{aligned}$$

As you continue your study of mathematics, you will find that forming a perfect square trinomial can sometimes be a useful tool for solving problems.

Example 3 Determine all values of k that make $25x^2 + kx + 49$ a perfect square trinomial.

$$25x^2 + kx + 49 = (5x)^2 + kx + (7)^2$$

In order for this to be a perfect square trinomial, kx must equal either $2(5x)(7)$ or $-2(5x)(7)$. *Why?*

$kx = 2(5x)(7)$	or	$kx = -2(5x)(7)$
$kx = 70x$		$kx = -70x$
$k = 70$		$k = -70$

Check to see if $25x^2 + 70x + 49$ and $25x^2 - 70x + 49$ are perfect square trinomials.

In this chapter, you have learned various methods to factor different types of polynomials. The following chart summarizes these methods and can help you decide when to use a specific method.

Check for:	Number of Terms		
	Two	Three	Four or More
greatest common factor	✓	✓	✓
difference of squares	✓		
perfect square trinomials		✓	
trinomial that has two binomial factors		✓	
pairs of terms that have a common monomial factor			✓

Whenever there is a GCF other than 1, always factor it out first. Then, check the appropriate factoring methods in the order shown in the table. Use these methods to factor until all of the factors are prime.

Example 4 **Factor each polynomial.**

a. $\mathbf{4k^2 - 100}$

First check for a GCF. Then, since the polynomial has two terms, check for the difference of squares.

$$4k^2 - 100 = 4(k^2 - 25) \quad \textit{The GCF is 4.}$$
$$= 4(k - 5)(k + 5) \quad \textit{$k^2 - 25$ is the difference of squares since $k \cdot k = k^2$ and $5 \cdot 5 = 25$.}$$

Therefore, $4k^2 - 25$ is completely factored as $4(k - 5)(k + 5)$.

b. $\mathbf{9x^2 - 3x - 20}$

The polynomial has three terms. The GCF is 1. $9x^2 = (3x)^2$, but -20 is not a perfect square. The trinomial is not a perfect square trinomial.

Are there two numbers whose product is $9(-20)$ or -180 and whose sum is -3? Yes, the product of -15 and 12 is -180, and their sum is -3.

$$9x^2 - 3x - 20 = 9x^2 - 15x + 12x - 20$$
$$= (9x^2 - 15x) + (12x - 20)$$
$$= 3x(3x - 5) + 4(3x - 5)$$
$$= (3x + 4)(3x - 5)$$

Therefore, $9x^2 - 3x - 20$ is completely factored as $(3x + 4)(3x - 5)$.

c. $\mathbf{4m^4n + 6m^3n - 16m^2n^2 - 24mn^2}$

Since the polynomial has four terms, first check for the GCF and then check for pairs of terms that have a common factor.

$$4m^4n + 6m^3n - 16m^2n^2 - 24mn^2 = 2mn(2m^3 + 3m^2 - 8mn - 12n)$$
$$= 2mn[(2m^3 + 3m^2) + (-8mn - 12n)]$$
$$= 2mn[m^2(2m + 3) + (-4n)(2m + 3)]$$
$$= 2mn(m^2 - 4n)(2m + 3)$$

Therefore, $4m^4n + 6m^3n - 16m^2n^2 - 24mn^2$ is completely factored as $2mn(m^2 - 4n)(2m + 3)$.

CHECK FOR UNDERSTANDING

Communicating Mathematics

Study the lesson. Then complete the following.

1. a. **Draw** a rectangle to show how to factor $4x^2 + 12x + 9$. Label the dimensions and the area of the rectangle.
   b. **Explain** why the name *perfect square trinomial* is appropriate for this trinomial.
2. a. **Write** a polynomial that is a perfect square trinomial.
   b. **Factor** your trinomial.
3. a. **Describe** the first step in factoring any polynomial.
   b. **Explain** why this step is important.
4. **You Decide** Robert says that $12a^4 - 8a^2 - 4$ is completely factored as $4(3a^2 + 1)(a^2 - 1)$. Samuel says that he can factor it further. Who is correct? Explain your answer.

MATH JOURNAL

5. **Assess Yourself** Describe the relationship between multiplying polynomials and factoring polynomials. Do you prefer to multiply polynomials or to factor polynomials? Explain.

Guided Practice

Complete.

6. $b^2 + 10b + 25 = (b + \underline{\ ?\ })^2$
7. $64a^2 - 16a + 1 = (\underline{\ ?\ } - 1)^2$
8. $81n^2 + 36n + 4 = (\underline{\ ?\ } + 2)^2$
9. $1 - 12c + 36c^2 = (1 - \underline{\ ?\ })^2$

Determine whether each trinomial is a perfect square trinomial. If so, factor it.

10. $t^2 + 18t + 81$
11. $4n^2 - 28n + 49$
12. $9y^2 + 30y - 25$
13. $16b^2 - 56bc + 49c^2$

Factor each polynomial, if possible. If the polynomial cannot be factored, write *prime*.

14. $15g^2 + 25$
15. $4a^2 - 36b^2$
16. $x^2 + 6x - 9$
17. $50g^2 + 40g + 8$
18. $9t^3 + 66t^2 - 48t$
19. $20a^2x - 4a^2y - 45xb^2 + 9yb^2$
20. a. Find the missing value that makes the following a perfect square trinomial.
   $$9x^2 + 24x + \underline{\ ?\ }$$
   b. Copy and complete the model for this trinomial.

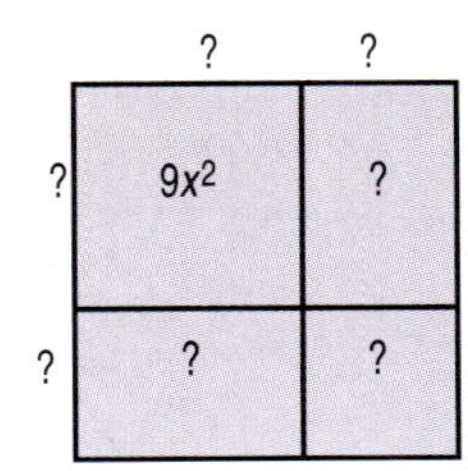

EXERCISES

Practice

Determine whether each trinomial is a perfect square trinomial. If so, factor it.

21. $r^2 - 8r + 16$
22. $d^2 + 50d + 225$
23. $49p^2 - 28p + 4$
24. $4y^2 + 12yz + 9z^2$
25. $49s^2 - 42st + 36t^2$
26. $25y^2 + 20yz - 4z^2$
27. $4m^2 + 4mn + n^2$
28. $81t^2 - 180t + 100$

Determine whether each trinomial is a perfect square trinomial. If so, factor it.

29. $2g^2 - 10g + 25$
30. $1 + 100h^2 + 20h$
31. $64b^2 - 72b + 81$
32. $9a^2 - 24a + 16$
33. $\frac{1}{4}a^2 + 3a + 9$
34. $\frac{4}{9}x^2 - \frac{16}{3}x + 16$

Factor each polynomial, if possible. If the polynomial cannot be factored, write *prime*.

35. $45a^2 - 32ab$
36. $c^2 - 5c + 6$
37. $v^2 - 30v + 225$
38. $m^2 - p^4$
39. $9a^2 + 12a - 4$
40. $3a^2b + 6ab + 9ab^2$
41. $3y^2 - 147$
42. $20n^2 + 34n + 6$
43. $18a^2 - 48a + 32$
44. $3m^3 + 48m^2n + 192mn^2$
45. $x^2y^2 - y^2 - z^2 + x^2z^2$
46. $5a^2 + 7a + 6b^2 - 4b$
47. $4a^3 + 3a^2b^2 + 8a + 6b^2$
48. $(x + y)^2 - (w - z)^2$
49. $0.7p^2 - 3.5pq + 4.2q^2$
50. $(x + 2y)^2 - 3(x + 2y) + 2$
51. $g^4 + 6g^3 + 9g^2 - 3g^2h - 18gh - 27h$
52. $12mp^2 - 15np^2 - 16m + 20np - 16mp + 20n$

Determine all values of *k* that make each of the following a perfect square trinomial.

53. $25t^2 - kt + 121$
54. $64x^2 - 16xy + k$
55. $ka^2 - 72ab + 144b^2$
56. $169n^2 + knp + 100p^2$

INTEGRATION
Geometry

57. The area of a circle is $(9y^2 + 78y + 169)\pi$ square centimeters. What is the diameter of the circle?
58. The volume of a rectangular prism is $(x^3y - 63y^2 + 7x^2 - 9xy^3)$ cubic inches. Find the dimensions of the prism, if its dimensions can be represented by binomials with integral coefficients.
59. The length of a rectangle is 3 centimeters greater than the length of a side of a square. The width of the rectangle is one-half the length of the side of the square. If the area of the square is $(16x^2 - 56x + 49)$ square centimeters, what is the area of the rectangle?
60. The area of a square is $(81 - 90x + 25x^2)$ square meters. If x is a positive integer, what is the least possible perimeter measure for the square?

LOOK BACK

You can refer to Lesson 2-8 to review square roots.

Critical Thinking

61. Consider the value of $\sqrt{a^2 - 2ab + b^2}$.
 a. Under what circumstances does the value equal $a - b$?
 b. Under what circumstances does the value equal $b - a$?
 c. Under what circumstances does the value equal $a - b$ and $b - a$?

Applications and Problem Solving

62. **Construction** The builders of an office complex are looking for a square lot. They found a vacant lot that was long enough. However, its length was 60 yards more than its width w, so it was not a square. It also did not have enough area; they needed 900 additional square yards. So they are still looking for a lot. Write an expression for the length of a side of the square lot they should be looking for.

63. **Investments** Tamara plans to invest some money in a certificate of deposit. After 2 years, the value of the certificate will be $p + 2pr + pr^2$, where p represents the amount of money invested and r represents the annual interest rate.
   a. If Tamara invests \$1000 at an annual interest rate of 8%, find the value of the certificate after 2 years.
   b. Factor the expression that represents the value of the certificate after 2 years.
   c. Suppose Tamara invests \$1000 at 7%. Use your expression in part b to find the value of the certificate after 2 years.
   d. Which form of the expression do you prefer to use to make your computations? Explain.

Mixed Review

64. Factor $45x^2 - 20y^2z^2$. (Lesson 10–4)

65. Simplify $2.5t(8t - 12) + 5.1(6t^2 + 10t - 20)$. (Lesson 9–6)

66. Simplify $(3a^2)(4a^3)$. (Lesson 9–1)

67. **Employment** Mike's parents allow him to work 30 hours a week. He would like to use this time to help out in his parents' hardware store, but it pays only \$5 per hour. He could mow lawns for \$7.50 per hour, but there is less than 20 hours of lawn work available. What is the maximum amount of time Mike can work in his parents' store and still make at least \$175 per week? (Lesson 8–5)

68. **Physical Science** A European-made hot tub is advertised to have a temperature of 35°C to 40°C, inclusive. What is the temperature range for the hot tub in degrees Fahrenheit? (*Hint:* Use $F = \frac{9}{5}C + 32$.) (Lesson 7–4)

Year	Median Income
1970	\$ 8734
1975	11,800
1980	17,710
1981	19,074
1982	20,191
1983	21,018
1984	22,415
1985	23,618
1986	24,897
1987	26,061
1988	27,225
1989	28,905
1990	29,943
1991	30,126
1992	30,786

Source: U.S. Census Bureau

69. **Statistics** The median incomes of American families since 1970 are shown in the table at the left. (Lesson 6–3)
   a. Make a scatter plot of the data.
   b. Can the data be approximated by a straight line? If so, graph the line and write an equation of this line.
   c. Estimate the median family income for this year.

70. Refer to Exercise 67 on page 586. Find the range and interquartile range of the state populations. (Lesson 5–7)

71. **Probability** If a card is selected at random from a deck of 52 cards, what are the odds of selecting a club? (Lesson 4–6)

72. **Geometry** ΔABC and ΔDEF are similar. If $a = 5$, $d = 11$, $f = 6$, and $e = 14$, find the missing measures. (Lesson 4–2)

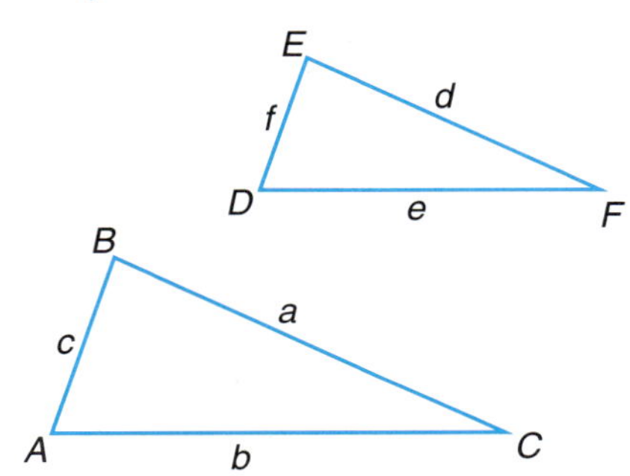

73. **National Landmarks** The Statue of Liberty and the pedestal on which it stands are 302 feet tall altogether. The pedestal is 2 feet shorter than the statue. How tall is the statue? (Lesson 3–3)

74. **Basketball** In 1962, Wilt Chamberlain set a professional basketball record by averaging 50.4 points per game for a few games. If he had been able to maintain this average over an 82-game season, how many total points would he have scored? Round to the nearest whole number. (Lesson 2–6)

10-6 Solving Equations by Factoring

What YOU'LL LEARN

- To use the zero product property to solve equations.

Why IT'S IMPORTANT

You can use equations to solve problems involving diving, history, and bridges.

APPLICATION

Diving

In Acapulco, Mexico, divers leap from La Quebrada, the "Break in the Rocks," diving headfirst into the Pacific Ocean 87 feet below. Because the base rocks extend out 21 feet from the starting point, the divers must jump outward 27 feet. The equation $h = 87 + 8t - 16t^2$ describes the height h (in feet) of a diver t seconds after leaping.

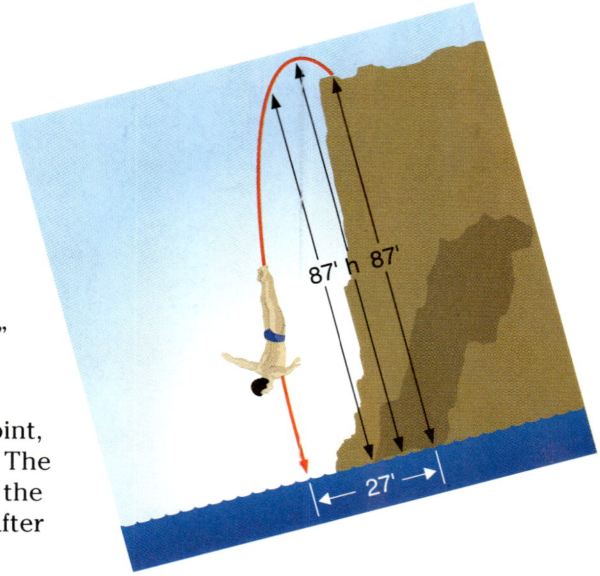

To find the time at which the diver reaches the highest point of the dive, you can find the time at which he will be 87 feet above the ocean on his way down. The diver springs upward at the beginning of the dive and will be at the highest point halfway between this time and the start of the dive.

$$87 = 87 + 8t - 16t^2$$

$$0 = 8t - 16t^2 \quad \textit{Subtract 87 from each side.}$$

$$0 = 8t(1 - 2t) \quad \textit{Factor } 8t - 16t^2.$$

To solve this equation, you need to find the values of t that make the product $8t(1 - 2t)$ equal to 0. Consider the following products.

$$8(0) = 0 \qquad 0(-17)(0) = 0 \qquad (29 - 11)(0) = 0 \qquad 0(2a - 3) = 0$$

Notice that in each case, *at least one* of the factors is zero. These examples illustrate the **zero product property.**

Zero Product Property	**For all numbers a and b, if $ab = 0$, then $a = 0$, $b = 0$, or both a and b equal 0.**

Thus, if an equation can be written in the form $ab = 0$, then the zero product property can be applied to solve that equation.

Use this information to solve the equation about the diver. If $0 = 8t(1 - 2t)$, then either $8t = 0$ or $(1 - 2t) = 0$.

$$8t = 0 \quad \text{or} \quad 1 - 2t = 0$$

$$t = 0 \qquad\qquad 1 = 2t$$

$$\frac{1}{2} = t$$

The diver will be 87 feet above the ocean at the start of the dive ($t = 0$) and $\frac{1}{2}$ second later. He will be at the highest point of the dive $\frac{1}{4}$ second after starting the dive. *You will solve more problems about this dive in Example 5.*

Example 1 **Solve each equation. Then check the solution.**

a. $(p - 8)(2p + 7) = 0$

If $(p - 8)(2p + 7) = 0$, then $p - 8 = 0$ or $2p + 7 = 0$. *Zero product property*

$p - 8 = 0$ or $2p + 7 = 0$

$p = 8$ $\qquad 2p = -7$

$p = -\frac{7}{2}$

Check: $(p - 8)(2p + 7) = 0$

$(8 - 8)[2(8) + 7] \stackrel{?}{=} 0$ or $\left(-\frac{7}{2} - 8\right)\left[2\left(-\frac{7}{2}\right) + 7\right] \stackrel{?}{=} 0$

$0(23) \stackrel{?}{=} 0$ $\qquad -\frac{23}{2}(0) \stackrel{?}{=} 0$

$0 = 0$ ✔ $\qquad 0 = 0$ ✔

The solution set is $\left\{8, -\frac{7}{2}\right\}$

b. $t^2 = 9t$

Write the equation in the form $ab = 0$.

$t^2 = 9t$

$t^2 - 9t = 0$

$t(t - 9) = 0$ *Factor out the GCF, t.*

$t = 0$ or $t - 9 = 0$ *Zero product property*

$t = 9$

Check: $t^2 = 9t$

$(0)^2 \stackrel{?}{=} 9(0)$ or $(9)^2 \stackrel{?}{=} 9(9)$

$0 = 0$ ✔ $\qquad 81 = 81$ ✔

The solution set is $\{0, 9\}$.

To solve $t^2 = 9t$ in Example 1b, you may be tempted to divide each side of the equation by t. If you did, the solution would be 9. Since it is not possible for an equation to have two different solutions, which process is correct? Recall that division by 0 is undefined. But when you divide each side by t, t is unknown. Thus, you may actually be dividing by 0. In fact, 0 is one of the solutions of this equation. To avoid situations like this, keep in mind that you cannot divide each side of an equation by an expression containing a variable unless you know that the value of the expression is not 0.

Example 2 **Solve $m^2 + 144 = 24m$. Then check the solution.**

$m^2 + 144 = 24m$

$m^2 - 24m + 144 = 0$ *Rewrite the equation.*

$(m - 12)^2 = 0$ *Factor $m^2 - 24m + 144$ as a perfect square trinomial.*

$(m - 12)(m - 12) = 0$

$m - 12 = 0$ or $m - 12 = 0$

$m = 12$ $\qquad m = 12$

(continued on the next page)

Check: $m^2 + 144 = 24m$

$$(12)^2 + 144 \stackrel{?}{=} 24(12)$$
$$144 + 144 \stackrel{?}{=} 288$$
$$288 = 288 \checkmark$$

The solution set is $\{12\}$.

You can apply the zero product property to an equation that is written as the product of any number of factors equal to zero.

Example 3 **Solve $5b^3 + 34b^2 = 7b$.**

$$5b^3 + 34b^2 = 7b$$

$5b^3 + 34b^2 - 7b = 0$ *Arrange the terms so the powers of b are in descending order.*

$b(5b^2 + 34b - 7) = 0$ *Factor the GCF, b.*

$b(5b - 1)(b + 7) = 0$ *Factor $5b^2 + 34b - 7$.*

$b = 0$ or $5b - 1 = 0$ or $b + 7 = 0$

$5b = 1$ $\quad$ $b = -7$

$b = \frac{1}{5}$

The solution set is $\left\{0, \frac{1}{5}, -7\right\}$. *Check this result.*

If an object is launched from ground level, it reaches its maximum height in the air at the time halfway between the launch and impact times. Its height above the ground after t seconds is given by the formula $h = vt - 16t^2$. In this formula, h represents the height of the object in feet, and v represents the object's initial upward velocity in feet per second.

Example 4 **A flare is launched from a life raft with an initial upward velocity of 144 feet per second. How long will the flare stay aloft? What will be the maximum height attained by the flare?**

APPLICATION
Rescue Missions

Explore You know the initial upward velocity of the flare is 144 feet per second. You need to determine the length of time the flare will be in the air and how high the flare will go.

Plan The flare will be in the air until the height is 0. Use the general formula $h = vt - 16t^2$ to determine how long the flare will be in the air. The flare will reach its maximum height halfway between the launch and impact times. Use the formula again to determine the height at the middle of its flight.

Solve

$h = vt - 16t^2$

$0 = 144t - 16t^2$ *Replace v with 144.*

$0 = 16t(9 - t)$

$16t = 0$ or $9 - t = 0$

$t = 0$ $\quad$ $9 = t$

Since 0 seconds is the launch time, the landing time is 9 seconds. The flare will be aloft for 9 seconds. It will reach its maximum height halfway through its flight time at $\frac{1}{2}(9)$ or 4.5 seconds.

$$h = 144t - 16t^2$$
$$= 144(4.5) - 16(4.5)^2 \quad \textit{Replace } t \textit{ with 4.5.}$$
$$= 648 - 324$$
$$= 324$$

The flare will reach its maximum height of 324 feet after 4.5 seconds.

Examine Check to see if the flare will actually be at a height of 0 feet after 9 seconds.

$$0 \stackrel{?}{=} 144(9) - 16(9)^2$$
$$0 \stackrel{?}{=} 1296 - 1296$$
$$0 = 0 \checkmark$$

The flare will be aloft for 9 seconds and the maximum height will be reached after 4.5 seconds.

Example 5 APPLICATION **Diving**

Refer to the application at the beginning of the lesson.

a. What is the diver's maximum height?

b. When will the diver enter the water?

a. The diver will reach the maximum height after $\frac{1}{4}$ second.

$$h = 87 + 8t - 16t^2$$
$$= 87 + 8\left(\frac{1}{4}\right) - 16\left(\frac{1}{4}\right)^2$$
$$= 87 + 2 - 1$$
$$= 88$$

The diver's maximum height is 88 feet. *Does this seem reasonable?*

b. When the diver reaches 88 feet, his upward motion has stopped and the diver begins to fall to the sea below. His velocity at this time is 0. Therefore, the vt term in the general formula $h = vt - 16t^2$ is also 0.

$$88 = 16t^2 \quad \textit{Why does 88 equal } 16t^2 \textit{ instead of } -16t^2\textit{?}$$
$$5.5 = t^2$$
$$2.35 \approx t$$

It takes the diver $\frac{1}{4}$ or 0.25 second to reach the maximum height and about another 2.35 seconds to reach the water. The diver will reach the water about 0.25 + 2.35 or 2.60 seconds after he starts his dive.

CHECK FOR UNDERSTANDING

Communicating Mathematics

Study the lesson. Then complete the following.

1. If the product of two or more factors is zero, what must be true of the factors?
2. **Describe** the type of equation that can be solved by using the zero-product property.
3. Can $(x + 3)(x - 5) = 0$ be solved by dividing each side of the equation by $x + 3$? Explain.
4. **You Decide** Diana says that if $(x + 2)(x - 3) = 8$, then $x + 2 = 8$ or $x - 3 = 8$. Caitlin disagrees. Who is correct?

Guided Practice

Solve each equation. Check your solutions.

5. $g(g + 5) = 0$
6. $(n - 4)(n + 2) = 0$
7. $5m = 3m^2$
8. $x^2 = 5x + 14$
9. $7r^2 = 70r - 175$
10. $a^3 - 29a^2 = -28a$
11. **Geometry** The dimensions of a rectangle are $(2x + 9)$ inches and $(2x - 1)$ inches. A square with side x inches is cut out of one of the corners. If the remaining area is 195 square inches, what is x?

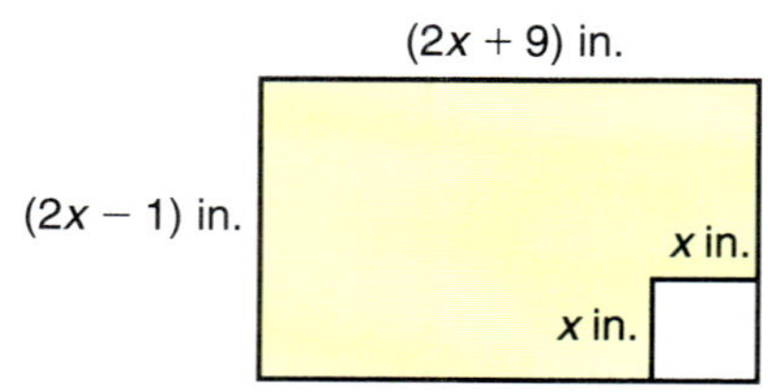

12. **Baseball** Nolan Ryan, the greatest strike-out pitcher in the history of baseball, had a fastball clocked at 103 miles per hour, which is 151 feet per second.
    a. If he threw the ball directly upward with the same velocity, how many seconds would it take for the ball to return to his glove? (*Hint:* Use the general formula $h = vt - 16t^2$.)
    b. How high above his glove would the ball travel?

Top Five List

First professional pitchers to throw a perfect game

1. Lee Pichmond, June 12, 1880
2. Monte Ward, June 17, 1880
3. Cy Young, May 5, 1904
4. Adrian Joss, Oct. 2, 1908
5. Charlie Robertson, Apr. 30, 1922

EXERCISES

Practice

Solve each equation. Check your solutions.

13. $x(x - 24) = 0$
14. $(q + 4)(3q - 15) = 0$
15. $(2x - 3)(3x - 8) = 0$
16. $(4a + 5)(3a - 7) = 0$
17. $a^2 + 13a + 36 = 0$
18. $x^2 - x - 56 = 0$
19. $y^2 - 64 = 0$
20. $5s - 2s^2 = 0$
21. $3z^2 = 12z$
22. $m^2 - 24m = -144$
23. $6q^2 + 5 = -17q$
24. $5b^3 + 34b^2 = 7b$
25. $\frac{x^2}{12} - \frac{2x}{3} - 4 = 0$
26. $t^2 - \frac{t}{6} = \frac{35}{6}$
27. $n^3 - 81n = 0$
28. $(x + 8)(x + 1) = -12$
29. $(r - 1)(r - 1) = 36$
30. $(3y + 2)(y + 3) = y + 14$

31. **Number Theory** Find two consecutive even integers whose product is 168.

32. **Number Theory** Find two consecutive odd integers whose product is 1023.

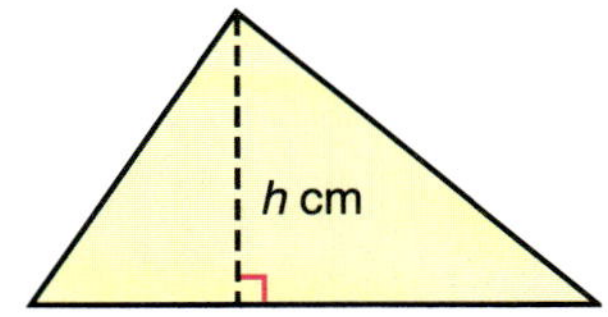

33. **Geometry** The triangle at the right has an area of 40 square centimeters. Find the height h of the triangle.

Critical Thinking

34. Write an equation with integral coefficients that has $\{-3, 0, 7\}$ as its solution set.

35. Consider the equations $a^2 + 5a = 6$ and $|2x + 5| = 7$.
    a. Solve each equation.
    b. What is the relationship between the two equations? What does that mean?

Applications and Problem Solving

36. **Gardening** LaKeesha has enough bricks to make a 30-foot-long border around the rectangular vegetable garden she is planning. The booklet she got from the plant nursery when she bought the seeds says the plants will need space to grow, and it advises that the seeds should be planted in an area of 54 square feet. What should the dimensions of her garden be?

37. **History** During the late 16th century, Galileo was a professor at the University of Pisa, Italy. During this time, he demonstrated that objects of different weights fell at the same velocity by dropping two objects of different weights from the top of the Leaning Tower of Pisa.
    a. If he dropped the objects from a height of 180 feet, how long did it take them to hit the ground?
    b. Research Galileo's life. Why was he criticized for experimenting with these weights? What other belief of his led to his trial by the Inquisition of 1633?

38. **Fountains** The tallest fountain in the world is at Fountain Hills, Arizona. When all three pumps are working, the nozzle speed of the water is 146.7 miles per hour (215.16 feet per second). It is claimed the water reaches a height of 625 feet. Do you agree or disagree with this claim? Explain.

FYI

Superman first appeared in a comic book in 1938 and in a newspaper strip in 1939. Jerry Seigel wrote these comics and Joe Shuster provided the artwork.

39. **Superheroes** A meteorite is headed towards Metropolis when Superman intercepts it. He takes it to the top of the *Daily Planet* (180 feet high) and tosses the meteorite into space with an upward velocity of 2400 feet per second. What height will the meteorite attain before returning to Earth?

40. **Bridges** The chart at the right compares the highest bridge in the world at Royal Gorge, Colorado with the highest railroad bridge in the world at Kolasin, Yugoslavia. If Elva accidentally drops her keys from the Royal Gorge Bridge, will the keys hit the Arkansas River below within 8 seconds?

High Bridges

Bridge	Height (ft)
Royal Gorge, Colorado	880
Kolasin, Yugoslavia	650

41. **Oil Leases** A drilling company has the oil rights for a rectangular piece of land that is 6 kilometers by 5 kilometers. According to a lease agreement, the company can only dig their wells in the inner two-thirds of the land. A uniform strip around the edge of the land must remain untouched. What is the width of the strip of land that must remain untouched?

Mixed Review

42. Factor $100x^2 + 20x + 1$. (Lesson 10–5)

43. Find $(5q + 2r)(8q - 3r)$. (Lesson 9–7)

44. Solve $9x + 4 < 7 - 13x$. (Lesson 7–3)

45. Determine the x- and y-intercepts of the graph of $2x - 7y = 28$. (Lesson 6–4)

46. **Patterns** Copy and complete the table below. (Lesson 5–5)

s	4	2	0	−2	−4
$r(s)$	19	11	3		

47. **World Records** The Huey P. Long Bridge in Metairie, Louisiana, is the longest railroad bridge in the world. If you were traveling on a train going 60 miles per hour across the 22,996-foot bridge, how long would it take you to cross it? (Lesson 4–7)

48. **Consumerism** Julio is offered two payment plans when he buys a sofa. Under one plan, he pays $400 down and x dollars per month for 9 months. Under the other plan, he pays no money down and $x + 25$ dollars per month for 12 months. How much does the sofa cost? (Lesson 3–5)

WORKING ON THE

In·ves·ti·ga·tion

Refer to the Investigation on pages 554–555.

the BRICKYARD

The perimeter P of a square is given by the formula $P = 4s$, where s is the length of the side of the square. The formula for the area A of a square is $A = s^2$. The perimeter of a rectangle is found using $P = 2\ell + 2w$, where ℓ is the length of the rectangle and w is the width. The formula for the area of the rectangle is $A = \ell w$.

1 Suppose the large square brick has a side x units long and the small square brick has a side y units long. What are the dimensions of the rectangular brick? What is the area of each of the bricks? Draw a diagram to illustrate the dimensions of each brick.

2 Refer to the drawings of all the rectangular brick patterns you found using 4, 5, 6, 7, 8, 9, and 10 bricks. Calculate the perimeter and area in terms of x and y of all of the patterns you discovered.

3 Create a table to record the linear dimensions, the perimeter, and the area of the brick patterns you found. Use the table to record the dimensions, perimeter, and area in terms of x and y. The table should be set up like the one below.

Add the results of your work to your Investigation Folder.

# of bricks in pattern	length of pattern	width of pattern	perimeter of pattern	area of pattern
4				
5				
6				

CHAPTER 10 HIGHLIGHTS

VOCABULARY

After completing this chapter, you should be able to define each term, property, or phrase and give an example or two of each.

Algebra

composite numbers (p. 558)

difference of squares (p. 581)

factored form (p. 559)

factoring or factored (pp. 564, 565)

factoring by grouping (p. 567)

greatest common factor (GCF) (p. 559)

perfect square trinomials (p. 587)

prime factorization (p. 558)

prime numbers (p. 558)

prime polynomial (p. 577)

Pythagorean triple (p. 583)

unique factorization theorem (p. 558)

zero product property (p. 594)

Problem Solving

guess and check (p. 574)

UNDERSTANDING AND USING THE VOCABULARY

State whether each sentence is *true* or *false*. If false, replace the underlined word or number to make a true sentence.

1. The number 27 is an example of a <u>prime</u> number.
2. <u>$2x$</u> is the greatest common factor (GCF) of $12x^2$ and $14xy$.
3. <u>66</u> is an example of a perfect square.
4. 61 is a <u>factor</u> of 183.
5. The prime factorization for 48 is <u>$3 \cdot 4^2$</u>.
6. $x^2 - 25$ is an example of a <u>perfect square trinomial</u>.
7. The number 35 is an example of a <u>composite</u> number.
8. <u>$x^2 - 3x - 70$</u> is an example of a prime polynomial.
9. The <u>unique factorization theorem</u> allows you to solve equations.
10. <u>$(b - 7)(b + 7)$</u> is the factorization of a difference of squares.

CHAPTER 10 STUDY GUIDE AND ASSESSMENT

SKILLS AND CONCEPTS

OBJECTIVES AND EXAMPLES

Upon completing this chapter, you should be able to:

- find the prime factorization of integers (Lesson 10–1)

Find the prime factorization of 180.

$$180 = 2 \cdot 90$$
$$= 2 \cdot 2 \cdot 45$$
$$= 2 \cdot 2 \cdot 3 \cdot 15$$
$$= 2 \cdot 2 \cdot 3 \cdot 3 \cdot 5$$

The prime factorization of 180 is $2 \cdot 2 \cdot 3 \cdot 3 \cdot 5$ or $2^2 \cdot 3^2 \cdot 5$.

REVIEW EXERCISES

Use these exercises to review and prepare for the chapter test.

State whether each number is *prime* or *composite*. If the number is composite, find its prime factorization.

11. 28

12. 33

13. 150

14. 301

15. 83

16. 378

- find the greatest common factors (GCF) for sets of monomials (Lesson 10–1)

Find the GCF of $15x^2y$ and $45xy^2$.

$$15x^2y = 3 \cdot 5 \cdot x \cdot x \cdot y$$
$$45xy^2 = 3 \cdot 3 \cdot 5 \cdot x \cdot y \cdot y$$

The GCF is $3 \cdot 5 \cdot x \cdot y$ or $15xy$.

Find the GCF of the given monomials.

17. 35, 30

18. 12, 18, 40

19. $12ab$, $-4a^2b^2$

20. $16mrt$, $30m^2r$

21. $20n^2$, $25np^5$

22. $60x^2y^2$, $35xz^3$

23. $56x^3y$, $49ax^2$

24. $6a^2$, $18b^2$, $9b^3$

- use the greatest common factor (GCF) and the distributive property to factor polynomials (Lesson 10–2)

Factor $12a^2 - 8ab$.

$$12a^2 - 8ab = 4a(3a) - 4a(2b)$$
$$= 4a(3a - 2b)$$

Factor each polynomial.

25. $13x + 26y$

26. $6x^2y + 12xy + 6$

27. $24a^2b^2 - 18ab$

28. $26ab + 18ac + 32a^2$

29. $36p^2q^2 - 12pq$

30. $a + a^2b + a^3b^3$

- use grouping techniques to factor polynomials with four or more terms (Lesson 10–2)

Factor $2x^2 - 3xz - 2xy + 3yz$.

$$2x^2 - 3xz - 2xy + 3yz = (2x^2 - 3xz) + (-2xy + 3yz)$$
$$= x(2x - 3z) - y(2x - 3z)$$
$$= (x - y)(2x - 3z)$$

Factor each polynomial.

31. $a^2 - 4ac + ab - 4bc$

32. $4rs + 12ps + 2mr + 6mp$

33. $16k^3 - 4k^2p^2 - 28kp + 7p^3$

34. $dm + mr + 7r + 7d$

35. $24am - 9an + 40bm - 15bn$

36. $a^3 - a^2b + ab^2 - b^3$

OBJECTIVES AND EXAMPLES

- factor quadratic trinomials (Lesson 10–3)

$a^2 - 3a - 4 = (a + 1)(a - 4)$

$$\begin{aligned} 4x^2 - 4xy - 15y^2 &= 4x^2 + (-10 + 6)xy - 15y^2 \\ &= 4x^2 - 10xy + 6xy - 15y^2 \\ &= (4x^2 - 10xy) + (6xy - 15y^2) \\ &= 2x(2x - 5y) + 3y(2x - 5y) \\ &= (2x - 5y)(2x + 3y) \end{aligned}$$

REVIEW EXERCISES

Factor each trinomial, if possible. If the trinomial cannot be factored using integers, write *prime*.

37. $y^2 + 7y + 12$

38. $x^2 - 9x - 36$

39. $6z^2 + 7z + 3$

40. $b^2 + 5b - 6$

41. $2r^2 - 3r - 20$

42. $3a^2 - 13a + 14$

- identify and factor binomials that are the differences of squares (Lesson 10–4)

$$\begin{aligned} a^2 - 9 &= (a)^2 - (3)^2 \\ &= (a - 3)(a + 3) \end{aligned}$$

$$\begin{aligned} 3x^3 - 75x &= 3x(x^2 - 25) \\ &= 3x(x - 5)(x + 5) \end{aligned}$$

Factor each polynomial, if possible. If the polynomial cannot be factored using integers, write *prime*.

43. $b^2 - 16$

44. $25 - 9y^2$

45. $16a^2 - 81b^4$

46. $2y^3 - 128y$

47. $9b^2 - 20$

48. $\frac{1}{4}n^2 - \frac{9}{16}r^2$

- identify and factor perfect square trinomials (Lesson 10–5)

$$\begin{aligned} &16z^2 - 8z + 1 \\ &= (4z)^2 - 2(4z)(1) + (1)^2 \\ &= (4z - 1)^2 \end{aligned}$$

$$\begin{aligned} 9x^2 + 24xy + 16y^2 &= (3x)^2 - 2(3x)(4y) + (4y)^2 \\ &= (3x + 4y)^2 \end{aligned}$$

Factor each polynomial, if possible. If the polynomial cannot be factored using integers, write *prime*.

49. $a^2 + 18a + 81$

50. $9k^2 - 12k + 4$

51. $4 - 28r + 49r^2$

52. $32n^2 - 80n + 50$

53. $6b^3 - 24b^2g + 24bg^2$

54. $49m^2 - 126m + 81$

55. $25x^2 - 120x + 144$

OBJECTIVES AND EXAMPLES	REVIEW EXERCISES
use the zero product property to solve equations (Lesson 10–6)	Solve each equation. Check your solution.

- use the zero product property to solve equations (Lesson 10–6)

Solve $b^2 - b - 12 = 0$.

$b^2 - b - 12 = 0$

$(b - 4)(b + 3) = 0$

If $(b - 4)(b + 3) = 0$, then $(b - 4) = 0$ or $(b + 3) = 0$.

$b - 4 = 0$ or $b + 3 = 0$

$b = 4$ $\quad$ $b = -3$

The solution set is $\{4, -3\}$.

REVIEW EXERCISES

Solve each equation. Check your solution.

56. $y(y + 11) = 0$

57. $(3x - 2)(4x + 7) = 0$

58. $2a^2 - 9a = 0$

59. $n^2 = -17n$

60. $\frac{3}{4}y = \frac{1}{2}y^2$

61. $y^2 + 13y + 40 = 0$

62. $2m^2 + 13m = 24$

63. $25r^2 + 4 = -20r$

APPLICATIONS AND PROBLEM SOLVING

64. Geometry The measure of the area of a rectangle is $4m^2 - 3mp + 3p - 4m$. If the dimensions of the rectangle are represented by polynomials with integral coefficients, find the dimensions of the rectangle. (Lesson 10–2)

65. Guess and Check Numero Uno says, "I am thinking of a three-digit number. If you multiply the digits together and then multiply the result by 4, the answer is the number I'm thinking of. What is my number?" (Lesson 10–3)

66. Photography To get a square photograph to fit into a rectangular frame, Li-Chih had to trim a 1-inch strip from one pair of opposite sides of the photo and a 2-inch strip from the other two sides. In all, he trimmed off 64 square inches. What were the original dimensions of the photograph? (Lesson 10–4)

67. Guess and Check Fill in each box below with a digit from 1 to 6 to make this multiplication work. Use each digit exactly once. (Lesson 10–3)

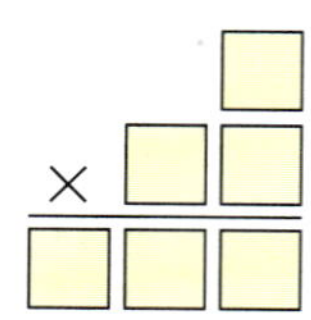

68. Geometry The measure of the area of a rectangle is $16x^2 - 9$. Find the measure of its perimeter. (Lesson 10–4)

69. Number Theory The product of two consecutive odd integers is 99. Find the integers. (Lesson 10–6)

A practice test for Chapter 10 is provided on page 796.

ALTERNATIVE ASSESSMENT

COOPERATIVE LEARNING PROJECT

Art and Framing In this project, you will determine what size mat and frame will be the most visually stimulating for an abstract print that you just bought on your trip to The Art Institute of Chicago. The print is 9 inches by 12 inches and can be cropped an inch on either side and not spoil its effect.

You called a friend to get some advice on how to mat and frame your print. This friend majored in art and works in the art industry, but he also enjoys puzzling you. He gave you two problems and told you to solve them and decide which you think would be the most appropriate dimensions for your mat and frame. Here are the two problems.

- The inside rectangle has a width four inches less than its length. The length of the larger rectangle is twice its width. Find the dimensions of each rectangle if the matted area is twice as much as the inside rectangle area and the perimeter of the inside rectangle is 32 inches less than the perimeter of the larger rectangle.
- The inside rectangle has a width four inches less than its length. The length of the larger rectangle is twice its width. Find the dimensions of each rectangle if the matted area is seven times as much in square inches as the perimeter of the smaller rectangle is in inches, and the width of the larger rectangle is two inches more than the length of the smaller rectangle.

Which problem will give you the dimensions that will best suit your print? What are the dimensions? Will you have to crop your print? If so, how much?

Follow these steps to determine the appropriate dimensions for the mat and frame.

- Illustrate each of the problems.
- Label each of the drawings with as much information as possible.
- Develop an equation for each problem that describes the situation.
- Investigate your answers and determine the appropriate dimensions for the mat and frame.
- If possible, find a 9-inch by 12-inch photograph or advertisement from a magazine. Have two color photocopies made of it and frame each with a cardboard frame that meets the specifications.
- Write a paragraph describing the two problems and how you determined the solution.

THINKING CRITICALLY

- A *nasty* number is a positive integer with at least four different factors such that the difference between the numbers in one pair of factors equals the sum of the numbers in another pair. The first nasty number is 6 since $6 = 6 \cdot 1 = 2 \cdot 3$ and $6 - 1 = 2 + 3$. Find the next five nasty numbers. (*Hint*: They are all multiples of 6.)
- Write an equation with integral coefficients that has $\left\{\frac{2}{3}, -1\right\}$ as the solution.

PORTFOLIO

When using the guess-and-check strategy for solving a math problem, if a first guess does not work, you must make a second guess. How do you make a second guess when the first one is incorrect? In making this second guess, you must know how and why the first guess was incorrect. Find a problem from your work in this chapter in which you used the guess-and-check strategy. Write a step-by-step description of why you chose each successive guess after the previous guess for that problem. Place this in your portfolio.

SELF EVALUATION

Having a strategy before solving a problem is helpful. It helps you to focus on the problem and the solution and to be organized in the solution of your problem. Using strategies or check lists are fundamental skills used in critical thinking.

Assess yourself. Do you determine a strategy for solving a problem before you delve into it? Do you stay with the initial plan or do you reevaluate after a time period and try a new strategy? Do you keep a record of your strategy and attempts so that you can refer back to it to determine if you are still on track? Give an example of a math problem in which a strategy is beneficial in order to keep track of what has been attempted. Also, give an example of a daily life problem in which you used a strategy to help organize your plan for a solution.

CUMULATIVE REVIEW

CHAPTERS 1–10

SECTION ONE: MULTIPLE CHOICE

There are nine multiple-choice questions in this section. After working each problem, write the letter of the correct answer on your paper.

1. The square of a number subtracted from 8 times the number is equal to twice the number. Find the number.

A. 0 or 6
B. 3
C. 2
D. 0 or 10

2. Choose the open sentence that represents the range of acceptable diameters for a lawn mower bolt that will work properly only if its diameter differs from 2 cm by no more than 0.04 cm.

A. $|d - 0.04| \geq 2$
B. $|d| < 1.96$
C. $|d - 2| \leq 0.04$
D. $|d| > 2.04$

3. Choose an expression for the area of the shaded region shown below.

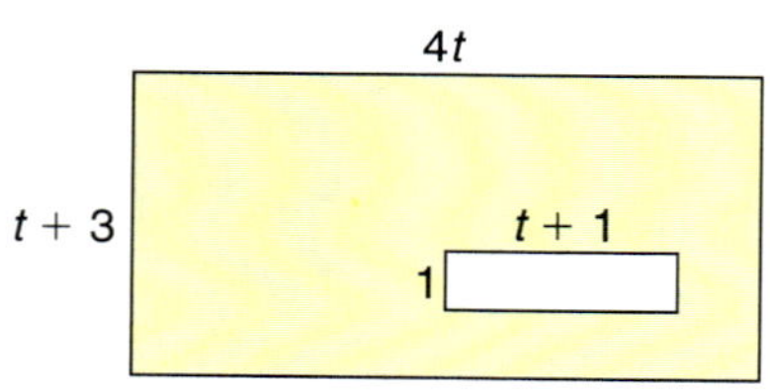

A. $(4t)(t + 3)$
B. $(4t - t)(t + 3) - (t + 1)$
C. $(t + 1)(t + 3) - (4t)(t)$
D. $(4t)(t + 3) - (t + 1)$

4. Choose the equivalent equation for $A = \frac{1}{2}h(a + b)$.

A. $h = \frac{2A}{a + b}$
B. $h = 2A - (a + b)$
C. $h = \frac{\frac{1}{2}(a + b)}{A}$
D. $h = \frac{A - b}{2a}$

5. Bob and Vicki took a trip to Zuma Beach. On the way there, their average speed was 42 miles per hour. On the way home, their average speed was 56 miles per hour. If their total travel time was 7 hours, find the distance to the beach.

A. 126 miles
B. 168 miles
C. 98 miles
D. 294 miles

6. Choose which statement is true.

A. The range is the difference between the greatest value and the lower quartile in a set of data.
B. An outlier will only affect the mean of a set of data.
C. Quartiles are values that divide a set of data into equal halves.
D. The interquartile range is the sum of the upper and lower quartiles in a set of data.

7. Choose the prime polynomial.

A. $y^2 + 12y + 27$
B. $6x^2 - 11x + 4$
C. $h^2 + 5h - 8$
D. $9k^2 + 30km + 25m^2$

8. Choose the equation of the line that passes through the points at (9, 5) and (−3, −4).

A. $y = -\frac{1}{12}x + \frac{23}{4}$
B. $y = \frac{4}{3}x$
C. $y = -\frac{7}{2}x - \frac{3}{4}$
D. $y = \frac{3}{4}x - \frac{7}{4}$

9. Carrie's bowling scores for four games are $b + 2$, $b + 3$, $b - 2$, and $b - 1$. What must her score be on her fifth game to average $b + 2$?

A. $b + 8$
B. b
C. $b - 2$
D. $b + 5$

SECTION TWO: SHORT ANSWER

This section contains ten questions for which you will provide short answers. Write your answer on your paper.

10. The measure of the perimeter of a square is $20m + 32p$. Find the measure of its area.

11. At a bake sale, cakes cost twice as much as pies. Pies were $4 more than triple the price of cookies. Darin bought a cake, three pies, and four cookies for $24.75. What is the price of each item?

12. Factor $3g^2 - 10gh - 8h^2$.

13. On the first day of school, 264 school notebooks were sold. Some sold for 95¢ each, and the rest sold for $1.25 each. How many of each were sold if the total sales were $297?

14. A rectangular photograph is 8 centimeters wide and 12 centimeters long. The photograph is enlarged by increasing the length and width by an equal amount. If the area of the new photograph is 69 square centimeters greater than the area of the original photograph, what are the dimensions of the new photograph?

15. Linda plans to spend at most $50 on shorts and blouses. She bought 2 pairs of shorts for $14.20 each. How much can she spend on blouses?

16. The difference of two numbers is 3. If the difference of their squares is 15, what is the sum of the numbers?

17. **Geometry** The length of a rectangle is eight times its width. If the length was decreased by 10 meters and the width was decreased by 2 meters, the area would be decreased by 162 square meters. Find the original dimensions.

18. Ben's car gets between 18 and 21 miles per gallon of gasoline. If his car's tank holds 15 gallons, what is the range of distance that Ben can drive his car on one tank of gasoline?

19. Find the measure of the third side of a triangle if the perimeter of the triangle is $8x^2 + x + 15$ and the measures of two of its sides can be represented by the expressions $2x^2 - 5x + 7$ and $x^2 - x + 11$.

SECTION THREE: OPEN-ENDED

This section contains two open-ended problems. Demonstrate your knowledge by giving a clear, concise solution to each problem. Your score on these problems will depend on how well you do the following.

- Explain your reasoning.
- Show your understanding of the mathematics in an organized manner.
- Use charts, graphs, and diagrams in your explanation.
- Show the solution in more than one way or relate it to other situations.
- Investigate beyond the requirements of the problem.

20. A tinsmith is going to make a box out of tin by cutting a square from each corner and folding up the sides. The box needs to be 3 inches high (so he will be cutting out 3-inch squares), and it needs to be twice as long as it is wide, so that it can hold two smaller square cardboard boxes. Finally, its volume needs to be 1350 cubic inches. What should the dimensions be?

21. The length of a rectangle is five times its width. If the length was increased by 7 meters and the width was decreased by 4 meters, the area would be decreased by 132 square meters. Find the original dimensions.

CHAPTER

11

Exploring Quadratic and Exponential Functions

Objectives

In this chapter, you will:

- find the equation of the axis of symmetry and the coordinates of the vertex of a parabola,
- graph quadratic and exponential functions,
- use estimation to find roots of quadratic equations by graphing,
- find roots of quadratic equations by using the quadratic formula,
- solve problems by looking for and using a pattern, and
- solve problems involving growth and decay.

Reaching Out to Help Others

Source: *Giving and Volunteering in the United States,* 1992 Edition

Dr. Robert Coles, a psychiatrist and Harvard professor, calls it "the call of service," men and women who volunteer their time to help others. Many teens would like to get involved in volunteer service, but may not know where to start. Some opportunities may be available in your own community—helping senior citizens, working as a Big Brother or Big Sister, or volunteering at a food pantry. Volunteering will help others and may help you feel great, too.

TIME *Line*

2100 B.C. Sumarian King Ur-Nammu builds the Ziggurat of Ur.

1482 Johannes Campanus's translation of Euclid's *Elements* is the first mathematical book of significance to be printed.

1245 Chin Chiu-Shao's *Mathematical treatise in nine sections* solves fourth-degree and higher-degree equations.

1654 Dutch inventor Christian Huygens develops the pendulum clock.

PEOPLE IN THE NEWS

A perfect example of a teenage volunteer is **Liz Alvarez** of St. Petersburg, Florida. She has been a community volunteer at St. Anthony's Hospital, giving more than 600 hours of her time to help the staff. She answers phones in the pastoral care department, does filing as an administrative assistant, and carries messages for staff members. She helps patients by delivering items to their rooms, works in the gift shop, and assists other volunteers.

She enjoys her time spent volunteering, is happy to help others, and believes that the experience is very rewarding. She encourages other teens to investigate the opportunities in their communities and join a volunteer team.

Chapter Project

Organizations in every community study the characteristics of those who volunteer their time. In this manner, they know what population to target when seeking volunteers for a particular project or event. Survey companies, such as the Gallup Organization, Inc., often provide statistics for these organizations.

One of the characteristics the Gallup Organization studied was the income of volunteers. They found the following information on income brackets and the percent of the people in each bracket who volunteer.

Income ($)	Percent of Population Volunteering
Under 10,000	31.6
10,000–19,999	37.9
20,000–29,999	51.3
30,000–39,999	56.4
40,000–49,999	67.4
50,000–59,999	67.7
60,000–74,999	55.0
75,000–99,999	62.8
100,000 +	73.7

Analyze these findings.

- Make a graph of the data.
- What type of behavior do these data present?
- Why do you think this behavior exists?
- Research in an almanac or statistical abstract to find the average income for the age groups listed in the graph on the previous page.
- Use your research, the graph on the previous page, and the table to make a conjecture about the characteristics of the average volunteer.

1940 U.S. photographer Helen Levitt chronicles life in the streets of New York City with her print *Children*.

1981 The Peace Corps becomes an independent agency, sending volunteers to improve living conditions in developing countries.

1940 1945 1950 1955 1960 1965 1970 1975 1980 1985 1990 1995 2000

1947 Dr. Bernardo A. Houssay receives the Nobel Prize for Medicine and Physiology for his research on the pituitary gland.

1991 Advances in music technology enable Natalie Cole to produce a duet album with her late father Nat "King" Cole.

11–1A Graphing Technology
Quadratic Functions

A Preview of Lesson 11–1

Equations in the form $y = ax^2 + bx + c$ are called **quadratic functions,** and their graphs are called **parabolas.** A parabola is a U-shaped curve that can open upward or downward. The maximum or minimum point of a parabola is called its **vertex.** You can use a graphing calculator to graph a quadratic function and find the coordinates of its vertex.

Example

Graph $y = \frac{1}{4}x^2 - 4x - 2$ and locate its vertex. Use the integer window.

A quadratic function is entered into the Y= list in the same way that you entered linear functions.

Enter: [Y=] .25 [X,T,θ,n] [x^2] [−] 4 [X,T,θ,n] [−] 2 *Enters the function.*

[ZOOM] 6 [ZOOM] 8 [ENTER] *Selects the integer window.*

Sometimes the coordinates of the vertex may not be integers. Use the ZOOM feature several times until you get coordinates that are fairly consistent (within three decimal places).

The parabola opens upward. The vertex is a minimum point.

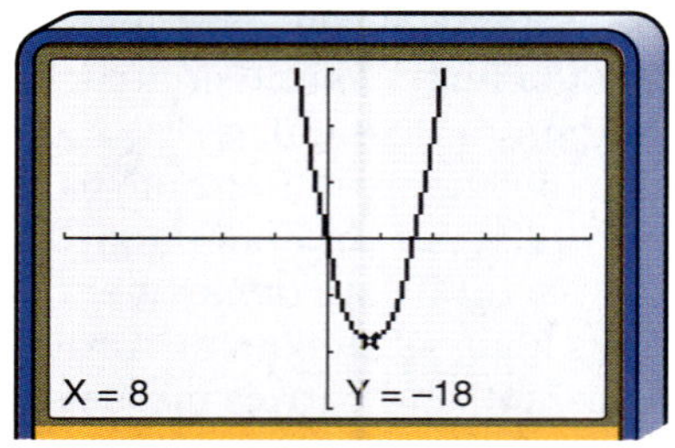

Method 1: Use TRACE.

Press [TRACE] and use the left and right arrow keys to move the cursor to the vertex. Watch the coordinates at the bottom of the screen as you move the cursor. The vertex will be the point of the least y value. *Why?*

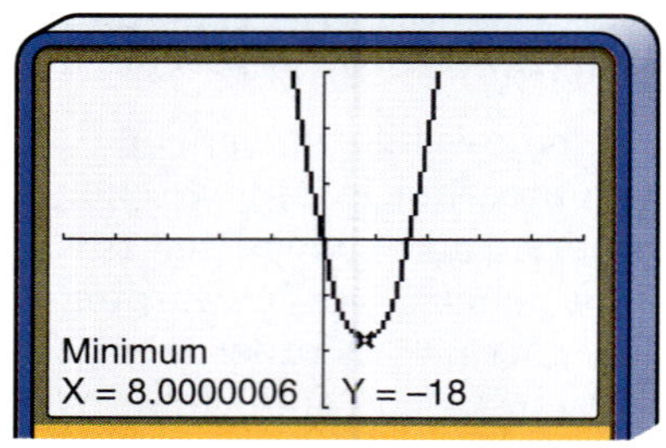

Method 2: Use CALC.

Since the parabola opens upward, the vertex is a minimum point. Press [2nd] [CALC] 3.

- A "Lower Bound?" prompt appears. Move the cursor to a location left of where you think the vertex is and press [ENTER].
- An "Upper Bound?" prompt appears. Move the cursor to a location right of where you think the vertex is and press [ENTER].
- When the "Guess?" prompt appears, move the cursor to your choice for the vertex and press [ENTER]. The screen will give you an approximation of the vertex coordinates.

You can also press [ENTER] at the Guess? prompt without entering a guess.

The coordinates of the vertex are (8, −18).

EXERCISES

Graph each function. Make a sketch of the graph and note the ordered pair representing the vertex on the graph.

1. $y = x^2 + 16x + 59$ **2.** $y = 12x^2 + 18x + 10$ **3.** $y = x^2 - 10x + 25$

4. $y = -2x^2 - 8x - 1$ **5.** $y = 2(x - 10)^2 + 14$ **6.** $y = -0.5x^2 - 2x + 3$

11–1 Graphing Quadratic Functions

What YOU'LL LEARN

- To find the equation of the axis of symmetry and the coordinates of the vertex of a parabola, and
- to graph quadratic functions.

Why IT'S IMPORTANT

You can graph quadratic functions to solve problems involving fireworks and football.

APPLICATION

Landmarks

The Gateway Arch of the Jefferson National Expansion Memorial in St. Louis, Missouri, is shaped like an upside-down U. This shape is actually a *catenary,* which resembles a geometric shape called a **parabola.** The shape of the arch can be approximated by the graph of the function $f(x) = -0.00635x^2 + 4.0005x - 0.07875$, where $f(x)$ is the height of the arch in feet and x is the horizontal distance from one base.

This type of function is an example of a **quadratic function.** A quadratic function can be written in the form $f(x) = ax^2 + bx + c$, where $a \neq 0$. Notice that this function has a degree of 2 and the exponents are positive.

Definition of a Quadratic Function	A quadratic function is a function that can be described by an equation of the form $y = ax^2 + bx + c$, where $a \neq 0$.

Since distance and height are involved, the domain and range must both be positive.

To graph a quadratic equation, you can use a table of values. The table at the right shows the distance (in 35-foot increments) from one base of the arch and the height of the arch at each increment (rounded to the nearest foot). Graph the ordered pairs and connect them with a smooth curve. The graph of $f(x) = -0.00635x^2 + 4.0005x - 0.07875$ is shown below.

x	f(x)
0	0
35	132
70	249
105	350
140	436
175	506
210	560
245	599
280	622
315	630
350	622
385	599
420	560
455	506
490	436
525	350
560	249
595	132
630	0

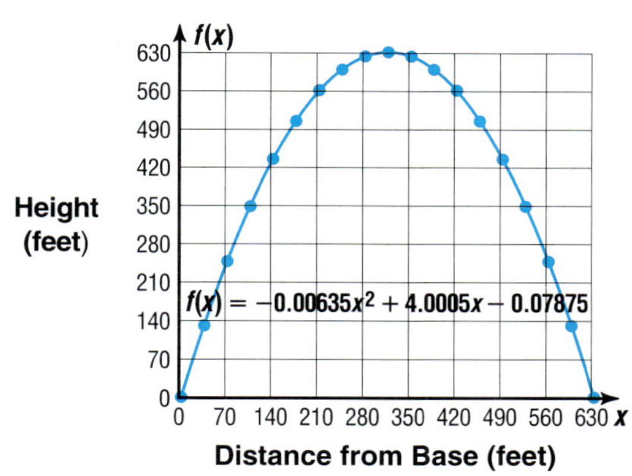

GLOBAL CONNECTIONS

The arch as an architectural form dates back to Egypt and Greece, but was first used extensively by the Romans in building bridges and aqueducts, like the Pont du Gard at Nimes, France. The architects in medieval times used majestic pointed arches in the construction of gothic cathedrals.

Notice that the value of a in this function is negative and the curve opens downward. The greatest value of $f(x)$ seems to be 630 feet, which occurs when the distance from the base is 315 feet. The point at (315, 630) would be the **vertex** of the parabola. For a parabola that opens downward, the vertex is a **maximum** point of the function. If the parabola opens upward, the vertex is a **minimum** point of the function.

Parabolas possess a geometric property called **symmetry.** Symmetrical figures are those in which the figure can be folded and each half matches the other exactly. The following activity explores the symmetry of a parabola.

MODELING MATHEMATICS

Symmetry of Parabolas

Materials: grid paper

Your Turn

a. Graph $y = x^2 - 6x + 5$ on grid paper.

b. Hold your paper up to the light and fold the parabola in half so the two sides match exactly.

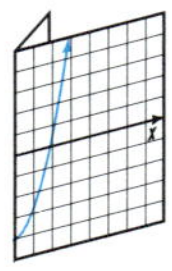

c. Unfold the paper. Which point on the parabola lies on the fold line?

d. Write an equation to describe the fold line

e. Write a few sentences to describe the symmetry of a parabola based on your findings in this activity.

The fold line in the activity above is called the **axis of symmetry** for the parabola. Each point on the parabola that is on one side of the axis of symmetry has a corresponding point on the parabola on the other side of the axis. The vertex is the only point on the parabola that is on the axis of symmetry. The equation for the axis of symmetry can be determined from the equation of the parabola.

Equation of the Axis of Symmetry of a Parabola	**The equation of the axis of symmetry for the graph of $y = ax^2 + bx + c$, where $a \neq 0$, is $x = -\frac{b}{2a}$.**

You can determine a lot of information about a parabola from its equation.

Example 1

Given the equation $y = x^2 - 4x + 5$,

a. find the equation of the axis of symmetry,

b. find the coordinates of the vertex of the parabola, and

c. graph the equation.

a. In the equation $y = x^2 - 4x + 5$, $a = 1$ and $b = -4$. Substitute these values into the equation of the axis of symmetry.

$$x = -\frac{b}{2a}$$

$$= -\frac{-4}{2(1)} \text{ or } 2$$

b. Since the equation for the axis of symmetry is $x = 2$ and the vertex lies on the axis, the x-coordinate for the vertex is 2.

$$y = x^2 - 4x + 5$$

$$= 2^2 - 4(2) + 5 \quad \textit{Replace x with 2.}$$

$$= 4 - 8 + 5 \text{ or } 1$$

The coordinates of the vertex are (2, 1).

You can use the TABLE feature on a graphing calculator to help you find ordered pairs that satisfy an equation.

c. You can use the symmetry of the parabola to help you draw its graph. Draw a coordinate plane. Graph the vertex and axis of symmetry. Choose a value less than 2, say 0, and find the *y*-coordinate that satisfies the equation.

$y = x^2 - 4x + 5$

$\quad = 0^2 - 4(0) + 5$ or 5

Graph (0, 5). Since the graph is symmetrical, you can find another point on the other side of the axis of symmetry. The point at (0, 5) is 2 units left of the axis. Go 2 units right of the axis and plot a point at (4, 5). Repeat this for several other points. Then sketch the parabola.

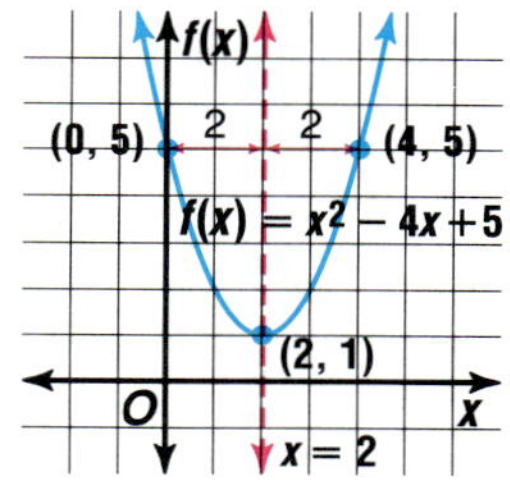

Check: Does (4, 5) satisfy the equation?

$y = x^2 - 4x + 5$

$5 \stackrel{?}{=} 4^2 - 4(4) + 5$

$5 \stackrel{?}{=} 16 - 16 + 5$

$5 = 5$ ✔

The point (4, 5) satisfies the equation $y = x^2 - 4x + 5$ and is part of the graph.

The graph of an equation describing the height of an object propelled into the air can be an example of a quadratic function. Because gravity overtakes the initial force of the object, the object falls back to Earth.

Example 2

APPLICATION

Pyrotechnics

FYI

The largest firework ever exploded was a 1543-pound shell called the Universe I Part II. It was used as part of the Lake Toya Festival in Hokkaido, Japan, on July 15, 1988, and had a burst 3937 feet in diameter.

In Cincinnati, Ohio, radio station WEBN and Rozzi's Famous Fireworks, Inc. team together to develop a large fireworks display for Labor Day. The fireworks are coordinated with recorded music compiled by the radio station's DJs. Mr. Rozzi assumes that each rocket (firework) explodes at approximately its highest point after being propelled from a barge in the Ohio River. The formula that describes the height *H*(*t*) of an object propelled into the air is $H(t) = v_0t - \frac{1}{2}gt^2 + h_0$, where v_0 represents the initial velocity in m/s, *t* represents time in seconds, *g* represents the acceleration of gravity (about 9.8 m/s^2), and h_0 is the initial height of the object at the time it is launched. A certain rocket has an initial velocity of 39.2 m/s and is launched 1.6 meters above the surface of the water.

a. Graph the equation representing the height of the rocket.

b. What is the maximum height that the rocket achieves?

c. One of these rockets is scheduled to explode 2 minutes and 28 seconds into the program. When should the rocket be fired from the barge?

(continued on the next page)

a. Use the given velocity and the force of gravity to determine the formula.

$H(t) = v_0 t - \frac{1}{2}gt^2 + h_0$

$= 39.2t - \frac{1}{2}(9.8)t^2 + 1.6$ *Replace v_0, g, and h_0 with the given values.*

$= 39.2t - 4.9t^2 + 1.6$ *Simplify.*

The values of a and b are -4.9 and 39.2, respectively.
$H(t)$ corresponds to $f(x)$ and t corresponds to x.

Find the equation of the axis of symmetry to help you locate the vertex.

$t = -\frac{b}{2a}$

$= -\frac{39.2}{2(-4.9)}$ or 4 seconds

Use a calculator to find $H(t)$ when $t = 4$.

$H(4) = 39.2(4) - 4.9(4)^2 + 1.6$ or 80 meters

The vertex of the graph is at (4, 80).

We can use a table of values to find other points that satisfy the equation.

The graph shows the height of the rocket at any given time. It does not show the path that the rocket took.

t	$H(t)$
0	1.6
1	35.9
2	60.4
3	75.1
4	80.0
5	75.1
6	60.4
7	35.9
8	1.6
9	−42.5

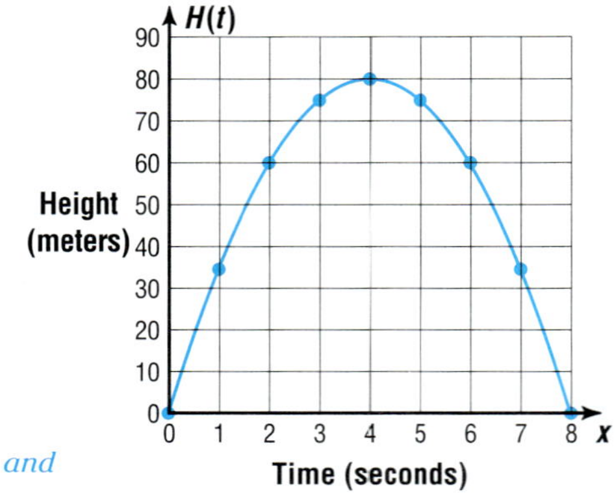

Since time is the independent variable and height is the dependent variable, the domain and range must both be positive.

b. The maximum height is at the vertex. This height is 80 meters.

c. Since the maximum height is achieved 4 seconds after launch, the rocket must be fired 4 seconds before its scheduled explosion at 2 minutes 28 seconds into the program. The rocket should be fired at 2 minutes 24 seconds into the program.

CHECK FOR UNDERSTANDING

Communicating Mathematics

Study the lesson. Then complete the following.

1. **Determine** the distance between the bases of the Gateway Arch.
2. **Explain** how you can use symmetry to help you graph a parabola.
3. **Write** a sentence to explain how you can write the equation of the axis of symmetry if you know the coordinates of the vertex of a parabola.
4. **You Decide** Lisa says that $y = -x^2$ is the same as $y = (-x)^2$. Angie says that they are different. Who is correct? Explain and include graphs.
5. How can you determine if the vertex is a maximum or minimum without graphing the equation first?
6. Graph $y = -x^2 + 4x - 4$. How does this graph differ from the one in the activity on page 612? Use paper folding to determine the axis of symmetry.

MODELING MATHEMATICS

Guided Practice

Write the equation of the axis of symmetry and find the coordinates of the vertex of the graph of each equation. State if the vertex is a maximum or minimum. Then graph the equation.

7. $y = x^2 + 2$

8. $y = -2x^2$

9. $y = x^2 + 4x - 9$

10. $y = x^2 - 14x + 13$

11. $y = -x^2 + 5x + 6$

12. $y = -2x^2 + 4x + 6.5$

13. Which equation describes the graph at the right?

a. $f(x) = x^2 - 6x + 9$

b. $f(x) = -x^2 + 6x + 9$

c. $f(x) = x^2 + 6x + 9$

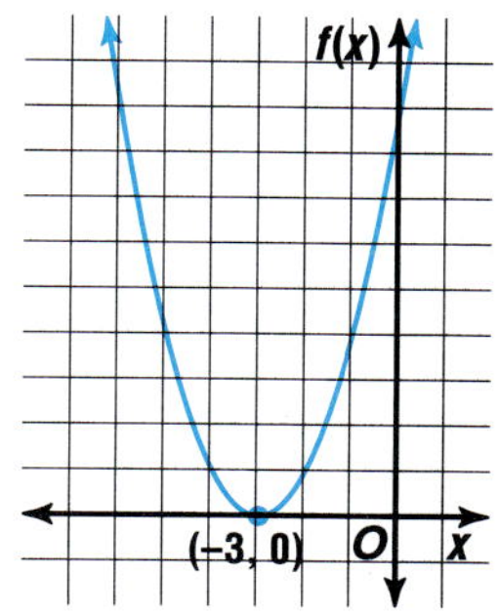

14. Tennis A tennis ball is propelled upward from the face of a racket at 40 ft/s. The racket face is 3 feet from the ground when it makes contact with the ball.

a. If the force of gravity is 32 ft/s^2, at what time after hitting the ball is it at its highest point?

b. How high does it go?

EXERCISES

Practice

Write the equation of the axis of symmetry and find the coordinates of the vertex of the graph of each equation. State if the vertex is a maximum or minimum. Then graph the equation.

15. $y = 4x^2$

16. $y = -x^2 + 4x - 1$

17. $y = x^2 + 2x + 18$

18. $y = x^2 - 3x - 10$

19. $y = x^2 - 5$

20. $y = 4x^2 + 16$

21. $y = 2x^2 + 12x - 11$

22. $y = 3x^2 + 24x + 80$

23. $y = x^2 - 25$

24. $y = 15 - 6x - x^2$

25. $y = -3x^2 - 6x + 4$

26. $y = 5 + 16x - 2x^2$

27. $y = 3(x + 1)^2 - 20$

28. $y = -(x - 2)^2 + 1$

29. $y = \frac{2}{3}(x + 1)^2 - 1$

Match each equation with its graph.

30. $f(x) = \frac{1}{2}x^2 + 1$

31. $f(x) = -\frac{1}{2}x^2 + 1$

32. $f(x) = \frac{1}{2}x^2 - 1$

a.

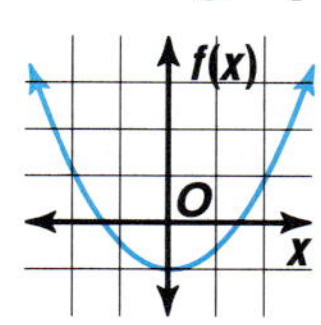

b.

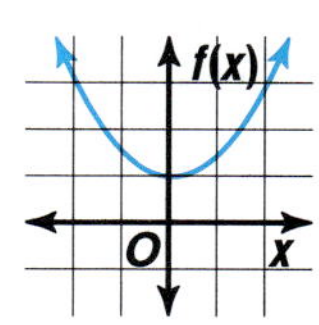

c.

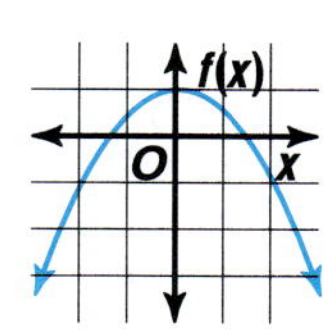

Graph each equation.

33. $y + 2 = x^2 - 10x + 25$

34. $y + 1 = 3x^2 + 12x + 12$

35. $y + 3 = -2(x - 4)^2$

36. $y - 5 = \frac{1}{3}(x + 2)^2$

37. What is the equation of the axis of symmetry of a parabola if its x-intercepts are -6 and 4?

38. The vertex of a parabola is at $(-4, -3)$. If one x-intercept is -11, what is the other x-intercept?

39. Two points on a parabola are at $(-8, 7)$ and $(12, 7)$. What is the equation of the axis of symmetry?

Graphing Calculator

You can draw the axis of symmetry on a graphed parabola by using the VERTICAL command on the DRAW menu. Press [2nd] [DRAW] 4 and use the arrow keys to move the line into place. To graph the axis of symmetry before the graph is drawn, enter the equation in the Y= list and press [2nd] [DRAW] 4 (the *x* value through which the line will pass) [ENTER]. Graph each equation and its axis of symmetry. Make a sketch of each graph on your paper, labeling the vertex of the graph.

40. $y = 8 - 4x - x^2$

41. $y = 20x^2 + 44x + 150$

42. $y = 0.023x^2 + 12.33x - 66.98$

43. $y = -78.23x^2 - 23.76x + 88.34$

Critical Thinking

44. Graph $y = x^2 + 2$ and $x + y = 8$ on the same coordinate plane. What are the coordinates of the points they have in common? Explain how you determined these points.

Applications and Problem Solving

45. **College** The cost of a college education is increasing every year. Many parents are starting college funds for their children before they are even born. The average tuition and fees for public college during the years 1970–1993 can be estimated using the function $U(t) = 2.97t^2 - 6.78t + 329.96$, where $U(t)$ represents tuition and fees (in dollars) for one year and t represents the number of years after 1970.

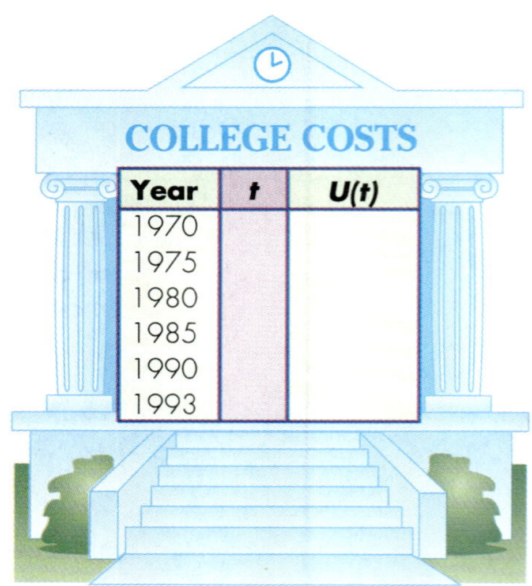

COLLEGE COSTS

Year	t	$U(t)$
1970		
1975		
1980		
1985		
1990		
1993		

a. Copy and complete the table at the right.

b. Determine the domain and range values for which this function makes sense.

c. Graph this function.

d. Assume that this function is a model for all years after 1993. How much will the tuition and fees for your first year of college be if you attend a public college?

46. **Football** When a football player punts a football, he hopes for a long "hang time," the total amount of time the ball stays in the air. Any hang time of more than about 4.5 seconds is usually good. Manuel is the punter for his high school team. He can kick the ball with an upward velocity of 80 ft/s, and his foot meets the ball 2 feet off the ground.

a. Write a quadratic equation to describe the height of the football at any given time t. Use 32 ft/s^2 as the acceleration of gravity.

b. How high is the ball after 1 second? 2 seconds? 3 seconds?

c. What is Manuel's hang time?

Mixed Review

47. **Agriculture** A field is 1.2 kilometers long and 0.9 kilometers wide. A farmer begins plowing the field by starting at the outer edge and going all the way around the field. When he stops for lunch, a strip of uniform width has been plowed on all sides of the field and half the field is plowed. What is the width of the strip? (Lesson 10–7)

48. Find $(x - 4)(x - 8)$. (Lesson 9–7)

49. **Astronomy** Mars, located 227,920,000 kilometers from the sun, has a diameter of 6.79×10^3 kilometers. (Lesson 9–3)

a. Write the diameter of Mars in decimal notation.

b. Write the distance Mars is from the sun in scientific notation.

50. Use elimination to solve the system of equations. (Lesson 8–4)

$3x + 4y = -25$

$2x - 3y = 6$

51. **Meteorology** The table below lists the record 24-hour precipitation for each state as of 1990. (Lesson 7–7)

State	Inches	State	Inches	State	Inches	State	Inches	State	Inches
AL	20.33	HI	38.00	MA	18.15	NM	11.28	SD	8.00
AK	15.20	ID	7.17	MI	9.78	NY	11.17	TN	11.00
AZ	11.40	IL	16.54	MN	10.84	NC	22.22	TX	43.00
AR	14.06	IN	10.50	MS	15.68	ND	8.10	UT	6.00
CA	26.12	IA	16.70	MO	18.18	OH	10.51	VT	8.77
CO	11.08	KS	12.59	MT	11.50	OK	15.50	VA	27.00
CT	12.77	KY	10.40	NE	13.15	OR	10.17	WA	12.00
DE	8.50	LA	22.00	NV	7.40	PA	34.50	WV	19.00
FL	38.70	ME	8.05	NH	10.38	RI	12.13	WI	11.72
GA	18.00	MD	14.75	NJ	14.81	SC	13.25	WY	6.06

Source: National Climatic Data Center

a. Make a box-and-whisker plot of the data.

b. Are there any outliers? If so, list them.

52. Graph $y = 3x + 4$. (Lesson 5–5)

53. Solve $3x = -15$. (Lesson 3–2)

54. **Patterns** Complete the pattern: 3, 6, 12, 24, __?__, __?__. (Lesson 1–2)

WORKING ON THE

In·ves·ti·ga·tion

Refer to the Investigation on pages 554–555.

the BRICKYARD

Examine the table you created in Lesson 10–7 that included the length, width, perimeter, and area of the rectangular brick patterns. Measure each of your models in millimeters to determine the values of x and y and record the measures.

1 Graph the data, plotting the length of the pattern on the horizontal axis and the area of the pattern on the vertical axis. What kind of a graph is it? What relationship does it show?

2 Make another graph, plotting the perimeter of the pattern on the horizontal axis and the area of the pattern on the vertical axis. What kind of a graph is it? What kind of relationship does it show?

3 What is the relationship between the measures of the area, length, and width? Why are there some rectangular patterns that have the same area but different perimeters?

Add the results of your work to your Investigation Folder.

11–1B Graphing Technology
Parent and Family Graphs

An Extension of Lesson 11–1

A family of graphs is a group of graphs that have at least one characteristic in common. In Lesson 6–5A, you learned about families of linear graphs that shared the same slope or y-intercept. Families of parabolas often fall into two categories—those that have the same vertex and those that have the same shape. Graphing calculators make it easy to study the characteristics of families of parabolas.

The parent function in each of these families is $y = x^2$.

LOOK BACK

Refer to Lesson 6-5A for an introduction to parent and family graphs.

Example 1 **Graph each group of equations on the same screen. Compare and contrast the graphs.**

a. $y = x^2, y = 2x^2, y = 3x^2$

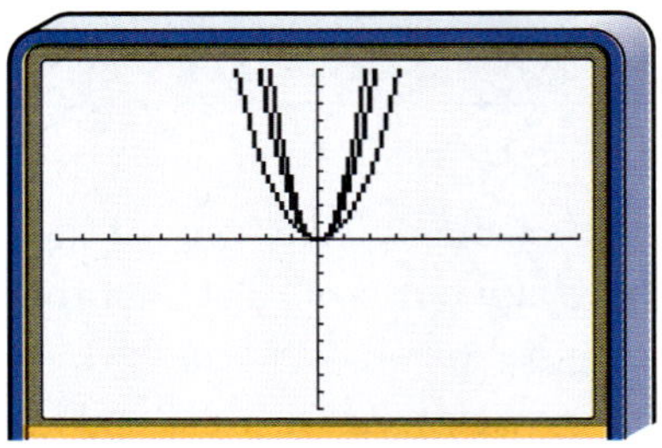

Each graph opens upward and has its vertex at the origin. The graphs of $y = 2x^2$ and $y = 3x^2$ are narrower than the graph of $y = x^2$.

b. $y = x^2, y = 0.5x^2, y = 0.3x^2$

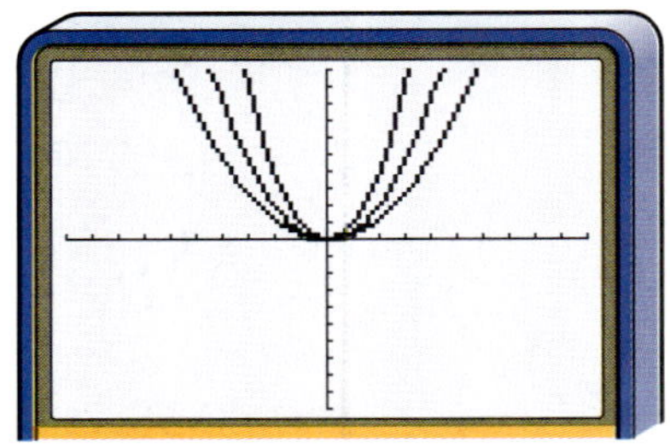

Each graph opens upward and has its vertex at the origin. The graphs of $y = 0.5x^2$ and $y = 0.3x^2$ are wider than the graph of $y = x^2$.

How does the value of a in $y = ax^2$ affect the shape of the graph?

c. $y = x^2, y = x^2 + 2,$ $y = x^2 - 3, y = x^2 - 5$

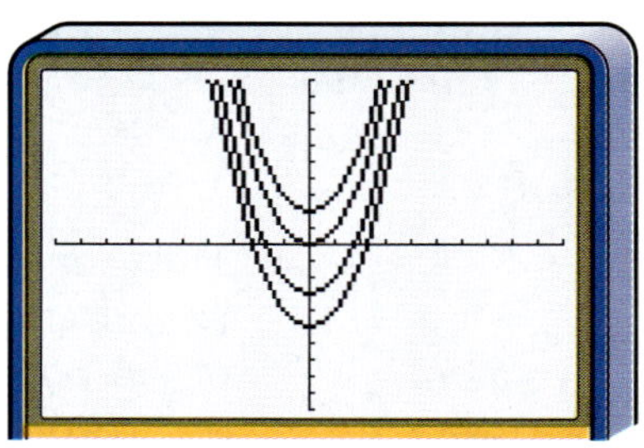

Each graph opens upward and has the same shape as $y = x^2$. However, each parabola has a different vertex, located along the y-axis. *How does the value of the constant affect the placement of the graph?*

d. $y = x^2, y = (x - 2)^2,$ $y = (x + 3)^2, y = (x + 1)^2$

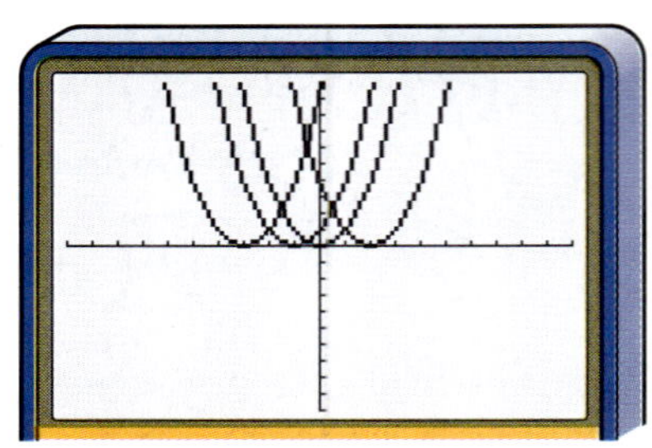

Each graph opens upward and has the same shape as $y = x^2$. However, each parabola has a different vertex, located along the x-axis. *How is the location of the vertex related to the equation of the graph?*

When analyzing or comparing the shapes of various graphs on different screens, it is important to compare the graphs using the same parameters. That is, the window used to compare the graphs should be the same, with the same scale factor. Suppose we graph the same equation using a different window for each. How will this affect the appearance of the graph?

Example 2 **Graph $y = x^2 - 5$ in each viewing window. What conclusions can you draw about the appearance of a graph in the window used?** *The scale is 1 unless otherwise noted.*

a. standard viewing window

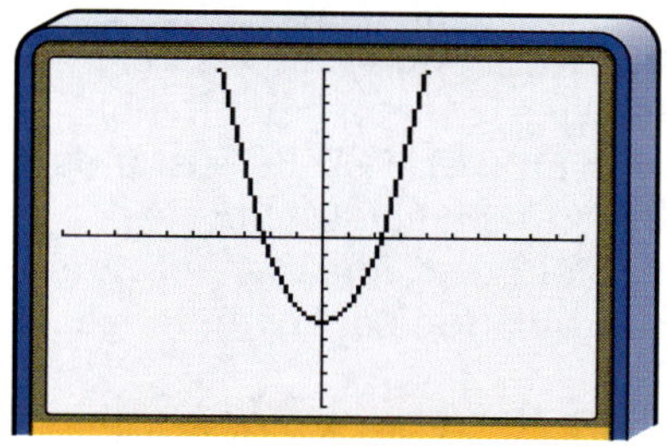

b. [−10, 10] by [−100, 100] Yscl: 20

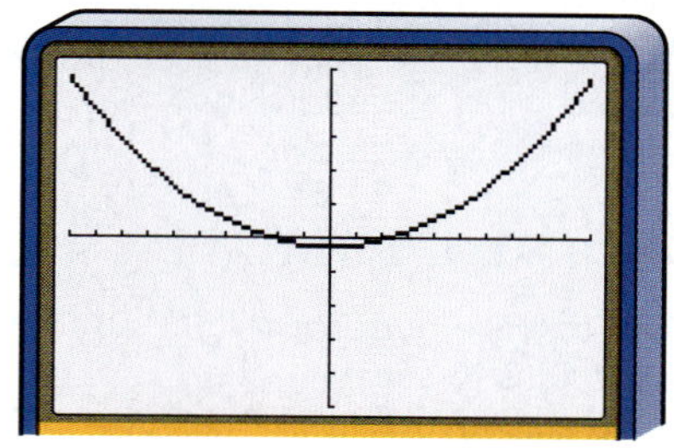

c. [−50, 50] Xscl: 5 by [−10, 10]

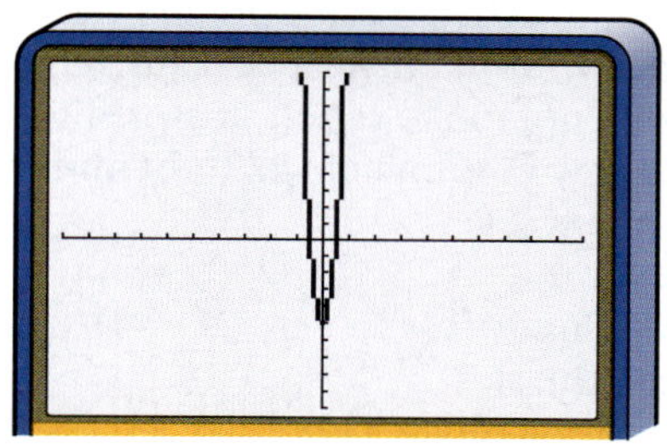

d. [−0.5, 0.5] Xscl: 0.1 by [−10, 10]

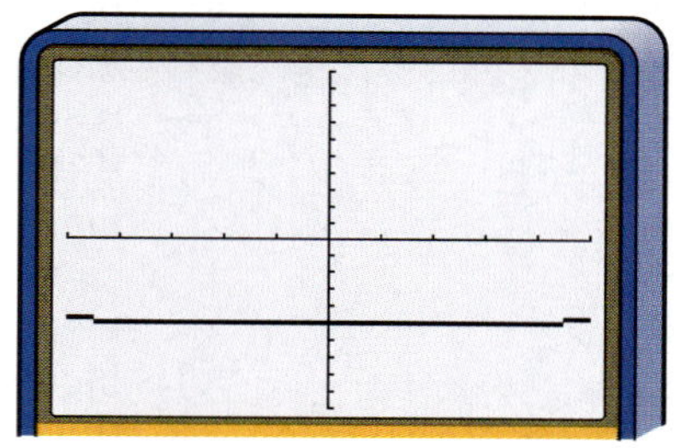

The window greatly affects the appearance of the parabola. Without knowing the window, graph b might be of the family $y = ax^2$, where $0 < a < 1$. Graph c makes the graph look like a member of $y = ax^2$, where $a > 1$. Graph d looks more like a line. However, all are graphs of the same equation.

EXERCISES

Graph each group of equations on the same screen. Make a sketch of the screen on grid paper, and compare and contrast the graphs.

1. $y = -x^2$; $y = -2x^2$; $y = -5x^2$
2. $y = -x^2$; $y = -0.3x^2$; $y = -0.7x^2$
3. $y = -x^2$; $y = -(x + 4)^2$; $y = -(x - 8)^2$
4. $y = -x^2$; $y = -x^2 + 6$; $y = -x^2 - 4$

Use the families of graphs that have appeared in this lesson to predict the appearance of the graph of each equation. Then sketch the graph.

5. $y = 4x^2$
6. $y = x^2 - 6$
7. $y = -0.1x^2$
8. $y = (x + 1)^2$
9. Describe how each change in the equation of $y = x^2$ would affect the graph of $y = x^2$. Be sure to consider all values of a and b.
   a. $y = ax^2$
   b. $y = x^2 + a$
   c. $y = (x + a)^2$
   d. $y = (x + a)^2 + b$

11-2 Solving Quadratic Equations by Graphing

What YOU'LL LEARN

- To use estimation to find roots of quadratic equations, and
- to find roots of quadratic equations by graphing.

Why IT'S IMPORTANT

You can use quadratic equations to solve problems involving architecture and number theory.

APPLICATION

Technology

In the United States, one of the fastest growing industries is the production of CD-ROMs for computers. CD-ROM stands for *Compact Disc-Read Only Memory*. CD-ROMs can hold text, music, photographic images, or combinations of any of these.

Any company that produces a product to sell finds that the profit they can make depends on the number of employees they have (among other things). The relationship between profit and the number of employees looks like the parabola drawn at right. The company does not make much of a profit if there are too few employees; as they hire more employees, the work can be done more efficiently, leading to higher profits. But if the company hires too many employees, it may not have room for them or enough work for them to do, yet they still have to be paid, causing lower profits.

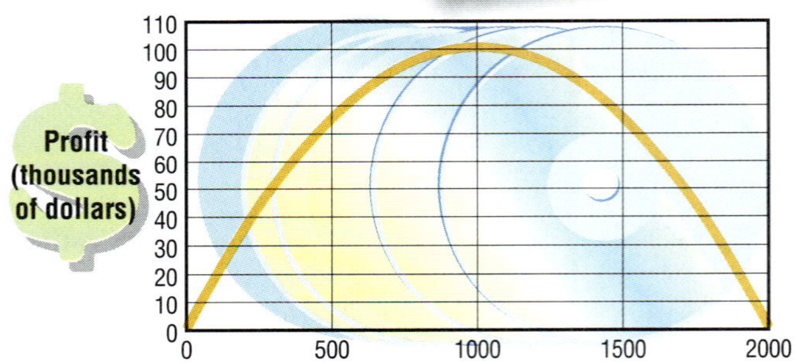

Since number of employees is the independent variable and profit is the dependent variable, the domain and range must both be positive.

Suppose a company that produces CD-ROMs can express its profit as $P(x) = -0.1x^2 + 200x$, where x is the number of employees in the company. As the personnel manager of the company, it is your job to determine the least number of employees the company should have in order to reach its goal of having \$75,000 in profit. *You will solve this problem in Exercise 4.*

A **quadratic equation** is an equation in which the value of the related quadratic function is 0. That is, for the quadratic equation $0 = x^2 + 6x - 7$, the related quadratic function is $f(x) = x^2 + 6x - 7$, where $f(x) = 0$. You have used factoring to solve equations like $x^2 + 6x - 7 = 0$. You can also use graphing to estimate the solutions to this equation.

The solutions of a quadratic equation are called the **roots** of the equation. The roots of a quadratic equation can be found by finding the x-intercepts or **zeros** of the related quadratic function.

Example 1 **Solve $x^2 - 2x - 3 = 0$ by graphing. Check by factoring.**

Graph the related function $f(x) = x^2 - 2x - 3$. The equation of the axis of symmetry is $x = 1$, and the coordinates of the vertex are $(1, -4)$. Make a table of values to find other points to sketch the graph of $f(x) = x^2 - 2x - 3$.

x	f(x)
−1	0
0	−3
1	−4
2	−3
3	0

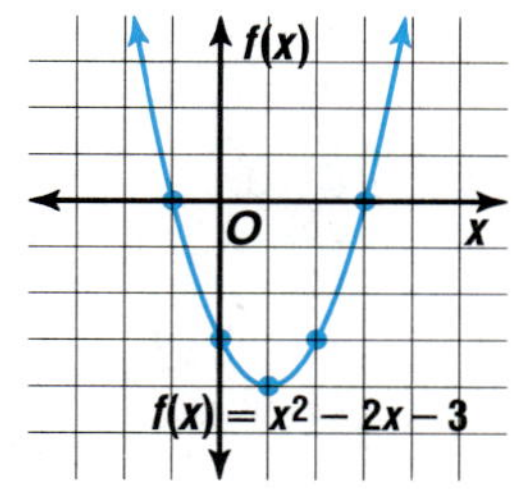

To solve the equation $x^2 - 2x - 3 = 0$, we need to know where the value of $f(x)$ is 0. On the graph, this occurs at the x-intercepts. The x-intercepts of the parabola appear to be -1 and 3.

LOOK BACK

You can refer to Lesson 10-6 for more information on the zero product property and solving equations by factoring.

Check: Solve by factoring.

$x^2 - 2x - 3 = 0$

$(x - 3)(x + 1) = 0$

Set each factor equal to 0.

$x - 3 = 0$ *Zero product property*

$x = 3$ *Add 3 to each side.*

$x + 1 = 0$ *Zero product property*

$x = -1$ *Add −1 to each side.*

The solutions of the equation are 3 and -1.

In Example 1, the zeros of the function were integers. Usually the zeros of a quadratic function are not integers. In these cases, use estimation to approximate the roots of the equation.

Example 2 **Solve $x^2 + 9x + 5 = 0$ by graphing. If integral roots cannot be found, estimate the roots by stating the consecutive integers between which the roots lie.**

Use a table of values to graph the related function $f(x) = x^2 + 9x + 5$.

Notice in the table of values that the value of the function changes from negative to positive between the x values of −9 and −8 and −1 and 0.

x	f(x)
−9	5
−8	−3
−7	−9
−6	−13
−5	−15
−4	−15
−3	−13
−2	−9
−1	−3
0	5

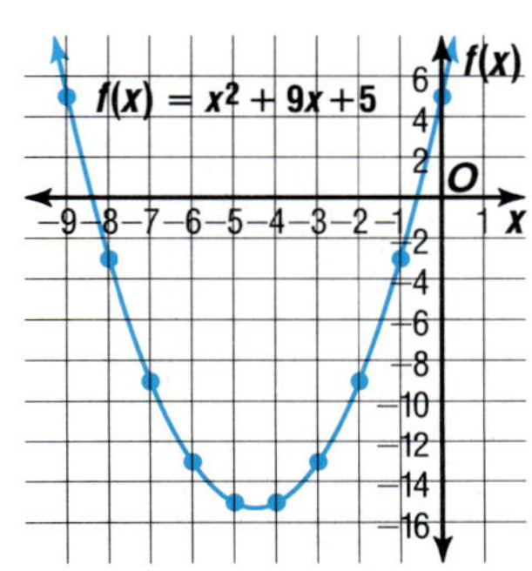

The x-intercepts of the graph are between -9 and -8 and between -1 and 0. So, one root of the equation is between -9 and -8, and the other root is between -1 and 0.

You can use a graphing calculator to find a more accurate estimate for the root of a quadratic equation than you can by using paper and pencil. One way to estimate the root is to ZOOM IN on the zero. Another method is to use the ROOT feature on the CALC menu.

EXPLORATION — GRAPHING CALCULATORS

Use a graphing calculator to solve $3x^2 - 6x - 2 = 0$ to the nearest hundredth.

Graph $y = 3x^2 - 6x - 2$ in the standard viewing window. To use the ROOT feature, you must use the cursor to define the interval in which the calculator will look. You define the interval in the same way the MAXIMUM and MINIMUM intervals are defined.

Enter: [2nd] [CALC] 2

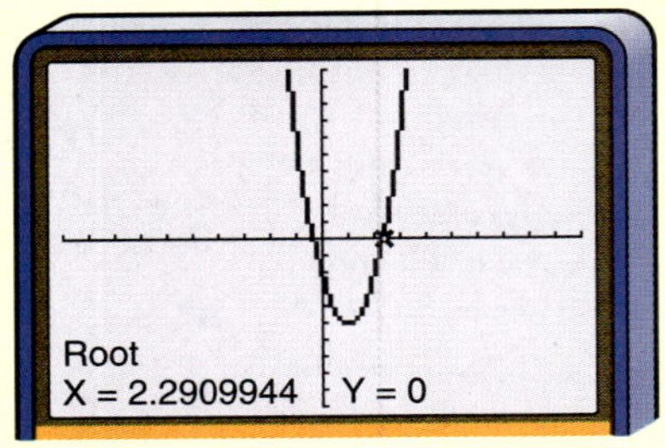

Now use the arrow keys to move the cursor to the left of one of the x-intercepts and press [ENTER] to define the lower bound. Then use the arrow keys to move the cursor to the right of that x-intercept and press [ENTER] to define the upper bound.

The y-coordinate value may appear as a decimal in scientific notation, such as −1E−12 rather than 0.

Press [ENTER] and the approximate coordinates of the root will appear. Repeat this process to find the coordinates of the other root.

Your Turn

Use a graphing calculator to estimate the roots of each equation.

a. $x^2 + 2x - 9 = 0$ **b.** $7.5x^2 - 9.5 = 0$ **c.** $6x^2 + 5x + 5 = 0$

d. Use a graphing calculator to solve $x^2 + 9x + 5 = 0$. Compare your results to those in Example 2. Which method of solution do you prefer?

Quadratic equations always have two roots. However, these roots may not be two distinct numbers.

Example 3 **Solve $x^2 - 12x + 36 = 0$ by graphing.**

Graph the related function $f(x) = x^2 - 12x + 36$.

x	$f(x)$
4	4
5	1
6	0
7	1
8	4

The equation of the axis of symmetry is $x = 6$. The vertex of the parabola is at (6, 0).

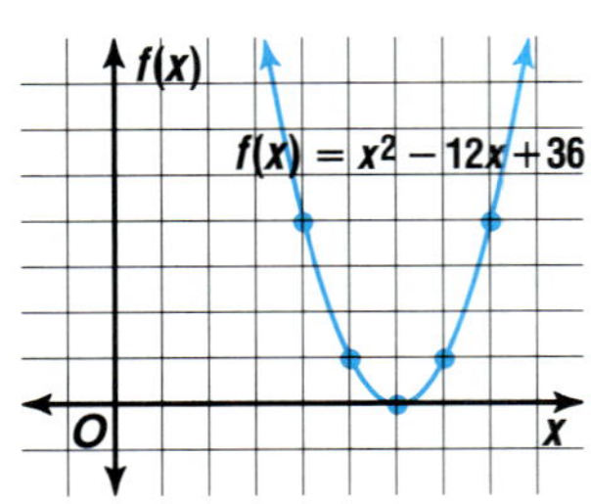

TECHNOLOGY Tip

If you graph a function with a graphing calculator and it appears that the vertex of a parabola is its x-intercept, use the ZOOM IN feature several times. You may find that the parabola actually does cross the x-axis twice.

Notice that the vertex of the parabola is the x-intercept. Thus, one solution is 6. What is the other solution?

Try solving by factoring.

$x^2 - 12x + 36 = 0$

$(x - 6)(x - 6) = 0$

Set each factor equal to 0.

$x - 6 = 0 \qquad x - 6 = 0$ *Zero product property*

$x = 6 \qquad x = 6$ *Add 6 to each side.*

There are two identical roots to this equation. So, there is only one distinct root. The solution for $x^2 - 12x + 36 = 0$ is 6.

Thus far, we have seen that quadratic equations can have two distinct real roots or one distinct real root. Is it possible that there may be no real roots?

Example 4 **Solve $x^2 + 2x + 5 = 0$ by graphing.**

Graph the function $f(x) = x^2 + 2x + 5$.

x	$f(x)$
−3	8
−2	5
−1	4
0	5
1	8

The equation of the axis of symmetry is $x = -1$. The vertex of the parabola is at $(-1, 4)$.

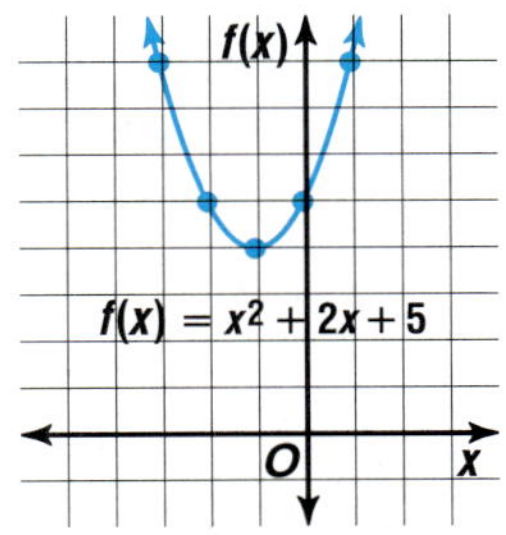

This graph has no x-intercept. Thus, there are no real number solutions for this equation.

The symbol ∅, indicating an empty set, is often used to represent no real solution.

Quadratic equations can be used to solve number problems.

Example 5 **Two numbers have a sum of 4. What are the numbers if their product is −12?**

INTEGRATION
Number Theory

Explore Let n represent one of the numbers. Then the other number is $4 - n$.

Plan A function that describes the product of these two numbers is $f(n) = n(4 - n)$ or $f(n) = -n^2 + 4n$. Find the value of n if $f(n)$ equals −12.

Solve Solve $f(n) = -n^2 + 4n$ if $f(n) = -12$.

$f(n) = -n^2 + 4n$

$-12 = -n^2 + 4n$ *$f(n) = -12$*

$0 = -n^2 + 4n + 12$ *Rewrite the equation so one side is 0.*

Graph the related function $f(n) = -n^2 + 4n + 12$.

n	$f(n)$
−3	−9
−2	0
−1	7
0	12
1	15
2	16
3	15
4	12
5	7
6	0
7	−9

The equation of the axis of symmetry is $n = 2$. The vertex of the parabola is at $(2, 16)$.

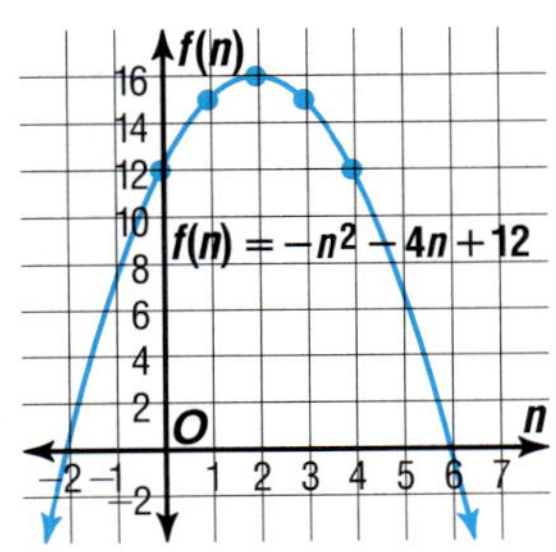

(continued on the next page)

The n-intercepts of the graph are -2 and 6. Use these values of n to find the value of the other number $4 - n$.

If $n = -2$, then $4 - n = 4 - (-2)$ or 6.

If $n = 6$, then $4 - n = 4 - 6$ or -2.

So the numbers are 6 and -2.

Examine Test to see if the numbers satisfy the problem.

The sum of the numbers is 4. The product of the numbers is -12.

$$-2 + 6 \stackrel{?}{=} 4 \qquad\qquad -2(6) \stackrel{?}{=} -12$$
$$4 = 4 \ ✓ \qquad\qquad -12 = -12 \ ✓$$

The two numbers are -2 and 6.

CHECK FOR UNDERSTANDING

Communicating Mathematics

Study the lesson. Then complete the following.

1. **Explain** why the x-intercepts of a quadratic function can be used to solve a quadratic equation.
2. **You Decide** Joshua says he likes to solve a quadratic equation by factoring rather than graphing. Hanna says that she likes graphing because she can always get an answer. Who is correct? Give examples to support your answer.
3. What is the related function you would use to solve $x^2 + 9x + 2 = 3x - 4$ by graphing?
4. Refer to the application at the beginning of the lesson. What is the least number of employees that would help the company make its goal of \$75,000 profit?

MATH JOURNAL

5. **Draw** an example of each type of situation that may occur when using graphing to find the solutions of a quadratic equation. Identify the number of real roots of the quadratic function in each situation.

Guided Practice

Determine the number of real roots for each quadratic equation whose related function is graphed below.

6.
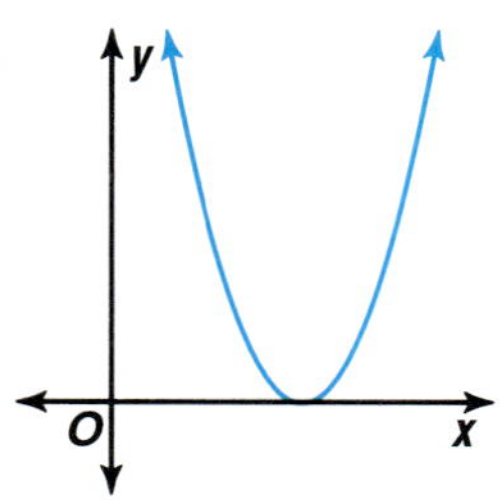

7.
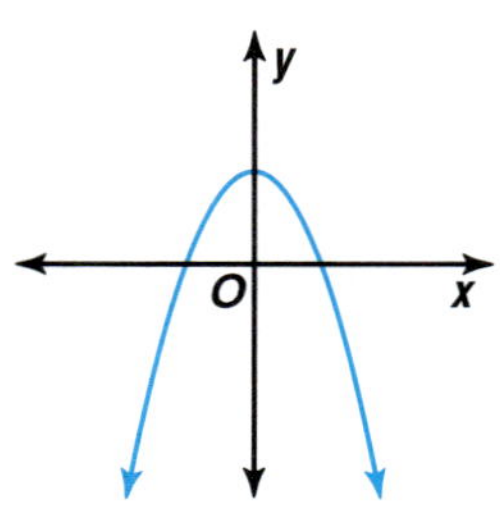

8.
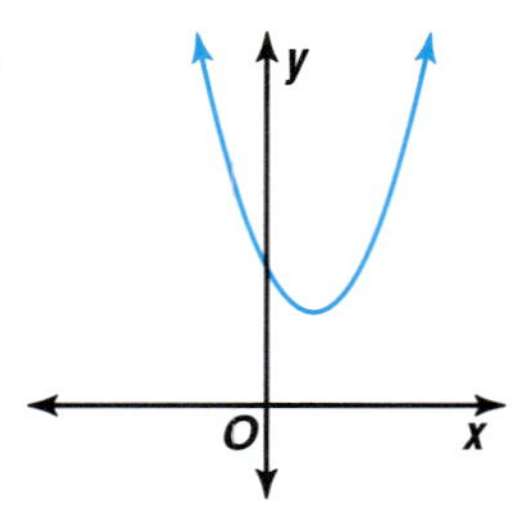

9. State the real roots of the quadratic equation whose related function is graphed at the right.

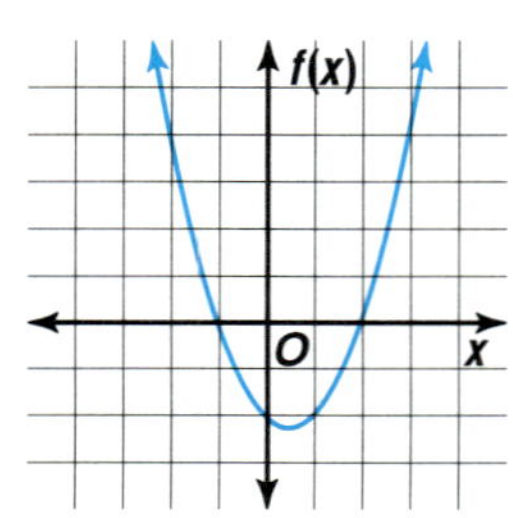

Solve each equation by graphing. If integral roots cannot be found, state the consecutive integers between which the roots lie.

10. $x^2 - 7x + 6 = 0$
11. $c^2 - 5c - 24 = 0$
12. $5n^2 + 2n + 6 = 0$
13. $w^2 - 3w = 5$
14. $b^2 - b + 4 = 0$
15. $a^2 - 10a = -25$

16. **Number Theory** Use a quadratic equation to find two real numbers whose sum is 5 and whose product is -24.

EXERCISES

Practice

State the real roots of each quadratic equation whose related function is graphed below.

17.

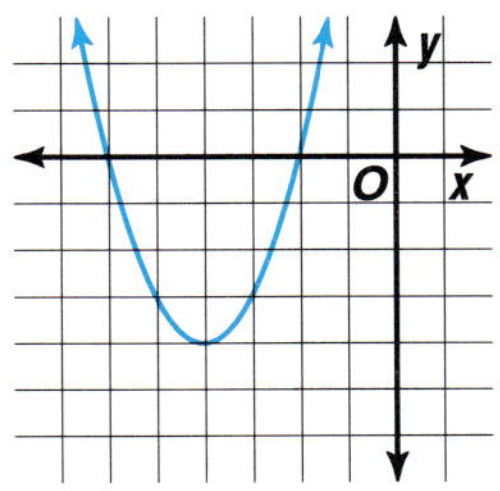

18.

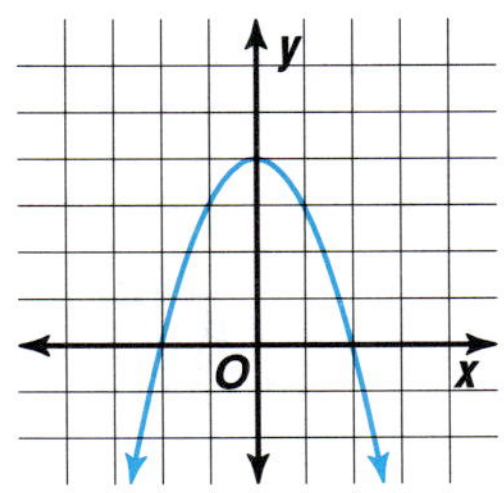

19.

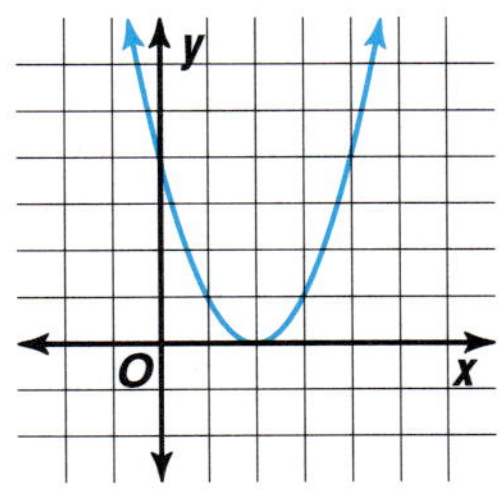

Solve each equation by graphing. If integral roots cannot be found, state the consecutive integers between which the roots lie.

20. $x^2 + 7x + 12 = 0$
21. $x^2 - 16 = 0$
22. $a^2 + 6a + 7 = 0$
23. $x^2 + 6x + 9 = 0$
24. $r^2 + 4r - 12 = 0$
25. $c^2 + 3 = 0$
26. $2c^2 + 20c + 32 = 0$
27. $3x^2 + 9x - 12 = 0$
28. $2x^2 - 18 = 0$
29. $p^2 + 16 = 8p$
30. $w^2 - 10w = -21$
31. $a^2 - 8a = 4$
32. $m^2 - 2\text{m} = -2$
33. $12n^2 - 26n = 30$
34. $4x^2 - 35 = -4x$

The roots of a quadratic equation are given. Graph the related quadratic function if it has the indicated maximum or minimum point.

35. roots: 0, -6
    maximum point: $(-3, 4)$
36. roots: -2, -6
    minimum point : $(-4, -2)$
37. roots: no real roots
    minimum point: $(2, 5)$
38. roots: $-4 < x < -3$, $1 < x < 2$
    maximum point: $(-1, 6)$

INTEGRATION
Number Theory

Use a quadratic equation to determine the two numbers that satisfy each situation.

39. Their difference is 4 and their product is 32.
40. Their sum is 9 and their product is 20.
41. Their sum is 4 and their product is 5.
42. They differ by 2. The sum of their squares is 130.

Estimate the *y*-intercepts of each quadratic equation by graphing.

43. $x = -0.75y^2 - 6y - 9$
44. $x = y^2 - 4y + 1$
45. $x = 3y^2 + 2y + 4$

Graphing Calculator

Use a graphing calculator to solve each equation to the nearest hundredth.

46. $4x^2 - 11 = 0$
47. $-2x^2 - x - 3 = 0$
48. $x^2 + 22x + 121 = 0$
49. $6x^2 - 12x + 3 = 0$
50. $5x^2 + 4x - 7 = 0$
51. $-4x^2 + 7x + 8 = 0$

Use a graphing calculator to find values for *k* for each equation so that it will have (a) one distinct root, (b) two real roots, and (c) no real roots.

52. $x^2 + 3x + k = 0$
53. $kx^2 + 4x - 2 = 0$

Critical Thinking

54. Suppose the value of a quadratic function is negative when $x = 10$ and positive when $x = 11$. Explain why it is reasonable to assume that the related equation has a solution between 10 and 11.

Applications and Problem Solving

55. **Architecture** A painter is hired to paint an art gallery whose walls are sculptured with arches that can be represented by the quadratic function $f(x) = -x^2 - 4x + 12$. The wall space under each arch is to be painted a different color from the arch itself. The painter can use the formula $A = \frac{2}{3}bh$ to estimate the area under a parabola, where b is the length of a horizontal segment connecting two points on the parabola and h is the height from that segment to the vertex. Suppose the horizontal segment is represented by the floor, which is the x-axis, and each unit represents 1 foot.

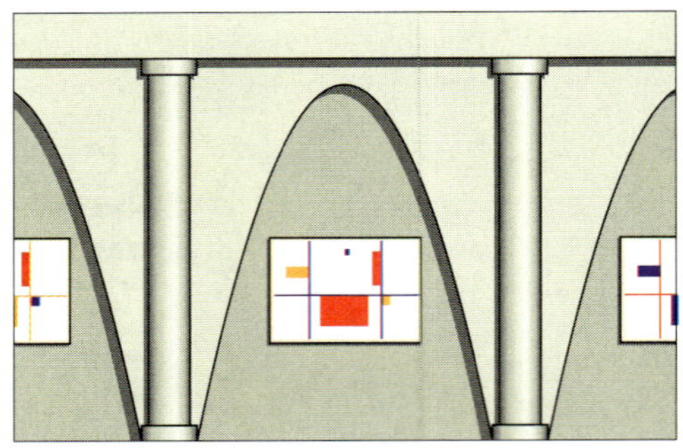

   a. Graph the quadratic function and determine its x-intercepts.
   b. What is the length of the segment along the floor?
   c. What is the height of the arch?
   d. How much wall space is there under each arch?
   e. How much would the paint cost to paint the walls under 12 arches if the paint is \$27/gallon, she applies two coats, and the manufacturer states that each gallon will cover 200 ft^2? *Remember you cannot buy part of a gallon.*

56. **Make a Drawing** Banneker Park has set aside a section of the park as a nature preserve with an observation deck and telescopes so that people can observe the wildlife and plants up close. To accommodate the increased number of visitors they expect, the park commission has received funding to double the parking area. The current lot is 64 yards by 96 yards, and they are going to add strips of equal width to the end and side of the lot to create a larger rectangle that is twice the size of the original.
   a. Make a drawing of the lot and the proposed additions.
   b. Write a quadratic equation to find x, the width of the strips, so that the area of the parking lot is doubled.
   c. How wide are the strips to be added?
   d. What are the dimensions of the new parking lot?

Top Five List

Most-Visited U.S. National Parks in 1993

Park	Visitors
1. Great Smoky Mountains	9,283,848
2. Grand Canyon	4,575,602
3. Yosemite	3,839,645
4. Yellowstone	2,912,193
5. Rocky Mountains	2,780,342

Mixed Review

57. Find the equation of the axis of symmetry and the coordinates of the vertex of the graph of $y = -3x^2 + 4$. (Lesson 11–1)

58. Solve $81x^3 + 36x^2 = -4x$. (Lesson 10–6)

59. **Geometry** The area of a rectangle is $(8x^2 - 10x + 3)$ square meters. What are the dimensions of the rectangle? (Lesson 10–3)

60. Find $(x - 2y)^3$. (Lesson 9–8)

61. Find the degree of $6x^2y + 5x^3y^2z - x + x^2y^2$. (Lesson 9–4)

62. Use graphing to solve the system of equations. (Lesson 8–1)
$x + y = 3$
$x + y = 4$

63. Solve $|3x + 4| < 8$. (Lesson 7–6)

64. Graph $y = -x + 6$. (Lesson 6–5)

65. **Commerce** Find the sale price of an item originally marked as \$33 with 25% off. (Lesson 4–4)

66. Find $-4 + 6 + (-10) + 8$. (Lesson 2–3)

WORKING ON THE In•ves•ti•ga•tion

Refer to the Investigation on pages 554–555.

the BRICKYARD

In order to best use the excess inventory of bricks, you are going to investigate the possible combinations that will use up the inventory at a steady rate.

1 Suppose you have four large square bricks and three small square bricks. How many rectangular bricks would you need to create a rectangular pattern? Is there more than one pattern that can be made if you change the number of rectangular bricks?
- What are the dimensions, perimeters, and areas of the rectangular patterns formed?
- Use the variables x and y as the length of the large square and the length of the small square, respectively. List the dimensions, perimeter, and area of each pattern in terms of x and y.
- Explain your findings. How do the perimeters and areas of these patterns relate in this matter?

2 If you had three large square bricks, five rectangular bricks, and two small square bricks, what size rectangular patterns can you make? Express the dimensions, perimeter, and area of each pattern in terms of x and y.

3 If you had two large bricks, six rectangular bricks, and four small bricks, what size rectangular patterns can you make? Express the dimensions, perimeter, and area of each pattern in terms of x and y.

4 Explain the method you used to solve these problems and any generalizations you found.

Add the results of your work to your Investigation Folder.

11-3 Solving Quadratic Equations by Using the Quadratic Formula

What YOU'LL LEARN

- To solve quadratic equations by using the quadratic formula.

Why IT'S IMPORTANT

You can use quadratic equations to solve problems involving hydraulics and civics.

CONNECTION

Civics

The number of citizens (in millions) voting in each presidential election since 1824 can be approximated by the quadratic function $V(t) = 0.0046t^2 - 0.185t + 3.30$, where t represents the number of years since 1824. For her history project, Marcela Ruiz needed to determine in what year the number of voters in a presidential election was approximately 55 million. She used the function above, replacing $V(t)$ with 55.

$$V(t) = 0.0046t^2 - 0.185t + 3.30$$
$$55 = 0.0046t^2 - 0.185t + 3.30$$
$$0 = 0.0046t^2 - 0.185t - 51.7$$

Marcela knew that she could use her graphing calculator to estimate the solutions of this equation, but she wondered how she could get a good estimate of t if she didn't have a graphing calculator. *You will estimate these solutions in Example 4.*

You can use the **quadratic formula** to solve any quadratic equation.

The Quadratic Formula	**The solutions of a quadratic equation in the form $ax^2 + bx + c = 0$, where $a \neq 0$, are given by the formula** $$x = \frac{-b \pm \sqrt{b^2 - 4ac}}{2a}.$$

The quadratic formula can be used to solve any quadratic equation involving any variable.

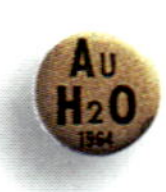

Example 1 **Use the quadratic formula to solve each equation.**

a. $x^2 - 6x - 40 = 0$

In the equation, $a = 1$, $b = -6$, and $c = -40$. Substitute these values into the quadratic formula.

The symbol ± means to evaluate the expression first using + and then evaluate it again using −. This provides for the two solutions of the equation.

$$x = \frac{-b \pm \sqrt{b^2 - 4ac}}{2a}$$
$$= \frac{-(-6) \pm \sqrt{(-6)^2 - 4(1)(-40)}}{2(1)} \quad a = 1,\ b = -6,\text{ and } c = -40$$
$$= \frac{6 \pm \sqrt{36 + 160}}{2}$$
$$= \frac{6 \pm \sqrt{196}}{2}$$
$$= \frac{6 \pm 14}{2}$$

You can also check the solution to any equation by substituting each value into the original equation.

$$x = \frac{6 + 14}{2} \quad \text{or} \quad x = \frac{6 - 14}{2}$$

$$= \frac{20}{2} \text{ or } 10 \qquad = -\frac{8}{2} \text{ or } -4$$

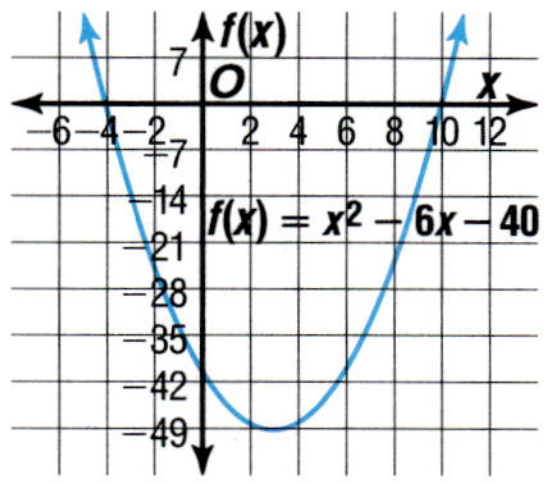

Check: Solve by graphing the related function $f(x) = x^2 - 6x - 40$. The x-intercepts appear to be 10 and −4. This agrees with the algebraic solution.

The solutions are 10 and −4.

b. $\mathbf{y^2 - 6y + 9 = 0}$

$$y = \frac{-b \pm \sqrt{b^2 - 4ac}}{2a}$$

$$= \frac{-(-6) \pm \sqrt{(-6)^2 - 4(1)(9)}}{2(1)} \quad \textit{a = 1, b = −6, and c = 9}$$

$$= \frac{6 \pm \sqrt{36 - 36}}{2}$$

$$= \frac{6 \pm \sqrt{0}}{2}$$

$$y = \frac{6 + 0}{2} \quad \text{or} \quad y = \frac{6 - 0}{2}$$

$$= 3 \qquad\qquad = 3$$

Check: Solve by factoring.

$$y^2 - 6y + 9 = 0$$

$$(y - 3)(y - 3) = 0$$

$$y - 3 = 0 \qquad y - 3 = 0 \quad \textit{Zero product property}$$

$$y = 3 \qquad y = 3 \quad \textit{Add 3 to each side.}$$

There is one distinct solution, 3.

LOOK BACK

You can refer to Lesson 2-8 for more information on irrational numbers.

Sometimes when you use the quadratic formula, you find the solutions are irrational numbers. It is helpful to use a calculator to estimate the values of the solutions in this case.

Example 2 **Use the quadratic formula to solve $2n^2 - 7n - 3 = 0$.**

$$n = \frac{-b \pm \sqrt{b^2 - 4ac}}{2a}$$

$$= \frac{-(-7) \pm \sqrt{(-7)^2 - 4(2)(-3)}}{2(2)} \quad \textit{a = 2, b = −7, and c = −3}$$

$$= \frac{7 \pm \sqrt{49 + 24}}{4}$$

$$= \frac{7 \pm \sqrt{73}}{4}$$

$\sqrt{73}$ is an irrational number. We can approximate the solutions by using a calculator to find a decimal value for $\sqrt{73}$.

$$n = \frac{7 + \sqrt{73}}{4} \approx 3.886 \qquad n = \frac{7 - \sqrt{73}}{4} \approx -0.386$$

The two solutions are approximately −0.386 and 3.886.

When we solved quadratic equations by graphing, we found that some quadratic equations have no real solutions. How does the quadratic formula work in this situation?

Example 3 **Use the quadratic formula to solve $z^2 - 5z + 12 = 0$.**

$$z = \frac{-b \pm \sqrt{b^2 - 4ac}}{2a}$$

$$= \frac{-(-5) \pm \sqrt{(-5)^2 - 4(1)(12)}}{2(1)} \quad a = 1,\ b = -5, \text{ and } c = 12$$

$$= \frac{5 \pm \sqrt{25 - 48}}{2}$$

$$= \frac{5 \pm \sqrt{-23}}{2}$$

Since there is no real number that is the square root of a negative number, this equation has no real solutions.

It is often helpful to use a calculator when using the quadratic formula to solve real-world problems. If there are no real solutions for the equation, the calculator will give you an error message.

Example 4

CONNECTION

Civics

Refer to the connection at the beginning of the lesson. Determine in what year the number of people voting in a presidential election was approximately 55 million.

Use a scientific calculator and the quadratic formula to find values for t. The values for a, b, and c are 0.0046, −0.185, and −51.7, respectively. Find the value of $\sqrt{b^2 - 4ac}$ and store it in the calculator's memory.

Enter: [( ] .185 [+/−] [x^2] [−] 4 [×] .0046 [×] 51.7 [+/−] [ )] [$\sqrt{x}$] [STO] 0.992726044

Now evaluate the quadratic formula.

Enter: [( ] [( ] .185 [+/−] [ )] [+/−] [+] [RCL] [ )] [÷] [( ] 2 [×] .0046 [ )] [=] 128.0137005

Enter: [( ] [( ] .185 [+/−] [ )] [+/−] [−] [RCL] [ )] [÷] [( ] 2 [×] .0046 [ )] [=] −87.79630922

The negative root has no meaning in this problem.

Since t represents the number of years since 1824, add 128 to 1824: $128 + 1824 = 1952$.

So, 1952 was the year in which approximately 55 million people voted.

CHECK FOR UNDERSTANDING

Communicating Mathematics

Study the lesson. Then complete the following.

1. **Explain** how you get two solutions when using the quadratic formula.
2. **Explain** what happens in the quadratic formula when there are no real solutions for the equation.
3. Refer to the connection at the beginning of the lesson.
   a. Predict how many will vote in the year 2000.
   b. Describe the domain and range of this relation.

MATH JOURNAL

4. **Assess Yourself** You have learned to use graphing, factoring, and the quadratic formula to solve quadratic equations. Which method do you prefer and why?

Guided Practice

State the values of *a*, *b*, and *c* for each quadratic equation. Then solve the equation by using the quadratic formula. Approximate irrational roots to the nearest hundredth.

5. $x^2 + 3x - 18 = 0$
6. $14 = 12 - 5x - x^2$
7. $4x^2 - 2x + 15 = 0$
8. $x^2 = 25$

Solve each equation by using the quadratic formula. Approximate roots to the nearest hundredth if necessary.

9. $4x^2 + 2x - 17 = 0$
10. $3b^2 + 5b + 11 = 0$
11. $x^2 + 7x + 6 = 0$
12. $z^2 - 13z = 32$
13. **Hydraulics** Cox's formula for measuring the velocity of water escaping from a reservoir through a horizontal pipe is $4v^2 + 5v - 2 = \frac{1200HD}{L}$, where v represents the velocity of the water in feet per second, H the height of the reservoir in feet, D the diameter of the pipe in inches, and L the length of the pipe in feet. How fast is water flowing through a pipe 20 feet long with a diameter of 6 inches that is draining a swimming pool with a depth of 10 feet? Round your answer to the nearest tenth.

EXERCISES

Practice

Solve each equation by using the quadratic formula. Approximate irrational roots to the nearest hundredth.

14. $x^2 - 2x - 24 = 0$
15. $a^2 + 10a + 12 = 0$
16. $c^2 + 12c + 20 = 0$
17. $5y^2 - y - 4 = 0$
18. $r^2 + 25 = 0$
19. $3b^2 - 7b - 20 = 0$
20. $y^2 + 12y + 36 = 0$
21. $2r^2 + r - 14 = 0$
22. $2x^2 + 4x = 30$
23. $2x^2 - 28x + 98 = 0$
24. $24x^2 - 14x = 6$
25. $6x^2 + 15 = -19x$
26. $12x^2 = 48$
27. $x^2 + 6x = 36 + 6x$
28. $1.34a^2 - 1.1a = -1.02$
29. $3m^2 - 2m = 1$
30. $24a^2 - 2a = 15$
31. $2w^2 = -(7w + 3)$
32. $a^2 - \frac{3}{5}a + \frac{2}{25} = 0$
33. $-2x^2 + 0.7x = -0.3$
34. $2y^2 - \frac{5}{4}y = \frac{1}{2}$

Without graphing, determine the *x*-intercepts of the graph of each function to the nearest tenth.

35. $f(x) = 2x^2 - 5x + 2$
36. $f(x) = 4x^2 - 9x + 4$
37. $f(x) = 13x^2 - 16x - 4$

Use the quadratic formula to determine values for *a*, *b*, and *c* if the given numbers are solutions of a quadratic equation. Then write the equation.

38. $-1 \pm \sqrt{3}$ **39.** $\frac{-5 \pm \sqrt{2}}{2}$ **40.** $\frac{4 \pm \sqrt{29}}{2}$

Programming

41. The graphing calculator program at the right determines what type of solutions a quadratic equation will have and then prints decimal approximations of the solutions if they exist.

```
PROGRAM:SOLUTIONS
: Prompt A,B,C
: B²−4AC→D
: If D<0
: Then
: Disp "NO REAL SOLUTIONS"
: Stop
: End
: If D=0
: Then
: Disp "1 DISTINCT SOLUTION",
  -B/(2A)
: Else
: Disp "2 REAL SOLUTIONS",
  (-B+√(D))/(2A), (-B−√(D))/(2A)
: End
```

Use the program to find the solutions of each equation.

a. $x^2 - 11x + 10 = 0$
b. $3x^2 - 2x + 1 = 0$
c. $4x^2 + 4x + 1 = 0$
d. $7x^2 + 2x - 5 = 0$

Critical Thinking

42. The expression $b^2 - 4ac$ is called the **discriminant** of a quadratic equation. The discriminant can help you determine what type of solutions to expect when you solve a quadratic equation. Copy and complete the table below.

Equation	$x^2 - 4x + 1 = 0$	$x^2 + 6x + 11 = 0$	$x^2 - 4x + 4 = 0$
Value of the Discriminant			
Graph of the Equation			
Number of *x*-intercepts			
Number of Real Solutions			

43. Use the results of Examples 1–3 and the table above to describe the discriminant of a quadratic equation for each type of solution.

a. two irrational solutions
b. two noninteger rational solutions
c. two integral solutions
d. 1 distinct integral solution

Applications and Problem Solving

44. Government Between 1980 and 1993, the income (billions of dollars) received by the federal government can be modeled by the quadratic function $I(t) = 0.26t^2 + 49.94t + 511.4$, where t represents the number of years since 1980.

a. Determine the domain and range values for which this function makes sense.

b. Determine the income in 1993.

c. Assume that the pattern continues to hold. What is the projected federal income for the year 2000?

d. Determine in which year the federal income was \$1000 billion or \$1 trillion.

45. **Medicine** The two rules that govern the amount of medicine you should give a child if you know the adult dosage are Young's rule, $c = \frac{ad}{a + 12}$, and Cowling's rule, $c = \frac{(a + 1)d}{24}$. In both formulas, a represents the age of the child (in years), d represents the amount of the adult dosage, and c represents the amount of the child's dosage.
   a. The adult dosage for a drug is 30 mg/day. Calculate the dosage for a 6-year-old using each rule.
   b. Write a quadratic equation that represents the age(s) at which the two rules give the same dosage. Then solve the equation.

Mixed Review

46. Solve $x^2 + 10x = -21$ by graphing. (Lesson 11–2)
47. Solve $4s^2 = -36s$. (Lesson 10–6)
48. Find $3a^2(a - 4) + 6a(3a^2 + a - 7) - 4(a - 7)$. (Lesson 9–6)
49. **Number Theory** The sum of two numbers is 42. Their difference is 6. Find the numbers. (Lesson 8–3)
50. Graph the solution set for $b > 5$ or $b \leq 0$. (Lesson 7–4)
51. Determine if the following relation is a function. (Lesson 5–5) $\{(3, 2), (-3, -2), (-4, -2), (4, -2)\}$
52. Solve $3x + 8 = 2x - 4$. (Lesson 3–5)
53. **Weather** The temperature at 8:00 A.M. was 36°F. A cold front went through that evening, and by 3:00 A.M. the next day, the temperature had fallen 40°. What was the temperature at 3:00 A.M.? (Lesson 2–1)

SELF TEST

Write the equation of the axis of symmetry and find the coordinates of the vertex of the graph of each equation. Then graph the equation. (Lesson 11–1)

1. $y = x^2 - x - 6$
2. $y = 2x^2 + 3$
3. $y = -x^2 + 7$

4. **Physics** The height h in feet of an experimental rocket t seconds after blast-off is given by the formula $h = -16t^2 + 2320t + 125$. (Lesson 11–1)
   a. Approximately how long after blast-off does the rocket reach a height of 84,225 feet?
   b. How much longer from this height does it take the rocket to reach its maximum height?

Solve each equation by graphing. If integral roots cannot be found, state the consecutive integers between which the roots lie. (Lesson 11–2)

5. $x^2 = 81$
6. $4x^2 = 35 - 4x$
7. $6x^2 + 36 = 0$

Solve each equation by using the quadratic formula. Approximate irrational roots to the nearest hundredth. (Lesson 11–3)

8. $a^2 + 7a = -6$
9. $y^2 + 6y + 10 = 0$
10. $z^2 - 13z - 32 = 0$

11–4A Graphing Technology
Exponential Functions

A Preview of Lesson 11–4

Graphing calculators can be used to graph many types of functions easily so patterns in the functions can be studied. This includes **exponential functions** of the form $y = a^x$, where $a > 0$ and $a \neq 1$.

Example

Graph each equation in the standard viewing window. Describe the graph.

a. $y = 3^x$

Enter the equation in the Y= list.

Enter: [Y=] 3 [^] [X,T,θ,n] [ZOOM] 6

Notice that the graph increases rapidly as x becomes greater. The graph passes through the point at (0, 1). The domain of the function is all real numbers, and the range is all positive real numbers.

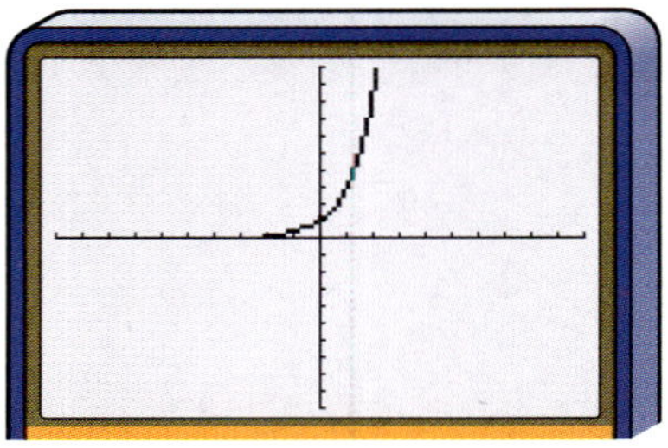

b. $y = \left(\frac{1}{3}\right)^x$

Enter: [Y=] [(] 1 [÷] 3 [)] [^] [X,T,θ,n] [GRAPH]

The graph decreases as x increases. The graph passes through the point at (0, 1). The domain is all real numbers, and the range is all positive real numbers.

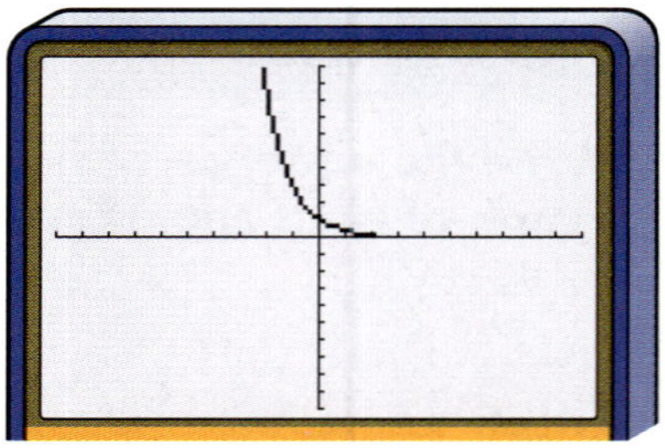

EXERCISES

Use a graphing calculator to graph each exponential equation. Sketch the graphs on a separate piece of paper.

1. $y = 2^x$ **2.** $y = 5^x$ **3.** $y = 0.1^x$

4. $y = \left(\frac{2}{3}\right)^x$ **5.** $y = 0.25^x$ **6.** $y = 1.6^x$

7. $y = 0.2^x$ **8.** $y = 0.5^{-x}$ **9.** $y = 10^x$

10. Solve $1.2^x = 10$ graphically. Explain how you solved the equation and write the solution accurately to the nearest hundredth.

11–4 Exponential Functions

What YOU'LL LEARN

- To graph exponential functions,
- to determine if a set of data displays exponential behavior, and
- to solve exponential equations.

Why IT'S IMPORTANT

You can use exponential equations to solve problems involving biology and archaeology.

APPLICATION

Folklore

A wise man asked his ruler to provide rice for feeding his people. Rather than receiving a constant daily supply of rice, the wise man asked the ruler to give him 2 grains of rice for the first square on a chessboard, 4 grains of rice for the second, 8 grains of rice for the third, 16 grains of rice for the fourth, and so on, doubling the amount of rice with each square of the board. How many grains of rice will he receive for the last (64th) square on the chessboard?

You could make a table and look for a pattern to determine how many grains of rice he received for each square of the chessboard.

Square	Grains	Pattern	Square	Grains	Pattern
1	2	2^1	19	524,288	2^{19}
2	4	2^2	20	1,048,576	2^{20}
3	8	2^3	21	2,097,152	2^{21}
4	16	2^4	22	4,194,304	2^{22}
5	32	2^5	23	8,388,608	2^{23}
6	64	2^6	24	16,777,216	2^{24}
7	128	2^7	25	33,554,432	2^{25}
8	256	2^8	26	67,108,864	2^{26}
9	512	2^9	27	134,217,728	2^{27}
10	1024	2^{10}	28	268,435,456	2^{28}
11	2048	2^{11}	29	536,870,912	2^{29}
12	4096	2^{12}	30	1,073,741,824	2^{30}
13	8192	2^{13}	31	2,147,483,648	2^{31}
14	16,384	2^{14}	32	4,294,967,296	2^{32}
15	32,768	2^{15}	33	8,589,934,592	2^{33}
16	65,536	2^{16}	34	17,179,869,184	2^{34}
17	131,072	2^{17}	35	34,359,738,368	2^{35}
18	262,144	2^{18}	36	68,719,476,736	2^{36}

FYI

There are approximately 24,000 grains of rice in 1 pound of rice.

Notice that when only 36 of the 64 squares are calculated, there are over 68 billion grains of rice. How many grains would there be for square 64? *You will answer this question in Exercise 1.*

Study the pattern column. Notice that the exponent number matches the number of the square on the chessboard. So we can write an equation to describe y, the number of grains of rice for any given square x as $y = 2^x$. This type of function, in which the variable is the exponent, is called an **exponential function.**

Definition of Exponential Function

An exponential function is a function that can be described by an equation of the form $y = a^x$, where $a > 0$ and $a \neq 1$.

You can use paper-folding to illustrate an exponential function.

Modeling an Exponential Function

Materials: large piece of paper

Your Turn

a. Fold a large rectangular piece of paper in half. Unfold it and record how many sections are formed by the creases. Refold the paper.

b. Fold the paper in half again. Record how many sections are formed by the creases. Refold the paper.

c. Continue folding in half and recording the number of sections until you can no longer fold the paper.

d. How many folds could you make?

e. How many sections were formed?

f. What exponential function is modeled by the folds and sections created?

As with other functions, you can use ordered pairs to graph an exponential function. Use a table of values and a calculator to find ordered pairs that satisfy $y = 2^x$. While the negative values of x have no meaning in the rice problem, they should be included in the graph of the function. Connect the points to form a smooth curve.

x	y
−5	0.03125
−4	0.0625
−3	0.125
−2	0.25
−1	0.5
0	1
1	2
2	4
3	8
4	16

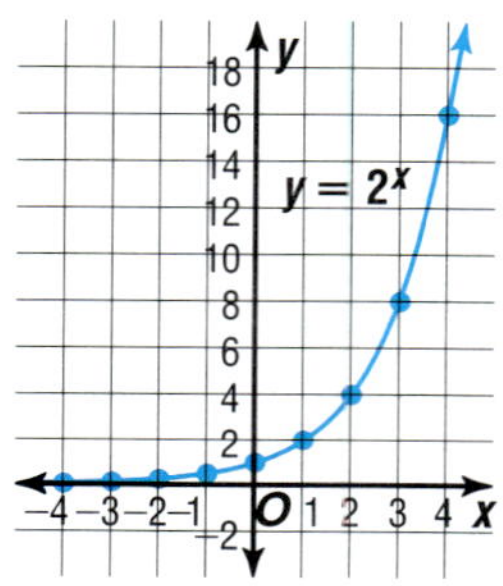

Notice that the graph has a y-intercept of 1. Does it have an x-intercept? *You will answer this question in Exercise 2.*

The graph shown above represents all real values of x and their corresponding values of y for $y = 2^x$.

You can use a scientific calculator to help you find ordered pairs to graph other exponential functions. For example, suppose $y = 3^x$ and $x = -2$.

Enter: 3 [y^x] 2 [+/−] [=] 0.111111111

Example 1 **Graph each function. State the y-intercept of each graph.**

a. $y = 3^x$

x	y
−3	0.037
−2	0.111
−1	0.333
0	1
1	3
2	9
3	27

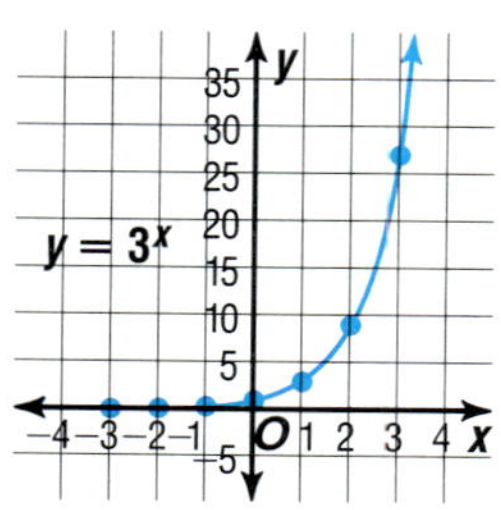

The y-intercept is 1.

b. $y = \left(\frac{1}{3}\right)^x$

x	y
−3	27
−2	9
−1	3
0	1
1	0.333
2	0.111
3	0.037
4	0.012

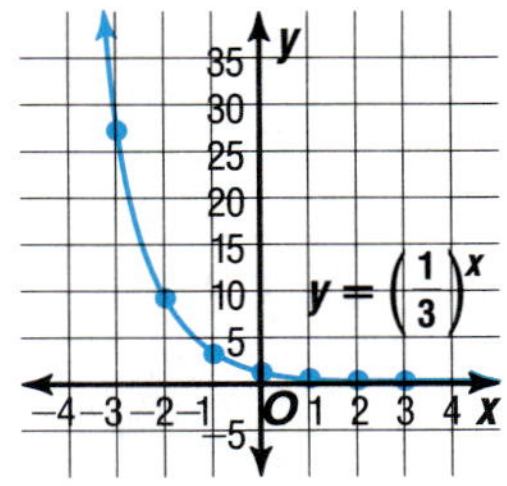

The y-intercept is 1.

Notice that the graph of $y = \left(\frac{1}{a}\right)^x$ decreases rapidly as x increases.

c. $y = 3^x - 7$

x	y
−3	−6.96
−2	−6.89
−1	−6.67
0	−6
1	−4
2	2
3	20
4	74

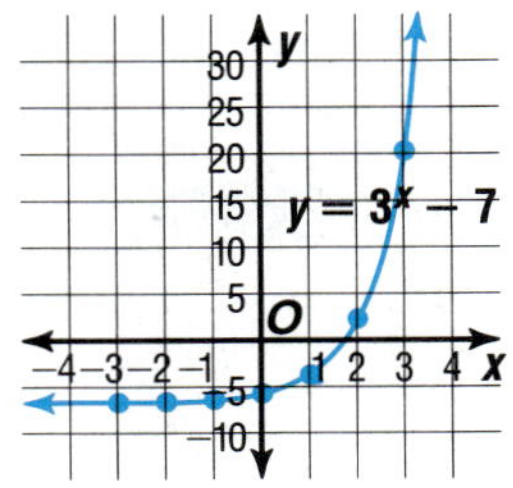

The y-intercept is −6.

LOOK BACK

You can refer to Lesson 10-1 for more information on factors.

How do you know if a set of data is exponential? One method is to observe the shape of the graph. But the graph of an exponential function may resemble part of the graph of a quadratic function. Another way is to **look for a pattern** in the data.

Example 2 **Determine whether each set of data displays exponential behavior.**

PROBLEM SOLVING

Look for a Pattern

TECHNOLOGY Tip

You could also use a graphing calculator to make a scatter plot of the data to observe the patterns.

a.

x	0	5	10	15	20	25
y	800	400	200	100	50	25

Method 1: Look for a Pattern

The domain values are at regular intervals of 5. Let's see if there is a common factor among the range values.

800 400 200 100 50 25

$\times\frac{1}{2}$ $\times\frac{1}{2}$ $\times\frac{1}{2}$ $\times\frac{1}{2}$ $\times\frac{1}{2}$

Since the domain values are at regular intervals and the range values have a common factor, the data are probably exponential. The equation for the data probably involves $\left(\frac{1}{2}\right)^x$.

Method 2: Graph the data.

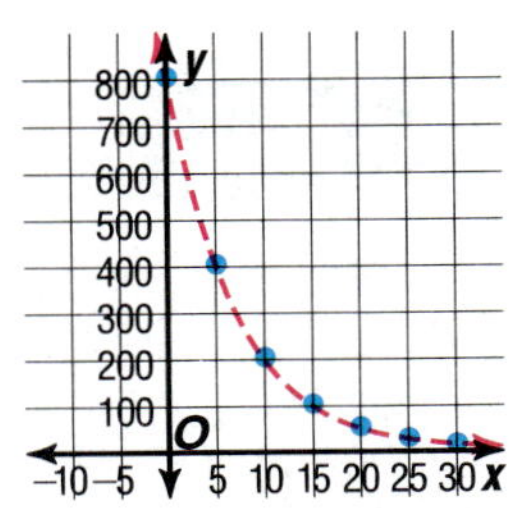

The graph shows a rapidly decreasing value of y as x increases. This is a characteristic of exponential behavior.

b.

x	0	5	10	15	20	25
y	3	6	9	12	15	18

Method 1: Look for a Pattern

The domain values are at regular intervals of 5. The range values have a common difference of 3.

3 6 9 12 15 18
+3 +3 +3 +3 +3

These data do not display exponential behavior, but rather linear behavior.

Method 2: Graph the data.

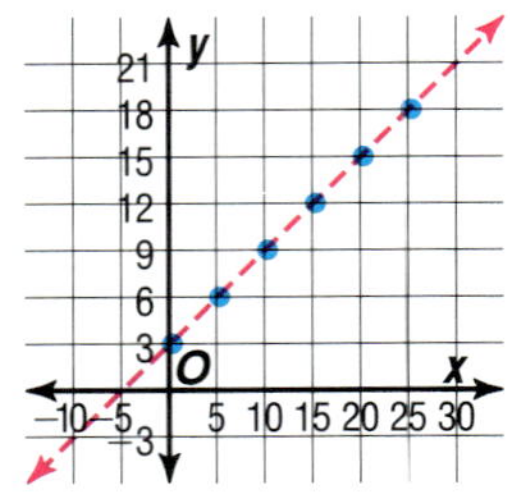

This is the graph of a line, not an exponential function.

FYI

Radiocarbon, or carbon-14, decays into nitrogen. It was first used in the late 1940s by Williard F. Libby to determine the age of an artifact. It has been used to date objects as old as 50,000 years.

Exponential functions are often used to describe real-life situations. In the late 1890s, Henri Becquerel discovered that fossils contain naturally-occurring radioactive atoms of carbon-14. When an organism is alive, it absorbs carbon-14 from the sun. When the organism dies, no more carbon-14 is absorbed, and the initial amount of carbon-14 begins to decay gradually into other elements.

The **half-life** of a radioactive element is defined as the time that it takes for one-half a quantity of the element to decay. Radioactive carbon-14 has a half-life of 5730 years. This means that after 5730 years, half the original amount of carbon-14 has decayed. In another 5730 years, half of the remaining half will decay, and so on. This pattern of decay can be described by $a = 0.5^t$, where a is the decay factor and t is the number of half-lives.

Half-life	Grams of Carbon-14 left	
0	64	$= 64 \times 0.5^0$
1	32	$= 64 \times 0.5^1$
2	16	$= 64 \times 0.5^2$
3	8	$= 64 \times 0.5^3$
4	4	$= 64 \times 0.5^4$
5	2	$= 64 \times 0.5^5$
6	1	$= 64 \times 0.5^6$
7	0.5	$= 64 \times 0.5^7$
8	0.25	$= 64 \times 0.5^8$
9	0.125	$= 64 \times 0.5^9$

Study the chart to see how 64 grams of carbon-14 decays over several half-lives. Notice its relationship to the exponential function $a = 0.5^t$.

Example 3

Archaeology

LOOK BACK

You can refer to Lesson 9-3 for more information on numbers written in scientific notation.

If the original concentration of carbon-14 in a living organism was 256 grams, determine the concentration of carbon-14 remaining in a fossil for each situation.

a. The organism lived 1000 years ago.

b. The organism lived 10,000 years ago.

a. First determine how many carbon-14 half-lives there are in 1 thousand years.

$$\frac{1000}{5730} \approx 0.1745 \text{ half-lives}$$

Then determine the value of the disintegration factor when $t = 0.1745$.

$$a = 0.5^t$$
$$= 0.5^{0.1745}$$
$$\approx 0.886 \quad \textit{Use a calculator.}$$

Multiply the original amount of carbon-14 by this factor.
256 grams $\times$ 0.886 = 226.8 grams

b. Find how many half-lives there are in 10,000 years.

$\frac{10{,}000}{5730} \approx 1.75$ half-lives

Determine the value of the disintegration factor when $t = 1.75$.

$a = 0.5^{1.75}$

≈ 0.297

Multiply the original amount of carbon-14 by this factor.
256 grams $\times$ 0.297 $\approx$ 76.0 grams

You can use algebra to solve equations involving exponential expressions by using the following rule.

Property of Equality for Exponential Functions	**Suppose a is a positive number other than 1. Then $a^{x_1} = a^{x_2}$ if and only if $x_1 = x_2$.**

The skills you learned when solving quadratic equations can be helpful when solving some exponential equations.

Example 4 **Solve $64^3 = 4^{x^2}$.**

LOOK BACK
You can refer to Lesson 9-1 for more information about properties of exponents.

Explore The two quantities do not have the same base, or value for a. However, 64 is a power of 4.

Plan In order to use the property of equality, we must rewrite the terms so that they have the same base. Then we can use the property of equality for exponential functions.

Solve

$64^3 = 4^{x^2}$

$(4^3)^3 = 4^{x^2}$ *$64 = 4 \cdot 4 \cdot 4$ or 4^3*

$4^9 = 4^{x^2}$ *Product of powers*

$9 = x^2$ *Property of equality for exponential functions*

$x^2 - 9 = 0$ *Rewrite the equation in standard form.*

$(x + 3)(x - 3) = 0$ *Factor.*

$x + 3 = 0$ $\quad$ $x - 3 = 0$ *Zero product property*

$x = -3$ $\quad$ $x = 3$

Examine Check each solution by substituting it into the original equation.

$64^3 = 4^{x^2}$ $\quad$ $64^3 = 4^{x^2}$

$64^3 \stackrel{?}{=} 4^{3^2}$ *$x = 3$* $\quad$ $64^3 \stackrel{?}{=} 4^{(-3)^2}$ *$x = -3$*

$262{,}144 \stackrel{?}{=} 4^9$ $\quad$ $262{,}144 \stackrel{?}{=} 4^9$

$262{,}144 = 262{,}144$ ✓ $\quad$ $262{,}144 = 262{,}144$ ✓

The solutions are 3 and -3.

CHECK FOR UNDERSTANDING

Communicating Mathematics

Study the lesson. Then complete the following.

1. **Refer** to the application at the beginning of the lesson.
   a. Use a calculator to determine how many grains there would be for the 64th square of the chessboard.
   b. How many tons of rice is this? (*Hint:* Recall that 1 T = 2000 lb.)
2. a. **Determine** whether the graph of $y = 2^x$ has an x-intercept.
   b. **Describe** your method.
   c. Is this true of all exponential functions?
3. a. **Determine** whether the graph of $y = 2^x$ has a vertex.
   b. **Describe** your method for answering part a.
   c. Is this true for all exponential functions?
4. **Explain** why $a \neq 1$ in the definitions and properties involving exponential functions.
5. **Write** a paragraph explaining why you think a graphing calculator might be a good tool to have when studying exponential functions.

MODELING MATHEMATICS

6. Refer to the Modeling Mathematics activity on page 636.
   a. The area of the large rectangle is 1. Find the area of each section after each set of folds. Record your findings in a table.
   b. Compare the number of folds to the area of each section. What pattern do you see?
   c. Write an exponential function relating the number of folds to the area of each section.

Guided Practice

Use a calculator to determine the approximate value of each expression to the nearest hundredth.

7. $3^{1.5}$
8. $3^{-0.9}$
9. $3^{2.3}$

Graph each function. State the y-intercept.

10. $y = 0.5^x$
11. $y = 2^x + 6$
12. Determine if the data in the table below displays exponential behavior. Describe the behavior.

x	0	1	2	3	4	5
y	1	6	36	216	1296	7776

Solve each equation.

13. $5^{3y+4} = 5^y$
14. $2^5 = 2^{2x-1}$
15. $3^x = 9^{x+1}$
16. **Biology** Suppose $B = 100 \cdot 2^t$ represents the number of bacteria B in a petri dish after t hours if you began with 100 bacteria. How long would it take to obtain 1000 bacteria?

EXERCISES

Practice

Use a calculator to determine the approximate value of each expression to the nearest hundredth.

17. $4^{1.7}$
18. $10^{-0.5}$
19. $\left(\frac{2}{3}\right)^{-1.2}$
20. $\left(\frac{1}{3}\right)^{4.1}$
21. $50(3^{-0.6})$
22. $10(3^{-1.8})$
23. $0.4(3^{0.7})$
24. $20(0.25^{-2.7})$

Graph each function. State the y-intercept.

25. $y = 2^x + 4$
26. $y = 2^{x+4}$
27. $y = 3\left(\frac{1}{3}\right)^x$
28. $y = 2 \cdot 3^x$
29. $y = 4^x$
30. $y = \left(\frac{1}{4}\right)^x$

Determine if the data in each table display exponential behavior. Explain why or why not.

31.

x	y
−2	−5
−1	−2
0	1
1	4

32.

x	y
0	1
1	0.5
2	0.25
3	0.125

33.

x	y
−1	−0.5
0	1.0
1	−2.0
2	4.0

Solve each equation.

34. $5^{3x} = 5^{-3}$
35. $2^{x+3} = 2^{-4}$
36. $5^x = 5^{3x+1}$
37. $10^x = 0.001$
38. $2^{2x} = \frac{1}{8}$
39. $\left(\frac{1}{6}\right)^q = 6^{q-6}$
40. $16^{x-1} = 64^x$
41. $81^x = 9^{x^2-3}$
42. $4^{x^2-2x} = 8^{x^2+1}$

Graphing Calculator

As with linear graphs and quadratic graphs, exponential graphs can form families of graphs. Graph each set of equations on the same screen. Sketch the graphs and discuss any similarities or differences.

43. $y = 3^x$
$y = 3^{x+4}$
$y = 3^{x-2}$

44. $y = \left(\frac{1}{3}\right)^x$
$y = \left(\frac{1}{3}\right)^x + 5$
$y = \left(\frac{1}{3}\right)^x - 3$

45. $y = 2^x$
$y = 2^{x-7}$
$y = 2^{x-2}$

46. $y = 6^x$
$y = 6^{3x}$
$y = 6^{8x}$

47. **a.** Use a graphing calculator to solve $2.5^x = 10$. Write the solution to the nearest hundredth.
b. Explain why you cannot solve this equation algebraically like you did the equation in Exercise 41.

Critical Thinking

48. Refer to the equations in Example 1. Use a calculator to find additional values to complete the following.
a. For $y = 3^x$, as x decreases, the value of y approaches what number?
b. For $y = \left(\frac{1}{3}\right)^x$, as x increases, the value of y approaches what number?
c. For $y = 3^x - 7$, as x decreases, the value of y approaches what number?
d. For any equation $y = a^x + c$, where $a > 1$, what value does y approach as x decreases?
e. For any equation $y = a^x + c$, where $0 < a < 1$, what value does y approach as x increases?

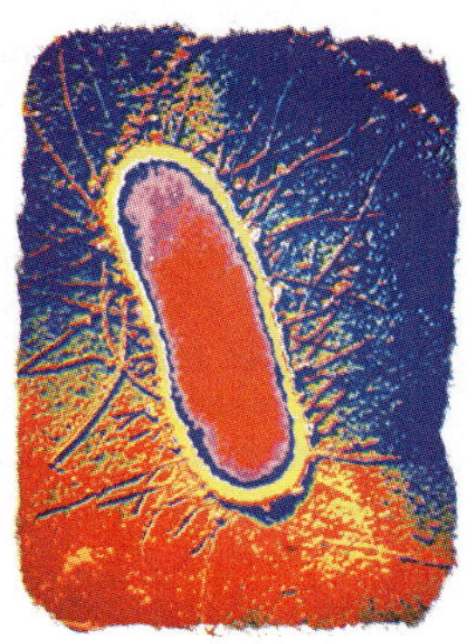

Applications and Problem Solving

49. **Biology** Mitosis is a process of cell reproduction in which one cell divides into two identical cells. *E. coli* is a fast-growing bacteria that is often responsible for food poisoning in uncooked meat. It can reproduce itself in 15 minutes. If you begin with 100 *e. coli* bacteria, how many bacteria will there be in 1 hour?

50. **Currency** In the United States between 1910 and 1994, the amount of currency in circulation $M(t)$ (billions of dollars) can be approximated by the function $M(t) = 2.08(1.06)^t$, where t represents the number of years since 1910.
   a. Determine $M(t)$ for the years 1920, 1950, 1980, and 2000.
   b. Determine the amount of currency in circulation in the years 1920, 1950, 1980, and 2000.

Mixed Review

51. Solve $2x^2 + 3 = -7x$ by using the quadratic formula. Check your solution by factoring. (Lesson 11–3)

52. **Geometry** A rectangle has an area of $(16p^2 - 40pr + 25r^2)$ square kilometers. (Lesson 10–5)
   a. Find the dimensions of the rectangle.
   b. Sketch the rectangle, labeling its dimensions.

53. Factor $\frac{4}{5}a^2b - \frac{3}{5}ab^2 - \frac{1}{5}ab$. (Lesson 10–2)

54. **City Planning** A section of Lithopolis is shaped like a trapezoid with an area of 81 square miles. The distance between Union Street and Lee Street is 9 miles. The length of Union Street is 14 miles less than 3 times the length of Lee Street. Find the length of Lee Street. Use $A = \frac{h(a + b)}{2}$. (Lesson 9–8)

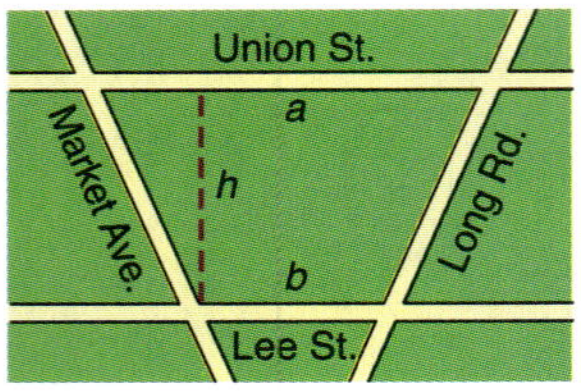

55. **Basketball** On December 13, 1983, the Nuggets and the Pistons broke the record for the highest score in a professional basketball game. The two teams scored a total of 370 points. If the Nuggets scored 2 points less than the Pistons, what was the Nuggets' final score? (Lesson 9–5)

56. Solve the system of inequalities by graphing. (Lesson 8–5)
$y \leq 2x + 2$
$y \geq -x - 1$

57. **Astronomy** The table at the right shows the relationship between the distance from the sun, measured in millions of miles, and the time to complete an orbit, measured in Earth years. (Lesson 6–3)

Planet	Distance from Sun	Years per Orbit
Mercury	36.0	0.241
Venus	67.0	0.615
Earth	93.0	1.000
Mars	141.5	1.880
Jupiter	483.0	11.900
Saturn	886.0	29.500
Uranus	1782.0	84.000
Neptune	2793.0	165.000
Pluto	3670.0	248.000

   a. Make a scatter plot of these data.
   b. Draw a best-fit line and write an equation for the line.
   c. Suppose a tenth planet was discovered at a distance of 4.1 billion miles from the sun. Use the scatter plot to estimate how long it would take it to orbit the sun.

58. **Geometry** Triangle ABC is similar to triangle ADE in the figure at the right. Find the value of s. (Lesson 4–2)

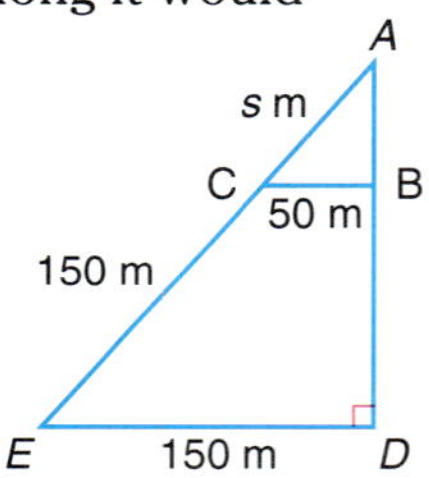

59. Find $(-2)(3)(-10)$. (Lesson 2–6)

fabulous FIRSTS

Clair C. Patterson (1922–1995)

Geochemist Clair Patterson, a professor at the California Institute of Technology, was the first scientist to establish Earth's age based on analysis of radioactive isotopes and their daughter products. In 1953, he established Earth's age to be 4.6 billion years.

11-5 Growth and Decay

What YOU'LL LEARN

- To solve problems involving growth and decay.

Why IT'S IMPORTANT

You can solve growth and decay problems to learn more about demographics and energy.

CAREER CHOICES

Urban, or **city, planners** use statistics on demographics, traffic patterns, and economics to help officials make decisions on social, economic, and environmental issues in their communities. A bachelors degree in urban or regional planning is required, and a masters degree in civil engineering or planning is helpful for advancement.

For further information, contact:

American Planning Association
1776 Massachusetts Ave., NW
Washington, DC 20036

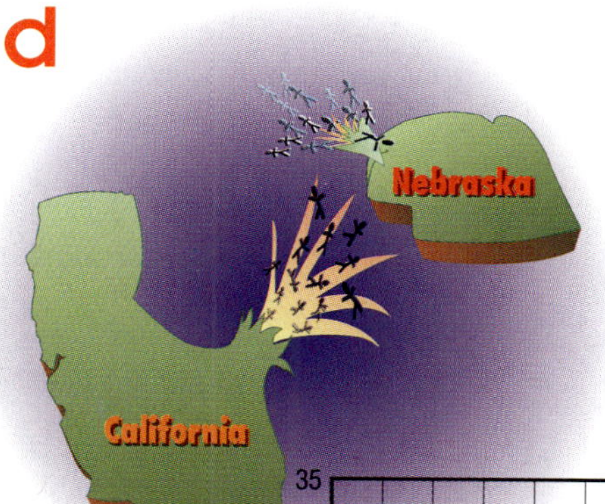

APPLICATION

Demographics

How quickly has the population of your state grown in the 20th century? Both California and Nebraska have grown in population during this century by a constant percent. The graph at the right shows the population of each state where t represents the number of years since 1900. Since 1900, the population in Nebraska has grown at a rate of 0.4% per year, while the population of California has grown at a rate of 3% per year.

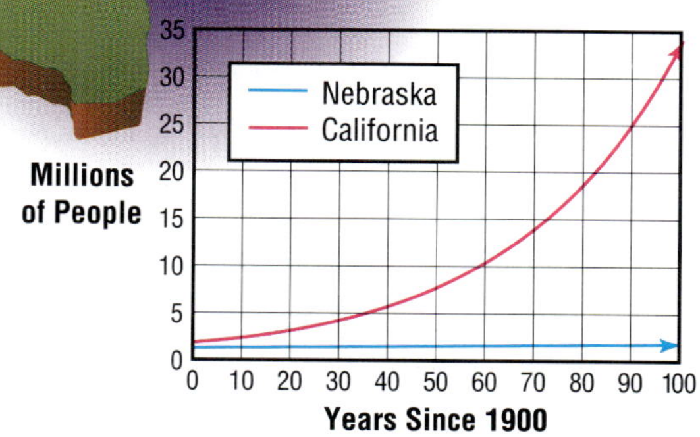

The exponential functions that model the growth of each state are given below.

California: $y = 1.77(1.03)^t$ *The population in 1900 was 1.77 million.*

Nebraska: $y = 1.14(1.004)^t$ *The population in 1900 was 1.14 million.*

Which state exhibits the more rapid growth? What will the population of each state be in the year 2000? *You will answer these questions in Exercise 1.*

The equations for the two states' populations are variations of the equation $y = C(1 + r)^t$. This is the **general equation for exponential growth** in which the initial amount C increases by the same percent r over a given period of time t. This equation can be applied to many kinds of growth applications.

One of these applications is monetary growth. When solving problems involving compound interest, the growth equation becomes $A = P\left(1 + \frac{r}{n}\right)^{nt}$, where A is the amount of the investment over a period of time, P is the principal (initial amount of the investment), r is the annual rate of interest expressed as a decimal, n is the number of times that the interest is compounded each year, and t is the number of years that the money is invested.

Example 1

APPLICATION

Finance

In the spring of 1994, Mr. and Mrs. Mitzu had $10,000 they wished to place in a bank certificate of deposit toward their retirement in the year 2004. The interest rate at that time was 2.5% compounded monthly. However, there were seven increases in the prime rate in a year so that in the spring of 1995, the interest rate had risen to 5.5%.

a. Determine the amount of their investment after 10 years if they invested the principal and let it remain at the 2.5% rate.

b. Determine the amount of the investment after 9 years if they waited and invested the principal at the 5.5% rate.

c. What are the best options for their investment?

(continued on the next page)

a. The interest rate r as a decimal is 0.025 and $n = 12$. *Why?*

$$A = P\left(1 + \frac{r}{n}\right)^{nt}$$

$$= 10{,}000\left(1 + \frac{0.025}{12}\right)^{12 \cdot 10} \quad \textit{P = 10,000, r = 0.025, n = 12, and t = 10}$$

Use a calculator.

Enter: 10000 [×] [(] 1 [+] [(] .025 [÷] 12 [)] [)] [y^x] 120 [=] 12836.91542

The amount of the account after 10 years at 2.5% is about \$12,836.92.

b. The interest rate as a decimal is 0.055, and t is 9 years.

$$A = P\left(1 + \frac{r}{n}\right)^{nt}$$

$$= 10{,}000\left(1 + \frac{0.055}{12}\right)^{12 \cdot 9} \quad \textit{P = 10,000, r = 0.055, n = 12, and t = 9}$$

$$\approx 16{,}386.44$$

c. If they waited until the rate went up, they would have had more money than leaving the money at the initial rate. However, if it is possible to reinvest the money each year, they could have invested the money for one year at 2.5% and then reinvested it the next year at 5.5%. That would yield even more money for their retirement in 2004.

A variation of the growth equation can be used as the **general equation for exponential decay.** In the formula $A = C(1 - r)^t$, A represents the final amount, C is the initial amount, r is the rate of decay, and t denotes time.

Example 2

APPLICATION

Demographics

The cities listed at the right have experienced declining populations since 1970.

City	1970 Population (thousands)	Annual Rate of Decrease
Baltimore, Maryland	894	1.029%
Cleveland, Ohio	733	1.055%

a. If t represents the number of years since 1970 and C represents the 1970 population, write an exponential decay equation for each city.

b. Assume that each city maintains the same decrease rate into the next century. Calculate the population of each city in the year 2070.

c. How do the projected populations of the cities in 2070 compare to the actual populations in 1970?

a. Baltimore

$C = 894$, $r = 0.01029$

$A = C(1 - r)^t$

$A = 894(1 - 0.01029)^t$

$A = 894(0.98971)^t$

Cleveland

$C = 733$, $r = 0.01055$

$A = C(1 - r)^t$

$A = 733(1 - 0.01055)^t$

$A = 733(0.98945)^t$

b. The year 2070 is 100 years later. Evaluate each decay equation for $t = 100$.

Baltimore	**Cleveland**
$A = 894(0.98971)^t$	$A = 733(0.98945)^t$
$A = 894(0.98971)^{100}$	$A = 733(0.98945)^{100}$
$A \approx 317.78$	$A \approx 253.80$

c. In 1970, the difference in the populations of Baltimore and Cleveland was 161,000. In 2070, the difference is only about 64,000. If the populations would continue to decrease at the same rates, they would grow even closer together.

Sometimes items decrease in value. For example, as equipment gets older, it *depreciates*. You can use the decay formula to determine the value of an item at a given time.

Example 3

APPLICATION
Consumerism

Hogan Blackburn is considering the purchase of a new car. He is faced with the decision to lease or buy. If he leases the car, he pays \$369 a month for 2 years and then has the option to buy the car for \$13,642. The price of the car now is \$16,893.

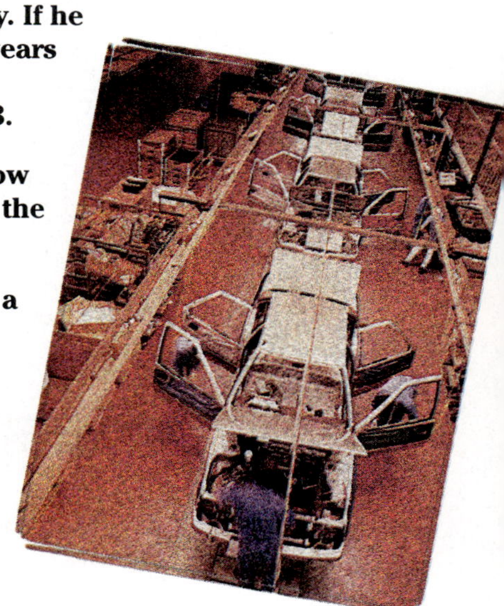

a. If the car depreciates at 17% per year, how will the depreciated price compare with the buyout price of the lease?

b. At the end of the lease, the dealer offers a loan for 3 years at a rate of \$435.79 per month. If he buys the car now, he will pay \$464.56 monthly for 4 years. Which is the best way to go if he plans to keep the car for at least 5 years?

a. Use the decay formula.

$$A = C(1 - r)^t$$
$$= 16{,}893(1 - 0.17)^2 \quad r = 0.17,\ C = 16{,}893,\ \text{and } t = 2$$
$$= 11{,}637.59$$

The depreciated value is \$2000 less than the buyout price.

b. Calculate the cost of each possibility over a 5-year period.

Lease and Buy: \$369(24 months) + \$435.79(36 months) = \$24,544.44

Buy: \$464.56(48 months) = \$22,298.88

The best way to go may depend on Hogan's financial status.

- Overall, the buy option costs less and lasts only 4 years while the lease and buy option costs more and lasts for 5 years.
- However, if Hogan really wants a new car and cannot afford the larger monthly payment now, the lease option may be best. However, he will eventually have to make the larger payment if he keeps the car.

You can use a spreadsheet to quickly evaluate different values for any exponential growth or decay formula.

EXPLORATION — SPREADSHEETS

Recall that in a spreadsheet you can refer to each cell by its name (A1 means column A, row 1). Suppose we set up a spreadsheet to evaluate the formula for monetary exponential growth.

- You can enter labels into the first row to identify the data in each column. Let column A contain the values of *P*, column *B* the values of *r*, column *C* the values of *n*, column *D* the value of *t*, and column *E* the values of *A*.

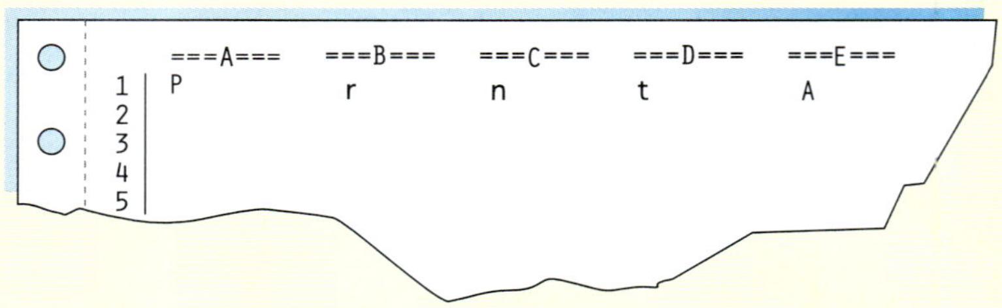

- You can enter a formula into cell E2 to evaluate the formula given the values entered into cells A2 through D2. The formula is A2 *(1 + (B2/C2))^(C2*D2).
- Copy this formula into the other cells in column E.

LOOK BACK

Refer to the Exploration in Lesson 6-1 for more information about spreadsheets.

Your Turn

a. Use the spreadsheet to evaluate the data in Example 1.

b. How would you change the spreadsheet to evaluate the general formula for decay?

CHECK FOR UNDERSTANDING

Communicating Mathematics

Study the lesson. Then complete the following.

1. Refer to the application at the beginning of the lesson.
   a. Which state exhibits more rapid growth?
   b. What will the population of each state be in the year 2000?
2. **Explain** how you could tell the difference between an exponential graph that shows 0.7% growth versus one that shows 7% growth.

Guided Practice

3. **State** the value of *n* in the monetary growth formula for each period of compounded interest.
   a. annually **b.** semi-annually **c.** quarterly **d.** daily

Determine whether each exponential equation represents growth or decay.

4. $y = 10(1.03)^x$
5. $y = 10(0.50)^x$
6. $y = 10(0.75)^x$

7. **History** In 1626, Peter Minuit, governor of the colony of New Netherland, bought the island of Manhattan from the Indians for beads, cloth, and trinkets worth 60 Dutch guilders ($24). If that $24 had been invested at 6% per year compounded annually, how much money would there be in the year 2000?

8. **Farming** Many self-employed individuals such as farmers can depreciate the value of the machinery they buy as a part of their income tax returns. Suppose a tractor valued at $50,000 depreciates 10% per year. Make a table to determine in how many years the value of the tractor would be less than $25,000.

EXERCISES

Applications and Problem Solving

Finance Determine the final amount from the investment for each situation.

	Initial Amount	Annual Interest Rate	Time	Type of Compounding
9.	$400	7.25%	7 years	quarterly
10.	$500	5.75%	25 years	monthly
11.	$10,000	6.125%	18 months	daily
12.	$250	10.3%	40 years	monthly

13. **Demographics** The population in 1994 and the growth rate for four countries is given below.

Country	Continent	Growth Rate	1994 Population
Ethiopia	Africa	2.5%	58.7 million
India	Asia	1.9%	919.9 million
Colombia	S. America	2.1%	35.6 million
Singapore	Asia	1.3%	2.9 million

a. Write an exponential equation for each country's growth.

b. Compute the estimated population for each country in the year 2000.

c. Exclude the data for India. Make a double-bar graph to show how the population in the other three countries in 1994 compares with the estimate for the year 2000.

14. **Energy** The Environmental Protection Agency (EPA) has called for businesses to find cleaner sources of energy as we approach the 21st century. Coal is not considered to be a clean source of energy. In 1950, the use of coal by residential and commercial users was 114.6 million tons. Since then, the use of coal has decreased by 6.6% per year.

a. Write an equation to represent the use of coal since 1950.

b. Suppose the use of coal continues to decrease at the same rate. Use a calculator to estimate in what year the use of coal will end.

15. **Insurance** The total amount of life insurance sold in 1950 was \$231.5 billion. Since then, the annual increase has been estimated at 9.63%.

a. Write an equation to represent the amount of insurance sold annually since 1950.

b. Find the estimated amount of life insurance that will be sold in the year 2010.

16. **Wildlife** In 1980, there were 1.2 million elephants living in Africa. Because the natural grazing lands for the elephant are disappearing due to increased population and cultivation of the land, the number of elephants in Africa has decreased by about 6.8% per year.

a. Write an equation to represent the population of elephants in Africa.

b. In what year did the population of African elephants drop to less than half of the number in 1980?

c. What factors might affect the rate of decline in elephant population?

17. **Savings** Sheena is investing her \$5000 inheritance in a saving certificate that matures in 4 years. The interest rate is 8.25% compounded quarterly.

a. Determine the balance in the account after 4 years.

b. Her friend, LaDonna, invests the same amount of money at the same interest rate but her bank compounds daily. Determine how much she will have after 4 years.

c. What is the difference in the amount Sheena and LaDonna have after 4 years?

d. Which type of compounding appears to be more profitable?

FYI

FM stations began surpassing AM stations in popularity during the 1970s. This may have been due to the FM waves producing a clearer signal that could be heard over a longer distance.

18. **Radio** FM broadcast frequencies range from 88 to 108 MHz in tenths. Before digital displays existed, you turned a knob and a bar slide from across the display or *dial* to find the station you wanted to hear. The equation that relates the MHz reading to position of the slide is $f(d) = 88(1.0137)^d$, where d is the distance from the left of the dial. Suppose someone didn't know the number of their favorite station, but knew it was about halfway across the dial. If the dial is 15 cm long, what station is their favorite ?

19. **Population** Research to find the population in your community for the past 50 years.

a. Make a graph to show the population change.

b. Does the population of your community show growth or decay?

c. Estimate what the population of your community will be when you are 50 years old.

Graphing Calculator

20. **Radioactivity** A formula for examining the decay of radioactive materials is $y = Ne^{kt}$, where N is the beginning amount in grams, $e \approx 2.72$, k is a negative constant for the substance, and t is the number of years. Use a graphing calculator to estimate each of the following.

a. How long will it take 250 grams of a radioactive substance to reduce to 50 grams if $k = -0.08042$?

b. In 10 years, 200 grams of a radioactive substance is reduced to 100 grams. Find an estimate for the constant k for this substance.

Critical Thinking

21. The general exponential formula for growth or decay is $y = Ca^x$. Determine what values of a describe growth or decay. What does x usually represent?

22. Consider the equation $y = C(1 + r)^x$. How do you determine the y-intercept of the graph of this equation without graphing or evaluating the function for values of x?

Mixed Review

23. Solve $3^y = 3^{3y+1}$. (Lesson 11–4)

24. Find $(n^2 + 5n + 3) - (2n^2 + 8n + 8)$. (Lesson 9–5)

25. Simplify $\frac{-6r^3s^5}{18r^{-7}s^5t^{-2}}$. (Lesson 9–2)

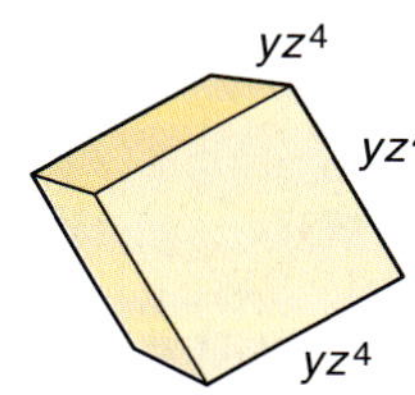

26. Geometry Find the volume of the cube shown at the right. (Lesson 9–2)

27. Geometry Write the equation of a line that passes through $(-2, 7)$ and is perpendicular to the line whose equation is $2x - 5y = 3$. Use slope-intercept form. (Lesson 6–6)

Mathematics and Society

Minimizing Computers

The following excerpt appeared in an article in *The New York Times* on November 22, 1994.

In a bold experiment that is provoking investigators to reconsider what a computer is and what it means to compute, a researcher has used DNA, the genetic material, as a sort of personal computer. Exploiting the extraordinary efficiency and speed of biological reactions, he translated a difficult mathematical problem into the language of molecular biology and solved it by carrying out a reaction in one-fiftieth of a teaspoon of solution in a test tube....Molecular computers can perform more than a trillion operations per second, which makes them a thousand times as fast as the fastest supercomputer. They are a billion times as energy efficient as conventional computers. And they can store information in a trillionth of the space required by ordinary computers. ■

1. Does the idea of a molecular computer in a test tube surprise you? Why or why not?
2. If biological systems can have computational abilities, what effects might this have on computer scientists, programmers, and mathematicians?
3. One class of problems that molecular computers could help solve involves finding one desired solution or path out of a huge number of possibilities. How could this be used if the problem was a defective gene causing the rate of a deadly disease to grow exponentially?

CLOSING THE

In·ves·ti·ga·tion

the BRICKYARD

Refer to the Investigation on pages 554–555.

Review the knowledge you have gained from your experiments working with the bricks. Review the instructions given to you by your manager as you begin to close this Investigation.

> Please create several patio designs that will utilize these bricks. Submit at least three different plans, explaining the materials required for each patio. I am anxious to see the different ways in which these bricks can be arranged to form rectangular patios. Is there a general formula or pattern we can use to design these in the future? I look forward to your report on helping us solve our inventory problems.

Analyze

You have conducted experiments and organized your data in various ways. It is now time to analyze your findings and state your conclusions.

1 Look over your data and complete a chart like the one on page 555 for each design. Use actual measurements.

2 What information does this chart reflect? Does it give information that can be used to generalize a method for forming future brick patio patterns? Explain.

PORTFOLIO ASSESSMENT

You may want to keep your work on this Investigation in your portfolio.

Write

The report to your manager should explain your process for investigating these rectangular brick patterns and what you found from your investigations.

3 What size rectangular brick patterns are possible? Draw sketches of the possible patterns. Describe the numbers of bricks used and include the dimensions, perimeter, and area of each pattern in terms of x and y.

4 Write procedures or generalizations that may be followed to find rectangular patterns in the following situations.
- You have a certain number of large squares and small squares. How many rectangular tiles are necessary to create a rectangular pattern?
- How can you find the dimensions of a pattern given the type and number of bricks available?
- How can you find the different possible patterns for any set number of bricks?
- How do you know that no possible rectangular pattern can be made given a set of the three types of bricks?

5 Summarize your findings and give recommendations for possible brick patterns. Explain methods for exploring more patterns in the future.

CHAPTER 11 HIGHLIGHTS

VOCABULARY

After completing this chapter, you should be able to define each term, property, or phrase and give an example or two of each.

Algebra

axis of symmetry (p. 612)
discriminant (p. 632)
exponential function (pp. 634, 635)
general equation for exponential decay (p. 644)
general equation for exponential growth (p. 643)
half-life (p. 638)
maximum (p. 611)
minimum (p. 611)
parabola (pp. 610, 611)
quadratic equation (p. 620)
quadratic formula (p. 628)
quadratic function (pp. 610, 611)
roots (p. 620)
symmetry (p. 612)
vertex (pp. 610, 611)
zeros (p. 620)

Problem Solving

look for a pattern (p. 637)

UNDERSTANDING AND USING THE VOCABULARY

Choose the letter of the term that best matches each equation or phrase.

1. $y = C(1 + r)^t$
2. $f(x) = ax^2 + bx + c$
3. a geometric property of parabolas
4. $x = \frac{-b}{2a}$
5. $y = a^x$
6. maximum or minimum point of a parabola
7. $A = C(1 - r)^t$
8. solutions of a quadratic equation
9. $x = \frac{-b \pm \sqrt{b^2 - 4ac}}{2a}$
10. the graph of a quadratic function

a. equation of axis of symmetry
b. exponential decay formula
c. exponential function
d. exponential growth formula
e. parabola
f. quadratic formula
g. quadratic function
h. roots
i. symmetry
j. vertex

CHAPTER 11 STUDY GUIDE AND ASSESSMENT

SKILLS AND CONCEPTS

OBJECTIVES AND EXAMPLES

Upon completing this chapter, you should be able to:

- find the equation of the axis of symmetry and the coordinates of the vertex of a parabola (Lesson 11–1)

In the equation $y = x^2 - 8x + 12$, $a = 1$ and $b = -8$.

The equation of the axis of symmetry is $x = -\frac{b}{2a} = -\frac{(-8)}{2(1)}$ or 4.

Use the value $x = 4$ to find the coordinates of the vertex.

$$y = x^2 - 8x + 12$$
$$= (4)^2 - 8(4) + 12$$
$$= 16 - 32 + 12 \text{ or } -4$$

The coordinates of the vertex are $(4, -4)$.

REVIEW EXERCISES

Use these exercises to review and prepare for the chapter test.

Write the equation of the axis of symmetry and find the coordinates of the vertex of the graph of each equation.

11. $y = -3x^2 + 4$
12. $y = x^2 - 3x - 4$
13. $y = 3x^2 + 6x - 17$
14. $y = 3(x + 1)^2 - 20$
15. $y = x^2 + 2x$

- graph quadratic functions (Lesson 11–1)

Graph $y = x^2 - 8x + 12$. Use the information above.

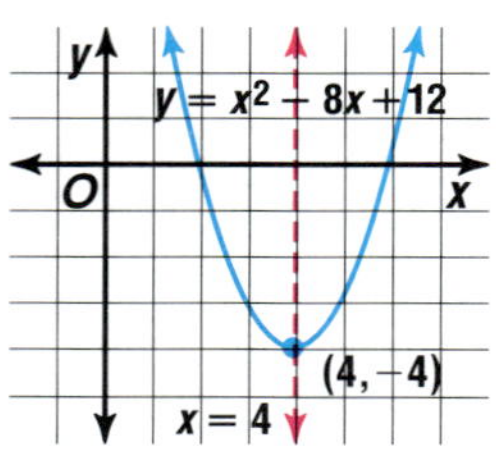

Using the results from Exercises 11–15, graph each equation.

16. $y = -3x^2 + 4$
17. $y = x^2 - 3x - 4$
18. $y = 3x^2 + 6x - 17$
19. $y = 3(x + 1)^2 - 20$
20. $y = x^2 + 2x$

- find roots of quadratic equations by graphing (Lesson 11–2)

Based on the graph of $y = x^2 - 8x + 12$ shown above, the roots of the equation $x^2 - 8x + 12 = 0$ are 2 and 6. This is because $y = 0$ at the x-intercepts, which appear to be at 2 and 6.

Substitute these values into the original equation.

$x^2 - 8x + 12 = 0$	$x^2 - 8x + 12 = 0$
$(2)^2 - 8(2) + 12 = 0$	$(6)^2 - 8(6) + 12 = 0$
$4 - 16 + 12 = 0$	$36 - 48 + 12 = 0$
$0 = 0$ ✓	$0 = 0$ ✓

The solutions of the equation are 2 and 6.

Solve each equation by graphing. If integral roots cannot be found, state the consecutive integers between which the roots lie.

21. $x^2 - x - 12 = 0$
22. $x^2 + 6x + 9 = 0$
23. $x^2 + 4x - 3 = 0$
24. $2x^2 - 5x + 4 = 0$
25. $x^2 - 10x = -21$
26. $6x^2 - 13x = 15$

OBJECTIVES AND EXAMPLES

- solve quadratic equations by using the quadratic formula (Lesson 11–3)

Solve $2x^2 + 7x - 15 = 0$.

In the equation, $a = 2$, $b = 7$, and $c = -15$. Substitute these values into the quadratic formula.

$$x = \frac{-(7) \pm \sqrt{(7)^2 - 4(2)(-15)}}{2(2)}$$

$$= \frac{-7 \pm \sqrt{169}}{4}$$

$$x = \frac{-7 + 13}{4} \quad \text{or} \quad x = \frac{-7 - 13}{4}$$

$$= \frac{3}{2} \qquad\qquad = -5$$

REVIEW EXERCISES

Solve each equation by using the quadratic formula. Approximate irrational roots to the nearest hundredth.

27. $x^2 - 8x = 20$

28. $r^2 + 10r + 9 = 0$

29. $4p^2 + 4p = 15$

30. $2y^2 + 3 = -8y$

31. $9k^2 - 13k + 4 = 0$

32. $9a^2 + 25 = 30a$

33. $-a^2 + 5a - 6 = 0$

34. $-2d^2 + 8d + 3 = 3$

35. $21a^2 + 5a - 7 = 0$

36. $2m^2 = \frac{17}{6}m - 1$

- graph exponential functions (Lesson 11–4)

Graph $y = 2^x - 3$.

x	y
−3	−2.875
−2	−2.75
−1	−2.5
0	−2
1	−1
2	1
3	5

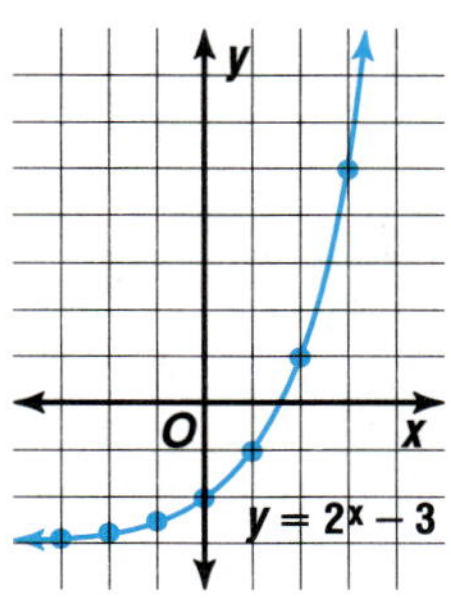

The y-intercept is −2.

Graph each function. State the y-intercept.

37. $y = 3^x + 6$

38. $y = 3^{x+2}$

39. $y = 2^x$

40. $y = 2\left(\frac{1}{2}\right)^x$

- solve exponential equations (Lesson 11–4)

Solve $25^{b+4} = \left(\frac{1}{5}\right)^{2b}$.

$$25^{b+4} = \left(\frac{1}{5}\right)^{2b}$$

$$(5^2)^{b+4} = (5^{-1})^{2b}$$

$$5^{2b+8} = 5^{-2b}$$

$$2b + 8 = -2b$$

$$8 = -4b$$

$$-2 = b$$

The solution is −2.

Solve each equation.

41. $3^{4x} = 3^{-12}$

42. $7^x = 7^{4x+9}$

43. $\left(\frac{1}{3}\right)^t = 27^{t+8}$

44. $0.01 = \left(\frac{1}{10}\right)^{4r}$

45. $64^{y-3} = \left(\frac{1}{16}\right)^{y^2}$

OBJECTIVES AND EXAMPLES

- solve problems involving growth and decay (Lesson 11–5)

Find the final amount from an investment of \$1500 invested at an interest rate of 7.5% compounded quarterly for 10 years.

$$A = P\left(1 + \frac{r}{n}\right)^{nt}$$

$$= 1500\left(1 + \frac{0.075}{4}\right)^{4 \cdot 10}$$

$$= 3153.523916$$

The amount of the account is about \$3153.52.

REVIEW EXERCISES

Determine the final amount from the investment for each situation.

	Initial Amount	Annual Interest Rate	Time	Type of Compounding
46.	\$2000	8%	8 years	quarterly
47.	\$5500	5.25%	15 years	monthly
48.	\$15,000	7.5%	25 years	monthly
49.	\$500	9.75%	40 years	daily

APPLICATIONS AND PROBLEM SOLVING

50. Archery The height h, in feet, that a certain arrow will reach t seconds after being shot directly upward is given by the formula $h = 112t - 16t^2$. What is the maximum height for this arrow? Assume the arrow is shot from ground level. (Lesson 11–1)

51. Physics A projectile is shot vertically up in the air from ground level. Its distance s, in feet, after t seconds is given by the equation $s = 96t - 16t^2$. Find the values of t when s is 96 feet. (Lesson 11–3)

52. Finance Kevin deposited \$1400 for 8 years at $6\frac{1}{2}$% interest compounded quarterly. How much will he have at the end of 8 years? (Lesson 11–5)

53. Diving Wyatt is diving from a 10-meter platform. His height h in meters above the water when he is x meters away from the platform is given by the formula $h = -x^2 + 2x + 10$. Approximately how far away from the platform is he when he enters the water? (Lesson 11–2)

54. Number Theory Find a number whose square is 168 greater than 2 times the number. (Lesson 11–3)

55. Decision Making Juanita wants to buy a new computer but she only has \$500. She decides to wait a year and invest her money. Should she put it in a 1-year CD with a rate of 8% compounded monthly or in a savings account with a rate of 6% compounded daily? Explain your answer. (Lesson 11–5)

A practice test for Chapter 11 is provided on page 797.

ALTERNATIVE ASSESSMENT

COOPERATIVE LEARNING PROJECT

Sightseeing Tours In this project, you will model a business's profit. The Wash Student Tour Company offers one week tours of Washington, D.C. in small groups. While some of Wash's cost per person go down as the number of people on the tour increases, other costs go up because they must reserve rooms in another motel and rent extra vans. Wash has a function that enables them to predict their profit per student. If x is the number of students on the tour, and $f(x)$ is the profit (in dollars) per student, then $f(x) = -0.6x^2 + 18x - 45$.

Write a summary, using this model that describes in detail the profit structure for the Tour Company. Find the number of students that will give Wash the largest profit per student. What is the maximum profit? What does this represent? The company will offer tours as long as they do not lose money. What is the least or greatest number of students they should accept?

Follow these steps to accomplish your task.

- Substitute various numbers of students into the function to determine the profit for each.
- Substitute various amounts of profits into the function to determine the number of students that must be on the tour.
- Graph the function.
- Using the model, discuss terms such as profit, loss, break even, and maximum or minimum.
- Write a summary.

THINKING CRITICALLY

- If the value of a quadratic function is negative when $x = 1$ and positive when $x = 2$, explain what this means in terms of the roots and why.
- In the quadratic equation $ax^2 - bx + c = 0$, if $ac < 0$, what must be true about the nature of the roots of the equation?

PORTFOLIO

Use the quadratic formula and factoring to solve several quadratic equations. As you solve each quadratic equation in both ways, compare the similarities and the differences, if there are any. Write a description of how the quadratic formula can be used to determine whether or not a quadratic polynomial is factorable. Place this in your portfolio.

SELF EVALUATION

While the solution to a problem may be unforeseen, a good problem solver can use the details of the problem to plan a method of solution. Those details can often be part of the solution or preliminary steps needed to arrive at the solution.

Assess yourself. Do you pay attention to detail? Do you organize and evaluate as you go through a problem? Once you have a solution, do you analyze the solution by looking at all options or do you only look for the most obvious? Give an example of a math-related problem and a daily life problem in which detail was essential and explain how it helped.

LONG-TERM PROJECT

In·ves·ti·ga·tion

A Growing Concern

MATERIALS NEEDED

- calculator
- cardboard
- construction paper
- flashlight
- glue
- markers
- modeling clay
- paint
- ruler
- scissors
- duct tape

You have a small landscape company that specializes in residential landscape design. One of your clients is the Sanchez family. Mr. and Dr. Sanchez have three children, ages 5, 11, and 15. They have just moved into a home on a lot that is one third of an acre (1 acre = 43,560 ft^2). Their one-story home and garage occupy 3425 square feet.

Dr. Sanchez loves to garden, and Mr. Sanchez likes to swim laps to keep in shape. So, the Sanchez family is interested in a backyard pool, hot tub, deck and/or patio, and a fairly good-sized lawn. They also want to leave room to later construct a play area for their youngest child and a garden for Dr. Sanchez. The front yard was fully landscaped by the construction company that built the house.

The family prefers a low-maintenance landscape, which consists mainly of lawn care. Because of the dry climate, daily watering must be done with a sprinkler system. They are also interested in concrete walkways, to match the driveway and the path to the front door.

For this job, the Sanchez family will request bids from several suppliers. They have asked your company to construct a model of your design, along with a bid, for them to view.

The Sanchezes are interested in a reasonably low price, but will choose a higher bid if they prefer the design and features. In either case, they plan to spend no more than $65,000.

When calculating bids, you must consider the cost of supplies, materials, labor, and a profit margin. Use the company's labor and material tables to estimate costs. Labor costs are determined either by the entire job or by the hour. This cost is dependent on the individual job. The profit margin is 20% of the total cost of materials, supplies, and labor.

Your design team consists of three people. Make an Investigation Folder in which you can store all of your work on this Investigation for future use.

THE PROPERTY

Use the dimensions given in the diagram below and your knowledge of geometry to design and create a *rough draft* of a landscaping plan for the Sanchez family's backyard. Be sure to include a pool, hot tub, lawn area, flower beds, trees, deck and/or patio, and concrete walkways in your design. Think about the dimensions of all of the features in your design. Be sure to leave ample space for a play area and garden to be developed later.

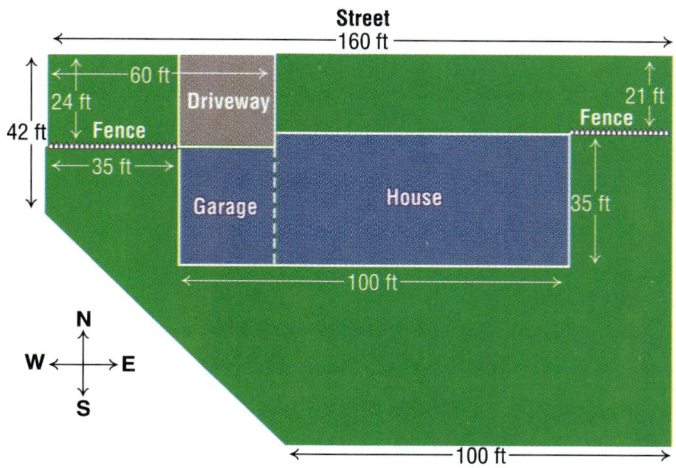

LABOR AND MATERIALS

POOL

Labor

digging: \$1/cu ft

pool construction: \$10/ft^2 of surface area

plumbing, filter, heating insulation: 8 h @ \$35/h

Materials

pool construction: \$18/ft^2 of surface area

plumbing and filter: \$1250

heater: \$1600

HOT TUB

Labor

digging: \$1/cu ft

hot tub construction: \$10/ft^2 of tub surface area

plumbing, filter, heating insulation: 8 h @ \$35/h (3 hours if installed with a pool)

Materials

tub construction: \$18/ft^2 of tub surface area

plumbing and filter: \$1250

plumbing without filter: \$250

heater: \$1600 (pool and hot tub can share heater and filter)

DECK

Labor

8 ft^2 of deck per hour @ \$25/h

Materials

redwood deck materials (4 ft × 1 ft): \$12

PLANTS and TREES

Labor

plants/trees: 4 per hour @ \$20/h

grass seed: 125 ft^2 per hour @ \$20/h

sprinkler installation: 20 ft per hour @ \$20/h

Materials

1 plant: \$6.25

1 tree: \$22.50

soil preparation: \$1.75 per ft^2 of seeded area

sprinkler: 14 ft of sprinkler for every 10 ft^2 of lawn @ \$1.50/ft

PATIO and WALKWAYS

Labor

12 ft^2 of patio or walkway per hour @ \$22/h

Materials

concrete: \$16/10 ft^2

You will continue working on this Investigation throughout Chapters 12 and 13.

Be sure to keep your designs, models, charts, and other materials in your Investigation Folder.

A Growing Concern Investigation

Working on the Investigation
Lesson 12–1, p. 665

Working on the Investigation
Lesson 12–7, p. 695

Working on the Investigation
Lesson 13–1, p. 718

Working on the Investigation
Lesson 13–5, p. 741

Closing the Investigation
End of Chapter 13, p. 748

CHAPTER 12

Exploring Rational Expressions and Equations

Objectives

In this chapter, you will:

- simplify rational expressions,
- add, subtact, multiply, and divide rational expressions,
- divide polynomials, and
- make organized lists to solve problems.

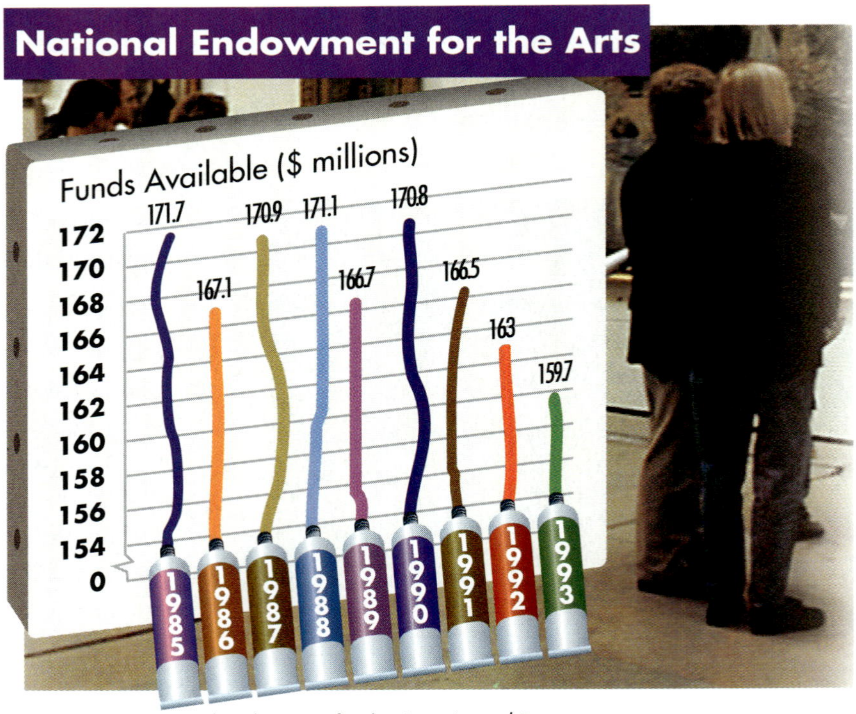

Source: U.S. National Endowment for the Arts, *Annual Report*

The term "starving artist" is not without merit. Many artists often have other jobs to survive while trying to pursue their careers as artists. The National Endowment for the Arts is authorized to assist individuals and nonprofit organizations financially in a wide range of artistic endeavors. Some of the artistic forms that are funded are music, museums, theater, dance, media arts, and visual arts.

TIME*Line*

1700 B.C. The great palace at Knossos in Crete is built. It is the legendary capital of King Minos.

64 The first dental drill is used by the Roman surgeon Archigenes. It was powered by a rope.

A.D. 1 Chinese mathematician Liu Hsin is the first to use decimal fractions.

1629 Albert Girard's *L'invention nouvelle en l'algebre* (The New Science of Algebra) asserts the fundamental theorem of algebra.

PEOPLE IN THE NEWS

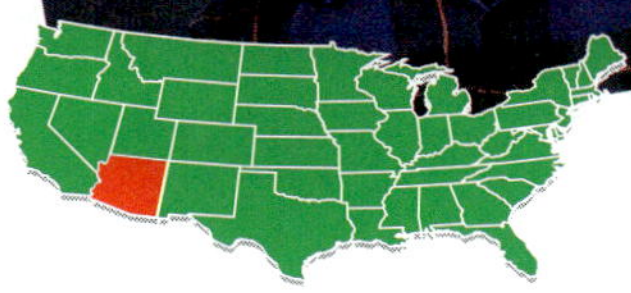

The expression of energy, vibrancy, and harmony are just some of the thoughts that flow through the creativity of **Joe Maktima** of Flagstaff, Arizona. The themes of his work in acrylic paints and mediums are deeply rooted in his pueblo culture. Joe began his artistic endeavors in high school as a hobby, but it was winning the Best of Show Award in a national competition of Native American high school art students that gave him the confidence to become a professional artist.

Chapter Project

Native American art also includes blanket weaving. Many of the designs include pictorial representations of everyday objects or characters from folklore about their ancestors.

- Design a 64″ × 80″ blanket. Choose either objects that represent you or some part of your personal history for the blanket's design.
- Make a drawing to represent your design. Include a scale expressed as a rational number to show the actual size of your blanket.
- Use yarn or construction paper to weave a portion of your design.
- Calculate how much yarn in each color you would need to create a real blanket.
- Estimate the cost of your blanket in materials and labor.

Suppose a blanket is priced at $375. How does this price compare with your estimate?

1928 American portrait photographer Berenice Abbott takes her famous picture of writer James Joyce.

1971 Aretha Franklin releases her live album *Aretha Live at Fillmore West.*

1983 A meter is officially redefined as the distance that light travels in $\frac{1}{299,792,458}$ of a second.

1990 Ellen Ochoa becomes the first Latina astronaut.

1915 1920 1925 1930 1935 1965 1970 1975 1980 1985 1990 1995 2000

12–1 Simplifying Rational Expressions

What YOU'LL LEARN

- To simplify rational expressions, and
- to identify values excluded from the domain of a rational expression.

Why IT'S IMPORTANT

You can use rational expressions to solve problems involving physics and carpentry.

CONNECTION Physical Science

Many bicyclists carry small tool kits in case they need to make adjustments to their bicycles while on the road. A wrench, for example, might be needed to tighten the bolts that keep the seat aligned. The force applied to one end of the wrench is multiplied so that the bolt at the other end of the wrench is made very secure.

A wrench is an example of a simple machine called a *lever*. In Lesson 7–2, you learned that to calculate the *mechanical advantage* (MA) of a lever, you find the ratio of the length of the effort arm to the length of the resistance arm. MA is usually expressed as a decimal value.

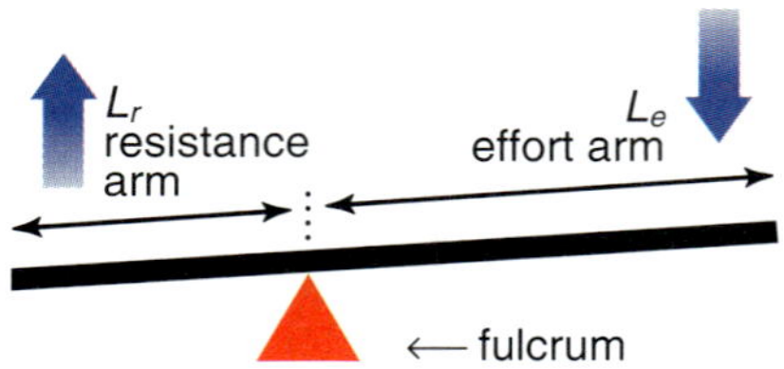

$$MA = \frac{\text{length of effort arm}}{\text{length of resistance arm}} = \frac{L_e}{L_r}$$

Suppose the total length of a lever is 6 feet. If the length of the resistance arm of the lever is x feet, then the length of the effort arm is $(6 - x)$ feet. The function $f(x) = \frac{6-x}{x}$ represents the mechanical advantage of the lever. The table and graph at the right represent this function. They illustrate how varying the length of the resistance arm affects the mechanical advantage. Notice that, as x increases, the mechanical advantage $f(x)$ decreases. The expression that defines this function, $\frac{6-x}{x}$, is an example of a **rational expression.**

x	f(x)
0	undefined
1	5.0
2	2.0
3	1.0
4	0.5
5	0.2
6	0.0

Definition of a Rational Expression	**A rational expression is an algebraic fraction whose numerator and denominator are polynomials.**

$f(x) = \frac{6-x}{x}$ is called a rational function.

Because a rational expression involves division, the denominator may not have a value of zero. Therefore, any values of a variable that result in a denominator of zero must be excluded from the domain of the variable. These are called **excluded values** of the rational expression.

For $\frac{6-x}{x}$, exclude $x = 0$.

For $\frac{5m+3}{m+6}$, exclude $m = -6$, since $-6 + 6 = 0$.

For $\frac{x^2-5}{x^2-5x+6}$, exclude $x = 2$ and $x = 3$. *Why?*

Example 1 **For each rational expression, state the values of the variable that must be excluded.**

a. $\frac{7b}{b+5}$

Exclude the values for which $b + 5 = 0$.

$b + 5 = 0$

$b = -5$

Therefore, b cannot equal -5.

b. $\frac{r^2 + 32}{r^2 + 9r + 8}$

Exclude the values for which $r^2 + 9r + 8 = 0$.

$r^2 + 9r + 8 = 0$

$(r + 1)(r + 8) = 0$

$r = -1$ or $r = -8$ *Zero product property*

Therefore, r cannot equal -1 or -8.

To simplify a rational expression, you must eliminate any common factors of the numerator and denominator. To do this, use their greatest common factor (GCF). Remember that $\frac{ab}{ac} = \frac{a}{a} \cdot \frac{b}{c}$ and $\frac{a}{a} = 1$. So, $\frac{ab}{ac} = 1 \cdot \frac{b}{c}$ or $\frac{b}{c}$.

Example 2 **Simplify $\frac{9x^2yz}{24xyz^2}$. State the excluded values of x, y, and z.**

$$\frac{9x^2yz}{24xyz^2} = \frac{(3xyz)(3x)}{(3xyz)(8z)}$$ *Factor; the GCF is 3xyz.*

$$= \frac{\overset{1}{\cancel{(3xyz)}}(3x)}{\underset{1}{\cancel{(3xyz)}}(8z)}$$ *Divide by the GCF.*

$$= \frac{3x}{8z}$$

Exclude the values for which $24xyz^2 = 0$: $x = 0$, $y = 0$, or $z = 0$. Therefore, neither x, y, nor z can equal 0.

You can use the same procedure to simplify a rational expression in which the numerator and denominator are polynomials.

Example 3 **Simplify $\frac{a+3}{a^2 + 4a + 3}$. State the excluded values of a.**

$$\frac{a+3}{a^2 + 4a + 3} = \frac{a+3}{(a+1)(a+3)}$$ *Factor the denominator.*

$$= \frac{\overset{1}{\cancel{a+3}}}{(a+1)\underset{1}{\cancel{(a+3)}}}$$ *The GCF is $a + 3$.*

$$= \frac{1}{a+1}$$

Exclude the values for which $a^2 + 4a + 3 = 0$.

$a^2 + 4a + 3 = 0$

$(a + 1)(a + 3) = 0$

$a = -1$ or $a = -3$

Therefore, a cannot equal -1 or -3.

EXPLORATION CALCULATORS

You can use a scientific or graphing calculator to evaluate rational expressions for given values of the variables. When you do this, you must be careful to use parentheses to group both the numerator and the denominator of the expression. For example, to evaluate $\frac{x^2 - 6x + 8}{x - 2}$ when $x = -3$, use a key sequence like this on a scientific calculator.

Enter: (3 +/− x^2 − 6 × 3 +/− + 8) ÷ (3 +/− − 2) = −7

The key sequence for a graphing calculator is very similar.

Enter: (((−) 3) x^2 − 6 × (−) 3 + 8) ÷ ((−) 3 − 2) ENTER −7

Your Turn

a. Copy and complete the table below.

x	−3	−2	−1	0	1	2	3
$\frac{x^2 - 6x + 8}{x - 2}$	−7						
$x - 4$							

b. For which value(s) of x is the value of $\frac{x^2 - 6x + 8}{x - 2}$ equal to the value of $x - 4$? Why does this result make sense?

c. For which value(s) of x is the value of $\frac{x^2 - 6x + 8}{x - 2}$ *not* equal to the value of $x - 4$? Why does this result make sense?

Example 4

CONNECTION Physical Science

To pry the lid off a paint can, a screwdriver that is 20.5 cm long is used as a lever. It is placed so that 0.5 cm of its length extends inward from the rim of the can. Then a force of 5 pounds is applied at the end of the screwdriver. What is the force placed on the lid?

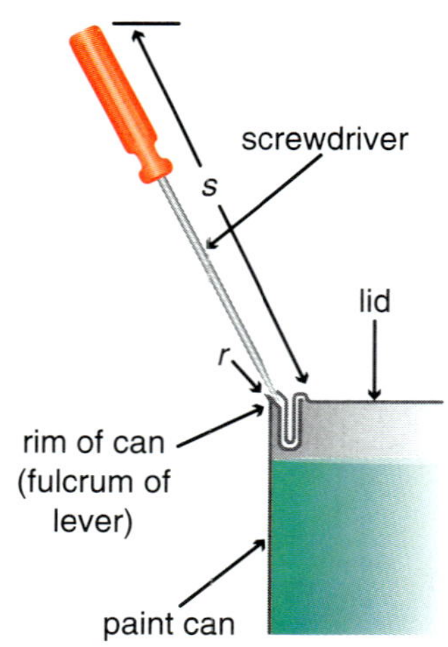

Let s represent the total length of the screwdriver.

Let r represent the length that extends inward from the rim. This is the length of the resistance arm of the lever.

Then $s - r$ represents the length that extends outward from the rim. This is the length of the effort arm of the lever.

Use the formula given in the connection at the beginning of the lesson to write an expression for mechanical advantage.

$$MA = \frac{\text{length of effort arm}}{\text{length of resistance arm}} \text{ or } \frac{s - r}{r}$$

Now evaluate the expression for the given values.

$$\frac{s - r}{r} = \frac{20.5 - 0.5}{0.5} \qquad s = 20.5 \text{ and } r = 0.5$$

$$= \frac{20}{0.5} \text{ or } 40 \qquad \textit{Simplify.}$$

The mechanical advantage is 40. The force placed on the lid is the product of this number and the force applied at the end of the screwdriver.

$40 \cdot 5$ pounds $= 200$ pounds

The force placed on the lid is 200 pounds.

CHECK FOR UNDERSTANDING

Communicating Mathematics

Study the lesson. Then complete the following.

1. **Explain** why $x = 2$ is excluded from the domain of $f(x) = \frac{x^2 + 7x + 12}{x - 2}$.
2. **Estimate** the mechanical advantage of the lever shown on page 660 using the graph if x is 1.5.
3. **Explain** how you would determine the values to be excluded from the domain of $f(x) = \frac{x + 5}{x^2 + 6x + 5}$.
4. **Write** a rational expression involving one variable for which the excluded values are -2 and 7.
5. **Write** the meaning of the term *mechanical advantage* in your own words.

Guided Practice

For each expression, find the GCF of the numerator and the denominator. Then simplify. State the excluded values of the variables.

6. $\frac{13a}{14ay}$
7. $\frac{-7a^2b^3}{21a^5b}$
8. $\frac{a(m + 3)}{a(m - 2)}$
9. $\frac{3b}{b(b + 5)}$
10. $\frac{(r + s)(r - s)}{(r - s)(r - s)}$
11. $\frac{m - 3}{m^2 - 9}$
12. Evaluate $\frac{x^2 + 7x + 12}{x + 3}$ if $x = 2$.
13. **Landscaping** To clear land for a garden, Chang needs to move some large rocks. He plans to use a 6-foot-long pinch bar as a lever. He positions it next to each rock as shown at the right.

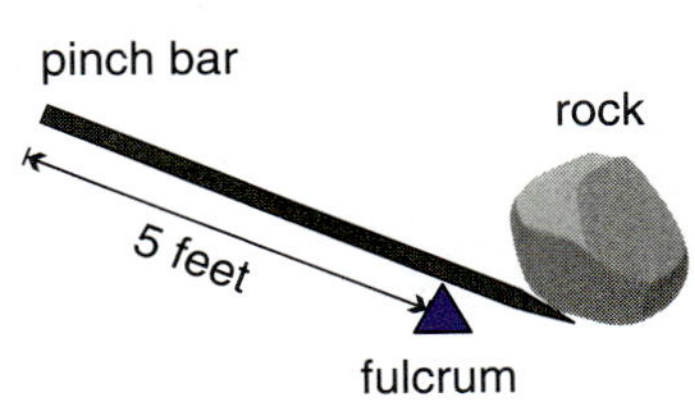

   a. Calculate the mechanical advantage.
   b. If Chang can apply a force of 150 pounds to the effort arm, what is the greatest weight he can lift?

EXERCISES

Practice

Simplify each rational expression. State the excluded values of the variables.

14. $\dfrac{15a}{39a^2}$ **15.** $\dfrac{35y^2z}{14yz^2}$ **16.** $\dfrac{28a^2}{49ab}$

17. $\dfrac{56x^2y}{70x^3y}$ **18.** $\dfrac{4a}{3a + a^2}$ **19.** $\dfrac{y + 3y^2}{3y + 1}$

20. $\dfrac{x^2 - 9}{2x + 6}$ **21.** $\dfrac{y^2 - 49x^2}{y - 7x}$ **22.** $\dfrac{x + 5}{x^2 + x - 20}$

23. $\dfrac{a - 3}{a^2 - 7a + 12}$ **24.** $\dfrac{3x - 15}{x^2 - 7x + 10}$ **25.** $\dfrac{x + 4}{x^2 + 8x + 16}$

26. $\dfrac{x^2 - 2x - 15}{x^2 - x - 12}$ **27.** $\dfrac{a^2 + 4a - 12}{a^2 + 2a - 8}$ **28.** $\dfrac{x^2 - 36}{x^2 + x - 30}$

29. $\dfrac{b^2 - 3b - 4}{b^2 - 13b + 36}$ **30.** $\dfrac{14x^2 + 35x + 21}{12x^2 + 30x + 18}$ **31.** $\dfrac{4x^2 + 8x + 4}{5x^2 + 10x + 5}$

Calculator

Use a calculator to evaluate each expression for the given values.

32. $\dfrac{x^2 - x}{3x}$, $x = -3$ **33.** $\dfrac{x^4 - 16}{x^4 - 8x^2 + 16}$, $x = -1$

34. $\dfrac{x + y}{x^2 + 2xy + y^2}$, $x = 3$, $y = 2$ **35.** $\dfrac{x^3y^3 + 5x^3y^2 + 6x^3y}{xy^5 + 5xy^4 + 6xy^3}$, $x = 1$, $y = -2$

Critical Thinking

36. Explain why $\dfrac{m^2 - 16}{m + 4}$ is not the same as $m - 4$.

Applications and Problem Solving

37. Carpentry A house mover can lift a house from its foundation using a *jackscrew* like the one shown at the right. As shown, the effort force is applied in a circular motion. The vertical distance that the jackscrew moves in one turn is called its *pitch*. You can use the following formula to calculate the mechanical advantage of the jackscrew.

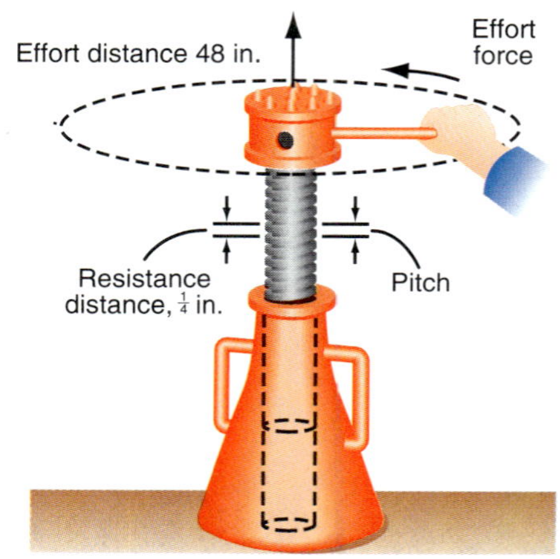

$$MA = \frac{\text{circumference of the circle}}{\text{pitch of the screw}}$$

a. Calculate the mechanical advantage for the jackscrew shown above.

b. Suppose the effort force is 20 pounds. What is the greatest weight the jackscrew can lift?

38. Aeronautics Aircraft engineers can use the following formula to calculate the atmospheric pressure P in pounds per square inch when an aircraft is flying at an altitude a in feet.

$$P = \frac{-9.05\left[\left(\frac{a}{1000}\right)^2 - \frac{65a}{1000}\right]}{\left(\frac{a}{1000}\right)^2 + 40\left(\frac{a}{1000}\right)}$$

a. Calculate the atmospheric pressure outside a plane flying at an altitude of 20,000 feet.

b. Calculate the atmospheric pressure outside a plane flying at an altitude of 40,000 feet.

c. Is your answer to part b twice that of part a? By how much do they differ?

FYI

Because altitude affects things like boiling temperatures, recipe cooking temperatures and times must be altered so that a cake, for example, will turn out correctly. Look on a box of cake mix to find the high altitude directions.

39. Physics At sea level, the boiling point of water is 212°F. At the top of Mt. Everest, the boiling point is 159.8°F. The top of Mt. Everest is 29,002 ft above sea level.

a. How many degrees does the boiling point drop for every mile up from sea level? Write the solution as a ratio involving units.

b. Simplify the expression you wrote in part a.

c. Draw a graph that represents the boiling point in degrees Fahrenheit as a function of altitude in miles.

Mixed Review

40. Finance In the compound interest formula $A = P\left(1 + \frac{r}{n}\right)^{nt}$, A represents the value of the investment in the future, P is the amount of the original investment, r is the annual interest rate, t is the number of years of the investment, and n is the number of times the interest is compounded each year. Find the total amount after $2500 is invested for 18 years at a rate of 6%, compounded quarterly. (Lesson 11–5)

41. Number Theory The square of a number decreased by 121 is 0. Find the number. (Lesson 10–7)

42. Find $3x(-5x^2 - 2x + 7)$. (Lesson 9–6)

43. Graph the system of inequalities. (Lesson 8–5)

$y \geq x - 2$

$y \leq 2x - 1$

44. Solve $4 + |x| = 12$. (Lesson 7–6)

45. Graph $y = 3x + 2$. (Lesson 5–4)

46. Solve $\frac{x}{4} + 7 = 6$. (Lesson 3–3)

WORKING ON THE

In•ves•ti•ga•tion

Refer to the Investigation on pages 656–657.

A Growing Concern

1 Use graph paper to make a scale drawing of the house, garage, driveway, boundary lines, and fences. This will serve as your template to which you will add the other details.

2 Develop a detailed plan for the pool and hot tub locations. Indicate the dimensions of both the pool and the hot tub. Explain why you chose the size, location, and orientation for the pool.

3 Figure the costs for materials, labor, and profit margin for construction of the pool and hot tub. Justify your costs and make a case for building the pool and hot tub as you have designed them.

4 Add the pool and hot tub to the scale drawing, indicating their measurements.

Add the results of your work to your Investigation Folder.

12–1B Graphing Technology
Rational Expressions

An Extension of Lesson 12–1

When simplifying rational expressions, you can use a graphing calculator to support your answer. You can also use a calculator to find the excluded values.

Example **Simplify** $\frac{3x^2 - 8x + 5}{x^2 - 1}$.

$$\frac{3x^2 - 8x + 5}{x^2 - 1} = \frac{(3x - 5)(x - 1)}{(x + 1)(x - 1)}$$ *Factor the numerator and denominator.*

$$= \frac{3x - 5}{x + 1}$$ *Divide the common factor $(x - 1)$.*

When $x = -1$ or $x = 1$, $x^2 - 1 = 0$. Therefore, x cannot equal -1 or 1.

Now use a graphing calculator. Graph $y = \frac{3x^2 - 8x + 5}{x^2 - 1}$ using the window $[-4.7, 4.7]$ by $[-10, 10]$ with scale factors of 1.

Enter: [Y=] [(] 3 [X,T,θ,n] [x^2] [−] 8 [X,T,θ,n] [+] 5 [)] [÷] [(] [X,T,θ,n] [x^2] [−] 1 [)] [GRAPH]

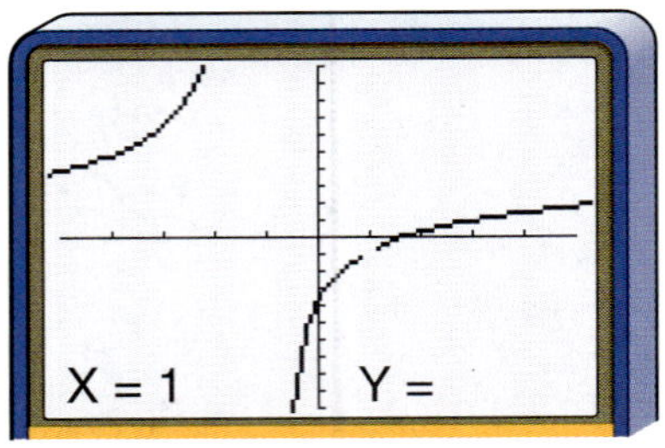

Use the TRACE key to observe the values of x and y. Notice that at $x = -1$ and $x = 1$, no value for y appears in the window. There are also "holes" in the graph at those points. These are the excluded values.

Now enter $y = \frac{3x - 5}{x + 1}$ as Y2 and observe the graphs.

Enter: [Y=] [(] 3 [X,T,θ,n] [−] 5 [)] [÷] [(] [X,T,θ,n] [+] 1 [)] [GRAPH]

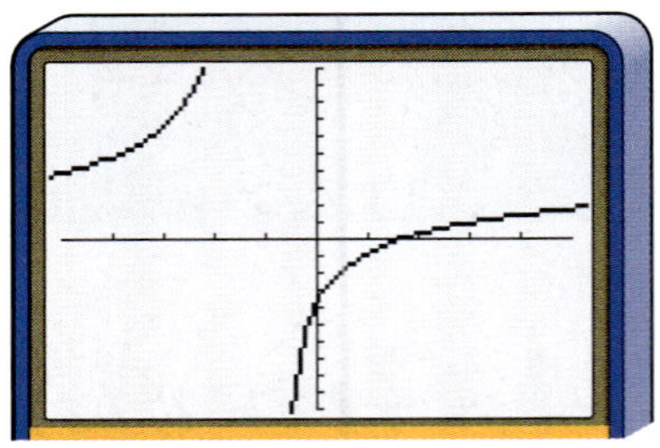

Notice that the two graphs appear to be identical. This means that the simplified expression is probably correct.

EXERCISES

Simplify each expression. Then verify your answer graphically. Name the excluded values.

1. $\frac{x^2 - 25}{x^2 + 10x + 25}$
2. $\frac{3x + 6}{x^2 + 7x + 10}$
3. $\frac{2x - 9}{4x^2 - 18x}$
4. $\frac{2x^2 - 4x}{x^2 + x - 6}$
5. $\frac{x^2 - 9x + 8}{x^2 - 16x + 64}$
6. $\frac{3x^2}{12x^2 + 192x}$
7. $\frac{-x^2 + 6x - 9}{x^2 - 6x + 9}$
8. $\frac{5x^2 + 10x + 5}{3x^2 + 6x + 3}$
9. $\frac{25 - x^2}{x^2 + x - 30}$

12-2 Multiplying Rational Expressions

What YOU'LL LEARN

- To multiply rational expressions.

Why IT'S IMPORTANT

You can use rational expressions to solve problems involving traffic and money.

APPLICATION

Traffic

On the Sunday after Thanksgiving in 1994, westbound traffic was backed up for 13 miles at one exit of the Massachusetts Turnpike. Assume that each vehicle occupied an average of 30 feet of space in a lane and that the turnpike has three lanes. You can use the expression below to estimate the number of vehicles involved in the backup.

$$3 \text{ lanes} \cdot \left(\frac{13 \text{ miles}}{\text{lane}}\right)\left(\frac{5280 \text{ feet}}{\text{mile}}\right)\left(\frac{1 \text{ vehicle}}{30 \text{ feet}}\right)$$

This expression will be simplified in Example 3.

LOOK BACK

You can refer to Lesson 2-6 for information about multiplying rational numbers.

This multiplication is similar to the multiplication of rational expressions. Recall that to multiply rational numbers that are expressed as fractions, you multiply numerators and multiply denominators. You can use this same method to multiply rational expressions. From this point on, you may assume that no denominator of a rational expression has a value of 0.

rational numbers

$$\frac{4}{5} \cdot \frac{3}{7} = \frac{4 \cdot 3}{5 \cdot 7} = \frac{12}{35}$$

rational expressions

$$\frac{3}{m} \cdot \frac{k}{4} = \frac{3 \cdot k}{m \cdot 4} = \frac{3k}{4m}$$

Example 1 Find $\frac{3x^2y}{2rs} \cdot \frac{24r^2s}{15xy^2}$.

Method 1: Divide by the common factors after multiplying.

$$\frac{3x^2y}{2rs} \cdot \frac{24r^2s}{15xy^2} = \frac{72r^2sx^2y}{30rsxy^2}$$

$$= \frac{\overset{1}{\cancel{6rsxy}}(12rx)}{\underset{1}{\cancel{6rsxy}}(5y)} \quad \textit{The GCF is } 6rsxy.$$

$$= \frac{12rx}{5y}$$

Method 2: Divide by the common factors before multiplying.

$$\frac{3x^2y}{2rs} \cdot \frac{24r^2s}{15xy^2} = \frac{\overset{1\,x\,1}{\cancel{3x^2y}}}{\underset{1\,1\,1}{\cancel{2rs}}} \cdot \frac{\overset{12\,r\,1}{\cancel{24r^2s}}}{\underset{5\,1\,y}{\cancel{15xy^2}}}$$

$$= \frac{12rx}{5y}$$

Sometimes you must factor a quadratic expression before you can simplify a product of rational expressions.

Example 2 **Find each product.**

a. $\dfrac{m+3}{5m} \cdot \dfrac{20m^2}{m^2+8m+15}$

$$\frac{m+3}{5m} \cdot \frac{20m^2}{m^2+8m+15} = \frac{m+3}{5m} \cdot \frac{20m^2}{(m+3)(m+5)} \quad \textit{Factor the denominator.}$$

$$= \frac{\overset{4}{\cancel{20}}\overset{m}{\cancel{m^2}}\overset{1}{\cancel{(m+3)}}}{\underset{1}{\cancel{5}}\underset{1}{\cancel{m}}\underset{1}{\cancel{(m+3)}}(m+5)} \quad \textit{The GCF is } 5m(m+3).$$

$$= \frac{4m}{m+5}$$

b. $\dfrac{3(x+5)}{4(2x^2+11x+12)} \cdot (2x+3)$

$$\frac{3(x+5)}{4(2x^2+11x+12)} \cdot (2x+3) = \frac{3(x+5)(2x+3)}{4(2x^2+11x+12)}$$

$$= \frac{3(x+5)(2x+3)}{4(2x+3)(x+4)} \quad \textit{Factor the denominator.}$$

$$= \frac{3(x+5)\overset{1}{\cancel{(2x+3)}}}{4\underset{1}{\cancel{(2x+3)}}(x+4)} \quad \textit{The GCF is } (2x+3).$$

$$= \frac{3(x+5)}{4(x+4)}$$

$$= \frac{3x+15}{4x+16} \quad \textit{Simplify the numerator and the denominator.}$$

When you multiply fractions that involve units of measure, you can divide by the units in the same way that you divide by variables. Recall that this process is called *dimensional analysis*.

Example 3 **APPLICATION** **Traffic**

Refer to the application at the beginning of the lesson. About how many vehicles were involved in the backup?

$$3 \text{ lanes} \cdot \left(\frac{13 \text{ miles}}{\text{lane}}\right)\left(\frac{5280 \text{ feet}}{\text{mile}}\right)\left(\frac{1 \text{ vehicle}}{30 \text{ feet}}\right)$$

$$= \frac{\overset{1}{\cancel{3 \text{ lanes}}}}{1} \cdot \left(\frac{13 \cancel{\text{ miles}}}{\cancel{\text{lane}}}\right)\left(\frac{\overset{528}{\cancel{5280 \text{ feet}}}}{\cancel{\text{mile}}}\right)\left(\frac{1 \text{ vehicle}}{\underset{1}{\cancel{30 \text{ feet}}}}\right) \quad \textit{Divide by common units.}$$

$$= 6864 \text{ vehicles}$$

The backup involved about 6900 vehicles.

CHECK FOR UNDERSTANDING

Communicating Mathematics

Study the lesson. Then complete the following.

1. **Write** two rational expressions whose product is $\dfrac{xy}{x-4}$.

2. **You Decide** The work of two students who simplified $\dfrac{4x+8}{4x-8} \cdot \dfrac{x^2+2x-8}{2x+8}$ is shown below. Which one is correct, and why?

   Matt: $\dfrac{\overset{1}{\cancel{4}}x + \overset{1}{\cancel{8}}}{\underset{1}{\cancel{4}}x - \underset{1}{\cancel{8}}} \cdot \dfrac{x^2 + \overset{1}{\cancel{2}}x - \overset{1}{\cancel{8}}}{\underset{1}{\cancel{2}}x + \underset{1}{\cancel{8}}} = x^2$

   Angie: $\dfrac{\overset{1}{\cancel{4}}(x+2)}{\underset{1}{\cancel{4}}\underset{1}{\cancel{(x-2)}}} \cdot \dfrac{\overset{1}{\cancel{(x-2)}}\overset{1}{\cancel{(x+4)}}}{2\underset{1}{\cancel{(x+4)}}} = \dfrac{x+2}{2}$

MATH JOURNAL

3. Write a paragraph explaining which is better—to simplify an expression first and then multiply, or to multiply and then simplify. Include examples to support your answers.

Guided Practice

Find each product. Assume that no denominator has a value of 0.

4. $\frac{12m^2y}{5r^2} \cdot \frac{r^2}{my}$

5. $\frac{16xy^2}{3m^2p} \cdot \frac{27m^3p}{32x^2y^3}$

6. $\frac{x-5}{r} \cdot \frac{r^2}{(x-5)(y+3)}$

7. $\frac{x+4}{4y} \cdot \frac{16y}{x^2+7x+12}$

8. $\frac{a^2+7a+10}{a+1} \cdot \frac{3a+3}{a+2}$

9. $\frac{4(x-7)}{3(x^2-10x+21)} \cdot (x-3)$

10. $3(x+6) \cdot \frac{x+3}{9(x^2+7x+6)}$

11. a. Multiply $\frac{2.54 \text{ centimeters}}{1 \text{ inch}} \cdot \frac{12 \text{ inches}}{1 \text{ foot}} \cdot \frac{3 \text{ feet}}{1 \text{ yard}}$. Then simplify.
    b. What does the simplified expression represent?

12. **Bicycling** Marisa says that bicycling at the rate of 20 miles per hour is equivalent to a rate of 1760 feet per minute. Is she correct? Write a product involving units of measure to justify your answer.

EXERCISES

Practice

Find each product. Assume that no denominator has a value of 0.

13. $\frac{7a^2}{5} \cdot \frac{15}{14a}$

14. $\frac{3m^2}{2m} \cdot \frac{18m^2}{9m}$

15. $\frac{10r^3}{6x^3} \cdot \frac{42x^2}{35r^3}$

16. $\frac{7ab^3}{11r^2} \cdot \frac{44r^3}{21a^2b}$

17. $\frac{64y^2}{5y} \cdot \frac{5y}{8y}$

18. $\frac{2a^2}{b} \cdot \frac{5bc}{6a}$

19. $\frac{m+4}{3m} \cdot \frac{4m^2}{m^2+9m+20}$

20. $\frac{m^2+8m+15}{a+b} \cdot \frac{7a+14b}{m+3}$

21. $\frac{5a+10}{10m^2} \cdot \frac{4m^3}{a^2+11a+18}$

22. $\frac{6r+3}{r+6} \cdot \frac{r^2+9r+18}{2r+1}$

23. $2(x+1) \cdot \frac{x+4}{x^2+5x+4}$

24. $4(a+7) \cdot \frac{12}{3(a^2+8a+7)}$

25. $\frac{x^2-y^2}{12} \cdot \frac{36}{x+y}$

26. $\frac{3a+9}{a} \cdot \frac{a^2}{a^2-9}$

27. $\frac{9}{3+2x} \cdot (12+8x)$

28. $(3x+3) \cdot \frac{x+4}{x^2+5x+4}$

29. $\frac{4x}{9x^2-25} \cdot (3x+5)$

30. $(b^2+12b+11) \cdot \frac{b+9}{b^2+20b+99}$

31. $\frac{4x+8}{x^2-25} \cdot \frac{x-5}{5x+10}$

32. $\frac{a^2-a-6}{a^2-9} \cdot \frac{a^2+7a+12}{a^2+4a+4}$

Multiply. Explain what each expression represents.

33. $\frac{32 \text{ feet}}{1 \text{ second}} \cdot \frac{60 \text{ seconds}}{1 \text{ minute}} \cdot \frac{60 \text{ minutes}}{1 \text{ hour}} \cdot \frac{1 \text{ mile}}{5280 \text{ feet}}$

34. $10 \text{ feet} \cdot 18 \text{ feet} \cdot 3 \text{ feet} \cdot \frac{1 \text{ yard}^3}{27 \text{ feet}^3}$

Simplify each expression.

35. **Heat** 20 grams at 540 Calories per gram

36. **Metal Refining** 4.025 grams per amp-hour at 2 amps for 5 hours

Critical Thinking

37. Find two different pairs of rational expressions whose product is $\frac{6x^2-6x-36}{x^2+3x-28}$.

Applications and Problem Solving

38. **Traffic** Refer to Example 3. Suppose there are eight toll collectors at the exit and it takes each an average of 24 seconds to collect the toll from one vehicle.
    a. Write a product involving units to estimate the time it would take in hours to collect tolls from all the vehicles in the backup.
    b. Simplify the product.

39. **Money** The chart at the right shows a recent foreign exchange rate table. It indicates how much of another country's currency you would receive in exchange for one American dollar at the time these rates were in effect.

Dollar Exchange

Country (Currency)	Equivalent to American Dollars
Canada (dollar)	0.7444
Hong Kong (dollar)	0.1292
Israel (shekel)	0.3281
France (franc)	0.1981
Mexico (peso)	0.1597

   a. Write a rational expression involving units of measure that indicates how many American dollars you would receive for one French franc. Write another expression that indicates how many French francs you would receive for one American dollar.
   b. Write a product involving units of measure that indicates how many French francs you would receive for 12,500 Mexican pesos. Then find the product.
   c. Explain how to determine an exchange rate between Canada's dollar and Hong Kong's dollar.

Mixed Review

40. **Cooking** The formula $t = \frac{40(25 + 1.85a)}{50 - 1.85a}$ relates the time t in minutes that it takes to bake an average-size potato in an oven that is at an altitude of a thousands of feet. (Lesson 12–1)
    a. What is the value of a for an altitude of 4500 feet?
    b. Calculate the time is takes to bake a potato at an altitude of 3500 feet.
    c. Calculate the time it takes to bake a potato at an altitude of 7000 feet.
    d. The altitude in part c is twice that of part b. How do your baking times compare for those two altitudes?

41. Find the value of y for $y = 3^{2x}$ if $x = 3$. (Lesson 11–4)
42. Solve $5x^2 + 30x + 45 = 0$ by factoring. (Lesson 10–6)
43. Find the degree of $6x^2yz + 5xyz - x^3$. (Lesson 9–4)
44. Solve the system of equations. (Lesson 8–3)
    $5 = 2x - 3y$
    $-1 = -4x + 3y$
45. Find the slope of the line that passes through $(-3, 5)$ and $(8, 5)$. (Lesson 5–1)
46. What is 45% of \$1567 to the nearest dollar? (Lesson 4–4)

12-3 Dividing Rational Expressions

What YOU'LL LEARN

- To divide rational expressions.

Why IT'S IMPORTANT

You can use rational expressions to solve problems involving construction and railroads.

LOOK BACK

You can refer to Lesson 2-7 for information about dividing rational numbers.

APPLICATION

Parades

A crowd watching the Tournament of Roses Parade in Pasadena, California, fills the sidewalks along the route for about 5.5 miles on each side. Suppose these sidewalks are 10 feet wide and each person occupies an average of 4 square feet of space. To estimate the number of people along this part of the route, you can use dimensional analysis and the following expression.

$$\left(5.5 \text{ miles} \cdot \frac{5280 \text{ ft}}{1 \text{ mile}} \cdot 10 \text{ feet}\right) \div \frac{4 \text{ ft}^2}{1 \text{ person}}$$ *This expression will be simplified in Example 4.*

This division is similar to the division of rational expressions. Recall that to divide rational numbers that are expressed as fractions you multiply by the reciprocal of the divisor. You can use this same method to divide algebraic rational expressions.

rational numbers

$$\frac{3}{2} \div \frac{2}{5} = \frac{3}{2} \cdot \frac{5}{2}$$ *The reciprocal of $\frac{2}{5}$ is $\frac{5}{2}$.*

$$= \frac{15}{4}$$

rational expressions

$$\frac{a}{b} \div \frac{c}{d} = \frac{a}{b} \cdot \frac{d}{c}$$ *The reciprocal of $\frac{c}{d}$ is $\frac{d}{c}$.*

$$= \frac{ad}{bc}$$

Example 1 **Find $\frac{2a}{a+3} \div \frac{a+7}{a+3}$.**

$$\frac{2a}{a+3} \div \frac{a+7}{a+3} = \frac{2a}{a+3} \cdot \frac{a+3}{a+7}$$ *The reciprocal of $\frac{a+7}{a+3}$ is $\frac{a+3}{a+7}$.*

$$= \frac{2a}{\cancel{a+3}_{1}} \cdot \frac{\overset{1}{\cancel{a+3}}}{a+7}$$ *Divide by the common factor $a + 3$.*

$$= \frac{2a}{a+7}$$

Sometimes a quotient of rational expressions involves a divisor that is a binomial.

Example 2 **Find $\frac{2m+6}{m+5} \div (m+3)$.**

$$\frac{2m+6}{m+5} \div (m+3) = \frac{2m+6}{m+5} \cdot \frac{1}{m+3}$$ *The reciprocal of $m + 3$ is $\frac{1}{m+3}$.*

$$= \frac{2(\overset{1}{\cancel{m+3}})}{(m+5)(\underset{1}{\cancel{m+3}})}$$ *Divide by the common factor $m + 3$.*

$$= \frac{2}{m+5}$$

Sometimes you must factor before you can simplify a quotient of rational expressions.

Example 3

Find $\frac{x}{x+2} \div \frac{x^2}{x^2+5x+6}$.

$$\frac{x}{x+2} \div \frac{x^2}{x^2+5x+6} = \frac{x}{x+2} \cdot \frac{x^2+5x+6}{x^2}$$

$$= \frac{\overset{1}{\cancel{x}}}{\underset{1}{\cancel{x+2}}} \cdot \frac{(\overset{1}{\cancel{x+2}})(x+3)}{\underset{x}{\cancel{x^2}}} \quad \textit{Divide by common factors.}$$

$$= \frac{x+3}{x}$$

Example 4

APPLICATION

Parades

Refer to the application at the beginning of the lesson. Estimate the number of people along the part of the parade route that is described.

$$\left(5.5 \text{ miles} \cdot \frac{5280 \text{ ft}}{1 \text{ mile}} \cdot 10 \text{ feet}\right) \div \frac{4 \text{ ft}^2}{1 \text{ person}}$$

The reciprocal of $\frac{4 \text{ ft}^2}{1 \text{ person}}$ is $\frac{1 \text{ person}}{4 \text{ ft}^2}$.

$$= \left(5.5 \text{ miles} \cdot \frac{5280 \text{ ft}}{1 \text{ mile}} \cdot 10 \text{ feet}\right) \cdot \frac{1 \text{ person}}{4 \text{ ft}^2}$$

$$= \frac{5.5 \cancel{\text{ miles}}}{1} \cdot \frac{\overset{1320}{\cancel{5280 \text{ ft}}}}{1 \cancel{\text{ mile}}} \cdot \frac{10 \cancel{\text{ ft}}}{1} \cdot \frac{1 \text{ person}}{\underset{1}{\cancel{4 \text{ ft}^2}}} \quad \textit{Divide by common units.}$$

$$= 72{,}600 \text{ people}$$

This means that there were about 72,600 people along *each side*. Since there were two sides, the total number of people along the route was about 2(72,600), or 145,200.

CHECK FOR UNDERSTANDING

Communicating Mathematics

Study the lesson. Then complete the following.

1. **Analyze** the solution shown below.

$$\frac{a^2-9}{3a} \div \frac{a+3}{a-3} = \frac{3a}{a^2-9} \cdot \frac{a+3}{a-3}$$

$$= \frac{3a}{(\underset{1}{\cancel{a+3}})(a-3)} \cdot \frac{(\overset{1}{\cancel{a+3}})}{a-3}$$

$$= \frac{3a}{(a-3)^2}$$

What error was made?

2. **Write** two rational expressions whose quotient is $\frac{10r}{d^2}$.

MATH JOURNAL

3. An expression for calculating the mass of 1 cubic meter of a substance is given below. Write a procedure for simplifying the expression.

$$\frac{5.96 \text{ grams}}{\text{centimeter}^3} \cdot \frac{1 \text{ kilogram}}{1000 \text{ grams}} \cdot \frac{100^3 \text{ centimeters}^3}{1 \text{ meter}^3} \cdot 1 \text{ meter}^3$$

Guided Practice

Find the reciprocal of each expression.

4. $\frac{m^2}{3}$
5. $\frac{x}{5}$
6. $\frac{-9}{4y}$
7. $\frac{x^2-9}{y+3}$
8. $m - 3$
9. $x^2 + 2x + 5$

Find each quotient. Assume that no denominator has a value of 0.

10. $\dfrac{x}{x+7} \div \dfrac{x-5}{x+7}$

11. $\dfrac{m^2+3m+2}{4} \div \dfrac{m+1}{m+2}$

12. $\dfrac{5a+10}{a+5} \div (a+2)$

13. $\dfrac{x^2+7x+12}{x+6} \div (x+3)$

Simplify each dimensional expression. State what you think the expression represents.

14. $(8 \text{ feet} \cdot 3 \text{ feet} \cdot 12 \text{ feet}) \div \dfrac{27 \text{ feet}^3}{1 \text{ yard}^3}$

15. $(12 \text{ inches} \cdot 18 \text{ inches} \cdot 4 \text{ inches}) \div \dfrac{1728 \text{ inches}^3}{1 \text{ feet}^3}$

16. **Railroading** Jaheem is a railroad buff who likes to watch trains. At the railroad crossing near his house in Menominee Falls, Wisconsin, a Chicago & North Western freight train passes by at 40 miles per hour. Suppose each railroad car is 48 feet long.
    a. Write an expression involving units that represents the number of cars that pass by him in one minute.
    b. Find how many railroad cars would pass by him per minute.

EXERCISES

Practice

Find each quotient. Assume that no denominator has a value of 0.

17. $\dfrac{a}{a+3} \div \dfrac{a+11}{a+3}$

18. $\dfrac{m+7}{m} \div \dfrac{m+7}{m+3}$

19. $\dfrac{a^2b^3c}{m^2y^2} \div \dfrac{a^2bc^3}{m^3y^2}$

20. $\dfrac{5x^2}{7} \div \dfrac{10x^3}{21}$

21. $\dfrac{3m+15}{m+4} \div \dfrac{3m}{m+4}$

22. $\dfrac{3x}{x+2} \div (x-1)$

23. $\dfrac{4z+8}{z+3} \div (z+2)$

24. $\dfrac{x+3}{x+1} \div (x^2+5x+6)$

25. $\dfrac{2x+4}{x^2+11x+18} \div \dfrac{x+1}{x^2+14x+45}$

26. $\dfrac{k+3}{m^2+4m+4} \div \dfrac{2k+6}{m+2}$

27. What is the quotient when $\dfrac{2x+6}{x+5}$ is divided by $\dfrac{2}{x+5}$?

28. Find the quotient when $\dfrac{m-8}{m+7}$ is divided by m^2-7m-8.

Find each quotient. Assume that no denominator has a value of 0.

29. $\dfrac{x^2+5x+6}{x^2-x-12} \div \dfrac{x+2}{x^2+x-20}$

30. $\dfrac{m^2+m-6}{m^2+8m+15} \div \dfrac{m^2-m-2}{m^2+9m+20}$

31. $\dfrac{2x^2+7x-15}{x+2} \div \dfrac{2x-3}{x^2+5x+6}$

32. $\dfrac{t^2-2t-8}{w-3} \div \dfrac{t-4}{w^2-7w+12}$

Simplify each expression. State what you think the expression represents.

33. $\left(\dfrac{60 \text{ miles}}{1 \text{ hour}} \cdot \dfrac{5280 \text{ feet}}{1 \text{ mile}} \div \dfrac{60 \text{ minutes}}{1 \text{ hour}}\right) \div \dfrac{60 \text{ seconds}}{1 \text{ minute}}$

34. $\dfrac{23.75 \text{ inches}}{1 \text{ revolution}} \cdot \dfrac{33\frac{1}{3} \text{ revolutions}}{1 \text{ minute}} \cdot 16.5 \text{ minutes}$

35. $(5 \text{ feet} \cdot 16.5 \text{ feet} \cdot 9 \text{ feet}) \div \dfrac{27 \text{ feet}^3}{1 \text{ yard}^3}$

36. $\left[\left(\dfrac{60 \text{ kilometers}}{1 \text{ hour}} \cdot \dfrac{1000 \text{ meters}}{1 \text{ kilometer}}\right) \div \dfrac{60 \text{ minutes}}{1 \text{ hour}}\right] \div \dfrac{60 \text{ seconds}}{1 \text{ minute}}$

Critical Thinking

37. Geometry The area of a rectangle is $\frac{x^2 - y^2}{2}$, and its length is $2x + 2y$. Find the width.

Applications and Problem Solving

38. Construction A construction supervisor needs to determine how many truckloads of earth must be removed from a site before a foundation can be poured. The bed of the truck has the shape shown at the right.

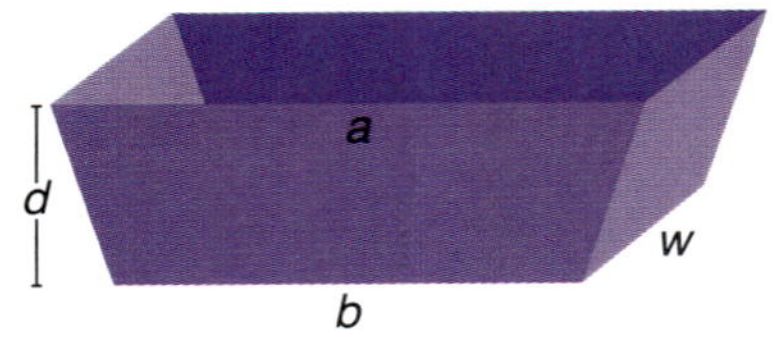

a. Use the formula $V = \frac{d(a + b)}{2} \cdot w$ to write an expression involving units that represents the volume of the truck bed in cubic yards if $a = 18$ ft, $b = 15$ ft, $w = 9$ ft, and $d = 5$ ft.

b. There are 20,000 cubic yards of earth that must be removed from the excavation site. Write an expression involving units that represents the number of truckloads that will be required to remove all the earth.

FYI

Phonograph records are played on a turntable that rotates at a constant speed. Each side of the record has a single groove, or *track*. As the record turns, the stylus of a *tone arm* vibrates in response to variations in the track. The vibration is converted to an electrical signal, which in turn is converted into sound.

39. Railroads The table at the right shows data about railroads in the United States.

Year	Miles of Track	Number of Freight Cars
1980	290,000	1,168,000
1985	257,000	867,000
1990	239,000	659,000
1992	227,000	605,000

a. If one freight car is 48 feet long on average, how many miles long would a train without a locomotive be if all the freight cars for 1992 were connected?

b. How many trains whose length is the answer to part a would it take to occupy all of the track in 1992?

c. Repeat parts a and b for the year 1980.

40. Music Many old phonograph records turn at a rate of $33\frac{1}{3}$ revolutions per minute. Suppose a record of this type plays for 16.5 minutes and the average of the radii of the grooves on the record is $3\frac{3}{4}$ inches.

a. Write an expression involving units that represents how many inches the needle travels while playing the record.

b. Find the distance the needle travels.

Mixed Review

41. Find $\frac{2m + 3}{4} \cdot \frac{32}{(2m + 3)(m - 5)}$. (Lesson 12–2)

42. Solve $x^2 + 6x + 8 = 0$ by graphing. (Lesson 11–2)

43. Factor $16a^2 - 24ab^2 + 9b^4$. (Lesson 10–5)

44. Health If your heart beats once every second and you live to be 78 years old, your heart will have beat about 2,460,000,000 times. Write this number in scientific notation. (Lesson 9–3)

45. Solve $-3x + 6 > 12$. (Lesson 7–3)

46. Find $-3 + 4 - 10$. (Lesson 2–3)

47. Use the numbers 7 and 2 to write a mathematical sentence illustrating the commutative property of addition. (Lesson 1–8)

12–4

Dividing Polynomials

What YOU'LL LEARN

- To divide polynomials by monomials, and
- to divide polynomials by binomials.

Why IT'S IMPORTANT

You can use polynomials to solve problems involving science and interior design.

APPLICATION

Interior Design

Tomi wants to put a decorative border waist-high around his dining room. The perimeter of the room is 52 feet, and the widths of the two windows and two doorways total $12\frac{3}{4}$ feet. To find the number of yards of border needed, he can use the expression $\frac{52 \text{ ft} - 12\frac{3}{4} \text{ ft}}{3 \text{ ft/yd}}$. The expression $\frac{52 \text{ ft}}{3 \text{ ft/yd}} - \frac{12\frac{3}{4} \text{ ft}}{3 \text{ ft/yd}}$ could also be used. In each case, each term of the numerator was divided by the denominator. *This expression will be simplified in Example 4.*

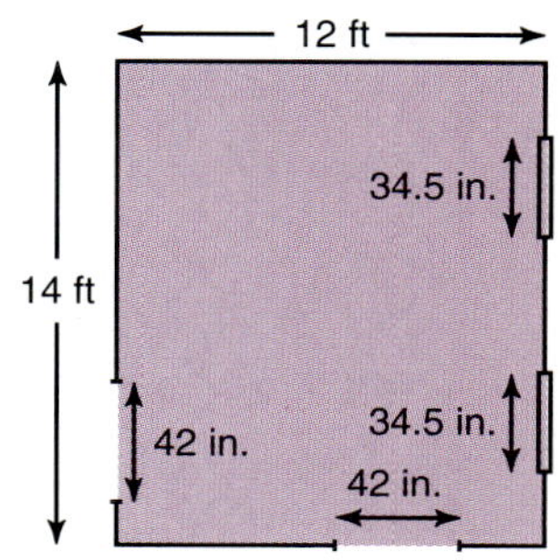

To divide a polynomial by a monomial, you divide each term of the polynomial by the monomial.

Example 1 **Find each quotient.**

a. $(3r^2 - 5) \div 12r$

$$(3r^2 - 5) \div 12r = \frac{3r^2 - 5}{12r} \qquad \textit{Write as a rational expression.}$$

$$= \frac{3r^2}{12r} - \frac{5}{12r} \qquad \textit{Divide each term by 12r.}$$

$$= \frac{\overset{1}{\cancel{3}}\overset{r}{\cancel{r^2}}}{\underset{4}{\cancel{12}}\underset{1}{\cancel{r}}} - \frac{5}{12r} \qquad \textit{Divide by the common factors.}$$

$$= \frac{r}{4} - \frac{5}{12r}$$

b. $(9n^2 - 15n + 24) \div 3n$

$$(9n^2 - 15n + 24) \div 3n = \frac{9n^2 - 15n + 24}{3n}$$

$$= \frac{9n^2}{3n} - \frac{15n}{3n} + \frac{24}{3n}$$

$$= \frac{\overset{3}{\cancel{9}}\overset{n}{\cancel{n^2}}}{\underset{1}{\cancel{3n}}} - \frac{\overset{5}{\cancel{15n}}}{\underset{1}{\cancel{3n}}} + \frac{\overset{8}{\cancel{24}}}{\underset{1}{\cancel{3}}n} \qquad \textit{Divide by the common factors.}$$

$$= 3n - 5 + \frac{8}{n}$$

Recall from Lesson 12–3 that, when you can factor, some divisions can be performed easily, as shown below.

$$(a^2 + 7a + 12) \div (a + 3) = \frac{a^2 + 7a + 12}{(a + 3)}$$

$$= \frac{\overset{1}{\cancel{(a + 3)}}(a + 4)}{\underset{1}{\cancel{(a + 3)}}} \qquad \textit{Factor the dividend.}$$

$$= a + 4$$

You can use algebra tiles to model some quotients of polynomials.

MODELING MATHEMATICS — Dividing Polynomials

Materials: algebra tiles   product mat

Use algebra tiles to find $(x^2 + 2x - 8) \div (x + 4)$.

a. Model the polynomial $x^2 + 2x - 8$.

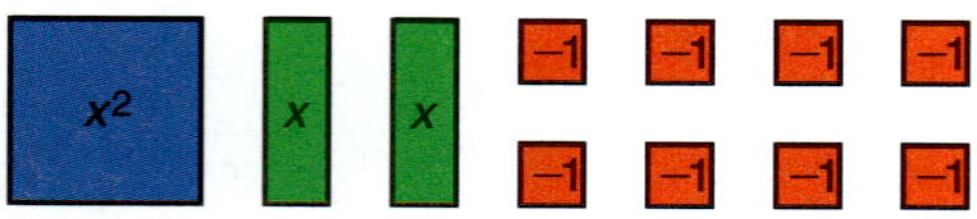

$x^2 + 2x + (-8)$

b. Place the x^2-tile at the corner of the mat. Arrange four of the 1-tiles as shown at the right, to make a length of $x + 4$.

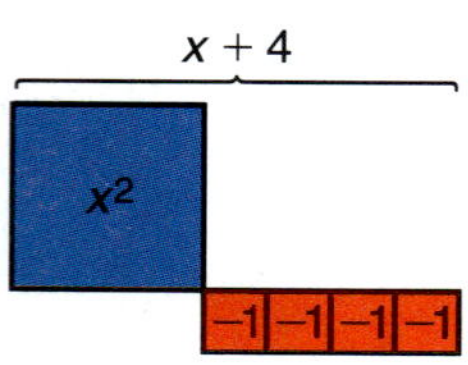

c. Use the remaining tiles to make a rectangular array. Recall that you can add zero-pairs without changing the value of the polynomial.

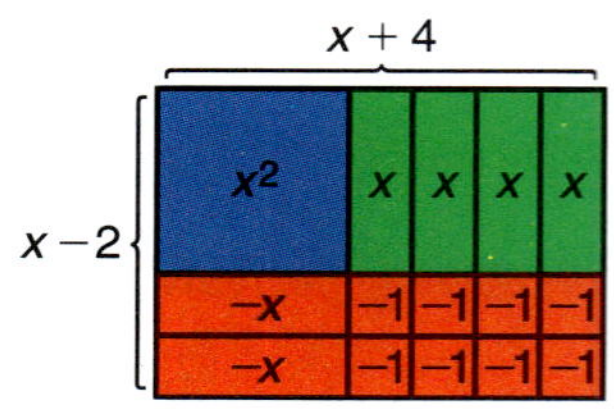

The width of the array, $x - 2$, is the quotient.

Your Turn

Use algebra tiles to find each quotient.

a. $(x^2 + 2x - 8) \div (x + 4)$

b. $(x^2 + 3x - 10) \div (x + 5)$

c. $(x^2 - 6x + 9) \div (x - 3)$

d. $(x^2 - 9) \div (x + 3)$

e. What happens when you try to model $(x^2 + 5x + 9) \div (x + 3)$? What do you think your result means?

When you cannot factor, you can use a long division process similar to the one you used in arithmetic. The division $(x^2 + 7x + 12) \div (x + 2)$ is shown below.

Step 1: To find the first term of the quotient, divide the first term of the dividend, x^2, by the first term of the divisor, x.

$$\begin{array}{rll} & x & \\ x + 2 \,\big)\!\! & \overline{x^2 + 7x + 12} & x^2 \div x = x \\ & \underline{(-)\ x^2 + 2x} & \textit{Multiply } x \textit{ and } x + 2. \\ & 5x & \textit{Subtract.} \end{array}$$

Step 2: To find the next term of the quotient, divide the first term of the partial dividend, $5x$, by the first term of the divisor, x.

$$\begin{array}{rll} & x + 5 & 5x \div x = 5. \\ x + 2 \,\big)\!\! & \overline{x^2 + 7x + 12} & \\ & \underline{(-)\ x^2 + 2x} & \\ & 5x + 12 & \textit{Bring down the 12.} \\ & \underline{(-)\ 5x + 10} & \textit{Multiply 5 and } x + 2. \\ & 2 & \textit{Subtract.} \end{array}$$

Therefore, the quotient when $x^2 + 7x + 12$ is divided by $x + 2$ is $x + 5$ with a remainder of 2. Since there is a nonzero remainder, the divisor is not a factor of the dividend. The remainder can be expressed as shown below.

$$\underbrace{(x^2 + 7x + 12)}_{\text{dividend}} \div \underbrace{(x + 2)}_{\text{divisor}} = \underbrace{x + 5 + \frac{2}{x+2}}_{\text{quotient}}$$

Example 2 **Find $(3k^2 - 7k - 6) \div (3k + 2)$.**

Method 1: Long Division

$$\begin{array}{r} k - 3 \\ 3k + 2 \overline{)3k^2 - 7k - 6} \\ (-)\ 3k^2 + 2k \\ \hline -9k - 6 \\ (-)\ -9k - 6 \\ \hline 0 \end{array}$$

Method 2: Factoring

$$\frac{3k^2 - 7k - 6}{3k + 2} = \frac{\overset{1}{\cancel{(3k+2)}}(k-3)}{\underset{1}{\cancel{3k+2}}}$$
$$= k - 3$$

The quotient is $k - 3$ with a remainder of 0.

When the dividend is an expression like $s^3 + 9$, there is no s^2 term or s term. In such situations, you must rename the dividend using 0 as the coefficient of the missing terms.

Example 3 **Find $(s^3 + 9) \div (s - 3)$.**

$$\begin{array}{r} s^2 + 3s + 9 \\ s - 3 \overline{)s^3 + 0s^2 + 0s + 9} \\ (-)\ s^3 - 3s^2 \qquad\qquad \\ \hline 3s^2 + 0s \qquad \\ (-)\ 3s^2 - 9s \qquad \\ \hline 9s + 9 \\ (-)\ 9s - 27 \\ \hline 36 \end{array} \qquad s^3 + 9 = s^3 + 0s^2 + 0s + 9$$

Therefore, $(s^3 + 9) \div (s - 3) = s^2 + 3s + 9 + \frac{36}{s-3}$.

Example 4 **Refer to the application at the beginning of the lesson. If the border comes in 5-yard rolls, how many rolls of border should Tomi buy?**

APPLICATION
Interior Design

First find the total number of yards needed.

$$\frac{52 \text{ ft} - 12\frac{3}{4} \text{ ft}}{3 \text{ ft/yd}} = \frac{52 \text{ ft}}{3 \text{ ft/yd}} - \frac{12\frac{3}{4} \text{ ft}}{3 \text{ ft/yd}}$$
$$= \frac{52 \cancel{\text{ft}}}{1} \cdot \frac{1 \text{ yd}}{3 \cancel{\text{ft}}} - \frac{\overset{17}{\cancel{51}}}{4} \cancel{\text{ft}} \cdot \frac{1 \text{ yd}}{\underset{1}{\cancel{3}} \cancel{\text{ft}}}$$
$$= 17\frac{1}{3} \text{ yd} - 4\frac{1}{4} \text{ yd or } 13\frac{1}{12} \text{ yd}$$

Two rolls are 10 yards, which is not enough. So, Tomi should buy 3 rolls of border.

You can use a graphing calculator to compare a rational expression with the quotient that results when you divide its numerator by its denominator.

EXPLORATION — GRAPHING CALCULATORS

Consider the following rational expression and its quotient.

rational expression *quotient*

$$\frac{2x}{x+5} = 2 - \frac{10}{x+5}$$

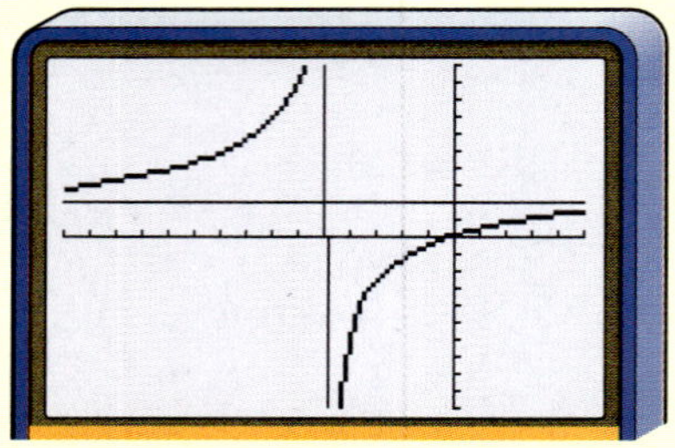

Use a graphing calculator to graph $y = \frac{2x}{x+5}$ and $y = 2$ on the same screen.

Use the viewing window $[-15, 5]$ by $[-10, 10]$.

Enter: [Y=] 2 [X,T,θ,n] [÷] [(] [X,T,θ,n] [+] 5 [)] [ENTER] 2 [GRAPH]

Your Turn

a. What can you say about the two graphs from examining the calculator screen?

b. Change Xmin and Xmax to -47 and 47. What can you say about the value of $\frac{2x}{x+5}$ and 2 as x gets larger and larger?

c. Use long division to find the quotient for $\frac{3x}{x-5}$.

d. What conclusion can you draw about the graph of $y = \frac{3x}{x-5}$ and the graph of $y = 3$?

CHECK FOR UNDERSTANDING

Communicating Mathematics

Study the lesson. Then complete the following.

1. Copy the division below and label the dividend, divisor, quotient, and remainder.

$$\frac{2x^2 - 11x - 20}{2x + 3} = x - 7 + \frac{1}{2x + 3}$$

2. **Explain** the meaning of a remainder of 0 in a long division of a polynomial by a binomial.
3. Refer to the application at the beginning of the lesson. Suppose Tomi decided to place the border at the bottom of the room above the baseboard, but below the windows. How many rolls of border should he buy?

MODELING MATHEMATICS

4. **a.** Use algebra tiles to model $2x^2 - 9x + 9$.
   b. Which of the following divisors of $2x^2 - 9x + 9$ results in a remainder of 0?
   $x + 3$ $x - 3$ $2x - 3$ $2x + 3$

Guided Practice

Find each quotient.

5. $(9b^2 - 15) \div 3$
6. $(a^2 + 5a + 13) \div 5a$
7. $(t^2 + 6t - 7) \div (t + 7)$
8. $(s^2 + 11s + 18) \div (s + 2)$
9. $\frac{2m^2 + 7m + 3}{m + 2}$
10. $\frac{3r^2 + 11r + 7}{r + 5}$

11. **Geometry** Find the length of a rectangle if its area is $(10x^2 + 29x + 21)$ square meters and its width is $(5x + 7)$ meters.

EXERCISES

Practice

Find each quotient.

12. $(x^3 + 2x^2 - 5) \div 2x$
13. $(b^2 + 9b - 7) \div 3b$
14. $(3a^2 + 6a + 2) \div 3a$
15. $(m^2 + 7m - 28) \div 7m$
16. $(9xy^2 - 15xy + 3) \div 3xy$
17. $(a^3 + 8a - 21) \div (a - 2)$
18. $(2b^2 + 3b - 5) \div (2b - 1)$
19. $(m^2 + 4m - 23) \div (m + 7)$
20. $(2x^2 - 7x - 16) \div (2x + 3)$
21. $(2x^2 - 8x - 41) \div (x - 7)$
22. $\dfrac{14a^2b^2 + 35ab^2 + 2a^2}{7a^2b^2}$
23. $\dfrac{12m^3k + 16mk^3 - 8mk}{4mk}$
24. $\dfrac{3r^2 + 20r + 11}{r + 6}$
25. $\dfrac{a^2 + 10a + 20}{a + 3}$
26. $\dfrac{4m^2 + 8m - 19}{2m + 7}$
27. $\dfrac{6x^2 + 5x + 15}{2x + 3}$
28. $\dfrac{y^2 - 19y + 9}{y - 4}$
29. $\dfrac{4t^2 + 17t - 1}{4t + 1}$
30. Find the quotient when $x^2 + 9x + 15$ is divided by $x + 3$.
31. What is the quotient when $56x^3 + 32x^2 - 63x$ is divided by $7x$?

Programming

32. The graphing calculator program at the right will help you find the quotient and remainder when you divide a polynomial of the form $ax^2 + bx + c$ by a binomial of the form $x - r$. You enter the values of a, b, c, and r when prompted.

```
PROGRAM; POLYDIV
: Disp "ENTER A,B,C"
: Prompt A: Prompt B:
  Prompt C
: Disp "ENTER R"
: Prompt R
: Disp "COEFFICIENTS"
: Disp "OF QUOTIENT:"
: Disp A
: Disp B+A*R
: Disp "REMAINDER:"
: Disp C+B*R+A*R^2
```

Run the program to find each quotient and remainder.

a. $(7x^2 + 5x - 3) \div (x + 2)$
b. $(x^2 - 14x - 25) \div (3x + 4)$

33. Modify the graphing calculator program given above so that you can use it to find each quotient.

a. $(x^3 + 2x^2 - 4x - 8) \div (x - 2)$
b. $(20t^3 - 27t^2 + t + 6) \div (4t - 3)$
c. $(2a^3 + 9a^2 + 5a - 12) \div (a + 3)$

Critical Thinking

34. Find the value of k if $x + 7$ is a factor of $x^2 - 2x - k$.
35. Find the value of k if $2m - 3$ is a factor of $2m^2 + 7m + k$.
36. Find the value of k if the remainder is 15 when $x^3 - 7x^2 + 4x + k$ is divided by $x - 2$.

Applications and Problem Solving

silver

37. Environment Due to concerns about air pollution, it is important to invest money on the reduction of pollutants. The equation $C = \frac{120{,}000p}{1 - p}$ models the expenditure C in dollars needed to reduce pollutants by p percent where p is the percent in decimal form. If a utility company wants to remove 80% of the pollutants their equipment emits, what expenditure must they make?

38. Science The *density* of a material is its mass per unit volume. A 2.48 g block of copper occupies 0.28 cm^3. For example, the density of copper is found from the quotient $\frac{2.48 \text{ g}}{0.28 \text{ cm}^3} \approx 8.9 \text{ g/cm}^3$.

Material	Mass(g)	Volume (cm^3)
aluminum	4.15	1.54
gold	2.32	0.12
silver	6.30	0.60
steel	7.80	1.00
iron	15.20	1.95
copper	2.48	0.28
blood	4.35	4.10
lead	11.30	1.00
brass	17.90	2.08
concrete	40.00	20.00

a. Make a table of densities for the materials above.

b. Make a line plot of the densities computed in part a. Use densities rounded to the nearest whole number.

c. Interpret the line plot made in part b.

raw copper

gold

Mixed Review

39. Find $\frac{x^2 - 16}{16 - x^2} \div \frac{7}{x}$. (Lesson 12–3)

40. Graph $y = -x^2 + 2x + 3$. (Lesson 11–1)

41. Factor $3x^2 - 6x - 105$. (Lesson 10–3)

42. **Geometry** Find the area of a rectangle if the length is $(2x + y)$ units and the width is $(x + y)$ units. (Lesson 9–7)

43. Solve the system of equations by graphing. (Lesson 8–1)

$y = 2x + 1$

$y = -2x + 5$

44. Write an equation for the relation $\{(2, 4), (3, 6), (-2, -4)\}$. (Lesson 5–6)

45. Graph $\{-2, -1, 4, 5\}$ on a number line. (Lesson 2–1)

SELF TEST

Simplify each rational expression. (Lesson 12–1)

1. $\frac{25x^3y^4}{36x^2y^5}$

2. $\frac{4x^2 - 9}{2x^2 + 13x - 15}$

Find each product or quotient. (Lessons 12–2 and 12–3)

3. $\frac{x^2 - 16}{x^2 + 5x + 6} \cdot \frac{4x^2 + 2x - 3}{x^2 - 5x + 4}$

4. $\frac{2x^2 - 5x + 2}{x^2 - 5x + 6} \div \frac{2x^2 + 9x - 5}{x^2 - 4x + 3}$

5. $(3x - 2) \cdot \frac{x - 5}{3x^2 + 10x - 8}$

6. $\frac{7x^2 + 36x + 5}{x - 5} \div (7x + 1)$

Find each quotient. (Lesson 12–4)

7. $(4x^2 - 18x + 20) \div (2x - 4)$

8. $\frac{3x^2 - 6x - 4}{x - 2}$

9. **Geometry** A rectangular field has an area of $12x^2 + 20x - 8$ square units and a width of $x + 2$ units. Find its length in terms of x. (Lesson 12–4)

10. **Travel** On the first day of a trip, Manuel drove 440 miles in 8 hours. The second day, he drove at the same speed but for only 6 hours. How far did he drive on the second day? (Lesson 12–2)

12–5 Rational Expressions with Like Denominators

What YOU'LL LEARN

- To add and subtract rational expressions with like denominators.

Why IT'S IMPORTANT

You can use rational expressions to solve problems involving history and geography.

CONNECTION

History

At 11:40 P.M. on the night of April 14, 1912, the lookout on the bridge of the *Titanic* spotted an iceberg directly ahead. Despite their heroic efforts, the crew could not steer clear of the iceberg, and a 300-foot gash was ripped in the side of the ship. The *Titanic* sank less than three hours later, and 1500 lives were lost.

The iceberg that the *Titanic* hit has been described as enormous. However, many people are surprised to learn that only about $\frac{1}{8}$ of any iceberg is visible above the surface of the water. This means the part of an iceberg that is submerged is about $1 - \frac{1}{8}$.

$$1 - \frac{1}{8} = \frac{8}{8} - \frac{1}{8} = \frac{8-1}{8} \text{ or } \frac{7}{8}$$

That is, about $\frac{7}{8}$, or 87.5% of the iceberg is submerged.

This example illustrates that, to add or subtract fractions with like denominators, you add or subtract the numerators and then write the sum or difference over the common denominator. You can use this same method to add or subtract rational expressions with like denominators.

rational numbers	*rational expressions*
$\frac{1}{9} + \frac{4}{9} = \frac{1+4}{9} = \frac{5}{9}$	$\frac{4}{y} + \frac{7}{y} = \frac{4+7}{y} = \frac{11}{y}$
$\frac{6}{7} - \frac{2}{7} = \frac{6-2}{7} = \frac{4}{7}$	$\frac{9}{5z} - \frac{6}{5z} = \frac{9-6}{5z} = \frac{3}{5z}$

Example 1 Find $\frac{a}{15m} + \frac{2a}{15m}$.

$\frac{a}{15m} + \frac{2a}{15m} = \frac{a+2a}{15m}$ *The common denominator is 15m.*

$= \frac{3a}{15m}$ *Add numerators.*

$= \frac{\overset{1}{\cancel{3}}a}{\underset{5}{\cancel{15}}m}$ *Divide by the common factors.*

$= \frac{a}{5m}$

LOOK BACK

You can refer to Lesson 2-5 for information about adding and subtracting rational numbers.

Sometimes the denominators of rational expressions are binomials. As long as each rational expression in a sum or difference has exactly the same binomial as its denominator, the process of adding or subtracting is the same.

Example 2 Find $\frac{4}{x+3} - \frac{1}{x+3}$.

$\frac{4}{x+3} - \frac{1}{x+3} = \frac{4-1}{x+3}$ *The common denominator is x + 3.*

$= \frac{3}{x+3}$ *Subtract numerators.*

Remember that, to subtract a polynomial, you add its additive inverse.

Example 3 **Find $\frac{2m + 3}{m - 4} - \frac{m - 2}{m - 4}$.**

$$\frac{2m + 3}{m - 4} - \frac{m - 2}{m - 4} = \frac{(2m + 3) - (m - 2)}{m - 4}$$

$$= \frac{2m + 3 + [-(m - 2)]}{m - 4} \quad \textit{The additive inverse of } m - 2 \textit{ is } -(m - 2).$$

$$= \frac{2m + 3 - m + 2}{m - 4}$$

$$= \frac{m + 5}{m - 4}$$

Sometimes you must factor in order to simplify a sum or difference of rational expressions. Also a factor may need to be rewritten as its additive inverse to recognize the common denominator.

Example 4 **Find $\frac{7k + 2}{4k - 3} + \frac{8 - k}{3 - 4k}$.**

The denominator $3 - 4k$ is the same as $-(-3 + 4k)$ or $-(4k - 3)$. Rewrite the second expression so that the denominator is the same as the first expression.

$$\frac{7k + 2}{4k - 3} + \frac{8 - k}{3 - 4k} = \frac{7k + 2}{4k - 3} - \frac{8 - k}{4k - 3}$$

$$= \frac{7k + 2 - (8 - k)}{4k - 3}$$

$$= \frac{8k - 6}{4k - 3}$$

$$= \frac{2(4k - 3)}{(4k - 3)} \quad \textit{Factor the numerator.}$$

$$= \frac{2\overset{1}{\cancel{(4k - 3)}}}{\underset{1}{\cancel{(4k - 3)}}} \quad \textit{Divide by the common factors.}$$

$$= 2$$

Example 5 **Find an expression for the perimeter of rectangle *ABCD*.**

INTEGRATION
Geometry

$$P = 2\ell + 2w$$

$$= 2\left(\frac{9r}{2r + 6s}\right) + 2\left(\frac{5r}{2r + 6s}\right)$$

$$= \frac{2(9r) + 2(5r)}{2r + 6s}$$

$$= \frac{18r + 10r}{2r + 6s}$$

$$= \frac{28r}{2r + 6s}$$

$$= \frac{28r}{2(r + 3s)} \quad \textit{Factor the denominator.}$$

$$= \frac{\overset{14}{\cancel{28}}r}{\underset{1}{\cancel{2}}(r + 3s)} \quad \textit{Divide by the common factors.}$$

$$= \frac{14r}{r + 3s}$$

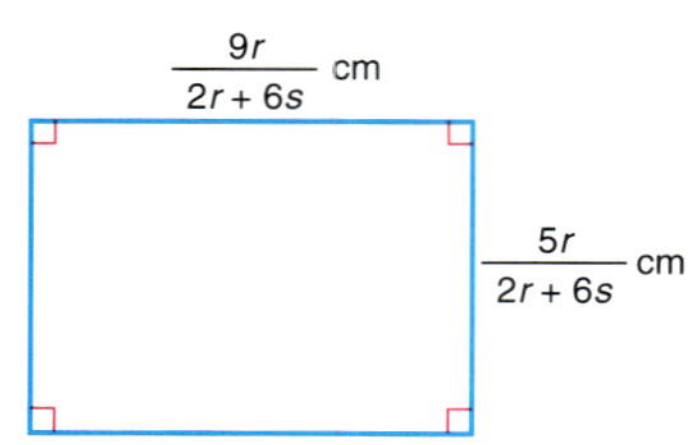

The perimeter of rectangle *ABCD* is $\left(\frac{14r}{r + 3s}\right)$ cm.

CHECK FOR UNDERSTANDING

Communicating Mathematics

Study the lesson. Then complete the following.

1. **Compare and contrast** two rational expressions whose sum is 0 with two rational expressions whose difference is 0.
2. **Summarize** the procedure for adding or subtracting two rational expressions whose denominators are the same.
3. **You Decide** Abigail wrote $\frac{7x-3}{2x+11} + \frac{3x-9}{2x+11} = \frac{10x-12}{4x+22}$. What mistake did she make?

Guided Practice

Find each sum or difference. Express in simplest form.

4. $\frac{5x}{7} + \frac{2x}{7}$
5. $\frac{3}{x} + \frac{7}{x}$
6. $\frac{7}{3m} - \frac{4}{3m}$
7. $\frac{3}{a+2} + \frac{7}{a+2}$
8. $\frac{2m}{m+3} - \frac{-6}{m+3}$
9. $\frac{3x}{x+4} - \frac{-12}{x+4}$
10. If the sum of $\frac{2x-1}{3x+2}$ and another rational expression with denominator $3x + 2$ is $\frac{5x-1}{3x+2}$, what is the numerator of the second rational expression?

EXERCISES

Practice

Find each sum or difference. Express in simplest form.

11. $\frac{m}{3} + \frac{2m}{3}$
12. $\frac{3y}{11} - \frac{8y}{11}$
13. $\frac{5a}{12} - \frac{7a}{12}$
14. $\frac{4}{3z} + \frac{-7}{3z}$
15. $\frac{x}{2} - \frac{x-4}{2}$
16. $\frac{a+3}{6} - \frac{a-3}{6}$
17. $\frac{2}{x+7} + \frac{5}{x+7}$
18. $\frac{2x}{x+1} + \frac{2}{x+1}$
19. $\frac{y}{y-2} + \frac{2}{2-y}$
20. $\frac{4m}{2m+3} + \frac{5}{2m+3}$
21. $\frac{-5}{3x-5} + \frac{3x}{3x-5}$
22. $\frac{3r}{r+5} + \frac{15}{r+5}$
23. $\frac{2x}{x+2} + \frac{2x}{x+2}$
24. $\frac{2m}{m-9} + \frac{18}{9-m}$
25. $\frac{2y}{y+3} + \frac{-6}{y+3}$
26. $\frac{3m}{m-2} - \frac{5}{m-2}$
27. $\frac{4x}{2x+3} - \frac{-6}{2x+3}$
28. $\frac{4t-1}{1-4t} + \frac{2t+3}{1-4t}$
29. If $\frac{3x-100}{2x+5}$ is added to the sum of $\frac{11x-5}{2x+5}$ and $\frac{11x+12}{2x+5}$, what is the result?
30. If $\frac{-3b+4}{2b+12}$ is subtracted from the sum of $\frac{b-15}{2b+12}$ and $\frac{-3b+12}{2b+12}$, what is the result?

INTEGRATION
Geometry

Find an expression for the perimeter of each rectangle.

31.

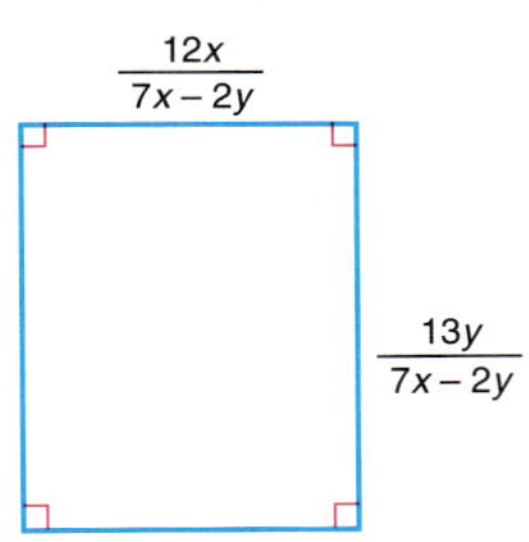

32.

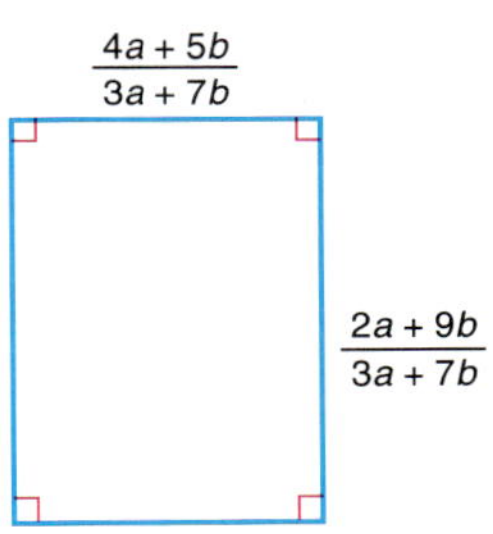

Critical Thinking

33. Which of the following rational numbers is not equivalent to the others?

a. $\frac{-3}{x-2}$ **b.** $-\frac{3}{2-x}$ **c.** $-\frac{3}{x-2}$ **d.** $\frac{3}{2-x}$

Applications and Problem Solving

34. Icebergs Water weighs 62.4 pounds per cubic foot. One cubic foot of water contains 7.48 gallons. Each cubic foot of ice yields 0.89 times as many gallons of water as a cubic foot of water.

a. How many gallons of water does one cubic foot of ice contain?

b. Some people have suggested moving icebergs from the North Atlantic to parts of the world that have little fresh water. If an iceberg is 1 mile wide, 2 miles long, and 800 feet thick, about how much fresh water would such an iceberg yield?

35. Utilities A person in the United States on the average uses 168 gallons of water each day. Suppose that 25% of the iceberg in Exercise 34 is lost as it is being moved to another location. How many days would the iceberg sustain the Atlanta, Georgia, metropolitan area, which has a population of about 3 million people?

Mixed Review

36. Engineering The Canadian Pacific Railroad constructed a track in the form of a circle so the train will spiral over itself as it passes through a mountain tunnel. This reduces the degree of incline for the train to climb. If we assume that the spiral is a circle one mile long, what would be the diameter of the circle in feet? (Lesson 12–4)

37. Solve $25x^2 = 36$ by factoring. (Lesson 10–6)

38. Geometry Find the perimeter of quadrilateral *MATH* shown at the right. (Lesson 9–5)

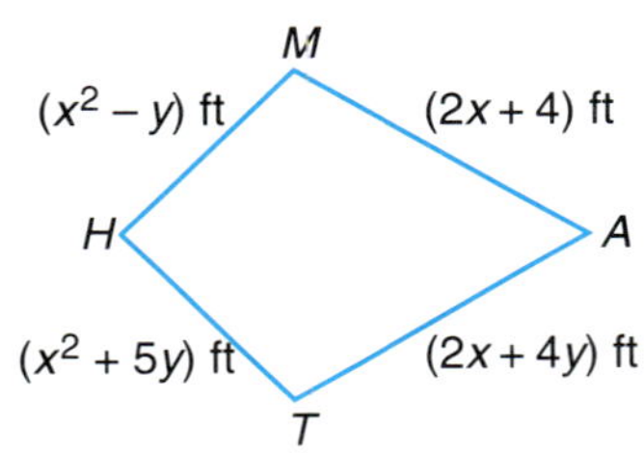

39. Use substitution to solve the system of equations. (Lesson 8–2)

$x + 2y = 5$

$x - 2y = -11$

40. Astronomy A *main sequence star* is a star that is in the neighborhood of the sun. The table below gives the names of the seven main sequence stars and the sun, their surface temperatures in thousands of °C, and their radii in multiples of the sun's radius. Draw a scatter plot with the temperatures on the horizontal axis and the radii on the vertical axis. (Lesson 6–3)

Stars	MU-1 Scorpii	Sirius A	Altair	Polycon A	Sun	61 Cygni A	Kueger 60	Barnard's Star
Surface Temp.	20	10.2	7.3	6.8	5.9	2.6	2.8	2.7
Radius	5.2	1.9	1.6	2.6	1.0	0.7	0.35	0.15

41. Probability A student rolls a die three times. What is the probability that each roll is a 1? (Lesson 4–6)

12-6 Rational Expressions with Unlike Denominators

What YOU'LL LEARN

- To add and subtract rational expressions with unlike denominators, and
- to make an organized list of possibilities to solve problems.

Why IT'S IMPORTANT

You can use rational expressions to solve problems involving astronomy and automobile maintenance.

CAREER CHOICES

Astronomers use the principles of physics and mathematics to try to discover the fundamental nature of the universe. They do research using computers and data gathered by satellites and observatories. A good foundation in mathematics and physics leading to a doctoral degree is the path to follow.

For more information, contact:

American Astronomical Society
Education Office
University of Texas
Dept. of Astronomy
Austin, TX 78712-1083

APPLICATION

Astronomy

Mars, Jupiter, and Saturn revolve around the sun approximately every 2 years, 12 years, and 30 years, respectively. The planets are said to be in *conjunction*, or alignment, when they appear close to one another in Earth's night sky. The last time this happened was in 1982. When will it happen again?

Mars will go through six revolutions for each one of Jupiter's. Mars will go through fifteen revolutions for each one of Saturn's. The times the planets align is related to the common multiples of 2, 12, and 30. In fact, the least number of years that will pass until the next alignment is the **least common multiple (LCM)** of these numbers. The least common multiple is the least number that is a common multiple of two or more numbers.

There are two methods you can use to find a least common multiple.

Method 1: Make an organized list.

You can often solve problems by listing the possibilities in an organized way. Use a systematic approach so you don't omit any important items.

Multiples of 2	Multiples of 12	Multiples of 30
$2 \cdot 0 = 0$ $2 \cdot 1 = 2$ $2 \cdot 2 = 4$ ⋮ $2 \cdot 30 = \mathbf{60}$	$12 \cdot 0 = 0$ $12 \cdot 1 = 12$ $12 \cdot 2 = 24$ ⋮ $12 \cdot 5 = \mathbf{60}$	$30 \cdot 0 = 0$ $30 \cdot 1 = 30$ $30 \cdot 2 = \mathbf{60}$

Compare the multiples in the table. Other than 0, the least number that is common to all three lists of multiples is 60. So, the LCM of 2, 12, and 30 is 60.

Method 2: Use prime factorization.

Find the prime factorization of each number.

$$2 = 2 \qquad 12 = 2 \cdot 2 \cdot 3 \qquad 30 = 2 \cdot 3 \cdot 5$$

Use each prime factor the greatest number of times it appears in any of the factorizations.

2 appears twice as a factor of 12. All other factors appear once.
Thus, the LCM of 2, 12, and 30 is $2 \cdot 2 \cdot 3 \cdot 5$ or 60.

Using either method, the LCM is 60. This means that the planets will be in alignment approximately 60 years after 1982, or about the year 2042.

You can use the same methods to find the LCM of two or more polynomials.

Example 1

PROBLEM SOLVING
List the Possibilities

Find the LCM of $15a^2b^2$ and $24a^2b$.

List the multiples of each coefficient and each variable expression.

15: 15, 30, 45, 60, 75, 90, 105, **120**, 135
24: 24, 48, 72, 96, **120**, 144
a^2: $\mathbf{a^2}$
b^2: $\mathbf{b^2}$, b^4, b^6
b: b, $\mathbf{b^2}$, b^3
LCM $= 120a^2b^2$

Example 2 Find the LCM of $x^2 - x - 6$ and $x^2 + 2x - 15$.

$x^2 - x - 6 = (x - 3)(x + 2)$ *Factor each expression.*

$x^2 + 2x - 15 = (x + 5)(x - 3)$

$\text{LCM} = (x - 3)(x + 2)(x + 5)$

To add or subtract fractions with unlike denominators, first rename the fractions so the denominators are alike. Any common denominator could be used. However, the computation usually is easier if you use the **least common denominator (LCD)**. Recall that the least common denominator is the LCM of the denominators.

You usually will use the following steps to add or subtract rational expressions with unlike denominators.

1. Find the LCD.
2. Change each rational expression into an equivalent expression with the LCD as the denominator.
3. Add or subtract as with rational expressions with like denominators.
4. Simplify if necessary.

Example 3 Find $\frac{7}{3m} + \frac{5}{6m^2}$.

$3m = 3 \cdot m$ *Factor each denominator.*

$6m^2 = 2 \cdot 3 \cdot m \cdot m$

$\text{LCM} = 2 \cdot 3 \cdot m \cdot m, \text{ or } 6m^2$

Since the denominator of $\frac{5}{6m^2}$ is already $6m^2$, only $\frac{7}{3m}$ needs to be renamed.

$$\frac{7}{3m} + \frac{5}{6m^2} = \frac{7(2m)}{3m(2m)} + \frac{5}{6m^2}$$ *Multiply $\frac{7}{3m}$ by $\frac{2m}{2m}$. Why?*

$$= \frac{14m}{6m^2} + \frac{5}{6m^2}$$

$$= \frac{14m + 5}{6m^2}$$ *Add the numerators.*

To combine rational expressions whose denominators are polynomials, follow the same procedure you use to combine expressions whose denominators are monomials.

Example 4 Find each sum or difference.

a. $\frac{s}{s + 3} + \frac{3}{s - 4}$

Since the denominators are $(s + 3)$ and $(s - 4)$, there are no common factors. The LCD is $(s + 3)(s - 4)$.

$$\frac{s}{s + 3} + \frac{3}{s - 4} = \frac{s}{s + 3} \cdot \frac{s - 4}{s - 4} + \frac{3}{s - 4} \cdot \frac{s + 3}{s + 3}$$

$$= \frac{s(s - 4)}{(s + 3)(s - 4)} + \frac{3(s + 3)}{(s + 3)(s - 4)}$$

$$= \frac{s^2 - 4s}{(s + 3)(s - 4)} + \frac{3s + 9}{(s + 3)(s - 4)}$$

$$= \frac{s^2 - 4s + 3s + 9}{(s + 3)(s - 4)}$$

$$= \frac{s^2 - s + 9}{(s + 3)(s - 4)}$$

b. $\dfrac{n-4}{(2-n)^2} - \dfrac{n-5}{n^2+n-6}$

$\dfrac{n-4}{(2-n)^2} - \dfrac{n-5}{n^2+n-6}$

$= \dfrac{n-4}{(2-n)^2} - \dfrac{n-5}{(n-2)(n+3)}$ *Factor the denominators.*

$= \dfrac{n-4}{(n-2)(n-2)} - \dfrac{n-5}{(n-2)(n+3)}$ *$(2-n)^2 = (n-2)^2$*

$= \dfrac{n-4}{(n-2)(n-2)} \cdot \dfrac{(n+3)}{(n+3)} - \dfrac{n-5}{(n-2)(n+3)} \cdot \dfrac{(n-2)}{(n-2)}$ *Rename each fraction using the LCD.*

$= \dfrac{\left(n^2+3n-4n-12\right) - \left(n^2-2n-5n+10\right)}{(n-2)(n-2)(n+3)}$ *Subtract numerators*

$= \dfrac{n^2-n-12-n^2+7n-10}{(n-2)^2(n+3)}$

$= \dfrac{6n-22}{(n-2)^2(n+3)}$

CHECK FOR UNDERSTANDING

Communicating Mathematics

Study the lesson. Then complete the following.

1. **You Decide** Kaylee simplified $\frac{16}{64}$ as $\frac{1\not{6}}{\not{6}4} = \frac{1}{4}$. Is her answer correct? Was her method of simplifying correct? Explain.
2. **Describe** a situation in which the LCD of two or more rational expressions is equal to the denominator of one of the rational expressions.

Guided Practice

Find the LCD for each pair of rational expressions.

3. $\frac{3}{x^2}, \frac{5}{x}$
4. $\frac{4}{a^2b}, \frac{3}{ab^2}$
5. $\frac{4}{15m^2}, \frac{7}{18mb^2}$
6. $\frac{6}{a+6}, \frac{7}{a+7}$
7. $\frac{5}{x-3}, \frac{4}{x+3}$
8. $\frac{9}{2x-8}, \frac{10}{x-4}$

Find each sum or difference.

9. $\frac{7}{15m^2} + \frac{3}{5m}$
10. $\frac{2}{x+3} + \frac{3}{x-2}$
11. $3x + 6 - \frac{9}{x+2}$
12. $\frac{m+2}{m^2+4m+3} - \frac{6}{m+3}$
13. $\frac{11}{3y^2} - \frac{7}{6y}$
14. $\frac{4}{2g-7} + \frac{5}{3g+1}$

15. **Parades** At the Veteran's Day parade, the local members of the Veterans of Foreign Wars (VFW) found that they could arrange themselves in rows of 6, 7, or 8, with no one left over. What was the least number of VFW members in the parade?

EXERCISES

Practice

Find each sum or difference.

16. $\frac{m}{4} + \frac{3m}{5}$
17. $\frac{x}{7} - \frac{2x}{9}$
18. $\frac{m+1}{m} + \frac{m-3}{3m}$
19. $\frac{7}{x} + \frac{3}{xyz}$
20. $\frac{7}{6a^2} - \frac{5}{3a}$
21. $\frac{2}{st^2} - \frac{3}{s^2t}$

Find each sum or difference.

22. $\frac{3}{7m} + \frac{4}{5m^2}$
23. $\frac{3}{z+5} + \frac{4}{z-4}$
24. $\frac{d}{d+4} + \frac{3}{d+3}$
25. $\frac{k}{k+5} - \frac{2}{k+3}$
26. $\frac{3}{y-3} - \frac{y}{y+4}$
27. $\frac{10}{3r-2} - \frac{9}{r-5}$
28. $\frac{4}{3a-6} + \frac{a}{2+a}$
29. $\frac{5}{2m-3} - \frac{m}{6-4m}$
30. $\frac{b}{3b+2} + \frac{2}{9b+6}$
31. $\frac{w}{5w+2} - \frac{4}{15w+6}$
32. $\frac{h-2}{h^2+4h+4} + \frac{h-2}{h+2}$
33. $\frac{n+2}{n^2+4n+3} - \frac{6}{n+3}$
34. $\frac{a}{5-a} - \frac{3}{a^2-25}$
35. Find the difference when $\frac{2}{t+3}$ is subtracted from $\frac{3}{10t-9}$.
36. Find the sum of $\frac{2y}{y^2+7y+12}$ and $\frac{y+2}{y+4}$.
37. Find the sum of $\frac{2}{v+4}$, $\frac{v}{v-1}$, and $\frac{5v}{v^2+3v-4}$.
38. Find the difference when $\frac{2}{a+1}$ is subtracted from $\frac{6}{a-2}$. Then find the difference when $\frac{6}{a-2}$ is subtracted from $\frac{2}{a+1}$. How are the differences related?

Critical Thinking

39. Copy and complete.
   a. $15 \cdot 24 = \underline{\ ?\ }$
   GCF of 15 and 24 = __?__
   LCM of 15 and 24 = __?__
   GCF · LCM = __?__
   b. $18 \cdot 30 = \underline{\ ?\ }$
   GCF of 18 and 30 = __?__
   LCM of 18 and 30 = __?__
   GCF · LCM = __?__
   c. Write a rule that describes the relationship between the GCF, the LCM, and the product of the two numbers.
   d. Use your rule to describe how to find the LCM of two numbers if you know their GCF.

Applications and Problem Solving

40. **List the Possibilities** Doug Paulsen, the choreographer of a Broadway musical, has asked the producer of the show to hire enough dancers so they can be arranged in groups of exactly three, six, or seven, with no dancer left out. What is the least number of dancers required?

41. **Automobiles** Car owners need to follow a regular maintenance schedule to keep their cars running smoothly. The table below shows several of the checkups that should be performed on a regular basis, according to the Spring, 1995, issue of a certain magazine.

If all these inspections and services are performed on April 20, 1996, and the owner follows the recommendations shown in the table, what is the next date on which they all should be performed again?

Source: *Know-How*

Inspection or Service	Frequency
engine oil and oil filter change	every 3000 miles (about 3 months)
transmission fluid level check	every oil change
brake system inspection	every oil change
chassis lubrication	every other oil change
power steering pump fluid level check	twice a year
tire and wheel rotation and inspection	every 15,000 miles

42. **Travel** Jaheed Toliver spent, in this order, a third of his life in the United States, a sixth of his life in Kenya, twelve years in Saudi Arabia, half the remainder in Australia, and as long in Canada as he spent in Hong Kong. How many years did Jaheed live if he spent his 45th birthday in Saudi Arabia and he spent a whole number of years in each country?

43. Find $\frac{8z+3}{3z+4} - \frac{2z-5}{3z+4}$. (Lesson 12–5)

Mixed Review

44. Simplify $\frac{x^2+7x+6}{3x^2+x-2}$. State the excluded values of x. (Lesson 12–1)

45. Solve $2x^2 - 3x - 4 = 0$ by using the quadratic formula. (Lesson 11–3)

46. Factor $3x^2y + 6xy + 9y^2$. (Lesson 10–1)

47. Find $(3a^2b)(-5a^4b^2)$. (Lesson 9–1)

48. Graph the solution set of $3x > -15$ and $2x \le 6$. (Lesson 7–4)

49. Solve $3n - 12 = 5n - 20$. (Lesson 3–5)

50. **Demographics** The populations of the capitals of some southern states are listed in the table below. Make a stem-and-leaf plot of the populations. (Lesson 1–4)

Capital	Population (thousands)	Capital	Population (thousands)
Atlanta, GA	394	Montgomery, AL	188
Austin, TX	466	Nashville, TN	488
Baton Rouge, LA	220	Oklahoma City, OK	445
Columbia, SC	98	Raleigh, NC	208
Frankfort, KY	26	Richmond, VA	203
Jackson, MS	197	Tallahassee, FL	125
Little Rock, AR	176		

Mathematics and SOCIETY

Reading the Labels

The excerpt below appeared in an article in *Aging Magazine*, issue number 366, 1994.

BY THIS SUMMER, ALMOST ALL PACKAGED foods found in your local supermarket included new, improved labels that make it easier to understand the nutritional information contained on them and to compare the nutritional value of different products. This revolution in food labeling is the result of years of work by consumer advocates who pressed for more complete, accurate, and pertinent information on food labels....The percent of daily fat consumption should be no more than 30 percent of calories....The labels also give percentages of daily allowances for sodium, sugar, fiber, and protein. ■

1. The food labels on items A, B, C, and D show fat contents of 25, 17, 4, and 33 grams per serving, respectively. If you are allowed a maximum daily allowance of 65 grams, which three-item combinations of these foods can you put together without exceeding the maximum allowance?

2. Numbers on the food labels are listed as "per serving" rather than per package, and the label also defines serving size. Do you think this is important? Explain your response.

3. When you shop for food, do you use the nutritional data on the labels in deciding what to buy? Why or why not?

12–7 Mixed Expressions and Complex Fractions

What YOU'LL LEARN

- To simplify mixed expressions and complex fractions.

Why IT'S IMPORTANT

You can use rational expressions to solve problems involving acoustics and statistics.

APPLICATION
Table Tennis

A table tennis ball weighs about $\frac{1}{10}$ of an ounce. How many table tennis balls weigh $1\frac{1}{2}$ pounds altogether? *This problem will be solved in Example 2.*

A number like $1\frac{1}{2}$ is a mixed number. Expressions like $a + \frac{b}{c}$ and $4 + \frac{x+y}{x-5}$ are **mixed expressions.** Changing mixed expressions to rational expressions is similar to changing mixed numbers to simple fractions (improper fractions).

mixed number to improper fraction

$$\begin{aligned} 5\frac{4}{7} &= 5 + \frac{4}{7} \\ &= \frac{5(7)+4}{7} \\ &= \frac{35+4}{7} \\ &= \frac{39}{7} \end{aligned}$$

mixed expression to rational expression

$$\begin{aligned} 4 + \frac{x+y}{x-5} &= \frac{4(x-5)}{x-5} + \frac{x+y}{x-5} \\ &= \frac{4(x-5)+(x+y)}{(x-5)} \\ &= \frac{4x-20+x+y}{x-5} \\ &= \frac{5x+y-20}{x-5} \end{aligned}$$

Example 1 **Simplify $7 + \frac{y-3}{y+4}$.**

$$\begin{aligned} 7 + \frac{y-3}{y+4} &= \frac{7(y+4)}{y+4} + \frac{y-3}{y+4} && \textit{The LCD is } y+4. \\ &= \frac{7(y+4)+y-3}{y+4} && \textit{Add the numerators.} \\ &= \frac{7y+28+y-3}{y+4} \\ &= \frac{8y+25}{y+4} && \textit{Simplify.} \end{aligned}$$

Now let's solve the table tennis ball problem.

Example 2

APPLICATION
Table Tennis

Refer to the applications at the beginning of the lesson. How many table tennis balls would weigh $1\frac{1}{2}$ pounds altogether?

$$\begin{aligned} \frac{1\frac{1}{2}\text{ pounds}}{\frac{1}{10}\text{ ounce}} &= \frac{\frac{3}{2}\text{ pounds}}{\frac{1}{10}\text{ ounce}} \\ &= \frac{\frac{3}{2}\text{ pounds}}{\frac{1}{10}\text{ ounce}} \cdot \frac{16\text{ ounces}}{1\text{ pound}} && \textit{Convert pounds to ounces. Divide by common units.} \\ &= \frac{24}{\frac{1}{10}} \text{ or } 240 \end{aligned}$$

It would take 240 table tennis balls to weigh $1\frac{1}{2}$ pounds.

Recall that if a fraction has one or more fractions in the numerator or denominator, it is called a *complex fraction.* Some complex fractions are shown below.

$$\frac{5\frac{1}{2}}{3\frac{3}{4}} \qquad \frac{9}{\frac{x}{y}} \qquad \frac{\frac{x+y}{y}}{\frac{x-y}{x}} \qquad \frac{\frac{1}{a}-\frac{1}{b}}{\frac{1}{a}+\frac{1}{b}}$$

You simplify an algebraic complex fraction in the same way you simplify a numerical complex fraction.

numerical

$$\frac{\frac{11}{2}}{\frac{15}{4}} = \frac{11}{2} \div \frac{15}{4}$$

$$= \frac{11}{2} \cdot \frac{4}{15}$$ *The reciprocal of $\frac{15}{4}$ is $\frac{4}{15}$.*

$$= \frac{22}{15}$$

algebraic

$$\frac{\frac{a}{b}}{\frac{c}{d}} = \frac{a}{b} \div \frac{c}{d}$$

$$= \frac{a}{b} \cdot \frac{d}{c}$$ *The reciprocal of $\frac{c}{d}$ is $\frac{d}{c}$.*

$$= \frac{ad}{bc}$$

Simplifying a Complex Fraction

Any complex fraction $\frac{\frac{a}{b}}{\frac{c}{d}}$, where $b \neq 0$, $c \neq 0$, and $d \neq 0$, can be expressed as $\frac{ad}{bc}$.

Example 3 **Simplify each rational expression.**

a. $\dfrac{1+\frac{4}{a}}{\frac{a}{6}+\frac{2}{3}}$

Simplify the numerator and denominator separately. Then divide.

$$\frac{1+\frac{4}{a}}{\frac{a}{6}+\frac{2}{3}} = \frac{\frac{1}{1}\cdot\frac{a}{a}+\frac{4}{a}}{\frac{a}{6}+\frac{2}{3}\cdot\frac{2}{2}}$$ *The LCD of the numerator is a.* *The LCD of the denominator is 6.*

$$= \frac{\frac{a+4}{a}}{\frac{a+4}{6}}$$ *Add to simplify both numerator and denominator.*

$$= \frac{a+4}{a} \div \frac{a+4}{6}$$ *Rewrite as a division sentence.*

$$= \frac{\overset{1}{\cancel{a+4}}}{a} \cdot \frac{6}{\underset{1}{\cancel{a+4}}}$$ *The reciprocal of $\frac{a+4}{6}$ is $\frac{6}{a+4}$.*

$$= \frac{6}{a}$$ *Divide by common factors.*

b. $\dfrac{m-\frac{m+5}{m-3}}{m+1}$

$$\frac{m-\frac{m+5}{m-3}}{m+1} = \frac{\frac{m(m-3)}{(m-3)}-\frac{m+5}{m-3}}{m+1}$$ *The LCD of the numerator is m – 3.* *The LCD of the denominator is m + 1.*

$$= \frac{\frac{m^2-3m-m-5}{m-3}}{m+1}$$ *Subtract to simplify the numerator.*

(continued on the next page)

$$= \frac{\frac{m^2 - 4m - 5}{m - 3}}{m + 1}$$ *Simplify.*

$$= \frac{\frac{(m + 1)(m - 5)}{m - 3}}{m + 1}$$ *Factor the numerator.*

$$= \frac{(m + 1)(m - 5)}{m - 3} \div (m + 1)$$ *Rewrite as a division sentence.*

$$= \frac{(m + 1)(m - 5)}{m - 3} \cdot \frac{1}{(m + 1)}$$ *The reciprocal of $m + 1$ is $\frac{1}{m + 1}$.*

$$= \frac{\overset{1}{\cancel{(m + 1)}}(m - 5)}{m - 3} \cdot \frac{1}{\underset{1}{\cancel{(m + 1)}}}$$ *Divide by the common factors.*

$$= \frac{m - 5}{m - 3}$$

You can use a graphing calculator to check the work you did in Example 3.

EXPLORATION — GRAPHING CALCULATORS

When you graph a function that involves rational expressions, remember to enclose every numerator and denominator in parentheses.

Your Turn

a. Graph $y = \frac{x - \frac{x + 5}{x - 3}}{x + 1}$. Use the window $[-1.4, 8]$ by $[-5, 5]$.

b. What are the excluded values of x in the expression in part a?

c. Graph $y = \frac{x - 5}{x - 3}$ on the same display used in part a.

d. What are the excluded values of x in the expression in part c?

e. Except for excluded values, do the graphs appear the same?

Example 4 **Simplify** $\frac{a - 2 + \frac{3}{a + 2}}{a + 1 - \frac{10}{a + 4}}$.

$$\frac{a - 2 + \frac{3}{a + 2}}{a + 1 - \frac{10}{a + 4}} = \frac{\frac{(a - 2)(a + 2)}{a + 2} + \frac{3}{a + 2}}{\frac{(a + 1)(a + 4)}{(a + 4)} - \frac{10}{a + 4}}$$ *The LCD of the numerator is $a + 2$.* *The LCD of the denominator is $a + 4$.*

$$= \frac{\frac{a^2 - 4 + 3}{a + 2}}{\frac{a^2 + 5a + 4 - 10}{(a + 4)}}$$ *Add to simplify the numerator.* *Subtract to simplify the denominator.*

$$= \frac{\frac{a^2 - 1}{(a + 2)}}{\frac{a^2 + 5a - 6}{(a + 4)}}$$ *Simplify.*

$$= \frac{\frac{(a + 1)(a - 1)}{(a + 2)}}{\frac{(a + 6)(a - 1)}{(a + 4)}}$$ *Factor to simplify the numerator and denominator.*

$$= \frac{(a + 1)\overset{1}{\cancel{(a - 1)}}}{(a + 2)} \cdot \frac{(a + 4)}{(a + 6)\underset{1}{\cancel{(a - 1)}}}$$ *Multiply by the reciprocal.*

$$= \frac{a^2 + 5a + 4}{a^2 + 8a + 12}$$ *Multiply.*

CHECK FOR UNDERSTANDING

Communicating Mathematics

Study the lesson. Then complete the following.

1. **Determine** the simplified form of $\dfrac{\frac{3}{(x+1)(x+2)(x+3)}}{\frac{4}{(x+3)(x+2)(x+1)}}$ mentally.
2. **a.** What is the LCD for the expression $3 + \frac{x}{2} + \frac{4}{x} + \frac{x^2 + 3x + 15}{x - 2}$?

   b. Write the expression in simplified form.

Guided Practice

Write each mixed expression as a rational expression.

3. $8 + \frac{3}{x}$
4. $5 + \frac{8}{3m}$
5. $3m + \frac{m+1}{2m}$

Simplify.

6. $\dfrac{4\frac{1}{3}}{5\frac{4}{7}}$
7. $\dfrac{6\frac{2}{5}}{3\frac{5}{9}}$
8. $\dfrac{\frac{3}{x}}{\frac{x}{3}}$
9. $\dfrac{\frac{5}{y}}{\frac{10}{y^2}}$
10. $\dfrac{\frac{x+4}{x-2}}{\frac{x+5}{x-2}}$
11. $\dfrac{\frac{a-b}{a+b}}{\frac{3}{a+b}}$
12. Nakita performed an operation on $\frac{x+2}{3x-1}$ and $\frac{2x^2-8}{3x-1}$ and got $\frac{1}{2(x-2)}$. What operation was it? Explain.

EXERCISES

Practice

Write each mixed expression as a rational expression.

13. $3 + \frac{6}{x+3}$
14. $11 + \frac{a-b}{a+b}$
15. $3 - \frac{4}{2x+1}$
16. $3 + \frac{x-4}{x+y}$
17. $5 + \frac{r-3}{r^2-9}$
18. $3 + \frac{x^2+y^2}{x^2-y^2}$

Simplify.

19. $\dfrac{7\frac{2}{3}}{5\frac{3}{4}}$
20. $\dfrac{6\frac{1}{7}}{8\frac{3}{5}}$
21. $\dfrac{\frac{a^3}{b}}{\frac{a^2}{b^2}}$
22. $\dfrac{\frac{x^2y^2}{a}}{\frac{x^2y}{a^3}}$
23. $\dfrac{2 + \frac{5}{x}}{\frac{x}{3} + \frac{5}{6}}$
24. $\dfrac{4 + \frac{3}{y}}{\frac{3}{8} + \frac{y}{2}}$
25. $\dfrac{a - \frac{15}{a-2}}{a+3}$
26. $\dfrac{x + \frac{35}{x+12}}{x+7}$
27. $\dfrac{\frac{x^2-4}{x^2+5x+6}}{x-2}$
28. $\dfrac{m + \frac{3m+7}{m+5}}{m+1}$
29. $\dfrac{m + 5 + \frac{2}{m+2}}{m + 1 + \frac{6}{m+6}}$
30. $\dfrac{a + 1 + \frac{3}{a+5}}{a + 1 + \frac{3}{a-1}}$
31. $\dfrac{y + 6 + \frac{3}{y+2}}{y + 11 + \frac{48}{y-3}}$
32. $\dfrac{x + 3 + \frac{4}{x-2}}{x - 1 - \frac{2}{x+3}}$
33. $\dfrac{t + 1 + \frac{1}{t+1}}{1 - t - \frac{1}{t+1}}$

34. What is the quotient when $b + \frac{1}{b}$ is divided by $a + \frac{1}{a}$?

35. What is the product when $\frac{2b^2}{5c}$ is multiplied by the quotient of $\frac{4b^3}{2c}$ and $\frac{7b^3}{8c^2}$?

36. Write $1 + \cfrac{1}{1 + \cfrac{1}{1 + \cfrac{1}{1 + \cfrac{1}{x}}}}$ in simplest form.

Graphing Calculator

37. a. Graph $y = \frac{\frac{x+3}{2x}}{\frac{3x+9}{4}}$. What are its excluded values?

b. Graph $\frac{x+3}{2x} \cdot \frac{4}{3x+9}$ on the same display used in part a. What are its excluded values?

c. Except for the excluded values, are the graphs the same?

Critical Thinking

38. Simplify $\frac{3}{1 - \frac{3}{3+y}} - \frac{3}{\frac{3}{3-y} - 1}$.

Applications and Problem Solving

39. **Acoustics** If a train is moving toward you at v miles per hour and blowing its whistle at a frequency of f, then you hear it as though it were blowing its whistle with a frequency h, which is defined as $h = \frac{f}{1 - \frac{v}{s}}$, where s is the speed of sound.

a. Simplify the right side of this formula.

b. Suppose a train whistle blows at 370 cycles per second (at the same frequency as the first F sharp (F#) above middle C on the piano). The train is moving toward you at a speed of 80 miles per hour. The speed of sound is 760 miles per hour. Find the frequency of the sound as you hear it.

c. The note F# and the notes to its right on the piano are listed with their frequencies in the table.

Note	F#	G	G#	A	A#	B	C	C#
Frequency	370.0	392.0	415.3	440.0	466.1	493.8	523.2	554.3

By approximately how many notes did the sound rise in part b?

d. Find the frequency of the same whistle as you would hear it from an approaching TGV, the French train that is the fastest in the world ($v = 236$ miles per hour). By approximately how many notes would it rise?

FYI

Have you noticed that the pitch (frequency) of a train whistle or a horn from a speeding car gets higher as it approaches you and lower as it moves away from you? This effect is known as the *Doppler effect,* named for the Austrian scientist Christian Doppler, who discovered it in 1842.

40. **Statistics** In 1993, New Jersey was the most densely populated state, and Alaska was the least densely populated. The population of New Jersey was 7,879,000, and the population of Alaska was 599,000. The land area of New Jersey is about 7419 square miles, and the land area of Alaska is about 570,374 square miles. How many more people were there per square mile in New Jersey than in Alaska in 1993?

Mixed Review

41. Find $\frac{4x}{2x+6} + \frac{3}{x+3}$. (Lesson 12–6)

42. Find $\frac{b-5}{b^2-7b+10} \cdot \frac{b-2}{3}$. (Lesson 12–2)

43. Factor $4x^2 - 1$. (Lesson 10–4)

44. Find $x^4y^5 \div xy^3$. (Lesson 9–2)

45. Solve the system of equations. (Lesson 8–4)

$3a + 4b = -25$
$2a - 3b = 6$

46. **Geometry** A quadrilateral has vertices $A(-1, -4)$, $B(2, -1)$, $C(5, -4)$, and $D(2, -7)$. (Lesson 6–6)
    a. Graph the quadrilateral and determine the relationship, if any, among its sides.
    b. What type of quadrilateral is $ABCD$?

47. Solve $P = 2\ell + 2w$ for w. (Lesson 3–6)

48. Find $\sqrt{225}$. (Lesson 2–8)

WORKING ON THE

In·ves·ti·ga·tion

Refer to the Investigation on pages 656–657.

A Growing Concern

1 Determine where the future play area and future garden should be placed. Mark off this space on your scale drawing. Justify your reasons for placing them where you did.

2 Develop a detailed plan for the deck and/or patio and walkways for the Sanchez family. Indicate the dimensions. Explain why you chose the placement and the type of materials for each place.

3 Figure the cost of materials, labor, and profit margin of the construction of the deck and/or patio. Justify your costs and make a case for building a deck and/or patio and the walkways as you designed them.

4 Be sure to add the deck and/or patio and the walkways to your drawing.

Add the results of your work to your Investigation Folder.

12-8 Solving Rational Equations

What YOU'LL LEARN

- To solve rational equations.

Why IT'S IMPORTANT

You can use rational equations to solve problems involving work, psychology, and electronics.

APPLICATION

Work

Tiko and Julio have decided to start a lawn care service in their neighborhood. In order to schedule their clients in an organized manner, they compared notes on how long it took each of them to mow the same yard. Tiko could mow and trim Mrs. Harris's lawn in 3 hours, while it took Julio 2 hours. How long would it take if they both worked together?

You can answer this question by solving a **rational equation**. A rational equation is an equation that contains rational expressions.

Explore Since it takes Tiko 3 hours to do the yard, he can finish $\frac{1}{3}$ of the yard in 1 hour. At his rate, Julio can finish $\frac{1}{2}$ of the yard in an hour. Use the following formula.

$$\underbrace{\text{rate of work}}_{r} \cdot \underbrace{\text{time}}_{t} = \underbrace{\text{work done}}_{w}$$

Plan In t hours, Tiko can do $t \cdot \frac{1}{3}$ or $\frac{t}{3}$ of the job and Julio can do $t \cdot \frac{1}{2}$ or $\frac{t}{2}$ of the job. Thus, $\frac{t}{3} + \frac{t}{2} = 1$, where 1 represents the finished job.

Solve

$$\frac{t}{3} + \frac{t}{2} = 1$$

$$6\left(\frac{t}{3} + \frac{t}{2}\right) = 6(1) \quad \textit{Multiply each side by the LCD, 3(2) or 6.}$$

$$2t + 3t = 6 \quad \textit{Use the distributive property.}$$

$$5t = 6$$

$$t = \frac{6}{5} \text{ or } 1\frac{1}{5} \quad \textit{Check this solution.}$$

Examine If Tiko and Julio work for $1\frac{1}{5}$ hours, will the whole yard get done?

$$\text{Tiko's } rt + \text{Julio's } rt \stackrel{?}{=} 1 \rightarrow \frac{1}{3} \cdot \frac{6}{5} + \frac{1}{2} \cdot \frac{6}{5} \stackrel{?}{=} 1$$

$$\frac{2}{5} + \frac{3}{5} \stackrel{?}{=} 1$$

$$1 = 1$$

Working together, Tiko and Julio can finish the yard in $1\frac{1}{5}$ hours.

Example 1 Solve $\mathbf{\frac{10}{3y} - \frac{5}{2y} = \frac{1}{4}}$.

$$\frac{10}{3y} - \frac{5}{2y} = \frac{1}{4}$$

$$12y\left(\frac{10}{3y} - \frac{5}{2y}\right) = 12y\left(\frac{1}{4}\right) \quad \textit{Multiply each side by the LCD, 12y.}$$

$$12y \cdot \frac{10}{3y} - 12y \cdot \frac{5}{2y} = 12y \cdot \frac{1}{4} \quad \textit{Use the distributive property.}$$

$$40 - 30 = 3y$$

$$10 = 3y$$

$$y = \frac{10}{3} \text{ or } 3\frac{1}{3}$$

Check: $\dfrac{10}{3\left(3\frac{1}{3}\right)} - \dfrac{5}{2\left(3\frac{1}{3}\right)} = \dfrac{1}{4}$

$$\frac{10}{10} - \frac{15}{20} \stackrel{?}{=} \frac{1}{4}$$

$$\frac{20}{20} - \frac{15}{20} \stackrel{?}{=} \frac{1}{4}$$

$$\frac{1}{4} = \frac{1}{4} \checkmark$$

The solution is $3\frac{1}{3}$.

Multiplying each side of an equation by the LCD of two rational expressions can yield results that are not solutions to the original equation. Such solutions are called **extraneous solutions** or "false" solutions.

GLOBAL CONNECTIONS

Algonquin Indians named the Mississippi River the "Father of Waters." Their phrase *Misi Sipi* meant big water. The Mississippi River drains one eighth of the North American continent, discharging 350 trillion gallons of water a day.

Example 2 **Solve $\dfrac{x}{x-1} + \dfrac{2x-3}{x-1} = 2$.**

$$\frac{x}{x-1} + \frac{2x-3}{x-1} = 2$$

$$(x-1)\left(\frac{x}{x-1} + \frac{2x-3}{x-1}\right) = (x-1)2 \quad \textit{Multiply each side by the LCD, } x-1.$$

$$(x-1)\left(\frac{x}{x-1}\right) + (x-1)\left(\frac{2x-3}{x-1}\right) = (x-1)2$$

$$x + 2x - 3 = 2x - 2$$

$$3x - 3 = 2x - 2$$

$$x = 1$$

The number 1 is not a solution, since 1 is an excluded value for x. Thus, the equation has no solution.

You can use the distance formula to solve real-world problems.

Example 3 **APPLICATION** **Commerce**

A grain barge operates between Minneapolis, Minnesota, and New Orleans, Louisiana, along the Mississippi River. The maximum speed of the barge in still water is 8 miles per hour. At this rate, a 30-mile trip downstream (with the current) takes as much time as an 18-mile trip upstream (against the current). What is the speed of the current?

Explore Let c = the speed of the current. The speed of the barge traveling downstream is 8 miles per hour plus the speed of the current, that is, $(8 + c)$ miles per hour. The speed of the barge traveling upstream is 8 miles per hour minus the speed of the current, that is, $(8 - c)$ miles per hour.

Plan To represent time t, solve $d = rt$ for t. Thus, $t = \frac{d}{r}$.

	d	r	$t = \frac{d}{r}$
downstream	30	$8 + c$	$\frac{30}{8 + c}$
upstream	18	$8 - c$	$\frac{18}{8 - c}$

(continued on the next page)

Top Five List

Longest Rivers in North America

River	Miles
1. Mackenzie-Peace	2635
2. Missouri-Red Rock	2540
3. Mississippi	2348
4. Missouri	2315
5. Yukon	1979

Solve

$$\frac{30}{8 + c} = \frac{18}{8 - c}$$

$$30(8 - c) = 18(8 + c) \quad \textit{Find the cross products.}$$

$$240 - 30c = 144 + 18c$$

$$96 = 48c$$

$$c = 2$$

Examine Check the value to see if it makes sense.
The barge goes downstream at (8 + 2) or 10 mph.
A 30-mile trip would take 30 ÷ 10 or 3 hours.
The barge goes upstream at (8 − 2) or 6 mph.
An 18-mile trip takes 18 ÷ 6 or 3 hours.
Both trips take the same amount of time, so the speed of the current must be 2 miles per hour.

Electricity can be described as the flow of electrons through a conductor, such as a copper wire. Electricity flows more freely through some conductors than others. The force opposing the flow is called *resistance*. The unit of resistance commonly used is the *ohm*.

Resistances can occur one after another, that is, *in series*. Resistances can also occur in branches with the conductor going in the same direction, or *in parallel*.

Series

$R_T = R_1 + R_2$

Parallel

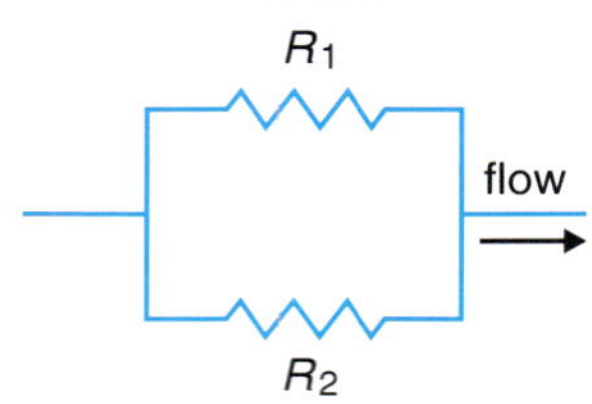

$\frac{1}{R_T} = \frac{1}{R_1} + \frac{1}{R_2}$

Example 4

APPLICATION

Electronics

Assume that R_1 = 4 ohms and R_2 = 3 ohms. Compute the total resistance of the conductor when the resistances are in series and in parallel.

series

$$R_T = R_1 + R_2$$

$$= 4 + 3 \text{ or } 7$$

parallel

$$\frac{1}{R_T} = \frac{1}{R_1} + \frac{1}{R_2}$$

$$\frac{1}{R_T} = \frac{1}{4} + \frac{1}{3}$$

$$\frac{1}{R_T} = \frac{7}{12}$$

$$12 = 7R_T \quad \textit{Cross products}$$

$$R_T = \frac{12}{7} \text{ or } 1\frac{5}{7}$$

A circuit, or path for the flow of electrons, often has some resistances connected in series and others in parallel.

Example 5 APPLICATION **Electronics**

A parallel circuit has one branch in series as shown at the right. Given that the total resistance is 2.25 ohms, $R_1 = 3$ ohms, and $R_2 = 4$ ohms, find R_3.

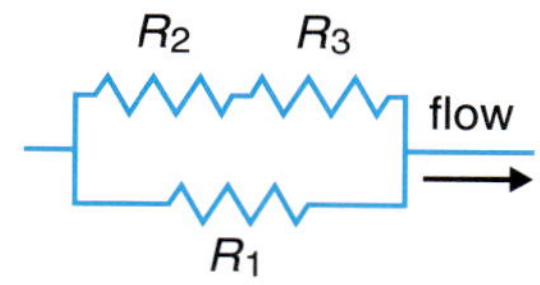

$$\frac{1}{R_T} = \frac{1}{R_1} + \frac{1}{R_2 + R_3}$$ *The total resistance of the branch in series is $R_2 + R_3$.*

$$\frac{1}{2.25} = \frac{1}{3} + \frac{1}{4 + R_3}$$ *$R_T = 2.25$, $R_1 = 3$, and $R_2 = 4$*

$$\frac{1}{2.25} - \frac{1}{3} = \frac{1}{4 + R_3}$$

$$\frac{4}{9} - \frac{3}{9} = \frac{1}{4 + R_3}$$

$$\frac{1}{9} = \frac{1}{4 + R_3}$$

$$4 + R_3 = 9$$ *Find the cross products.*

$$R_3 = 5$$

Thus, R_3 is 5 ohms.

CHECK FOR UNDERSTANDING

Communicating Mathematics

Study the lesson. Then complete the following.

1. Refer to the application at the beginning of the lesson. How would the solution be different if Julio takes 6 hours to complete the lawn?
2. **You Decide** Antoinette solved $\frac{2m}{1-m} + \frac{m+3}{m^2-1} = 1$ and claimed that 1 and $-\frac{4}{3}$ were the solutions. Joel says that $-\frac{4}{3}$ is the only solution. Who is correct, and why?
3. **Define** a rational equation and distinguish it from a linear equation.

MATH JOURNAL

4. **Assess Yourself**
   a. Describe an activity that you and a friend do together that each can complete separately. Estimate the time it would take for each of you to complete it working alone.
   b. Use the math you have learned to find out how long it would take to complete the activity if the two of you worked together.

Guided Practice

Solve each equation.

5. $\frac{1}{4} + \frac{4}{x} = \frac{1}{x}$
6. $\frac{1}{5} + \frac{3}{2y} = \frac{3}{3y}$
7. $\frac{4}{x+5} = \frac{4}{3(x+2)}$
8. $\frac{x}{2} = \frac{3}{x+1}$
9. $\frac{a-1}{a+1} - \frac{2a}{a-1} = -1$
10. $\frac{w-2}{w} - \frac{w-3}{w-6} = \frac{1}{w}$
11. **Work** Olivia can wash and wax her car, vacuum the interior, and wash the insides of the windows in 5 hours. What part of the job can she do in
    a. 1 hour? b. 3 hours? c. x hours?

12. **Recreation** Sally and her brother rented a boat to go fishing in Jones Creek. The maximum speed of the boat in still water was 3 miles per hour. At this rate, a 9-mile trip downstream (with the current) took the same amount of time as a 3-mile trip upstream. Let c = the speed of the current. Copy and complete the table below.

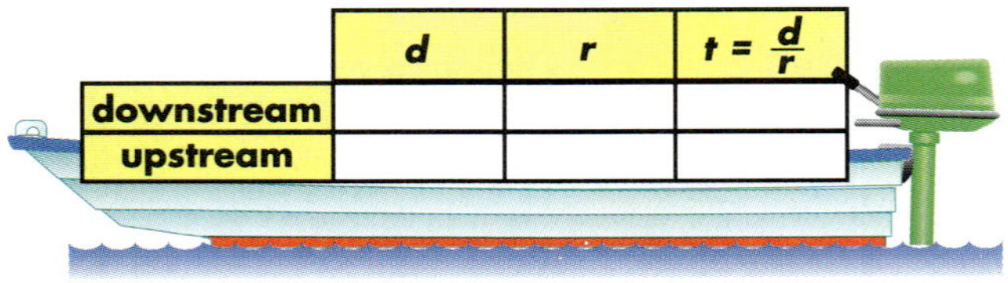

	d	r	$t = \frac{d}{r}$
downstream			
upstream			

   a. Write an equation that represents the conditions in the problem.
   b. Find the speed of the current.

Electronics: Exercises 13–15 refer to the diagram below.

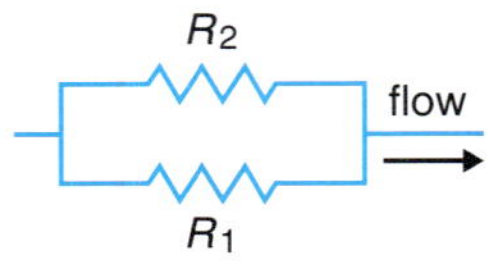

13. Find the total resistance, R_T, given that $R_1 = 8$ ohms and $R_2 = 6$ ohms.
14. Find R_1, given that R_T is $2.\overline{2}$ ohms and $R_2 = 5$ ohms.
15. Find R_1 and R_2, given that the total resistance is $2.\overline{6}$ ohms and R_1 is twice as great as R_2.

EXERCISES

Practice

Solve each equation.

16. $\frac{1}{4} + \frac{3}{x} = \frac{1}{x}$
17. $\frac{1}{5} - \frac{4}{3m} = \frac{2}{m}$
18. $x + 3 = -\frac{2}{x}$
19. $\frac{m+1}{m} + \frac{m+4}{m} = 6$
20. $\frac{x}{x+1} + \frac{5}{x-1} = 1$
21. $\frac{m-1}{m+1} - \frac{2m}{m-1} = -1$
22. $\frac{-4}{a+1} + \frac{3}{a} = 1$
23. $\frac{3x}{10} - \frac{1}{5x} = \frac{1}{2}$
24. $\frac{b}{4} + \frac{1}{b} = \frac{-5}{3}$
25. $\frac{-4}{n} = 11 - 3n$
26. $\frac{x-3}{x} = \frac{x-3}{x-6}$
27. $\frac{7}{a-1} = \frac{5}{a+3}$
28. $\frac{3}{r+4} - \frac{1}{r} = \frac{1}{r}$
29. $\frac{3}{x} + \frac{4x}{x-3} = 4$
30. $\frac{1}{4m} + \frac{2m}{m-3} = 2$
31. $\frac{a-2}{a} - \frac{a-3}{a-6} = \frac{1}{a}$
32. $\frac{x+3}{x+5} + \frac{2}{x-9} = \frac{5}{2x+10}$
33. $\frac{-1}{w+2} = \frac{w^2-7w-8}{3w^2+2w-8}$

Electronics: Refer to the diagram at the right.

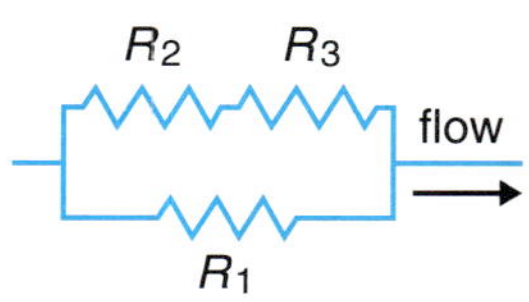

34. Find R_T, given that $R_1 = 5$ ohms, $R_2 = 4$ ohms, and $R_3 = 3$ ohms.
35. Find R_1, given that $R_T = 2\frac{10}{13}$ ohms, $R_2 = 3$ ohms, and $R_3 = 6$ ohms.
36. Find R_2, given that $R_T = 3.5$ ohms, $R_1 = 5$ ohms, and $R_3 = 4$ ohms.

Electronics: Solve each formula for the variable indicated.

37. $\frac{1}{R_T} = \frac{1}{R_1} + \frac{1}{R_2}$, for R_1

38. $I = \frac{E}{r + R}$, for R

39. $I = \frac{nE}{nr + R}$, for n

40. $I = \frac{E}{\frac{r}{n} + R}$, for r

Critical Thinking

41. What number would you add to both the numerator and denominator of $\frac{4}{11}$ to make a fraction equivalent to $\frac{2}{3}$?

42. Refer to the diagram at the right.
    a. Write an equation for the total resistance for the diagram.
    b. Find the total resistance, given that R_1 = 5 ohms, R_2 = 4 ohms, and R_3 = 6 ohms.

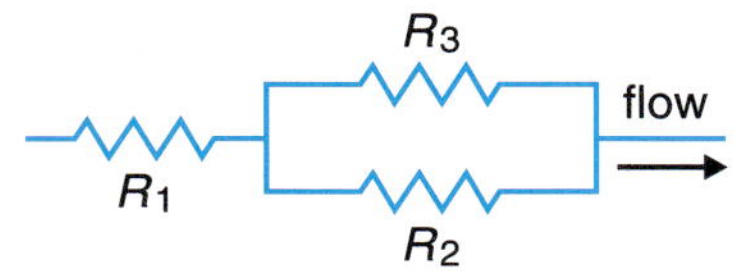

Applications and Problem Solving

43. **Electricity** Eight lights on a decorated tree are connected in series. Each has a resistance of 12 ohms. What is the total resistance?

44. **Electricity** Three appliances are connected in parallel: a lamp with a resistance of 60 ohms, an iron with a resistance of 20 ohms, and a heating coil with a resistance of 80 ohms. Find the total resistance.

45. **Air Travel** The flying distance from Honolulu, Hawaii, to San Francisco, California, is approximately 2400 miles. The air speed of a 747-100 airplane is 520 miles per hour. A strong tailwind blows at 120 miles per hour. At 1000 miles into the trip (1400 miles from San Francisco), the aircraft loses power in one engine. As a navigator for the aircraft, you must answer the following questions.
    a. How long would it take to return to Honolulu?
    b. How long would it take to continue on to San Francisco?
    c. What is the point-of-no-return? That is, at what point into the flight (in miles) would it be quicker to continue the flight to San Francisco than return to Honolulu?

46. **Bicycling** The Lake Pontchartrain Causeway in Louisiana is 24 miles long.
    a. Suppose Todd starts cycling at one end at 20 miles per hour and Kristie starts at the other end at 16 miles per hour. How long would it take them to meet? At what distance from either end would they meet?
    b. Todd's rate with no wind is 20 miles per hour, while Kristie's is 16 miles per hour. If Todd cycles against the wind, while Kristie cycles with the wind, and they meet at the midpoint of the bridge, what is the wind speed?

    c. The causeway consists of two parallel bridges. Assume Todd starts to bicycle from one end in one direction at 20 miles per hour. Kristie starts from the other end on the parallel bridge, bicycling at 16 miles per hour in the opposite direction. They pedal in a continuous loop on the two parallel causeways. How long does it take Todd to catch up with Kristie? (*Note:* She has a 24-mile head start.)

fabulous FIRSTS

Jim Thorpe (1886–1953)

James Francis Thorpe was the first American-Indian sports hero, winner of Olympic Gold medals in 1912, a professional baseball and football player, and the first president of the American Professional Football Association, which later became the NFL. In 1950, he was selected by sportswriters and broadcasters as the greatest athlete of the first half of the 20th century.

47. Anthropology The formula $c = \frac{100w}{\ell}$ provides a measure called the cephalic index c. Anthropologists use this index to identify skulls by their ethnic characteristics. You calculate the cephalic index by using the width w of a person's head, ear to ear, and the length ℓ of the head from face to back.

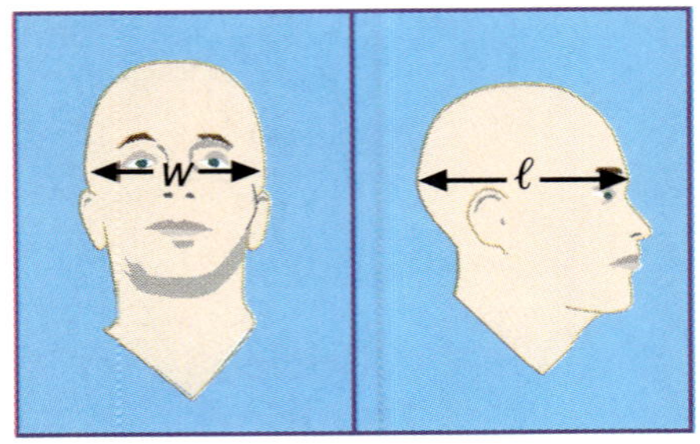

a. Solve the formula for w in terms of c and ℓ.

b. Solve the formula for ℓ in terms of c and w.

48. Psychology The formula $i = \frac{100m}{c}$ provides a measure i of intelligence, called the intelligence quotient, or I.Q. In the formula, m represents the person's mental age, and c represents the person's chronological age.

a. Solve the formula for m in terms of i and c.

b. Solve the formula for c in terms of i and m.

49. Baseball Chang has 32 hits in 128 times at bat. His current batting average is $\frac{32}{128} = 0.250$. How many consecutive hits must he get in his next x times at bat in order to get his average up to 0.300?

Mixed Review

50. Simplify $\dfrac{\frac{x^2 - 5x}{x^2 + x - 30}}{\frac{x^2 + 2x}{x^2 + 9x + 18}}$. (Lesson 12–7)

51. Simplify $\frac{a + 2}{b^2 + 4b + 4} \div \frac{4a + 8}{b + 4}$. (Lesson 12–3)

52. Find $(0.5a + 0.25b)^2$. (Lesson 9–8)

53. Sales The amounts in the picture at the right are the cash register totals of 20 customers on the Wednesday before Thanksgiving. Make a box-and-whisker plot of these data. (Lesson 7–7)

54. Statistics Refer to the data in Exercise 53. Find the range, median, upper quartile, lower quartile, and interquartile range of the data. Identify any outliers. (Lesson 5–7)

55. Write 12 pounds to 100 ounces as a fraction in simplest form. (Lesson 4–1)

56. Solve $3x = -15$. (Lesson 3–2)

57. Find $(-2)(3)(-3)$. (Lesson 2–6)

58. Complete: $3(2 + x) = 6 + \underline{\ ?\ }$. (Lesson 1–7)

CHAPTER 12 HIGHLIGHTS

VOCABULARY

After completing this chapter, you should be able to define each term, property, or phrase and give an example or two of each.

Algebra

excluded values (p. 660)

extraneous solutions (p. 697)

least common denominator (LCD) (p. 686)

least common multiple (LCM) (p. 685)

mixed expressions (p. 690)

rational equation (p. 696)

rational expression (p. 660)

Problem Solving

make an organized list (p. 685)

UNDERSTANDING AND USING THE VOCABULARY

State whether each sentence is *true* or *false*. If false, replace the underlined word or number to make a true sentence.

1. A <u>mixed</u> expression is an algebraic fraction whose numerator and denominator are polynomials.
2. The complex fraction $\frac{\frac{4}{5}}{\frac{2}{3}}$ can be simplfied as $\underline{\frac{6}{5}}$.
3. The equation $\frac{x}{x-1} + \frac{2x-3}{x-1} = 2$ has an extraneous solution of $\underline{1}$.
4. The mixed expression $6 - \frac{a-2}{a+3}$ can be rewritten as the rational expression $\underline{\frac{5a+16}{a+3}}$.
5. The least common multiple for $(x^2 - 144)$ and $(x + 12)$ is $\underline{x + 12}$.
6. The excluded values for $\frac{4x}{x^2 - x - 12}$ are $\underline{-3 \text{ and } 4}$.
7. The least common denominator is the <u>greatest common factor</u> of the denominators.

CHAPTER 12 STUDY GUIDE AND ASSESSMENT

SKILLS AND CONCEPTS

OBJECTIVES AND EXAMPLES

Upon completing this chapter, you should be able to:

- simplify rational expressions (Lesson 12–1)

Simplify $\frac{x+y}{x^2+3xy+2y^2}$.

$$\frac{x+y}{x^2+3xy+2y^2} = \frac{\cancel{x+y}^{\,1}}{\cancel{(x+y)}_{1}(x+2y)} = \frac{1}{x+2y}$$

REVIEW EXERCISES

Use these exercises to review and prepare for the chapter test.

Simplify each rational expression. State the excluded values of the variables.

8. $\frac{3x^2y}{12xy^3z}$
9. $\frac{z^2-3z}{z-3}$
10. $\frac{a^2-25}{a^2+3a-10}$
11. $\frac{3a^3}{3a^3+6a^2}$
12. $\frac{x^2+10x+21}{x^3+x^2-42x}$
13. $\frac{b^2-5b+6}{b^4-13b^2+36}$

- multiply rational expressions (Lesson 12–2)

$$\frac{1}{x^2+x-12}\cdot\frac{x-3}{x+5} = \frac{1}{(x+4)\cancel{(x-3)}_{1}}\cdot\frac{\cancel{x-3}^{\,1}}{x+5} = \frac{1}{(x+4)(x+5)} = \frac{1}{x^2+9x+20}$$

Find each product. Assume that no denominator has a value of 0.

14. $\frac{7b^2}{9}\cdot\frac{6a^2}{b}$
15. $\frac{5x^2y}{8ab}\cdot\frac{12a^2b}{25x}$
16. $(3x+30)\cdot\frac{10}{x^2-100}$
17. $\frac{3a-6}{a^2-9}\cdot\frac{a+3}{a^2-2a}$
18. $\frac{x^2+x-12}{x+2}\cdot\frac{x+4}{x^2-x-6}$
19. $\frac{b^2+19b+84}{b-3}\cdot\frac{b^2-9}{b^2+15b+36}$

- divide rational expressions (Lesson 12–3)

$$\frac{y^2-16}{y^2-64}\div\frac{y+4}{y-8} = \frac{y^2-16}{y^2-64}\cdot\frac{y-8}{y+4}$$

$$= \frac{(y-4)\cancel{(y+4)}^{\,1}}{\cancel{(y-8)}_{1}(y+8)}\cdot\frac{\cancel{y-8}^{\,1}}{\cancel{y+4}_{1}} = \frac{y-4}{y+8}$$

Find each quotient. Assume that no denominator has a value of 0.

20. $\frac{p^3}{2q}\div\frac{p^2}{4q}$
21. $\frac{y^2}{y+4}\div\frac{3y}{y^2-16}$
22. $\frac{3y-12}{y+4}\div(y^2-6y+8)$
23. $\frac{2m^2+7m-15}{m+5}\div\frac{9m^2-4}{3m+2}$

OBJECTIVES AND EXAMPLES

- divide a polynomial by a binomial. (Lesson 12–4)

$$\begin{array}{r} x^2 + \quad x - 19 \\ x - 3\overline{)x^3 - 2x^2 - 22x + 21} \\ \underline{x^3 - 3x^2} \qquad\qquad \\ x^2 - 22x \qquad \\ \underline{x^2 - \quad 3x} \qquad \\ -19x + 21 \\ \underline{-19x + 57} \\ -36 \end{array}$$

The quotient is $x^2 + x - 19 - \frac{36}{x-3}$.

REVIEW EXERCISES

Find each quotient.

24. $(4a^2b^2c^2 - 8a^3b^2c + 6abc^2) \div (2ab^2)$
25. $(x^3 + 7x^2 + 10x - 6) \div (x + 3)$
26. $(x^3 - 7x + 6) \div (x - 2)$
27. $(x^4 + 3x^3 + 2x^2 - x + 6) \div (x - 2)$
28. $(48b^2 + 8b + 7) \div (12b - 1)$

OBJECTIVES AND EXAMPLES

- add and subtract rational expressions with like denominators. (Lesson 12–5)

$$\frac{m^2}{m+4} - \frac{16}{m+4} = \frac{m^2 - 16}{m+4}$$

$$= \frac{(m-4)\overset{1}{\cancel{(m+4)}}}{\underset{1}{\cancel{m+4}}}$$

$$= m - 4$$

REVIEW EXERCISES

Find each sum or difference. Express in simplest form.

29. $\frac{7a}{m^2} - \frac{5a}{m^2}$
30. $\frac{2x}{x-3} - \frac{6}{x-3}$
31. $\frac{m+4}{5} + \frac{m-1}{5}$
32. $\frac{-5}{2n-5} + \frac{2n}{2n-5}$
33. $\frac{a^2}{a-b} + \frac{-b^2}{a-b}$
34. $\frac{m^2}{m-n} - \frac{2mn - n^2}{m-n}$

OBJECTIVES AND EXAMPLES

- add and subtract rational expressions with unlike denominators (Lesson 12–6)

$$\frac{x}{x+3} - \frac{5}{x-2} = \frac{x}{x+3} \cdot \frac{x-2}{x-2} - \frac{5}{x-2} \cdot \frac{x+3}{x+3}$$

$$= \frac{x(x-2)}{(x+3)(x-2)} - \frac{5(x+3)}{(x+3)(x-2)}$$

$$= \frac{x^2 - 2x}{(x+3)(x-2)} - \frac{5x + 15}{(x+3)(x-2)}$$

$$= \frac{x^2 - 2x - 5x - 15}{(x+3)(x-2)}$$

$$= \frac{x^2 - 7x - 15}{x^2 + x - 6}$$

REVIEW EXERCISES

Find each sum or difference.

35. $\frac{7n}{3} - \frac{9n}{7}$
36. $\frac{7}{3a} - \frac{3}{6a^2}$
37. $\frac{2c}{3d^2} + \frac{3}{2cd}$
38. $\frac{2a}{2a+8} - \frac{4}{5a+20}$
39. $\frac{r^2 + 21r}{r^2 - 9} + \frac{3r}{r+3}$
40. $\frac{3a}{a-2} + \frac{5a}{a+1}$

OBJECTIVES AND EXAMPLES

- simplify mixed expressions and complex fractions. (Lesson 12–7)

$$\frac{y - \frac{40}{y-3}}{y+5} = \frac{\frac{y(y-3)}{(y-3)} - \frac{40}{y-3}}{y+5}$$

$$= \frac{\frac{y^2 - 3y - 40}{y-3}}{y+5}$$

$$= \frac{\frac{(y-8)(y+5)}{y-3}}{y+5}$$

$$= \frac{(y-8)(y+5)}{y-3} \div (y+5)$$

$$= \frac{(y-8)\overset{1}{\cancel{(y+5)}}}{y-3} \cdot \frac{1}{\underset{1}{\cancel{y+5}}}$$

$$= \frac{y-8}{y-3}$$

REVIEW EXERCISES

Write each mixed expression as a rational expression.

41. $4 + \frac{m}{m-2}$

42. $2 - \frac{x+2}{x^2-4}$

Simplify.

43. $\frac{\frac{x^2}{y^3}}{\frac{3x}{9y^2}}$

44. $\frac{5 + \frac{4}{a}}{\frac{a}{2} - \frac{3}{4}}$

45. $\frac{x - \frac{35}{x+2}}{x + \frac{42}{x+13}}$

46. $\frac{y + 9 - \frac{6}{y+4}}{y + 4 + \frac{2}{y+1}}$

OBJECTIVES AND EXAMPLES

- solve rational equations (Lesson 12–8)

$$\frac{3}{x} + \frac{1}{x-5} = \frac{1}{2x}$$

$$2x(x-5)\left(\frac{3}{x} + \frac{1}{x-5}\right) = \left(\frac{1}{2x}\right)2x(x-5)$$

$$6(x-5) + 2x = x - 5$$

$$6x - 30 + 2x = x - 5$$

$$7x = 25$$

$$x = \frac{25}{7}$$

REVIEW EXERCISES

Solve each equation.

47. $\frac{4x}{3} + \frac{7}{2} = \frac{7x}{12} - \frac{1}{4}$

48. $\frac{11}{2x} - \frac{2}{3x} = \frac{1}{6}$

49. $\frac{2}{3r} - \frac{3r}{r-2} = -3$

50. $\frac{x-2}{x} - \frac{x-3}{x-6} = \frac{1}{x}$

51. $-\frac{5}{m} = 19 - 4m$

52. $\frac{1}{h+1} + 2 = \frac{2h+3}{h-1}$

APPLICATIONS AND PROBLEM SOLVING

53. List Possibilities Wacky Wheels carries bicycles, tricycles, and wagons. They have an equal number of tricycles and wagons in stock. If there are 60 pedals and 180 wheels, how many bicycles, tricycles, and wagons are there in stock? (Lesson 12–6)

54. Electronics Assume that $R_1 = 4$ ohms and $R_2 = 6$ ohms. What is the total resistance of the conductor if R_1 and R_2 are: (Lesson 12–8)

a. connected in series?

b. connected in parallel?

55. Finance Barrington High School is raising money to build a house for Habitat for Humanity by doing lawn work for friends and neighbors. Scott can rake a lawn and bag the leaves in 5 hours, while Kalyn can do it in 3 hours. If Scott and Kalyn work together, how long will it take them to rake a lawn and bag the leaves? (Lesson 12–8)

A practice test for Chapter 12 is provided on page 798.

ALTERNATIVE ASSESSMENT

COOPERATIVE LEARNING PROJECT

Fun Puzzle In this project, you will determine the mathematical equation that is used for a puzzle. Mara developed a puzzle in which the number that you start with ends up being the number that you end with. Edwin was intrigued by this and wanted to determine why it works and if it will work all the time.

Use the steps below to develop the algebraic equation for a puzzle. Then prove that it works by simplifying it. Will it work if the number chosen is zero? Will it work if the number chosen is a fraction? If not, find a counterexample. Will it always work?

1. Choose any whole number.
2. Multiply by three.
3. Add fifteen.
4. Multiply by four.
5. Subtract twice the chosen number.
6. Multiply by five.
7. Add ten times the chosen number.
8. Divide by six.
9. Subtract three times the chosen number.
10. Add thirteen.
11. Divide by seven.
12. Subtract nine.

Consider these ideas while accomplishing your task.

- Read the sequence and determine your variable.
- Develop the algebraic equation expressed by the sequence.
- Determine a plan for simplifying the algebraic equation.
- Simplify the equation.
- Determine when it works and when it doesn't work.

Write a report showing why it works and explaining if it works all the time.

THINKING CRITICALLY

- Write three different rational equations whose solution is the set of all real numbers except a.
- For all real numbers a, b, and x, tell whether each statement is *always true*, *sometimes true*, or *never true*. Give a reason.

  $\frac{x}{x} = 1$

  $\frac{ab^2}{b^2} = ab^3$

  $\frac{x^2 + 6x - 5}{2x + 2} = \frac{x + 5}{2}$

PORTFOLIO

In the last chapter, you learned how to solve quadratic equations. Think about that process. Now choose a quadratic equation from your work in that lesson and solve it. Choose a rational equation from your work from this lesson and solve it right next to the quadratic equation that you solved. Refer to these two processes and compare and contrast solving quadratic equations and solving rational equations. Place this in your portfolio.

SELF EVALUATION

Applying a previous skill to help in developing a new skill is often a useful procedure. This can be refered to as building on a firm foundation. If a new idea is difficult to comprehend, stopping and relating it to a skill that has already been mastered can be helpful. The new skill is then "not so new" anymore and becomes more familiar.

Assess yourself. Do you build your skills? When developing a new idea, do you go back to something familiar and then build, or do you start from scratch? Give an example of when you could easily apply this method in learning a new skill in mathematics and in your daily life.

CUMULATIVE REVIEW

CHAPTERS 1–12

SECTION ONE: MULTIPLE CHOICE

There are eight multiple-choice questions in this section. After working each problem, write the letter of the correct answer on your paper.

1. **Geometry** The measure of the area of a square is 129 square inches. What is the perimeter of this square, rounded to the nearest hundredth?

   A. 11.36 in. B. 32.25 in.
   C. 45.43 in. D. 1040.06 in.

2. Express the relation shown as a set of ordered pairs.

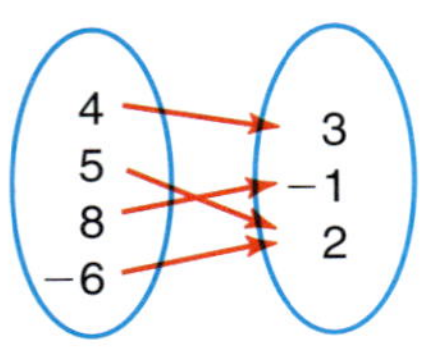

   A. {(3, 4), (−1, 8), (2, 5), (2, −6)}
   B. {(4, 3), (5, 2), (−1, 8), (−6, 2)}
   C. {4, 5, 8, −6, 3, −1, 2}
   D. {(4, 3), (5, 2), (8, −1), (−6, 2)}

3. **Geometry** Find the measure of the area of the rectangle shown below in simplest form.

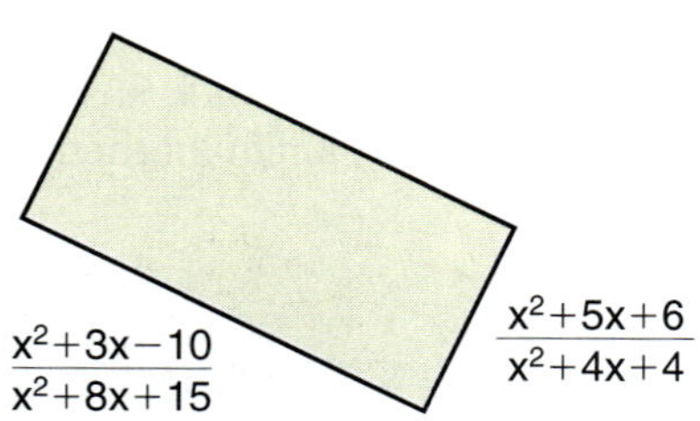

   A. $\frac{15}{32}x^2 - 1$ B. $\frac{x-2}{x+2}$
   C. $\frac{15x^2 - 32x - 60}{32x^2 + 92x + 60}$ D. $\frac{9x^2 - 42x + 49}{16x^2}$

4. **Probability** If a card is selected at random from a deck of 52 cards, what is the probability that it is not a face card?

   A. $\frac{3}{13}$ B. 3:10
   C. $\frac{13}{25}$ D. $\frac{10}{13}$

5. **Physics** Rafael threw a rock up from the edge of a cliff with an initial velocity of 15 meters per second. The rock was 10 meters above the ground level below the cliff when it left his hand. To the nearest tenth of a second, determine when the rock will hit the ground by using the formula $H = -4.9t^2 + vt + h$.

   A. 3.6 s B. 3.1 s
   C. 4 s D. 3.9 s

6. Simplify $\dfrac{\frac{x^2 + 8x + 15}{x^2 + x - 6}}{\frac{x^2 + 2x - 15}{x^2 - 2x - 3}}$.

   A. $\frac{23}{30}$ B. $\frac{x^2 + 4x + 3}{x^2 + x - 6}$
   C. $\frac{x^2 + 10x + 25}{x^2 - x - 2}$ D. $\frac{x+1}{x-2}$

7. **Geometry** What is the value of x if the perimeter of a square is 60 cm and its area is $4x^2 - 28x + 49$ cm^2?

   A. 4 only B. 11 only
   C. 4 and 11 D. −4 and 11

8. **Physics** The distance a force can move an object is $\frac{2a}{6a^2 - 17a - 3}$ yards. The distance a second force can move the same object is $\frac{a+2}{a^2 - 9}$ yards. How much farther did the object move when the second force was applied than when the first force was applied?

   A. $\frac{4a^2 + 7a + 2}{(a-3)(a+3)(6a+1)}$ B. $\frac{a+2}{5a^2 + 17a - 6}$
   C. $\frac{4a^2 + 17a - 2}{(a-3)(a+3)(6a-1)}$ D. $\frac{10a^2 + 11a + 1}{(3a-2)(2a+1)}$

SECTION TWO: SHORT ANSWER

This section contains nine questions for which you will provide short answers. Write your answer on your paper.

9. Evaluate
$42 \div 7 - 1 - 5 + 8 \cdot 2 + 14 \div 2 - 8$.

10. The rectangular penguin pond at the Bay Park Zoo is 12 meters long by 8 meters wide. The zoo wants to double the area of the pond by increasing the length and width by the same amount. By how much should the length and width be increased?

11. Determine the slope, y-intercept, and x-intercept of the graph of $2x - 3y = 13$.

12. Find the value of k if the remainder is 15 when $x^3 - 7x^2 + 4x + k$ is divided by $(x - 2)$.

13. The tens digit of a two-digit number exceeds twice its units digit by 1. If the digits are reversed, the number is 4 more than 3 times the sum of the digits. Find the number.

14. A long-distance cyclist pedaling at a steady rate travels 30 miles with the wind. He can travel only 18 miles against the wind in the same amount of time. If the rate of the wind is 3 miles per hour, what is the cyclist's rate without the wind?

15. Solve $-2 \leq 2x + 4 < 6$ and graph the solution set.

16. **Biology** The 2-inch long hummingbird flaps its wings about forty to fifty times each second. At this rate, how many times does it flap its wings in half of an hour? Express your answer in scientific notation.

17. **Construction** Muturi has 120 meters of fence to make a rectangular pen for his rabbits. If a shed is used as one side of the pen, what would be the maximum area of the pen?

SECTION THREE: OPEN-ENDED

This section contains three open-ended problems. Demonstrate your knowledge by giving a clear, concise solution to each problem. Your score on these problems will depend on how well you do the following.

- Explain your reasoning.
- Show your understanding of the mathematics in an organized manner.
- Use charts, graphs, and diagrams in your explanation.
- Show the solution in more than one way or relate it to other situations.
- Investigate beyond the requirements of the problem.

18. Mrs. Bloom bought some impatiens and petunias for her landscaping business for \$111.25. How many flats of each did she buy if each flat of impatiens was \$10.00, each flat of petunias was \$8.75, and if two fewer flats of impatiens than petunias were bought?

19. Graph the quadratic function $y = -x^2 + 6x + 16$. Include the equation of the axis of symmetry, the coordinates of the vertex, and the roots of the related quadratic equation.

20. Solve the system of equations below by graphing. Explain how you determined the solution, and name at least three ordered pairs that satisfy the system.

$y \leq x + 3$

$2x - 2y < 8$

$2y + 3x > 4$

CHAPTER

13 Exploring Radical Expressions and Equations

Objectives

In this chapter, you will:

- use the Pythagorean theorem to solve problems,
- simplify radical expressions,
- solve problems involving radical equations,
- solve quadratic equations by completing the square, and
- solve problems by identifying subgoals.

Teens Talk to Parents

Teens rate the following things as important for parents to do
for children who are 12 years old or younger: ○
For people their own age: ■

	Very important	Somewhat important	Not too important
Help them with their homework	○ 74%	22%	4%
	■ 42%	38%	20%
Give them a hug at least once a week	○ 70%	34%	8%
	■ 46%	34%	19%
Talk with their teachers regularly	○ 43%	44%	13%
	■ 32%	42%	25%
Be active in school activities like the PTA	○ 39%	43%	17%
	■ 24%	42%	34%

Source: *Oakland Press,* 1995

Almost everyone agrees that people who can communicate, who really listen to one another, have the healthiest relationships. This is certainly true when talking about teenagers and their parents. Kids can learn much from the experiences of their parents, and adults can benefit from the fresh ideas they share with their teens. What is the communication like in your home? What topics do you think are important to discuss with your parents?

TIME Line

1475 B.C. Cleopatra's Needles, two red granite obelisks covered with hieroglyphic writing, are built and raised in Heliopolis, Egypt.

1522 Cuthbert Tunstall publishes the first book on arithmetic in England.

1600 B.C. | 1500 | 1400 | A.D. 600 | 700 | 800 | 900 | 1300 | 1400 | 1500 | 1600 | 1700 | 1800

A.D. 605 Decimal notation is used in India.

1687 The coffee grinder is invented for the new drink in Europe.

PEOPLE IN THE NEWS

At age 12, **Ryan Holladay** of Arlington, Virginia, is already a published author. His book *What Preteens Want Their Parents to Know* contains about 180 tips for parents on subjects from discipline and homework to love and respect. "It's tough growing up from being a little kid to a teenager," says Holladay. "I noticed lots of advice books written by adults, but none by kids. So I began writing one myself." Holladay surveyed children aged 9 to 12 for more ideas for his book, which took two years to complete. Since his book was published, Holladay has been on TV and radio shows to talk about it. His best advice to parents and children: "Be flexible."

Chapter Project

Form teams and conduct your own survey of what teens want from their parents or guardians. You can use the questions from the chart on page 710 or add your own. Keep track of the age, gender, and number of people questioned and their responses. See if you can make conclusions about the attitude of teens toward their parents' communication with them. Create charts or graphs using your data and report to the class on your findings.

1968 Luis W. Alvarez wins the Nobel Prize for Physics for his discovery of resonance particles.

1994 Kim Campbell becomes Canada's first female prime minister.

1880 1890 1900 1910 1920 1930 1940 1950 1960 1970 1980 1990 2000

1963 Charles Moore takes his famous photograph for *Life* magazine, *Birmingham Riots,* during the civil rights struggle in Alabama.

1987 The African-American experience is portrayed in the photograph *Basket of Millet* by artist Elisabeth Sunday.

MODELING MATHEMATICS

A Preview of Lesson 13–1

13–1A The Pythagorean Theorem

Materials: geoboard dot paper

In this activity, you will use the Pythagorean theorem to build squares on a geoboard or dot paper.

Activity **Make a square with an area of 2 square units.**

Step 1 Start with a right triangle like the one shown below.

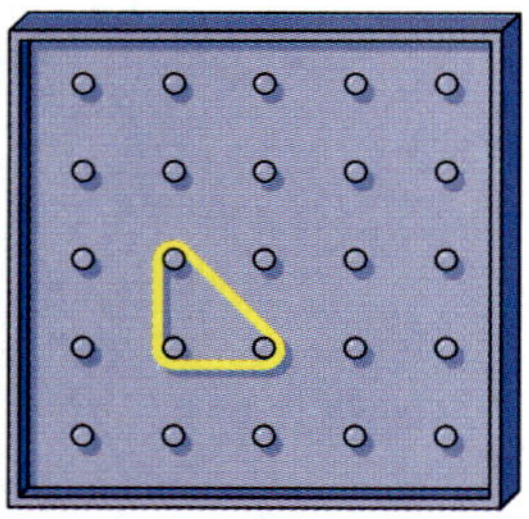

Step 2 Build squares on the two legs. Each square has an area of 1 square unit.

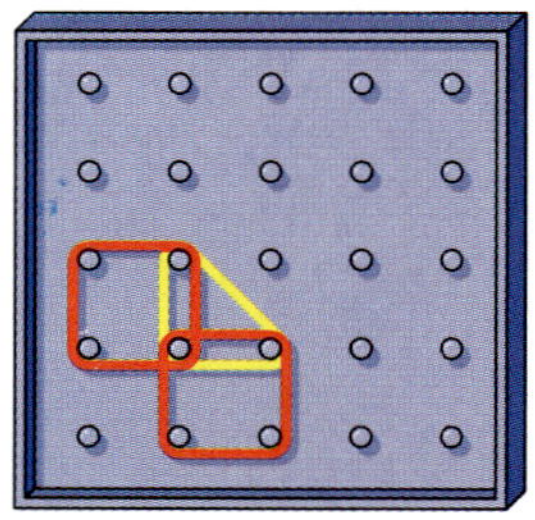

Step 3 Now build a square on the hypotenuse.

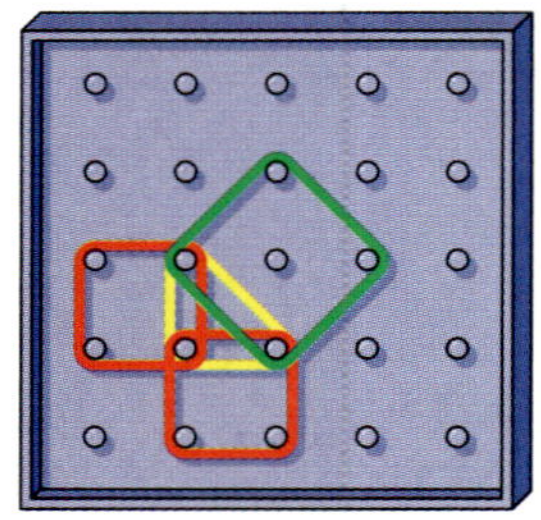

You can find the area of the square on the hypotenuse by using the Pythagorean theorem. Let c represent the measure of the hypotenuse and a and b represent the measures of the legs.

$$c^2 = a^2 + b^2$$
$$= 1^2 + 1^2 \quad \textit{Replace a with 1 and b with 1.}$$
$$= 1 + 1 \text{ or } 2$$

The area of the square on the hypotenuse is 2 square units.

Model **Build squares on each side of the triangles shown below using a geoboard or dot paper. Record the area of each square.**

1.

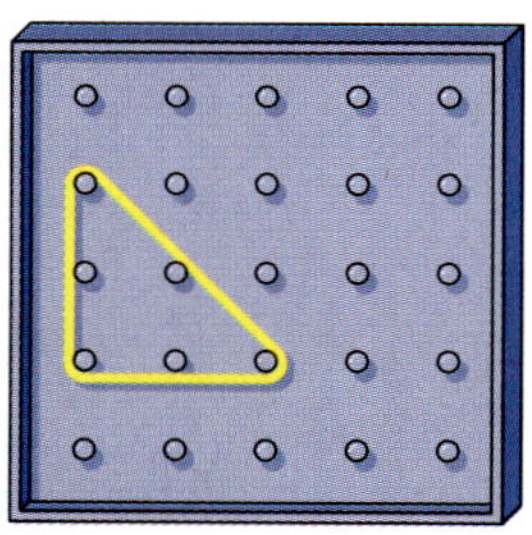

2.

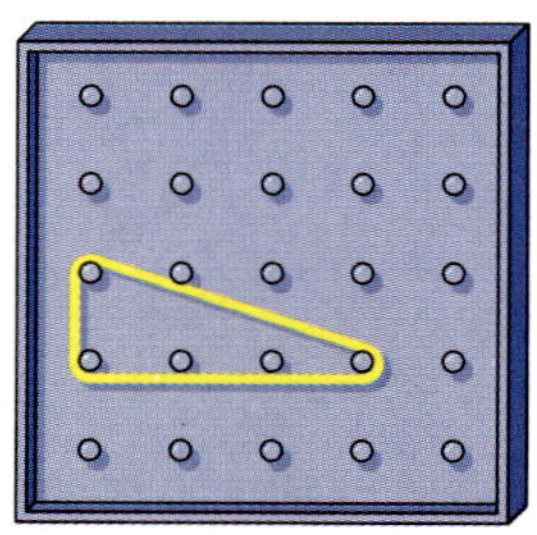

3.

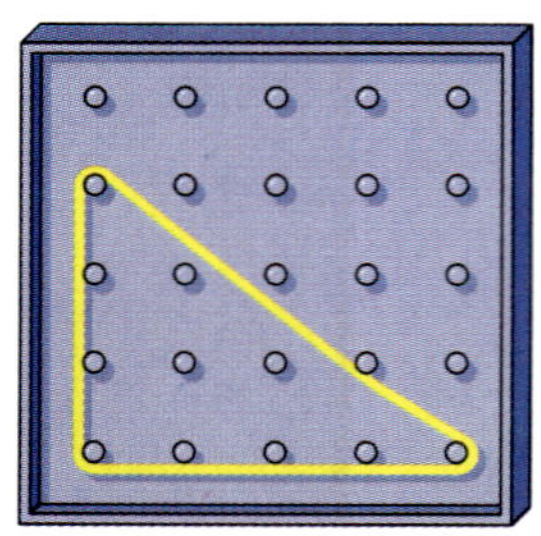

Draw **Draw a square on dot paper having each area.**

4. 4 square units
5. 9 square units
6. 8 square units
7. 13 square units
8. 17 square units
9. 32 square units

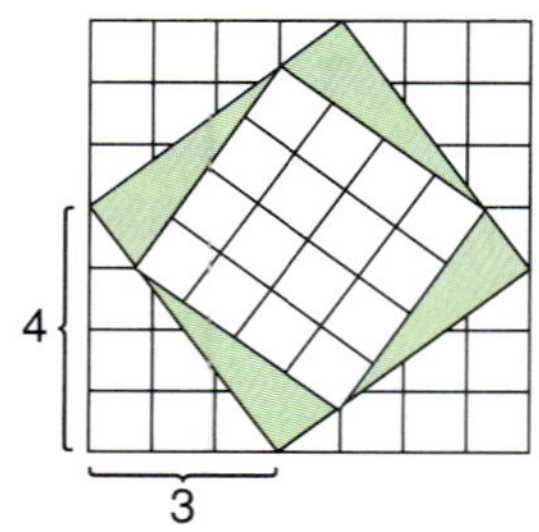

Write

10. Write a paragraph explaining how to find the total area of the shaded triangles in the drawing at the right.

13-1 Integration: Geometry
The Pythagorean Theorem

What YOU'LL LEARN

- To use the Pythagorean theorem to solve problems.

Why IT'S IMPORTANT

You can use the Pythagorean theorem to solve problems involving sailing and travel.

FYI

Nearly 700 women applied for positions on the *America*[3] team. The final crew consisted of 28 women of various backgrounds, including an areospace engineer, a body builder, and a student.

APPLICATION

Sailing

One of the most prestigious sailboat races in the world is the America's Cup. In 1995, for the first time in the 144-year history of the race, one of the sailboats, *America*[3], had an all-woman crew. Theirs was one of three U.S. boats vying for the most prized trophy in sailing.

A sailboat's *mast* and *boom* form a right angle. The sail itself, called a *mainsail*, is in the shape of a right triangle.

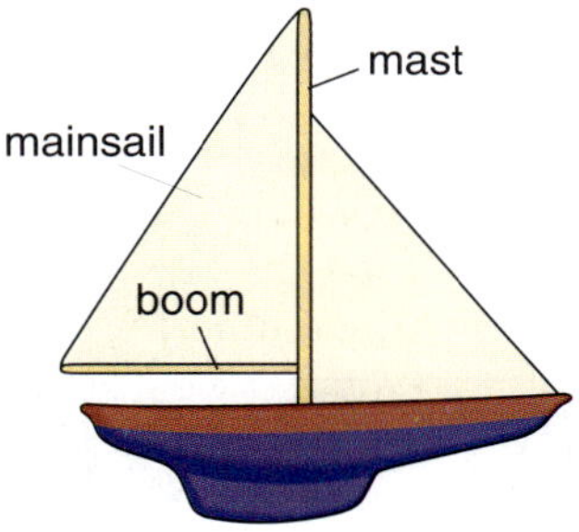

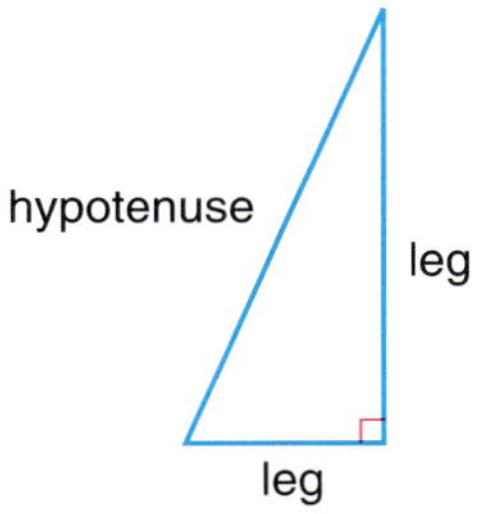

Recall that the side opposite the right angle in a right triangle is called the *hypotenuse*. This side is always the longest side of a right triangle. The other two sides are called the *legs* of the triangle.

To find the length of any side of a right triangle when the lengths of the other two are known, you can use a formula named for the Greek mathematician Pythagoras.

The Pythagorean Theorem	If a and b are the measures of the legs of a right triangle and c is the measure of the hypotenuse, then $c^2 = a^2 + b^2$.

You can use the Pythagorean theorem to find the length of the hypotenuse of a right triangle when the lengths of the legs are known.

LOOK BACK

Refer to Lesson 2-8 to review square roots.

Example 1 Find the length of the hypotenuse of a right triangle if $a = 12$ and $b = 5$.

$c^2 = a^2 + b^2$ *Pythagorean theorem*

$c^2 = 12^2 + 5^2$ *$a = 12$ and $b = 5$*

$c^2 = 144 + 25$

$c^2 = 169$

$c = \pm\sqrt{169}$

$c = \pm 13$ *Disregard -13. Why?*

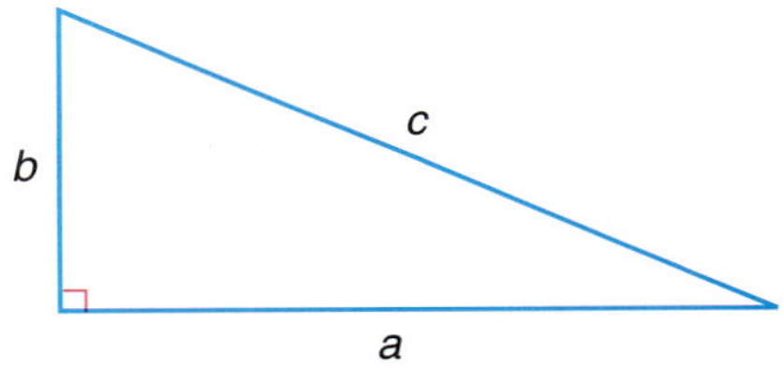

The length of the hypotenuse is 13 units.

Example 2

Find the length of side a if $b = 9$ and $c = 21$. Round to the nearest hundredth.

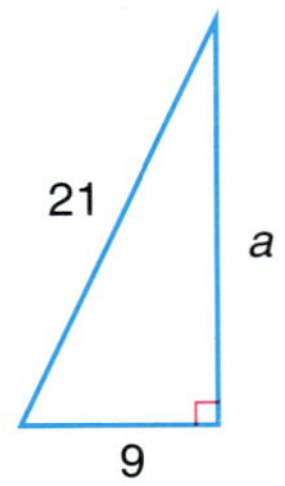

$$c^2 = a^2 + b^2 \quad \textit{Pythagorean theorem}$$
$$21^2 = a^2 + 9^2 \quad b = 9 \textit{ and } c = 21$$
$$441 = a^2 + 81$$
$$360 = a^2$$
$$\pm\sqrt{360} = a \quad \textit{Use a calculator to approximate } \sqrt{360} \textit{ to the nearest hundredth.}$$
$$18.97 \approx a \quad \textit{Only the positive value of c has meaning in this situation.}$$

The length of the leg, to the nearest hundredth, is 18.97 units.

The following corollary, based on the Pythagorean theorem, can be used to determine whether a triangle is a right triangle.

Corollary to the Pythagorean Theorem	**If c is the measure of the longest side of a triangle and $c^2 \neq a^2 + b^2$, then the triangle is not a right triangle.**

Example 3

Determine whether the following side measures would form right triangles.

a. 6, 8, 10

Since the measure of the longest side is 10, let $c = 10$, $a = 6$, and $b = 8$. Then determine whether $c^2 = a^2 + b^2$.

$$10^2 \stackrel{?}{=} 6^2 + 8^2$$
$$100 \stackrel{?}{=} 36 + 64$$
$$100 = 100 \checkmark$$

Since $c^2 = a^2 + b^2$, the triangle is a right triangle.

b. 7, 9, 12

Since the measure of the longest side is 12, let $c = 12$, $a = 7$, and $b = 9$. Then determine whether $c^2 = a^2 + b^2$.

$$12^2 \stackrel{?}{=} 7^2 + 9^2$$
$$144 \stackrel{?}{=} 49 + 81$$
$$144 \neq 130$$

Since $c^2 \neq a^2 + b^2$, the triangle is not a right triangle.

GLOBAL CONNECTIONS

One of the earliest inventions was the sail, and it was the most important means of powering boats for most of maritime history. Boats with sails appear in Egyptian rock carvings near the Nile, dating from 3300 B.C.

Example 4

APPLICATION

World Cultures

Agriculture was very important in ancient Aztec culture. Aztec farmers kept records of their farms including calculations of the dimensions and area. Because the terrain was so rough, very few of the farms were rectangular. Yet, by using measuring ropes that measured length with a unit called a *quahuitl* (about 2.5 meters), they were able to make accurate calculations. In the farm shown at the right, the farmer measured three sides of his farm. He had trouble measuring the fourth side because it was located in a dense forest. Find the measure of the fourth side.

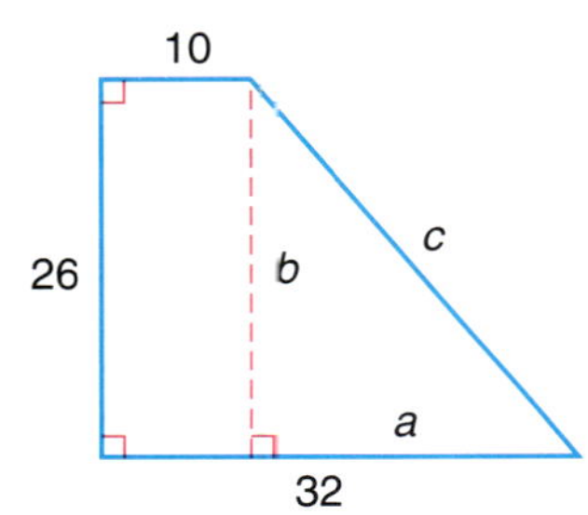

Explore Let c represent the length of the fourth side of the farm. Note that it is the hypotenuse of a right triangle.

Plan Use the Pythagorean theorem to find c. Let $a = 32 - 10$ or 22 and $b = 26$. Then solve the resulting equation.

Solve
$$c^2 = (22)^2 + (26)^2$$
$$c^2 = 484 + 676$$
$$c^2 = 1160$$
$$c \approx 34.06$$

The length of the forest side of the farm is approximately 34.06 quahuitls.

Examine Check the solution by substituting 34.06 for c in the Pythagorean theorem.
$$c^2 = a^2 + b^2$$
$$(34.06)^2 \stackrel{?}{=} (22)^2 + (26)^2$$
$$1160 = 1160 \checkmark$$

CHECK FOR UNDERSTANDING

Communicating Mathematics

Study the lesson. Then complete the following.

1. **Draw** a right triangle and label each side with a letter.
2. **Explain** how you can determine whether a triangle is a right triangle if you know the lengths of the three sides.
3. In 1955, Greece issued the stamp shown at the left to honor the 2500th anniversary of the Pythagorean School. Notice that there is a triangle bordered on each side by a checkerboard pattern.
   a. Count the number of squares along each side of the triangle.
   b. Use the Pythagorean theorem to show that it is a right triangle.
4. When taking the square root of a number, you can get a positive and a negative number. Why then, when using the Pythagorean theorem, is only the positive value used? Explain.

MODELING MATHEMATICS

5. Use a geoboard or dot paper to build squares on each side of the triangle at the right. Record the areas of the squares.

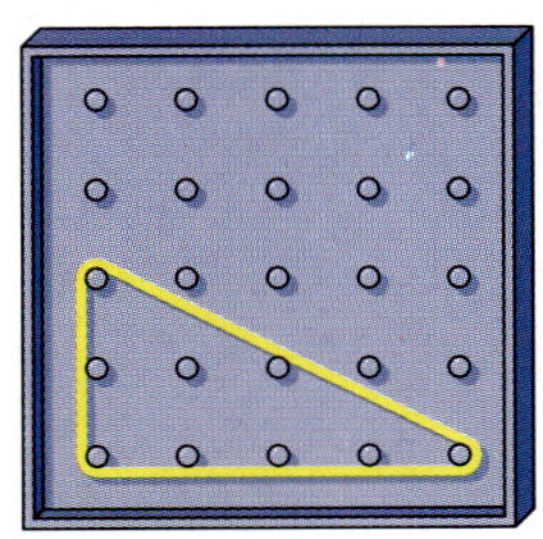

Guided Practice

Solve each equation. Assume each variable represents a positive number.

6. $5^2 + 12^2 = c^2$
7. $a^2 + 24^2 = 25^2$
8. $16^2 + b^2 = 20^2$

Find the length of each missing side. Round to the nearest hundredth.

9. 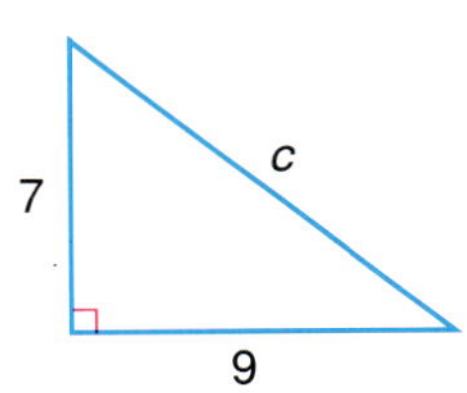

10. 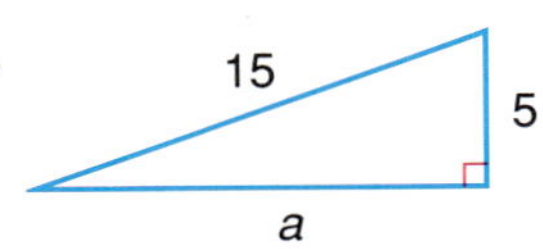

If c is the measure of the hypotenuse of a right triangle, find each missing measure. Round answers to the nearest hundredth, if necessary.

11. $a = 9, b = 12, c = ?$

12. $a = \sqrt{11}, c = 6, b = ?$

13. $b = \sqrt{30}, c = \sqrt{34}, a = ?$

14. $a = 7, b = 4, c = ?$

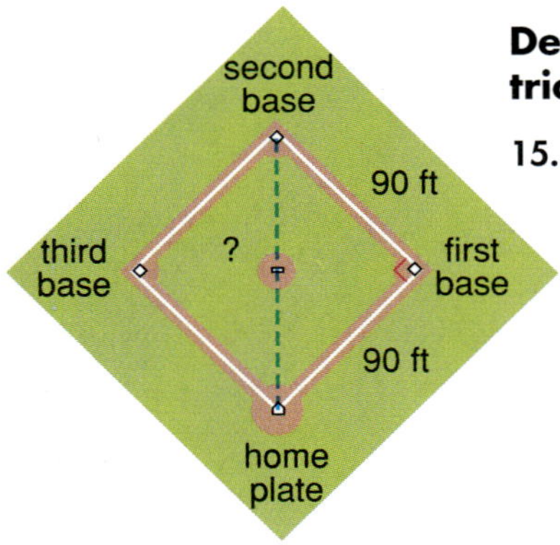

Determine whether the following side measures would form right triangles. Explain why or why not.

15. 12, 16, 20

16. 2, 8, 8

17. Baseball A baseball scout uses many different tests to determine whether or not to draft a particular player. One test for catchers is to see how quickly they can throw a ball from home plate to second base. On a baseball diamond, the distance from one base to the next is 90 feet. What is the distance from home plate to second base?

EXERCISES

Practice

Find the length of each missing side. Round to the nearest hundredth.

18.

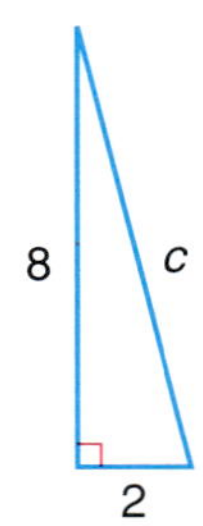

19.

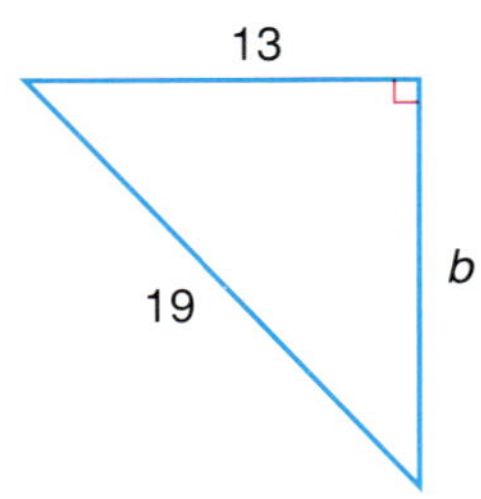

20.

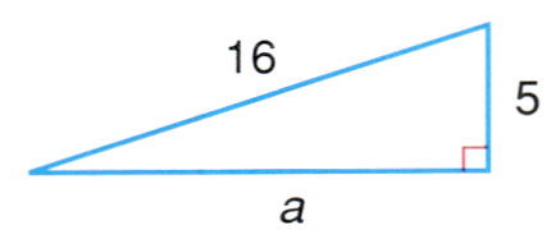

21.

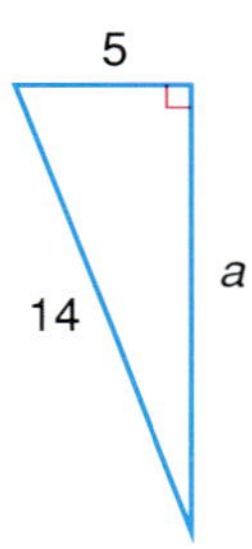

22.

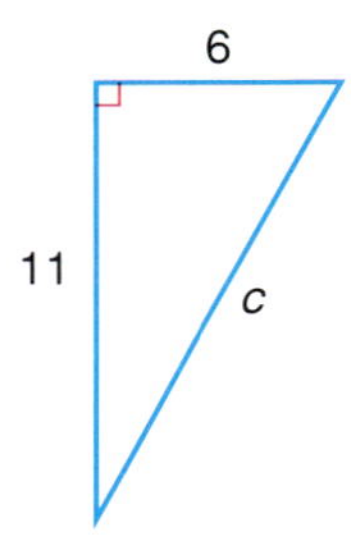

23.

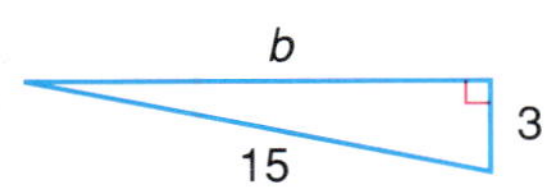

If c is the measure of the hypotenuse of a right triangle, find each missing measure. Round answers to the nearest hundredth.

24. $a = 16, b = 30, c = ?$

25. $a = 11, c = 61, b = ?$

26. $b = 13, c = \sqrt{233}, a = ?$

27. $a = \sqrt{7}, b = \sqrt{9}, c = ?$

28. $a = 6, b = 3, c = ?$

29. $b = \sqrt{77}, c = 12, a = ?$

30. $b = 10, c = 11, a = ?$

31. $a = 4, b = \sqrt{11}, c = ?$

32. $a = 15, b = \sqrt{28}, c = ?$

33. $a = 12, c = 17, b = ?$

Determine whether the following side measures would form right triangles. Explain why or why not.

34. 6, 9, 12

35. 45, 60, 75

36. 30, 40, 50

37. 11, 12, 15

38. 16, $\sqrt{32}$, 20

39. 15, $\sqrt{31}$, 16

INTEGRATION
Geometry

Use an equation to solve each problem. Round answers to the nearest hundredth.

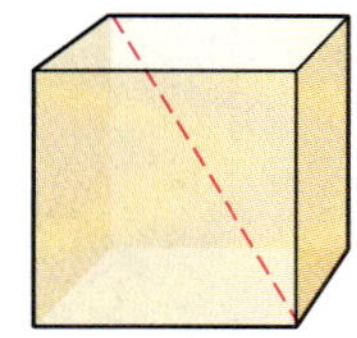

40. Find the length of the diagonal of a square if its area is 128 cm^2.

41. Find the length of the diagonal of a cube if each side of the cube is 5 inches long.

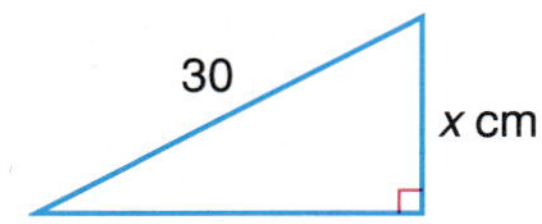

42. A right triangle has one leg that is 6 centimeters longer than the other. The hypotenuse is 30 centimeters long.
  a. Write an equation to find the length of the legs.
  b. Find the length of each leg of the triangle.

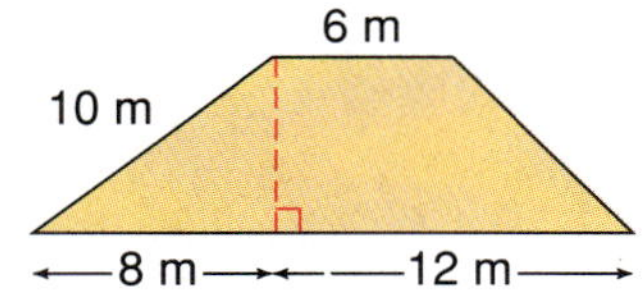

43. Look at the trapezoid at the right.
  a. Find the perimeter. (*Hint:* Drawing a second height will be helpful.)
  b. Find the area.

Programming

44. The graphing calculator program at the right calculates the hypotenuse of a right triangle and displays the right triangle being measured.

```
PROGRAM:PYTH
:FnOff
:AxesOff
:−1→Xmin
:−1→Ymin
:2→Xscl
:2→Yscl
:ClrDraw
:ClrHome
:Split
:Input "SIDE A", A
:Line (0, A, 0, 0)
:Input "SIDE B", B
:Line (B, 0, 0, 0)
:√ (A² + B²)→C
:Line (B, 0, 0, A)
:Text (1, 1,
 "HYPOTENUSE IS", C)
:Shade (0,
 (−A/B)X+A, 1, 0, B)
```

Find the hypotenuse *c* of each right triangle below, given the measures of sides *a* and *b*. Round to the nearest hundredth.

a. $a = 2, b = 7$
b. $a = 9, b = 12$
c. $a = 13, b = 15$
d. $a = 6, b = 9$
e. $a = 12, b = 16$

Critical Thinking

45. The window in Julia's attic was a square with an area of 1 square foot. After she remodeled her home, the width and height of the new attic window were the same as the original, but its area was half that of the original window. If the new window is also a square, explain how this is possible. Include a drawing.

Applications and Problem Solving

46. Sailing Refer to the application at the beginning of the lesson. If the edge of the mainsail that is attached to the mast is 100 feet long and the edge of the mainsail that is attached to the boom is 60 feet long, what is the length of the longest edge of the mainsail?

47. Construction The walls of the Downtown Recreation Center are being covered with paneling. The doorway into one room is 0.9 meters wide and 2.5 meters high. What is the length of the longest rectangular panel that can be taken through this doorway diagonally?

48. **Travel** The cruise ship M.S. Starward has a right triangle-shaped dance floor on the cabaret deck. The lengths of the two shortest sides of the dance floor are equal, and the longest side next to the stage is 36 feet long. How long is one side of the dance floor?

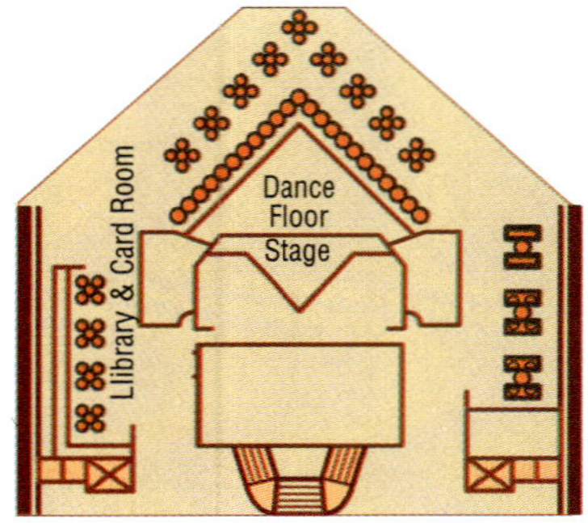

Mixed Review

49. Solve $\frac{a+2}{a} + \frac{a+5}{a} = 1$. (Lesson 12–8)

50. Find an equation of the axis of symmetry and the coordinates of the vertex of the graph of $y = x^2 - 6x + 8$. Then draw the graph. (Lesson 11–1)

51. Simplify $(4r^5)(3r^2)$. (Lesson 9–1)

52. **Number Theory** The sum of two numbers is 38. Their difference is 6. Find the numbers. (Lesson 8–3)

53. Solve $5c - 2 \geq c$. (Lesson 7–2)

54. State the slope and y-intercept of the line graphed at the right. Then write an equation of the line in slope-intercept form. (Lesson 6–4)

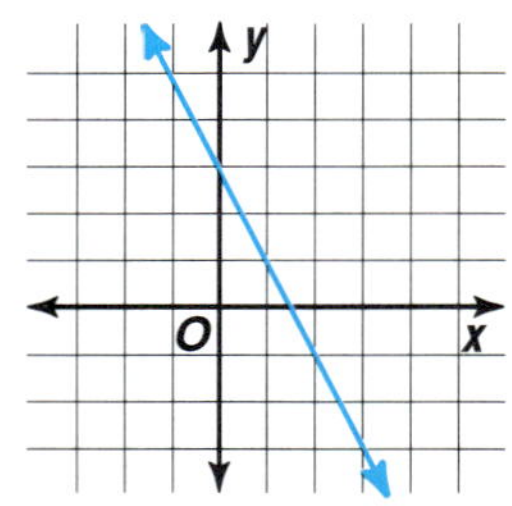

55. Given $f(x) = 2x^2 - 5x + 8$, find $f(-3)$. (Lesson 5–5)

56. Solve $-\frac{5}{6}y = 15$. (Lesson 3–2)

WORKING ON THE In·ves·ti·ga·tion

Refer to the Investigation on pages 656–657.

A Growing Concern

1 Develop a detailed plan for planting the lawn, plants, and trees for the Sanchez family's yard. Indicate the dimensions of the lawn area as well as the location of the plants and trees you selected. Mark the length of each property line on the drawing.

2 Research the plants and trees that you feel would be good specimens for the areas in which you indicated that they would be planted. Explain why you chose those plants and trees. Think about all four seasons and which plants best suit each season. Also consider the amount of sunlight each area receives during the day.

3 Calculate the cost of materials, labor, and profit margin of planting these items and laying the sprinkler system. Justify your costs and make a case for the quantity and location of the plants, trees, and lawn area in your design.

4 Be sure to add the plants, trees, and sprinkler system to your overall design.

Add the results of your work to your Investigation Folder.

13–2 Simplifying Radical Expressions

What YOU'LL LEARN

- To simplify square roots, and
- to simplify radical expressions.

Why IT'S IMPORTANT

You can use radical expressions to solve problems involving physics and racing.

CONNECTION Physics

The period of a pendulum is the time in seconds that it takes the pendulum to make one complete swing back and forth. The formula for the period P of a pendulum is $P = 2\pi\sqrt{\frac{\ell}{32}}$, where ℓ is the length of the pendulum in feet. Suppose a clock makes one "tick" after each complete swing back and forth of a 2-foot-long pendulum. How many ticks would the clock make in one minute? *This problem will be solved in Example 4.*

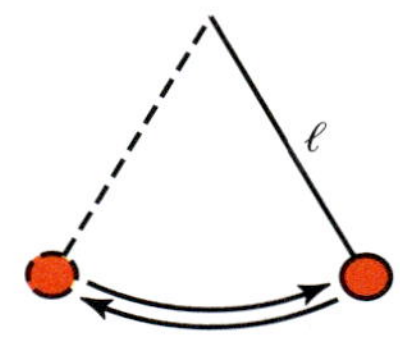

Can $2\pi\sqrt{\frac{\ell}{32}}$ be simplified? One rule used for simplifying radical expressions is that a radical expression is in *simplest form* if the **radicand,** the expression under the radical sign, contains no perfect square factors other than one. The following property can be used to simplify square roots.

Product Property of Square Roots	**For any numbers *a* and *b*, where $a \geq 0$ and $b \geq 0$, $\sqrt{ab} = \sqrt{a} \cdot \sqrt{b}$.**

The product property of square roots and prime factorization can be used to simplify radical expressions in which the radicand is not a perfect square.

Example 1 **Simplify.**

a. $\sqrt{18}$

$$\begin{aligned} \sqrt{18} &= \sqrt{3 \cdot 3 \cdot 2} && \textit{Prime factorization of 18} \\ &= \sqrt{3^2} \cdot \sqrt{2} && \textit{Product property of square roots} \\ &= 3\sqrt{2} \end{aligned}$$

b. $\sqrt{140}$

$$\begin{aligned} 140 &= \sqrt{2 \cdot 2 \cdot 5 \cdot 7} && \textit{Prime factorization of 140} \\ &= \sqrt{2^2} \cdot \sqrt{5 \cdot 7} && \textit{Product property of square roots} \\ &= 2\sqrt{35} \end{aligned}$$

When finding the principal square root of an expression containing variables, be sure that the result is not negative. Consider the expression $\sqrt{x^2}$. Its simplest form is not x since, for example, $\sqrt{(-4)^2} \neq -4$. For radical expressions like $\sqrt{x^2}$, use absolute value to ensure nonnegative results.

$\sqrt{x^2} = |x|$ $\quad \sqrt{x^3} = |x|\sqrt{x}$ $\quad \sqrt{x^4} = x^2$ $\quad \sqrt{x^5} = x^2\sqrt{x}$ $\quad \sqrt{x^6} = |x^3|$

For $\sqrt{x^3}$, absolute value is not necessary. If x were negative, then x^3 would be negative, and $\sqrt{x^3}$ would not be defined as a real number. *Why is absolute value not necessary for $\sqrt{x^4}$?*

Example 2 **Simplify $\sqrt{72x^3y^4z^5}$.**

$$\begin{aligned}\sqrt{72x^3y^4z^5} &= \sqrt{2^3 \cdot 3^2 \cdot x^3 \cdot y^4 \cdot z^5} && \textit{Prime factorization}\\ &= \sqrt{2^2} \cdot \sqrt{2} \cdot \sqrt{3^2} \cdot \sqrt{x^2} \cdot \sqrt{x} \cdot \sqrt{y^4} \cdot \sqrt{z^4} \cdot \sqrt{z} && \textit{Product property}\\ &= 2 \cdot 3 \cdot |x| \cdot y^2 \cdot z^2 \cdot \sqrt{2xz} && \textit{Simplify.}\\ &= 6|x|y^2z^2\sqrt{2xz} && \textit{The absolute value of x ensures a nonegative result.}\end{aligned}$$

The product property can also be used to multiply square roots.

Example 3 **Simplify $\sqrt{5} \cdot \sqrt{35}$.**

$$\begin{aligned}\sqrt{5} \cdot \sqrt{35} &= \sqrt{5} \cdot \sqrt{5} \cdot \sqrt{7} && \textit{Product property of square roots}\\ &= \sqrt{5^2} \cdot 7\\ &= 5\sqrt{7}\end{aligned}$$

You can use a graphing calculator to explore and analyze radical expressions.

EXPLORATION — GRAPHING CALCULATORS

The formula $Y = 91.4 - (91.4 - T)[0.478 + 0.301(\sqrt{x} - 0.02x)]$ can be used to calculate the windchill factor. In this formula, Y represents the windchill, T represents the outside Fahrenheit temperature, and x represents the wind speed in miles per hour. When a meteorologist says that the temperature is 12 degrees, but it feels like 18 degrees below zero because of the wind, you can use the formula to find how fast the wind is blowing. Set the range at [0, 40] by 2 and [−50, 40] by 5.

Enter: [Y=] 91.4 [−] [(] 91.4 [−] [ALPHA] [T] [)] [(] .478 [+] .301 [(] [2nd] [√] [X,T,θ,n] [−] .02 [X,T,θ,n] [)] [)] [ENTER] [2nd] [QUIT]

Store 12 into T by pressing 12 [STO▸] [ALPHA] [T] [ENTER]. Graph the function and trace along the graph until Y is about −18. The value of X will be about 10.2. So the wind is blowing at approximately 10 miles per hour.

Your Turn

a. Use the graph to find the wind speed if the temperature feels like −7°.

b. Enter the formula into Y1, Y2, and Y3 using different variables for T. Store three different temperatures for these variables and graph them simultaneously.

c. Analyze and compare the graphs.

CAREER CHOICES

A **meteorologist** studies the atmosphere, its physical characteristics, motions, processes, and effects on the environment.

A bachelor's degree in meteorology is required, but a graduate degree is needed for advancement.

For more information, contact:

American Meteorological Society
45 Beacon St.
Boston, MA 02108-3693

Example 4

CONNECTION
Physics

Refer to the connection at the beginning of the lesson. How many ticks would the clock make in one minute? Use 3.14 for π and round to the nearest whole number.

Explore The clock makes one "tick" after each complete swing back and forth of its 2-foot-long pendulum. The formula for the period P of a pendulum is $P = 2\pi\sqrt{\frac{\ell}{32}}$.

Plan First find P, the number of seconds it takes for the pendulum to go back and forth one time. Then find $\frac{60}{P}$, the number of times the clock's pendulum swings back and forth in one minute.

Solve

$$P = 2\pi\sqrt{\frac{\ell}{32}}$$

$$\approx 2(3.14)\sqrt{\frac{2}{32}} \quad \pi \approx 3.14,\ \ell = 2$$

$$\approx 6.28 \cdot \sqrt{\frac{1}{16}}$$

$$\approx 6.28 \cdot \frac{1}{4} \text{ or } 1.57$$

So it takes about 1.57 seconds for the pendulum to go back and forth once.

$$\frac{60}{1.57} \approx 38.22$$

Thus, the clock makes about 38 ticks per minute.

Examine Since 38.22×1.57 is about 40×1.5 or 60, the answer seems reasonable.

You can divide square roots and simplify radical expressions that involve division by using the quotient property of square roots.

Quotient Property of Square Roots	**For any numbers a and b, where $a \geq 0$ and $b > 0$, $\sqrt{\frac{a}{b}} = \frac{\sqrt{a}}{\sqrt{b}}$.**

A fraction containing radicals is in simplest form if no radicals are left in the denominator.

Example 5

a. Simplify $\frac{\sqrt{56}}{\sqrt{7}}$ and $\sqrt{\frac{34}{25}}$.

b. Compare the expressions using <, >, or =.

a. $\frac{\sqrt{56}}{\sqrt{7}} = \sqrt{\frac{56}{7}}$ *Quotient property of square roots*

$$= \sqrt{8}$$

$$= \sqrt{4} \cdot \sqrt{2}$$

$$= 2\sqrt{2}$$

$$\sqrt{\frac{34}{25}} = \frac{\sqrt{34}}{\sqrt{25}}$$

$$= \frac{\sqrt{34}}{5}$$

FYI

The world's largest pendulum clock is in Tokyo, Japan. It is part of a water-mill clock and is 73 feet 9.75 inches long.

b. You can compare these expressions by estimating their values and then using a scientific calculator to find approximations for each simplified expression.

Estimate: *$2\sqrt{2} \rightarrow$ Since 2 is a little more than 1, $2\sqrt{2}$ will be a little more than 2.*

$\frac{\sqrt{34}}{5} \rightarrow \frac{\sqrt{36}}{5} = \frac{6}{5}$ This will be a little more than 1. So, $2\sqrt{2} > \frac{\sqrt{34}}{5}$.

Verify by using a calculator.

Enter: 2 [X] 2 [√x] [=] 2.828427125

Enter: 34 [√x] [÷] 5 [=] 1.166190379

Since 2.8 > 1.2, then $\frac{\sqrt{56}}{\sqrt{7}} > \sqrt{\frac{34}{25}}$.

PEANUTS®

In the cartoon above, Woodstock simplified the radical expression by **rationalizing the denominator.** This method may be used to remove or eliminate radicals from the denominator of a fraction.

Example 6 **Simplify.**

a. $\frac{\sqrt{5}}{\sqrt{3}}$

$$\frac{\sqrt{5}}{\sqrt{3}} = \frac{\sqrt{5}}{\sqrt{3}} \cdot \frac{\sqrt{3}}{\sqrt{3}} \quad \textit{Note that } \frac{\sqrt{3}}{\sqrt{3}} = 1.$$

$$= \frac{\sqrt{15}}{3}$$

b. $\frac{\sqrt{7}}{\sqrt{12}}$

$$\frac{\sqrt{7}}{\sqrt{12}} = \frac{\sqrt{7}}{\sqrt{2 \cdot 2 \cdot 3}}$$

$$= \frac{\sqrt{7}}{\sqrt{2 \cdot 2 \cdot 3}} \cdot \frac{\sqrt{3}}{\sqrt{3}}$$

$$= \frac{\sqrt{7}\sqrt{3}}{2 \cdot 3}$$

$$= \frac{\sqrt{21}}{6}$$

Binomials of the form $a\sqrt{b} + c\sqrt{d}$ and $a\sqrt{b} - c\sqrt{d}$ are called **conjugates** of each other. For example, $6 + \sqrt{2}$ and $6 - \sqrt{2}$ are conjugates. Conjugates are useful when simplifying radical expressions because their product is always a rational number with no radicals.

$$(6 + \sqrt{2})(6 - \sqrt{2}) = 6^2 - (\sqrt{2})^2$$
$$= 36 - 2$$
$$= 34$$

Use the pattern $(a - b)(a + b) = a^2 - b^2$ to simplify the product.

This is true because of the following.

$$(\sqrt{2})^2 = \sqrt{2} \cdot \sqrt{2}$$
$$= \sqrt{2 \cdot 2}$$
$$= \sqrt{2^2} \text{ or } 2$$

Conjugates are often used to rationalize the denominators of fractions containing square roots.

Example 7 **Simplify $\frac{4}{4-\sqrt{3}}$.**

To rationalize the denominator, multiply both the numerator and denominator by $4+\sqrt{3}$, which is the conjugate of $4-\sqrt{3}$.

$$\frac{4}{4-\sqrt{3}} = \frac{4}{4-\sqrt{3}} \cdot \frac{4+\sqrt{3}}{4+\sqrt{3}}$$ *Notice that $\frac{4+\sqrt{3}}{4+\sqrt{3}} = 1$.*

$$= \frac{4(4)+4\sqrt{3}}{4^2-\left(\sqrt{3}\right)^2}$$ *Use the distributive property to multiply numerators. Use the pattern $(a-b)(a+b) = a^2 - b^2$ to multiply denominators.*

$$= \frac{16+4\sqrt{3}}{16-3}$$

$$= \frac{16+4\sqrt{3}}{13}$$

When simplifying radical expressions, check the following conditions to determine if the expression is in simplest form.

Simplest Radical Form	**A radical expression is in simplest form when the following three conditions have been met.** **1. No radicands have perfect square factors other than 1.** **2. No radicands contain fractions.** **3. No radicals appear in the denominator of a fraction.**

CHECK FOR UNDERSTANDING

Communicating Mathematics

Study the lesson. Then complete the following.

1. **Explain** why absolute values are sometimes needed when simplifying radical expressions containing variables.
2. **Describe** the steps you take to rationalize a denominator.
3. **You Decide** Niara showed the following equations to her friend Melanie and said, "I know that 6 can't equal 10, but all these steps make sense!" Melanie said, "One of the steps must be wrong." Who is correct? Can you explain the mistake?

$-60 = -60$	*Reflexive property of equality*
$36 - 96 = 100 - 160$	*Rewrite −60 as 36 − 96 and 100 − 160.*
$36 - 96 + 64 = 100 - 160 + 64$	*Add 64 to each side.*
$(6-8)^2 = (10-8)^2$	*Factor.*
$6 - 8 = 10 - 8$	*Take the square root of each side.*
$6 - 8 + 8 = 10 - 8 + 8$	*Add 8 to each side.*
$6 = 10$	*Simplify.*

MATH JOURNAL

4. Refer to the cartoon on page 722. Obviously, Woodstock realized that rationalizing the denominator is important. What are other steps that you may have to use to simplify a radical expression?

Guided Practice

State the conjugate of each expression. Then multiply the expression by its conjugate.

5. $5 + \sqrt{2}$
6. $\sqrt{3} - \sqrt{7}$

State the fraction by which each expression should be multiplied to rationalize the denominator.

7. $\frac{4}{\sqrt{7}}$
8. $\frac{2\sqrt{5}}{4 - \sqrt{3}}$

Simplify. Leave in radical form and use absolute value symbols when necessary.

9. $\sqrt{18}$
10. $\frac{\sqrt{20}}{\sqrt{5}}$
11. $\sqrt{\frac{3}{7}}$
12. $\sqrt{\frac{2}{3}} \cdot \sqrt{\frac{5}{2}}$
13. $(\sqrt{2} + 4)(\sqrt{2} + 6)$
14. $(y - \sqrt{5})(y + \sqrt{5})$
15. $\frac{6}{3 - \sqrt{2}}$
16. $\sqrt{80a^2b^3}$

Compare each pair of expressions using <, >, or =.

17. $4\sqrt{3} \cdot \sqrt{3}, \sqrt{48} + \sqrt{8}$
18. $\sqrt{\frac{12}{7}}, \frac{\sqrt{18} \cdot \sqrt{2}}{\sqrt{7} \cdot \sqrt{3}}$

19. **Water Supply** There is a relationship between a city's capacity to supply water to its citizens and the city's size. Suppose a city has a population P (in thousands). Then the number of gallons per minute that are required to assure water adequacy is given by the expression $1020\sqrt{P}(1 - 0.01\sqrt{P})$. If a city has a population of 55,000 people, how many gallons per minute must the city's pumping stations be able to supply?

EXERCISES

Practice

Simplify. Leave in radical form and use absolute value symbols when necessary.

20. $\sqrt{75}$
21. $\sqrt{80}$
22. $\sqrt{280}$
23. $\sqrt{500}$
24. $\frac{\sqrt{7}}{\sqrt{3}}$
25. $\frac{\sqrt{5}}{\sqrt{10}}$
26. $\sqrt{\frac{2}{7}}$
27. $\sqrt{\frac{11}{32}}$
28. $5\sqrt{10} \cdot 3\sqrt{10}$
29. $7\sqrt{30} \cdot 2\sqrt{6}$
30. $\sqrt{\frac{3}{5}} \cdot \sqrt{\frac{7}{3}}$
31. $\sqrt{\frac{1}{6}} \cdot \sqrt{\frac{6}{11}}$
32. $\sqrt{40b^4}$
33. $\sqrt{54a^2b^2}$
34. $\sqrt{60m^2y^4}$
35. $\sqrt{147x^5y^7}$
36. $\sqrt{\frac{t}{8}}$
37. $\sqrt{\frac{27}{p^2}}$
38. $\sqrt{\frac{5n^5}{4m^5}}$
39. $\frac{\sqrt{9x^5y}}{\sqrt{12x^2y^6}}$
40. $(1 + 2\sqrt{5})^2$
41. $(y - \sqrt{7})^2$
42. $(\sqrt{m} + \sqrt{20})^2$
43. $\frac{14}{\sqrt{8} - \sqrt{5}}$
44. $\frac{9a}{6 + \sqrt{a}}$
45. $\frac{2\sqrt{5}}{-4 + \sqrt{8}}$
46. $\frac{3\sqrt{7}}{5\sqrt{3} + 3\sqrt{5}}$
47. $\frac{\sqrt{c} - \sqrt{d}}{\sqrt{c} + \sqrt{d}}$
48. $(\sqrt{2x} - \sqrt{6})(\sqrt{2x} + \sqrt{6})$
49. $(x - 4\sqrt{3})(x - \sqrt{3})$

Compare each pair of expressions using <, >, or =.

50. $\sqrt{\frac{8}{9}} \cdot \frac{2}{\sqrt{8}}, \frac{2}{\sqrt{51}} \cdot \sqrt{\frac{17}{3}}$

51. $\sqrt{10} \cdot \sqrt{30}, \frac{10}{\sqrt{5}+9}$

52. $\frac{2}{\sqrt{6}-\sqrt{5}}, \frac{20}{6+\sqrt{3}}$

53. $\frac{3\sqrt{2}-\sqrt{7}}{2\sqrt{3}-5\sqrt{2}}, \frac{4\sqrt{5}-3\sqrt{7}}{\sqrt{6}}$

Critical Thinking

54. Determine whether $\sqrt{a \cdot b} = \sqrt{a} \cdot \sqrt{b}$ is true for negative real numbers. Give examples or counterexamples to support your answer.

Applications and Problem Solving

55. **Racing** In yacht racing from 1958 to 1987, 12-meter boats were not really 12 meters long, but the formula that governed their design contained numbers that equaled 12. In the expression $\frac{\sqrt{S}+L-F}{2.37}$, S is the area of the sails, L is the waterline length, and F is the distance from the deck of the boat to the waterline. The result must be less than or equal to 12 for a boat to be classified as a 12-meter boat. Determine if a boat for which $S = 158$ m^2, $L = 17.5$ m, and $F = 2$ m could be classified as a 12-meter boat.

56. **Electricity** The voltage V required for a circuit is given by $V = \sqrt{PR}$ where P is the power in watts and R is the resistance in ohms. Find the volts needed to light a 75-watt bulb with a resistance of 110 ohms.

Mixed Review

57. **Geometry** Find the length of the missing side of the triangle shown at the right. Round to the nearest hundredth. (Lesson 13–1)

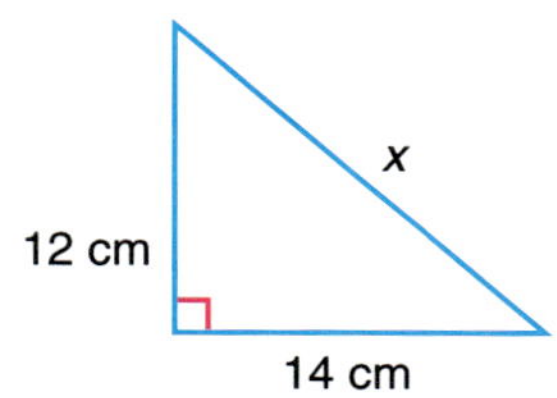

58. Simplify $\frac{2a^2+11a-6}{a^2-2a-48}$. State the excluded values of a. (Lesson 12–1)

59. Solve $3x^2 - 5x + 2 = 0$ by using the quadratic formula. (Lesson 11–3)

60. Factor $12a^2b^3 - 28ab^2c^2$. (Lesson 10–2)

61. **Forests** The largest forested areas in the world are located in northern Russia. They cover 2,700,000,000 acres, and they make up 25% of the world's forests. Express the number of acres in scientific notation. (Lesson 9–3)

62. Solve $4 - 2.3t < 17.8$. (Lesson 7–3)

63. **Geometry** Write an equation of the line that is perpendicular to the graph of $y = -5x + 2$ and passes through the point at (0, 6). (Lesson 6–6)

64. Express the relation shown in the graph at the right as a set of ordered pairs. Then state the domain and range of the relation. (Lesson 5–2)

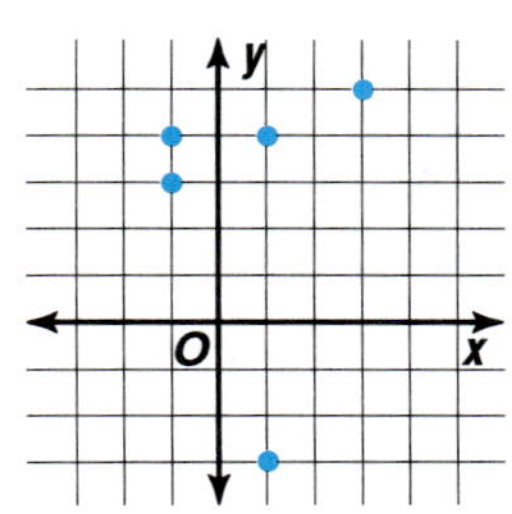

65. Solve $6(x + 3) = 3x$. (Lesson 3–5)

66. Write an algebraic expression for the verbal expression *one-fourth the square of a number.* (Lesson 1–1)

13–2B Graphing Technology
Simplifying Radical Expressions

An Extension of Lesson 13–2

The built-in square root feature of a graphing calculator allows us to simplify and approximate values of expressions containing radicals. In addition to obtaining approximate values for expressions, this feature is also useful for checking algebraic computations.

Example **Simplify each expression algebraically. Then check with a graphing calculator.**

a. $\sqrt{\frac{3}{5}}$

$$\sqrt{\frac{3}{5}} = \sqrt{\frac{3}{5}} \cdot \frac{\sqrt{5}}{\sqrt{5}}$$
$$= \frac{\sqrt{3 \cdot 5}}{5} \text{ or } \frac{\sqrt{15}}{5}$$

Verify with the calculator.

Enter: [2nd] [√] [(] 3 [÷] 5 [)]
[ENTER] .7745966692
[2nd] [√] 15 [÷] 5
[ENTER] .7745966692

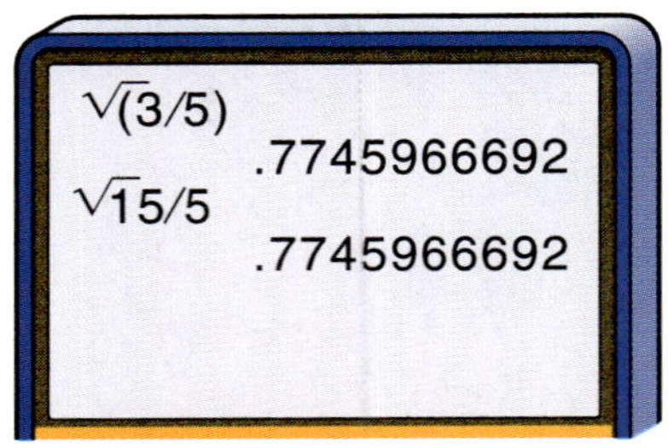

b. $\frac{1}{\sqrt{2} - 3}$

$$\frac{1}{\sqrt{2} - 3} = \frac{1}{\sqrt{2} - 3} \cdot \frac{\sqrt{2} + 3}{\sqrt{2} + 3}$$
$$= \frac{\sqrt{2} + 3}{\left(\sqrt{2}\right)^2 - 3^2} \text{ or } \frac{\sqrt{2} + 3}{-7}$$

Verify with the calculator.

Enter: 1 [÷] [(] [2nd] [√] 2 [−]
3 [)] [ENTER] −.6306019375
[(] [2nd] [√] 2 [+] 3 [)]
[÷] [(−)] 7 [ENTER]
−.6306019375

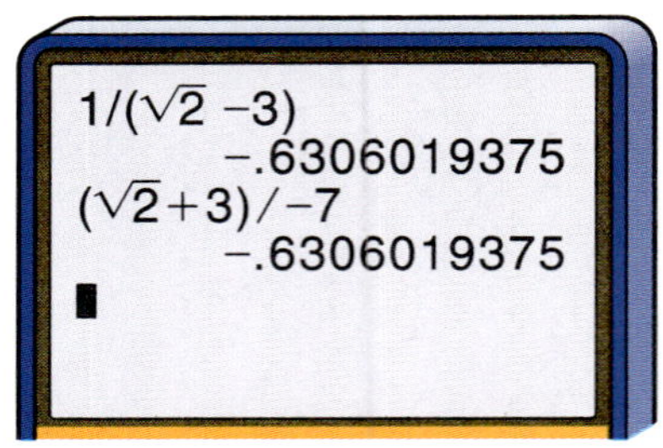

EXERCISES

Simplify each expression. Then check with a graphing calculator. Round answers to the nearest hundredth.

1. $\sqrt{1372}$
2. $\sqrt{32} \cdot \sqrt{12}$
3. $\sqrt{2}(\sqrt{6} + 3)$
4. $\sqrt{\frac{5}{6}}$
5. $\frac{4}{\sqrt{7}}$
6. $\frac{2}{\sqrt{11} + 8}$
7. $\sqrt{12} + \sqrt{3}$
8. $\frac{4}{5}\sqrt{2} + \frac{3}{5}\sqrt{2}$
9. $\frac{\sqrt{3}}{2} - \frac{\sqrt{5}}{3} + \sqrt{18}$
10. $\sqrt{18} + \sqrt{108} + \sqrt{50}$
11. $\sqrt{\frac{2}{3}} + \frac{\sqrt{6}}{3} - 6\sqrt{6}$

13–3 Operations with Radical Expressions

What YOU'LL LEARN

- To simplify radical expressions involving addition, subtraction, and multiplication.

Why IT'S IMPORTANT

You can use radical expressions to solve problems involving travel and construction.

Top Five List

Largest Passenger Ships in the World (gross tonnage)

1. *Norway, 76,049*
2. *Majesty of the Seas, 73,937*
2. *Monarch of the Seas, 73,937*
4. *Sovereign of the Seas, 73,192*
5. *Sensation, 70,367*
5. *Ecstasy, 70,367*
5. *Fantasy, 70,367*

APPLICATION

Travel

The Norway cruise ship is the largest passenger ship in the Caribbean. Suppose the captain of the ship is on the star deck, which is 48 feet above the pool deck. The pool deck is 72 feet above the water. The captain sees the next island, but the passengers on the pool deck cannot. The equation $d = \sqrt{\frac{3h}{2}}$ represents the distance d in miles a person h feet high can see. So, $\sqrt{\frac{3(120)}{2}} - \sqrt{\frac{3(72)}{2}}$ describes how much farther the captain can see than the passengers. *You will find the value of this expression in Example 3.*

Radical expressions in which the radicands are alike can be added or subtracted in the same way that monomials are added or subtracted.

Monomials	**Radical Expressions**
$4x + 5x = (4 + 5)x$	$4\sqrt{5} + 5\sqrt{5} = (4 + 5)\sqrt{5}$
$= 9x$	$= 9\sqrt{5}$
$18y - 7y = (18 - 7)y$	$18\sqrt{2} - 7\sqrt{2} = (18 - 7)\sqrt{2}$
$= 11y$	$= 11\sqrt{2}$

Notice that the distributive property was used to simplify each radical expression.

Example 1 **Simplify each expression.**

a. $\mathbf{6\sqrt{7} + 5\sqrt{7} - 3\sqrt{7}}$

$$\begin{aligned} 6\sqrt{7} + 5\sqrt{7} - 3\sqrt{7} &= (6 + 5 - 3)\sqrt{7} \\ &= 8\sqrt{7} \end{aligned}$$

b. $\mathbf{5\sqrt{6} + 3\sqrt{7} + 4\sqrt{7} - 2\sqrt{6}}$

$$\begin{aligned} 5\sqrt{6} + 3\sqrt{7} + 4\sqrt{7} - 2\sqrt{6} &= 5\sqrt{6} - 2\sqrt{6} + 3\sqrt{7} + 4\sqrt{7} \\ &= (5 - 2)\sqrt{6} + (3 + 4)\sqrt{7} \\ &= 3\sqrt{6} + 7\sqrt{7} \end{aligned}$$

In Example 1b, the expression $3\sqrt{6} + 7\sqrt{7}$ cannot be simplified further because the radicands are different. There are no common factors, and each radicand is in simplest form.

If the radicals in a radical expression are not in simplest form, simplify them first. Then use the distributive property wherever possible to further simplify the expression.

Example 2 **Simplify $4\sqrt{27} + 5\sqrt{12} + 8\sqrt{75}$. Then use a scientific calculator to verify your answer.**

$$\begin{aligned} 4\sqrt{27} + 5\sqrt{12} + 8\sqrt{75} &= 4\sqrt{3^2 \cdot 3} + 5\sqrt{2^2 \cdot 3} + 8\sqrt{5^2 \cdot 3} \\ &= 4(\sqrt{3^2} \cdot \sqrt{3}) + 5(\sqrt{2^2} \cdot \sqrt{3}) + 8(\sqrt{5^2} \cdot \sqrt{3}) \\ &= 4(3\sqrt{3}) + 5(2\sqrt{3}) + 8(5\sqrt{3}) \\ &= 12\sqrt{3} + 10\sqrt{3} + 40\sqrt{3} \\ &= 62\sqrt{3} \end{aligned}$$

The exact answer is $62\sqrt{3}$. Now, use a calculator to verify.

First, find a decimal approximation for the original expression.

Enter: 4 [×] 27 [√x] [+] 5 [×] 12 [√x] [+] 8 [×] 75 [√x] [=] 107.3871501

Next, find a decimal approximation for the simplified expression.

Enter: 62 [×] 3 [√x] [=] 107.3871501

Since the approximations are equal, the results have been verified.

Example 3

APPLICATION

Travel

Refer to the application at the beginning of the lesson. How much farther is the captain able to see than the passengers on the pool deck?

$$\begin{aligned} d &= \sqrt{\frac{3(120)}{2}} - \sqrt{\frac{3(72)}{2}} \\ &= \sqrt{\frac{360}{2}} - \sqrt{\frac{216}{2}} \\ &= \sqrt{180} - \sqrt{108} \\ &= \sqrt{6^2 \cdot 5} - \sqrt{6^2 \cdot 3} \\ &= 6\sqrt{5} - 6\sqrt{3} \\ &\approx 3.02 \end{aligned}$$

The captain can see about 3 miles farther.

In the last lesson, you multiplied conjugates and expressions with like radicands. Multiplying two radical expressions with different radicands is similar to multiplying two binomials.

Example 4 **Simplify $(2\sqrt{3} - \sqrt{5})(\sqrt{10} + 4\sqrt{6})$.**

> **LOOK BACK**
> Refer to Lesson 9-7 to review multiplying polynomials.

$(2\sqrt{3} - \sqrt{5})(\sqrt{10} + 4\sqrt{6})$

$$= \underbrace{(2\sqrt{3})(\sqrt{10})}_{\text{First terms}} + \underbrace{(2\sqrt{3})(4\sqrt{6})}_{\text{Outer terms}} + \underbrace{(-\sqrt{5})(\sqrt{10})}_{\text{Inner terms}} + \underbrace{(-\sqrt{5})(4\sqrt{6})}_{\text{Last terms}}$$

$= 2\sqrt{30} + 8\sqrt{18} - \sqrt{50} - 4\sqrt{30}$ *Multiply.*

$= 2\sqrt{30} + 24\sqrt{2} - 5\sqrt{2} - 4\sqrt{30}$ *Simplify each term.*

$= -2\sqrt{30} + 19\sqrt{2}$ *Combine like terms.*

CHECK FOR UNDERSTANDING

Communicating Mathematics

Study the lesson. Then complete the following.

1. **Write** three radical expressions that have the same radicand.
2. **Explain** why you should simplify each radical in a radical expression before adding or subtracting.
3. **Explain** why $\sqrt{x} + \sqrt{y} \neq \sqrt{x + y}$. Give an example using numbers.

MATH JOURNAL

4. Explain how you use the distributive property to simplify like radicands that are added or subtracted.

Guided Practice

Name the expressions in each group that will have the same radicand after each expression is written in simplest form.

5. $3\sqrt{5}, 5\sqrt{6}, 3\sqrt{20}$
6. $-5\sqrt{7}, 2\sqrt{28}, 6\sqrt{14}$
7. $\sqrt{24}, \sqrt{12}, \sqrt{18}, \sqrt{28}$
8. $9\sqrt{32}, 2\sqrt{50}, \sqrt{48}, 3\sqrt{200}$

Simplify.

9. $3\sqrt{6} + 10\sqrt{6}$
10. $2\sqrt{5} - 5\sqrt{2}$
11. $8\sqrt{7x} + 4\sqrt{7x}$

Simplify. Then use a calculator to verify your answer.

12. $8\sqrt{5} + 3\sqrt{5}$
13. $8\sqrt{3} - 2\sqrt{2} + 3\sqrt{2} + 5\sqrt{3}$
14. $2\sqrt{3} + \sqrt{12}$
15. $\sqrt{7} + \sqrt{\frac{1}{7}}$

Simplify.

16. $\sqrt{2}(\sqrt{18} + 4\sqrt{3})$
17. $(4 + \sqrt{5})(4 - \sqrt{5})$
18. **Geometry** Find the exact measures of the perimeter and area in simplest form for the rectangle at the right.

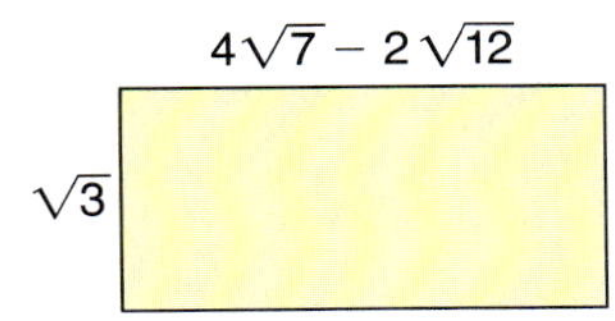

EXERCISES

Practice

Simplify.

19. $25\sqrt{13} + \sqrt{13}$
20. $7\sqrt{2} - 15\sqrt{2} + 8\sqrt{2}$
21. $2\sqrt{6} - 8\sqrt{3}$
22. $2\sqrt{11} - 6\sqrt{11} - 3\sqrt{11}$
23. $18\sqrt{2x} + 3\sqrt{2x}$
24. $3\sqrt{5m} - 5\sqrt{5m}$

Simplify. Then use a calculator to verify your answer.

25. $4\sqrt{3} + 7\sqrt{3} - 2\sqrt{3}$
26. $5\sqrt{5} + 3\sqrt{5} - 18\sqrt{5}$
27. $\sqrt{6} + 2\sqrt{2} + \sqrt{10}$
28. $4\sqrt{6} + \sqrt{7} - 6\sqrt{2} + 4\sqrt{7}$
29. $3\sqrt{7} - 2\sqrt{28}$
30. $2\sqrt{50} - 3\sqrt{32}$
31. $3\sqrt{27} + 5\sqrt{48}$
32. $2\sqrt{20} - 3\sqrt{24} - \sqrt{180}$
33. $\sqrt{80} + \sqrt{98} + \sqrt{128}$
34. $\sqrt{10} - \sqrt{\frac{2}{5}}$
35. $3\sqrt{3} - \sqrt{45} + 3\sqrt{\frac{1}{3}}$
36. $6\sqrt{\frac{7}{4}} + 3\sqrt{28} - 10\sqrt{\frac{1}{7}}$

Simplify.

37. $\sqrt{5}(2\sqrt{10} + 3\sqrt{2})$
38. $\sqrt{6}(\sqrt{3} + 5\sqrt{2})$
39. $(2\sqrt{10} + 3\sqrt{15})(3\sqrt{3} - 2\sqrt{2})$
40. $(\sqrt{5} - \sqrt{2})(\sqrt{14} + \sqrt{35})$
41. $(\sqrt{6} + \sqrt{8})(\sqrt{24} + \sqrt{2})$
42. $(5\sqrt{2} + 3\sqrt{5})(2\sqrt{10} - 3)$

Critical Thinking

43. Explain why the simplified form of $\sqrt{(x-5)^2}$ must have an absolute value sign, but $\sqrt{(x-5)^4}$ does not need one.

Applications and Problem Solving

44. **Construction** *Slip forming* is the fastest method of erecting tall concrete buildings. With this method, the 1815-foot CN Tower in Toronto, Canada, was built at an average speed of 20 feet per day. At the beginning of the week, construction workers were 530 feet above the ground. After one week of construction, they were 670 feet above the ground. How many more miles could they see from the top of the building at the end of the week than at the beginning? Write your answer in exact form and as an approximation to the nearest hundredth. (*Hint:* Use the formula from the application at the beginning of the lesson.)

45. **Construction** A wire is stretched from the top of a 12-foot pole to a stake in the ground and then to the base of the pole. If a total of 20 feet of wire is needed, how far is the stake from the pole? (*Hint:* In the figure, $a + b = 20$.)

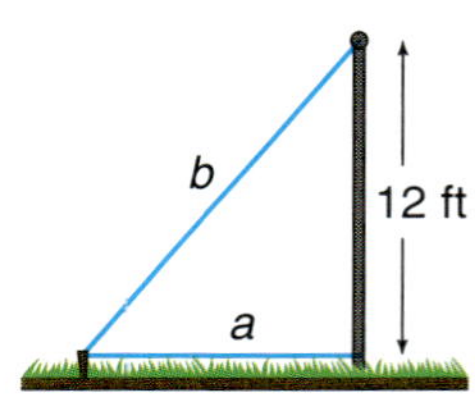

Mixed Review

46. Simplify $\frac{\sqrt{3}}{\sqrt{6}}$. (Lesson 13–2)

47. Find $\frac{x^2 - y^2}{3} \cdot \frac{9}{x + y}$. (Lesson 12–2)

48. Factor $3a^2 + 19a - 14$. (Lesson 10–3)

49. Find the degree of $16s^3t^2 + 3s^2t + 7s^6t$. (Lesson 9–4)

50. **Statistics** Tim's scores on the first four of five 50-point quizzes were 47, 45, 48, and 45. What score must he receive on the fifth quiz to have an average of at least 46 points for all the quizzes? (Lesson 7–3)

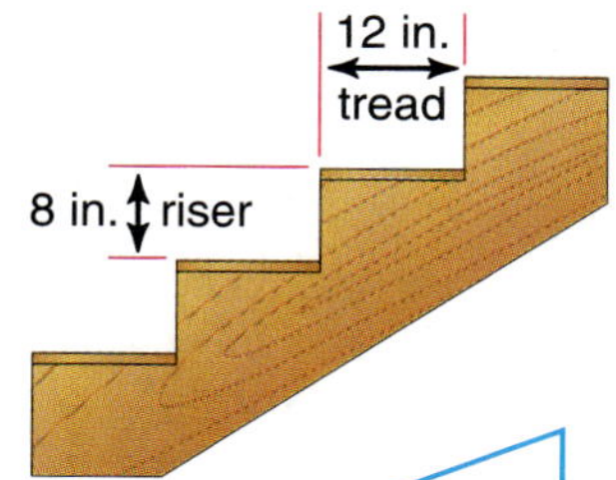

51. **Carpentry** When building a stairway, a carpenter considers the ratio of riser to tread. Write a ratio to describe the steepness of the stairs. (Lesson 6–1)

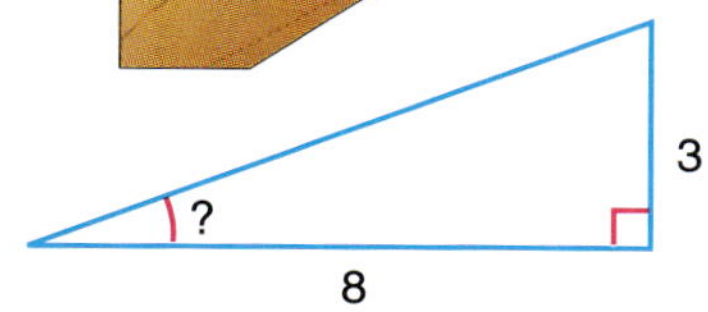

52. **Geometry** Find the measure of the marked acute angle to the nearest degree. (Lesson 4–3)

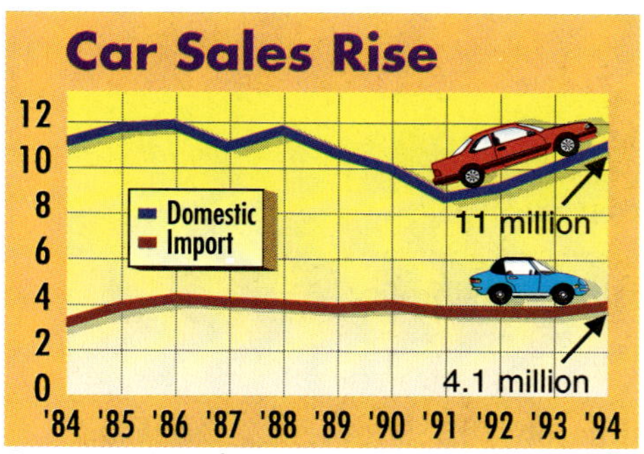

Source: Autodata

53. **Interpret Graphs** The graph at the left compares domestic and import brand auto sales from 1984 to 1994. (Lesson 1–9)
   a. During the ten-year period, when were domestic car sales the lowest? How many domestic cars were sold during that year?
   b. In 1990, how many more domestic cars were sold than imports?

SELF TEST

If c is the measure of the hypotenuse of a right triangle, find each missing measure. Round answers to the nearest hundredth. (Lesson 13–1)

1. $a = 21, b = 28, c = ?$
2. $a = \sqrt{41}, c = 8, b = ?$
3. $b = 28, c = 54, a = ?$

Simplify. Leave in radical form and use absolute value symbols when necessary. (Lesson 13–2)

4. $\sqrt{20}$
5. $2\sqrt{5} \cdot \sqrt{5}$
6. $\frac{\sqrt{42x^2}}{\sqrt{6y^3}}$

Simplify. (Lesson 13–3)

7. $8\sqrt{6} + 3\sqrt{6}$
8. $10\sqrt{17} + 9\sqrt{7} - 8\sqrt{17} + 6\sqrt{7}$
9. $(6 + \sqrt{3})(2\sqrt{5} - \sqrt{3})$

10. **Geometry** Find the perimeter and area of the figure at the right. Round answers to the nearest hundredth. (Lesson 13–1)

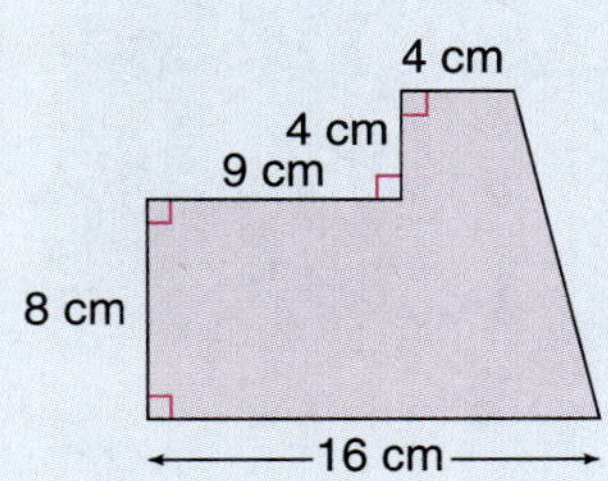

13-4 Radical Equations

What YOU'LL LEARN

- To solve radical equations.

Why IT'S IMPORTANT

You can use radical equations to solve problems involving oceanography and recreation.

FYI

A tsunami may begin as a 2-foot high wave. After traveling hundreds of miles across the ocean at speeds of 450 to 500 miles per hour, it could approach shallow coastal waters as a towering 50-foot wall of water, capable of destroying anything in its path.

Topographical map of the ocean surface

APPLICATION

Oceanography

The Tonga Trench in the Pacific Ocean is a potential source for a *tsunami* (su-nom'-ee), a large ocean wave generated by an undersea earthquake. The formula for a tsunami's speed s in meters per second is $s = 3.1\sqrt{d}$, where d is the depth of the ocean in meters.

Equations like $s = 3.1\sqrt{d}$ that contain radicals with variables in the radicand are called **radical equations**. To solve these equations, first isolate the radical on one side of the equation. Then square each side of the equation to eliminate the radical.

Find the depth of the Tonga Trench if a tsunami's speed is 322 meters per second.

$322 = 3.1\sqrt{d}$ *Replace s with 322.*

$\frac{322}{3.1} = \frac{3.1\sqrt{d}}{3.1}$ *Divide each side by 3.1.*

$\left(\frac{322}{3.1}\right)^2 = \left(\sqrt{d}\right)^2$ *Square each side of the equation.*

$\left(\frac{322}{3.1}\right)^2 = d$ Use a scientific calculator to simplify $\left(\frac{322}{3.1}\right)^2$.

Enter: (322 ÷ 3.1) x^2 10789.17794

The depth of the Tonga Trench is approximately 10,789 meters. *Check this result by substituting 10,789 for d into the original formula.*

Example 1 **Solve each equation.**

a. $\sqrt{x} + 4 = 7$

$\sqrt{x} + 4 = 7$

$\sqrt{x} + 4 - 4 = 7 - 4$ *Subtract 4 from each side.*

$\sqrt{x} = 3$ *Simplify.*

$\left(\sqrt{x}\right)^2 = 3^2$ *Square each side.*

$x = 9$ The solution is 9.

Check:

$\sqrt{x} + 4 = 7$

$\sqrt{9} + 4 \stackrel{?}{=} 7$ *x = 9*

$3 + 4 = 7$ ✔

b. $\sqrt{x + 3} + 5 = 9$

$\sqrt{x + 3} + 5 = 9$

$\sqrt{x + 3} + 5 - 5 = 9 - 5$ *Subtract 5 from each side.*

$\sqrt{x + 3} = 4$ *Simplify.*

$\left(\sqrt{x + 3}\right)^2 = 4^2$ *Square each side.*

$x + 3 = 16$

$x + 3 - 3 = 16 - 3$ *Subtract 3 from each side.*

$x = 13$ The solution is 13. *Check this result.*

Squaring each side of an equation does not necessarily produce results that satisfy the original equation. Therefore, you must check all solutions when you solve radical equations.

Example 2 **Solve $\sqrt{3x - 5} = x - 5$.**

$$\begin{aligned} \sqrt{3x-5} &= x-5 \\ (\sqrt{3x-5})^2 &= (x-5)^2 && \textit{Square each side.} \\ 3x-5 &= x^2 - 10x + 25 && \textit{Simplify.} \\ 3x - 3x - 5 + 5 &= x^2 - 10x + 25 - 3x + 5 && \textit{Add } -3x \textit{ and 5 to each side.} \\ 0 &= x^2 - 13x + 30 && \textit{Simplify.} \\ 0 &= (x-10)(x-3) && \textit{Factor.} \\ x - 10 = 0 \quad &\text{or} \quad x - 3 = 0 && \textit{Use the zero product property.} \\ x = 10 \quad & \quad\quad x = 3 \end{aligned}$$

Check:

$$\begin{aligned} \sqrt{3x-5} &= x-5 \\ \sqrt{3(10)-5} &\stackrel{?}{=} 10-5 \\ \sqrt{30-5} &\stackrel{?}{=} 5 \\ \sqrt{25} &\stackrel{?}{=} 5 \\ 5 &= 5 \ ✔ \end{aligned} \qquad \begin{aligned} \sqrt{3x-5} &= x-5 \\ \sqrt{3(3)-5} &\stackrel{?}{=} 3-5 \\ \sqrt{9-5} &\stackrel{?}{=} -2 \\ \sqrt{4} &\stackrel{?}{=} -2 \\ 2 &\neq -2 \end{aligned}$$

Since 3 does not satisfy the original equation, 10 is the only solution.

You can use the *Mathematics Exploration Toolkit* (*MET*) to solve equations involving square roots.

EXPLORATION — GRAPHING SOFTWARE

The CALC commands below will be used.

ADD (add)	SUBTRACT (sub)	MULTIPLY (mult)
DIVIDE (div)	FACTOR (fac)	RAISETO (rai)
SIMPLIFY (simp)	STORE (sto)	SUBSTITUTE (subs)

To enter the square root symbol, type &.

Solve $\sqrt{x - 2} = x - 4$.

Enter:	**Result:**
&(x − 2) = x − 4	$\sqrt{x-2} = x - 4$
sto *a*	Saves the equation as *a*.
rai 2	$\left(\sqrt{x-2}\right)^2 = (x-4)^2$
simp	$x - 2 = x^2 - 8x + 16$
sub $x - 2$	$x - 2 - (x - 2) = x^2 - 8x + 16 - (x - 2)$
simp	$0 = x^2 - 9x + 18$
fac	$0 = (x - 6)(x - 3)$

By inspection, the solutions are $x = 6$ or $x = 3$. However, 3 does not satisfy the original equation. Therefore, 6 is the only solution.

Your Turn

Use CALC to solve each equation.

a. $3 + \sqrt{2x} = 7$

b. $\sqrt{x+1} = x - 1$

c. $\sqrt{x} + 6 = 1$

d. $\sqrt{3x - 8} = 5$

e. $x + \sqrt{6 - x} = 4$

f. $\sqrt{3x - 9} = 2x + 6$

Example 3 The geometric mean of a and b is x if $\frac{a}{x} = \frac{x}{b}$. Find two numbers that have a geometric mean of 8 given that one number is 12 more than the other.

INTEGRATION
Number Theory

Explore Let n represent the lesser number.
Then $n + 12$ represents the greater number.

Plan Use the equation $\frac{a}{x} = \frac{x}{b}$. Replace each variable with the appropriate value.

$$\frac{n}{8} = \frac{8}{n + 12}$$ *The geometic mean of the numbers is 8.*

Solve

$$n^2 + 12n = 64$$

$$n^2 + 12n - 64 = 0$$

$$(n + 16)(n - 4) = 0$$ *Factor.*

$$n + 16 = 0 \quad \text{or} \quad n - 4 = 0$$ *Zero product property*

$$n = -16 \qquad n = 4$$

If $n = -16$, then $n + 12 = -4$. If $n = 4$, then $n + 12 = 16$.

Thus, the numbers are -16 and -4, or 4 and 16.

Examine $\frac{-16}{8} \stackrel{?}{=} \frac{8}{-4}$ or $\frac{4}{8} \stackrel{?}{=} \frac{8}{16}$

$64 = 64$ ✔ $\qquad$ $64 = 64$ ✔

CHECK FOR UNDERSTANDING

Communicating Mathematics

Study the lesson. Then complete the following.

1. **Explain** the first step you should do when solving a radical equation.
2. **Write** an expression for the geometric mean of 7 and y.
3. Refer to the application at the beginning of the lesson.
   a. Solve $s = 3.1\sqrt{d}$ for d.
   b. Use the equation you found in part a to find the depth of the ocean in meters if the speed of the tsunami is 400 meters per second.
4. **You Decide** Alberto says that if you have an equation that contains a radical, you can always get a real solution by squaring each side of the equation. Ellen disagrees. Who is correct? Explain.

MATH JOURNAL

5. a. **Assess Yourself** Explain in your own words the process or steps needed to solve a radical equation.
   b. Explain why it is important to check your answers when solving equations containing radicals.

Guided Practice

Square each side of the following equations.

6. $\sqrt{x} = 6$
7. $\sqrt{a + 3} = 2$
8. $13 = \sqrt{2y - 5}$

Solve each equation. Check your solution.

9. $\sqrt{m} = 4$
10. $\sqrt{b} = -3$
11. $-\sqrt{x} = -6$
12. $\sqrt{7x} = 7$
13. $\sqrt{-3a} = 6$
14. $\sqrt{y - 2} = 8$

15. **Engineering** It is possible to measure the speed of water using an L-shaped tube. You can find the speed V of the water in miles per hour by measuring the height h of the column of water above the surface in inches and by using the formula $V = \sqrt{2.5h}$. If you take the tube into a river and the height of the column is 6 inches, what is the speed of the water to the nearest tenth of a mile per hour?

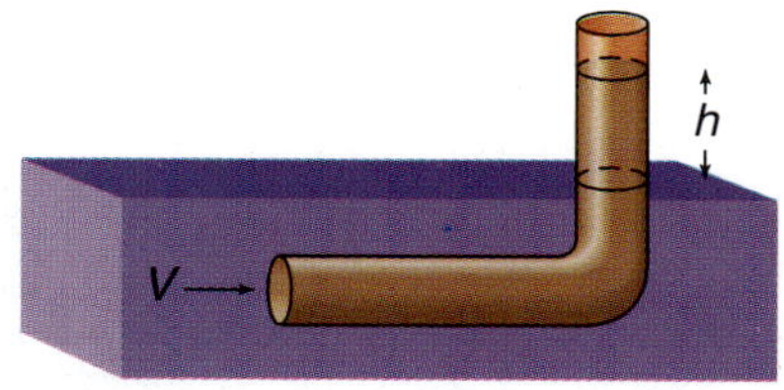

EXERCISES

Practice

Solve each equation. Check your solution.

16. $\sqrt{a} = 5\sqrt{2}$
17. $3\sqrt{7} = \sqrt{-x}$
18. $\sqrt{m} - 4 = 0$
19. $\sqrt{2d} + 1 = 0$
20. $10 - \sqrt{3y} = 1$
21. $3 + 5\sqrt{n} = 12$
22. $\sqrt{8s + 1} = 5$
23. $\sqrt{4b + 1} - 3 = 0$
24. $\sqrt{3r - 5} + 7 = 3$
25. $\sqrt{\frac{w}{6}} = 2$
26. $\sqrt{\frac{4x}{5}} - 9 = 3$
27. $5\sqrt{\frac{4t}{3}} - 2 = 0$
28. $\sqrt{2x^2 - 121} = x$
29. $7\sqrt{3z^2 - 15} = 7$
30. $\sqrt{x + 2} = x - 4$
31. $\sqrt{5x^2 - 7} = 2x$
32. $\sqrt{1 - 2m} = 1 + m$
33. $4 + \sqrt{b - 2} = b$

INTEGRATION
Number Theory

34. The geometric mean of a certain number and 6 is 24. Find the number.
35. Find two numbers with a geometric mean of $\sqrt{30}$ given that one number is 7 more than the other.
36. Find two numbers with a geometric mean of 12 given that one number is 11 less than three times the other.

Solve each equation. Check your solution.

37. $\sqrt{x - 12} = 6 - \sqrt{x}$
38. $\sqrt{x} + 4 = \sqrt{x + 16}$
39. $\sqrt{x + 7} = 7 + \sqrt{x}$

Solve each system of equations.

40. $2\sqrt{a} + 5\sqrt{b} = 6$
    $3\sqrt{a} - 5\sqrt{b} = 9$
41. $-3\sqrt{x} + 3\sqrt{y} = 1$
    $-4\sqrt{x} + 6\sqrt{y} = 3$
42. $s = 4t$
    $\sqrt{s} - 5\sqrt{t} = -6$

Critical Thinking

43. Solve for x if $x + 2 = x\sqrt{3}$.
44. Find two numbers such that the square root of their sum is 5 and the square root of their product is 12.

Applications and Problem Solving

45. **Recreation** The rangers at an aid station received a distress call from a group camping 60 miles east and 10 miles south of the station. A jeep sent to the campsite travels directly east for some number of miles and then turns and heads directly to the campsite. If the jeep traveled a total of 66 miles to get to the campsite, for how many miles did it travel due east?

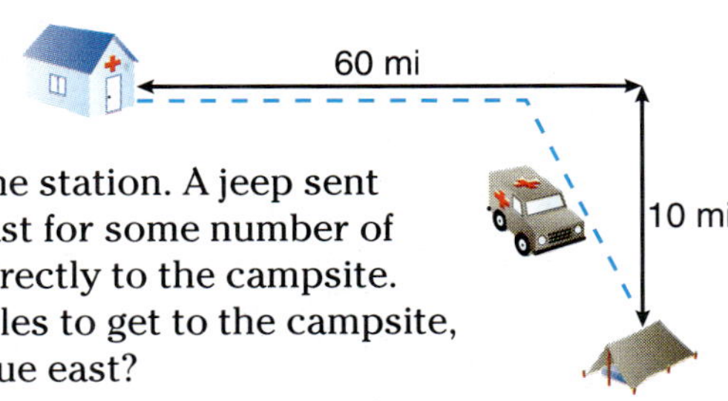

46. **Sound** The speed of sound near Earth's surface can be found with the equation $V = 20\sqrt{t + 273}$, where t is the surface temperature in degrees Celsius.
    a. Find the temperature if the speed of sound V is 356 meters per second.
    b. The speed of sound at Earth's surface is often given as 340 meters per second, but that's really only true at a certain temperature. On what temperature is the 340 m/s figure based?

47. **Travel** The speed s that a car is traveling in miles per hour, and the distance d in feet that it will skid when the brakes are applied, are related by the formula $s = \sqrt{30fd}$. In this formula, f is the coefficient of friction, which depends on the type and condition of the road. Sylvia Kwan told police she was traveling at about 30 miles per hour when she applied the brakes and skidded on a wet concrete road. The length of her skid marks was measured at 110 feet.

a. If $f = 0.4$ for a wet concrete road, should Ms. Kwan's car have skidded that far when she applied the brakes?

b. How fast was she traveling?

Mixed Review

48. Simplify $5\sqrt{6} - 11\sqrt{3} - 8\sqrt{6} + \sqrt{27}$. (Lesson 13–3)

49. Find $(6b^2 + 4b + 20) \div (b + 5)$. (Lesson 12–4)

50. Find the roots of $x^2 - 2x - 8 = 0$ by graphing its related function. (Lesson 11–2)

51. Find the GCF of $12x^2y^3$ and $42xy^4$. (Lesson 10–1)

52. Find $(6a - 2m) - (4a + 7m)$. (Lesson 9–5)

53. Use substitution to solve the system of equations. (Lesson 8–2)
$x + 4y = 16$
$3x + 6y = 18$

54. Write an equation in slope-intercept form of the line that passes through the points at $(6, -1)$ and $(3, 2)$. (Lesson 6–4)

55. **Probability** If the odds that an event will occur are 8:5, what is the probability that the event will occur? (Lesson 4–6)

56. Find $\frac{3}{7} + \left(-\frac{4}{9}\right)$. (Lesson 2–5)

Mathematics and SOCIETY

Nonlinear Math

The excerpt below appeared in an article in *Business Week* on September 5, 1994.

ABOVE ALL ELSE, ENGINEERS ARE practical. If developing the perfect camera or oil refinery takes too long, they settle for a design that's "good enough." Increasingly, though, this no longer suffices. In companies driven by competition... engineers are being forced to dip into a new mathematics toolbox.... The new tools are called nonlinear equations, and the name says it all. These equations are used for precisely describing the behavior of things with an unpredictable facet. That's nearly everything—from the workings of car engines to the actions of DNA molecules. Even baking a cake is nonlinear: turning up the oven's temperature twice as high won't bake the cake twice as fast. And with some industrial recipes, such as those for making drugs and plastics, a tiny change in ingredients or processing conditions can mean a huge difference in the finished product. Nonlinear math can help explain such lopsided effects. ■

1. In nonlinear processes, you can't be sure how changes in input will affect the result. Therefore, what can you conclude about the number of variations you will need to enter into the equations you are solving?

2. Because of the huge number of variables that can be involved, solving nonlinear equations can require many millions of calculations. Why do you think the use of these equations has only recently begun to expand into many industries?

13–5 Integration: Geometry
The Distance Formula

What YOU'LL LEARN

- To find the distance between two points in the coordinate plane.

Why IT'S IMPORTANT

You can use the distance formula to solve problems involving art and communication.

INTEGRATION
Geometry

In a coordinate plane, consider the points $A(-2, 6)$ and $B(5, 3)$. These two points do not lie on the same horizontal or vertical line. Therefore, you cannot find the distance between them by simply subtracting the x- or y-coordinates. A different method must be used.

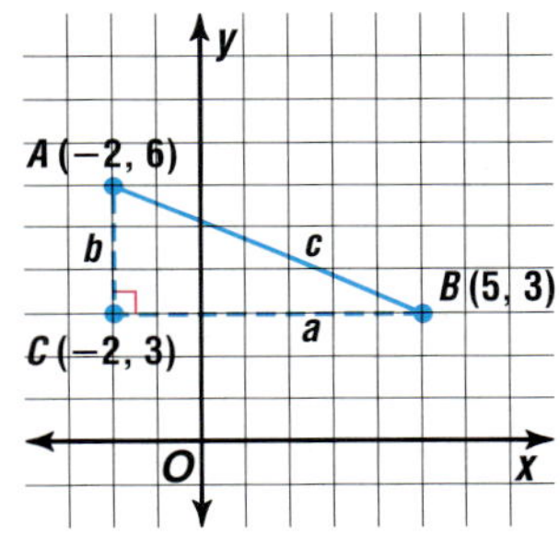

Notice that a right triangle can be formed by drawing lines parallel to the axes through points at $(-2, 6)$ and $(5, 3)$. These lines intersect at $C(-2, 3)$. The measure of side b is the difference of the y-coordinates of the endpoints, $6 - 3$ or 3. The measure of side a is the difference of the x-coordinates of the endpoints, $5 - (-2)$ or 7.

Now the Pythagorean theorem can be used to find c, the distance between $A(-2, 6)$ and $B(5, 3)$.

$$c^2 = a^2 + b^2 \quad \textit{Pythagorean theorem}$$
$$c^2 = 7^2 + 3^2 \quad \textit{Replace a with 7 and b with 3.}$$
$$c^2 = 49 + 9$$
$$c^2 = 58$$
$$c = \sqrt{58}$$
$$c \approx 7.62$$

The distance between points A and B is approximately 7.62 units.

The method used for finding the distance between $A(-2, 6)$ and $B(5, 3)$ can also be used to find the distance between any two points in the coordinate plane. This method can be described by the following formula.

The Distance Formula

The distance d between any two points with coordinates (x_1, y_1) and (x_2, y_2) is given by the following formula.

$$d = \sqrt{(x_2 - x_1)^2 + (y_2 - y_1)^2}$$

Example 1 **Find the distance between the points with coordinates (3, 5) and (6, 4).**

$$d = \sqrt{(x_2 - x_1)^2 + (y_2 - y_1)^2}$$
$$= \sqrt{(6 - 3)^2 + (4 - 5)^2} \quad (x_1, y_1) = (3, 5) \text{ and } (x_2, y_2) = (6, 4)$$
$$= \sqrt{3^2 + (-1)^2}$$
$$= \sqrt{9 + 1}$$
$$= \sqrt{10} \text{ or about 3.16 units}$$

Example 2 INTEGRATION Geometry

Determine if triangle ABC with vertices $A(-3, 4)$, $B(5, 2)$, and $C(-1, -5)$ is an isosceles triangle.

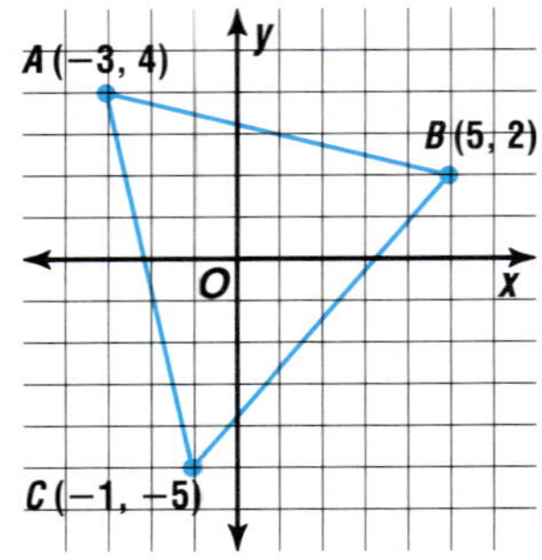

A triangle is isosceles if at least two sides are congruent. Find AB, BC, and AC.

$$AB = \sqrt{[5-(-3)]^2 + (2-4)^2}$$
$$= \sqrt{8^2 + (-2)^2} \text{ or } \sqrt{68}$$

$$BC = \sqrt{(-1-5)^2 + (-5-2)^2}$$
$$= \sqrt{(-6)^2 + (-7)^2} \text{ or } \sqrt{85}$$

$$AC = \sqrt{[-1-(-3)]^2 + (-5-4)^2}$$
$$= \sqrt{2^2 + (-9)^2} \text{ or } \sqrt{85}$$

Since $\overline{BC}$ and $\overline{AC}$ have the same length, $\sqrt{85}$, they are congruent. So, triangle ABC is an isosceles triangle.

Suppose you know the coordinates of a point, one coordinate of another point, and the distance between the two points. You can use the distance formula to find the missing coordinate.

Example 3

Find the value of a if the distance between the points with coordinates $(-3, -2)$ and $(a, -5)$ is 5 units.

$$d = \sqrt{(x_2 - x_1)^2 + (y_2 - y_1)^2}$$
$$5 = \sqrt{[a-(-3)]^2 + [-5-(-2)]^2} \quad \textit{Let } x_2 = a,\ x_1 = -3,\ y_2 = -5,\ y_1 = -2, \textit{ and } d = 5.$$
$$5 = \sqrt{(a+3)^2 + (-3)^2}$$
$$5 = \sqrt{a^2 + 6a + 9 + 9}$$
$$5 = \sqrt{a^2 + 6a + 18}$$
$$(5)^2 = \left(\sqrt{a^2 + 6a + 18}\right)^2 \quad \textit{Square each side.}$$
$$25 = a^2 + 6a + 18$$
$$0 = a^2 + 6a - 7$$
$$0 = (a+7)(a-1) \quad \textit{Factor.}$$
$$a + 7 = 0 \quad \text{or} \quad a - 1 = 0 \quad \textit{Zero product property}$$
$$a = -7 \qquad\qquad a = 1$$

The value of a is -7 or 1.

CHECK FOR UNDERSTANDING

Communicating Mathematics

Study the lesson. Then complete the following.

1. **Explain** why the value calculated under the radical sign in the distance formula will never be negative.
2. a. **Write** two ordered pairs and label them $A(x_1, y_1)$ and $B(x_2, y_2)$. Does it matter which ordered pair is first when using the distance formula? Explain.
   b. Find the distance between A and B.

3. a. **Explain** how you can find the distance between $X(12, 4)$ and $Y(3, 4)$ without using the distance formula.

   b. **Explain** how you can find the distance between $S(-2, 7)$ and $T(-2, -5)$ without using the distance formula.

4. Refer to Example 3. Check your answer by using the distance formula.

Guided Practice

Find the distance between each pair of points whose coordinates are given. Express answers in simplest radical form and as decimal approximations rounded to the nearest hundredth if necessary.

5. $(6, 8), (3, 4)$
6. $(3, 7), (-2, -5)$
7. $(2, 2), (5, -1)$
8. $(2, 7), (10, -4)$

Find the value of *a* if the points with the given coordinates are the indicated distance apart.

9. $(4, 7), (a, 3); d = 5$
10. $(5, a), (6, 1); d = \sqrt{10}$

11. **Communication** Alpha Corporation is having a fiber optic cable system installed between two new offices. Alphatower I is 4 miles east and 5 miles north of Alpha Central. Alphatower II is 5 miles west and 2 miles north of Alpha Central. How many miles of cable will be needed to connect the new offices? (*Hint:* Alpha Central is located at (0, 0).)

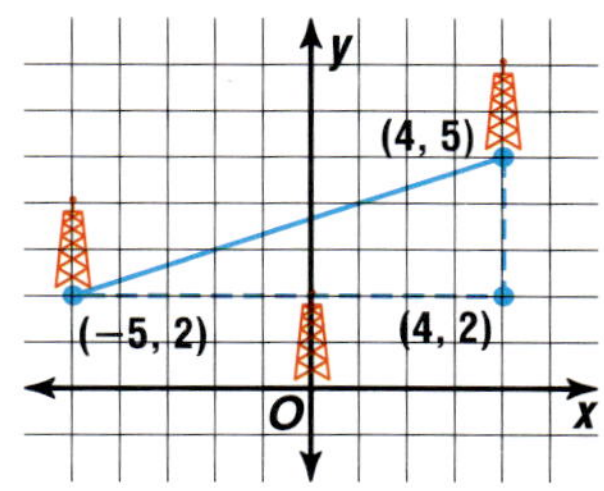

EXERCISES

Practice

Find the distance between each pair of points whose coordinates are given. Express answers in simplest radical form and as decimal approximations rounded to the nearest hundredth if necessary.

12. $(5, -1), (11, 7)$
13. $(-4, 2), (4, 17)$
14. $(-3, 8), (5, 4)$
15. $(-8, -4), (-3, -8)$
16. $(9, -2), (3, -6)$
17. $(4, 2), \left(6, -\frac{2}{3}\right)$
18. $\left(3, \frac{3}{7}\right), \left(4, -\frac{2}{7}\right)$
19. $\left(\frac{4}{5}, -1\right), \left(2, -\frac{1}{2}\right)$
20. $(4\sqrt{5}, 7), (6\sqrt{5}, 1)$
21. $(5\sqrt{2}, 8), (7\sqrt{2}, 10)$

Find the value of *a* if the points with the given coordinates are the indicated distance apart.

22. $(3, -1), (a, 7); d = 10$
23. $(-4, a), (4, 2); d = 17$
24. $(a, 5), (-7, 3); d = \sqrt{29}$
25. $(6, -3), (-3, a); d = \sqrt{130}$
26. $(10, a), (1, -6); d = \sqrt{145}$
27. $(20, -5), (a, 9); d = \sqrt{340}$

INTEGRATION Geometry

Determine if the triangles with the following vertices are isosceles triangles.

28. $L(7, -4), M(-1, 2), N(5, -6)$
29. $T(1, -8), U(3, 5), V(-1, 7)$

30. Find the perimeter of square $QRST$ if two of the vertices are $Q(6, 7)$ and $R(-3, 4)$.

31. If the diagonals of a trapezoid have the same length, then the trapezoid is isosceles. Find the lengths of the diagonals of the trapezoid with vertices $A(-2, 2)$, $B(10, 6)$, $C(9, 8)$, and $D(0, 5)$ to determine if it is isosceles.

Programming

32. The program at the right calculates the distance between a pair of points whose coordinates are given.

```
PROGRAM: DISTANCE
:ClrDraw
:Input "X1=",Q
:Input "Y1=",R
:Input "X2=",S
:Input "Y2=",T
:Line (Q,R,S,T)
:√((Q-S)² + (R-T)²)→D
:Text (5,50,"DIST=",D)
```

Find the distance between each pair of points.

a. $A(6, -3)$, $B(12, 5)$
b. $M(-3, 5)$, $N(12, -2)$
c. $S(6.8, 9.9)$, $T(-5.9, 4.3)$

Critical Thinking

33. Use the distance formula to show that the triangle with vertices at $(3, -2)$, $(-3, 7)$, and $(-9, 3)$ is a right triangle.

Applications and Problem Solving

34. **Art** Egyptian artists about 5000 years ago decorated tombs of pharaohs by painting their pictures on the walls. The artists used small sketches on grids as a reference. In Egypt, the main standard of length was the cubit. It was the length of a man's forearm from the elbow to the tip of the outstretched fingers. Use the grid at the right to find the length of a cubit to the nearest inch if each unit represents 3.3 inches.

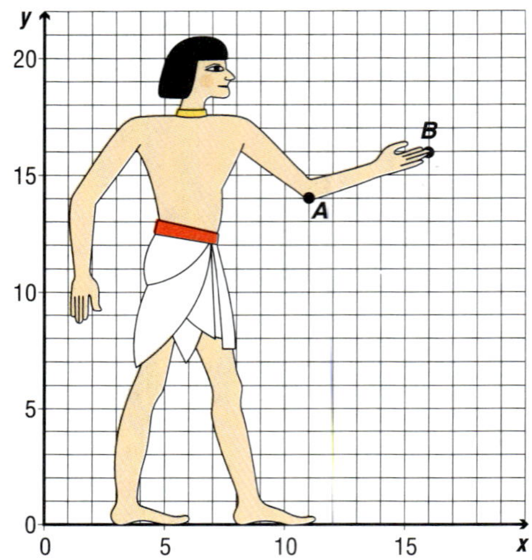

35. **Telecommunications** In order to set long distance rates, phone companies first superimpose an imaginary coordinate grid over the United States. Then the location of each exchange is represented by an ordered pair on the grid. The units of this grid are approximately equal to 0.316 miles. So, a distance of 3 units on the grid equals an actual distance of about 3(0.316) or 0.948 miles. Suppose the exchanges in two cities are at (132, 428) and (254, 105). Find the actual distance between these cities to the nearest mile.

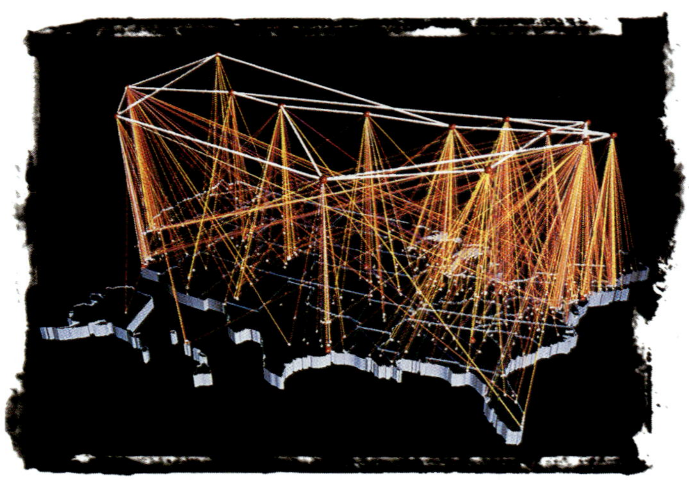

fabulous FIRSTS

Granville T. Woods (1856–1910)

Granville T. Woods patented an improved telephone transmitter in 1884. This was the first of more than twenty patents that he received for his inventions.

Mixed Review

36. **Physics** The time t, in seconds, it takes an object to drop d feet is given by the formula $4t = \sqrt{d}$. Jessica and Lu-Chan each dropped a stone at the same time, but Jessica dropped hers from a spot higher than Lu-Chan's. Lu-Chan's stone hit the ground 1 second before Jessica's. If Jessica's stone dropped 112 feet farther than Lu-Chan's, how long did it take her stone to hit the ground? (Lesson 13–4)

37. Simplify $\sqrt{\frac{8}{9}}$. (Lesson 13–2)

38. Find $\frac{4p^3}{p-1} \div \frac{p^2}{p-1}$. (Lesson 12–3)

39. Graph the system of equations. Then determine whether the system has *one* solution, *no* solution, or *infinitely many* solutions. (Lesson 8–1)
$4x - y = 2$
$y - 4x = 4$

40. **Consumerism** Jackie wanted to buy a new coat that cost \$145. If she waited until the coat went on sale for 30% off the original price, how much money did Jackie save? (Lesson 4–5)

41. **Air Conditioning** The formula for determining the BTU (British Thermal Units) rating of the air conditioner necessary to cool a room is BTU = Area (sq ft) × Exposure Factor × Climate Factor. Use this formula to determine the BTU necessary to cool each of the rooms described in the following chart. (Lesson 2–6)

	Room Dimensions (feet)	Exposure Factor	Climate Factor
a.	22 by 16	North: 20	Buffalo: 1.05
b.	13 by 12	West: 25	Portland: 0.95
c.	17 by 14	East: 25	Topeka: 1.05
d.	26 by 18	South: 30	San Diego: 1.00
e.	23.5 by 15.3	North: 20	Tacoma: 0.95

WORKING ON THE In·ves·ti·ga·tion

Refer to the Investigation on pages 656–657.

A Growing Concern

1 Review your scale drawing. Make sure you have included everything that you think the Sanchez family wanted or will want in the future. Make any changes that you feel need to be made now that the plan is complete.

2 The Sanchez family had asked for a 3-dimensional model of the design. On a piece of cardboard, draw the boundary lines of the Sanchez property. Use modeling clay, construction paper, paint, markers, and whatever else you need to create a 3-dimensional model of your design.

3 Use a flashlight to model the sun's movement during the day. Note the patterns and the length of time certain areas are shaded.

Add the results of your work to your Investigation Folder.

MODELING MATHEMATICS

A Preview of Lesson 13–6

13–6A Completing the Square

Materials: algebra tiles equation mat

One way to solve a quadratic equation is by **completing the square.** To use this method, the quadratic expression on one side of the equation must be a perfect square. You can use algebra tiles as a model for completing the square.

Activity Use algebra tiles to complete the square for the equation $x^2 + 4x + 1 = 0$.

Step 1 Subtract 1 from each side of the equation.

$$x^2 + 4x + 1 - 1 = 0 - 1$$
$$x^2 + 4x = -1$$

Then model the equation $x^2 + 4x = -1$.

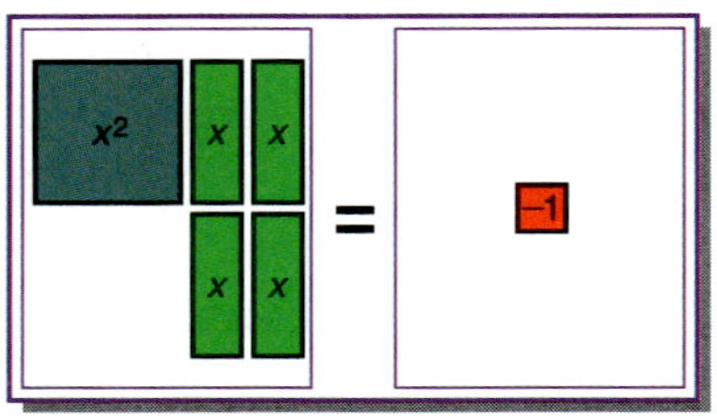

Step 2 Begin to arrange the x^2-tile and the x-tiles into a square.

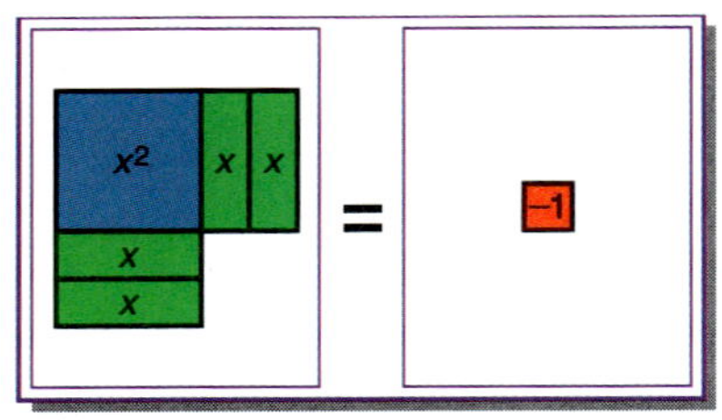

Step 3 In order to complete the square, you need to add 4 1-tiles to the left side of the mat. Since you are modeling an equation, add 4 1-tiles to the right side of the mat.

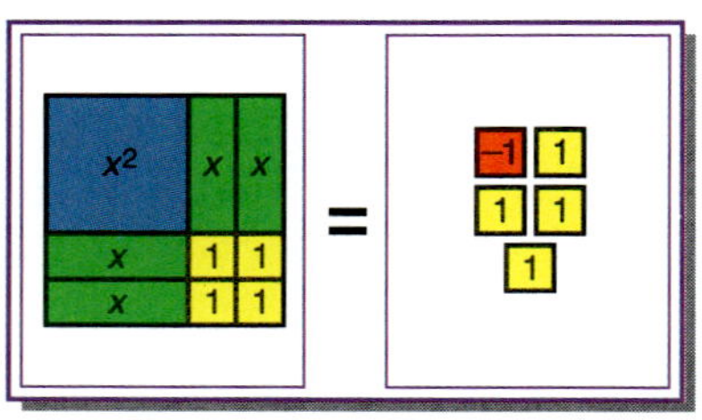

$x^2 + 4x + 4 = -1 + 4$

Step 4 Remove the zero pair on the right side of the mat. You have completed the square, and the equation is $x^2 + 4x + 4 = 3$ or $(x + 2)^2 = 3$.

Model Use algebra tiles to complete the square for each equation.

1. $x^2 + 4x + 3 = 0$ **2.** $x^2 - 6x + 5 = 0$ **3.** $x^2 + 4x - 1 = 0$

4. $x^2 - 2x + 5 = 3$ **5.** $x^2 - 4x + 7 = 8$ **6.** $0 = x^2 + 8x - 3$

Draw

7. In the equations shown above, the coefficient of x was always an even number. Sometimes you have an equation like $x^2 + 3x - 1 = 0$ in which the coefficient of x is an odd number. Complete the square by making a drawing.

Write

8. Write a paragraph explaining how you could complete the square with models without first rewriting the equation. Include a drawing.

13–6 Solving Quadratic Equations by Completing the Square

***What* YOU'LL LEARN**

- To solve quadratic equations by completing the square, and
- to solve problems by identifying subgoals.

***Why* IT'S IMPORTANT**

You can solve quadratic equations to solve problems involving geography and construction.

CONNECTION

Geography

The greatest flow of any river in the world is that of the Amazon, which discharges an average of 4.2 million cubic feet of water per second into the Atlantic Ocean. The rate at which water flows in a river varies depending on the distance from the shore.

Amazon River

Suppose the Castillos have a home on the bank of a river that is 40 yards wide. The rate of the river is given by the equation $y = -0.01x^2 + 0.4x$. Mr. and Mrs. Castillo do not want their children to wade in the water if the current is greater than 3 miles per hour. Find how many yards from shore the water flows at 3 miles per hour. *This problem will be solved in Example 4.*

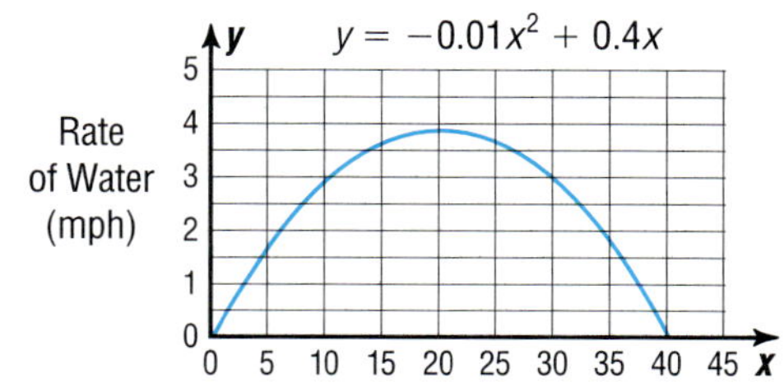

You can solve some quadratic equations by taking the square root of each side.

Example 1 **Solve $x^2 - 6x + 9 = 7$.**

$x^2 - 6x + 9 = 7$

$(x - 3)^2 = 7$ — *$x^2 - 6x + 9$ is a perfect square trinomial.*

$\sqrt{(x - 3)^2} = \sqrt{7}$ — *Take the square root of each side.*

$|x - 3| = \sqrt{7}$

$x - 3 = \pm\sqrt{7}$ — *Why is this the case?*

$x = 3 \pm \sqrt{7}$ — *Add 3 to each side.*

The solution set is $\{3 + \sqrt{7}, 3 - \sqrt{7}\}$.

To use the method shown in Example 1, the quadratic expression on one side of the equation must be a perfect square. However, few quadratic expressions are perfect squares. To make any quadratic expression a perfect square, a method called **completing the square** may be used.

Consider the pattern for squaring a binomial such as $x + 5$.

$$(x + 5)^2 = x^2 + 2(5)x + 5^2$$
$$= x^2 + 10x + 25$$
$$\left(\frac{10}{2}\right)^2 \rightarrow 5^2$$

Notice that one half of 10 is 5 and 5^2 is 25.

To complete the square for a quadratic expression of the form $x^2 + bx$, you can follow the steps below.

Step 1 Find $\frac{1}{2}$ of b, the coefficient of x.

Step 2 Square the result of Step 1.

Step 3 Add the result of Step 2 to $x^2 + bx$, the original expression.

Example 2 **Find the value of c that makes each trinomial a perfect square.**

a. $x^2 + 20x + c$

Step 1	Find $\frac{1}{2}$ of 20.	$\frac{20}{2} = 10$
Step 2	Square the result of Step 1.	$10^2 = 100$
Step 3	Add the result of Step 2 to $x^2 + 20x$.	$x^2 + 20x + 100$

Thus, $c = 100$. Notice that $x^2 + 20x + 100 = (x + 10)^2$.

b. $x^2 - 15x + c$

Step 1	Find $\frac{1}{2}$ of -15.	$\frac{-15}{2} = -7.5$
Step 2	Square the result of Step 1.	$(-7.5)^2 = 56.25$
Step 3	Add the result of Step 2 to $x^2 - 15x$.	$x^2 - 15x + 56.25$

Thus, $c = 56.25$. Notice that $x^2 - 15x + 56.25 = (x - 7.5)^2$.

Example 3 **Solve $x^2 + 8x - 18 = 0$ by completing the square.**

$x^2 + 8x - 18 = 0$ *Notice that $x^2 + 8x - 18$ is not a perfect square.*

$x^2 + 8x = 18$ *Add 18 to each side. Then complete the square.*

$x^2 + 8x + 16 = 18 + 16$ *Since $\left(\frac{8}{2}\right)^2 = 16$, add 16 to each side.*

$(x + 4)^2 = 34$ *Factor $x^2 + 8x + 16$.*

$x + 4 = \pm\sqrt{34}$ *Take the square root of each side.*

$x = -4 \pm \sqrt{34}$ *Subtract 4 from each side.*

$x = -4 + \sqrt{34}$ or $x = -4 - \sqrt{34}$

The solution set is $\{-4 + \sqrt{34}, -4 - \sqrt{34}\}$. *Check this result.*

The method for solving quadratic equations cannot be used unless the coefficient of the first term is 1. To solve a quadratic equation in which the leading coefficient is not 1, divide each term by the coefficient.

Example 4 **Refer to the application at the beginning of the lesson. How far from shore will the rate of the current be 3 miles per hour?**

CONNECTION
Geography

$y = -0.01x^2 + 0.4x$

$3 = -0.01x^2 + 0.4x$ *Replace y with 3 since the rate is 3 mph.*

$-300 = x^2 - 40x$ *Divide each side by -0.01.*

$-300 + 400 = x^2 - 40x + 400$ *Complete the square. $\left(\frac{-40}{2}\right)^2 = 400$*

$100 = (x - 20)^2$ *Factor $x^2 - 40x + 400$.*

$\pm 10 = x - 20$ *Take the square root of each side.*

$20 \pm 10 = x$ *Add 20 to each side.*

The solutions are 20 + 10 or 30 and 20 − 10 or 10. Thus, the children should not be allowed to wade more than 10 yards from the shore; between 10 and 30 yards from the shore the water is flowing too fast.

Check this result with a graphing calculator by graphing the equation $y = -0.01x^2 + 0.4x$, and then estimating.

Sometimes finding the solution to a problem requires several steps. An important strategy for solving such problems is to **identify subgoals.** This strategy involves taking steps that will either produce part of the solution or make the problem easier to solve.

Example 5 **Show how to derive the quadratic formula by solving the equation $ax^2 + bx + c = 0$.**

PROBLEM SOLVING
Identify Subgoals

The first subgoal is to choose a method for solving the equation. Since the coefficients are variables, we cannot solve by graphing. It is possible, however, to solve for x by completing the square.

The second subgoal is to complete the square to find the value of x.

$$ax^2 + bx + c = 0$$

$$x^2 + \frac{b}{a}x + \frac{c}{a} = 0 \quad \text{Divide each side by } a.\ a \neq 0$$

$$x^2 + \frac{b}{a}x = -\frac{c}{a} \quad \text{Subtract } \frac{c}{a} \text{ from each side.}$$

$$x^2 + \frac{b}{a}x + \frac{b^2}{4a^2} = -\frac{c}{a} + \frac{b^2}{4a^2} \quad \text{Complete the square. } \left(\frac{b}{2a}\right)^2 = \frac{b^2}{4a^2}$$

$$\left(x + \frac{b}{2a}\right)^2 = \frac{-4ac + b^2}{4a^2} \quad \text{Factor } x^2 + \frac{b}{a}x + \frac{b^2}{4a^2}.$$

$$x + \frac{b}{2a} = \pm\frac{\sqrt{b^2 - 4ac}}{2a} \quad \text{Find the square root of each side.}$$

$$x = \frac{-b \pm \sqrt{b^2 - 4ac}}{2a} \quad \text{Subtract } \frac{b}{2a} \text{ from each side.}$$

Thus, we have derived the quadratic formula by completing the square.

CHECK FOR UNDERSTANDING

Communicating Mathematics

Study the lesson. Then complete the following.

1. **Explain** which method for solving a quadratic equation always produces an exact solution, graphing or completing the square.
2. **Explain** the three steps used to complete the square for the expression $x^2 + bx$.
3. **Write** a quadratic equation that has no real solutions. After completing the square, explain how you could tell it had no real solutions.

Modeling Mathematics

4. Use algebra tiles to complete the square for the equation $x^2 + 6x + 2 = 0$.

Guided Practice

Find the value of *c* that makes each trinomial a perfect square.

5. $x^2 + 16x + c$
6. $a^2 - 7a + c$

Solve each equation by completing the square. Leave irrational roots in simplest radical form.

7. $x^2 + 4x + 3 = 0$
8. $d^2 - 8d + 7 = 0$
9. $a^2 - 4a = 21$
10. $4x^2 - 20x + 25 = 0$
11. $r^2 - 4r = 2$
12. $2t^2 + 3t - 20 = 0$

13. **Sports** The dimensions of a regulation high school basketball court are 50 feet by 84 feet. The builders of an indoor sports arena can afford to construct an arena of 5600 square feet. They want it to have a regulation basketball court and walkways the same width around the court. Find the dimensions of the walkway.

EXERCISES

Practice

Find the value of *c* that makes each trinomial a perfect square.

14. $x^2 - 6x + c$
15. $b^2 + 8b + c$
16. $m^2 - 5m + c$
17. $a^2 + 11a + c$
18. $9t^2 - 18t + c$
19. $\frac{1}{2}x^2 - 4x + c$

Solve each equation by completing the square. Leave irrational roots in simplest radical form.

20. $x^2 + 7x + 10 = -2$
21. $a^2 - 5a + 2 = -2$
22. $r^2 + 14r - 9 = 6$
23. $9b^2 - 42b + 49 = 0$
24. $x^2 - 24x + 9 = 0$
25. $t^2 + 4 = 6t$
26. $m^2 - 8m = 4$
27. $p^2 - 10p = 23$
28. $x^2 - \frac{7}{2}x + \frac{3}{2} = 0$
29. $5x^2 + 10x - 7 = 0$
30. $\frac{1}{2}d^2 - \frac{5}{4}d - 3 = 0$
31. $0.3t^2 + 0.1t = 0.2$
32. $b^2 + 0.25b = 0.5$
33. $3p^2 - 7p - 3 = 0$
34. $2r^2 - 5r + 8 = 7$

Find the value of *c* that makes each trinomial a perfect square.

35. $x^2 + cx + 81$
36. $4x^2 + cx + 225$
37. $cx^2 + 30x + 75$
38. $cx^2 - 18x + 36$

Solve each equation by completing the square. Leave irrational roots in simplest radical form.

39. $x^2 - 4x + c = 0$
40. $x^2 + bx + c = 0$
41. $x^2 + 4bx + b^2 = 0$

Critical Thinking

42. **Geometry** Consider the quadratic function $y = x^2 - 8x + 15$.
    a. Write the function in the form $y = (x - h)^2 + k$.
    b. Graph the function.
    c. What is the relationship of the point (h, k) to the graph?

Applications and Problem Solving

43. **Identify Subgoals** Two trains left the same station at the same time. One was traveling due north at a speed that was 10 mph faster than the other train, which was traveling due east. After one hour, the trains were 71 miles apart. How fast, to the nearest mile per hour, was each train traveling? (*Hint:* Use the Pythagorean theorem.)

44. **Construction** Arlando's Restaurant wants to add an outdoor café on the side of the restaurant. They are having a special water fountain shipped in that is 10 by 15 feet, and Arlando can afford to buy 1800 square feet of space next to his restaurant. He wishes to have a dining area around the fountain, of equal width all around.

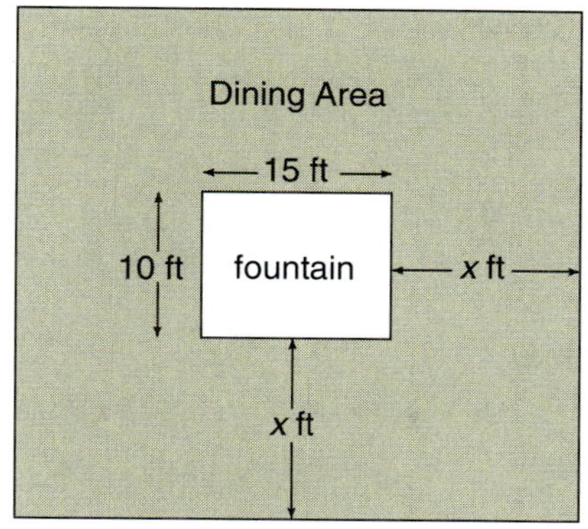

a. Write an equation for x, the width of the dining area around the fountain and solve it.

b. What should be the length and width of the piece of land Arlando buys for the café?

Mixed Review

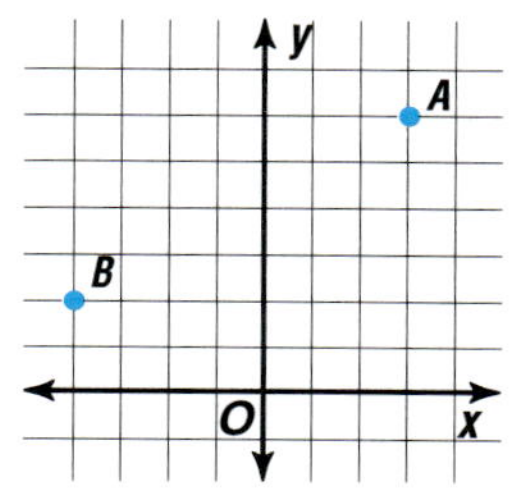

45. **Geometry** Find the distance between points A and B graphed at the right. Round your answer to the nearest hundredth. (Lesson 13–5)

46. **Geometry** The measures of the sides of a triangle are 5, 7, and 9. Determine whether this triangle is a right triangle. (Lesson 13–1)

47. **Astronomy** Earth, Jupiter, and Saturn revolve around the Sun about once every 1, 12, and 30 years, respectively. The last time Jupiter and Saturn appeared close to each other in Earth's night sky was in 1982. When will this happen again? (Lesson 12–6)

48. Find $(5y - 3)(y + 2)$. (Lesson 9–7)

49. Use elimination to solve the system of equations. (Lesson 8–4)

$5y - 4x = 2$

$2y + x = 6$

50. If the graph of $P(x, y)$ satisfies the given conditions, name the quadrant in which point P is located. (Lesson 5–1)

a. $x > 0, y < 0$ b. $x < 0, y = 3$ c. $x = -1, y < 0$

51. **Food** The chart at the right compares the Calorie content of regular tacos and the light tacos at a Mexican fast-food chain. (Lesson 3–7)

a. Find the mean number of Calories for the regular tacos.

b. Find the mean number of Calories for the light tacos.

Item	Calories in Regular Tacos	Calories in Light Tacos
Taco	180	140
Soft Taco	220	180
Taco Deluxe	230	160
Soft Taco Deluxe	270	200
Chicken Soft Taco	223	180

52. Evaluate $|a| + |4b|$ if $a = -3$ and $b = -6$. (Lesson 2–3)

CLOSING THE

In•ves•ti•ga•tion

A Growing Concern

Refer to the Investigation on pages 656–657.

When landscape businesses prepare a proposal for a client, they prepare all the specifications for the bid and include a sketch of the proposal and a photo display of other work they have done for individuals or companies. They also include a list of references that they give to prospective clients. These clients can then call these people and see other work the company has done in order to verify their credentials. What else might be good to include in a sales presentation to a prospective client?

Analyze

You have made a scale drawing of your design and organized your computations in various ways. It is now time to analyze your design and verify your conclusions.

> **PORTFOLIO ASSESSMENT**
>
> You may want to keep your work on this Investigation in your portfolio.

1 Look over your scale drawing of the landscape design and verify the dimensions and placement of each item.

2 Refer to your data on the shade patterns in the yard. Review your knowledge of the plants and trees that you suggested and verify the amount of sun and/or shade that they will get or that they need. Make any necessary changes.

3 Organize a detailed financial bid for the Sanchez family's backyard design. The bid must include the cost of supplies, materials, labor costs, and a profit margin for each phase of the project.

Present

Select members of your class to represent the Sanchez family. Present your proposal, scale drawing, model, and written report as you would for the real Sanchez family.

4 Begin the presentation by stating the requirements that the Sanchez family had specified that they wanted or needed for their backyard design.

5 Explain the process you used to develop your plan. Justify your design and fully explain your bid costs.

6 Prepare a detailed plan for the Sanchez family. Submit in this plan one scale drawing, the model, a written description of the backyard design, and a detailed financial bid.

7 Make sure that each aspect of the design is justified in writing. Include any options that may negate the terms of the proposal, such as a change in the types of plants used.

8 Summarize your plan with a sales statement that details why your plan is superior.

CHAPTER 13 HIGHLIGHTS

VOCABULARY

After completing this chapter, you should be able to define each term, property, or phrase and give an example or two of each.

Algebra

completing the square (pp. 742, 743)
conjugate (p. 722)
distance formula (p. 737)
product property of square roots (p. 719)
quotient property of square roots (p. 721)
radical equations (p. 732)
radicand (p. 719)
rationalizing the denominator (p. 722)
simplest radical form (p. 723)

Geometry

Pythagorean theorem (p. 713)

Problem Solving

identify subgoals (p. 745)

UNDERSTANDING AND USING THE VOCABULARY

State whether each sentence is *true* or *false*. If false, replace the underlined word or number to make a true sentence.

1. The binomials $-3 + \sqrt{7}$ and $\underline{3 - \sqrt{7}}$ are conjugates.
2. In the expression $-4\sqrt{5}$, the radicand is $\underline{5}$.
3. The rational expression $\frac{1 + \sqrt{3}}{2 - \sqrt{5}}$ becomes $\underline{2 + 2\sqrt{3} + \sqrt{5} + \sqrt{15}}$ when the denominator is rationalized.
4. The value of c that makes the trinomial $t^2 - 3t + c$ a perfect square is $\underline{9}$.
5. The <u>longest</u> side of a right triangle is the hypotenuse.
6. The distance formula can be expressed using the equation $\underline{d^2 = (x_2 - x_1)^2 + (y_2 - y_1)^2}$.
7. After the first step in solving the rational equation $\sqrt{3x + 19} = x + 3$, you would have the equation $\underline{3x + 19 = x^2 + 9}$.
8. The two sides that form the right angle in a right triangle are called the <u>legs</u> of the triangle.
9. The expression $\underline{\frac{2x\sqrt{3x}}{\sqrt{6y}}}$ is in simplest radical form.
10. To verify whether a triangle with sides having lengths of 25, 20, and 15 is a right triangle, the Pythagorean Theorem would be used: $\underline{15^2 = 25^2 + 20^2}$.

CHAPTER 13 STUDY GUIDE AND ASSESSMENT

SKILLS AND CONCEPTS

OBJECTIVES AND EXAMPLES

Upon completing this chapter, you should be able to:

- use the Pythagorean theorem to solve problems (Lesson 13–1)

Find the length of the missing side.

$c^2 = a^2 + b^2$

$25^2 = 15^2 + b^2$

$625 = 225 + b^2$

$400 = b^2$

$20 = b$

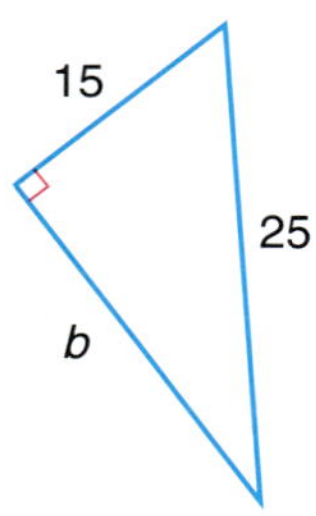

REVIEW EXERCISES

Use these exercises to review and prepare for the chapter test.

If *c* is the measure of the hypotenuse of a right triangle, find each missing measure. Round answers to the nearest hundredth.

11. $a = 30, b = 16, c = ?$

12. $a = 6, b = 10, c = ?$

13. $a = 10, c = 15, b = ?$

14. $b = 4, c = 56, a = ?$

15. $a = 18, c = 30, b = ?$

16. $a = 1.2, b = 1.6, c = ?$

Determine whether the following side measures would form right triangles. Explain why or why not.

17. 9, 16, 20

18. 20, 21, 29

19. 9, 40, 41

20. 18, $\sqrt{24}$, 30

OBJECTIVES AND EXAMPLES

- simplify radical expressions (Lesson 13–2)

$$\sqrt{343x^2y^3} = \sqrt{7 \cdot 7^2 \cdot x^2 \cdot y \cdot y^2}$$
$$= \sqrt{7} \cdot \sqrt{7^2} \cdot \sqrt{x^2} \cdot \sqrt{y} \cdot \sqrt{y^2}$$
$$= 7|x|y\sqrt{7y}$$

$$\frac{3}{5-\sqrt{2}} = \frac{3}{5-\sqrt{2}} \cdot \frac{5+\sqrt{2}}{5+\sqrt{2}}$$
$$= \frac{3(5)+3\sqrt{2}}{5^2-(\sqrt{2})^2}$$
$$= \frac{15+3\sqrt{2}}{25-2}$$
$$= \frac{15+3\sqrt{2}}{23}$$

REVIEW EXERCISES

Simplify. Leave in radical form and use absolute value symbols when necessary.

21. $\sqrt{480}$

22. $\sqrt{\frac{60}{y^2}}$

23. $\sqrt{44a^2b^5}$

24. $\sqrt{96x^4}$

25. $(3 - 2\sqrt{12})^2$

26. $\frac{9}{3+\sqrt{2}}$

27. $\frac{2\sqrt{7}}{3\sqrt{5}+5\sqrt{3}}$

28. $\frac{\sqrt{3a^3b^4}}{\sqrt{8ab^{10}}}$

OBJECTIVES AND EXAMPLES	REVIEW EXERCISES

- simplify radical expressions involving addition, subtraction, and multiplication (Lesson 13–3)

$\sqrt{6} - \sqrt{54} + 3\sqrt{12} + 5\sqrt{3}$
$= \sqrt{6} - \sqrt{3^2 \cdot 6} + 3\sqrt{2^2 \cdot 3} + 5\sqrt{3}$
$= \sqrt{6} - (\sqrt{3^2} \cdot \sqrt{6}) + 3(\sqrt{2^2} \cdot \sqrt{3}) + 5\sqrt{3}$
$= \sqrt{6} - 3\sqrt{6} + 3(2\sqrt{3}) + 5\sqrt{3}$
$= \sqrt{6} - 3\sqrt{6} + 6\sqrt{3} + 5\sqrt{3}$
$= -2\sqrt{6} + 11\sqrt{3}$

Simplify. Then use a calculator to verify your answer.

29. $2\sqrt{6} - \sqrt{48}$
30. $2\sqrt{13} + 8\sqrt{15} - 3\sqrt{15} + 3\sqrt{13}$
31. $4\sqrt{27} + 6\sqrt{48}$
32. $5\sqrt{18} - 3\sqrt{112} - 3\sqrt{98}$
33. $\sqrt{8} + \sqrt{\frac{1}{8}}$
34. $4\sqrt{7k} - 7\sqrt{7k} + 2\sqrt{7k}$

- solve radical equations (Lesson 13–4)

Solve $\sqrt{5 - 4x} - 6 = 7$.

$\sqrt{5 - 4x} - 6 = 7$
$\sqrt{5 - 4x} = 13$
$(\sqrt{5 - 4x})^2 = (13)^2$
$5 - 4x = 169$
$-4x = 164$
$x = -41$

Solve each equation. Check your solution.

35. $\sqrt{3x} = 6$
36. $\sqrt{t} = 2\sqrt{6}$
37. $\sqrt{7x - 1} = 5$
38. $\sqrt{x + 4} = x - 8$
39. $\sqrt{r} = 3\sqrt{5}$
40. $\sqrt{3x - 14} + x = 6$
41. $\sqrt{\frac{4a}{3}} - 2 = 0$
42. $9 = \sqrt{\frac{5n}{4}} - 1$
43. $10 + 2\sqrt{b} = 0$
44. $\sqrt{a + 4} = 6$

- find the distance between two points in the coordinate plane (Lesson 13–5)

Find the distance between the pair of points with coordinates $(-5, 1)$ and $(1, 5)$.

$d = \sqrt{(x_2 - x_1)^2 + (y_2 - y_1)^2}$
$= \sqrt{(1 - (-5))^2 + (5 - 1)^2}$
$= \sqrt{6^2 + 4^2}$
$= \sqrt{36 + 16}$ or $\sqrt{52} \approx 7.21$

Find the distance between each pair of points whose coordinates are given.

45. $(9, -2), (1, 13)$
46. $(4, 2), (7, -9)$
47. $(4, -6), (-2, 7)$
48. $(2\sqrt{5}, 9), (4\sqrt{5}, 3)$

Find the value of *a* if the points with the given coordinates are the indicated distance apart.

49. $(-3, 2), (1, a); d = 5$
50. $(5, -2), (a, -3); d = \sqrt{170}$
51. $(1, 1), (4, a); d = 5$

OBJECTIVES AND EXAMPLES

- solve quadratic equations by completing the square (Lesson 13–6)

Solve $y^2 + 6y + 2 = 0$ by completing the square.

$$y^2 + 6y + 2 = 0$$
$$y^2 + 6y = -2$$
$$y^2 + 6y + 9 = -2 + 9 \quad \textit{Complete the square.}$$
$$(y + 3)^2 = 7 \quad \textit{Since } \left(\tfrac{6}{2}\right)^2 = 9\textit{, add 9 to}$$
$$y + 3 = \pm\sqrt{7} \quad \textit{each side}$$
$$y = -3 \pm \sqrt{7}$$

The solution set is $-3 + \sqrt{7}$ and $-3 - \sqrt{7}$.

REVIEW EXERCISES

Find the value of c that makes each trinomial a perfect square.

52. $y^2 - 12y + c$
53. $m^2 + 7m + c$
54. $b^2 + 18b + c$
55. $p^2 - \frac{2}{3}p + c$

Solve each equation by completing the square. Leave irrational roots in simplest radical form.

56. $x^2 - 16x + 32 = 0$
57. $m^2 - 7m = 5$
58. $4a^2 + 16a + 15 = 0$
59. $\frac{1}{2}y^2 + 2y - 1 = 0$
60. $n^2 - 3n + \frac{5}{4} = 0$

APPLICATIONS AND PROBLEM SOLVING

61. **Geometry** The sides of a triangle measure $4\sqrt{24}$ cm, $5\sqrt{6}$ cm, and $3\sqrt{54}$ cm. What is the perimeter of the triangle? (Lesson 13–3)

62. **Sight Distance** In a movie about baseball, Roger decides to climb a tree in order to be able to see the Angels game better. The formula $V = 3.5\sqrt{h}$ relates height and distance, where h is your height in meters above the ground and V is the distance in kilometers that you can see. (Lesson 13–4)
    a. How far could Roger see if he had climbed 9 meters to the top of a tree?
    b. How high would someone have to be if she wanted to be able to see 56 kilometers?

63. **Geometry** What kind of triangle has vertices at (4, 2), (−3, 1), and (5, −4)? (Lesson 13–5)

64. **Number Theory** When 6 is subtracted from 10 times a number, the result is equal to 4 times the square of the number. Find the numbers. (Lesson 13–6)

65. **Nature** An 18-foot tall tree is broken by the wind. The top of the tree falls and touches the ground 12 feet from its base. How many feet from the base of the tree did the break occur? (Lesson 13–1)

66. **Physics** The time T (in seconds) required for a pendulum of length L (in feet) to make one complete swing back and forth is given by the formula $T = 2\pi\sqrt{\frac{L}{32}}$. How long does it take a pendulum 4 feet long to make one complete swing? (Lesson 13–2)

67. **Law Enforcement** Lina told the police officer that she was traveling at 55 mph when she applied the brakes and skidded. The skid marks at the scene were 240 feet long. Should Lina's car have skidded that far if it was traveling at 55 mph? Use the formula $s = \sqrt{15d}$. (Lesson 13–4)

A practice test for Chapter 13 is provided on page 799.

ALTERNATIVE ASSESSMENT

COOPERATIVE LEARNING PROJECT

Games Ryan and Nicholas enjoy playing a game in which the location of ships on a grid must be determined. They determine the lengths of five ships that they will draw on their grids. Each time a ship intersects a grid coordinate, that is one of the points where the ship can be attacked and hit. A ship can be placed on the grid horizontally or vertically. When all of the grid coordinates for a ship are hit, the ship is sunk. The goal is to sink all of the other person's ships first.

For their first game, Ryan and Nicholas decided on $2\sqrt{5}$ units, 3 units, $\sqrt{13}$ units, $\sqrt{2}$ units, and 2 units for their ship lengths. Place these five ships on the grid below making sure that they have the above stated lengths. How many hits would another player have to get in order to sink all of the ships on your grid?

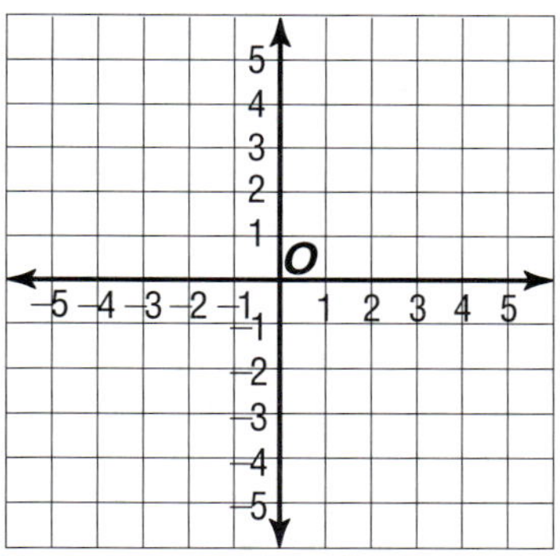

Follow these guidelines for your game.

- Determine whether each of the ships with the specified lengths have to be drawn horizontally or vertically.
- Devise a chart that will be helpful in organizing the data you will need; for example, length of ship, length of legs of triangle formed by diagonal ships, and number of grid coordinates for each ship.
- Create a grid that will incorporate the above specifications for the ships.
- Write a summary of the above game.
- Play the game with a fellow classmate.

THINKING CRITICALLY

- Is the sum of two irrational numbers always an irrational number? Explain.
- For any real number n, $\sqrt{n^2} = |n|$. What rule would be true for $\sqrt{n^t}$ if t were odd?

PORTFOLIO

Visualizing a concept or skill is a good way to help understand a concept. Using colored pencils is one way to visualize steps that need to be remembered or aid in "seeing" items that are easy to forget. When simplifying a rational expression, write the perfect square number or variables using colored pencils. This will serve to remind you what needs to be written outside the radical sign and what needs to stay inside the radical sign. Use one of the exercises in this chapter and use colored pencils to simplify it. Write how you chose what to put in color and how it aided you in the problem-solving process. Place this in your portfolio.

SELF EVALUATION

When solving a problem, one may look for alternative methods to use. The same method may not work in every situation. Being open-minded about a different process is a positive value. Comparing methods can also be beneficial.

Assess yourself. Are you a person that sticks to the same method for a solution or do you also look for other means? Do you compare methods or not? Think of two problems that you have had, one from your daily life and one from your mathematical experiences, where you used two different methods to solve each of them.

STUDENT HANDBOOK

For Additional Assessment

For Reference

EXTRA PRACTICE

Lesson 1-1 Write an algebraic expression for each verbal expression.

1. the product of x and 7
2. the quotient of r and s
3. the sum of b and 21
4. a number t decreased by 6
5. a number a to the third power
6. sixteen squared

Write a verbal expression for each algebraic expression.

7. $n - 7$
8. xy
9. m^5
10. 8^4
11. $6r^2$
12. $z^7 + 2$

Write each expression as an expression with exponents.

13. $5 \cdot 5 \cdot 5$
14. $7 \cdot a \cdot a \cdot a \cdot a$
15. $2(m)(m)(m)$
16. $5 \cdot 5 \cdot 5 \cdot x \cdot x \cdot y$
17. $p \cdot p \cdot p \cdot p \cdot p \cdot p$
18. $4 \cdot 4 \cdot 4 \cdot t \cdot t$

Evaluate each expression.

19. 2^4
20. 8^2
21. 7^3
22. 10^4
23. 3^6
24. 4^5

Lesson 1-2 Give the next two items for each pattern.

1.

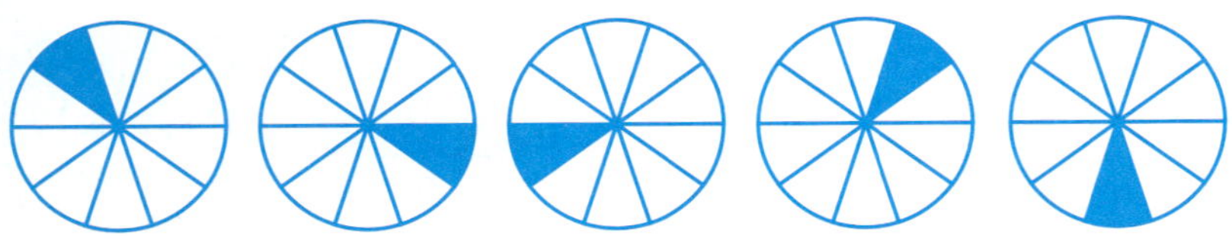

2.

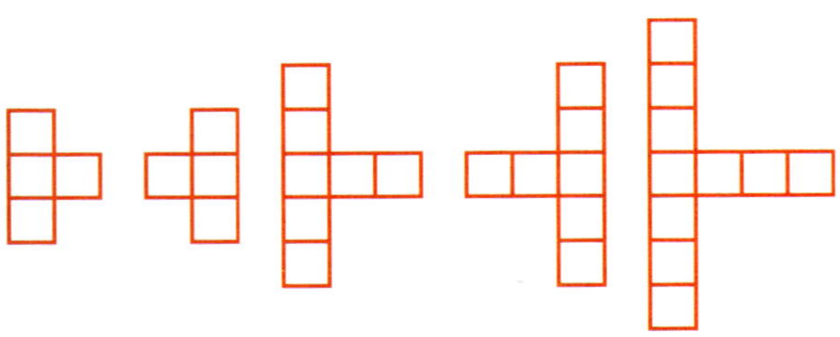

3. 12, 23, 34, 45, ...
4. 39, 33, 27, 21, ...
5. 6, 7.2, 8.4, 9.6, ...
6. 86, 81.5, 77, 72.5, ...
7. 4, 8, 16, 32, ...
8. 3125, 625, 125, 25, ...
9. 15, 16, 18, 21, 25, 30, ...
10. $w - 2, w - 4, w - 6, w - 8, \ldots$
11. 13, 10, 11, 8, 9, 6, ...

Lesson 1-3 Evaluate each expression.

1. $3 + 8 \div 2 - 5$
2. $4 + 7 \cdot 2 + 8$
3. $5(9 + 3) - 3 \cdot 4$
4. $4(11 + 7) - 9 \cdot 8$
5. $5^3 + 6^3 - 5^2$
6. $16 \div 2 \cdot 5 \cdot 3 \div 6$
7. $7(5^3 + 3^2)$
8. $\frac{9 \cdot 4 + 2 \cdot 6}{7 \cdot 7}$
9. $25 - \frac{1}{3}(18 + 9)$

Evaluate each expression when $a = 2$, $b = 5$, $x = 4$, and $n = 10$.

10. $8a + b$
11. $12x + ab$
12. $a(6 - 3n)$
13. $bx + an$
14. $x^2 - 4n$
15. $3b + 16a - 9n$
16. $n^2 + 3(a + 4)$
17. $(2x)^2 + an - 5b$
18. $[a + 8(b - 2)]^2 \div 4$

Lesson 1-4 **Suppose the number 16,782 is rounded to 16,800 and plotted using stem 16 and leaf 8. Write the stem and leaf for each number below if the numbers are part of the same set of data.**

1. 24,640
2. 35,788
3. 4239
4. 5865
5. 611
6. 17,903
7. The stem-and-leaf plot at the right gives the average weekly earnings for various occupations in 1993. Use the plot to answer each question.
   a. What were the highest weekly earnings?
   b. What were the lowest weekly earnings?
   c. How many occupations have weekly earnings of at least $500?
   d. What does 5 | 1 represent?

Average Weekly Earnings

Stem	Leaf
2	6 7
3	1 2 8 9
4	1 3 6 8 8 8 9
5	0 1 6
6	
7	1 2 4

3 | 8 = $380–$389

Lesson 1-5 **State whether each equation is *true* or *false* for the value of the variable given.**

1. $b + \frac{2}{3} = \frac{3}{4} + \frac{1}{3}, b = \frac{1}{2}$
2. $\frac{2 + 13}{y} = \frac{3}{5}y, y = 5$
3. $x^8 = 9^4, x = 3$
4. $4t^2 - 5(3) = 9, t = 7$
5. $\frac{3^2 - 5x}{3^2 - 1} \leq 2, x = 4$
6. $a^6 \div 4 \div a^3 \div a < 3, a = 2$

Find the solution set for each inequality if the replacement set for *x* is {4, 5, 6, 7, 8} and for *y* is {10, 12, 14, 16}.

7. $x + 2 > 7$
8. $x - 1 > 3$
9. $2y - 15 \leq 17$
10. $y + 12 < 25$
11. $\frac{y + 12}{7} \geq 4$
12. $\frac{2(x - 2)}{3} < \frac{4}{7 - 5}$
13. $x - 4 > \frac{x + 2}{3}$
14. $y^2 - 100 \geq 4y$
15. $9x - 20 \geq x^2$
16. $0.3(x + 4) \leq 0.4(2x + 3)$
17. $1.3x - 12 < 0.9x + 4$
18. $1.2y - 8 \leq 0.7y - 3$

Solve each equation.

19. $x = \frac{17 + 9}{2}$
20. $3(8) + 4 = b$
21. $\frac{18 - 7}{13 - 2} = y$
22. $28 - (-14) = z$
23. $20.4 - 5.67 = t$
24. $t = 91.8 \div 27$
25. $-\frac{5}{8}\left(-\frac{4}{5}\right) = c$
26. $8\frac{1}{12} - 5\frac{5}{12} = e$
27. $\frac{3}{4} - \frac{9}{16} = s$
28. $\frac{5}{8} + \frac{1}{4} = y$
29. $n = \frac{84 \div 7}{18 \div 9}$
30. $d = 3\frac{1}{2} \div 2$

Lesson 1-6 **Name the property or properties illustrated by each statement.**

1. If $8 \cdot 3 = 24$, then $24 = 8 \cdot 3$.
2. $6 + (4 + 1) = 6 + 5$
3. $(12 - 3)(7) = 9(7)$
4. $qrs = 1qrs$
5. $\left(\frac{8}{9}\right)\left(\frac{9}{8}\right) = 1$
6. $4\left(6^2 \cdot \frac{1}{36}\right) = 4$
7. $0 + 45 = 45$
8. If $5 = 9 - 4$, then $9 - 4 = 5$.
9. $2(0) = 0$
10. $16 + 37 = 16 + 37$
11. $1(57) = 57$
12. $0 + h = h$
13. If $9 + 1 = 10$ and $10 = 5(2)$, then $9 + 1 = 5(2)$.

Lesson 1-7 **Use the distributive property to rewrite each expression without parentheses.**

1. $3(5 + w)$
2. $(h - 8)7$
3. $6(y + 4)$
4. $9(3n + 5)$
5. $32\left(x - \frac{1}{8}\right)$
6. $c(7 - d)$

Use the distributive property to find each product.

7. $6 \cdot 55$
8. $\left(4\frac{1}{18}\right) \times 18$
9. $15(108)$
10. $14(3.7)$
11. $689 \cdot 5$
12. 7×314

Simplify each expression, if possible. If not possible, write *in simplest form*.

13. $13a + 5a$
14. $21x - 10x$
15. $8(3x + 7)$
16. $4m - 4n$
17. $3(5am - 4)$
18. $15x^2 + 7x^2$
19. $9y^2 + 13y^2 + 3$
20. $11a^2 - 11a^2 + 12a^2$
21. $6a + 7a + 12b + 8b$

Lesson 1-8 **Name the property illustrated by each statement.**

1. $1 \cdot a^2 = a^2$
2. $x^2 + (y + z) = x^2 + (z + y)$
3. $ax + 2b = xa + 2b$
4. $29 + 0 = 29$
5. $5(a + 3b) = 5a + 15b$
6. $5a + 3b = 3b + 5a$
7. $(4 \cdot c) \cdot d = 4 \cdot (c \cdot d)$
8. $(6x^3) \cdot 0 = 0$
9. $(4 + 1)x + 2 = 5x + 2$
10. $(a + b) + 3 = a + (b + 3)$
11. $5(ab) = (5a)b$
12. $5a + \left(\frac{1}{2}b + c\right) = \left(5a + \frac{1}{2}b\right) + c$

Simplify.

13. $5a + 6b + 7a$
14. $8x + 4y + 9x$
15. $3a + 5b + 2c + 8b$
16. $\frac{2}{3}x^2 + 5x + x^2$
17. $(4p - 7q) + (5q - 8p)$
18. $8q + 5r - 7q - 6r$
19. $4(2x + y) + 5x$
20. $9r^5 + 2r^2 + r^5$
21. $12b^3 + 12 + 12b^3$
22. $7 + 3(uv - 6) + u$
23. $3(x + 2y) + 4(3x + y)$
24. $6.2(a + b) + 2.6(a + b) + 3a$
25. $3 + 8(st + 3w) + 3st$
26. $5.4(s - 3t) + 3.6(s - 4)$
27. $3[4 + 5(2x + 3y)]$

Lesson 1-9 **Match each description with the most appropriate graph.**

Graph 1

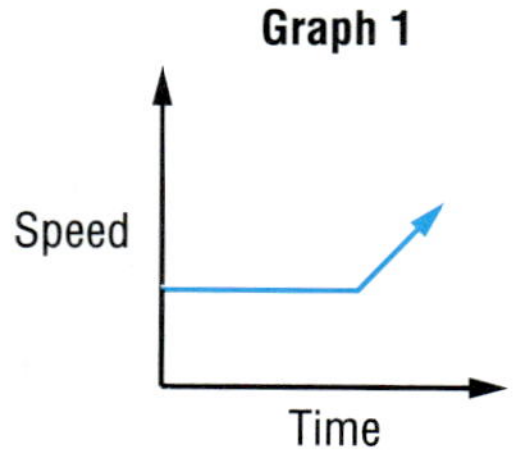

Graph 2

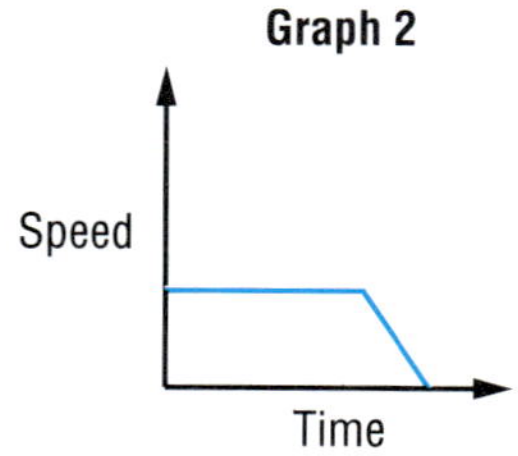

Graph 3

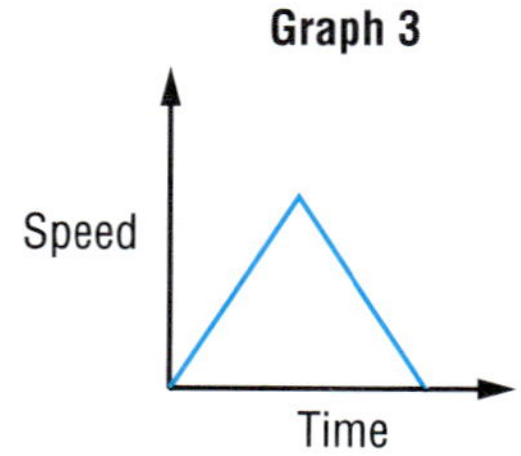

Graph 4

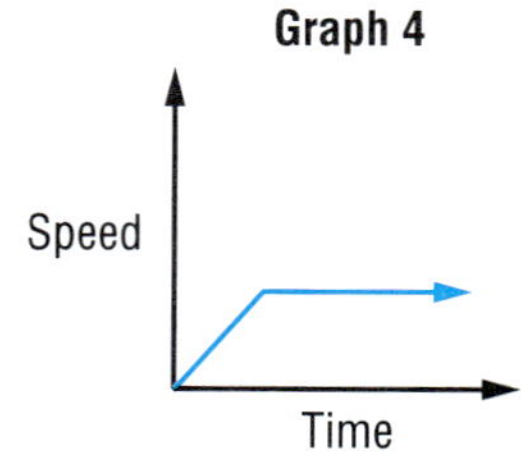

1. Jeremy picks up his speed while jogging down a hill. Then he slows down until he comes to a stop.
2. Ilene jogs up a hill at a steady speed. Then she runs down the hill and picks up her speed.
3. Casey runs down a hill and picks up his speed. Then he continues to jog at a steady pace.
4. Luisa jogs along a road at a steady speed. Then she slows down until she comes to a stop.

Lesson 2-1 Name the set of numbers graphed.

1. 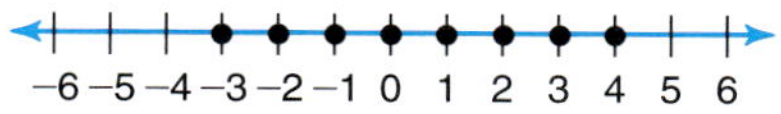

2. 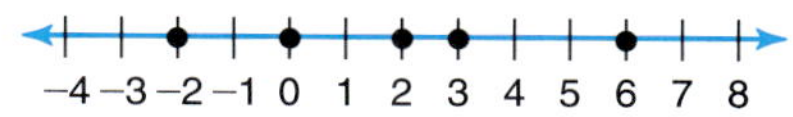

3. 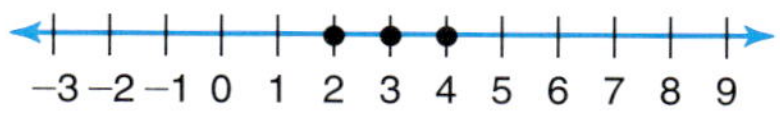

4. 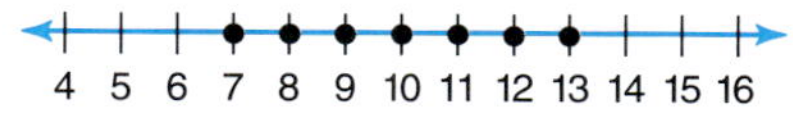

5. 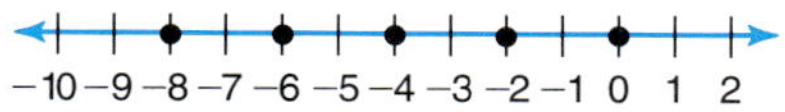

6. 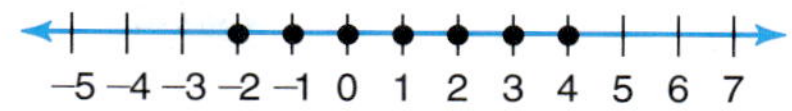

Graph each set of numbers on a number line.

7. $\{-2, -4, -6\}$
8. $\{\ldots, -3, -2, -1, 0\}$
9. {integers greater than -1}
10. {integers less than -5 and greater than -10}
11. {integers less than or equal to 3}
12. {integers less than 0 and greater than or equal to -6}

Lesson 2-2 Use the line plot below to answer each question.

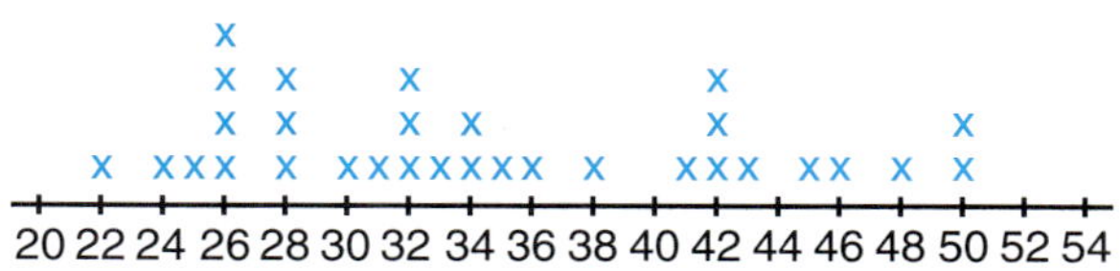

1. What was the highest score on the test?
2. What was the lowest score on the test?
3. How many students took the test?
4. How many students scored in the 40s?
5. What score was received by the most students?

Make a line plot for each set of data.

6. 134, 167, 137, 138, 120, 134, 145, 155, 152, 159, 164, 135, 144, 156
7. 19, 12, 11, 11, 7, 7, 8, 13, 12, 12, 9, 9, 8, 15, 11, 4, 12, 7, 7, 6
8. 66, 74, 72, 78, 68, 75, 80, 69, 62, 65, 63, 78, 81, 78, 76, 87, 80, 69, 81, 76, 79, 70, 62, 73, 85, 87, 70
9. 152, 156, 133, 154, 129, 146, 174, 138, 185, 141, 169, 176, 179, 168, 185, 154, 199, 200

Lesson 2-3 Find each sum or difference.

1. $-3 + 16$
2. $27 - 19$
3. $8 - 13$
4. $14 + (-9)$
5. $-18 + (-11)$
6. $-25 + 47$
7. $19m - 12m$
8. $8h - 23h$
9. $24b - (-9b)$
10. $97 + (-79)$
11. $4 + (-12) + (-18)$
12. $7 + (-11) + 32$
13. $|-28 + (-67)|$
14. $|-89 + 46|$
15. $|-285 + (-641)|$
16. $-35 - (-12)$
17. $24 + (-15)$
18. $-15 + (-13)$
19. $-7 + (-21)$
20. $8 - 17 + (-3)$
21. $27 - 14 - (-19)$
22. $|-9 + 15|$
23. $\begin{bmatrix} 5 & -4 \\ 0 & 3 \end{bmatrix} + \begin{bmatrix} -3 & 4 \\ -2 & -4 \end{bmatrix}$
24. $\begin{bmatrix} 1 & -4 \\ 5 & -6 \end{bmatrix} - \begin{bmatrix} 4 & -3 \\ 7 & -1 \end{bmatrix}$

EXTRA PRACTICE

Lesson 2-4 Replace each ___?___ with <, >, or = to make each sentence true.

1. $6 \underline{\ ?\ } -4$
2. $12 \underline{\ ?\ } -21$
3. $-4 \underline{\ ?\ } -10$
4. $4 \underline{\ ?\ } 14$
5. $-13 \underline{\ ?\ } -8$
6. $-5 + 2 \underline{\ ?\ } -3$
7. $7 \underline{\ ?\ } 13 - (-6)$
8. $3.4 - 5.7 \underline{\ ?\ } -2$
9. $\frac{18}{-6} \underline{\ ?\ } -3$
10. $\frac{8}{13} \underline{\ ?\ } \frac{9}{14}$
11. $\frac{25}{-8} \underline{\ ?\ } \frac{-28}{7}$
12. $6\left(\frac{5}{3}\right) \underline{\ ?\ } \left(\frac{3}{2}\right)6$
13. $\frac{0.6}{7} \underline{\ ?\ } \frac{1.8}{12}$
14. $24.6 \underline{\ ?\ } 13.8 - (-12.8)$
15. $-54 + 26.5 \underline{\ ?\ } 27.5$
16. $\frac{5.4}{18} \underline{\ ?\ } -4 + 1$
17. $(4.1)(0.2) \underline{\ ?\ } 8.4$
18. $-\frac{12}{17} \underline{\ ?\ } -\frac{9}{14}$

Lesson 2-5 Find each sum or difference.

1. $-\frac{11}{9} + \left(-\frac{7}{9}\right)$
2. $\frac{5}{11} - \frac{6}{11}$
3. $\frac{2}{7} - \frac{3}{14}$
4. $-4.8 + 3.2$
5. $-1.7 - 3.9$
6. $-72.5 - 81.3$
7. $-\frac{3}{5} + \frac{5}{6}$
8. $\frac{3}{8} + \left(-\frac{7}{12}\right)$
9. $-\frac{7}{15} + \left(-\frac{5}{12}\right)$
10. $-4.5 - 8.6$
11. $89.3 - (-14.2)$
12. $-0.007 + 0.06$
13. $-\frac{2}{7} + \frac{3}{14} + \frac{3}{7}$
14. $-\frac{3}{5} + \frac{6}{7} + \left(-\frac{2}{35}\right)$
15. $\frac{7}{3} + \left(-\frac{5}{6}\right) + \left(-\frac{2}{3}\right)$
16. $-4.13 + (-5.18) + 9.63$
17. $6.7 + (-8.1) + (-7.3)$
18. $\frac{3}{4} + \left(-\frac{5}{8}\right) + \frac{3}{32}$
19. $1.9 - (-7)$
20. $-1.8 - 3.7$
21. $-18 - (-1.3)$

Lesson 2-6 Find each product.

1. $5(12)$
2. $(-6)(11)$
3. $(-7)(-5)$
4. $\left(-\frac{7}{8}\right)\left(-\frac{1}{3}\right)$
5. $(-5)\left(-\frac{2}{5}\right)$
6. $(-6)(4)(-3)$
7. $(4)(-2)(-1)(-3)$
8. $(-6.8)(-5.415)(3.1)$
9. $(-5.34)(3.2)$
10. $\left(\frac{3}{5}\right)\left(-\frac{5}{7}\right)$
11. $-\frac{7}{15}\left(\frac{9}{14}\right)$
12. $(4.2)(-5.1)(3.6)$
13. $-6\left(\frac{5}{3}\right)\left(\frac{9}{10}\right)$
14. $(3)(-6)(0)(-1)$
15. $(-21)(-2)(-1)$

Lesson 2-7 Simplify.

1. $\frac{-48}{8}$
2. $-49 \div (-7)$
3. $-64 \div 8$
4. $-\frac{3}{4} \div 9$
5. $-9 \div \left(-\frac{10}{17}\right)$
6. $\frac{-450n}{10}$
7. $\frac{-36a}{-6}$
8. $\frac{63a}{-9}$
9. $8 \div \left(-\frac{5}{4}\right)$
10. $\frac{\frac{7}{8}}{-10}$
11. $\frac{12}{\frac{-8}{5}}$
12. $\frac{6a + 24}{6}$
13. $\frac{20a + 30b}{-2}$
14. $\frac{\frac{11}{5}}{-6}$
15. $\frac{70a - 42b}{-14}$
16. $\frac{-32x + 12y}{-4}$
17. $-\frac{7}{12} \div \frac{1}{18}$
18. $\frac{5}{\frac{15}{-7}}$

Lesson 2-8 Find each square root. Use a calculator if necessary. Round to the nearest hundredth if the result is not a whole number.

1. $-\sqrt{81}$
2. $\sqrt{0.0016}$
3. $\pm\sqrt{206}$
4. $\pm\sqrt{\frac{81}{64}}$
5. $\sqrt{85}$
6. $-\sqrt{\frac{36}{196}}$
7. $-\sqrt{149}$
8. $\pm\sqrt{961}$
9. $\sqrt{10.24}$

Evaluate each expression. Use a calculator if necessary. Round to the nearest hundredth if the result is not a whole number.

10. $\sqrt{m}$, if $m = 529$
11. $-\sqrt{c - d}$, if $c = 1.097$ and $d = 1.0171$
12. $-\sqrt{ab}$, if $a = 1.2$ and $b = 2.7$
13. $\pm\sqrt{\frac{x}{y}}$, if $x = 144$ and $y = 1521$

Lesson 2-9 Translate each sentence into an equation, inequality, or formula.

1. The square of a decreased by the cube of b is equal to c.
2. Twenty-nine decreased by the product of x and y is less than z.
3. The perimeter P of a parallelogram is twice the sum of the lengths of two adjacent sides a and b.
4. Four-fifths of the product of m, n, and the square of p is greater than 26.
5. Thirty increased by the quotient of s and t is equal to v.
6. The area A of a trapezoid is half the product of the height h and the sum of the two parallel bases a and b.

Lesson 3-1 Solve each equation. Then check your solution.

1. $-2 + g = 7$
2. $9 + s = -5$
3. $-4 + y = -9$
4. $m + 6 = 2$
5. $t + (-4) = 10$
6. $v - 7 = -4$
7. $a - (-6) = -5$
8. $-2 - x = -8$
9. $d + (-44) = -61$
10. $e - (-26) = 41$
11. $p - 47 = 22$
12. $-63 - f = -82$
13. $c + 5.4 = -11.33$
14. $-6.11 + b = 14.321$
15. $-5 = y - 22.7$
16. $-5 - q = 1.19$
17. $n + (-4.361) = 59.78$
18. $t - (-46.1) = -3.673$
19. $\frac{7}{10} - a = \frac{1}{2}$
20. $f - \left(-\frac{1}{8}\right) = \frac{3}{10}$
21. $-4\frac{5}{12} = t - \left(-10\frac{1}{36}\right)$
22. $x + \frac{3}{8} = \frac{1}{4}$
23. $1\frac{7}{16} + s = \frac{9}{8}$
24. $17\frac{8}{9} = d + \left(-2\frac{5}{6}\right)$

Lesson 3-2 Solve each equation. Then check your solution.

1. $-5p = 35$
2. $-3x = -24$
3. $62y = -2356$
4. $\frac{a}{-6} = -2$
5. $\frac{c}{-59} = -7$
6. $\frac{f}{14} = -63$
7. $84 = \frac{x}{97}$
8. $\frac{w}{5} = 3$
9. $\frac{q}{9} = -3$
10. $\frac{2}{5}x = \frac{4}{7}$
11. $\frac{z}{6} = -\frac{5}{12}$
12. $-\frac{5}{9}r = 7\frac{1}{2}$
13. $2\frac{1}{6}j = 5\frac{1}{5}$
14. $3 = 1\frac{7}{11}q$
15. $-1\frac{3}{4}p = -\frac{5}{8}$
16. $57k = 0.1824$
17. $0.0022b = 0.1958$
18. $5j = -32.15$
19. $\frac{w}{-2} = -2.48$
20. $\frac{z}{2.8} = -6.2$
21. $\frac{x}{-0.063} = 0.015$
22. $15\frac{3}{8} = -5.125p$
23. $-7.25 = -3\frac{5}{8}g$
24. $-18\frac{1}{4} = 2.50x$

Lesson 3-3 Solve each equation. Then check your solution.

1. $2x - 5 = 3$
2. $4t + 5 = 37$
3. $7a + 6 = -36$
4. $47 = -8g + 7$
5. $-3c - 9 = -24$
6. $5k - 7 = -52$
7. $5s + 4s = -72$
8. $3x - 7 = 2$
9. $8 + 3x = 5$
10. $-3y + 7.569 = 24.069$
11. $7 - 9.1f = 137.585$
12. $6.5 = 2.4m - 4.9$
13. $\frac{e}{5} + 6 = -2$
14. $\frac{d}{4} - 8 = -5$
15. $-\frac{4}{13}y - 7 = 6$
16. $\frac{p + 10}{3} = 4$
17. $\frac{h - 7}{6} = 1$
18. $\frac{5f + 1}{8} = -3$
19. $\frac{4n - 8}{-2} = 12$
20. $\frac{2a}{7} + 9 = 3$
21. $\frac{-3t - 4}{2} = 8$

Lesson 3-4 Find the complement of each angle measure.

1. $15°$
2. $79°$
3. $88°$
4. $a°$
5. $(3c)°$
6. $(b - 15)°$

Find the supplement of each angle measure.

7. $156°$
8. $94°$
9. $21°$
10. $a°$
11. $(3c)°$
12. $(b - 15)°$

Find the measure of the third angle of each triangle in which the measures of two angles of the triangle are given.

13. $90°, 2°$
14. $34°, 132°$
15. $111°, 28°$
16. $a°, b°$
17. $a°, (a - 15)°$
18. $b°, (3b - 2)°$

Lesson 3-5 Solve each equation. Then check your solution.

1. $6(y - 5) = 18$
2. $-21 = 7(p - 10)$
3. $3(h + 2) = 12$
4. $-3(x + 2) = -18$
5. $11.2n + 6 = 5.2n$
6. $2m + 5 - 6m = 25$
7. $3z - 1 = 23 - 3z$
8. $5a - 5 = 7a - 19$
9. $5b + 12 = 3b - 6$
10. $3x - 5 = 7x + 7$
11. $1.9s + 6 = 3.1 - s$
12. $2.85y - 7 = 12.85y - 2$
13. $2.9m + 1.7 = 3.5 + 2.3m$
14. $3(x + 1) - 5 = 3x - 2$
15. $4(2y - 1) = -10(y - 5)$
16. $\frac{6v - 9}{3} = v$
17. $\frac{3t + 1}{4} = \frac{3}{4}t - 5$
18. $\frac{2}{5}y + \frac{y}{2} = 9$
19. $3y - \frac{4}{5} = \frac{1}{3}y$
20. $\frac{3}{4}x - 4 = 7 + \frac{1}{2}x$
21. $\frac{x}{2} - \frac{1}{3} = \frac{x}{3} - \frac{1}{2}$

Lesson 3-6 Solve each equation for x.

1. $x + r = q$
2. $ax + 4 = 7$
3. $2bx - b = -5$
4. $\frac{x - c}{c + a} = a$
5. $\frac{x + y}{c} = d$
6. $\frac{ax + 1}{2} = b$
7. $\frac{x + t}{4} = d$
8. $6x - 7 = -r$
9. $kx + 4y = 5z$
10. $ax - 6 = t$
11. $\frac{2}{3}x + a = b$
12. $q(x + 1) = 5$
13. $\frac{x - y}{z} = 8$
14. $\frac{7a + b}{x} = 1$
15. $\frac{4cx + t}{7} = 2$
16. $\frac{9x - 4c}{z} = z$
17. $cx + a = bx$
18. $\frac{12q - x}{5} = t$

Lesson 3-7

1. **Geography** The areas in square miles of the 20 largest natural U.S. lakes are given below. Find the mean, median, and mode of the areas.

31,700 1697 242 700 22,300 451 374 432 23,000 207
1000 1361 315 625 9910 215 458 360 7550 435

2. **Work** Each number below represents the number of days that each employee of the Cole Corporation was absent during 1996. Find the mean, median, and mode of the number of days absent.

0 10 8 5 8 9 3 3 2 9 7 0 4 2 4 6 2
9 13 3 1 5 5 7 2 6 5 3 4 7 1 1 5 3
3 1 4 5 1 2

3. **Football** Tailback Michael Anderson, of the West High Bears, averaged 137.6 yards rushing per game for the first five games of the season. He rushes for 155 yards in the sixth game. What is his new rushing average?

4. **Olympic Games** One of the events in the Winter Olympics is the men's 500-meter speed skating. The winning times for this event are shown at the right. Find the mean, median, and mode of the times.

Year	Time(s)	Year	Time(s)
1932	43.4	1968	40.3
1936	43.4	1972	39.4
1948	43.1	1976	39.2
1952	43.2	1980	38.0
1956	40.2	1984	38.2
1960	40.2	1988	36.5
1964	40.1	1992	37.1

Lesson 4-1 Solve each proportion.

1. $\frac{4}{5} = \frac{x}{20}$
2. $\frac{b}{63} = \frac{3}{7}$
3. $\frac{y}{5} = \frac{3}{4}$
4. $\frac{7}{4} = \frac{3}{a}$
5. $\frac{t-5}{4} = \frac{3}{2}$
6. $\frac{x}{9} = \frac{0.24}{3}$
7. $\frac{n}{3} = \frac{n+4}{7}$
8. $\frac{12q}{-7} = \frac{30}{14}$
9. $\frac{1}{y-3} = \frac{3}{y-5}$
10. $\frac{r-1}{r+1} = \frac{3}{5}$
11. $\frac{a-3}{8} = \frac{3}{4}$
12. $\frac{6p-2}{7} = \frac{5p+7}{8}$
13. $\frac{2}{9} = \frac{k+3}{2}$
14. $\frac{5m-3}{4} = \frac{5m+3}{6}$
15. $\frac{w-5}{4} = \frac{w+3}{3}$
16. $\frac{96.8}{t} = \frac{12.1}{7}$
17. $\frac{x}{6.03} = \frac{4}{17.42}$
18. $\frac{4n+5}{5} = \frac{2n+7}{7}$

Lesson 4-2 Determine whether each pair of triangles is similar. Justify your answer.

1.
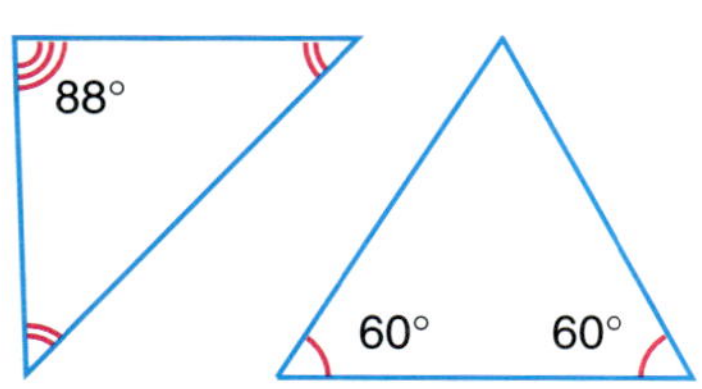

2.
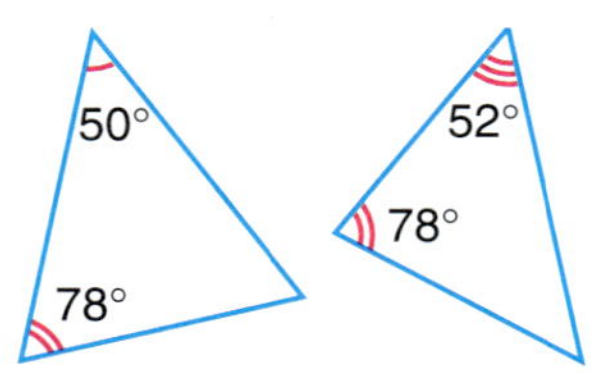

3.
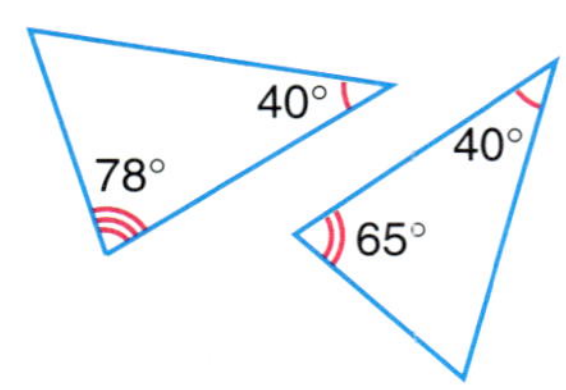

4.
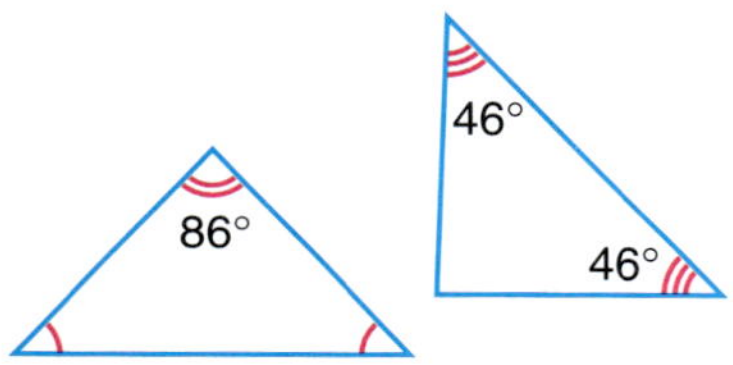

5.
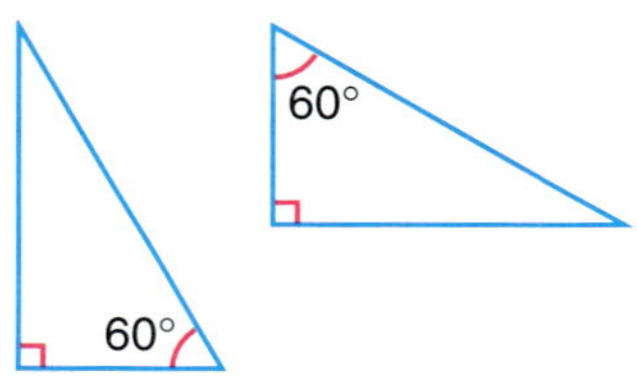

6.
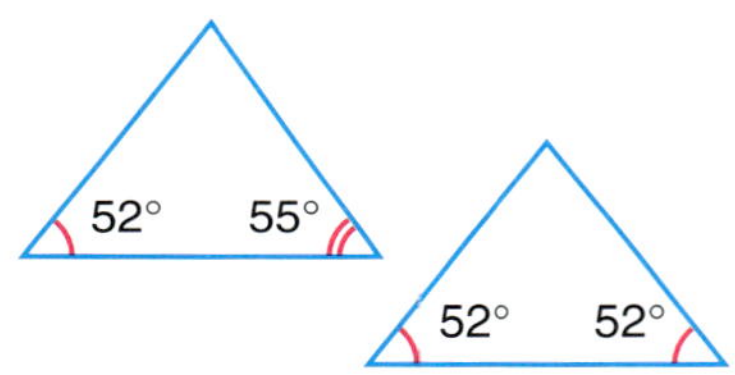

Lesson 4-3 For each triangle, find sin N, cos N, and tan N to the nearest thousandth.

1. 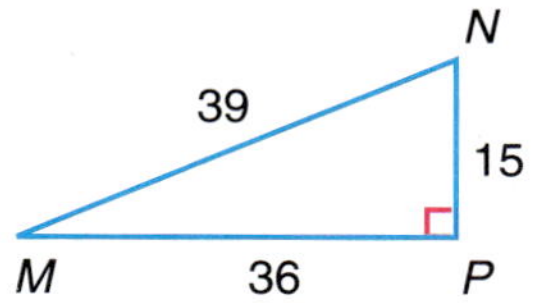

2. 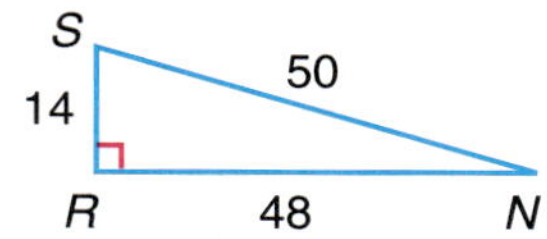

3. 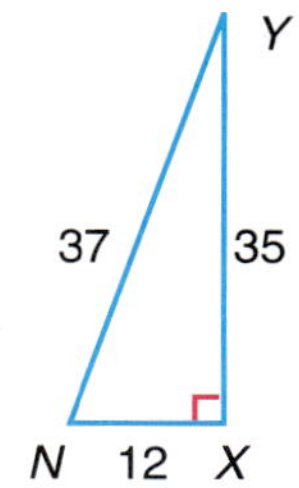

Use a calculator to find the value of each trigonometric ratio to the nearest ten thousandth.

4. cos 25°
5. tan 31°
6. sin 71°
7. cos 64°
8. tan 9°
9. sin 2°

Use a calculator to find the measure of each angle to the nearest degree.

10. $\tan B = 0.5427$
11. $\cos A = 0.8480$
12. $\sin J = 0.9654$
13. $\cos Q = 0.3645$
14. $\sin R = 0.2104$
15. $\tan V = 0.956$

Lesson 4-4 Write each ratio as a percent and then as a decimal.

1. $\frac{1}{4}$
2. $\frac{34}{100}$
3. $\frac{4}{25}$
4. $\frac{3}{20}$
5. $\frac{7}{8}$
6. $\frac{9}{10}$
7. $\frac{24}{40}$
8. $\frac{4}{50}$
9. $\frac{7}{15}$
10. $\frac{4}{9}$
11. $\frac{36}{15}$
12. $\frac{18}{4}$

Use a proportion to answer each question.

13. Twenty-four is what percent of 48?
14. What percent of 70 is 14?
15. Nine is what percent of 72?
16. Fourteen is 17.5% of what number?
17. What percent of 16 is 5.12?
18. What number is 25% of 64?
19. What percent of 80 is 2?
20. Forty-five is what percent of 112.5?

Lesson 4-5 State whether each percent of change is a percent of increase or a percent of decrease. Then find the percent of increase or decrease. Round to the nearest whole percent.

1. original: $100
   new: $67
2. original: 62 acres
   new: 98 acres
3. original: 322 people
   new: 289 people
4. original: 78 pennies
   new: 36 pennies
5. original: $212
   new: $230
6. original: 35 mph
   new: 65 mph

Find the final price of each item. When there is a discount and sales tax, first compute the discount price and then compute the sales tax and final price.

7. television: $299
   sales tax: 4.5%
8. boots: $49.99
   discount: 15%
   sales tax: 3.5%
9. backpack: $28.95
   discount: 10%
   sales tax: 5%
10. software: $36.99
    sales tax: 6.25%
11. jacket: $65
    discount: 30%
    sales tax: 4%
12. book: $15.95
    sales tax: 7%

Lesson 4–6 **Determine the probability of each event.**

1. a coin will land tails up
2. There is a December 1 this year.
3. A baby will be a girl.
4. Next year will have 400 days.
5. This is an algebra book.
6. Today is Wednesday.

Find the probability of each outcome if a computer randomly chooses a letter in the word "success."

7. the letter e
8. P(not c)
9. the letter s
10. the letter b
11. P(vowel)
12. the letters u or c

Find the odds of each outcome if a die is rolled.

13. a 4
14. a number greater than 3
15. a multiple of 3
16. a number less than 5
17. an odd number
18. not a 6

Lesson 4–7

1. **Advertising** An advertisement for an orange drink claims that the drink contains 10% orange juice. How much pure orange juice would have to be added to 5 quarts of the drink to obtain a mixture containing 40% orange juice?
2. **Finance** Jane Pham is investing $6000 in two accounts, part at 4.5% and the remainder at 6%. If the total annual interest earned from the two accounts is $279, how much did Jane deposit at each rate?
3. **Entertainment** At the Golden Oldies Theater, tickets for adults cost $5.50 and tickets for children cost $3.50. How many of each kind of ticket was purchased if 21 tickets were bought for $83.50?
4. **Automotives** A car radiator has a capacity of 14 quarts and is filled with a 20% antifreeze solution. How much must be drained off and replaced with pure antifreeze to obtain a 40% antifreeze solution?
5. **Nutrition** A liter of cream has 9.2% butterfat. How much skim milk containing 2% butterfat should be added to the cream to obtain a mixture with 6.4% butterfat?

Lesson 4–8 **Determine which equations represent inverse variations and which represent direct variations. Then find the constant of variation.**

1. $ab = 6$
2. $\frac{50}{y} = x$
3. $\frac{1}{5}a = d$
4. $s = 3t$
5. $14 = cd$
6. $2x = y$

Solve. Assume that y varies directly as x.

7. If $y = 45$ when $x = 9$, find y when $x = 7$.
8. If $y = 18$ when $x = 27$, find x when $y = 8$.
9. If $y = 450$ when $x = 6$, find y when $x = 10$.
10. If $y = 6$ when $x = 48$, find y when $x = 20$.
11. If $y = 25$ when $x = 20$, find x when $y = 35$.
12. If $y = 100$ when $x = 40$, find y when $x = 16$.
13. If $y = -7$ when $x = -1$, find x when $y = -84$.
14. If $y = 5$ when $x = -10$, find y when $x = 50$.
15. If $y = 24$ when $x = 6$, find y when $x = 14$.
16. If $y = -10$ when $x = -4$, find x when $y = -15$.

Solve. Assume that y varies inversely as x.

17. If $y = 54$ when $x = 4$, find x when $y = 27$.
18. If $y = 18$ when $x = 6$, find x when $y = 12$.
19. If $y = 2$ when $x = 26$, find y when $x = 4$.
20. If $y = 3$ when $x = 8$, find x when $y = 4$.
21. If $y = 12$ when $x = 24$, find x when $y = 9$.
22. If $y = 8$ when $x = -8$, find y when $x = -16$.
23. If $y = 3$ when $x = -8$, find y when $x = 4$.
24. If $y = 27$ when $x = \frac{1}{3}$, find y when $x = \frac{3}{4}$.
25. If $y = 19.5$ when $x = 6.3$, find x when $y = 10.5$.
26. If $y = 4.8$ when $x = 10$, find y when $x = 19.2$.

Lesson 5-1 **Refer to the coordinate plane below. Write the ordered pair for each point. Name the quadrant in which the point is located.**

1. B
2. T
3. P
4. Q
5. A
6. K
7. J
8. L
9. S
10. D
11. M
12. N

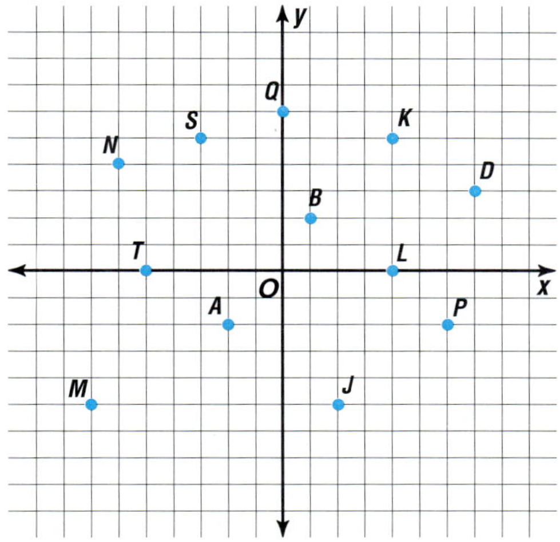

Graph each point.

13. $A(2, -4)$
14. $B(3, 5)$
15. $C(-4, 0)$
16. $D(-4, 3)$
17. $E(-5, -5)$
18. $F(-1, 1)$
19. $G(0, -3)$
20. $H(2, 3)$

Lesson 5-2 **State the domain and range of each relation.**

1. $\{(5, 2), (0, 0), (-9, -1)\}$
2. $\{(-4, 2), (-2, 0), (0, 2), (2, 4)\}$
3. $\{(7, 5), (-2, -3), (4, 0), (5, -7), (-9, 2)\}$
4. $\{(3.1, -1), (-4.7, 3.9), (2.4, -3.6), (-9, 12.12)\}$

Express the relation shown in each table, mapping, or graph as a set of ordered pairs. Then state the domain, range, and inverse of the relation.

5.

x	y
1	3
2	4
3	5
4	6
5	7

6.

x	y
−4	1
−2	3
0	1
2	3
4	1

7. 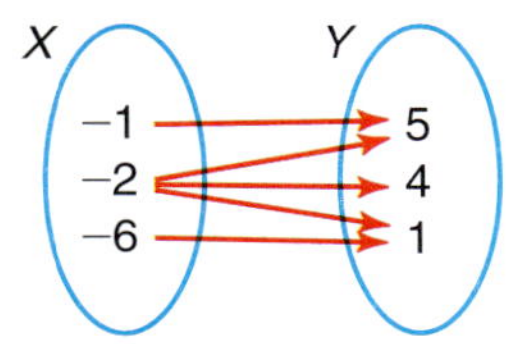

8. 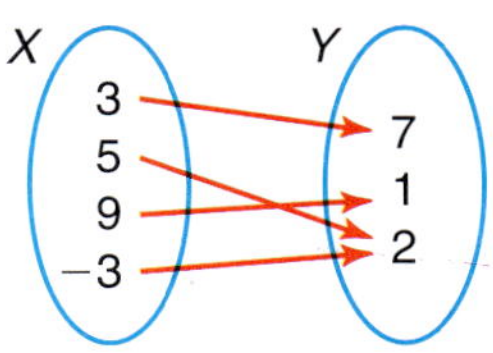

9. 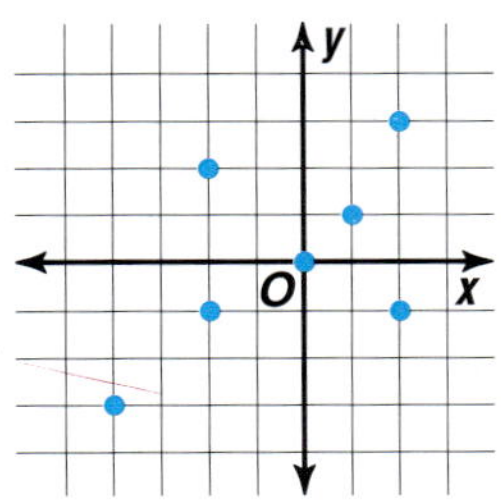

10. 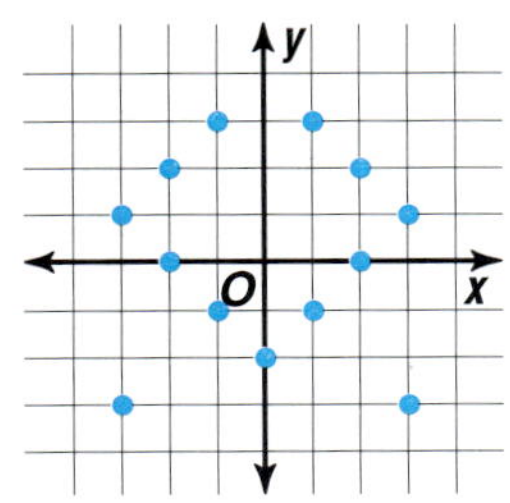

Lesson 5-3 **Which ordered pairs are solutions of each equation?**

1. $3r = 8s - 4$ a. $\left(\frac{2}{3}, \frac{3}{4}\right)$ b. $\left(0, \frac{1}{2}\right)$ c. $(4, 2)$ d. $(2, 4)$
2. $3y = x + 7$ a. $(2, 4)$ b. $(2, -1)$ c. $(2, 3)$ d. $(-1, 2)$
3. $4x = 8 - 2y$ a. $(2, 0)$ b. $(0, 2)$ c. $(0.5, -3)$ d. $(1, -2)$
4. $3n = 10 - 4m$ a. $(0, 3)$ b. $(-2, 6)$ c. $(1, 2)$ d. $(2, 1)$

Solve each equation if the range is $\{-3, -1, 0, 2, 3\}$.

5. $y = 2x$
6. $y = 5x + 1$
7. $2a + b = 4$
8. $4r + 3s = 13$
9. $5b = 8 - 4a$
10. $6m - n = -3$

EXTRA PRACTICE

Lesson 5-4 Determine whether each equation is a linear equation. If an equation is linear, rewrite it in the form $Ax + By = C$.

1. $3x = 2y$
2. $2x - 3 = y^2$
3. $3x - 2y = 8$
4. $5x - 7y = 2x - 7$
5. $2x + 5x = 7y$
6. $\frac{1}{x} + \frac{5}{y} = -4$

Graph each equation.

7. $3x + y = 4$
8. $y = 3x + 1$
9. $3x - 2y = 12$
10. $2x - y = 6$
11. $3x - 2y = 8$
12. $y = \frac{3}{4}$
13. $y = 5x - 7$
14. $x + \frac{1}{3}y = 6$
15. $x = -\frac{5}{2}$
16. $5x - 2y = 8$
17. $4x + 2y = 9$
18. $4x + 3y = 12$

Lesson 5-5 Determine whether each relation is a function.

1.

x	y
1	3
2	5
1	−7
2	9
3	3

2.

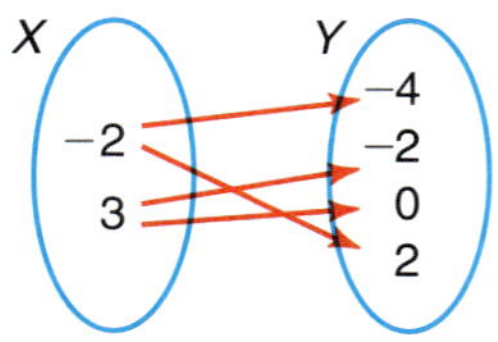

3.

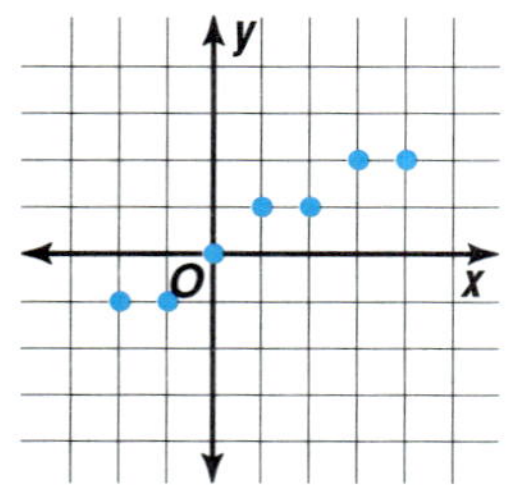

4.

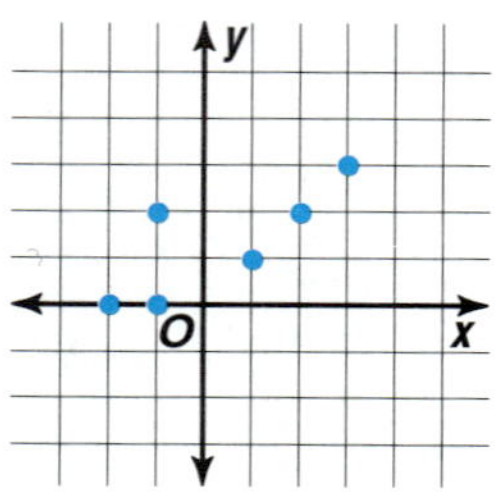

5.

a	b
1	−2
3	−4
5	−6
9	−4
10	1

6.

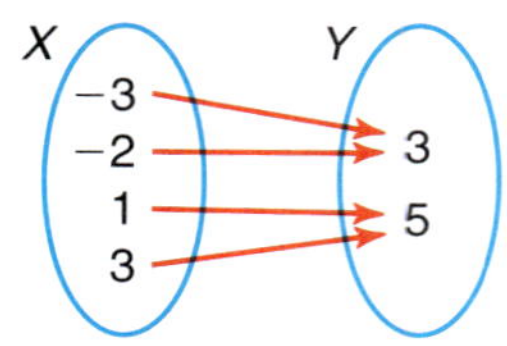

7. $\{(-2, 4), (1, 3), (5, 2), (1, 4)\}$
8. $\{(5, 4), (-6, 5), (4, 5), (0, 4)\}$
9. $\{(3, 1), (5, 1), (7, 1)\}$
10. $\{(3, -2), (4, 7), (-2, 7), (4, 5)\}$
11. $y = 2$
12. $x^2 + y = 11$

Lesson 5-6 Write an equation for each relation.

1.

x	2	4	6	8	10
f(x)	−4	−3	−2	−1	0

2.

x	−2	−1	0	1	2
f(x)	0	−3	−4	−3	0

3.

x	1	2	3	4	5
f(x)	7	11	15	19	23

4.

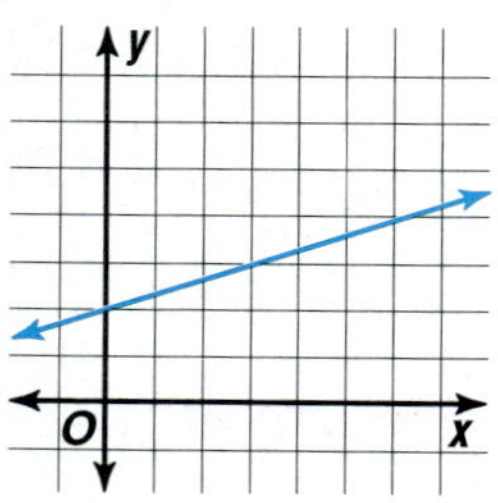

5.

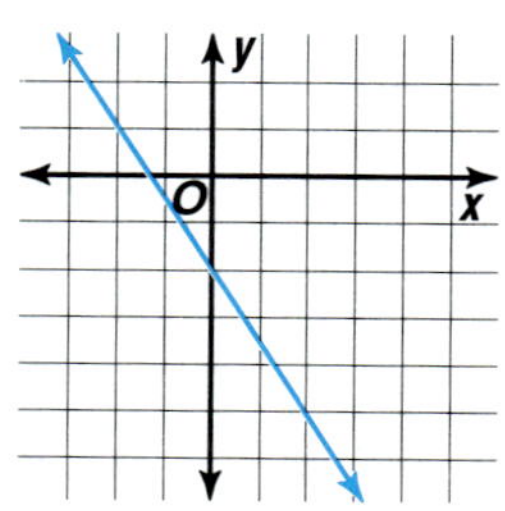

6.

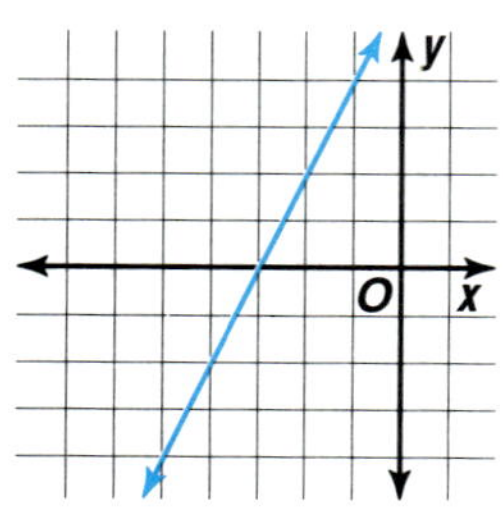

7. $\{(3, 12), (4, 14), (5, 16), (6, 18), (7, 20)\}$
8. $\{(1, 4), (2, 8), (3, 12), (-2, -8), (-3, -12)\}$
9. $\{(-6, -8), (-3, -6), (0, -4), (3, -2), (6, 0)\}$
10. $\{(-3, 9), (-2, 7), (1, 1), (4, -5), (6, -9)\}$

EXTRA PRACTICE

Lesson 5-7 **Find the range, median, upper quartile, lower quartile, and interquartile range for each set of data.**

1. 56, 45, 37, 43, 10, 34
2. 77, 78, 68, 96, 99, 84, 65
3. 30, 90, 40, 70, 50, 100, 80, 60
4. 4, 5.2, 1, 3, 2.4, 6, 3.7, 8, 1.3, 7.1, 9
5. 25°, 56°, 13°, 44°, 0°, 31°, 73°, 66°, 4°, 29°, 37°
6. 234, 648, 369, 112, 527, 775, 406, 268, 400

7.

Stem	Leaf
0	0 2 3
1	1 7 9
2	2 3 5 6
3	3 4 4 5 9
4	0 7 8 8

$2|2 = 22$

8.

Stem	Leaf
7	3 4 7 8
8	0 0 3 5 7
9	4 6 8
10	0 1 8
11	1 9

$9|4 = 9.4$

9.

Stem	Leaf
25	0 3 7 9
26	1 3 4 5 5 6
27	1 5 6 6 9
28	1 2 3 5 8
29	2 5 6 9

$27|5 = 2750$

Lesson 6-1 **Determine the slope of each line.**

1. *a*
2. *b*
3. *c*
4. *d*
5. *e*
6. *f*
7. *g*
8. *h*

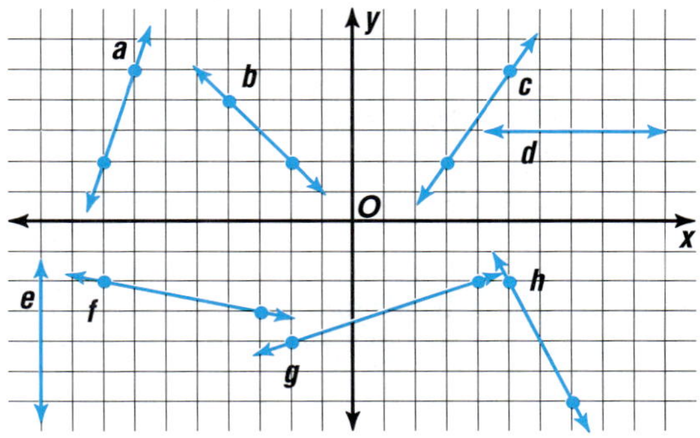

Determine the slope of the line that passes through each pair of points.

9. (−2, 2), (3, −3)
10. (−2, −8), (1, 4)
11. (3, 4), (4, 6)
12. (−5, 4), (−1, 11)
13. (18, −4), (6, −10)
14. (−4, −6), (−4, −8)

Determine the value of *r* so the line that passes through each pair of points has the given slope.

15. (−1, *r*), (1, −4), $m = -5$
16. (−2, 1), (*r*, 4), $m = \frac{3}{5}$
17. (−1, 3), (−3, *r*), $m = -3$
18. (3, *r*), (7, −2), $m = \frac{1}{2}$
19. (*r*, −2), (−7, −1), $m = -\frac{1}{4}$
20. (−3, 2), (7, *r*), $m = \frac{2}{3}$

Lesson 6-2 **Write the point-slope form of an equation of the line that passes through the given point and has the given slope.**

1. (5, −2), $m = 3$
2. (5, 4), $m = -5$
3. (−2, −4), $m = \frac{3}{4}$
4. (−3, 1), $m = 0$
5. (−1, 0), $m = \frac{2}{3}$
6. (0, 6), $m = -2$

Write the standard form of an equation of the line that passes through the given point and has the given slope.

7. (−6, −3), $m = -\frac{1}{2}$
8. (4, −3), $m = 2$
9. (5, 4), $m = -\frac{2}{3}$
10. (1, 3), m = undefined
11. (−2, 6), $m = 0$
12. (6, −2), $m = \frac{4}{3}$

Lesson 6–3 **Explain whether a scatter plot for each pair of variables would probably show a *positive*, *negative*, or *no* correlation between the variables.**

1. playing time of a basketball game and points scored
2. age of a car and its value
3. heights of mothers and sons
4. temperature of the water in an outdoor swimming pool and the temperature outside
5. the weight of a person's car and the amount they pay to use a turnpike
6. the number of guests at a birthday party and the amount of food remaining after the party
7. The scatter plot at the right compares the number of hours per week people watched television to the number of hours per week they spent doing some physical activity.
   a. As people watched more television, what happened to the number of hours they spend doing some physical activity?
   b. Is there a correlation between the variables? Is it positive or negative?

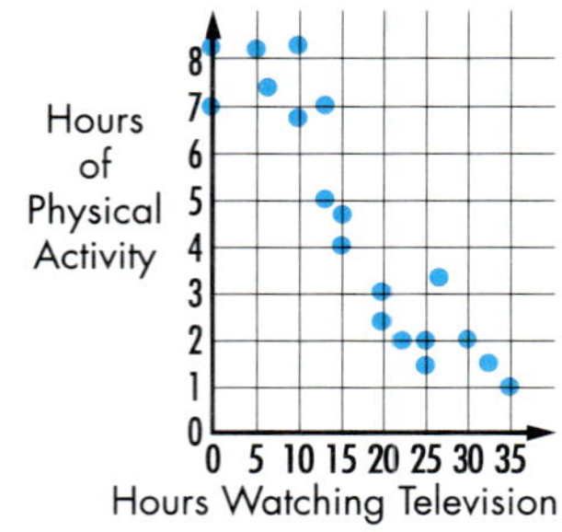

Lesson 6–4 **Find the *x*- and *y*-intercepts of the graph of each equation.**

1. $3x + 2y = 6$
2. $5x + y = 10$
3. $2x + 5y = -11$
4. $3y = 12$
5. $y - 6x = 5$
6. $x = -2$

Write an equation in slope-intercept form of a line with the given slope and *y*-intercept. Then write the equation in standard form.

7. $m = -\frac{2}{5}, b = 2$
8. $m = 5, b = -15$
9. $m = -\frac{7}{4}, b = 2$
10. $m = -\frac{4}{3}, b = \frac{5}{3}$
11. $m = -6, b = 15$
12. $m = 12, b = -24$

Find the slope and *y*-intercept of the graph of each equation.

13. $y - \frac{3}{5}x = -\frac{1}{4}$
14. $y = 3x - 7$
15. $\frac{2}{3}x + \frac{1}{6}y = 2$
16. $2x + 3y = 5$
17. $3y = 8x + 2$
18. $5y = -8x - 2$

Write an equation in standard form for a line that passes through each pair of points.

19. $(-1, 7), (8, -2)$
20. $(6, 0), (0, 4)$
21. $(8, -1), (7, -1)$
22. $(1, 0), (0, 1)$
23. $(5, 7), (-1, 6)$
24. $(-3, -5), (3, -15)$

Lesson 6–5 **Graph each equation.**

1. $4x + y = 8$
2. $2x - y = 8$
3. $3x - 2y = 6$
4. $6x - 3y = 6$
5. $x + \frac{1}{2}y = 4$
6. $4x + 5y = 20$
7. $y + 3 = -2(x + 4)$
8. $y - 1 = 3(x - 5)$
9. $y + 6 = -\frac{2}{3}(x + 1)$
10. $y - 5 = 4(x + 6)$
11. $y - 2 = (x + 7)$
12. $3(x - 1) = y + \frac{4}{5}$
13. $y = \frac{3}{4}x + 4$
14. $y = 4x - 1$
15. $-4x + y = 6$
16. $-2x + y = 3$
17. $5y - 6 = 3x$
18. $y = \frac{3}{2}x - 5$

Lesson 6-6 Determine whether the graphs of each pair of equations are *parallel, perpendicular,* or *neither.*

1. $2x + 3y = -12$; $2x + 3y = 6$
2. $-4x + 3y = 12$; $x + 3y = 12$
3. $y = -3x + 9$; $y + 3x = 14$
4. $y = 0.5x + 8$; $2y = -8x - 3$
5. $y = 7x + 2$; $y = 2x + 7$
6. $y + 5 = -9$; $y + x = y - 6$

Write an equation in slope-intercept form of the line that passes through the given point and is parallel to the graph of each equation.

7. $(1, 6), y = 4x - 2$
8. $(4, 6), y = 2x - 7$
9. $(-3, 0), y = \frac{2}{3}x + 1$
10. $(2, 3), x - 5y = 7$
11. $(0, 4), 3x + 8y = 4$
12. $(5, -2), y = -3x - 7$

Write an equation in slope-intercept form of the line that passes through the given point and is perpendicular to the graph of each equation.

13. $(0, -1), y = -\frac{3}{5}x + 4$
14. $(-2, 3), 6x + y = 4$
15. $(0, 0), y = \frac{3}{4}x - 1$
16. $(4, 0), 4x - 3y = 2$
17. $(6, 7), 3x - 5y = 1$
18. $(5, -1), 8x + 4y = 15$

Lesson 6-7 Find the coordinates of the midpoint of a segment with each pair of endpoints.

1. $L(12, 2), M(8, 4)$
2. $S(9, 5), T(17, 3)$
3. $D(17, 9), E(11, -3)$
4. $F(4, 2), G(8, -6)$
5. $M(19, -3), N(11, 5)$
6. $B(-6, 5), C(8, -11)$
7. $T(-11, 6), U(13, 4)$
8. $A(-6, 1), B(8, 9)$
9. $J(6.4, -3), K(1.8, -3)$
10. $R(19, 5), S(7, 4)$
11. $G(8, 10), H(16, -6)$
12. $C(7.6, 8.3), D(-5, 6.1)$

Find the coordinates of the other endpoint of a segment given one endpoint and the midpoint *M*.

13. $P(9, 3), M(1, 2)$
14. $C(3, 5), M(5, -7)$
15. $G(5, -9), M\left(8, -\frac{15}{2}\right)$
16. $J(4, -7), M(-2, -3)$
17. $A(-3, 8), M(3, -5)$
18. $F(5, 7), M(5, 6)$
19. $T(-6, 12), M(4, 1)$
20. $D(-8, 5), M\left(-\frac{1}{2}, 2\right)$
21. $S(16, -9), M\left(\frac{3}{2}, -\frac{13}{2}\right)$
22. $U(-9, 14), M(0, 3)$
23. $F(21, 18), M(19, 11)$
24. $X\left(\frac{1}{4}, \frac{1}{3}\right), M\left(\frac{3}{16}, \frac{1}{3}\right)$

Lesson 7-1 Solve each inequality. Then check your solution.

1. $c + 9 \leq 3$
2. $d - (-3) < 13$
3. $z - 4 > 20$
4. $h - (-7) > -2$
5. $-11 > d - 4$
6. $2x > x - 3$
7. $2x - 3 \geq x$
8. $16 + w < -20$
9. $14p > 5 + 13p$
10. $-7 < 16 - z$
11. $-5 + 14b \leq -4 + 15b$
12. $2s - 6.5 \geq -11.4 + s$
13. $1.1v - 1 > 2.1v - 3$
14. $\frac{1}{2}t + \frac{1}{4} \geq \frac{3}{2}t - \frac{2}{3}$
15. $9x < 8x - 2$
16. $-2 + 9n \leq 10n$
17. $a - 2.3 \geq -7.8$
18. $5z - 6 > 4z$

Lesson 7-2 Solve each inequality. Then check your solution.

1. $7b \geq -49$
2. $-5j < -60$
3. $\frac{w}{3} > -12$
4. $\frac{p}{5} < 8$
5. $-8f < 48$
6. $\frac{t}{-4} \geq -10$
7. $\frac{128}{-g} < 4$
8. $-4.3x < -2.58$
9. $4c \geq -6$
10. $6 \leq 0.8n$
11. $\frac{2}{3}m \geq -22$
12. $-25 > \frac{a}{-6}$
13. $-15a < -28$
14. $-\frac{7}{9}x < 42$
15. $\frac{3y}{8} \leq 32$
16. $-7y \geq 91$
17. $0.8t > 0.96$
18. $\frac{4}{7}z \leq -\frac{2}{5}$

Lesson 7-3 Solve each inequality. Then check your solution.

1. $3y - 4 > -37$
2. $7s - 12 < 13$
3. $-5e + 9 > 24$
4. $-6v - 3 \geq -33$
5. $-2k + 12 < 30$
6. $-2x + 1 < 16 - x$
7. $15t - 4 > 11t - 16$
8. $13 - y \leq 29 + 2y$
9. $5q + 7 \leq 3(q + 1)$
10. $2(w + 4) \geq 7(w - 1)$
11. $-4t - 5 > 2t + 13$
12. $\frac{2t + 5}{3} < -9$
13. $\frac{z}{4} + 7 \geq -5$
14. $13r - 11 > 7r + 37$
15. $8c - (c - 5) > c + 17$
16. $-5(k + 4) \geq 3(k - 4)$
17. $9m + 7 < 2(4m - 1)$
18. $3(3y + 1) < 13y - 8$
19. $5x \leq 10(3x + 4)$
20. $3\left(a + \frac{2}{3}\right) \geq a - 1$
21. $0.7(n - 3) \leq n - 0.6(n + 5)$

Lesson 7-4 Solve each compound inequality. Then graph the solution set.

1. $2 + x < -5$ or $2 + x > 5$
2. $-4 + t > -5$ or $-4 + t < 7$
3. $3 \leq 2g + 7$ and $2g + 7 \leq 15$
4. $2v - 2 \leq 3v$ and $4v - 1 \geq 3v$
5. $3b - 4 \leq 7b + 12$ and $8b - 7 \leq 25$
6. $-9 < 2z + 7 < 10$
7. $5m - 8 \geq 10 - m$ or $5m + 11 < -9$
8. $12c - 4 \leq 5c + 10$ or $-4c - 1 \leq c + 24$
9. $2h - 2 \leq 3h \leq 4h - 1$
10. $3p + 6 < 8 - p$ and $5p + 8 \geq p + 6$
11. $2r + 8 > 16 - 2r$ and $7r + 21 < r - 9$
12. $4j + 3 < j + 22$ and $j - 3 < 2j - 15$
13. $2(q - 4) \leq 3(q + 2)$ or $q - 8 \leq 4 - q$
14. $\frac{1}{2}w + 5 \geq w + 2 \geq \frac{1}{2}w + 9$

Lesson 7-5

1. **Food** For breakfast at Paul's Place, you can select one item from each of the following categories for $1.99.

Meat	Potato	Bread	Beverage
ham sausage bacon	hash browns country potatoes	toast muffin bagel biscuit	juice coffee

   a. What is the probability that a customer will have ham for breakfast?

   b. What is the probability of selecting a biscuit and hash browns?

   c. What is the probability of having a bagel, country potatoes, and coffee?

2. **Music** In order to raise money for a trip to the opera, the music club has set up a lottery using two-digit numbers. The first digit will be a numeral from 1 to 4. The second digit will be a numeral from 3 to 8. The first digit in Trudy's lottery number is 2, but she can't remember the second digit. If only one two-digit lottery number is drawn, and that number has 2 as the first digit, what is the probability that Trudy will win?

3. **Law** A three-judge panel is being used to settle a dispute. Both sides in the dispute have decided that a majority decision will be upheld. If each judge will render a favorable decision based on the evidence presented two-thirds of the time, what is the probability that the correct side will win the dispute?

Lesson 7-6 **Solve each open sentence. Then graph the solution set.**

1. $|a - 5| = -3$
2. $|g + 6| > 8$
3. $|t - 5| \leq 3$
4. $|a + 5| \geq 0$
5. $|14 - 2z| = 16$
6. $|y - 9| < 19$
7. $|2m - 5| > 13$
8. $|14 - w| \geq 20$
9. $|13 - 5y| = 8$
10. $|3p + 5| \leq 23$
11. $|6b - 12| \leq 36$
12. $|25 - 3x| < 5$
13. $|7 + 8x| > 39$
14. $|4c + 5| \geq 25$
15. $|4 - 5s| > 46$

Lesson 7-7

1. **Travel** Speeds of the fastest train runs in the U.S. and Canada are given below in miles per hour. Make a box-and-whisker plot of the data.

93.5	82.5	89.3	83.8	81.8	86.8
90.8	84.9	95.0	83.1	83.2	88.2

2. **Basketball** The numbers below represent the 20 highest points-scored-per-game averages for a season in the NBA from 1947 to 1990. Make a box-and-whisker plot of this data.

35.0	33.5	32.5	37.9	31.2	38.4	34.5	34.7	32.9	44.8
31.7	37.1	36.5	34.0	50.4	32.3	33.6	34.8	33.1	35.6

3. **Baseball** The stem-and-leaf plot at the right shows the number of home runs hit by the home run leaders in the National League in 1990.

   a. Find the median, upper quartile, lower quartile, and interquartile range.

   b. Are there any outliers? If so, name them.

   c. Draw a box-and-whisker plot of the data.

Stem	Leaf
2	2 3 3 4 4 4 4 5 5 6 7 7 8
3	2 2 3 3 5 7
4	0

$3|3 = 33$

EXTRA PRACTICE

Lesson 7-8 **Graph each inequality.**

1. $y \leq -2$
2. $x < 4$
3. $x + y < -2$
4. $x + y > -4$
5. $y > 4x - 1$
6. $3x + y > 1$
7. $3y - 2x \leq 2$
8. $x < y$
9. $3x + y > 4$
10. $5x - y < 5$
11. $-4x + 3y \geq 12$
12. $-x + 3y \leq 9$
13. $y > -3x + 7$
14. $3x + 8y \leq 4$
15. $5x - 2y \geq 6$

Lesson 8-1 **Graph each system of equations. Then determine whether the system has *one* solution, *no* solution, or *infinitely many* solutions. If the system has one solution, name it.**

1. $y = 3x$; $4x + 2y = 30$
2. $x = -2y$; $3x + 5y = 21$
3. $y = x + 4$; $3x + 2y = 18$
4. $x + y = 6$; $x - y = 2$
5. $x + y = 6$; $3x + 3y = 3$
6. $y = -3x$; $4x + y = 2$
7. $x + y = 8$; $x - y = 2$
8. $\frac{1}{5}x - y = \frac{12}{5}$; $3x - 5y = 6$
9. $x + 2y = 0$; $y + 3 = -x$
10. $x + 2y = -9$; $x - y = 6$
11. $x + \frac{1}{2}y = 3$; $y = 3x - 4$
12. $\frac{2}{3}x + \frac{1}{2}y = 2$; $4x + 3y = 12$
13. $y = x - 4$; $x + \frac{1}{2}y = \frac{5}{2}$
14. $2x + y = 3$; $4x + 2y = 6$
15. $12x - y = -21$; $\frac{1}{2}x + \frac{2}{3}y = -3$

Lesson 8-2 **Use substitution to solve each system of equations. If the system *does not* have exactly one solution, state whether it has *no* solution or *infinitely many* solutions.**

1. $y = x$; $5x = 12y$
2. $y = 7 - x$; $2x - y = 8$
3. $x = 5 - y$; $3y = 3x + 1$
4. $3x + y = 6$; $y + 2 = x$
5. $x - 3y = 3$; $2x + 9y = 11$
6. $3x = -18 + 2y$; $x + 3y = 4$
7. $x + 2y = 10$; $-x + y = 2$
8. $2x = 3 - y$; $2y = 12 - x$
9. $6y - x = -36$; $y = -3x$
10. $\frac{3}{4}x + \frac{1}{3}y = 1$; $x - y = 10$
11. $x + 6y = 1$; $3x - 10y = 31$
12. $3x - 2y = 12$; $\frac{3}{2}x - y = 3$
13. $2x + 3y = 5$; $4x - 9y = 9$
14. $x = 4 - 8y$; $3x + 24y = 12$
15. $3x - 2y = -3$; $25x + 10y = 215$

Lesson 8-3 State whether addition, subtraction, or substitution would be most convenient to solve each system of equations. Then solve the system.

1. $x + y = 7$
   $x - y = 9$
2. $2x - y = 32$
   $2x + y = 60$
3. $-y + x = 6$
   $y + x = 5$
4. $s + 2t = 6$
   $3s - 2t = 2$
5. $x = y - 7$
   $2x - 5y = -2$
6. $3x + 5y = -16$
   $3x - 2y = -2$
7. $x - y = 3$
   $x + y = 3$
8. $x + y = 8$
   $2x - y = 6$
9. $2s - 3t = -4$
   $s = 7 - 3t$
10. $-6x + 16y = -8$
    $6x - 42 = 16y$
11. $3x + 0.2y = 7$
    $3x = 0.4y + 4$
12. $9x + 2y = 26$
    $1.5x - 2y = 13$
13. $\frac{2}{3}x - \frac{1}{2}y = 14$
    $\frac{5}{6}x - \frac{1}{2}y = 18$
14. $4x - \frac{1}{3}y = 8$
    $5x + \frac{1}{3}y = 6$
15. $2x - y = 3$
    $\frac{2}{3}x - y = -1$

Lesson 8-4 Use elimination to solve each system of equations.

1. $x + 8y = 3$
   $4x - 2y = 7$
2. $4x - y = 4$
   $x + 2y = 3$
3. $3y - 8x = 9$
   $y - x = 2$
4. $x + 4y = 30$
   $2x - y = -6$
5. $3x - 2y = 0$
   $4x + 4y = 5$
6. $9x - 3y = 5$
   $x + y = 1$
7. $-3x + 2y = 10$
   $-2x - y = -5$
8. $2x + 5y = 13$
   $4x - 3y = -13$
9. $5x + 3y = 4$
   $-4x + 5y = -18$
10. $2x - 7y = 9$
    $-3x + 4y = 6$
11. $2x - 6y = -16$
    $5x + 7y = -18$
12. $6x - 3y = -9$
    $-8x + 2y = 4$
13. $\frac{1}{3}x - y = -1$
    $\frac{1}{5}x - \frac{2}{5}y = -1$
14. $3x - 5y = 8$
    $4x - 7y = 10$
15. $x - 0.5y = 1$
    $0.4x + y = -2$

Lesson 8-5 Solve each system of inequalities by graphing.

1. $x > 3$
   $y < 6$
2. $y > 2$
   $y > -x + 2$
3. $x \leq 2$
   $y - 3 \geq 5$
4. $x + y \leq -1$
   $2x + y \leq 2$
5. $y \geq 2x + 2$
   $y \geq -x - 1$
6. $y \leq x + 3$
   $y \geq x + 2$
7. $x + 3y \geq 4$
   $2x - y < 5$
8. $y - x > 1$
   $y + 2x \leq 10$
9. $5x - 2y > 15$
   $2x - 3y < 6$
10. $4x + 3y > 4$
    $2x - y < 0$
11. $4x + 5y \geq 20$
    $y \geq x + 1$
12. $-4x + 10y \leq 5$
    $-2x + 5y < -1$

Lesson 9-1 Simplify.

1. $a^5(a)(a^7)$
2. $(r^3t^4)(r^4t^4)$
3. $(x^3y^4)(xy^3)$
4. $(bc^3)(b^4c^3)$
5. $(-3mn^2)(5m^3n^2)$
6. $[(3^3)^2]^2$
7. $(3s^3t^2)(-4s^3t^2)$
8. $x^3(x^4y^3)$
9. $(1.1g^2h^4)^3$
10. $-\frac{3}{4}a(a^2b^3c^4)$
11. $\left(\frac{1}{2}w^3\right)^2(w^4)^2$
12. $\left(\frac{2}{3}y^3\right)(3y^2)^3$
13. $[(-2^3)^3]^2$
14. $(10s^3t)(-2s^2t^2)^3$
15. $(-0.2u^3w^4)^3$

Lesson 9-2 Simplify. Assume no denominator is equal to zero.

1. $\frac{b^6c^5}{b^3c^2}$
2. $\frac{(-a)^4b^8}{a^4b^7}$
3. $\frac{(-x)^3y^3}{x^3y^6}$
4. $\frac{12ab^5}{4a^4b^3}$
5. $\frac{24x^5}{-8x^2}$
6. $\frac{-9h^2k^4}{18h^5j^3k^4}$
7. $\frac{a^0}{2a^{-3}}$
8. $\frac{9a^2b^7c^3}{2a^5b^4c}$
9. $\frac{-15xy^5z^7}{-10x^4y^6z^4}$
10. $\frac{(u^{-3}v^3)^2}{(u^3v)^{-3}}$
11. $\frac{(-r)s^5}{r^{-3}s^{-4}}$
12. $\frac{28a^{-4}b^0}{14a^3b^{-1}}$
13. $\frac{(j^2k^3l)^4}{(jk^4)^{-1}}$
14. $\left(\frac{-2x^4y}{4y^2}\right)^0$
15. $\frac{3m^7n^2p^4}{9m^2np^3}$

Lesson 9-3 Express each number in scientific notation.

1. 6500
2. 953.56
3. 0.697
4. 843.5
5. 568,000
6. 0.0000269
7. 0.121212
8. 543×10^4
9. 739.9×10^{-5}
10. 6480×10^{-2}
11. 0.366×10^{-7}
12. 167×10^3

Evaluate. Express each result in scientific and standard notation.

13. $(2 \times 10^5)(3 \times 10^{-8})$
14. $\frac{4.8 \times 10^3}{1.6 \times 10^1}$
15. $(4 \times 10^2)(1.5 \times 10^6)$
16. $\frac{8.1 \times 10^2}{2.7 \times 10^{-3}}$
17. $\frac{7.8 \times 10^{-5}}{1.3 \times 10^{-7}}$
18. $(2.2 \times 10^{-2})(3.2 \times 10^5)$
19. $(3.1 \times 10^4)(4.2 \times 10^{-3})$
20. $(78 \times 10^6)(0.01 \times 10^3)$
21. $\frac{2.31 \times 10^{-2}}{3.3 \times 10^{-3}}$

Lesson 9-4 State whether each expression is a polynomial. If the expression is a polynomial, identify it as a *monomial,* a *binomial,* or a *trinomial* and find the degree of the polynomial.

1. $5x^2y + 3xy + 7$
2. 0
3. $\frac{5}{k} - k^2y$
4. $3a^2x - 5a$
5. $a + \frac{5}{c}$
6. $14abcd - 6d^3$
7. $\frac{a^3}{3}$
8. $-4h^3$
9. $x^2 - \frac{x}{2} + \frac{1}{3}$

Arrange the terms of each polynomial so that the powers of x are in descending order.

10. $5x^2 - 3x^3 + 7 + 2x$
11. $-6x + x^5 + 4x^3 - 20$
12. $5b + b^3x^2 + \frac{2}{3}bx$
13. $21p^2x + 3px^3 + p^4$
14. $3ax^2 - 6a^2x^3 + 7a^3 - 8x$
15. $\frac{1}{3}s^2x^3 + 4x^4 - \frac{2}{5}s^4x^2 + \frac{1}{4}x$

Lesson 9-5 Find each sum or difference.

1. $\begin{array}{rrrr} & -7t^2 & +\ 4ts & -\ 6s^2 \\ (+) & -5t^2 & -\ 12ts & +\ 3s^2 \\ \hline \end{array}$
2. $\begin{array}{rrrr} & 6a^2 & -\ 7ab & -\ 4b^2 \\ (-) & 2a^2 & +\ 5ab & +\ 6b^2 \\ \hline \end{array}$
3. $\begin{array}{rrrrrr} & 4a^2 & -\ 10b^2 & +\ 7c^2 & & \\ & -5a^2 & & +\ 2c^2 & & +\ 2b \\ (+) & & 7b^2 & -\ 7c^2 & +\ 7a & \\ \hline \end{array}$
4. $\begin{array}{rrrr} & z^2 & +\ 6z & -\ 8 \\ (-) & 4z^2 & -\ 7z & -\ 5 \\ \hline \end{array}$
5. $(4d + 3e - 8f) - (-3d + 10e - 5f + 6)$
6. $(7g + 8h - 9) + (-g - 3h - 6k)$
7. $(9x^2 - 11xy - 3y^2) - (x^2 - 16xy + 12y^2)$
8. $(-3m + 9mn - 5n) + (14m - 5mn - 2n)$
9. $(4x^2 - 8y^2 - 3z^2) - (7x^2 - 14z^2 - 12)$
10. $(17z^4 - 5z^2 + 3z) - (4z^4 + 2z^3 + 3z)$
11. $(6 - 7y + 3y^2) + (3 - 5y - 2y^2) + (-12 - 8y + y^2)$
12. $(-3x^2 + 2x - 5) + (2x - 6) + (5x^2 + 3) + (-9x^2 - 7x + 4)$

Lesson 9-6 Find each product.

1. $-3(8x + 5)$
2. $3b(5b + 8)$
3. $1.1a(2a + 7)$
4. $\frac{1}{2}x(8x - 6)$
5. $7xy(5x^2 - y^2)$
6. $5y(y^2 - 3y + 6)$
7. $-ab(3b^2 + 4ab - 6a^2)$
8. $4m^2(9m^2n + mn - 5n^2)$
9. $4st^2(-4s^2t^3 + 7s^5 - 3st^3)$
10. $-\frac{1}{3}x(9x^2 + x - 5)$
11. $-2mn(8m^2 - 3mn + n^2)$
12. $-\frac{3}{4}ab^2\left(\frac{1}{3}b^2 - \frac{4}{9}b + 1\right)$

Solve.

13. $-3(2a - 12) + 48 = 3a - 3$
14. $-6(12 - 2w) = 7(-2 - 3w)$
15. $a(a - 6) + 2a = 3 + a(a - 2)$
16. $11(a - 3) + 5 = 2a + 44$
17. $q(2q + 3) + 20 = 2q(q - 3)$
18. $w(w + 12) = w(w + 14) + 12$
19. $x(x + 8) - x(x + 3) - 23 = 3x + 11$
20. $y(y - 12) + y(y + 2) + 25 = 2y(y + 5) - 15$
21. $x(x - 3) + 4x - 3 = 8x + 4 + x(3 + x)$
22. $c(c - 3) + 4(c - 2) = 12 - 2(4 + c) - c(1 - c)$

EXTRA PRACTICE

Lesson 9-7 Find each product.

1. $(d + 2)(d + 3)$
2. $(z + 7)(z - 4)$
3. $(m - 8)(m - 5)$
4. $(2x - 5)(x + 6)$
5. $(7a - 4)(2a - 5)$
6. $(4x + y)(2x - 3y)$
7. $(7v + 3)(v + 4)$
8. $(7s - 8)(3s - 2)$
9. $(4g + 3h)(2g - 5h)$
10. $(4a + 3)(2a - 1)$
11. $(7y - 1)(2y - 3)$
12. $(2x + 3y)(5x + 2y)$
13. $(12r - 4s)(5r + 8s)$
14. $(x - 2)(x^2 + 2x + 4)$
15. $(3x + 5)(2x^2 - 5x + 11)$
16. $(4s + 5)(3s^2 + 8s - 9)$
17. $(3a + 5)(-8a^2 + 2a + 3)$
18. $(5x - 2)(-5x^2 + 2x + 7)$
19. $(x^2 - 7x + 4)(2x^2 - 3x - 6)$
20. $(a^2 + 2a + 5)(a^2 - 3a - 7)$
21. $(5x^4 - 2x^2 + 1)(x^2 - 5x + 3)$

Lesson 9-8 Find each product.

1. $(t + 7)^2$
2. $(w - 12)(w + 12)$
3. $(q - 4h)^2$
4. $(10x + 11y)(10x - 11y)$
5. $(4e + 3)^2$
6. $(2b - 4d)(2b + 4d)$
7. $(a + 2b)^2$
8. $(4x + y)^2$
9. $(6m + 2n)^2$
10. $(5c - 2d)^2$
11. $(5b - 6)(5b + 6)$
12. $(1 + x)^2$
13. $(4x - 9y)^2$
14. $(8a - 2b)(8a + 2b)$
15. $\left(\frac{1}{2}a + b\right)^2$
16. $(5a - 12b)^2$
17. $(a - 3b)^2$
18. $(7a^2 + b)(7a^2 - b)$
19. $(x + 2)(x - 2)(2x + 5)$
20. $(4x - 1)(4x + 1)(x - 4)$
21. $(x - 3)(x + 3)(x - 4)(x + 4)$

Lesson 10-1 Find the factors of each number.

1. 17
2. 21
3. 81
4. 24
5. 18
6. 22

State whether each number is *prime* or *composite*. If the number is composite, find its prime factorization.

7. 39
8. 89
9. 72
10. 41
11. 57
12. 60

Factor each expression completely. Do not use exponents.

13. -64
14. -26
15. -240
16. -231
17. $44rs^2t^3$
18. $756(mn)^2$

Find the GCF of the given monomials.

19. 16, 60
20. 15, 50
21. -80, 45
22. 29, -58
23. 305, 55
24. 252, 126
25. 128, 245
26. $7y^2$, $14y^2$
27. $4xy$, $-6x$
28. $35t^2$, $7t$
29. $16pq^2$, $12p^2q$
30. 5, 15, 10
31. $12mn$, $10mn$, $15mn$
32. 14, 12, 20
33. $26jk^4$, $16jk^3$, $8j^2$

Lesson 10-2 Complete. In exercises with two blanks, both blanks represent the same expression.

1. $6x + 3y = 3(\underline{?} + y)$
2. $8x^2 - 4x = 4x(2x - \underline{?})$
3. $12a^2b + 6a = 6a(\underline{?} + 1)$
4. $14r^2t - 42t = 14t(\underline{?} - 3)$
5. $24x^2 + 12y^2 = 12(\underline{?} + y^2)$
6. $12xy + 12x^2 = \underline{?}\,(y + x)$
7. $(bx + by) + (3ax + 3ay) = b(\underline{?}) + 3a(\underline{?})$
8. $(10x^2 - 6xy) + (15x - 9y) = 2x(\underline{?}) + 3(\underline{?})$
9. $(6x^3 + 6x) + (7x^2y + 7y) = 6x(\underline{?}) + 7y(\underline{?})$

Factor each polynomial.

10. $10a^2 + 40a$
11. $15wx - 35wx^2$
12. $27a^2b + 9b^3$
13. $11x + 44x^2y$
14. $16y^2 + 8y$
15. $14mn^2 + 2mn$
16. $25a^2b^2 + 30ab^3$
17. $2m^3n^2 - 16m^2n^3 + 8mn$
18. $2ax + 6xc + ba + 3bc$
19. $6mx - 4m + 3rx - 2r$
20. $3ax - 6bx + 8b - 4a$
21. $a^2 - 2ab + a - 2b$
22. $8ac - 2ad + 4bc - bd$
23. $2e^2g + 2fg + 4e^2h + 4fh$

Lesson 10-3 Complete.

1. $p^2 + 9p - 10 = (p + \underline{?})(p - 1)$
2. $y^2 - 2y - 35 = (y + 5)(y - \underline{?})$
3. $4a^2 + 4a - 63 = (2a - 7)(2a \underline{?} 9)$
4. $4r^2 - 25r + 6 = (r - 6)(\underline{?} - 1)$
5. $b^2 + 12b + 35 = (b + 5)(b + \underline{?})$
6. $3x^2 - 7x - 6 = (3x + 2)(x \underline{?} 7)$
7. $3a^2 - 2a - 21 = (a \underline{?} 3)(3a + 7)$
8. $4y^2 + 11y + 6 = (\underline{?} + 3)(y + 2)$
9. $2z^2 - 11z + 15 = (\underline{?} - 5)(z - 3)$
10. $6n^2 + 7n - 3 = (2n + \underline{?})(3n - 1)$

Factor each trinomial, if possible. If the trinomial cannot be factored using integers, write *prime*.

11. $5x^2 - 17x + 14$
12. $a^2 - 9a - 36$
13. $x^2 + 2x - 15$
14. $n^2 - 8n + 15$
15. $b^2 + 22b + 21$
16. $c^2 + 2c - 3$
17. $x^2 - 5x - 24$
18. $2n^2 - 11n + 7$
19. $8m^2 - 10m + 3$
20. $z^2 + 15z + 36$
21. $s^2 - 13st - 30t^2$
22. $6y^2 + 2y - 2$
23. $2r^2 + 3r - 14$
24. $5x - 6 + x^2$
25. $x^2 - 4xy - 5y^2$
26. $5r^2 - 3r + 15$
27. $18v^2 + 42v + 12$
28. $4k^2 + 2k - 12$

Lesson 10-4 Factor each polynomial, if possible. If the polynomial cannot be factored, write *prime*.

1. $x^2 - 9$
2. $a^2 - 64$
3. $t^2 - 49$
4. $4x^2 - 9y^2$
5. $1 - 9z^2$
6. $16a^2 - 9b^2$
7. $8x^2 - 12y^2$
8. $a^2 - 4b^2$
9. $x^2 - y^2$
10. $75r^2 - 48$
11. $x^2 - 36y^2$
12. $3a^2 - 16$
13. $12t^2 - 75$
14. $9x^2 - 100y^2$
15. $49 - a^2b^2$
16. $12a^2 - 48$
17. $169 - 16t^2$
18. $8r^2 - 4$
19. $-45m^2 + 5$
20. $9x^4 - 16y^2$
21. $36b^2 - 64$
22. $5g^2 - 20h^2$
23. $\frac{1}{4}n^2 - 16$
24. $\frac{1}{4}t^2 - \frac{4}{9}p^2$
25. $(r - t)^2 + t^2$
26. $12x^3 - 27xy^2$
27. $0.01n^2 - 1.69r^2$
28. $0.04m^2 - 0.09n^2$
29. $(x - y)^2 - y^2$
30. $162m^4 - 32n^8$

EXTRA PRACTICE

EXTRA PRACTICE

Lesson 10-5 Determine whether each trinomial is a perfect square trinomial. If so, factor it.

1. $x^2 + 12x + 36$
2. $n^2 - 13n + 36$
3. $a^2 + 4a + 4$
4. $b^2 - 14b + 49$
5. $x^2 + 20x - 100$
6. $y^2 - 10y + 100$
7. $9b^2 - 6b + 1$
8. $4x^2 + 4x + 1$
9. $2n^2 + 17n + 21$
10. $9x^2 - 10x + 4$
11. $9y^2 + 8y - 16$
12. $4a^2 - 20a + 25$

Factor each polynomial, if possible. If the polynomial cannot be factored, write *prime*.

13. $n^2 - 8n + 16$
14. $4k^2 - 4k + 1$
15. $x^2 + 16x + 64$
16. $t^2 - 4t + 1$
17. $x^2 + 22x + 121$
18. $s^2 + 30s + 225$
19. $1 - 10z + 25z^2$
20. $9p^2 - 56p + 49$
21. $9n^2 - 36nm + 36m^2$
22. $16a^2 + 81 - 72a$
23. $9x^2 + 12xy + 4y^2$
24. $m^2 + 16mn + 64n^2$
25. $8t^4 + 56t^3 + 98t^2$
26. $4p^2 + 12pr + 9r^2$
27. $16m^4 - 72m^2n^2 + 81n^4$

Lesson 10-6 Solve each equation. Check your solutions.

1. $y(y - 12) = 0$
2. $2x(5x - 10) = 0$
3. $7a(a + 6) = 0$
4. $(b - 3)(b - 5) = 0$
5. $(p - 5)(p + 5) = 0$
6. $(4t + 4)(2t + 6) = 0$
7. $(3x - 5)^2 = 0$
8. $x^2 - 6x = 0$
9. $n^2 + 36n = 0$
10. $2x^2 + 4x = 0$
11. $2x^2 = x^2 - 8x$
12. $7y - 1 = -3y^2 + y - 1$
13. $\frac{1}{2}y^2 - \frac{1}{4}y = 0$
14. $\frac{5}{6}x^2 - \frac{1}{3}x = \frac{1}{3}x$
15. $\frac{2}{3}x = \frac{1}{3}x^2$
16. $\frac{3}{4}a^2 + \frac{7}{8}a = a$
17. $n^2 - 3n = 0$
18. $3x^2 - \frac{3}{4}x = 0$
19. $8a^2 = -4a$
20. $(2y + 8)(3y + 24) = 0$
21. $(4x - 7)(3x + 5) = 0$

Lesson 11-1 Write the equation of the axis of symmetry and find the coordinates of the vertex of the graph of each equation. State if the vertex is a maximum or minimum. Then graph the equation.

1. $y = x^2 + 6x + 8$
2. $y = -x^2 + 3x$
3. $y = -x^2 + 7$
4. $y = x^2 + x + 3$
5. $y = -x^2 + 4x + 5$
6. $y = 3x^2 + 6x + 16$
7. $y = -x^2 + 2x - 3$
8. $y = 3x^2 + 24x + 80$
9. $y = x^2 - 4x - 4$
10. $y = 5x^2 - 20x + 37$
11. $y = 3x^2 + 6x + 3$
12. $y = 2x^2 + 12x$
13. $y = x^2 - 6x + 5$
14. $y = \frac{1}{2}x^2 + 3x + \frac{9}{2}$
15. $y = \frac{1}{4}x^2 - 4x + \frac{15}{4}$
16. $y = 4x^2 - 1$
17. $y = -2x^2 - 2x + 4$
18. $y = 6x^2 - 12x - 4$
19. $y = x^2 - 1$
20. $y = -x^2 + x + 1$
21. $y = -5x^2 - 3x + 2$
22. $y = x^2 - x - 6$
23. $y = 2x^2 + 5x - 2$
24. $y = -3x^2 - 18x - 15$

Lesson 11-2 State the real roots of each quadratic equation whose related function is graphed below.

1. 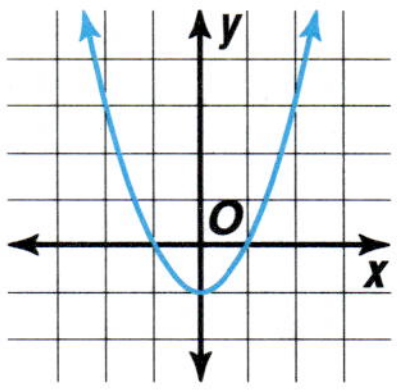

2. 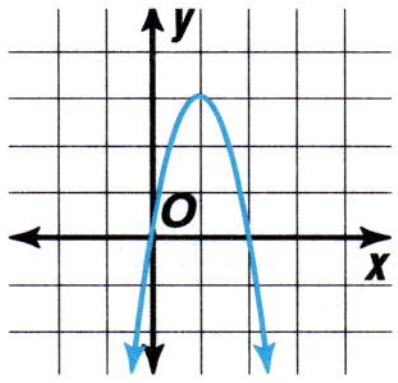

3. 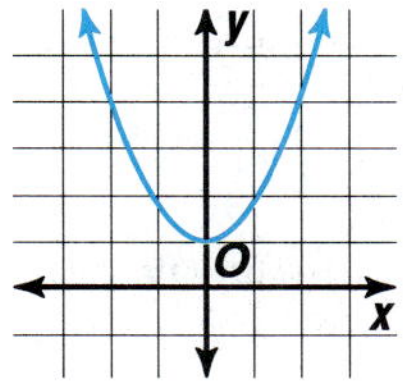

4. 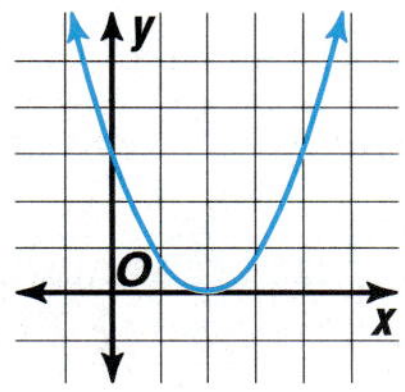

Solve each equation by graphing. If exact roots cannot be found, state the consecutive integers between which the roots lie.

5. $x^2 + 2x - 3 = 0$ **6.** $-x^2 + 6x - 5 = 0$ **7.** $-a^2 - 2a + 3 = 0$

8. $2r^2 - 8r + 5 = 0$ **9.** $-3x^2 + 6x - 9 = 0$ **10.** $c^2 + c = 0$

11. $3t^2 + 2 = 0$ **12.** $-b^2 + 5b + 2 = 0$ **13.** $3x^2 + 7x = 1$

14. $x^2 + 5x - 24 = 0$ **15.** $8 - k^2 = 0$ **16.** $x^2 - 7x = 18$

17. $a^2 + 12a + 36 = 0$ **18.** $64 - x^2 = 0$ **19.** $-4x^2 + 2x = -1$

Lesson 11-3 Solve each equation by using the quadratic formula. Approximate irrational roots to the nearest hundredth.

1. $x^2 - 8x - 4 = 0$ **2.** $x^2 + 7x + 6 = 0$ **3.** $x^2 + 5x - 6 = 0$

4. $y^2 - 7y - 8 = 0$ **5.** $m^2 - 2m = 35$ **6.** $4n^2 - 20n = 0$

7. $m^2 + 4m + 2 = 0$ **8.** $2t^2 - t - 15 = 0$ **9.** $5t^2 = 125$

10. $t^2 + 16 = 0$ **11.** $-4x^2 + 8x = -3$ **12.** $3k^2 + 2 = -8k$

13. $8t^2 + 10t + 3 = 0$ **14.** $3x^2 - \frac{5}{4}x - \frac{1}{2} = 0$ **15.** $-5b^2 + 3b - 1 = 0$

16. $s^2 + 8s + 7 = 0$ **17.** $d^2 - 14d + 24 = 0$ **18.** $3k^2 + 11k = 4$

19. $n^2 - 3n + 1 = 0$ **20.** $2z^2 + 5z - 1 = 0$ **21.** $3h^2 = 27$

22. $3f^2 + 2f = 6$ **23.** $2x^2 = 0.7x + 0.3$ **24.** $3w^2 - 8w + 2 = 0$

25. $2r^2 - r - 3 = 0$ **26.** $x^2 - 9x = 5$ **27.** $6t^2 - 4t - 9 = 0$

Lesson 11-4 Use a calculator to determine the approximate value of each expression to the nearest hundredth.

1. $3^{1.6}$ **2.** $10^{-0.2}$ **3.** $\left(\frac{1}{3}\right)^{-1.4}$

4. $\left(\frac{2}{3}\right)^{5.1}$ **5.** $40(2^{-0.5})$ **6.** $10(2^{-1.6})$

7. $0.3(4^{0.8})$ **8.** $30(0.75^{-3.6})$ **9.** $5^{1.75}$

Graph each function. State the *y*-intercept.

10. $y = 3^x + 1$ **11.** $y = 2^x - 5$ **12.** $y = 2^{x+3}$

13. $y = 3^{x+1}$ **14.** $y = \left(\frac{1}{4}\right)^x$ **15.** $y = 5\left(\frac{2}{5}\right)^x$

16. $y = 3 \cdot 2^x$ **17.** $y = 4 \cdot 5^x$ **18.** $y = 6^x$

19. $y = 3^x$ **20.** $y = \left(\frac{1}{8}\right)^x$ **21.** $y = \left(\frac{3}{4}\right)^x$

Solve each equation.

22. $6^{3x-4} = 6^x$ **23.** $3^4 = 3^{2x+2}$ **24.** $4^x = 4^{5x+8}$

25. $2^x = 4^{x+1}$ **26.** $5^{4x} = 5^{-4}$ **27.** $2^{x+3} = 2^{-5}$

EXTRA PRACTICE

Lesson 11-5 Determine whether each exponential equation represents growth or decay.

1. $y = 3.89(1.05)^x$
2. $y = 476(0.35)^x$
3. $y = 19{,}520(0.98)^x$
4. $y = 16(1.0432)^x$
5. $y = 1.01(1.099)^x$
6. $y = 84(0.03)^x$

7. **Education** Marco withdrew all of the $2500 in his savings account to pay the tuition for his first semester at college. The account had earned 12% interest compounded monthly, and no withdrawals or additional deposits were made.
   a. If Marco's original deposit was $1250, how long ago did he open the account?
   b. If Marco's original deposit was $1500, how long ago did he open the account?
8. **Finance** Erin saved $500 of the money she earned working at the Dairy Dream last summer. She deposited the money in a certificate of deposit that earns 8.75% interest compounded monthly. If she rolls over the CD at the same rate each year, when will Erin's CD have a balance of $800?
9. **Demographics** In 1994, the metropolitan area of Pensacola, Florida, had a population of 371,000. The growth rate from 1990 to 1994 was 7.7%.
   a. Write an exponential equation for the area's growth.
   b. Compute the estimated population for Pensacola in the year 2000.

Lesson 12-1 Simplify each rational expression. State the excluded values of the variables.

1. $\frac{13a}{39a^2}$
2. $\frac{38x^2}{42xy}$
3. $\frac{14y^2z}{49yz^3}$
4. $\frac{p+5}{2(p+5)}$
5. $\frac{79a^2b}{158a^3bc}$
6. $\frac{a+b}{a^2-b^2}$
7. $\frac{y+4}{(y-4)(y+4)}$
8. $\frac{c^2-4}{(c+2)^2}$
9. $\frac{a^2-a}{a-1}$
10. $\frac{(w-4)(w+4)}{(w-2)(w-4)}$
11. $\frac{m^2-2m}{m-2}$
12. $\frac{x^2+4}{x^4-16}$
13. $\frac{r^3-r^2}{r-1}$
14. $\frac{3m^3}{6m^2-3m}$
15. $\frac{4t^2-8}{4t-4}$
16. $\frac{6y^3-12y^2}{12y^2-18}$
17. $\frac{x-3}{x^2+x-12}$
18. $\frac{5x^2+10x+5}{3x^2+6x+3}$

Lesson 12-2 Find each product. Assume that no denominator has a value of 0.

1. $\frac{a^2b}{b^2c} \cdot \frac{c}{d}$
2. $\frac{6a^2n}{8n^2} \cdot \frac{12n}{9a}$
3. $\frac{2a^2d}{3bc} \cdot \frac{9b^2c}{16ad^2}$
4. $\frac{10n^3}{6x^3} \cdot \frac{12n^2x^4}{25n^2x^2}$
5. $\left(\frac{2a}{b}\right)^2 \cdot \frac{5c}{6a}$
6. $\frac{6m^3n}{10a^2} \cdot \frac{4a^2m}{9n^3}$
7. $\frac{5n-5}{3} \cdot \frac{9}{n-1}$
8. $\frac{a^2}{a-b} \cdot \frac{3a-3b}{a}$
9. $\frac{2a+4b}{5} \cdot \frac{25}{6a+8b}$
10. $\frac{4t}{4t+40} \cdot \frac{3t+30}{2t}$
11. $\frac{3k+9}{k} \cdot \frac{k^2}{k^2-9}$
12. $\frac{7xy^3}{11z^2} \cdot \frac{44z^3}{21x^2y}$
13. $\frac{3}{x-y} \cdot \frac{(x-y)^2}{6}$
14. $\frac{x+5}{3x} \cdot \frac{12x^2}{x^2+7x+10}$
15. $\frac{a^2-b^2}{4} \cdot \frac{16}{a+b}$
16. $\frac{4a+8}{a^2-25} \cdot \frac{a-5}{5a+10}$
17. $\frac{r^2}{r-s} \cdot \frac{r^2-s^2}{s^2}$
18. $\frac{a^2-b^2}{a-b} \cdot \frac{7}{a+b}$

Lesson 12-3 Find each quotient. Assume that no denominator has a value of 0.

1. $\frac{5m^2n}{12a^2} \div \frac{30m^4}{18an}$
2. $\frac{25g^7h}{28t^3} \div \frac{5g^5h^2}{42s^2t^3}$
3. $\frac{6a + 3b}{36} \div \frac{3a + 2b}{45}$
4. $\frac{x^2y}{18z} \div \frac{2yz}{3x^2}$
5. $\frac{p^2}{14qr^3} \div \frac{2r^2p}{7q}$
6. $\frac{5e - f}{5e + f} \div (25e^2 - f^2)$
7. $\frac{t^2 - 2t - 15}{t - 5} \div \frac{t + 3}{t + 5}$
8. $\frac{5x + 10}{x + 2} \div (x + 2)$
9. $\frac{3d}{2d^2 - 3d} \div \frac{9}{2d - 3}$
10. $\frac{3v^2 - 27}{15v} \div \frac{v + 3}{v^2}$
11. $\frac{3g^2 + 15g}{4} \div \frac{g + 5}{g^2}$
12. $\frac{b^2 - 9}{4b} \div (b - 3)$
13. $\frac{p^2}{y^2 - 4} \div \frac{p}{2 - y}$
14. $\frac{k^2 - 81}{k^2 - 36} \div \frac{k - 9}{k + 6}$
15. $\frac{2a^3}{a + 1} \div \frac{a^2}{a + 1}$
16. $\frac{x^2 - 16}{16 - x^2} \div \frac{7}{x}$
17. $\frac{y}{5} \div \frac{y^2 - 25}{5 - y}$
18. $\frac{3m}{m + 1} \div (m - 2)$

Lesson 12-4 Find each quotient.

1. $(2x^2 - 11x - 20) \div (2x + 3)$
2. $(a^2 + 7a + 12) \div (a + 3)$
3. $(m^2 + 9m + 20) \div (m + 5)$
4. $(x^2 - 2x - 35) \div (x - 7)$
5. $(c^2 + 12c + 36) \div (c + 9)$
6. $(y^2 - 2y - 30) \div (y + 7)$
7. $(3t^2 - 14t - 24) \div (3t + 4)$
8. $(2r^2 - 3r - 35) \div (2r + 7)$
9. $\frac{12n^2 + 36n + 15}{6n + 3}$
10. $\frac{10x^2 + 29x + 21}{5x + 7}$
11. $\frac{4t^3 + 17t^2 - 1}{4t + 1}$
12. $\frac{2a^3 + 9a^2 + 5a - 12}{a + 3}$
13. $\frac{4m^3 + 5m - 21}{2m - 3}$
14. $\frac{6t^3 + 5t^2 + 12}{2t + 3}$
15. $\frac{27c^2 - 24c + 8}{9c - 2}$
16. $\frac{3b^3 + 8b^2 + b - 7}{b + 2}$
17. $\frac{t^3 - 19t + 9}{t - 4}$
18. $\frac{9d^3 + 5d - 8}{3d - 2}$

Lesson 12-5 Find each sum or difference. Express in simplest form.

1. $\frac{4}{z} + \frac{3}{z}$
2. $\frac{a}{12} + \frac{2a}{12}$
3. $\frac{5}{2t} + \frac{-7}{2t}$
4. $\frac{y}{2} + \frac{y}{2}$
5. $\frac{b}{x} + \frac{2}{x}$
6. $\frac{5x}{24} - \frac{3x}{24}$
7. $\frac{7p}{p} - \frac{8p}{p}$
8. $\frac{8k}{5m} - \frac{3k}{5m}$
9. $\frac{y}{2} + \frac{y - 6}{2}$
10. $\frac{a + 2}{6} - \frac{a + 3}{6}$
11. $\frac{8}{m - 2} - \frac{6}{m - 2}$
12. $\frac{x}{x + 1} + \frac{1}{x + 1}$
13. $\frac{2n}{2n - 5} + \frac{5}{5 - 2n}$
14. $\frac{y}{b + 6} - \frac{2y}{b + 6}$
15. $\frac{x - y}{2 - y} + \frac{x + y}{y - 2}$
16. $\frac{r^2}{r - s} + \frac{s^2}{r - s}$
17. $\frac{12n}{3n + 2} + \frac{8}{3n + 2}$
18. $\frac{6x}{x + y} + \frac{6y}{x + y}$

EXTRA PRACTICE

Lesson 12-6 Find each sum or difference.

1. $\frac{s}{3} + \frac{2s}{7}$
2. $\frac{5}{2a} + \frac{-3}{6a}$
3. $\frac{2n}{5} - \frac{3m}{4}$
4. $\frac{6}{5x} + \frac{7}{10x^2}$
5. $\frac{3z}{7w^2} - \frac{2z}{w}$
6. $\frac{s}{t^2} - \frac{r}{3t}$
7. $\frac{5}{xy} + \frac{6}{yz}$
8. $\frac{2}{t} + \frac{t+3}{s}$
9. $\frac{a}{a-b} + \frac{b}{2b+3a}$
10. $\frac{a}{a^2-4} - \frac{4}{a+2}$
11. $\frac{4a}{2a+6} + \frac{3}{a+3}$
12. $\frac{m}{1(m-n)} - \frac{5}{m}$
13. $\frac{-3}{a-5} + \frac{-6}{a^2-5a}$
14. $\frac{3t+2}{3t-6} - \frac{t+2}{t^2-4}$
15. $\frac{y+5}{y-5} + \frac{2y}{y^2-25}$
16. $\frac{-18}{y^2-9} + \frac{7}{3-y}$
17. $\frac{c}{c^2-4c} - \frac{5c}{c-4}$
18. $\frac{t+10}{t^2-100} + \frac{1}{t-10}$

Lesson 12-7 Write each mixed expression as a rational expression.

1. $4 + \frac{2}{x}$
2. $8 + \frac{5}{3t}$
3. $3b + \frac{b+1}{2b}$
4. $2n + \frac{4+n}{n}$
5. $a^2 + \frac{2}{a-2}$
6. $3r^2 + \frac{4}{2r+1}$

Simplify.

7. $\frac{3\frac{1}{2}}{4\frac{3}{4}}$
8. $\frac{\frac{x^2}{y}}{\frac{y}{x^3}}$
9. $\frac{\frac{t^4}{u}}{\frac{t^3}{u^2}}$
10. $\frac{\frac{x^3}{y^2}}{\frac{x+y}{x-y}}$
11. $\frac{\frac{y}{3}+\frac{5}{6}}{2+\frac{5}{y}}$
12. $\frac{\frac{1}{x}+\frac{1}{y}}{\frac{1}{y}-\frac{1}{x}}$
13. $\frac{t-2}{\frac{t^2-4}{t^2+5t+6}}$
14. $\frac{\frac{y^2-1}{y^2+3y-4}}{y+1}$

Lesson 12-8 Solve each equation.

1. $\frac{k}{6} + \frac{2k}{3} = -\frac{5}{2}$
2. $\frac{3x}{5} + \frac{3}{2} = \frac{7x}{10}$
3. $\frac{18}{b} = \frac{3}{b} + 3$
4. $\frac{3}{5x} + \frac{7}{2x} = 1$
5. $\frac{2a-3}{6} = \frac{2a}{3} + \frac{1}{2}$
6. $\frac{x+1}{x} + \frac{x+4}{x} = 6$
7. $\frac{2b-3}{7} - \frac{b}{2} = \frac{b+3}{14}$
8. $\frac{2y}{y-4} - \frac{3}{5} = 3$
9. $\frac{2t}{t+3} + \frac{3}{t} = 2$
10. $\frac{5x}{x+1} + \frac{1}{x} = 5$
11. $\frac{r-1}{r+1} - \frac{2r}{r-1} = -1$
12. $\frac{m}{m+1} + \frac{5}{m-1} = 1$
13. $\frac{5}{5-p} - \frac{p^2}{5-p} = -2$
14. $\frac{14}{b-6} = \frac{1}{2} + \frac{6}{b-8}$
15. $\frac{r}{3r+6} - \frac{r}{5r+10} = \frac{2}{5}$
16. $\frac{4x}{2x+3} - \frac{2x}{2x-3} = 1$
17. $\frac{2a-3}{a-3} - 2 = \frac{12}{a+2}$
18. $\frac{z+3}{z-1} + \frac{z+1}{z-3} = 2$

Lesson 13-1

If c is the measure of the hypotenuse of a right triangle, find each missing measure. Round answers to the nearest hundredth.

1. $b = 20, c = 29, a = ?$
2. $a = 7, b = 24, c = ?$
3. $a = 2, b = 6, c = ?$
4. $b = 10, c = \sqrt{200}, a = ?$
5. $a = 3, c = 3\sqrt{2}, b = ?$
6. $a = 6, c = 14, b = ?$
7. $a = \sqrt{11}, c = \sqrt{47}, b = ?$
8. $a = \sqrt{13}, b = 6, c = ?$
9. $a = \sqrt{6}, b = 3, c = ?$
10. $b = \sqrt{75}, c = 10, a = ?$
11. $b = 9, c = \sqrt{130}, a = ?$
12. $a = 9, c = 15, b = ?$
13. $b = 5, c = 11, a = ?$
14. $a = \sqrt{33}, b = 4, c = ?$

Determine whether the following side measures would form right triangles.

15. 14, 48, 50
16. 20, 30, 40
17. 21, 72, 75
18. 5, 12, $\sqrt{119}$
19. 15, 39, 36
20. $\sqrt{5}$, 12, 13
21. 10, 12, $\sqrt{22}$
22. 2, 3, 4
23. $\sqrt{7}$, 8, $\sqrt{71}$

Lesson 13-2

Simplify. Leave in radical form and use absolute value symbols when necessary.

1. $\sqrt{50}$
2. $\sqrt{20}$
3. $\sqrt{162}$
4. $\sqrt{700}$
5. $\frac{\sqrt{3}}{\sqrt{5}}$
6. $\frac{\sqrt{72}}{\sqrt{6}}$
7. $\sqrt{\frac{8}{7}}$
8. $\sqrt{\frac{7}{32}}$
9. $\sqrt{10} \cdot \sqrt{20}$
10. $\sqrt{7} \cdot \sqrt{3}$
11. $6\sqrt{2} \cdot \sqrt{3}$
12. $5\sqrt{6} \cdot 2\sqrt{3}$
13. $\sqrt{4x^4y^3}$
14. $\sqrt{200m^2y^3}$
15. $\sqrt{12ts^3}$
16. $\sqrt{175a^4b^6}$
17. $\sqrt{\frac{54}{g^2}}$
18. $\sqrt{99x^3y^7}$
19. $\sqrt{\frac{32c^5}{9d^2}}$
20. $\sqrt{\frac{27p^4}{3p^2}}$
21. $\frac{1}{3 + \sqrt{5}}$
22. $\frac{2}{\sqrt{3} - 5}$
23. $\frac{\sqrt{3}}{\sqrt{3} - 5}$
24. $\frac{\sqrt{6}}{7 - 2\sqrt{3}}$
25. $(\sqrt{p} + \sqrt{10})^2$
26. $(2\sqrt{5} + \sqrt{7})(2\sqrt{5} - \sqrt{7})$
27. $(t - 2\sqrt{3})(t - \sqrt{3})$

Lesson 13-3

Simplify.

1. $3\sqrt{11} + 6\sqrt{11} - 2\sqrt{11}$
2. $6\sqrt{13} + 7\sqrt{13}$
3. $2\sqrt{12} + 5\sqrt{3}$
4. $9\sqrt{7} - 4\sqrt{2} + 3\sqrt{2} + 5\sqrt{7}$
5. $3\sqrt{5} - 5\sqrt{3}$
6. $4\sqrt{8} - 3\sqrt{5}$
7. $2\sqrt{27} - 4\sqrt{12}$
8. $8\sqrt{32} + 4\sqrt{50}$
9. $\sqrt{45} + 6\sqrt{20}$
10. $2\sqrt{63} - 6\sqrt{28} + 8\sqrt{45}$
11. $14\sqrt{3t} + 8\sqrt{3t}$
12. $7\sqrt{6x} - 12\sqrt{6x}$
13. $5\sqrt{7} - 3\sqrt{28}$
14. $7\sqrt{8} - \sqrt{18}$
15. $7\sqrt{98} + 5\sqrt{32} - 2\sqrt{75}$
16. $4\sqrt{6} + 3\sqrt{2} - 2\sqrt{5}$
17. $-3\sqrt{20} + 2\sqrt{45} - \sqrt{7}$
18. $4\sqrt{75} + 6\sqrt{27}$
19. $10\sqrt{\frac{1}{5}} - \sqrt{45} - 12\sqrt{\frac{5}{9}}$
20. $\sqrt{15} - \sqrt{\frac{3}{5}}$
21. $3\sqrt{\frac{1}{3}} - 9\sqrt{\frac{1}{12}} + \sqrt{243}$

Lesson 13–4 **Solve each equation. Check your solution.**

1. $\sqrt{5x} = 5$
2. $4\sqrt{7} = \sqrt{-m}$
3. $\sqrt{t} - 5 = 0$
4. $\sqrt{3b} + 2 = 0$
5. $\sqrt{x-3} = 6$
6. $5 - \sqrt{3x} = 1$
7. $2 + 3\sqrt{y} = 13$
8. $\sqrt{3g} = 6$
9. $\sqrt{a} - 2 = 0$
10. $\sqrt{2j} - 4 = 8$
11. $5 + \sqrt{x} = 9$
12. $\sqrt{5y+4} = 7$
13. $7 + \sqrt{5c} = 9$
14. $2\sqrt{5t} = 10$
15. $\sqrt{44} = 2\sqrt{p}$
16. $4\sqrt{x-5} = 15$
17. $4 - \sqrt{x-3} = 9$
18. $\sqrt{10x^2 - 5} = 3x$
19. $\sqrt{2a^2 - 144} = a$
20. $\sqrt{3y+1} = y - 3$
21. $\sqrt{2x^2 - 12} = x$
22. $\sqrt{b^2 + 16} + 2b = 5b$
23. $\sqrt{m+2} + m = 4$
24. $\sqrt{3 - 2c} + 3 = 2c$

Lesson 13–5 **Find the distance between each pair of points whose coordinates are given. Express answers in simplest radical form and as decimal approximations rounded to the nearest hundredth.**

1. $(4, 2), (-2, 10)$
2. $(-5, 1), (7, 6)$
3. $(4, -2), (1, 2)$
4. $(-2, 4), (4, -2)$
5. $(3, 1), (-2, -1)$
6. $(-2, 4), (7, -8)$
7. $(-5, 0), (-9, 6)$
8. $(5, -1), (5, 13)$
9. $(2, -3), (10, 8)$
10. $(-7, 5), (2, -7)$
11. $(-6, -2), (-5, 4)$
12. $(8, -10), (3, 2)$
13. $(4, -3), (7, -9)$
14. $(6, 3), (9, 7)$
15. $(10, 0), (9, 7)$
16. $(2, -1), (-3, 3)$
17. $(-5, 4), (3, -2)$
18. $(0, -9), (0, 7)$
19. $(-1, 7), (8, 4)$
20. $(-9, 2), (3, -3)$
21. $(3\sqrt{2}, 7), (5\sqrt{2}, 9)$
22. $(6, 3), (10, 0)$
23. $(3, 6), (5, -5)$
24. $(-4, 2), (5, 4)$

Lesson 13–6 **Find the value of c that makes each trinomial a perfect square.**

1. $a^2 + 6a + c$
2. $x^2 + 10x + c$
3. $t^2 + 12t + c$
4. $y^2 - 9y + c$
5. $p^2 - 14p + c$
6. $b^2 + 5b + c$

Solve each equation by completing the square. Leave irrational roots in simplest radical form.

7. $x^2 - 4x = 5$
8. $t^2 + 12t - 45 = 0$
9. $b^2 + 4b - 12 = 0$
10. $a^2 - 8a - 84 = 0$
11. $c^2 + 6 = -5c$
12. $t^2 - 7t = -10$
13. $p^2 - 8p + 5 = 0$
14. $a^2 + 4a + 2 = 0$
15. $2y^2 + 7y - 4 = 0$
16. $t^2 + 3t = 40$
17. $x^2 + 8x - 9 = 0$
18. $y^2 + 5y - 84 = 0$
19. $x^2 + 2x - 6 = 0$
20. $t^2 + 12t + 32 = 0$
21. $2x - 3x^2 = -8$
22. $2y^2 - y - 9 = 0$
23. $2z^2 - 5z - 4 = 0$
24. $4t^2 - 6t - \frac{1}{2} = 0$

CHAPTER 1 TEST

Write an algebraic expression for each verbal expression.

1. the sum of a number x and 13
2. the reciprocal of a number x squared
3. the cube of a number x decreased by 7
4. the product of 5 and a number x squared

Find the next two items for each pattern.

5. 
6. 4, 7, 10, 13, . . .
7. 2, 5, 10, 17, . . .

Evaluate each expression.

8. $5^2 - 12$
9. $(0.5)^3 + 2 \cdot 7$
10. $\frac{2}{5}(16 - 9)$

Evaluate each expression when $a = 2$, $b = 0.5$, $c = 3$, and $d = \frac{4}{3}$.

11. $a^2b + c$
12. $(cd)^3$
13. $(a + d)c$

Solve each equation.

14. $y = (4.5 + 0.8) - 3.2$
15. $4^2 - 3(4 - 2) = y$
16. $\frac{2^3 - 1^3}{2 + 1} = y$

Name the property illustrated by each statement.

17. $a = a + 0$
18. $\frac{1}{a} \cdot a = 1$
19. If $a = b$, and $b = c$, then $a = c$.
20. $a(bc) = (ab)c$
21. $8(st) = 8(ts)$
22. $7y + 5x - 4y = 5x + 7y - 4y$

Simplify each expression.

23. $2m + 3m$
24. $4x + 2y - 2x + y$
25. $3(2a + b) - 1.5a - 1.5b$

Use the stem-and-leaf plot below to complete Exercises 26–27.

Stem	Leaf
1	1 4 6 8 8
2	0 3 3 3 5 7 9
3	0 0 2 6

$2|4 = 24$

26. List the set of data represented by the plot on the left.
27. Which number is used most frequently?

Sketch a reasonable graph for each situation.

28. A basketball is shot from the free throw line and falls through the net.
29. A slammer is dropped on a stack of pogs and bounces off.
30. An infant grows through adulthood.

Solve.

31. **Travel** If a car travels at an average speed of 50 miles per hour, how far can the car travel in 5 hours? Use the distance formula $d = r \cdot t$.
32. **Geometry** If the area of a circle is given by the equation $A = \pi r^2$, find the area if the radius is 4 in. (Use 3.14 for π.)
33. If a farmer wants to put a fence around his rectangular garden that measures 11 yards by 14 yards, how many yards of fencing will he need?

CHAPTER 2 TEST

CHAPTER TEST

Find each sum or difference.

1. $12 - 19$
2. $-21 + (-34)$
3. $1.654 + (-2.367)$
4. $-\frac{7}{16} - \frac{3}{8}$
5. $18b + 13xy - 46b$
6. $6.32 - (-7.41)$
7. $\frac{5}{8} + \left(-\frac{3}{16}\right) + \left(-\frac{3}{4}\right)$
8. $32y + (-73y)$
9. $|-28 + (-13)|$
10. $\begin{bmatrix} -8 & 5 \\ 2 & -3 \end{bmatrix} + \begin{bmatrix} 3 & 6 \\ -4 & -7 \end{bmatrix}$
11. $\begin{bmatrix} 1 & 0 \\ -9 & 3 \end{bmatrix} - \begin{bmatrix} 5 & 8 \\ -4 & 2 \end{bmatrix}$

Evaluate each expression.

12. $-x - 38$, if $x = -2$
13. $\left|-\frac{1}{2} + z\right|$, if $z = \frac{1}{4}$
14. $mp - k$, if $m = -12$, $p = 1.5$, and $k = -8$
15. $w^2 - 15$, if $w = 5$

Replace each __?__ with <, >, or = to make each sentence true.

16. -14 __?__ -15
17. $\frac{9}{20}$ __?__ $\frac{7}{15}$
18. -4.65 __?__ -4.45

Find a number between the given numbers.

19. $-\frac{2}{3}$ and $-\frac{9}{14}$
20. $\frac{4}{7}$ and $\frac{9}{4}$
21. $\frac{12}{7}$ and $\frac{15}{8}$

Simplify.

22. $\frac{8(-3)}{2}$
23. $(-5)(-2)(-2) - (-6)(-3)$
24. $\frac{2}{3}\left(\frac{1}{2}\right) - \left(-\frac{3}{2}\right)\left(-\frac{2}{3}\right)$
25. $\frac{70x - 30y}{-5}$
26. $\frac{7}{\frac{-2}{5}}$
27. $\frac{3}{4}(8x + 12y) - \frac{5}{7}(21x - 35y)$

Find each square root. Use a calculator if necessary. Round to the nearest hundredth if the result is not a whole number.

28. $\pm\sqrt{\frac{16}{81}}$
29. $\sqrt{40}$
30. $\sqrt{2.89}$

31. **Statistics** The height, in inches, of the students in a health class are 65, 63, 68, 66, 72, 61, 62, 63, 59, 58, 61, 74, 65, 63, 71, 60, 62, 63, 71, 70, 59, 66, 61, 62, 68, 69, 64, 63, 70, 61, 68, and 67.
    a. Make a line plot of the data on the heights of the students in health class.
    b. What was the most common height for the students in this class?

32. Define a variable and write an equation for the following problem. Do *not* solve.
    Each week for several weeks, Save-a-Buck stores reduced the price of a sofa by \$18.25. The original price was \$380.25. The final reduced price was \$252.50. For how many weeks was the sofa on sale?

33. Translate $r = (a - b)^3$ into a verbal sentence.

Solve each equation. Then check your solution.

1. $-15 - k = 8$
2. $-1.2x = 7.2$
3. $\frac{3}{4}y = -27$
4. $\frac{t-7}{4} = 11$
5. $-12 = 7 - \frac{y}{3}$
6. $k - 16 = -21$
7. $t - (-3.4) = -5.3$
8. $-3(x + 5) = 8x + 18$
9. $2 - \frac{1}{4}(b - 12) = 9$
10. $\frac{r}{5} - 3 = \frac{2r}{5} + 16$
11. $25 - 7w = 46$
12. $-w + 11 = 4.6$

Find the mean, median, and mode for each set of data.

13. 67, 31, 15, 49, 31, 35, 42, 27

14.

Stem	Leaf
18	0 5 8
19	3 3 4 4
20	8 8 9
21	4 5 5 5 9 $19 \mid 4 = 194$

Define a variable, write an equation, and solve each problem.

15. The sum of two integers is -23. One integer is -84. Find the other integer.
16. Negative two thirds of a number is eight fifths. What is the number?
17. What number decreased by 37 is -65?
18. The measures of two angles of a triangle are 23° and 121°. Find the measure of the third angle.
19. Find two consecutive odd integers whose sum is 172.

Solve each equation or formula for the variable specified.

20. $h = at - 0.25vt^2$, for a
21. $A = \frac{1}{2}(b + B)h$, for h

Solve.

22. **Geometry** One of two supplementary angles measures 37° less than four times the other. Find the measure of each angle.
23. **Grades** James had a cumulative score of 338 points after his first four tests, each worth 100 points. What is the least that he would need to score on his next chapter test in order to have a mean score of 82%?
24. **Merchandise Stock** A store has 49 cartons of yogurt, some plain, some with blueberry flavoring. There are six times as many cartons of plain yogurt as flavored yogurt. How many cartons of plain yogurt are there?
25. **Consumerism** Teri went to SuperValue to buy some groceries. Her total bill was \$8.51. She bought 2 pounds of grapes at \$0.99 per pound, a gallon of milk for \$2.59, and three cans of orange juice. She used a coupon worth 50¢ for the three cans of orange juice. How much was each can of orange juice?

CHAPTER 4 TEST

Solve each proportion.

1. $\frac{2}{5} = \frac{x-3}{-2}$
2. $\frac{n}{4} = \frac{3.25}{52}$
3. $\frac{x-3}{x+5} = \frac{9}{11}$
4. $\frac{x+1}{-3} = \frac{x-4}{5}$

Solve.

5. Find 6.5% of 80.
6. 42 is what percent of 126?
7. 84 is 60% of what number?
8. What number decreased by 20% is 16?
9. 24 is what percent of 8?
10. 54 is 20% more than what number?
11. A price decreased from \$60 to \$45. Find the percent of decrease.
12. The price in dollars p minus a 15% discount is \$3.40. Find p.

ΔABC and ΔJKH are similar. For each set of measures given, find the measures of the remaining sides.

13. $c = 20, h = 15, k = 16, j = 12$
14. $c = 12, b = 13, a = 6, h = 10$
15. $k = 5, c = 6.5, b = 7.5, a = 4.5$
16. $h = 1\frac{1}{2}, c = 4\frac{1}{2}, k = 2\frac{1}{4}, a = 3$

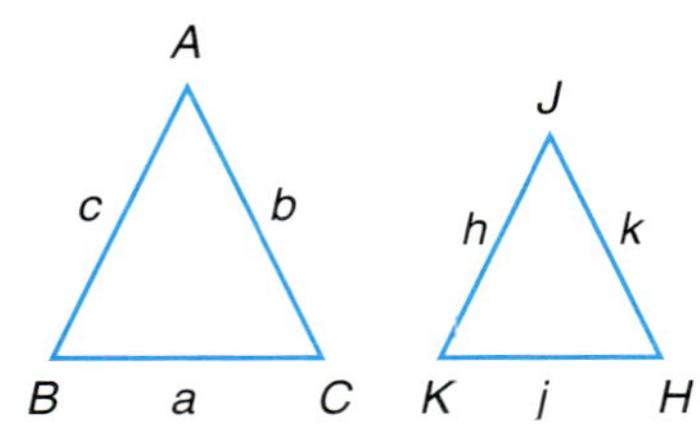

Solve each right triangle. State the side lengths to the nearest tenth and the angle measures to the nearest degree.

17.
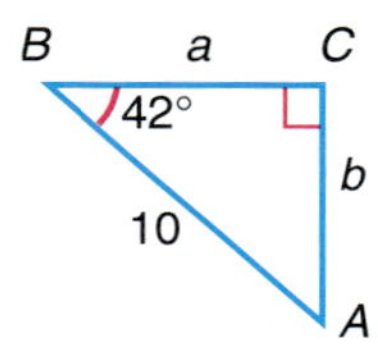

18.
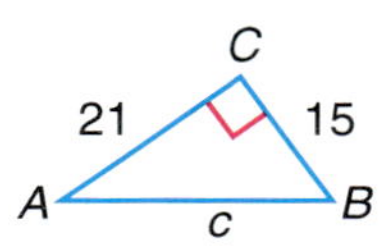

19.
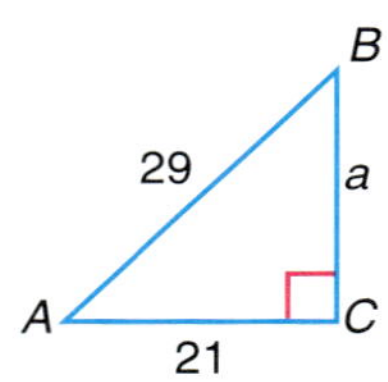

20.
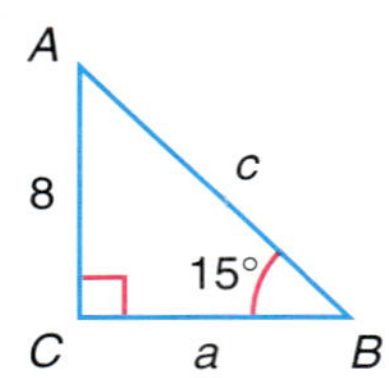

Solve.

21. **Music** During a 20-song sequence on a popular radio station, 8 soft-rock, 7 hard-rock, and 5 rap songs are played at random. You tune in to the station.
    a. What is the probability that a hard-rock song is playing?
    b. What are the odds that a rap song is playing?
    c. What is the probability that a soft-rock song or a hard-rock song is playing?

22. Two buildings are separated by an alley. Joe is looking out of a window 60 feet above the ground in one building. He observes the measurement of the angle of depression of the base of the second building to be 50° and the angle of elevation of the top to be 40°. How high is the second building?

23. **Finance** Gladys deposited an amount of money in the bank at 6.5% annual interest. After 6 months, she received \$7.80 interest. How much money had Gladys deposited in the bank?

24. **Stereo** Larry is buying a stereo that costs \$399. Since he is an employee of the store, he receives a 15% discount. He also has to pay 6% sales tax. If the discount is computed first, what is the total cost of Larry's stereo?

25. **Travel** At the same time Kris leaves Washington, D.C., for Detroit, Michigan, Amy leaves Detroit for Washington, D.C. The distance between the cities is 510 miles. Amy's average speed is 5 miles per hour faster than Kris's. How fast is Kris's average speed if they pass each other in 6 hours?

1. Graph $K(0, -5)$, $M(3, -5)$, and $N(-2, -3)$.

2. Name the quadrant in which $P(-5, 1)$ is located.

Express the relations shown in each table, mapping, or graph as a set of ordered pairs. Then state the domain, range, and inverse of the relation.

3.

x	$f(x)$
0	−1
2	4
4	5
6	10

4. 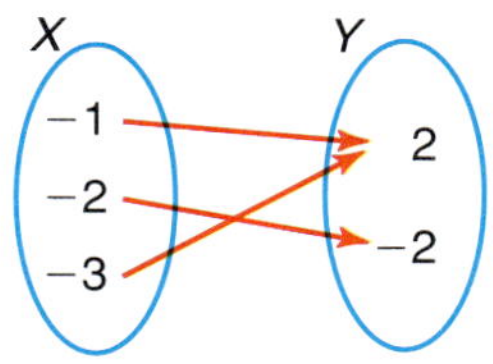

5. 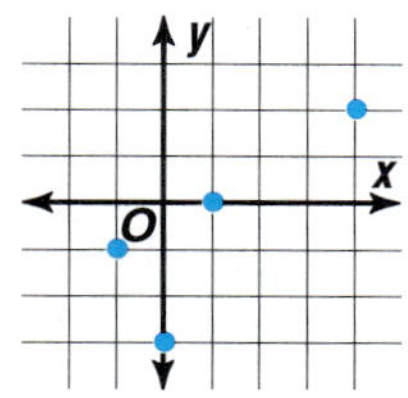

Solve each equation if the domain is {−2, −1, 0, 2, 4}.

6. $y = -4x + 10$

7. $4 - 2x = 5y$

8. $-x + 3y = 1$

Graph each equation.

9. $x + 2y = -1$

10. $-3x = 5 - y$

11. $-4 = x - \frac{1}{2}y$

Determine whether each relation is a function.

12. $\{(2, 4), (3, 2), (4, 6), (5, 4)\}$

13. $8y = 7 + 3x$

If $f(x) = -2x + 5$ and $g(x) = x^2 - 4x + 1$, find each value.

14. $f\left(\frac{1}{2}\right)$

15. $g(-2)$

16. $-2g(3)$

Write an equation for each relation.

17.

x	1	2	3	4	7
y	3	8	13	18	33

18.

x	1	3	5	7	9	11	13
y	5	17	29	41	53	65	77

Solve.

19. **School** Art and Gina's test scores in algebra are given below.
Art: 87, 54, 78, 97, 65, 82, 75, 68, 82, 73, 66, 75
Gina: 70, 80, 57, 100, 73, 74, 65, 77, 91, 69, 71, 76
   a. Find the range and interquartile range for each set of scores.
   b. Identify any outliers.
   c. Which one had the more consistent scores?

20. **Sales** When you use Jay's Taxi Service, a two-mile trip costs \$6.30, a five-mile trip costs \$11.25, and a ten-mile trip costs \$19.50. Write an equation to describe this relationship and use it to find the cost of a one-mile trip.

CHAPTER 6 TEST

Determine the slope of the line that passes through each pair of points.

1. (5, 8), (−3, 7)
2. (−2, 5), (2, 9)

Find the slope and x- and y-intercepts of the graph of each equation.

3. $x - 8y = 3$
4. $3x - 2y = 9$
5. $y = 7$

Graph each equation.

6. $4x - 3y = 24$
7. $2x + 7y = 16$
8. $y = \frac{2}{3}x + 3$

Determine whether the graphs of each pair of equations are *parallel, perpendicular,* or *neither.*

9. $y = 4x - 11$
   $2y + 1 = 8x$
10. $-7y = 4x + 14$
    $7x - 4y = -12$

Write an equation in standard form of the line that satisfies the given conditions.

11. passes through (2, 5) and (8, −3)
12. passes through (−2, −1) and (6, −4)
13. has slope of 2 and y-intercept = 3
14. has y-intercept = −4 and passes through (5, −3)
15. slope = $\frac{3}{4}$ and passes through (6, −2)
16. parallel to $6x - y = 7$ and passes through (−2, 8)

Write an equation in slope-intercept form of the line that satisfies the given conditions.

17. passes through (4, −2) and the origin
18. passes through (−2, −5) and (8, −3)
19. passes through (6, 4) with y-intercept = −2
20. slope = $-\frac{2}{3}$ and y-intercept = 5
21. slope = 6 and passes through (−3, −4)
22. perpendicular to $5x - 3y = 9$ and passes through the origin
23. parallel to $3x + 7y = 4$ and passes through (5, −2)
24. perpendicular to $x + 3y = 7$ and passes through (5, 2)
25. Find the coordinates of the other endpoint of segment AB given $A(-2, -7)$ and midpoint $M(6, -5)$.
26. The table below shows the number of students per computer in American classrooms since 1983.

School Year	Students per Computer	School Year	Students per Computer
1983–84	125	1989–90	22
1984–85	75	1990–91	20
1985–86	50	1991–92	18
1986–87	37	1992–93	16
1987–88	32	1993–94	14
1988–89	25	1994–95	12

a. Make a scatter plot of the data.
b. Describe the correlation between the variables.
c. Are these data best modeled by a line? Explain your answer.

Solve each inequality. Then check your solution.

1. $-12 \le d + 7$
2. $7x < 6x - 11$
3. $z - 1 \ge 2z - 3$
4. $5 - 4b > -23$
5. $-\frac{2}{3}r \le \frac{7}{12}$
6. $8y + 3 < 13y - 9$
7. $8(1 - 2z) \le 25 + z$
8. $0.3(m + 4) > 0.5(m - 4)$
9. $\frac{2n - 3}{-7} \le 5$
10. $y + \frac{5}{8} > \frac{11}{24}$

Solve each compound inequality. Then graph the solution set.

11. $x + 1 > -2$ and $3x < 6$
12. $2n + 1 \ge 15$ or $2n + 1 \le -1$
13. $8 + 3t > 2$ and $-12 > 11t - 1$
14. $|2x - 1| < 5$
15. $|5 - 3b| \ge 1$
16. $|3 - 5y| < 8$

Define a variable, write an inequality, and solve each problem. Then check your solution.

17. Twice a number subtracted from 12 is no less than the number increased by 27.
18. Seven less than twice a number is between 71 and 83.
19. The product of two integers is no less than 30. One of the integers is 6. What is the other integer?
20. The average of four consecutive odd integers is less than 20. What are the greatest integers that satisfy this condition?

Graph each inequality.

21. $y \ge 5x + 1$
22. $x - 2y > 8$
23. $3x - 2y < 6$

Solve.

24. **Business** Two men and three women are each waiting for a job interview. There is only enough time to interview two people before lunch. Two people are chosen at random.
    a. What is the probability that both people are women?
    b. What is the probability that at least one person is a woman?
    c. Which is more likely, one of the people is a woman and the other is a man, or both people are either men or women?

25. **Fire Safety** The city council of McBride is investigating the efficiency of the fire department. The time taken by the fire department to respond to a fire alarm was surveyed. It was found that the response times in minutes for 17 alarms were as follows.

    1, 3, 2, 2, 1, 9, 4, 6, 1, 10, 1, 4, 5, 10, 1, 3, 6

    a. Draw a box-and-whisker plot of the data.
    b. Between what two values of the data is the middle 50% of the data?

CHAPTER 8 TEST

Graph each system of equations. Then determine whether the system has *one* solution, *no* solution, or *infinitely many* solutions. If the system has one solution, name it.

1. $y = x + 2$
   $y = 2x + 7$
2. $x + 2y = 11$
   $x = 14 - 2y$
3. $2x + 5y = 16$
   $5x - 2y = 11$
4. $3x + y = 5$
   $2y - 10 = -6x$
5. $y + 2x = -1$
   $y - 4 = -2x$
6. $2x + y = -4$
   $5x + 3y = -6$

Use substitution or elimination to solve each system of equations.

7. $y = 7 - x$
   $x - y = -3$
8. $x = 2y - 7$
   $y - 3x = -9$
9. $x + y = 8$
   $x - y = 2$
10. $3x - y = 11$
    $x + 2y = -36$
11. $3x + y = 10$
    $3x - 2y = 16$
12. $5x - 3y = 12$
    $-2x + 3y = -3$
13. $2x + 5y = 12$
    $x - 6y = -11$
14. $x + y = 6$
    $3x - 3y = 13$
15. $3x + \frac{1}{3}y = 10$
    $2x - \frac{5}{3}y = 35$
16. $8x - 6y = 14$
    $6x - 9y = 15$
17. $5x - y = 1$
    $y = -3x + 1$
18. $7x + 3y = 13$
    $3x - 2y = -1$

Solve each system of inequalities by graphing.

19. $y \leq 3$
    $y > -x + 2$
20. $x \leq 2y$
    $2x + 3y \leq 7$
21. $x > y + 1$
    $2x + y \geq -4$

Solve.

22. **Number Theory** The units digit of a two-digit number exceeds twice the tens digit by 1. Find the number if the sum of its digits is 10.
23. **Geometry** The difference between the length and width of a rectangle is 7 cm. Find the dimensions of the rectangle if its perimeter is 50 cm.
24. **Finance** Last year, Jodi invested $10,000, part at 6% annual interest and the rest at 8% annual interest. If she received $760 in interest at the end of the year, how much did she invest at each rate?
25. **Organize Data** Joey sold 30 peaches from his fruit stand for a total of $7.50. He sold small ones for 20 cents each and large ones for 35 cents each. How many of each kind did he sell?

Simplify. Assume that no denominator is equal to zero.

1. $(a^2b^4)(a^3b^5)$
2. $(-12abc)(4a^2b^4)$
3. $\left(\frac{3}{5}m\right)^2$
4. $(-3a)^4(a^5b)^2$
5. $(-5a^2)(-6b^3)^2$
6. $(5a)^2b + 7a^2b$
7. $\frac{y^{11}}{y^6}$
8. $\frac{mn^4}{m^3n^2}$
9. $\frac{9a^2bc^2}{63a^4bc}$
10. $\frac{48a^2bc^5}{(3ab^3c^2)^2}$
11. $\frac{14ab^{-3}}{21a^2b^{-5}}$
12. $\frac{(10a^2bc^4)^{-2}}{(5^{-1}a^{-1}b^{-5})^2}$

Express each number in scientific notation.

13. 46,300
14. 0.003892
15. 284×10^3
16. 0.0031×10^4

Evaluate. Express each result in scientific notation.

17. $(3 \times 10^3)(2 \times 10^4)$
18. $\frac{2.5 \times 10^3}{5 \times 10^{-3}}$
19. $\frac{14.72 \times 10^{-4}}{3.2 \times 10^{-3}}$
20. $(15 \times 10^{-7})(3.1 \times 10^4)$
21. Find the degree of $5ya^3 - 7 - y^2a^2 + 2y^3a$ and arrange the terms so that the powers of y are in descending order.

Find each sum or difference.

22.
$$\begin{array}{r} 5ax^2 + 3a^2x - 7a^3 \\ \underline{(+)\ 2ax^2 - 8a^2x \qquad\quad + 4} \end{array}$$

23.
$$\begin{array}{r} x^3 - 3x^2y + 4xy^2 + y^3 \\ \underline{(-)\ 7x^3 + x^2y - 9xy^2 + y^3} \end{array}$$

24. $(n^2 - 5n + 4) - (5n^2 + 3n - 1)$
25. $(ab^3 - 4a^2b^2 + ab - 7) + (-2ab^3 + 4ab^2 + 3ab + 2)$

Simplify.

26. $(h - 5)^2$
27. $(2x - 5)(7x + 3)$
28. $(4x - y)(4x + y)$
29. $(2a^2b + b^2)^2$
30. $3x^2y^3(2x - xy^2)$
31. $(4m + 3n)(2m - 5n)$
32. $x^2(x - 8) - 3x(x^2 - 7x + 3) + 5(x^3 - 6x^2)$
33. $(x - 6)(x^2 - 4x + 5)$

CHAPTER 10 TEST

CHAPTER TEST

Find the GCF of the given monomials.

1. 48, 64
2. $18a^2b$, $28a^3b^2$
3. $6x^2y^3$, $12x^2y^2z$, $15x^2y$

Factor each polynomial, if possible. If the polynomial cannot be factored using integers, write *prime*.

4. $25y^2 - 49w^2$
5. $t^2 - 16t + 64$
6. $x^2 + 14x + 24$
7. $28m^2 + 18m$
8. $a^2 - 11ab + 18b^2$
9. $12x^2 + 23x - 24$
10. $2h^2 - 3h - 18$
11. $6x^3 + 15x^2 - 9x$
12. $4my - 20m + 3py - 15p$
13. $x^3 - 4x^2 - 9x + 36$
14. $36a^2b^3 - 45ab^4$
15. $36m^2 + 60mn + 25n^2$
16. $\frac{1}{4}a^2 - \frac{4}{9}$
17. $64p^2 - 63p + 16$
18. $15a^2b + 5a^2 - 10a$
19. $6y^2 - 5y - 6$
20. $4s^2 - 100t^2$
21. $2d^2 + d - 1$
22. $3g^2 + g + 1$
23. $2xz + 2yz - x - y$

Solve each equation. Check your solutions.

24. $(4x - 3)(3x + 2) = 0$
25. $18s^2 + 72s = 0$
26. $4x^2 = 36$
27. $t^2 + 25 = 10t$
28. $a^2 - 9a - 52 = 0$
29. $x^3 - 5x^2 - 66x = 0$
30. $2x^2 = 9x + 5$
31. $3b^2 + 6 = 11b$

Solve.

32. **Geometry** A rectangle is 4 inches wide by 7 inches long. When the length and width are increased by the same amount, the area is increased by 26 square inches. What are the dimensions of the new rectangle?

33. **Construction** A rectangular lawn is 24 feet wide by 32 feet long. A sidewalk will be built along the inside edges of all four sides. The remaining lawn will have an area of 425 square feet. How wide will the walk be?

CHAPTER 11 TEST

Write the equation of the axis of symmetry and find the coordinates of the vertex of the graph of each equation. State if the vertex is a maximum or minimum. Then graph the equation.

1. $y = x^2 - 4x + 13$
2. $y = -3x^2 - 6x + 4$
3. $y = 2x^2 + 3$
4. $y = -1(x - 2)^2 + 1$

Solve each equation by graphing. If exact roots cannot be found, state the consecutive integers between which the roots lie.

5. $x^2 - 2x + 2 = 0$
6. $x^2 + 6x = -7$
7. $x^2 + 24x + 144 = 0$
8. $2x^2 - 8x = 42$

Solve each equation.

9. $x^2 + 7x + 6 = 0$
10. $2x^2 - 5x - 12 = 0$
11. $6n^2 + 7n = 20$
12. $3k^2 + 2k = 5$
13. $y^2 - \frac{3y}{5} + \frac{2}{25} = 0$
14. $-3x^2 + 5 = 14x$
15. $4^{x - 2} = 16^{2x + 5}$
16. $1000^x = 10{,}000^{6x + 4}$
17. $5^{x^2} = 5^{15 - 2x}$
18. $\left(\frac{1}{2}\right)^{x - 2} = 4^{5x}$

Graph each function. State the *y*-intercept.

19. $y = \left(\frac{1}{2}\right)^x$
20. $y = 4 \cdot 2^x$
21. $y = \left(\frac{1}{3}\right)^x - 3$

Solve.

22. **Automobile** Adina Ley needs to replace her car. If she leases a car, she will pay \$410 a month for 2 years and then has the option to buy the car for \$14, 458. The price of the car now is \$17,369. If the car depreciates at 16% per year, how will the depreciated price compare with the buyout price of the lease?

23. **Geometry** The area of a certain square is one-half the area of the rectangle formed if the length of one side of the square is increased by 2 cm and the length of an adjacent side is increased by 3 cm. What are the dimensions of the square?

24. **Number Theory** Find two integers whose sum is 21 and whose product is 90.

25. **Investment** After 6 years, a certain investment is worth \$8479. If the money was invested at 9% interest compounded semiannually, find the original amount that was invested.

CHAPTER 12 TEST

Simplify each rational expression. State the excluded values of the variables.

1. $\dfrac{5-2m}{6m-15}$

2. $\dfrac{3+x}{2x^2+5x-3}$

3. $\dfrac{4c^2+12c+9}{2c^2-11c-21}$

Simplify each expression.

4. $\dfrac{1-\frac{9}{t}}{1-\frac{81}{t^2}}$

5. $\dfrac{\frac{5}{6}+\frac{u}{t}}{\frac{2u}{t}-3}$

6. $\dfrac{x+4+\frac{5}{x-2}}{x+6+\frac{15}{x-2}}$

Perform the indicated operations.

7. $\dfrac{2x}{x-7}-\dfrac{14}{x-7}$

8. $\dfrac{n+3}{2n-8}\cdot\dfrac{6n-24}{2n+1}$

9. $(10m^2+9m-36)\div(2m-3)$

10. $\dfrac{x^2+4x-32}{x+5}\cdot\dfrac{x-3}{x^2-7x+12}$

11. $\dfrac{z^2+2z-15}{z^2+9z+20}\div(z-3)$

12. $\dfrac{4x^2+11x+6}{x^2-x-6}\div\dfrac{x^2+8x+16}{x^2+x-12}$

13. $(10z^4+5z^3-z^2)\div 5z^3$

14. $\dfrac{y}{7y+14}+\dfrac{6}{3y+6}$

15. $\dfrac{x+5}{x+2}+6$

16. $\dfrac{x^2-1}{x+1}-\dfrac{x^2+1}{x-1}$

17. $\dfrac{-3}{a-5}+\dfrac{15}{a^2-5a}$

18. $\dfrac{8}{m^2}\cdot\left(\dfrac{m^2}{2c}\right)^2$

Solve each equation.

19. $\dfrac{2}{3t}+\dfrac{1}{2}=\dfrac{3}{4t}$

20. $\dfrac{2e}{e-4}-2=\dfrac{4}{e+5}$

21. $\dfrac{4}{h-4}=\dfrac{3h}{h+3}$

Solve each formula for the variable indicated.

22. $F=G\left(\dfrac{Mm}{d^2}\right)$, for G

23. $\dfrac{1}{R_T}=\dfrac{1}{R_1}+\dfrac{1}{R_2}$, for R_2

Solve.

24. **Keyboarding** Willie can type a 200 word essay in 6 hours. Myra can type the same essay in $4\frac{1}{2}$ hours. If they work together, how long will it take them to type the essay?

25. **Electronics** Three appliances are connected in parallel: a lamp of resistance 120 ohms, a toaster of resistance 20 ohms, and an iron of resistance 12 ohms. Find the total resistance.

CHAPTER 13 TEST

Simplify. Leave in radical form and use absolute value symbols when necessary.

1. $\sqrt{480}$

2. $\sqrt{72} \cdot \sqrt{48}$

3. $\sqrt{54x^4y}$

4. $\sqrt{\frac{32}{25}}$

5. $\sqrt{\frac{3x^2}{4n^3}}$

6. $\sqrt{6} + \sqrt{\frac{2}{3}}$

7. $\left(x + \sqrt{3}\right)^2$

8. $\frac{7}{7 + \sqrt{5}}$

9. $3\sqrt{50} - 2\sqrt{8}$

10. $\sqrt{\frac{10}{3}} \cdot \sqrt{\frac{4}{30}}$

11. $2\sqrt{27} + \sqrt{63} - 4\sqrt{3}$

12. $\left(1 - \sqrt{3}\right)\left(3 + \sqrt{2}\right)$

Find the distance between each pair of points whose coordinates are given. Express answers in simplest radical form.

13. $(4, 7), (4, -2)$

14. $(-9, 2), \left(\frac{2}{3}, \frac{1}{2}\right)$

15. $(-1, 1), (1, -5)$

Find the length of each missing side. Round to the nearest hundredth.

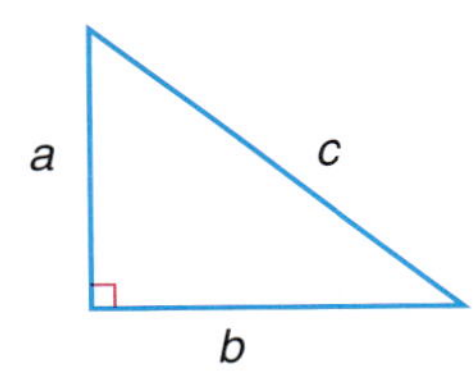

16. $a = 8, b = 10, c = ?$

17. $a = 12, c = 20, b = ?$

18. $a = 6\sqrt{2}, c = 12, b = ?$

19. $b = 13, c = 17, a = ?$

Solve each equation. Check your solution.

20. $\sqrt{4x + 1} = 5$

21. $\sqrt{4x - 3} = 6 - x$

22. $y^2 - 5 = -8y$

23. $2x^2 - 10x - 3 = 0$

Solve.

24. Geometry Find the measures of the perimeter and area, in simplest form, for the rectangle shown at the right.

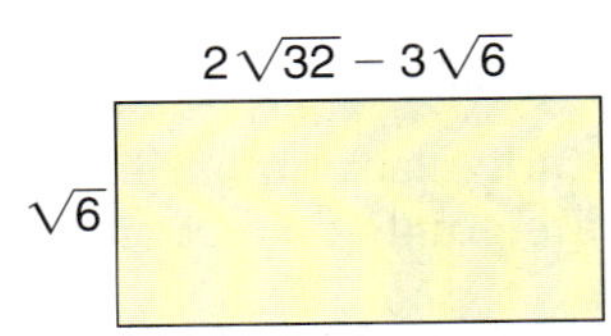

25. Sports A hiker leaves her camp in the morning. How far is she from camp after walking 9 miles due west and then 12 miles due north?

GLOSSARY

A

absolute value (85) The absolute value of a number is its distance from zero on a number line.

acute triangle (165) In an acute triangle, all of the angles measure less than 90 degrees.

adding integers (86)

1. To add integers with the *same* sign, add their absolute values. Give the result the same sign as the integers.
2. To add integers with *different* signs, subtract the lesser absolute value from the greater absolute value. Give the result the same sign as the integer with the greater absolute value.

addition property for inequality (385) For all numbers a, b, and c, the following are true:
1. if $a > b$, then $a + c > b + c$.
2. if $a < b$, then $a + c < b + c$.

addition property of equality (144) For any numbers a, b, and c, if $a = b$, then $a + c = b + c$.

additive identity (37) For any number a, $a + 0 = 0 + a = a$.

additive inverse property (87) For any number a, $a + (-a) = 0$.

algebraic expression (6) An expression consisting of one or more numbers and variables along with one or more arithmetic operations.

angle of depression (208) An angle of depression is formed by a horizontal line and a line of sight below it.

angle of elevation (208) An angle of elevation is formed by a horizontal line and a line of sight above it.

associative property (51) For any numbers a, b, and c, $(a + b) + c = a + (b + c)$ and $(ab)\,c = a(bc)$.

axes (254) Two perpendicular number lines that are used to locate points on a coordinate plane.

axis of symmetry (612) The equation of the axis of symmetry for the graph of $y = ax^2 + bx + c$, where $a \neq 0$, is $x = -\frac{b}{2a}$.

B

back-to-back stem-and-leaf plot (27) A back-to-back stem-and-leaf plot is used to compare two sets of data. The same stem is used for the leaves of both plots.

base **1.** (7) In an expression of the form x^n, the base is x. **2.** (215) The number that is divided into the percentage in the percent proportion.

best-fit line (341) A line drawn on a scatter plot that passes close to most of the data points.

binomial (514) The sum of two monomials.

boundary (437) A boundary of an inequality is a line that separates the coordinate plane into half-planes.

box-and-whisker plot (427) A type of diagram or graph that shows the quartiles and extreme values of data.

C

coefficient (47) The numerical factor in a term.

commutative property (51) For any numbers a and b, $a + b = b + a$ and $ab = ba$.

comparison property (94) For any two numbers a and b, exactly one of the following sentences is true.

$a < b \qquad a = b \qquad a > b$

complementary angles (163) Two angles are complementary if the sum of their measures is 90 degrees.

complete graph (278) A complete graph shows the origin, the points at which the graph crosses the x- and y-axes, and other important characteristics of the graph.

completeness property (121) Each real number corresponds to exactly one point on the number line. Each point on the number line corresponds to exactly one real number.

completeness property for points in the plane (256)

1. Exactly one point in the plane is named by a given ordered pair of numbers.

2. Exactly one ordered pair of numbers names a given point in the plane.

completing the square (742, 743) To add a constant term to a binomial of the form $x^2 + bx$ so that the resulting trinomial is a perfect square.

complex fraction (114) If a fraction has one or more fractions in the numerator or denominator, it is called a complex fraction.

composite numbers (558) A whole number, greater than 1, that is not prime.

compound event (414) A compound event consists of two or more simple events.

compound inequality (405) Two inequalities connected by *and* or *or*.

congruent angles (164) Angles that have the same measure.

conjugates (722) Two binomials of the form $a\sqrt{b} + c\sqrt{d}$ and $a\sqrt{b} - c\sqrt{d}$.

consecutive integers (158) Consecutive integers are integers in counting order.

consistent (455) A system of equations is said to be consistent when it has at least one ordered pair that satisfies both equations.

constant of variation (239) The number k in equations of the form $y = kx$ and $xy = k$.

constants (496) Monomials that are real numbers.

coordinate (73) The number that corresponds to a point on a number line.

coordinate plane (254) The plane containing the x- and y-axes.

corresponding angles (201) Matching angles in similar triangles, which have equal measures.

corresponding sides (201) The sides opposite the corresponding angles in similar triangles.

cosine (206) In a right triangle with acute angle A, the cosine of angle $A = \frac{\text{measure of leg adjacent to angle } A}{\text{measure of hypotenuse}}$.

cross products (94) When two fractions are compared, the cross products are the products of the terms on the diagonals.

D

data (25) Numerical information.

defining the variable (127) Choosing a variable to represent one of the unspecified numbers in a problem.

degree 1. (515) The degree of a monomial is the sum of the exponents of its variables. 2. (516) The degree of a polynomial is the degree of the term of the greatest degree.

density property (96) Between every pair of distinct rational numbers, there are infinitely many rational numbers.

dependent (456) A system of equations that has an infinite number of solutions.

dependent variable (58) The variable in a function whose value is determined by the independent variable.

difference of squares (545) Two perfect squares separated by a subtraction sign, $a^2 - b^2 = (a + b)(a - b)$.

dimensional analysis (174) The process of carrying units throughout a computation.

direct variation (239) A direct variation is described by an equation of the form $y = kx$, where $k \neq 0$.

discrete mathematics (88) A branch of mathematics that deals with finite or discontinuous quantities.

discriminant (632) In the quadratic formula, the expression $b^2 - 4ac$.

distance formula (737) The distance d between any two points with coordinates (x_1, y_1) and (x_2, y_2) is given by the following formula.

$$d = \sqrt{(x_2 - x_1)^2 + (y_2 - y_1)^2}$$

distributive property (46) For any numbers a, b, and c:

1. $a(b + c) = ab + ac$ and $(b + c)a = ba + ca$.
2. $a(b - c) = ab - ac$ and $(b - c)a = ba - ca$.

dividing rational numbers (112) The quotient of two rational numbers having the same sign is positive. The quotient of two rational numbers having different signs is negative.

division property for inequality (393) For all numbers a, b, and c, the following are true:

1. If c is positive and $a < b$, then $\frac{a}{c} < \frac{b}{c}$, and if c is positive and $a > b$, then $\frac{a}{c} > \frac{b}{c}$.
2. If c is negative and $a < b$, then $\frac{a}{c} > \frac{b}{c}$, and if c is negative and $a > b$, then $\frac{a}{c} < \frac{b}{c}$.

division property of equality (151) For any numbers a, b, and c, with $c \neq 0$, if $a = b$, then $\frac{a}{c} = \frac{b}{c}$.

domain (263) The set of all first coordinates from the ordered pairs in a relation.

draw a diagram (406) A problem-solving strategy that is often used as an organizational tool.

E

element (33) A member of a set.

elimination (469) The elimination method of solving a system of equations is a method that uses addition or subtraction to eliminate one of the variables to solve for the other variable.

equally likely (229) Outcomes that have an equal chance of occurring.

equation (33) A mathematical sentence that contains an equals sign, =.

equation in two variables (271) An equation in two variables contains two unknown values.

equilateral triangle (164) A triangle in which all the sides have the same length and all the angles have the same measure.

equivalent equation (144) Equations that have the same solution.

equivalent expressions (47) Expressions that denote the same number.

evaluate (8) To find the value of an expression when the values of the variables are known.

excluded value (660) A value is excluded from the domain of a variable because if that value were substituted for the variable, the result would have a denominator of zero.

exponent (7) In an expression of the form x^n, the exponent is n.

exponential function (634, 635) A function that can be described by an equation of the form $y = a^x$, where $a > 0$ and $a \neq 1$.

extraneous solutions (697) Solutions derived from an equation that are not solutions of the original equation.

extreme values (427) The least value and the greatest value in a set of data.

extremes (196) *See* proportion.

F

factored form (559) A monomial is written in factored form when it is expressed as the product of prime numbers and variables where no variable has an exponent greater than 1.

factoring (564) To express a polynomial as the product of monomials and polynomials.

factoring by grouping (567) A method of factoring polynomials with four or more terms.

factors (6) In a multiplication expression, the quantities being multiplied are called factors.

family of graphs (354) A family of graphs includes graphs and equations of graphs that have at least one characteristic in common.

FOIL method (537) To multiply two binomials, find the sum of the products of

F the first terms,
O the outside terms,
I the inside terms, and
L the last terms.

formula (128) An equation that states a rule for the relationship between certain quantities.

function **1.** (56) A relationship between input and output in which the output depends on the input. **2.** (287) A relation in which each element of the domain is paired with exactly one element of the range.

functional notation (289) In functional notation, the equation $y = x + 5$ is written as $f(x) = x + 5$.

G

general equation for exponential decay (644) The general equation for exponential decay is represented by the formula $A = C(1 - r)^t$.

general equation for exponential growth (643) The general equation for exponential growth is represented by the formula $A = C(1 + r)^t$.

graph (73, 255) To draw, or plot, the points named by certain numbers or ordered pairs on a number line or coordinate plane, respectively.

greatest common factor (GCF) (559) The greatest common factor of two or more integers is the greatest number that is a factor of all the integers.

guess and check (574) A problem-solving strategy in which several values or combinations of values are tried in order to find a solution to a problem.

H

half-life (638) The half-life of an element is defined as the time it takes for one-half a quantity of a radioactive element to decay.

half-plane (437) The region of a graph on one side of a boundary is called a half-plane.

horizontal axis (56) The horizontal line in a graph that represents the independent variable.

hypotenuse (206) The side of a right triangle opposite the right angle.

I

identify subgoals (745) A problem-solving strategy that uses a series of small steps, or subgoals.

identity (170) An equation that is true for every value of the variable.

inconsistent (456) A system of equations is said to be inconsistent when it has no ordered pair that satisfies both equations.

independent (456) A system of equations is said to be independent if the system has exactly one solution.

independent variable (58) The variable in a function whose value is subject to choice is the independent variable. The independent variable affects the value of the dependent variable.

inequality (33) A mathematical sentence having the symbols $<$, $\leq$, $>$, or $\geq$.

integers (73) The set of numbers represented as $\{..., -3, -2, -1, 0, 1, 2, 3, ...\}$.

interquartile range (304, 306) The difference between the upper quartile and the lower quartile of a set of data. It represents the middle half, or 50%, of the data in the set.

intersection (406) The intersection of two sets A and B is the set of elements common to both A and B.

inverse of a relation (264) The inverse of any relation is obtained by switching the coordinates in each ordered pair.

inverse variation (241) An inverse variation is described by an equation of the form $xy = k$, where $k \neq 0$.

irrational numbers (120) A number that cannot be expressed in the form $\frac{a}{b}$, where a and b are integers and $b \neq 0$.

isosceles triangle (164) In an isosceles triangle, at least two angles have the same measure and at least two sides have the same length.

L

least common denominator (LCD) (686) The least common denominator is the least common multiple of the denominators of two or more fractions.

least common multiple (LCM) (685) The least common multiple of two or more integers is the least positive integer that is divisible by each of the integers.

legs (206) The sides of a right triangle that are not the hypotenuse.

like terms (47) Terms that contain the same variables, with corresponding variables with the same power.

linear equation (280) An equation whose graph is a line.

linear function (278) An equation whose graph is a nonvertical line.

line plot (78) Numerical data displayed on a number line.

look for a pattern (13, 497, 637) A problem-solving strategy often involving the use of tables to organize information so that a pattern may be determined.

lower quartile (306) The lower quartile divides the lower half of a set of data into two equal parts.

M

make an organized list (685) A problem-solving strategy that uses an organized list to arrange and evaluate data in order to determine a solution.

mapping (263) A mapping pairs one element in the domain with one element in the range.

matrix (88) A matrix is a rectangular arrangement of elements in rows and columns.

maximum (611) The highest point on the graph of a curve, such as the vertex of parabola that opens downward.

mean (178) The mean of a set of data is the sum of the numbers in the set divided by the number of numbers in the set.

means (196) *See* proportion.

measures of central tendency (178) Numbers known as measures of central tendency are often used to describe sets of data because they represent a centralized, or middle, value.

measures of variation (306) Measures of variation are used to describe the distribution of data.

median (178) The median is the middle number of a set of data when the numbers are arranged in numerical order.

midpoint (369) A point that is halfway between the endpoints of a segment.

minimum (611) The lowest point on the graph of a curve, such as the vertex of parabola that opens upward.

mixed expression (690) An algebraic expression that contains a monomial and a rational expression.

mode (178) The mode of a set of data is the number that occurs most often in the set.

monomial (496) A monomial is a number, a variable, or a product of a number and one or more variables.

multi-step equations (157) Multi-step equations are equations that need more than one operation to solve them.

multiplicative identity property (38) For any number a, $a \cdot 1 = 1 \cdot a = a$.

multiplicative inverse property (38) For every nonzero number $\frac{a}{b}$, where $a \cdot b \neq 0$, there is exactly one number $\frac{b}{a}$ such that $\frac{a}{b} \cdot \frac{b}{c} = 1$.

multiplication property for inequality (393) For all numbers a, b, and c, the following are true.

1. If c is positive and $a < b$, then $ac < bc$, $c \neq 0$, and if c is positive and $a > b$, then $ac > bc$, $c \neq 0$.
2. If c is negative and $a < b$, then $ac > bc$, $c \neq 0$, and if c is negative and $a > b$, then $ac < bc$, $c \neq 0$.

multiplicative property of −1 (107) The product of any number and −1 is its additive inverse.

$$-1(a) = -a \text{ and } a(-1) = -a$$

multiplicative property of equality (150) For any numbers a, b, and c, if $a = b$, then $a \cdot c = b \cdot c$.

multiplicative property of zero (38) For any number a, $a \cdot 0 = 0 \cdot a = 0$.

N

negative correlation (340) There is a negative correlation between x and y if the values are related in opposite ways.

negative exponent (503) For any nonzero number a and any integer n, $a^{-n} = \frac{1}{a^n}$.

negative number (73) Any number that is less than zero.

number line (72) A line with equal distances marked off to represent numbers.

number theory (158) The study of numbers and the relationships between them.

O

obtuse triangle (165) An obtuse triangle has one angle with measure greater than 90 degrees.

odds (229) The odds of an event occurring is the ratio of the number of ways the event can occur (successes) to the number of ways the event cannot occur (failures).

open sentences (32) Mathematical statements with one or more variables, or unknown numbers.

opposites (87) The opposite of a number is its additive inverse.

order of operations (19)

1. Simplify the expressions inside grouping symbols, such as parentheses, brackets, and braces, and as indicated by fraction bars.
2. Evaluate all powers.
3. Do all multiplications and divisions from left to right.
4. Do all additions and subtractions from left to right.

ordered pair (57) Pairs of numbers used to locate points in the coordinate plane.

organize data (464) Organizing data is useful before solving a problem. Some ways to organize data are to use tables, charts, different types of graphs, or diagrams.

origin (254) The point of intersection of the two axes in the coordinate plane.

outcomes (413) Outcomes are all possible combinations of a counting problem.

outlier (307) In a set of data, a value that is much greater or much less than the rest of the data can be called an outlier.

P

parabola (610, 611) The general shape of the graph of a quadratic function.

parallel lines (362) Lines in the plane that never intersect. Nonvertical parallel lines have the same slope.

parallelogram (362) A quadrilateral in which opposite sides are parallel.

parent graph (354) The simplest of the graphs in a family of graphs.

percent (215) A percent is a ratio that compares a number to 100.

percentage (215) The number that is divided by the base in a percent proportion.

percent of decrease (222) The ratio of an amount of decrease to the previous amount, expressed as a percent.

percent of increase (222) The ratio of an amount of increase to the previous amount, expressed as a percent.

percent proportion (215) $\frac{\text{Percentage}}{\text{Base}} = \frac{r}{100}$

perfect square (119) A rational number whose square root is a rational number.

perfect square trinomial (587) A trinomial which, when factored, has the form $(a + b)^2 = (a + b)(a + b)$ or $(a - b)^2 = (a - b)(a - b)$.

perpendicular lines (362) Lines that meet to form right angles.

point-slope form (333) For any point (x_1, y_1) on a nonvertical line having slope m, the point-slope form of a linear equation is as follows:

$$y - y_1 = m(x - x_1).$$

polynomial (513, 514) A polynomial is a monomial or a sum of monomials.

positive correlation (340) There is a positive correlation between x and y if the values are related in the same way.

power (7) An expression of the form x^n is known as a power.

power of a monomial (498) For any numbers a and b, and any integers m, n, and p, $(a^mb^n)^p = a^{mp}b^{np}$.

power of a power (498) For any number a, and all integers m and n, $(a^m)^n = a^{mn}$.

power of a product (498) For all numbers a and b, and any integer m, $(ab)^m = a^mb^m$.

prime factorization (558) A whole number expressed as a product of factors that are all prime numbers.

prime number (558) A prime number is a whole number, greater than 1, whose only factors are 1 and itself.

prime polynomial (577) A polynomial that cannot be written as a product of two polynomials with integral coefficients is called a prime polynomial.

principal square root (119) The nonnegative square root of an expression.

probability (228) The ratio that tells how likely it is that an event will take place.

$$P(\text{event}) = \frac{\text{number of favorable outcomes}}{\text{total number of possible outcomes}}$$

problem-solving plan (126)

1. Explore the problem.
2. Plan the solution.
3. Solve the problem.
4. Examine the solution.

product (6) The result of multiplication.

product of powers (497) For any number a, and all integers m and n, $a^m \cdot a^n = a^{m+n}$.

product property of square roots (719) For any number a and b, where $a \geq 0$ and $b \geq 0$, $\sqrt{ab} = \sqrt{a} \cdot \sqrt{b}$.

proportion (195) In a proportion, the product of the extremes is equal to the product of the means. If $\frac{a}{b} = \frac{c}{d}$, then $ad = bc$.

Pythagorean theorem (713) If a and b are the measures of the legs of a right triangle and c is the measure of the hypotenuse, then $c^2 = a^2 + b^2$.

Pythagorean triple (583) Three whole numbers a, b, and c such that $a^2 + b^2 = c^2$.

Q

quadrant (254) One of the four regions into which the x- and y-axes separate the coordinate plane.

quadratic equation (620) A quadratic equation is one in which the value of the related quadratic function is 0.

quadratic formula (628) The roots of a quadratic equation in the form $ax^2 + bx + c = 0$, where $a \neq 0$, are given by the formula $x = \frac{-b \pm \sqrt{b^2 - 4ac}}{2a}$.

quadratic function (610, 611) A quadratic function is a function that can be described by an equation of the form $y = ax^2 + bx + c$, where $a \neq 0$.

quartiles (304, 306) In a set of data, the quartiles are values that divide the data into four equal parts.

quotient of powers (501) For all integers m and n and any nonzero number a, $\frac{a^m}{a^n} = a^{m-n}$.

quotient property of square roots (721) For any numbers a and b, where $a > 0$ and $b > 0$, $\sqrt{\frac{a}{b}} = \frac{\sqrt{a}}{\sqrt{b}}$.

R

radical equations (732) Equations that contain radicals with variables in the radicand.

radical sign (119) The symbol $\sqrt{}$, indicating the principal or nonnegative root of an expression.

radicand (719) The radicand is the expression under the radical sign.

random (229) When an outcome is chosen without any preference, the outcome occurs at random.

range **1.** (263) The set of all second coordinates from the ordered pairs in the relation. **2.** (306) The difference between the greatest and the least values of a set of data.

rate **1.** (197) The ratio of two measurements having different units of measure. **2.** (215) In the percent proportion, the rate is the fraction with a denominator of 100.

ratio (195) A ratio is a comparison of two numbers by division.

rational equation (696) A rational equation is an equation that contains rational expressions.

rational expression (660) A rational expression is an algebraic fraction whose numerator and denominator are polynomials.

rational numbers (93) A rational number is a number that can be expressed in the form $\frac{a}{b}$, where a and b are integers and $b \neq 0$.

rationalizing the denominator (722) Rationalizing the denominator of a radical expression is a method used to remove or eliminate the radicals from the denominator of a fraction.

real numbers (121) The set of rational numbers and the set of irrational numbers together form the set of real numbers.

reciprocal (38) The multiplicative inverse of a number.

reflexive property of equality (39) For any number a, $a = a$.

regression line (342) The most accurate best-fit line for a set of data, and can be determined with a graphing calculator or computer.

relation (260, 263) A relation is a set of ordered pairs.

replacement set (33) A set of numbers from which replacements for a variable may be chosen.

right triangle (165) A right triangle has one angle with a measure of 90 degrees.

rise (325) The vertical change in a line.

roots (620) The solutions of a quadratic equation.

run (325) The horizontal change in a line.

S

scalar multiplication (108) In scalar multiplication, each element of a matrix is multiplied by a constant.

scale (197) A ratio called a scale is used when making a model to represent something that is too large or too small to be conveniently drawn at actual size.

scatter plot (339) In a scatter plot, the two sets of data are plotted as ordered pairs in the coordinate plane.

scientific notation (506) A number is expressed in scientific notation when it is in the form $a \times 10^n$, where $1 \leq a < 10$ and n is an integer.

set (33) A collection of objects or numbers.

set-builder notation (385) A notation used to describe the members of a set. For example, $\{y \mid y < 17\}$ represents the set of all numbers y such that y is less than 17.

sequence (13) A set of numbers in a specific order.

similar triangles (201) If two triangles are similar, the measures of their corresponding sides are proportional, and the measures of their corresponding angles are equal.

simple events (414) A single event in a probability problem.

simple interest (217) The amount paid or earned for the use of money. The formula $I = prt$ is used to solve simple interest problems.

simplest form (47) An expression is in simplest form when it is replaced by an equivalent expression having no like terms and no parentheses.

simplest radical form (723) A radical expression is in simplest radical form when the following three conditions have been met.

1. No radicands have perfect square factors other than one.
2. No radicands contain fractions.
3. No radicals appear in the denominator of a fraction.

sine (206) In a right triangle with acute angle A, sine of angle $A = \frac{\text{measure of leg opposite angle } A}{\text{measure of the hypotenuse}}$.

slope (324, 325) The ratio of the rise to the run as you move from one point to another along a line.

slope-intercept form (347) An equation of the form $y = mx + b$, where m is the slope and b is the y-intercept of a given line.

solution (32) A replacement for the variable in an open sentence that results in a true sentence.

solution of an equation in two variables (271) If a true statement results when the numbers in an ordered pair are substituted into an equation in two variables, then the ordered pair is a solution of the equation.

solution set (33) The set of all replacements for the variable in an open sentence that result in a true sentence.

solve an equation (145) To solve an equation means to isolate the variable having a coefficient of 1 on one side of the equation.

solving an open sentence (32) Finding a replacement for the variable that results in a true sentence.

solving a triangle (208) Finding the measures of all sides and angles of a right triangle.

square of a difference (544) If a and b are any numbers, $(a - b)^2 = (a - b)(a - b) = a^2 - 2ab + b^2$.

square of a sum (543) If a and b are any numbers, $(a + b)^2 = (a + b)(a + b) = a^2 + 2ab + b^2$.

square root (118, 119) One of two identical factors of a number.

standard form (333) The standard form of a linear equation is $Ax + By = C$, where A, B, and C are integers, $A \geq 0$, and A and B are not both zero.

statistics (25) A branch of mathematics concerned with methods of collecting, organizing, and interpreting data.

stem-and-leaf plot (26) In a stem-and-leaf plot, each piece of data is separated into two numbers that are used to form a stem and a leaf. The data are organized into two columns. The column on the left contains the stem and the column on the right contains the leaves.

substitution (462) The substitution method of solving a system of equations is a method that uses substitution of one equation into the other equation to solve for the other variable.

substitution property of equality (39) If $a = b$, then a may be replaced by b in any expression.

subtracting integers (87) To subtract a number, add its additive inverse. For any numbers a and b, $a - b = a + (-b)$.

subtraction property for inequality (385) For all numbers a, b, and c, the following are true:

1. if $a > b$, then $a - c > b - c$.
2. if $a < b$, then $a - c < b - c$.

subtraction property of equality (146) For any numbers a, b, and c, if $a = b$, then $a - c = b - c$.

supplementary angles (162) Two angles are supplementary if the sum of their measures is 180 degrees.

symmetric property of equality (39) For any numbers a and b, if $a = b$, then $b = a$.

symmetry (612) Symmetrical figures are those in which the figure can be folded and each half matches the other exactly.

system of equations (455) A set of equations with the same variables.

system of inequalities (482) A set of inequalities with the same variables.

GLOSSARY

T

tangent (206) In a right triangle, the tangent of angle $A = \frac{\text{measure of leg opposite angle } A}{\text{measure of leg adjacent to angle } A}$.

term **1.** (13) A number in a sequence. **2.** (47) A number, a variable, or a product or quotient of numbers and variables.

transitive property of equality (39) For any numbers a, b, and c, if $a = b$ and $b = c$, then $a = c$.

tree diagram (413) A tree diagram is a diagram used to show the total number of possible outcomes.

triangle (163) A triangle is a polygon with three sides and three angles.

trigonometric ratios (206) $m\angle C = 90$

$\sin A = \frac{a}{c}$ $\cos A = \frac{b}{c}$ $\tan A = \frac{a}{b}$

trinomials (514) A trinomial is the sum of three monomials.

U

uniform motion (235) When an object moves at a constant speed, or rate, it is said to be in uniform motion.

union (408) The union of two sets A and B is the set of elements contained in both A or B.

unique factorization theorem (558) The prime factorization of every number is unique except for the order in which the factors are written.

unit cost (95) The cost of one unit of something.

upper quartile (306) The upper quartile divides the upper half of a set of data into two equal parts.

use a model (339) A problem-solving strategy that uses models, or simulations, of mathematical situations that are difficult to solve directly.

use a table (255) A problem-solving strategy that uses tables to organize and solve problems.

V

variable (6) Variables are symbols that are used to represent unspecified numbers.

Venn diagrams (73) Venn diagrams are diagrams that use circles or ovals inside a rectangle to show relationships of sets.

vertex (610, 611) The maximum or minimum point of a parabola.

vertical axis (56) The vertical line in a graph that represents the dependent variable.

vertical line test (289) If any vertical line passes through no more than one point of the graph of a relation, then the relation is a function.

W

weighted average (233) The weighted average M of a set of data is the sum of the product of each number in the set and its weight divided by the sum of all the weights.

whiskers (428) The whiskers of a box-and-whisker plot are the segments that are drawn from the lower quartile to the least value and from the upper quartile to the greatest value.

whole numbers (72) The set of whole numbers is represented by $\{0, 1, 2, 3, \ldots\}$.

work backward (156) A problem-solving strategy that uses inverse operations to determine an original value.

X

***x*-axis** (254) The horizontal number line.

***x*-coordinate** (254) The first number in an ordered pair.

***x*-intercept** (346) The coordinate at which a graph intersects the x-axis.

Y

***y*-axis** (254) The vertical number line.

***y*-coordinate** (254) The second number in an ordered pair.

***y*-intercept** (346) The coordinate at which a graph intersects the y-axis.

Z

zero exponent (502) For any nonzero number a, $a^0 = 1$.

zero product property (594) For all numbers a and b, if $ab = 0$, then $a = 0$, $b = 0$, or both a and b equal 0.

zeros (620) The zeros of a function are the roots, or x-intercepts, of the function.

SPANISH GLOSSARY

A

absolute value/valor absoluto (85) El valor absoluto de un número equivale al número de unidades que dicho número dista de cero en la recta numérica.

acute triangle/triángulo agudo (165) En un triángulo agudo, todos los ángulos miden menos de 90°.

adding integers/suma de enteros (86)

1. Para sumar enteros del *mismo* signo, suma los valores absolutos de los números. Da al resultado el mismo signo de los números.
2. Para sumar enteros de *distinto* signo, resta el valor menor del valor mayor. Da al resultado el mismo signo que el número con el mayor valor absoluto.

addition property of equality/propiedad de adición de la igualdad (144) Para cualquiera de los números a, b y c, si $a = b$, entonces $a + c = b + c$.

addition property of inequality/propiedad de adición de la desigualdad (385) Para todos los números a, b y c:

1. si $a > b$, entonces $a + c > b + c$;
2. si $a < b$, entonces $a + c < b + c$.

additive identity/identidad aditiva (37) Para cualquier número a, $a + 0 = 0 + a = a$.

additive inverse property/propiedad del inverso de la adición (87) Para cualquier número a, $a + (-a) = 0$.

algebraic expression/expresión algebraica (6) Una expresión que consiste de uno o más números y variables, además de una o más operaciones aritméticas.

angle of depression/ángulo de depresión (208) El ángulo de depresión se forma por una línea horizontal y una línea visual por debajo de la misma.

angle of elevation/ángulo de elevación (208) Un ángulo de elevación se forma por una línea horizontal y una línea visual por encima de la misma.

associative property/propiedad asociativa (51) Para cualquiera de los números a, b, y c, $(a + b) + c = a + (b + c)$ y $(ab)c = a(bc)$.

axes/ejes (254) Dos rectas numéricas perpendiculares que se usan para ubicar puntos en un plano de coordenadas.

axis of symmetry/eje de simetría (612) La ecuación para el eje de simetría de la gráfica $y = ax^2 + bx + c$, en la cual $a \neq 0$ y $x = -\frac{b}{2a}$.

B

back-to-back stem-and-leaf plot/diagrama de tallo y hojas consecutivo (27) Un diagrama de tallo y hojas consecutivo se usa para comparar dos conjuntos de datos. El mismo tallo se usa para las hojas de ambos diagramas.

base/base **1.** (7) En una expresión de la forma x^n, la base es x. **2.** (215) El número que se divide entre el porcentaje en una proporción de porcentaje.

best-fit line/línea de mejor encaje (341) Es una línea que se dibuja en un diagrama de dispersión y que pasa cerca de la mayoría de los puntos de datos.

binomial/binomio (514) La suma de dos monomios.

boundary/frontera (437) La frontera de una desigualdad es una línea que separa el plano de coordenadas en dos mitades de planos.

box-and-whisker plot/diagrama de caja y patillas (427) Un tipo de diagrama o gráfica que muestra los valores cuartílicos y los extremos de los datos.

C

coefficient/coeficiente (47) El factor numérico de un término.

commutative property/propiedad conmutativa (51) Para cualquiera de los números a y b, $a + b = b + a$ y $ab = ba$.

comparison property/propiedad de comparación (94) Para cualquier par de números a y b, exactamente una de las siguientes operaciones es válida.

$$a < b \qquad a = b \qquad a > b$$

complementary angles/ángulos complementarios (163) Dos ángulos son complementarios si la suma de sus medidas es 90 grados.

complete graph/gráfica completa (278) Una gráfica completa muestra el origen, los puntos en donde la gráfica cruza el eje de coordenadas x y el eje de coordenadas y, además de otras características importantes en la gráfica.

completeness property/propiedad del completo (121) Cada número real corresponde exactamente a un punto en la recta numérica. Cada punto en la recta numérica corresponde exactamente a un número real.

completeness property for points in the plane/propiedad del completo de los puntos en el plano (256)

1. Exactamente un punto en el plano es nombrado por un par ordenado de números dado.

2. Exactamente un par ordenado de números nombra un punto dado en el plano.

completing the square/completar el cuadrado (742, 743) Sumar un término constante a un binomio de la forma $x^2 = bx$, de modo que el trinomio resultante sea un cuadrado perfecto.

complex fraction/fracción compleja (114) Si una fracción tiene uno o más fracciones en el numerador o denominador, entonces se llama una fracción compleja.

composite number/número compuesto (558) Un número entero, mayor de 1, que no es un número primo.

compound event/evento compuesto (414) Un evento compuesto consiste de dos o más eventos simples.

compound inequality/desigualdad compuesta (405) Dos desigualdades conectadas por *y* u *o*.

congruent angles/ángulos congruentes (164) Ángulos que tienen la misma medida.

conjugates/conjugados (722) Dos binomios de la forma $a\sqrt{b} + c\sqrt{d}$ y $a\sqrt{b} - c\sqrt{d}$.

consecutive integers/números enteros consecutivos (158) Son los números enteros en el orden de contar.

consistent/consistente (455) Se dice que un sistema de ecuaciones es consistente cuando tiene por lo menos un par ordenado que satisface ambas ecuaciones.

constant of variation/constante de variación (239) El número k en ecuaciones de la forma $y = kx$ y $xy = k$.

constants/constantes (469) Los monomios que son números reales.

coordinate/coordenada (73) El número que corresponde a un punto en una recta numérica.

coordinate plane/plano de coordenadas (254) El plano que contiene el eje de coordenadas x y el eje de coordenadas y.

corresponding angles/ángulos correspondientes (201) Ángulos que encajan en triángulos semejantes y que tienen medidas iguales.

corresponding sides/lados correspondientes (201) Los lados opuestos a los ángulos correspondientes en triángulo semejantes.

cosine/coseno (206) En un triángulo rectángulo con ángulo agudo A, el coseno del

$$\text{ángulo } A = \frac{\text{medida del cateto adyacente al ángulo } A}{\text{medida de la hipotenusa}}.$$

cross products/productos cruzados (94) Cuando se comparan dos fracciones, los productos cruzados son los productos de los términos en diagonales.

D

data/datos (25) La información numérica.

defining the variable/definir la variable (127) El escoger una variable para representar uno de los números no especificados en un problema.

degree/grado 1. (515) El grado de un monomio es la suma de los exponentes de sus variables. 2. (516) El grado de un polinomio es el grado del término con el grado más alto.

density property/propiedad de la densidad (96) Entre cada par de números racionales distintos, existe una infinidad de números racionales.

dependent/dependiente (456) Un sistema de ecuaciones que tiene un número infinito de soluciones.

dependent variable/variable dependiente (58) La variable en una función cuyo valor lo determina la variable independiente.

difference of squares/diferencia de cuadrados (545) Dos cuadrados perfectos separados por un signo de sustracción, $a^2 - b^2 = (a + b)(a - b)$.

dimensional analysis/análisis dimensional (174) El proceso de llevar unidades a lo largo de un cómputo.

direct variation/variación directa (239) Una función lineal descrita por una ecuación de la forma $y = kx$, en que $k \neq 0$.

discrete mathematics/matemáticas de números discretos (88) Una rama de las matemáticas que estudia los conjuntos de números finitos o interrumpidos.

discriminant/discriminante (632) En la fórmula cuadrática, la expresión $b^2 - 4ac$ se denomina la discriminante.

distance formula/fórmula de distancia (737) La distancia d entre cualquier par de puntos con coordenadas (x_1, y_1) y (x_2, y_2) es dada por la siguiente fórmula.

$$d = \sqrt{(x_2 - x_1)^2 + (y_2 - y_1)^2}.$$

distributive property/propiedad distributiva (46) Para cualquiera de los números a, b y c:

1. $a(b + c) = ab + ac$ y $(b + c)a = ba + ca$.
2. $a(b - c) = ab - ac$ y $(b - c)a = ba - ca$.

dividing rational numbers/división de números racionales (112) El cociente de dos números racionales que tienen el mismo signo es positivo. El cociente de dos números racionales que tienen diferente signo es negativo.

division property of equality/propiedad de división de la igualdad (151) Para cualquiera de los números a, b y c, en que $c \neq 0$, si $a = b$, entonces $\frac{a}{c} = \frac{b}{c}$.

division property of inequality/propiedad de división de la desigualdad (393) Para cualquiera de los números reales a, b y c:

1. si c es positivo y $a < b$, entonces $\frac{a}{c} < \frac{b}{c}$, y
   si c es positivo y $a > b$, entonces $\frac{a}{c} > \frac{b}{c}$.
2. si c es negativo y $a < b$, entonces $\frac{a}{c} > \frac{b}{c}$, y
   si c es negativo y $a > b$, entonces $\frac{a}{c} < \frac{b}{c}$.

domain/dominio (263) El conjunto de todas las primeras coordenadas de los pares ordenados de una relación.

draw a diagram/trazar un diagrama (406) Una estrategia para resolver problemas que a menudo se usa como una herramienta organizadora.

E

element/elemento (33) Un miembro de un conjunto.

elimination/eliminación (469) El método de eliminación para resolver un sistema de ecuaciones es un método que usa adición o sustracción para eliminar una de las variables y así despejar la otra variable.

equally likely/igualmente verosímil (229) Respuestas que tienen igual posibilidad de ocurrir.

equation/ecuación (33) Un enunciado matemático que contiene un signo de igualdad, =.

equation in two variables/ecuación en dos variables (271) Una ecuación en dos variables contiene dos valores desconocidos.

equilateral triangle/triángulo equilátero (164) Un triángulo en el cual todos los lados y todos los ángulos tienen la misma medida.

equivalent equation/ecuación equivalente (144) Ecuaciones que tienen la misma solución.

equivalente expressions/expresiones equivalentes (47) Expresiones que denotan el mismo número.

evaluate/evaluar (8) El método de hallar el valor de una expresión cuando se conocen los valores de las variables.

excluded value/valor excluido (660) Se excluye un valor del dominio de una variable porque si se sustituyera ese valor por la variable, el resultado tendría un cero en el denominador.

exponent/exponente (7) En una expresión de la forma x^n, el exponente es n.

exponential function/función exponencial (634, 635) Una función que se puede describir por una ecuación de la forma $y = a^x$, en que $a > 0$ y $a \neq 1$.

extraneous solutions/soluciones extrañas (697) Soluciones obtenidas de una ecuación y las cuales no son soluciones aceptables para la ecuación original.

extreme values/valores extremos (427) Los valores extremos son el menor valor y el mayor valor en un conjunto de datos.

extremes/extremos (196) *Ver* proporción.

F

factored form/forma factorial (559) Un monomio está escrito en forma factorial cuando está expresado como el producto de números primos y variables y las variables no tienen un exponente mayor de 1.

factoring/factorizar (564) Expresar un polinomio como el producto de monomios o polinomios.

factoring by grouping/factorizando por grupos (567) Un método de factorización de polinomios de cuatro o más términos.

factors/factores (6) En una expresión de multiplicación, los factores son las cantidades que se multiplican.

family of graphs/familia de gráficas (354) Una familia de gráficas incluye gráficas y ecuaciones de gráficas que tienen por lo menos una característica en común.

FOIL method/método FOIL (537) Para multiplicar dos binomios, halla la suma de los productos de los primeros términos, los términos de afuera, los términos de adentro y los últimos términos.

formula/fórmula (128) Una ecuación que enuncia una regla para la relación entre ciertas cantidades.

function/función **1.** (56) Una relación entre los datos de entrada y de salida, en que los datos de salida dependen de los datos de entrada. **2.** (287) Una relación en que cada elemento del dominio se aparea exactamente con un elemento de la amplitud.

functional notation/notación funcional (289) En notación funcional, la ecuación $y = x + 5$ se escribe $f(x) = x + 5$.

G

general equation for exponential decay/ ecuación general para la disminución exponencial (644) La ecuación general para la disminución exponencial está representada por $A = C(1 - r)^t$.

general equation for exponential growth/ ecuación general para el crecimiento exponencial (643) La ecuación general para el crecimiento exponencial está representada por $A = C(1 + r)^t$.

graph/gráfica (73, 255) Consiste en dibujar, o trazar sobre una recta numérica o plano de coordenadas, los puntos nombrados por ciertos números o pares ordenados.

greatest common factor (GCF)/máximo común divisor (MCD) (559) El máximo común divisor de dos o más números enteros es el número mayor que es un factor de todos los números.

guess and check/conjetura y cotejo (574) Una estrategia para resolver problemas en la cual se prueban varios valores o combinaciones de valores para hallar una solución al problema.

H

half-life/media vida (638) La media vida de un elemento radioactivo es el tiempo que tarda en desintegrarse la mitad del elemento.

half-plane/medio plano (437) La región de un plano en un lado de una recta en el plano.

horizontal axis/eje horizontal (56) La recta horizontal en una gráfica que representa la variable independiente.

hypotenuse/hipotenusa (206) El lado de un triángulo rectángulo opuesto al ángulo recto.

I

identify subgoals/identificación de submetas (745) Una estrategia para resolver problemas que utiliza una serie de pasos secundarios o submetas.

identity/identidad (170) Una ecuación que es cierta para cualquier valor de la variable.

inconsistent/inconsistente (456) Se dice que un sistema de ecuaciones es inconsistente cuando no tiene pares ordenados que satisfacen ambas ecuaciones.

independent/independiente (456) Se dice que un sistema de ecuaciones es independiente si el sistema tiene exactamente una solución.

independent variable/variable independiente (58) La variable en una función cuyo valor está sujeto a elección se dice que es una variable independiente. La variable independiente determina el valor de la variable dependiente.

inequality/desigualdad (33) Un enunciado matemático que contiene los símbolos $<$, $\leq$, $>$, o $\geq$.

integers/enteros (73) El conjunto de enteros representados por $\{\ldots, -3, -2, -1, 0, 1, 2, 3, \ldots\}$.

interquartile range/amplitud intercuartílica (304, 306) La diferencia entre el cuartil superior y el inferior de un conjunto de datos. Representa la mitad inferior, ó 50%, de los datos en un conjunto.

intersection/intersección (406) Para dos conjuntos A y B, es el conjunto de elementos comunes a ambos A y B.

inverse of a relation/inverso de una relación (264) El inverso de cualquier relación se obtiene intercambiando las coordenadas en cada par ordenado.

inverse variation/variación inversa (241) Una variación inversa se describe por una ecuación de la forma $xy = k$, en que $k \neq 0$.

irrational number/números irracional (120) Un número que no se puede expresar en la forma $\frac{a}{b}$, en que a y b son números enteros y $b \neq 0$.

isosceles triangle/triángulo isósceles (164) En un triángulo isósceles, por lo menos dos ángulos tienen la misma medida y por lo menos dos lados tienen la misma longitud.

L

least common denominator (LCD)/mínimo común denominador (MCD) (686) El mínimo común múltiplo de los denominadores de dos o más fracciones.

least common multiple (LCM)/mínimo común múltiplo (MCM) (685) Para dos o más enteros, el MCM es el menor número entero positivo divisible entre cada uno de los enteros.

legs/catetos (206) Los lados de un triángulo rectángulo que forman el ángulo recto.

like terms/términos semejantes (47) Términos que contienen las mismas variables, con variables correspondientes que tienen la misma potencia.

line plot/esquema lineal (78) Datos numéricos desplegados sobre una recta numérica.

linear equation/ecuación lineal (280) Una ecuación que puede escribirse de la forma $Ax + By = C$, en que A y B no son ambos iguales a cero. La gráfica de una ecuación lineal es una recta.

linear function/función lineal (278) Ecuación cuya gráfica es una recta no vertical.

look for a pattern/busca un patrón (13, 497, 637) Una estrategia para resolver problemas que a menudo involucra el uso de tablas para organizar la información de manera que se pueda determinar un patrón.

lower quartile/cuartil inferior (306) El cuartil inferior divide la mitad inferior de un conjunto de datos en dos partes iguales.

M

make an organized list/haz una lista organizada (685) Una estrategia para resolver problemas que utiliza una lista organizada para arreglar y evaluar los datos y determinar una solución.

mapping/relación (263) Una relación aparea un elemento en el dominio con un elemento en la amplitud.

matrix/matriz (88) Una matriz es un arreglo rectangular de elementos en hileras y columnas.

maximum/máximo (611) El punto más alto en la gráfica de una curva, tal como el vértice de la parábola que se abre hacia abajo.

mean/media (178) La media de un conjunto de datos es la suma de los números en el conjunto dividida entre el número de números en el conjunto.

means/media proporcional (196) *Ver* proporción.

measures of central tendency/medidas de tendencia central (178) Los números que se usan a menudo para describir conjuntos de datos porque estos representan un valor centralizado o en el medio.

measures of variation/medidas de variación (306) Números usados para describir la amplitud o distribución de los datos.

median/mediana (178) La mediana es el número en el centro de un conjunto de datos cuando los números se organizan en orden numérico.

midpoint/punto medio (369) El punto medio de un segmento es el punto equidistante entre los extremos del segmento.

minimum/mínimo (611) El punto más bajo en la gráfica de una curva, tal como el vértice de una parábola que se abre hacia arriba.

mixed expression/expresión mixta (690) Una expresión algebraica que contiene un monomio y una expresión racional.

mode/modal (178) El número que ocurre con más frecuencia en un conjunto.

monomial/monomio (496) Un número, una variable o el producto de un número y una o más variables.

multi-step equations/ecuaciones múltiples (157) Ecuaciones que requieren más de una operación para resolverlas.

multiplicative identity/identidad de multiplicación (38) Para cualquier número a, $a \cdot 1 = 1 \cdot a = a$.

multiplicative inverse/inverso multiplicativo (38) Para cualquier número no cero a, hay exactamente un número $\frac{1}{a}$, tal que $a \cdot \frac{1}{a} = \frac{1}{a} \cdot a = 1$.

multiplicative property of −1/propiedad multiplicativa de −1 (107) El producto de cualquier número y −1 es el inverso aditivo del número.

$$-1(a) = -a \text{ y } a(-1) = -a.$$

multiplicative property of equality/propiedad multiplicativa de la igualdad (150) Para cualquiera de los números a, b y c, si $a = b$, entonces $a \cdot c = b \cdot c$.

multiplication property of inequality/propiedad de multiplicación de la desigualdad (393) Para todos los números a, b y c, lo siguiente es cierto:

1. Si c es positivo y $a < b$, entonces $ac < bc$, y si c es positivo y $a > b$, entonces $ac > bc$.
2. Si c es negativo y $a < b$, entonces $ac > bc$, y si c es negativo y $a > b$, entonces $ac < bc$.

multiplicative property of zero/propiedad multiplicativa de cero (38) Para cualquier número a, $a \cdot 0 = 0 \cdot a = 0$.

N

negative correlation/correlación negativa (340) Existe una correlación negativa entre x y y si los valores están relacionados de maneras opuestas.

negative exponent/exponente negativo (503) Para cualquiera de los números no cero a y cualquier número entero n, $a^{-n} = \frac{1}{a^n}$

negative number/número negativo (73) Cualquier número que es menos de cero.

number line/recta numérica (72) Una recta con marcas equidistantes que se usa para representar números.

number theory/teoría de números (158) El estudio de los números y de las relaciones entre los mismos.

O

obtuse triangle/triángulo obtuso (165) Un triángulo obtuso tiene un ángulo cuya medida es mayor de 90 grados.

odds/posibilidades (229) Las posibilidades de que un evento ocurra son la proporción del número de formas en que el evento puede ocurrir (éxitos) comparada con el número de formas en que puede no ocurrir (fracasos).

open sentences/enunciados abiertos (32) Enunciado matemático que contiene una o más variables, o incógnitas.

opposites/opuestos (87) El opuesto de un número es su inverso aditivo.

order of operations/orden de operaciones (19)

1. Simplifica las expresiones dentro de los símbolos de agrupación, tales como paréntesis, corchetes y como lo indiquen las barras de fracción.
2. Evalúa todas las potencias.
3. Realiza todas las multiplicaciones y las divisiones de izquierda a derecha.
4. Realiza todas las sumas y las restas de izquierda a derecha.

ordered pair/par ordenado (57) Pares de números que se usan para ubicar puntos en el plano de coordenadas.

organize data/organizar datos (464) Una estrategia útil antes de resolver un problema. Algunas formas de organizar los datos son el uso de tablas, esquemas, diferentes tipos de gráficas o diagramas.

origin/origen (254) El punto de intersección de los dos ejes en el plano de coordenadas.

outcomes/resultados (413) Todas las maneras en que puede ocurrir un evento.

outlier/valor atípico (307) Cualquier elemento en un conjunto de datos que es por lo menos 1.5 veces el valor de la amplitud intercuartílica mayor que el cuartil superior, o menor que el cuartil inferior.

P

parabola/parábola (610, 611) La forma general de la gráfica de una función cuadrática.

parallel lines/rectas paralelas (362) Rectas en el plano que nunca se intersecan. Las rectas paralelas no verticales tienen la misma pendiente.

parallelogram/paralelogramo (362) Un cuadrilátero cuyos lados opuestos son paralelos.

parent graph/gráfica principal (354) La gráfica más simple en una familia de gráficas.

percent/por ciento (215) Un por ciento es una proporción que compara un número con 100.

percentage/porcentaje (215) El número que se divide entre la base en un por ciento de proporción.

percent of decrease/porcentaje de disminución (222) La proporción de una cantidad de disminución comparada con una cantidad previa, expresada en forma de por ciento.

percent of increase/porcentaje de aumento (222) La proporción de una cantidad de aumento comparada con una cantidad previa, expresada en forma de por ciento.

percent proportion/proporción de porcentaje (215)

$$\frac{\text{Percentaje}}{\text{Base}} = \frac{r}{100}$$

perfect square/cuadrado perfecto (119) Un número racional cuya raíz cuadrada es un número racional.

perfect square trinomial/cuadrado perfecto trinómico (587) Un trinomio que al factorizarse tiene la forma $(a + b)^2 = (a + b)(a + b)$ o $(a - b)^2 = (a - b)(a - b)$.

perpendicular lines/rectas perpendiculares (362) Rectas que se encuentran para formar ángulos rectos.

point-slope form/forma punto–pendiente (333) Para cualquier punto (x_1, y_1) sobre una recta no vertical cuya pendiente es m, la forma punto–pendiente de una ecuación lineal es la siguiente:

$$y - y_1 = m(x - x_1).$$

polynomial/polinomio (513, 514) Un polinomio es un monomio o la suma de monomios.

positive correlation/correlación positiva (340) Existe una correlación positiva entre x y y si los valores están relacionados de la misma forma.

power/potencia (7) Una expresión de la forma x^n se conoce como una potencia.

power of a monomial/potencia de un monomio (498) Para cualquiera de los números a y b, y para todos los números enteros m, n y p, $(a^m b^n)^p = a^{mp} b^{np}$.

power of a power/potencia de una potencia (498) Para cualquier número a y todos los números enteros m y n, $(a^m)^n = a^{mn}$.

power of a product/potencia de un producto (498) Para todos los números a y b y cualquier número entero m, $(ab)^m = a^m b^m$.

prime factorization/factorización prima (558) Un número entero expresado como un producto de factores que son todos números primos.

prime number/número primo (558) Un número primo es un número entero mayor que 1 cuyos únicos factores son 1 y el número mismo.

prime polynomial/polinomio primo (577) Un polinomio que no se puede escribir como el producto de dos polinomios con coeficientes integrales se llama un polinomio primo.

principal square root/raíz cuadrada principal (119) La raíz cuadrada no negativa de una expresión.

probability/probabilidad (228) Una razón que expresa la posibilidad de que algún evento suceda.

$$P(\text{evento}) = \frac{\text{número de resultados favorables}}{\text{número de resultados posibles}}$$

problem-solving plan/plan para solucionar problemas (126)

1. Explorar el problema.
2. Planificar la solución.
3. Resolver el problema.
4. Examinar la solución.

product/producto (6) El resultado de la multiplicación.

product of powers/producto de potencias (497) Para cualquiera de los números a y todos los números enteros m y n, $a^m \cdot a^n = a^{m+n}$.

product property of square roots/propiedad del producto de raíces cuadradas (719) Para cualquiera de los números a y b, en que $a \geq 0$ y $b \geq 0$, $\sqrt{ab} = \sqrt{a} \cdot \sqrt{b}$.

proportion/proporción (195) En una proporción, el producto de los extremos es igual al producto de las medias. Si $\frac{a}{b} = \frac{c}{d}$, entonces $ad = bc$.

Pythagorean theorem/teorema de Pitágoras (713) Si a y b son las medidas de los catetos de un triángulo rectángulo y c es la medida de la hipotenusa, entonces, $c^2 = a^2 + b^2$.

Pythagorean triple/triplete de Pitágoras (583) Tres números enteros a, b, y c, tales que $a^2 + b^2 = c^2$.

Q

quadrant/cuadrante (254) Una de las cuatro regiones en que el eje x y el eje y separan el plano de coordenadas.

quadratic equation/ecuación cuadrática (620) Una ecuación cuadrática es una en que el valor de la función cuadrática relacionada es 0.

quadratic formula/fórmula cuadrática (628) Las raíces de una ecuación cuadrática en la forma $ax^2 + bx + c = 0$, en la cual $a \neq 0$, son dadas por la fórmula

$$x = \frac{-b \pm \sqrt{b^2 - 4ac}}{2a}.$$

quadratic function/función cuadrática (610, 611) Función que se puede describir con una equación de la forma $ax^2 + bx + c = 0$, en la cual $a \neq 0$.

quartiles/cuartiles (304, 306) En un conjunto de datos, los cuartiles son valores que dividen los datos en cuatro partes iguales.

quotient of powers/cociente de potencias (501) Para todos los números enteros m y n y todo número no cero a, $\frac{a^m}{a^n} = a^{m-n}$.

quotient property of square roots/propiedad del cociente de raíces cuadradas (721) Para cualquiera de los números a y b, en que $a > 0$ y $b > 0$, $\sqrt{\frac{a}{b}} = \frac{\sqrt{a}}{\sqrt{b}}$.

R

radical equations/ecuaciones radicales (732) Ecuaciones que contienen radicales con variables en el radicando.

radical sign/signo radical (119) El símbolo $\sqrt{}$ que se usa para indicar la raíz cuadrada principal no negativa de una expresión.

radicand/radicando (719) El radicando es la expresión debajo del signo radical.

random/al azar (229) Cuando se escoge un resultado sin ninguna preferencia, el resultado ocurre al azar.

range/amplitud **1.** (263) El conjunto de todas las segundas coordenadas de los pares ordenados de una relación. **2.** (306) La diferencia entre los valores mayor y menor en un conjunto de datos.

rate/razón (197) La proporción de dos medidas que se dan en diferentes unidades de medida.

rate/tasa (215) En una proporción de por ciento, la tasa es la fracción con 100 como denominador.

ratio/razón (195) Una razón es una comparación de dos números mediante división.

rational equation/ecuación racional (696) Una ecuación racional es una ecuación que contiene expresiones racionales.

rational expression/expresión racional (660) Una expresión racional es una fracción algebraica cuyo numerador y cuyo denominador son polinomios.

rational number/número racional (93) Un número racional es un número que se puede expresar en la forma $\frac{a}{b}$, en que a y b son números enteros y $b \neq 0$.

rationalizing the denominator/racionalizando el denominador (722) Un proceso que se usa para quitar o eliminar radicales del denominador de una fracción, en una expresión radical.

real numbers/números reales (121) El conjunto de números irracionales junto con los números racionales.

reciprocal/recíproco (38) El inverso multiplicativo de un número.

reflexive property of equality/propiedad reflexiva de la igualdad (39) Para cualquier número a, $a = a$.

regression line/línea de regresión (342) La línea más exacta de mejor ajuste para un conjunto de datos. Se puede determinar con una calculadora de gráficar o una computadora.

relation/relación (260, 263) Una relación es un conjunto de pares ordenados.

replacement set/conjunto de substitución (33) Un conjunto de números de los cuales se pueden escoger números para reemplazar una variable.

right triangle/triángulo rectángulo (165) Un triángulo que tiene un ángulo con una medida de 90 grados.

rise/altura (325) El cambio vertical en una recta.

roots/raíces (620) Las soluciones para una ecuación cuadrática.

run/carrera (325) El cambio horizontal en una recta.

S

scalar multiplication/multiplicación escalar (108) En multiplicación escalar, cada elemento de una matriz se multiplica por una constante.

scale/escala (197) Una razón llamada una escala se usa en la construcción de un modelo para representar algo que es muy grande o muy pequeño para ser dibujado a su tamaño real.

scatter plot/diagrama de dispersión (339) Gráfica que muestra dos conjuntos de datos trazados como puntos (pares ordenados) en el plano de coordenadas.

scientific notation/notación científica (506) Un número está expresado en notación científica cuando está en la forma de $a \times 10^n$, en que $1 \leq a < 10$ y n es un número entero.

set/conjunto (33) Una colección de objetos o números.

set-builder notation/notación de construcción de conjuntos (385) Una notación que se usa para describir los miembros de un conjunto. Por ejemplo, $\{y \mid y < 17\}$ representa el conjunto de todos los números y de modo que y es menor que 17.

sequence/sucesión (13) Un conjunto de números en un orden específico.

similar triangles/triángulos semejantes (201) Si dos triángulos son semejantes, las medidas de sus lados correspondientes son proporcionales y las medidas de sus ángulos correspondientes son iguales.

simple event/evento simple (414) Evento sencillo en un problema de probabilidad.

simple interest/interés simple (217) La cantidad pagada o ganada por el uso de una cantidad de dinero. La fórmula $I = prt$ se usa para resolver problemas de interés simple.

simplest form/forma reducida (47) Una expresión está en su forma reducida cuando ha sido reemplazada por una expresión similar que no tiene términos semejantes ni paréntesis.

simplest radical form/forma radical reducida (723) Una expresión radical se encuentra en forma reducida cuando se satisfacen las siguientes condiciones:

1. Ningún radicando tiene factores cuadrados perfectos además de uno.
2. Ningún radicando contiene fracciones.
3. No aparece ningún radical en el denominador de una fracción.

sine/seno (206) En un triángulo rectángulo con ángulo agudo A, el seno del ángulo $A = \frac{\text{medida del cateto opuesto al ángulo } A}{\text{medida de la hipotenusa}}$.

slope/pendiente (324, 325) El cambio vertical (altura) al cambio horizontal (carrera) a medida que te mueves de un punto a otro a lo largo de la recta.

slope-intercept form/forma pendiente-intersección (347) Una ecuación de la forma $y = mx + b$, en que m es la pendiente y b es la intersección en y de una recta dada.

solution/solución (32) Una sustitución por una variable en una ecuación que resulta en una ecuación válida.

solution of an equation in two variables/ solución de una ecuación de dos variables (271) Si al sustituir los números en un par ordenado se satisface una ecuación de dos variables, entonces el par ordenado es una solución de la ecuación.

solution set/conjunto de solución (33) El conjunto de todos los sustitutos para una variable en un enunciado abierto que satisfacen el enunciado.

solve an equation/resuelve una ecuación (145) Resolver una ecuación quiere decir aislar la variable cuyo coeficiente es 1, en un lado de la ecuación.

solving an open sentence/resolviendo un enunciado abierto (32) Hallar un sustituto que satisface la variable.

solving a triangle/resolviendo un triángulo (208) El proceso de hallar las medidas de todos los lados y ángulos de un triángulo rectángulo.

square of a difference/cuadrado de una diferencia (544) Si a y b son cualquier par de números, $(a - b)^2 = (a - b)(a - b) = a^2 - 2ab + b^2$.

square of a sum/cuadrado de una suma (543) Si a y b son cualquier par de números, $(a + b)^2 = (a + b)(a + b) = a^2 + 2ab + b^2$.

square root/raíz cuadrada (118, 119) Uno de los dos factores idénticos de un número.

standard form/forma estándar (333) La forma estándar de una ecuación lineal es $Ax + By = C$, en la cual A, B y C son números enteros, $A \geq 0$ y A y B no son ceros ambos.

statistics/estadística (25) Una rama de las matemáticas que tiene que ver con los métodos de recolección, organización e interpretación de datos.

stem-and-leaf plot/gráfica de tallo y hojas (26) En una gráfica de tallo y hojas, cada dato se separa en dos números que se usan para formar un tallo y las hojas. Los datos se organizan en dos columnas. La columna de la izquierda contiene el tallo y la columna de la derecha las hojas.

substitution/sustitución (462) El método de sustitución para resolver un sistema de ecuaciones es un método que sustituye una ecuación en la otra ecuación para despejar la otra variable.

substitution property of equality/propiedad de sustitución de la igualdad (39) Si $a = b$, entonces, a se puede reemplazar por b en cualquier expresión.

subtracting integers/sustracción de enteros (87) Para restar un entero, suma su inverso aditivo. Para cualquiera de los enteros a y b, $a - b = a + (-b)$.

subtraction property of equality/propiedad de sustracción de la igualdad (146) Para cualquiera de los números a, b y c, si $a = b$, entonces $a - c = b - c$.

subtraction property of inequality/propiedad de sustracción de la desigualdad (385) Para todos los números a, b y c los siguientes son ciertos:

1. si $a > b$, entonces $a - c > b - c$;
2. si $a < b$, entonces $a - c < b - c$.

supplementary angles/ángulos suplementarios (162) Dos ángulos son suplementarios si la suma de sus medidas es 180 grados.

symmetric property of equality/propiedad simétrica de la igualdad (39) Para cualquiera de los números a y b, si $a = b$, entonces $b = a$.

symmetry/simetría (612) Las figuras simétricas son aquellas en que la figura se puede doblar y cada mitad es exactamente igual a la otra.

system of equations/sistema de ecuaciones (455) Un conjunto de ecuaciones con las mismas variables.

system of inequalities/sistema de desigualdades (482) Un conjunto de desigualdades con las mismas variables.

T

tangent/tangente (206) En un triángulo rectángulo con ángulo agudo A, la tangente del ángulo $A = \frac{\text{medida del cateto opuesto al ángulo } A}{\text{medida del cateto adyacente al ángulo } A}$.

term/término 1. (13) Un número en una sucesión. 2. (47) Un número, una variable o un producto o cociente de números y variables.

transitive property of equality/propiedad transitiva de la igualdad (39) Para cualquiera de los números a, b y c, si $a = b$ y $b = c$, entonces $a = c$.

tree diagram/diagrama de árbol (413) Un diagrama de árbol es un diagrama que se usa para mostrar el número total de posibles resultados.

triangle/triángulo (163) Un triángulo es un polígono con tres lados y tres ángulos.

trigonometric ratios/razones trigonométricas (206) Para el triángulo rectángulo ABC con ángulo agudo A, el seno $A = \frac{a}{c}$, coseno $A = \frac{b}{c}$, tangente $A = \frac{a}{b}$.

trinomial/trinomio (514) La suma de tres monomios.

U

uniform motion/movimiento uniforme (235) Cuando un objeto se mueve a una velocidad, o a un ritmo constante, se dice que se mueve en movimiento uniforme.

union/unión (408) Para dos conjuntos A y B, el conjunto de los elementos contenidos en ambos A o B o A y B.

unique factorization theorem/teorema de la factorización única (558) La factorización prima de cada número es única excepto por el orden en que se escriben los factores.

unit cost/costo unitario (95) El costo de una unidad de un artículo.

upper quartile/cuartil superior (306) El cuartil superior divide la parte superior de un conjunto de datos en dos partes iguales.

use a model/usa un modelo (339) Una estrategia para resolver problemas que usa modelos, o simulaciones, de situaciones matemáticas difíciles de resolver directamente.

use a table/usa una tabla (255) Una estrategia para resolver problemas que usa tablas para organizar y resolver problemas.

V

variable/variable (6) Las variables son símbolos que se usan para representar números desconocidos.

Venn diagrams/diagramas de Venn (73) Los diagramas de Venn son diagramas que usan círculos u óvalos dentro de un rectángulo para mostrar relaciones de conjuntos.

vertex/vértice (610, 611) El punto máximo o mínimo de una parábola.

vertical axis/eje vertical (56) La recta vertical en una gráfica que representa la variable dependiente.

vertical line test/prueba de recta vertical (289) Si cualquier recta vertical pasa por un solo punto de la gráfica de una relación, entonces la relación es una función.

W

weighted average/promedio ponderado (233) El promedio ponderado M de un conjunto de datos es la suma del producto de cada número en el conjunto y su peso divididos entre la suma de todos los pesos.

whiskers/patillas (428) Las patillas de un diagrama de caja y patillas son los segmentos que se dibujan desde el cuartil inferior hasta el mínimo valor y desde el cuartil superior hasta el máximo valor.

whole numbers/números enteros (72) El conjunto de números enteros se representa por $\{0,1,2,3,...\}$.

work backward/trabaja al revés (156) Una estrategia para resolver problemas que usa operaciones inversas para determinar un valor inicial.

X

x*-axis/eje *x (254) La recta numérica horizontal en el plano de coordenadas.

x*-coordinate/coordenada *x (254) El primer número en un par ordenado.

x*-intercept/intersección con el eje *x (346) La coordenada x de un punto donde una gráfica interseca el eje x.

Y

y*-axis/eje *y (254) La recta numérica vertical en el plano de coordenadas.

y*-coordinate/coordenada *y (254) El segundo número en un par ordenado.

y*-intercept/intersección con el eje *y (346) La coordenada y de un punto donde una gráfica interseca el eje y.

Z

zero exponent/exponente cero (502) Para cualquier número no cero a, $a^0 = 1$.

zero product property/propiedad del producto cero (594) Para todos los números a y b, si $ab = 0$, entonces $a = 0$, $b = 0$, o ambos a y b son iguales a cero.

zeros/ceros (620) Las raíces, o intersecciones con el eje x de la gráfica de una función.

SELECTED ANSWERS

CHAPTER 1 EXPLORING EXPRESSIONS, EQUATIONS, AND FUNCTIONS

Pages 9–11 Lesson 1–1

7. $3y^2 - 6$ **9.** 3 times x squared increased by 4 **11.** a^7 **13.** 32 **15.** $k + 20$ **17.** a^7 **19.** $\frac{2x^2}{3}$ or $\frac{2}{3}x^2$ **21.** $b + 8$ **23.** 4 times m to the fifth power **25.** c squared plus 23 **27.** 2 times 4 times 5 squared **29.** 8^2 **31.** 4^7 **33.** z^5 **35.** 49 **37.** 64 **39.** 16 **41.** $3(55 - w^3)$ **43.** $a + b + \frac{a}{b}$ **45.** $y + 10x$ **47.** 16; 16 **47a.** They are equal; no; no. **47b.** no; for example, $2^3 \neq 3^2$ **49a.** $3.5x$ **49b.** $3.5y$ **49c.** $3.5x + 3.5y$

Pages 15–18 Lesson 1–2

5.

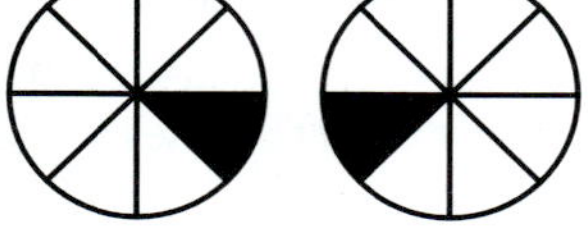

7. $5x + 1$, $6x + 1$

9a.

4^1	4^2	4^3	4^4	4^5
4	16	64	256	1024

9b. 6; $4^6 = 4096$ **9c.** 4; When the exponent is odd, 4 is in the ones place. **11.**

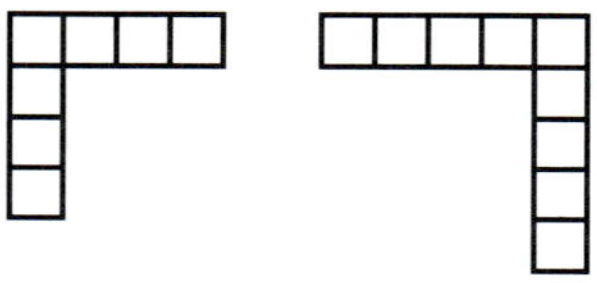

13. 48, 96 **15.** 25, 36 **17.** $a + 7$, $a + 9$

19a.

19b. White; even-numbered figures are white.
19c. 12 sides; The shapes come in pairs. Since $19 \div 2 = 9.5$, the 19th figure will be part of the 10th pair. The 10th pair will have 10 + 2, or 12 sides. **21a.** 4; 9; 16; 25 **21b.** The sums are perfect square numbers; that is 1^2, 2^2, 3^2, 4^2, 5^2, ... **21c.** 10,000 **21d.** x^2 **23a.** 1,999,998; 2,999,997; 3,999,996; 4,999,995 **23b.** 8,999,991 **25.** 4, 7, 10, 13, 16 **27.** 1:13 P.M. **29a.** 100 cards **31.** x cubed divided by 9 **33.** 4^3; 64 cubes **35.** $x + \frac{1}{11}x$

Pages 22–24 Lesson 1–3

5. 173 **7.** 4 **9.** 25 **11.** $a^2 - a$ **13.** 14 **15.** 14 **17.** 9 **19.** 60 **21.** $\frac{11}{18}$ **23.** 6 **25.** 126 **27.** 147 **29.** 126 **31.** $r^2 + 3s$; 19 **33.** $(r + s)t^2$; $\frac{7}{4}$ **35.** 19.5 mm **37.** 22 in. **39.** 16.62 **41.** 3.77 **43a.** Sample answer: $(4 - 2)5 \div (3 + 2)$ **43b.** $4 \times 2 \times 5 \times 3 \times 2$ **45a.** $\frac{1}{3}Bh$ **45b.** 198,450 m^3 **47.** 16, 19.5 **49.** June 18 **51.** $t + 3$ **53.** 9 more than two times y

Pages 28–31 Lesson 1–4

5. stem 12, leaf 2 **7.** stem 126, leaf 9 **9a.** 35 tickets sold one day **9b.** 31 tickets **9c.** 75 tickets **9d.** 1043 tickets **11.** stem 13, leaf 3 **13.** stem 44, leaf 3 **15.** stem 111, leaf 3 **17.** stem 14, leaf 3 **19.** stem 111, leaf 4 **21.** rounded to the nearest hundred: 9, 12, 24, 27, 38, 39, 40 **23a.** Possible answer: Both teens and young adults had similar distribution of responses. **23b.** Sample answer: The market research shows that the new game is equally appealing to teens and young adults. Therefore, we should concentrate our marketing efforts towards both teens and young adults.

25a.

1980	Stem	1993
4	1	3
6	2	4
8 5 1	3	3 7 7
	4	6
1	5	

3 | 7 = 3700

25b. 3000 to 3900; 3000 to 3900 **25c.** Sample answer: Farm sizes seem to be shrinking. **27.** 15 **29a.** $\frac{s}{5}$ **29b.** 2 miles; yes

31.

Pages 34–36 Lesson 1–5

7. false **9.** {1, 3, 5} **11.** 75 **13.** false **15.** true **17.** true **19.** {5} **21.** $\left\{\frac{1}{2}, \frac{3}{4}\right\}$ **23.** {10, 15, 20} **25.** 3 **27.** 2 **29.** $4\frac{5}{6}$ **31.** Sample answer: $p = 1$ and $q = 2$, $p = 2$ and $q = 10$, $p = 3$ and $q = 8$, $p = 4$ and $q = 20$, and $p = 5$ and $q = 15$ **33a.** $C = \frac{3500 \cdot 4}{14}$ **33b.** 1000 Calories **35.** 2, 5, 6, 7, 9 **37.** 8 **39.** 5 less than x to the fifth power

Page 36 Self Test

1. $3a + b^2$ **3.** 11:04, 11:08, 11:51, 11:55 **5.** 408

7.

Stem	Leaf
4	8
5	4
6	7
7	7
8	5 9

6 | 7 = 67

9. {6, 7, 8}

Pages 41–43 Lesson 1–6

7. $\frac{2}{9}$ **9.** c **11.** e **13.** d **15.** f

17.

$6(12 - 48 \div 4) + 9 \cdot 1$	
$= 6(12 - 12) + 9 \cdot 1$	*Substitution (=)*
$= 6(0) + 9 \cdot 1$	*Substitution (=)*
$= 0 + 9 \cdot 1$	*Multiplicative property of 0*
$= 0 + 9$	*Multiplicative identity*
$= 9$	*Additive identity*

19a. $4(20) + 7$

19b.

$4(20) + 7$	
$= 80 + 7$	*Substitution (=)*
$= 87$	*Substitution (=)*

19c. 87 years **21.** 9 **23.** $\frac{1}{p}$ **25.** $\frac{2}{3}$ **27.** substitution (=) **29.** multiplicative identity **31.** multiplicative inverse, multiplicative identity **33.** symmetric (=) **35.** reflexive (=) **37.** substitution (=); substitution (=); multiplicative identity; multiplicative inverse; substitution (=) **39.** substitution (=); substitution (=); substitution (=); multiplicative identity

41. $(15 - 8) \div 7 \cdot 25$
$= 7 \div 7 \cdot 25$ *Substitution(=)*
$= 1 \cdot 25$ *Substitution (=)*
$= 25$ *Multiplicative identity*

43. $(2^5 - 5^2) + (4^2 - 2^4)$
$= (32 - 25) + (16 - 16)$ *Substitution (=)*
$= 7 + 0$ *Substitution (=)*
$= 7$ *Additive identity*

45. $5^3 + 9\left(\frac{1}{3}\right)^2$
$= 125 + 9\left(\frac{1}{9}\right)$ *Substitution (=)*
$= 125 + 1$ *Multiplicative inverse*
$= 126$ *Substitution (=)*

47a. $[21(12 \cdot 2)] + [23(15 \cdot 2)] + [67(10 \cdot 2)]$

47b. $[21(12 \cdot 2)] + [23(15 \cdot 2)] + [67(10 \cdot 2)]$
$= [21(24)] + [23(30)] + 67(20)]$ *Substitution (=)*
$= 504 + 690 + 1340$ *Substitution (=)*
$= 2534$ *Substitution (=)*

47c. \$25.34 **49.** true **51.** false **55.** 36 **57.** $12y$

Page 44 Lesson 1-7A

1. $2x + 2$ **3.** $4x + 2$ **5.** false;

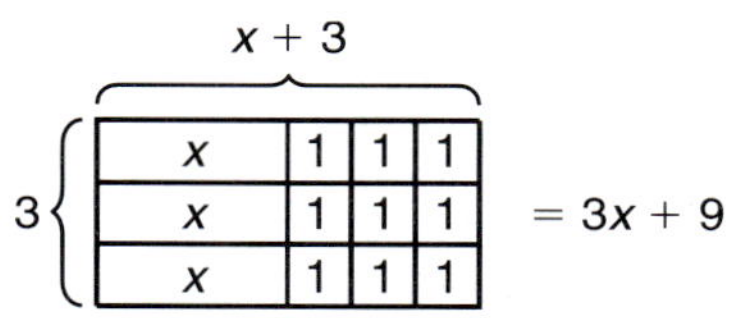

7a. Adita **7b.** Answers will vary. Answers should include the concept that multiplication by 3 is distributed over both terms in parentheses.

Pages 48–50 Lesson 1-7

5. b **7.** a **9.** c **11.** $2a - 2b$ **13.** 60 **15.** 7 **17.** $4y^4, y^4$ **19.** $3t^2 + 4t$ **21.** $23a^2b + 3ab^2$ **23.** 5.35(24) + 5.35(32); 5.35(24 + 32) **25.** $5g - 45$ **27.** $24m + 48$ **29.** $5a - ab$ **31.** 52 **33.** 60 **35.** 645 **37.** in simplest form **39.** $12a + 15b$ **41.** in simplest form **43.** $3x + 4y$ **45.** $1\frac{3}{5}a$ **47.** $9x + 5y$

49. no; sample counterexample: $2 + (4 \cdot 5) \neq (2 + 4)(2 + 5)$ **51a.** $2[x + (x + 14)] = 4x + 28$ **51b.** 96 **51c.** 527 ft^2 **53.** multiplicative property of 0 **55a.** $d = (1129)(2)$ **55b.** 2258 ft **57.** 2 **59.** 8 years

Pages 53–55 Lesson 1-8

7. commutative (+) **9.** associative (×) **11.** $5a + 2b$ **13.** $14x + 3y$

15. $6z^2 + (7 + z^2 + 6)$
$= 6z^2 + (z^2 + 7 + 6)$ *Commutative (+)*
$= (6z^2 + z^2) + (7 + 6)$ *Associative (+)*
$= (6 + 1)z^2 + (7 + 6)$ *Distributive property*
$= 7z^2 + 13$ *Substitution (=)*

17. multiplicative identity **19.** associative (×) **21.** distributive property **23.** commutative (×) **25.** associative (+) **27.** $10x + 5y$ **29.** $7x + 10y$ **31.** $10x + 2y$ **33.** $32a^2 + 16$ **35.** $5x$ **37.** $\frac{3}{4} + \frac{5}{3}m + \frac{4}{3}n$

39. $2(s + t) - s$
$= 2s + 2t - s$ *Distributive property*
$= 2t + 2s - s$ *Commutative (+)*
$= 2t + (2s - s)$ *Associative (+)*
$= 2t + (2s - 1s)$ *Multiplicative identity*
$= 2t + (2 - 1)s$ *Distributive property*
$= 2t + 1s$ *Substitution (=)*
$= 2t + s$ *Multiplicative identity*

41. $5xy + 3xy$
$= (5 + 3)xy$ *Distributive property*
$= 8xy$ *Substitution (=)*

43. $\frac{1}{100}$; Each denominator and the following numerator represent the number 1. The resulting expression is 1 in the numerator and 100 in the denominator multiplied by numerous 1s. Since 1 is the multiplicative identity, the product is $\frac{1}{100}$. **45.** no; Sample example: Let $a = 1$ and b = 2, then 1 * 2 = 1 + 2(2) or 5 and 2 * 1 = 2 + 2(1) or 4. **47a.** $G = 3.73$ **49.** $100d + 80d + 8d$, $188d$ **51.** $\frac{3}{2}$

53.

Stem	Leaf
10	0 0 0 1 1 1 1 3
9	5 7 7 9 9 9

10|3 = 103

55. 

Pages 59–62 Lesson 1-9

5a. Graph 3 **5b.** Graph 4 **5c.** Graph 2 **5d.** Graph 1 **7a.** False, A is the younger player, but B runs the mile in less time. **7b.** False, A made more 3-point shots, but B made more 2-point shots. **7c.** True, B is the older player and B made more 2-point shots. **7d.** True, A is the younger player and A made more free-throw shots. **9.** Graph a; An average person makes no money as a child, then his or her income rises for several years, and finally levels off. **11a.** Graph 5 **11b.** Graph 3 **11c.** Graph 1 **11d.** Graph 4 **11e.** Graph 6 **11f.** Graph 2

13.

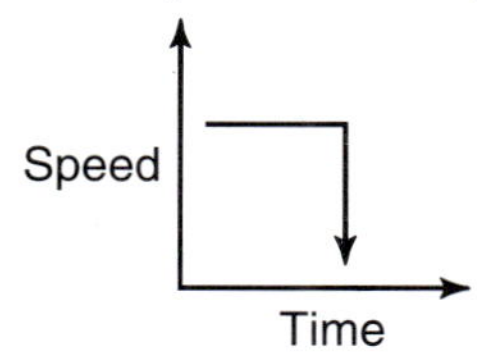

15.

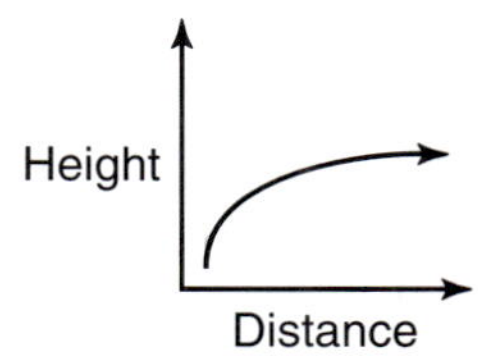

17a. horizontal axis: time in years; vertical axis: millions of dollars **17b.** In 1991 the telethon raised 45 million dollars. **17c.** Money raised in the telethon decreased, then increased steadily. **17d.** The money raised increased. **19.** $7p + 11q + 9$ **21.** 14 **23.** $\frac{1}{3}Bh$

Page 63 Chapter 1 Highlights

1. a **3.** e **5.** f **7.** g **9.** b

Pages 64–66 Chapter 1 Study Guide and Assessment

11. x^5 **13.** $5x^2$ **15.** three times a number m to the fifth power **17.** the difference of four times m squared and twice m **19.** 32, 64 **21.** $4x + y$, $5x + y$ **23.** 10^1, 10^2, 10^3, 10^4 **25.** 11 **27.** 9 **29.** 26 **31.** 2.4 **33.** 9.2 **35.** 90

37. No; some former presidents are still living. **39.** false **41.** true **43.** $13\frac{1}{2}$ **45.** $\frac{1}{3}$ **47.** 5 **49.** additive identity **51.** $2 \times 4 + 2 \times 7$ **53.** $1 - 3p$ **55.** 294 **57.** $8m + 8n$ **59.** commutative (+) **61.** commutative (×) **63.** $5x + 5y$ **65.** $3pq$ **67.** Graph c **69a.** $80s$ **69b.** 320 **69c.** 640 **71a.** $3 + 4 > 5, 4 + 5 > 3, 3 + 5 > 4$ **71b.** $x < 9$ ft and $x > 3$ ft

CHAPTER 2 EXPLORING RATIONAL NUMBERS

Pages 75–77 Lesson 2–1

7. $\{-1, 0, 1, 2, \ldots\}$

9.

11. $-4 + (-3) = -7$ **13.** -5 **15.** 9-yard gain **17.** $\{-4, -3, -2, -1\}$ **19.** $\{-7, -3\}$ **21.** $\{\ldots, -5, -4, -3, -2, -1, 0\}$

23.

25.

27.

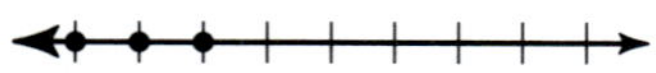

29.

31. 13 **33.** -5 **35.** -12 **37.** 6 **39.** -23 **41.** $-17 + 82 = 65$; 65°F **43a.** 4°F **43b.** -31°F **43c.** -15°F **43d.** 9°F

45.

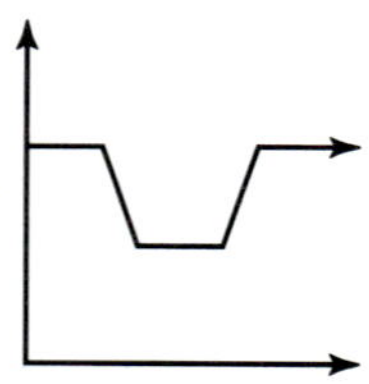

47. commutative (×) **49.** substitution (=) **51.** 13.9

Pages 80–83 Lesson 2–2

5. from 35 to 80;

7a.

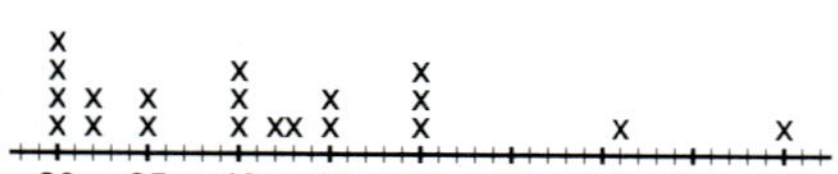

7b. 70 mph; cheetah **7c.** 30 mph **7d.** 30 mph **7e.** 12 **7f.** 4 **9a.** from 20 to 75 by 5;

9b. yes; 25 and 42 **11a.** Ms. Martinez's **11b.** No; in Ms. Martinez's class, the hours that the students talked on the phone were close to each other (4 ± 2 hours). In Mr. Thomas' class, the students had a wider range of hours spent talking on the phone. The range was from 0 to 8 hours, with no hours clustered around a certain number. **13.** Mr. Thomas', 3.6 hours; Ms. Martinez's, 3.7 hours; yes **15.** associative (×) **17.** 2

Page 84 Lesson 2–3A

1. 6 **3.** -2 **5.** 2 **7.** 6 **9.** false **11.** true **13.** Answers should include using the number line.

Pages 90–92 Lesson 2–3

7. $-7, 7$ **9.** 0, 0 **11.** -4 **13.** -11 **15.** 0 **17.** $40c$ **19.** -4 **21.** 3 **23.** $\begin{bmatrix} -1 & 4 \\ 6 & -6 \end{bmatrix}$ **25.** $-12, 12$ **27.** 302, 302 **29.** 0 **31.** -32 **33.** -16 **35.** -70 **37.** -15 **39.** -5 **41.** $40b$ **43.** $-29p$ **45.** $26d$ **47.** -4 **49.** -15 **51.** 5 **53.** 8 **55.** 99 **57.** -59 **59.** $\begin{bmatrix} 0 & 3 \\ 2 & 2 \end{bmatrix}$ **61.** $\begin{bmatrix} -4 & -5 \\ -4 & -5 \\ 10 & -3 \end{bmatrix}$ **63.** 24th floor

65a.

Monday	*Sesame*	*Poppy*	*Blue*	*Plain*
East Store	120	80	64	75
West Store	65	105	77	53

Tuesday	*Sesame*	*Poppy*	*Blue*	*Plain*
East Store	112	76	56	74
West Store	69	95	82	50

65b.

Monday + Tuesday	*Sesame*	*Poppy*	*Blue*	*Plain*
East Store	232	156	120	149
West Store	134	200	159	103

65c.

Monday − Tuesday	*Sesame*	*Poppy*	*Blue*	*Plain*
East Store	8	4	8	1
West Store	−4	10	−5	3

This matrix represents the difference between Monday's and Tuesday's sales in each category. **67a.** from 100 to 146

67b.

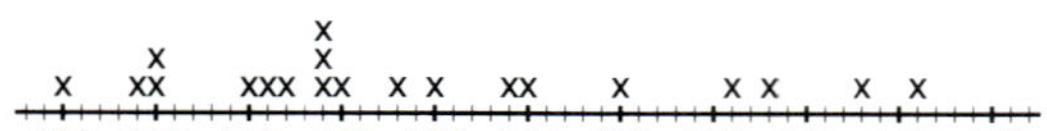

67c. yes; 114 **67d.** Siberian Elm; American Elm

69.

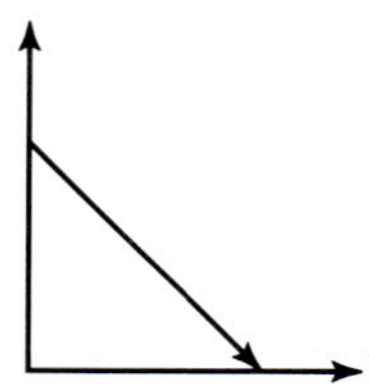

71. $55y^2$ **73.** symmetric (=) **75.** 14, 20, 29, 34, 37, 38, 43, 59, 64, 74, 84 **77.** 24

Pages 97–99 Lesson 2–4

7. < **9.** = **11.** $-0.5, \frac{3}{4}, \frac{7}{8}, 2.5$ **15.** > **17.** < **19.** < **21.** > **23.** $\frac{3}{8}, \frac{2}{3}, \frac{6}{7}$ **25.** $\frac{3}{23}, \frac{8}{42}, \frac{4}{14}$ **27.** $-\frac{2}{5}, -0.2, 0.2$ **29.** a 16-ounce drink for \$0.59 **31.** a package of 75 paper plates for \$3.29 **33.** Sample answer: $\frac{2}{3}$ **35.** Sample answer: $\frac{7}{20}$ **37.** Sample answer: $\frac{1}{6}$ **39.** $E = \frac{4}{14}$ or $\frac{2}{7}$; $G = \frac{10}{14}$ or $\frac{5}{7}$; $H = \frac{13}{14}$ **41.** 0.375 inch **43.** $-9, 9$

45. 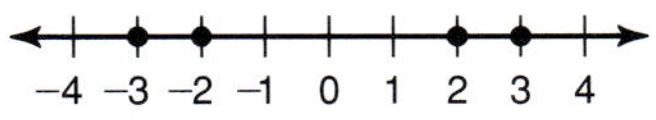

47. $m + 2n + \frac{3}{2}$ **49.** two times x squared plus six

Page 99 Self Test

1. 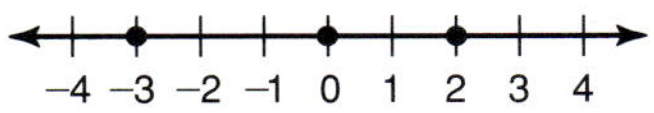

3. -17 **5.** 55

7a. 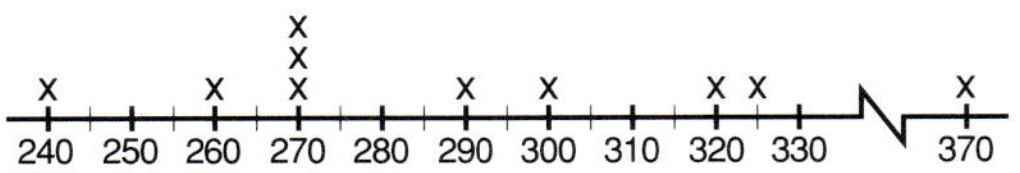

7b. yes; \$270 **9.** $<$

Pages 102–104 Lesson 2–5

5. $-\frac{1}{9}$ **7.** $-2\frac{5}{8}$ **9.** 0.88 **11.** 5.75 **13a.** $+\frac{1}{2}$

13b. 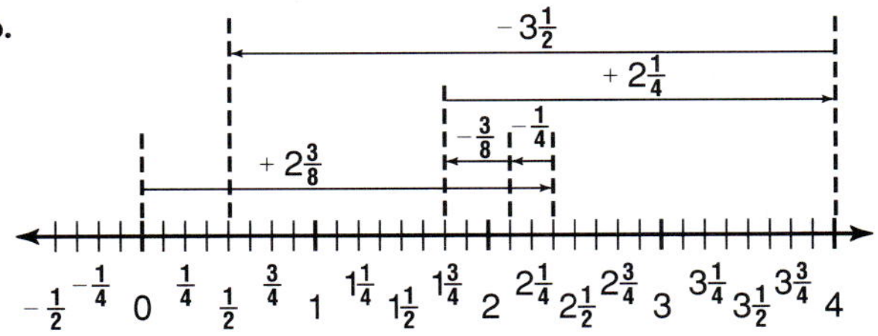

15. $-\frac{11}{16}$ **17.** -1.3 **19.** $\frac{4}{9}$ **21.** -0.2007 **23.** $-8\frac{5}{8}$

25. 0.0485 **27.** -22.94 **29.** -2.17 **31.** 1 **33.** -3.5

35. -16.7 **37.** $-\frac{52}{21}$ **39.** $\begin{bmatrix} -3.8 & -0.1 \\ 1.7 & 2.9 \end{bmatrix}$ **41.** $\begin{bmatrix} \frac{1}{4} & 11 \\ -5 & 8 \\ \frac{1}{2} & -12 \end{bmatrix}$

43. Answers will vary. Sample answer: $\begin{bmatrix} 5 & 3 \\ 1 & 7 \end{bmatrix}, \begin{bmatrix} 4 & -3 \\ 1 & 2 \end{bmatrix},$ $\begin{bmatrix} 9 & 0 \\ 2 & 9 \end{bmatrix}, \begin{bmatrix} 18 & 0 \\ 4 & 18 \end{bmatrix}; \begin{bmatrix} 5 & 3 \\ 1 & 7 \end{bmatrix} + \begin{bmatrix} 4 & -3 \\ 1 & 2 \end{bmatrix} = \begin{bmatrix} 9 & 0 \\ 2 & 9 \end{bmatrix} = \begin{bmatrix} 4 & -3 \\ 1 & 2 \end{bmatrix} +$ $\begin{bmatrix} 5 & 3 \\ 1 & 7 \end{bmatrix}; \left(\begin{bmatrix} 5 & 3 \\ 1 & 7 \end{bmatrix} + \begin{bmatrix} 4 & -3 \\ 1 & 2 \end{bmatrix}\right) + \begin{bmatrix} 9 & 0 \\ 2 & 9 \end{bmatrix} = \begin{bmatrix} 18 & 0 \\ 4 & 18 \end{bmatrix} =$ $\begin{bmatrix} 5 & 3 \\ 1 & 7 \end{bmatrix} + \left(\begin{bmatrix} 4 & -3 \\ 1 & 2 \end{bmatrix} + \begin{bmatrix} 9 & 0 \\ 2 & 9 \end{bmatrix}\right)$ **45a.** 9.01, 10.13, 11.25

45b. 1.12 **45c.** $-2, -\frac{5}{4}, -\frac{1}{2}, \frac{1}{4}, 1; -2\frac{1}{2}$ **47.** $<$

49a. 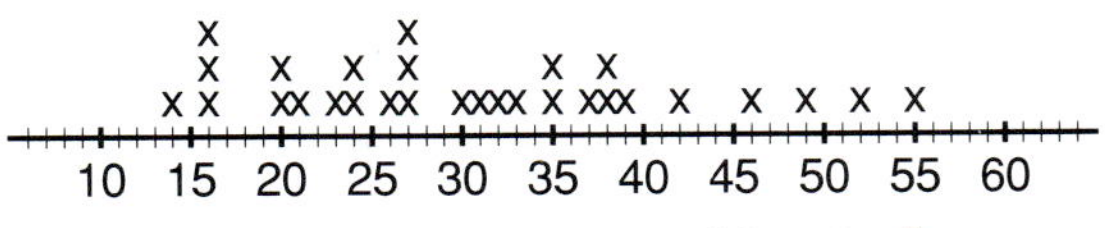

49b. no **51.** multiplicative property of 0 **53.** $\frac{7}{24}$

Page 105 Lesson 2–6A

3. -10 **5.** -10 **7.** 10

Pages 109–111 Lesson 2–6

5. -18 **7.** 24 **9.** $-\frac{4}{5}$ **11.** -4 **13.** $-46st$ **15.** $\begin{bmatrix} -6 & 12 \\ -3 & 15 \end{bmatrix}$

17. \$28.65 **19.** -60 **21.** -1 **23.** 2 **25.** 0.00879 **27.** $-\frac{6}{5}$

29. $-\frac{9}{17}$ **31.** 85.7095 **33.** 3 **35.** -6 **37.** $\frac{13}{12}$ **39.** $-\frac{179}{24}$

41. $\frac{25}{24}$ **43.** $-30rt + 4s$ **45.** $21x$ **47.** $16.48x - 5.3y$

49. $\begin{bmatrix} 2 & 6 & 3 \\ \frac{5}{2} & 5 & 1 \end{bmatrix}$ **51.** $\begin{bmatrix} -9 & 22.68 \\ -22.4 & -10 \\ 28.8 & 11.12 \end{bmatrix}$ **53.** $\begin{bmatrix} 6 & 18 & 4 \\ 0 & 2 & \frac{8}{3} \end{bmatrix}$

55. It is negative. **57a.** No; it meets the requirement that no dimensions can be less than 20 feet, but the minimum of 1250 square feet is not met because this yard would have 1216 square feet. **57b.** No; it meets the requirement that yards must have a minimum of 1250 square feet because it would have 1330 square feet, but the requirement that no dimension can be less than 20 feet is not met because it has a side of length 19 feet. **57c.** Answers will vary. Sample answer: 30 feet.

59. -2.2 **61.** -20 **63.** -7 **65.** $\{6, 7\}$ **67.** 408

Pages 115–117 Lesson 2–7

5. -4 **7.** $-\frac{3}{32}$ **9.** $-\frac{5}{48}$ **11.** $-6x$ **13.** about 2 minutes

15. 6 **17.** $-\frac{1}{18}$ **19.** $-\frac{1}{16}$ **21.** -6 **23.** $-\frac{1}{12}$ **25.** $\frac{243}{10}$

27. $-\frac{35}{3}$ **29.** $-65m$ **31.** $r + 3$ **33.** $-20a - 25b$

35. $-14c + 6d$ **37.** $-a - 4b$ **39.** -1.2 **41.** $-0.8\overline{3}$ **43.** 4

45a. 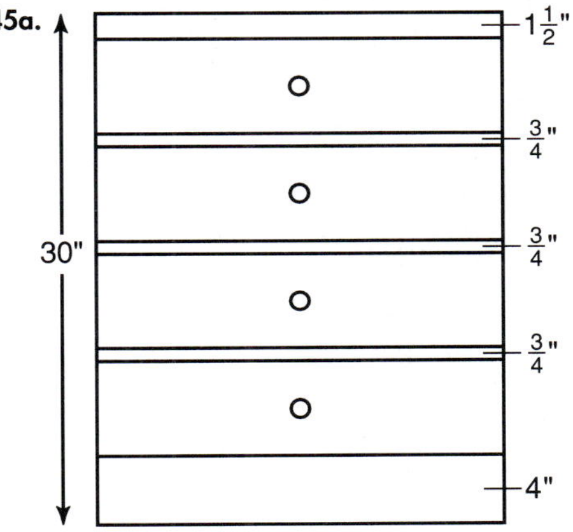

45b. $5\frac{9}{16}$ inches **47a.** 17.4 ± 0.161 cm **47b.** 0.161 cm

49. $\frac{13}{12}$ **51a.** $\begin{bmatrix} -2 & 4 \\ 3 & 12 \end{bmatrix}$ **51b.** $\begin{bmatrix} 4 & 4 \\ 7 & 2 \end{bmatrix}$ **53.** $20b + 24$

55a.

Stem	Leaf
13	0
15	4
17	2 3
19	4
20	0
22	0 2
24	5
25	1 4
27	9
29	0
30	4 7
33	0
34	6
52	5

13|0 = 13,000

55b. \$13,000 **55c.** \$52,500 **55d.** 9

Page 118 Lesson 2–8A

1. 4–5 **3.** 13–14 **5.** 1–2

Pages 123–125 Lesson 2–8

7. 8 **9.** 11.05 **11.** 16 **13.** Q **15.** Q

17. 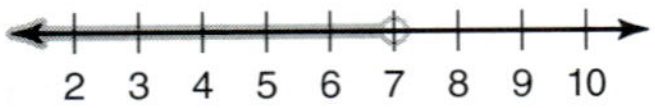

19. 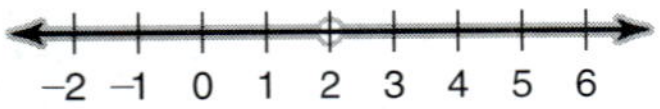

21. 13 **23.** $\frac{2}{3}$ **25.** 20.49 **27.** 15 **29.** −25 **31.** $\frac{3}{5}$ **33.** 9.33 **35.** −47 **37.** −20 **39.** Z, Q **41.** Q **43.** Q **45.** Q **47.** I **49.** Q **51.** 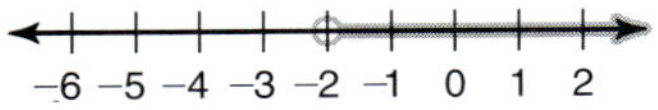

53. 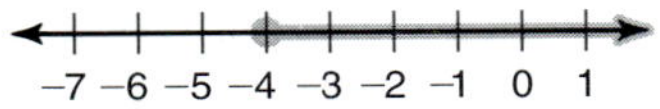

55. 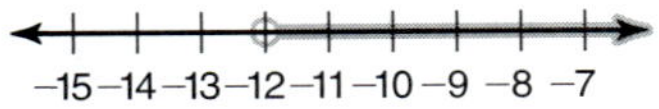

57. 

59. 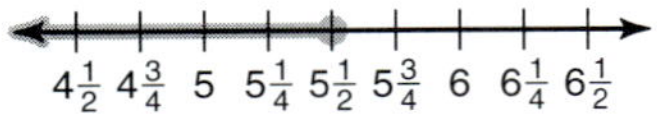

61. Yes; it lies between 27 and 28. **63a.** $d = 1.4\sqrt{1275}$; Estimates should be close to 50. **63b.** 49.989999 **65.** Fibonacci **67.** −12 **69.** a 1-pound package of lunch meat for $1.95 **71.** from 500 to 520 by 5s;

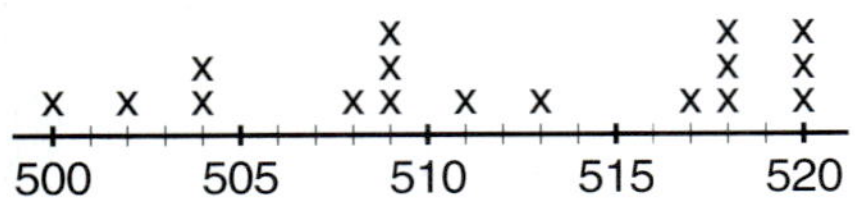

73. b **75a.** to the nearest ten thousand **75b.** 10 **75c.** $690,000 **77.** 26, 32

Pages 130–132 Lesson 2–9

5a. 4 points **5b.** 15 questions **5c.** 86 **5d.** 6 points **5e.** $15 - n$ **5f.** $4n$ **7.** $n + 5 \geq 48$ **9.** Let s = average speed; $s = \frac{189}{3} = 63$. **11.** The product of a times the sum of y and 1 is b. **13a.** 640 feet **13b.** $y - 80$ **13c.** $\ell + \ell + w + w$ or $2\ell + 2w$ **13d.** 200 ft **13e.** 24,000 ft^2 **13f.** Is there enough space to build the playground as designed? **15.** $a^2 + b^3 = 25$ **17.** $x < (a - 4)^2$ **19.** $\frac{7}{8}(a + b + c^2) = 48$

21. Sample answer: x = first number
$x + 25$ = second number
$25 + 2x = 106$

23. Sample answer:
y = how much money Hector saves
$y = 2(7)(50)$

25. V is equal to the quotient of a times h and three. **27.** Sample answer: Three times the number of miles home is from school is 36. How many miles away from home is the school? **29.** Sample answer: The number of minutes spent waiting for a doctor in the waiting room is 5 minutes more than 6 times the number of appointments she has. How long would you have to wait for a doctor with d appointments?

31. $ab + cd + 2d - 8$

33. Sample answer: $4.5 + x + x = 24 + x$
$x = 19.5$

35a. $A = \frac{1}{2}h(a + b)$ **35b.** $A = 108\frac{1}{2}$ ft^2 **37.** −8

39. $\begin{bmatrix} 8 & -1.6 \\ 12 & -20 \end{bmatrix}$ **41.** −25, 25 **43.** {2, 3, 4, 5}

Page 133 Chapter 2 Highlights

1. true **3.** true **5.** false, sample answer: $\frac{\frac{1}{2}}{5}$ **7.** true **9.** true

Pages 134–136 Chapter 2 Study Guide and Assessment

11. 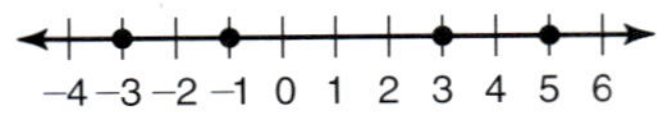

13. 

15. −5 **17.** −4 **19.** −5 **21.** 56% **23.** 8 **25.** −2 **27.** 4 **29.** −5 **31.** > **33.** < **35.** Sample answer: 0 **37.** −1 **39.** 12.37 **41.** −13.26 **43.** −99 **45.** $-\frac{3}{7}$

47. −90 **49.** −9 **51.** $\frac{-4}{35}$ **53.** −109 **55.** 14 **57.** −30

59a. 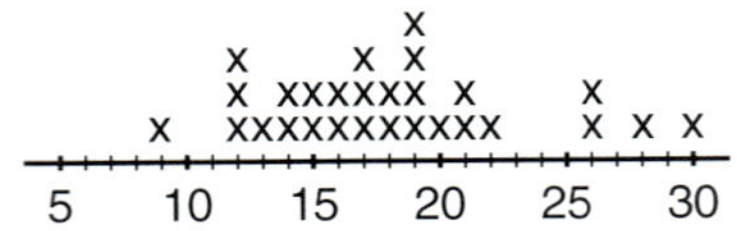

59b. 14 detergents **61.** 1.25 liters of soda for $1.31 **63a.** They both saw a gain of $\frac{1}{4}$ for the week. **63b.** CompNet **63c.** It changed $-\frac{3}{4}$ from Wednesday to Thursday. **65.** Let n = the number; $3n - 21 = 57$.

CHAPTER 3 SOLVING LINEAR EQUATIONS

Page 143 Lesson 3–1A

1. 1 **3.** −11 **5.** 8 **7.** 4 **9.** no **11.** yes

Pages 148–149 Lesson 3–1

7. −17 **9.** −12 **11.** −14 **13.** $n + (-56) = -82$; −26 **15.** −9 **17.** −1.3 **19.** 1.4 **21.** −3 **23.** −6 **25.** −7 **27.** 24 **29.** $1\frac{1}{4}$ **31.** $-\frac{1}{10}$ **33.** $n + 5 = 34$; 29 **35.** $n - (-23) = 35$; 12 **37.** $n + (-35) = 98$; 133 **39a.** $203{,}600 + s = 19{,}300{,}000$; 19,096,400 subscribers **39b.** Sample answer: 25 million **41a.** 24 years old **41b.** 24 years **41c.** 78 years **41d.** 34 years old **41e.** 24 years **43.** −5 **45.** $-0.73x$ **47.** 48

Pages 152–154 Lesson 3–2

7. 17 **9.** 48 **11.** $\frac{11}{15}$ **13.** $-7n = 1.477$; −0.211 **15.** −9

17. −17.33 or $-17\frac{1}{3}$ **19.** −14 **21.** 12.81 **23.** 600

25. −275 **27.** −25 **29.** $8\frac{6}{13}$ **31.** −8 **33.** $-12n = -156$; 13

35. $\frac{4}{3}n = 4.82$; 3.615 **37.** 45 **39.** 30 **41.** 12 **43a.** $7\ell = 350$, 50 people; $7\ell = 583$, ≈ 83 people **43b.** $\frac{p}{7} = 65$; 455 people **45a.** $0.10m = 2.30$; 23 minutes **45b.** $0.10(18) = c$; $1.80 **47.** $17 + 1\frac{1}{2}y = 33\frac{1}{2}$; 11 years **49.** $\frac{19}{28}$ **51a.** The number of bags increased during the day. **51b.** The machine was refilled. **53.** 31

Page 155 Lesson 3–3A

1. 5 **3.** −2 **5.** 2 **7.** 4 **9.** −2

Pages 159–161 Lesson 3–3

9. −6 **11.** 35 **13.** −17 **15.** $n + (n + 2) + (n + 4) = 21$;

5, 7, 9 **17.** -1 **19.** -2 **21.** -42.72 **23.** $12\frac{2}{3}$ **25.** -6

27. -48 **29.** 30 **31.** 57 **33.** $4\frac{3}{7}$ **35.** $12 - 2n = -7; 9\frac{1}{2}$

37. $n + (n + 1) + (n + 2) + (n + 3) = 86$; 20, 21, 22, 23 **39.** $n + (n + 2) + (n + 4) = 39$; 11 m, 13 m, 15 m **41.** 28 **43.** -38 **45.** $(3n - 1) + (3n + 1) + (3n + 3)$ **47.** $2a + 2 = 26$; 12 letters **51.** I **53.** -5 **55.** 5

Page 161 Self Test

1. 44 **3.** 6 **5.** $-8\frac{1}{3}$ **7.** $23 - n = 42; -19$ **9.** $n + (n + 2) = 126$; 62, 64

Pages 165–167 Lesson 3–4

7. 79°, 169° **9.** $(90 - 3x)°$, $(180 - 3x)°$ **11.** $(110 - x)°$, $(200 - x)°$ **13.** 85° **15.** $(c - 38) + c = 90$; 26°, 64° **17.** 48°, 138° **19.** none, 55° **21.** 69°, 159° **23.** none, 81° **25.** $(90 - 3a)°$, $(180 - 3a)°$ **27.** $(128 - b)°$, $(218 - b)°$ **29.** 70° **31.** 105° **33.** 138° **35.** $(190 - 2p)°$ **37.** 45° **39.** $x + (x - 30) = 180$; 75° **41.** $x + (30 + 3x) = 90$; 15°, 75° **43.** $x + 3x + 4x = 180$; 22.5°, 67.5°, 90° **45.** 60° **47.** 40° **49a.** \$80 **49b.** \$74.75 **51.** $7t$

53a.

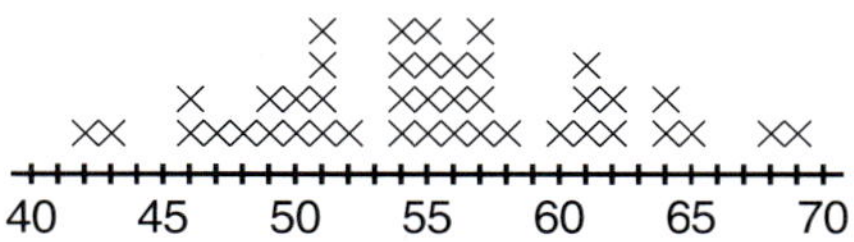

53b. yes; 51, 54, 55, and 57

55.

Stem	Leaf
4	2 3 6 6 7 8 9 9
5	0 0 1 1 1 1 2 4
	4 4 4 5 5 5 5 6
	6 6 7 7 7 7 8
6	0 1 1 1 2 2 4 4
	5 8 9

5|2 = 52

Pages 170–172 Lesson 3–5

5. $-\frac{1}{2}$; Add $4x$ to each side, subtract 10 from each side, then divide each side by 14. **7.** -25; Subtract $\frac{1}{5}$ from each side, subtract 3 from each side, then multiply by $\frac{5}{2}$. **9.** all numbers **11.** $2(n + 2) = 3n - 13$; 17, 19 **13.** $\frac{1}{2}n + 16 = \frac{2}{3}n - 4$; 120 **15.** no solution **17.** -2 **19.** 5.6 **21.** -16 **23.** no solution **25.** 4 **27.** 2.6 or $2\frac{3}{5}$ **29.** 8 **31.** 2 **33.** all numbers **35.** $\frac{1}{5}n + 5n = 7n - 18$; 10 **37.** $n + (n + 2) + (n + 4) = 180$; 58°, 60°, 62° **39a.** $4x + 6 = 4x + 6$; identity **39b.** $5x - 7 = x + 3$; 2.5 **39c.** $-3x + 6 = 3x - 6$; 2 **39d.** $5.4x + 6.8 = 4.6x + 2.8$; -5 **39e.** $2x - 8 = 2x - 6$; no solution **41a.** 6.827 years **41b.** Air conditioner sales are decreasing while fan sales are increasing. **43.** 148° **45.** -2.7 **47.** $\frac{11}{9}$ **49.** 11.05

Pages 175–177 Lesson 3–6

5. $\frac{3x - 7}{4}$ **7.** $\frac{c - b}{2}$ **9.** $\frac{2S - nt}{n}$ **11.** $\frac{b}{9}$ **13.** $3c - a$ **15.** $\frac{v - r}{t}$ **17.** $\frac{I}{pt}$ **19.** $\frac{H}{0.24I^2t}$ **21.** $\frac{-t + 5}{4}$ **23.** $\frac{4}{3}(c - b)$ **25.** $\frac{5x + y}{2}$ **27.** $2x + 12 = 3y - 31$; $\frac{3y - 43}{2}$ **29.** $\frac{2}{3}x + 5 = \frac{1}{2}y - 3$; $\frac{3}{4}y - 12$ **31.** \$900 **33a.** 36 words per minute **33b.** Clarence, with 74 words per minute **35.** 5° **37.** $x \neq 2$ **39.** {8}

Pages 181–183 Lesson 3–7

11. 8.2; 8; 8 **13.** Sample answer: 20, 20, 30, 50, 90, 90 **15a.** 3.857; 3; 3 **15b.** mean **17.** 96.8; 50; none **19.** 9; 9; none **21.** 5.69; 4.56; none **23.** 212.94; 218; 219 **25.** 14 **27a.** mean **27b.** Yes, because the article indicates that the median value is in the middle of the data set. **27c.** No, he should have used the term *mean* since the mean can be affected by extremely high values, causing the majority to be below the mean value. **29.** $1660\frac{3}{5}$; $1076\frac{1}{2}$; none **31.** 37.5 mph **33.** 16 **35.** -20 **37.** $5 + 9ac + 14b$

Page 185 Chapter 3 Highlights

1. b **3.** i **5.** d **7.** k **9.** a **11.** g

Pages 186–188 Chapter 3 Study Guide and Assessment

13. -16 **15.** 21 **17.** -10 **19.** -32 **21.** -116 **23.** 7 **25.** $83\frac{1}{3}$ **27.** 10 **29.** -16 **31.** 3 **33.** -153 **35.** 11 **37.** 50 **39.** 16, 17 **41.** 21°; 111° **43.** $(70 - y)°$; $(160 - y)°$ **45.** 30° **47.** 15° **49.** $180° - (z + z - 30°)$ or $(210° - 2z)$ **51.** -30 **53.** 2 **55.** $\frac{y}{5}$ **57.** $\frac{a}{y - c}$ **59.** 21; 21; 21 **61a.** 25.5 years **63.** $13\frac{3}{4}$ years

CHAPTER 4 USING PROPORTIONAL REASONING

Pages 198–200 Lesson 4–1

5. = **7.** 12 **9.** 5 **11.** 4.62 **13.** 9.5 gallons **15.** = **17.** ≠ **19.** = **21.** 9 **23.** $\frac{8}{5}$; 1.6 **25.** 0.84 **27.** $-\frac{149}{6}$; -24.8 **29.** 11 **31.** 2.28 **33.** 1.251

35a.

Louis' age	1	2	3	6	10	20	30
Mariah's age	9	**10**	**11**	**14**	**18**	**28**	**38**

35b. 9, 5, $3.\overline{6}$, $2.\overline{3}$, 1.8, 1.4, $1.2\overline{6}$ **35c.** $r = \frac{y + 8}{y}$ **35d.** The ratio gets smaller. **35e.** No; if the ratio equaled 1, Mariah and Louis would be the same age. **37.** 85 movies **39.** 23; 19; 18 **41.** $4x - 2x = 100$; 50 **43a.** 93 **43b.** \$9695 **43c.** more than 40 **43d.** $93 - p$ **43e.** yes **45.** 10

Pages 203–205 Lesson 4–2

5. ΔDEF **7.** yes **9.** $\ell = 12, m = 6$ **11.** 27 feet high **13.** ΔDFE **15.** no **17.** yes **19.** no **21.** $a = \frac{55}{6}, b = \frac{22}{3}$ **23.** $d = \frac{51}{5}, e = 9$ **25.** $a = 2.78, c = 4.24$ **27.** $b = 16.2, d = 6.3$ **29.** $e = \frac{7}{2}, d = \frac{17}{8}$

31. Sample answer:

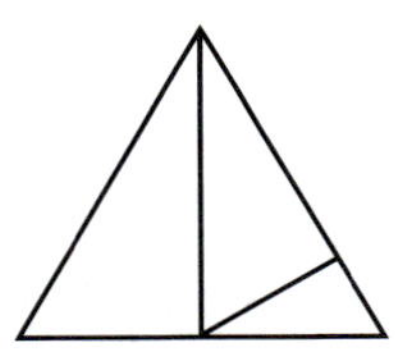

33a. $\frac{3}{9} = \frac{d}{d + 39}$; $d = 19.5$ ft; yes **33b.** When the ball is

served from 8 feet, $d = 23.4$ ft, and the serve is a fault. When the ball is served from 10 feet, $d = 16.7$ ft. Therefore, tall players have an easier time serving. **35.** $16\frac{1}{2}$ feet by 21 feet **37.** 160 **39.** 60 million; 420 million
41. 23;
$(19 - 12) \div 7 \cdot 23$
$= 7 \div 7 \cdot 23$ *Substitution (=)*
$= 1 \cdot 23$ *Substitution (=)*
$= 23$ *Multiplicative identity*

Pages 211–214 Lesson 4–3
7. $\sin Y = 0.600$, $\cos Y = 0.800$, $\tan Y = 0.750$ **9.** 0.8192 **11.** 0.1228 **13.** 46° **15.** 36° **17.** $m\angle B = 50°$, $AC = 12.3$ m, $BC = 10.3$ m **19.** $m\angle A = 30°$, $AC = 13.9$ m, $BC = 8$ m **21.** $\sin G = 0.600$, $\cos G = 0.800$, $\tan G = 0.750$ **23.** $\sin G = 0.471$, $\cos G = 0.882$, $\tan G = 0.533$ **25.** $\sin G = 0.923$, $\cos G = 0.385$, $\tan G = 2.4$ **27.** 0.3584 **29.** 0.9703 **31.** 0.3746 **33.** 33° **35.** 22° **37.** 62° **39.** 77° **41.** 58° **43.** 18° **45.** $m\angle B = 60°$, $AC = 12.1$ m, $BC = 7$ m **47.** $m\angle A = 45°$, $AC = 6$ ft, $AB = 8.5$ ft **49.** $m\angle A = 63°$, $AC = 9.1$ in., $BC = 17.8$ in. **51.** $m\angle A = 23°$, $m\angle B = 67°$, $AB \approx 12.8$ ft **53.** $m\angle A = 30°$, $m\angle B = 60°$, $AC = 5.2$ cm **55a.** true; $\sin C = \frac{c}{a}$, $\cos B = \frac{c}{a}$ **55b.** $\cos B = \frac{c}{a}$, $\frac{1}{\sin B} = \frac{a}{b}$ **55c.** $\tan C = \frac{c}{b}$, $\frac{\cos C}{\sin C} = \frac{b}{a} \div \frac{c}{a} = \frac{b}{c}$ **55d.** true; $\tan C = \frac{c}{b}$, $\frac{\sin C}{\cos C} = \frac{c}{a} \div \frac{b}{a} = \frac{c}{b}$ **55e.** true; $\sin B = \frac{b}{a}$, $(\tan B)(\cos B) = \frac{b}{c} \cdot \frac{c}{a} = \frac{b}{a}$ **57.** 2229 ft **59.** 3 **61.** 10 **63.** N, W, Z, Q **65.** $\frac{2}{15}$ **67.** $9x + 2y$ **69.** 125

Pages 218–221 Lesson 4–4
7. 43%, 0.43 **9.** 55% **11.** 15 **13.** \$52.50 **15.** \$1200 at 10%, \$6000 at 14% **17.** 30%, 0.30 **19.** 70%, 0.70 **21.** 180%, 1.8 **23.** $62\frac{1}{2}$%; 0.625 **25.** 50% **27.** $12\frac{1}{2}$%, 12.5% **29.** 400% **31.** 2.5% **33.** 72.3 **35.** 702.4 **37.** 28% **39.** 25.92 **41.** 12% **43.** \$3125 **45.** \$2400 **47.** 39%, 34%, 15%, 12% **49.** 11.5% **51.** \$5.45 **53a.** about 54 people; about 23 people **53b.** Respondents could choose more than one entree. **55.** about 277 feet **57.** $\frac{77}{4}$; 19.25 **59.** −4.7 **61.** $-28y$ **63.** 2

Page 221 Self Test
1. 5 **3.** 5 **5.** $m\angle B = 34°$, $b \approx 11.5$, $c \approx 20.5$ **7.** no **9.** $62\frac{1}{2}$%, 62.5%

Pages 225–227 Lesson 4–5
5. I; 40% **7.** D; 50% **9.** \$85.85 **11.** \$196 **13.** I; 69% **15.** D; 55% **17.** D; 27% **19.** I; 2% **21.** \$233.24 **23.** \$19.90 **25.** \$85.39 **27.** \$16.59 **29.** \$30.09 **31.** no **33.** 133% **35.** 8.6% **37.** an increase of more than 22% **39.** 11% **41.** 65 ft **43.** 11 **45.** heavy, 571; light, 286

Pages 230–232 Lesson 4–6
7. $\frac{1}{2}$ **9.** $\frac{2}{3}$ **11.** 5:1 **13.** $\frac{1}{2}$ **15.** $\frac{1}{2}$ **17.** $\frac{1}{2}$ **19.** $\frac{2}{11}$ **21.** 0 **23.** $\frac{8}{11}$ **25.** 1:5 **27.** 4:11 **29.** 23:7 **31.** $\frac{1}{2}$ **33.** 1:3 **35.** $\frac{8}{13}$ **37.** $\frac{1}{7}$ **39a.** 1:14 **39b.** $\frac{1}{27}$ **41a.** $\frac{3}{26}$ **41b.** $\frac{4}{13}$ **41c.** 3:23 **43.** 9° **45.** \$50 **47.** $\frac{4}{21}$ **49.** 75

Pages 236–238 Lesson 4–7
5. 226 dozen chocolate chip; 311 dozen peanut butter **7.** 11:30 A.M. **9.** 5 quarters **11.** 3 hours **13.** 2.5 hours **15.** 46 mph **17.** 67 mph **19a.** 7 **19b.** 16 **21.** Sample answer: How much pure antifreeze must be mixed with a 20% solution to produce 40 quarts of a 28% solution? **23.** 0 **25.** \$11,000 **27.** 49 **29.** associative (+)

Pages 243–244 Lesson 4–8
5. I, 5 **7.** 10 **9.** 99 **11.** 20 inches from the 8-ounce weight, 16 inches from the 10-ounce weight **13.** I, 15 **15.** I, 9 **17.** D, 4 **19.** $26\frac{1}{4}$ **21.** −8 **23.** 12 **25.** 6.075 **27.** 8.3875 **29.** $\frac{1}{4}$ **31.** 18 pounds **33.** 1.6 feet **35.** 2:1 **37.** \$4300 at 5%, \$7400 at 7% **39.** −12

Page 245 Chapter 4 Highlights
1. angle of elevation **3.** equal, proportional **5.** legs **7.** odds **9.** inverse variation

Pages 246–248 Chapter 4 Study Guide and Assessment
11. = **13.** ≠ **15.** 18 **17.** 16 **19.** $d = \frac{45}{8}$, $e = \frac{27}{4}$ **21.** $b = \frac{44}{3}$, $d = 6$ **23.** 0.528 **25.** 0.849 **27.** 1.607 **29.** 39° **31.** 80° **33.** $m\angle B = 45°$, $AB = 8.5$, $BC = 6$ **35.** $m\angle A \approx 66°$, $AB \approx 9.8$, $m\angle B \approx 24°$ **37.** 48 **39.** 87.5% **41.** 0.1881 **43.** decrease, 13% **45.** increase, 6% **47.** decrease, 10% **49.** \$85.66 **51.** \$9272.23 **53.** $\frac{1}{12}$ **55.** $\frac{5}{6}$ **57.** 10:39 **59.** 34:15 **61.** 21 **63.** 6 **65.** 21 **67.** 48 **69.** 450 mph and 530 mph

CHAPTER 5 GRAPHING RELATIONS AND FUNCTIONS

Pages 257–259 Lesson 5–1
5. (−3, −1); III **7.** (0, −2); none
8–11.

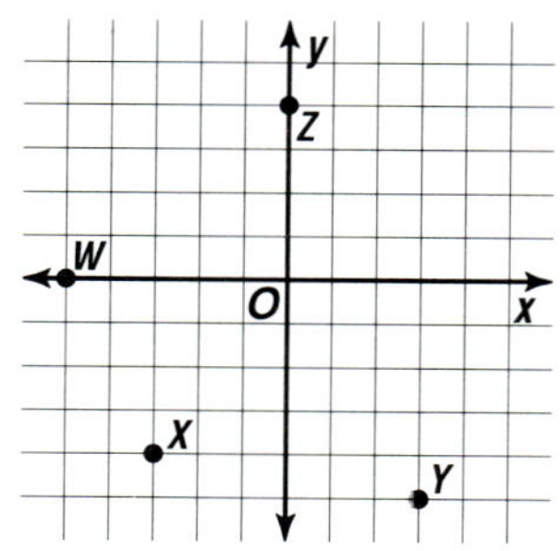

13. (−1, −3); III **15.** (0, 3); none **17.** (0, 0); none **19.** (3, −2); IV **21.** (2, 2); I **23.** (−5, 4); II
25–36.

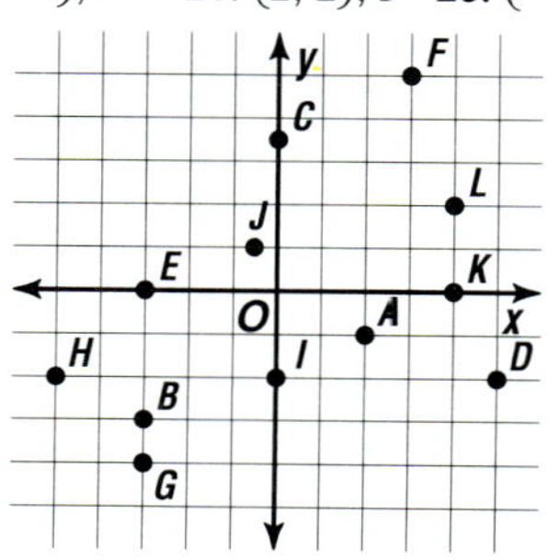

37.

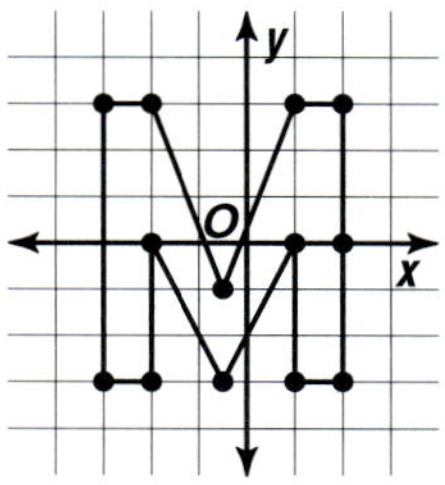

41a. New Orleans **41b.** Oregon **41c.** Sample answer: $(75°, 40°)$ **41d.** Honolulu, Hawaii **41f.** Sample answer: The longitude lines are not the same distance apart; they meet at the poles. **45.** $3\frac{1}{2}$ hours **47.** 4; 3; none **49.** $-a - 5$ **51.** $31a + 21b$

Page 261 Lesson 5–2A

1–6.

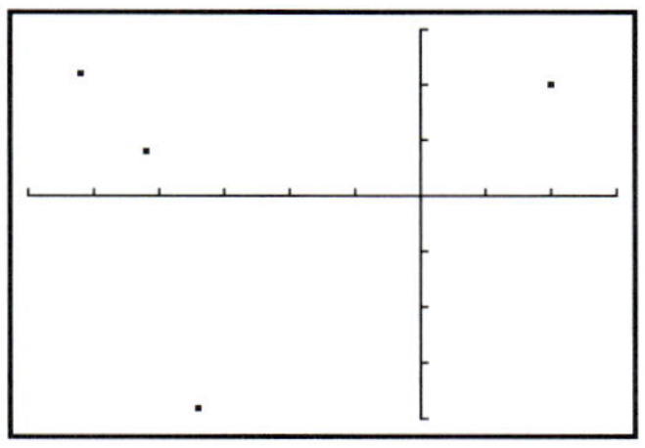

7. They are points on the axes.

Pages 266–269 Lesson 5–2

5. D = {0, 1, 2}; R = {2, −2, 4} **7.** {(1, 3), (2, 4), (3, 5), (5, 7)}; D = {1, 2, 3, 5}; R = {3, 4, 5, 7}; Inv = {(3, 1), (4, 2), (5, 3), (7, 5)} **9.** {(1, 3), (2, 2), (4, 9), (6, 5)}; D = {1, 2, 4, 6}; R = {2, 3, 5, 9}; Inv = {(3, 1), (2, 2), (9, 4), (5, 6)} **11.** {(−2, 2), (−1, 1), (0, 1), (1, 1), (1, −1), (2, −1), (3, 1)}; D = {−2, −1, 0, 1, 2, 3}; R = {−1, 1, 2}; Inv = {(2, −2), (1, −1), (1, 0), (1, 1), (−1, 1), (−1, 2), (1, 3)}

13.

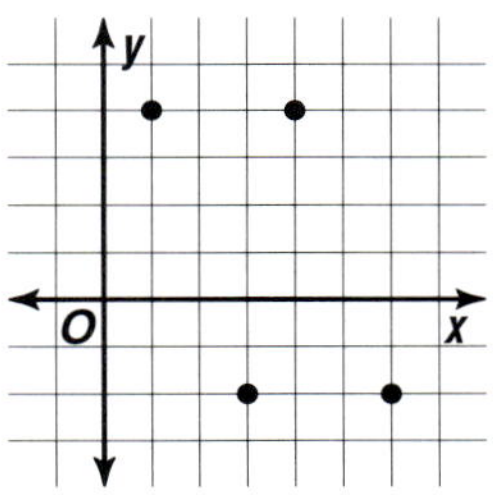

15b. 5.6% **15c.** Except for the first 6 months of 1992, the unemployment rate seems to be decreasing. **17.** D = {−5, −2, 1, 3}; R = {7} **19.** D = $\left\{-5\frac{1}{4}, -3, \frac{1}{2}, 1\frac{1}{2}\right\}$; R = $\left\{-6\frac{2}{7}, -\frac{2}{3}, \frac{1}{4}, \frac{2}{5}\right\}$ **21.** {(6, 4), (4, −2), (3, 4), (1, −2)}; D = {1, 3, 4, 6}; R = {−2, 4}; Inv = {(4, 6), (−2, 4), (4, 3), (−2, 1)} **23.** {(6, 0), (−3, 5), (2, −2), (−3, 3)}; D = {−3, 2, 6}, R = {−2, 0, 3, 5}; Inv = {(0, 6), (5, −3), (−2, 2), (3, −3)} **25.** (3, 4), (3, 2), (2, 9), (5, 4), (5, 8), (−7, 2)}; D = {−7, 2, 3, 5}; R = {2, 4, 8, 9}; Inv = {(4, 3), (2, 3), (9, 2), (4, 5), (8, 5), (2, −7)} **27.** {(0, 25), (1, 50), (2, 75), (3, 100)}; D = {0, 1, 2, 3}; R = {25, 50, 75, 100}; Inv = {(25, 0), (50, 1), (75, 2), (100, 3)} **29.** {(−3, 4), (−2, 2), (−1, −2), (2, 2)}; D = {−3, −2, −1, 2}; R = {−2, 2, 4}; Inv = {(4, −3), (2, −2), (−2, −1), (2, 2)} **31.** {(−3, 3), (−3, −3), (3, 3), (3, −3), (0, 0)}; D = {−3, 0, 3}; R = {−3, 0, 3}; Inv = {(3, −3), (−3, −3), (3, 3), (−3, 3), (0, 0)} **33.** {(−3, 1), (−1, 1), (2, 1), (3, 1), (4, 1)}; D = {−3, −1, 2, 3, 4}; R = {1}; Inv = {(1, −3), (1, −1), (1, 2), (1, 3), (1, 4)}

35.

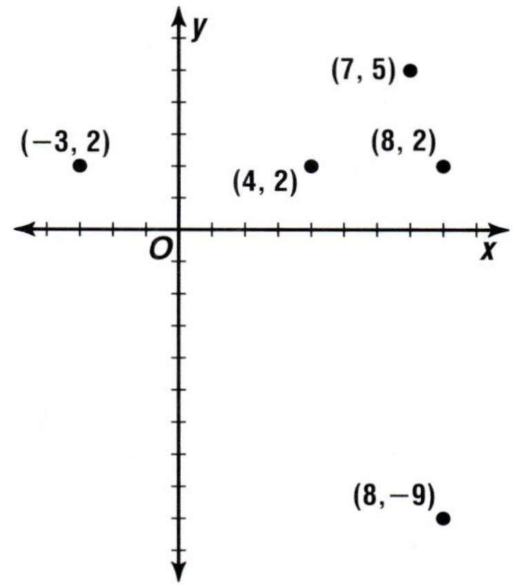

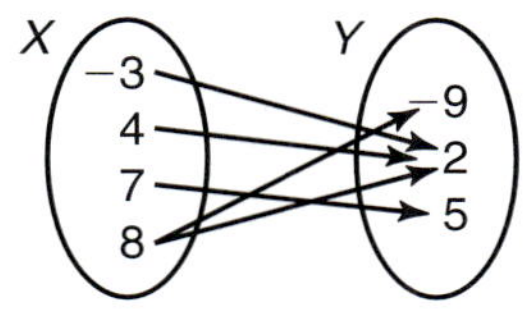

37.

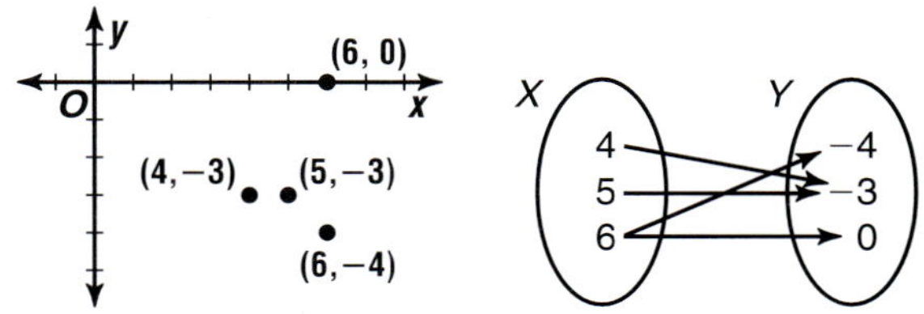

39a. [−10, 10] by [−10, 10]

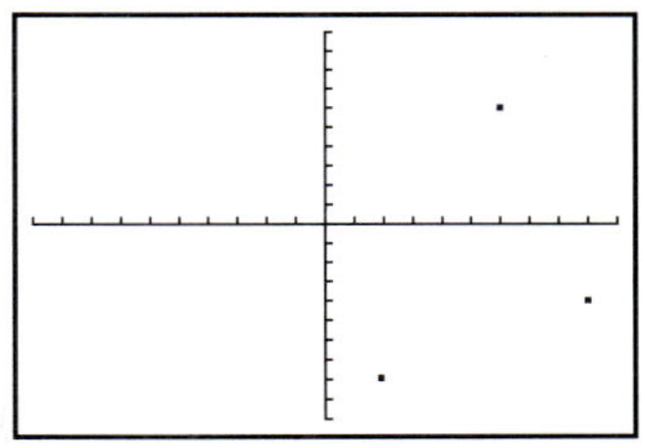

39b. {(10, 0), (−8, 2), (6, 6), (−4, 9)}

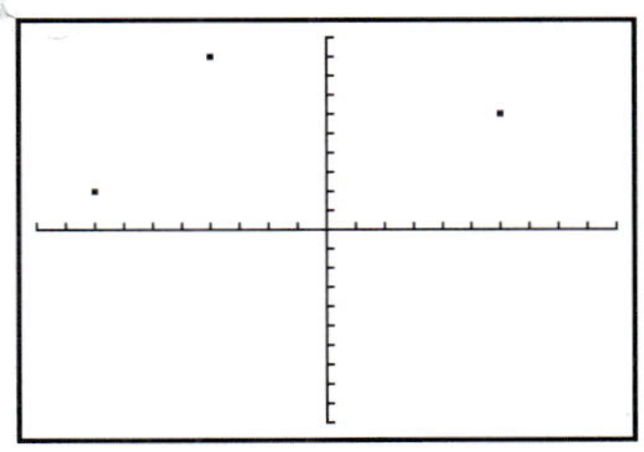

39c.

(x, y)	Quadrant	Inverse's Quadrant
(0, 10)	I	I
(2, −8)	IV	II
(6, 6)	I	I
(9, −4)	IV	II

41. If a point lies in Quadrants I or III, its inverse will lie in the same quadrant as the point. If a point lies in Quadrant II, its inverse lies in Quadrant IV, and vice versa. If a point lies on the *x*-axis, its inverse lies on the *y*-axis and vice versa. **43.** Sample answers: **a.** 157 billion, 191 billion

b. Retail sales have increased from 1992 to 1994.
c. As unemployment decreases, retail sales increase, because people have more money to spend.

45a.

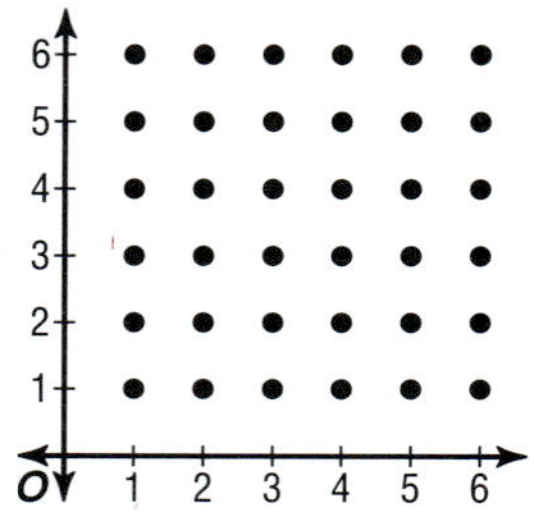

D = R = {1, 2, 3, 4, 5, 6} **45b.** D = R = {1, 2, 3, 4, 5, 6}; relation = inverse
45c. 11 possible sums

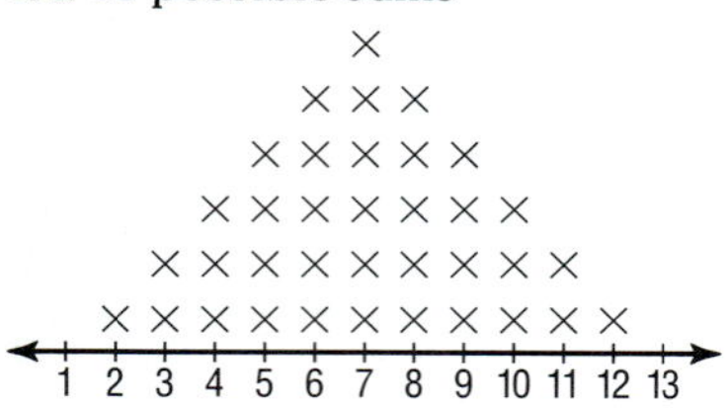

45d.

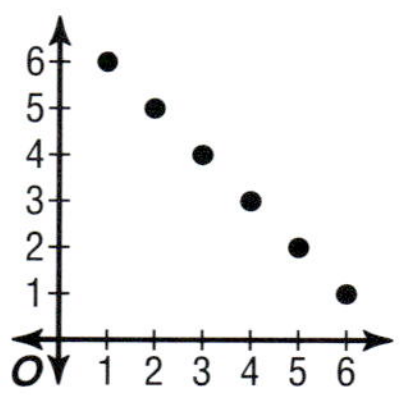

45e. $\frac{6}{36}$ or $\frac{1}{6}$; There are 6 out of 36 ways to roll a sum of 7.

47. 32 **49.** \$480 **51.** 2214, 2290 **53.** $4 + 80x + 32y$

Page 270 Lesson 5–3A
1. {(−3, −19), (−2, −15), (−1, −11), (0, −7), (1, −3), (2, −1), (3, 5)} **3.** {(−3, −10.4), (−2, −9.2), (−1, −8), (0, −6.8), (1, −5.6), (2, −4.4), (3, −3.2)}

Pages 274–277 Lesson 5–3
7. {(−2, −1), (−1, 1), (0, 3), (1, 5), (2, 7), (3, 9)} **9.** a, d
11. {(−2, 8), (−1, 7.5), (0, 7), (1, 6.5), (2, 6)}

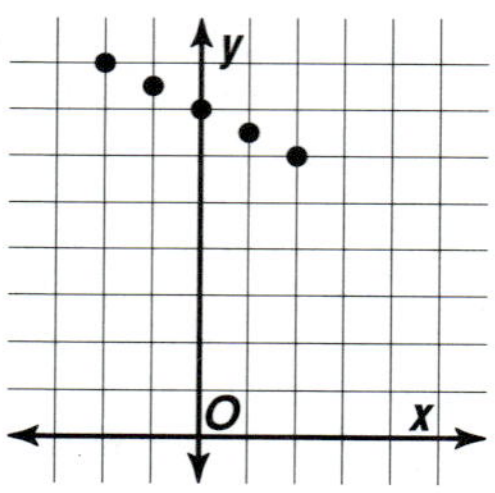

13. a, c **15.** a, b **17.** c **19.** {(−3, −12), (−2, −8), (0, 0), (3, 12), (6, 24)} **21.** {(−3, 10), (−2, 9), (0, 7), (3, 4), (6, 1)} **23.** {(−3, 11), (−2, 9.5), (0, 6.5), (3, 2), (6, −2.5)} **25.** {(−3, −12), (−2, −7), (0, 3), (3, 18), (6, 33)} **27.** {(−3, 1.8), (−2, 1.4), (0, 0.6), (3, −0.6), (6, −1.8)}

29.

x	y
−5	−9
−3	−5
0	1
1	3
3	7
6	13

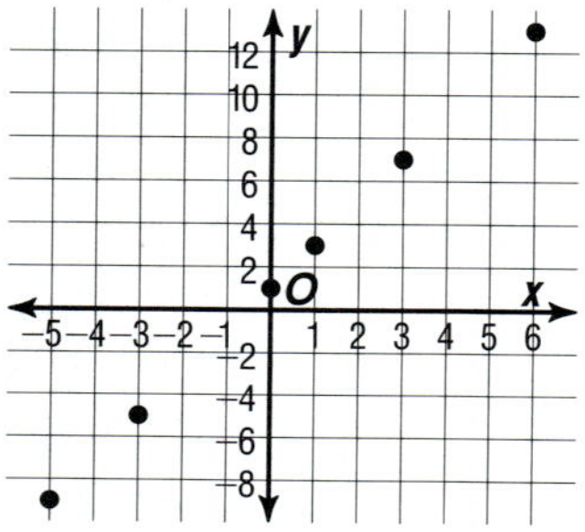

31.

a	b
−2	4.5
−1	3.25
0	2.00
1	0.75
3	−1.75
4	−3.00
5	−4.25

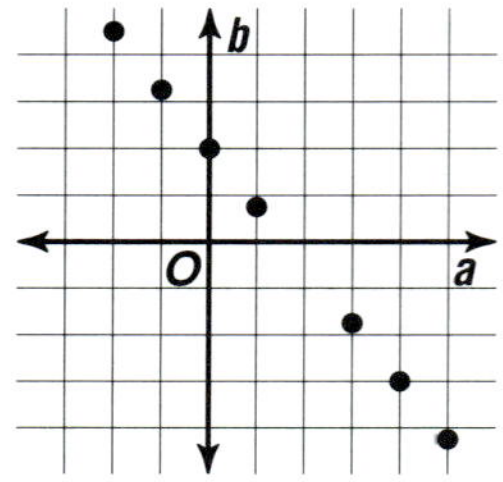

33a. $3x + 4y = 180$ **33b.** $y = 45 - \frac{3}{4}x$ **33c.** Sample answer: (1, 44.25), (2, 43.5), (3, 42.75), (4, 42), (5, 41.25)

35. $\left\{-\frac{2}{3}, -\frac{1}{3}, 0, \frac{2}{3}, 1\right\}$ **37.** $\left\{-\frac{7}{4}, -\frac{1}{2}, 2, \frac{13}{4}, \frac{9}{2}\right\}$

39.

x	y
−2	−8
−1	−1
0	0
1	1
2	8

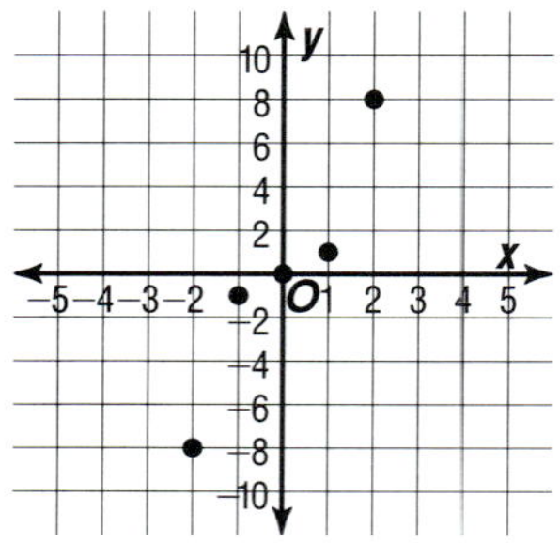

41. {(−2.5, −4.26), (−1.75, −3.21), (0, −0.76), (1.25, 0.99), (3.333, 3.902)} **43.** [(−100, 350), (−30, $116.\overline{6}$), (0, $16.\overline{6}$), (120, $-383.\overline{3}$), (360, $-1183.\overline{3}$), (720, $-2383.\overline{3}$)}
45a. {−6, −4, 0, 4, 6} **45b.** {−13, −8, −4, 4, 8, 13}
45c. {−5, 0, 4, 8, 13} **47a.** $D = \frac{m}{V}$ **47b.** silver and gasoline

49. Women

L	S	(L, S)
$9\frac{1}{3}$	6	$\left(9\frac{1}{3}, 6\right)$
$9\frac{5}{6}$	$7\frac{1}{2}$	$\left(9\frac{5}{6}, 7\frac{1}{2}\right)$
$10\frac{1}{6}$	$8\frac{1}{2}$	$\left(10\frac{1}{6}, 8\frac{1}{2}\right)$
$10\frac{2}{3}$	10	$\left(10\frac{2}{3}, 10\right)$

Men

L	S	(L, S)
$11\frac{1}{3}$	8	$\left(11\frac{1}{3}, 8\right)$
$11\frac{5}{6}$	$9\frac{1}{2}$	$\left(11\frac{5}{6}, 9\frac{1}{2}\right)$
$12\frac{1}{3}$	11	$\left(12\frac{1}{3}, 11\right)$
$12\frac{5}{6}$	$12\frac{1}{2}$	$\left(12\frac{5}{6}, 12\frac{1}{2}\right)$

51a.

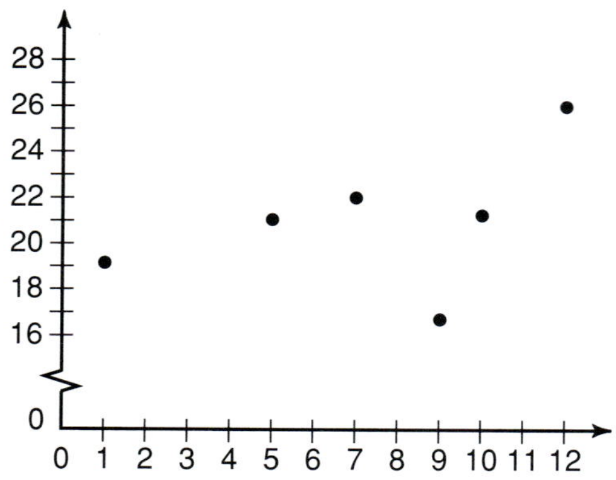

51b. The more years played, the higher the point per game average of the player. **53.** \$467.50 **55.** \$18,000
57a. $2w + 2\ell = 148$ **57b.** w, 14.25 in.; ℓ, 59.75 in.
59. −7.976

Page 280 Lesson 5–4A

1.

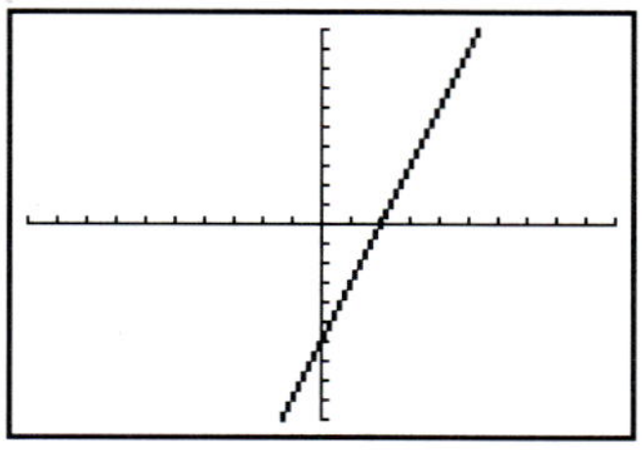

3.

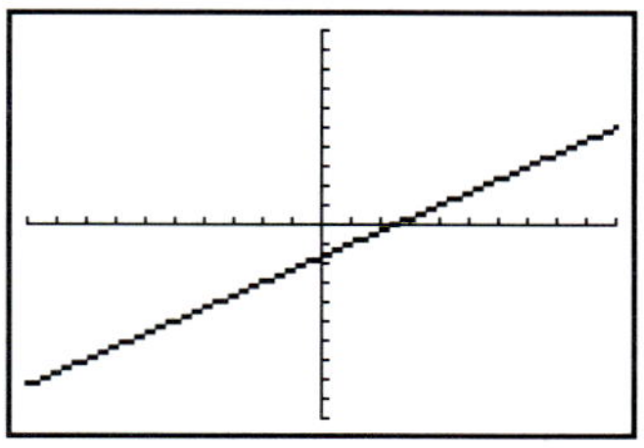

5.

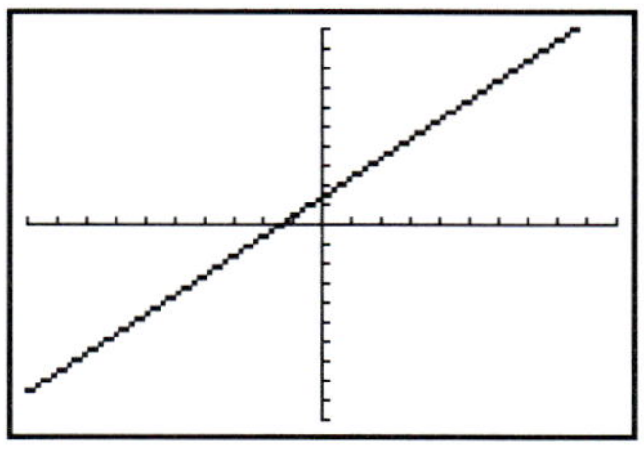

7a. Sample answer: $[-10, 110]$ by $[-5, 15]$

7b.

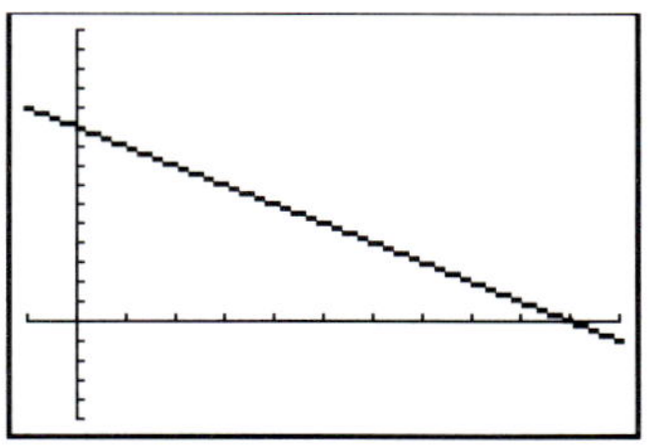

7c. Sample answer: (0, 10), (100, 0), (10, 9)

9a. Sample answer: $[-2.5, 0.5]$ by $[-0.05, 0.05]$

9b.

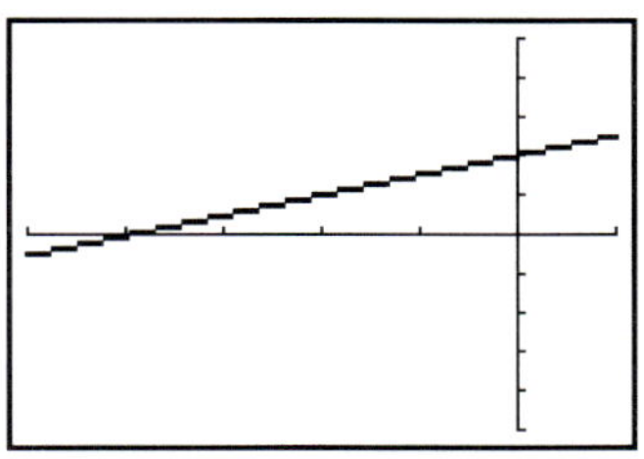

9c. Sample answer: $(-2, 0)$, (0, 0.02), (1, 0.03)

Pages 283–286 Lesson 5–4

7. yes; $2x + y = 6$ **9.** yes; $3x + 2y = 7$

11.

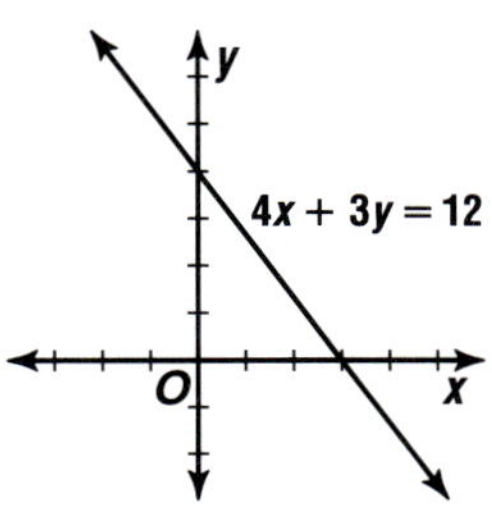

13.

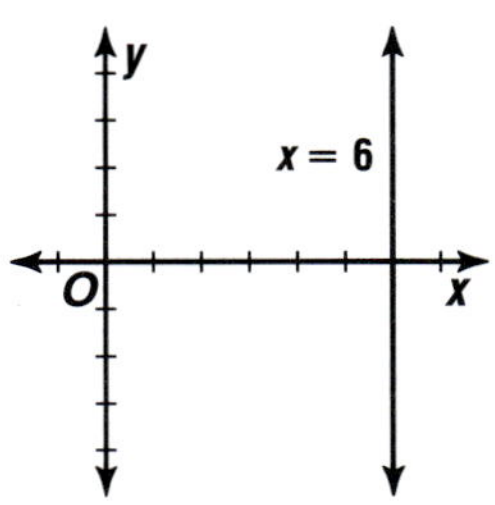

15.

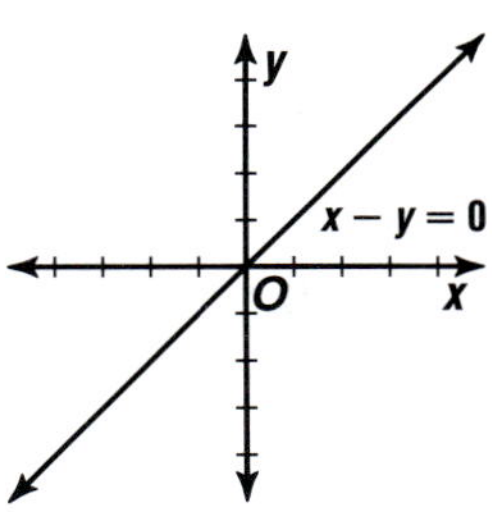

17. yes; $\frac{3}{5}x - \frac{2}{3}y = 5$ **19.** no **21.** yes; $3x - 2y = 8$ **23.** yes; $7x - 7y = 0$ **25.** yes; $3m - 2n = 0$ **27.** yes; $6a - 7b = -5$

29.

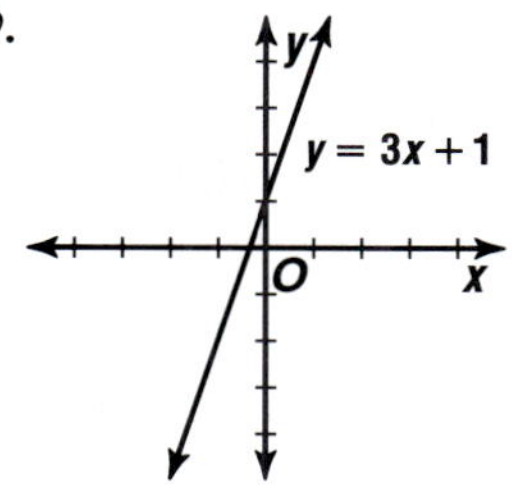

33.

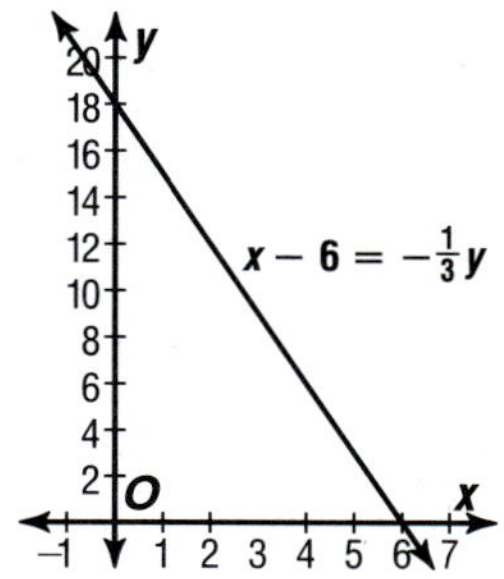

37.

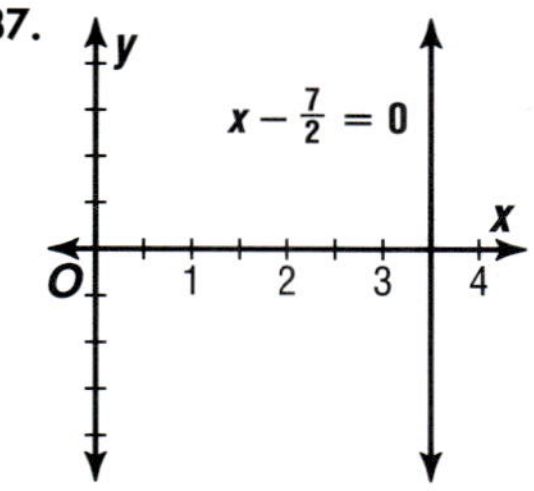

41.

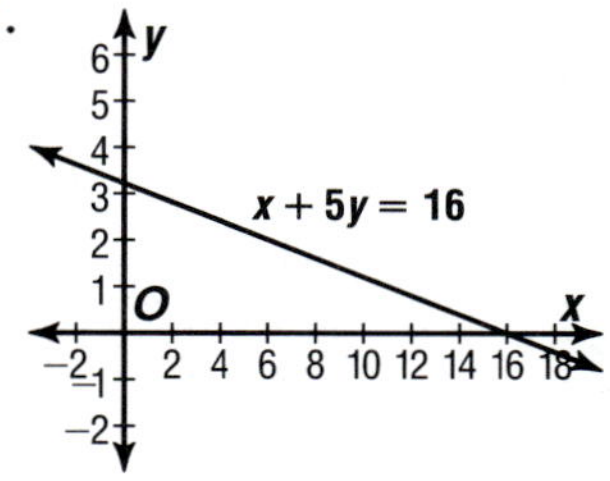

45.

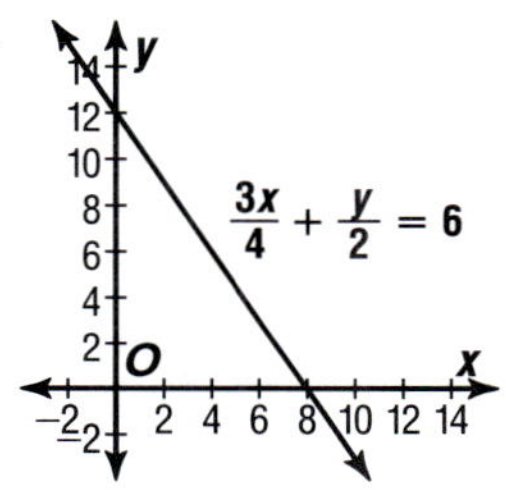

47. -5, 7.5 **49.** 6, 9, 10

51. $[-5, 15]$ by $[-10, 10]$, Xscl: 1, Yscl: 1

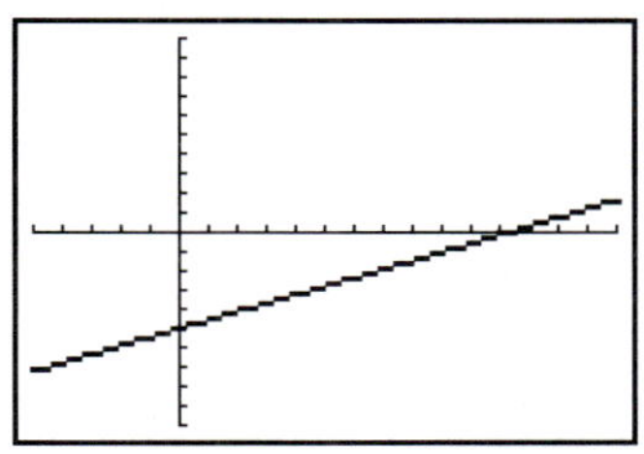

53. $[-10, 10]$ by $[-2, 2]$, Xscl: 1, Yscl: 0.25

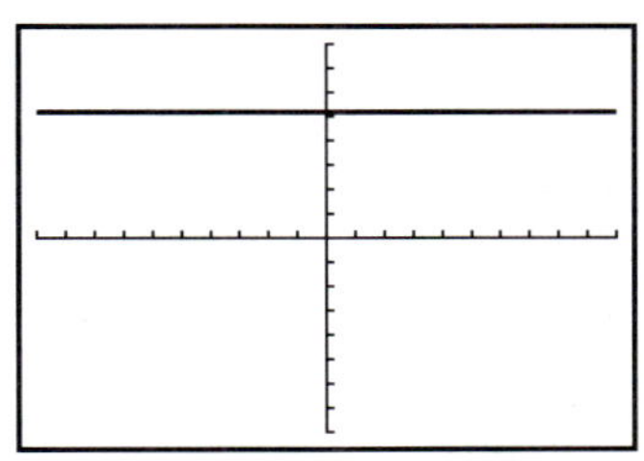

55. $[-5, 25]$ by $[-20, 5]$, Xscl: 5, Yscl: 5

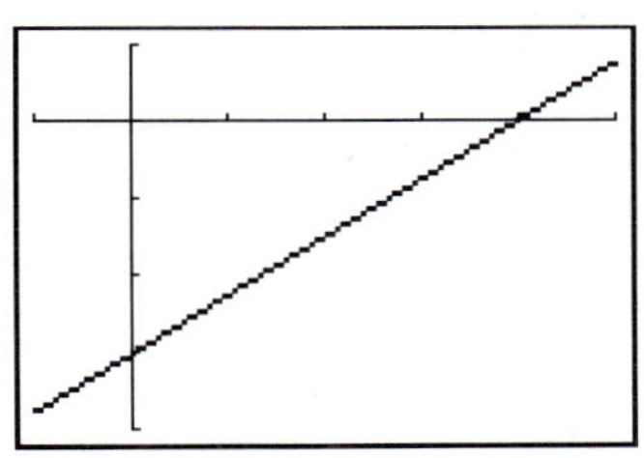

57a. Sample answer: Parallel lines that slant upward and intersect the x-axis at -7, -2.5, 0, and 4.5.

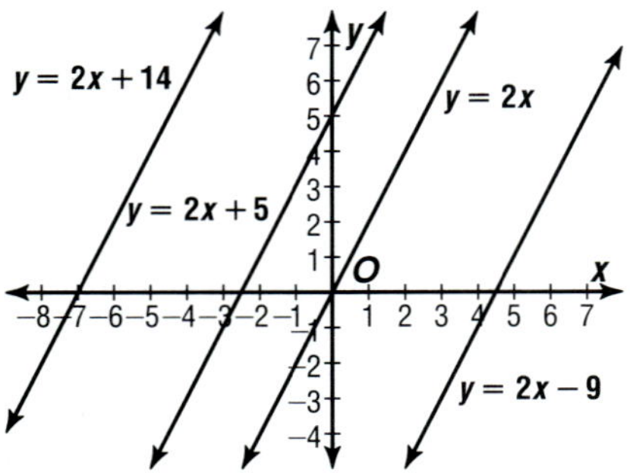

57b. Sample answer: Parallel lines that slant downward and intersect the x-axis at 0, $1\frac{1}{3}$, $2\frac{1}{3}$, and $-3\frac{1}{3}$.

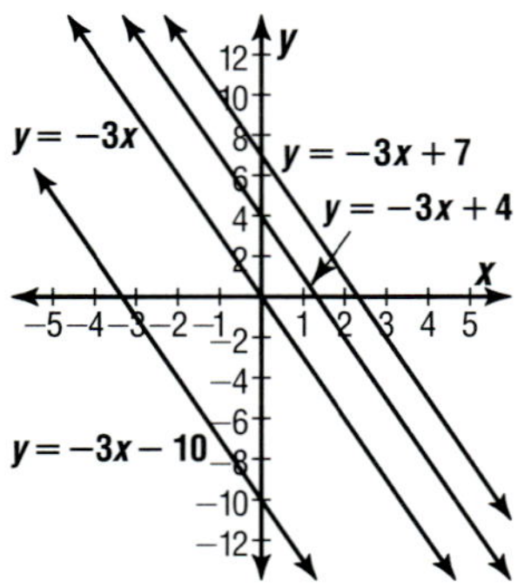

59a.

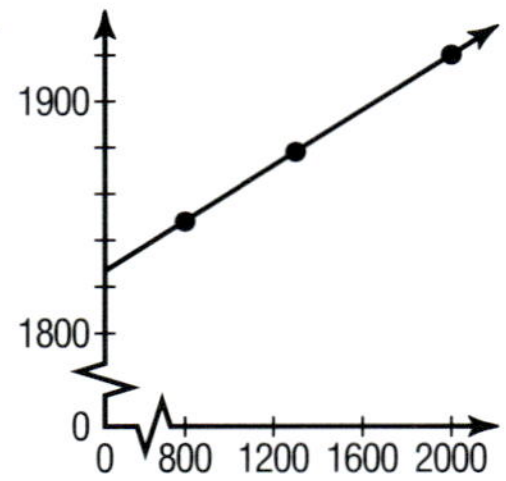

59b. yes, but only if her sales are \$1300 or \$2000 over target **61.** $y = 3 - 4x$

63a.

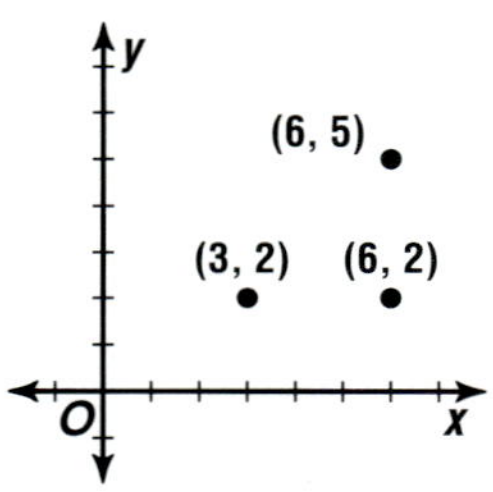

63b. (3, 5) **63c.** 12 inches **65.** 15% **67.** 120° **69.** $\frac{1}{48}$

Page 286 Self Test

1.

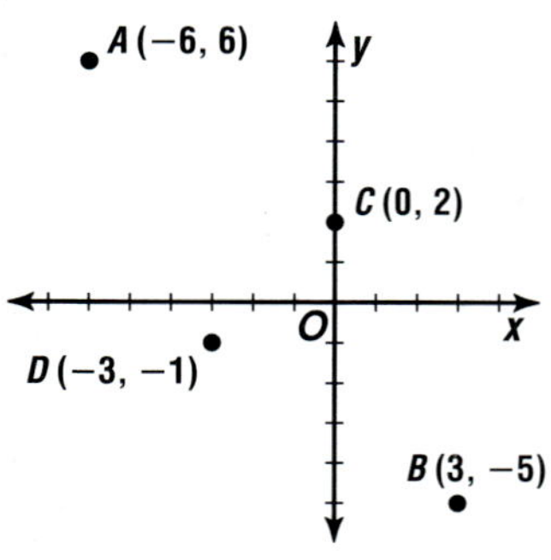

3. $\{(-5, -3), (-1, 4), (4, 4), (4, -3)\}$, D = $\{-5, -1, 4\}$, R = $\{-3, 4\}$, Inv = $\{(-3, -5), (4, -1), (4, 4), (-3, 4)\}$

5. $b = 3 - \frac{2}{3}a$: $\left\{\left(-2, 4\frac{1}{3}\right), \left(-1, 3\frac{2}{3}\right), (0, 3), \left(1, 2\frac{1}{3}\right), (3, 1)\right\}$

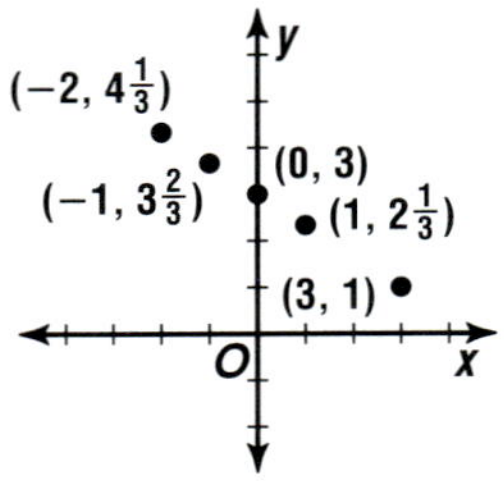

7.

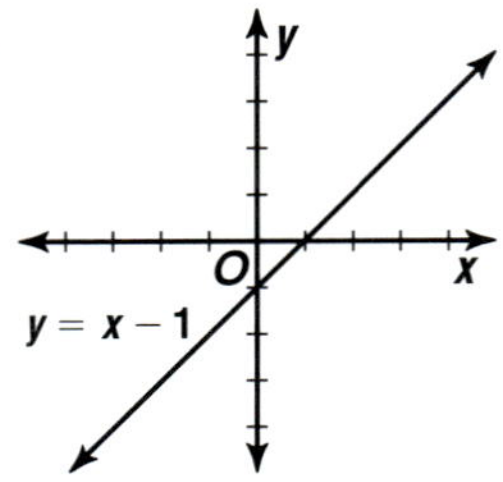

9.

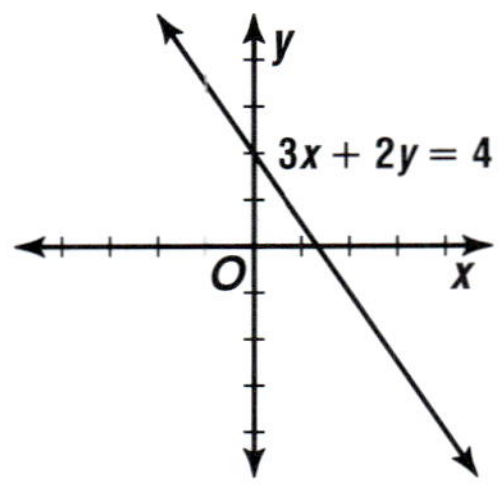

Pages 291–294 Lesson 5–5

7. no **9.** yes **11.** yes **13.** no **15.** -10 **17.** $3w + 2$ **19.** yes **21.** no **23.** yes **25.** yes **27.** yes **29.** yes **31.** yes **33.** no **35.** -14 **37.** $-\frac{9}{25}$ **39.** 5.25 **41.** -18 **43.** $9b^2 - 6b$ **45.** 3 **47.** $5a^4 - 10a^2$ **49.** $24p - 36$ **51a.** Sample answer: $f(x) = x$. **51b.** Sample answer: $f(x) = x^2$ **53.** a; sample answer: because they have a single price per shirt, and since you cannot have a fraction of a shirt, you must use points instead of lines. It is a function.

55a. D: $0 \le k \le 24$; R: $0 \le g \le 100$

55b.

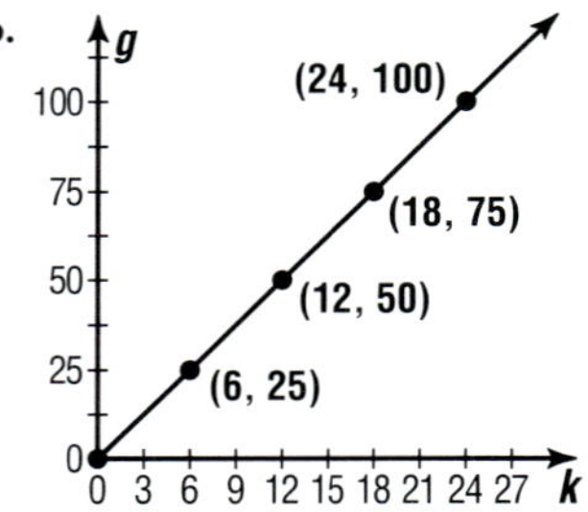

It is a line.

55c. 24 karats **57a.** \$260.87 **57b.** Sample equation: $B = \frac{3}{23}P$ **59.** $\{-16, -13, 5, 11\}$ **61.** $\frac{3}{13}$ **63.** 45° **65.** -48

67a.

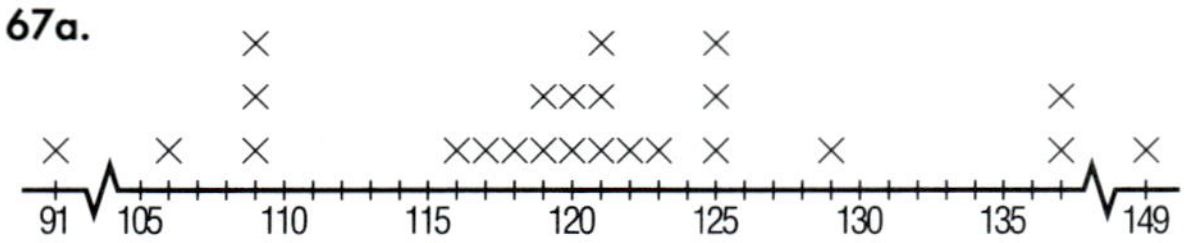

67b. 149 **67c.** 91 **67d.** 121 and 125 **67e.** 13 players

Pages 299–302 Lesson 5–6

5. $f(x) = 2x + 6$ **7.** $y = \frac{1}{2}x - \frac{3}{2}$ **9.** -6 **11.** 48, 60 **13.** 8, -2 **15.** $f(x) = 5x$ **17.** $g(x) = 11 - x$ **19.** $h(x) = \frac{1}{3}x - 2$ **21.** $y = -3x$ **23.** $y = \frac{1}{2}x$ **25.** $y = 2x - 10$ **27.** $xy = -24$ **29.** $y = x^3$ **31.** y-intercept: $f(0)$, x-intercept: $f(x) = 0$ **33a.** $f(x) = 34x - 34$ **33b.** You must go deeper in fresh water to get the same pressure as in ocean water. **35a.** 1514 C **35b.** 11.04 C/min

Page 355 Lesson 6–5A

1. All graphs are of the family $y = -ax + 0$, where a represents different negative slopes.

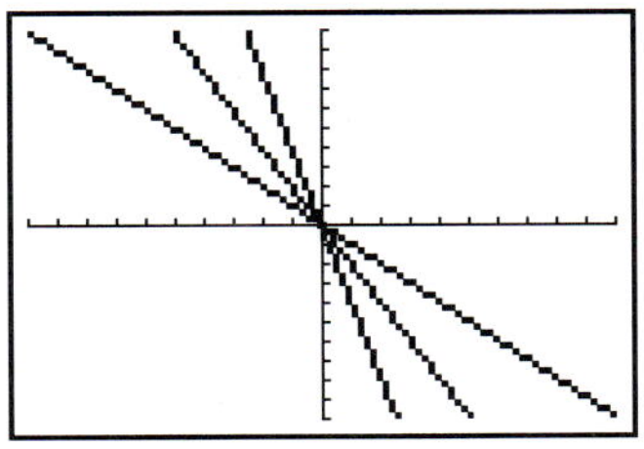

3. All graphs have the same slope, -1, but have different y-intercepts.

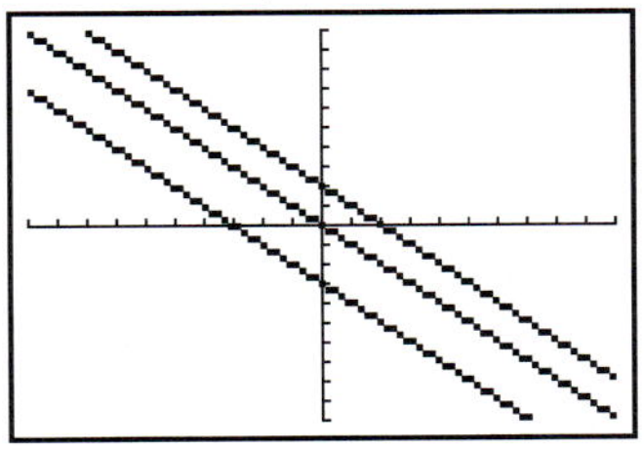

5.

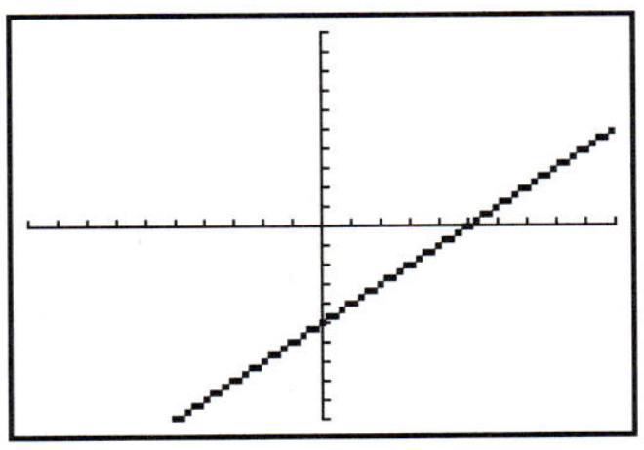

7.

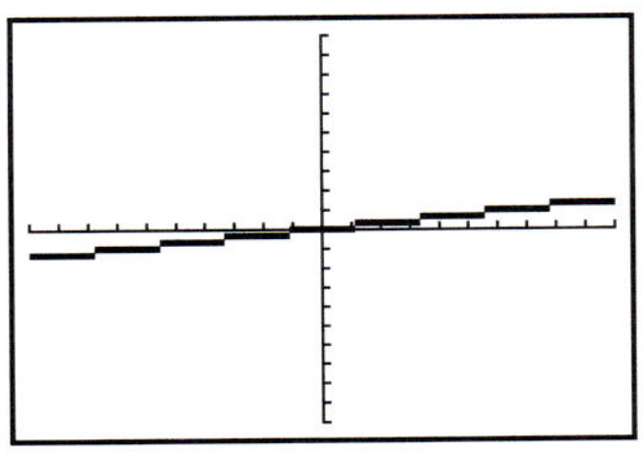

9. $y = -x + 2.5$

Pages 359–360 Lesson 6–5

7.

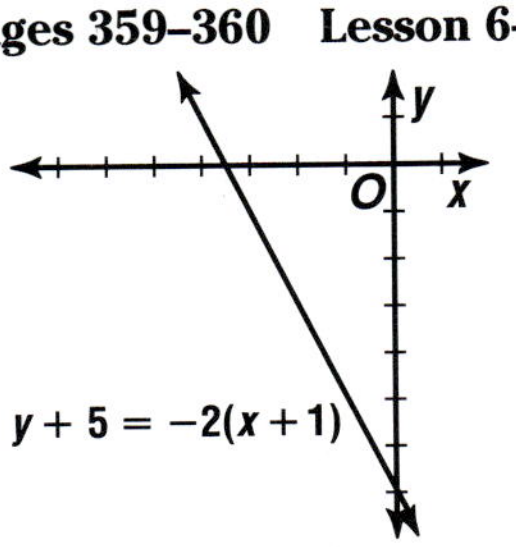

9.

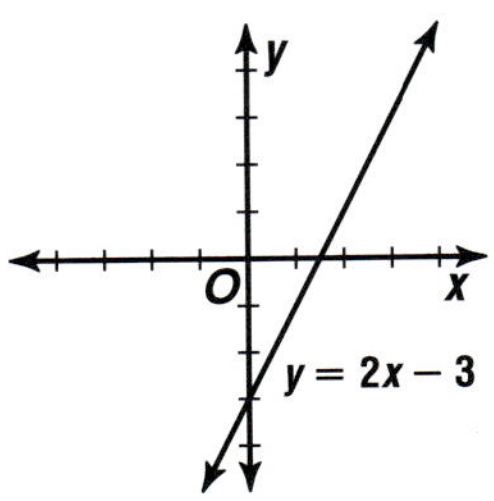

11.

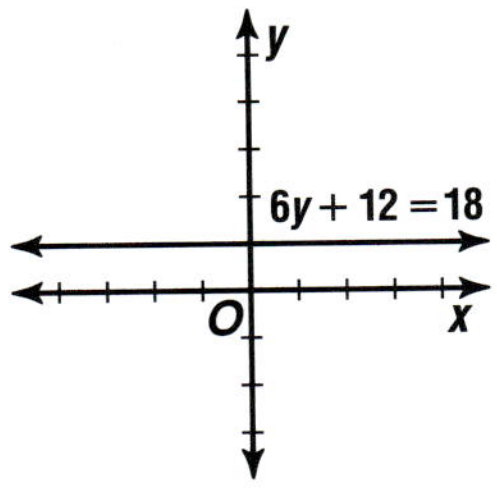

13a.

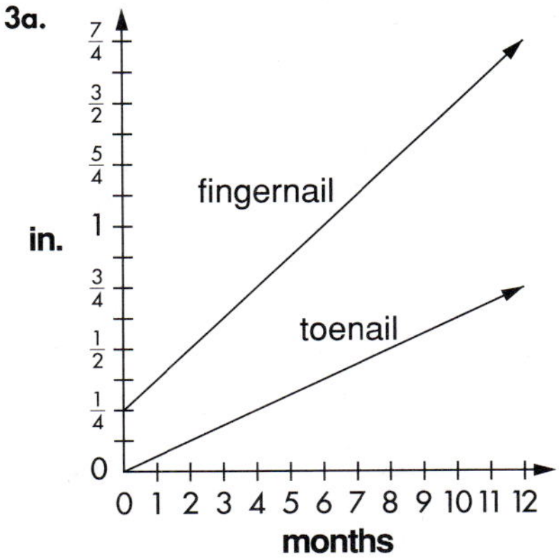

13b. $1\frac{3}{4}$ inches **13c.** $\frac{1}{16}$ inch **13d.** See 13a.

13e. the rate of growth per month

15.

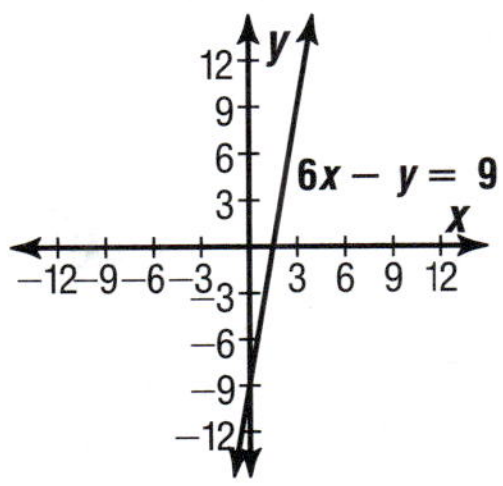

19.

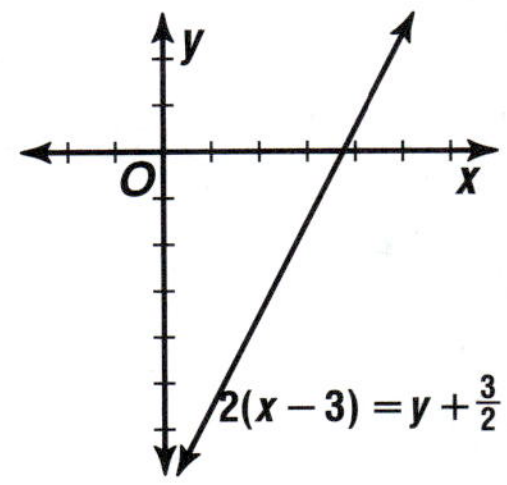

23.

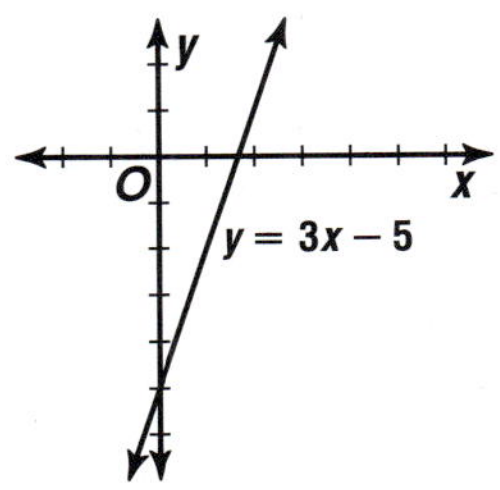

27.

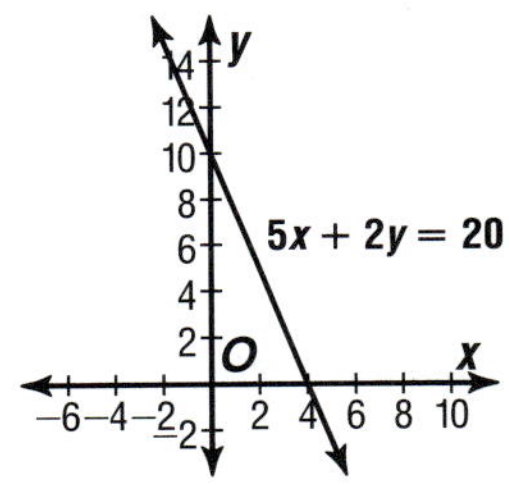

31.

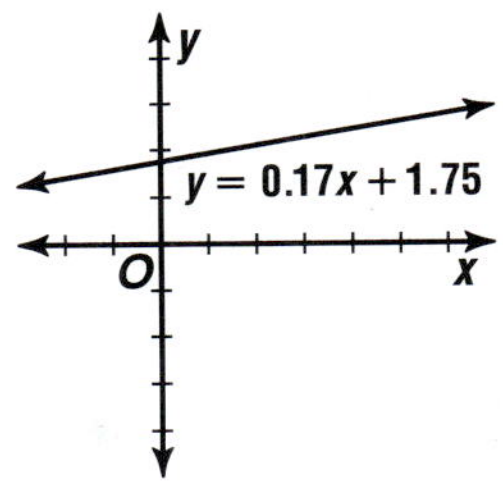

35.

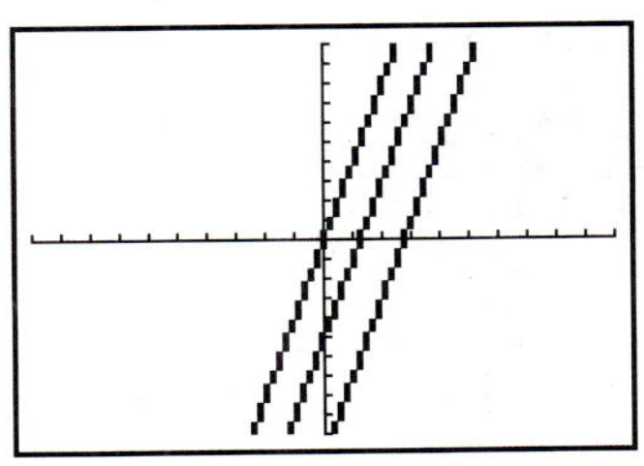

All lines have the same slope 4.

37a.

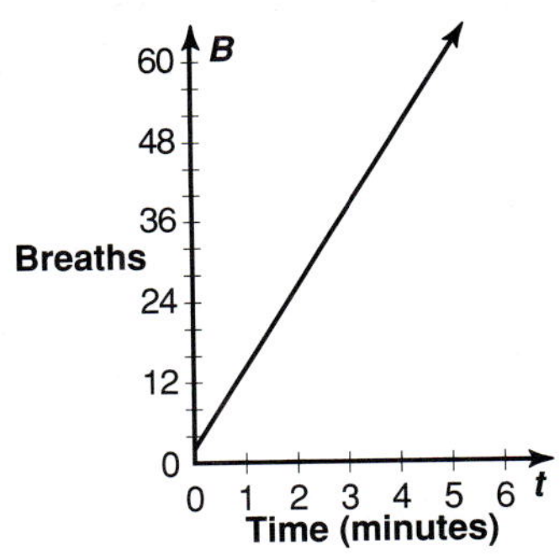

37b. 122 breaths

39. $y = \frac{2}{5}x + 12$

41. 4:30 P.M. **43.** 1.8

45. a number m minus 1

Pages 366–368 Lesson 6–6

7. $\frac{2}{3}, -\frac{3}{2}$ **9.** perpendicular **11.** $y = \frac{5}{6}x - \frac{21}{2}$

13. $y = x - 9$ **15.** $y = \frac{9}{5}x$ **17.** perpendicular

19. parallel **21.** perpendicular **23.** perpendicular

25. $y = x + 1$ **27.** $y = \frac{8}{7}x + \frac{2}{7}$ **29.** $y = 2.5x - 5$

31. $y = \frac{2}{3}x + 4$ **33.** $y = -\frac{9}{2}x + 14$ **35.** $y = 3x - 19$

37. $y = -\frac{1}{5}x - 1$ **39.** $y = -\frac{7}{2}x + 11$ **41.** $y = -3$

43. $y = \frac{5}{4}x$ **45.** $y = \frac{1}{3}x - 6$ **47.** No, because the slope of $\overline{AC}$ is $\frac{6}{7}$ and the slope of $\overline{BC}$ is $-\frac{2}{3}$. These slopes are not negative reciprocals of each other, so the lines are not perpendicular and the figure is not a rhombus. **49a.** $y = \frac{1}{2}x + \frac{7}{2}$, $y = -2x + 11$ **49b.** right or 90° angle

51.

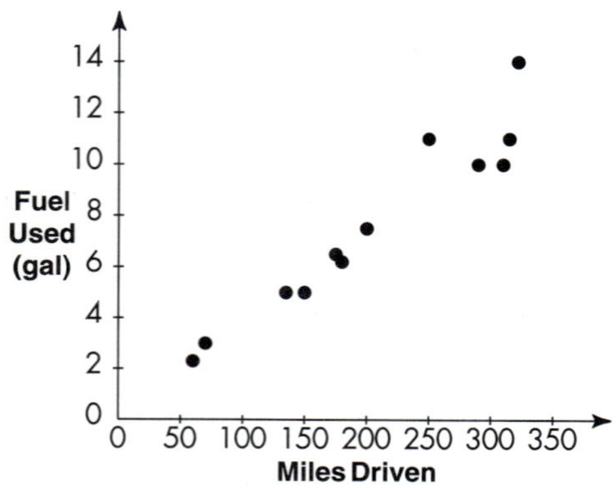

53. \$242.80 **55a.** $\frac{5}{12}; \frac{7}{12}$ **55b.** 16-karat gold

57. multiplicative identity

Pages 372–374 Lesson 6–7

5. (1.5, 6) **7.** (−6, 1) **9.** (−11, 7) **11.** (8, 9.8)

13. (12.5, 6) **15.** (1, 5) **17.** (3, 2) **19.** $\left(\frac{1}{2}, 1\right)$

21. (0.8, 2.7) **23.** (4*x*, 9*y*) **25.** (−7, 0) **27.** (21, −6)

29. (9, 10) **31.** $\left(\frac{5}{6}, \frac{1}{3}\right)$ **33.** *B*(2.3, 6.8) **35.** *P*(6.65, −1.85)

37. (−1, 5) **39.** $\left(1, \frac{5}{2}\right)$ **41a.** *N*(6, 3), *M*(10, 3)

41b. parallel, $MN = \frac{1}{2}AB$ **43a.** *P*(−4, 1), *Q*(10, −1), *R*(2, 9) **43b.** 62 square units; Sample answer: The area of the smaller triangle is $\frac{1}{2}bh$. Since the base of the larger triangle is twice that of the smaller one and the height is also twice the length of the small one, the area of the larger is $\frac{1}{2}(2b)(2h)$, or $2bh$. This is 4 times the area of the small one. **45.** $y = -\frac{7}{9}x - \frac{8}{3}$ **47.** yes; $9x - 6y = 7$

49. −20 **51.** $3.1x + 1.54$

Page 375 Chapter 6 Highlights

1. parallel **3.** midpoint **5.** perpendicular

7. slope-intercept **9.** slope

Pages 376–378 Chapter 6 Study Guide and Assessment

11. $-\frac{1}{3}$ **13.** $\frac{2}{5}$ **15.** $\frac{25}{3}$ **17.** $y + 3 = -2(x - 4)$

19. $y - 7 = 0$ **21.** $y - 3 = \frac{3}{5}x$ **23.** $y - 1 = -\frac{6}{7}(x - 4)$

25. $3x - y = 18$ **27.** $3x - 4y = 22$ **29.** $y = 5$ **31.** $x = -2$

33a. Yes; it is positive **33b.** Sample answer: 35 stories

33c. $y = 0.03x + 21$

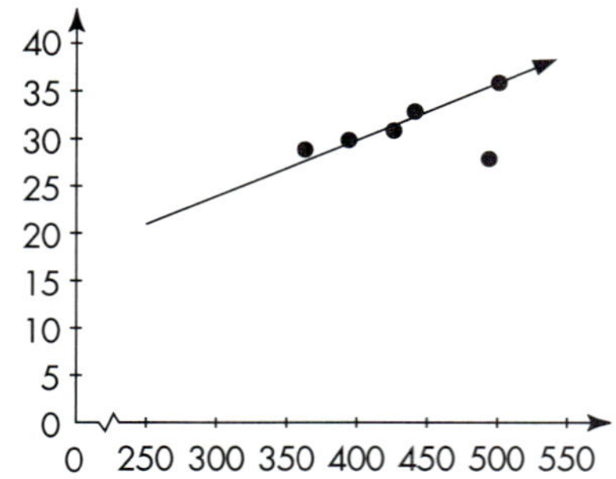

35. $y = -3x$

37. $y = 5.5$

39. −8, 4

41. −2, 12

43.

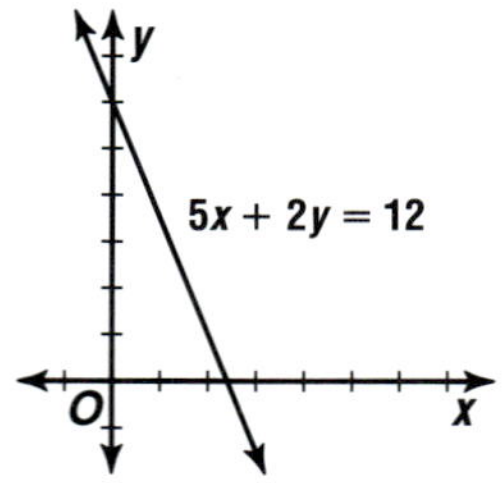

45.

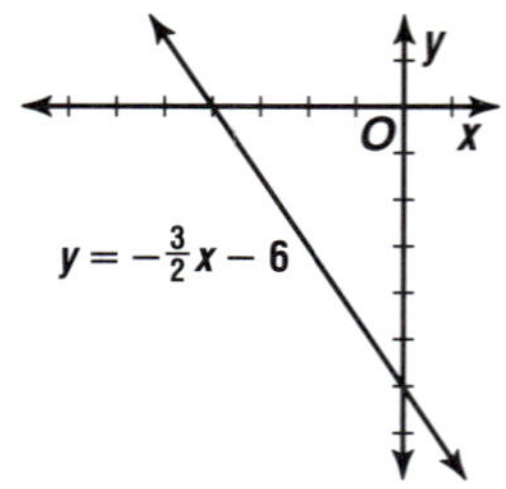

47.

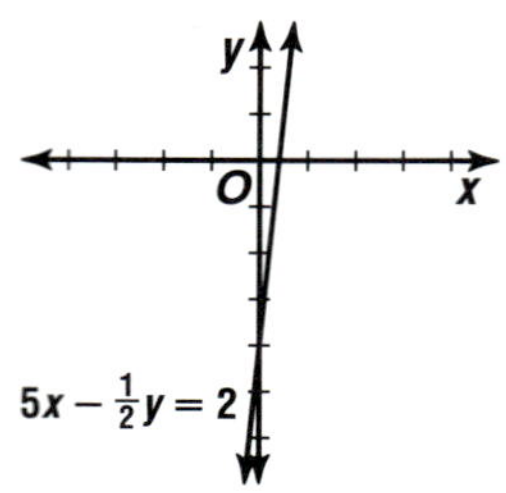

49.

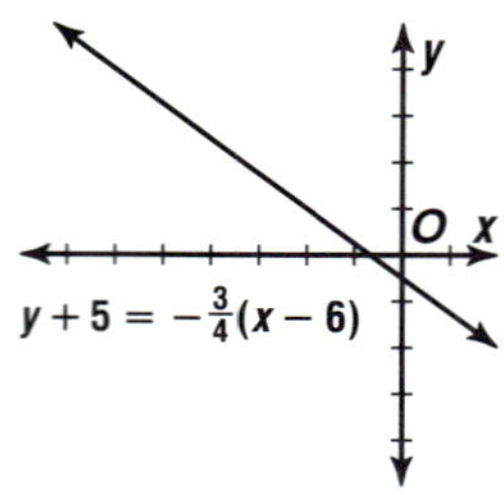

51. $y = -\frac{7}{2}x - 14$ **53.** $y = -\frac{3}{8}x \div \frac{13}{2}$ **55.** $y = 5x - 15$

57. $\left(1, -\frac{5}{2}\right)$ **59.** $\left(5, \frac{11}{2}\right)$ **61.** $\left(\frac{7}{2}, -\frac{3}{2}\right)$ **63.** (13, 11)

65. (−5, 20) **67.** $d = 45t - 10$

CHAPTER 7 SOLVING LINEAR EQUATIONS

Pages 388–390 Lesson 7–1

7. c **9.** d **11.** $\{x \mid x > -5\}$ **13.** $\{y \mid y < -5\}$

15. $x - 17 < -13$, $\{x \mid x < 4\}$

17. $\{a \mid a < 18\}$

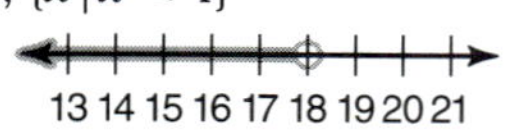

19. $\{x \mid x \le 1\}$

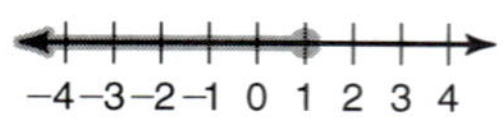

21. $\left\{x \mid x > \frac{11}{3}\right\}$

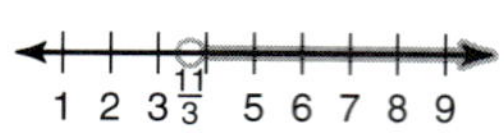

23. $\{x \mid x > 2\}$

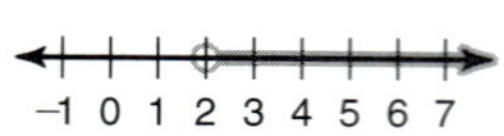

25. $\left\{x \mid x < \frac{3}{8}\right\}$ **27.** $\{x \mid x \le 15\}$ **29.** $\{x \mid x < 0.98\}$

31. $\{r \mid r < 10\}$ **33.** $x - (-4) \ge 9$, $\{x \mid x \ge 5\}$ **35.** $3x < 2x + 8$, $\{x \mid x < 8\}$ **37.** $20 + x < 53$, $\{x \mid x < 33\}$ **39.** $2x > x - 6$, $\{x \mid x > -6\}$ **41.** 12 **43.** −2 **45a.** no **45b.** yes **45c.** yes **45d.** yes **47.** The value of *x* falls between −2.4 and 3.6. **49a.** $x \le \$12.88$ **49b.** Sample answer: There may be sales tax on his purchases. **51.** $y = -3x + 3$ **53.** 42, 131, 145, 159, 28 **55.** 12 **57.** $<$

Page 391 Lesson 7–2A

1. Sample answer: The variable remains on the left, but the inequality symbol is reversed. **3.** When the coefficient of x is positive, you can solve the inequality like an equation and retain the same inequality symbol. If the coefficient of x is negative, you can solve like an equation, but the symbol must be reversed.

Pages 396–398 Lesson 7–2

9. multiply by $-\frac{1}{6}$ or divide by -6; yes; $\{y \mid y \leq 4\}$ **11.** multiply by 4; no; $\{x \mid x < -20\}$ **13.** $\{x \mid x < 30\}$ **15.** $\{t \mid t \leq -30\}$ **17.** $\frac{1}{5}x \leq 4.025$; $\{x \mid x \leq 20.125\}$ **19.** $s \geq 12$ **21.** $\{b \mid b > -12\}$ **23.** $\{x \mid x \geq -44\}$ **25.** $\{r \mid r < -6\}$ **27.** $\{t \mid t < 169\}$ **29.** $\{g \mid g \geq 7.5\}$ **31.** $\{x \mid x \geq -0.7\}$ **33.** $\left\{r \mid r < -\frac{1}{20}\right\}$ **35.** $\{x \mid x < -27\}$ **37.** $\{m \mid m \geq -24\}$ **39.** $36 \geq \frac{1}{2}x$; $\{x \mid x \leq 72\}$ **41.** $\frac{3}{4}x \leq -24$; $\{x \mid x \leq -32\}$ **43.** $-8x \leq 144$; -18 or greater **45.** $y < 7.14$ meters **47.** $\geq$ **49.** $<$ **51.** up to 416 miles **53.** at least 5883 signatures **55.** $(-1, 1)$ **57.** -2 **59.** \$155.64 **61.** 65 yd by 120 yd

Pages 402–404 Lesson 7–3

7. c **9.** $\{x \mid x > 2\}$ **11.** $\{d \mid d > -125\}$ **13.** $\{2, 3\}$ **15a.** $x + (x + 2) > 75$ **15b.** $x > 36.5$ **15c.** Sample answer: 38 and 40. **17.** $\{-10, -9, \ldots, 2, 3\}$ **19.** $\{-10, -9, \ldots, -5, -4\}$ **21.** $\{t \mid t > 3\}$ **23.** $\{w \mid w \leq 15\}$ **25.** $\{n \mid n > -9\}$ **27.** $\{m \mid m < 15\}$ **29.** $\{x \mid x < -15\}$ **31.** $\left\{p \mid p \leq \frac{14}{3}\right\}$ **33.** $\{x \mid x > -10\}$ **35.** $\{k \mid k \leq -1\}$ **37.** $\{y \mid y < -1\}$ **39.** $3(x + 7) > 5x - 13$; $\{x \mid x < 17\}$ **41.** $2x + 2 \leq 18$ for $x > 0$; 7 and 9; 5 and 7; 3 and 5; 1 and 3 **43.** no solution $\{\varnothing\}$ **45a.** $x \leq -8$ **45b.** $x > 8$ **45c.** $x > 2$ **45d.** $x \leq -1$ **47.** $x + 0.04x + 0.15(x + 0.04x) \leq \$50$, $x \leq \$41.80$ **49.** at least \$571,428.57 **51a.** at most 2.9 weeks **51b.** no change **51c.** at most 4.1 weeks **53.** $\{y \mid y > 10\}$ **55.** $3x + 2y = 14$ **57.** $\{-5, -3, -2, 4, 16\}$ **59.** 25.1; 23.5; no mode

Pages 409–412 Lesson 7–4

7. $0 \leq x \leq 9$ 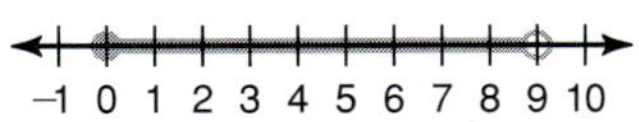

9. $-3 < x \leq 1$ **11.** The solution is the empty set. There are no numbers greater than 5 but less than -3.

13. $\{h \mid h \leq -7$ or $h \geq 1\}$ 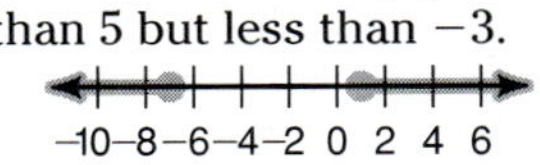

15. $\{w \mid 1 > w \geq -5\}$ 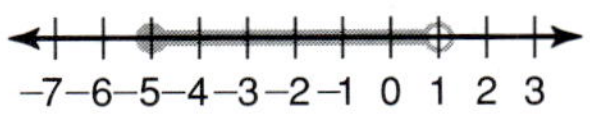

17. Drawings will vary; 16 pieces. **19.** $\varnothing$

21. 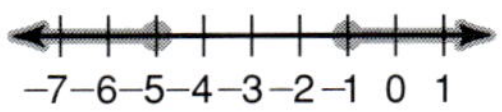 **23.** 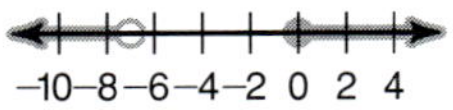

25. $-4 \leq x \leq 5$ **27.** $x \leq -2$ or $x > 1$

29. $\{x \mid -1 < x < 5\}$ 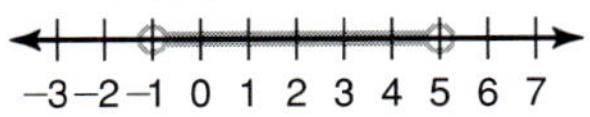

31. $\{x \mid x < -2$ or $x > 3\}$ 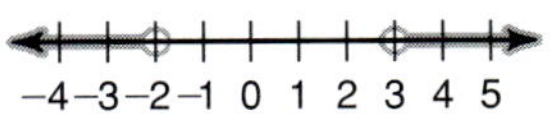

33. $\{c \mid c < 7\}$ 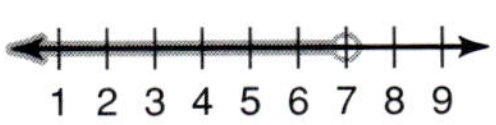

35. $\varnothing$

37. $\{x \mid x$ is a real number.$\}$ 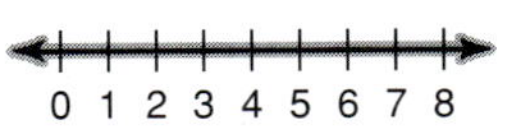

39. $\{y \mid y > 3$ and $y \neq 6\}$ 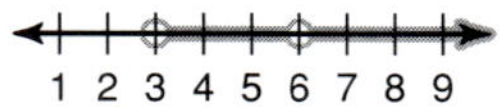

41. $\{x \mid x$ is a real number.$\}$ 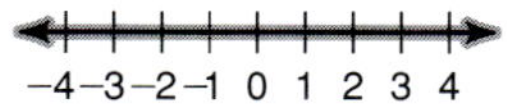

43. $\{w \mid w < 4\}$ 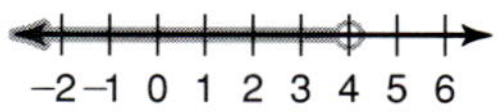

45. Sample answer: $x > 5$ and $x < -4$ **47.** $n + 2 \leq 6$ or $n + 2 \geq 10$; $\{n \mid n \leq 4$ or $n \geq 8\}$ **49.** $31 \leq 6n - 5 \leq 37$; $\{n \mid 6 \leq n \leq 7\}$

51. $\{m \mid -4 < m < 1\}$ 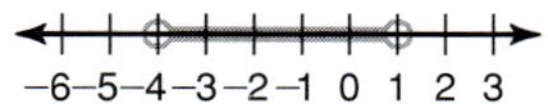

53a. $\{x \mid x < -7$ or $x > 1\}$ **53b.** $\{x \mid -5 \leq x < 1\}$ **55.** $-4 \leq x \leq -1.5$ or $x \geq 2$ **57.** $4.4 < x < 6.7$ **59.** $\left\{m \mid m \geq \frac{44}{3}\right\}$ **61.** -5

63.

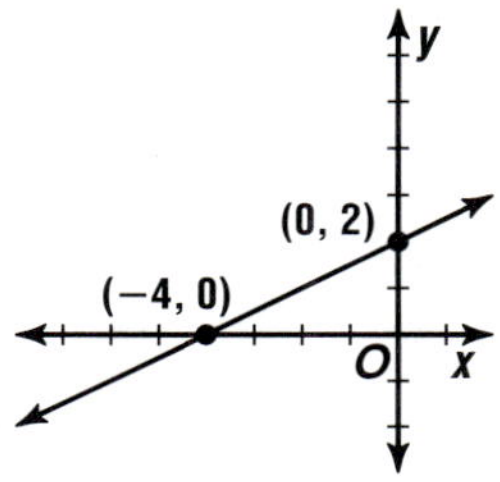

65. a little more than half a mile **67.** $18px - 15bg$

Page 412 Self Test

1. $\{y \mid y \geq -17\}$ **3.** $\{n \mid n < 4\}$ **5.** $\{g \mid g < -5\}$ **7.** c **9.** more than 17 points

Pages 415–419 Lesson 7–5

7a. outcomes from tree diagram: burger, soup, lemonade; burger, soup, soft drink; burger, salad, lemonade; burger, salad, soft drink; burger, french fries, lemonade; burger, french fries, soft drink; sandwich, soup, lemonade; sandwich, soup, soft drink; sandwich, salad, lemonade; sandwich, salad, soft drink; sandwich, french fries, lemonade; sandwich, french fries, soft drink; taco, soup, lemonade; taco, soup, soft drink; taco, salad, lemonade; taco, salad, soft drink; taco, french fries, lemonade; taco, french fries, soft drink; pizza, soup, lemonade; pizza, soup, soft drink; pizza, salad, lemonade; pizza, salad, soft drink; pizza, french fries, lemonade; pizza, french fries, soft drink **7b.** $\frac{1}{3}$ or $0.\overline{3}$ **7c.** $\frac{1}{12}$ or $0.08\overline{3}$ **7d.** $\frac{1}{24}$ or $0.041\overline{6}$ **9a.** 15 **9b.** $\frac{1}{5}$ or 0.2 **11.** $\frac{1}{3}$ or $0.\overline{3}$ **13a.** R3-G5, R3-R10, R3-B10, R3-G1, R3-Y14, B3-G5, B3-R10, B3-B10, B3-G1, B3-Y14, R5-G5, R5-R10, R5-B10, R5-G1, R5-Y14, R14-G5, R14-R10, R14-B10, R14-G1, R14-Y14, Y10-G5, Y10-R10, Y10-B10, Y10-G1, Y10-Y14 **13b.** $\frac{3}{25}$ or 0.12 **13c.** $\frac{2}{25}$ or 0.08 **13d.** 0 **13e.** $\frac{14}{25}$ or 0.56 **15a.** about 5.6% **15b.** about 26.3% **17.** 32% **19.** between 83 and 99, inclusive **21.** 3; -9 **23a.** 50° **23b.** 130° **23c.** yes

Pages 423–426 Lesson 7–6

5. c **7.** c **9.** d

11. $\{m \mid m \leq -5$ or $m \geq 5\}$ 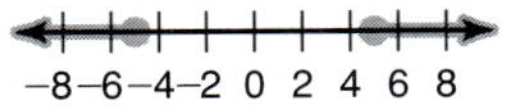

13. $\{r \mid -9 < r < 3\}$ 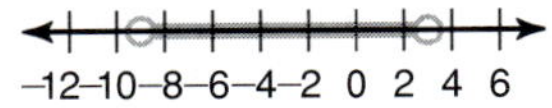

15. $|x| = 2$

17. $\{-2, 6\}$ 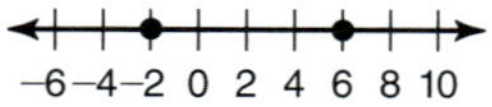

19. $\varnothing$

21. $\{y \mid 1 \leq y \leq 3\}$ 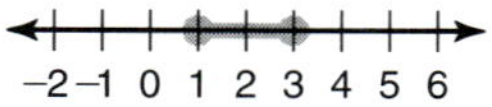

23. $\varnothing$

25. $\left\{e \mid \frac{5}{3} < e < 3\right\}$ 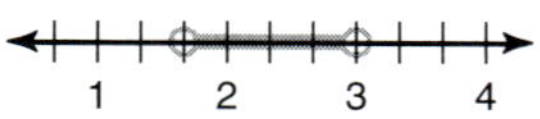

27. $\{y \mid y$ is a real number.$\}$ 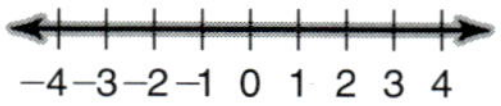

29. $\{w \mid 0 \leq w \leq 18\}$ 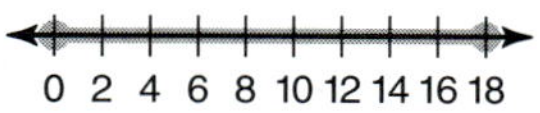

31. $\{-2, 3\}$ 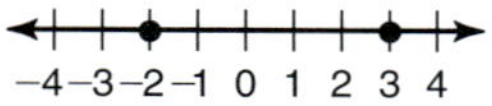

33. $\left\{x \mid x \leq -\frac{8}{3} \text{ or } x \geq 4\right\}$ 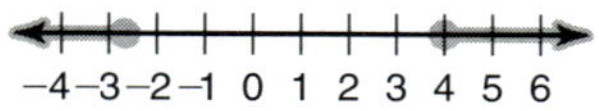

35. $|p - 1| \leq 0.01$ **37.** $|t - 50| > 50$ **39.** $|x + 1| = 3$ **41.** $|x - 1| \leq 1$ **43.** $|x - 8| \geq 3$ **45.** $\{-2, -1, 0, 1, 2\}$ **47.** $2a + 1$ **49.** always; never; $|a| \geq 0$, so $-|a| \leq 0$ **51.** $\frac{8}{13}$ or 0.61 **53.** no; $52 \leq s \leq 66$ **55.** $\$16{,}500 \leq p \leq \$18{,}000$ **57a.** Outcomes from tree diagram: BBBB, BBBG, BBGB, BBGG, BGBB, BGBG, BGGB, BGGG, GBBB, GBBG, GBGB, GBGG, GGBB, GGBG, GGGB, GGGG **57b.** $\frac{1}{16}$ or 0.0625, regardless of gender **57c.** $\frac{3}{8}$ or 0.375 **59.** $\{x \mid x \geq -1\}$ **61.** $\{k \mid k \geq -15\}$

63.

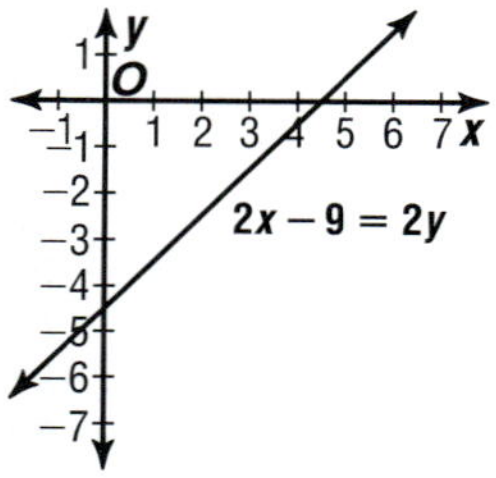

65. $m = -6 - \frac{n}{2}$

Pages 430–432 Lesson 7–7

7a. A; 25, 65, 30, 60, 40; B; 20, 70, 40, 60, 45 **7b.** B **7c.** A **7d.** B **9a.** Q2 = 6.5, Q3 = 16, Q1 = 5, IQR = 11 **9b.** no

9c.

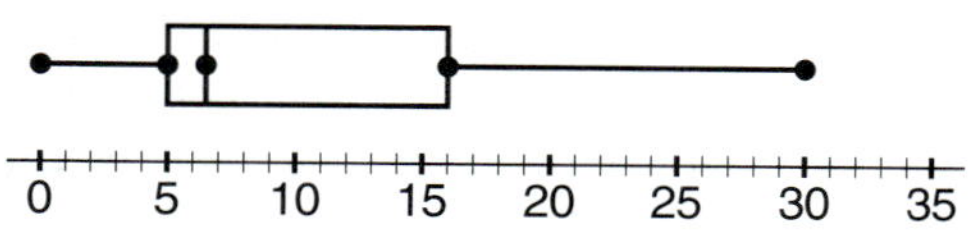

11a.

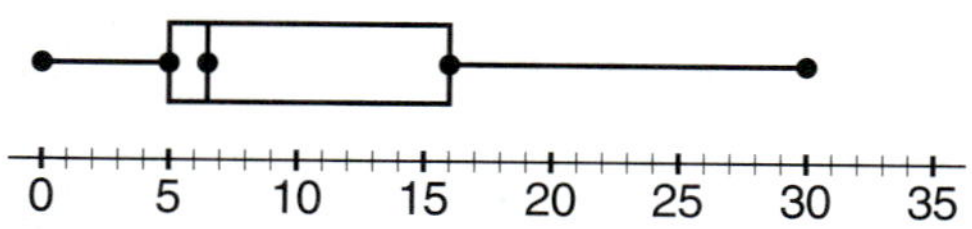

11b. clustered with lots of outliers **11c.** There are four western states that have more American Indian people than other states. **11d.** It is greater than the median.

13a.

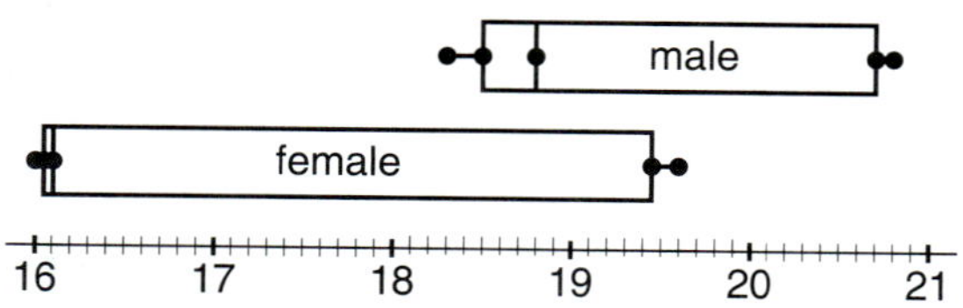

13b. 1990 **15.** Sample answer: Class A appears to be a more difficult class than B because the students don't do as well. **17.** $\{m \mid m > 1\}$

19.

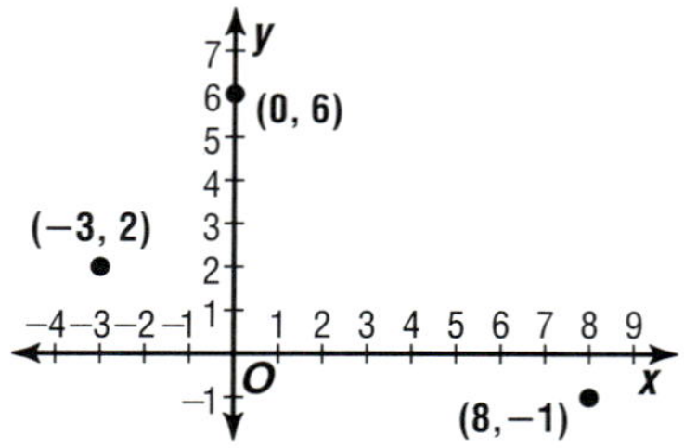

Page 434 Lesson 7–7B

1. women identifying objects with their left hands **3.** The left hand data are more clustered. **5.** males

Page 435 Lesson 7–8A

1.

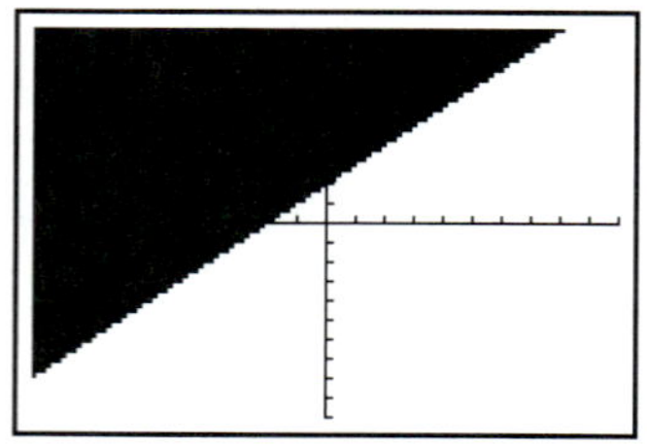

3.

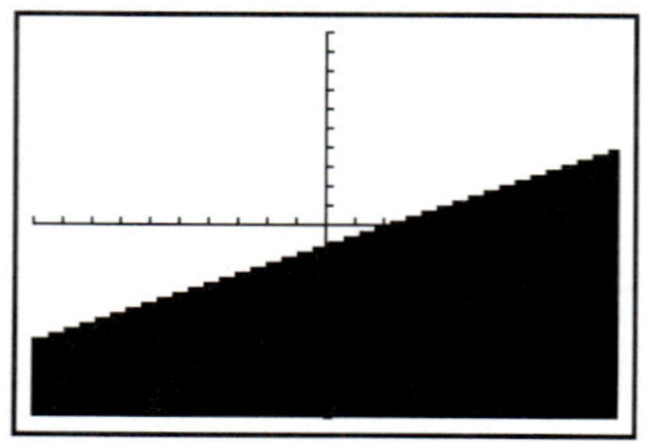

5.

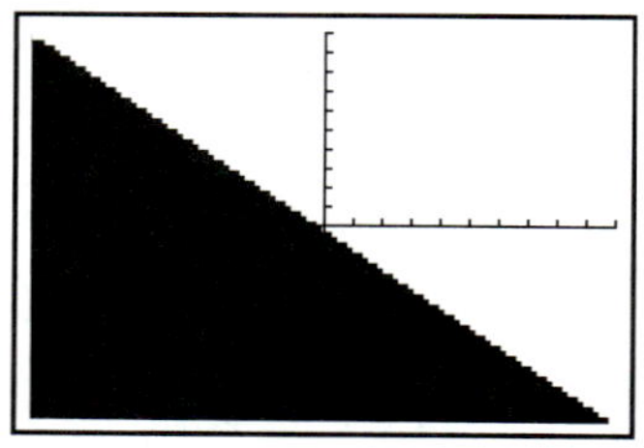

7.

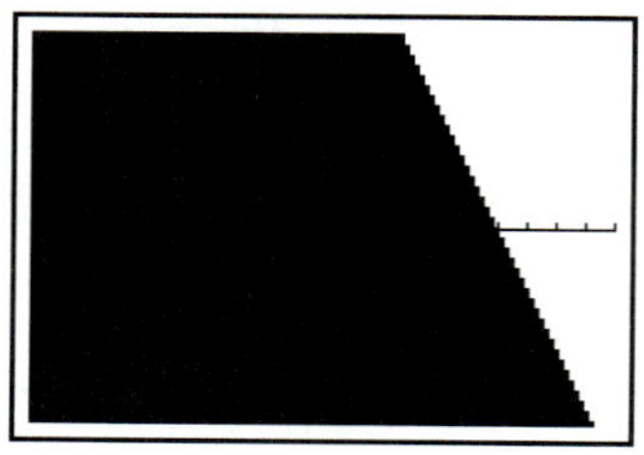

9.

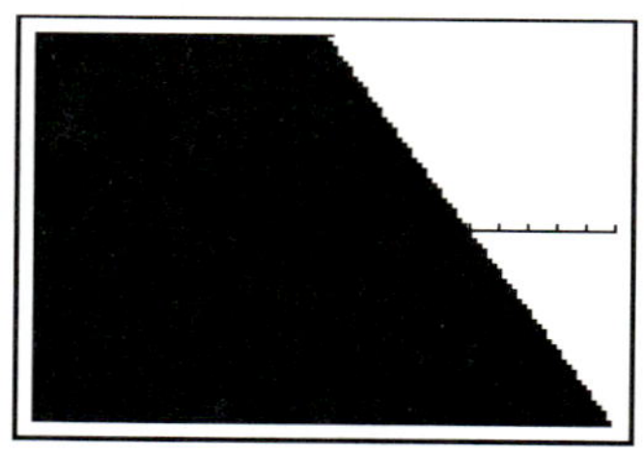

Page 439–441 Lesson 7–8

5. a **7.** b **9.** a, c; no

11. 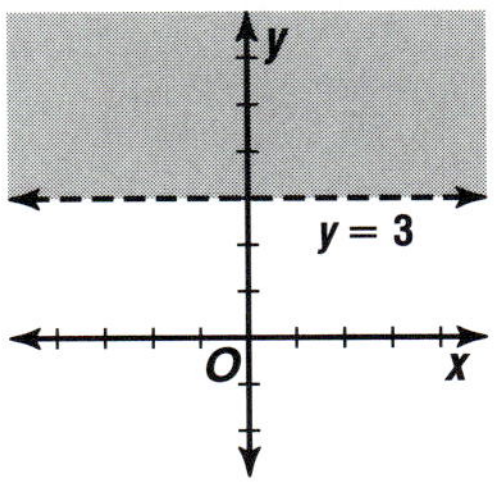

13. 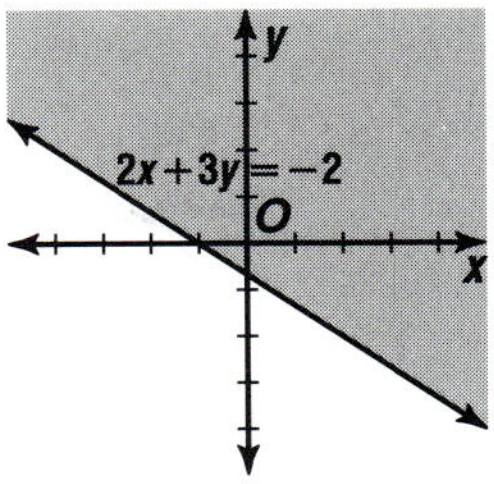

15. 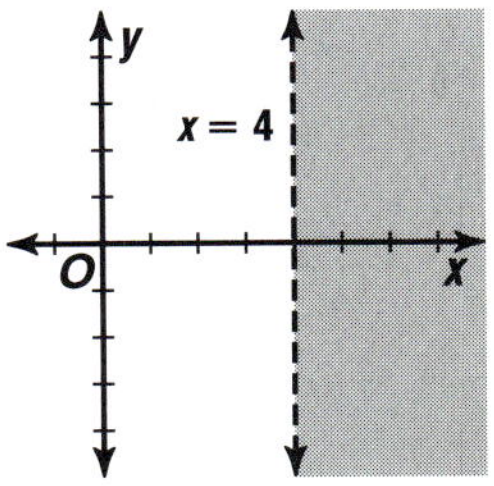

17. 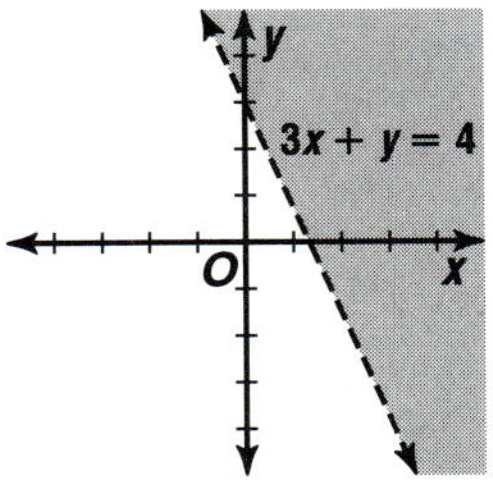

19. {(1, 1), (1, 2)} **21.** ∅

23. 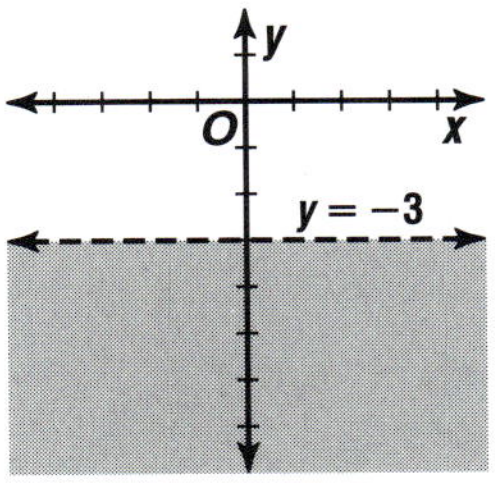

25. 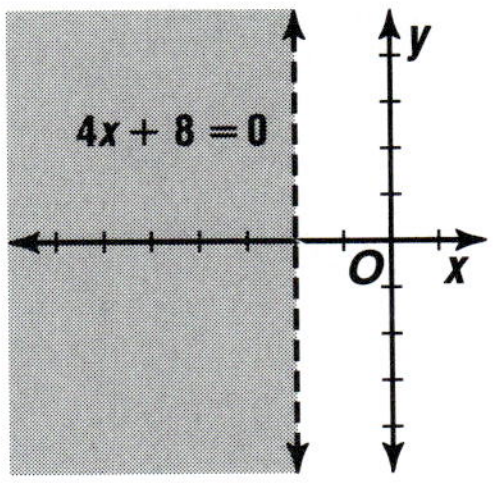

27. 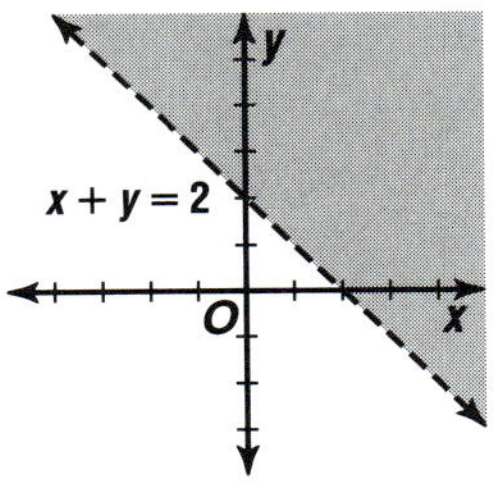

29. 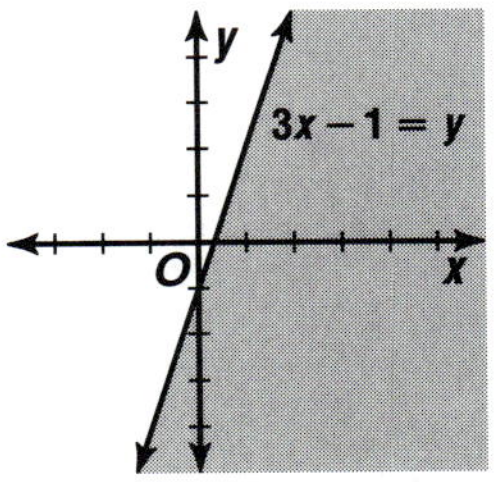

31. 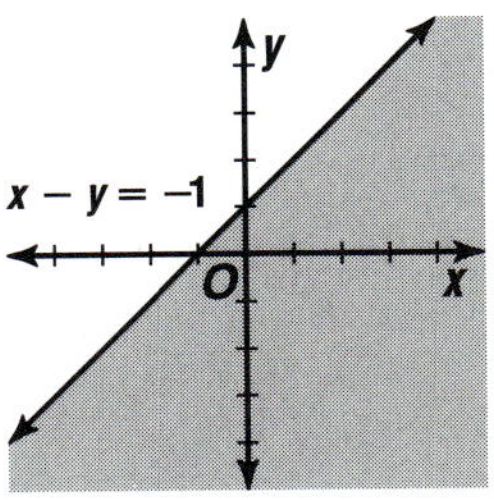

33. 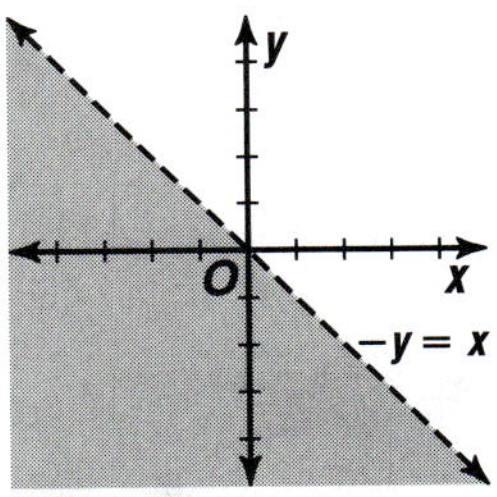

35. 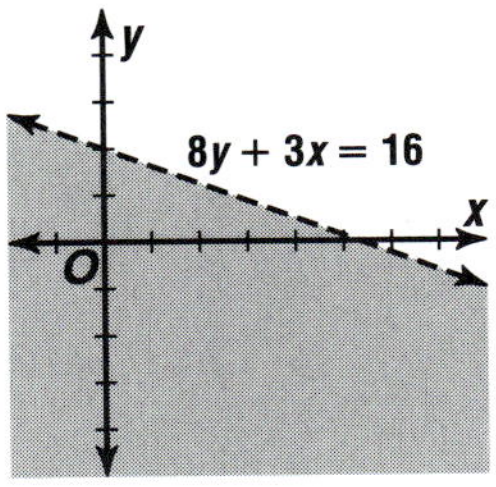

37. 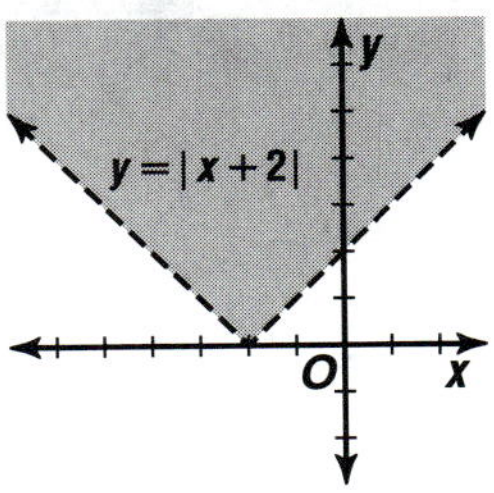

39. 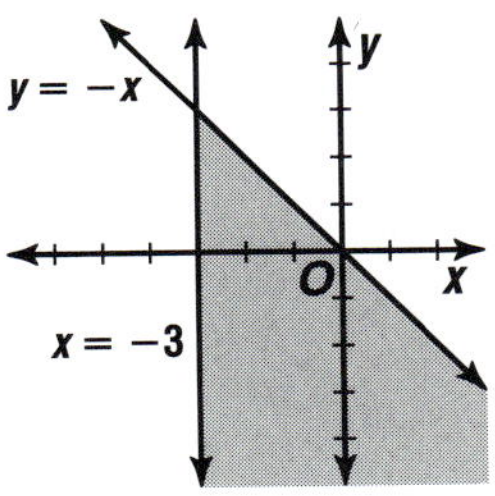

41. 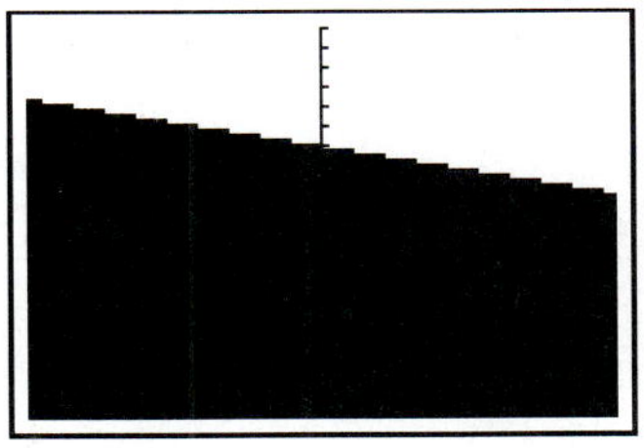

43. c **45.** a, b, d **47a.** $0.7(220 - a) \leq z \leq 0.8(220 - a)$ **47b.** $32 \leq z \leq 37$ **47c.** improve cardiovascular conditioning

49. 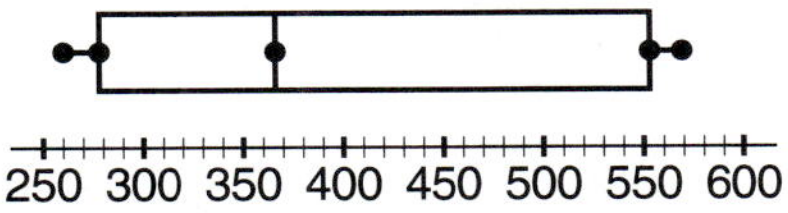

51. $y = 4x - 2$

53. 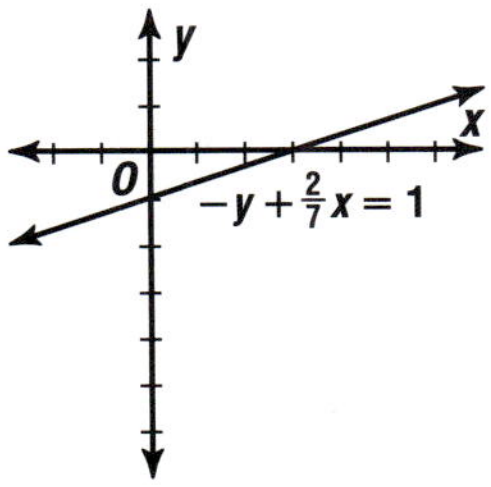

55. \$138.22

Page 443 Chapter 7 Highlights

1. h **3.** i **5.** c, f **7.** d **9.** g **11.** a

Pages 444–446 Chapter 7 Study Guide and Assessment

13. $\{n \mid n > -35\}$ **15.** $\{p \mid p \leq -18\}$ **17.** $3n > 4n - 8$, $\{n \mid n < 8\}$ **19.** $\{w \mid w \leq -15\}$ **21.** $\{x \mid x > 32\}$ **23.** $-\frac{3}{4}n \leq 30$, $\{n \mid n \geq -40\}$ **25.** $\{-5, -4, \ldots 0, 1\}$

27. $\left\{y \mid y \leq -\frac{9}{2}\right\}$ **29.** $\left\{x \mid x > -\frac{5}{2}\right\}$ **31.** $\{z \mid z \leq 20\}$

33. $\{a \mid a$ is a real number$\}$ 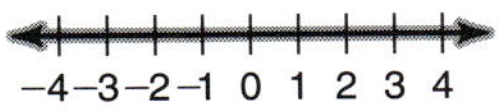

35. $\{b \mid b \leq 5\}$ 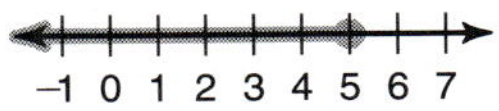

37a. $\frac{2}{7}$ **37b.** $\frac{1}{2}$ **37c.** $\frac{2}{7}$ **37d.** 0 **37e.** $\frac{3}{14}$ **37f.** $\frac{1}{14}$

39. $\{y \mid y > -5$ or $y < -5\}$ 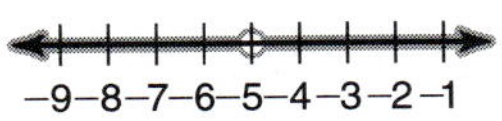

41. $\{k \mid 3 \geq k \geq -4\}$ 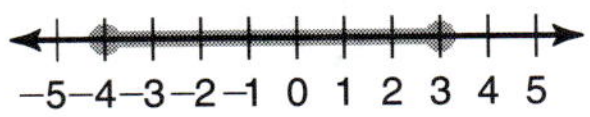

43. $\left\{y \mid y \geq \frac{21}{5}\text{ or } y \leq 1\right\}$ 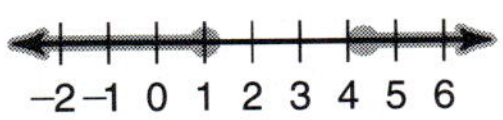

45. 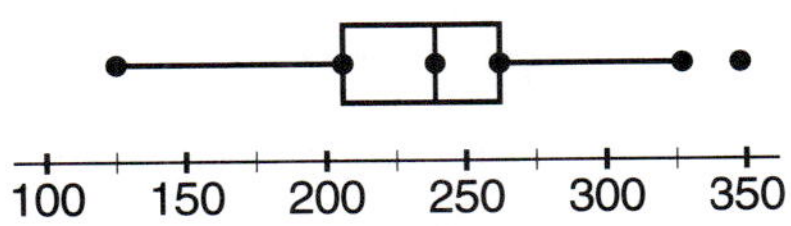

47. {(2, −1), (−1, 1)} **49.** {(5, 10), (3, 6)}

51. 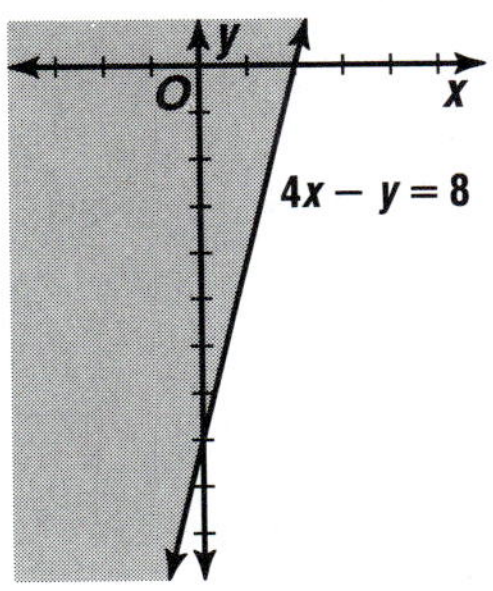

53. 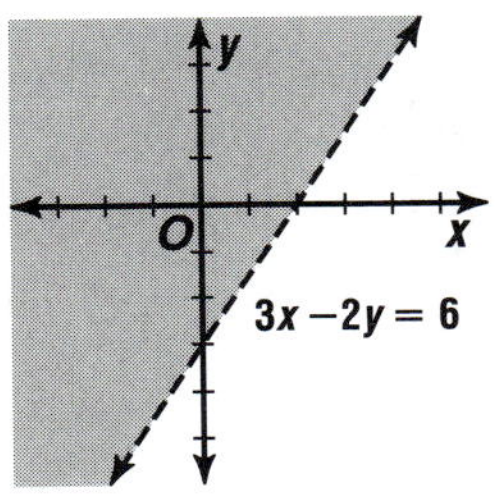

55. 17 to 20 books

CHAPTER 8 SYSTEMS OF LINEAR EQUATIONS AND INEQUALITIES

Page 453 Lesson 8–1A
1. (1, 8) **3.** (2.86, 4.57) **5.** (2.28, 3.08) **7.** (−2.9, 5.6) **9.** (1.14, −3.29)

Pages 458–461 Lesson 8-1
9. no solution **11.** one; (−6, 2) **13.** yes
15. (3, 5)

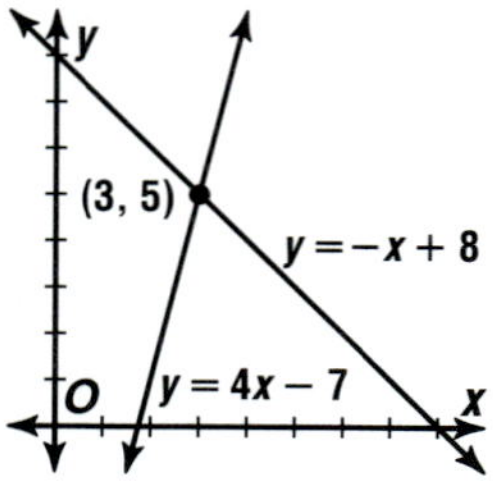

17. (2, −6)

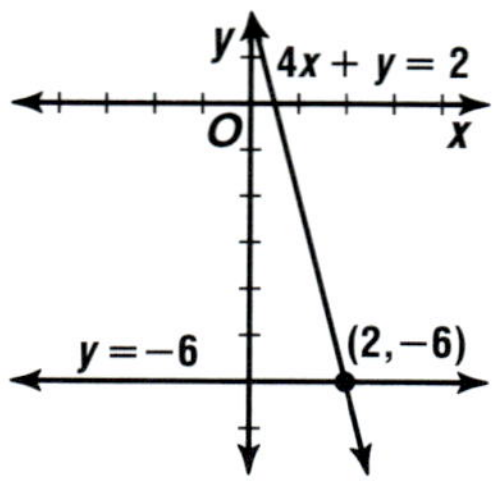

19. (−6, 8)

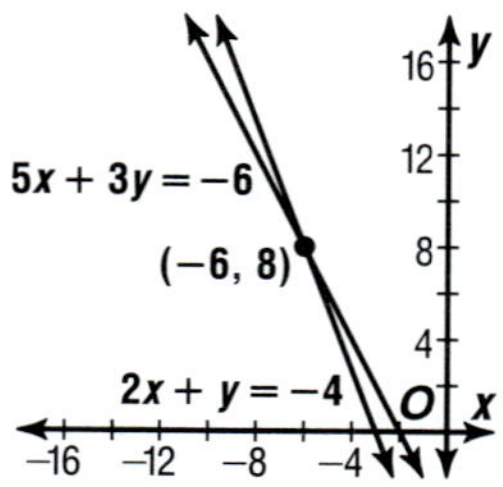

21. one, (3, −1) **23.** no solution **25.** one, (3, 3)

27. (2, −2)

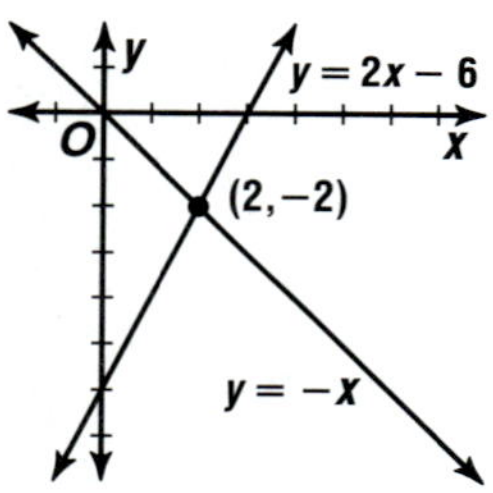

29. (−1, 3)

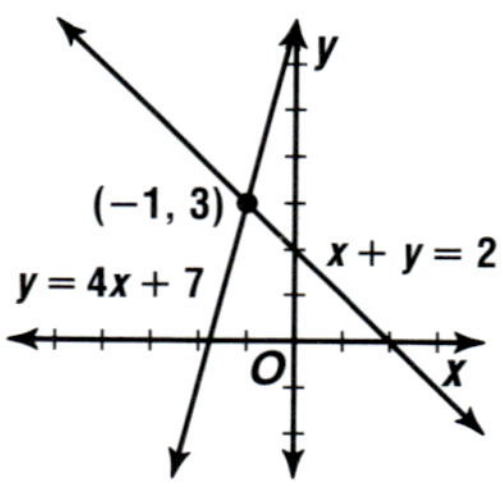

31. (−2, 4)

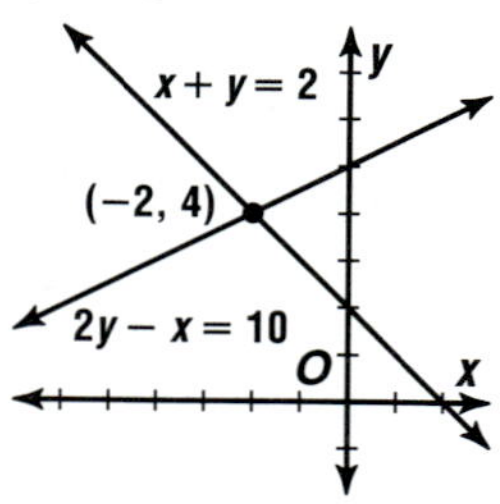

33. (2, 0)

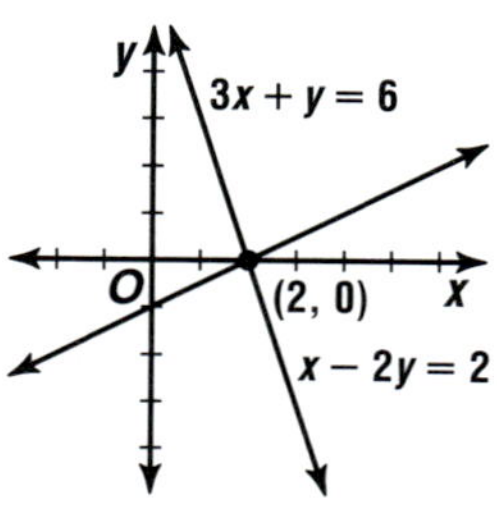

35. infinitely many

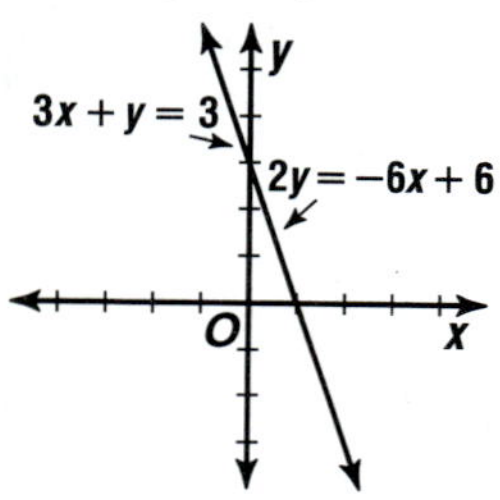

37. no solution

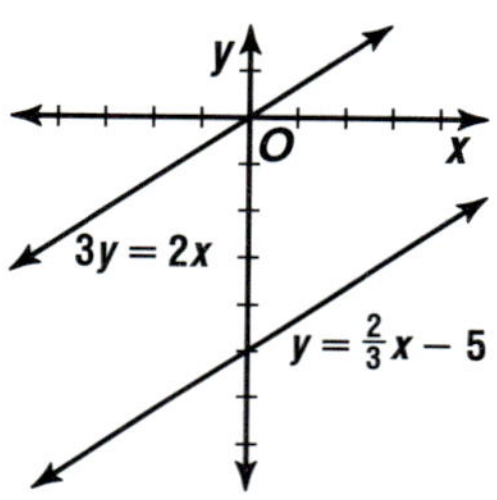

39. (8, 6)

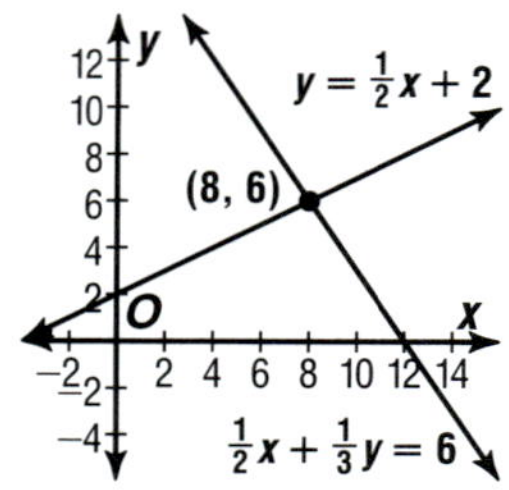

41. infinitely many

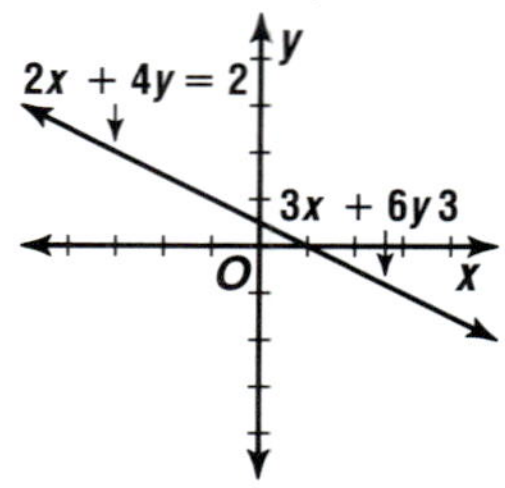

43. 15 square units

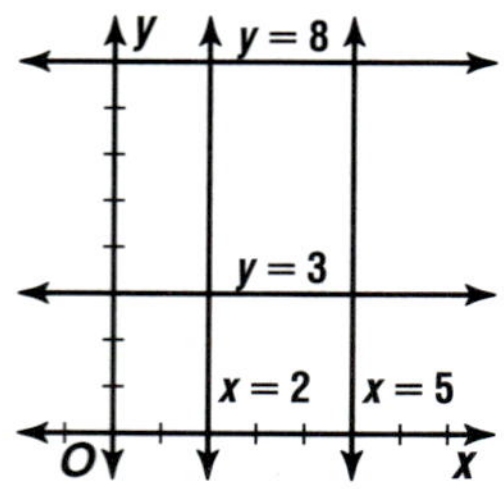

45. (1.71, −2.57)
47. (−0.25, −3.25)
49. $A = -3, B = 2$

51. A.D. 376

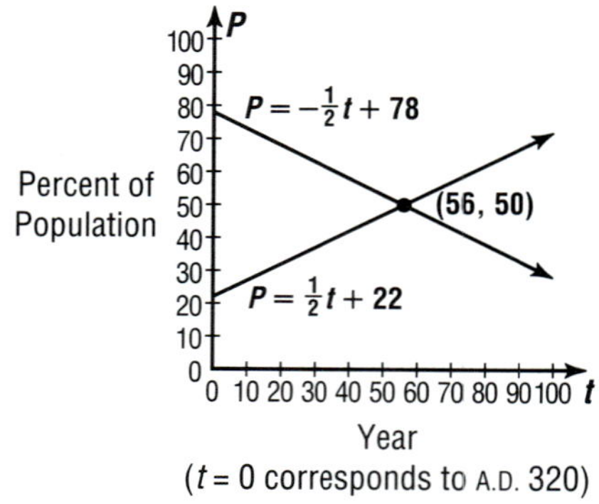

53. −1.5, −13.5 **55.** $y = -2x + 2$ **57.** $7\frac{1}{2}\%$ **59a.** how many three- and four-bedroom homes will be built **59b.** $100 - h$ **59c.** 80 homes

Pages 466–468 Lesson 8–2
7. $x = 8 - 4y; y = 2 - \frac{1}{4}x$ **9.** $x = -\frac{0.75}{0.8}y - 7.5; y = -\frac{0.8}{0.75}x - 8$
11. $\left(3, \frac{3}{2}\right)$ **13.** no solution **15.** infinitely many **17.** (3, 1)
19. (−4, 4) **21.** (4, −1) **23.** (2, 0) **25.** (9, 1) **27.** (2, 5)
29. (4, 2) **31.** (5, 2) **33.** $\left(\frac{8}{3}, \frac{13}{3}\right)$ **35.** (36, −6, −84)
37. (14, 27, −6) **39a.** $y = 1000 + 5x, y = 13x$ **39b.** 125 tickets **41a.** 26.5 years **41b.** 33.8 seconds
43a.

	75% Gold (18-carat)	50% Gold (12-carat)	58% Gold (14-carat)
Total Grams	x	y	300
Grams of Pure Gold	$0.75x$	$0.50y$	0.58(300)

43b. $x + y = 300;\ 0.75x + 0.50y = 0.58(300)$ **43c.** 96 grams of 18-carat gold, 204 grams of 12-carat gold **45.** 37 shares **47.** {(−1, −7), (4, 8), (7, 17), (13, 35)} **49.** −3 **51.** $m - 12$

Pages 472–474 Lesson 8–3
5. addition, (1, 0) **7.** subtraction, $\left(-\frac{5}{2}, -2\right)$
9. substitution, (1, 4) **11.** 8, 48 **13.** (1, −4), (1.29, −4.05)
15. +; (6, 2) 17. −; (4, −1) **19.** −; (4, −7) **21.** +; (5, 1)
23. sub; infinitely many **25.** −; (−2, 3) **27.** −; $\left(\frac{1}{2}, 1\right)$

29. +; (10, −15) **31.** +; (1.75, 2.5) **33.** 11, 53 **35.** 5, 8 **37.** (2, 3, 7) **39.** (14, 27, −6) **41.** Ling, 1.45 hours or 1 hour, 27 minutes; José, 1.15 hours, or 1 hour, 9 minutes **43.** 320 gal of 25% and 180 gal of 50% **45.** −3 **47.** $-\frac{7}{6}$ **49.** substitution (=)

Page 474 Self Test

1. (1, −2)

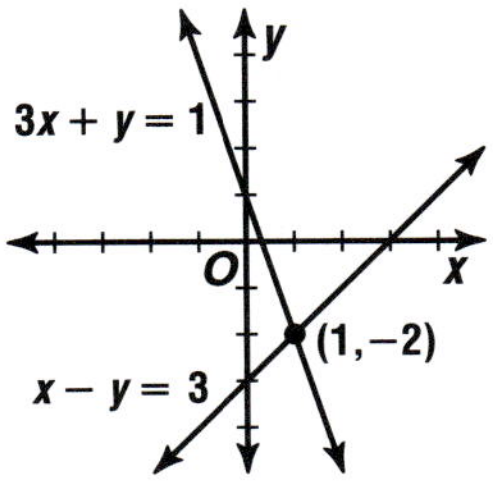

3. infinitely many

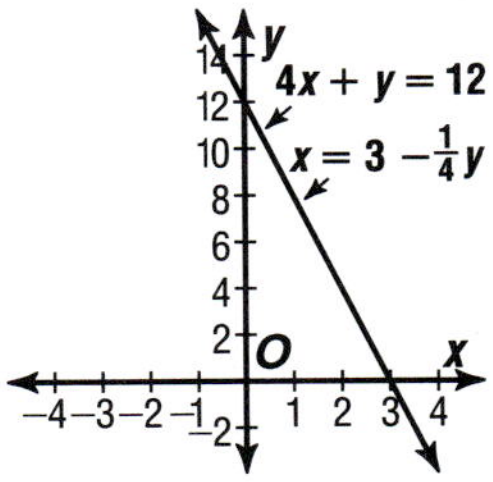

5. (−9, −7) **7.** (10, 15) **9.** (4, −2)

Pages 478–481 Lesson 8–4

5. (−1, 1); Multiply the first equation by −3, then add. **7.** (−9, −13); Multiply the second equation by 5, then add. **9.** (−1, −2); Multiply the first equation by 5, multiply the second equation by −8, then add. **11.** b; (2, 0) **13.** c; (4, 1) **15.** (2, 1) **17.** (5, −2) **19.** (2, −5) **21.** (−4, −7) **23.** (−1, −2) **25.** (4, −6) **27.** (13, −2) **29.** (10, 12) **31.** 6, 9 **33.** elimination, addition; $\left(2, \frac{1}{8}\right)$ **35.** substitution or elimination, multiplication; infinitely many **37.** elimination, subtraction; (24, 4) **39.** (11, 12) **41.** $\left(\frac{1}{3}, \frac{1}{6}\right)$ **43.** (−2, 7), (2, 2), (7, 5) **45.** 6 2-seat tables, 11 4-seat tables **47.** (3, −4) **49.** $\frac{1}{3}$ **51.** 165 yd **53.** 2 cups

Pages 485–486 Lesson 8–5

7.

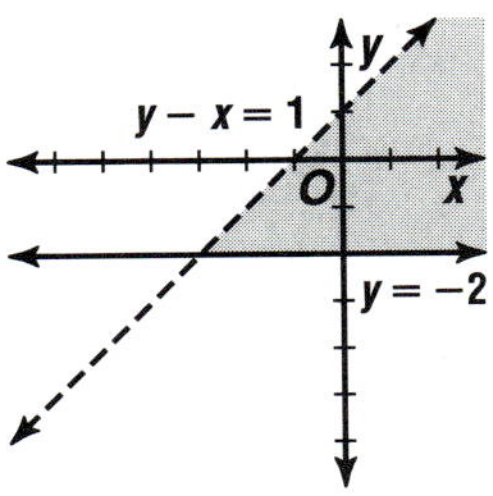

9.

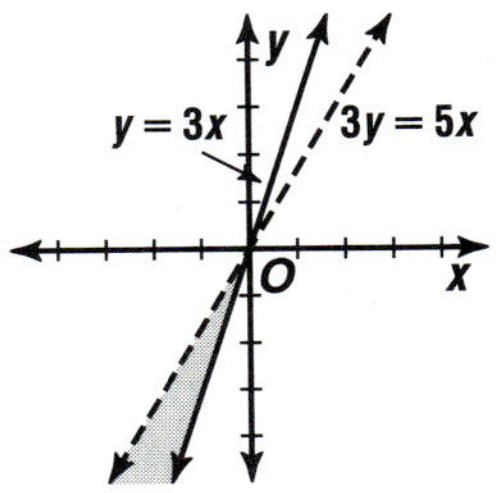

11.

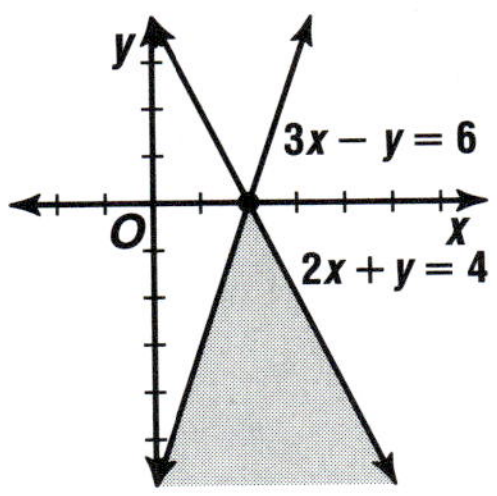

13. $y > x, y \leq x + 4$

15.

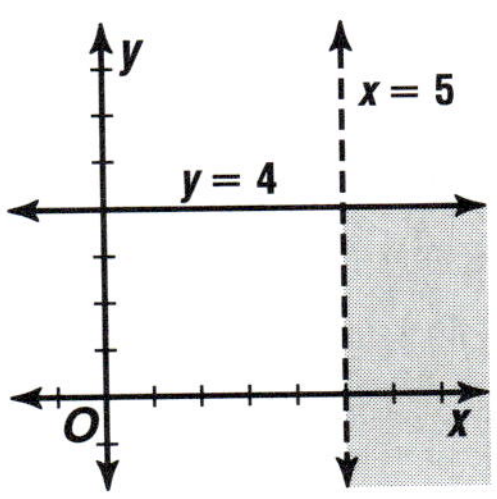

17.

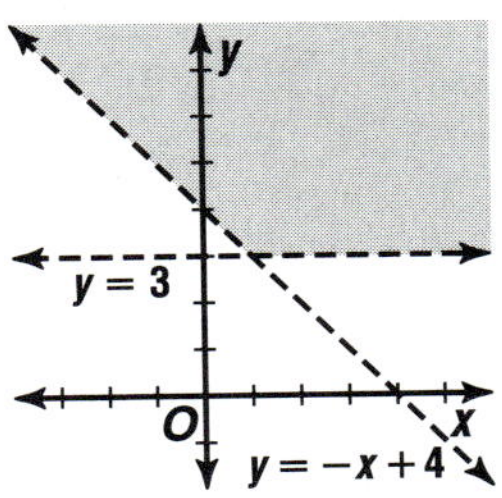

19.

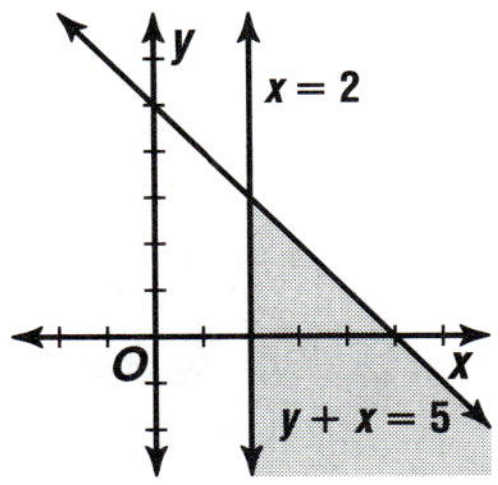

21.

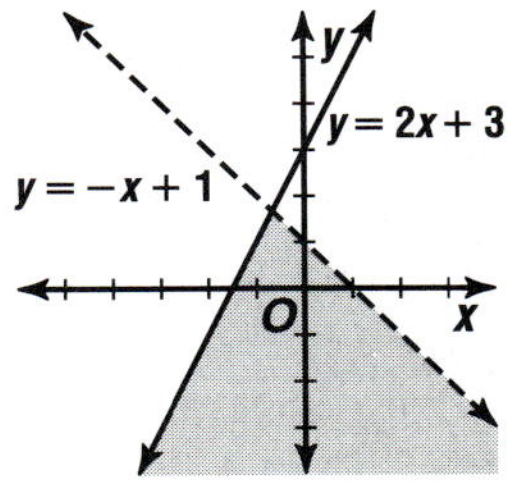

23.

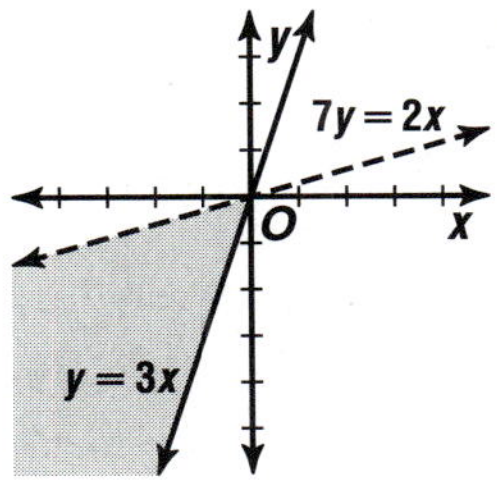

25.

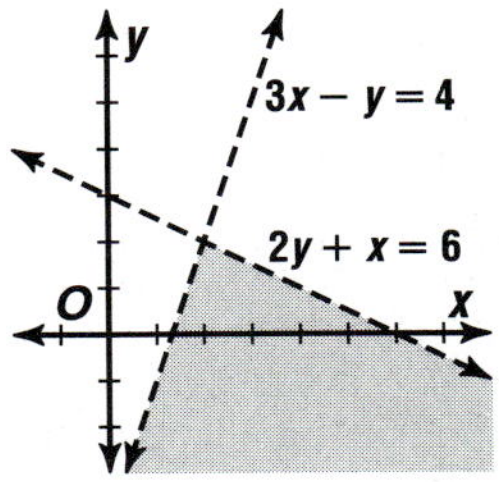

27.

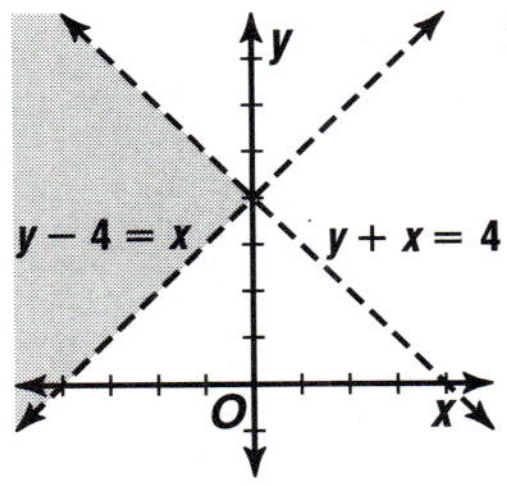

29.

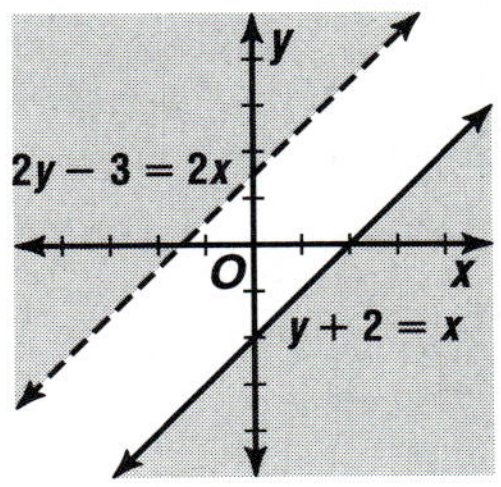

31.

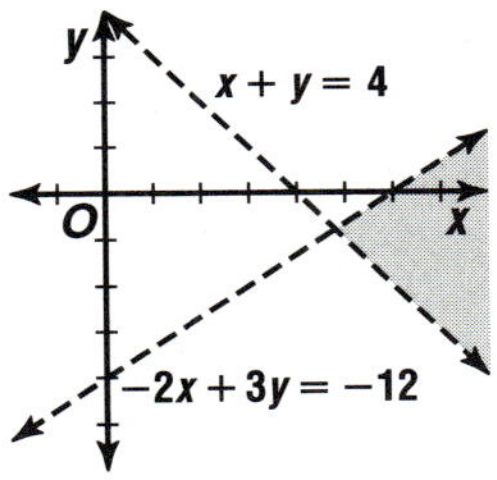

33. $y > -1, x \geq -2$ **35.** $y \leq x, y > x - 3$ **37.** $x \geq 0, y \geq 0, x + 2y \leq 6$

39.

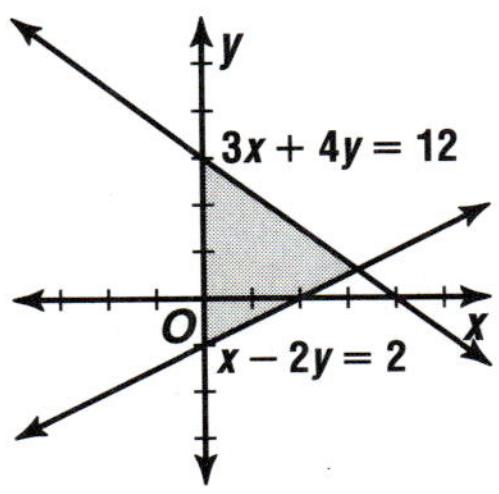

41.

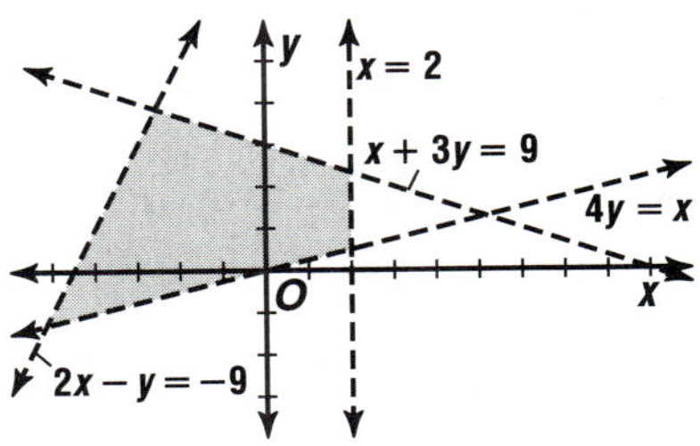

43.

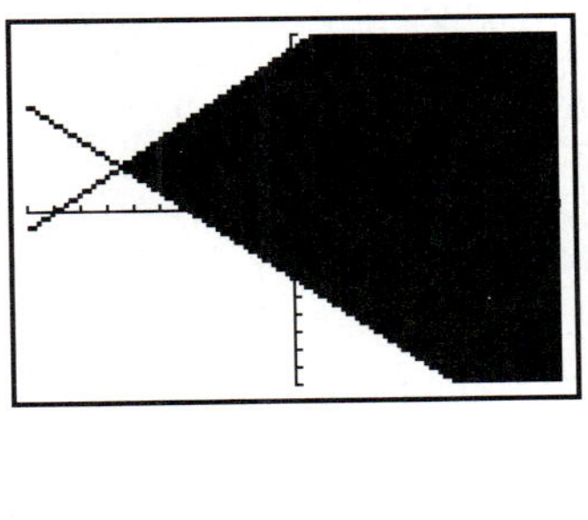

45.

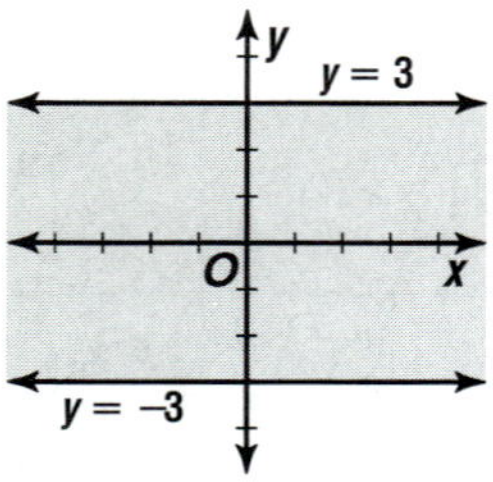

47. Sample answer: walk, 15 min, jog, 15 min; walk, 10 min, jog, 20 min; walk, 5 min, jog, 25 min. **49.** 4 \$5 bills, 8 \$20 bills **51.** $y = -\frac{1}{2}x + \frac{9}{2}$ **53.** 10 **55.** Let y = the number of yards gained in both games; $y = 134 + (134 - 17)$

Page 487 Chapter 8 Highlights

1. substitution **3.** inconsistent **5.** elimination **7.** infinitely many **9.** no **11.** second

Pages 488–490 Chapter 8 Study Guide and Assessment

13. no solution

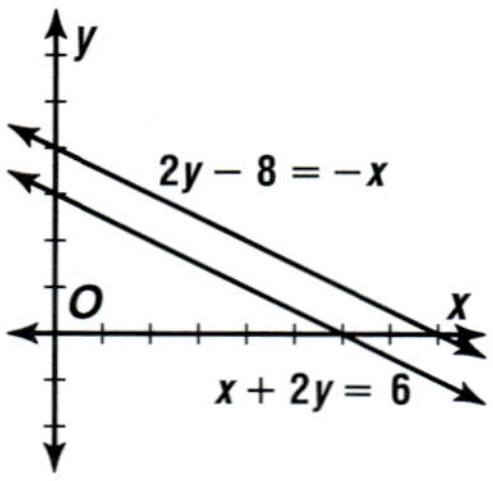

15. $(-2, -7)$

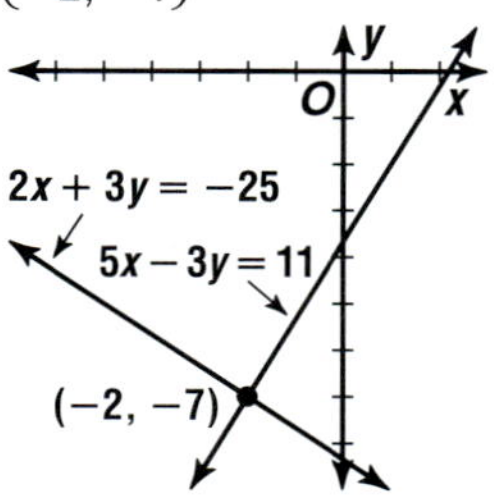

17. no solution

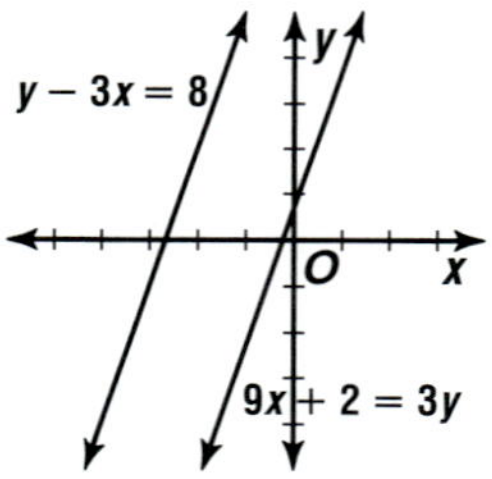

19. one, $(2, -2)$

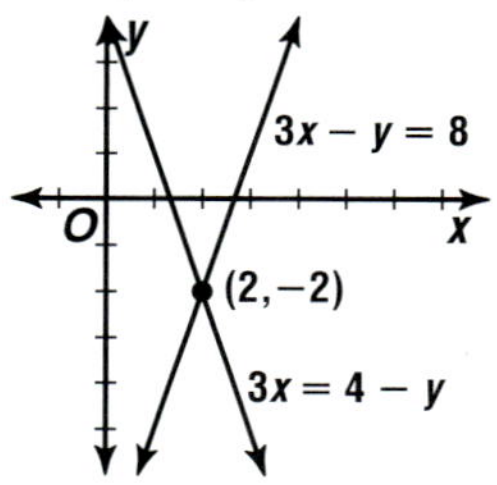

21. $(0, 2)$ **23.** $\left(\frac{1}{2}, \frac{1}{2}\right)$ **25.** $(2, -1)$ **27.** $(5, 1)$ **29.** $(8, -2)$ **31.** $(-9, -7)$ **33.** $\left(\frac{3}{5}, 3\right)$ **35.** $(2, -1)$ **37.** $\left(\frac{7}{9}, 0\right)$ **39.** $(0, 0)$ **41.** $(13, -2)$

43.

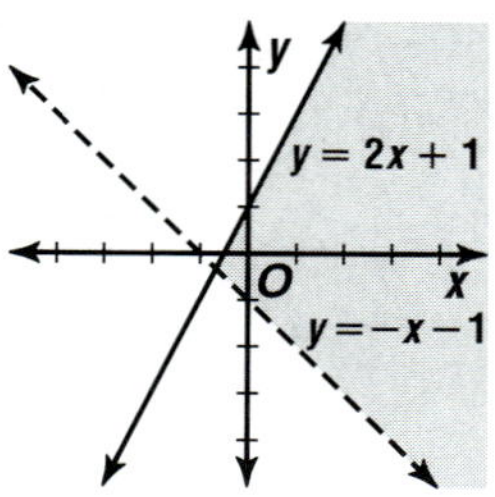

45.

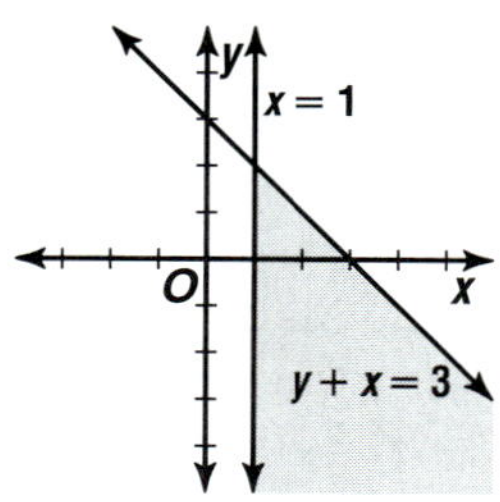

47.

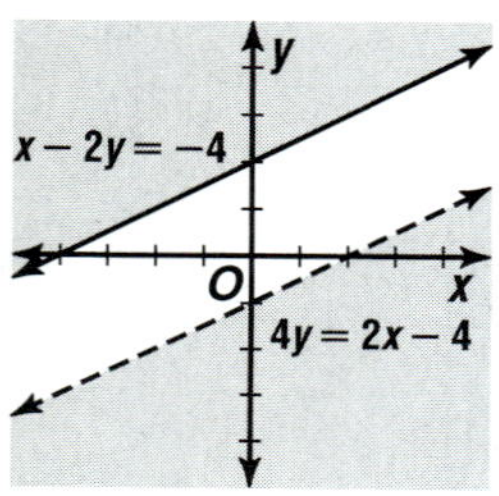

49. 35 **51a.** \$75 **51b.** \$15

CHAPTER 9 EXPLORING POLYNOMIALS

Pages 499–500 Lesson 9–1

5. no **7.** no **9.** a^{12} **11.** 3^{16} or 43,046,721 **13.** $9a^2y^6$ **15.** $15a^4b^3$ **17.** m^4n^3 **19.** 2^{12} or 4096 **21.** $a^{12}x^8$ **23.** $6x^4y^4z^4$ **25.** $a^2b^2c^2$ **27.** $\frac{4}{25}d^2$ **29.** $0.09x^6y^4$ **31.** $90y^{10}$ **33.** $4a^3b^5$ **35.** $-520x^9$ **37.** -2^4 equals $-(2)(2)(2)(2)$ or -16 and $(-2)^4$ equals $(-2)(-2)(-2)(-2)$ or 16. **39.** 301 parts **41.** one; $(-6, 3)$

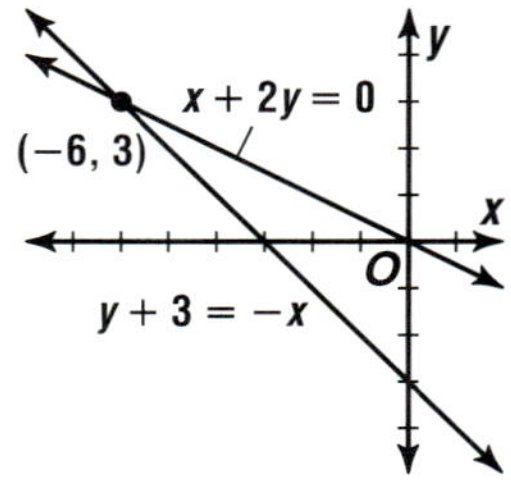

43. $n = 2m + 1$

m	−3	−2	−1	0	1
n	−5	−3	−1	1	3

45. 136° **47.** $1.11y + 0.06$

Pages 504–505 Lesson 9–2

7. $\frac{1}{121}$ **9.** 36 **11.** $\frac{6}{r^4}$ **13.** $\frac{\pi}{4}$ **15.** a^2 **17.** m^6 **19.** $\frac{m^3}{3}$ **21.** $\frac{c^3}{b^8}$ **23.** b^8 **25.** $-s^6$ **27.** $-\frac{4b^3}{c^3}$ **29.** $\frac{1}{64a^6}$ **31.** $\frac{s^3}{r^3}$ **33.** $\frac{a}{4c^2}$ **35.** m^{3+n} **37.** 3^{4x-6} **39.** $\frac{1}{q^{18}}$ **41.** \$1257.14 **43.** $98a^5b^4$ **45.** $|x + 1| < 3$ **47.** $(3, -5)$ **49.** $\frac{52}{41}$

Pages 509–512 Lesson 9–3

5. 43,400,000; 1.515×10^3 **7.** 507,000,000; 4.4419×10^4 **9.** 4,551,400,000; 7.14×10^2 **11.** 1.672×10^{-21} mg **13.** 4×10^{-6} in. **15.** 6.2×10^{-7}; 0.00000062 **17.** 6×10^7; 60,000,000 **19.** 9.5×10^{-3} **21.** 8.76×10^{10} **23.** 3.1272×10^8 **25.** 9.0909×10^{-2} **27.** 7.86×10^4 **29.** 7×10^{-10} **31.** 9.9×10^{-6} **33.** 6×10^{-3}; 0.006 **35.** 8.992×10^{-7}; 0.0000008992 **37.** 4×10^{-2}; 0.04 **39.** 6.5×10^{-6}; 0.0000065 **41.** 6.6×10^{-6}; 0.0000066 **43.** 1.2×10^{-4}; 0.00012 **45.** 2.4336×10^{-1} **47.** 2.8×10^5 **49a.** Sample answer: overflow **49b.** Multiply 3.7 and 5.6 and multiply 10^{112} and 10^{10}. Then write the product in scientific notation. **49c.** 2.072×10^{123} **51.** 1,000,000,000,001 **53.** 6.75×10^{18} molecules **55a.** about 0.25 kg

57.

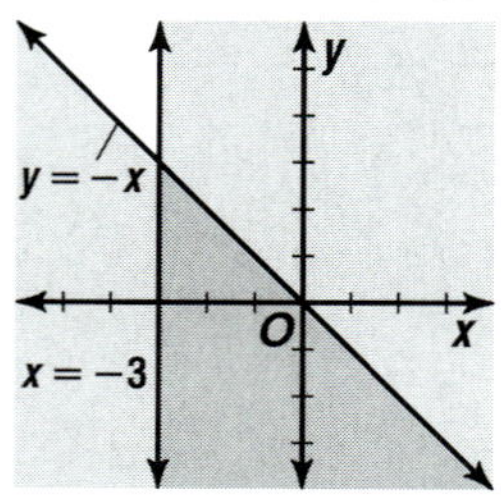

59. 25% **61.** $y = x + 5$ **63.** yes **65.** 27° **67.** −163

Page 513 Lesson 9–4A

1.

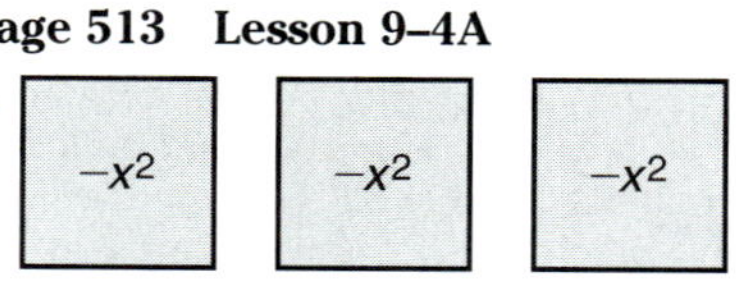

3.

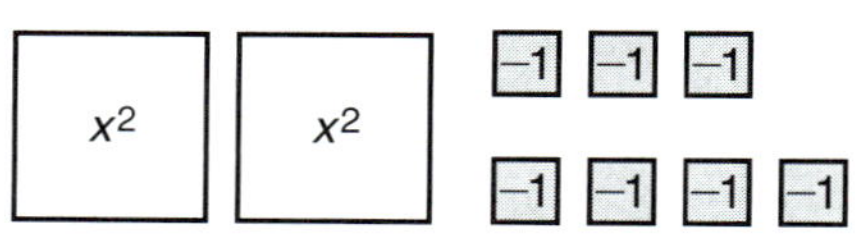

5. $x^2 - 3x + 2$ **7.** $2x^2 - x - 5$ **9.** x^2, x, and 1 represent the areas of the tiles.

Pages 517–519 Lesson 9–4
5. yes; trinomial **7.** yes; binomial **9.** 0 **11.** $x^8 - 12x^6 + 5x^3 - 11x$ **13a.** $\ell w - \pi r^2 - s^2$ **13b.** about 91.43 square units **15.** yes; trinomial **17.** yes; binomial **19.** yes; trinomial **21.** 5 **23.** 3 **25.** 9 **27.** 4 **29.** $x^5 + 3x^3 + 5$ **31.** $-x^7 + abx^2 - bcx + 34$ **33.** $1 + x^2 + x^3 + x^5$ **35.** $7a^3x + \frac{2}{3}x^2 - 8a^3x^3 + \frac{1}{5}x^5$ **37.** $2ab + \pi b^2$; about 353.10 square units **39.** $ab - 4x^2$; 116 square units **41b.** $8a^4 + 9a^3 + 4a^2 + 3a^1 + 5a^0$ **43.** about 153 eggs **45.** 4.235×10^4 **47.** 7, 8, 9 **49.** $\{(-3, 8), (1, \frac{8}{3}), (3, 0), (9, -8)\}$ **51.** \$38.75

Page 521 Lesson 9–5A
1. $-x^2 + 6$ **3.** $-2x^2 - 6x$ **5.** $3x^2 - x + 4$
7. true

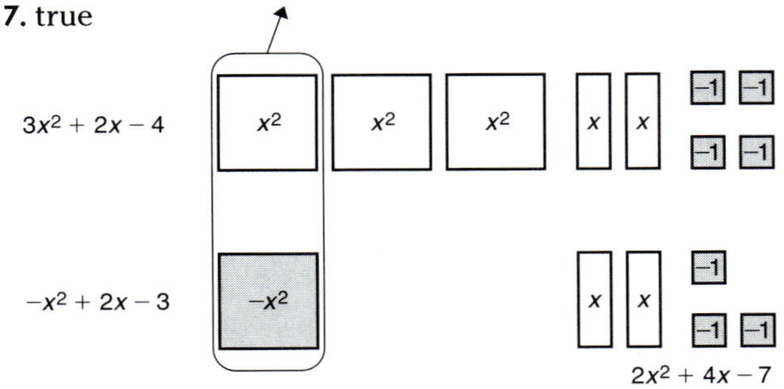

9. Method from Activity 2:

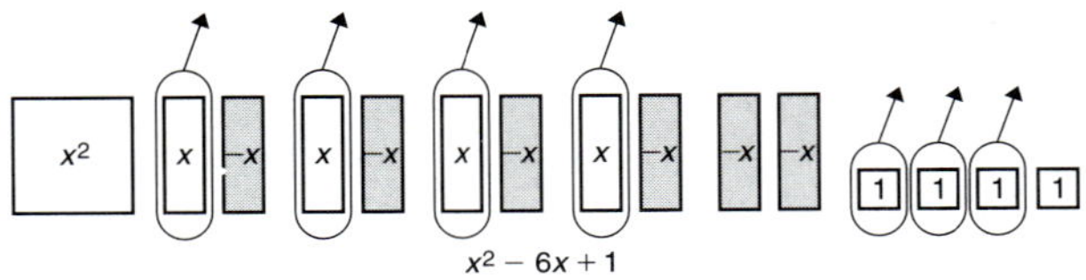

You need to add zero-pairs so that you can remove 4 green x-tiles.
Method from Activity 4:

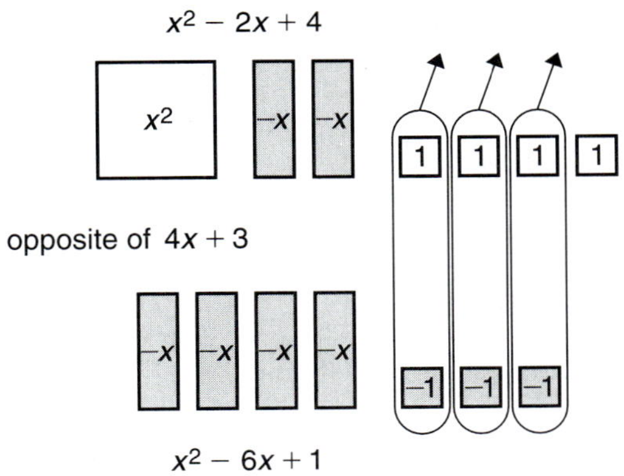

You remove all zero-pairs to find the difference in simplest form.

Pages 524–527 Lesson 9–5
7. $6a^2 - 3$ **9.** $4x^2 + 3y^2 - 8y - 7x$ **11.** $-8y^2$ and $3y^2$; $2x$ and $4x$ **13.** $3p^3q$ and $10p^3q$; $-2p$ and $-p$ **15.** $6m^2n^2 + 8mn - 28$ **17.** $-4y^2 + 5y + 3$ **19.** $7p^3 - 3p^2 - 2p - 7$ **21.** $10x^2 + 13xy$ **23.** $4a^3 + 2a^2b - b^2 + b^3$ **25.** $-4a + 6b - 5c$ **27.** $3a - 11m$ **29.** $-2n^2 + 7n + 5$ **31.** $13x - 2y$ **33.** $-y^3 + 3y + 3$ **35.** $4z^3 - 2z^2 + z$ **37.** $2x + 3y$ **39.** $353 - 18x$ **41.** $-2n^2 - n + 4$ **43.** $719x^2$ cubic stories **45.** $-3x - 2x^3 + 4x^5$
47. (3, 1)

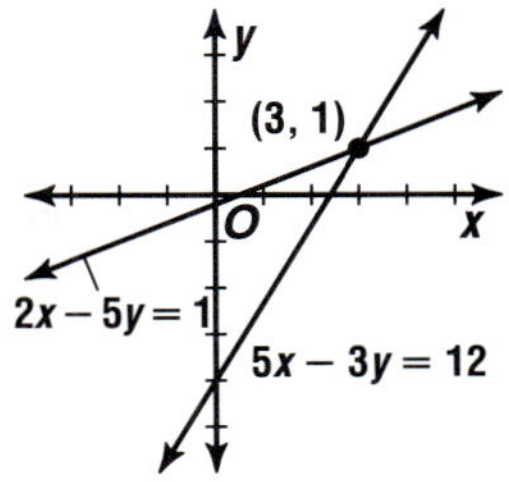

49. Sample answer: Let h = the number of hours for the repair and let c = the total charge; $c = 34h + 15$.
51. $-\frac{50}{3}$

Page 527 Self Test
1. $-6n^5y^7$ **3.** $-12ab^4$ **5.** 5.67×10^6 **7.** about 1.53×10^4 seconds or 4.25 hours **9.** $5x^2 - 4x - 14$

Page 528 Lesson 9–6A
1. $x^2 + 2x$ **3.** $2x^2 + 2x$ **5.** $2x^2 + x$
7. true

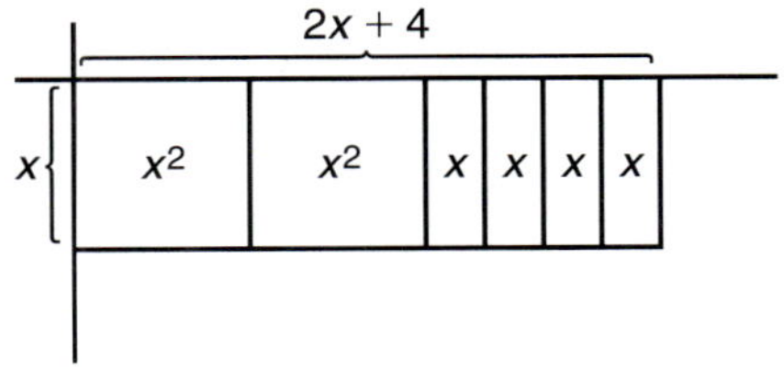

9a. $3x$ and $x + 15$
9b. $(3x^2 + 45x)$ square feet

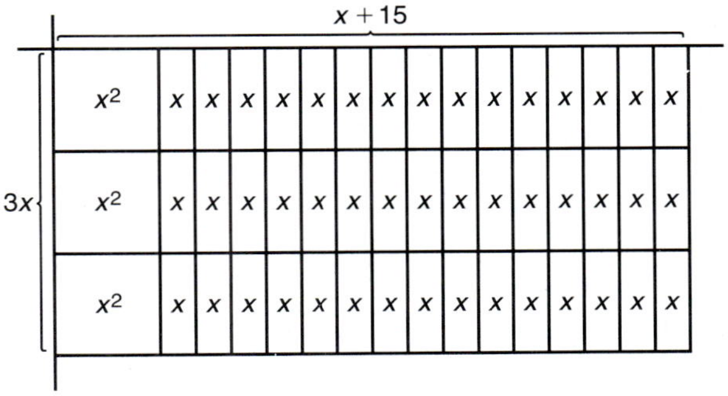

Pages 531–533 Lesson 9–6
5. $-63b^4c - 7b$ **7.** $10y^2 - 26y$ **9.** $3w^2 - 2w$ **11.** $\frac{103}{19}$ **13a.** $a^2 + a$ **13b.** $a^2 + 2a$ **15.** $\frac{1}{3}x^2 - 9x$ **17.** $-20m^5 - 8m^4$ **19.** $30m^5 - 40m^4n + 60m^3n^3$ **21.** $-28d^3 + 16d^2 - 12d$ **23.** $-32r^2s^2 - 56r^2s + 112rs^3$ **25.** $\frac{36}{5}x^3y + x^3 - 24x^2y$ **27.** $36t^2 - 42$ **29.** $61y^3 - 16y^2 + 167y - 18$ **31.** $53a^3 - 57a^2 + 7a$ **33.** $-\frac{77}{8}$ **35.** 0 **37.** $\frac{23}{24}$ **39.** 2 **41.** $15p^2 + 32p$ **43.** Sample answer: $1(8a^2b + 18ab)$, $a(8ab + 18b)$, $b(8a^2 + 18a)$, $2(4a^2b + 9ab)$, $(2a)(4ab + 9b)$, $(2b)(4a^2 + 9a)$, $(ab)(8a + 18)$, $(2ab)(4a + 9)$
45. $1.50t + 1.25mt$
47a.

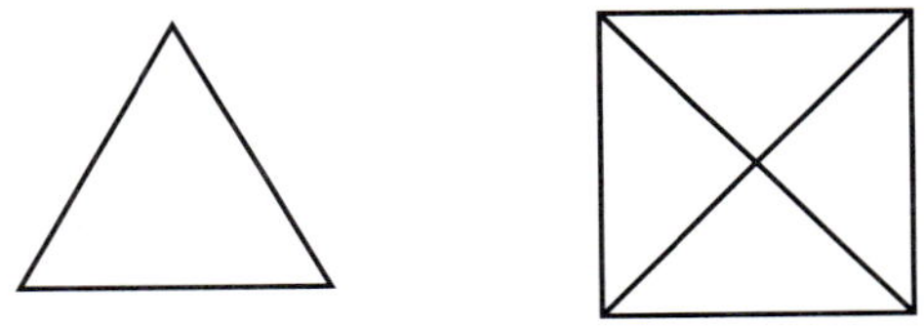

0 diagonals
$\frac{1}{2}(3)(3 - 3) = \frac{1}{2}(3)(0)$
$= 0$

2 diagonals
$\frac{1}{2}(4)(4 - 3) = \frac{1}{2}(4)(1)$
$= 2$

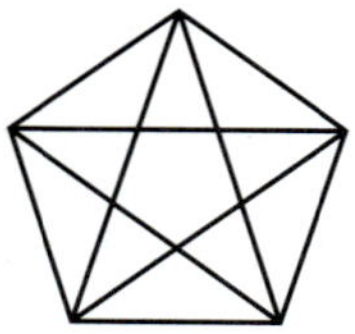

5 diagonals

$\frac{1}{2}(5)(5-3) = \frac{1}{2}(5)(2)$

$= 5$

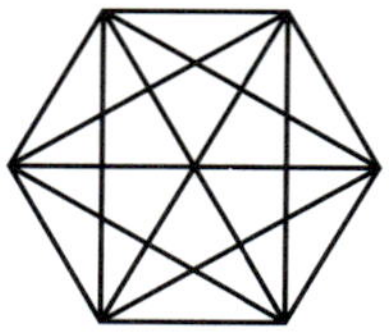

9 diagonals

$\frac{1}{2}(6)(6-3) = \frac{1}{2}(6)(3)$

$= 9$

47b. $\frac{1}{2}n^2 - \frac{3}{2}n$ **47c.** 90 diagonals **49.** 75 gal of 50%, 25 gal of 30% **51.** $a^2 - 1$ **53.** 11 days **55.** 25.7

Page 535 Lesson 9–7A

1. $x^2 + 3x + 2$ **3.** $x^2 - 6x + 8$ **5.** $2x^2 - 2$

7. false

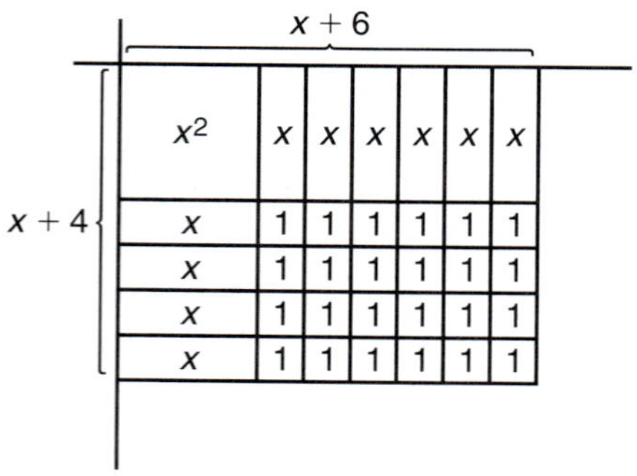

9. false

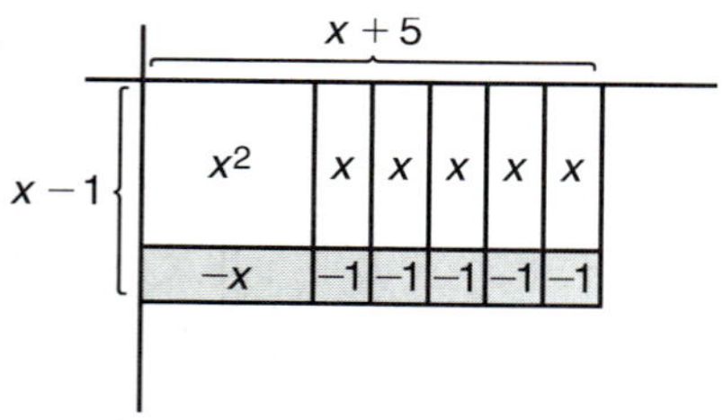

11. By the distributive property, $(x + 3)(x + 2) = x(x + 2) + 3(x + 2)$. The top row represents $x(x + 2)$ or $x^2 + 2x$. The bottom row represents $3(x + 2)$ or $3x + 6$.

Pages 539–541 Lesson 9–7

5. $d^2 + 10d + 16$ **7.** $y^2 - 4y - 21$ **9.** $2x^2 + 9x - 5$ **11.** $10a^2 + 11ab - 6b^2$ **13a.** $a^3 + 3a^2 + 2a$ **13c.** The result is the same as the product in part b. **15.** $c^2 - 10c + 21$ **17.** $w^2 - 6w - 27$ **19.** $10b^2 - b - 3$ **21.** $169x^2 - 9$ **23.** $0.15v^2 - 2.9v - 14$ **25.** $\frac{2}{3}a^2 + \frac{1}{18}ab - \frac{1}{3}b^2$ **27.** $0.63p^2 + 3.9pq + 6q^2$ **29.** $6x^3 + 11x^2 - 68x + 55$ **31.** $9x^3 - 45x^2 + 62x - 16$ **33.** $20d^4 - 9d^3 + 73d^2 - 39d + 99$ **35.** $10x^4 + 3x^3 + 51x^2 - 16x - 48$ **37.** $a^4 - a^3 - 8a^2 - 29a - 35$ **39.** $63y^3 - 57y^2 - 36y$ **41a.** 28 cm, 20 cm, 16 cm **41b.** 8960 cm^3 **41c.** 8960 **41d.** They are the same measure. **43.** $-8x^4 - 6x^3 + 24x^2 - 12x + 80$ **45.** $-3x^3 - 5x^2 - 6x + 24$ **47a.** Sample answer: $x - 2$, $x + 3$ **47b.** Sample answer: $x^2 + x - 6$ **47c.** larger, 2 sq ft **49.** $\{y \mid y < -6\}$ **51.** $y = 2x + 1$ **53.** $a = 4, y = 9$ **55.** 15°C

Pages 546–547 Lesson 9–8

7. $m^2 - 6mn + 9n^2$ **9.** $m^4 + 8m^2n + 16n^2$ **11.** $25 - 10x + x^2$ **13.** $x^2 + 8xy + 16y^2$ **15.** $9b^2 - 6ab + a^2$ **17.** $81p^2 - 4q^2$ **19.** $25b^2 - 120ab + 144a^2$ **21.** $x^6 + 2x^3a^2 + a^4$ **23.** $64x^4 - 9y^2$ **25.** $1.21g^2 + 2.2gh^5 + h^{10}$ **27.** $\frac{16}{9}x^4 - y^2$ **29.** $9x^3 - 45x^2 - x + 5$ **31.** $a^3 + 9a^2b + 27ab^2 + 27b^3$ **33.** $x^2 + y^2 + z^2 + 2xy + 2yz + 2xz$

	x	y	z
x	x^2	xy	xz
y	xy	y^2	yz
z	xz	yz	z^2

35a. $2\pi s + 7\pi$ square meters **35b.** about 28.27 square meters **35c.** about 40.84 square meters **37.** $6t^2 - 3t - 3$

39a.

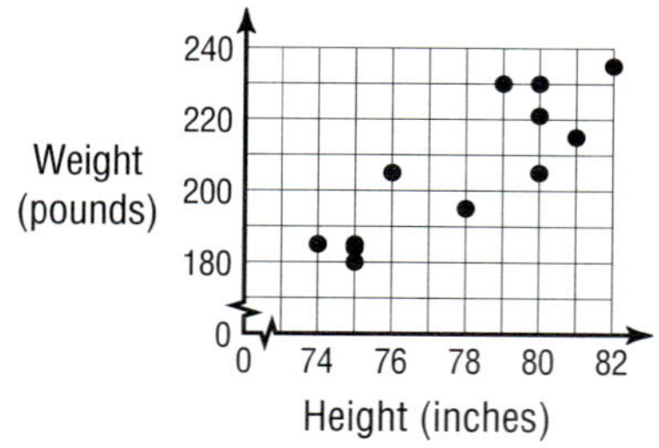

39b. the taller the player, the greater the weight

41.

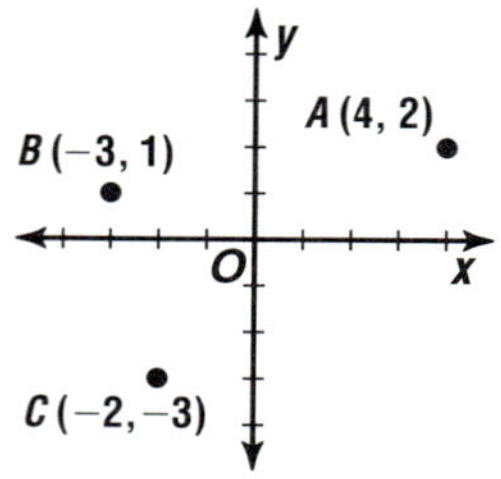

43. 5

Page 549 Chapter 9 Highlights

1. e **3.** h **5.** i **7.** f **9.** a

Pages 550–552 Chapter 9 Study Guide and Assessment

11. y^7 **13.** $20a^5x^5$ **15.** $576x^5y^2$ **17.** $-\frac{1}{2}m^4n^8$ **19.** y^4 **21.** $3b^3$ **23.** $\frac{a^4}{2b}$ **25.** 2.4×10^5 **27.** 4.88×10^9 **29.** 7.96×10^5 **31.** 6×10^{11} **33.** 6×10^{-1} **35.** 1.68×10^{-1} **37.** 2 **39.** 5 **41.** 4 **43.** $3x^4 + x^2 - x - 5$ **45.** $-3x^3 + x^2 - 5x + 5$ **47.** $16m^2n^2 - 2mn + 11$ **49.** $21m^4 - 10m - 1$ **51.** $12a^3b - 28ab^3$ **53.** $8x^5y - 12x^4y^3 + 4x^2y^5$ **55.** $2x^2 - 17xy^2 + 10x + 10y^2$ **57.** $r^2 + 4r - 21$ **59.** $4x^2 + 13x - 12$ **61.** $18x^2 - 0.125$ **63.** $2x^3 + 15x^2 - 11x - 9$ **65.** $x^2 - 36$ **67.** $16x^2 + 56x + 49$ **69.** $25x^2 - 9y^2$ **71.** $36a^2 - 60ab + 25b^2$ **73.** $305.26 **75.** no; after 6 years

CHAPTER 10 USING FACTORING

Pages 561–563 Lesson 10–1

5. 1, 2, 4 **7.** prime **9.** $-1 \cdot 2 \cdot 3 \cdot 5$ **11.** 4 **13.** $6d$ **15.** $4gh$ **17.** 40 in. **19.** 1, 67 **21.** 1, 2, 4, 5, 8, 10, 16, 20, 40, 80 **23.** 1, 2, 5, 10, 19, 25, 38, 50, 95, 190, 475, 950 **25.** composite; $3^2 \cdot 7$ **27.** prime **29.** composite; $2^2 \cdot 5 \cdot 7 \cdot 11$ **31.** $-1 \cdot 3 \cdot 3 \cdot 13$ **33.** $2 \cdot 2 \cdot b \cdot b \cdot b \cdot d \cdot d$ **35.** $-1 \cdot 2 \cdot 7 \cdot 7 \cdot a \cdot a \cdot b$ **37.** 9 **39.** 1 **41.** 19 **43.** $7pq$ **45.** $15r^2t^2$ **47.** 12 **49.** 6 **51.** $8m^2n$ **53.** $-12x^3yz^2$ **55.** $3m^2n$ **57.** 29 cm by 47 cm **59.** 3, 5; 5, 7; 11, 13; 17, 19; 29, 31; 41, 43; 59, 61; 71, 73

61a. false; counterexample: $a = 2$, $b = 4$
61b. True; if 8 is a factor of ab, then the prime factorization of ab must contain $2 \cdot 2 \cdot 2$. So $2 \cdot 2$ or 4 must be a factor of either a or b.
61c. false; counterexample: $a = 4$, $b = 14$
63. 1500 squares of sod **65.** $3b$
67.

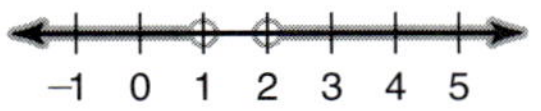

69. $x = 4$ **71.** $9\frac{3}{5}$ ft **73.** -4

Page 564 Lesson 10–2A
1. $3(x + 3)$ **3.** $x(3x + 4)$
5. no

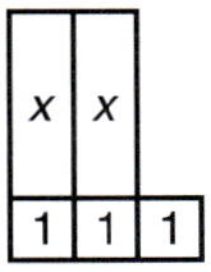

7. yes

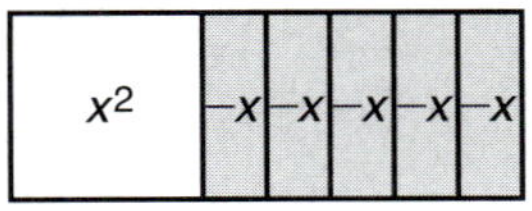

9. Binomials can be factored if they can be represented by a rectangle. Examples: $4x + 4$ can be factored and $4x + 3$ cannot be factored.

Pages 569–571 Lesson 10–2
7. 3 **9.** 1 **11.** $4xy^2$ **13.** $(a + b)(x + y)$ **15.** $(x - y)(3a + 4b)$ **17.** $3t$ **19.** $x(29y - 3)$ **21.** $3c^2d(1 - 2d)$
23. $(r + k)(x + 2y)$ **25a.** $g = \frac{1}{2}n(n - 1)$ **25b.** 91 games
25c. 63 games **27.** $8rs$ **29.** $2y - 5$ **31.** $5k - 7p$
33. $2xz(7 - 9z)$ **35.** $a(17 - 41ab)$ **37.** $(m + x)(2y + 7)$
39. $3xy(x^2 - 3y + 12)$ **41.** $(2x^2 - 5y^2)(x - y)$ **43.** $(2x - 5y)(2a - 7b)$ **45.** $7abc(4abc + 3ac - 2)$ **47.** $2(2m + r)(3x - 2)$ **49.** $(7x + 3t - 4)(a + b)$ **51.** $8a - 4b + 8c + 16d + ab + 64$ **53.** $4r^2(4 - \pi)$ **55.** $(4z + 3m)$ cm by $(z - 6)$ cm **57.** Sample answer: $(3a + 2b)(ab + 6)$, $(3a + ab)(2b + 6)$, $(2b + ab)(3a + 6)$ **59.** $(2s - 3)(s + 8)$ **61.** A and C sharp **63.** 9 **65.** $\{z \mid z \geq -1.654\}$ **67.** $\left\{(-3, 10), \left(0, \frac{11}{2}\right), (1, 4), \left(2, \frac{5}{2}\right), (5, -2)\right\}$ **69.** $y = -\frac{4}{3}x + \frac{7}{3}$ **71.** 7

Page 573 Lesson 10–3A
1. $(x + 1)(x + 5)$ **3.** $(x + 3)(x + 4)$ **5.** $(x - 1)(x - 2)$
7. $(x - 1)(x + 5)$
9. yes

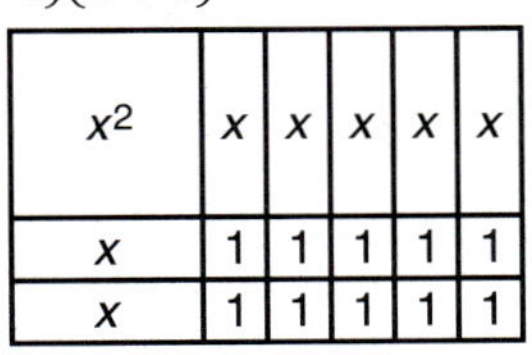

11. no

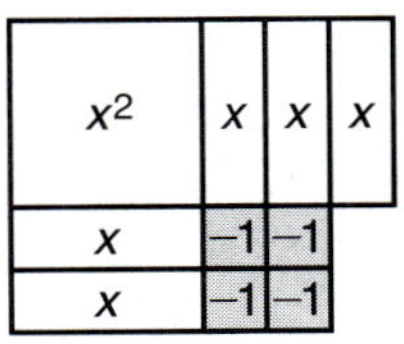

13. Trinomials can be factored if they can be represented by a rectangle. Sample answers: $x^2 + 4x + 4$ can be factored and $x^2 + 6x + 4$ cannot be factored.

Pages 578–580 Lesson 10–3
5. 3, 8 **7.** 8, 5 **9.** -2, -6 **11.** – **13.** $(t + 3)(t + 4)$
15. $2(y + 2)(y - 3)$ **17.** prime **19.** 9, -9, 15, -15
21. $(3x^2 + 2x)$ m^2 **23.** – **25.** 5 **27.** 5 **29.** $(m - 4)(m - 10)$
31. prime **33.** $(2x + 7)(x - 3)$ **35.** $(2x + 3)(x - 4)$
37. $(2n - 7)(2n + 5)$ **39.** $(2 + 3m)(5 + 2m)$ **41.** prime
43. $2x(3x + 8)(2x - 5)$ **45.** $2a^2b(5a - 7b)(2a - 3b)$
47. 7, -7, 11, -11 **49.** 1, -1, 11, -11, 19, -19, 41, -41
51. 6, 4 **53.** r cm, $(5r + 6)$ cm, $(3r - 7)$ cm **55.** no; $(2x + 3)(x - 1)$ **57.** no; $(x - 3)(x - 3)$ **59.** 27 ft^3
61. $(3x - 10)$ shares **63.** $(5, -2)$ **65.** $y = -\frac{2}{3}x + \frac{14}{3}$
67. D = {0, 1, 2}; R = {2, -2, 4} **69.** 90° **71.** $3x + 4y$

Page 580 Self Test
1. $10n^2$ **3.** $6xy(3y - 4x)$ **5.** $(2q + 3)(q - 6)$ **7.** $(3y - 5)(y - 1)$ **9.** 41,312,432 or 23,421,314

Pages 584–586 Lesson 10–4
7. yes **9.** no **11.** d **13.** a **15.** $(1 - 4g)(1 + 4g)$
17. $5(2m - 3n)(2m + 3n)$ **19.** $(x - y)(x + y)(x^2 + y^2)$
21. 5 **23.** $(2 - v)(2 + v)$ **25.** $(10d - 1)(10d + 1)$
27. $2(z - 7)(z + 7)$ **29.** prime **31.** $17(1 - 2k)(1 + 2k)$
33. prime **35.** prime **37.** $(ax - 0.8y)(ax + 0.8y)$
39. $\frac{1}{2}(3a - 7b)(3a + 7b)$ **41.** $(a + b - c - d)(a + b + c + d)$ **43.** $(x^2 - 2y)(x^2 + 2y)(x^4 + 4y^2)$ **45.** $(a^2 + 5b^2)(a - 2b)(a + 2b)$ **47.** 624 **49.** $(2a - b)$ in., $(2a + b)$ in.
51. $(x - 2)$ ft, $(x + 4)$ ft **53.** $(a - 5b)$ in., $(a + 5b)$ in., $(5a + 3b)$ in. **55a.** square **55b.** 25 cm^2 **57.** 9, 12, 15
59. \$3.16, \$1.50, \$1.25, \$1.20 **61.** (4, 16)
63.

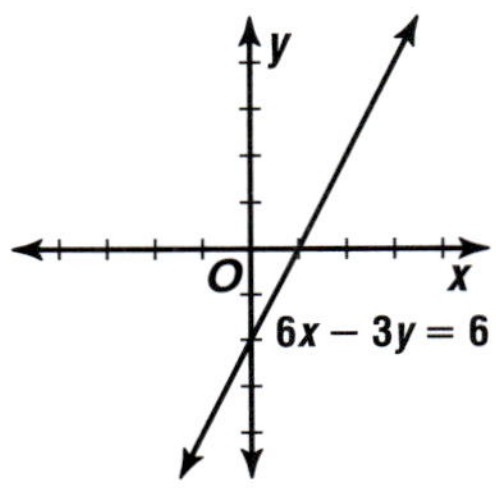

65.

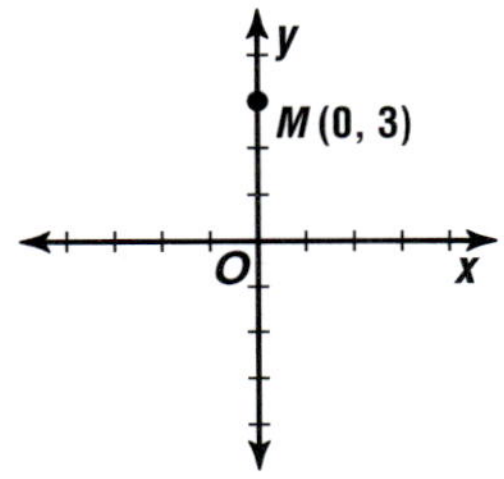

67. 5.14, 3.6, 0.6

Pages 591–593 Lesson 10–5
7. 8a **9.** 6c **11.** yes; $(2n - 7)^2$ **13.** yes; $(4b - 7c)^2$
15. $4(a - 3b)(a + 3b)$ **17.** $2(5g + 2)^2$ **19.** $(2a - 3b)(2a + 3b)(5x - y)$ **21.** yes; $(r - 4)^2$ **23.** yes; $(7p - 2)^2$ **25.** no
27. yes; $(2m + n)^2$ **29.** no **31.** no **33.** yes; $\left(\frac{1}{2}a + 3\right)^2$
35. $a(45a - 32b)$ **37.** $(v - 15)^2$ **39.** prime **41.** $3(y - 7)(y + 7)$ **43.** $2(3a - 4)^2$ **45.** $(y^2 + z^2)(x - 1)(x + 1)$
47. $(a^2 + 2)(4a + 3b^2)$ **49.** $0.7(p - 3q)(p - 2q)$
51. $(g^2 - 3h)(g + 3)^2$ **53.** -110, 110 **55.** 9 **57.** $(6y + 26)$ cm **59.** $(8x^2 - 22x + 14)$ cm^2 **61a.** $a \geq b$ **61b.** $a \leq b$
61c. $a = b$ **63a.** \$1166.40 **63b.** $p(1 + r)^2$ **63c.** \$1144.90
65. $50.6t^2 + 21t - 102$ **67.** 20 hours
69a.

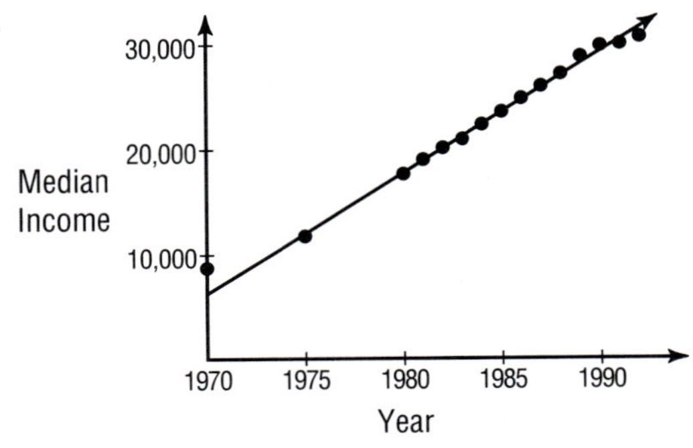

69b. Sample answer: Yes; $I = 1200y + 6000$, where I is the median income and y is the number of years since 1970.
71. 1:3 **73.** 152 ft

Pages 598–600 Lesson 10–6
5. {0, −5} **7.** $\left\{0, \frac{5}{3}\right\}$ **9.** {5} **11.** 6 **13.** {0, 24} **15.** $\left\{\frac{3}{2}, \frac{8}{3}\right\}$ **17.** {−9, −4} **19.** {−8, 8} **21.** {0, 4} **23.** $\left\{-\frac{1}{3}, -\frac{5}{2}\right\}$ **25.** {12, −4} **27.** {−9, 0, 9} **29.** {−5, 7} **31.** −14 and −12 or 12 and 14 **33.** 5 cm **35a.** {−6, 1}; {−6, 1} **35b.** They are equivalent; they have the same solution. **37a.** about 3.35 s **37b.** His ideas about falling objects differed from what most people thought to be true. He believed that Earth is a moving planet and that the sun and planets do not revolve around Earth. **39.** about 90,180 ft or 17 mi **41.** 0.5 km **43.** $40q^2 + rq - 6r^2$ **45.** 14; −4 **47.** 4.355 minutes or about 4 minutes 21 seconds

Page 601 Chapter 10 Highlights
1. false; composite **3.** false; sample answer: 64 **5.** false; $2^4 \cdot 3$ **7.** true **9.** false; zero product property

Pages 602–604 Chapter 10 Study Guide and Assessment
11. composite, $2^2 \cdot 7$ **13.** composite, $2 \cdot 3 \cdot 5^2$ **15.** prime **17.** 5 **19.** $4ab$ **21.** $5n$ **23.** $7x^2$ **25.** $13(x + 2y)$ **27.** $6ab(4ab - 3)$ **29.** $12pq(3pq - 1)$ **31.** $(a - 4c)(a + b)$ **33.** $(4k - p^2)(4k^2 - 7p)$ **35.** $(8m - 3n)(3a + 5b)$ **37.** $(y + 3)(y + 4)$ **39.** prime **41.** $(r - 4)(2r + 5)$ **43.** $(b - 4)(b + 4)$ **45.** $(4a - 9b^2)(4a + 9b^2)$ **47.** prime **49.** $(a + 9)^2$ **51.** $(2 - 7r)^2$ **53.** $6b(b - 2g)^2$ **55.** $(5x - 12)^2$ **57.** $\left\{\frac{2}{3}, -\frac{7}{4}\right\}$ **59.** {0, −17} **61.** {−5, −8} **63.** $\left\{-\frac{2}{5}\right\}$ **65.** 384 **67.**

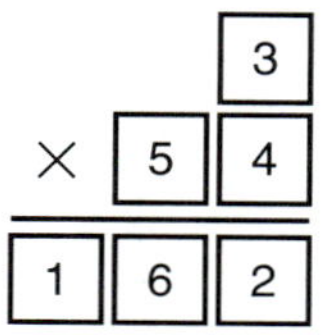

69. 9, 11; −11, −9

CHAPTER 11 EXPLORING QUADRATIC AND EXPONENTIAL FUNCTIONS

Page 610 Lesson 11–1A
1. (−8, −5)

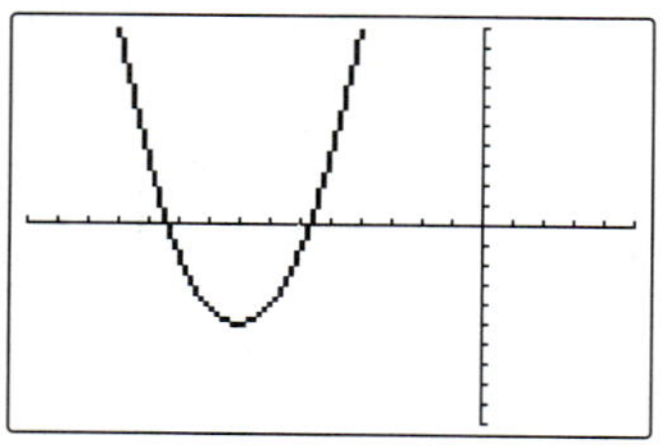

3. (5, 0)

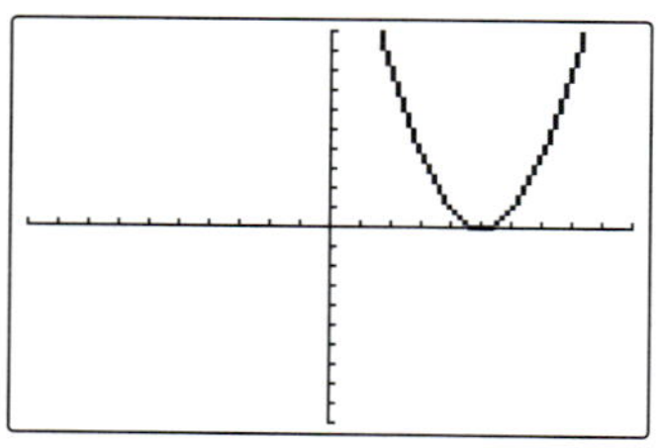

5. (10, 14)

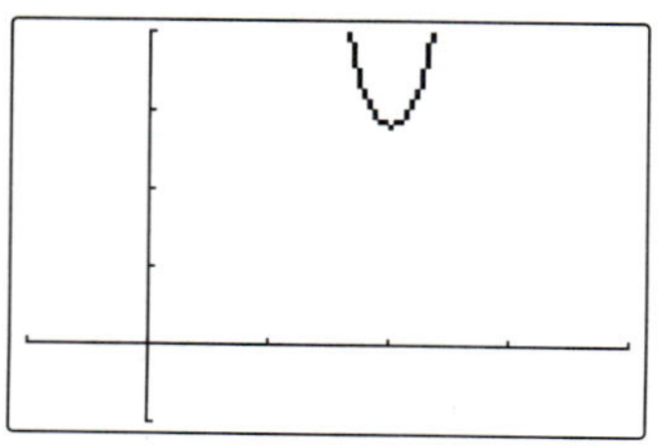

Pages 615–617 Lesson 11–1
7. $x = 0$, (0, 2), min.

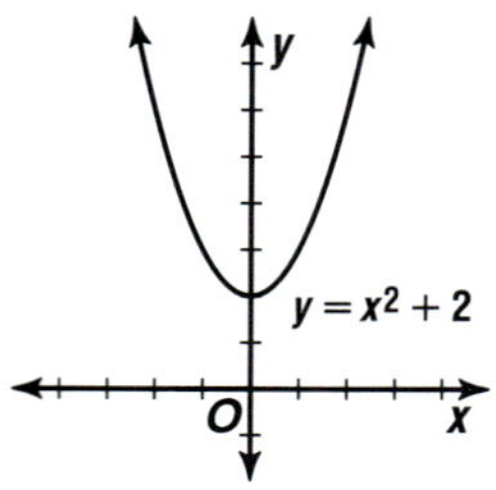

9. $x = -2$, (−2, −13), min.

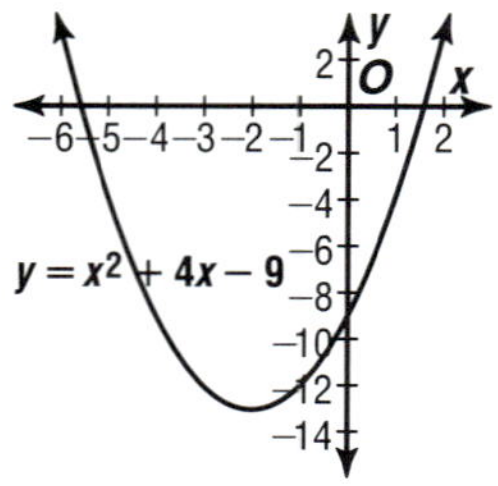

11. $x = 2.5$, (2.5, 12.25), max.

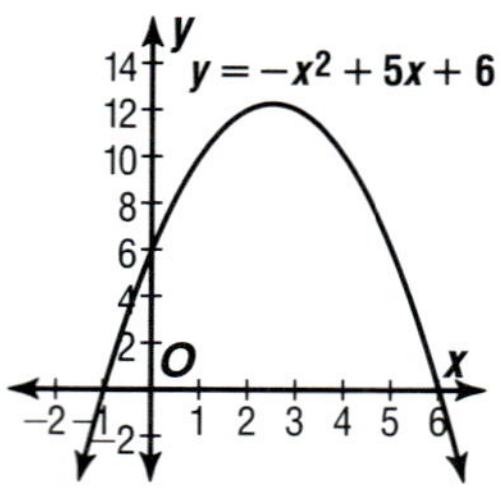

13. c

15. $x = 0$, (0, 0), min.

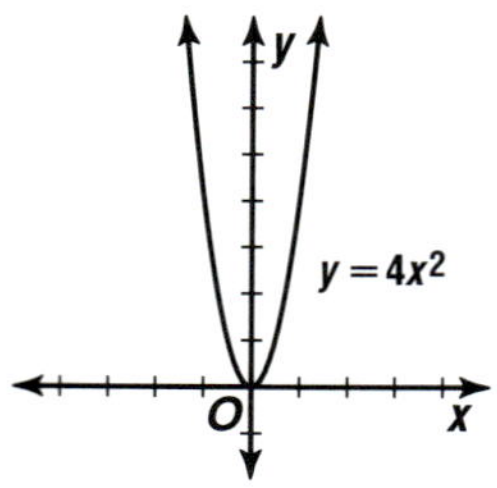

17. $x = -1$, (−1, 17), min.

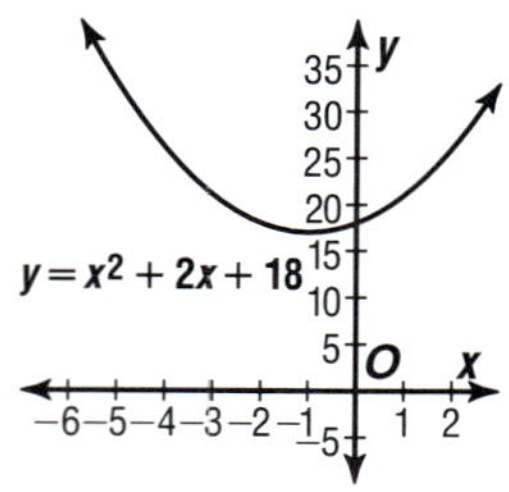

19. $x = 0$, (0, −5), min.

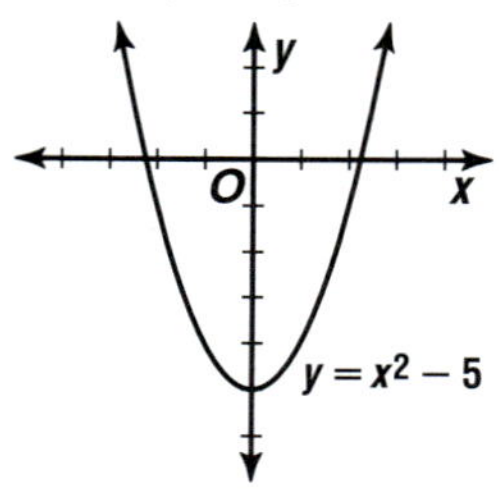

21. $x = -3$, (−3, −29), min.

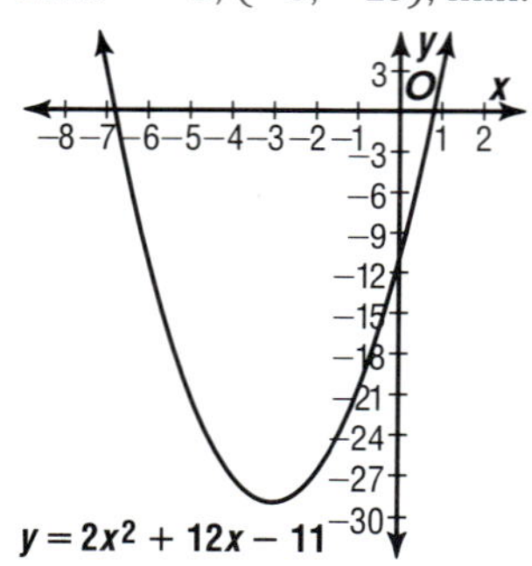

23. $x = 0$, (0, −25), min.

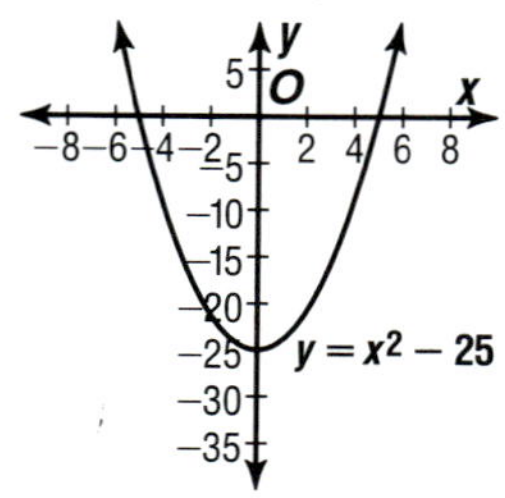

25. $x = -1$, (−1, 7), max.

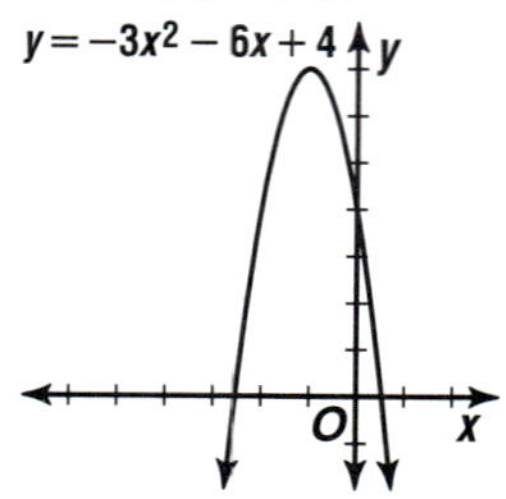

27. $x = -1$, (−1, −20), min.

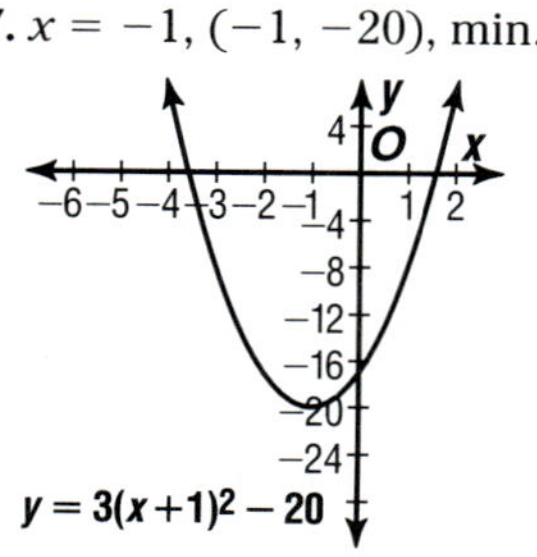

29. $x = -1$, (−1, −1), min.

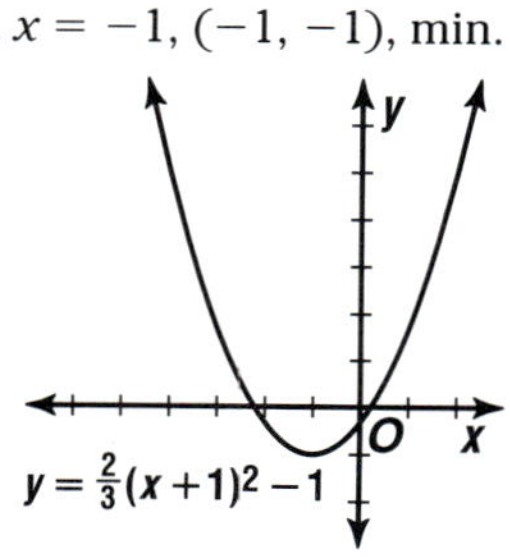

31. *c* **33.**

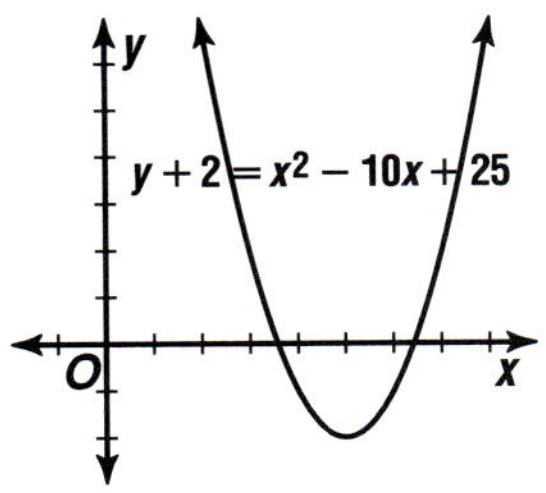

35.

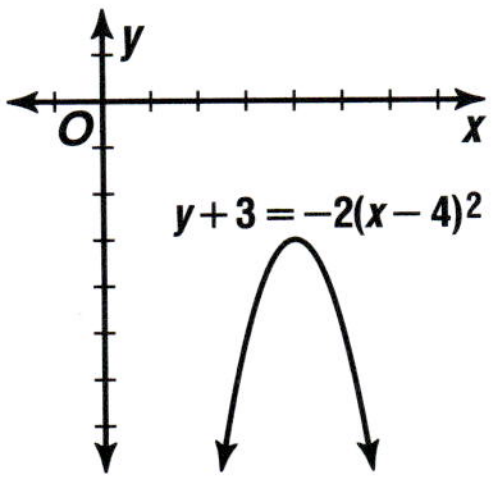

37. $x = -1$ **39.** $x = 2$

41. $(-1.10, 125.8)$

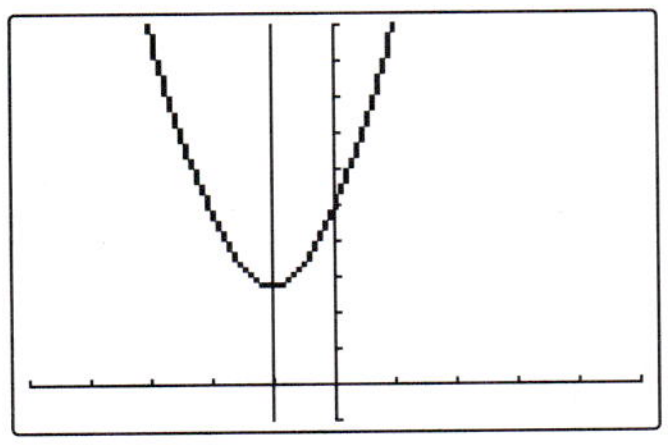

43. $(-0.15, 90.14)$

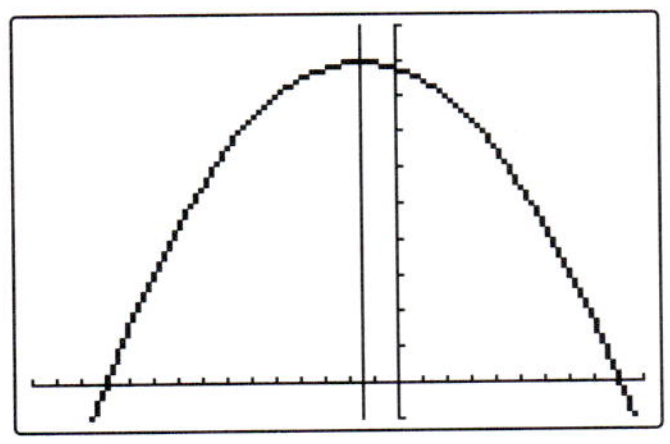

45a.

Year	t	U(t)
1970	0	329.96
1975	5	370.31
1980	10	559.16
1985	15	896.51
1990	20	1382.36
1993	23	1745.15

45b. D: $0 \leq t \leq 23$; R: $326 < U(t) < 1746$

45c.

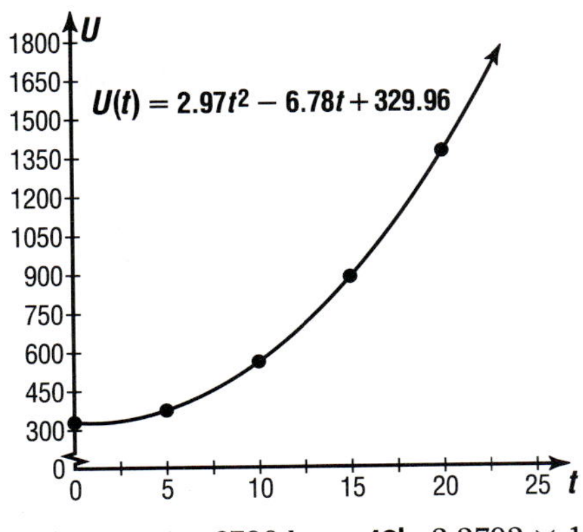

47. 0.15 km **49a.** 6790 km **49b.** 2.2792×10^8 km

51a.

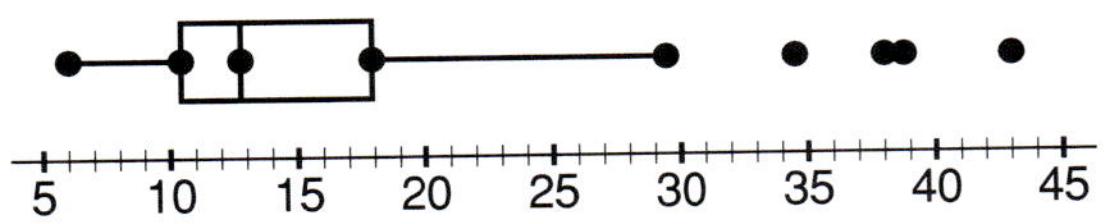

51b. 34.5, 38, 38.7, 43 **53.** -5

Page 619 Lesson 11–1B

1. All the graphs open downward from the origin. $y = -2x^2$ is narrower than $y = -x^2$ and $y = -5x^2$ is the narrowest.

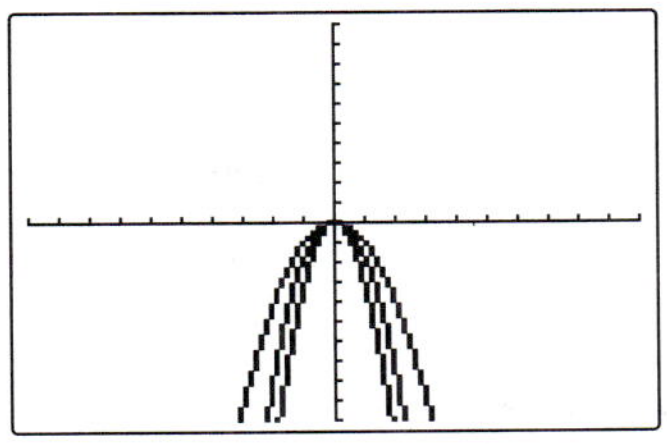

3. All open downward, have the same shape, and have vertices along the x-axis. However, each vertex is different.

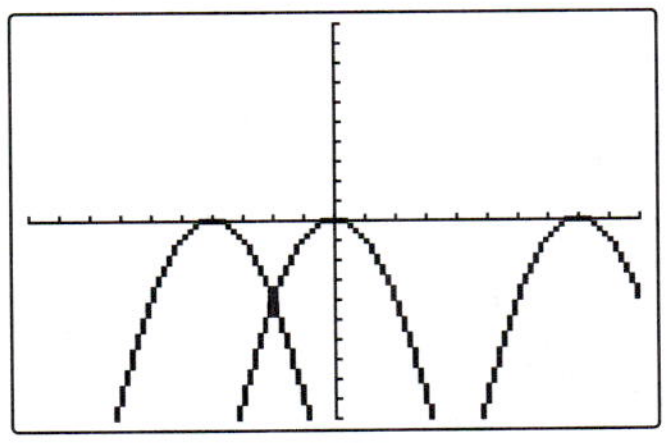

5. It will open upward, have a vertex at the origin, and be narrower than $y = x^2$.

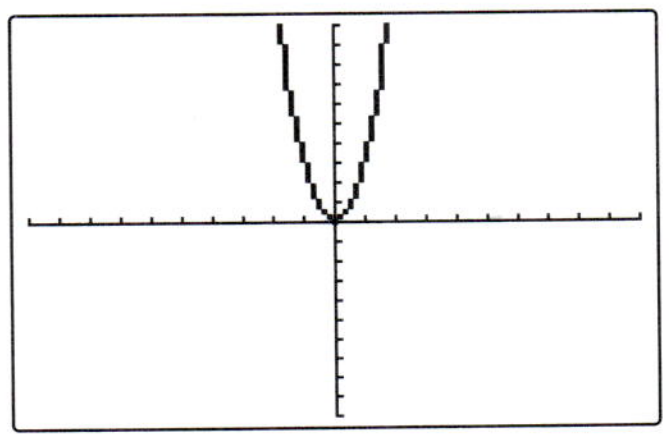

7. It will have vertex at the origin, open downward, and be wider than $y = x^2$.

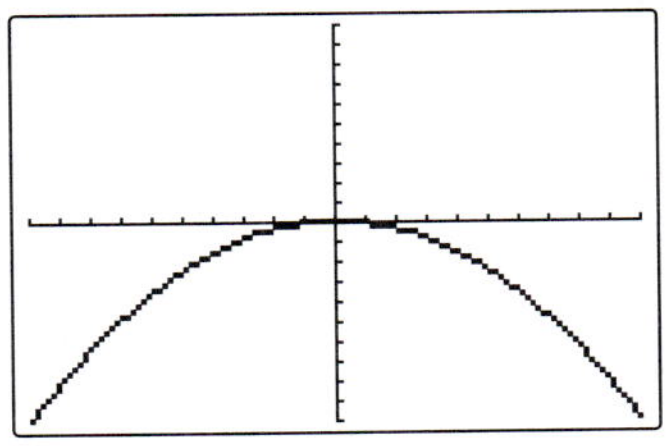

9a. If $|a| > 1$, the graph is narrower than the graph of $y = x^2$. If $0 < |a| < 1$, the graph is wider than the graph of $y = x^2$. If $a < 0$, it opens downward; if $a > 0$, it opens upward. **9b.** The graph has the same shape as $y = x^2$, but is shifted a units (up if $a > 0$, down if $a < 0$). **9c.** The graph has the same shape as $y = x^2$, but is shifted a units (left if $a > 0$, right if $a < 0$). **9d.** The graph has the same shape as $y = x^2$ but is shifted a units left or right and b units up or down as prescribed in 9b and 9c.

Pages 624–627 Lesson 11–2

7. 2 real roots **9.** $-1, 2$

11. $-3, 8$

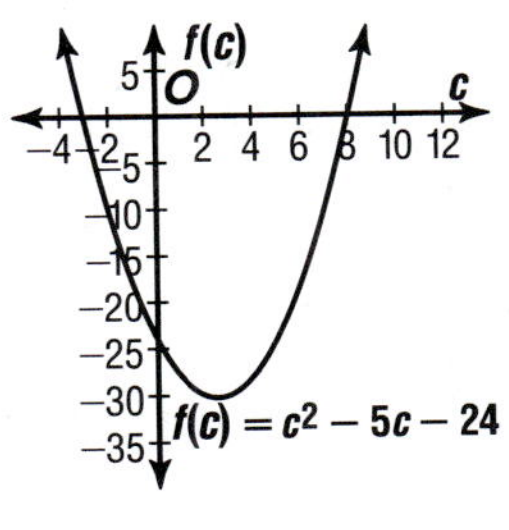

13. $-2 < w < -1, 4 < w < 5$

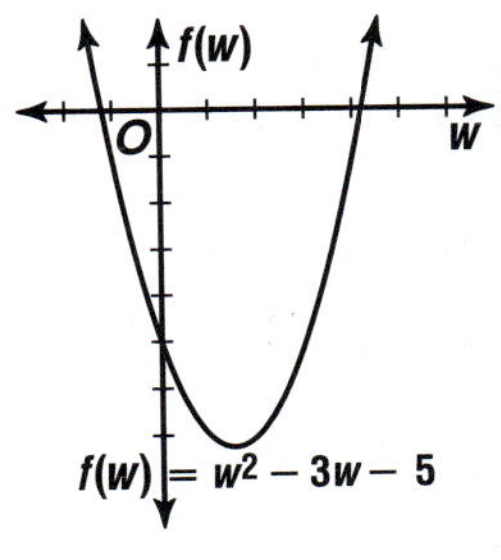

15. 5

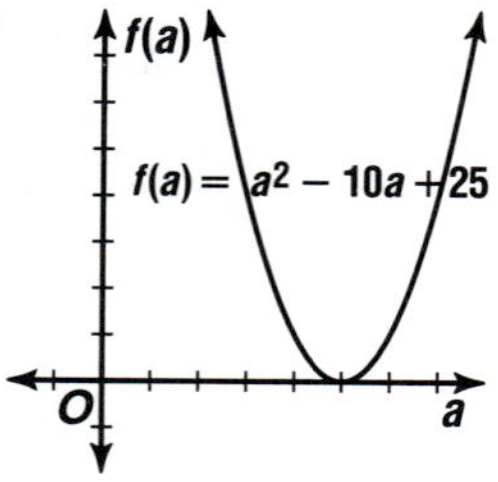

17. $-2, -6$ **19.** 2 **21.** $-4, 4$ **23.** -3 **25.** $\varnothing$ **27.** $-4, 1$ **29.** 4 **31.** $8 < a < 9, -1 < a < 0$ **33.** $3, -1 < n < 0$

35.

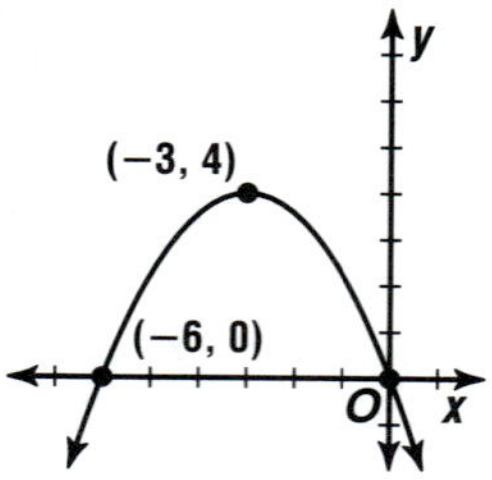

37.

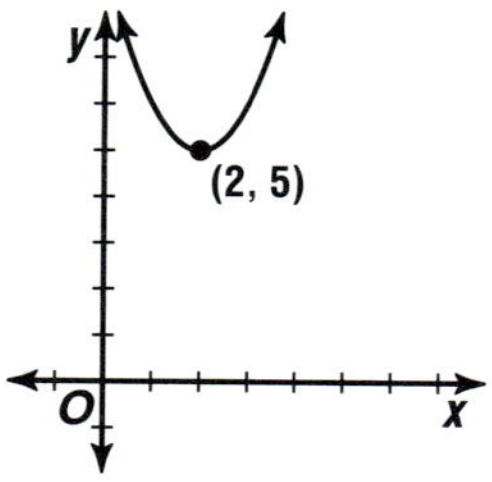

39. $-4, -8$ or $4, 8$ **41.** no solution **43.** $-2, -6$ **45.** no y-intercepts **47.** no real roots **49.** 0.29, 1.71 **51.** $-0.79, 2.54$ **53.** $-2, k > -2, k < -2$

55a.

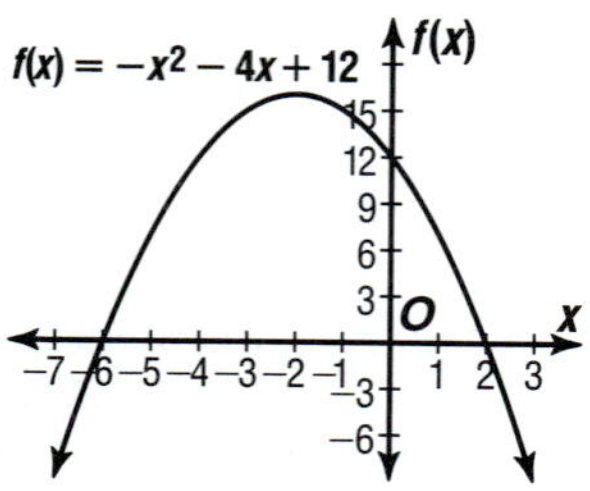

55b. 8 feet **55c.** 16 feet **55d.** $85\frac{1}{3}$ ft^2 **55e.** \$297

57. $x = 0$; $(0, 4)$

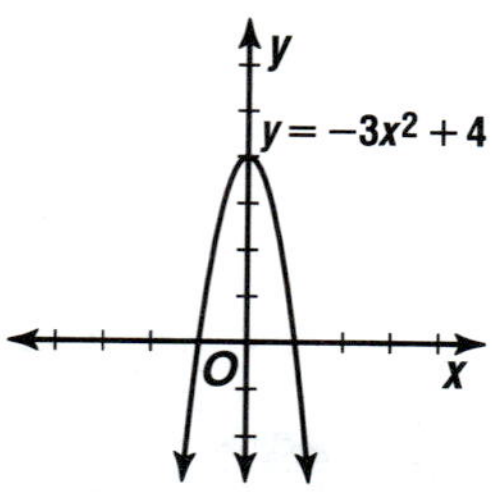

59. $(4x - 3)$ m by $(2x - 1)$ m **61.** 6 **63.** $-4 < x < \frac{4}{3}$ **65.** \$24.75

Pages 631–633 Lesson 11–3

5. $1, 3, -18; 3, -6$ **7.** $4, -2, 15$; no real roots **9.** $1.83, -2.33$ **11.** $-1, -6$ **13.** about 29.4 ft/s **15.** $-8.61, -1.39$ **17.** $-\frac{4}{5}, 1$ **19.** $-\frac{5}{3}, 4$ **21.** $-2.91, 2.41$ **23.** 7 **25.** $-\frac{3}{2}, -\frac{5}{3}$ **27.** $-6, 6$ **29.** $-\frac{1}{3}, 1$ **31.** $-3, -\frac{1}{2}$ **33.** $0.60, -0.25$ **35.** 0.5, 2 **37.** $-0.2, 1.4$ **39.** Sample answer: 4, 20, 23; $4x^2 + 20x + 23 = 0$ **41a.** 10, 1 **41b.** none **41c.** -0.5 **41d.** $-1, 0.7142857143$ **43a.** Discriminant is not a perfect square. **43b.** Discriminant is a perfect square but the expression is not an integer **43c.** Discriminant is a perfect square and the equation can be factored. **43d.** Discriminant is 0 and the equation is a perfect square. **45a.** Y, 10 mg; C, 8.75 mg **45b.** $0 = a^2 - 11a + 12$; 1.2 yr, 9.8 yr **47.** $\{0, -9\}$ **49.** 24, 18 **51.** yes **53.** $-4°$F

Page 633 Self Test

1. $x = \frac{1}{2}, \left(\frac{1}{2}, -\frac{25}{4}\right)$

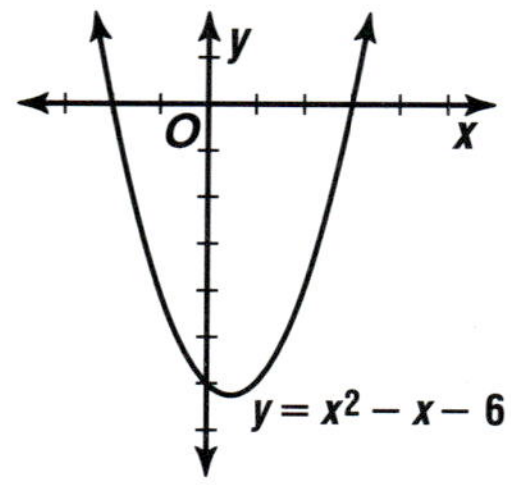

3. $x = 0, (0, 7)$

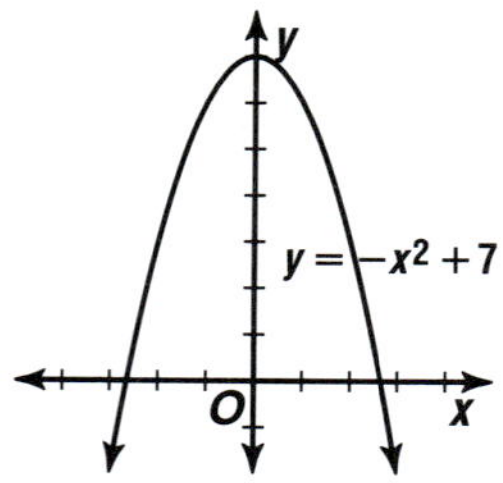

5. $-9, 9$

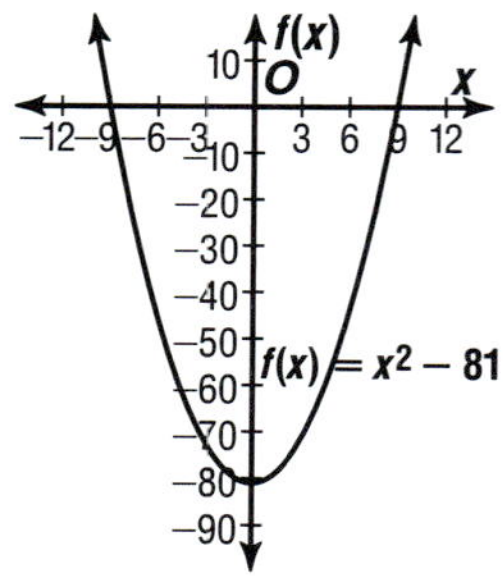

7. $\varnothing$

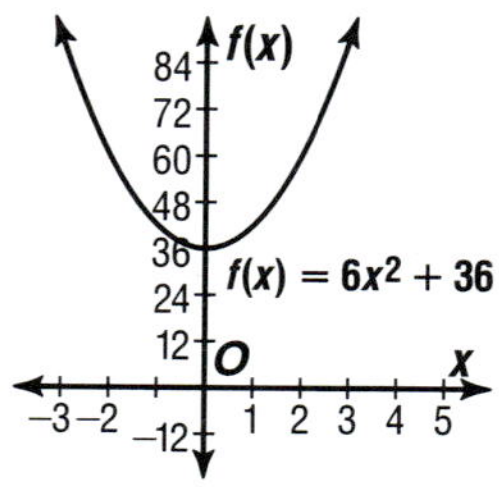

9. $\varnothing$

Page 634 Lesson 11–4A

1.

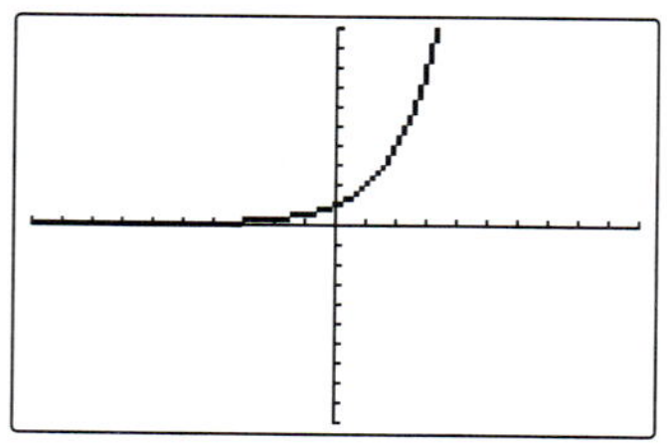

3.

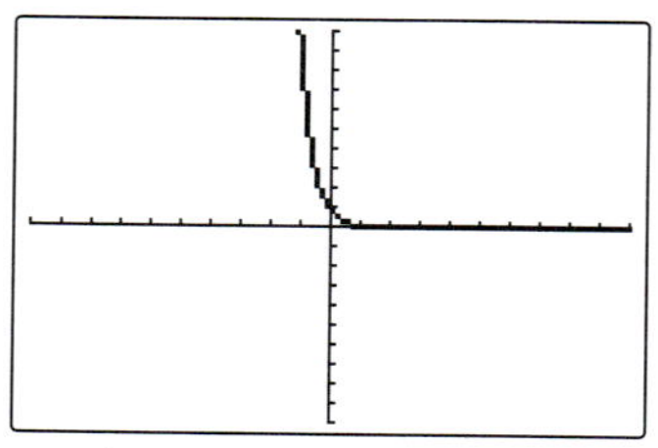

5.

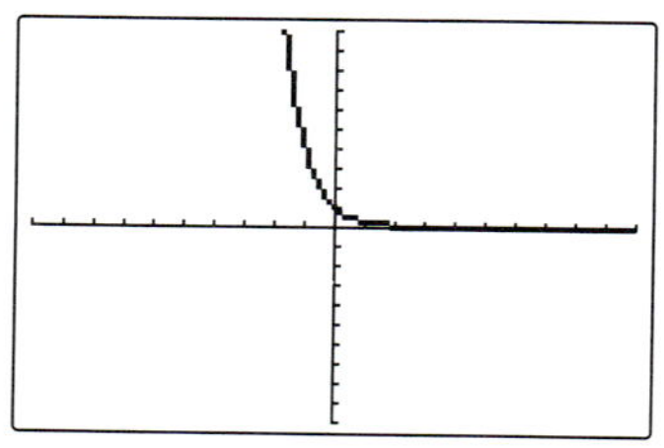

7.
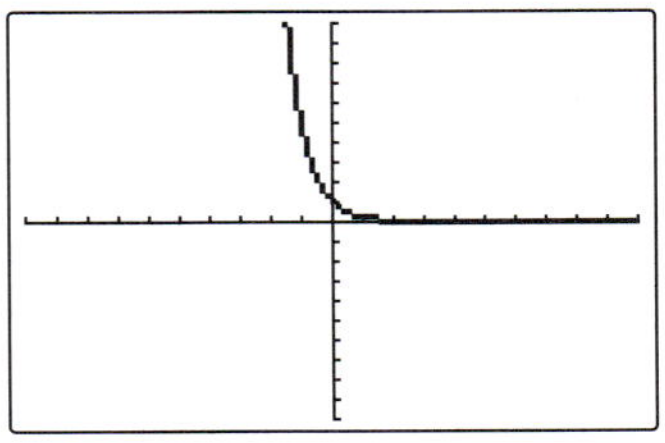

9.
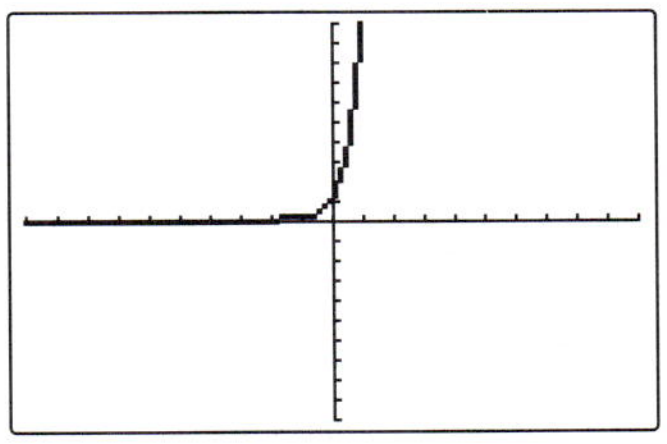

Pages 640–642 Lesson 11–4

7. 5.20 **9.** 12.51

11. 7

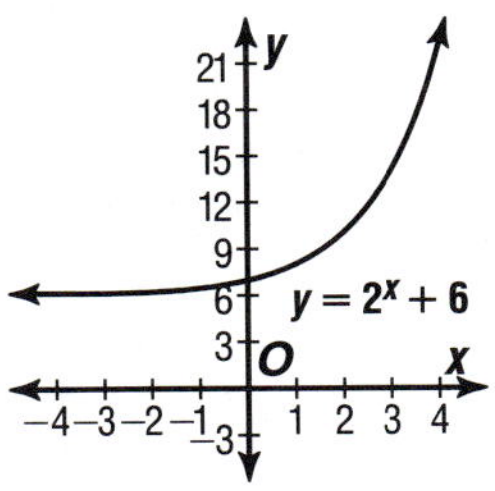

13. −2 **15.** −2 **17.** 10.56 **19.** 1.63 **21.** 25.86 **23.** 0.86

25. 5

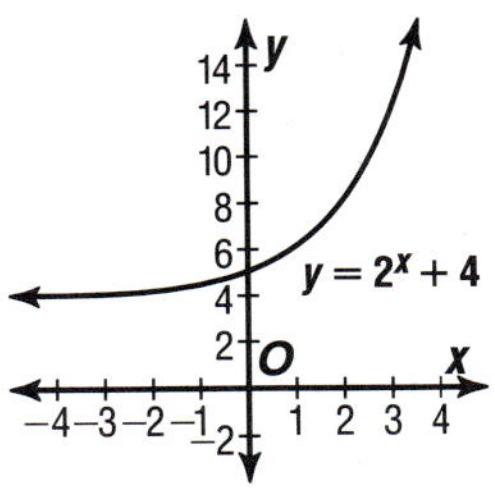

27. 3

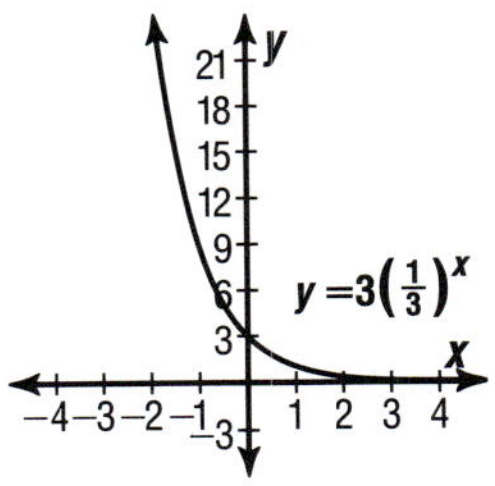

29. 1

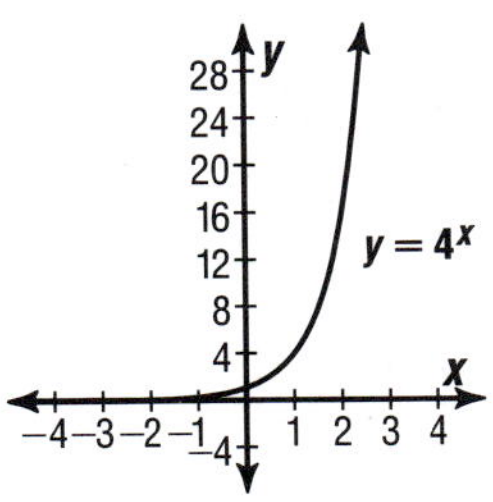

31. no, linear **33.** no, no pattern **35.** −7 **37.** −3 **39.** 3 **41.** 3, −1

43. All have the same shape but different y-intercepts.

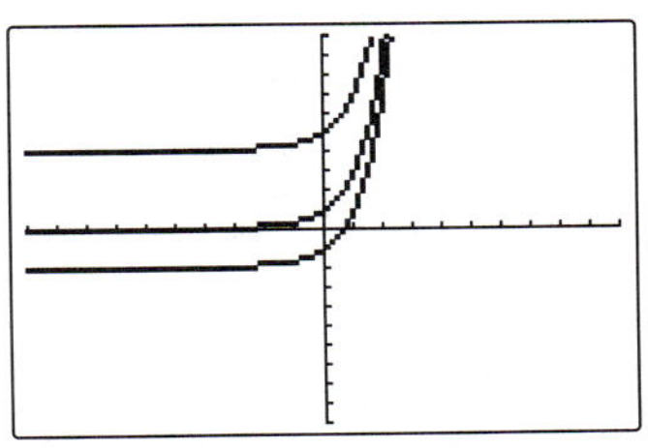

45. All have the same shape but are positioned at different places along the x-axis.

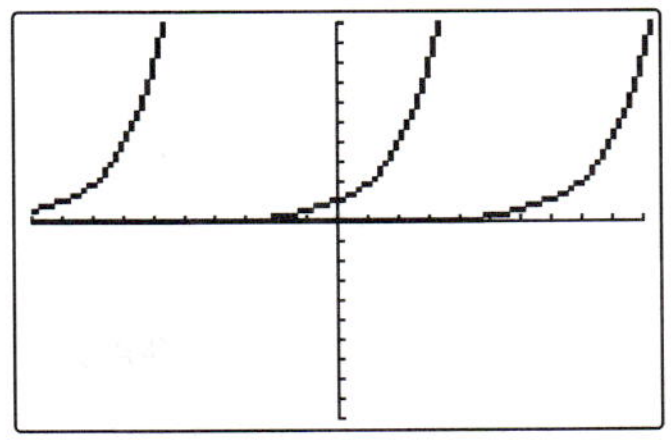

47a. 2.51 **47b.** You cannot write 10 as a power or 2.5. **49.** 1600 bacteria **51.** $-3, -\frac{1}{2}$ **53.** $\frac{1}{5}ab(4a - 3b - 1)$ **55.** 184

57a–b.

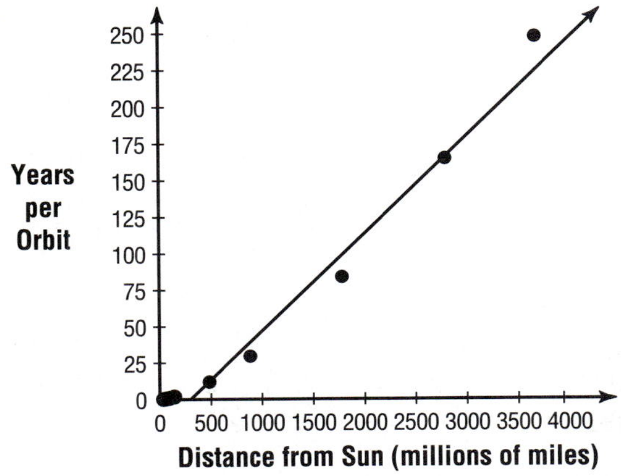

Sample answer: $y = 0.07x - 12$ **57c.** 275 years **59.** 60

Pages 646–649 Lesson 11–5

3a. 1 **3b.** 2 **3c.** 4 **3d.** 365 **5.** decay **7.** about \$70,000,000,000 **9.** \$661.44 **11.** \$10,962.19 **13a.** Each equation represents growth and t is the number of years since 1994. $y = 58.7(1.025)^t$, $y = 919.9(1.019)^t$, $y = 35.6(1.021)^t$, $y = 2.9(1.013)^t$ **13b.** 68.1 million, 1029.9 million, 40.3 million, 3.1 million

13c.

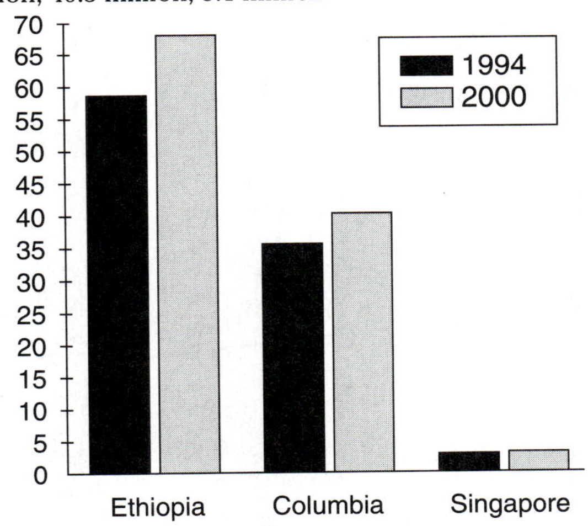

15a. $y = 231.5(1.0963)^t$, t = years since 1950, growth **15b.** 57.6 trillion **17a.** \$6931.53 **17b.** \$6954.58 **17c.** \$23.05 **17d.** daily **21.** $a > 1$, growth; $0 < a < 1$, decay; x represents time **23.** $-\frac{1}{2}$ **25.** $-\frac{r^{10}t^2}{3}$ **27.** $y = -2.5x + 2$

Page 651 Chapter 11 Highlights

1. d **3.** i **5.** c **7.** b **9.** f

Pages 652–654 Chapter 11 Study Guide and Assessment

11. $x = 0$; (0, 4) **13.** $x = -1$; (−1, −20) **15.** $x = -1$; (−1, −1)

17.
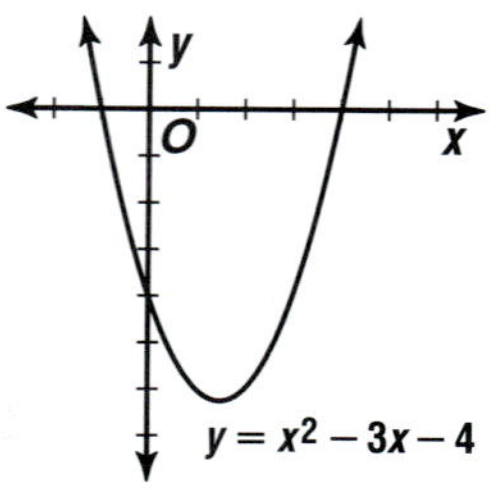

19.
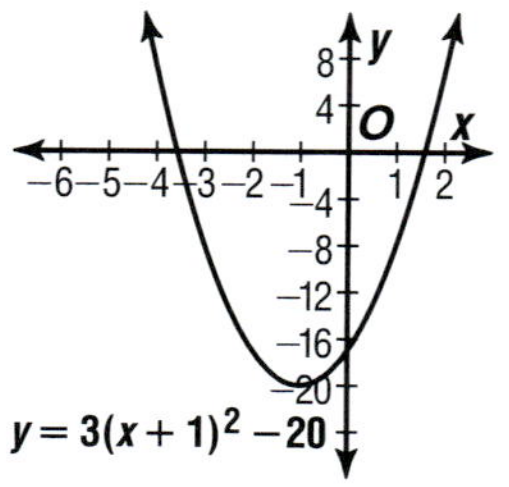

21. $-3, 4$ **23.** $-5 < x < -4, 0 < x < 1$ **25.** 3, 7 **27.** $10, -2$ **29.** $\frac{3}{2}, -\frac{5}{2}$ **31.** $1, \frac{4}{9}$ **33.** 2, 3 **35.** $0.47, -0.71$

37. 7
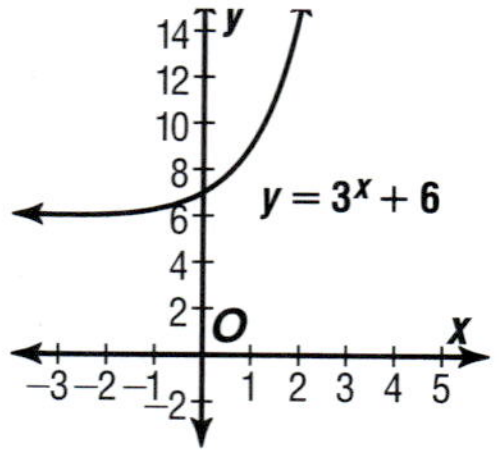

39. 1
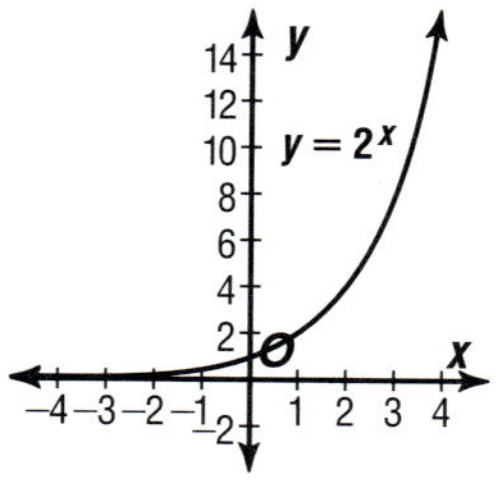

41. -3 **43.** -6 **45.** $-3, \frac{3}{2}$ **47.** \$12,067.68 **49.** \$24,688.37 **51.** 1.3 seconds and 4.7 seconds **53.** between 4 meters and 5 meters **55.** CD, which yields \$541.50 vs. savings at \$530.92

CHAPTER 12 EXPLORING RATIONAL EXPRESSIONS AND EQUATIONS

Pages 663–665 Lesson 12–1

7. $7a^2b$; $\frac{-b^2}{3a^3}$; $a \neq 0, b \neq 0$ **9.** b; $\frac{3}{b+5}$; $b \neq 0, b \neq -5$ **11.** $m - 3$; $\frac{1}{m+3}$; $m \neq \pm 3$ **13a.** 5 **13b.** 750 lb **15.** $\frac{5y}{2z}$; $y \neq 0, z \neq 0$ **17.** $\frac{4}{5x}$; $x \neq 0, y \neq 0$ **19.** y; $y \neq -\frac{1}{3}$ **21.** $y + 7x$; $y \neq 7x$ **23.** $\frac{1}{a-4}$; $a \neq 4, 3$ **25.** $\frac{1}{x+4}$; $x \neq -4$ **27.** $\frac{a+6}{a+4}$; $a \neq -4, 2$ **29.** $\frac{b+1}{b-9}$; $b \neq 9, 4$ **31.** $\frac{4}{5}$; $x \neq -1$ **33.** $-\frac{5}{3}$ **35.** not possible, $y \neq -2$ **37a.** 192 **37b.** 3840 lb **39a.** 9.5°/mile **39b.** $-\frac{95}{10} = -\frac{19}{2}$

39c.
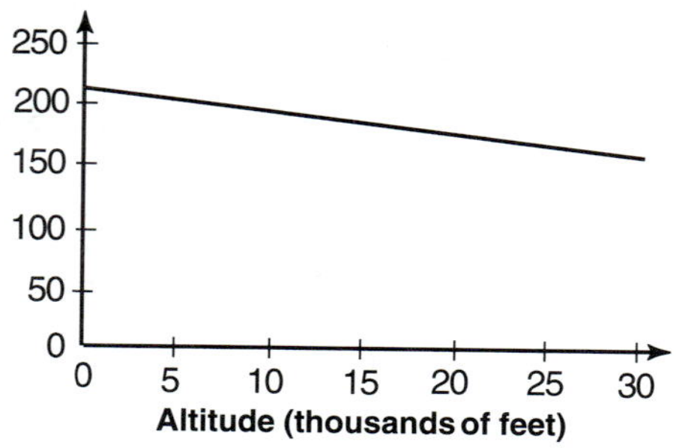

41. ± 11

43.
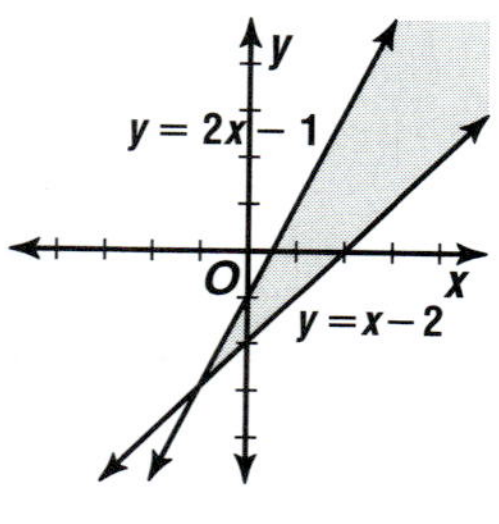

45.
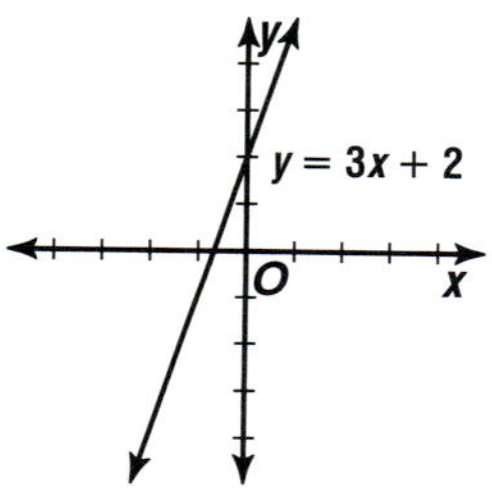

Page 666 Lesson 12–1B

1. $\frac{x-5}{x+5}$; -5 **3.** $\frac{1}{2x}$; 0, 4.5 **5.** $\frac{x-1}{x-8}$; 8 **7.** -1; 3 **9.** $-\frac{x+5}{x+6}$; $-6, 5$

Pages 669–670 Lesson 12–2

5. $\frac{9m}{2xy}$ **7.** $\frac{4}{x+3}$ **9.** $\frac{4}{3}$ **11a.** 91.44 cm/yd **11b.** changing centimeters to yards **13.** $\frac{3a}{2}$ **15.** $\frac{2}{x}$ **17.** $8y$ **19.** $\frac{4m}{3(m+5)}$ **21.** $\frac{2m}{a+9}$ **23.** 2 **25.** $3(x - y)$ **27.** 36 **29.** $\frac{4x}{3x-5}$ **31.** $\frac{4}{5(x+5)}$ **33.** 21.8 mph; converts ft/s to mph **35.** 10,800 Calories **37.** Sample answer: $\frac{3(x+2)}{x+7} \cdot \frac{2(x-3)}{x-4}$; $\frac{6}{x+7} \cdot \frac{x^2-x-6}{x-4}$ **39a.** $\frac{\text{1 franc}}{\text{0.1981 dollars}}$; $\frac{\text{1 dollar}}{\text{5.05 francs}}$ **39b.** 12,500 pesos $\cdot \frac{\text{0.1597 dollars}}{\text{1 peso}} \cdot \frac{\text{1 franc}}{\text{0.1981 dollars}}$; about 10,077 francs **39c.** Convert to American dollars and then to Hong Kong's dollar. **41.** 729 **43.** 4 **45.** 0

Pages 672–674 Lesson 12–3

5. $\frac{5}{x}$ **7.** $\frac{y+3}{x^2-9}$ **9.** $\frac{1}{x^2+2x+5}$ **11.** $\frac{(m+2)^2}{4}$ **13.** $\frac{x+4}{x+6}$ **15.** 0.5 ft^3 **17.** $\frac{a}{a+11}$ **19.** $\frac{b^2m}{c^2}$ **21.** $\frac{m+5}{m}$ **23.** $\frac{4}{z+3}$ **25.** $\frac{2(x+5)}{x+1}$ **27.** $x + 3$ **29.** $x + 5$ **31.** $(x + 5)(x + 3)$ **33.** 88 ft/s; sample answer: changes 60 mph to ft/s **35.** 27.5 yd^3; changes ft^3 to yd^3 **37.** $\frac{x-y}{4}$ **39a.** 5500 miles **39b.** 41.3 trains **39c.** 10,618.2 miles; 27.3 trains **41.** $\frac{8}{m-5}$ **43.** $(4a - 3b^2)^2$ **45.** $x < -2$ **47.** $7 + 2 = 2 + 7$

Pages 678–680 Lesson 12–4

5. $3b^2 - 5$ **7.** $t - 1$ **9.** $2m + 3 + \frac{-3}{m+2}$ **11.** $(2x + 3)$ m **13.** $\frac{b}{3} + 3 - \frac{7}{3b}$ **15.** $\frac{m}{7} + 1 - \frac{4}{m}$ **17.** $a^2 + 2a + 12 + \frac{3}{a-2}$ **19.** $m - 3 - \frac{2}{m+7}$ **21.** $2x + 6 + \frac{1}{x-7}$ **23.** $3m^2 + 4k^2 - 2$ **25.** $a + 7 - \frac{1}{a+3}$ **27.** $3x - 2 + \frac{21}{2x+3}$ **29.** $t + 4 - \frac{5}{4t+1}$ **31.** $8x^2 + \frac{32x}{7} - 9$ **33a.** $x^2 + 4x + 4$ **33b.** $5t^2 - 3t - 2$ **33c.** $2a^2 + 3a - 4$ **35.** -15 **37.** \$480,000 **39.** $-\frac{x}{7}$ **41.** $3(x - 7)(x + 5)$ **43.** (1, 3)

45.
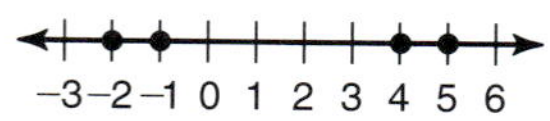

Page 680 Self Test

1. $\frac{25x}{36y}$ **3.** $\frac{(x+4)(4x^2+2x-3)}{(x+3)(x+2)(x-1)}$ **5.** $\frac{x-5}{x+4}$ **7.** $2x - 5$ **9.** $4(3x - 1)$ or $(12x - 4)$ units

Pages 683–684 Lesson 12–5

5. $\frac{10}{x}$ **7.** $\frac{10}{a+2}$ **9.** 3 **11.** m **13.** $-\frac{a}{6}$ **15.** 2 **17.** $\frac{7}{x+7}$ **19.** 1 **21.** 1 **23.** $\frac{4x}{x+2}$ **25.** $\frac{2y-6}{y+3}$ **27.** 2 **29.** $\frac{25x-93}{2x+5}$ **31.** $\frac{24x+26y}{7x-2y}$ **33.** b **35.** 442 days **37.** $\pm\frac{6}{5}$ **39.** $-3, 4$ **41.** $\frac{1}{216}$

Pages 687–689 Lesson 12–6

3. x^2 **5.** $90m^2b^2$ **7.** $(x-3)(x+3)$ **9.** $\frac{7+9m}{15m^2}$

11. $\frac{-20}{3(x+2)}$ **13.** $\frac{22-7y}{6y^2}$ **15.** 168 members **17.** $\frac{-5x}{63}$

19. $\frac{7yz+3}{xyz}$ **21.** $\frac{2s-3t}{s^2t^2}$ **23.** $\frac{7z+8}{(z+5)(z-4)}$ **25.** $\frac{k^2+k-10}{(k+5)(k+3)}$

27. $\frac{-17r-32}{(3r-2)(r-5)}$ **29.** $\frac{10+m}{2(2m-3)}$ **31.** $\frac{3w-4}{3(5w+2)}$

33. $\frac{-5n-4}{(n+3)(n+1)}$ **35.** $\frac{-17t+27}{(t+3)(10t-9)}$ **37.** $\frac{v^2+11v-2}{(v+4)(v-1)}$

39a. 360, 3, 120, 360 **39b.** 540, 6, 90, 540 **39c.** The GCF times the LCM of two numbers is equal to the product of the two numbers. **39d.** Divide the GCF into the product of the two numbers to find the LCM. **41.** 30 months later or October 20, 1998 **43.** 2 **45.** $\frac{3 \pm \sqrt{41}}{4} \approx 2.35$ or -0.85 **47.** $-15a^6b^3$ **49.** 4

Pages 693–695 Lesson 12–7

3. $\frac{8x+3}{x}$ **5.** $\frac{6m^2+m+1}{2m}$ **7.** $\frac{9}{5}$ **9.** $\frac{y}{2}$ **11.** $\frac{a-b}{3}$

13. $\frac{3x+15}{x+3}$ **15.** $\frac{6x-1}{2x+1}$ **17.** $\frac{5r^2+r-48}{r^2-9}$ **19.** $\frac{4}{3}$ **21.** ab

23. $\frac{6}{x}$ **25.** $\frac{a-5}{a-2}$ **27.** $\frac{1}{x+3}$ **29.** $\frac{m+6}{m+2}$ **31.** $\frac{y-3}{y+2}$

33. $\frac{t^2+2t+2}{-t^2}$ **35.** $\frac{32b^2}{35}$ **37a.** $x \neq 0, x \neq -3$ **37b.** $x \neq 0$, $x \neq -3$ **37c.** yes **39a.** $\frac{fs}{s-v}$ **39b.** 413.5 **39c.** 2 **39d.** 6

41. $\frac{2x+3}{x+3}$ **43.** $(2x+1)(2x-1)$ **45.** $(-3, 4)$

47. $w = \frac{P-2\ell}{2}$

Pages 700–702 Lesson 12–8

5. -12 **7.** $-\frac{1}{2}$ **9.** 0 **11a.** $\frac{1}{5}$ **11b.** $\frac{3}{5}$ **11c.** $\frac{x}{5}$ **13.** 3.429 ohms **15.** 8 ohms, 4 ohms **17.** $\frac{50}{3}$ **19.** $\frac{5}{4}$ **21.** 0

23. 2 or $-\frac{1}{3}$ **25.** 4 or $-\frac{1}{3}$ **27.** -13 **29.** $\frac{3}{5}$ **31.** 3 **33.** 6

35. 4 ohms **37.** $R_1 = \frac{R_2R_T}{R_2-R_T}$ **39.** $n = \frac{IR}{E-Ir}$ **41.** 10

43. 96 ohms **45a.** 2.5 hours **45b.** 2.19 hours **45c.** after 923 miles **47a.** $w = \frac{c\ell}{100}$ **47b.** $\ell = \frac{100w}{c}$ **49.** 10

51. $\frac{b+4}{4(b+2)^2}$

53.

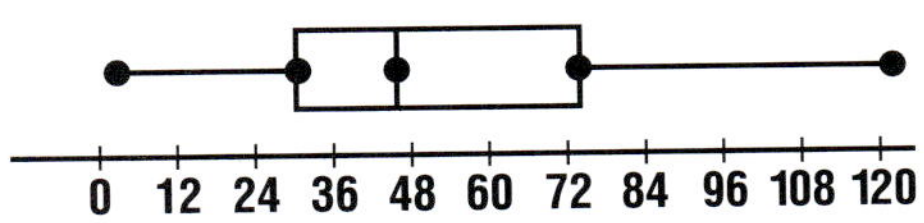

55. $\frac{48}{25}$ **57.** 18

Page 703 Chapter 12 Highlights

1. false, rational **3.** true **5.** false, $x^2 - 144$ **7.** false, least common multiple

Pages 704–706 Chapter 12 Study Guide and Assessment

9. $z, z \neq 3$ **11.** $\frac{a}{a+2}, a \neq 0, -2$ **13.** $\frac{1}{(b+3)(b+2)}$, $b \neq \pm 2, \pm 3$ **15.** $\frac{3axy}{10}$ **17.** $\frac{3}{a^2-3a}$ **19.** $b+7$

21. $\frac{y^2-4y}{3}$ **23.** $\frac{2m-3}{3m-2}$ **25.** x^2+4x-2 **27.** $x^3+5x^2+12x+23+\frac{52}{x-2}$ **29.** $\frac{2a}{m^2}$ **31.** $\frac{2m+3}{5}$ **33.** $a+b$

35. $\frac{22n}{21}$ **37.** $\frac{4c^2+9d}{6cd^2}$ **39.** $\frac{4r}{r-3}$ **41.** $\frac{5m-8}{m-2}$ **43.** $\frac{3x}{y}$

45. $\frac{x^2+8x-65}{x^2+8x+12}$ **47.** -5 **49.** $-\frac{1}{4}$ **51.** 5, $-\frac{1}{4}$ **53.** 6 bicycles, 24 tricycles, and 24 wagons **55.** $1\frac{7}{8}$ hours

CHAPTER 13 EXPLORING RADICAL EXPRESSIONS AND EQUATIONS

Page 712 Lesson 13–1A

1. $4+4=8$ **3.** $16+9=25$

5.

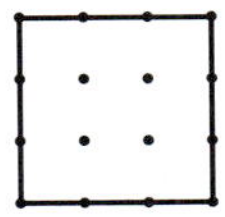

7.

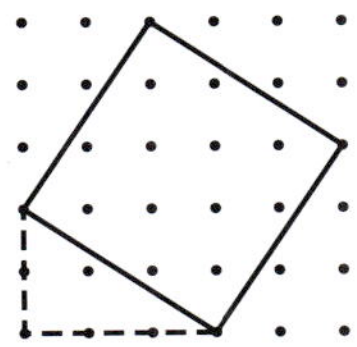

9.

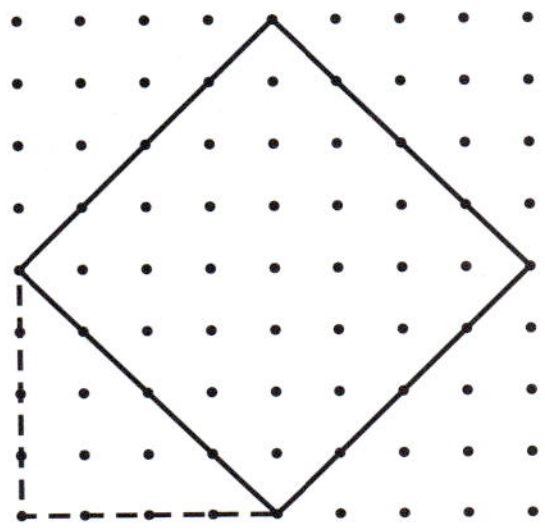

Pages 715–718 Lesson 13–1

7. 7 **9.** 11.40 **11.** 15 **13.** 2 **15.** yes **17.** 127.28 ft **19.** 13.86 **21.** 13.08 **23.** 14.70 **25.** 60 **27.** 4 **29.** $\sqrt{67} \approx 8.19$ **31.** $\sqrt{27} \approx 5.20$ **33.** $\sqrt{145} \approx 12.04$ **35.** yes **37.** no; $11^2 + 12^2 \neq 15^2$ **39.** yes **41.** $\sqrt{75}$ in. or about 8.66 in. **43a.** 44.49 m **43b.** 78 m^2

45.

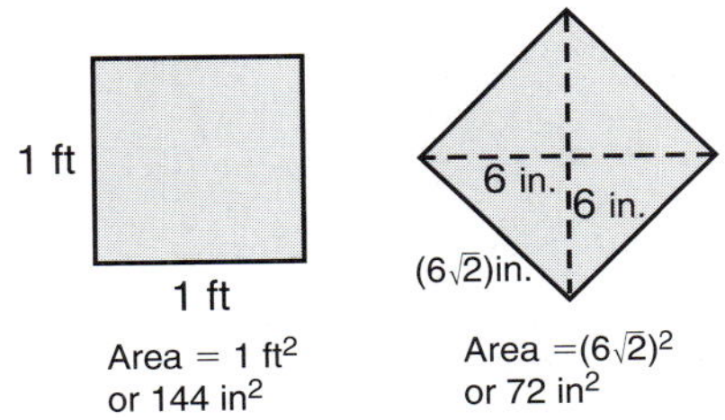

47. about 2.66 m **49.** -7 **51.** $12r^7$ **53.** $\left\{c \mid c \geq \frac{1}{2}\right\}$ **55.** 41

Pages 724–725 Lesson 13–2

5. $5-\sqrt{2}$; 23 **7.** $\frac{\sqrt{7}}{\sqrt{7}}$ **9.** $3\sqrt{2}$ **11.** $\frac{\sqrt{21}}{7}$ **13.** $10\sqrt{2}+26$ **15.** $\frac{18+6\sqrt{2}}{7}$ **17.** > **19.** about 7003.5 gal/min

21. $4\sqrt{5}$ **23.** $10\sqrt{5}$ **25.** $\frac{\sqrt{2}}{2}$ **27.** $\frac{\sqrt{22}}{8}$ **29.** $84\sqrt{5}$

31. $\frac{\sqrt{11}}{11}$ **33.** $3|ab|\sqrt{6}$ **35.** $7x^2y^3\sqrt{3xy}$ **37.** $\frac{3\sqrt{3}}{|p|}$

39. $\frac{x\sqrt{3xy}}{2y^3}$ **41.** $y^2 - 2y\sqrt{7} + 7$ **43.** $\frac{28\sqrt{2}+14\sqrt{5}}{3}$

45. $\frac{-2\sqrt{5}-\sqrt{10}}{2}$ **47.** $\frac{c-2\sqrt{cd}+d}{c-d}$ **49.** $x^2 - 5x\sqrt{3} + 12$

51. > **53.** < **55.** Yes; the result is about 11.84. **57.** 18.44 cm **59.** 1, $\frac{2}{3}$ **61.** 2.7×10^9 acres

63. $y = \frac{1}{5}x + 6$ **65.** -6

Page 726 Lesson 13–2B

1. $14\sqrt{7}$ or 37.04 **3.** $2\sqrt{3} + 3\sqrt{2}$ or 7.71 **5.** $\frac{4\sqrt{7}}{7}$ or 1.51 **7.** $3\sqrt{3}$ or 5.20 **9.** $\frac{\sqrt{3}}{2} - \frac{\sqrt{5}}{3} + 3\sqrt{2}$ or 4.36 **11.** $\frac{-16\sqrt{6}}{3}$ or -13.06

Pages 729–731 Lesson 13–3

5. $3\sqrt{5}, 3\sqrt{20}$ **7.** none **9.** $13\sqrt{6}$ **11.** $12\sqrt{7x}$ **13.** $13\sqrt{3} + \sqrt{2}$; 23.93 **15.** $\frac{8}{7}\sqrt{7}$; 3.02 **17.** 11 **19.** $26\sqrt{13}$ **21.** in simplest form **23.** $21\sqrt{2x}$ **25.** $9\sqrt{3}$; 15.59 **27.** $\sqrt{6} + 2\sqrt{2} + \sqrt{10}$; 8.44 **29.** $-\sqrt{7}$; -2.65 **31.** $29\sqrt{3}$; 50.23 **33.** $4\sqrt{5} + 15\sqrt{2}$; 30.16 **35.** $4\sqrt{3} - 3\sqrt{5}$; 0.22 **37.** $10\sqrt{2} + 3\sqrt{10}$ **39.** $19\sqrt{5}$ **41.** $10\sqrt{3} + 16$ **43.** Both $(x - 5)^2$ and $(x - 5)^4$ must be nonnegative, but $x - 5$ may be negative. **45.** $6\frac{2}{5}$ ft **47.** $3x - 3y$ **49.** 7 **51.** $\frac{2}{3}$ **53a.** 1991; about 9 million **53b.** 6 million

Page 731 Self Test

1. 35 **3.** 46.17 **5.** 10 **7.** $11\sqrt{6}$ **9.** $12\sqrt{5} - 6\sqrt{3} + 2\sqrt{15} - 3$

Pages 734–736 Lesson 13–4

7. $a + 3 = 4$ **9.** 16 **11.** 36 **13.** -12 **15.** 3.9 mph **17.** -63 **19.** no real solution **21.** $\frac{81}{25}$ **23.** 2 **25.** 24 **27.** $\frac{3}{25}$ **29.** $\pm\frac{4}{3}\sqrt{3}$ **31.** $\sqrt{7}$ **33.** 6 **35.** $-3, -10$ or $3, 10$ **37.** 16 **39.** no real solution **41.** $\left(\frac{1}{4}, \frac{25}{36}\right)$ **43.** $\sqrt{3} + 1$ **45.** $54\frac{2}{3}$ mi **47a.** No, at 30 mph, her car should have skidded 75 feet after the breaks were applied and not 110 feet. **47b.** about 36 miles per hour **49.** $6b - 26 + \frac{150}{b + 5}$ **51.** $6xy^3$ **53.** $(-4, 5)$ **55.** $\frac{8}{13}$

Pages 739–741 Lesson 13–5

5. 5 **7.** $3\sqrt{2}$ or 4.24 **9.** 7 or 1 **11.** about 9.49 mi **13.** 17 **15.** $\sqrt{41}$ or 6.40 **17.** $\frac{10}{3}$ or 3.33 **19.** $\frac{13}{10}$ or 1.30 **21.** $2\sqrt{3}$ or 3.46 **23.** 17 or -13 **25.** -10 or 4 **27.** 8 or 32 **29.** no **31.** $\sqrt{157} \neq \sqrt{101}$; Trapezoid is not isosceles. **33.** The distance between $(3, -2)$ and $(-3, 7)$ is $3\sqrt{13}$ units. The distance between $(-3, 7)$ and $(-9, 3)$ is $2\sqrt{13}$ units. The distance between $(3, -2)$ and $(-9, 3)$ is 13 units. Since $\left(3\sqrt{13}\right)^2 + \left(2\sqrt{13}\right)^2 = 13^2$, the triangle is a right triangle. **35.** 109 miles **37.** $\frac{2\sqrt{2}}{3}$

39. no solution

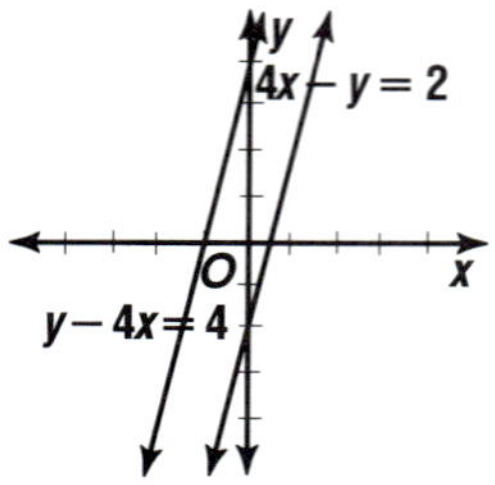

41a. 7392 BTU **41b.** 3705 BTU **41c.** 6247.5 BTU **41d.** 14,040 BTU **41e.** 6831.45 BTU

Page 742 Lesson 13–6A

1. $(x + 2)^2 = 1$ **3.** $(x + 2)^2 = 5$ **5.** $(x - 2)^2 = 5$ **7.** $(x + 1.5)^2 = 3.25$

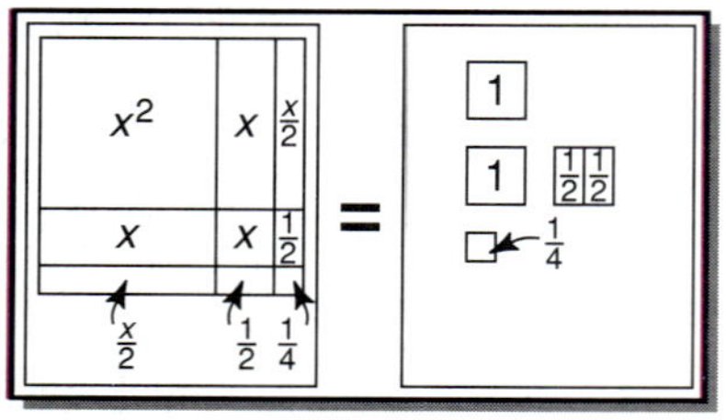

Pages 746–747 Lesson 13–6

5. 64 **7.** $-1, -3$ **9.** $7, -3$ **11.** $2 \pm \sqrt{6}$ **13.** 4.9 ft **15.** 16 **17.** $\frac{121}{4}$ **19.** 8 **21.** 4, 1 **23.** $\frac{7}{3}$ **25.** $3 \pm \sqrt{5}$ **27.** $5 \pm 4\sqrt{3}$ **29.** $\frac{-5 \pm 2\sqrt{15}}{5}$ **31.** $\frac{2}{3}, -1$ **33.** $\frac{7 \pm \sqrt{85}}{6}$ **35.** $18, -18$ **37.** 3 **39.** $2 \pm \sqrt{4 - c}$ **41.** $b(-2 \pm \sqrt{3})$ **43.** 45 mph, 55 mph **45.** 8.06 **47.** 2042 **49.** $(2, 2)$ **51a.** 224.6 **51b.** 172

Page 749 Chapter 13 Highlights

1. false, $-3 - \sqrt{7}$ **3.** false, $-2 - 2\sqrt{3} - \sqrt{5} - \sqrt{15}$ **5.** true **7.** false, $3x + 19 = x^2 + 6x + 9$ **9.** false, $\frac{x\sqrt{2xy}}{y}$

Pages 750–752 Chapter 13 Study Guide and Assessment

11. 34 **13.** $5\sqrt{5} \approx 11.18$ **15.** 24 **17.** no; $9^2 + 16^2 \neq 20^2$ **19.** yes **21.** $4\sqrt{30}$ **23.** $2|a|b^2\sqrt{11b}$ **25.** $57 - 24\sqrt{3}$ **27.** $\frac{3\sqrt{35} - 5\sqrt{21}}{-15}$ **29.** $2\sqrt{6} - 4\sqrt{3}$ **31.** $36\sqrt{3}$ **33.** $\frac{9\sqrt{2}}{4}$ **35.** 12 **37.** $\frac{26}{7}$ **39.** 45 **41.** 3 **43.** no solution **45.** 17 **47.** $\sqrt{205} \approx 14.32$ **49.** 5 or -1 **51.** 5 or -3 **53.** $\frac{49}{4}$ **55.** $\frac{1}{9}$ **57.** $\frac{7 \pm \sqrt{69}}{2}$ **59.** $-2 \pm \sqrt{6}$ **61.** $22\sqrt{6} \approx 53.9$ **63.** scalene triangle **65.** 5 ft **67.** No, it should skid about 201.7 ft.

PHOTO CREDITS

Cover (t)FPG, (b)Nawrocki Stock, (bkgd)Superstock; **iii** (t)courtesy Home of the Hamburger, Inc., (b)Aaron Haupt; **viii** (l)Terry Eiler, (r)Paul L. Ruben **ix** (t)Geoff Butler, (b)Skip Comer; **x** (t)Stephen Webster, (bl)Aaron Haupt, (br)Mark Peterson/Tony Stone Images; **xi** Tom Tietz/Tony Stone Images; **xii** (t)Stan Fellerman/The Stock Market, (b)Aaron Haupt; **xiii** (t)Tom McCarthy/The Stock Market, (c)Geoff Butler, (b)Charles H. Kuhn Collection, The Ohio State University Cartoon,Graphic and Photgraphic Arts Research Library/Reprinted with Special Permission of King Features Syndicate; **xiv** (t)Clark James Mishler/The Stock Market, (b)Julian Baum/Science Photo Library/Photo Researchers; **xv** (t)Jonathan Daniel/Allsport USA, (c)Steve Niedorf/The Image Bank, (b)Jody Dole/The Image Bank; **xvi** Tate Gallery, London/Art Resource, NY; **xvii** (t)Morton & White, (b)NCSA, University of IL/Science Photo Library/Photo Researchers, **4** (l)E. Hobson/Ancient Art & Architecture Collection, (r)David Ball/The Stock Market; **5** (tl)John Neubauer, (tr)Scott Cunningham, (bl)Ron Sheridan/Ancient Art & Architecture Collection, (br)Ulf Anderson/Gamma Liaison; **6** Doug Martin; **10** (l)Aaron Haupt, (r)KS Studio; **11** (t)Ted Rice, (b)courtesy Math Association Of America; **12** Terry Eiler; **18** Aaron Haupt; **19** Dennis O'Clair/Tony Stone Images; **24** (t)Stephen Studd/Tony Stone Images, (b)Ken Reid/FPG; **27** (t)Cynthia Johnson/Gamma Liaison, (bl br)KS Studio; **30** (t)KS Studio, (b)Bruce Hands/Tony Stone Images; **31** Phil Degginger/Tony Stone Images; **32** courtesy Home of the Hamburger, Inc.; **36** Gail Shumwat/FPG; **37** Duomo/Steven E. Sutton; **40** Doug Martin; **41** Mary Ann Evans; **43, 45** Aaron Haupt; **46** David Madison; **50** Eugene G. Schulz; **52** Kenji Kerins; **54** Doug Martin; **55** (l)KS Studio, (r)Paul L. Ruben; **57** Ken Huang/The Image Bank; **58** Aaron Haupt; **59** HERMAN ©1975 Jim Unger. Reprinted with permission of UNIVERSAL PRESS SYNDICATE. All rights reserved. **60** J. Parker/Westlight; **61** Aaron Haupt; **62** Sonderegger/Westlight; **67** (l)Aaron Haupt, (r)Eclipse Studios; **70** (t)Geoff Butler, (b)Frank Lerner; **71** (tl)James Wasserman, (tr)Doug Martin, (cl)Archive Photos, (cr)courtesy Gae Veit, (b)courtesy Nestle USA; **72-73** Geoff Butler **75** KS Studio; **76** Geoff Butler; **77** Kenji Kerins; **78** James Avery/Everett Collection; **79** Geoff Butler; **80** (l)Mark Petersen/Tony Stone Images, (r)R.B. Sanchez/The Stock Market; **82** Geoff Butler; **83** Focus on Sports; **85** AP/NASA/Wide World Photos; **88** Doug Martin; **89** Geoff Butler; **91** (t)American Photo Bank, (b)Geoff Butler; **92** William Clark/Tony Stone Images; **95** (t)Duomo/Paul Sutton, (b)Aaron Haupt; **97** Aaron Haupt; **98** (l)UPI/Corbis-Bettmann, (r)Warren Morgan/Westlight; **99** Doug Martin; **100** (t)Westlight, (b)Stewart Cohen/Tony Stone Images; **102** Archive Photos; **103** James Marshall/The Stock Market; **104** (t)Aaron Haupt, (c)Gary Mortimore/Allsport USA, (b)Geoff Butler; **106** R. Foulds/Washington Stock Photos; **110** P. Saloutos/The Stock Market, (inset)Aaron Haupt; **112** (t)Holmes-Lebel/FPG, (b)Corbis-Bettmann; **113** Kenji Kerins, (inset)Aaron Haupt; **116** Aaron Haupt; **117** (l)David Stoecklein/The Stock Market, (r)David Woods/The Stock Market; **119** Johnny Johnson/Tony Stone Images; **122** CLOSE TO HOME ©1994 John McPherson/Dist. of UNIVERSAL PRESS SYNDICATE. Reprinted with permission. All rights reserved. **124** (t)Joe Towers/The Stock Market, (c)Nick Nicholson/The Image Bank, (b)Aaron Haupt; **125** (l)Aaron Haupt, (r)David Cannon/Allsport USA; **126** (t)Ian R. Howarth, (cl)Charles W. Melton, (cr)Roy Morsch/The Stock Market, (bl)Meryl Joseph/The Stock Market (br)William J. Weber; **127** (t)Elaine Shay, (b)John Neubauer; **129, 130** Aaron Haupt; **131** Bob Daemmrich; **132** Doug Martin; **136** Mark Burnett; **140** (t,chart)Mark Scott/FPG, (c b)Ron Sheridan/Ancient Art & Architecture Collection, (b,chart)Frank Cezus; **141** (tl)courtesy Marianne Ragins, (tr)David Woods/The Stock Market, (bl)Ron Sheridan/Ancient Art & Architecture Collection, (bc)Corbis-Bettmann, (br)Gamma Liaison; **149** Rick Weber; **150** AP/Wide World Photos; **153** Rick Weber; **154** Dave Lawrence/The Stock Market; **156** (t)Wide World Photos, (b)H.G. Ross/FPG; **157** Archive Photos; **160** Benn Mitchell/The Image Bank; **161** Skip Comer; **162** Ralph Cowan/Tony Stone Images; **163** Allsport USA **167** (t)StudiOhio, (b)Rick Weber; **168** (l)UPI/Corbis-Bettmann, (r)LPI/M. Yada/FPG; **170** E. Alan McGee/FPG; **172** Paul Barton/The Stock Market; **174** Rick Weber; **176** Aaron Haupt; **177** Bruce Ayres/Tony Stone Images; **178** David M. Grossman/Photo Researchers; **180** Archive Photos/Martin Keene; **181** Focus On Sports; **183** Aaron Haupt; **184** (l)David M. Dennis, (r)NASA; **189** Rick Weber; **190** James Meyer/The Image Bank; **191** Morton & White, (bkgd)James Meyer/The Image Bank; **192** (t)Tim Courlas, (cl)Corbis-Bettmann, (cr)Glencoe photo, (b)Archive Photos; **193** (t)John Karl Breun, (c)KS Studio, (bl)Corbis-Bettmann, (br)UPI/Corbis-Bettmann **195** Morton & White; **196** Larry Hamill; **197** (t)Universal Pictures/Shooting Star, (b)Phil Schofield/Tony Stone Images; **198** (l)David R. Frazier Photolibrary, (r)Glencoe photo; **199** (t)Biophoto Associates/Photo Researchers, (b)Morton & White; **200** Kenji Kerins; **201** (t)Gus Chan, (c)TJ Collection/Shooting Star, (b)AP/Wide World Photos; **202** Aaron Haupt; **203** James N. Westwater; **205** (t)Mike Yamashita/Westlight, (b)Scott Padgett/Tradd Street Stock; **206** (t)John Elk III, (b)Jurgen Vogt/The Image Bank; **209** AP Photo/Luc Novovitch/Wide World Photos; **213** (t)Ulf Wallin/The Image Bank, (b)Doug Martin; **214** (t)Focus on Sports, (b)courtesy Ryan Morgan; **215** (t)Doug Martin, (b)Morton & White; **217** (t)Amanita Pictures, (bl br)Morton & White; **218** Leo Nason/The Image Bank; **219** KS Studio; **220** (t)Elaine Shay, (tc tb)Morton & White, (b)John Mead/Science Photo Library/Photo Researchers; **222** (bkgd)Morton & White, (t)Dr. E.R. Degginger/Color-Pic, (b)Charles Cangialosi/ Westlight; **223, 224** Morton & White; **226** (t)Morton & White, (b)KS Studios; **227** Kenji Kerins; **228** (t)Roger Dons/People Weekly, (b)Morton & White; **229, 230, 231** Morton & White; **232** (t)Everett Collection, (b)Morton & White, (c)Chris Hackett/The Image Bank; **233** Everett Collection; **234** (t)Don Mason/The Stock Market, (b)Morton & White; **236** Skip Comer; **237** (t)Morton & White Photographic, (b)Chuck Bankuti/Shooting Star; **238** (t)Kenji Kerins, (b)Morton & White; **239** KS Studios; **240** Matt Meadows; **241** Morton & White; **242** Photo Researchers; **244** NASA; **248-249** KS Studio; **252** (t)Terry Vine/Tony Stone Images, (c)Ronald Sheridan/Ancient Art & Architecture Collection, (b)Corbis-Bettmann; **253** (tl)Weldon McDougal, (tr)David W. Hamiliton/The Image Bank, (cl)Jim Cornfield/Westlight, (cr)Glencoe photo, (br)courtesy Council for the Traditional Arts; **254** (t)Mimi Ostendorf-Smith, (b)James Blank/The Stock Market; **262** (t)Tom Tietz/Tony Stone Images, (c)Daniel J. Cox/Tony Stone Iamges, (b)Tim Davis/Tony Stone Images; **264** James P. Rowan/Tony Stone Images; **266** Stephen Marks/The Image Bank; **269** Stephen Webster; **271** (t)Doug Martin, (c)Brent Turner/BLT Productions, (b)Aaron Haupt; **273, 277** Aaron Haupt; **280** Eclipse Studios; **281** (t)Doug Martin, (b)Tom McGuire; **282** KS Studio; **284** Ruth Dixon; **285** (t)KS Studio, (b)Aaron Haupt; **286** Bob Daemmrich; **287** David O. Hill/Photo Researchers; **290** KS Studio; **293** Stephen Marks/The Image Bank; **294** (l)Duomo/Al Tielemans, (r)Duomo/Bryan Yablonsky; **295** Alese & Mort Pecher/The Stock Market; **301** (t)Smithsonian Institution, (b)David Madison; **302** MAK-1; **304** KS Studio; **306** (t)Aaron Haupt, (b)Doug Martin; **308** David Barnes/The Stock Market; **309** KS Studio; **310** Aaron Haupt; **311** Aaron Haupt; **313** (t)Aaron Haupt, (b)Harald Sund The Image Bank; **314** (t)Eric Lars Bakke/Allsport USA, (c b)In Fisherman Magazine; **318** Aaron Haupt; **319** Denis Valentine/The Stock Market; **321** (t)Matt Meadows, (b)Morton & White; **322** (t)Corbis-Bettmann, (b)Culver Pictures; **323** (tl)courtesy Jorge Arturo Pineda Aguilar, (tr)Morton & White. (cl)National Portrait Gallery, Washington, D.C./Art Resource, NY, (cr)Archive Photos/Consolidated News, (b)Alan S. Weiner/People Weekly; **325, 328** Morton & White; **330** J. Coolidge/The Image Bank; **331** (tl)John M. Roberts/The Stock Market, (tc)Andrea Pistolesi/The Image Bank, (tr)Dallas & John Heaton/Westlight, (cl)Tom Walker/Tony Stone Images, (cr)Art Wolfe/Tony Stone Images,(bl)UPI/Corbis-Bettmann, (br)Gail Shumway/FPG; **332** (t)Grant V. Faint/The Image Bank, (c)Scott Markewitz/FPG, (b)Van Bucher/Photo Researchers; **335, 337** Doug Martin; **338** Morton & White; **339** Aaron Haupt; **340** (t)Tom Stack/Tom Stack & Associates, (c)Bob Daemmrich, (b)Tracy I. Borland; **342** Stan Fellerman/The Stock Market; **343** (t)Doug Martin, (b)Morton & White; **344-345** Morton & White Photographic; **349** Corbis-Bettmann; **350** John McDermott/Tony Stone Images; **353** Morton & White; **354** Dick Luria/FPG; **356** Morton & White; **358** E.R. Degginger/Color-Pic; **360** Gabe Palmer/The Stock Market; **362** (t)E. Alan McGee/FPG, (b)Bob Taylor/FPG; **364** Terry Qing/FPG; **368** Bryan Peterson/The Stock Market; **369, 372** Morton & White; **374** Rainer Grosskopf/Tony Stone Images; **379** Life Images; **382** (t)Bob Daemmrich/Tony Stone Images, (b)Ron Sheridan/Ancient Art & Architecture Collection; **383** (tl)Phil Matt, (tr)Ken Edward/Science Source/Photo Researchers, (cl)John Berry/courtesy Center for Forensic Science, Univ. of New Haven, CT, (cr)courtesy University of TX at Brownsville, (bl)Culver Pictures, (br)US Justice Department; **384, 386** Aaron Haupt; **390** (bkgd)KS Studio, (t)Doug Martin; **392** The Gordon Hart Collection, Bluffton, IN; **394** Life Images; **395** Kenji Kerins; **397** (l)courtesy the office of Congresswoman Patsy Mink, (r)Doug Martin; **398** (l)Duomo/Paul Sutton, (r)Mark Lawrence/The Stock Market; **399** Aaron Haupt; **404** (t)Kenji Kerins, (b)Doug Martin; **405** (t)Alain Evrard/Photo Researchers, (c)Nikolas/Konstantinou/Tony Stone Images, (b)Norbert Wu/Tony Stone Images; **407** Aaron Haupt;

411 Pal Hermansen/Tony Stone Images; **413** (t)Suzanne Murphy-Larronde/FPG (b)Bill Ross/Westlight; **415** (bkgd)Duomo/William Sallaz,(t)KS Studio; **416** Travelpix/FPG; **417** (t)KS Studio, (b)Matt Meadows; 418 (t)Eclipse Studios, (b)Skip Comer; **419** Aaron Haupt; **420** (t)Joseph Drivas/The Image Bank, (bl)Michael Salas/The Image Bank; **422** Aaron Haupt; **423** Scott Cunningham; **425** (t)David R. Frazier/Photo Researchers, (b)MAK-1; **429** C.T. Tracy/FPG; **430** Gary Buss/FPG; **431** Lawrence Migdale; **432** courtesy The White House; **433** KS Studio; **436** Lori Adamski Peek/Tony Stone Images; **438** Court Mast/FPG; **440** Kenji Kerins; **442** (bkgd)Jane Shemilt/Science Photo Library/Photo Researchers, (t)Aaron Haupt, (b)Photo Researchers; **449** Steve Lissau; **450** (t)David Madison, (bl)Ronald Sheridan/Ancient Art & Architecture Collection, (br)Corbis-Bettmann; **451** (tl)Tom Lynn/Sports Illustrated, (tr)AP Photo/Elise Amendola/Wide World Photos, (cl)Corbis-Bettmann, (cr)Reuters/Corbis-Bettmann, (b)Corbis-Bettmann; **455** AP Photo/Mark Lenniham/Wide World Photos; **460** (t)Dinodia/Jagdish Agarwal, (b)Dinodia/Jagdish Agarwal; **461** Matt Meadows; **462** Clark James Mishler/The Stock Market; **465** (t)Bob Daemmrich/Tony Stone Images , (b)Aaron Haupt; **467** PEANUTS reprinted by permission of United Feature Syndicate, Inc.; **468** (t)Ronald Johnson/The Image Bank, (b)Brian Brake/Photo Researchers; **469** (t)Archive Photos, (l)Charles H. Kuhn Collection, The Ohio State University Cartoon,Graphic, and Photographic Arts Research Library/Reprinted with Special Permission of King Features Syndicate; **471** Doug Martin; **473** M. Gerber/LGI Photo Agency; **475** J-L Charmet/Science Photo Library/Photo Researchers; **477** (t)Bob Daemmrich, (b)AP/Wide World Photos; **481** (t)Aaron Haupt, (b)Tim Courlas, **482** Aaron Haupt; **483** James Blank/FPG; **485** Nino Mascardi/The Image Bank; **486** Elaine Shay **490** Tracy Borland; **494** (c)Corbis-Bettmann, (b)Corbis-Bettmann; **495** (t)Richard Lee/Detroit Free Press, (c)Gary Buss/FPG, (b)Culver Pictures; **496** (t)People Weekly ©1995 Keith Philpott, (b)AP/Wide World Photos; **500** (t)Will Crocker/The Image Bank, (b)Doug Martin; **501** (t)Aaron Haupt; **505** (t,inset)Aaron Haupt, (t)Julie Marcotte/Westlight, (b)Kenji Kerins; **506** (t)Aaron Haupt, (b)Mason Morfit/FPG; **507** David R. Frazier Photolibrary; **508** (t)Julian Baum/Science Photo Library/Photo Researchers, (b)Archive Photos/PA News; **509** Centers For Disease Control; **510** (l)Demmie Todd/Shooting Star, (r)Adam Hart-Davis/Science Photo Library/Photo Researchers; **511** (t)Prof. Aaron Pollack/Science Photo Library/Photo Researchers, (b)Doug Martin; **512** (t)Co Rentmeester/The Image Bank, (b)Garry Gay/The Image Bank; **514** (t)Tate Gallery, London/Art Resource, N.Y., (bl)The Metropolitan Museum of Art, Gift of Adele R. Levy, 1958/Malcolm Varon, (br)Erich Lessing/Art Resource, NY; **515** David R. Frazier/Photo Researchers; **518** Gene Frazier; **519** Scott Cunningham; **522** (t)Aaron Haupt, (b)Doug Martin; **526** Bill Ross/Westlight; **527** (r)Aaron Haupt, (l)Richard Hutchings/Photo Researchers; **529** (t)Aaron Haupt, (b)Jeff Spielman/The Image Bank; **531** (t)Robert Tringali/Sportschrome East/West, (b)Mark Gibson/The Stock Market; **533** (t)Eric A. Wessman/Viesti Associates, (b)Charlotte Raymond/Photo Researchers; **536** (t)Jon Blumb, (b)Mark Burnett/Photo Researchers; **540** Steve Elmore/The Stock Market; **541** Aaron Haupt; **542** (t)Larry Lefever from Grant Heilman, (b)Aaron Haupt; **547** Aaron Haupt; **548** Steve Lissau; **553** (l)Geoff Butler, (r)Morton & White; **555** (l)Ira Block/The Image Bank, (r)David R. Frazier Photolibrary; **556** Corbis-Bettmann; **557** (t)Everett Collection, (ct)Morton & White, (cb)NASA, (b)UPI/Corbis-Bettmann; **558** Morton & White; **559** National Archives; **560** (t)Archive Photos, (b)Morton & White; **561-562** Morton & White; **563** (t)Morton & White, (b)Jeff Shallit; **565** (t)Barros & Barros/The Image Bank, (b)KS Studio; **566** Kenji Kerins; **569** (r)Larry Hamill, (l)Otto Greule/Allsport USA; **570** Kenji Kerins; **571** (l)National Portrait Gallery, Smithsonian Institution, Gift of TIME, Inc./Art Resource, NY; **579** Derek Berwin/The Image Bank; **583** (t)Corbis-Bettmann, (b)Ron Sheridan/Ancient Art & Architecture Collection; **586** Brent Turner/BLT Productions; **593** L.D.Gordon/The Image Bank; **594** Piffret/Photo Researchers; **596** Janeart LTD./The Image Bank; **597** (t)Joe Towers/The Stock Market, (b)Roy Marsch/The Stock Market; **598** (l)Steve Niedorf/The Image Bank; **599** (l)Chuck Doyle, (r)Archive Photos; **600** Kenji Kerins; **608** (t)Tim Courlas, (c)North Wind Picture Archive, (b)Corbis-Bettmann; **609** (t)Kathleen Cabble/St. Petersburg Times, (c bl)Archive Photos, (br)Archive Photos/Frank Edwards; **611** Arteaga Photo Ltd.; **613** (l)American Photo Library, (r)Ed & Chris Kumler; **615** Morton & White; **616** (t)Mark Burnett, (b)Morton & White; **620** Aaron Haupt; **626** David R. Frazier Photolibrary; **628** (t)Library of Congress, (b)Aaron Rezny/The Stock Market; **631** Harald Sund/The Image Bank; **633** (t)Marc Grimberg/The Image Bank, (b)Morton & White; **635** Morton & White; **638** David M. Dennis; **641** Howard Sochurek/The Stock Market; **642** (t)Jody Dole/The Image Bank, (b)courtesy Bob Paz/Caltech; **645** (t)Michael Melford/The Image Bank, (c)James N. Westwater, (b)Gary Cralle/The Image Bank; **646** Culver Pictures; **647** Elaine Shay; **648** (t)Herbert Schaible/The Image Bank, (b)Hans Wol/The Image Bank; **650** (t)Morton & White, (bl)John Phelan/The Stock Market, (br)John Maher/The Stock Market; **654** (l)Doug Martin, (r)Co Rentmeester/The Image Bank; **655** (l)Mark Burnett, (c)G. Petrov/Washington Stock Photo, (r)M. Winn/Washington Stock Photo; **657** Tony Freeman/PhotoEdit; **658** (t)Lou Jacobs Jr. from Grant Heilman, (b)Ron Sheridan/Ancient Art & Architecture Collection; **659** (t)courtesy Joe Maktima, (cl)Lawrence Migdale, (cr)M. Miller/H. Armstrong Roberts, (b)NASA; **660** (t)Morton & White, (b)MAK-1; **662, 663** Morton & White; **664** (t)Ron Watts/Westlight, (b)Doug Martin; **665** (t)Ned Gillette/The Stock Market, (b)Lynn Campbell; **667** Benjamin Rondel/The Stock Market; **669** (t)KS Studio, (b)Morton & White; **670** (t)Morton & White, (b)Bob Mullenix; **671** (l)Stephen Dunn/Allsport USA, (r)Brett Palmer/The Stock Market; **672** (l)Mark Gibson/The Stock Market, (r)Larry Hamill; **674** Aaron Haupt; **675, 677** KS Studio; **680** (t)Ward's Natural Science, (bl br)Aaron Haupt; **681** Corbis-Bettmann; **684** Dave Merrill & Co./National Geographic Society; **685** (br)CalTech & Carnegie Institution, (others)NASA; **687** Roy Morsch/The Stock Market; **689** (t)GK & Vikki Hart/The Image Bank, (b)Morton & White; **690** Morton & White; **694** Andrew Unangst/The Image Bank; **696** Kenji Kerins; **697** (l)Patrick W. Stoll/Westlight, (r)Morton & White; **698** Doug Martin; **701** (l)Morton & White, (r)Guido Alberto Rossi/The Image Bank; **702** Archive Photos; **707** Morton & White; **710** (t)Glencoe photo, (c)Ron Sheridan/Ancient Art & Architecture Collection, (b)Matt Meadows; **711** (tl)Annie Griffiths Belt, (tr)Doug Martin, (cl)University of California/Lawrence Berkeley Laboratory, (cr)Archive Photos/Reuters/Peter Jones, (b)Lucille Day/Black Star; **713** Stock Newport/Daniel Forster; **715** (t)Ulrike Welsch/Photo Researchers, (b)Glencoe photo; **717** David R. Frazier Photolibrary; **718** Archive Photos/David Lees; **719** W. Warren/Westlight; **720** Doug Martin; **721** Gerard Photography; **722** PEANUTS reprinted by permission of United Feature Syndicate, Inc.; **723** Bob Daemmrich; **724** (l)Flip Chalfant/The Image Bank, (r)Glencoe photo; **725** KS Studio; **727** (t)Tom Bean/The Stock Market, (b)D. Logan/H. Armstrong Roberts; **728** William Kennedy/The Image Bank; **730** K. Scholz/H. Armstrong Roberts; **732** (t)Kaz Mori/The Image Bank, (c)DLR, ESA/Science Photo Library/Photo Researchers, (b)Greg Davis/The Stock Market; **736** (t)Joe Azzara/The Image Bank, (b)KS Studio; **739** Ken Davies/Masterfile; **740** (l)Glencoe photo, (r)NCSA, University of IL/Science Photo Library/Photo Researchers; **743** (t)David R. Frazier Photolibrary, (c)Dallas & John Heaton/Westlight, (b)Wong How Man/Westlight; **746** Doug Martin; **747** Sylvain Grandadam/Photo Researchers; **748** David R. Frazier Photolibrary; **752** The Walt Disney Co./Shooting Star; **753** Aaron Haupt; **755** (tl)Ken Edwards/Science Source/Photo Researchers, (tr)Kaz Mori/The Image Bank, (bl)David Ball/The Stock Market, (br)E. Alan McGee/FPG.

APPLICATIONS & CONNECTIONS INDEX

A

B

C

D

E

INDEX

D

E

F

G

H

I

J

K

L

M

N

O

P

Q

R

FORMULA CHART

Perimeter	square	$P = 4s$
	rectangle	$P = 2(\ell + w)$ or $P = 2\ell + 2w$
Circumference	circle	$C = 2\pi r$ or $C = \pi d$
Area	square	$A = s^2$
	rectangle	$A = \ell w$ or $A = bh$
	parallelogram	$A = bh$
	triangle	$A = \frac{1}{2}bh$
	trapezoid	$A = \frac{1}{2}(b_1 + b_2)h$
	circle	$A = \pi r^2$
Surface Area	cube	$S = 6s^2$
	cylinder (lateral)	$S = 2\pi rh$
Volume	rectangular prism	$V = \ell wh$
	cylinder	$V = \pi r^2 h$
	cube	$V = s^3$
	cone	$V = \frac{1}{3}\pi r^2 h$
	pyramid	$V = \frac{1}{3}Bh$
	sphere	$V = \frac{4}{3}\pi r^3$
Pythagorean Theorem	right triangle	$a^2 + b^2 = c^2$
Distance Formula	any two points with coordinates (x_1, y_1) and (x_2, y_2)	$d = \sqrt{(x_2 - x_1)^2 + (y_2 - y_1)^2}$
Quadratic Formula	quadratic equation of the form $ax^2 + bx + c = 0$, where $a \neq 0$	$x = \frac{-b \pm \sqrt{b^2 - 4ac}}{2a}$
Temperature	Fahrenheit to Celsius	$C = \frac{5}{9}(F - 32)$
	Celsius to Fahrenheit	$F = \frac{9}{5}C + 32$